Prentice Hall Literature Portfolio

Edited by

Christy Desmet
University of Georgia

D. Alexis Hart
Virginia Military Institute

Deborah Church Miller
University of Georgia

Upper Saddle River, New Jersey 07458

KH

Library of Congress Cataloging-in-Publication Data
Desmet, Christy
Prentice Hall Literature Portfolio / Christy Desmet, D. Alexis Hart, Deborah Church Miller.
p.cm.
Includes bibliographical references and index.
ISBN 0-13-193508-9
1. English language—Rhetoric—Problems, exercises, etc. 2. Literature—History and criticism—Theory, etc. 3. Critical thinking—Problems, exercises, etc. 4. Fiction—History and criticism—Problems, exercises, etc. 5. Criticism—Authorship—Problems, exercises, etc. 6. Academic writing—Problems, exercises, etc. 7. College readers. I. Hart, D. Alexis. II. Miller, Deborah Church. III. Title.
PE 1479.C47 2007
808.0668—dc22

2006045337

Editor-in-Chief: Leah Jewell
Acquisitions Editor: Vivian Garcia
Editorial Assistant: Christina Volpe
Production Liaison: Joanne Hakim
Marketing Manager: Vivian Garcia
Marketing Assistant: Vicki DeVita
Manufacturing Buyer: Christina Amato
Permissions Specialist: Robyn Renahan
Cover Art Director: Jayne Conte
Cover Design: Bruce Kenselaar
Cover Photo/Illustration: Don Li-Leger and Canadian Art Prints
Director, Image Resource Center: Melinda Patelli
Manager, Rights and Permissions: Zina Arabia
Manager, Visual Research: Beth Brenzel
Manager, Cover Visual Research & Permissions: Karen Sanatar
Image Permission Coordinator: Craig Jones
Photo Researcher: Kathy (Beaura) Ringrose
Composition/Full-Service Project Management: GGS Book Services
Printer/Binder: The Courier Companies

Credits and acknowledgments borrowed from other sources and reproduced, with permission, in this textbook appear on page 1319.

Pearson Education LTD., London
Pearson Education Singapore, Pte. Ltd
Pearson Education, Canada, Ltd
Pearson Education–Japan
Pearson Education Australia PTY, Limited
Pearson Education North Asia Ltd
Pearson Educación de Mexico, S.A. de C.V.
Pearson Education Malaysia, Pte. Ltd
Pearson Education, Upper Saddle River, New Jersey

10 9 8 7 6 5 4 3 2 1
ISBN 0-13-193508-9

2/15/08

Contents

Acknowledgments

Christy Desmet would like to thank David Schiller, Rosemary Desmet, and ILY for their forbearance and encouragement during the year that it took to put together this book. Alexis Hart would like to thank Mike and Amelia. Deborah Miller would like to thank Chris and Laura for library time; her Spring 2005 ENGL 1102 students, who gave her valuable feedback on the book's contents and writing assignments; and Maggie and Allison, for being themselves.

Thank you to the following reviewers for their thoughtful comments: Margaret V. Gardineer, Felician College; Stephen Bernstein, University of Michigan-Flint; A. J. Mittendorf, College of New Caledonia; Joni Schockett, Wentworth Institute; Keith O'Neill, Dutchess Community College; Abby Coykendall, Eastern Michigan University; and Matthew G. J. Rolph, Plymouth State University.

Collectively, the authors would like to thank their patient editor, Vivian Garcia; one another; Bob Cummings; and Administrative Assistant extraordinaire Jane Barroso, without whose bibliographical talents nothing would have been possible.

CHAPTER 1

Introduction

One of the short stories printed in *Prentice Hall Literature Portfolio* is "Arturo's Flight," by Judith Ortiz Cofer. The young hero of this story feels "trapped in a school that's like an insane asylum" (Cofer 27). One source of Arturo's discomfort is the literature that he is forced to read and recite in school. Author Ortiz Cofer has studied (and loves) traditional English literature. For the fictional Arturo, however, the encounter is not a pleasant one, for a school incident involving Donne's seduction poem, "The Flea"—also printed in this textbook—earns Arturo the unappreciated nickname of the "purple flea."

In the story, Arturo runs away from home, abandoning both the barrio and his traditional literary education. During his flight, Arturo meets an elderly survivor of the holocaust who gives him a new perspective on life and human relations. At the end of the story, Arturo returns home, but first retrieves—from the dumpster where he had thrown it in disgust—his copy of Shakespeare's *Sonnets*. This gesture signals the young man's new understanding of life, people, and literature. In *Prentice Hall Literature Portfolio*, we recognize that our readers, like the fictional Arturo, may find literature intimidating. At the same time, we hope that you, like Arturo, will take away from the experience a sense of how literature can provide both pleasure and insight into life's ups and downs.

Why do you read literature? When asked this question, most people would probably reply, "for fun." Relaxation, enjoyment, an escape from everyday routines—these are all powerful motives for reading fiction, poetry, drama, and other kinds of literature. When you walk into a bookstore and see people seated in comfortable chairs browsing through books, you will recognize at once the importance of reading for pleasure as well as information. But other motives for reading literature exist, as well. A class of students studying works of English Literature before 1700 or American Multicultural Literature might well reply that they read this literature to learn about unfamiliar peoples and times, to understand human nature, or to become a "well-rounded person" and "informed citizen." Over the years, many of our students have articulated all of these reasons.

The belief that fiction can bring history vividly before our eyes or take us to places we will never visit in person is felt deeply by many cultures. So too is the conviction that literature can contribute to readers' ethical, political, or religious development. Sociologists, philosophers, theologians, and even legal theorists turn to literature for exemplary human problems and solutions that can be studied according to the principles of more abstract disciplines. Teachers in classrooms at all levels also use literature to convey lessons of ethics, politics, or religion. Still other readers enjoy thinking critically about how works of literature are put together, how they reflect the events and cultures that produced them, and how they are related to other works of their time or type. These readers are literary critics, or to put it more simply, students of literature. Literary critics are concerned particularly with the qualities of writing that make a text "literary" rather than just a "story." Some of these features—poetic form and meter, metaphor and symbolism, scenic structure—may be familiar to you. Others may not be familiar, but this book is constructed to help you learn about them and to appreciate how they contribute to literature's power.

In *Prentice Hall Literature Portfolio*, we invite you to act as a critic or student of literature. We hope that you will read the selections offered here for both pleasure and profit, and we proceed on the assumption that these goals are enhanced rather than diminished by understanding how works of literature are put together, who wrote them, and how they reflect or challenge the culture in which they were produced. The text is designed to help initiate and sustain a critical conversation about literature.

First, we have organized the anthology according to three traditional genres: short story, poetry, and drama. This organizational method helps you to understand the essential features that define each genre. Within the genres, selections are organized within broad chronological periods. Although literary history is not the anthology's primary focus, this organizational choice can help you see how each of the genres develops over time. Head notes provide biographical information about the author, selected information about her or his relation to literary history and specific movements, and a brief consideration of the work's thematic, rhetorical, or literary features. They also suggest other pieces of literature from throughout the anthology that might, for historical, thematic, or rhetorical reasons, be considered in relation to this text. Words that appear in **bold type** in the head notes or in the following chapters are explained at further length in the Glossary at the back of the book. Together, the head notes and glossary seek to provide both individual readers and groups of students with a "way into" the literature reproduced here—not a definitive interpretation of any author or text, but a starting point for analysis, conversation, and writing.

Second, in *Prentice Hall Literature Portfolio* we consider the processes of reading and writing about literature together, as complementary acts. The French critic Roland Barthes has suggested that every act of reading is also an act of rewriting a text (Barthes, 142–48). More mundanely, we might say that the two processes reinforce one another: reading closely and carefully sharpens the argument of our own writing, while writing about a text records the progress of our thoughts about that text. The relation is recursive, or circular. The better we read, the better we write, and vice versa. In Chapter 3, we offer a general discussion of the writing process. In the chapters about reading and writing within genres, we consider particular problems and opportunities offered to writers about these particular genres. In Chapter 10, we address methods for incorporating and documenting the voices of other critics and artists. Finally, in Chapter 11, we discuss strategies for comparing texts and for working across genres. *Prentice Hall Literature Portfolio* seeks to offer readers, students, and critics a compact, affordable introduction to great literature in the three major genres, with focused suggestions for analytic reading and writing that, we hope, will allow the literature to do what it was meant to do—in Sir Philip Sidney's adaptation of a formula from the Latin poet Horace—to "teach and delight" (Sidney 10).

WORKS CITED

Barthes, Roland. "The Death of the Author." *Image, Music, Text.* Trans. Stephen Heath. New York: Hill and Wang, 1977. 142–48.

Cofer, Judith Ortiz. "Arturo's Flight." *An Island Like You: Stories of the Barrio.* New York: Puffin Books, 1996. 27–40.

Sidney, Philip. *The Defense of Poesy*. Ed. Lewis Soens. Lincoln: U of Nebraska P, 1970.

CHAPTER 2

Reading to Become "Symbol-Wise"

INTRODUCTION

The Introduction to *Prentice Hall Literature Portfolio* identifies literature's goal as to "teach and delight." But how exactly does this process work? **Didactic literature** attempts to inculcate ethical or religious lessons directly. The fifteenth-century play *Everyman* exemplifies most clearly the tradition of didactic literature, presenting through the aptly named figure of Everyman the path to dying well by living well. But although the Anglo-American tradition has long embraced didactic literature as suitable for young readers—those texts in which good children are rewarded and the wicked severely punished—most literature does not go about educating audiences so directly.

TO TEACH

In oral cultures, where information must be rehearsed constantly to stay alive in public memory, literature can hardly be differentiated from history. Homer's *Iliad* is, at one level, a history of war between the Greeks and Trojans. Within the **epic**, we find information that after the advent of writing, could be simply written down and archived—for instance, Homer's famous catalogue of Greek ships. Ancient Greek drama also has a strongly historical dimension: *Antigone*, for instance, represents one episode in the ongoing disintegration of the House of Thebes. More broadly, Greek drama, like epic, enacts and reinforces basic cultural values. *Antigone*, once again, dramatizes the competing claims of the law and family piety, or Antigone's love for her brother. This play, we might say, offers a forum for exploring ethics rather than the direct moral instruction offered by didactic literature. Later texts can also address broader questions of philosophy, ethics, religion, and politics. William Blake's illustrated poems evolve with their author's complex personal mythology and thoughts about religion. John Donne's sonnet "Batter My Heart" and George Herbert's "The Collar" are intellectually complex and artfully constructed poems, but both are also spiritual meditations by serious-minded churchmen. Judith Ortiz Cofer and Susan Glaspell capture aspects of regional domestic life, but in their work we also see evidence of a **feminist** consciousness. Langston Hughes's poems, for instance "Theme for English B," often reflect on social issues. And Arthur Miller's masterpiece of **realism**, *Death of a Salesman*, owes much to the author's commitment to social justice.

TO DELIGHT

The advent of writing as a technology in Western culture meant that knowledge could be separated from concrete performances, allowing the goal of "delight" to play a greater role in literary experience. In oral epic performance, according to Eric Havelock, there is an intense identification between speaker and audience that is at once intellectual and emotional, and so strong as to be almost pathological (Havelock 20–35). As drama evolved out of epic in literate Greece, the emotional dynamic of literature changed. Aristotle's *Poetics*, probably the best-known treatise on literature ever written, says that tragedy works by arousing in spectators the twin emotions of fear and pity in the face of the tragic hero's fate: we feel pity because the hero does not deserve his very harsh fate and experience fear because we can imagine the same fate for ourselves. The **catharsis** of the drama is the ultimate purging of those negative emotions to leave the spectator in a state of satisfaction.

IDENTIFICATION

A broader, post-Aristotelian term for the emotional charge that is produced in audiences by the experience of literature is **identification**: not merely empathy with the main character of a literary work, but a broader resonance between the situations depicted in a literary work and our own. Literary texts need not imitate life as we know it directly; indeed, some of literature's power comes from its representations of the exotic or unfamiliar. As defined by rhetorician Kenneth Burke, the concept of identification acknowledges similarities, but also differences between the literary situation and that of the audience (Burke, *Rhetoric* 19–23 and *passim*). Some of the difference is a matter of social context and individual nature. White and black spectators, or rural Southerners and Northern urbanites, might bring to August Wilson's *The Piano Lesson* different understandings of family dynamics. Or they might not. A fourteen-year-old girl in suburban Maryland might find the life portrayed in Ibsen's *A Doll House* suffocating and repressive. Or wonderfully romantic. Or, for better or worse, just like home.

Although literature does not erase cultural differences—indeed, **multicultural** writers work from the position that there is no universal human experience—readers achieve a sense of identification, paradoxically enough, through literature's tendency to paint human experience with broad brushstrokes. Literature, as Burke puts it, is a "stylized answer" to important questions that arise in the course of human life (Burke, "Philosophy" 1). These questions and answers may be hyperbolic, larger than life. This is certainly the case in a play like *Antigone*. Who expects to choose between death and burying your dead? This is also the case in Samuel Taylor Coleridge's "The Rime of the Ancient Mariner," in which both mariner and wedding guest find themselves in unpleasantly extreme positions. In some works of literature, the effect of stylization can result from a discrepancy between subject matter and manner of representation. Edgar Allan Poe's short stories, for instance, set us on edge by the tension between their **gothic** events and matter-of-fact narration. The same might be said for sung ballads such as "Lord Randall." In many texts, such as Elizabeth Bishop's "One Art," we find a related tension between a highly structured poetic form and raw emotion. Finally, literature can also transform the ordinary through the beauty of language. August Wilson is well known for capturing the musical cadences of ordinary conversation, William Wordsworth for the delicacy of his poetic diction when describing the evanescent moods of man in nature.

Of course, it is impossible to detach the twin functions of literature—to teach and delight—from one another. The proportions of each motive may vary according to author, reader, context, or even the time of day, but they always work together to create literary experience. Sidney's venerable formula, however, cannot define completely the centrality of literature to human experience. At different times and places, thinkers from such diverse fields as philosophy, sociology, anthropology, cognitive linguistics, and theology have arrived at the conclusion that literature does not just mirror reality, but actively helps to construct both human identity and the outside world.

BECOMING "SYMBOL-WISE," OR THE USES OF LITERATURE

This short chapter cannot do justice to the body of thought on the complex relation between literature and life, but can outline key points in the argument. Kenneth Burke, once again, provides a starting point. He begins his book *Permanence and Change* with the premise that "all living things are critics" (Burke, *Permanence* 5). In this statement, Burke is not taking a stand in the debate about whether animals such as chimpanzees can master language. Rather, with this provocative declaration he points to the fact that **interpretation**—not literary criticism per se, but the simple ability to read signs and symbols—is fundamental to existing in the world. Even so lowly an organism as a fish can "read" and interpret signs that are crucial to its survival. Say that one kind of fish is preyed upon by another kind, which is distinguished by a bright red spot on its back. Members of the first species learn to avoid these predators not just by blind instinct, but by "reading" the red spot as a sign of "danger." In its humble way, the fish is acting as a "critical organism."

Teaching us how to read signs is what literature does best. Leaving aside the critical capabilities of fish, we can turn to contemporary linguists such as George Lakoff and Mark Turner, who would generally agree with Burke that there is a connection between interpreting the world and interpreting literature because ordinary language is already more literary than we recognize. In *More Than Cool Reason: A Field Guide to Poetic Metaphor*, Lakoff and Turner argue that **metaphor** is a tool that we use constantly and unconsciously (Lakoff and Turner). Some literary texts offer us richly developed **symbols** as a starting point for unraveling the meaning of an entire work. Consider, for instance, the chrysanthemums in John Steinbeck's short story of that name, the lavishly carved musical instrument in August Wilson's *The Piano Lesson*, and the chilling central metaphor (or **simile**) of Margaret Atwood's poem "You Fit Into Me." But metaphors do not have to become full-fledged literary symbols to impart meaning to literature. Sometimes the basic, deeply embedded metaphors that structure ordinary experience are reproduced and elaborated on by literary texts: think, for instance, of how one basic metaphor, "life is a journey" with death as its destination, is reworked by

Everyman or Emily Dickinson's "Because I could not stop for death." Coming to understand how signs, symbols, and metaphors structure literary texts and the world means becoming what Burke calls "symbol-wise." In this way, reading literature critically functions as a dress rehearsal for life.

At times, literature asks us to think self-consciously not just about what words and signs mean, or even *how* they mean, but about the *process* of creating meaning through art and even the metaphysical question of whether meaning is possible. This kind of literature is called **metafiction**, or fiction about the process of reading and writing literature. (In the case of plays, the relevant term is **metadrama**.) In some cases, texts will make us think about the materiality of the written or printed word. George Herbert's "Easter Wings," for instance, uses poetic shape to imitate the poem's subject; the poems of e. e. cummings jolt us out of the habit of looking through the typography of poems to their underlying "meaning." "Since feeling is first" becomes metafiction by going one step further. Working through a device we might call "anti-metaphor" (life is *not* a paragraph), the poem calls into question our tendency to accept without question poetic metaphors (e.g., love is like a red rose). This poem is not "about" anything other than art; in it, cummings takes a long, hard look at the commonplace assumptions that we bring to literature.

Shakespeare's *Hamlet*, although not a completely **metadramatic** work, brings to the foreground how drama works in the scene where Hamlet counsels the actors on fine points of delivery (3.2). Hamlet also offers a soliloquy (2.2) lamenting that the actor who has given a long speech about the Trojan Queen Hecuba's pain and suffering is able to cry for her while Hamlet, the injured son of a murdered father, cannot "act" in either sense of the word. Hamlet brings to our attention the potency and limitations of the idea that "life is a play" and man an actor. At this moment, *Hamlet* becomes a play about drama, or a **metadrama**.

Some examples of **magic realism**, such as Gabriel Garcia Marquez's "The Handsomest Drowned Man in the World," use their fantastic plots as platforms for exploring the art of constructing meaning. In this story, the appearance of the drowned man, who is finally nothing more than a corpse, becomes through the imaginations of the people a powerful symbol of the village itself. Even in literature that does not foreground the methods of art and the making of meaning, we can find glimpses of self-conscious examination of language. Take, for instance, Elizabeth Bishop's "The Fish," which examines the hapless fish's anatomy through metaphor, but ends with a renunciation of art when the speaker releases the fish, acknowledging its material existence and right to live. Judith Ortiz Cofer's short story "More Room" performs a similar operation by showing how the simple act of adding on a new room to the family house changes in meaning when a woman takes charge of her body.

TAKING A POSITION AS A READER

The subject of how reading works as a process has been debated since the Medieval period and has even produced a contemporary school of thought called **reader-response criticism**. When we read, we are constantly shifting position in relation to the text we hold in our hands and to the producer(s) of that text, but these movements generally go on below the level of consciousness. When acting

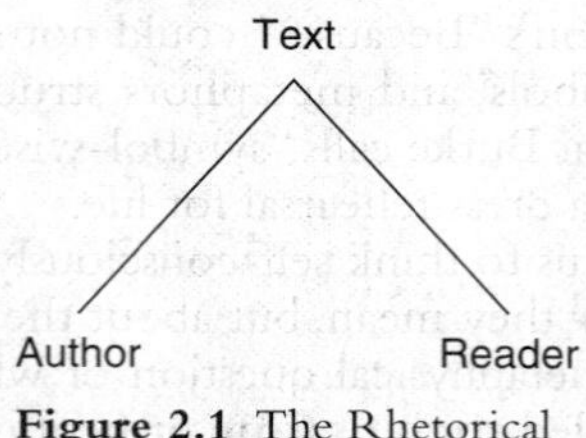

Figure 2.1 The Rhetorical Triangle

as students or critics of literature, we bring the dynamics of reading to the foreground, becoming self-conscious about not only why, but also how we read literature. This is all part of the process of moving from reading to **interpretation**, of being a student or critic of literature.

We can visualize the reading process in different ways. The simplest model is a variation on the structure commonly called the **rhetorical triangle**. Usually traced to Aristotle (although he never actually uses the term), the rhetorical triangle establishes a carefully balanced tension among author, reader, and text as active forces in the reading process.

But as discussed previously, how any act of reading unfolds is variable; this is particularly true when we read "symbol-wise." In some cases, the figure of the author comes to the foreground, destabilizing the triangle by capturing the reader's interest and attention. When we read poetry for biography—for instance, learning about John Milton's blindness by reading his sonnet, "When I consider how my light is spent"—the author takes precedence over text and reader in the rhetorical triangle. Some forms of **psychoanalytic criticism** (although by no means all) focus on the figure of the author. Sometimes, just attending a public reading—where the author is present to answer questions—shifts the triangle in favor of the author.

In yet another variation on the basic triangle, the reader takes precedence over author and text. This dynamic can occur, for instance, when a student makes the teacher see a work in a totally new way. "I've never thought of 'A Rose for Emily' that way," she might say. Landmark critical essays achieve the same effect. Once we have read them, we never see the work of literature they discuss the same way again. The reader also takes precedence in the triangle when she or he feels resistance to a text or author. Negative feelings, such as irritation at an author's treatment of sexuality or misogyny, can produce reader-oriented experiences; so too can a rush of appreciation, a feeling that a John Edgar Wideman story, for instance, has opened up new worlds for you. Finally, the reader can take precedence whenever she thinks self-consciously about reading or interpretation *as a process*.

At times, the text itself becomes the focus of attention. **Pattern poems** such as "Easter Wings" or unusual typography, as in the poetry of e.e. cummings or Carolyn Forché's "The Colonel," can make the text interpose itself between reader and writer, asking readers to focus on the materiality of art. **Metafiction** and **metadrama** also direct attention to the features of the text. And in particularly dense poetry, such as the **modernist** poetry of T. S. Eliot, the text poses an active challenge to readers by its sheer difficulty.

Figure 2.2 The Rabbit-Duck Illusion

This section of Chapter 2 is entitled "Taking a Position as a Reader," but the phrase does not imply that readers necessarily control their own processes. They may equally well "find" themselves in one position or another, for the simple reason that reading is not a completely intentional process. No activity that involves imagination can be. Rhetorician and literary scholar Richard Lanham offers a simple way to think of the rhetorical triangle's instability by positing the existence of a mental "switch" that, in the process of going off and on, alters the dynamics of the rhetorical triangle. One minute we may be stalking the author, and the next stymied by the impenetrable surface of the text (Lanham 199–225). The change happens with a simple flip of the "switch." An even more concrete way to imagine the shift in attitude is through a perceptual trick such as the well-known "rabbit-duck" illusion.

When you look at the figure in one way, it seems to be a rabbit; look again, and you see a duck. You can see either figure at different times, but never both at once. The dynamics of reading, although obviously more complicated, are equally volatile and transformative. Each time you come to a short story, poem, or play in this anthology, you may discover either a rabbit or a duck, metaphorically speaking, but never both at once. This dynamic quality is what makes reading literature critically so rewarding—and yes, downright fun.

WORKS CITED

Burke, Kenneth. *Permanence and Change: An Anatomy of Purpose*. 3rd ed. 1954. Berkeley: U of California P, 1984.

———. "The Philosophy of Literary Form." *The Philosophy of Literary Form: Studies in Symbolic Action*. 3rd ed. 1941. Berkeley: U of California P, 1973.

———. *A Rhetoric of Motives*. 1950. Berkeley: U of California P, 1969.

Havelock, Eric A. *Preface to Plato*. Cambridge, Mass.: Harvard UP, 1963.

Lakoff, George, and Mark Turner. *More Than Cool Reason: A Field Guide to Poetic Metaphor*. Chicago: U of Chicago P, 1989.

Lanham, Richard. "Opaque and Transparent Styles." *Analyzing Prose*. New York: Scribner, 1983. 199–225.

CHAPTER 3

Writing about Literature

True ease in writing comes from art, not chance,
As those move easiest who have learn'd to dance.
—ALEXANDER POPE

You write with ease to show your breeding,
But easy writing's curst hard reading.
—RICHARD BRINSLEY SHERIDAN

INTRODUCTION

As was discussed in the Introduction to *Prentice Hall Literature Portfolio*, reading and writing are complementary acts: the better we read, the better we write, and vice versa. Once you have finished reading a literary text—interacted with, reacted to, and discussed it in class with your teacher and peers—you can begin to write an essay about it. Writing, of course, can take place at all stages of encounters with literature. Often, we write journal entries on the class reading as preparation for talking about a literary work; other kinds of writing, both in and out of class, can feed both thought and formal essays. Writing helps you to clarify your interpretation of the text, to unravel its meaning, or to link it to life outside the text. In later chapters, we talk about particular ways to use writing both as an aid to learning and as a way of presenting formally your thoughts when working with texts from different literary genres. In this chapter, by contrast, we focus more generally on the writing process and on some procedures that can help you write essays about literature.

Of course, we have all been confronted with that initial sense of panic as we stare at the blank screen or page; but, if you follow the strategies of a careful and active reader (see the following chapters for tips on reading strategies), you will have already begun the informal process of **prewriting**; that is, you will have already begun to organize, sharpen, and articulate your responses to your reading in written form. We recommend that you try to get an early start on focusing and formalizing your initial ideas into a polished essay and that you leave ample time to draft and revise. In other words, don't wait until the night before the essay is due! Here are some steps you can follow to set in motion the process of moving from prewriting to a polished, formal written assignment.

Finding a unified thesis statement

ESTABLISHING THE REQUIREMENTS OF THE ASSIGNMENT

Often, your instructor or professor will give you a list of essay topics from which to choose; alternatively, she may offer you the opportunity to develop your own topic. We discuss some of the more common kinds of essay assignments you might encounter later in this chapter. But whether you choose from a list of possible topics or devise your own, you must first narrow your focus enough so that you can write a compelling essay that addresses the subject sufficiently within the assignment's constraints of time (due date) and space (page or word limit).

A consistent requirement for essays about literature is a clear, strong **thesis statement**. The literary thesis statement is a *focused, clearly defined, and arguable* assertion about a literary work—a poem, story, play, or creative essay. Your thesis statement should declare your paper's focus (or *topic*) and your *purpose* in exploring the topic. A thesis statement is not a statement of fact ("At the end of *Hamlet*, all the principal characters die"), nor should it be purely a statement of intention ("In this essay, I will prove that . . ."). A strong thesis should tell something more than the writer's position. A thesis statement, for instance, might give reasons *why* the "To be or not to be" soliloquy is critical to understanding *Hamlet* ("Hamlet's 'To be or not to be' soliloquy is the key speech in the play because . . ."); or it might indicate how an analysis of the soliloquy's importance will revise current views of *Hamlet* ("A close analysis of Hamlet's 'To be or not to be' speech shows that Hamlet's problem is less a reluctance to take revenge than a vivid understanding of the afterlife").

Many writers like to come up with a provisional or working thesis before going on to develop their arguments. However, a powerful thesis may need to develop over time, as a result of further thought, research, rereading, or rewriting. Sometimes a thesis is not completely formulated until the essay has gone through several drafts. As you strive to narrow your topic to a defined and specific working thesis, consider the important issues that you noticed while reading and that you focused on during class discussions; think about the difficult questions you, your classmates, and your instructor addressed and disagreed about; reread passages about intriguing events or characters; look for connections between the texts you have read; and try asking the reporter's questions formally—Who? What? Where? When? Why? How? Once you have an idea or a question that you want to develop into a working thesis, ask yourself if *you* are interested and engaged enough in the topic to spend time writing about it. What is it about the topic and the literary text(s) that holds *your* attention and makes *you* want to delve deeper? Then ask yourself "so what?" That is, try to clarify for yourself how your essay will give you and your audience some interesting insight into the literary text or provide you with new ways of interpreting it.

PREWRITING

To help yourself determine the answers to these questions, you might try some of the following **prewriting** techniques.

Brainstorming

Once you have picked a working thesis for your writing project, or to discover or invent a topic, get out a piece of paper—or open your word-processing program—and begin to record all of the ideas, reactions, and comments about the literary text that you can think of as they come to you, in no particular order, and with no concern for complete sentences or grammatical structures. During brainstorming activities, your only concern is to generate material for a potential essay.

Here is an example of a brainstorm about Flannery O'Connor's story "Good Country People":

What is the significance of the title "Good Country People"?

- Who is a "good country person"?
  - Mrs. Freeman (a "lady")
  - Glynese Freeman has "common sense," Freeman girls "two of the finest," care about appearance and manners
  - Mr. Freeman a "good farmer"
  - Bible salesman "just a country boy"?
  - Mrs. Hopewell a good Christian, can't be rude to anyone
  - Joy/Hulga doesn't fit in—Ph.D. in philosophy, bad attitude, poor manners
- Who has the authoritative definition of a "good country person"?
  - Mrs. Hopewell?
  - Bible salesman?
  - Joy/Hulga?

After you have completed your brainstorming session, take a breather. When you review your results, look for "nuggets" of information that may help you narrow your focus, develop your working **thesis** (your main assertion), and/or organize your essay. If you have not generated much writing or see little that you are interested in pursuing further, try brainstorming again on a different topic or on a different text.

Freewriting

Immediately upon rereading a story, sit down for five or ten *uninterrupted* minutes and write down all of your thoughts in a loose, informal paragraph. Do not pause in your writing to reflect or to go back and reread the topic, your notes, or passages from the text. The point of freewriting is to compose new thoughts continually without interruption, to turn off the critical part of your brain that might censor ideas. When you freewrite, you do not stop writing to edit or review. If you find that you are having trouble writing without editing in your word-processing program (if those squiggly red and green lines are too distracting), turn off your monitor and continue to type "blind" until your five or ten allotted minutes are up.

When you have completed your freewriting, scan it for "nuggets" worth keeping. Underline or highlight the places where they appear. If you like, you can

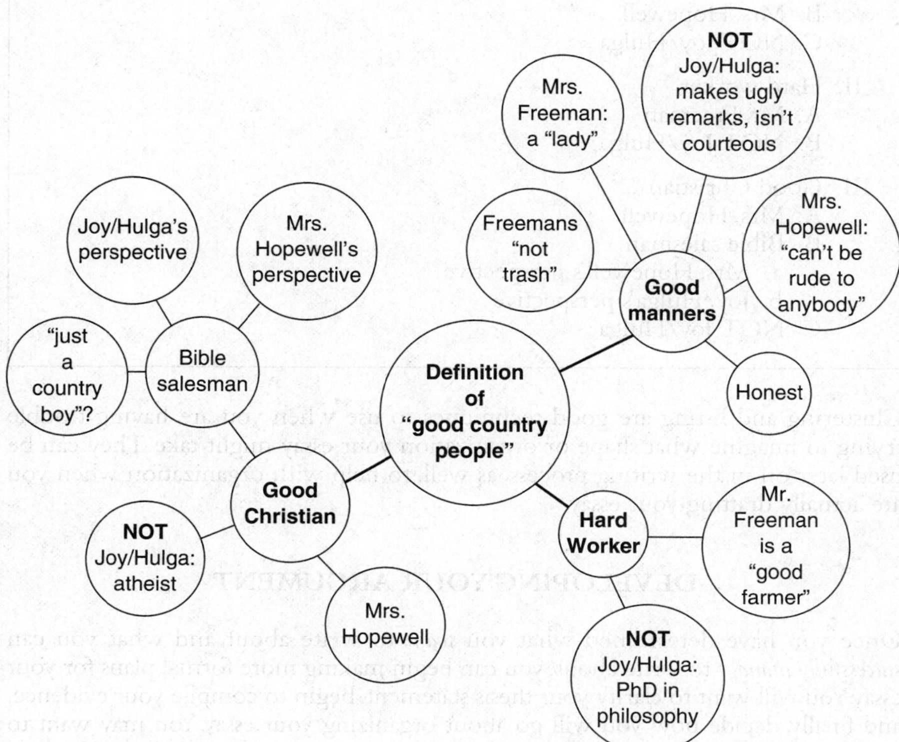

Figure 3.1 Clustering

use these "nuggets" as starting places for additional freewriting sessions, or you can move on to drafting your essay.

Making Clusters or Lists

If you are a spatial thinker, you may want to try prewriting by clustering or listing. A cluster begins with an initial box or bubble, in which you write the topic or the idea that you hope to develop. (You may want to begin with the "nuggets" from your brainstorming or freewriting.) As ideas occur to you, write them in their own boxes or bubbles and connect them with lines to the existing ideas with which they are most closely associated. A cluster might look something like our example of such an exercise.

A list, on the other hand, looks more like an outline:

Topic: Definition of "good country people"

I. Good manners
  A. Freemans
    a. Mrs. Freeman
    b. Freeman girls
  B. Mrs. Hopewell
  C. NOT Joy/Hulga

II. Hard worker
  A. Mr. Freeman
  B. NOT Joy/Hulga

III. Good Christian
  A. Mrs. Hopewell
  B. Bible salesman
    a. Mrs. Hopewell's perspective
    b. Joy/Hulga's perspective
  C. NOT Joy/Hulga

Clustering and listing are good techniques to use when you are having trouble trying to imagine what shape or organization your essay might take. They can be used later on in the writing process, as well, to help with organization when you are actually drafting your essay.

DEVELOPING YOUR ARGUMENT

Once you have determined what you *want* to write about and what you can *successfully manage* to write about, you can begin making more formal plans for your essay. You will want to clarify your thesis statement, begin to compile your evidence, and finally, decide how you will go about organizing your essay. You may want to begin by looking through your prewriting for passages, words, and dialogue that you have already noted as being significant. (See the "Strategies for Reading" sections in the following chapters for more prewriting ideas.)

Once you have settled on a preliminary working **thesis**, you will want to start finding evidence or support for that thesis. Although for some assignments you may do outside reading and research, any thesis about a piece of literature requires *textual support*. At this stage of the process, it is a good idea to go through your chosen text systematically, from beginning to end, to find quotations and pieces of text that can be used to support your thesis. (It is also useful to note evidence that contradicts your claim; close reading of this kind helps you refine and strengthen your essay's thesis!)

To help you discover and interpret textual support for your thesis, you might want to use a double-entry journal. (Although particularly useful for developing your argument once you have completed prewriting and settled on a working thesis, the double-entry journal can also be used as a reading aid or prewriting strategy.) To make a double-entry journal, simply draw a line down the middle of several sheets of paper and label one side "Evidence" and the other "Comment." As you reread the passage or passages you intend to write about, in the "Evidence" column write down every word, phrase, sentence, or passage (and any identifying page or line numbers) that applies to the *topic* of your paper. On the "Comment" side, briefly describe how the selected section fits into its text and add a brief description of how this word, phrase, or passage might relate to your paper's *purpose* or argument. You should collect *every* passage that clearly relates to your topic. For example, if you wanted to write on the topic of color in Hawthorne's short story, "Young Goodman Brown," making the claim that physical color can symbolize a character's moral nature, you would reread the story carefully, collecting every reference to color. As you collect quotations for the "Evidence" column, add comments in the "Comment" column, explaining how each reference to color fits within the story, noting interesting parallels or repetitions, and, if you spot a relationship at this point, jotting down thoughts about the way your "evidence" might correspond to your working thesis, that is, your overall intended purpose or argument; keep in mind the fact that your working thesis is only provisional and may change several times during the writing process.

Evidence	**Comment**
". . . letting the wind play with the *pink* ribbons of her cap while she called to Goodman *Brown*." (3)	This is the second sentence of the story and our first look at Faith. Faith has either put her head out the window or the door to give her husband a "parting kiss." Faith's color is pink? YGB is brown? What do these colors connote?
" 'Then God bless you!' said Faith, with the *pink* ribbons, . . ." (3)	Halfway down the first page, and again the pink ribbons are mentioned along with Faith.
". . . likeness of a great *black* snake . . ."	The next mention of a specific color (other than Brown's last name) is Goodman's companion's staff—which seems very lifelike—it "twist and wriggles." This is in the first really substantial paragraph after YGB meets his companion and very early in the story.

After you have sorted through and mulled over your textual evidence, it is time to devise a plan for structuring your argument. First, it is a good idea to revisit the essay's thesis, which may have changed some in the process of being developed and supported with textual evidence. Then you will need to decide how best to *organize* your essay in support of that thesis. Although every argument demands its own logical structure—which you may discover by looking back at your brainstorming sessions, lists, or clustering activities—different genres of literary essays have different modes of organization that traditionally are associated with them. (For some standard kinds of literary essay, see the end of this chapter.)

Many—although certainly not all—writers make an outline to guide the drafting process. Outlines vary from the barest of topical lists to a complete and complex map of a future essay's points. For more spatial or visual thinkers, listing and clustering can also be used to imagine an appropriate organization for an essay. Only you can tell whether an outline or other structuring device will help you organize your thoughts or simply stifle your creativity. If you *are* the kind of writer who benefits from having an outline, you can speed up the drafting process by using a word-processed outline as the backbone of your actual paper, constructing paragraphs and even topic sentences around the significant words and phrases in your outline.

DRAFTING YOUR ESSAY

Once you have a general plan for your essay and have gathered some initial evidence, you can begin shaping your ideas into a formal essay. (Note: At this point, you may want to turn off the automatic spelling and grammar checkers on your word-processing program so that you can concentrate on generating content rather than on surface-level editing.) Your anthology underlinings, reading notes, and double-entry notebook probably follow, in chronological order, the text's events and language; for each of these exercises, you start at the beginning and move on to the end of the story, poem, or play. Essays, by contrast, make an argument and are designed for a reader. For both of these reasons, unless your essay analyzes your own reading process, the organization of your essay should never simply follow the shape of your reading notes. You need to shape the essay as an argument.

While your thesis statement establishes your central argument, the body of your essay explains and supports your assertion. Just as the thesis statement provides the main idea for the essay, each paragraph should include a **topic sentence** that functions as a sort of "mini-thesis" for that paragraph. The topic sentence need not be the first sentence of the paragraph, although often it is. The rest of the paragraph should consist of supporting details, examples, and evidence to back up the topic sentence's claim *and* should provide your own explanations and interpretations of those supporting details. Generally, you should avoid ending paragraphs with a quotation. Remember, you are trying to convince your audience to accept *your* point of view, so you'll want to get into the habit of "having the last word" in each of your paragraphs. Avoiding quotations at the ends of paragraphs will also help you create more effective transitions between paragraphs.

Despite your planning, your first draft may end up looking a lot like your earlier freewriting. That's OK. As you begin to draft your essay, you may also discover that your ideas are changing or that you need additional evidence to support some of your assertions. Or, as we noted above, you may find your thesis changing in radical or subtle ways. That's OK, too. The drafting stage is still a stage of exploration, and you may compose several drafts before you have a document that even begins to resemble your final essay. Furthermore, because writing is a recursive, or circular, process, you may find yourself returning to the drafting stage several times throughout the course of generating the essay. In the age of word processing, you may be tempted just to tinker in places with your existing draft; but you should not be afraid to throw out, if necessary, large chunks of what you have produced or even to start over with a clean, blank document.

REVIEWING YOUR ESSAY

Once you have composed a fairly well-formed rough draft, get some distance from your writing so that when you return to it you can "re-view" it with fresh eyes. Imagine, if you can, that you are an outside reader, or that a member of your audience is reading over your shoulder and asking you questions. Try to see what kinds of connections are missing, what assumptions have been made that need to be stated outright, what points need further development or clarification, and what assertions need more support. At this stage, you'll want to ensure that you haven't just retold, or **summarized**, the text or simply described the major events, but instead that you have offered to your readers some fresh perspective on or unique insight about the text. Generally, you can assume that your readers are fellow "students of literature" who are familiar with the text (though they may need to be reminded of key details) and who are hoping to learn or discover something about it that you have seen but that they have overlooked or have not considered.

You may find that your instructor will organize the members of your class into peer review groups so that you can receive the benefit of responses and comments from classmates who have engaged in the same intellectual process as you have. At this stage, you should ask your peer reviewer to concentrate on the larger issues of content and organization, rather than on surface details of grammar and punctuation. If your instructor has not assigned formal groups, you can still ask one of your classmates to review your draft and take on the role of an audience member. Remember to ask him or her to read critically, with an eye toward content and organization, rather than as a proofreader or copy editor. If your school has a Writing Center, it too can be a valuable resource. Be aware, however, that while the Writing Center tutors may help you find and recognize patterns of error, generally they will not proofread or edit your paper for you. Finally, don't forget that your instructor is also an experienced reader who is willing to schedule a conference with you to review and discuss your draft—just don't expect him or her to correct your paper or to tell you what grade he or she thinks you will earn on it!

REVISING YOUR ESSAY

Once your rough draft has been reviewed thoroughly, you can begin revising your essay. Revision often takes place over several drafts or stages. Most writers cannot focus on all facets of writing at once; it would also be a waste to polish sentences that later are deleted in order to tighten organization. Generally, you will want to focus first on the essay as a whole and then, for subsequent reviews and revisions, narrow your focus further to different sections of the paper (if your essay is long enough), paragraphs, and, finally, sentences and individual words. Using notes from your own review, peer reviewers, or your teacher as a starting place, ask yourself questions pertinent to the stage of review or revision in which you are engaged.

First, ask yourself if the focus of your essay is clear and if you have adequately developed and supported your points while keeping a particular audience in mind.

Remember, your task is not to provide "the right answer" to the topic, but rather, to provide a thoughtful interpretation of your chosen text that is sufficiently backed up by adequate and appropriate evidence, much of which will come directly from the literary text itself. You'll also want to ensure that your essay is well organized and that your sentences and paragraphs are well connected, with smooth transitions between ideas. Finally, look closely at your word and sentence choices. Are they appropriate and effective? Have you avoided vague generalizations and clichés? Have you been overly repetitious? Have you made an effort to vary your sentence structures to aid your readers' comprehension and to sustain their interest?

A particular convention of critical writing about literature is that both fictional events and the writing itself are referred to in the present tense. (When writing about literature, you should only use the past tense to refer to events in the text that took place in the past or to relate historical facts.) Most literature teachers also urge their students not to rely too heavily on the **passive voice**, which can make sentences loose and "flabby" and even encourage grammatical errors. You may also want to read your essay aloud to see how it sounds, or have someone else read it to you. Listen for places that seem awkward or wordy or areas that require further clarification. The more time that you give yourself, the more extensively you can revise.

Many writers use a checklist to focus their attention on specific features of their writing. Here is an example of such a checklist:

A Revision Checklist for Writing about Literature

1. The Essay
   - Is the thesis complete and does it adequately summarize the essay's argument?
   - Is the supporting evidence adequate and appropriate?
   - Is the essay well organized? Are any parts or paragraphs out of place?
2. The Paragraph
   - Are individual paragraphs complete and well developed? Are any too short or thin?
   - Do topic sentences reflect the main idea of each paragraph?
   - Are there strong and logical transitions between paragraphs?
3. The Sentence
   - Are your sentences well constructed? Are there any that are too long, too convoluted, or simply do not make sense?
   - Are fictional events and descriptions of writing described in the present tense?
   - Is there excessive use of passive voice?
4. The Word
   - Are any words or phrases incorrect or unidiomatic?
   - Are there vague generalizations and clichés?
   - Is the diction repetitive? Alternatively, does it sound like you rely too much on the thesaurus?

For any given assignment, however, you and your teacher may decide on other criteria than those listed above.

In the age of computing and word processors, revision is a much speedier and less burdensome process than it was in any time period between the age of manuscripts and the reign of the typewriter. But the same rules apply to revision as to drafting: don't be afraid to throw away words, sentences, even whole paragraphs; and don't be afraid, if necessary, simply to start over. Some very successful and thoughtful writers use successive drafts not only to change their thesis, but to rework, from the ground up, their ideas, organization, and sentences.

When revising, you can also use the word processor's flexibility to "see" your prose in a new and different light. For instance, try highlighting your thesis statement and topic sentences. Then copy and paste these sentences into a new document to create an ex-post-facto outline of your essay. (Indeed, many writers find the outline more useful for the revision than for the drafting stage.) When you read through this "skeleton" of your essay, you should be able to follow the logical thread of its argument. The ex-post-facto outline can help you find logical gaps in your argument, identify paragraphs that are out of place, and pinpoint weak transitions.

For later stages of revision, the word processor can help you develop stronger paragraphs. Use the "Enter" key to put a blank line between each paragraph. Look, first of all, to see if there are any paragraphs that are much shorter than any of the others. Are these paragraphs underdeveloped? Could they stand to have more support? To improve a weak, undeveloped paragraph, try adding a blank space after the topic sentence and another before the concluding sentence. Then fill in further analysis and evidence.

On the sentence level, you can use the word processor's highlighter function to isolate each sentence's main verb, making sure that you are describing events in the present tense and avoiding excessive use of the passive voice. You might want to check whether your sentences are varied in length, a quality that gives rhythm and voice to critical prose. Simply hit the "Enter" key after every period to put a hard return between each sentence. Your prose will now make a "bar graph" that indicates whether or not your sentences vary in length. Look especially hard at very long sentences to see if they should be revised or even just cut into two or more sentences. The great virtue of the word processor is its ability to support the writing process at the same time that it produces well-formed writing products, and you should take advantage of the machine's flexibility. Use your imagination to think up other ways to exploit the computer's flexibility and smooth visual surface to "re-view" and revise your writing.

A Note about Using and Incorporating Quotations

We discuss the research paper (and therefore the use of quotations from critical sources) in a later chapter, but because textual evidence is so important when writing about literature, it is worthwhile to talk briefly about using quotations as evidence and about incorporating quotations from literary texts into your essay. For literary essays, descriptions of literary events and direct quotations of a text generally provide evidence in support of *your* thesis. In other words, quotations should not overwhelm your own thoughts and statements. Look at your paragraphs. Is there more quotation than analysis? If so, your argument probably could use strengthening. Alternatively, by using some of the tactics outlined below, you might streamline your quotations. Because quotations exist to support *your* argument or analysis, only rarely do paragraphs begin with quotations, and, as noted earlier, paragraphs that end with quotations often end weakly and lack a suitable transition to the next paragraph. Think generally of units of support as consisting of "quotation + explanation of the quote's significance to the paragraph's argument."

You can alter the proportion of discussion to quotation within your paragraphs in a number of ways. **Quotations**, to state the obvious, can be either long or short. Long quotations are produced as indented block quotations, whereas shorter quotations are marked off with quotation marks, but integrated directly into your paragraph. You should save block quotations for passages that are important to your thesis and that will therefore receive extensive analysis or commentary. Shorter quotations generally are better than long ones, because they focus the reader's attention on the exact phrases, and even words, that you want to discuss.

One method is to **paraphrase** relatively unimportant portions of the passage under consideration and to quote only those phrases or words that are crucial to your argument. Look back, for instance, at the exemplary double-entry notebook on colors in "Young Goodman Brown" and imagine a paragraph that discusses the symbolic colors associated with Faith and Young Goodman Brown. In such a paragraph, we might find the following development from the first entry in our imaginary double-entry notebook:

> From the very beginning of the story, Faith and Young Goodman Brown are opposed to one another by the colors associated with their characters. As early as the second sentence, for instance, Faith kisses her husband goodbye, "letting the wind play with the pink ribbons of her cap while she call[s] to Goodman Brown" (3). At this early stage, Brown's name does not seem to be particularly symbolic, and Faith's pink ribbons are merely a descriptive detail. But as the story progresses, Faith is continually associated with the light color pink, while Brown's character takes on morally darker associations.

Note, first of all, that the author paraphrases rather than quotes less important background information (Faith is kissing her husband goodbye). Note as well that our author follows the quotation from Hawthorne with an explanation of its significance. Finally, look at how the quotation is "trimmed" so that it can be incorporated smoothly into the essay author's sentence, without a loss of comprehension or violation of normal grammar rules. If you want to check on whether your quotations make grammatical and logical sense in the context of your own sentence, eliminate the quotation marks (either mentally or physically) and read the sentence aloud. Does it sound like normal English?

Another way to incorporate quotations properly is to quote entire sentences, which are separated from the introductory prose by a colon—for instance,

> Not much further down the same page, the narrator's gaze focuses on the appearance of Young Goodman Brown's wife, even as he repeats her exact words: "'Then God bless you!' said Faith, with the pink ribbons" (3). While Faith evokes her faith, the narrator is distracted by her "pink ribbons."

One mistake that writers sometimes make is just to "drop in" quotations in their paragraphs as freestanding sentences. In the example above, replacing the colon with a period would make the quotation a separate sentence. We do not recommend this method of quotation because it makes it difficult for the reader to tell where your voice ends and the voice of the literary text begins. Using a colon to introduce the quotation serves as a visual reminder that the quotation is supporting *your* argument.

Occasionally you will need to make minor alterations in a quotation for the sake of clarity or grammatical correctness, and specific conventions exist for acknowledging these changes. Words eliminated from the beginning or end of a quotation do not require ellipses [. . .] to indicate that text has been excised. But if you take out words from the middle of a quote, indicate that excision with ellipsis marks in brackets—for example,

> Faith moved toward the door, "letting the wind play with the pink ribbons [. . .] while she called to Goodman Brown" (3).

If you change a word to make it fit grammatically into your sentence, put that word in brackets as well—for instance,

> As Faith moved toward the door, she "[let] the wind play with the pink ribbons of her cap while she called to Goodman Brown" (3).

Finally, if you really are interested in particular words and are doing a fair amount of quotation within a given paragraph, limit your direct quotation to those words:

> While in the second sentence of Hawthorne's story, Young Goodman "Brown"'s name seems merely conventional, we already get a sense that Faith's "pink ribbons" are symbolic of her inner self.

The conventions for incorporating and documenting quotations from different genres—poetry, short stories, and drama—will be covered in Chapter 10, "Literary Research and Documentation." But generally, the art of quotation consists of deciding what portions of a text need to be quoted directly; incorporating those quotations into your own prose intelligibly and grammatically; acknowledging through correct punctuation exactly what words of the author you are reproducing, changing, or eliminating; and varying the length and manner of introducing your quotations to keep your prose rhythm moving along in a pleasing manner.

EDITING AND PROOFREADING

Once you are satisfied with your argument, organization, content, and style, you will want to proofread your essay and edit it for grammar, mechanics, documentation style (see Chapter 10), and format (e.g., headings, page numbers, font size and type, line spacing). You might want to begin by running the spelling and grammar checkers on your word-processing program. Be cautious, however, about automatically accepting all of the suggested changes. Take note of the advice, and then use your own best judgment. Don't hesitate to crosscheck with your dictionary, grammar handbook, or instructor.

You might also try reading your essay from back to front, forcing yourself to stop and pay close attention to each sentence. Take a proactive interest in proofreading. If you know that you have trouble with commas, for example, circle every comma and then review the comma rules in your handbook. If you know that you have a tendency to overuse imprecise "to be" verbs, circle each one or use your word processor's "Find" function and then see if you can replace some of the "to be" verbs with stronger, more precise ones. Check your pronouns to make sure that each one has a clear antecedent. Ensure that you have properly documented all of your quotations and that you have introduced them or incorporated them within the context of the paragraph, rather than just dropping them in and expecting them to stand on their own. Check to see that you primarily have used the present tense when writing about the literary text. Finally, when you think that you have found every error you can in your essay, put the paper away for a couple of hours and then do one final proofreading. We guarantee that you will see mistakes and typos that you did not see before!

COMMON WRITING ASSIGNMENTS

In *Prentice Hall Literature Portfolio*, we consider writing as a mode both for learning about literature and for presenting arguments about literature to other readers. The chapters on reading and writing in different genres consider writing from both perspectives and talk about writing projects that are particularly congenial to a given genre. In this introductory chapter, we have focused more generally on the writing process and on the traditional, thesis-driven essay frequently assigned in literature classrooms. So that you can understand the assignments your teacher gives to you, we conclude by taking a look at some common subgenres of the literary essay.

Response Essay

As you were reading, you responded and reacted to the story or stories in particular ways. A response essay offers you an opportunity to make connections between the text and your reactions to it. As an individual reader, you bring a unique perspective to the story based on your personal history and experiences. Your purpose in a response essay is to show your audience the particular meaning that the literary text held for you, based on your distinctive characteristics (age, gender, race, religion, class, hobbies, location, etc.). When composing a **reader-response** essay, you analyze your reactions and the elements of the story that induced your response, and you try to convince your audience that they ought to take your reading into consideration and understand the story from your perspective.

Analysis

When you write an essay of analysis, you scrutinize the text by focusing generally on a *single* element (e.g., **plot, setting, character, theme, symbolism**, language). For example, you might choose to write about how one particular character contributes to the resolution of conflict in a story, how a poet's word choice influences how the poem is interpreted, or how a particular dramatic scene sets in motion the events that occur throughout the rest of a play. Although your **thesis statement** will focus on the function of one particular element, you should also demonstrate how your analysis of that single feature contributes to the meaning of the work as a whole. Remember, your thesis should be disputable, and an analysis is not merely a summary or paraphrase of the text.

Evaluation

An essay of evaluation focuses on assessing the effectiveness of the literary text. You will judge the text's effectiveness by gauging it against certain standards within the genre. You might determine, for instance, that a particular short story fails to be effective because its characters or situations are unbelievable or because its plot is insufficiently developed; alternatively, you might argue that a poem fails to carry sufficient impact due to its forced and artificial rhyme scheme. You might also evaluate the strength or weakness of a text's expression of certain values or themes.

Comparison and Contrast

A comparison-and-contrast essay requires you to compare and contrast two works in terms of their similarities and differences. (See "Strategies for Writing about Poems" in Chapter 6 for more suggestions about writing a comparison-and-contrast essay.) Although the point may be self-evident, this genre of essay works only when the two texts genuinely have something in common. The "loosest," although still legitimate, form of comparison is based on thematic similarities. Comparing two love poems, for instance, or two short stories that deal with loss of faith would be a thematic comparison. More tightly focused comparisons might be two poems by the same author or a comparison of Renaissance and contemporary uses of the **sonnet** form. Another intriguing form of comparison involves the influence of one author on another, or even an author's deliberate imitation of, response to, or **parody** of an earlier work.

Although you will want to evaluate your comparisons and contrasts within the context of the complete texts, you will probably want to focus your essay on a particular element, such as the psychological impact of death in Edgar Allan Poe's "The Cask of Amontillado" and Faulkner's "A Rose for Emily" or the role played by father figures in "A Rose for Emily" and Theodore Roethke's "My Papa's Waltz." (See Chapter 11, "Reading and Writing Intertextually and across Genres" for more ideas about comparing and contrasting works from different genres.) As you proceed through your essay, you may choose to treat first one text and then the other in alternating paragraphs, or you may choose to examine a particular feature of both texts within each paragraph. Regardless of your organizational pattern, however, your essay must go beyond simply pointing out similarities and differences between two or more texts; it must use the comparison to draw some conclusions about the works; that is, your essay must have an argumentative **thesis**.

Writing from a Particular Critical Stance

From about 1970 on, literary criticism has exploded into a variety of "schools" or methods of criticism: **feminist** and gender criticism, **psychoanalytic criticism, archetypal criticism**, **Marxist criticism**, stylistics, **reader-response** or subjective criticism, deconstruction, performance or reception study, New Historical criticism, and so on. Each of these schools has a particular focus or critical method. For example, feminist critics examine the way stereotypes about and cultural conditions of women have impacted the writers, the writing, and the reception of literary texts; such a stance might be useful for writing about stories such as Kate Chopin's "The Story of an Hour" or Adrienne Rich's "Diving into the Wreck." Reader response, or subjective, critics turn their focus away from the text and the author and, instead, turn their attention to the reader's response to a text. Archetypal or Jungian critics draw out the universal, "archetypal" motifs and characters in stories and poems across cultures. An archetypal critic might compare the traditional motif of the **bildungsroman**, or coming of age story, in James Joyce's "Araby" and John Updike's "A&P." Marxist critics might focus on the class differences that literature exposes—think, for instance, of Toni Cade Bambara's "The Lesson." Performance or reception critics focus on the way a particular work's performance or reception has varied over time. If you choose to write from one of these critical stances, you'll need to spend some time familiarizing yourself with the methods of criticism used by the particular critical school of thought, and you'll want to read some essays that have been written from that particular critical perspective. Confer with your instructor on how best to go about this familiarization process.

Research

A research assignment requires you to find information about the story from sources other than the original text and to incorporate this information from outside sources into your essay. For example, you might conduct some additional research on the biography of the writer or the historical period in which the story is set, or you might read existing critical essays about the story and use these interpretations to broaden your assessment or to serve as counterarguments to your reading. For more ideas about how to write a research essay, see "Writing about Poetry with Research" in Chapter 6. To learn more about the processes of literary research and documentation in general, see Chapter 10.

CONCLUSION

Whatever kinds of essays you write, we hope that the experience of writing about literature will bring you both pleasure and knowledge. Part of the fun of studying literature comes from mastering the craft of writing about it and thus of engaging with other readers in lively argument and dialogue. Writing about literature allows you to share your pleasure and insights with a wider audience and, at the same time, to grow as an individual.

CHAPTER 4

Reading and Writing about Short Stories

A story can serve as "an axe to break up the frozen sea within us."
—Franz Kafka

Telling stories helps us "arrive at some kind of spiritual truth that one can't discover simply by recording the world-as-it-is. We're inventing and using the imagination for sublime reasons—to get at the essence of things, not merely the surface."
—Tim O'Brien

INTRODUCTION

Telling stories is an intrinsic part of all human cultures. In all likelihood, soon after our ancestors began to speak, and certainly long before they began to write, they started telling stories—stories that explained natural events, stories about their skirmishes and hunts, and stories about their origins. You, too, probably began to tell stories soon after you began to speak—stories about how you went to visit your grandparents or stories about how the dog, and not you, knocked over the lamp. Furthermore, some of your earliest memories may be of bedtime stories and fairy tales. In other words, the concept of stories and storytelling is familiar to you, as is the sense that stories are different from other **genres** of literature, such as poems and plays.

WHAT IS A SHORT STORY?

Many of the earliest forms of oral narratives were **myths** that helped the storytellers and their listeners describe and attempt to understand themselves and the world around them. Chinua Achebe's story "Why the Tortoise's Shell is Not Smooth" is an example of a myth that, like other myths, unscientifically, yet imaginatively, explains why something in the world is the way that it is; in this case, the story explains why tortoises' shells are ridged and bumpy.

Other early storytellers were less concerned with explaining natural phenomena and more concerned with providing lessons about human behavior. The stories they told, called **parables**, impart religious or spiritual guidance; their lessons, often not overtly stated, are rewarding, yet difficult, to untangle. Isaac Bashevis Singer's short story "Gimpel the Fool," for example, can be read as a parable of faith because

Gimpel meets each act of deceit, betrayal, and ridicule steadfastly, and, despite his cruel treatment by others, accepts these trials while maintaining his faith in his religion, in his God, and in basic human goodness.

Unlike parables, **fables** are meant to be transparent, with explicitly stated "aha!" lessons in their endings, as in the well-known tales of Aesop. Fables often feature animals with human characteristics and present lessons about everyday behavior or manners rather than offering nonspecific spiritual advice.

Fairy tales and **folktales** frequently explore cultural fears, rituals, or superstitions or are designed to combat them, often drawing on fantastic elements such as giants and witches, extraordinary transformations, or legendary heroes. Gabriel Garcia Marquez's story "The Handsomest Drowned Man in the World" incorporates several aspects of fantasy and magic, as do the stories about María Sabida in Judith Ortiz Cofer's story "Tales Told under the Mango Tree."

Although storytelling has been around for thousands of years, prose fictions (such as novels, novellas, and short stories) were not "officially" recognized as literary forms until relatively recently. Early works of written literature were usually composed in **verse** (poems) or **dialogue** (plays), and it was not until the late eighteenth century that the novel emerged in England as a distinctive literary form (Hoffman and Murphy 4–5).

Once prose fiction established its place alongside the previously privileged forms of poetry and drama, however, it quickly gained status and popularity, which may be why so many of us today think first of novels when we think of "literature." Although the novel had its origins in England, the short story is considered the first literary genre to be "invented" in America. Perhaps this explains why Americans often find short stories to be the most familiar and accessible genre of literature. Because you are probably already fairly comfortable with this fictional form, we have chosen to begin your exploration of literary genres with Nathaniel Hawthorne's and Edgar Allan Poe's "tales" from the late nineteenth century, which are often considered to be the original American short stories.

ELEMENTS OF SHORT STORIES

Short stories share with poetry an economy of scale in which every detail counts. Writer Grace Paley contends that short stories "are closer to poetry than they are to the novel because they are shorter, and second, because they are more concentrated, more economical" (Charters). On the other hand, short stories, like novels, are written in prose rather than verse and share many narrative techniques with the novel. Short stories concentrate these techniques by focusing on a single episode or on a series of connected events, or, in some cases, by focusing on a principal character—a character experiencing a change, a **conflict**, or a unique experience. Writer Margaret Atwood compares writing short stories to telling **riddles** and jokes, since all three require "the same mystifying buildup, the same surprising twist, the same impeccable sense of timing" (quoted in Charters and Charters 33). This is not to say, however, that all short stories involve a conflict or a "twist," nor that they all end with tidy resolutions of the action or with the main character experiencing some kind of enlightenment or momentous change. In fact, many present-day short story authors consciously resist these neat conclusions, conveying, instead, the uncertainties of contemporary society (see, for example, Louise Erdrich's "The Red Convertible" and John Edgar Wideman's "What We Cannot Speak About We Must Pass Over in Silence"). Even so, most short stories do share several basic elements; the most common of these elements—setting, plot, character, point of view, style, and theme—are explained below.

Setting

The historical time, the social and cultural situation, and the environment in which the actions of a story take place establish its **setting**. By creating a vivid setting, the author creates certain expectations for the readers. In other words, the general setting of the story, as well as the specific settings of the fictional events, provide the readers with a mental picture of the places and the characters they are about to encounter. Think of the opening sequence of the *Star Wars* movies, for example. When we see the words "A long time ago, in a galaxy far, far away" scroll past us into the vastness of space, we assume that the events we are about to witness will involve alien beings and space travel.

The setting also places limits on the characters' options and opportunities for action. The story "Gimpel the Fool," for example, is set in an imaginary, small, rural Jewish village (or *shtetl*). Consequently, Gimpel must abide by the customs of that religious community, such as obtaining the approval of the rabbis before making many of his decisions.

Finally, the setting provides an **atmosphere** or **mood** for the story. Think about how the comic strip character Snoopy tries to create dramatic intensity and a sense of mystery by beginning all of his stories with the clichéd phrase "It was

Oak tree and barn in fog

a dark and stormy night . . ." A similarly intense and foreboding mood is created in this description of the Salinas Valley from the opening paragraphs of John Steinbeck's story "The Chrysanthemums":

> The high grey-flannel fog of winter closed off the Salinas Valley from the sky and from all the rest of the world. On every side it sat like a lid on the mountains and made of the great valley a closed pot . . . there was no sunshine in the valley now in December. . . . It was a time of quiet and of waiting.

As you read this description, can you imagine yourself drawing your neck down deeper into your collar to combat the effects of the fog, and do you start to wonder what might await those who are still and patient? Contrast this somber mood with the homey and secure atmosphere described at the beginning of Alice Walker's story "Everyday Use," where the narrator stands in a yard that "is more comfortable than most people know. It is not just a yard. It is like an extended living room." Doesn't this "extended living room" sound like a more welcoming place than the "closed pot" of Steinbeck's story?

Plot

The **plot** of a story consists of the sequence of events or narrative episodes that give the story its shape and that help you understand *what* is happening and *why* it is happening. A typical romance plot might go something like this: boy meets girl, boy falls in love with girl, boy performs heroic actions to win girl's heart, girl falls in love with boy, girl marries boy, girl and boy live "happily ever after."

In a short story, the plot is tightly constructed, and the events are carefully selected and presented so that the reader can quickly make sense of the unfolding action, although not always on a first reading. Some plots, such as the plot of Judith Ortiz Cofer's story "Arturo's Flight," adhere closely to the traditional sequence of establishing a background for the action (Arturo's sense of entrapment in his school and home), describing a primary setting (a New York tenement and an old church), developing a series of actions (Arturo's escape from the tenement to the church, his memory of his poetry recital, his decision to toss his Shakespeare text in the dumpster), leading to a **climax** or turning point (listening to Johann's life story), and finally creating a series of actions (recovering Shakespeare from the dumpster) that lead to a **resolution** ("Revenge, Shakespearean-style"). Few short story plots, however, abide strictly by this pattern. For example, the series of events may not be presented in chronological order. The characters may have **flashbacks** to prior moments, as happens in Anton Chekhov's story "Vanka," William Faulkner's "A Rose for Emily," and Trudy Lewis's "Limestone Diner." The story also might not lead to a turning point or a resolution at all, as in Jamaica Kincaid's story "Girl," in which the reader never finds out whether or not the daughter heeds her mother's advice. As you read a story, try to note any places where the plot structure deviates from the standard pattern and ask yourself what might be the effect of that deviation.

Character

Characters are those fictional persons who engage in the events that take place in the story. Although these characters are generally humans, they may be animals, such as the tortoise in Achebe's "Why the Tortoise's Shell is Not Smooth" or the bug, Gregor Samsa, in Franz Kafka's "Metamorphosis." An inanimate object may be **anthropomorphized**, or given the characteristics of a human, and take an active role in determining the course of events in the story, as do the discarded flowers in Steinbeck's "The Chrysanthemums" and the dumpster (the "green monster") in Ortiz Cofer's "Arturo's Flight." In these stories, the objects transform from simple background components into agents with recognizable human or animal qualities.

Typically, characters are identified according to certain principles. One distinction among characters was made by E. M. Forster, an English author and literary critic in the late nineteenth and early twentieth centuries. In his work *Aspects of the Novel*, he distinguishes between *static* (or flat) characters and *dynamic* (or round) characters. A **static character** is one-dimensional and remains relatively unchanged throughout the story. A **dynamic character**, on the other hand, is multidimensional and complex, often undergoing some sort of change as the story progresses. In John Steinbeck's "The Chrysanthemums," Elisa is a dynamic character whereas the traveling salesman is static.

Minor or **secondary characters**—characters described with fewer details since they partake in less of the action—may contribute to the plot as well. Some minor characters serve to highlight and emphasize the principal characters' habits and behaviors (e.g., Elisa's husband Henry in "The Chrysanthemums," who wonders at the change in her demeanor and pointedly asks, "What's the matter, Elisa?"), whereas others act as **foils**, or contrasts, to the main characters (e.g., the baker's apprentice in Singer's "Gimpel the Fool" who, unlike Gimpel, is able to sleep with and impregnate Gimpel's wife, Elka). Of course, sometimes minor characters are included only to contribute to the verisimilitude, or "realness," of the setting (e.g., shoppers in a market, restaurant staff, and prison guards).

An important distinction is also made between the **protagonist**—the central character with whom the reader is meant to empathize—and the **antagonist**, or the character who opposes the protagonist. The differences between them are not always clear, however, for your sympathies may change as the story develops or after you complete a second or third reading.

Point of View

Point of view concerns the manner in which a story is told, the viewpoint through which you encounter and experience a story's setting, characters, plot, or other details. One of the most common ways to present the various elements of a story is through the use of a **narrator**.

A **third-person narrator** recounts the details from a position outside the story, referring to the characters by name or, more generally, by pronouns such as "he," "she," or "they." A third-person narrator may be **omniscient**, or in other words, a narrator who has access to the internal thoughts and feelings of *all* the characters and who can observe and comment on events happening in more than one place or at more than one time. In contrast, a **limited-omniscient narrator** only has access the thoughts and feelings of one or two characters. The narrator of Franz Kafka's "The Metamorphosis," for example, has access to Gregor's thoughts, but can only report on the external actions and dialogue of the other characters. Finally, a **limited narrator** has no access to the internal thoughts and feelings of the characters at all and only observes, reports, and comments on the characters' external actions and speeches.

A **first-person narrator** uses the pronoun "I" when speaking about him- or herself. However, the first-person narrator and the author of the story should not be equated with one another automatically, since stories are fictional accounts, not autobiographies. Although authors may draw on personal experience to help define some of the characters or describe some of the settings and events, they primarily use their imagination to create stories. Think of the disclaimers that you see at the beginnings of some films and TV shows: "The characters and events in this story are purely fictional, and any resemblance to actual people and/or events is purely coincidental." In addition, a first-person account is necessarily subjective, limited by the narrator's observations and experiences, so, as a reader, you must make a judgment about his or her trustworthiness as a storyteller and consider his or her motivations for including or excluding certain details. A **reliable narrator** is a narrator who can be trusted to observe and report events accurately without obvious bias. A reliable narrator generally shares the values of the author and the reader and thus gains your trust and sympathy. An **unreliable narrator**'s account, on the other hand, cannot be accepted at face value either because he is too naïve, inexperienced, or mentally unbalanced to give an accurate report or because she has an ulterior motive for distorting events.

Style

How a story is written—the words, sentence structures, and grammatical constructions the author chooses, and the language characters use to express themselves—determines a story's **style**. Think about the differing answers you might get from two friends after asking them about a movie they just saw. The first might respond to your question, "How was the movie?" with a simple, "Good. You should see it." The other friend, however, might gush, "It was amazing! The cinematography was spectacular! The characters were truly three-dimensional, and the soundtrack rocked!" Both of these responses might convince you to go see the movie yourself, but the second response is clearly more detailed and expressive.

Now compare these two descriptions of setting:

> It was late and every one had left the café except an old man who sat in the shadow the leaves of the tree made against the electric light. In the day time the street was dusty, but at night the dew settled the dust. . . .

> It was a big, squarish frame house that had once been white, decorated with cupolas and spires and scrolled balconies in the heavily lightsome style of the seventies, set on what had once been our most select street. But garages and cotton gins had encroached and obliterated even the august names of that neighborhood; only Miss Emily's house was left, lifting its

> stubborn and coquettish decay above the cotton wagons and the gasoline pumps—an eyesore among eyesores.

The first example, from Ernest Hemingway's story "A Clean, Well-Lighted Place," uses simple words and sentences that are strung together by repeated use of the connector "and." The second example, from William Faulkner's "A Rose for Emily," uses more sophisticated vocabulary and more complex sentences composed of numerous added clauses and phrases. Notice how, although both descriptions effectively provide the reader with a mental image of a specific place, their varying diction and grammar also suggest something about the characters in the scenes. Hemingway's details are sparse and straightforward, reflecting the old man's isolation, whereas Faulkner's vivid, colorful comparison of Miss Emily's house to the others on the street emphasizes her decrepitude and peculiarity.

Style is also reflected in the language that the characters use. Compare these two excerpts of dialogue:

> My love and my Faith, of all nights in the year, this one night I must tarry away from thee.

> Hey, I'm going to buy that there.
> That there? You don't even know what it is, stupid.
> I do so . . . It's a microscope.
> Whatcha gonna do with a microscope, fool?

The first excerpt, from Nathaniel Hawthorne's "Young Goodman Brown," is fittingly formal and biblical for a nineteenth-century Puritan. The second example, from Toni Cade Bambara's "The Lesson," appropriately reflects an informal, slightly mocking, conversation between two young, urban, African American schoolchildren in the late twentieth century. Consider the fact that you wouldn't write a letter of application for a job in the same way that you would write an instant message to a friend ("thx 4 havin yr ppl look at my app. i no this job'll b gr8"). Likewise, imagine how strange and unrealistic the two preceding conversations would sound if the characters' grammar, diction, and rhythm of speaking were reversed.

Theme

The **theme** of a story is a synopsis of the central idea (or ideas) that it explores and the issues that it raises. The theme should not be confused with the plot, which is the sequence of events that make up the action of the story. The theme is the implicit or underlying topic of a story that offers insight into the world or reveals something about humanity. In both "Young Goodman Brown" and "Gimpel the Fool," for example, spiritual faith is a central theme; each story allows us to consider how faith affects Goodman Brown's and Gimpel's lives and how the presence or absence of faith might also affect our own lives and the lives of our leaders, our enemies, and our friends. Of course, a story may have more than one theme, and the theme(s) may not always be readily accessible; in these cases, readers and critics have to infer the thematic concerns from the story. Even when the themes seem obvious, however, readers and critics may disagree about how the theme(s) should be interpreted.

STRATEGIES FOR READING SHORT STORIES

Now that you have learned more about what short stories are and about the elements from which they are constructed, you are ready to think about how to go about reading the stories you have been assigned. We hope that you will get as much enjoyment from reading these stories as you did from listening to the bedtime stories and fairy tales of your childhood and from reading novels, stories, comic books, magazines, and Web sites of your own choosing. However, you will be doing more than simply reading and enjoying the short stories in this collection; you will be studying the stories as you read, engaging actively with their texts, discussing them with your classmates and instructor, and preparing to write about them in a thoughtful way. You will need to read these stories carefully, and you'll want to read them more than once or twice. This more intensive kind of reading requires effort, but the rewards will be well worth it. As the philosopher John Locke noted, "Reading furnishes the mind with materials of knowledge; it is thinking that makes what we read ours" (quoted in Barnet and Bedau 33). Here are some suggestions for how you can go about reading a short story in order to make it "yours."

Head Notes

A good place to begin your reading process is with the head notes that precede each of the selections. The head notes provide an initial context for your reading by presenting some biographical information about the author: you may find it helpful, for instance, to know that Nathaniel Hawthorne was raised in a Puritan household or that Flannery O'Connor was a Catholic Southerner. The head notes also provide some information about common aspects of the author's works: you will discover, for example, that Katherine Anne Porter's fiction often features strong female figures who struggle for independence in a predominately male society and that Edgar Allan Poe's short stories are famous for their **gothic** settings. The head notes, of course, cannot replace a close and careful reading of the whole story, but they can give you some preliminary hints about the elements and ideas that you might want to keep an eye out for, especially on your first reading.

Annotating the Text

The first time you read a story, you will probably want to read it straight through from beginning to end so that you can establish "the big picture" before you go back to do a closer, more critical reading. In preparation for your critical reading, make sure that you have a pencil or pen close at hand. As long as you have purchased this text, you are welcome to write in it as you please (don't worry, you can still return it as a used book at the end of the class if you want to!). As you read, write notes to yourself in the margins, or, if you prefer, write your comments on sticky notes and attach them to the margins of the text instead. Record your reactions and responses. Jot down questions. Note turning points or other important plot shifts (for more ideas about creating **marginalia**, see "Strategies for Reading Poetry" in Chapter 6). Underline passages that seem particularly important, particularly confusing, or particularly revealing, and highlight key words, descriptions, and dialogue. Circle words or phrases that are unfamiliar to you, look them up in a dictionary, and jot down brief definitions in the margins or on a sticky note so that you remember them later. These annotations will not only help you engage with the text and participate in class discussions, but also serve as a mode of **prewriting**, or early, informal, idea-generating writing.

Keep a Reading Journal

Since your marginal annotations will necessarily be limited, you probably will want to have a place in which you can develop your ideas more fully, add depth to your analyses, and record answers to your questions: A reading journal serves as an informal writing space for just such purposes. In addition to expanding on your marginal notes, you may want to record or list information about each of the formal elements of the story: setting, plot, characters, point of view, style, and theme(s). You may want to pull out and list key words or significant quotes from the text. You can also use some of the pages in your reading journal for the double-entry notes mentioned in Chapter 3. These notes will be helpful later as you compile supporting evidence for your formal essay.

You can also interact and familiarize yourself with the text by writing a **summary** or **paraphrase** (see "Strategies for Writing about Poems" in Chapter 6 to learn more about other innovative ways to "rewrite" a text, such as parodying and creative responses). You might think of a summary as a shortened version of the story that could be told to someone in the time it takes to ride up a long escalator in a large department store or in an airport terminal. A paraphrase, on the other hand, might be as long as the original story, but it is composed in your own words. Like your marginal annotations, the reading journal will serve as an important piece of prewriting as you approach the formal writing stage.

WAYS OF WRITING ABOUT SHORT STORIES

You may have noticed that the reading strategies discussed above already involve quite a bit of writing. The writing that you do to assist your close and careful reading is informal, however, and only preparatory to the formation of an essay. As we mentioned in Chapter 3, you may be given a list of essay topics by your instructor, or you may be asked to devise an essay topic on your own. In Chapter 3, we also introduced you to some common essay assignments. The following are some suggestions for using those general assignments to write about short stories specifically.

Writing about Plots

Plots are tricky subjects for critical papers, and when we try to explore plot in essays, we can fall into the trap of merely summarizing the story. Ask yourself two questions when you begin to examine a story's plot for potential paper topics: What are the important conflicts in the story? What is causing these conflicts? If the answers are not immediately obvious, or if your answers are obviously arguable, you may have an excellent paper topic on plot. Prepare for writing a paper about a story's plot by drawing a timeline that places the story's major events into a chronology that corresponds with "real time" and then one that follows "story time," or if you are more visually inclined, you could sketch a "storyboard" like the ones used to illustrate and summarize movie plots for directors. You can use the timeline or storyboard to help you remember to incorporate key plot developments in your essay much as you would use the double-entry journal recommended in Chapter 3.

In your introductory paragraph, you should name the conflict that you will examine and explain why this particular conflict is a key to understanding the story's underlying theme. In the body, you need to describe each plot point that contributes to this conflict and explain how the causes of the conflict, its participants, their responses, and the ways in which the conflict is either resolved or not *all* point toward an underlying theme. If you remember to stay focused on conflict, you will remain close to the plot.

Focusing on a Character

Many times when you read a short story, your imagination or interest is captured by a particular character, and if so you may want to select this character as the focus of an analytic essay. Because your analysis must be organized around an argumentative thesis that is supported by evidence from the text, it must go beyond a simple description of the character's traits or a summary of the character's actions.

A character analysis might proceed inductively; that is, you might begin by introducing the specific example of one or more of the character's traits and proceed to use your examination of this character's growth or education to draw a general conclusion about the work as a whole. A character analysis might also proceed sequentially, following the plot of the story closely to demonstrate that the character fails to develop or gain insight, a failure which, in turn, mirrors the overall theme of the story.

Studies of characters also lend themselves readily to comparison-and-contrast essays. You might focus your comparison on a particular type of character, such as fathers, mothers, workers, travelers, or athletes. You might also choose to compare and contrast two characters facing similar conflicts who resolve their conflicts in different ways. As with the analysis essay, a comparison-and-contrast essay should be driven by an argumentative thesis. It should use the supporting evidence of the similarities and differences between the characters to assert a particular claim: that one of the characters is more believable or more sympathetic than the other, for example.

Finally, because characters often narrate the stories in which they participate, character studies often provide good starting points for essays about point of view. Review the section above on identifying point of view. If the point of view is hard to pinpoint, confusing, shifting, influenced by the personality or motives of the narrating character, or in any way surprising, you may have already identified an interesting paper topic. Your essay will reveal the narrative point of view as it operates in a story's key passages and will also provide an argument that explains how and in what way this point of view influences the story's theme.

Examining a Theme

Earlier, we admitted to you that readers and critics often disagree on the overall purpose or theme of a story. Such disagreements lend themselves readily to argumentative essays. In an essay that examines a story's theme, you try to convince your audience that your understanding of the prevailing theme is valid. In the body of the essay, you will show how the other elements of the story (plot, characters, setting) contribute to the development of the theme. To conclude, you may want to make a claim about the effect the theme has on the readers of the story. It may, for instance, dismantle stereotypes or strengthen deep-rooted beliefs. To begin your study of a story's theme, pay particularly close attention to the opening and closing words and sentences of the story and to the story's title; more often than not, short story authors address key issues, themes, and conflicts in these parts of their creation.

Considering the Historical Context

Each of the stories that you will read was written in a specific time period and location, and may therefore reflect or defy prevailing social attitudes, political situations, economic conditions, or environmental circumstances of the times. If a character has a particular mindset or takes a position on an issue that you find offensive or mystifying, you could do research about the historical context of the story and argue that although the character may have acted within the acceptable social norms of his or her day, such actions ought to be censured today. Or you might make an argument about how similar characters living in a different period would have behaved differently. Be sure to consult your teacher or a reference librarian who can help you find resources that will help you characterize a particular time period with regard to its political, social, economic, and environmental values.

CONCLUSION

After reading this chapter, you should realize that you have taken part in listening to, reading, and discussing various types of literature or stories since your infancy. In this chapter, we have also introduced you to some literary terms to help you discuss the anthologized stories in a more formal manner and have provided you with some writing strategies to help you organize your thoughts and present them to your audience with a specific purpose in mind. These tools should assist you in your role as a "student of literature" as you contribute your arguments to the ongoing critical conversation about these literary texts.

WORKS CITED

Barnet, Sylvan, and Hugo Bedau, eds. *Current Issues and Enduring Questions*. 7th ed. Boston: Bedford/St. Martin's, 2005.

Charters, Ann. "Grace Paley: Open Destiny of Life." 2004. *PEN American Center*. 11 May 2005. <http://www.pen.org/viewmedia.php/prmMID/98/prmID/515>.

Charters, Ann, and Samuel Charters, eds. *Literature and Its Writers*. Boston: Bedford/St. Martin's, 2004.

Hoffman, Michael, and Patrick Murphy, eds. *Essentials of the Theory of Fiction*. Durham, NC: Duke UP, 1988.

CHAPTER 5

An Anthology of Short Stories

NATHANIEL HAWTHORNE (1804–1864) was born in Salem, Massachusetts on July 4, an appropriately American holiday for someone whose ancestors had been among the first to settle in the "New World" and who is regarded among the first distinctly American writers. The influences of Hawthorne's Puritan ancestors and New England upbringing are reflected clearly in his writing. He was especially interested in the limitations of postlapsarian (after the fall in the Garden of Eden) human beings and in humankind's inherently sinful nature. Rather than distinguishing clearly between good and evil, Hawthorne's fiction explores the significance of this dualism, especially for individuals who cannot reconcile this ambiguity within themselves or their fellow human beings and thus become isolated from the larger human community. Hawthorne's works often incorporate supernatural and **mythical** elements, and many can be read as **allegories**.

Hawthorne graduated from Bowdoin College in 1825 and began his career as a writer soon after. He submitted his stories to various periodicals, and his first collection of stories, *Twice Told Tales,* was published in 1837. His next collection of "tales" was published as *Mosses from an Old Manse* in 1846. Although he was a prolific short story writer and children's author, he may be best known for his novel *The Scarlet Letter*, published in 1850. Hawthorne's skill as a writer was lauded by Herman Melville, and he received as well positive reviews from Edgar Allan Poe and Henry Wadsworth Longfellow. Of Hawthorne, Melville wrote in a review of *Mosses* that he possessed "a great, deep intellect" along with a "great power of blackness."[1]

This blackness manifests itself in both of the **allegorical** tales included here. In "Young Goodman Brown" (1846), the "good man" of the title journeys into the blackness of the forest and, after witnessing an evil ceremony that implicates his wife, Faith, in sin, he returns from the journey with blackness in his soul. Like Young Goodman Brown, the character of the scientist in "The Birthmark" (1843) wants the central female character of the story to be pure and flawless; therefore, he cannot abide by her physical imperfection, the "crimson hand" that marks her cheek.

Related Works: Everyman; Blake, "The Lamb" and "The Tiger"; Singer, "Gimpel the Fool"; Garcia, "Why I Left the Church"; Ibsen, *A Dollhouse.*

NOTE

1. Herman Melville, review of Nathaniel Hawthorne, *Mosses from an Old Manse, The Literary World*, 17 (24 August, 1850): 243.

Young Goodman Brown

Young Goodman Brown came forth at sunset into the street of Salem village; but put his head back, after crossing the threshold, to exchange a parting kiss with his young wife. And Faith, as the wife was aptly named, thrust her own pretty head into the street, letting the wind play with the pink ribbons of her cap while she called to Goodman Brown.

"Dearest heart," whispered she, softly and rather sadly, when her lips were close to his ear, "prithee put off your journey until sunrise and sleep in your own bed to-night. A lone woman is troubled with such dreams and such thoughts that she's afeard of herself sometimes. Pray tarry with me this night, dear husband, of all nights in the year."

"My love and my Faith," replied young Goodman Brown, "of all nights in the year, this one night must I tarry away from thee. My journey, as thou callest it, forth and back again, must needs be done 'twixt now and sunrise. What, my sweet, pretty wife, dost thou doubt me already, and we but three months married?"

"Then God bless you!" said Faith, with the pink ribbons; "and may you find all well when you come back."

"Amen!" cried Goodman Brown. "Say thy prayers, dear Faith, and go to bed at dusk, and no harm will come to thee."

So they parted; and the young man pursued his way until, being about to turn the corner by the meeting house, he looked back and saw the head of Faith still peeping after him with a melancholy air, in spite of her pink ribbons.

"Poor little Faith!" thought he, for his heart smote him. "What a wretch am I to leave her on such an errand! She talks of dreams, too. Methought as she spoke there was trouble in her face, as if a dream had warned her what work is to be done to-night. But no, no; 'twould kill her to think it. Well, she's a blessed angel on earth; and after this one night I'll cling to her skirts and follow her to heaven."

With this excellent resolve for the future, Goodman Brown felt himself justified in making more haste on his present evil purpose. He had taken a dreary road, darkened by all the gloomiest trees of the forest, which barely stood aside to let the narrow path creep through, and closed immediately behind. It was all as lonely as could be; and there is this peculiarity in such a solitude, that the traveller knows not who may be concealed by the innumerable trunks and the thick boughs overhead; so that with lonely footsteps he may yet be passing through an unseen multitude.

"There may be a devilish Indian behind every tree," said Goodman Brown to himself; and he glanced fearfully behind him as he added, "What if the devil himself should be at my very elbow!"

His head being turned back, he passed a crook of the road, and, looking forward again, beheld the figure of a man, in grave and decent attire, seated at the foot of an old tree. He arose at Goodman Brown's approach and walked onward side by side with him.

"You are late, Goodman Brown," said he. "The clock of the Old South was striking as I came through Boston; and that is full fifteen minutes agone."

"Faith kept me back a while," replied the young man, with a tremor in his voice, caused by the sudden appearance of his companion, though not wholly unexpected.

It was now deep dusk in the forest, and deepest in that part of it where these two were journeying. As nearly as could be discerned, the second traveller was about fifty years old, apparently in the same rank of life as Goodman Brown, and bearing a considerable resemblance to him, though perhaps more in expression than features. Still they might have been taken for father and son. And yet, though the elder person was as simply clad us the younger and as simple in manner too, he had an indescribable air of one who knew the world, and who would not have felt abashed at the governor's dinner table or in King William's court, were it possible that his affairs should call him thither. But the only thing about him that could be fixed upon as remarkable was his staff, which bore the likeness of a great black snake, so curiously wrought that it might almost be seen to twist and wriggle itself like a living serpent. This, of course, must have been an ocular deception, assisted by the uncertain light.

"Come, Goodman Brown," cried his fellow-traveller, "this is a dull pace for the beginning of a journey. Take my staff, if you are so soon weary."

"Friend," said the other, exchanging his slow pace for a full stop, "having kept covenant by meeting thee here, it is my purpose now to return whence I came. I have scruples touching the matter thou wot'st of."

"Sayest thou so?" replied he of the serpent, smiling apart. "Let us walk on, nevertheless, reasoning as we go; and if I convince thee not thou shalt turn back. We are but a little way in the forest yet."

"Too far! too far!" exclaimed the goodman, unconsciously resuming his walk. "My father never went into the woods on such an errand, nor his father before him. We have been a race of honest men and good Christians since the days of the martyrs; and shall I be the first of the name of Brown that ever took this path and kept———"

"Such company, thou wouldst say," observed the elder person, interpreting his pause. "Well said, Goodman Brown! I have been as well acquainted with your family as with ever a one among the Puritans; and that's no trifle to say. I helped your grandfather, the constable, when he lashed the Quaker woman so smartly through the streets of Salem; and it was I that brought your father a pitch-pine knot, kindled at my own hearth, to set fire to an Indian village, in King Philip's war. They were my good friends, both; and many a pleasant walk have we had along this path, and returned merrily after midnight. I would fain be friends with you for their sake."

"If it be as thou sayest," replied Goodman Brown, "I marvel they never spoke of these matters; or, verily, I marvel not, seeing that the least rumor of the sort would have driven them from New England. We are a people of prayer, and good works to boot, and abide no such wickedness."

"Wickedness or not," said the traveller with the twisted staff, "I have a very general acquaintance here in New England. The deacons of many a church have drunk the communion wine with me; the selectmen of divers towns make me their chairman; and a majority of the Great and General Court are firm supporters of my interest. The governor and I, too———But these are state secrets."

"Can this be so?" cried Goodman Brown, with a stare of amazement at his undisturbed companion. "Howbeit, I have nothing to do with the governor and council; they have their own ways, and are no rule for a simple husbandman like me. But, were I to go on with thee, how should I meet the eye of that good old man, our minister, at Salem village? O, his voice would make me tremble both Sabbath day and lecture day."

Thus far the elder traveller had listened with due gravity; but now burst into a fit of irrepressible mirth, shaking himself so violently that his snakelike staff actually seemed to wriggle in sympathy.

"Ha! ha! ha!" shouted he again and again; then composing himself. "Well, go on, Goodman Brown, go on; but, prithee, don't kill me with laughing."

"Well, then, to end the matter at once," said Goodman Brown, considerably nettled, "there is my wife, Faith. It would break her dear little heart; and I'd rather break my own."

"Nay, if that be the case," answered the other, "e'en go thy ways, Goodman Brown. I would not for twenty old women like the one hobbling before us that Faith should come to any harm."

As he spoke, he pointed his staff at a female figure on the path, in whom Goodman Brown recognized a very pious and exemplary dame, who had taught him his catechism in youth, and was still his moral and spiritual adviser, jointly with the minister and Deacon Gookin.

"A marvel, truly, that Goody Cloyse should be so far in the wilderness at nightfall," said he. "But, with your leave, friend, I shall take a cut through the woods until we have left this Christian woman behind. Being a stranger to you, she might ask whom I was consorting with and whither I was going."

"Be it so," said his fellow-traveller. "Betake you to the woods, and let me keep the path."

Accordingly the young man turned aside, but took care to watch his companion, who advanced softly along the road until he had come within a staff's length of the old dame. She, meanwhile, was making the best of her way, with singular speed for so aged a woman, and mumbling some indistinct words—a prayer, doubtless—as she went. The traveller put forth his staff and touched her withered neck with what seemed the serpent's tail.

"The devil!" screamed the pious old lady.

"Then Goody Cloyse knows her old friend?" observed the traveller, confronting her and leaning on his writhing stick.

"Ah, forsooth, and is it your worship indeed?" cried the good dame. "Yea, truly is it, and in the very image of my old gossip, Goodman Brown, the grandfather of the silly fellow that now is. But—would your worship believe it?—my broomstick hath strangely disappeared, stolen, as I suspect, by that unhanged witch, Goody Cory, and that, too, when I was all anointed with the juice of smallage, and cinquefoil, and wolf's bane———"

"Mingled with fine wheat and the fat of a new-born babe," said the shape of old Goodman Brown.

"Ah, your worship knows the recipe," cried the old lady, cackling aloud. "So, as I was saying, being all ready for the meeting, and no horse to ride on, I made up my mind to foot it; for they tell me there is a nice young man to be taken into communion to-night. But now your good worship will lend me your arm, and we shall be there in a twinkling."

"That can hardly be," answered her friend. "I may not spare you my arm, Goody Cloyse; but here is my staff, if you will."

So saying, he threw it down at her feet, where, perhaps, it assumed life, being one of the rods which its owner had formerly lent to the Egyptian magi. Of this fact, however, Goodman Brown could not take cognizance. He had cast up his eyes in astonishment, and, looking down again, beheld neither Goody Cloyse nor the serpentine staff, but his fellow-traveller alone, who waited for him as calmly as if nothing had happened.

"That old woman taught me my catechism," said the young man; and there was a world of meaning in this simple comment.

They continued to walk onward, while the elder traveller exhorted his companion to make good speed and persevere in the path, discoursing so aptly that his arguments seemed rather to spring up in the bosom of his auditor than to be suggested by himself. As they went, he plucked a branch of maple to serve for a walking stick, and began to strip it of the twigs and little boughs, which were wet with evening dew. The moment his fingers touched them they became strangely withered and dried up as with a week's sunshine. Thus the pair proceeded, at a good free pace, until suddenly, in a gloomy hollow of the road, Goodman Brown sat himself down on the stump of a tree and refused to go any farther.

"Friend," said he, stubbornly, "my mind is made up. Not another step will I budge on this errand. What if a wretched old woman do choose to go to the devil when I thought she was going to heaven; is that any reason why I should quit my dear Faith and go after her?"

"You will think better of this by and by," said his acquaintance, composedly. "Sit here and rest yourself a while; and when you feel like moving again, there is my staff to help you along."

Without more words, he threw his companion the maple stick, and was as speedily out of sight as if he had vanished into the deepening gloom. The young man sat a few moments by the roadside, applauding himself greatly, and thinking with how clear a conscience he should meet the minister in his morning walk, nor shrink from the eye of good old Deacon Gookin. And what calm sleep would be his that very night, which was to have been spent so wickedly, but so purely and sweetly now, in the arms of Faith! Amidst these pleasant and praiseworthy meditations, Goodman Brown heard the tramp of horses along the road, and deemed it advisable to conceal himself within the verge of the forest, conscious of the guilty purpose that had brought him thither, though now so happily turned from it.

On came the hoof tramps and the voices of the riders, two grave old voices, conversing soberly as they drew near. These mingled sounds appeared to pass along the road, within a few yards of the young man's hiding place; but, owing doubtless to the depth of the gloom at that particular spot, neither the travellers nor their steeds were visible. Though their figures brushed the small boughs by the wayside, it could not be seen that they intercepted, even for a moment, the faint gleam from the strip of bright sky athwart which they must have passed. Goodman Brown alternately crouched and stood on tiptoe, pulling aside the branches and thrusting forth his head as far as he durst without discerning so much as a shadow. It vexed him the more, because he could have sworn, were such a thing possible, that he recognized the voices of the minister and Deacon Gookin, jogging along quietly, as they were wont to do, when bound to some ordination or ecclesiastical council. While yet within hearing, one of the riders stopped to pluck a switch.

"Of the two, reverend sir," said the voice like the deacon's, "I had rather miss an ordination dinner than to-night's meeting. They tell me that some of our community are to be here from Falmouth and beyond, and others from Connecticut and Rhode Island, besides several of the Indian powwows, who, after their fashion, know almost as much deviltry as the best of us. Moreover, there is a goodly young woman to be taken into communion."

"Mighty well, Deacon Gookin!" replied the solemn old tones of the minister. "Spur up, or we shall be late. Nothing can be done, you know, until I get on the ground."

The hoofs clattered again; and the voices, talking so strangely in the empty air, passed on through the forest, where no church had ever been gathered or solitary Christian prayed. Whither, then, could these holy men be journeying so deep into the heathen wilderness? Young Goodman Brown caught hold of a tree for support, being ready to sink down on the ground, faint and overburdened with the heavy sickness of his heart. He looked up to the sky, doubting whether there really was a heaven above him. Yet there was the blue arch, and the stars brightening in it.

"With heaven above and Faith below, I will yet stand firm against the devil!" cried Goodman Brown.

While he still gazed upward into the deep arch of the firmament and had lifted his hands to pray, a cloud, though no wind was stirring, hurried across the zenith and hid the brightening stars. The blue sky was still visible except directly overhead, where this black mass of cloud was sweeping swiftly northward. Aloft in the air, as if from the depths of the cloud, came a confused and doubtful sound of voices. Once the listener fancied that he could distinguish the accents of townspeople of his own, men and women, both pious and ungodly, many of whom he had met at the communion table, and had seen others rioting at the tavern. The next moment, so indistinct were the sounds, he doubted whether he had heard aught but the murmur of the old forest, whispering without a wind. Then came a stronger swell of those familiar tones, heard daily in the sunshine at Salem village, but never until now from a cloud of night. There was one voice, of a young woman, uttering lamentations, yet with an uncertain sorrow, and entreating for some favor, which, perhaps, it would grieve her to obtain; and all the unseen multitude, both saints and sinners, seemed to encourage her onward.

"Faith!" shouted Goodman Brown, in a voice of agony and desperation; and the echoes of the forest mocked him, crying, "Faith! Faith!" as if bewildered wretches were seeking her all through the wilderness.

The cry of grief, rage, and terror was yet piercing the night, when the unhappy husband held his breath for a response. There was a scream, drowned immediately in a louder murmur of voices, fading into far-off laughter, as the dark cloud swept away, leaving the clear and silent sky above Goodman Brown. But something fluttered lightly down through the air and caught on the branch of a tree. The young man seized it, and beheld a pink ribbon.

"My Faith is gone!" cried he, after one stupefied moment. "There is no good on earth; and sin is but a name. Come, devil; for to thee is this world given."

And, maddened with despair, so that he laughed loud and long, did Goodman Brown grasp his staff and set forth again, at such a rate that he seemed to fly along the forest path rather than to walk or run. The road grew wilder and drearier and more faintly traced, and vanished at length, leaving him in the heart of the dark wilderness, still rushing onward with the instinct that guides mortal man to evil. The whole forest was peopled with frightful sounds—the creaking of the trees, the howling of wild beasts, and the yell of Indians; while sometimes the wind tolled like a distant church bell, and sometimes gave a broad roar around the traveller, as if all Nature were laughing him to scorn. But he was himself the chief horror of the scene, and shrank not from its other horrors.

"Ha! ha! ha!" roared Goodman Brown when the wind laughed at him. "Let us hear which will laugh loudest. Think not to frighten me with your deviltry. Come witch, come wizard, come Indian powwow, come devil himself, and here comes Goodman Brown. You may as well fear him as he fear you."

In truth, all through the haunted forest there could be nothing more frightful than the figure of Goodman Brown. On he flew among the black pines, brandishing his staff with frenzied gestures, now giving vent to an inspiration of horrid blasphemy, and now shouting forth such laughter as set all the echoes of the forest laughing like demons around him. The fiend in his own shape is less hideous than when he rages in the breast of man. Thus sped the demoniac on his course, until, quivering among the trees, he saw a red light before him, as when the felled trunks and branches of a clearing have been set on fire, and throw up their lurid blaze against the sky, at the hour of midnight. He paused, in a lull of the tempest that had driven him onward, and heard the swell of what seemed a hymn, rolling solemnly from a distance with the weight of many voices. He knew the tune; it was a familiar one in the choir of the village meeting house. The verse died heavily away, and was lengthened by a chorus, not of human voices, but of all the sounds of the benighted wilderness pealing in awful harmony together. Goodman Brown cried out; and his cry was lost to his own ear by its unison with the cry of the desert.

In the interval of silence he stole forward until the light glared full upon his eyes. At one extremity of an open space, hemmed in by the dark wall of the forest, arose a rock bearing some rude, natural resemblance either to an alter or a pulpit, and surrounded by four blazing pines, their tops aflame, their stems untouched, like candles at an evening meeting. The mass of foliage that had overgrown the summit of the rock was all on fire, blazing high into the night and fitfully illuminating the whole field. Each pendent twig and leafy festoon was in a blaze. As the red light arose and fell, a numerous congregation alternately shone forth, then disappeared in shadow, and again grew, as it were, out of the darkness, peopling the heart of the solitary woods at once.

"A grave and dark-clad company," quoth Goodman Brown.

In truth they were such. Among them, quivering to and fro between gloom and splendor, appeared faces that would be seen next day at the council board of the province, and others which, Sabbath after Sabbath, looked devoutly heavenward, and benignantly over the crowded pews, from the holiest pulpits in the land. Some affirm that the lady of the governor was there. At least there were high dames well known to her, and wives of honored husbands, and widows, a great multitude, and ancient maidens, all of excellent repute, and fair young girls, who trembled lest their mothers should espy them. Either the sudden gleams of light flashing over the obscure field bedazzled Goodman Brown, or he recognized a score of the church members of Salem village famous for their especial sanctity. Good old Deacon Gookin had arrived, and waited at the skirts of that venerable saint, his revered pastor. But, irreverently consorting with these grave, reputable, and pious people, these elders of the church, these chaste dames and dewy virgins, there were men of dissolute lives and women of spotted fame, wretches given over to all mean and filthy vice, and suspected even of horrid crimes. It was strange to see that the good shrank not from the wicked, nor were the sinners abashed by the saints. Scattered also among their palefaced enemies were the Indian priests, or powwows, who had often scared their native forest with more hideous incantations than any known to English witchcraft.

"But where is Faith?" thought Goodman Brown; and, as hope came into his heart, he trembled.

Another verse of the hymn arose, a slow and mournful strain, such as the pious love, but joined to words which expressed all that our nature can conceive of sin, and darkly hinted at far more. Unfathomable to mere mortals is the lore of fiends. Verse after verse was sung; and still the chorus of the desert swelled between like the deepest tone of a mighty organ; and with the final peal of that dreadful anthem there came a sound, as if the roaring wind, the rushing streams, the howling beasts, and every other voice of the unconverted wilderness were mingling and according with the voice of guilty man in homage to the prince of all. The four blazing pines threw up a loftier flame, and obscurely discovered shapes and visages of horror on the smoke wreaths above the impious assembly. At the same moment the fire on the rock shot redly forth and formed a glowing arch above its base, where now appeared a figure. With reverence be it spoken, the figure bore no slight similitude, both in garb and manner, to some grave divine of the New England churches.

"Bring forth the converts!" cried a voice that echoed through the field and rolled into the forest.

At the word, Goodman Brown stepped forth from the shadow of the trees and approached the congregation, with whom he felt a loathful brotherhood by the sympathy of all that was wicked in his heart. He could have well nigh sworn that the shape of his own dead father beckoned him to advance, looking downward from a smoke wreath, while a woman, with dim features of despair, threw out her hand to warn him back. Was it his mother? But he had no power to retreat one step, nor to resist, even in thought, when the minister and good old Deacon Gookin seized his arms and led him to the blazing rock. Thither came also the slender form of a veiled female, led between Goody Cloyse, that pious teacher of the catechism, and Martha Carrier, who had received the devil's promise to be queen of hell. A rampant hag was she. And there stood the proselytes beneath the canopy of fire.

"Welcome, my children," said the dark figure, "to the communion of your race. Ye have found thus young your nature and your destiny. My children, look behind you!"

They turned; and flashing forth, as it were, in a sheet of flame, the fiend worshippers were seen; the smile of welcome gleamed darkly on every visage.

"There," resumed the sable form, "are all whom ye have reverenced from youth. Ye deemed them holier than yourselves, and shrank from your own sin, contrasting it with their lives of righteousness and prayerful aspirations heavenward. Yet here are they all in my worshipping assembly. This night it shall be granted you to know their secret deeds; how hoary-bearded elders of the church have whispered wanton words to the young maids of their households; how many a woman, eager for widows' weeds, has given her husband a drink at bedtime and let him sleep his last sleep in her bosom; how beardless youths have made haste to inherit their fathers' wealth; and how fair damsels—blush not, sweet ones—have dug little graves in the garden, and bidden me, the sole guest, to an infant's funeral. By the sympathy of your human hearts for sin ye shall scent out all the places—whether in church, bed chamber, street, field, or forest—where crime has been committed, and shall exult to behold the whole earth one stain of guilt, one mighty blood spot. Far more than this. It shall be yours to penetrate, in every bosom, the deep mystery of sin, the fountain of all wicked arts, and which inexhaustibly supplies more evil impulses than human power—than my power at its utmost—can make manifest in deeds. And now, my children, look upon each other."

They did so; and, by the blaze of the hell-kindled torches, the wretched man beheld his Faith, and the wife her husband, trembling before that unhallowed altar.

"Lo, there ye stand my children," said the figure, in a deep and solemn tone, almost sad with its despairing awfulness, as if his once angelic nature could yet mourn for our miserable race. "Depending upon one another's hearts, ye had still hoped that virtue were not all a dream. Now are ye undeceived. Evil is the nature of mankind. Evil must be your only happiness. Welcome again, my children, to the communion of your race."

"Welcome," repeated the fiend worshippers, in one cry of despair and triumph.

And there they stood, the only pair, as it seemed, who were yet hesitating on the verge of wickedness in this dark world. A basin was hollowed, naturally, in the rock. Did it contain water, reddened by the lurid light? or was it blood? or, perchance, a liquid flame? Herein did the shape of evil dip his hand and prepare to lay the mark of baptism upon their foreheads, that they might be partakers of the mystery of sin, more conscious of the secret guilt of others, both in deed and thought, than they could now be of their own. The husband cast one look at his pale wife, and Faith at him. What polluted wretches would the next glance show them to each other, shuddering alike at what they disclosed and what they saw!

"Faith! Faith!" cried the husband, "look up to heaven, and resist the wicked one."

Whether Faith obeyed, he knew not. Hardly had he spoken when he found himself amid calm night and solitude, listening to a roar of the wind which died heavily away through the forest. He staggered against the rock, and felt it chill and damp; while a hanging twig, that had been all on fire, besprinkled his cheek with the coldest dew.

The next morning young Goodman Brown came slowly into the street of Salem village, staring around him like a bewildered man. The good old minister was taking a walk along the graveyard to get an appetite for breakfast and meditate his sermon, and bestowed a blessing, as he passed, on Goodman Brown. He shrank from the venerable saint as if to avoid an anathema. Old Deacon Gookin was at domestic worship, and the holy words of his prayer were heard through the open window. "What God doth the wizard pray to?" quoth Goodman Brown. Goody Cloyse, that excellent old Christian, stood in the early sunshine at her own lattice, catechizing a little girl who had brought her a pint of morning's milk. Goodman Brown snatched away the child as from the grasp of the fiend himself. Turning the corner by the meeting house, he spied the head of Faith, with the pink ribbons, gazing anxiously forth, and bursting into such joy at sight of him that she skipped along the street and almost kissed her husband before the whole village. But Goodman Brown looked sternly and sadly into her face, and passed on without a greeting.

Had Goodman Brown fallen asleep in the forest and only dreamed a wild dream of a witch meeting?

Be it so, if you will; but, alas! it was a dream of evil omen for young Goodman Brown. A stern, a sad, a darkly meditative, a distrustful, if not a desperate man did he become from the night of that fearful dream. On the Sabbath day, when the congregation were singing a holy psalm, he could not listen, because an anthem of sin rushed loudly upon his ear and drowned all the blessed strain. When the minister spoke from the pulpit, with power and fervid eloquence and with his hand on the open Bible, of the sacred truths of our religion, and of saintlike lives and triumphant deaths, and of future bliss or misery unutterable, then did Goodman Brown turn pale, dreading lest the roof should thunder down upon the gray blasphemer and his hearers. Often, awaking suddenly at midnight, he shrank from the bosom of Faith; and at morning or eventide, when the family knelt down at prayer, he scowled, and muttered to himself, and gazed sternly at his wife, and turned away. And when he had lived long, and was borne to his grave, a hoary corpse, followed by Faith, an aged woman, and children and grandchildren, a goodly procession, besides neighbors not a few, they carved no hopeful verse upon his tombstone; for his dying hour was gloom.

NATHANIEL HAWTHORNE

The Birthmark

In the latter part of the last century there lived a man of science, an eminent proficient in every branch of natural philosophy, who not long before our story opens had made experience of a spiritual affinity more attractive than any chemical one. He had left his laboratory to the care of an assistant, cleared his fine countenance from the furnace smoke, washed the stain of acids from his fingers, and persuaded a beautiful woman to become his wife. In those days when the comparatively recent discovery of electricity and other kindred mysteries of Nature seemed to open paths into the region of miracle, it was not unusual for the love of science to rival the love of woman in its depth and absorbing energy. The higher intellect, the imagination, the spirit, and even the heart might all find their congenial ailment in pursuits which, as some of their ardent votaries believed, would ascend from one step of powerful intelligence to another, until the philosopher should lay his hand on the secret of creative force and perhaps make new worlds for himself. We know not whether Aylmer possessed this degree of faith in man's ultimate control over Nature. He had devoted himself, however, too unreservedly to scientific studies ever to be weaned from them by any second passion. His love for his young wife might prove the stronger of the two; but it could only be by intertwining itself with his love of science, and uniting the strength of the latter to his own.

Such a union accordingly took place, and was attended with truly remarkable consequences and a deeply impressive moral. One day, very soon after their marriage, Aylmer sat gazing at his wife with a trouble in his countenance that grew stronger until he spoke.

"Georgiana," said he, "has it ever occurred to you that the mark upon your cheek might be removed?"

"No, indeed," said she, smiling; but perceiving the seriousness of his manner, she blushed deeply. "To tell you the truth it has been so often called a charm that I was simple enough to imagine it might be so."

"Ah, upon another face perhaps it might," replied her husband; "but never on yours. No, dearest Georgiana, you came so nearly perfect from the hand of Nature that this slightest possible defect, which we hesitate whether to term a defect or a beauty, shocks me, as being the visible mark of earthly imperfection."

"Shocks you, my husband!" cried Georgiana, deeply hurt; at first reddening with momentary anger, but then bursting into tears. "Then why did you take me from my mother's side? You cannot love what shocks you!"

To explain this conversation it must be mentioned that in the center of Georgiana's left cheek there was a singular mark, deeply interwoven, as it were, with the texture and substance of her face. In the usual state of her complexion—a healthy though delicate bloom—the mark wore a tint of deeper crimson, which imperfectly defined its shape amid the surrounding rosiness. When she blushed it gradually became more indistinct, and finally vanished amid the triumphant rush of blood that bathed the whole cheek with its brilliant glow. But if any shifting motion caused her to turn pale, there was the mark again, a crimson stain upon the snow, in what Aylmer sometimes deemed an almost fearful distinctness. Its shape bore not a little similarity to the human hand, though of the smallest pygmy size. Georgiana's lovers were wont to say that some fairy at her birth hour had laid her tiny hand upon the infant's cheek, and left this impress there in token of the magic endowments that were to give her such sway over all hearts. Many a desperate swain would have risked life for the privilege of pressing his lips to the mysterious hand. It must not be concealed, however, that the impression wrought by this fairy sign manual varied exceedingly, according to the difference of temperament in the beholders. Some fastidious persons—but they were exclusively of her own sex—affirmed that the bloody hand, as they chose to call it, quite destroyed the effect of Georgiana's beauty, and rendered her countenance even hideous. But it would be as reasonable to say that one of those small blue stains which sometimes occur in the purest statuary marble would convert the Eve of Powers* to a monster. Masculine observers, if the birthmark did not heighten their admiration, contented themselves with wishing it away, that the world might possess one living specimen of ideal loveliness without the semblance of a flaw. After his marriage,—for he thought little or nothing of the matter before,—Aylmer discovered that this was the case with himself.

Had she been less beautiful,—if Envy's self could have found aught else to sneer at,—he might have felt his affection heightened by the prettiness of this mimic hand, now vaguely portrayed, now lost, now stealing forth again and glimmering to and fro with every pulse of emotion that throbbed within her heart; but seeing her otherwise so perfect, he found this one defect grow more and more intolerable with every moment of their united lives. It was the fatal flaw of humanity which Nature, in one shape or another, stamps ineffaceably on all her productions, either to imply that they are temporary and finite, or that their perfection must be wrought by toil and pain. The crimson hand expressed the ineludible gripe† in which mortality clutches the highest and purest of earthly mold, degrading them into kindred with the lowest, and even with the very

---

*A statue, *Eve before the Fall*, by Hiram Powers (1805–1873), a sculptor known for his idealized portraits of feminine purity.

†Grip.

brutes, like whom their visible frames return to dust. In this manner, selecting it as the symbol of his wife's liability to sin, sorrow, decay, and death, Aylmer's somber imagination was not long in rendering the birthmark a frightful object, causing him more trouble and horror than ever Georgiana's beauty, whether of soul or sense, had given him delight.

At all the seasons which should have been their happiest, he invariably and without intending it, nay, in spite of a purpose to the contrary, reverted to this one disastrous topic. Trifling as it at first appeared, it so connected itself with innumerable trains of thought and modes of feeling that it became the central point of all. With the morning twilight Aylmer opened his eyes upon his wife's face and recognized the symbol of imperfection; and when they sat together at the evening hearth his eyes wandered stealthily to her cheek, and beheld, flickering with the blaze of the wood fire, the spectral hand that wrote mortality where he would fain have worshiped. Georgiana soon learned to shudder at his gaze. It needed but a glance with the peculiar expression that his face often wore to change the roses of her cheek into a deathlike paleness, amid which the crimson hand was brought strongly out, like a bas-relief of ruby on the whitest marble.

Late one night when the lights were growing dim, so as hardly to betray the stain on the poor wife's cheek, she herself, for the first time, voluntarily took up the subject.

"Do you remember, my dear Aylmer," said she, with a feeble attempt at a smile, "have you any recollection of a dream last night about this odious hand?"

"None! none whatever!" replied Aylmer, starting; but then he added, in a dry, cold tone, affected for the sake of concealing the real depth of his emotion, "I might well dream of it; for before I fell asleep it had taken a pretty firm hold of my fancy."

"And you did dream of it?" continued Georgiana hastily, for she dreaded lest a gush of tears should interrupt what she had to say. "A terrible dream! I wonder that you can forget it. Is it possible to forget this one expression?—'It is in her heart now; we must have it out!' Reflect, my husband; for by all means I would have you recall that dream."

The mind is in a sad state when Sleep, the all-involving, cannot confine her specters within the dim region of her sway, but suffers them to break forth, affrighting this actual life with secrets that perchance belong to a deeper one. Aylmer now remembered his dream. He had fancied himself with his servant Aminadab, attempting an operation for the removal of the birthmark; but the deeper went the knife, the deeper sank the hand, until at length its tiny grasp appeared to have caught hold of Georgiana's heart; whence, however, her husband was inexorably resolved to cut or wrench it away.

When the dream had shaped itself perfectly in his memory, Aylmer sat in his wife's presence with a guilty feeling. Truth often finds its way to the mind close muffled in robes of sleep, and then speaks with uncompromising directness of matters in regard to which we practice an unconscious self-deception during our waking moments. Until now he had not been aware of the tyrannizing influence acquired by one idea over his mind, and of the lengths which he might find in his heart to go for the sake of giving himself peace.

"Aylmer," resumed Georgiana solemnly, "I know not what may be the cost to both of us to rid me of this fatal birthmark. Perhaps its removal may cause cureless deformity; or it may be the stain goes as deep as life itself. Again: do we know that there is a possibility, on any terms, of unclasping the firm grip of this little hand which was laid upon me before I came into the world?"

"Dearest Georgiana, I have spent much thought upon the subject," hastily interrupted Aylmer. "I am convinced of the perfect practicability of its removal."

"If there be the remotest possibility of it," continued Georgiana, "let the attempt be made at whatever risk. Danger is nothing to me; for life, while this hateful mark makes me the object of your horror and disgust,—life is a burden which I would fling down with joy. Either remove this dreadful hand, or take my wretched life! You have deep science. All the world bears witness of it. You have achieved great wonders. Cannot you remove this little, little mark, which I cover with the tips of two small fingers? Is this beyond your power, for the sake of your own peace, and to save your poor wife from madness?"

"Noblest, dearest, tenderest wife," cried Aylmer rapturously, "doubt not my power. I have already given this matter the deepest thought—thought which might almost have enlightened me to create a being less perfect than yourself. Georgiana, you have led me deeper than ever into the heart of science. I feel myself fully competent to render this dear cheek as faultless as its fellow; and then, most beloved, what will be my triumph when I shall have corrected what Nature left imperfect in her fairest work! Even Pygmalion* when his sculptured woman assumed life, felt not greater ecstasy than mine will be."

"It is resolved, then," said Georgiana, faintly smiling, "And, Aylmer, spare me not, though you should find the birthmark take refuge in my heart at last."

Her husband tenderly kissed her cheek—her right cheek—not that which bore the impress of the crimson hand.

The next day Aylmer apprised his wife of a plan that he had formed whereby he might have opportunity for the intense thought and constant watchfulness which the proposed operation would require; while Georgiana, likewise, would enjoy the perfect repose essential to its success. They were to seclude themselves in the extensive apartments occupied by Aylmer as a laboratory, and where, during his toilsome youth, he had made discoveries in the elemental powers of Nature that had roused the admiration of all the learned societies in Europe. Seated calmly in this laboratory, the pale philosopher had investigated the secrets of the highest cloud region and of the profoundest mines; he had satisfied himself of the causes that kindled and kept alive the fires of the volcano; and had explained the mystery of fountains, and how it is that they gush forth, some so bright and pure, and others with such rich medicinal virtues, from the dark bosom of the earth. Here, too, at an earlier period, he had studied the wonders of the human frame, and attempted to fathom the very process by which Nature assimilates all her precious influences from earth and air, and from the spiritual world, to create and foster man, her masterpiece. The latter pursuit, however, Aylmer had long laid aside in unwilling recognition of the truth—against which all seekers sooner or later stumble—that our great creative Mother, while she amuses us with apparently working in the broadest sunshine, is yet severely careful to keep her own secrets, and, in spite of her pretended openness, shows us nothing but results. She permits us, indeed, to mar, but seldom to mend, and, like a jealous patentee,

---

*The king of Cyprus in Greek mythology, who fell in love with a statue he had sculpted. Aphrodite, the goddess of love, brought the statue to life for him.

on no account to make. Now, however, Aylmer resumed these half-forgotten investigations,—not, of course, with such hopes or wishes as first suggested them, but because they involved much physiological truth and lay in the path of his proposed scheme for the treatment of Georgiana.

As he led her over the threshold of the laboratory, Georgiana was cold and tremulous. Aylmer looked cheerfully into her face, with intent to reassure her, but was so startled with the intense glow of the birthmark upon the whiteness of her cheek that he could not restrain a strong convulsive shudder. His wife fainted.

"Aminadab! Aminadab!" shouted Aylmer, stamping violently on the floor.

Forthwith there issued from an inner apartment a man of low stature, but bulky frame, with shaggy hair hanging about his visage, which was grimed with the vapors of the furnace. This personage had been Aylmer's underworker during his whole scientific career, and was admirably fitted for that office by his great mechanical readiness, and the skill with which, while incapable of comprehending a single principle, he executed all the details of his master's experiments. With his vast strength, his shaggy hair, his smoky aspect and the indescribable earthiness that encrusted him, he seemed to represent man's physical nature; while Aylmer's slender figure, and pale, intellectual face, were no less apt a type of the spiritual element.

"Throw open the door of the boudoir, Aminadab," said Aylmer, "and burn a pastille."*

"Yes, master," answered Aminadab, looking intently at the lifeless form of Georgiana; and then he muttered to himself, "If she were my wife, I'd never part with that birthmark."

When Georgiana recovered consciousness she found herself breathing an atmosphere of penetrating fragrance, the gentle potency of which had recalled her from her deathlike faintness. The scene around her looked like enchantment. Aylmer had converted those smoky, dingy, somber rooms, where he had spent his brightest years in recondite pursuits, into a series of beautiful apartments not unfit to be the secluded abode of a lovely woman. The walls were hung with gorgeous curtains, which imparted the combination of grandeur and grace that no other species of adornment can achieve; and as they fell from the ceiling to the floor, their rich and ponderous folds, concealing all angles and straight lines, appeared to shut in the scene from infinite space. For aught Georgiana knew, it might be a pavilion among the clouds. And Aylmer, excluding the sunshine, which would have interfered with his chemical processes, had supplied its place with perfumed lamps, emitting flames of various hue, but all uniting in a soft, empurpled radiance. He now knelt by his wife's side, watching her earnestly, but without alarm; for he was confident in his science, and felt that he could draw a magic circle round her within which no evil might intrude.

"Where am I? Ah, I remember," said Georgiana faintly; and she placed her hand over her cheek to hide the terrible mark from her husband's eyes.

"Fear not, dearest!" exclaimed he. "Do not shrink from me! Believe me, Georgiana, I even rejoice in this single imperfection, since it will be such a rapture to remove it."

---

*Incense.

"Oh, spare me!" sadly replied his wife. "Pray do not look at it again. I never can forget that convulsive shudder."

In order to soothe Georgiana, and, as it were, to release her mind from the burden of actual things, Aylmer now put in practice some of the light and playful secrets which science had taught him among its profounder lore. Airy figures, absolutely bodiless ideas, and forms of unsubstantial beauty came and danced before her, imprinting their momentary footsteps on beams of light. Though she had some indistinct idea of the method of these optical phenomena, still the illusion was almost perfect enough to warrant the belief that her husband possessed sway over the spiritual world. Then again, when she felt a wish to look forth from her seclusion, immediately, as if her thoughts were answered, the procession of external existence flitted across a screen. The scenery and the figures of actual life were perfectly represented, but with that bewitching, yet indescribable difference which always makes a picture, an image, or a shadow so much more attractive than the original. When wearied of this, Aylmer bade her cast her eyes upon a vessel containing a quantity of earth. She did so, with little interest at first; but was soon startled to perceive the germ of a plant shooting upward from the soil. Then came the slender stalk; the leaves gradually unfolded themselves; and amid them was a perfect and lovely flower.

"It is magical!" cried Georgiana. "I dare not touch it."

"Nay, pluck it," answered Aylmer: "pluck it, and inhale its brief perfume while you may. The flower will wither in a few moments and leave nothing save its brown seed vessels; but thence may be perpetuated a race as ephemeral as itself."

But Georgiana had no sooner touched the flower than the whole plant suffered a blight, its leaves turning coal-black as if by the agency of fire.

"There was too powerful a stimulus," said Aylmer thoughtfully.

To make up for this abortive experiment, he proposed to take her portrait by a scientific process of his own invention. It was to be effected by rays of light striking upon a polished plate of metal. Georgiana assented; but, on looking at the result, was affrighted to find the features of the portrait blurred and indefinable; while the minute figure of a hand appeared where the cheek should have been. Aylmer snatched the metallic plate and threw it into a jar of corrosive acid.

Soon, however, he forgot these mortifying failures. In the intervals of study and chemical experiment he came to her flushed and exhausted, but seemed invigorated by her presence, and spoke in glowing language of the resources of his art. He gave a history of the long dynasty of the alchemists,* who spent so many ages in quest of the universal solvent by which the golden principle might be elicited from all things vile and base. Aylmer appeared to believe that, by the plainest scientific logic, it was altogether within the limits of possibility to discover this long-sought medium; "but," he added, "a philosopher who should go deep enough to acquire the power would attain too lofty a wisdom to stoop to the exercise of it." Not less singular were his opinions in regard to the elixir vitae. He more than intimated that it was at his option to concoct a liquid that should prolong life for years, perhaps interminably; but that it would produce a discord in Nature which all the world, and chiefly the quaffer of the immortal nostrum, would find cause to curse.

---

*Medieval scientists who attempted to create an elixir that would prolong life indefinitely.

"Aylmer, are you in earnest?" asked Georgiana, looking at him with amazement and fear. "It is terrible to possess such power, or even to dream of possessing it."

"Oh, do not tremble, my love," said her husband. "I would not wrong either you or myself by working such inharmonious effects upon our lives; but I would have you consider how trifling, in comparison, is the skill requisite to remove this little hand."

At the mention of the birthmark, Georgiana, as usual, shrank as if a red-hot iron had touched her cheek.

Again Aylmer applied himself to his labors. She could hear his voice in the distant furnace-room giving directions to Aminadab, whose harsh, uncouth, misshapen tones were audible in response, more like the grunt or growl of a brute than human speech. After hours of absence, Aylmer reappeared and proposed that she should now examine his cabinet of chemical products and natural treasures of the earth. Among the former he showed her a small vial, in which, he remarked, was contained a gentle yet most powerful fragrance, capable of impregnating all the breezes that blow across a kingdom. They were of inestimable value, the contents of that little vial; and, as he said so, he threw some of the perfume into the air and filled the room with piercing and invigorating delight.

"And what is this?" asked Georgiana, pointing to a small crystal globe containing a gold-colored liquid. "It is so beautiful to the eye that I could imagine it the elixir of life."

"In one sense it is," replied Aylmer; "or rather, the elixir of immortality. It is the most precious poison that ever was concocted in this world. By its aid I could apportion the lifetime of any mortal at whom you might point your finger. The strength of the dose would determine whether he were to linger out years, or drop dead in the midst of a breath. No king on his guarded throne could keep his life if I, in my private station, should deem that the welfare of millions justified me in depriving him of it."

"Why do you keep such a terrific drug?" inquired Georgiana in horror.

"Do not mistrust me, dearest," said her husband, smiling: "its virtuous potency is yet greater than its harmful one. But see! here is a powerful cosmetic. With a few drops of this in a vase of water, freckles may be washed away as easily as the hands are cleansed. A stronger infusion would take the blood out of the cheek, and leave the rosiest beauty a pale ghost."

"Is it with this lotion that you intend to bathe my cheek?" asked Georgiana, anxiously.

"Oh, no," hastily replied her husband; "this is merely superficial. Your case demands a remedy that shall go deeper."

In his interviews with Georgiana, Aylmer generally made minute inquiries as to her sensations and whether the confinement of the rooms and the temperature of the atmosphere agreed with her. These questions had such a particular drift that Georgiana began to conjecture that she was already subjected to certain physical influences, either breathed in with the fragrant air or taken with her food. She fancied likewise, but it might be altogether fancy, that there was a stirring up of her system—a strange, indefinite sensation creeping through her veins, and tingling, half painfully, half pleasurably, at her heart. Still, whenever she dared to look into the mirror, there she beheld herself pale as a white rose and with the crimson birthmark stamped upon her cheek. Not even Aylmer now hated it so much as she.

To dispel the tedium of the hours which her husband found it necessary to devote to the processes of combination and analysis, Georgiana turned over the volumes of his scientific library. In many dark old tomes she met with chapters full of romance and poetry. They were the works of the philosophers of the middle ages, such as Albertus Magnus, Cornelius Agrippa, Paracelsus, and the famous friar who created the prophetic Brazen Head.* All these antique naturalists stood in advance of their centuries, yet were imbued with some of their credulity, and therefore were believed, and perhaps imagined themselves to have acquired from the investigation of Nature a power above Nature, and from physics a sway over the spiritual world. Hardly less curious and imaginative were the early volumes of the Transactions of the Royal Society, in which the members, knowing little of the limits of natural possibility, were continually recording wonders or proposing methods whereby wonders might be wrought.

But to Georgiana the most engrossing volume was a large folio from her husband's own hand, in which he had recorded every experiment of his scientific career, its original aim, the methods adopted for its development, and its final success or failure, with the circumstances to which either event was attributable. The book, in truth, was both the history and emblem of his ardent, ambitious, imaginative, yet practical and laborious life. He handled physical details as if there were nothing beyond them; yet spiritualized them all, and redeemed himself from materialism by his strong and eager aspiration towards the infinite. In his grasp the veriest clod of earth assumed a soul. Georgiana, as she read, reverenced Aylmer and loved him more profoundly than ever, but with a less entire dependence on his judgment than heretofore. Much as he had accomplished, she could not but observe that his most splendid successes were almost invariably failures, if compared with the ideal at which he aimed. His brightest diamonds were the merest pebbles, and felt to be so by himself, in comparison with the inestimable gems which lay hidden beyond his reach. The volume, rich with achievements that had won renown for its author, was yet as melancholy a record as ever mortal hand had penned. It was the sad confession and continual exemplification of the shortcomings of the composite man, the spirit burdened with clay and working in matter, and of the despair that assails the higher nature of finding itself so miserably thwarted by the earthly part. Perhaps every man of genius in whatever sphere might recognize the image of his own experience in Aylmer's journal.

So deeply did these reflections affect Georgiana that she laid her face upon the open volume and burst into tears. In this situation she was found by her husband.

"It is dangerous to read in a sorcerer's books," said he with a smile, though his countenance was uneasy and displeased. "Georgiana, there are pages in that volume which I can scarcely glance over and keep my senses. Take heed lest it prove as detrimental to you."

"It has made me worship you more than ever," said she.

"Ah, wait for this one success," rejoined he, "then worship me if you will. I shall deem myself hardly unworthy of it. But come, I have sought you for the luxury of your voice. Sing to me, dearest."

So she poured out the liquid music of her voice to quench the thirst of his spirit. He then took his leave with a boyish exuberance of gaiety, assuring her that

---

*An English scientist and philosopher, Friar Roger Bacon, was reputed to have created a brass head that could speak.

her seclusion would endure but a little longer, and that the result was already certain. Scarcely had he departed when Georgiana felt irresistibly impelled to follow him. She had forgotten to inform Aylmer of a symptom which for two or three hours past had begun to excite her attention. It was a sensation in the fatal birthmark, not painful, but which induced a restlessness throughout her system. Hastening after her husband, she intruded for the first time into the laboratory.

The first thing that struck her eye was the furnace, that hot and feverish worker, with the intense glow of its fire, which by the quantities of soot clustered above it seemed to have been burning for ages. There was a distilling apparatus in full operation. Around the room were retorts, tubes, cylinders, crucibles, and other apparatus of chemical research. An electrical machine stood ready for immediate use. The atmosphere felt oppressively close, and was tainted with gaseous odors which had been tormented forth by the process of science. The severe and homely simplicity of the apartment, with its naked walls and brick pavement, looked strange, accustomed as Georgiana had become to the fantastic elegance of her boudoir. But what chiefly, indeed almost solely, drew her attention, was the aspect of Aylmer himself.

He was pale as death, anxious and absorbed, and hung over the furnace as if it depended upon his utmost watchfulness whether the liquid which it was distilling should be the draught of immortal happiness or misery. How different from the sanguine and joyous mien that he had assumed for Georgiana's encouragement!

"Carefully now, Aminadab; carefully, thou human machine; carefully, thou man of clay!" muttered Aylmer, more to himself than his assistant. "Now, if there be a thought too much or too little, it is all over."

"Ho! ho!" mumbled Aminadab. "Look, master! look!"

Aylmer raised his eyes hastily, and at first reddened, then grew paler than ever, on beholding Georgiana. He rushed towards her and seized her arm with a gripe that left the print of his fingers upon it.

"Why do you come hither? Have you no trust in your husband?" cried he impetuously. "Would you throw the blight of that fatal birthmark over my labors? It is not well done. Go, prying woman, go!"

"Nay, Aylmer," said Georgiana with the firmness of which she possessed no stinted endowment, "it is not you that have a right to complain. You mistrust your wife; you have concealed the anxiety with which you watch the development of this experiment. Think not so unworthily of me, my husband. Tell me all the risk we run, and fear not that I shall shrink; for my share in it is far less than your own."

"No, no, Georgiana!" said Aylmer impatiently; "it must not be."

"I submit," replied she calmly. "And, Aylmer, I shall quaff whatever draught you bring me; but it will be on the same principle that would induce me to take a dose of poison if offered by your hand."

"My noble wife," said Aylmer, deeply moved, "I knew not the height and depth of your nature until now. Nothing shall be concealed. Know, then, that this crimson hand, superficial as it seems, has clutched its grasp into your being with a strength of which I had no previous conception. I have already administered agents powerful enough to do aught except to change your entire physical system. Only one thing remains to be tried. If that fails us we are ruined."

"Why did you hesitate to tell me this?" asked she.

"Because, Georgiana," said Aylmer in a low voice, "there is danger."

"Danger? There is but one danger—that this horrible stigma shall be left upon my cheek!" cried Georgiana. "Remove it, remove it, whatever be the cost, or we shall both go mad!"

"Heaven knows your words are too true," said Aylmer sadly. "And now, dearest, return to your boudoir. In a little while all will be tested."

He conducted her back and took leave of her with a solemn tenderness which spoke far more than his words how much was now at stake. After his departure Georgiana became rapt in musings. She considered the character of Aylmer, and did it completer justice than at any previous moment. Her heart exulted, while it trembled, at his honorable love—so pure and lofty that it would accept nothing less than perfection nor miserably make itself contented with an earthlier nature than he had dreamed of. She felt how much more precious was such a sentiment than that meaner kind which would have borne with the imperfection for her sake, and have been guilty of treason to holy love by degrading its perfect idea to the level of the actual; and with her whole spirit she prayed that, for a single moment, she might satisfy his highest and deepest conception. Longer than one moment she well knew it could not be; for his spirit was ever on the march, ever ascending, and each instant required something that was beyond the scope of the instant before.

The sound of her husband's footsteps aroused her. He bore a crystal goblet containing a liquor colorless as water, but bright enough to be the draught of immortality. Aylmer was pale; but it seemed rather the consequence of a highly wrought state of mind and tension of spirit than of fear or doubt.

"The concoction of the draught has been perfect," said he, in answer to Georgiana's look. "Unless all my science have deceived me, it cannot fail."

"Save on your account, my dearest Aylmer," observed his wife, "I might wish to put off this birthmark of mortality by relinquishing mortality itself in preference to any other mode. Life is but a sad possession to those who have attained precisely the degree of moral advancement at which I stand. Were I weaker and blinder it might be happiness. Were I stronger, it might be endured hopefully. But, being what I find myself, methinks I am of all mortals the most fit to die."

"You are fit for heaven without tasting death!" replied her husband, "But why do we speak of dying? The draught cannot fail. Behold its effect upon this plant."

On the window seat there stood a geranium diseased with yellow blotches, which had overspread all its leaves. Aylmer poured a small quantity of the liquid upon the soil in which it grew. In a little time, when the roots of the plant had taken up the moisture, the unsightly blotches began to be extinguished in a living verdure.

"There needed no proof," said Georgiana quietly. "Give me the goblet. I joyfully stake all upon your word."

"Drink, then, thou lofty creature!" exclaimed Aylmer, with fervid admiration. "There is no taint of imperfection on thy spirit. Thy sensible frame, too, shall soon be all perfect."

She quaffed the liquid and returned the goblet to his hand.

"It is grateful," said she, with a placid smile, "Methinks it is like water from a heavenly fountain; for it contains I know not what of unobtrusive fragrance and deliciousness. It allays a feverish thirst that had parched me for many days. Now, dearest, let me sleep. My earthly senses are closing over my spirit like the leaves around the heart of a rose at sunset."

She spoke the last words with a gentle reluctance, as if it required almost more energy than she could command to pronounce the faint and lingering syllables.

Scarcely had they loitered through her lips ere she was lost in slumber. Aylmer sat by her side, watching her aspect with the emotions proper to a man the whole value of whose existence was involved in the process now to be tested. Mingled with this mood, however, was the philosophic investigation characteristic of the man of science. Not the minutest symptom escaped him. A heightened flush of the cheek, a slight irregularity of breath, a quiver of the eyelid, a hardly perceptible tremor through the frame,—such were the details which, as the moments passed, he wrote down in his folio volume. Intense thought had set its stamp upon every previous page of that volume, but the thoughts of years were all concentrated upon the last.

While thus employed, he failed not to gaze often at the fatal hand, and not without a shudder. Yet once, by a strange and unaccountable impulse, he pressed it with his lips. His spirit recoiled, however, in the very act; and Georgiana, out of the midst of her deep sleep, moved uneasily and murmured as if in remonstrance. Again Aylmer resumed his watch. Nor was it without avail. The crimson hand, which at first had been strongly visible upon the marble paleness of Georgiana's cheek, now grew more faintly outlined. She remained not less pale than ever; but the birthmark, with every breath that came and went, lost somewhat of its former distinctness. Its presence had been awful; its departure was more awful still. Watch the stain of the rainbow fading out of the sky, and you will know how that mysterious symbol passed away.

"By Heaven! it is well-nigh gone!" said Aylmer to himself, in almost irrepressible ecstasy. "I can scarcely trace it now. Success! success! And now it is like the faintest rose color. The lightest flush of blood across her cheek would overcome it. But she is so pale!"

He drew aside the window curtain and suffered the light of natural day to fall into the room and rest upon her check. At the same time he heard a gross, hoarse chuckle, which he had long known as his servant Aminadab's expression of delight.

"Ah, clod! ah, earthly mass!" cried Aylmer, laughing in a sort of frenzy, "you have served me well! Matter and spirit—earth and heaven—have both done their part in this! Laugh, thing of the senses! You have earned the right to laugh."

These exclamations broke Georgiana's sleep. She slowly unclosed her eyes and gazed into the mirror which her husband had arranged for that purpose. A faint smile flitted over her lips when she recognized how barely perceptible was now that crimson hand which had once blazed forth with such disastrous brilliancy as to scare away all their happiness. But then her eyes sought Aylmer's face with a trouble and anxiety that he could by no means account for.

"My poor Aylmer!" murmured she.

"Poor? Nay, richest, happiest, most favored!" exclaimed he. "My peerless bride, it is successful! You are perfect!"

"My poor Aylmer," she repeated, with a more than human tenderness, "you have aimed loftily; you have done nobly. Do not repent that with so high and pure a feeling, you have rejected the best the earth could offer. Aylmer, dearest Aylmer, I am dying!"

Alas! it was too true! The fatal hand had grappled with the mystery of life, and was the bond by which an angelic spirit kept itself in union with a mortal frame. As the last crimson tint of the birthmark—that sole token of human imperfection—faded from her cheek, the parting breath of the now perfect woman passed into the atmosphere, and her soul, lingering a moment near her husband, took its heavenward flight. Then a hoarse, chuckling laugh was heard again! Thus ever does the gross fatality of earth exult in its invariable triumph over the immortal essence which, in this dim sphere of half development, demands the completeness of a higher state. Yet, had Aylmer reached a profounder wisdom, he need not thus have flung away the happiness which would have woven his mortal life of the selfsame texture with the celestial. The momentary circumstance was too strong for him; he failed to look beyond the shadowy scope of time, and, living once for all in eternity, to find the perfect future in the present.

EDGAR ALLAN POE (1809–1849) was the son of two itinerant actors: a father who abandoned him and a mother who died when Poe was not quite three. He was raised, but never legally adopted, by a childless Richmond couple. He was educated in private academies in Virginia and England, and he attended the University of Virginia, but left due to gambling debts. He enlisted for a time in the Army and spent a semester at West Point before leaving it under dubious circumstances. In 1833, after winning a prize for his story "A MS. Found in a Bottle," he became the editor of the *Southern Literary Messenger*. He would later edit other periodicals, to which he often submitted his own works.

Poe's short fiction runs the gamut from the comic and **satiric** to the **grotesque** and the terrifying. His first collection of short stories appeared in 1840 under the title *Tales of the Grotesque and Arabesque*. "The Raven," perhaps his best-known poem, and other poems were printed in a collection *The Raven and Other Poems* in 1845. That same year, he published his second collection of stories, simply titled *Tales*. In addition to being a fiction writer and a poet, Poe was a respected literary critic who, when writing a review of Nathaniel Hawthorne's *Twice Told Tales*, developed a theory that helped to distinguish the short story from the novel.

"The Tell-Tale Heart" (1843), "The Cask of Amontillado" (1846), and "The Black Cat" (1843) are horror stories that examine the psychological effects of repressed morality and forces beyond human control, which in turn reveal the irrational in all of us. "The Purloined Letter" (1845) is a modern **ratiocinative** detective story. Poe's detective Dupin was the predecessor of the fabled Sherlock Holmes.

Related Works: "The Cask of Amontillado," "The Tell-Tale Heart," and "The Black Cat"; Faulkner, "A Rose for Emily"; Forché, "The Colonel"; Hardy, "'Ah, Are you digging on my grave?'"; Heaney, "Punishment" and "Digging"; Robert Browning, "My Last Duchess." "The Purloined Letter" and "The Black Cat"; Wideman, "What We Cannot Speak About We Must Pass Over in Silence"; Plath, "Metaphors"; Old English Riddles; Shakespeare, *Hamlet.*

The Tell-Tale Heart

True!—nervous—very, very dreadfully nervous I had been and am; but why *will* you say that I am mad? The disease had sharpened my senses—not destroyed—not dulled them. Above all was the sense of hearing acute. I heard all things in the heaven and in the earth. I heard many things in hell. How, then, am I mad? Hearken! and observe how healthily—how calmly I can tell you the whole story.

It is impossible to say how first the idea entered my brain; but once conceived, it haunted me day and night. Object there was none. Passion there was none. I loved the old man. He had never wronged me. He had never given me insult. For his gold I had no desire. I think it was his eye! yes, it was this! One of his eyes resembled that of a vulture—a pale blue eye, with a film over it. Whenever it fell upon me, my blood ran cold; and so by degrees—very gradually—I made up my mind to take the life of the old man, and thus rid myself of the eye for ever.

Now this is the point. You fancy me mad. Madmen know nothing. But you should have seen *me*. You should have seen how wisely I proceeded—with what caution—with what foresight—with what dissimulation I went to work! I was never kinder to the old man than during the whole week before I killed him. And every night, about midnight, I turned the latch of his door and opened it—oh, so gently! And then, when I had made an opening sufficient for my head, I put in a dark lantern, all closed, closed, so that no light shone out, and then I thrust in my head. Oh, you would have laughed to see how cunningly I thrust it in! I moved it slowly—very, very slowly, so that I might not disturb the old man's sleep. It took me an hour to place my whole head within the opening so far that I could see him as he lay upon his bed. Ha!—would a madman have been so wise as this? And then, when my head was well in the room, I undid the lantern cautiously—oh, so cautiously—cautiously (for the hinges creaked)—I undid it just so much that a single thin ray fell upon the vulture eye. And this I did for seven long nights—every night just at midnight—but I found the eye always closed; and so it was impossible to do the work; for it was not the old man who vexed me, but his Evil Eye. And every morning, when the day broke, I went boldly into the chamber, and spoke courageously to him, calling him by name in a hearty tone, and inquiring how he had passed the night. So you see he would have been a very profound old man, indeed, to suspect that every night, just at twelve, I looked in upon him while he slept.

Upon the eighth night I was more than usually cautious in opening the door. A watch's minute hand moves more quickly than did mine. Never before that night had I *felt* the extent of my own powers—of my sagacity. I could scarcely contain my feelings of triumph. To think that there I was, opening the door, little by little, and he not even to dream of my secret deeds or thoughts. I fairly chuckled at the idea; and perhaps he heard me; for he moved on the bed suddenly, as if startled. Now you may think that I drew back—but no. His room was as black as pitch with the thick darkness, (for the shutters were close fastened, through fear of robbers,) and so I knew that he could not see the opening of the door, and I kept pushing it on steadily, steadily.

I had my head in, and was about to open the lantern, when my thumb slipped upon the tin fastening, and the old man sprang up in the bed, crying out—"Who's there?"

I kept quite still and said nothing. For a whole hour I did not move a muscle, and in the meantime I did not hear him lie down. He was still sitting up in the bed listening;—just as I have done, night after night, hearkening to the death watches in the wall.

Presently I heard a slight groan, and I knew it was the groan of mortal terror. It was not a groan of pain or of grief—oh, no!—it was the low stifled sound that arises from the bottom of the soul when overcharged with awe. I knew the sound well. Many a night, just at midnight, when all the world slept, it has welled up from my own bosom, deepening, with its dreadful echo, the terrors that distracted me. I say I knew it well. I knew what the old man felt, and pitied him, although I chuckled at heart. I knew that he had been lying awake ever since the first slight noise, when he had turned in the bed. His fears had been ever since growing upon him. He had been trying to fancy them causeless, but could not. He had been saying to himself—"It is nothing but the wind in the chimney—it is only a mouse, crossing the floor," or "it is merely a cricket which has made a single chirp." Yes, he has been trying to comfort himself with these suppositions; but he had found all in vain, *All in vain*; because Death, in approaching him, had stalked with his black shadow before him, and enveloped the victim. And it was the mournful influence of the unperceived shadow that caused him to feel—although he neither saw nor heard—to *feel* the presence of my head within the room.

When I had waited a long time, very patiently, without hearing him lie down, I resolved to open a little—a very, very little crevice in the lantern. So I opened it—you cannot imagine how stealthily, stealthily—until, at length, a single dim ray, like the thread of the spider, shot from out the crevice and full upon the vulture eye.

It was open—wide, wide open—and I grew furious as I gazed upon it. I saw it with perfect distinctness—all a dull blue, with a hideous veil over it that chilled the very marrow in my bones; but I could see nothing else of the old man's face or person: for I had directed the ray as if by instinct, precisely upon the damned spot.

And now have I not told you that what you mistake for madness is but over-acuteness of the senses?—now, I say, there came to my ears a low, dull, quick sound, such as a watch makes when enveloped in cotton. I knew *that* sound well too. It was the beating of the old man's heart. It increased my fury, as the beating of a drum stimulates the soldier into courage.

But even yet I refrained and kept still. I scarcely breathed. I held the lantern motionless, I tried how steadily I could maintain the ray upon the eye. Meantime the hellish tattoo of the heart increased. It grew quicker and quicker, and louder and louder every instant. The old man's terror *must* have been extreme! It grew louder, I say, louder every moment!—do you mark me well? I have told you that I am nervous: so I am. And now at the dead hour of the night, amid the dreadful silence of that old house, so strange a noise as this excited me to uncontrollable terror. Yet, for some minutes longer I refrained and stood still. But the beating grew louder, louder! I thought the heart must burst. And now a new anxiety seized me—the sound would be heard by a neighbor! The old man's hour had come! With a loud yell, I threw open the lantern and leaped into the room. He shrieked once—once only. In an instant I dragged him to the floor, and pulled the heavy bed over him. I then smiled gaily, to find the deed so far done. But, for many minutes, the heart beat on with a muffled sound. This, however, did not vex me; it would not be heard through the wall. At length it ceased. The old man was dead. I removed the bed and examined the corpse. Yes, he was stone, stone dead. I placed my hand upon the heart and held it there many minutes. There was no pulsation. He was stone dead. His eye would trouble me no more.

If still you think me mad, you will think so no longer when I describe the wise precautions I took for the concealment of the body. The night waned, and

I worked hastily, but in silence. First of all I dismembered the corpse. I cut off the head and the arms and the legs.

I then took up three planks from the flooring of the chamber, and deposited all between the scantlings. I then replaced the boards so cleverly, so cunningly, that no human eye—not even *his*—could have detected any thing wrong. There was nothing to wash out—no stain of any kind—no blood-spot whatever. I had been too wary for that. A tub had caught all—ha! ha!

When I had made an end of these labors, it was four o'clock—still dark as midnight. As the bell sounded the hour, there came a knocking at the street door. I went down to open it with a light heart,—for what had I *now* to fear? There entered three men, who introduced themselves, with perfect suavity, as officers of the police. A shriek had been heard by a neighbor during the night; suspicion of foul play had been aroused; information had been lodged at the police office, and they (the officers) had been deputed to search the premises.

I smiled,—for *what* had I to fear? I bade the gentlemen welcome. The shriek, I said, was my own in a dream. The old man, I mentioned, was absent in the country. I took my visitors all over the house. I bade them search—search *well.* I led them, at length, to *his* chamber. I showed them his treasures, secure, undisturbed. In the enthusiasm of my confidence, I brought chairs into the room, and desired them *here* to rest from their fatigues, while I myself, in the wild audacity of my perfect triumph, placed my own seat upon the very spot beneath which reposed the corpse of the victim.

The officers were satisfied. My *manner* had convinced them. I was singularly at ease. They sat, and while I answered cheerily, they chatted familiar things. But, ere long, I felt myself getting pale and wished them gone. My head ached, and I fancied a ringing in my ears: but still they sat and still chatted. The ringing became more distinct:—it continued and became more distinct: I talked more freely to get rid of the feeling: but it continued and gained definitiveness—until, at length, I found that the noise was *not* within my ears.

No doubt I now grew *very* pale;—but I talked more fluently, and with a heightened voice. Yet the sound increased—and what could I do? It was *a low, dull, quick sound—much such a sound as a watch makes when enveloped in cotton.* I gasped for breath—and yet the officers heard it not. I talked more quickly—more vehemently; but the noise steadily increased. I arose and argued about trifles, in a high key and with violent gesticulations, but the noise steadily increased. Why *would* they not be gone? I paced the floor to and fro with heavy strides, as if excited to fury by the observation of the men—but the noise steadily increased. Oh God! what *could* I do? I foamed—I raved—I swore! I swung the chair upon which I had been sitting, and grated it upon the boards, but the noise arose over all and continually increased. It grew louder—louder—*louder!* And still the men chatted pleasantly, and smiled. Was it possible they heard not? Almighty God!—no, no! They heard!—they suspected!—they *knew!*—they were making a mockery of my horror!—this I thought, and this I think. But any thing was better than this agony! Any thing was more tolerable than this derision! I could bear those hypocritical smiles no longer! I felt that I must scream or die!—and now—again!—hark! louder! louder! louder! *louder!*—

"Villains!" I shrieked, "dissemble no more! I admit the deed!—tear up the planks!—here, here!—it is the beating of his hideous heart!"

EDGAR ALLAN POE

The Cask of Amontillado

The thousand injuries of Fortunato I had borne as I best could; but when he ventured upon insult, I vowed revenge. You, who so well know the nature of my soul, will not suppose, however, that I gave utterance to a threat. *At length* I would be avenged; this was a point definitively settled—but the very definitiveness with which it was resolved, precluded the idea of risk. I must not only punish, but punish with impunity. A wrong is unredressed when retribution overtakes its redresser. It is equally unredressed when the avenger fails to make himself felt as such to him who has done the wrong.

It must be understood, that neither by word nor deed had I given Fortunato cause to doubt my good-will. I continued, as was my wont, to smile in his face, and he did not perceive that my smile *now* was at the thought of his immolation.

He had a weak point—this Fortunato—although in other regards he was a man to be respected and even feared. He prided himself on his connoisseurship in wine. Few Italians have the true virtuoso spirit. For the most part their enthusiasm is adopted to suit the time and opportunity—to practise imposture upon the British and Austrian *millionaires*. In painting and gemmary Fortunato, like his countrymen, was a quack—but in the matter of old wines he was sincere. In this respect I did not differ from him materially: I was skilful in the Italian vintages myself, and bought largely whenever I could.

It was about dusk, one evening during the supreme madness of the carnival season, that I encountered my friend. He accosted me with excessive warmth, for he had been drinking much. The man wore motley. He had on a tight-fitting parti-striped dress, and his head was surmounted by the conical cap and bells. I was so pleased to see him, that I thought I should never have done wringing his hand.

I said to him: "My dear Fortunato, you are luckily met. How remarkably well you are looking to-day! But I have received a pipe of what passes for Amontillado, and I have my doubts."

"How?" said he. "Amontillado? A pipe? Impossible! And in the middle of the carnival!"

"I have my doubts," I replied; "and I was silly enough to pay the full Amontillado price without consulting you in the matter. You were not to be found, and I was fearful of losing a bargain."

"Amontillado!"

"I have my doubts."

"Amontillado!"

"And I must satisfy them."

"Amontillado!"

"As you are engaged, I am on my way to Luchesi. If any one has a critical turn, it is he. He will tell me————"

"Luchesi cannot tell Amontillado from Sherry."

"And yet some fools will have it that his taste is a match for your own."

"Come, let us go."

"Whither?"

"To your vaults."

"My friend, no; I will not impose upon your good nature. I perceive you have an engagement. Luchesi———"

"I have no engagement;—come."

"My friend, no. It is not the engagement, but the severe cold with which I perceive you are afflicted. The vaults are insufferably damp. They are encrusted with nitre."

"Let us go, nevertheless. The cold is merely nothing. Amontillado! You have been imposed upon. And as for Luchesi, he cannot distinguish Sherry from Amontillado."

Thus speaking, Fortunato possessed himself of my arm. Putting on a mask of black silk, and drawing a *roquelaire* closely about my person, I suffered him to hurry me to my palazzo.

There were no attendants at home; they had absconded to make merry in honor of the time. I had told them that I should not return until the morning, and had given them explicit orders not to stir from the house. These orders were sufficient, I well knew, to insure their immediate disappearance, one and all, as soon as my back was turned.

I took from their sconces two flambeaux, and giving one to Fortunato, bowed him through several suites of rooms to the archway that led into the vaults. I passed down a long and winding staircase, requesting him to be cautious as he followed. We came at length to the foot of the descent, and stood together on the damp ground of the catacombs of the Montresors.

The gait of my friend was unsteady, and the bells upon his cap jingled as he strode.

"The pipe?" said he.

"It is farther on," said I; "but observe the white webwork which gleams from these cavern walls."

He turned toward me, and looked into my eyes with two filmy orbs that distilled the rheum of intoxication.

"Nitre?" he asked, at length.

"Nitre," I replied. "How long have you had that cough?"

"Ugh! ugh! ugh!—ugh! ugh! ugh!—ugh! ugh! ugh!—ugh! ugh! ugh!—ugh! ugh! ugh!"

My poor friend found it impossible to reply for many minutes.

"It is nothing," he said, at last.

"Come," I said, with decision, "we will go back; your health is precious. You are rich, respected, admired, beloved; you are happy, as once I was. You are a man to be missed. For me it is no matter. We will go back; you will be ill, and I cannot be responsible. Besides, there is Luchesi———"

"Enough," he said; "the cough is a mere nothing; it will not kill me. I shall not die of a cough."

"True—true," I replied; "and, indeed, I had no intention of alarming you unnecessarily; but you should use all proper caution. A draught of this Medoc will defend us from the damps."

Here I knocked off the neck of a bottle which I drew from a long row of its fellows that lay upon the mould.

"Drink," I said, presenting him the wine.

He raised it to his lips with a leer. He paused and nodded to me familiarly, while his bells jingled.

"I drink," he said, "to the buried that repose around us."

"And I to your long life."

He again took my arm, and we proceeded.

"These vaults," he said, "are extensive."

"The Montresors," I replied, "were a great and numerous family."

"I forget your arms."

"A huge human foot d' or, in a field azure; the foot crushes a serpent rampant whose fangs are imbedded in the heel."

"And the motto?"

"*Nemo me impune lacessit*."†

"Good!" he said.

The wine sparkled in his eyes and the bells jingled. My own fancy grew warm with the Medoc. We had passed through walls of piled bones, with casks and puncheons intermingling, into the inmost recesses of the catacombs. I paused again, and this time I made bold to seize Fortunato by an arm above the elbow.

"The nitre!" I said; "see, it increases. It hangs like moss upon the vaults. We are below the river's bed. The drops of moisture trickle among the bones. Come, we will go back ere it is too late. Your cough——"

"It is nothing," he said; "let us go on. But first, another draught of the Medoc."

I broke and reached him a flagon of De Grâve. He emptied it at a breath. His eyes flashed with a fierce light. He laughed and threw the bottle upward with a gesticulation I did not understand.

I looked at him in surprise. He repeated the movement—a grotesque one.

"You do not comprehend?" he said.

"Not I," I replied.

"Then you are not of the brotherhood."

"How?"

"You are not of the masons."

"Yes, yes," I said; "yes, yes."

"You? Impossible! A mason?"

"A mason," I replied.

"A sign," he said.

"It is this," I answered, producing a trowel from beneath the folds of my *roquelaire*.

"You jest," he exclaimed, recoiling a few paces. "But let us proceed to the Amontillado."

"Be it so," I said, replacing the tool beneath the cloak, and again offering him my arm. He leaned upon it heavily. We continued our route in search of the Amontillado. We passed through a range of low arches, descended, passed on, and descending again, arrived at a deep crypt, in which the foulness of the air caused our flambeaux rather to glow than flame.

At the most remote end of the crypt there appeared another less spacious. Its walls had been lined with human remains, piled to the vault overhead, in the fashion of the great catacombs of Paris. Three sides of this interior crypt were still

---

† "*No one insults me with impurity*" (Latin)

ornamented in this manner. From the fourth the bones had been thrown down, and lay promiscuously upon the earth, forming at one point a mound of some size. Within the wall thus exposed by the displacing of the bones, we perceived a still interior recess, in depth about four feet, in width three, in height six or seven. It seemed to have been constructed for no especial use within itself, but formed merely the interval between two of the colossal supports of the roof of the catacombs, and was backed by one of their circumscribing walls of solid granite.

It was in vain that Fortunato, uplifting his dull torch, endeavored to pry into the depth of the recess. Its termination the feeble light did not enable us to see.

"Proceed," I said; "herein is the Amontillado. As for Luchesi———"

"He is an ignoramus," interrupted my friend, as he stepped unsteadily forward, while I followed immediately at his heels. In an instant he had reached the extremity of the niche, and finding his progress arrested by the rock, stood stupidly bewildered. A moment more and I had fettered him to the granite. In its surface were two iron staples, distant from each other about two feet, horizontally. From one of these depended a short chain, from the other a padlock. Throwing the links about his waist, it was but the work of a few seconds to secure it. He was too much astounded to resist. Withdrawing the key I stepped back from the recess.

"Pass your hand," I said, "over the wall; you cannot help feeling the nitre. Indeed it is *very* damp. Once more let me *implore* you to return. No? Then I must positively leave you. But I must first render you all the little attentions in my power."

"The Amontillado!" ejaculated my friend, not yet recovered from his astonishment.

"True," I replied; "the Amontillado."

As I said these words I busied myself among the pile of bones of which I have before spoken. Throwing them aside, I soon uncovered a quantity of building stone and mortar. With these materials and with the aid of my trowel, I began vigorously to wall up the entrance of the niche.

I had scarcely laid the first tier of the masonry when I discovered that the intoxication of Fortunato had in a great measure worn off. The earliest indication I had of this was a low moaning cry from the depth of the recess. It was *not* the cry of a drunken man. There was then a long and obstinate silence. I laid the second tier, and the third, and the fourth; and then I heard the furious vibrations of the chain. The noise lasted for several minutes, during which, that I might hearken to it with the more satisfaction, I ceased my labors and sat down upon the bones. When at last the clanking subsided, I resumed the trowel, and finished without interruption the fifth, the sixth, and the seventh tier. The wall was now nearly upon a level with my breast. I again paused, and holding the flambeaux over the mason-work, threw a few feeble rays upon the figure within.

A succession of loud and shrill screams, bursting suddenly from the throat of the chained form, seemed to thrust me violently back. For a brief moment I hesitated—I trembled. Unsheathing my rapier, I began to grope with it about the recess; but the thought of an instant reassured me. I placed my hand upon the solid fabric of the catacombs, and felt satisfied. I reapproached the wall. I replied to the yells of him who clamored. I re-echoed—I aided—I surpassed them in volume and in strength. I did this, and the clamorer grew still.

It was now midnight, and my task was drawing to a close. I had completed the eighth, the ninth, and the tenth tier. I had finished a portion of the last and the eleventh; there remained but a single stone to be fitted and plastered in. I struggled with its weight; I placed it partially in its destined position. But now there came from out the niche a low laugh that erected the hairs upon my head. It was succeeded by a sad voice, which I had difficulty in recognizing as that of the noble Fortunato. The voice said—

"Ha! ha! ha!—he! he!—a very good joke indeed—an excellent jest. We will have many a rich laugh about it at the palazzo—he! he! he!—over our wine—he! he! he!"

"The Amontillado!" I said.

"He! he! he!—he! he! he!—yes, the Amontillado. But is it not getting late? Will not they be awaiting us at the palazzo, the Lady Fortunato and the rest? Let us be gone."

"Yes," I said, "let us be gone."

"*For the love of God, Montresor!*"

"Yes," I said, "for the love of God!"

But to these words I hearkened in vain for a reply. I grew impatient. I called aloud;

"Fortunato!"

No answer. I called again;

"Fortunato!"

No answer still. I thrust a torch through the remaining aperture and let it fall within. There came forth in return only a jingling of the bells. My heart grew sick—on account of the dampness of the catacombs. I hastened to make an end of my labor. I forced the last stone into its position; I plastered it up. Against the new masonry I re-erected the old rampart of bones. For the half of a century no mortal has disturbed them. *In pace requiescat*!

EDGAR ALLAN POE

The Black Cat

For the most wild yet most homely narrative which I am about to pen, I neither expect nor solicit belief. Mad indeed would I be to expect it in a case where my very senses reject their own evidence. Yet, mad am I not—and very surely do I not dream. But tomorrow I die, and today I would unburden my soul. My immediate purpose is to place before the world, plainly, succinctly, and without comment, a series of mere household events. In their consequences, these events have terrified—have tortured—have destroyed me. Yet I will not attempt to expound them. To me, they have presented little but horror—to many they will seem less terrible than *baroques*. Hereafter, perhaps, some intellect may be found which will reduce my phantasm to the commonplace—some intellect more calm, more logical, and far less excitable than my own, which will perceive in the circumstances I detail with awe, nothing more than an ordinary succession of very natural causes and effects.

From my infancy I was noted for the docility and humanity of my disposition. My tenderness of heart was even so conspicuous as to make me the jest of my companions. I was especially fond of animals, and was indulged by my parents with a great variety of pets. With these I spent most of my time, and never was so happy as when feeding and caressing them. This peculiarity of character grew with my growth, and, in my manhood, I derived from it one of my principal sources of pleasure. To those who have cherished an affection for a faithful and sagacious dog, I need hardly be at the trouble of explaining the nature or the intensity of the gratification this derivable. There is something in the unselfish and self-sacrificing love of brute, which goes directly to the heart of him who has had frequent occasion to test the paltry friendship and gossamer fidelity of mere *Man*.

I married early and was happy to find in my wife a disposition not uncongenial with my own. Observing my partiality for domestic pets, she lost no opportunity of procuring those of the most agreeable land. We had birds gold-fish, a fine dog, rabbits, a small monkey, and a *cat*.

This latter was a remarkably large and beautiful animal, entirely black and sagacious to an astonishing degree. In speaking of his intelligence my wife, who at heart was not a little tinctured with superstition, made frequent allusion to the ancient popular notion, which regarded all black cats as witches in disguise. Not that she was ever *serious* upon this point—and I mention the matter at all for no better reason than that it happens, just now, to be remembered.

Pluto—this was the cat's name—was my favorite pet and playmate. I alone fed him, and he attended me wherever I went about the house. It was even with difficulty that I could prevent him from following me through the streets.

Our friendship lasted in this manner, for several years, during which my general temperament and character—through the instrumentality of the Fiend Intemperance—had (I blush to confess it) experienced a radical alteration for the worse. I grew, day by day, more moody, more irritable, more regardless of the feelings of others. I suffered myself to use intemperate language to my wife. At length, I even offered her personal violence. My pets, of course, were made to feel the change in my disposition. I not only neglected, but ill-used them. For Pluto, however, I still retained sufficient regard to restrain me from maltreating him, as I made no scruple of maltreating the rabbits, the monkey, or even the dog, when by accident or through affection, they came in my way. But my disease grew upon me—for what disease is like Alcohol!—and at length even Pluto, who was now becoming old, and consequently somewhat peevish—even Pluto began to experience the effects of my ill temper.

One night, returning home, much intoxicated from one of my haunts about town, I fancied that the cat avoided my presence. I seized him; when, in his fright at my violence, he inflicted a slight wound upon my hand with his teeth. The fury of a demon instantly possessed me; I knew myself no longer. My original soul seemed, at once, to take its flight from my body; and a more than fiendish malevolence, gin-nurtured, thrilled every fibre of my frame. I took from my waistcoat pocket a penknife, opened it, grasped the poor beast by the throat, and deliberately cut one of its eyes from the socket! I blush, I burn, I shudder, while I pen the damnable atrocity.

When reason returned with the morning—when I had slept off the fumes of the night's debauch—I experienced a sentiment half of horror, half of remorse, for the crime of which I had been guilty, but it was, at best, a feeble and equivocal feeling, and the soul remained untouched. I again plunged into excess, and soon drowned in wine all memory of the deed.

In the meantime the cat slowly recovered. The socket of the lost eye presented, it is true, a frightful appearance, but he no longer appeared to suffer any pain. He went about the house as usual, but, as might be expected, fled in extreme terror at my approach. I had so much of my old heart left, as to be at first grieved by this evident dislike on the part of a creature which had once so loved me. But this feeling soon gave place to irritation. And then came, as if to my final and irrevocable overthrow, the spirit of PERVERSENESS. Of this spirit philosophy takes no account. Yet I am not more sure that my soul lives, than I am that perverseness is one of the primitive impulses of the human heart—one of the indivisible primary faculties, or sentiments, which give direction to the character of Man. Who has not, a hundred times, found himself committing a vile or a stupid action, for no other reason than because he knows he should *not?* Have we not a perpetual inclination, in the teeth of our best judgment, to violate that which is *Law*, merely because we understand it to be such? This spirit of perverseness, I say, came to my final overthrow. It was this unfathomable longing of the soul *to vex itself*—to offer violence to its own nature—to do wrong for the wrong's sake only—that urged me to continue and finally to consummate the injury I had inflicted upon the unoffending brute. One morning, in cold blood, I slipped a noose about its neck and hung it to the limb of a tree;—hung it with the tears streaming from my eyes, and with the bitterest remorse at my heart;—hung it *because* I knew that it had loved me, and *because* I felt it had given me no reason of offence—hung it *because* I knew that in so doing I was committing a sin—a deadly sin that would so jeopardize my immortal soul as to place it—if such a thing were possible—even beyond the reach of the infinite mercy of the Most Merciful and Most Terrible God.

On the night of the day on which this most cruel deed was done, I was aroused from sleep by the cry of fire. The curtains of my bed were in flames. The whole house was blazing. It was with great difficulty that my wife, a servant, and myself, made our escape from the conflagration. The destruction was complete. My entire worldly wealth was swallowed up, and I resigned myself thenceforward to despair.

I am above the weakness of seeking to establish a sequence of cause and effect, between the disaster and the atrocity. But I am detailing a chain of facts—and wish not to leave even a possible link imperfect. On the day succeeding the fire, I visited the ruins. The walls, with one exception, had fallen in. This exception was found in a compartment wall, not very thick, which stood about the middle of the house, and against which had rested the head of my bed. The plastering had here, in great measure, resisted the action of the fire—a fact which I attributed to its having been recently spread. About this wall a dense crowd were collected, and many persons seemed to be examining a particular portion of it with very minute and eager attention. The words "strange!" "singular!" and other similar expressions, excited my curiosity. I approached and saw, as if graven in *bas relief*, upon the white surface, the figure of a gigantic *cat*. The impression was given with an accuracy truly marvellous. There was a rope about the animal's neck.

When I first beheld this apparition—for I could scarcely regard it as less—my wonder and my terror were extreme. But at length reflection came to my aid. The cat, I remembered, had been hung in a garden adjacent to the house. Upon the alarm of fire, this garden had been immediately filled by the crowd—by some one of whom the animal must have been cut from the tree and thrown, through an open window, into my chamber. This had probably been done with the view of arousing me from sleep. The falling of other walls had compressed the victim of my cruelty into the substance of the freshly-spread plaster; the lime of which, with the flames, and the *ammonia* from the carcass, had then accomplished the portraiture as I saw it.

Although I thus readily accounted to my reason if not altogether to my conscience, for the startling fact just detailed, it did not the less fail to make a deep impression upon my fancy. For months I could not rid myself of the phantasm of the cat; and, during this period, there came back into my spirit a half-sentiment that seemed, but was not, remorse. I went so far as to regret the loss of the animal, and to look about me, among the vile haunts which I now habitually frequented, for another pet of the same species and of somewhat similar appearance, with which to supply its place.

One night as I sat, half stupefied, in a den of more than infamy, my attention was suddenly drawn to some black object, reposing upon the head of one of the immense hogsheads of gin, or of rum, which constituted the chief furniture of the apartment. I had been looking steadily at the top of this hogshead for some minutes, and what now caused me surprise was the fact that I had not sooner perceived the object thereupon. I approached it, and touched it with my hand. It was a black cat—a very large one—fully as large as Pluto, and closely resembling him in every respect but one. Pluto had not a white hair upon any portion of his body; but this cat had a large although indefinite splotch of white, covering nearly the whole region of the breast.

Upon my touching him, he immediately arose, purred loudly, rushed against my hand, and appeared delighted with my notice. This, then, was the very creature of which I was in search. I at once offered to purchase it of the landlord, but this person made no claim to it—knew nothing of it—had never seen it before.

I continued my caresses, and when I prepared to go home, the animal evinced a disposition to accompany me. I permitted it to do so, occasionally stooping and patting it as I proceeded. When it reached the house, it domesticated itself at once, and became immediately a great favorite with my wife.

For my own part, I soon found a dislike to it arising within me. This was just the reverse of what I had anticipated; but—I know not how or why it was—its evident fondness for myself rather disgusted and annoyed me. By slow degrees these feelings of disgust and annoyance rose into the bitterness of hatred. I avoided the creature; a certain sense of shame, and the remembrance of my former deed of cruelty, preventing me from physically abusing it. I did not, for some weeks, strike, or otherwise violently ill use it; but gradually—very gradually—I came to look upon it with unutterable loathing, and to flee silently from its odious presence, as from the breath of a pestilence.

What added, no doubt, to my hatred of the beast, was the discovery, on the morning after I brought it home, that like Pluto, it also had been deprived of one of its eyes. This circumstance, however, only endeared it to my wife, who, as I have already said, possessed, in a high degree, that humanity of feeling which had once been my distinguishing trail, and the source of many of my simplest and purest pleasures.

With my aversion to this cat, however, its partiality for myself seemed to increase. It followed my footsteps with a pertinacity which it would be difficult to make the reader comprehend. Whenever I sat, it would crouch beneath my chair, or spring upon my knees covering me with its loathsome caresses. If I arose to walk it would get between my feet and thus nearly throw me down, or, fastening its long and sharp claws in my dress, clamber, in this manner to my breast. At such times although I longed to destroy it with a blow, I was yet withheld from so doing, partly by a memory of my former crime, but chiefly—let me confess it at once—by absolute *dread* of the beast.

This dread was not exactly a dread of physical evil—and yet I should be at a loss how otherwise to define it. I am almost ashamed to own—yes, even in this felon's cell, I am almost ashamed to own—that the terror and horror with which the animal inspired me, had been heightened by one of the merest chimeras it would be possible to conceive. My wife had called my attention, more than once, to the character of the mark of white hair, of which I have spoken, and which constituted the sole visible difference between the strange beast and the one I had destroyed. The reader will remember that this mark, although large, had been originally very indefinite, but, by slow degrees—degrees nearly imperceptible, and which for a long time my reason struggled to reject as fanciful—it had, at length, assumed a rigorous distinction of outline. It was now the representation of an object that I shudder to name—and for this, above all, I loathed and dreaded, and would have rid myself of the monster *had I dared*—it was now, I say, the image of a hideous—of a ghastly thing—of the GALLOWS!—oh, mournful and terrible engine of Horror and of Crime—of Agony and of Death!

And now was I indeed wretched beyond the wretchedness of mere Humanity. And *a brute beast*—whose fellow I had contemptuously destroyed—*a brute beast* to work out for *me*—for me, a man fashioned in the image of the High God—so much of insufferable woe! Alas! neither by day nor by night knew I the blessing of rest any more! During the former the creature left me no moment alone, and in the latter I started hourly from dreams of unutterable fear to find the hot breath of *the thing* upon my face, and its vast weight—an incarnate nightmare that I had no power to shake off—incumbent eternally upon my *heart*!

Beneath the pressure of torments such as these the feeble remnant of the good within me succumbed. Evil thoughts became my sole intimates—the darkest and most evil of thoughts. The moodiness of my usual temper increased to hatred of all things and of all mankind; while from the sudden, frequent, and ungovernable outbursts of a fury to which I now blindly abandoned myself, my uncomplaining wife, alas, was the most usual and the most patient of sufferers.

One day she accompanied me, upon some household errand, into the cellar of the old building which our poverty compelled us to inhabit. The cat followed me down the steep stairs, and, nearly throwing me headlong, exasperated me to madness. Uplifting an axe, and forgetting in my wrath the childish dread which had hitherto stayed my hand, I aimed a blow at the animal, which, of course, would have proved instantly fatal had it descended as I wished. But this blow was arrested by the hand of my wife. Goaded by the interference into a rage more than demoniacal, I withdrew my arm from her grasp and buried the axe in her brain. She fell dead upon the spot without a groan.

This hideous murder accomplished, I set myself forthwith, and with entire deliberation, to the task of concealing the body. I knew that I could not remove it from the house, either by day or by night, without the risk of being observed by the neighbors. Many projects entered my mind. At one period I thought of cutting the corpse into minute fragments, and destroying them by fire. At another, I resolved to dig a grave for it in the floor of the cellar. Again, I deliberated about casting it in the well in the yard—about packing it in a box, as if merchandise, with the usual arrangements, and so getting a porter to take it from the house. Finally I hit upon what I considered a far better expedient than either of these. I determined to wall it up in the cellar, as the monks of the Middle Ages are recorded to have walled up their victims.

For a purpose such as this the cellar was well adapted. Its walls were loosely constructed, and had lately been plastered throughout with a rough plaster, which the dampness of the atmosphere had prevented from hardening. Moreover, in one of the walls was a projection, caused by a false chimney, or fireplace that had been filled up and made to resemble the rest of the cellar. I made no doubt that I could readily displace the bricks at this point, insert the corpse, and wall the whole up as before, so that no eye could detect any thing suspicious.

And in this calculation I was not deceived. By means of a crowbar I easily dislodged the bricks, and, having carefully deposited the body against the inner wall, I propped it in that position, while with little trouble I relaid the whole structure as it originally stood. Having procured mortar, sand, and hair, with every possible precaution, I prepared a plaster which could not be distinguished from the old and with this I very carefully went over the new brick-work. When I had finished, I felt satisfied that all was right. The wall did not present the slightest appearance of having been disturbed. The rubbish on the floor was picked up with the minutest care. I looked around triumphantly, and said to myself, "Here at least, then, my labor has not been in vain."

My next step was to look for the beast which had been the cause of so much wretchedness, for I had, at length, firmly resolved to put it to death. Had I been able to meet with it at the moment, there could have been no doubt of its fate; but it appeared that the crafty animal had been alarmed at the violence of my previous anger, and forbore to present itself in my present mood. It is impossible to describe or to imagine the deep, the blissful sense of relief which the absence of the detested creature occasioned in my bosom. It did not make its appearance during the night; and thus for one night, at least, since its introduction into the house, I soundly and tranquilly slept, aye, *slept* even with the burden of murder upon my soul.

The second and the third day passed, and still my tormentor came not. Once again I breathed as a free man. The monster, in terror, had fled the premises for ever! I should behold it no more! My happiness was supreme! The guilt of my dark deed disturbed me but little. Some few inquiries had been made, but these had been readily answered. Even a search had been instituted—but of course nothing was to be discovered. I looked upon my future felicity as secured.

Upon the fourth day of the assassination, a party of the police came, very unexpectedly, into the house, and proceeded again to make rigorous investigation of the premises. Secure, however, in the inscrutability of my place of concealment, I felt no embarrassment whatever. The officers bade me accompany them in their search. They left no nook or corner unexplored. At length, for the third or fourth time, they descended into the cellar. I quivered not in a muscle. My heart beat calmly as that of one who slumbers in innocence. I walked the cellar from end to end. I folded my arms upon my bosom, and roamed easily to and fro. The police were thoroughly satisfied and prepared to depart. The glee at my heart was too strong to be restrained. I burned to say if but one word, by way of triumph, and to render doubly sure their assurance of my guiltlessness.

"Gentlemen," I said at last, as the party ascended the steps, "I delight to have allayed your suspicions. I wish you all health and a little more courtesy. By the bye, gentlemen, this—this is a very well-constructed house," (in the rabid desire to say something easily, I scarcely knew what I uttered at all),—"I may say an *excellently* well-constructed house. These walls—are you going, gentlemen?—these walls are solidly put together"; and here, through the mere frenzy of bravado, I rapped heavily with a cane which I held in my hand, upon that very portion of the brick-work behind which stood the corpse of the wife of my bosom.

But may God shield and deliver me from the fangs of the Arch-Fiend! No sooner had the reverberation of my blows sunk into silence, than I was answered by a voice from within the tomb!—by a cry, at first muffled and broken, like the sobbing of a child, and then quickly swelling into one long loud, and continuous scream, utterly anomalous and inhuman—a howl—a wailing shriek, half of horror and half of triumph, such as might have arisen only out of hell, conjointly from the throats of the damned in their agony and of the demons that exult in the damnation.

Of my own thoughts it is folly to speak. Swooning, I staggered to the opposite wall. For one instant the party on the stairs remained motionless, through extremity of terror and awe. In the next a dozen stout arms were toiling at the wall. It fell bodily. The corpse, already greatly decayed and clotted with gore, stood erect before the eyes of the spectators. Upon its head, with red extended mouth and solitary eye of fire, sat the hideous beast whose craft had seduced me into murder, and whose informing voice had consigned me to the hangman. I had walled the monster up within the tomb.

EDGAR ALLAN POE

The Purloined Letter

Nil sapientiae odiosius acumine nimio.—*Seneca.*

At Paris, just after dark one gusty evening in the autumn of 18——, I was enjoying the twofold luxury of meditation and a meerschaum, in company with my friend, C. Auguste Dupin, in his little back library, or book-closet, *au troisième*, No. 33 *Rue Dunôt, Faubourg St. Germain*. For one hour at least we had maintained a profound silence; while each, to any casual observer, might have seemed intently and exclusively occupied with the curling eddies of smoke that oppressed the atmosphere of the chamber. For myself, however, I was mentally discussing certain topics which had formed matter for conversation between us at an earlier period of the evening; I mean the affair of the Rue Morgue, and the mystery attending the murder of Marie Rogêt. I looked upon it, therefore, as something of a coincidence, when the door of our apartment was thrown open and admitted our old acquaintance, Monsieur G——, the Prefect of the Parisian police.

We gave him a hearty welcome; for there was nearly half as much of the entertaining as of the contemptible about the man, and we had not seen him for several years. We had been sitting in the dark, and Dupin now arose for the purpose of lighting a lamp, but sat down again, without doing so, upon G.'s saying that he had called to consult us, or rather to ask the opinion of my friend, about some official business which had occasioned a great deal of trouble.

"If it is any point requiring reflection," observed Dupin, as he forebore to enkindle the wick, "we shall examine it to better purpose in the dark."

"That is another of your odd notions," said the Prefect, who had the fashion of calling every thing "odd" that was beyond his comprehension, and thus lived amid an absolute legion of "oddities."

"Very true," said Dupin, as he supplied his visitor with a pipe, and rolled toward him a comfortable chair.

"And what is the difficulty now?" I asked. "Nothing more in the assassination way I hope?"

"Oh, no; nothing of that nature. The fact is, the business is *very* simple indeed, and I make no doubt that we can manage it sufficiently well ourselves; but then I thought Dupin would like to hear the details of it, because it is so excessively *odd*."

"Simple and odd," said Dupin.

"Why, yes; and not exactly that either. The fact is, we have all been a good deal puzzled because the affair *is* so simple, and yet baffles us altogether."

"Perhaps it is the very simplicity of the thing which puts you at fault," said my friend.

"What nonsense you *do* talk!" replied the Prefect, laughing heartily.

"Perhaps the mystery is a little *too* plain," said Dupin.

"Oh, good heavens! who ever heard of such an idea?"

"A little *too* self-evident."

"Ha! ha! ha!—ha! ha! ha!—ho! ho! ho!" roared our visitor, profoundly amused, "oh, Dupin, you will be the death of me yet!"

"And what, after all, *is* the matter on hand?" I asked.

"Why, I will tell you," replied the Prefect, as he gave a long, steady, and contemplative puff, and settled himself in his chair. "I will tell you in a few words; but, before I begin, let me caution you that this is an affair demanding the greatest secrecy, and that I should most probably lose the position I now hold, were it known that I confided it to any one."

"Proceed," said I.

"Or not," said Dupin.

"Well, then; I have received personal information, from a very high quarter, that a certain document of the last importance has been purloined from the royal apartments. The individual who purloined it is known; this beyond a doubt; he was seen to take it. It is known, also, that it still remains in his possession."

"How is this known?" asked Dupin.

"It is clearly inferred," replied the Prefect, "from the nature of the document, and from the non-appearance of certain results which would at once arise from its passing *out* of the robber's possession—that is to say, from his employing it as he must design in the end to employ it."

"Be a little more explicit," I said.

"Well, I may venture so far as to say that the paper gives its holder a certain power in a certain quarter where such power is immensely valuable." The Prefect was fond of the cant of diplomacy.

"Still I do not quite understand," said Dupin.

"No? Well; the disclosure of the document to a third person, who shall be nameless, would bring in question the honor of a personage of most exalted station; and this fact gives the holder of the document an ascendancy over the illustrious personage whose honor and peace are so jeopardized."

"But this ascendancy," I interposed, "would depend upon the robber's knowledge of the loser's knowledge of the robber. Who would dare—"

"The thief," said G., "is the Minister D——, who dares all things, those unbecoming as well as those becoming a man. The method of the theft was not less ingenious than bold. The document in question—a letter, to be frank—had been received by the personage robbed while alone in the royal *boudoir*. During its perusal she was suddenly interrupted by the entrance of the other exalted personage from whom especially it was her wish to conceal it. After a hurried and vain endeavor to thrust it in a drawer, she was forced to place it, open as it was, upon a table. The address, however, was uppermost, and, the contents thus unexposed, the letter escaped notice. At this juncture enters the Minister D——. His lynx eye immediately perceives the paper, recognizes the handwriting of the address, observes the confusion of the personage addressed, and fathoms her secret. After some business transactions, hurried through in his ordinary manner, he produces a letter somewhat similar to the one in question, opens it, pretends to read it, and then places it in close juxtaposition to the other. Again he converses, for some fifteen minutes, upon the public affairs. At length, in taking leave, he takes also from the table the letter to which he had no claim. Its rightful owner saw, but, of course, dared not call attention to the act, in the presence of the third personage who stood at her elbow. The minister decamped; leaving his own letter—one of no importance—upon the table."

"Here, then," said Dupin to me, "you have precisely what you demand to make the ascendancy complete—the robber's knowledge of the loser's knowledge of the robber."

"Yes," replied the Prefect; "and the power thus attained has, for some months past, been wielded, for political purposes, to a very dangerous extent. The personage robbed is more thoroughly convinced, every day, of the necessity of reclaiming her letter. But this, of course, cannot be done openly. In fine, driven to despair, she has committed the matter to me."

"Than whom," said Dupin, amid a perfect whirlwind of smoke, "no more sagacious agent could, I suppose, be desired, or even imagined."

"You flatter me," replied the Prefect; "but it is possible that some such opinion may have been entertained."

"It is clear," said I, "as you observe, that the letter is still in the possession of the minister; since it is this possession, and not any employment of the letter, which bestows the power. With the employment the power departs."

"True," said G.; "and upon this conviction I proceeded. My first care was to make thorough search of the minister's hotel; and here my chief embarrassment lay in the necessity of searching without his knowledge. Beyond all things, I have been warned of the danger which would result from giving him reason to suspect our design."

"But," said I, "you are quite *au fait* in these investigations. The Parisian police have done this thing often before."

"Oh, yes; and for this reason I did not despair. The habits of the minister gave me, too, a great advantage. He is frequently absent from home all night. His servants are by no means numerous. They sleep at a distance from their master's apartment, and, being chiefly Neapolitans, are readily made drunk. I have keys, as you know, with which I can open any chamber or cabinet in Paris. For three months a night has not passed, during the greater part of which I have not been engaged, personally, in ransacking the D——— Hotel. My honor is interested, and, to mention a great secret, the reward is enormous. So I did not abandon the search until I had become fully satisfied that the thief is a more astute man than myself. I fancy that I have investigated every nook and corner of the premises in which it is possible that the paper can be concealed."

"But is it not possible," I suggested, "that although the letter may be in possession of the minister, as it unquestionably is, he may have concealed it elsewhere than upon his own premises?"

"This is barely possible," said Dupin, "The present peculiar condition of affairs at court, and especially of those intrigues in which D——— is known to be involved, would render the instant availability of the document—its susceptibility of being produced at a moment's notice—a point of nearly equal importance with its possession."

"Its susceptibility of being produced?" said I.

"That is to say, of being *destroyed*," said Dupin.

"True," I observed; "the paper is clearly then upon the premises. As for its being upon the person of the minister, we may consider that as out of the question."

"Entirely," said the Prefect. "He has been twice waylaid, as if by footpads, and his person rigidly searched under my own inspection."

"You might have spared yourself this trouble," said Dupin. "D———, I presume, is not altogether a fool, and, if not, must have anticipated these waylayings, as a matter of course."

"Not *altogether* a fool," said G., "but then he is a poet, which I take to be only one remove from a fool."

"True," said Dupin, after a long and thoughtful whiff from his meerschaum, "although I have been guilty of certain doggrel myself."

"Suppose you detail," said I, "the particulars of your search."

"Why, the fact is, we took our time, and we searched *everywhere*. I have had long experience in these affairs. I took the entire building, room by room; devoting the nights of a whole week to each. We examined, first, the furniture of each apartment. We opened every possible drawer; and I presume you know that, to a properly trained police-agent, such a thing as a '*secret*' drawer is impossible. Any man is a dolt who permits a 'secret' drawer to escape him in a search of this kind. The thing is *so* plain. There is a certain amount of bulk—of space—to be accounted for in every cabinet. Then we have accurate rules. The fiftieth part of a line could not escape us. After the cabinets we took the chairs. The cushions we probed with the fine long needles you have seen me employ. From the tables we removed the tops."

"Why so?"

"Sometimes the top of a table, or other similarly arranged piece of furniture, is removed by the person wishing to conceal an article; then the leg is excavated, the article deposited within the cavity, and the top replaced. The bottoms and tops of bedposts are employed in the same way."

"But could not the cavity be detected by sounding?" I asked.

"By no means, if, when the article is deposited, a sufficient wadding of cotton be placed around it. Besides, in our case, we were obliged to proceed without noise."

"But you could not have removed—you could not have taken to pieces *all* articles of furniture in which it would have been possible to make a deposit in the manner you mention. A letter may be compressed into a thin spiral roll, not differing much in shape or bulk from a large knitting-needle, and in this form it might be inserted into the rung of a chair, for example. You did not take to pieces all the chairs?"

"Certainly not; but we did better—we examined the rungs of every chair in the hotel, and, indeed, the jointings of every description of furniture, by the aid of a most powerful microscope. Had there been any traces of recent disturbance we should not have failed to detect it instantly. A single grain of gimlet-dust, for example, would have been as obvious as an apple. Any disorder in the gluing—any unusual gaping in the joints—would have sufficed to insure detection."

"I presume you looked to the mirrors, between the boards and the plates, and you probed the beds and the bedclothes, as well as the curtains and carpets."

"That of course; and when we had absolutely completed every particle of the furniture in this way, then we examined the house itself. We divided its entire surface into compartments, which we numbered, so that none might be missed; then we scrutinized each individual square inch throughout the premises, including the two houses immediately adjoining, with the microscope, as before."

"The two houses adjoining!" I exclaimed; "you must have had a great deal of trouble."

"We had; but the reward offered is prodigious."

"You include the *grounds* about the houses?"

"All the grounds are paved with brick. They gave us comparatively little trouble. We examined the moss between the bricks, and found it undisturbed."

"You looked among D———'s papers, of course, and into the books of the library?"

"Certainly; we opened every package and parcel; we not only opened every book, but we turned over every leaf in each volume, not contenting ourselves with a mere shake, according to the fashion of some of our police officers. We also measured the thickness of every book-*cover*, with the most accurate admeasurement, and applied to each the most jealous scrutiny of the microscope. Had any of the bindings been recently meddled with, it would have been utterly impossible that the fact should have escaped observation. Some five or six volumes, just from the hands of the binder, we carefully probed, longitudinally, with the needles."

"You explored the floors beneath the carpets?"

"Beyond doubt. We removed every carpet, and examined the boards with the microscope."

"And the paper on the walls?"

"Yes."

"You looked into the cellars?"

"We did."

"Then," I said, "you have been making a miscalculation, and the letter is *not* upon the premises, as you suppose."

"I fear you are right there," said the Prefect. "And now, Dupin, what would you advise me to do?"

"To make a thorough research of the premises."

"That is absolutely needless," replied G———. "I am not more sure that I breathe than I am that the letter is not at the hotel."

"I have no better advice to give you," said Dupin. "You have, of course, an accurate description of the letter?"

"Oh, yes!"—And here the Prefect, producing a memorandum-book, proceeded to read aloud a minute account of the internal, and especially of the external, appearance of the missing document. Soon after finishing the perusal of this description, he took his departure, more entirely depressed in spirits than I had ever known the good gentleman before.

In about a month afterward he paid us another visit, and found us occupied very nearly as before. He took a pipe and a chair and entered into some ordinary conversation. At length I said:

"Well, but G———, what of the purloined letter? I presume you have at last made up your mind that there is no such thing as overreaching the Minister?"

"Confound him, say I—yes; I made the re-examination, however, as Dupin suggested—but it was all labor lost, as I knew it would be."

"How much was the reward offered, did you say?" asked Dupin.

"Why, a very great deal—a *very* liberal reward—I don't like to say how much, precisely; but one thing I *will* say, that I wouldn't mind giving my individual check for fifty thousand francs to any one who could obtain me that letter. The fact is, it is becoming of more and more importance every day; and the reward has been lately doubled. If it were trebled, however, I could do no more than I have done."

"Why, yes," said Dupin, drawlingly, between the whiffs of his meerschaum, "I really—think, G———, you have not exerted yourself—to the utmost in this matter. You might—do a little more, I think, eh?"

"How?—in what way?"

"Why—puff, puff—you might—puff, puff—employ counsel in the matter, eh?—puff, puff, puff. Do you remember the story they tell of Abernethy?"

"No; hang Abernethy!"

"To be sure! hang him and welcome. But, once upon a time, a certain rich miser conceived the design of spunging upon this Abernethy for a medical opinion. Getting up, for this purpose, an ordinary conversation in a private company, he insinuated his case to the physician, as that of an imaginary individual.

"'We will suppose,' said the miser, 'that his symptoms are such and such; now, doctor, what would *you* have directed him to take?'

"'Take!' said Abernethy, 'why, take *advice*, to be sure.'"

"But," said the Prefect, a little discomposed, "*I* am *perfectly* willing to take advice, and to pay for it. I would *really* give fifty thousand francs to any one who would aid me in the matter."

"In that case," replied Dupin, opening a drawer, and producing a check-book, "you may as well fill me up a check for the amount mentioned. When you have signed it, I will hand you the letter."

I was astounded. The Prefect appeared absolutely thunder-stricken. For some minutes he remained speechless and motionless, looking incredulously at my friend with open mouth, and eyes that seemed starting from their sockets; then apparently recovering himself in some measure, he seized a pen, and after several pauses and vacant stares, finally filled up and signed a check for fifty thousand francs, and handed it across the table to Dupin. The latter examined it carefully and deposited it in his pocket-book; then, unlocking an *escritoire*, took thence a letter and gave it to the Prefect. This functionary grasped it in a perfect agony of joy, opened it with a trembling hand, cast a rapid glance at its contents, and then, scrambling and struggling to the door, rushed at length unceremoniously from the room and from the house, without having uttered a syllable since Dupin had requested him to fill up the check.

When he had gone, my friend entered into some explanations.

"The Parisian police," he said, "are exceedingly able in their way. They are persevering, ingenious, cunning, and thoroughly versed in the knowledge which their duties seem chiefly to demand. Thus, when G—— detailed to us his mode of searching the premises at the Hotel D——, I felt entire confidence in his having made a satisfactory investigation—so far as his labors extended."

"So far as his labors extended?" said I.

"Yes," said Dupin. "The measures adopted were not only the best of their kind, but carried out to absolute perfection. Had the letter been deposited within the range of their search, these fellows would, beyond a question, have found it."

I merely laughed—but he seemed quite serious in all that he said.

"The measures, then," he continued, "were good in their kind, and well executed; their defect lay in their being inapplicable to the case and to the man. A certain set of highly ingenious resources are, with the Prefect, a sort of Procrustean bed, to which he forcibly adapts his designs. But he perpetually errs by being too deep or too shallow for the matter in hand; and many a school-boy is a better reasoner than he. I knew one about eight years of age, whose success at guessing in the game of 'even and odd' attracted universal admiration. This game is simple, and is played with marbles. One player holds in his hand a number of these toys, and demands of another whether that number is even or odd. If the guess is right, the guesser wins one; if wrong, he loses one. The boy to whom I allude won all the marbles of the school. Of course he had some principle of guessing; and this lay in mere observation and admeasurement of the astuteness of his opponents. For example, an arrant simpleton is his opponent, and, holding up his closed hand, asks, 'Are they even or odd?' Our school-boy replies, 'Odd,' and loses; but upon the second trial he wins, for he then says to himself: 'The simpleton had them even upon the first trial, and his amount of cunning is just sufficient to make him have them odd upon the second; I will therefore guess odd';—he guesses odd, and wins. Now, with a simpleton a degree above the first, he would have reasoned thus: 'This fellow finds that in the first instance I guessed odd, and, in the second, he will propose to himself, upon the first impulse, a simple variation from even to odd, as did the first simpleton; but then a second thought will suggest that this is too simple a variation, and finally he will decide upon putting it even as before. I will therefore guess even';—he guesses even, and wins. Now this mode of reasoning in the school-boy, whom his fellows termed 'lucky,'—what, in its last analysis, is it?"

"It is merely," I said, "an identification of the reasoner's intellect with that of his opponent."

"It is," said Dupin; "and, upon inquiring of the boy by what means he effected the *thorough* identification in which his success consisted, I received answer as follows: 'When I wish to find out how wise, or how stupid, or how good, or how wicked is any one, or what are his thoughts at the moment, I fashion the expression of my face, as accurately as possible, in accordance with the expression of his, and then wait to see what thoughts or sentiments arise in my mind or heart, as if to match or correspond with the expression.' This response of the school-boy lies at the bottom of all the spurious profundity which has been attributed to Rochefoucault, to La Bougive, to Machiavelli, and to Campanella."

"And the identification," I said, "of the reasoner's intellect with that of his opponent, depends, if I understand you aright, upon the accuracy with which the opponent's intellect is admeasured."

"For its practical value it depends upon this," replied Dupin; "and the Prefect and his cohort fail so frequently, first, by default of this identification, and, secondly, by ill-admeasurement, or rather through non-admeasurement, of the intellect with which they are engaged. They consider only their *own* ideas of ingenuity; and, in searching for any thing hidden, advert only to the modes in which *they* would have hidden it. They are right in this much—that their own ingenuity is a faithful representative of that of *the mass*; but when the cunning of the individual felon is diverse in character from their own, the felon foils them, of course. This always happens when it is above their own, and very usually when it is below. They have no variation of principle in their investigations; at best, when urged by some unusual emergency—by some extraordinary reward—they extend or exaggerate their old modes of *practice*, without touching their principles. What, for example, in this case of D———, has been done to vary the principle of action? What is all this boring, and probing, and sounding, and scrutinizing with the microscope, and dividing the surface of the building into registered square inches—what is it all but an exaggeration *of the application* of the one principle or set of principles of search, which are based upon the one set of notions regarding human ingenuity, to which the Prefect, in the long routine of his duty, has been accustomed? Do you not see he has taken it for granted that *all* men proceed to conceal a letter, not exactly in a gimlet-hole bored in a chair-leg, but, at least, in *some* out-of-the-way hole or corner suggested by the same tenor of thought which would urge a man to secrete a letter in a gimlet-hole bored in a chair-leg? And do you not see also, that such *recherchés* nooks for concealment are adapted only for ordinary occasions, and would be adopted only by ordinary intellects; for, in all cases of concealment, a disposal of the article concealed—a disposal of it in this *recherché* manner,—is, in the very first instance, presumable and presumed; and thus its discovery depends, not at all upon the acumen, but altogether upon the mere care, patience, and determination of the seekers; and where the case is of importance—or, what amounts to the same thing in the political eyes, when the reward is of magnitude,—the qualities in question have *never* been known to fail. You will now understand what I meant in suggesting that, had the purloined letter been hidden anywhere within the limits of the Prefect's examination—in other words, had the principle of its concealment been comprehended within the principles of the Prefect—its discovery would have been a matter altogether beyond question. This functionary, however, has been thoroughly mystified; and the remote source of his defeat lies in the supposition that the Minister is a fool, because he has acquired renown as a poet. All fools are poets; this the Prefect *feels*; and he is merely guilty of a *non distributio medii* in thence inferring that all poets are fools."

"But is this really the poet?" I asked. "There are two brothers, I know; and both have attained reputation in letters. The minister I believe has written learnedly on the Differential Calculus. He is a mathematician, and no poet."

"You are mistaken; I know him well; he is both. As poet *and* mathematician, he would reason well; as mere mathematician, he could not have reasoned at all, and thus would have been at the mercy of the Prefect."

"You surprise me," I said, "by these opinions, which have been contradicted by the voice of the world. You do not mean to set at naught the well-digested idea of centuries. The mathematical reason has long been regarded as *the* reason *par excellence*."

"'*Il y a à parièr,*'" replied Dupin, quoting from Chamfort, "'*que toute idée publique, toute convention reçue, est une sottise, car elle a convenue au plus grand nombre.*' The mathematicians, I grant you, have done their best to promulgate the popular error to which you allude, and which is none the less an error for its promulgation as truth. With an art worthy a better cause, for example, they have insinuated the term 'analysis' into application to algebra. The French are the originators of this particular deception; but if a term is of any importance—if words derive any value from applicability—then 'analysis' conveys 'algebra' about as much as, in Latin, '*ambitus*' implies 'ambition,' '*religio*' 'religion,' or '*homines honesti*' a set of *honorable* men."

"You have a quarrel on hand, I see," said I, "with some of the algebraists of Paris; but proceed."

"I dispute the availability, and thus the value, of that reason which is cultivated in any especial form other than the abstractly logical. I dispute, in particular, the reason educed by mathematical study. The mathematics are the science of form and quantity; mathematical reasoning is merely logic applied to observation upon form and quantity. The great error lies in supposing that even the truths of what is called *pure* algebra are abstract or general truths. And this error is so egregious that I am confounded at the universality with which it has been received. Mathematical axioms are *not* axioms of general truth. What is true of *relation*—of form and quantity—is often grossly false in regard to morals, for example. In this latter science it is very usually *un*true that the aggregated parts are equal to the whole. In chemistry also the axiom fails. In the consideration of motive it fails; for two motives, each of a given value, have not, necessarily, a value when united, equal to the sum of their values apart. There are numerous other mathematical truths which are only truths within the limits of *relation*. But the mathematician argues from his *finite truths*, through habit, as if they were of an absolutely general applicability—as the world indeed imagines them to be. Bryant, in his very learned 'Mythology,' mentions an analogous source of error, when he says that 'although the pagan fables are not believed, yet we forget ourselves continually, and make inferences from them as existing realities.' With the algebraists, however, who are pagans themselves, the pagan fables' *are* believed, and the inferences are made, not so much through lapse of memory as through an unaccountable addling of the brains. In short, I never yet encountered the mere mathematician who could be trusted out of equal roots, or one who did not clandestinely hold it as a point of his faith that $x^2 + px$ was absolutely and unconditionally equal to q. Say to one of these gentlemen, by way of experiment, if you please, that you believe occasions may occur where $x^2 + px$ is *not* altogether equal to q, and, having made him understand what you mean, get out of his reach as speedily as convenient, for, beyond doubt, he will endeavor to knock you down.

"I mean to say," continued Dupin, while I merely laughed at his last observations, "that if the minister had been no more than a mathematician, the Prefect would have been under no necessity of giving me this check. I knew him, however, as both mathematician and poet, and my measures were adapted to his capacity, with reference to the circumstances by which he was surrounded. I knew him as a courtier, too, and as a bold *intriguant*. Such a man, I considered, could not fail to be aware of the ordinary policial modes of action. He could not have failed to anticipate—and events have proved that he did not fail to anticipate—the waylayings to which he was subjected. He must have foreseen, I reflected, the secret investigations of his premises. His frequent absences from home at night, which were hailed by the Prefect as certain aids to his success, I regarded only as *ruses*, to afford opportunity for thorough search to the police, and thus the sooner to impress them with the conviction to which G———, in fact, did finally arrive—the conviction that the letter was not upon the premises. I felt, also, that the whole train of thought, which I was at some pains in detailing to you just now, concerning the invariable principle of policial action in searches for articles concealed—I felt that this whole train of thought would necessarily pass through the mind of the minister. It would imperatively lead him to despise all the ordinary *nooks* of concealment. *He* could not, I reflected, be so weak as not to see that the most intricate and remote recess of his hotel would be as open as his commonest closets to the eyes, to the probes, to the gimlets, and to the microscopes of the Prefect. I saw, in fine, that he would be driven, as a matter of course, to *simplicity*, if not deliberately induced to it as a matter of choice. You will remember, perhaps, how desperately the Prefect laughed when I suggested, upon our first interview, that it was just possible this mystery troubled him so much on account of its being so *very* self-evident."

"Yes," said I, "I remember his merriment well. I really thought he would have fallen into convulsions."

"The material world," continued Dupin, "abounds with very strict analogies to the immaterial; and thus some color of truth has been given to the rhetorical dogma, that metaphor, or simile, may be made to strengthen an argument as well as to embellish a description. The principle of the *vis inertiæ*, for example, seems to be identical in physics and metaphysics. It is not more true in the former, that a large body is with more difficulty set in motion than a smaller one, and that its subsequent *momentum* is commensurate with this difficulty, than it is, in the latter, that intellects of the vaster capacity, while more forcible, more constant, and more eventful in their movements than those of inferior grade, are yet the less readily moved, and more embarrassed, and full of hesitation in the first few steps of their progress. Again: have you ever noticed which of the street signs, over the shop doors, are the most attractive of attention?"

"I have never given the matter a thought," I said.

"There is a game of puzzles," he resumed, "which is played upon a map. One party playing requires another to find a given word—the name of town, river, state, or empire—any word, in short, upon the motley and perplexed surface of the chart. A novice in the game generally seeks to embarrass his opponents by giving them the most minutely lettered names; but the adept selects such words as stretch, in large characters, from one end of the chart to the other. These, like the over-largely lettered signs and placards of the street, escape observation by dint of being excessively obvious; and here the physical oversight is precisely analogous with the moral inapprehension by which the intellect suffers to pass unnoticed those considerations which are too obtrusively and too palpably self-evident. But this is a point, it appears, somewhat above or beneath the understanding of the Prefect. He never once thought it probable, or possible, that the minister had deposited the letter immediately beneath the nose of the whole world, by way of best preventing any portion of that world from perceiving it.

"But the more I reflected upon the daring, dashing, and discriminating ingenuity of D———; upon the fact that the document must always have been *at hand*, if he intended to use it to good purpose; and upon the decisive evidence, obtained by the Prefect, that it was not hidden within the limits of that dignitary's ordinary search—the more satisfied I became that, to conceal this letter, the minister had resorted to the comprehensive and sagacious expedient of not attempting to conceal it at all.

"Full of these ideas, I prepared myself with a pair of green spectacles, and called one fine morning, quite by accident, at the Ministerial hotel. I found D——— at home, yawning, lounging, and dawdling, as usual, and pretending to be in the last extremity of *ennui*. He is, perhaps, the most really energetic human being now alive—but that is only when nobody sees him.

"To be even with him, I complained of my weak eyes, and lamented the necessity of the spectacles, under cover of which I cautiously and thoroughly surveyed the whole apartment, while seemingly intent only upon the conversation of my host.

"I paid especial attention to a large writing-table near which he sat, and upon which lay confusedly, some miscellaneous letters and other papers, with one or two musical instruments and a few books. Here, however after a long and very deliberate scrutiny, I saw nothing to excite particular suspicion.

"At length my eyes, in going the circuit of the room, fell upon a trumpery filigree card-rack of pasteboard, that hung dangling by a dirty blue ribbon, from a little brass knob just beneath the middle of the mantel-piece. In this rack, which had three or four compartments, were five or six visiting cards and a solitary letter. This last was much soiled and crumpled. It was torn nearly in two, across the middle—as if a design, in the first instance, to tear it entirely up as worthless, had been altered, or stayed, in the second. It had a large black seal, bearing the D——— cipher *very* conspicuously, and was addressed, in a diminutive female hand, to D———, the minister, himself. It was thrust carelessly, and even, as it seemed, contemptuously, into one of the uppermost divisions of the rack.

"No sooner had I glanced at this letter than I concluded it to be that of which I was in search. To be sure, it was, to all appearance, radically different from the one of which the Prefect had read us so minute a description. Here the seal was large and black, with the D——— cipher; there it was small and red, with the ducal arms of the S——— family. Here, the address, to the minister, was diminutive and feminine; there the superscription, to a certain royal personage, was markedly bold and decided; the size alone formed a point of correspondence. But, then, the *radicalness* of these differences, which was excessive; the dirt; the soiled and torn condition of the paper, so inconsistent with the *true* methodical habits of D———, and so suggestive of a design to delude the beholder into an idea of the worthlessness of the document;—these things, together with the hyperobtrusive situation of this document, full in the view of every visitor, and thus exactly in accordance with the conclusions to which I had previously arrived; these things, I say, were strongly corroborative of suspicion, in one who came with the intention to suspect.

"I protracted my visit as long as possible, and, while I maintained a most animated discussion with the minister, upon a topic which I knew well had never failed to interest and excite him, I kept my attention really riveted upon the letter. In this examination, I committed to memory its external appearance and arrangement in the rack; and also fell, at length, upon a discovery which set at rest whatever trivial doubt I might have entertained. In scrutinizing the edges of the paper, I observed them to be more *chafed* than seemed necessary. They presented the *broken* appearance which is manifested when a stiff paper, having been once folded and pressed with a folder, is refolded in a reversed direction, in the same creases or edges which had formed the original fold. This discovery was sufficient. It was clear to me that the letter had been turned, as a glove, inside out, re-directed and re-sealed. I bade the minister good-morning, and took my departure at once, leaving a gold snuff-box upon the table.

"The next morning I called for the snuff-box, when we resumed, quite eagerly, the conversation of the preceding day. While thus engaged, however, a loud report, as if of a pistol, was heard immediately beneath the windows of the hotel, and was succeeded by a series of fearful screams, and the shoutings of a terrified mob. D—— rushed to a casement, threw it open, and looked out. In the meantime I stepped to the card-rack, took the letter, put it in my pocket, and replaced it by a *fac-simile*, (so far as regards externals) which I had carefully prepared at my lodgings—imitating the D—— cipher, very readily, by means of a seal formed of bread.

"The disturbance in the street had been occasioned by the frantic behavior of a man with a musket. He had fired it among a crowd of women and children. It proved, however, to have been without ball, and the fellow was suffered to go his way as a lunatic or a drunkard. When he had gone, D—— came from the window, whither I had followed him immediately upon securing the object in view. Soon afterward I bade him farewell. The pretended lunatic was a man in my own pay."

"But what purpose had you," I asked, "in replacing the letter by a *fac-simile?* Would it not have been better, at the first visit, to have seized it openly, and departed?"

"D——," replied Dupin, "is a desperate man, and a man of nerve. His hotel, too, is not without attendants devoted to his interests. Had I made the wild attempt you suggest, I might never have left the Ministerial presence alive. The good people of Paris might have heard of me no more. But I had an object apart from these considerations. You know my political prepossessions. In this matter, I act as a partisan of the lady concerned. For eighteen months the minister has had her in his power. She has now him in hers—since, being unaware that the letter is not in his possession, he will proceed with his exactions as if it was. Thus will he inevitably commit himself, at once, to his political destruction. His downfall, too, will not be more precipitate than awkward. It is all very well to talk about the *facilis descensus Averni*; but in all kinds of climbing, as Catalani said of singing, it is far more easy to get up than to come down. In the present instance I have no sympathy—at least no pity—for him who descends. He is that *monstrum horrendum*, an unprincipled man of genius. I confess, however, that I should like very well to know the precise character of his thoughts, when, being defied by her whom the Prefect terms 'a certain personage,' he is reduced to opening the letter which I left for him in the card rack."

"How? did you put any thing particular in it?"

"Why—it did not seem altogether right to leave the interior blank—that would have been insulting. D——, at Vienna once, did me an evil turn, which I told him, quite good-humoredly, that I should remember. So, as I knew he would feel some curiosity in regard to the identity of the person who had outwitted him, I thought it a pity not to give him a clew. He is well acquainted with my MS., and I just copied into the middle of the blank sheet the words—

"'— —Un dessein si funeste,
S' il n' est digne d' Atrée, est digne de Thyeste.'

They are to be found in Crébillon's 'Atrée.'"

Herman Melville (1819–1891) was born in New York City. After attending the Albany Classical School, he left home in search of adventure. After serving as a cabin boy on a whaling ship, enlisting in the navy, working as clerk and bookkeeper in Hawaii, and living in the Marquesas Islands and in Tahiti, he returned home to write about his adventures. His early adventure stories "Typee" (1846) and "Omoo" (1847) gained him an avid readership. His masterpiece, *Moby Dick* (1851), was not well-received by critics and did not initially gain a wide audience, but it has come to be recognized as one of the great masterpieces of American literature.

In the years following the publication of *Moby Dick*, Melville suffered from financial and personal difficulties. After a lecture tour that was not very successful, he obtained steady employment as a customs inspector in New York, earning an income that allowed him to continue writing. Melville's death in 1891 went largely unnoticed. His novella *Billy Budd*, unfinished at the time of his death, was first published in 1924.

"Bartleby, the Scrivener: A Story of Wall Street" (1853) was first published as a magazine serial in two volumes of *Putnam's Monthly*. Narrated by a nameless lawyer who employs the title character, "Bartleby" tells the story of a law copyist on Wall Street. Bartleby completes his work "silently, palely, and mechanically," in physical and symbolic isolation. When asked to work with a partner to verify the accuracy of his copies against the original documents, Bartleby consistently responds, "I would prefer not to," and withdraws within the **symbolic** walls of his "hermitage."

Related Works: Eliot, "Love Song of J. Alfred Prufrock"; Hemingway, "A Clean, Well-Lighted Place"; Kafka, "The Metamorphosis"; Miller, *Death of a Salesman*; Norman, *'Night, Mother*.

HERMAN MELVILLE

Bartleby, the Scrivener

A Story of Wall Street

I am a rather elderly man. The nature of my avocations, for the last thirty years, has brought me into more than ordinary contact with what would seem an interesting and somewhat singular set of men, of whom, as yet, nothing, that I know of, has ever been written—I mean, the law-copyists, or scriveners. I have known very many of them, professionally and privately, and, if I pleased, could relate divers histories, at which good-natured gentlemen might smile, and sentimental souls might weep. But I waive the biographies of all other scriveners, for a few passages in the life of Bartleby, who was a scrivener, the strangest I ever saw, or heard of. While, of other law-copyists, I might write the complete life, of Bartleby nothing of that sort can be done. I believe that no materials exist, for a full and satisfactory biography of this man. It is an irreparable loss to literature. Bartleby was one of those beings of whom nothing is ascertainable, except from the original sources, and, in his case, those are very small. What my own astonished eyes saw of

Bartleby, *that* is all I know of him, except, indeed, one vague report, which will appear in the sequel.

Ere introducing the scrivener, as he first appeared to me, it is fit I make some mention of myself, my *employés*, my business, my chambers, and general surroundings, because some such description is indispensable to an adequate understanding of the chief character about to be presented. Imprimis:* I am a man who, from his youth upwards, has been filled with a profound conviction that the easiest way of life is the best. Hence, though I belong to a profession proverbially energetic and nervous, even to turbulence, at times, yet nothing of that sort have I ever suffered to invade my peace. I am one of those unambitious lawyers who never address a jury, or in any way draw down public applause; but, in the cool tranquillity of a snug retreat, do a snug business among rich men's bonds, and mortgages, and title-deeds. All who know me, consider me an eminently *safe* man. The late John Jacob Astor, † a personage little given to poetic enthusiasm, had no hesitation in pronouncing my first grand point to be prudence; my next, method. I do not speak it in vanity, but simply record the fact, that I was not unemployed in my profession by the late John Jacob Astor; a name which, I admit, I love to repeat; for it hath a rounded and orbicular sound to it, and rings like unto bullion. I will freely add, that I was not insensible to the late John Jacob Astor's good opinion.

Some time prior to the period at which this little history begins, my avocations had been largely increased. The good old office, now extinct in the State of New York, of a Master in Chancery, had been conferred upon me. It was not a very arduous office, but very pleasantly remunerative. I seldom lose my temper; much more seldom indulge in dangerous indignation at wrongs and outrages; but I must be permitted to be rash here and declare, that I consider the sudden and violent abrogation of the office of Master in Chancery, by the new Constitution, as a——premature act; inasmuch as I had counted upon a life-lease of the profits, whereas I only received those of a few short years. But this is by the way.

My chambers were up stairs, at No.—Wall Street. At one end, they looked upon the white wall of the interior of a spacious skylight shaft, penetrating the building from top to bottom.

This view might have been considered rather tame than otherwise, deficient in what landscape painters call "life." But, if so, the view from the other end of my chambers offered, at least, a contrast, if nothing more. In that direction, my windows commanded an unobstructed view of a lofty brick wall, black by age and everlasting shade; which wall required no spyglass to bring out its lurking beauties, but, for the benefit of all near-sighted spectators, was pushed up to within ten feet of my window-panes. Owing to the great height of the surrounding buildings, and my chambers being on the second floor, the interval between this wall and mine not a little resembled a huge square cistern.

At the period just preceding the advent of Bartleby, I had two persons as copyists in my employment, and a promising lad as an office-boy. First, Turkey; second, Nippers; third, Ginger Nut. These may seem names, the like of which are not usually found in the Directory. In truth, they were nicknames, mutually conferred upon each other by my three clerks, and were deemed expressive of

---

**Imprimis:* In the first place.

†*John Jacob Astor* (1763–1848): An enormously wealthy American capitalist.

their respective persons or characters. Turkey was a short, pursy Englishman, of about my own age—that is, somewhere not far from sixty. In the morning, one might say, his face was of a fine florid hue, but after twelve o'clock, meridian—his dinner hour—it blazed like a grate full of Christmas coals; and continued blazing—but, as it were, with a gradual wane—till six o'clock, P.M., or thereabouts; after which, I saw no more of the proprietor of the face, which, gaining its meridian with the sun, seemed to set with it, to rise, culminate, and decline the following day, with the like regularity and undiminished glory. There are many singular coincidences I have known in the course of my life, not the least among which was the fact, that, exactly when Turkey displayed his fullest beams from his red and radiant countenance, just then, too, at that critical moment, began the daily period when I considered his business capacities as seriously disturbed for the remainder of the twenty-four hours. Not that he was absolutely idle, or averse to business then; far from it. The difficulty was, he was apt to be altogether too energetic. There was a strange, inflamed, flurried, flighty recklessness of activity about him. He would be incautious in dipping his pen into his inkstand. All his blots upon my documents were dropped there after twelve o'clock, meridian. Indeed, not only would he be reckless, and sadly given to making blots in the afternoon, but, some days, he went further, and was rather noisy. At such times, too, his face flamed with augmented blazonry, as if cannel coal had been heaped on anthracite. He made an unpleasant racket with his chair; spilled his sand-box; in mending his pens, impatiently split them all to pieces, and threw them on the floor in a sudden passion; stood up, and leaned over his table, boxing his papers about in a most indecorous manner, very sad to behold in an elderly man like him. Nevertheless, as he was in many ways a most valuable person to me, and all the time before twelve o'clock, meridian, was the quickest, steadiest creature, too, accomplishing a great deal of work in a style not easily to be matched—for these reasons, I was willing to overlook his eccentricities, though, indeed, occasionally, I remonstrated with him. I did this very gently, however, because, though the civilest, nay, the blandest and most reverential of men in the morning, yet, in the afternoon, he was disposed, upon provocation, to be slightly rash with his tongue—in fact, insolent. Now, valuing his morning services as I did, and resolved not to lose them—yet, at the same time, made uncomfortable by his inflamed ways after twelve o'clock—and being a man of peace, unwilling by my admonitions to call forth unseemly retorts from him, I took upon me, one Saturday noon (he was always worse on Saturdays) to hint to him, very kindly, that, perhaps, now that he was growing old, it might be well to abridge his labors; in short, he need not come to my chambers after twelve o'clock, but, dinner over, had best go home to his lodgings, and rest himself till tea-time. But no; he insisted upon his afternoon devotions. His countenance became intolerably fervid, as he oratorically assured me—gesticulating with a long ruler at the other end of the room—that if his services in the morning were useful, how indispensable, then, in the afternoon?

"With submission, sir," said Turkey, on this occasion. "I consider myself your right-hand man. In the morning I but marshal and deploy my columns; but in the afternoon I put myself at their head, and gallantly charge the foe, thus"—and he made a violent thrust with the ruler.

"But the blots, Turkey," intimated I.

"True; but, with submission, sir, behold these hairs! I am getting old. Surely, sir, a blot or two of a warm afternoon is not to be severely urged against gray hairs. Old age—even if it blot the page—is honorable. With submission, sir, we *both* are getting old."

This appeal to my fellow-feeling was hardly to be resisted. At all events I saw that go he would not. So, I made up my mind to let him stay, resolving, nevertheless, to see to it that, during the afternoon, he had to do with my less important papers.

Nippers, the second on my list, was a whiskered, sallow, and, upon the whole, rather piratical-looking young man, of about five-and-twenty. I always deemed him the victim of two evil powers—ambition and indigestion. The ambition was evinced by a certain impatience of the duties of a mere copyist, an unwarrantable usurpation of strictly professional affairs such as the original drawing up of legal documents. The indigestion seemed betokened in an occasional nervous testiness and grinning irritability, causing the teeth to audibly grind together over mistakes committed in copying; unnecessary maledictions, hissed, rather than spoken, in the heat of business; and especially by a continual discontent with the height of the table where he worked. Though of a very ingenious mechanical turn, Nippers could never get this table to suit him. He put chips under it, blocks of various sorts, bits of pasteboard, and at last went so far as to attempt an exquisite adjustment, by final pieces of folded blotting-paper. But no invention would answer. If, for the sake of easing his back, he brought the table-lid at a sharp angle well up towards his chin and wrote there like a man using the steep roof of a Dutch house for his desk, then he declared that it stopped the circulation in his arms. If now he lowered the table to his waistbands, and stooped over it in writing, then there was a sore aching in his back. In short, the truth of the matter was, Nippers knew not what he wanted. Or, if he wanted anything, it was to be rid of a scrivener's table altogether. Among the manifestations of his diseased ambition was a fondness he had for receiving visits from certain ambiguous-looking fellows in seedy coats, whom he called his clients. Indeed, I was aware that not only was he, at times, considerable of a ward-politician, but he occasionally did a little business at the justices' courts, and was not unknown on the steps of the Tombs.* I have good reason to believe, however, that one individual who called upon him at my chambers, and who, with a grand air, he insisted was his client, was no other than a dun, and the alleged title-deed, a bill. But, with all his failings, and the annoyances he caused me, Nippers, like his compatriot Turkey, was a very useful man to me; wrote a neat, swift hand; and, when he chose, was not deficient in a gentlemanly sort of deportment. Added to this, he always dressed in a gentlemanly sort of way; and so, incidentally, reflected credit upon my chambers. Whereas, with respect to Turkey, I had much ado to keep him from being a reproach to me. His clothes were apt to look oily, and smell of eating-houses. He wore his pantaloons very loose and baggy in summer. His coats were execrable, his hat not to be handled. But while the hat was a thing of indifference to me, inasmuch as his natural civility and deference, as a dependent Englishman, always led him to doff it the moment he entered the room, yet his coat was another matter. Concerning his coats, I reasoned with him; but with no effect. The truth was, I suppose, that a man with so small an income could not afford to sport such a lustrous face and a

---

**the Tombs:* A jail in New York City.

lustrous coat at one and the same time. As Nippers once observed, Turkey's money went chiefly for red ink. One winter day, I presented Turkey with a highly respectable-looking coat of my own—a padded gray coat, of a most comfortable warmth, and which buttoned straight up from the knee to the neck. I thought Turkey would appreciate the favor, and abate his rashness and obstreperousness of afternoons. But no; I verily believe that buttoning himself up in so downy and blanket-like a coat had a pernicious effect upon him—upon the same principle that too much oats are bad for horses. In fact, precisely as a rash, restive horse is said to feel his oats, so Turkey felt his coat. It made him insolent. He was a man whom prosperity harmed.

Though, concerning the self-indulgent habits of Turkey, I had my own private surmises, yet, touching Nippers, I was well persuaded that, whatever might be his faults in other respects, he was, at least, a temperate young man. But indeed, nature herself seemed to have been his vintner, and, at his birth, charged him so thoroughly with an irritable, brandy-like disposition, that all subsequent potations were needless. When I consider how, amid the stillness of my chambers, Nippers would sometimes impatiently rise from his seat, and stooping over his table, spread his arms wide apart, seize the whole desk, and move it, and jerk it, with a grim, grinding motion on the floor, as if the table were a perverse voluntary agent, intent on thwarting and vexing him; I plainly perceive that, for Nippers, brandy-and-water were altogether superfluous.

It was fortunate for me that, owing to its peculiar cause—indigestion—the irritability and consequent nervousness of Nippers were mainly observable in the morning, while in the afternoon he was comparatively mild. So that, Turkey's paroxysms only coming on about twelve o'clock, I never had to do with their eccentricities at one time. Their fits relieved each other, like guards. When Nippers' was on, Turkey's was off; and *vice versa*. This was a good natural arrangement, under the circumstances.

Ginger Nut, the third on my list, was a lad, some twelve years old. His father was a carman, ambitious of seeing his son on the bench instead of a cart, before he died. So he sent him to my office, as student at law, errand-boy, cleaner, and sweeper, at the rate of one dollar a week. He had a little desk to himself, but he did not use it much. Upon inspection, the drawer exhibited a great array of the shells of various sorts of nuts. Indeed, to this quick-witted youth, the whole noble science of the law was contained in a nutshell. Not the least among the employments of Ginger Nut, as well as one which he discharged with the most alacrity, was his duty as cake and apple purveyor for Turkey and Nippers. Copying lawpapers being proverbially a dry, husky sort of business, my two scriveners were fain to moisten their mouths very often with Spitzenbergs, to be had at the numerous stalls nigh the Custom House and Post Office. Also, they sent Ginger Nut very frequently for that peculiar cake—small, flat, round, and very spicy—after which he had been named by them. Of a cold morning, when business was but dull, Turkey would gobble up scores of these cakes, as if they were mere wafers—indeed, they sell them at the rate of six or eight for a penny—the scrape of his pen blending with the crunching of the crisp particles in his mouth. Of all the fiery afternoon blunders and flurried rashness of Turkey, was his once moistening a ginger-cake between his lips, and clapping it on to a mortgage, for a seal. I came within an ace of dismissing him then. But he mollified me by making an oriental bow, and saying—

"With submission, sir, it was generous of me to find you in stationery on my own account."

Now my original business—that of a conveyancer and title hunter, and drawer-up of recondite documents of all sorts—was considerably increased by receiving the Master's office. There was now great work for scriveners. Not only must I push the clerks already with me, but I must have additional help.

In answer to my advertisement, a motionless young man one morning stood upon my office threshold, the door being open, for it was summer. I can see that figure now—pallidly neat, pitiably respectable, incurably forlorn! It was Bartleby.

After a few words touching his qualifications, I engaged him, glad to have among my corps of copyists a man of so singularly sedate an aspect, which I thought might operate beneficially upon the flighty temper of Turkey, and the fiery one of Nippers.

I should have stated before that ground-glass folding-doors divided my premises into two parts, one of which was occupied by my scriveners, the other by myself. According to my humor, I threw open these doors, or closed them. I resolved to assign Bartleby a corner by the folding-doors, but on my side of them, so as to have this quiet man within easy call, in case any trifling thing was to be done. I placed his desk close up to a small side-window in that part of the room, a window which originally had afforded a lateral view of certain grimy brickyards and bricks, but which, owing to subsequent erections, commanded at present no view at all, though it gave some light. Within three feet of the panes was a wall, and the light came down from far above, between two lofty buildings, as from a very small opening in a dome. Still further to a satisfactory arrangement, I procured a high green folding screen, which might entirely isolate Bartleby from my sight, though not remove him from my voice. And thus, in a manner, privacy and society were conjoined.

At first, Bartleby did an extraordinary quantity of writing. As if long famishing for something to copy, he seemed to gorge himself on my documents. There was no pause for digestion. He ran a day and night line, copying by sunlight and by candle-light. I should have been quite delighted with his application, had he been cheerfully industrious. But he wrote on silently, palely, mechanically.

It is, of course, an indispensable part of a scrivener's business to verify the accuracy of his copy, word by word. Where there are two or more scriveners in an office, they assist each other in this examination, one reading from the copy, the other holding the original. It is a very dull, wearisome, and lethargic affair. I can readily imagine that, to some sanguine temperaments; it would be altogether intolerable. For example, I cannot credit that the mettlesome poet, Byron, would have contentedly sat down with Bartleby to examine a law document of, say five hundred pages, closely written in a crimpy hand.

Now and then, in the haste of business, it had been my habit to assist in comparing some brief document myself, calling Turkey or Nippers for this purpose. One object I had in placing Bartleby so handy to me behind the screen, was, to avail myself of his services on such trivial occasions. It was on the third day, I think, of his being with me, and before any necessity had arisen for having his own writing examined, that, being much hurried to complete a small affair I had in hand, I abruptly called to Bartleby. In my haste and natural expectancy of instant compliance, I sat with my head bent over the original on my desk, and my right hand sideways, and somewhat nervously extended with the copy, so that, immediately upon emerging from his retreat, Bartleby might snatch it and proceed to business without the least delay.

In this very attitude did I sit when I called to him, rapidly stating what it was I wanted him to do—namely, to examine a small paper with me. Imagine my surprise, nay, my consternation, when, without moving from his privacy, Bartleby, in a singularly mild, firm voice, replied, "I would prefer not to."

I sat awhile in perfect silence, rallying my stunned faculties. Immediately it occurred to me that my ears had deceived me, or Bartleby had entirely misunderstood my meaning. I repeated my request in the clearest tone I could assume; but in quite as clear a one came the previous reply, "I would prefer not to."

"Prefer not to," echoed I, rising in high excitement, and crossing the room with a stride. "What do you mean? Are you moonstruck? I want you to help me compare this sheet here—take it," and I thrust it towards him.

"I would prefer not to," said he.

I looked at him steadfastly. His face was leanly composed; his gray eye dimly calm. Not a wrinkle of agitation rippled him. Had there been the least uneasiness, anger, impatience, or impertinence in his manner; in other words, had there been anything ordinarily human about him, doubtless I should have violently dismissed him from the premises. But as it was, I should have as soon thought of turning my pale plaster-of-paris bust of Cicero out of doors. I stood gazing at him awhile, as he went on with his own writing, and then reseated myself at my desk. This is very strange, thought I. What had one best do? But my business hurried me. I concluded to forget the matter for the present, reserving it for my future leisure. So, calling Nippers from the other room, the paper was speedily examined.

A few days after this, Bartleby concluded four lengthy documents, being quadruplicates of a week's testimony taken before me in my High Court of Chancery. It became necessary to examine them. It was an important suit, and great accuracy was imperative. Having all things arranged, I called Turkey, Nippers, and Ginger Nut, from the next room, meaning to place the four copies in the hands of my four clerks, while I should read from the original. Accordingly, Turkey, Nippers, and Ginger Nut had taken their seats in a row, each with his document in his hand, when I called to Bartleby to join this interesting group.

"Bartleby! quick, I am waiting."

I heard a slow scrape of his chair legs on the uncarpeted floor, and soon he appeared standing at the entrance of his hermitage.

"What is wanted?" said he, mildly.

"The copies, the copies," said I, hurriedly. "We are going to examine them. There"—and I held towards him the fourth quadruplicate.

"I would prefer not to," he said, and gently disappeared behind the screen.

For a few moments I was turned into a pillar of salt, standing at the head of my seated column of clerks. Recovering myself, I advanced towards the screen, and demanded the reason for such extraordinary conduct.

"*Why* do you refuse?"

"I would prefer not to."

With any other man I should have flown outright into a dreadful passion, scorned all further words, and thrust him ignominiously from my presence. But there was something about Bartleby that not only strangely disarmed me, but, in a wonderful manner, touched and disconcerted me. I began to reason with him.

"These are your own copies we are about to examine. It is labor saving to you, because one examination will answer for your four papers. It is common usage. Every copyist is bound to help examine his copy. Is it not so? Will you not speak? Answer!"

"I prefer not to," he replied in a flute-like tone. It seemed to me that, while I had been addressing him, he carefully revolved every statement that I made; fully comprehended the meaning; could not gainsay the irresistible conclusion: but, at the same time, some paramount consideration prevailed with him to reply as he did.

"You are decided, then, not to comply with my request—a request made according to common usage and common sense?"

He briefly gave me to understand, that on that point my judgment was sound. Yes; his decision was irreversible.

It is not seldom the case that, when a man is browbeaten in some unprecedented and violently unreasonable way, he begins to stagger in his own plainest faith. He begins, as it were, vaguely to surmise that, wonderful as it may be, all the justice and all the reason is on the other side. Accordingly, if any disinterested persons are present, he turns to them for some reinforcement for his own faltering mind.

"Turkey," said I, "what do you think of this? Am I not right?"

"With submission, sir," said Turkey, in his blandest tone. "I think that you are."

"Nippers," said I, "what do *you* think of it?"

"I think I should kick him out of the office."

(The reader of nice perceptions will have perceived that, it being morning. Turkey's answer is couched in polite and tranquil terms, but Nippers replies in ill-tempered ones. Or, to repeat a previous sentence, Nippers' ugly mood was on duty, and Turkey's off.)

"Ginger Nut," said I, willing to enlist the smallest suffrage in my behalf, "what do *you* think of it?"

"I think, sir, he's a little *luny*," replied Ginger Nut, with a grin.

"You hear what they say," said I, turning towards the screen, "come forth and do your duty."

But he vouchsafed no reply. I pondered a moment in sore perplexity. But once more business hurried me. I determined again to postpone the consideration of this dilemma to my future leisure. With a little trouble we made out to examine the papers without Bartleby, though at every page or two Turkey deferentially dropped his opinion, that this proceeding was quite out of the common; while Nippers, twitching in his chair with a dyspeptic nervousness, ground out, between his set teeth, occasional hissing maledictions against the stubborn oaf behind the screen. And for his (Nippers) part, this was the first and the last time he would do another man's business without pay.

Meanwhile Bartleby sat in his hermitage, oblivious to everything but his own peculiar business there.

Some days passed, the scrivener being employed upon another lengthy work. His late remarkable conduct led me to regard his ways narrowly. I observed that he never went to dinner; indeed, that he never went anywhere. As yet I had never, of my personal knowledge, known him to be outside of my office. He was a perpetual sentry in the corner. At about eleven o'clock though, in the morning, I noticed that Ginger Nut would advance toward the opening in Bartleby's screen, as if silently beckoned thither by a gesture invisible to me where I sat. The boy would then leave the office, jingling a few pence, and reappear with a handful of ginger-nuts, which he delivered in the hermitage, receiving two of the cakes for his trouble.

He lives, then, on ginger-nuts, thought I, never eats a dinner, properly speaking; he must be a vegetarian, then, but no; he never eats even vegetables, he eats nothing but ginger-nuts. My mind then ran on in reveries concerning the probable effects upon the human constitution of living entirely on ginger-nuts. Ginger-nuts are so called, because they contain ginger as one of their peculiar constituents, and the final flavoring one. Now, what was ginger? A hot, spicy thing. Was Bartleby hot and spicy? Not at all. Ginger, then, had no effect upon Bartleby. Probably he preferred it should have none.

Nothing so aggravates an earnest person as a passive resistance. If the individual so resisted be of a not inhumane temper, and the resisting one perfectly harmless in his passivity, then, in the better moods of the former, he will endeavor charitably to construe to his imagination what proves impossible to be solved by his judgment. Even so, for the most part, I regarded Bartleby and his ways. Poor fellow! thought I, he means no mischief; it is plain he intends no insolence; his aspect sufficiently evinces that his eccentricities are involuntary. He is useful to me. I can get along with him. If I turn him away, the chances are he will fall in with some less indulgent employer, and then he will be rudely treated, and perhaps driven forth miserably to starve. Yes. Here I can cheaply purchase a delicious self-approval. To befriend Bartleby; to humor him in his strange wilfulness, will cost me little or nothing, while I lay up in my soul what will eventually prove a sweet morsel for my conscience. But this mood was not invariable with me. The passiveness of Bartleby sometimes irritated me. I felt strangely goaded on to encounter him in new opposition—to elicit some angry spark from him answerable to my own. But, indeed, I might as well have essayed to strike fire with my knuckles against a bit of Windsor soap. But one afternoon the evil impulse in me mastered me, and the following little scene ensued:

"Bartleby," said I, "when those papers are all copied, I will compare them with you."

"I would prefer not to."

"How? Surely you do not mean to persist in that mulish vagary?"

No answer.

I threw open the folding-doors nearby, and turning upon Turkey and Nippers, exclaimed:

"Bartleby a second time says, he won't examine his papers. What do you think of it, Turkey?"

It was afternoon, be it remembered. Turkey sat glowing like a brass boiler; his bald head steaming; his hands reeling among his blotted papers.

"Think of it?" roared Turkey. "I think I'll just step behind his screen, and black his eyes for him!"

So saying, Turkey rose to his feet and threw his arms into a pugilistic position. He was hurrying away to make good his promise, when I detained him, alarmed at the effect of incautiously rousing, Turkey's combativeness after dinner.

"Sit down, Turkey," said I, "and hear what Nippers has to say. What do you think of it, Nippers? Would I not be justified in immediately dismissing Bartleby?"

"Excuse me, that is for you to decide, sir. I think his conduct quite unusual, and, indeed, unjust, as regards Turkey and myself. But it may only be a passing whim."

"Ah," exclaimed I, "You have strangely changed your mind, then—you speak very gently of him now."

"All beer," cried Turkey, "gentleness is effects of beer—Nippers and I dined together to-day. You see how gentle *I* am, sir. Shall I go and black his eyes?"

"You refer to Bartleby, I suppose. No, not to-day, Turkey," I replied; "pray, put up your fists."

I closed the doors, and again advanced towards Bartleby. I felt additional incentives tempting me to my fate. I burned to be rebelled against again. I remembered that Bartleby never left the office.

"Bartleby," said I, "Ginger Nut is away, just step around to the Post Office, won't you?" (it was but a three minutes' walk) "and see if there is anything for me."

"I would prefer not to."

"You *will* not?"

"I *prefer* not."

I staggered to my desk, and sat there in a deep study. My blind inveteracy returned. Was there any other thing in which I could procure myself to be ignominiously repulsed by this lean, penniless wight?—my hired clerk? What added thing is there, perfectly reasonable, that he will be sure to refuse to do?

"Bartleby!"

No answer.

"Bartleby," in a louder tone.

No answer.

"Bartleby," I roared.

Like a very ghost, agreeably to the laws of magical invocation at the third summons, he appeared at the entrance of his hermitage.

"Go to the next room, and tell Nippers to come to me."

"I prefer not to," he respectfully and slowly said, and mildly disappeared.

"Very good, Bartleby," said I, in a quiet sort of serenely-severe self-possessed tone, intimating the unalterable purpose of some terrible retribution very close at hand. At the moment I half intended something of the kind. But upon the whole, as it was drawing towards my dinner-hour, I thought it best to put on my hat and walk home for the day, suffering much from perplexity and distress of mind.

Shall I acknowledge it? The conclusion of this whole business was, that it soon became a fixed fact of my chambers, that a pale young scrivener, by the name of Bartleby, had a desk there: that he copied for me at the usual rate of four cents a folio (one hundred words); but he was permanently exempt from examining the work done by him, that duty being transferred to Turkey and Nippers, out of compliment, doubtless, to their superior acuteness: moreover, said Bartleby was never on any account to be dispatched on the most trivial errand of any sort; and that even if entreated to take upon him such a matter, it was generally understood that he would "prefer not to"—in other words, that he would refuse point-blank.

As days passed on, I became considerably reconciled to Bartleby. His steadiness, his freedom from all dissipation, his incessant industry (except when he chose to throw himself into a standing revery behind his screen), his great stillness, his unalterableness of demeanor under all circumstances, made him a valuable acquisition. One prime thing was this—*he was always there*—first in the morning, continually through the day, and the last at night. I had a singular confidence in his honesty. I felt my most precious papers perfectly safe in his hands. Sometimes to be sure, I could not, for the very soul of me, avoid falling into sudden spasmodic passions with him. For it was exceeding difficult to bear in mind all the time those strange peculiarities, privileges, and unheard-of exemptions, forming the tacit stipulations on Bartleby's part under which he remained in my office. Now and then, in the eagerness of dispatching pressing business, I would inadvertently summon Bartleby, in a short, rapid tone, to put his finger, say, on the incipient tie of a bit of red tape with which I was about compressing some papers. Of course, from behind the screen the usual answer, "I prefer not to," was sure to come; and then, how could a human creature, with the common infirmities of our nature, refrain from bitterly exclaiming upon such perverseness—such unreasonableness? However, every added repulse of this sort which I received only tended to lessen the probability of my repeating the inadvertence.

Here it must be said, that, according to the custom of most legal gentlemen occupying chambers in densely populated law buildings, there were several keys to my door. One was kept by a woman residing in the attic, which person weekly scrubbed and daily swept and dusted my apartments. Another was kept by Turkey for convenience sake. The third I sometimes carried in my own pocket. The fourth I knew not who had.

Now, one Sunday morning I happened to go to Trinity Church, to hear a celebrated preacher, and finding myself rather early on the ground I thought I would walk round to my chambers for a while. Luckily I had my key with me; but upon applying it to the lock, I found it resisted by something inserted from the inside. Quite surprised, I called out, when to my consternation a key was turned from within; and thrusting his lean visage at me, and holding the door ajar, the apparition of Bartleby appeared, in his shirt-sleeves, and otherwise in a strangely tattered *deshabille*, saying quietly that he was sorry, but he was deeply engaged just then, and—preferred not admitting me at present. In a brief word or two, he moreover added, that perhaps I had better walk round the block two or three times, and by that time he would probably have concluded his affairs.

Now, the utterly unsurmised appearance of Bartleby, tenanting my law-chambers of a Sunday morning, with his cadaverously gentlemanly *nonchalance*, yet withal firm and self-possessed, had such a strange effect upon me, that incontinently I slunk away from my own door, and did as desired. But not without sundry twinges of impotent rebellion against the mild effrontery of this unaccountable scrivener. Indeed, it was his wonderful mildness chiefly, which not only disarmed me, but unmanned me, as it were. For I consider that one, for the time, is sort of unmanned when he tranquilly permits his hired clerk to dictate to him, and order him away from his own premises. Furthermore, I was full of uneasiness as to what Bartleby could possibly be doing in my office in his shirt-sleeves, and in an otherwise dismantled condition of a Sunday morning. Was anything amiss going on? Nay, that was out of the question. It was not to be thought of for a moment that Bartleby was an immoral person. But what could he be doing there?—copying? Nay again, whatever might be his eccentricities, Bartleby was an eminently decorous person. He would be the last man to sit down to his desk in any state approaching to nudity. Besides, it was Sunday; and there was something about Bartleby that forbade the supposition that he would by any secular occupation violate the proprieties of the day.

Nevertheless, my mind was not pacified; and full of a restless curiosity, at last I returned to the door. Without hindrance I inserted my key, opened it, and entered. Bartleby was not to be seen. I looked round anxiously, peeped behind his screen; but it was very plain that he was gone. Upon more closely examining the place, I surmised that for an indefinite period Bartleby must have ate, dressed, and slept in my office, and that too without plate, mirror, or bed. The cushioned seat of a rickery old sofa in one corner bore the faint impress of a lean, reclining form. Rolled away under his desk, I found a blanket; under the empty grate, a blacking box and brush; on a chair, a tin basin, with soap and a ragged towel; in a newspaper a few crumbs of ginger-nuts and a morsel of cheese. Yes, thought I, it is evident enough that Bartleby has been making his home here, keeping bachelor's hall all by himself. Immediately then the thought came sweeping across me, what miserable friendlessness and loneliness are here revealed! His poverty is great; but his solitude, how horrible! Think of it. Of a Sunday, Wall Street is deserted as Petra;* and every night of every day it is an emptiness. This building, too, which of week-days hums with industry and life, at nightfall echoes with sheer vacancy, and all through Sunday is forlorn. And here Bartleby makes his home; sole spectator of a solitude which he has seen all populous—a sort of innocent and transformed Marius brooding among the ruins of Carthage?†

For the first time in my life a feeling of overpowering stinging melancholy seized me. Before, I had never experienced aught but a not unpleasing sadness. The bond of a common humanity now drew me irresistibly to gloom. A fraternal melancholy! For both I and Bartleby were sons of Adam. I remembered the bright silks and sparkling faces I had seen that day, in gala trim swan-like sailing down the Mississippi of Broadway; and I contrasted them with the pallid copyist, and thought to myself, Ah, happiness courts the light, so we deem the world is gay; but misery hides aloof, so we deem that misery there is none. These sad fancyings—chimeras, doubtless, of a sick and silly brain—led on to other and more special thoughts, concerning the eccentricities of Bartleby. Presentiments of strange discoveries hovered round me. The scrivener's pale form appeared to me laid out, among uncaring strangers, in its shivering winding-sheet.

Suddenly I was attracted by Bartleby's closed desk, the key in open sight left in the lock.

I mean no mischief, seek the gratification of no heartless curiosity, thought I; besides, the desk is mine, and its contents, too, so I will make bold to look within. Everything was methodically arranged, the papers smoothly placed. The pigeon-holes were deep, and removing the files of documents, I groped into their recesses. Presently I felt something there, and dragged it out. It was an old bandanna handkerchief, heavy and knotted. I opened it, and saw it was a saving's bank.

I now recalled all the quiet mysteries which I had noted in the man. I remembered that he never spoke but to answer; that, though at intervals he had considerable time to himself, yet I had never seen him reading—no, not even a newspaper; that for long periods he would stand looking out, at his pale window behind the screen, upon the dead brick wall; I was quite sure he never visited any refectory or eating-house; while his pale face clearly indicated that he never drank beer like Turkey; or tea and coffee even, like other men; that he never went anywhere in particular that I could learn; never went out for a walk, unless, indeed, that was the case at present; that he had declined telling who he was, or whence he came, or whether he had any relatives in the world; that though so thin and pale, he never

---

**Petra:* An ancient Arabian city whose ruins were discovered intact.

†*Marius . . . of Carthage:* Gaius Marius (157–86 B.C.), an exiled Roman general, sought refuge in the African city-state of Carthage, which was destroyed by the Romans in the Third Punic War.

complained of ill-health. And more than all, I remembered a certain unconscious air of pallid—how shall I call it?—of pallid haughtiness, say, or rather an austere reserve about him, which had positively awed me into my tame compliance with his eccentricities, when I had feared to ask him to do the slightest incidental thing for me, even though I might know, from his long-continued motionlessness, that behind his screen he must be standing in one of those dead-wall reveries of his.

Revolving all these things, and coupling them with the recently discovered fact, that he made my office his constant abiding place and home, and not forgetful of his morbid moodiness; revolving all these things, a prudential feeling began to steal over me. My first emotions had been those of pure melancholy and sincerest pity; but just in proportion as the forlornness of Bartleby grew and grew to my imagination, did that same melancholy merge into fear, that pity into repulsion. So true it is, and so terrible, too, that up to a certain point the thought or sight of misery enlists our best affections; but, in certain special cases, beyond that point it does not. They err who would assert that invariably this is owing to the inherent selfishness of the human heart. It rather proceeds from a certain hopelessness of remedying excessive and organic ill. To a sensitive being, pity is not seldom pain. And when at last it is perceived that such pity cannot lead to effectual succor, common sense bids the soul be rid of it. What I saw that morning persuaded me that the scrivener was the victim of innate and incurable disorder. I might give alms to his body; but his body did not pain him; it was his soul that suffered, and his soul I could not reach.

I did not accomplish the purpose of going to Trinity Church that morning. Somehow the things I had seen disqualified me for the time from church-going. I walked homeward, thinking what I would do with Bartleby. Finally, I resolved upon this—I would put certain calm questions to him the next morning, touching his history, etc., and if he declined to answer them openly and unreservedly (and I supposed he would prefer not), then to give him a twenty dollar bill over and above whatever I might owe him, and tell him his services were no longer required; but that if in any other way I could assist him, I would be happy to do so, especially if he desired to return to his native place, wherever that might be, I would willingly help to defray the expenses. Moreover, if, after reaching home, he found himself at any time in want of aid, a letter from him would be sure of a reply.

The next morning came.

"Bartleby," said I, gently calling to him behind his screen.

No reply.

"Bartleby," said I, in a still gentler tone. "come here; I am not going to ask you to do anything you would prefer not to do—I simply wish to speak to you."

Upon this he noiselessly slid into view.

"Will you tell me, Bartleby, where you were born?"

"I would prefer not to."

"Will you tell me *anything* about yourself?"

"I would prefer not to."

"But what reasonable objection can you have to speak to me? I feel friendly towards you."

He did not look at me while I spoke, but kept his glance fixed upon my bust of Cicero, which, as I then sat, was directly behind me, some six inches above my head.

"What is your answer, Bartleby?" said I after waiting a considerable time for a reply, during which his countenance remained immovable, only there was the faintest conceivable tremor of the white attenuated mouth.

"At present I prefer to give no answer," he said, and retired into his hermitage.

It was rather weak in me I confess, but his manner, on this occasion, nettled me. Not only did there seem to lurk in it a certain calm disdain, but his perverseness seemed ungrateful, considering the undeniable good usage and indulgence he had received from me.

Again I sat ruminating what I should do. Mortified as I was at his behavior, and resolved as I had been to dismiss him when I entered my office, nevertheless I strangely felt something superstitious knocking at my heart, and forbidding me to carry out my purpose, and denouncing me for a villain if I dared to breathe one bitter word against this forlornest of mankind. At last, familiarly drawing my chair behind his screen, I sat down and said: "Bartleby, never mind, then, about revealing your history; but let me entreat you as a friend, to comply as far as may be with the usages of this office. Say now, you will help to examine papers tomorrow or next day; in short, say now, that in a day or two you will begin to be a little reasonable:—say so. Bartleby."

"At present I would prefer not to be a little reasonable," was his mildly cadaverous reply.

Just then the folding-doors opened, and Nippers approached. He seemed suffering from an unusually bad night's rest, induced by severer indigestion than common. He overheard those final words of Bartleby.

"*Prefer not*, eh?" gritted Nippers—"I'd *prefer* him, if I were you, sir," addressing me—"I'd *prefer* him; I'd give him preferences, the stubborn mule! What is it, sir, pray, that he *prefers* not to do now?"

Bartleby moved not a limb.

"Mr. Nippers," said I, "I'd prefer that you would withdraw for the present."

Somehow, of late, I had got into the way of involuntarily using this word "prefer" upon all sorts of not exactly suitable occasions. And I trembled to think that my contact with the scrivener had already and seriously affected me in a mental way. And what further and deeper aberration might it not yet produce? This apprehension had not been without efficacy in determining me to summary measures.

As Nippers, looking very sour and sulky, was departing, Turkey blandly and deferentially approached.

"With submission, sir," said he, "yesterday I was thinking about Bartleby here, and I think that if he would but prefer to take a quart of good ale every day, it would do much towards mending him, and enabling him to assist in examining his papers."

"So you have got the word, too," said I, slightly excited.

"With submission, what word, sir?" asked Turkey respectfully crowding himself into the contracted space behind the screen and by so doing, making me jostle the scrivener. "What word, sir?"

"I would prefer to be left alone here," said Bartleby, as if offended at being mobbed in his privacy.

"*That's* the word, Turkey," said I—"*that's* it."

"Oh, *prefer*? oh yes—queer word. I never use it myself. But, sir, as I was saying, if he would but prefer—"

"Turkey," interrupted I, "you will please withdraw."

"Oh certainly, sir, if you prefer that I should."

As he opened the folding-door to retire, Nippers at his desk caught a glimpse of me, and asked whether I would prefer to have a certain paper copied on blue paper or white. He did not in the least roguishly accent the word "prefer." It was plain that it involuntarily rolled from his tongue. I thought to myself, surely I must get rid of a demented man, who already has in some degree turned the tongues, if not the heads of myself and clerks. But I thought it prudent not to break the dismission at once.

The next day I noticed that Bartleby did nothing but stand at his window in his dead-wall revery. Upon asking him why he did not write he said that he had decided upon doing no more writing.

"Why, how now? what next?" exclaimed I, "do no more writing?"

"No more."

"And what is the reason?"

"Do you not see the reason for yourself?" he indifferently replied.

I looked steadfastly at him, and perceived that his eyes looked dull and glazed. Instantly it occurred to me, that his unexampled diligence in copying by his dim window for the first few weeks of his stay with me might have temporarily impaired his vision.

I was touched. I said something in condolence with him. I hinted that of course he did wisely in abstaining from writing for a while; and urged him to embrace that opportunity of taking wholesome exercise in the open air. This however, he did not do. A few days after this, my other clerks being absent, and being in a great hurry to dispatch certain letters by the mail, I thought that, having nothing else earthly to do, Bartleby would surely be less inflexible than usual, and carry these letters to the Post Office. But he blankly declined. So, much to my inconvenience, I went myself.

Still added days went by. Whether Bartleby's eyes improved or not, I could not say. To all appearance, I thought they did. But when I asked him if they did, he vouchsafed no answer. At all events, he would do no copying. At last, in replying to my urgings, he informed me that he had permanently given up copying.

"What!" exclaimed I; "suppose your eyes should get entirely well—better than ever before—would you not copy then?"

"I have given up copying," he answered, and slid aside.

He remained as ever, a fixture in my chamber. Nay—if that were possible—he became still more of a fixture than before. What was to be done? He would do nothing in the office; why should he stay there? In plain fact, he had now become a millstone to me, not only useless as a necklace, but afflictive to bear. Yet I was sorry for him. I speak less than truth when I say that, on his own account, he occasioned me uneasiness. If he would but have named a single relative or friend, I would instantly have written, and urged their taking the poor fellow away to some convenient retreat. But he seemed alone, absolutely alone in the universe. A bit of wreck in the mid-Atlantic. At length, necessities connected with my business tyrannized over all other considerations. Decently as I could, I told Bartleby that in six days' time he must unconditionally leave the office. I warned him to take measures, in the interval, for procuring some other abode. I offered to assist him in this endeavor, if he himself would but take the first step towards a removal. "And when you finally quit me, Bartleby," added I, "I shall see that you go not away entirely unprovided. Six days from this hour, remember."

At the expiration of that period, I peeped behind the screen and lo! Bartleby was there.

I buttoned up my coat, balanced myself; advanced slowly towards him, touched his shoulder, and said, "The time has come; you must quit this place: I am sorry for you; here is money; but you must go."

"I would prefer not," he replied, with his back still towards me.

"You *must*."

He remained silent.

Now I had an unbounded confidence in this man's common honesty. He had frequently restored to me sixpences and shillings carelessly dropped upon the floor, for I am apt to be very reckless in such shirt-button affairs. The proceeding, then, which followed will not be deemed extraordinary.

"Bartleby," said I, "I owe you twelve dollars on account; here are thirty-two, the odd twenty are yours—Will you take it?" and I handed the bills towards him.

But he made no motion.

"I will leave them here, then," putting them under a weight on the table. Then taking my hat and cane and going to the door, I tranquilly turned and added—"After you have removed your things from these offices, Bartleby, you will of course lock the door—since every one is now gone for the day but you—and if you please, slip your key underneath the mat, so that I may have it in the morning. I shall not see you again; so good-bye to you. If, hereafter, in your new place of abode, I can be of any service to you, do not fail to advise me by letter. Good-bye, Bartleby, and fare you well."

But he answered not a word; like the last column of some ruined temple, he remained standing mute and solitary in the middle of the otherwise deserted room.

As I walked home in a pensive mood, my vanity got the better of my pity. I could not but highly plume myself on my masterly management in getting rid of Bartleby. Masterly I call it, and such it must appear to any dispassionate thinker. The beauty of my procedure seemed to consist in its perfect quietness. There was no vulgar bullying, no bravado of any sort, no choleric hectoring, and striding to and fro across the apartment, jerking out vehement commands for Bartleby to bundle himself off with his beggarly traps. Nothing of the kind. Without loudly bidding Bartleby depart—as an inferior genius might have done—I *assumed* the ground that depart he must; and upon that assumption built all I had to say. The more I thought over my procedure, the more I was charmed with it. Nevertheless, next morning, upon awakening, I had my doubts—I had somehow slept off the fumes of vanity. One of the coolest and wisest hours a man has, is just after he awakes in the morning. My procedure seemed as sagacious as ever—but only in theory. How it would prove in practice—there was the rub. It was truly a beautiful thought to have assumed Bartleby's departure; but, after all, that assumption was simply my own, and none of Bartleby's. The great point was, not whether I had assumed that he would quit me, but whether he would prefer to do so. He was more a man of preferences than assumptions.

After breakfast, I walked down town, arguing the probabilities *pro* and *con*. One moment I thought it would prove a miserable failure, and Bartleby would be found all alive at my office as usual; the next moment it seemed certain that I should find his chair empty. And so I kept veering about. At the corner of Broadway and Canal Street, I saw quite an excited group of people standing in earnest conversation.

"I'll take odds he doesn't," said a voice as I passed.

"Doesn't go?—done!" said I, "put up your money."

I was instinctively putting my hand in my pocket to produce my own, when I remembered that this was an election day. The words I had overheard bore no reference to Bartleby, but to the success or non-success of some candidate for the mayoralty. In my intent frame of mind, I had, as it were, imagined that all Broadway shared in my excitement, and were debating the same question with me. I passed on, very thankful that the uproar of the street screened my momentary absent-mindedness.

As I had intended, I was earlier than usual at my office door. I stood listening for a moment. All was still. He must be gone. I tried the knob. The door was locked. Yes, my procedure had worked to a charm; he indeed must be vanished. Yet a certain melancholy mixed with this: I was almost sorry for my brilliant success. I was fumbling under the door mat for the key, which Bartleby was to have left there for me, when accidentally my knee knocked against a panel, producing a summoning sound, and in response a voice came to me from within—"Not yet: I am occupied."

It was Bartleby.

I was thunderstruck. For an instant I stood like the man who, pipe in mouth, was killed one cloudless afternoon long ago in Virginia, by summer lightning; at his own warm open window he was killed, and remained leaning out there upon the dreamy afternoon, till some one touched him, when he fell.

"Not gone!" I murmured at last. But again obeying that wondrous ascendancy which the inscrutable scrivener had over me, and from which ascendancy, for all my chafing, I could not completely escape, I slowly went down stairs and out into the street, and while walking round the block, considered what I should next do in this unheard-of perplexity. Turn the man out by an actual thrusting I could not; to drive him away by calling him hard names would not do; calling in the police was an unpleasant idea; and yet, permit him to enjoy his cadaverous triumph over me—this, too, I could not think of. What was to be done? or, if nothing could be done, was there anything further that I could *assume* in the matter? Yes, as before I had prospectively assumed that Bartleby would depart, so now I might retrospectively assume that departed he was. In the legitimate carrying out of this assumption, I might enter my office in a great hurry, and pretending not to see Bartleby at all, walk straight against him as if he were air. Such a proceeding would in a singular degree have the appearance of a home-thrust. It was hardly possible that Bartleby could withstand such an application of the doctrine of assumption. But upon second thoughts the success of the plan seemed rather dubious. I resolved to argue the matter over with him again.

"Bartleby," said I, entering the office, with a quietly severe expression. "I am seriously displeased. I am pained, Bartleby. I had thought better of you. I had imagined you of such a gentlemanly organization, that in any delicate dilemma a slight hint would suffice—in short, an assumption. But it appears I am deceived. Why," I added, unaffectedly starting, "you have not even touched that money yet," pointing to it, just where I had left it the evening previous.

He answered nothing.

"Will you, or will you not, quit me?" I now demanded in a sudden passion, advancing close to him.

"I would prefer *not* to quit you," he replied, gently emphasizing the *not*.

"What earthly right have you to stay here? Do you pay any rent? Do you pay my taxes? Or is this property yours?"

He answered nothing.

"Are you ready to go on and write now? Are your eyes recovered? Could you copy a small paper for me this morning? or help examine a few lines or step round to the Post Office? In a word, will you do anything at all, to give a coloring to your refusal to depart the premises?"

He silently retired into his hermitage.

I was now in such a state of nervous resentment that I thought it but prudent to check myself at present from further demonstrations. Bartleby and I were alone. I remembered the tragedy of the unfortunate Adams and the still more unfortunate Colt* in the solitary office of the latter; and how poor Colt, being dreadfully incensed by Adams, and imprudently permitting himself to get wildly excited, was at unawares hurried into his fatal act—an act which certainly no man could possibly deplore more than the actor himself. Often it had occurred to me in my ponderings upon the subject that had that altercation taken place in the public street, or at a private residence, it would not have terminated as it did. It was the circumstance of being alone in a solitary office, up stairs, of a building entirely unhallowed by humanizing domestic associations—an uncarpeted office, doubtless, of a dusty haggard sort of appearance—this it must have been, which greatly helped to enhance the irritable desperation of the hapless Colt.

But when this old Adam of resentment rose in me and tempted me concerning Bartleby, I grappled him and threw him. How? Why, simply by recalling the divine injunction: "A new commandment give I unto you, that ye love one another." Yes, this it was that saved me. Aside from higher considerations, charity often operates as a vastly wise and prudent principle—a great safeguard to its possessor. Men have committed murder for jealousy's sake, and anger's sake, and hatred's sake, and selfishness' sake, and spiritual pride's sake but no man, that ever I heard of, ever committed a diabolical murder for sweet charity's sake. Mere self-interest, then, if no better motive can be enlisted, should, especially with high-tempered men, prompt all beings to charity and philanthropy. At any rate, upon the occasion in question, I strove to drown my exasperated feelings towards the scrivener by benevolently construing his conduct. Poor fellow, poor fellow! thought I, he don't mean anything; and besides, he has seen hard times, and ought to be indulged.

I endeavored, also, immediately to occupy myself, and at the same time to comfort my despondency. I tried to fancy that in the course of the morning, at such time as might prove agreeable to him, Bartleby, of his own free accord, would emerge from his hermitage and take up some decided line of march in the direction of the door. But no. Half-past twelve o'clock came. Turkey began to glow in the face, overturn his inkstand, and become generally obstreperous. Nippers abated down into quietude and courtesy; Ginger Nut munched his noon apple; and Bartleby remained standing at his window in one of his profoundest dead wall reveries. Will it be credited? Ought I to acknowledge it? That afternoon I left the office without saying one further word to him.

**Adams . . . Colt:* Samuel Adams was killed by John C. Colt, brother of the gun maker, during a quarrel in 1842. After a sensational court case, Colt committed suicide just before he was to be hanged.

Some days now passed, during which, at leisure intervals I looked a little into. "Edwards on the Will," and "Priestley on Necessity."[*] Under the circumstances, those books induced a salutary feeling. Gradually I slid into the persuasion that these troubles of mine, touching the scrivener, had been all predestined from eternity, and Bartleby was billeted upon me for some mysterious purpose of an all-wise Providence, which it was not for a mere mortal like me to fathom. Yes, Bartleby, stay there behind your screen, thought I; I shall persecute you no more; you are harmless and noiseless as any of these old chairs; in short, I never feel so private as when I know you are here. At last I see it, I feel it; I penetrate to the predestined purpose of my life. I am content. Others may have loftier parts to enact; but my mission in this world, Bartleby, is to furnish you with office-room for such period as you may see fit to remain.

I believe that this wise and blessed frame of mind would have continued with me, had it not been for the unsolicited and uncharitable remarks obtruded upon me by my professional friends who visited the rooms. But thus it often is, that the constant friction of illiberal minds wears out at last the best resolves of the more generous. Though to be sure, when I reflected upon it, it was not strange that people entering my office should be struck by the peculiar aspect of the unaccountable Bartleby, and so be tempted to throw out some sinister observations concerning him. Sometimes an attorney, having business with me, and calling at my office, and finding no one but the scrivener there, would undertake to obtain some sort of precise information from him touching my whereabouts; but without heeding his idle talk, Bartleby would remain standing immovable in the middle of the room. So after contemplating him in that position for a time, the attorney would depart, no wiser than he came.

Also, when a Reference was going on, and the room full of lawyers and witnesses, and business driving fast, some deeply-occupied legal gentleman present, seeing Bartleby wholly unemployed, would request him to run round to his (the legal gentleman's) office and fetch some papers for him. Thereupon, Bartleby would tranquilly decline, and yet remain idle as before. Then the lawyer would give a great stare, and turn to me. And what could I say? At last I was made aware that all through the circle of my professional acquaintance, a whisper of wonder was running round, having reference to the strange creature I kept at my office. This worried me very much. And as the idea came upon me of his possibly turning out a long-lived man, and keeping occupying my chambers, and denying my authority; and perplexing my visitors; and scandalizing my professional reputation; and casting a general gloom over the premises; keeping soul and body together to the last upon his savings (for doubtless he spent but half a dime a day), and in the end perhaps outlive me, and claim possession of my office by right of his perpetual occupancy; as all these dark anticipations crowded upon me more and more, and my friends continually intruded their relentless remarks upon the apparition in my room; a great change was wrought in me. I resolved to gather all my faculties together, and forever rid me of this intolerable incubus.

Ere revolving any complicated project, however, adapted to this end, I first simply suggested to Bartleby the propriety of his permanent departure. In a calm and serious tone, I commended the idea to his careful and mature consideration.

[*]"*Edwards . . . Necessity*": Jonathan Edwards, in *Freedom of the Will* (1754) and Joseph Priestley, in *Doctrine of Philosophical Necessity* (1777), both argued that human beings do not have free will.

But, having taken three days to meditate upon it, he apprised me, that his original determination remained the same; in short, that he still preferred to abide with me.

What shall I do? I now said to myself, buttoning up my coat to the last button. What shall I do? what ought I to do? what does conscience say I *should* do with this man, or, rather, ghost. Rid myself of him, I must; go, he shall. But how? You will not thrust him, the poor, pale, passive mortal—you will not thrust such a helpless creature out of your door? you will not dishonor yourself by such cruelty? No, I will not, I cannot do that. Rather would I let him live and die here, and then mason up his remains in the wall. What, then, will you do? For all your coaxing, he will not budge. Bribes he leaves under your own paperweight on your table; in short, it is quite plain that he prefers to cling to you.

Then something severe, something unusual must be done. What! surely you will not have him collared by a constable, and commit his innocent pallor to the common jail? And upon what ground could you procure such a thing to be done?—a vagrant, is he? What! he a vagrant, a wanderer, who refuses to budge? It is because he will *not* be a vagrant, then, that you seek to count him *as* a vagrant. That is too absurd. No visible means of support: there I have him. Wrong again: for indubitably he *does* support himself, and that is the only unanswerable proof that any man can show of his possessing the means so to do. No more, then. Since he will not quit me, I must quit him. I will change my offices: I will move elsewhere, and give him fair notice, that if I find him on my new premises I will then proceed against him as a common trespasser.

Acting accordingly, next day I thus addressed him. "I find these chambers too far from the City Hall; the air is unwholesome. In a word, I propose to remove my offices next week, and shall no longer require your services. I tell you this now, in order that you may seek another place."

He made no reply, and nothing more was said.

On the appointed day I engaged carts and men proceeded to my chambers, and having but little furniture, everything was removed in a few hours. Throughout, the scrivener remained standing behind the screen, which I directed to be removed the last thing. It was withdrawn and, being folded up like a huge folio, left him the motionless occupant of a naked room. I stood in the entry watching him a moment, while something from within me upbraided me.

I re-entered, with my hand in my pocket—and—and my heart in my mouth.

"Good-bye, Bartleby: I am going—good-bye, and God some way bless you, and take that," slipping something in his hand. But it dropped upon the floor, and then—strange to say—I tore myself from him whom I had so longed to be rid of.

Established in my new quarters, for a day or two I kept the door locked, and started at every footfall in the passages. When I returned to my rooms, after any little absence, I would pause at the threshold for an instant, and attentively listen, ere applying my key. But these fears were needless. Bartleby never came nigh me.

I thought all was going well, when a perturbed-looking stranger visited me, inquiring whether I was the person who had recently occupied rooms at No.— Wall Street.

Full of forebodings, I replied that I was.

"Then, sir," said the stranger, who proved a lawyer, "you are responsible for the man you left there. He refuses to do any copying; he refuses to do anything; he says he prefers not to; and he refuses to quit the premises.

"I am very sorry, sir," said I, with assumed tranquillity but an inward tremor, "but, really, the man you allude to is nothing to me—he is no relation or apprentice of mine, that you should hold me responsible for him."

"In mercy's name, who is he?"

"I certainly cannot inform you. I know nothing about him. Formerly I employed him as a copyist; but he has done nothing for me now for some time past."

"I shall settle him, then—good morning, sir."

Several days passed, and I heard nothing more; and, though I often felt a charitable prompting to call at the place and see poor Bartleby, yet a certain squeamishness, of I know not what, withheld me.

All is over with him, by this time, thought I at last, when, through another week, no further intelligence reached me. But, coming to my room the day after, I found several persons waiting at my door in a high state of nervous excitement.

"That's the man—here he comes," cried the foremost one, whom I recognized as the lawyer who had previously called upon me alone.

"You must take him away, sir, at once," cried a portly person among them, advancing upon me, and whom I knew to be the landlord of No.—Wall Street. "These gentlemen, my tenants, cannot stand it any longer. Mr. B——," pointing to the lawyer, "has turned him out of his room and he now persists in haunting the building generally, sitting upon the banisters of the stairs by day, and sleeping in the entry by night. Everybody is concerned; clients are leaving the offices; some fears are entertained of a mob; something you must do, and that without delay."

Aghast at this torrent, I fell back before it and would fain have locked myself in my new quarters. In vain I persisted that Bartleby was nothing to me—no more than to any one else. In vain—I was the last person known to have anything to do with him, and they held me to the terrible account. Fearful, then, of being exposed in the papers (as one person present obscurely threatened), I considered the matter, and, at length said, that if the lawyer would give me a confidential interview with the scrivener, in his (the lawyer's) own room, I would, that afternoon, strive my best to rid them of the nuisance they complained of.

Going up stairs to my old haunt, there was Bartleby silently sitting upon the banister at the landing.

"What are you doing here, Bartleby?" said I.

"Sitting upon the banister," he mildly replied.

I motioned him into the lawyer's room, who then left us.

"Bartleby," said I, "are you aware that you are the cause of great tribulation to me, by persisting in occupying the entry after being dismissed from the office?"

No answer.

"Now one of two things must take place. Either you must do something, or something must be done to you. Now what sort of business would you like to engage in? Would you like to re-engage in copying for some one?"

"No; I would prefer not to make any change."

"Would you like a clerkship in a dry-goods store?"

"There is too much confinement about that. No, I would not like a clerkship; but I am not particular."

"Too much confinement," I cried, "why, you keep yourself confined all the time!"

"I would prefer not to take a clerkship," he rejoined as if to settle that little item at once.

"How would a bar-tender's business suit you? There is no trying of the eyesight in that."

"I would not like it at all; though, as I said before, I am not particular."

His unwonted wordiness inspirited me. I returned to the charge.

"Well, then, would you like to travel through the country collecting bills for the merchants? That would improve your health."

"No, I would prefer to be doing something else."

"How, then, would going as a companion to Europe, to entertain some young gentleman with your conversation—how would that suit you?"

"Not at all. It does not strike me that there is anything definite about that. I like to be stationary. But I am not particular."

"Stationary you shall be then," I cried, now losing all patience, and, for the first time in all my exasperating connection with him, fairly flying into a passion. "If you do not go away from these premises before night, I shall feel bound—indeed, I *am* bound—to—to quit the premises myself!" I rather absurdly concluded, knowing not with what possible threat to try to frighten his immobility into compliance. Despairing of all further efforts, I was precipitately leaving him, when a final thought occurred to me—one which had not been wholly unindulged before.

"Bartleby," said I, in the kindesttone I could assume under such exciting circumstances, "will you go home with me now—not to my office, but my dwelling—and remain there till we can conclude upon some convenient arrangement for you at our leisure? Come let us start now, right away."

"No: at present I would prefer not to make any change at all."

I answered nothing; but, effectually dodging every one by the suddenness and rapidity of my flight, rushed from the building, ran up Wall Street towards Broadway, and, jumping into the first omnibus, was soon removed from pursuit. As soon as tranquillity returned, I distinctly perceived that I had now done all that I possibly could, both in respect to the demands of the landlord and his tenants, and with regard to my own desire and sense of duty, to benefit Bartleby, and shield him from rude persecution. I now strove to be entirely care-free and quiescent; and my conscience justified me in the attempt, though, indeed, it was not so successful as I could have wished. So fearful was I of being again hunted out by the incensed landlord and his exasperated tenants, that, surrendering my business to Nippers, for a few days, I drove about the upper part of the town and through the suburbs, in my rockaway; crossed over to Jersey City and Hoboken, and paid fugitive visits to Manhattanville and Astoria. In fact, I almost lived in my rockaway for the time.

When again I entered my office, lo, a note from the landlord lay upon the desk. I opened it with trembling hands. It informed me that the writer had sent to the police, and had Bartleby removed to the Tombs as a vagrant. Moreover, since I knew more about him than any one else, he wished me to appear at that place, and make a suitable statement of the facts. These tidings had a conflicting effect upon me. At first I was indignant; but, at last, almost approved. The landlord's energetic, summary disposition, had led him to adopt a procedure which I do not think I would have decided upon myself: and yet, as a last resort, under such peculiar circumstances, it seemed the only plan.

As I afterwards learned, the poor scrivener, when told that he must be conducted to the Tombs, offered not the slightest obstacle, but, in his pale, unmoving way, silently acquiesced.

Some of the compassionate and curious by-standers joined the party; and headed by one of the constables arm-in-arm with Bartleby, the silent procession filed its way through all the noise, and heat, and joy of the roaring thoroughfares at noon.

The same day I received the note, I went to the Tombs; or, to speak more properly, the Halls of Justice. Seeking the right officer, I stated the purpose of my call, and was informed that the individual I described was, indeed, within. I then assured the functionary that Bartleby was a perfectly honest man, and greatly to be compassionated, however unaccountably eccentric. I narrated all I knew, and closed by suggesting the idea of letting him remain in as indulgent confinement as possible, till something less harsh might be done—though, indeed, I hardly knew what. At all events, if nothing else could be decided upon, the almshouse must receive him. I then begged to have an interview.

Being under no disgraceful charge, and quite serene and harmless in all his ways, they had permitted him freely to wander about the prison, and, especially, in the inclosed grass-platted yards thereof. And so I found him there, standing all alone in the quietest of the yards, his face towards a high wall, while all around, from the narrow slits of the jail windows, I thought I saw peering out upon him the eyes of murderers and thieves.

"Bartleby!"

"I know you," he said, without looking round—"and I want nothing to say to you."

"It was not I that brought you here, Bartleby," said I, keenly pained at his implied suspicion. "And to you, this should not be so vile a place. Nothing reproachful attaches to you by being here. And see, it is not so sad a place as one might think. Look, there is the sky, and here is the grass."

"I know where I am," he replied, but would say nothing more, and so I left him.

As I entered the corridor again, a broad meat-like man, in an apron, accosted me, and, jerking his thumb over his shoulder, said—"Is that your friend?"

"Yes."

"Does he want to starve? If he does, let him live on the prison fare, that's all."

"Who are you?" asked I, not knowing what to make of such an unofficially speaking person in such a place.

"I am the grub-man. Such gentlemen as have friends here, hire me to provide them with something good to eat."

"Is this so?" said I, turning the turnkey.

He said it was.

"Well, then," said I, slipping some silver into the grub-man's hands (for so they called him), "I want you to give particular attention to my friend there; let him have the best dinner you can get. And you must be as polite to him as possible."

"Introduce me, will you?" said the grub-man, looking at me with an expression which seemed to say he was all impatience for an opportunity to give a specimen of his breeding.

Thinking it would prove of benefit to the scrivener, I acquiesced; and, asking the grub-man his name, went up with him to Bartleby.

"Bartleby, this is a friend; you will find him very useful to you."

"Your sarvant, sir, your sarvant," said the grub-man, making a low salutation behind his apron. "Hope you find it pleasant here, sir; nice grounds—cool apartments—hope you'll stay with us some time—try to make it agreeable. What will you have for dinner to day?"

"I prefer not to dine to-day," said Bartleby, turning away. "It would disagree with me; I am unused to dinners." So saying, he slowly moved to the other side of the inclosure, and took up a position fronting the deadwall.

"How's this?" said the grub-man, addressing me with a stare of astonishment. "He's odd, ain't he?"

"I think he is a little deranged," said I, sadly.

"Deranged? deranged is it? Well, now, upon my word, I thought that friend of yourn was a gentleman forger; they are always pale and genteel-like, them forgers. I can't help pity 'em—can't help it, sir. Did you know Monroe Edwards?" he added, touchingly, and paused. Then, laying his hand piteously on my shoulder, sighed, "he died of consumption at Sing-Sing. So you weren't acquainted with Monroe?"

"No, I was never socially acquainted with any forgers. But I cannot stop longer. Look to my friend yonder. You will not lose by it. I will see you again."

Some few days after this, I again obtained admission to the Tombs, and went through the corridors in quest of Bartleby; but without finding him.

"I saw him coming from his cell not long ago," said a turnkey, "may be he's gone to loiter in the yards."

So I went in that direction.

"Are you looking for the silent man?" said another turnkey, passing me. "Yonder he lies—sleeping in the yard there. 'Tis not twenty minutes since I saw him lie down."

The yard was entirely quiet. It was not accessible to the common prisoners. The surrounding walls, of amazing thickness, kept off all sounds behind them. The Egyptian character of the masonry weighed upon me with its gloom. But a soft imprisoned turf grew under foot; The heart of the eternal pyramids, it seemed, wherein, by some strange magic, through the clefts, grass-seed, dropped by birds, had sprung.

Strangely huddled at the base of the wall, his knees drawn up, and lying on his side, his head touching the cold stones, I saw the wasted Bartleby. But nothing stirred. I paused; then went close up to him; stooped over, and saw that his dim eyes were open; otherwise he seemed profoundly sleeping. Something prompted me to touch him. I felt his hand, when a tingling shiver ran up my arm and down my spine to my feet.

The round face of the grub-man peered upon me now. "His dinner is ready. Won't he dine to-day, either? Or does he live without dining?"

"Lives without dining," said I, and closed the eyes.

"Eh!—He's asleep, ain't he?"

"With kings and counselors,"* murmured I.

There would seem little need for proceeding further in this history. Imagination will readily supply the meagre recital of poor Bartleby's interment.

*"*With kings and counselors*": From Job 3:13–14: "then had I been at rest,/With kings and counselors of the earth,/which built desolate places for themselves."

But, ere parting with the reader, let me say, that if this little narrative has sufficiently interested him, to awaken curiosity as to who Bartleby was, and what manner of life he led prior to the present narrator's making his acquaintance, I can only reply, that in such curiosity I fully share, but am wholly unable to gratify it. Yet here I hardly know whether I should divulge one little item of rumor, which came to my ear a few months after the scrivener's decease. Upon what basis it rested, I could never ascertain; and hence, how true it is I cannot now tell. But, inasmuch as this vague report has not been without a certain suggestive interest to me, however sad, it may prove the same with some others; and so I will briefly mention it. The report was this: that Bartleby had been a subordinate clerk in the Dead Letter Office at Washington, from which he had been suddenly removed by a change in the administration. When I think over this rumor, hardly can I express the emotions which seize me. Dead letters! does it not sound like dead men? Conceive a man by nature and misfortune prone to a pallid hopelessness, can any business seem more fitted to heighten it than that of continually handling these dead letters, and assorting them for the flames? For by the cart-load they are annually burned. Sometimes from out the folded paper the pale clerk takes a ring—the finger it was meant for, perhaps, moulders in the grave; a bank-note sent in swiftest charity—he whom it would relieve, nor eats nor hungers any more; pardon for those who died despairing; hope for those who died unhoping; good tidings for those who died stifled by unrelieved calamities. On errands of life, these letters speed to death.

Ah, Bartleby! Ah, humanity!

SARAH ORNE JEWETT (1849–1909) was born in South Berwick, Maine. Her father was a country doctor, whom Jewett frequently accompanied on house calls. Her father also shared with her his love of classic fiction and his knowledge of nature. After being schooled at home as a young girl, Jewett graduated from Berwick Academy in 1865. In 1901 she was the first woman to receive an honorary Litt. D. degree from Bowdoin College. She published her first short story, "Jenny Garrow's Lovers" (1868), under the pseudonym A. C. Eliot, and soon thereafter began to write stories about the area with which she was most familiar—rural Maine. The first of these Maine stories, "The Shorehouse," was published in the *Atlantic Monthly* in 1873. Before a debilitating carriage accident in 1902, Jewett wrote prolifically, publishing over 150 stories in magazines and collected volumes, as well as numerous children's stories and a handful of novels, including *A Country Doctor* (1884), and was critically recognized as a prominent writer of regional fiction.

In 1886, Jewett joined the Massachusetts Audubon Society, which had dedicated itself to saving the white heron, a bird that was being killed in great numbers to provide feathers for women's hats. Jewett drew upon this experience when writing "A White Heron" (1886), the title story of the collection *A White Heron, and Other Stories*; the story is part **bildungsroman**, part romantic fantasy, and part **nature writing**.

Related Works: Joyce, "Araby"; Updike, "A&P"; Bambara, "The Lesson"; Berry, "The Peace of Wild Things"; Bishop, "The Fish"; Cofer, "Arturo's Flight"; Kinnell, "The Bear"; Stafford, "Traveling in the Dark"; Steinbeck, "The Chrysanthemums."

SARAH ORNE JEWETT
A White Heron

1

The woods were already filled with shadows one June evening, just before eight o'clock, though a bright sunset still glimmered faintly among the trunks of the trees. A little girl was driving home her cow, a plodding, dilatory, provoking creature in her behavior, but a valued companion for all that. They were going away from whatever light there was, and striking deep into the woods, but their feet were familiar with the path, and it was no matter whether their eyes could see it or not.

There was hardly a night the summer through when the old cow could be found waiting at the pasture bars; on the contrary, it was her greatest pleasure to hide herself away among the huckleberry bushes, and though she wore a loud bell she had made the discovery that if one stood perfectly still it would not ring. So Sylvia had to hunt for her until she found her, and call Co'! Co'! with never an answering Moo, until her childish patience was quite spent. If the creature had not given good milk and plenty of it, the case would have seemed very different to her owners. Besides, Sylvia had all the time there was, and very little use to make of it. Sometimes in pleasant weather it was a consolation to look upon the cow's pranks as an intelligent attempt to play hide and seek, and as the child had no playmates she lent herself to this amusement with a good deal of zest. Though this chase had been so long that the wary animal herself had given an unusual signal of her whereabouts, Sylvia had only laughed when she came upon Mistress Moolly at the swampside, and urged her affectionately homeward with a twig of birch leaves. The old cow was not inclined to wander farther, she even turned in the right direction for once as they left the pasture, and stepped along the road at a good pace. She was quite ready to be milked now, and seldom stopped to browse. Sylvia wondered what her grandmother would say because they were so late. It was a great while since she had left home at half-past five o'clock, but everybody knew the difficulty of making this errand a short one. Mrs. Tilley had chased the hornéd torment too many summer evenings herself to blame any one else for lingering, and was only thankful as she waited that she had Sylvia, nowadays, to give such valuable assistance. The good woman suspected that Sylvia loitered occasionally on her own account; there never was such a child for straying about out-of-doors since the world was made! Everybody said that it was a good change for a little maid who had tried to grow for eight years in a crowded manufacturing town, but, as for Sylvia herself, it seemed as if she never had been alive at all before she came to live at the farm. She thought often with wistful compassion of a wretched geranium that belonged to a town neighbor.

"'Afraid of folks,'" old Mrs. Tilley said to herself, with a smile, after she had made the unlikely choice of Sylvia from her daughter's houseful of children, and was returning to the farm. "'Afraid of folks,' they said! I guess she won't be troubled no great with 'em up to the old place!" When they reached the door of the lonely house and stopped to unlock it, and the cat came to purr loudly, and rub against them, a deserted pussy, indeed, but fat with young robins, Sylvia whispered that this was a beautiful place to live in, and she never should wish to go home.

The companions followed the shady woodroad, the cow taking slow steps and the child very fast ones. The cow stopped long at the brook to drink, as if the pasture were not half a swamp, and Sylvia stood still and waited, letting her bare feet cool themselves in the shoal water, while the great twilight moths struck softly against her. She waded on through the brook as the cow moved away, and listened to the thrushes with a heart that beat fast with pleasure. There was a stirring in the great boughs overhead. They were full of little birds and beasts that seemed to be wide awake, and going about their world, or else saying good-night to each other in sleepy twitters. Sylvia herself felt sleepy as she walked along. However, it was not much farther to the house, and the air was soft and sweet. She was not often in the woods so late as this, and it made her feel as if she were a part of the gray shadows and the moving leaves. She was just thinking how long it seemed since she first came to the farm a year ago and wondering if everything went on in the noisy town just the same as when she was there; the thought of the great red-faced boy who used to chase and frighten her made her hurry along the path to escape from the shadow of the trees.

Suddenly this little woods-girl is horror-stricken to hear a clear whistle not very far away. Not a bird's-whistle, which would have a sort of friendliness, but a boy's whistle, determined, and somewhat aggressive. Sylvia left the cow to whatever sad fate might await her, and stepped discreetly aside into the bushes, but she was just too late. The enemy had discovered her, and called out in a very cheerful and persuasive tone, "Halloa, little girl, how far is it to the road?" and trembling Sylvia answered almost inaudibly, "A good ways."

She did not dare to look boldly at the tall young man, who carried a gun over his shoulder, but she came out of her bush and again followed the cow, while he walked alongside.

"I have been hunting for some birds," the stranger said kindly, "and I have lost my way, and need a friend very much. Don't be afraid," he added gallantly. "Speak up and tell me what your name is, and whether you think I can spend the night at your house, and go out gunning early in the morning."

Sylvia was more alarmed than before. Would not her grandmother consider her much to blame? But who could have foreseen such an accident as this? It did not seem to be her fault, and she hung her head as if the stem of it were broken, but managed to answer "Sylvy," with much effort when her companion again asked her name.

Mrs. Tilley was standing in the doorway when the trio came into view. The cow gave a loud moo by way of explanation.

"Yes, you'd better speak up for yourself, you old trial! Where'd she tucked herself away this time, Sylvy?" But Sylvia kept an awed silence; she knew by instinct that her grandmother did not comprehend the gravity of the situation. She must be mistaking the stranger for one of the farmer-lads of the region.

The young man stood his gun beside the door, and dropped a lumpy gamebag beside it; then he bade Mrs. Tilley good-evening, and repeated his wayfarer's story, and asked if he could have a night's lodging.

"Put me anywhere you like," he said. "I must be off early in the morning, before day; but I am very hungry, indeed. You can give me some milk at any rate that's plain."

"Dear sakes, yes," responded the hostess, whose long slumbering hospitality seemed to be easily awakened. "You might fare better if you went out to the main road a mile or so, but you're welcome to what we've got. I'll milk right off, and you make yourself at home. You can sleep on husks or feathers," she proffered graciously. "I raised them all myself. There's good pasturing for geese just below here towards the ma'sh. Now step round and set a plate for the gentleman, Sylvy!" And Sylvia promptly stepped. She was glad to have something to do, and she was hungry herself.

It was a surprise to find so clean and comfortable a little dwelling in this New England wilderness. The young man had known the horrors of its most primitive housekeeping, and the dreary squalor of that level of society which does not rebel at the companionship of hens. This was the best thrift of an old-fashioned farmstead, though on such a small scale that it seemed like a hermitage. He listened eagerly to the old woman's quaint talk, he watched Sylvia's pale face and shining gray eyes with ever growing enthusiasm, and insisted that this was the best supper he had eaten for a month, and afterward the new-made friends sat down in the door-way together while the moon came up.

Soon it would be berry-time, and Sylvia was a great help at picking. The cow was a good milker, though a plaguy thing to keep track of, the hostess gossiped frankly, adding presently that she had buried four children, so Sylvia's mother, and a son (who might be dead) in California were all the children she had left. "Dan, my boy, was a great hand to go gunning," she explained sadly. "I never wanted for pa'tridges or gray squer'ls while he was to home. He's been a great wand'rer, I expect, and he's no hand to write letters. There, I don't blame him, I'd ha' seen the world myself if it had been so I could."

"Sylvy takes after him," the grandmother continued affectionately, after a minute's pause. "There ain't a foot o' ground she don't know her way over, and the wild creatures counts her one o' themselves. Squer'ls she'll tame to come an' feed right out o' her hands, and all sorts o' birds. Last winter she got the jaybirds to bangeing* here, and I believe she'd 'a' scanted herself of her own meals to have plenty to throw out amongst 'em, if I hadn't kep' watch. Anything but crows, I tell her, I'm willin' to help support—though Dan he had a tamed one o' them that did seem to have reason same as folks. It was round here a good spell after he went away. Dan an' his father they didn't hitch,—but he never held up his head ag'in after Dan had dared him an gone off."

The guest did not notice this hint of family sorrows in his eager interest in something else.

"So Sylvy knows all about birds, does she?" he exclaimed, as he looked round at the little girl who sat, very demure but increasingly sleepy, in the moonlight. "I am making a collection of birds myself. I have been at it ever since I was a boy." (Mrs. Tilley smiled.) "There are two or three very rare ones I have been hunting for these five years. I mean to get them on my own ground if they can be found."

**bangeing:* New England slang for loafing.

"Do you cage 'em up?" asked Mrs. Tilley doubtfully, in response to this enthusiastic announcement.

"Oh no, they're stuffed and preserved, dozens and dozens of them," said the ornithologist, "and I have shot or snared every one myself. I caught a glimpse of a white heron a few miles from here on Saturday, and I have followed it in this direction. They have never been found in this district at all. The little white heron, it is," and he turned again to look at Sylvia with the hope of discovering that the rare bird was one of her acquaintances.

But Sylvia was watching a hop-toad in the narrow footpath.

"You would know the heron if you saw it," the stranger continued eagerly. "A queer tall white bird with soft feathers and long thin legs. And it would have a nest perhaps in the top of a high tree, made of sticks, something like a hawk's nest."

Sylvia's heart gave a wild beat; she knew that strange white bird, and had once stolen softly near where it stood in some bright green swamp grass, away over at the other side of the woods. There was an open place where the sunshine always seemed strangely yellow and hot, where tall, nodding rushes grew, and her grandmother had warned her that she might sink in the soft black mud underneath and never be heard of more. Not far beyond were the salt marshes just this side the sea itself, which Sylvia wondered and dreamed much about, but never had seen, whose great voice could sometimes be heard above the noise of the woods on stormy nights.

"I can't think of anything I should like so much as to find that heron's nest," the handsome stranger was saying. "I would give ten dollars to anybody who could show it to me," he added desperately, "and I mean to spend my whole vacation hunting for it if need be. Perhaps it was only migrating, or had been chased out of its own region by some bird of prey."

Mrs. Tilley gave amazed attention to all this, but Sylvia still watched the toad, not divining, as she might have done at some calmer time, that the creature wished to get to its hole under the door-step, and was much hindered by the unusual spectators at that hour of the evening. No amount of thought, that night, could decide how many wished for treasures the ten dollars, so lightly spoken of, would buy.

The next day the young sportsman hovered about the woods, and Sylvia kept him company, having lost her first fear of the friendly lad, who proved to be most kind and sympathetic. He told her many things about the birds and what they knew and where they lived and what they did with themselves. And he gave her a jack-knife, which she thought as great a treasure as if she were a desert-islander. All day long he did not once make her troubled or afraid except when he brought down some unsuspecting singing creature from its bough. Sylvia would have liked him vastly better without his gun; she could not understand why he killed the very birds he seemed to like so much. But as the day waned, Sylvia still watched the young man with loving admiration. She had never seen anybody so charming and delightful; the woman's heart, asleep in the child, was vaguely thrilled by a dream of love. Some premonition of that great power stirred and swayed these young creatures who traversed the solemn woodlands with soft-footed silent care. They stopped to listen to a bird's song; they pressed forward again eagerly, parting the branches—speaking to each other rarely and in whispers; the young man going first and Sylvia following, fascinated, a few steps behind, with her gray eyes dark with excitement.

She grieved because the longed-for white heron was elusive, but she did not lead the guest, she only followed, and there was no such thing as speaking first. The sound of her own unquestioned voice would have terrified her—it was hard enough to answer yes or no when there was need of that. At last evening began to fall, and they drove the cow home together, and Sylvia smiled with pleasure when they came to the place where she heard the whistle and was afraid only the night before.

II

Half a mile from home, at the farther edge of the woods, where the land was highest, a great pine-tree stood, the last of its generation. Whether it was left for a boundary mark, or for what reason, no one could say; the wood-choppers who had felled its mates were dead and gone long ago, and a whole forest of sturdy trees, pines and oaks and maples, had grown again. But the stately head of this old pine towered above them all and made a landmark for sea and shore miles and miles away. Sylvia knew it well. She had always believed that whoever climbed to the top of it could see the ocean; and the little girl had often laid her hand on the great rough trunk and looked up wistfully at those dark boughs that the wind always stirred, no matter how hot and still the air might be below. Now she thought of the tree with a new excitement, for why, if one climbed it at break of day could not one see all the world, and easily discover from whence the white heron flew, and mark the place, and find the hidden nest?

What a spirit of adventure, what wild ambition. What fancied triumph and delight and glory for the later morning when she could make known the secret! It was almost too real and too great for the childish heart to bear.

All night the door of the little house stood open and the whippoorwills came and sang upon the very step. The young sportsman and his old hostess were sound asleep, but Sylvia's great design kept her broad awake and watching. She forgot to think of sleep. The short summer night seemed as long as the winter darkness, and at last when the whippoorwills ceased, and she was afraid the morning would after all come too soon, she stole out of the house and followed the pasture path through the woods, hastening toward the open ground beyond, listening with a sense of comfort and companionship to the drowsy twitter of a half-awakened bird, whose perch she had jarred in passing. Alas, if the great wave of human interest which flooded for the first time this dull little life should sweep away the satisfactions of an existence heart to heart with nature and the dumb life of the forest!

There was the huge tree asleep yet in the paling moonlight, and small and silly Sylvia began with utmost bravery to mount to the top of it, with tingling, eager blood coursing the channels of her whole frame, with her bare feet and fingers, that pinched and held like bird's claws to the monstrous ladder reaching up, up, almost to the sky itself. First she must mount the white oak tree that grew alongside, where she was almost lost among the dark branches and the green leaves heavy and wet with dew; a bird fluttered off its nest, and a red squirrel ran to and fro and scolded pettishly at the harmless housebreaker. Sylvia felt her way easily. She had often climbed there, and knew that higher still one of the oak's upper branches chafed against the pine trunk, just where its lower boughs were set close together. There, when she made the dangerous pass from one tree to the other, the great enterprise would really begin.

She crept out along the swaying oak limb at last, and took the daring step across into the old pine tree. The way was harder than she thought; she must reach far and hold fast, the sharp dry twigs caught and held her and scratched her like angry talons, the pitch made her thin little fingers clumsy and stiff as she went round and round the tree's great stem, higher and higher upward. The sparrows and robins in the woods below were beginning to wake and twitter to the dawn, yet it seemed much lighter there aloft in the pine-tree, and the child knew she must hurry if her project were to be of any use.

The tree seemed to lengthen itself out as she went up, and to reach farther and farther upward. It was like a great main-mast to the voyaging earth; it must truly have been amazed that morning through all its ponderous frame as it felt this determined spark of human spirit wending its way from higher branch to branch. Who knows how steadily the least twigs held themselves to advantage this light, weak creature on her way. The old pine must have loved his new dependent. More than all the hawks, and bats, and moths, and even the sweet voiced thrushes, was the brave, beating heart of the solitary gray-eyed child. And the tree stood still and frowned away the winds that June morning while the dawn grew bright in the east.

Sylvia's face was like a pale star, if one had seen it from the ground, when the last thorny bough was past, and she stood trembling and tired but wholly triumphant, high in the treetop. Yes, there was the sea with the dawning sun making a golden dazzle over it, and toward that glorious east flew two hawks with slow-moving pinions. How low they looked in the air from that height when one had only seen them before far up, and dark against the blue sky. Their gray feathers were as soft as moths; they seemed only a little way from the tree, and Sylvia felt as if she too could go flying away among the clouds. Westward, the woodlands and farms reached miles and miles into the distance; here and there were church steeples, and white villages, truly it was a vast and awesome world!

The birds sang louder and louder. At last the sun came up bewilderingly bright. Sylvia could see the white sails of ships out at sea, and the clouds that were purple and rose-colored and yellow at first began to fade away. Where was the white heron's nest in the sea of green branches, and was this wonderful sight and pageant of the world the only reward for having climbed to such a giddy height? Now look down again, Sylvia, where the green marsh is set among the shining birches and dark hemlocks; there where you saw the white heron once you will see him again: look, look! a white spot of him like a single floating feather comes up from the dead hemlock and grows larger, and rises, and comes close at last, and goes by the landmark pine with steady sweep of wing and outstretched slender neck and crested head. And wait! wait! do not move a foot or a finger, little girl, do not send an arrow of light and consciousness from your two eager eyes, for the heron has perched on a pine bough not far beyond yours, and cries back to his mate on the nest and plumes his feathers for the new day!

The child gives a long sigh a minute later when a company of shouting cat-birds comes also to the tree, and vexed by their fluttering and lawlessness the solemn heron goes away. She knows his secret now, the wild, light, slender bird that floats and wavers, and goes back like an arrow presently to his home in the green world beneath. Then Sylvia, well satisfied, makes her perilous way down again not daring to look far below the branch she stands on, ready to cry sometimes because her fingers ache and her lamed feet slip. Wondering over and over again what the stranger would say to her, and what he would think when she told him how to find his way straight to the heron's nest.

"Sylvy, Sylvy!" called the busy old grandmother again and again, but nobody answered, and the small husk bed was empty and Sylvia had disappeared.

The guest waked from a dream, and remembering his day's pleasure hurried to dress himself that might it sooner begin. He was sure from the way the shy little girl looked once or twice yesterday that she had at least seen the white heron, and now she must really be made to tell. Here she comes now, paler than ever, and her worn old frock is torn and tattered, and smeared with pine pitch. The grandmother and the sportsman stand in the door together and question her, and the splendid moment has come to speak of the dead hemlock-tree by the marsh.

But Sylvia does not speak after all, though the old grandmother fretfully rebukes her, and the young man's kind, appealing eyes are looking straight in her own. He can make them rich with money; he has promised it, and they are poor now. He is so well worth making happy, and he waits to hear the story she can tell.

No, she must keep silence! What is it that suddenly forbids her and makes her dumb? Has she been nine years growing and now, when the great world for the first time puts out a hand to her, must she thrust it aside for a bird's sake? The murmur of the pine's green branches is in her ears, she remembers how the white heron came flying through the golden air and how they watched the sea and the morning together, and Sylvia cannot speak; she cannot tell the heron's secret and give its life away.

Dear loyalty, that suffered a sharp pang as the guest went away disappointed later in the day, that could have served and followed him and loved him as a dog loves! Many a night Sylvia heard the echo of his whistle haunting the pasture path as she came home with the loitering cow. She forgot even her sorrow at the sharp report of his gun and the sight of thrushes and sparrows dropping silent to the ground, their songs hushed and their pretty feathers stained and wet with blood. Were birds better friends than their hunter might have been,—who can tell? Whatever treasures were lost to her, woodlands and summer-time, remember! Bring your gifts and graces and tell your secrets to this lonely country child!

LEO TOLSTOY (1828–1910) was born near Tula, Russia, on the family estate of his aristocratic parents. Raised by an aunt following the early death of both parents, Tolstoy was privately tutored before entering the University of Kazan in 1844. By 1847, the period of his formal education over, he returned home to manage his estates. In 1851, Tolstoy joined the Russian army as a volunteer to fight the hill tribes in the Caucasus and then served with distinction as an artillery officer during the Crimean War, most notably at the famous siege of Sevastapol in 1855. Tolstoy's first published work, *Childhood*, a fresh and authentic semifictional narrative based on his own experiences, appeared in 1852, followed by two sequels, *Boyhood* (1854) and *Youth* (1857). These works, together with *Sevastapol*

Stories (1855), the legacy of his Crimean experiences, won Tolstoy a measure of recognition, as did his short novel *The Cossacks* (1862), a humanistic study of peasant life in the Caucasus.

Following two trips to western Europe in 1857 and 1861, Tolstoy returned to his estates, where for the next fifteen years he settled down to a life of farming, teaching peasant children, rearing his own family, and writing. Tolstoy's two great novels of Russian aristocratic life, *War and Peace* and *Anna Karenina*, were published in 1869 and 1877, after which he passed through a deep personal and religious crisis. His later works, including "The Death of Ivan Ilych" (1886), *Master and Man* (1895), and *Resurrection* (1899), reflect his disenchantment with bourgeois society, his rejection of orthodox religion, and his own hard-won conception of Christian salvation. These beliefs, and the struggle leading up to them, resulted in the publication of such nonfiction as *What Men Live By* (1881), *My Confession* (1882), *What I Believe* (1884), and *The Kingdom of God Is Within You* (1893).

In "The Death of Ivan Ilych," the title character's **epiphany** in the throes of dying represents the **moral** of the story: a lesson in how one ought to live one's life and a hope that it's never too late to change one's ways and die at peace.

Related Works: Joyce, "Araby"; Robinson, "Richard Cory"; Milton, "When I consider how my light is spent"; Singer, "Gimpel the Fool."

LEO TOLSTOY

The Death of Ivan Ilych

Translated by Louise and Aylmer Maude

I

During an interval in the Melvinski trial in the large building of the Law Courts, the members and public prosecutor met in Ivan Egorovich Shebek's private room, where the conversation turned on the celebrated Krasovski case. Fëdor Vasilievich warmly maintained that it was not subject to their jurisdiction, Ivan Egorovich maintained the contrary, while Peter Ivanovich, not having entered into the discussion at the start, took no part in it but looked through the *Gazette* which had just been handed in.

"Gentlemen," he said, "Ivan Ilych has died!"

"You don't say so!"

"Here, read it yourself," replied Peter Ivanovich, handing Fëdor Vasilievich the paper still damp from the press. Surrounded by a black border were the words: "Praskovya Fëdorovna Golovinà, with profound sorrow, informs relatives and friends of the demise of her beloved husband Ivan Ilych Golovin, Member of the Court of Justice, which occurred on February the 4th of this year 1882. The funeral will take place on Friday at one o'clock in the afternoon."

Ivan Ilych had been a colleague of the gentlemen present and was liked by them all. He had been ill for some weeks with an illness said to be incurable. His post had been kept open for him, but there had been conjectures that in case of his death Alexeev might receive his appointment, and that either Vinnikov or Shtabel would succeed Alexeev. So on receiving the news of Ivan Ilych's death the first thought of each of the gentlemen in that private room was of the changes and promotions it might occasion among themselves or their acquaintances.

"I shall be sure to get Shtabel's place or Vinnikov's," thought Fëdor Vasilievich. "I was promised that long ago, and the promotion means an extra eight hundred rubles a year for me besides the allowance."

"Now I must apply for my brother-in-law's transfer from Kaluga," thought Peter Ivanovich. "My wife will be very glad, and then she won't be able to say that I never do anything for her relations."

"I thought he would never leave his bed again," said Peter Ivanovich aloud. "It's very sad."

"But what really was the matter with him?"

"The doctors couldn't say—at least they could, but each of them said something different. When last I saw him I thought he was getting better."

"And I haven't been to see him since the holidays. I always meant to go."

"Had he any property?"

"I think his wife had a little—but something quite trifling."

"We shall have to go to see her, but they live so terribly far away."

"Far away from you, you mean. Everything's far away from your place."

"You see, he never can forgive my living on the other side of the river," said Peter Ivanovich, smiling at Shebek. Then, still talking of the distances between different parts of the city, they returned to the Court.

Besides considerations as to the possible transfers and promotions likely to result from Ivan Ilych's death, the mere fact of the death of a near acquaintance aroused, as usual, in all who heard of it the complacent feeling that "it is he who is dead and not I."

Each one thought or felt, "Well, he's dead but I'm alive!" But the more intimate of Ivan Ilych's acquaintances, his so-called friends, could not help thinking also that they would now have to fulfil the very tiresome demands of propriety by attending the funeral service and paying a visit of condolence to the widow.

Fëdor Vasilievich and Peter Ivanovich had been his nearest acquaintances. Peter Ivanovich had studied law with Ivan Ilych and had considered himself to be under obligations to him.

Having told his wife at dinner-time of Ivan Ilych's death and of his conjecture that it might be possible to get her brother transferred to their circuit, Peter Ivanovich sacrificed his usual nap, put on his evening clothes, and drove to Ivan Ilych's house.

At the entrance stood a carriage and two cabs. Leaning against the wall in the hall downstairs near the cloak-stand was a coffin-lid covered with cloth of gold, ornamented with gold cord and tassels, that had been polished up with metal powder. Two ladies in black were taking off their fur cloaks. Peter Ivanovich recognized one of them as Ivan Ilych's sister, but the other was a stranger to him. His colleague Schwartz was just coming downstairs, but on seeing Peter Ivanovich enter he stopped and winked at him, as if to say: "Ivan Ilych has made a mess of things—not like you and me."

Schwartz's face with his Piccadilly whiskers and his slim figure in evening dress had as usual an air of elegant solemnity which contrasted with the playfulness of his character and had a special piquancy here, or so it seemed to Peter Ivanovich.

Peter Ivanovich allowed the ladies to precede him and slowly followed them upstairs. Schwartz did not come down but remained where he was, and Peter Ivanovich understood that he wanted to arrange where they should play bridge that evening. The ladies went upstairs to the widow's room, and Schwartz with seriously compressed lips but a playful look in his eyes, indicated by a twist of his eyebrows the room to the right where the body lay.

Peter Ivanovich, like everyone else on such occasions, entered feeling uncertain what he would have to do. All he knew was that at such times it is always safe to cross oneself. But he was not quite sure whether one should make obeisances while doing so. He therefore adopted a middle course. On entering the room he began crossing himself and made a slight movement resembling a bow. At the same time, as far as the motion of his head and arm allowed, he surveyed the room. Two young men—apparently nephews, one of whom was a high-school pupil—were leaving the room, crossing themselves as they did so. An old woman was standing motionless, and a lady with strangely arched eyebrows was saying something to her in a whisper. A vigorous, resolute Church Reader, in a frock-coat, was reading something in a loud voice with an expression that precluded any contradiction. The butler's assistant, Gerasim, stepping lightly in front of Peter Ivanovich, was strewing something on the floor. Noticing this, Peter Ivanovich was immediately aware of a faint odor of a decomposing body.

The last time he had called on Ivan Ilych, Peter Ivanovich had seen Gerasim in the study. Ivan Ilych had been particularly fond of him and he was performing the duty of a sick nurse.

Peter Ivanovich continued to make the sign of the cross, slightly inclining his head in an intermediate direction between the coffin, the Reader, and the icons on the table in a corner of the room. Afterwards, when it seemed to him that this movement of his arm in crossing himself had gone on too long, he stopped and began to look at the corpse.

The dead man lay, as dead men always lie, in a specially heavy way, his rigid limbs sunk in the soft cushions of the coffin, with the head forever bowed on the pillow. His yellow waxen brow with bald patches over his sunken temples was thrust up in the way peculiar to the dead, the protruding nose seeming to press on the upper lip. He was much changed and had grown even thinner since Peter Ivanovich had last seen him, but, as is always the case with the dead, his face was handsomer and above all more dignified than when he was alive. The expression on the face said that what was necessary had been accomplished, and accomplished rightly. Besides this there was in that expression a reproach and a warning to the living. This warning seemed to Peter Ivanovich out of place, or at least not applicable to him. He felt a certain discomfort and so he hurriedly crossed himself once more and turned and went out the door—too hurriedly and too regardless of propriety, as he himself was aware.

Schwartz was waiting for him in the adjoining room with legs spread wide apart and both hands toying with his top-hat behind his back. The mere sight of that playful, well-groomed, and elegant figure refreshed Peter Ivanovich. He felt that Schwartz was above all these happenings and would not surrender to any depressing influences. His very look said that this incident of a church service for Ivan Ilych could not be a sufficient reason for infringing the order of the session—in other words, that it would certainly not prevent his unwrapping a new pack of cards and shuffling them that evening while a footman placed four fresh candles on the table: in fact, that there was no reason for supposing that this incident would hinder their spending the evening agreeably. Indeed he said this in a whisper as Peter Ivanovich passed him, proposing that they should meet for a game at Fëdor Vasilievich's. But apparently Peter Ivanovich was not destined to play bridge that evening. Praskovya Fëdorovna (a short, fat woman who despite all efforts to the contrary had continued to broaden steadily from her shoulders downwards and who had the same extraordinarily arched eyebrows as the lady who had been standing by the coffin), dressed all in black, her head covered with lace, came out of her own room with some other ladies, conducted them to the room where the dead body lay, and said: "The service will begin immediately. Please go in."

Schwartz, making an indefinite bow, stood still, evidently neither accepting nor declining this invitation. Praskovya Fëdorovna, recognizing Peter Ivanovich, sighed, went close up to him, took his hand, and said: "I know you were a true friend to Ivan Ilych . . ." and looked at him awaiting some suitable response. And Peter Ivanovich knew that, just as it had been the right thing to cross himself in that room, so what he had to do here was to press her hand, sigh, and say, "Believe me. . . ." So he did all this and as he did it felt that the desired result had been achieved: that both he and she were touched.

"Come with me. I want to speak to you before it begins," said the widow. "Give me your arm."

Peter Ivanovich gave her his arm and they went to the inner rooms, passing Schwartz, who winked at Peter Ivanovich compassionately.

"That does for our bridge! Don't object if we find another player. Perhaps you can cut in when you do escape," said his playful look.

Peter Ivanovich sighed still more deeply and despondently, and Praskovya Fëdorovna pressed his arm gratefully. When they reached the drawing-room, upholstered in pink cretonne and lighted by a dim lamp, they sat down at the table—she on a sofa and Peter Ivanovich on a low pouffe, the springs of which yielded spasmodically under his weight. Praskovya Fëdorovna had been on the point of warning him to take another seat, but felt that such a warning was out of keeping with her present condition and so changed her mind. As he sat down on the pouffe Peter Ivanovich recalled how Ivan Ilych had arranged this room and had consulted him regarding this pink cretonne with green leaves. The whole room was full of furniture and knick-knacks, and on her way to the sofa the lace of the widow's black shawl caught on the carved edge of the table. Peter Ivanovich rose to detach it, and the springs of the pouffe, relieved of his weight, rose also and gave him a push. The widow began detaching her shawl herself, and Peter Ivanovich again sat down, suppressing the rebellious springs of the pouffe under him. But the widow had not quite freed herself and Peter Ivanovich got up again, and again the pouffe rebelled and even creaked. When this was all over she took out a clean cambric handkerchief and began to weep. The episode with the shawl and the struggle with the pouffe had cooled Peter Ivanovich's emotions and he sat there with a sullen look on his face. This awkward situation was interrupted by Sokolov, Ivan Ilych's butler, who came to report that the plot in the cemetery that

Praskovya Fëdorovna had chosen would cost two hundred rubles. She stopped weeping and, looking at Peter Ivanovich with the air of a victim, remarked in French that it was very hard for her. Peter Ivanovich made a silent gesture signifying his full conviction that it must indeed be so.

"Please smoke," she said in a magnanimous yet crushed voice, and turned to discuss with Sokolov the price of the plot for the grave.

Peter Ivanovich while lighting his cigarette heard her inquiring very circumstantially into the prices of different plots in the cemetery and finally decide which she would take. When that was done she gave instructions about engaging the choir. Sokolov then left the room.

"I look after everything myself," she told Peter Ivanovich, shifting the albums that lay on the table; and noticing that the table was endangered by his cigarette-ash, she immediately passed him an ashtray, saying as she did so: "I consider it an affectation to say that my grief prevents my attending to practical affairs. On the contrary, if anything can—I won't say console me, but—distract me, it is seeing to everything concerning him." She again took out her handkerchief as if preparing to cry, but suddenly, as if mastering her feeling, she shook herself and began to speak calmly. "But there is something I want to talk to you about."

Peter Ivanovich bowed, keeping control of the springs of the pouffe, which immediately began quivering under him.

"He suffered terribly the last few days."

"Did he?" said Peter Ivanovich.

"Oh, terribly! He screamed unceasingly, not for minutes but for hours. For the last three days he screamed incessantly. It was unendurable. I cannot understand how I bore it; you could hear him three rooms off. Oh, what I have suffered!"

"Is it possible that he was conscious all that time?" asked Peter Ivanovich.

"Yes," she whispered. "To the last moment. He took leave of us a quarter of an hour before he died, and asked us to take Vasya away."

The thought of the sufferings of this man he had known so intimately, first as a merry little boy, then as a school-mate, and later as a grown-up colleague, suddenly struck Peter Ivanovich with horror, despite an unpleasant consciousness of his own and this woman's dissimulation. He again saw that brow, and that nose pressing down on the lip, and felt afraid for himself.

"Three days of frightful suffering and then death! Why, that might suddenly, at any time, happen to me," he thought, and for a moment felt terrified. But—he did not himself know how—the customary reflection at once occurred to him that this had happened to Ivan Ilych and not to him, and that it should not and could not happen to him, and that to think that it could would be yielding to depression which he ought not to do, as Schwartz's expression plainly showed. After which reflection Peter Ivanovich felt reassured, and began to ask with interest about the details of Ivan Ilych's death, as though death was an accident natural to Ivan Ilych but certainly not to himself.

After many details of the really dreadful physical sufferings Ivan Ilych had endured (which details he learnt only from the effect those sufferings had produced on Praskovya Fëdorovna's nerves) the widow apparently found it necessary to get to business.

"Oh, Peter Ivanovich, how hard it is! How terribly, terribly hard!" and she again began to weep.

Peter Ivanovich sighed and waited for her to finish blowing her nose. When she had done so he said, "Believe me . . ." and she again began talking and brought out what was evidently her chief concern with him—namely, to question him as to how she could obtain a grant of money from the government on the occasion of her husband's death. She made it appear that she was asking Peter Ivanovich's advice about her pension, but he soon saw that she already knew about that to the minutest detail, more even than he did himself. She knew how much could be got out of the government in consequence of her husband's death, but wanted to find out whether she could not possibly extract something more. Peter Ivanovich tried to think of some means of doing so, but after reflecting for a while and, out of propriety, condemning the government for its niggardliness, he said he thought that nothing more could be got. Then she sighed and evidently began to devise means of getting rid of her visitor. Noticing this, he put out his cigarette, rose, pressed her hand, and went out into the anteroom.

In the dining-room where the clock stood that Ivan Ilych had liked so much and had bought at an antique shop, Peter Ivanovich met a priest and a few acquaintances who had come to attend the service, and he recognized Ivan Ilych's daughter, a handsome young woman. She was in black and her slim figure appeared slimmer than ever. She had a gloomy, determined, almost angry expression, and bowed to Peter Ivanovich as though he were in some way to blame. Behind her, with the same offended look, stood a wealthy young man, an examining magistrate, whom Peter Ivanovich also knew and who was her fiancé, as he had heard. He bowed mournfully to them and was about to pass into the death-chamber, when from under the stairs appeared the figure of Ivan Ilych's schoolboy son, who was extremely like his father. He seemed a little Ivan Ilych, such as Peter Ivanovich remembered when they studied law together. His tear-stained eyes had in them the look that is seen in the eyes of boys of thirteen or fourteen who are not pureminded. When he saw Peter Ivanovich he scowled morosely and shamefacedly. Peter Ivanovich nodded to him and entered the death-chamber. The service began: candles, groans, incense, tears, and sobs. Peter Ivanovich stood looking gloomily down at his feet. He did not look once at the dead man, did not yield to any depressing influence, and was one of the first to leave the room. There was no one in the anteroom, but Gerasim darted out of the dead man's room, rummaged with his strong hands among the fur coats to find Peter Ivanovich's, and helped him on with it.

"Well, friend Gerasim," said Peter Ivanovich, so as to say something. "It's a sad affair, isn't it?"

"It's God's will. We shall all come to it some day," said Gerasim, displaying his teeth—the even, white teeth of a healthy peasant—and, like a man in the thick of urgent work, he briskly opened the front door, called the coachman, helped Peter Ivanovich into the sledge, and sprang back to the porch as if in readiness for what he had to do next.

Peter Ivanovich found the fresh air particularly pleasant after the smell of incense, the dead body, and carbolic acid.

"Where to, sir?" asked the coachman.

"It's not too late even now . . . I'll call round on Fëdor Vasilievich."

He accordingly drove there and found them just finishing the first rubber, so that it was quite convenient for him to cut in.

II

Ivan Ilych's life had been most simple and most ordinary and therefore most terrible.

He had been a member of the Court of Justice, and died at the age of forty-five. His father had been an official who after serving in various ministries and departments in Petersburg had made the sort of career which brings men to positions from which by reason of their long service they cannot be dismissed, though they are obviously unfit to hold any responsible position, and for whom therefore posts are specially created, which though fictitious carry salaries of from six to ten thousand rubles that are not fictitious, and in receipt of which they live on to a great age.

Such was the Privy Councillor and superfluous member of various superfluous institutions, Ilya Epimovich Golovin.

He had three sons, of whom Ivan Ilych was the second. The eldest son was following in his father's footsteps only in another department, and was already approaching that stage in the service at which a similar sinecure would be reached. The third son was a failure. He had ruined his prospects in a number of positions and was now serving in the railway department. His father and brothers, and still more their wives, not merely disliked meeting him, but avoided remembering his existence unless compelled to do so. His sister had married Baron Greff, a Petersburg official of her father's type. Ivan Ilych was *le phénix de la famille** as people said. He was neither as cold and formal as his elder brother nor as wild as the younger, but was a happy mean between them—an intelligent, polished, lively, and agreeable man. He had studied with his younger brother at the School of Law, but the latter had failed to complete the course and was expelled when he was in the fifth class. Ivan Ilych finished the course well. Even when he was at the School of Law he was just what he remained for the rest of his life: a capable, cheerful, good-natured, and sociable man, though strict in the fulfillment of what he considered to be his duty: and he considered his duty to be what was so considered by those in authority. Neither as a boy nor as a man was he a toady, but from early youth was by nature attracted to people of high station as a fly is drawn to the light, assimilating their ways and views of life and establishing friendly relations with them. All the enthusiasms of childhood and youth passed without leaving much trace on him; he succumbed to sensuality, to vanity, and latterly among the highest classes to liberalism, but always within limits which his instinct unfailingly indicated to him as correct.

At school he had done things which had formerly seemed to him very horrid and made him feel disgusted with himself when he did them; but when later on he saw that such actions were done by people of good position and that they did not regard them as wrong, he was able not exactly to regard them as right, but to forget about them entirely or not be at all troubled at remembering them.

Having graduated from the School of Law and qualified for the tenth rank of the civil service, and having received money from his father for his equipment, Ivan Ilych ordered himself clothes at Scharmer's, the fashionable tailor, hung a medallion inscribed *respice finem*† on his watch-chain, took leave of his professor

---

**le phénix de la famille:* French for "the prize of the family."

†*respice finem:* Latin for "Think of the end (of your life)."

and the prince who was patron of the school, had a farewell dinner with his comrades at Donon's first-class restaurant, and with his new and fashionable portmanteau, linen, clothes, shaving and other toilet appliances, and a traveling rug all purchased at the best shops, he set off for one of the provinces where, through his father's influence, he had been attached to the Governor as an official for special service.

In the province Ivan Ilych soon arranged as easy and agreeable a position for himself as he had had at the School of Law. He performed his official tasks, made his career, and at the same time amused himself pleasantly and decorously. Occasionally he paid official visits to country districts, where he behaved with dignity both to his superiors and inferiors, and performed the duties entrusted to him, which related chiefly to the sectarians,* with an exactness and incorruptible honesty of which he could not but feel proud.

In official matters, despite his youth and taste for frivolous gaiety, he was exceedingly reserved, punctilious, and even severe; but in society he was often amusing and witty, and always good-natured, correct in his manner, and *bon enfant*,† as the Governor and his wife—with whom he was like one of the family—used to say of him.

In the province he had an affair with a lady who made advances to the elegant young lawyer, and there was also a milliner; and there were carousals with aides-de-camp who visited the district, and after-supper visits to a certain outlying street of doubtful reputation; and there was too some obsequiousness to his chief and even to his chief's wife, but all this was done with such a tone of good breeding that no hard names could be applied to it. It all came under the heading of the French saying: "*Il faut que jeunesse se passe.*"‡ It was all done with clean hands, in clean linen, with French phrases, and above all among people of the best society and consequently with the approval of people of rank.

So Ivan Ilych served for five years and then came a change in his official life. The new and reformed judicial institutions were introduced, and new men were needed. Ivan Ilych became such a new man. He was offered the post of examining magistrate, and he accepted it though the post was in another province and obliged him to give up the connections he had formed and to make new ones. His friends met to give him a send-off: they had a group-photograph taken and presented him with a silver cigarette-case, and he set off to his new post.

As examining magistrate Ivan Ilych was just as *comme il faut*§ and decorous a man, inspiring general respect and capable of separating his official duties from his private life, as he had been when acting as an official on special service. His duties now as examining magistrate were far more interesting and attractive than before. In his former position it had been pleasant to wear an undress uniform made by Scharmer, and to pass through the crowd of petitioners and officials who were timorously awaiting an audience with the Governor, and who envied him as with free and easy gait he went straight into his chief's private room to have a cup of tea and a cigarette with him. But not many people had been directly dependent

---

**sectarians:* dissenters from the Orthodox Church.

†*bon enfant:* French for "a well-behaved child."

‡"*Il faut que jeunesse se passe*": "Youth doesn't last."

§*comme il faut:* "as required," rule-abiding.

on him—only police officials and the sectarians when he went on special missions—and he liked to treat them politely, almost as comrades, as if he were letting them feel that he who had the power to crush them was treating them in this simple, friendly way. There were then but few such people. But now, as an examining magistrate, Ivan Ilych felt that everyone without exception, even the most important and self-satisfied, was in his power, and that he need only write a few words on a sheet of paper with a certain heading, and this or that important self-satisfied person would be brought before him in the role of an accused person or a witness, and if he did not choose to allow him to sit down, would have to stand before him and answer his questions. Ivan Ilych never abused his power; he tried on the contrary to soften its expression, but the consciousness of it and of the possibility of softening its effect, supplied the chief interest and attraction of his office. In his work itself, especially in his examinations, he very soon acquired a method of eliminating all considerations irrelevant to the legal aspect of the case, and reducing even the most complicated case to a form in which it would be presented on paper only in its externals, completely excluding his personal opinion of the matter, while above all observing every prescribed formality. The work was new and Ivan Ilych was one of the first men to apply the new Code of 1864.*

On taking up the post of examining magistrate in a new town, he made new acquaintances and connections, placed himself on a new footing, and assumed a somewhat different tone. He took up an attitude of rather dignified aloofness towards the provincial authorities, but picked out the best circle of legal gentlemen and wealthy gentry living in the town and assumed a tone of slight dissatisfaction with the government, of moderate liberalism, and of enlightened citizenship. At the same time, without at all altering the elegance of his toilet, he ceased shaving his chin and allowed his beard to grow as it pleased.

Ivan Ilych settled down very pleasantly in this new town. The society there, which inclined towards opposition to the Governor, was friendly, his salary was larger, and he began to play *vint*,† which he found added not a little to the pleasure of life, for he had a capacity for cards, played good-humoredly, and calculated rapidly and astutely, so that he usually won.

After living there for two years he met his future wife, Praskovya Fëdorovna Mikhel, who was the most attractive, clever, and brilliant girl of the set in which he moved, and among other amusements and relaxations from his labors as examining magistrate, Ivan Ilych established light and playful relations with her.

While he had been an official on special service he had been accustomed to dance, but now as an examining magistrate it was exceptional for him to do so. If he danced now, he did it as if to show that though he served under the reformed order of things, and had reached the fifth official rank, yet when it came to dancing he could do it better than most people. So at the end of an evening he sometimes danced with Praskovya Fëdorovna, and it was chiefly during these dances that he captivated her. She fell in love with him. Ivan Ilych had at first no definite intention of marrying, but when the girl fell in love with him he said to himself: "Really, why shouldn't I marry?"

**Code of 1864:* The emancipation of the serfs in 1861 was followed by a thorough all-round reform of judicial proceedings. [Translator's note.]

†*vint:* a form of bridge. [Translators' note.]

Praskovya Fëdorovna came of a good family, was not bad-looking, and had some little property. Ivan Ilych might have aspired to a more brilliant match, but even this was good. He had his salary, and she, he hoped, would have an equal income. She was well connected, and was a sweet, pretty, and thoroughly correct young woman. To say that Ivan Ilych married because he fell in love with Praskovya Fëdorovna and found that she sympathized with his views of life would be as incorrect as to say that he married because his social circle approved of the match. He was swayed by both these considerations; the marriage gave him personal satisfaction, and at the same time it was considered the right thing by the most highly placed of his associates.

So Ivan Ilych got married.

The preparations for marriage and the beginning of married life, with its conjugal caresses, the new furniture, new crockery, and new linen, were very pleasant until his wife became pregnant—so that Ivan Ilych had begun to think that marriage would not impair the easy, agreeable, gay, and always decorous character of his life, approved of by society and regarded by himself as natural, but would even improve it. But from the first months of his wife's pregnancy, something new, unpleasant, depressing, and unseemly, and from which there was no way of escape, unexpectedly showed itself.

His wife, without any reason—*de gaieté de coeur** as Ivan Ilych expressed it to himself—began to disturb the pleasure and propriety of their life. She began to be jealous without any cause, expected him to devote his whole attention to her, found fault with everything, and made coarse and ill-mannered scenes.

At first Ivan Ilych hoped to escape from the unpleasantness of this state of affairs by the same easy and decorous relation to life that had served him heretofore: he tried to ignore his wife's disagreeable moods, continued to live in his usual easy and pleasant way, invited friends to his house for a game of cards, and also tried going out to his club or spending his evenings with friends. But one day his wife began upbraiding him so vigorously, using such coarse words, and continued to abuse him every time he did not fulfil her demands, so resolutely and with such evident determination not to give way till he submitted—that is, till he stayed at home and was bored just as she was—that he became alarmed. He now realized that matrimony—at any rate with Praskovya Fëdorovna—was not always conducive to the pleasures and amenities of life, but on the contrary often infringed both comfort and propriety, and that he must therefore entrench himself against such infringement. And Ivan Ilych began to seek for means of doing so. His official duties were the one thing that imposed upon Praskovya Fëdorovna, and by means of his official work and the duties attached to it he began struggling with his wife to secure his own independence.

With the birth of their child, the attempts to feed it and the various failures in doing so, and with the real and imaginary illnesses of mother and child, in which Ivan Ilych's sympathy was demanded but about which he understood nothing, the need of securing for himself an existence outside his family life became still more imperative.

As his wife grew more irritable and exacting and Ivan Ilych transferred the center of gravity of his life more and more to his official work, so did he grow to like his work better and became more ambitious than before.

**de gaieté de coeur:* "from pure whim."

Very soon, within a year of his wedding, Ivan Ilych had realized that marriage, though it may add some comforts to life, is in fact a very intricate and difficult affair towards which in order to perform one's duty, that is, to lead a decorous life approved of by society, one must adopt a definite attitude just as towards one's official duties.

And Ivan Ilych evolved such an attitude towards married life. He only required of it those conveniences—dinner at home, housewife, and bed—which it could give him, and above all that propriety of external forms required by public opinion. For the rest he looked for light-hearted pleasure and propriety, and was very thankful when he found them, but if he met with antagonism and querulousness he at once retired into his separate fenced-off world of official duties, where he found satisfaction.

Ivan Ilych was esteemed a good official, and after three years was made Assistant Public Prosecutor. His new duties, their importance, the possibility of indicting and imprisoning anyone he chose, the publicity his speeches received, and the success he had in all these things, made his work still more attractive.

More children came. His wife became more and more querulous and ill-tempered, but the attitude Ivan Ilych had adopted towards his home life rendered him almost impervious to her grumbling.

After seven years service in that town he was transferred to another province as Public Prosecutor. They moved, but were short of money and his wife did not like the place they moved to. Though the salary was higher the cost of living was greater, besides which two of their children died and family life became still more unpleasant for him.

Praskovya Fëdorovna blamed her husband for every inconvenience they encountered in their new home. Most of the conversations between husband and wife, especially as to the children's education, led to topics which recalled former disputes, and those disputes were apt to flare up again at any moment. There remained only those rare periods of amorousness which still came to them at times but did not last long. These were islets at which they anchored for a while and then again set out upon that ocean of veiled hostility which showed itself in their aloofness from one another. This aloofness might have grieved Ivan Ilych had he considered that it ought not to exist, but he now regarded the position as normal, and even made it the goal at which he aimed in family life. His aim was to free himself more and more from those unpleasantnesses and to give them a semblance of harmlessness and propriety. He attained this by spending less and less time with his family, and when obliged to be at home he tried to safeguard his position by the presence of outsiders. The chief thing, however, was that he had his official duties. The whole interest of his life now centered in the official world and that interest absorbed him. The consciousness of his power, being able to ruin anybody he wished to ruin, the importance, even the external dignity of his entry into court, or meetings with his subordinates, his success with superiors and inferiors, and above all his masterly handling of cases, of which he was conscious—all this gave him pleasure and filled his life, together with chats with his colleagues, dinners, and bridge. So that on the whole Ivan Ilych's life continued to flow as he considered it should do—pleasantly and properly.

So things continued for another seven years. His eldest daughter was already sixteen, another child had died, and only one son was left, a schoolboy and a subject of dissension. Ivan Ilych wanted to put him in the School of Law, but to spite him Praskovya Fëdorovna entered him at the High School. The daughter had been educated at home and had turned out well; the boy did not learn badly either.

III

So Ivan Ilych lived for seventeen years after his marriage. He was already a Public Prosecutor of long standing, and had declined several proposed transfers while awaiting a more desirable post, when an unanticipated and unpleasant occurrence quite upset the peaceful course of his life. He was expecting to be offered the post of presiding judge in a University town, but Happe somehow came to the front and obtained the appointment instead. Ivan Ilych became irritable, reproached Happe, and quarreled both with him and with his immediate superiors—who became colder to him and again passed him over when other appointments were made.

This was in 1880, the hardest year of Ivan Ilych's life. It was then that it became evident on the one hand that his salary was insufficient for them to live on, and on the other that he had been forgotten, and not only this, but that what was for him the greatest and most cruel injustice appeared to others a quite ordinary occurrence. Even his father did not consider it his duty to help him. Ivan Ilych felt himself abandoned by everyone, and that they regarded his position with a salary of 3,500 rubles as quite normal and even fortunate. He alone knew that with the consciousness of the injustices done him, with his wife's incessant nagging, and with the debts he had contracted by living beyond his means, his position was far from normal.

In order to save money that summer he obtained leave of absence and went with his wife to live in the country at her brother's place.

In the country, without his work, he experienced *ennui* for the first time in his life, and not only *ennui* but intolerable depression, and he decided that it was impossible to go on living like that, and that it was necessary to take energetic measures.

Having passed a sleepless night pacing up and down the veranda, he decided to go to Petersburg and bestir himself, in order to punish those who had failed to appreciate him and to get transferred to another ministry.

Next day, despite many protests from his wife and her brother, he started for Petersburg with the sole object of obtaining a post with a salary of five thousand rubles a year. He was no longer bent on any particular department, or tendency, or kind of activity. All he now wanted was an appointment to another post with a salary of five thousand rubles, either in the administration, in the banks, with the railways, in one of the Empress Marya's Institutions,* or even in the customs—but it had to carry with it a salary of five thousand rubles and be in a ministry other than that in which they had failed to appreciate him.

And this quest of Ivan Ilych's was crowned with remarkable and unexpected success. At Kursk an acquaintance of his, F. I. Ilyin, got into the first-class carriage, sat down beside Ivan Ilych, and told him of a telegram just received by the Governor of Kursk announcing that a change was about to take place in the ministry: Peter Ivanovich was to be superseded by Ivan Semënovich.

The proposed change, apart from its significance for Russia, had a special significance for Ivan Ilych, because by bringing forward a new man, Peter Petrovich,

**Empress Marya's Institutions:* orphanages.

and consequently his friend Zachar Ivanovich, it was highly favorable for Ivan Ilych, since Zachar Ivanovich was a friend and colleague of his.

In Moscow this news was confirmed, and on reaching Petersburg Ivan Ilych found Zachar Ivanovich and received a definite promise of an appointment in his former department of Justice.

A week later he telegraphed to his wife: "Zachar in Miller's place. I shall receive appointment on presentation of report."

Thanks to this change of personnel, Ivan Ilych had unexpectedly obtained an appointment in his former ministry which placed him two stages above his former colleagues besides giving him five thousand rubles salary and three thousand five hundred rubles for expenses connected with his removal. All his ill humor towards his former enemies and the whole department vanished, and Ivan Ilych was completely happy.

He returned to the country more cheerful and contented than he had been for a long time. Praskovya Fëdorovna also cheered up and a truce was arranged between them. Ivan Ilych told of how he had been feted by everybody in Petersburg, how all those who had been his enemies were put to shame and now fawned on him, how envious they were of his appointment, and how much everybody in Petersburg had liked him.

Praskovya Fëdorovna listened to all this and appeared to believe it. She did not contradict anything, but only made plans for their life in the town to which they were going. Ivan Ilych saw with delight that these plans were his plans, that he and his wife agreed, and that, after a stumble, his life was regaining its due and natural character of pleasant lightheartedness and decorum.

Ivan Ilych had come back for a short time only, for he had to take up his new duties on the 10th of September. Moreover, he needed time to settle into the new place, to move all his belongings from the province, and to buy and order many additional things; in a word, to make such arrangements as he had resolved on, which were almost exactly what Praskovya Fëdorovna too had decided on.

Now that everything had happened so fortunately, and that he and his wife were at one in their aims and moreover saw so little of one another, they got on together better than they had done since the first years of marriage. Ivan Ilych had thought of taking his family away with him at once, but the insistence of his wife's brother and her sister-in-law, who had suddenly become particularly amiable and friendly to him and his family, induced him to depart alone.

So he departed, and the cheerful state of mind induced by his success and by the harmony between his wife and himself, the one intensifying the other, did not leave him. He found a delightful house, just the thing both he and his wife had dreamt of. Spacious, lofty reception rooms in the old style, a convenient and dignified study, rooms for his wife and daughter, a study for his son—it might have been specially built for them. Ivan Ilych himself superintended the arrangements, chose the wallpapers, supplemented the furniture (preferably with antiques which he considered particularly *comme il faut*), and supervised the upholstering. Everything progressed and progressed and approached the ideal he had set himself; even when things were only half completed they exceeded his expectations. He saw what a refined and elegant character, free from vulgarity, it would all have when it was ready. On falling asleep he pictured to himself how the reception-room would look. Looking at the yet unfinished drawing-room he could see the fireplace, the screen, the what not, the little chairs dotted here and there, the dishes and plates on the walls, and the bronzes, as they would be when everything was in place. He was pleased by the thought of how his wife and daughter, who shared his taste in this matter, would be impressed by it. They were certainly not expecting as much. He had been particularly successful in finding, and buying cheaply, antiques which gave a particularly aristocratic character to the whole place. But in his letters he intentionally understated everything in order to be able to surprise them. All this so absorbed him that his new duties—though he liked his official work—interested him less than he had expected. Sometimes he even had moments of absentmindedness during the Court Sessions, and would consider whether he should have straight or curved cornices for his curtains. He was so interested in it all that he often did things himself, rearranging the furniture, or rehanging the curtains. Once when mounting a stepladder to show the upholsterer, who did not understand, how he wanted the hangings draped, he made a false step and slipped, but being a strong and agile man he clung on and only knocked his side against the knob of the window frame. The bruised place was painful but the pain soon passed, and he felt particularly bright and well just then. He wrote: "I feel fifteen years younger." He thought he would have everything ready by September, but it dragged on till mid-October. But the result was charming not only in his eyes but to everyone who saw it.

In reality it was just what is usually seen in the houses of people of moderate means who want to appear rich, and therefore succeed only in resembling others like themselves: there were damasks, dark wood, plants, rugs, and dull and polished bronzes—all the things people of a certain class have in order to resemble other people of that class. His house was so like the others that it would never have been noticed, but to him it all seemed to be quite exceptional. He was very happy when he met his family at the station and brought them to the newly furnished house all lit up, where a footman in a white tie opened the door into the hall decorated with plants, and when they went on into the drawing-room and the study uttering exclamations of delight. He conducted them everywhere, drank in their praises eagerly, and beamed with pleasure. At tea that evening, when Praskovya Fëdorovna among other things asked him about his fall, he laughed and showed them how he had gone flying and had frightened the upholsterer.

"It's a good thing I'm a bit of an athlete. Another man might have been killed, but I merely knocked myself, just there; it hurts when it's touched, but it's passing off already—it's only a bruise."

So they began living in their new home—in which, as always happens, when they got thoroughly settled in they found they were just one room short—and with the increased income, which as always was just a little (some five hundred rubles) too little, but it was all very nice.

Things went particularly well at first, before everything was finally arranged and while something had still to be done: this thing bought, that thing ordered, another thing moved, and something else adjusted. Though there were some disputes between husband and wife, they were both so well satisfied and had so much to do that it all passed off without any serious quarrels. When nothing was left to arrange it became rather dull and something seemed to be lacking, but they were then making acquaintances, forming habits, and life was growing fuller.

Ivan Ilych spent his mornings at the law courts and came home to dinner, and at first he was generally in a good humor, though he occasionally became irritable just on account of his house. (Every spot on the tablecloth or the upholstery, and every broken window-blind string, irritated him. He had devoted so much trouble to arranging it all that every disturbance of it distressed him.) But on the whole his life ran its course as he believed life should do; easily, pleasantly, and decorously.

He got up at nine, drank his coffee, read the paper, and then put on his undress uniform and went to the law courts. There the harness in which he worked had already been stretched to fit him and he donned it without a hitch: petitioners, inquiries at the chancery, the chancery itself, and the sittings public and administrative. In all this the thing was to exclude everything fresh and vital, which always disturbs the regular course of official business, and to admit only official relations with people, and then only on official grounds. A man would come, for instance, wanting some information. Ivan Ilych, as one in whose sphere the matter did not lie, would have nothing to do with him; but if the man had some business with him in his official capacity, something that could be expressed on officially stamped paper, he would do everything, positively everything he could within the limits of such relations, and in doing so would maintain the semblance of friendly human relations, that is, would observe the courtesies of life. As soon as the official relations ended, so did everything else. Ivan Ilych possessed this capacity to separate his real life from the official side of affairs and not mix the two, in the highest degree, and by long practice and natural aptitude had brought it to such a pitch that sometimes, in the manner of a virtuoso, he would even allow himself to let the human and official relations mingle. He let himself do this just because he felt that he could at any time he chose resume the strictly official attitude again and drop the human relation. And he did it all easily, pleasantly, correctly, and even artistically. In the intervals between the sessions he smoked, drank tea, chatted a little about politics, a little about general topics, a little about cards, but most of all about official appointments. Tired, but with the feelings of a virtuoso—one of the first violins who has played his part in an orchestra with precision—he would return home to find that his wife and daughter had been out paying calls, or had a visitor, and that his son had been to school, had done his homework with his tutor, and was duly learning what is taught at High Schools. Everything was as it should be. After dinner, if they had no visitors, Ivan Ilych sometimes read a book that was being much discussed at the time, and in the evening settled down to work, that is, read official papers, compared the depositions of witnesses, and noted paragraphs of the Code applying to them. This was neither dull nor amusing. It was dull when he might have been playing bridge, but if no bridge was available it was at any rate better than doing nothing or sitting with his wife. Ivan Ilych's chief pleasure was giving little dinners to which he invited men and women of good social position, and just as his drawing-room resembled all other drawing-rooms so did his enjoyable little parties resemble all other such parties.

Once they even gave a dance. Ivan Ilych enjoyed it and everything went off well, except that it led to a violent quarrel with his wife about the cakes and sweets. Praskovya Fëdorovna had made her own plans, but Ivan Ilych insisted on getting everything from an expensive confectioner and ordered too many cakes, and the quarrel occurred because some of those cakes were left over and the confectioner's bill came to forty-five rubles. It was a great and disagreeable quarrel. Praskovya Fëdorovna called him "a fool and an imbecile," and he clutched at his head and made angry allusions to divorce.

But the dance itself had been enjoyable. The best people were there, and Ivan Ilych had danced with Princess Trufonova, a sister of the distinguished founder of the Society "Bear My Burden."

The pleasures connected with his work were pleasures of ambition; his social pleasures were those of vanity; but Ivan Ilych's greatest pleasure was playing bridge. He acknowledged that whatever disagreeable incident happened in his life, the pleasure that beamed like a ray of light above everything else was to sit down to bridge with good players, not noisy partners, and of course to four-handed bridge (with five players it was annoying to have to stand out, though one pretended not to mind), to play a clever and serious game (when the cards allowed it), and then to have supper and drink a glass of wine. After a game of bridge, especially if he had won a little (to win a large sum was unpleasant), Ivan Ilych went to bed in specially good humor.

So they lived. They formed a circle of acquaintances among the best people and were visited by people of importance and by young folk. In their views as to their acquaintances, husband, wife, and daughter were entirely agreed, and tacitly and unanimously kept at arm's length and shook off the various shabby friends and relations who, with much show of affection, gushed into the drawing-room with its Japanese plates on the walls. Soon these shabby friends ceased to obtrude themselves and only the best people remained in the Golovins' set.

Young men made up to Lisa, and Petrishchev, an examining magistrate and Dmitri Ivanovich Petrishchev's son and sole heir, began to be so attentive to her that Ivan Ilych had already spoken to Praskovya Fëdorovna about it, and considered whether they should not arrange a party for them, or get up some private theatricals.

So they lived, and all went well, without change, and life flowed pleasantly.

IV

They were all in good health. It could not be called ill health if Ivan Ilych sometimes said that he had a queer taste in his mouth and felt some discomfort in his left side.

But this discomfort increased and, though not exactly painful, grew into a sense of pressure in his side accompanied by ill humor. And his irritability became worse and worse and began to mar the agreeable, easy, and correct life that had established itself in the Golovin family. Quarrels between husband and wife became more and more frequent, and soon the ease and amenity disappeared and even the decorum was barely maintained. Scenes again became frequent, and very few of those islets remained on which husband and wife could meet without an explosion. Praskovya Fëdorovna now had good reason to say that her husband's temper was trying. With characteristic exaggeration she said he had always had a dreadful temper, and that it had needed all her good nature to put up with it for twenty years. It was true that now the quarrels were started by him. His bursts of temper always came just before dinner, often just as he began to eat his soup. Sometimes he noticed that a plate or dish was chipped, or the food was not right, or his son put his elbow on the table, or his daughter's hair was not done as he liked it, and for all this he blamed Praskovya Fëdorovna. At first she retorted and said disagreeable things to him, but once or twice he fell into such a rage at the beginning of dinner that she realized it was due to some physical derangement brought on by taking food, and so she restrained herself and did not answer, but only hurried to get the dinner over. She regarded this self-restraint as highly praiseworthy. Having come to the conclusion that her husband had a dreadful temper and made her life miserable, she began to feel sorry for herself, and the more she pitied herself the more she hated her husband. She began to wish he would die; yet she did not want him to die because then his salary would cease. And this irritated her against him still more. She considered herself dreadfully unhappy just because not even his death could save her, and though she concealed her exasperation, that hidden exasperation of hers increased his irritation also.

After one scene in which Ivan Ilych had been particularly unfair and after which he had said in explanation that he certainly was irritable but that it was due to his not being well, she said that if he was ill it should be attended to, and insisted on his going to see a celebrated doctor.

He went. Everything took place as he had expected and as it always does. There was the usual waiting and the important air assumed by the doctor, with which he was so familiar (resembling that which he himself assumed in court), and the sounding and listening, and the questions which called for answers that were foregone conclusions and were evidently unnecessary, and the look of importance which implied that "if only you put yourself in our hands we will arrange everything—we know indubitably how it has to be done, always in the same way for everybody alike." It was all just as it was in the law courts. The doctor put on just the same air towards him as he himself put on towards an accused person.

The doctor said that so-and-so indicated that there was so-and-so inside the patient, but if the investigation of so-and-so did not confirm this, then he must assume that and that. If he assumed that and that, then . . . and so on. To Ivan Ilych only one question was important: was his case serious or not? But the doctor ignored that inappropriate question. From his point of view it was not the one under consideration, the real question was to decide between a floating kidney, chronic catarrh, or appendicitis. It was not a question of Ivan Ilych's life or death, but one between a floating kidney and appendicitis. And that question the doctor solved brilliantly, as it seemed to Ivan Ilych, in favor of the appendix, with the reservation that should an examination of the urine give fresh indications the matter would be reconsidered. All this was just what Ivan Ilych had himself brilliantly accomplished a thousand times in dealing with men on trial. The doctor summed up just as brilliantly, looking over his spectacles triumphantly and even gaily at the accused. From the doctor's summing up Ivan Ilych concluded that things were bad, but that for the doctor, and perhaps for everybody else, it was a matter of indifference, though for him it was bad. And this conclusion struck him painfully, arousing in him a great feeling of pity for himself and of bitterness towards the doctor's indifference to a matter of such importance.

He said nothing of this, but rose, placed the doctor's fee on the table, and remarked with a sigh: "We sick people probably often put inappropriate questions. But tell me, in general, is this complaint dangerous, or not? . . ."

The doctor looked at him sternly over his spectacles with one eye, as if to say: "Prisoner, if you will not keep to the questions put to you, I shall be obliged to have you removed from the court."

"I have already told you what I consider necessary and proper. The analysis may show something more." And the doctor bowed.

Ivan Ilych went out slowly, seated himself disconsolately in his sledge, and drove home. All the way home he was going over what the doctor had said, trying to translate those complicated, obscure, scientific phrases into plain language and find in them an answer to the question: "Is my condition bad?

Is it very bad? Or is there as yet nothing much wrong?" And it seemed to him that the meaning of what the doctor had said was that it was very bad. Everything in the streets seemed depressing. The cabmen, the houses, the passers-by, and the shops, were dismal. His ache, this dull gnawing ache that never ceased for a moment, seemed to have acquired a new and more serious significance from the doctor's dubious remarks. Ivan Ilych now watched it with a new and oppressive feeling.

He reached home and began to tell his wife about it. She listened, but in the middle of his account his daughter came in with her hat on, ready to go out with her mother. She sat down reluctantly to listen to this tedious story, but could not stand it long, and her mother too did not hear him to the end.

"Well, I am very glad," she said. "Mind now to take your medicine regularly. Give me the prescription and I'll send Gerasim to the chemist's." And she went to get ready to go out.

While she was in the room Ivan Ilych had hardly taken time to breathe, but he sighed deeply when she left it.

"Well," he thought, "perhaps it isn't so bad after all."

He began taking his medicine and following the doctor's directions, which had been altered after the examination of the urine. But then it happened that there was a contradiction between the indications drawn from the examination of the urine and the symptoms that showed themselves. It turned out that what was happening differed from what the doctor had told him, and that he had either forgotten, or blundered, or hidden something from him. He could not, however, be blamed for that, and Ivan Ilych still obeyed his orders implicitly and at first derived some comfort from doing so.

From the time of his visit to the doctor, Ivan Ilych's chief occupation was the exact fulfillment of the doctor's instructions regarding hygiene and the taking of medicine, and the observation of his pain and his excretions. His chief interests came to be people's ailments and people's health. When sickness, deaths, or recoveries were mentioned in his presence, especially when the illness resembled his own, he listened with agitation which he tried to hide, asked questions, and applied what he heard to his own case.

The pain did not grow less, but Ivan Ilych made efforts to force himself to think that he was better. And he could do this so long as nothing agitated him. But as soon as he had any unpleasantness with his wife, any lack of success in his official work, or held bad cards at bridge, he was at once acutely sensible of his disease. He had formerly borne such mischances, hoping soon to adjust what was wrong, to master it and attain success, or make a grand slam. But now every mischance upset him and plunged him into despair. He would say to himself: "There now, just as I was beginning to get better and the medicine had begun to take effect, comes this accursed misfortune, or unpleasantness. . . ." And he was furious with the mishap, or with the people who were causing the unpleasantness and killing him, for he felt that this fury was killing him but could not restrain it. One would have thought that it should have been clear to him that this exasperation with circumstances and people aggravated his illness, and that he ought therefore to ignore unpleasant occurrences. But he drew the very opposite conclusion: he said that he needed peace, and he watched for everything that might disturb it and became irritable at the slightest infringement of it. His condition was rendered worse by the fact that he read medical books and consulted doctors.

The progress of his disease was so gradual that he could deceive himself when comparing one day with another—the difference was so slight. But when he consulted the doctors it seemed to him that he was getting worse, and even very rapidly. Yet despite this he was continually consulting them.

That month he went to see another celebrity, who told him almost the same as the first had done but put his questions rather differently, and the interview with this celebrity only increased Ivan Ilych's doubts and fears. A friend of a friend of his, a very good doctor, diagnosed his illness again quite differently from the others, and though he predicted recovery, his questions and suppositions bewildered Ivan Ilych still more and increased his doubts. A homeopathist diagnosed the disease in yet another way, and prescribed medicine which Ivan Ilych took secretly for a week. But after a week, not feeling any improvement and having lost confidence both in the former doctor's treatment and in this one's, he became still more despondent. One day a lady acquaintance mentioned a cure effected by a wonder-working icon. Ivan Ilych caught himself listening attentively and beginning to believe that it had occurred. This incident alarmed him. "Has my mind really weakened to such an extent?" he asked himself. "Nonsense! It's all rubbish. I mustn't give way to nervous fears but having chosen a doctor must keep strictly to his treatment. That is what I will do. Now it's all settled. I won't think about it, but will follow the treatment seriously till summer, and then we shall see. From now there must be no more of this wavering!" This was easy to say but impossible to carry out. The pain in his side oppressed him and seemed to grow worse and more incessant, while the taste in his mouth grew stranger and stranger. It seemed to him that his breath had a disgusting smell, and he was conscious of a loss of appetite and strength. There was no deceiving himself; something terrible, new, and more important than anything before in his life, was taking place within him of which he alone was aware. Those about him did not understand or would not understand it, but thought everything in the world was going on as usual. That tormented Ivan Ilych more than anything. He saw that his household, especially his wife and daughter who were in a perfect whirl of visiting, did not understand anything of it and were annoyed that he was so depressed and so exacting, as if he were to blame for it. Though they tried to disguise it he saw that he was an obstacle in their path, and that his wife had adopted a definite line in regard to his illness and kept to it regardless of anything he said or did. Her attitude was this: "You know," she would say to her friends, "Ivan Ilych can't do as other people do, and keep to the treatment prescribed for him. One day he'll take his drops and keep strictly to his diet and go to bed in good time, but the next day unless I watch him he'll suddenly forget his medicine, eat sturgeon—which is forbidden—and sit up playing cards till one o'clock in the morning.

"Oh, come, when was that?" Ivan Ilych would ask in vexation. "Only once at Peter Ivanovich's."

"And yesterday with Shebek."

"Well, even if I hadn't stayed up, this pain would have kept me awake."

"Be that as it may you'll never get well like that, but will always make us wretched."

Praskovya Fëdorovna's attitude to Ivan Ilych's illness, as she expressed it both to others and to him, was that it was his own fault and was another of the annoyances he caused her. Ivan Ilych felt that this opinion escaped her involuntarily—but that did not make it easier for him.

At the law courts too, Ivan Ilych noticed, or thought he noticed, a strange attitude towards himself. It sometimes seemed to him that people were watching him inquisitively as a man whose place might soon be vacant. Then again, his friends would suddenly begin to chaff him in a friendly way about his low spirits, as if the awful, horrible, and unheard of thing that was going on within him, incessantly gnawing at him and irresistibly drawing him away, was a very agreeable subject for jests. Schwartz in particular irritated him by his jocularity, vivacity, and *savoir-faire*, which reminded him of what he himself had been ten years ago.

Friends came to make up a set and they sat down to cards. They dealt, bending the new cards to soften them, and he sorted the diamonds in his hand and found he had seven. His partner said "No trumps" and supported him with two diamonds. What more could be wished for? It ought to be jolly and lively. They would make a grand slam. But suddenly Ivan Ilych was conscious of that gnawing pain, that taste in his mouth, and it seemed ridiculous that in such circumstances he should be pleased to make a grand slam.

He looked at his partner Mikhail Mikhaylovich, who rapped the table with his strong hand and instead of snatching up the tricks pushed the cards courteously and indulgently towards Ivan Ilych that he might have the pleasure of gathering them up without the trouble of stretching out his hand for them. "Does he think I am too weak to stretch out my arm?" thought Ivan Ilych, and forgetting what he was doing he over-trumped his partner, missing the grand slam by three tricks. And what was most awful of all was that he saw how upset Mikhail Mikhaylovich was about it but did not himself care. And it was dreadful to realize why he did not care.

They all saw that he was suffering, and said: "We can stop if you are tired. Take a rest." Lie down? No, he was not at all tired, and he finished the rubber. All were gloomy and silent. Ivan Ilych felt that he had diffused this gloom over them and could not dispel it. They had supper and went away, and Ivan Ilych was left alone with the consciousness that his life was poisoned and was poisoning the lives of others, and that this poison did not weaken but penetrated more and more deeply into his whole being.

With this consciousness, and with physical pain besides the terror, he must go to bed, often to lie awake the greater part of the night. Next morning he had to get up again, dress, go to the law courts, speak, and write; or if he did not go out, spend at home those twenty-four hours a day each of which was a torture. And he had to live thus all alone on the brink of an abyss, with no one who understood or pitied him.

V

So one month passed and then another. Just before the New Year his brother-in-law came to town and stayed at their house. Ivan Ilych was at the law courts and Praskovya Fëdorovna had gone shopping. When Ivan Ilych came home and entered his study he found his brother-in-law there—a healthy, florid man—unpacking his portmanteau himself. He raised his head on hearing Ivan Ilych's footsteps and looked up at him for a moment without a word. That stare told Ivan Ilych everything. His brother-in-law opened his mouth to utter an exclamation of surprise but checked himself, and that action confirmed it all.

"I have changed, eh?"

"Yes, there is a change."

And after that, try as he would to get his brother-in-law to return to the subject of his looks, the latter would say nothing about it. Praskovya Fëdorovna came home and her brother went out to her. Ivan Ilych locked the door and began to examine himself in the glass, first full face, then in profile. He took up a portrait of himself taken with his wife, and compared it with what he saw in the glass. The change in him was immense. Then he bared his arms to the elbow, looked at them, drew the sleeves down again, sat down on an ottoman, and grew blacker than night.

"No, no, this won't do!" he said to himself, and jumped up, went to the table, took up some law papers, and began to read them, but could not continue. He unlocked the door and went into the reception-room. The door leading to the drawing-room was shut. He approached it on tiptoe and listened.

"No, you are exaggerating!" Praskovya Fëdorovna was saying.

"Exaggerating! Don't you see it? Why, he's a dead man! Look at his eyes—there's no light in them. But what is it that is wrong with him?"

"No one knows. Nikolaevich said something, but I don't know what. And Leshchetitsky* said quite the contrary . . ."

Ivan Ilych walked away, went to his own room, lay down, and began musing: "The kidney, a floating kidney." He recalled all the doctors had told him of how it detached itself and swayed about. And by an effort of imagination he tried to catch that kidney and arrest it and support it. So little was needed for this, it seemed to him. "No, I'll go to see Peter Ivanovich† again." He rang, ordered the carriage, and got ready to go.

"Where are you going, Jean?" asked his wife, with a specially sad and exceptionally kind look.

This exceptionally kind look irritated him. He looked morosely at her.

"I must go to see Peter Ivanovich."

He went to see Peter Ivanovich, and together they went to see his friend, the doctor. He was in, and Ivan Ilych had a long talk with him.

Reviewing the anatomical and physiological details of what in the doctor's opinion was going on inside him, he understood it all.

There was something, a small thing, in the vermiform appendix. It might all come right. Only stimulate the energy of one organ and check the activity of another, then absorption would take place and everything would come right. He got home rather late for dinner, ate his dinner, and conversed cheerfully, but could not for a long time bring himself to go back to work in his room. At last, however, he went to his study and did what was necessary, but the consciousness that he had put something aside—an important, intimate matter which he would revert to when his work was done—never left him. When he had finished his work he remembered that this intimate matter was the thought of his vermiform appendix. But he did not give himself up to it, and went to the drawing-room for tea. There were callers there, including the examining magistrate who was a desirable match for his daughter, and they were conversing, playing the piano, and singing. Ivan Ilych, as Praskovya Fëdorovna remarked, spent that evening more cheerfully than usual, but he never for a moment forgot that he had postponed the important

---

**Nikolaevich, Leshchetitsky:* two doctors, the latter a celebrated specialist. [Translators' note.]

†*Peter Ivanovich:* That was the friend whose friend was a doctor. [Translators' note.]

matter of the appendix. At eleven o'clock he said good-night and went to his bedroom. Since his illness he had slept alone in a small room next to his study. He undressed and took up a novel by Zola, but instead of reading it he fell into thought, and in his imagination that desired improvement in the vermiform appendix occurred. There was the absorption and evacuation and the re-establishment of normal activity. "Yes, that's it!" he said to himself. "One need only assist nature, that's all." He remembered his medicine, rose, took it, and lay down on his back watching for the beneficent action of the medicine and for it to lessen the pain. "I need only take it regularly and avoid all injurious influences. I am already feeling better, much better." He began touching his side; it was not painful to the touch. "There, I really don't feel it. It's much better already." He put out the light and turned on his side . . . "The appendix is getting better, absorption is occurring." Suddenly he felt the old, familiar, dull, gnawing pain, stubborn and serious. There was the same familiar loathsome taste in his mouth. His heart sank and he felt dazed. "My God! My God!" he muttered. "Again, again! and it will never cease." And suddenly the matter presented itself in a quite different aspect. "Vermiform appendix! Kidney!" he said to himself. "It's not a question of appendix or kidney, but of life and . . . death. Yes, life was there and now it is going, going and I cannot stop it. Yes. Why deceive myself? Isn't it obvious to everyone but me that I'm dying, and that it's only a question of weeks, days . . . it may happen this moment. There was light and now there is darkness. I was here and now I'm going there! Where?" A chill came over him, his breathing ceased, and he felt only the throbbing of his heart.

"When I am not, what will there be? There will be nothing. Then where shall I be when I am no more? Can this be dying? No, I don't want to!" He jumped up and tried to light the candle, felt for it with trembling hands, dropped candle and candlestick on the floor, and fell back on his pillow.

"What's the use? It makes no difference," he said to himself, staring with wide-open eyes into the darkness. "Death. Yes, death. And none of them know or wish to know it, and they have no pity for me. Now they are playing." (He heard through the door the distant sound of a song and its accompaniment.) "It's all the same to them, but they will die too! Fools! I first, and they later, but it will be the same for them. And now they are merry . . . the beasts!"

Anger choked him and he was agonizingly, unbearably miserable. "It is impossible that all men have been doomed to suffer this awful horror!" He raised himself.

"Something must be wrong. I must calm myself—must think it all over from the beginning." And he again began thinking. "Yes, the beginning of my illness: I knocked my side, but I was still quite well that day and the next. It hurt a little, then rather more. I saw the doctors, then followed despondency and anguish, more doctors, and I drew nearer to the abyss. My strength grew less and I kept coming nearer and nearer, and now I have wasted away and there is no light in my eyes. I think of the appendix—but this is death! I think of mending the appendix, and all the while here is death! Can it really be death?" Again terror seized him and he gasped for breath. He leant down and began feeling for the matches, pressing with his elbow on the stand beside the bed. It was in his way and hurt him, he grew furious with it, pressed on it still harder, and upset it. Breathless and in despair he fell on his back, expecting death to come immediately.

Meanwhile the visitors were leaving. Praskovya Fëdorovna was seeing them off. She heard something fall and came in.

"What has happened?"

"Nothing. I knocked it over accidentally."

She went out and returned with a candle. He lay there panting heavily, like a man who has run a thousand yards, and stared upwards at her with a fixed look.

"What is it, Jean?"

"No . . . o . . . thing. I upset it." ("Why speak of it? She won't understand," he thought.)

And in truth she did not understand. She picked up the stand, lit his candle, and hurried away to see another visitor off. When she came back he still lay on his back, looking upwards.

"What is it? Do you feel worse?"

"Yes."

She shook her head and sat down.

"Do you know, Jean, I think we must ask Leshchetitsky to come and see you here."

This meant calling in the famous specialist, regardless of expense. He smiled malignantly and said "No." She remained a little longer and then went up to him and kissed his forehead.

While she was kissing him he hated her from the bottom of his soul and with difficulty refrained from pushing her away.

"Good-night. Please God you'll sleep."

"Yes."

VI

Ivan Ilych saw that he was dying, and he was in continual despair.

In the depth of his heart he knew he was dying, but not only was he not accustomed to the thought, he simply did not and could not grasp it.

The syllogism he had learnt from Kiezewetter's Logic: "Caius is a man, men are mortal, therefore Caius is mortal," had always seemed to him correct as applied to Caius, but certainly not as applied to himself. That Caius—man in the abstract—was mortal, was perfectly correct, but he was not Caius, not an abstract man, but a creature quite, quite separate from all others. He had been little Vanya, with a mamma and a papa, with Mitya and Volodya, with the toys, a coachman and a nurse, afterwards with Katenka and with all the joys, griefs, and delights of childhood, boyhood, and youth. What did Caius know of the smell of that striped leather ball Vanya had been so fond of? Had Caius kissed his mother's hand like that, and did the silk of her dress rustle so for Caius? Had he rioted like that at school when the pastry was bad? Had Caius been in love like that? Could Caius preside at a session as he did? "Caius really was mortal, and it was right for him to die; but for me, little Vanya, Ivan Ilych, with all my thoughts and emotions, it's altogether a different matter. It cannot be that I ought to die. That would be too terrible."

Such was his feeling.

"If I had to die like Caius I should have known it was so. An inner voice would have told me so, but there was nothing of the sort in me and I and all my friends felt that our case was quite different from that of Caius. And now here it is!" he said to himself. "It can't be. It's impossible! But here it is. How is this? How is one to understand it?"

He could not understand it, and tried to drive this false, incorrect, morbid thought away and to replace it by other proper and healthy thoughts. But that thought, and not the thought only but the reality itself, seemed to come and confront him.

And to replace that thought he called up a succession of others, hoping to find in them some support. He tried to get back into the former current of thoughts that had once screened the thought of death from him. But strange to say, all that had formerly shut off, hidden, and destroyed his consciousness of death, no longer had that effect. Ivan Ilych now spent most of his time in attempting to re-establish that old current. He would say to himself: "I will take up my duties again—after all I used to live by them." And banishing all doubts he would go to the law courts, enter into conversation with his colleagues, and sit carelessly as was his wont, scanning the crowd with a thoughtful look and leaning both his emaciated arms on the arms of his oak chair; bending over as usual to a colleague and drawing his papers nearer he would interchange whispers with him, and then suddenly raising his eyes and sitting erect would pronounce certain words and open the proceedings. But suddenly in the midst of those proceedings the pain in his side, regardless of the stage the proceedings had reached, would begin its own gnawing work. Ivan Ilych would turn his attention to it and try to drive the thought of it away, but without success. *It* would come and stand before him and look at him, and he would be petrified and the light would die out of his eyes, and he would again begin asking himself whether *It* alone was true. And his colleagues and subordinates would see with surprise and distress that he, the brilliant and subtle judge, was becoming confused and making mistakes. He would shake himself, try to pull himself together, manage somehow to bring the sitting to a close, and return home with the sorrowful consciousness that his judicial labors could not as formerly hide from him what he wanted them to hide, and could not deliver him from *It*. And what was worst of all was that *It* drew his attention to itself not in order to make him take some action but only that he should look at *It*, look it straight in the face: look at it and, without doing anything, suffer inexpressibly.

And to save himself from this condition Ivan Ilych looked for consolation—new screens—and new screens were found and for a while seemed to save him, but then they immediately fell to pieces or rather became transparent, as if *It* penetrated them and nothing could veil *It*.

In these latter days he would go into the drawing-room he had arranged—that drawing-room where he had fallen and for the sake of which (how bitterly ridiculous it seemed) he had sacrificed his life—for he knew that his illness originated with that knock. He would enter and see that something had scratched the polished table. He would look for the cause of this and find that it was the bronze ornamentation of an album, that had got bent. He would take up the expensive album which he had lovingly arranged, and feel vexed with his daughter and her friends for their untidiness—for the album was torn here and there and some of the photographs turned upside down. He would put it carefully in order and bend the ornamentation back into position. Then it would occur to him to place all those things in another corner of the room, near the plants. He could call the footman, but his daughter or wife would come to help him. They would not agree, and his wife would contradict him, and he would dispute and grow angry. But that was all right, for then he did not think about *It*. *It* was invisible.

But then, when he was moving something himself, his wife would say: "Let the servants do it. You will hurt yourself again." And suddenly *It* would flash through the screen and he would see it. It was just a flash, and he hoped it would disappear, but he would involuntarily pay attention to his side. "It sits there as before, gnawing just the same!" And he could no longer forget *It*, but could distinctly see it looking at him from behind the flowers. "What is it all for?"

"It really is so! I lost my life over that curtain as I might have done when storming a fort. Is that possible? How terrible and how stupid. It can't be true! It can't, but it is."

He would go to his study, lie down, and again be alone with *It*: face to face with *It*. And nothing could be done with *It* except to look at it and shudder.

VII

How it happened it is impossible to say because it came about step by step, unnoticed, but in the third month of Ivan Ilych's illness, his wife, his daughter, his son, his acquaintances, the doctors, the servants, and above all he himself, were aware that the whole interest he had for other people was whether he would soon vacate his place, and at last release the living from the discomfort caused by his presence and be himself released from his sufferings.

He slept less and less. He was given opium and hypodermic injections of morphine, but this did not relieve him. The dull depression he experienced in a somnolent condition at first gave him a little relief, but only as something new, afterwards it became as distressing as the pain itself or even more so.

Special foods were prepared for him by the doctors' orders, but all those foods became increasingly distasteful and disgusting to him.

For his excretions also special arrangements had to be made, and this was a torment to him every time—a torment from the uncleanliness, the unseemliness, and the smell, and from knowing that another person had to take part in it.

But just through this most unpleasant matter, Ivan Ilych obtained comfort. Gerasim, the butler's young assistant, always came in to carry the things out. Gerasim was a clean, fresh peasant lad, grown stout on town food and always cheerful and bright. At first the sight of him, in his clean Russian peasant costume, engaged on that disgusting task embarrassed Ivan Ilych.

Once when he got up from the commode too weak to draw up his trousers, he dropped into a soft armchair and looked with horror at his bare, enfeebled thighs with the muscles so sharply marked on them.

Gerasim with a firm light tread, his heavy boots emitting a pleasant smell of tar and fresh winter air, came in wearing a clean Hessian apron, the sleeves of his print shirt tucked up over his strong, bare young arms; and refraining from looking at his sick master out of consideration for his feelings, and restraining the joy of life that beamed from his face, he went up to the commode.

"Gerasim!" said Ivan Ilych in a weak voice.

Gerasim started, evidently afraid he might have committed some blunder, and with a rapid movement turned his fresh, kind, simple young face which just showed the first downy signs of a beard.

"Yes, sir?"

"That must be very unpleasant for you. You must forgive me, I am helpless."

"Oh, why, sir," and Gerasim's eyes beamed and he showed his glistening white teeth, "what's a little trouble? It's a case of illness with you, sir."

And his deft strong hands did their accustomed task, and he went out of the room stepping lightly. Five minutes later he as lightly returned.

Ivan Ilych was still sitting in the same position in the armchair.

"Gerasim," he said when the latter had replaced the freshly washed utensil. "Please come here and help me." Gerasim went up to him. "Lift me up. It is hard for me to get up, and I have sent Dmitri away."

Gerasim went up to him, grasped his master with his strong arms deftly but gently, in the same way that he stepped—lifted him, supported him with one hand, and with the other drew up his trousers and would have set him down again, but Ivan Ilych asked to be led to the sofa. Gerasim, without an effort and without apparent pressure, led him, almost lifting him, to the sofa, and placed him on it.

"Thank you. How easily and well you do it all!"

Gerasim smiled again and turned to leave the room. But Ivan Ilych felt his presence such a comfort that he did not want to let him go.

"One thing more, please move up that chair. No, the other one—under my feet. It is easier for me when my feet are raised."

Gerasim brought the chair, set it down gently in place, and raised Ivan Ilych's legs on to it. It seemed to Ivan Ilych that he felt better while Gerasim was holding up his legs.

"It's better when my legs are higher," he said, "Place that cushion under them."

Gerasim did so. He again lifted the legs and placed them, and again Ivan Ilych felt better while Gerasim held his legs. When he set them down Ivan Ilych fancied he felt worse.

"Gerasim," he said. "Are you busy now?"

"Not at all, sir," said Gerasim, who had learnt from the townsfolk how to speak to gentlefolk.

"What have you still to do?"

"What have I to do? I've done everything except chopping the logs for tomorrow."

"Then hold my legs up a bit higher, can you?"

"Of course I can. Why not?" And Gerasim raised his master's legs higher and Ivan Ilych thought that in that position he did not feel any pain at all.

"And how about the logs?"

"Don't trouble about that, sir. There's plenty of time."

Ivan Ilych told Gerasim to sit down and hold his legs, and began to talk to him. And strange to say it seemed to him that he felt better while Gerasim held his legs up.

After that Ivan Ilych would sometimes call Gerasim and get him to hold his legs on his shoulders, and he liked talking to him. Gerasim did it all easily, willingly, simply, and with a good nature that touched Ivan Ilych. Health, strength, and vitality in other people were offensive to him, but Gerasim's strength and vitality did not mortify but soothed him.

What tormented Ivan Ilych most was the deception, the lie, which for some reason they all accepted, that he was not dying but was simply ill, and that he only need keep quiet and undergo a treatment and then something very good would result. He, however, knew that do what they would nothing would come of it, only still more agonizing suffering and death. This deception tortured him—their not wishing to admit what they all knew and what he knew, but wanting to lie to him concerning his terrible condition, and wishing and forcing him to participate in that lie. Those lies—lies enacted over him on the eve of his death and destined to degrade this awful, solemn act to the level of their visitings, their curtains, their sturgeon for dinner—were a terrible agony for Ivan Ilych. And strangely enough, many times when they were going through their antics over him he had been within a hair-breadth of calling out to them: "Stop lying! You know and I know that I am dying. Then at least stop lying about it." But he had never had the spirit to do it. The awful, terrible act of his dying was, he could see, reduced by those about him to the level of a casual, unpleasant, and almost indecorous incident (as if someone entered a drawing-room diffusing an unpleasant odor) and this was done by that very decorum which he had served all his life long. He saw that no one felt for him, because no one even wished to grasp his position. Only Gerasim recognized it and pitied him. And so Ivan Ilych felt at ease only with him. He felt comforted when Gerasim supported his legs (sometimes all night long) and refused to go to bed, saying: "Don't you worry, Ivan Ilych. I'll get sleep enough later on," or when he suddenly became familiar and exclaimed: "If you weren't sick it would be another matter, but as it is, why should I grudge a little trouble?" Gerasim alone did not lie; everything showed that he alone understood the facts of the case and did not consider it necessary to disguise them, but simply felt sorry for his emaciated and enfeebled master. Once when Ivan Ilych was sending him away he even said straight out: "We shall all of us die, so why should I grudge a little trouble?"—expressing the fact that he did not think his work burdensome, because he was doing it for a dying man and hoped someone would do the same for him when his time came.

Apart from this lying, or because of it, what most tormented Ivan Ilych was that no one pitied him as he wished to be pitied. At certain moments after prolonged suffering he wished most of all (though he would have been ashamed to confess it) for someone to pity him as a sick child is pitied. He longed to be petted and comforted. He knew he was an important functionary, that he had a beard turning grey, and that therefore what he longed for was impossible, but still he longed for it. And in Gerasim's attitude towards him there was something akin to what he wished for, and so that attitude comforted him. Ivan Ilych wanted to weep, wanted to be petted and cried over, and then his colleague Shebek would come, and instead of weeping and being petted, Ivan Ilych would assume a serious, severe, and profound air, and by force of habit would express his opinion on a decision of the Court of Cassation and would stubbornly insist on that view. This falsity around him and within him did more than anything else to poison his last days.

VIII

It was morning. He knew it was morning because Gerasim had gone, and Peter the footman had come and put out the candles, drawn back one of the curtains, and begun quietly to tidy up. Whether it was morning or evening, Friday or Sunday, made no difference, it was all just the same: the gnawing, unmitigated, agonizing pain, never ceasing for an instant, the consciousness of life inexorably waning but not yet extinguished, the approach of that ever dreaded and hateful

Death which was the only reality, and always the same falsity. What were days, weeks, hours, in such a case?

"Will you have some tea, sir?"

"He wants things to be regular, and wishes the gentlefolk to drink tea in the morning," thought Ivan Ilych, and only said "No."

"Wouldn't you like to move onto the sofa, sir?"

"He wants to tidy up the room, and I'm in the way. I am uncleanliness and disorder," he thought, and said only:

"No, leave me alone."

The man went on bustling about. Ivan Ilych stretched out his hand. Peter came up, ready to help.

"What is it, sir?"

"My watch."

Peter took the watch which was close at hand and gave it to his master.

"Half-past eight. Are they up?"

"No, sir, except Vasily Ivanovich" (the son) "who has gone to school. Praskovya Fëdorovna ordered me to wake her if you asked for her. Shall I do so?"

"No, there's no need to." "Perhaps I'd better have some tea," he thought, and added aloud: "Yes, bring me some tea."

Peter went to the door, but Ivan Ilych dreaded being left alone. "How can I keep him here? Oh yes, my medicine." "Peter, give me my medicine." "Why not? Perhaps it may still do me some good." He took a spoonful and swallowed it. "No, it won't help. It's all tomfoolery, all deception," he decided as soon as he became aware of the familiar, sickly, hopeless taste. "No, I can't believe in it any longer. But the pain, why this pain? If it would only cease just for a moment!" And he moaned. Peter turned towards him. "It's all right. Go and fetch me some tea."

Peter went out. Left alone Ivan Ilych groaned not so much with pain, terrible though that was, as from mental anguish. Always and forever the same, always these endless days and nights. If only it would come quicker! If only *what* would come quicker? Death, darkness? . . . No, no! Anything rather than death!

When Peter returned with the tea on a tray, Ivan Ilych stared at him for a time in perplexity, not realizing who and what he was. Peter was disconcerted by that look and his embarrassment brought Ivan Ilych to himself.

"Oh, tea! All right, put it down. Only help me to wash and put on a clean shirt."

And Ivan Ilych began to wash. With pauses for rest, he washed his hands and then his face, cleaned his teeth, brushed his hair, and looked in the glass. He was terrified by what he saw, especially by the limp way in which his hair clung to his pallid forehead.

While his shirt was being changed he knew that he would be still more frightened at the sight of his body, so he avoided looking at it. Finally he was ready. He drew on a dressing-gown, wrapped himself in a plaid, and sat down in the armchair to take his tea. For a moment he felt refreshed, but soon as he began to drink the tea he was again aware of the same taste, and the pain also returned. He finished it with an effort, and then lay down stretching out his legs, and dismissed Peter.

Always the same. Now a spark of hope flashes up, then a sea of despair rages, and always pain; always pain, always despair, and always the same. When alone he had a dreadful and distressing desire to call someone, but he knew beforehand that with others present it would be still worse. "Another dose of morphine—to lose consciousness. I will tell him, the doctor, that he must think of something else. It's impossible, impossible, to go on like this."

An hour and another pass like that. But now there is a ring at the door bell. Perhaps it's the doctor? It is. He comes in fresh, hearty, plump, and cheerful, with that look on his face that seems to say: "There now, you're in a panic about something, but we'll arrange it all for you directly!" The doctor knows this expression is out of place here, but he has put it on once for all and can't take it off—like a man who has put on a frock-coat in the morning to pay a round of calls.

The doctor rubs his hands vigorously and reassuringly.

"Brr! How cold it is! There's such a sharp frost; just let me warm myself!" he says, as if it were only a matter of waiting till he was warm, and then he would put everything right.

"Well now, how are you?"

Ivan Ilych feels that the doctor would like to say: "Well, how are our affairs?" but that even he feels that this would not do, and says instead: "What sort of a night have you had?"

Ivan Ilych looks at him as much as to say: "Are you really never ashamed of lying?" But the doctor does not wish to understand this question, and Ivan Ilych says: "Just as terrible as ever. The pain never leaves me and never subsides. If only something . . ."

"Yes, you sick people are always like that. . . . There, now I think I am warm enough. Even Praskovya Fëdorovna, who is so particular, could find no fault with my temperature. Well, now I can say good-morning," and the doctor presses his patient's hand.

Then, dropping his former playfulness, he begins with a most serious face to examine the patient, feeling his pulse and taking his temperature, and then begins the sounding and auscultation.

Ivan Ilych knows quite well and definitely that all this is nonsense and pure deception, but when the doctor, getting down on his knee, leans over him, putting his ear first higher then lower, and performs various gymnastic movements over him with a significant expression on his face, Ivan Ilych submits to it all as he used to submit to the speeches of the lawyers, though he knew very well that they were all lying and why they were lying.

The doctor, kneeling on the sofa, is still sounding him when Praskovya Fëdorovna's silk dress rustles at the door and she is heard scolding Peter for not having let her know of the doctor's arrival.

She comes in, kisses her husband, and at once proceeds to prove that she has been up a long time already, and only owing to a misunderstanding failed to be there when the doctor arrived.

Ivan Ilych looks at her, scans her all over, sets against her the whiteness and plumpness and cleanness of her hands and neck, the gloss of her hair, and the sparkle of her vivacious eyes. He hates her with his whole soul. And the thrill of hatred he feels for her makes him suffer from her touch.

Her attitude towards him and his disease is still the same. Just as the doctor had adopted a certain relation to his patient which he could not abandon, so had she formed one towards him—that he was not doing something he ought to do and was himself to blame, and that she reproached him lovingly for this—and she could not now change that attitude.

"You see he doesn't listen to me and doesn't take his medicine at the proper time. And above all he lies in a position that is no doubt bad for him—with his legs up."

She described how he made Gerasim hold his legs up.

The doctor smiled with a contemptuous affability that said: "What's to be done? These sick people do have foolish fancies of that kind, but we must forgive them."

When the examination was over the doctor looked at his watch, and then Praskovya Fëdorovna announced to Ivan Ilych that it was of course as he pleased, but she had sent today for a celebrated specialist who would examine him and have a consultation with Michael Danilovich (their regular doctor).

"Please don't raise any objections, I am doing this for my own sake," she said ironically, letting it be felt that she was doing it all for his sake and only said this to leave him no right to refuse. He remained silent, knitting his brows. He felt that he was so surrounded and involved in a mesh of falsity that it was hard to unravel anything.

Everything she did for him was entirely for her own sake, and she told him she was doing for herself what she actually was doing for herself, as if that was so incredible that he must understand the opposite.

At half-past eleven the celebrated specialist arrived. Again the sounding began and the significant conversations in his presence and in another room, about the kidneys and the appendix, and the questions and answers, with such an air of importance that again, instead of the real question of life and death which now alone confronted him, the question arose of the kidney and appendix which were not behaving as they ought to and would now be attacked by Michael Danilovich and the specialist and forced to amend their ways.

The celebrated specialist took leave of him with a serious though not hopeless look, and in reply to the timid question Ivan Ilych, with eyes glistening with fear and hope, put to him as to whether there was a chance of recovery, said that he could not vouch for it but there was a possibility. The look of hope with which Ivan Ilych watched the doctor out was so pathetic that Praskovya Fëdorovna, seeing it, even wept as she left the room to hand the doctor his fee.

The gleam of hope kindled by the doctor's encouragement did not last long. The same room, the same pictures, curtains, wallpaper, medicine bottles, were all there, and the same aching suffering body, and Ivan Ilych began to moan. They gave him a subcutaneous injection and he sank into oblivion.

It was twilight when he came to. They brought him his dinner and he swallowed some beef tea with difficulty, and then everything was the same again and night was coming on.

After dinner, at seven o'clock, Praskovya Fëdorovna came into the room in evening dress, her full bosom pushed up by her corset, and with traces of powder on her face. She had reminded him in the morning that they were going to the theater. Sarah Bernhardt was visiting the town and they had a box, which he had insisted on their taking. Now he had forgotten about it and her toilet offended him, but he concealed his vexation when he remembered that he had himself insisted on their securing a box and going because it would be an instructive and aesthetic pleasure for the children.

Praskovya Fëdorovna came in, self-satisfied but yet with a rather guilty air. She sat down and asked how he was, but, as he saw, only for the sake of asking and not in order to learn about it, knowing that there was nothing to learn—and then went on to what she really wanted to say: that she would not on any account have gone but that the box had been taken and Helen and their daughter were going, as well as Petrishchev (the examining magistrate, their daughter's fiancé), and that it was out of the question to let them go alone; but that she would have much preferred to sit with him for a while; and he must be sure to follow the doctor's orders while she was away.

"Oh, and Fëdor Petrovich" (the fiancé) "would like to come in. May he? And Lisa?"

"All right."

Their daughter came in in full evening dress, her fresh young flesh exposed (making a show of that very flesh which in his own case caused so much suffering), strong, healthy, evidently in love, and impatient with illness, suffering, and death, because they interfered with her happiness.

Fëdor Petrovich came in too, in evening dress, his hair curled *à la Capoul,** a tight stiff collar round his long sinewy neck, an enormous white shirtfront, and narrow black trousers tightly stretched over his strong thighs. He had one white glove tightly drawn on, and was holding his opera hat in his hand.

Following him the schoolboy crept in unnoticed, in a new uniform, poor little fellow, and wearing gloves. Terribly dark shadows showed under his eyes, the meaning of which Ivan Ilych knew well.

His son had always seemed pathetic to him, and now it was dreadful to see the boy's frightened look of pity. It seemed to Ivan Ilych that Vasya was the only one besides Gerasim who understood and pitied him.

They all sat down and again asked how he was. A silence followed. Lisa asked her mother about the opera-glasses, and there was an altercation between mother and daughter as to who had taken them and where they had been put. This occasioned some unpleasantness.

Fëdor Petrovich inquired of Ivan Ilych whether he had ever seen Sarah Bernhardt. Ivan Ilych did not at first catch the question, but then replied: "No, have you seen her before?"

"Yes, in *Adrienne Lecouvreur.*"

Praskovya Fëdorovna mentioned some roles in which Sarah Bernhardt was particularly good. Her daughter disagreed. Conversation sprang up as to the elegance and realism of her acting—the sort of conversation that is always repeated and is always the same.

In the midst of the conversation Fëdor Petrovich glanced at Ivan Ilych and became silent. The others also looked at him and grew silent. Ivan Ilych was staring with glittering eyes straight before him, evidently indignant with them. This had to be rectified, but it was impossible to do so. The silence had to be broken, but for a time no one dared to break it and they all became afraid that the conventional deception would suddenly become obvious and the truth become plain to all. Lisa was the first to pluck up courage and break that silence, but by trying to hide what everybody was feeling, she betrayed it.

"Well, if we are going it's time to start," she said, looking at her watch, a present from her father, and with a faint and significant smile at Fëdor Petrovich relating to something known only to them. She got up with a rustle of her dress.

They all rose, said good-night, and went away.

When they had gone it seemed to Ivan Ilych that he felt better; the falsity had gone with them. But the pain remained—that same pain and that same fear

**à la Capoul:* imitating the hairdo of Victor Capoul, a contemporary French singer.

that made everything monotonously alike, nothing harder and nothing easier. Everything was worse.

Again minute followed minute and hour followed hour. Everything remained the same and there was no cessation. And the inevitable end of it all became more and more terrible.

"Yes, send Gerasim here," he replied to a question Peter asked.

IX

His wife returned late at night. She came in on tiptoe, but he heard her, opened his eyes, and made haste to close them again. She wished to send Gerasim away and to sit with him herself, but he opened his eyes and said: "No, go away."

"Are you in great pain?"

"Always the same."

"Take some opium."

He agreed and took some. She went away.

Till about three in the morning he was in a state of stupefied misery. It seemed to him that he and his pain were being thrust into a narrow, deep black sack, but though they were pushed further and further in they could not be pushed to the bottom. And this, terrible enough in itself, was accompanied by suffering. He was frightened yet wanted to fall through the sack, he struggled but yet cooperated. And suddenly he broke through, fell, and regained consciousness. Gerasim was sitting at the foot of the bed dozing quietly and patiently, while he himself lay with his emaciated stockinged legs resting on Gerasim's shoulders; the same shaded candle was there and the same unceasing pain.

"Go away, Gerasim," he whispered.

"It's all right, sir. I'll stay a while."

"No. Go away."

He removed his legs from Gerasim's shoulders, turned sideways onto his arm, and felt sorry for himself. He only waited till Gerasim had gone into the next room and then restrained himself no longer but wept like a child. He wept on account of his helplessness, his terrible loneliness, the cruelty of man, the cruelty of God, and the absence of God.

"Why hast Thou done all this? Why hast Thou brought me here? Why, why dost Thou torment me so terribly?"

He did not expect an answer and yet wept because there was no answer and could be none. The pain grew more acute, but he did not stir and did not call. He said to himself: "Go on! Strike me! But what is it for? What have I done to Thee? What is it for?"

Then he grew quiet and not only ceased weeping but even held his breath and became all attention. It was as though he was listening not to an audible voice but to the voice of his soul, to the current of thoughts arising within him.

"What is it you want?" was the first clear conception capable of expression in words, that he heard.

"What do you want? What do you want?" he repeated to himself.

"What do I want? To live and not to suffer," he answered.

And again he listened with such concentrated attention that even his pain did not distract him.

"To live? How?" asked his inner voice.

"Why, to live as I used to—well and pleasantly."

"As you lived before, well and pleasantly?" the voice repeated.

And in imagination he began to recall the best moments of his pleasant life. But strange to say none of those best moments of his pleasant life now seemed at all what they had then seemed—none of them except the first recollections of childhood. There, in childhood, there had been something really pleasant with which it would be possible to live if it could return. But the child who had experienced that happiness existed no longer, it was like a reminiscence of somebody else.

As soon as the period began which had produced the present Ivan Ilych, all that had then seemed joys now melted before his sight and turned into something trivial and often nasty.

And the further he departed from childhood and the nearer he came to the present the more worthless and doubtful were the joys. This began with the School of Law. A little that was really good was still found there—there was lightheartedness, friendship, and hope. But in the upper classes there had already been fewer of such good moments. Then during the first years of his official career, when he was in the service of the Governor, some pleasant moments again occurred: they were the memories of love for a woman. Then all became confused and there was still less of what was good; later on again there was still less that was good, and the further he went the less there was. His marriage, a mere accident, then the disenchantment that followed it, his wife's bad breath and the sensuality and hypocrisy; then the deadly official life and those preoccupations about money, a year of it, and two, and ten, and twenty, and always the same thing. And the longer it lasted the more deadly it became. "It is as if I had been going downhill while I imagined I was going up. And that is really what it was. I was going up in public opinion, but to the same extent life was ebbing away from me. And now it is all done and there is only death."

"Then what does it mean? Why? It can't be that life is so senseless and horrible. But if it really has been so horrible and senseless, why must I die and die in agony? There is something wrong!"

"Maybe I did not live as I ought to have done," it suddenly occurred to him. "But how could that be, when I did everything properly?" he replied, and immediately dismissed from his mind this, the sole solution of all the riddles of life and death, as something quite impossible.

"Then what do you want now? To live? Live how? Live as you lived in the law courts when the usher proclaimed 'The judge is coming!' The judge is coming, the judge!" he repeated to himself. "Here he is, the judge. But I am not guilty!" he exclaimed angrily. "What is it for?" And he ceased crying, but turning his face to the wall continued to ponder on the same question: Why, and for what purpose, is there all this horror? But however much he pondered he found no answer. And whenever the thought occurred to him, as it often did, that it all resulted from his not having lived as he ought to have done, he at once recalled the correctness of his whole life and dismissed so strange an idea.

X

Another fortnight passed. Ivan Ilych now no longer left his sofa. He would not lie in bed but lay on the sofa, facing the wall nearly all the time. He suffered ever the same unceasing agonies and in his loneliness pondered always on the same insoluble question: "What is this? Can it be that it is Death?" And the inner voice answered: "Yes, it is Death."

"Why these sufferings?" And the voice answered, "For no reason—they just are so." Beyond and besides this there was nothing.

From the very beginning of his illness, ever since he had first been to see the doctor, Ivan Ilych's life had been divided between two contrary and alternating moods: now it was despair and the expectation of this uncomprehended and terrible death, and now hope and an intently interested observation of the functioning of his organs. Now before his eyes there was only a kidney or an intestine that temporarily evaded its duty, and now only that incomprehensible and dreadful death from which it was impossible to escape.

These two states of mind had alternated from the very beginning of his illness, but the further it progressed the more doubtful and fantastic became the conception of the kidney, and the more real the sense of impending death.

He had but to call to mind what he had been three months before and what he was now, to call to mind with what regularity he had been going downhill, for every possibility of hope to be shattered.

Latterly during that loneliness in which he found himself as he lay facing the back of the sofa, a loneliness in the midst of a populous town and surrounded by numerous acquaintances and relations but that yet could not have been more complete anywhere—either at the bottom of the sea or under the earth—during that terrible loneliness Ivan Ilych had lived only in memories of the past. Pictures of his past rose before him one after another. They always began with what was nearest in time and then went back to what was most remote—to his childhood—and rested there. If he thought of the stewed prunes that had been offered him that day, his mind went back to the raw shrivelled French plums of his childhood, their peculiar flavor and the flow of saliva when he sucked their stones, and along with the memory of that taste came a whole series of memories of those days: his nurse, his brother, and their toys. "No, I mustn't think of that. . . . It is too painful." Ivan Ilych said to himself, and brought himself back to the present—to the button on the back of the sofa and the creases in its morocco. "Morocco is expensive, but it does not wear well: there had been a quarrel about it. It was a different kind of quarrel and a different kind of morocco that time when we tore father's portfolio and were punished, and mamma brought us some tarts. . . ." And again his thoughts dwelt on his childhood, and again it was painful and he tried to banish them and fix his mind on something else.

Then again together with that chain of memories another series passed through his mind—of how his illness had progressed and grown worse. There also the further back he looked the more life there had been. There had been more of what was good in life and more of life itself. The two merged together. "Just as the pain went on getting worse and worse, so my life grew worse and worse," he thought. "There is one bright spot there at the back, at the beginning of life, and afterwards all becomes blacker and proceeds more and more rapidly—in inverse ratio to the square of the distance from death," thought Ivan Ilych. And the example of a stone falling downwards with increasing velocity entered his mind. Life, a series of increasing sufferings, flies further and further towards its end—the most terrible suffering. "I am flying. . . ." He shuddered, shifted himself, and tried to resist, but was already aware that resistance was impossible, and again, with eyes weary of gazing but unable to cease seeing what was before them, he stared at the back of the sofa and waited—awaiting that dreadful fall and shock and destruction.

"Resistance is impossible!" he said to himself. "If I could only understand what it is all for! But that too is impossible. An explanation would be possible if it could be said that I have not lived as I ought to. But it is impossible to say that," and he remembered all the legality, correctitude, and propriety of his life. "That at any rate can certainly not be admitted," he thought, and his lips smiled ironically as if someone could see that smile and be taken in by it. "There is no explanation! Agony, death. . . . What for?"

XI

Another two weeks went by in this way and during that fortnight an event occurred that Ivan Ilych and his wife had desired. Petrishchev formally proposed. It happened in the evening. The next day Praskovya Fëdorovna came into her husband's room considering how best to inform him of it, but that very night there had been a fresh change for the worse in his condition. She found him still lying on the sofa but in a different position. He lay on his back, groaning and staring fixedly straight in front of him.

She began to remind him of his medicines, but he turned his eyes towards her with such a look that she did not finish what she was saying; so great an animosity, to her in particular, did that look express.

"For Christ's sake let me die in peace!" he said.

She would have gone away, but just then their daughter came in and went up to say good morning. He looked at her as he had done at his wife, and in reply to her inquiry about his health said dryly that he would soon free them all of himself. They were both silent and after sitting with him for a while went away.

"Is it our fault?" Lisa said to her mother. "It's as if we were to blame! I am sorry for papa, but why should we be tortured?"

The doctor came at his usual time. Ivan Ilych answered "Yes" and "No," never taking his angry eyes from him, and at last said: "You know you can do nothing for me, so leave me alone."

"We can ease your sufferings."

"You can't even do that. Let me be."

The doctor went into the drawing-room and told Praskovya Fëdorovna that the case was very serious and that the only resource left was opium to allay her husband's sufferings, which must be terrible.

It was true, as the doctor said, that Ivan Ilych's physical sufferings were terrible, but worse than the physical sufferings were his mental sufferings, which were his chief torture.

His mental sufferings were due to the fact that one night, as he looked at Gerasim's sleepy, good-natured face with its prominent checkbones, the question suddenly occurred to him: "What if my whole life has really been wrong?"

It occurred to him that what had appeared perfectly impossible before, namely that he had not spent his life as he should have done, might after all be true. It occurred to him that his scarcely perceptible attempts to struggle against what was considered good by the most highly placed people, those scarcely noticeable impulses which he had immediately suppressed, might have been the real thing, and all the rest false. And his professional duties and the whole arrangement of his life and of his family, and all his social and official interests, might all have been false. He tried to defend all those things to himself and suddenly felt the weakness of what he was defending. There was nothing to defend.

"But if that is so," he said to himself, "and I am leaving this life with the consciousness that I have lost all that was given me and it is impossible to rectify it—what then?"

He lay on his back and began to pass his life in review in quite a new way. In the morning when he saw first his footman, then his wife, then his daughter, and then the doctor, their every word and movement confirmed to him the awful truth that had been revealed to him during the night. In them he saw himself—all that for which he had lived—and saw clearly that it was not real at all, but a terrible and huge deception which had hidden both life and death. This consciousness intensified his physical suffering tenfold. He groaned and tossed about, and pulled at his clothing which choked and stifled him. And he hated them on that account.

He was given a large dose of opium and became unconscious, but at noon his sufferings began again. He drove everybody away and tossed from side to side.

His wife came to him and said:

"Jean, my dear, do this for me. It can't do any harm and often helps. Healthy people often do it."

He opened his eyes wide.

"What? Take communion? Why? It's unnecessary! However . . ."

She began to cry.

"Yes, do, my dear. I'll send for our priest. He is such a nice man."

"All right. Very well," he muttered.

When the priest came and heard his confession, Ivan Ilych was softened and seemed to feel a relief from his doubts and consequently from his sufferings, and for a moment there came a ray of hope. He again began to think of the vermiform appendix and the possibility of correcting it. He received the sacrament with tears in his eyes.

When they laid him down again afterwards he felt a moment's ease, and the hope that he might live awoke in him again. He began to think of the operation that had been suggested to him. "To live! I want to live!" he said to himself.

His wife came in to congratulate him after his communion, and when uttering the usual conventional words she added:

"You feel better, don't you?"

Without looking at her he said, "Yes."

Her dress, her figure, the expression of her face, the tone of her voice, all revealed the same thing. "This is wrong, it is not as it should be. All you have lived for and still live for is falsehood and deception, hiding life and death from you." And as soon as he admitted that thought, his hatred and his agonizing physical suffering again sprang up, and with that suffering a consciousness of the unavoidable, approaching end. And to this was added a new sensation of grinding shooting pain and a feeling of suffocation.

The expression of his face when he uttered that "yes" was dreadful. Having uttered it, he looked her straight in the eyes, turned on his face with a rapidity extraordinary in his weak state and shouted:

"Go away! Go away and leave me alone!"

XII

From that moment the screaming began that continued for three days, and was so terrible that one could not hear it through two closed doors without horror. At the moment he answered his wife he realized that he was lost, that there was no return, that the end had come, the very end, and his doubts were still unsolved and remained doubts.

"Oh! Oh! Oh!" he cried in various intonations. He had begun by screaming "I won't!" and continued screaming on the letter O.

For three whole days, during which time did not exist for him, he struggled in that black sack into which he was being thrust by an invisible, resistless force. He struggled as a man condemned to death struggles in the hands of the executioner, knowing that he cannot save himself. And every moment he felt that despite all his efforts he was drawing nearer and nearer to what terrified him. He felt that his agony was due to his being thrust into that black hole and still more to his not being able to get right into it. He was hindered from getting into it by his conviction that his life had been a good one. That very justification of his life held him fast and prevented his moving forward, and it caused him most torment of all.

Suddenly some force struck him in the chest and side, making it still harder to breathe, and he fell through the hole and there at the bottom was a light. What had happened to him was like the sensation one sometimes experiences in a railway carriage when one thinks one is going backwards while one is really going forwards and suddenly becomes aware of the real direction.

"Yes, it was all not the right thing," he said to himself, "but that's no matter. It can be done. But what *is* the right thing?" he asked himself, and suddenly grew quiet.

This occurred at the end of the third day, two hours before his death. Just then his schoolboy son had crept softly in and gone up to the bedside. The dying man was still screaming desperately and waving his arms. His hand fell on the boy's head, and the boy caught it, pressed it to his lips, and began to cry.

At that very moment Ivan Ilych fell through and caught sight of the light, and it was revealed to him that though his life had not been what it should have been, this could still be rectified. He asked himself, "What *is* the right thing?" and grew still, listening. Then he felt that someone was kissing his hand. He opened his eyes, looked at his son, and felt sorry for him. His wife came up to him and he glanced at her. She was gazing at him open-mouthed, with undried tears on her nose and cheek and a despairing look on her face. He felt sorry for her too.

"Yes, I am making them wretched," he thought. "They are sorry, but it will be better for them when I die." He wished to say this but had not the strength to utter it. "Besides, why speak? I must act," he thought. With a look at his wife he indicated his son and said: "Take him away . . . sorry for him . . . sorry for you too. . . ." He tried to add, "Forgive me," but said "forgo" and waved his hand, knowing that He whose understanding mattered would understand.

And suddenly it grew clear to him that what had been oppressing him and would not leave him was all dropping away at once from two sides, from ten sides, and from all sides. He was sorry for them, he must act so as not to hurt them: release them and free himself from these sufferings. "How good and how simple!" he thought. "And the pain?" he asked himself. "What has become of it? Where are you, pain?"

He turned his attention to it.

"Yes, here it is. Well, what of it? Let the pain be."

"And death . . . where is it?"

He sought his former accustomed fear of death and did not find it. "Where is it? What death?" There was no fear because there was no death.

In place of death there was light.

"So that's what it is!" he suddenly exclaimed aloud. "What joy!"

To him all this happened in a single instant, and the meaning of that instant did not change. For those present his agony continued for another two hours. Something rattled in his throat, his emaciated body twitched, then the gasping and rattle became less and less frequent.

"It is finished!" said someone near him.

He heard these words and repeated them in his soul.

"Death is finished," he said to himself. "It is no more!"

He drew in a breath, stopped in the midst of a sigh, stretched out, and died.

MARK TWAIN, the pen name of Samuel Langhorne Clemens (1835–1910), was born to John and Jane Clemens and reared primarily in Hannibal, Missouri, where according to Twain all the boys wanted to become steamboat captains on the Mississippi River. After the death of his father when he was only twelve years old, Twain worked at a wide range of jobs, including as a printer's apprentice, silver prospector, riverboat pilot, and journalist. Twain also served briefly in the Confederate Army before running away to join his brother in the Northwest. In 1870, Twain married Olivia Langdon, known as Livy, and took up residence first in Buffalo, New York, and then Hartford, Connecticut. The couple had four children. Although the family spent a brief time living in Paris, Twain mostly called Hartford home for the rest of his life. When Mark Twain died, he was financially comfortable, but had become increasingly misanthropic and gloomy in his later years.

At the present time, Twain is best known for his children's books, such as *The Adventures of Huckleberry Finn* (1884), *The Adventures of Tom Sawyer* (1876), and *The Prince and the Pauper* (1881). But in his own time, Mark Twain was first and foremost a travel writer, and his first work in this genre, *The Innocents Abroad* (1869), offered a view of Europe, the Old World, from the confident, and often satiric, perspective of an American. There followed *Roughing It* (1872), which explored the far West of the United States, and *Life on the Mississippi* (1883). While he was in the West after having deserted from the Confederate Army, Twain claims, he heard the story about a man and frog that lies at the heart of "The Celebrated Jumping Frog of Calaveras County." The piece was published in a New York newspaper in 1865, under the title "Jim Smiley and His Jumping Frog," and was featured as the title piece of Twain's first book, *The Celebrated Jumping Frog of Calaveras County and Other Sketches* (1867).

Like much of Twain's fiction, "The Celebrated Jumping Frog of Calaveras County" combines **realism** with **local color** to create a humorous effect. Twain's readers are drawn into Simon Wheeler's outlandish anecdotes, and they share the narrator's **satiric** attitude toward his storytelling prowess. As in the work of writers such as Achebe and Faulkner, appreciating the art of narration becomes part of the story's point.

Related Works: Achebe, "Why the Tortoise's Shell Is Not Smooth"; Cofer, "Tales Told Under the Mango Tree"; Faulkner, "A Rose for Emily"; Márquez, "The Handsomest Drowned Man in the World."

MARK TWAIN

The Celebrated Jumping Frog of Calaveras County

In compliance with the request of a friend of mine, who wrote me from the East, I called on good-natured, garrulous old Simon Wheeler, and inquired after my friend's friend, *Leonidas W.* Smiley, as requested to do, and I hereunto append the result. I have a lurking suspicion that *Leonidas W.* Smiley is a myth; that my friend never knew such a personage; and that he only conjectured that, if I asked old Wheeler about him, it would remind him of his infamous *Jim* Smiley, and he would go to work and bore me nearly to death with some infernal reminiscence of him as long and tedious as it should be useless to me. If that was the design, it certainly succeeded.

I found Simon Wheeler dozing comfortably by the bar-room stove of the old, dilapitated tavern in the ancient mining camp of Angel's, and I noticed that he was fat, and bald-headed, and had an expression of winning gentleness and simplicity upon his tranquil countenance. He roused up and gave me good day. I told him a friend of mine had commissioned me to make some inquiries about a cherished companion of his boyhood, named *Leonidas W.* Smiley—*Rev. Leonidas W.* Smiley, a young minister of the gospel, who he had heard was at one time a resident of Angel's Camp. I added that, if Mr. Wheeler could tell me anything about this Rev. Leonidas W. Smiley, I would feel under many obligations to him.

Simon Wheeler backed me into a corner, and blockaded me there with his chair, and then sat me down and reeled off the monotonous narrative which follows this paragraph. He never smiled, he never frowned, he never changed his voice from the gentle-flowing key to which he tuned the initial sentence, he never betrayed the slightest suspicion of enthusiasm; but all through the interminable narrative there ran a vein of impressive earnestness and sincerity, which showed me plainly that, so far from his imagining that there was anything ridiculous or funny about his story, he regarded it as a really important matter, and admired its two heroes as men of transcendent genius in *finesse*. To me, the spectacle of a man drifting serenely along through such a queer yarn without ever smiling, was exquisitely absurd. As I said before, I asked him to tell me what he knew of Rev. Leonidas W. Smiley, and he replied as follows. I let him go on in his own way, and never interrupted him once:

There was a feller here once by the name of *Jim* Smiley in the winter of '49—or may be it was the spring of '50—I don't recollect exactly, somehow, though what makes me think it was one or the other is because I remember the big flume wasn't finished when he first came to the camp; but anyway, he was the curiosest man about, always betting on anything that turned up you ever see, if he could get anybody to bet on the other side; and if he couldn't, he'd change sides. Anyway that suited the other man would suit him—anyway just so's he got a bet, *he* was satisfied. But still he was lucky, uncommon lucky; he most always come out winner. He was always ready and laying for a chance; there couldn't be no solitary thing mentioned but that feller'd offer to bet on it, and take any side you please, as I was just telling you. If there was a horse-race, you'd find him flush, or you'd find him busted at the end of it; if there was a dog-fight, he'd bet on it; if there was a cat-fight, he'd bet on it; if there was a chicken-fight, he'd bet on it; why, if there was two birds sitting on a fence, he would bet you which one would fly first; or if there was a camp-meeting, he would be there reg'lar, to bet on Parson Walker, which he judged to be the best exhorter about here, and so he was, too, and a good man. If he even seen a straddle-bug start to go anywheres, he would bet you how long it would take him to get wherever he was going to, and if you took him up, he would foller that straddle-bug to Mexico, but what he would find out where he was bound for and how long he was on the road. Lots of the boys here has seen that Smiley, and can tell you about him. Why it never made no difference to *him*—he would bet on *any* thing—the dangdest feller. Parson Walker's wife laid very sick once, for a good while, and it seemed as if they warn't going to save her; but one morning he come in, and Smiley asked how she was, and he said she was considerable better—thank the Lord for his infinite mercy—and coming on so smart that, with the blessing of Prov'dence, she'd get well yet; and Smiley, before he thought, says, "Well, I'll risk two-and-a-half that she don't, anyway."

Thish-yer Smiley had a mare—the boys called her the fifteen-minute nag, but that was only in fun, you know, because, of course, she was faster than that—and he used to win money on that horse, for all she was so slow and always had the asthma, or the distemper, or the consumption, or something of that kind. They used to give her two or three hundred yards' start, and then pass her under way; but always at the fag-end of the race she'd get excited and desperate-like, and come cavorting and straddling up, and scattering her legs around limber, sometimes in the air, and sometimes out to one side amongst the fences, and kicking up m-o-r-e dust and raising m-o-r-e racket with her coughing and sneezing and blowing her nose—and always fetch up at the stand, just about a neck ahead, as near as you could cipher it down.

And he had a little small bull-pup, that to look at him you'd think he warn't worth a cent, but to set around and look ornery, and lay for a chance to steal something. But as soon as money was upon him, he was a different dog; his under-jaw'd begin to stick out like the fo'castle of a steamboat and his teeth would uncover, and shine savage like the furnaces. And a dog might tackle him, and bully-rag him, and bite him, and throw him over his shoulder two or three times, and Andrew Jackson—which was the name of the pup—Andrew Jackson would never let on but what *he* was satisfied, and hadn't expected nothing else—and the bets being doubled and doubled on the other side all the time, till the money was all up; and then all of a sudden he would grab that other dog jest by the j'int of his hind leg and freeze to it—not chaw, you understand, but only jest grip and hang on till they throwed up the sponge, if it was a year. Smiley always come out winner on that pup, till he harnessed a dog once that didn't have no hind legs, because they'd been saw'd off by a circular saw, and when the thing had gone along far enough, and the money was all up, and he come to make a snatch for his pet holt, he saw in a minute how he'd been imposed on, and how the other dog had him in the door, so to speak, and he 'peared surprised, and then he looked sorter discouraged-like, and didn't try no more to win the fight, and so he got shucked out bad. He gave Smiley a look, as much as to say his heart was broke, and it was *his* fault, for putting up a dog that hadn't no hind legs for him to take holt of, which was his main dependence in a fight, and then he limped off a piece and laid down and died. It was a good pup, was that Andrew Jackson, and would have made a name for hisself if he'd lived, for the stuff was in him, and he had genius—I know it, because he hadn't had no opportunities to speak of, and it don't stand to reason that a dog could make such a fight as he could under them circumstances, if he hadn't no talent. It always makes me feel sorry when I think of that last fight of his'n, and the way it turned out.

Well, thish-yer Smiley had rat-tarriers, and chicken-cocks, and tom-cats, and all them kind of things, till you couldn't rest, and you couldn't fetch nothing for him to bet on but he'd match you. He ketched a frog one day, and took him home, and said he cal'klated to edercate him; and so he never done nothing for three months but set in his back yard and learn that frog to jump. And you bet you he *did* learn him, too. He'd give him a little punch behind, and the next minute you'd see that frog whirling in the air like a doughnut—see him turn one summerset, or maybe a couple, if he got a good start, and come down flat-footed and all right, like a cat. He got him up so in the matter of catching flies, and kept him in practice so constant, that he'd nail a fly every time as far as he could see him. Smiley said all a frog wanted was education, and he could do most anything—and I believe him. Why, I've seen him set Dan'l Webster down here on this floor—Dan'l Webster was the name of the frog—and sing out, "Flies, Dan'l, flies!" and quicker'n you could wink, he'd spring straight up, and snake a fly off'n the counter there, and flop down on the floor again as solid as a gob of mud, and fall to scratching the side of his head with his hind foot as indifferent as if he hadn't no idea he'd been doin' any more'n any frog might do. You never see a frog so modest and straightfor'ard as he was, for all he was so gifted. And when it come to fair and square jumping on a dead level, he could get over more ground at one straddle than any animal of his breed you ever see. Jumping on a dead level was his strong suit, you understand; and when it come to that, Smiley would ante up money on him as long as he had a red. Smiley was monsterous proud of his frog, and well he might be, for fellers that had travelled and been everywheres, all said he laid over any frog that ever *they* see.

Well, Smiley kept the beast in a little lattice box, and he used to fetch him down sometimes and lay for a bet. One day a feller—a stranger in the camp, he was—come across him with his box, and says;

"What might it be that you've got in the box?"

And Smiley says, sorter indifferent like, "It might be a parrot, or it might be a canary, maybe, but it ain't—it's only just a frog."

And the feller took it, and looked at it careful, and turned it round this way and that, and says, "H'm—so 'tis. Well, what's *he* good for?"

"Well," Smiley says, easy and careless, "he's good enough for *one* thing, I should judge—he can outjump any frog in Calaveras County."

The feller took the box again, and took another long, particular look, and gave it back to Smiley, and says, very deliberate, "Well, I don't see no p'ints about that frog that's any better'n any other frog."

"Maybe you don't," Smiley says. "Maybe you understand frogs, and maybe you don't understand 'em; maybe you've had experience, and maybe you ain't only a amateur, as it were. Anyways, I've got *my* opinion, and I'll risk forty dollars that he can outjump any frog in Calaveras Country."

And the feller studied a minute, and then says, kinder sad like, "Well, I'm only a stranger here, and I ain't got no frog; but if I had a frog, I'd bet you."

And then Smiley says, "That's all right—that's all right—if you'll hold my box a minute, I'll go and get you a frog." And so the feller took the box, and put up his forty dollars along with Smiley's, and set down to wait.

So he set there a good while thinking and thinking to hisself, and then he got the frog out and prized his mouth open and took a teaspoon and filled him full of quail shot—filled him pretty near up to his chin—and set him on the floor. Smiley he went to the swamp and slopped around in the mud for a long time, and finally he ketched a frog, and fetched him in, and gave him to this feller, and says: "Now if you're ready, set him alongside of Dan'l, with his forepaws just even with Dan'l's, and I'll give the word." Then he says, "One—two—three—jump!" and him and the feller touched up the frogs from behind, and the new frog hopped off, but Dan'l give a heave, and hysted up his shoulders—so—like a Frenchman, but it warn't no use—he couldn't budge; he was planted as solid as an anvil, and he couldn't no more stir than if he was anchored out. Smiley was a good deal surprised, and he was disgusted too, but he didn't have no idea what the matter was, of course.

The feller took the money and started away; and when he was going out at the door, he sorter jerked his thumb over his shoulder—this way—at Dan'l, and says again, very deliberate, "Well, *I* don't see no p'ints about that frog that's any better'n any other frog."

Smiley he stood scratching his head and looking down at Dan'l a long time, and at last he says, "I do wonder what in the nation that frog throwed off for—I wonder if there ain't something the matter with him—he 'pears to look mighty baggy, somehow." And he ketched Dan'l by the nap of the neck, and lifted him up and says, "Why, blame my cats, if he don't weigh five pound!" and turned him upside down, and he belched out a double handful of shot. And then he see how it was, and he was the maddest man— he set the frog down and took out after that feller, but he never ketched him. And——

[Here Simon Wheeler heard his name called from the front yard, and got up to see what was wanted.] And turning to me as he moved away, he said: "Just set where you are, stranger, and rest easy—I ain't going to be gone a second."

But, by your leave, I did not think that a continuation of the history of the enterprising vagabond *Jim* Smiley would be likely to afford me much information concerning the *Rev. Leonidas W.* Smiley, and so I started away.

At the door I met the sociable Wheeler returning, and he button-holed me and recommenced:

"Well, thish-yer Smiley had a yaller one-eyed cow that didn't have no tail, only just a short stump like a bannanner, and—"

"Oh! hang Smiley and his afflicted cow!" I muttered, good-naturedly, and bidding the old gentleman good day, I departed.

ANTON CHEKHOV (1860–1904) was born in a small town in southwest Russia. His grandfather was a serf who had purchased his own freedom, and his father owned a small general store in which Chekhov and his brothers worked. Eventually, the family moved to Moscow, where Chekhov received a medical degree from Moscow University. Although he was a prolific writer of short stories as well as a novelist, playwright, and humorist, Chekhov also used his degree to practice medicine and was intensely interested in the latest scientific theories. He was moved by the conditions of the poor and therefore philanthropically offered his medical services to them.

Perhaps inspired by his brother Aleksandr's minor successes as an author, Chekhov chose to become a professional writer rather than pursue a career in medicine. He began by publishing humorous pieces in newspapers under various pseudonyms and eventually published his short story collection *Motley Tales* in 1886. In 1888, he won a Pushkin Prize for his collection of stories *In the Twilight* (1887). Chekhov's works reflect his social consciousness. His **realistic** tales tend to portray life in all its seeming simplicity and to avoid overt morals or social messages, yet his portrayals of the sufferings of the poor and the inefficiencies of government bureaucracy serve to raise their readers' consciousness just the same.

In "Vanka" (1886), an orphaned boy who has been sent to apprentice with a shoemaker in Moscow surreptitiously composes a letter to his grandfather on Christmas Eve, begging him for rescue and relief from his suffering at the hands of the shoemaker and his wife. As he weaves his **pathetic** tale, he reminisces about his life prior to his apprenticeship.

Related Works: Lewis, "Limestone Diner"; Ellison, "Battle Royal"; Joyce, "Araby"; Rios, "Nani."

Vanka

Nine-year-old Vanka Zhukov, who had been apprentice to the shoemaker Aliakhin for three months, did not go to bed the night before Christmas. He waited till the master and mistress and the assistants had gone out to an early church-service, to procure from his employer's cupboard a small phial of ink and a penholder with a rusty nib; then, spreading a crumpled sheet of paper in front of him, he began to write.

Before, however, deciding to make the first letter, he looked furtively at the door and at the window, glanced several times at the sombre ikon, on either side of which stretched shelves full of lasts, and heaved a heart-rending sigh. The sheet of paper was spread on a bench, and he himself was on his knees in front of it.

"Dear Grandfather Konstantin Makarych," he wrote, "I am writing you a letter. I wish you a Happy Christmas and all God's holy best. I have no mamma or papa, you are all I have."

Vanka gave a look towards the window in which shone the reflection of his candle, and vividly pictured to himself his grandfather, Konstantin Makarych, who was night-watchman, at Messrs. Zbivarev. He was a small, lean, unusually lively and active old man of sixty-five, always smiling and blear-eyed. All day he slept in the servants' kitchen or trifled with the cooks. At night, enveloped in an ample sheepskin coat, he strayed round the domain, tapping with his cudgel. Behind him, each hanging its head, walked the old bitch Kashtanka, and the dog Viun, so named because of his black coat and long body and his resemblance to a loach. Viun was an unusually civil and friendly dog, looking as kindly at a stranger as at his masters, but he was not to be trusted. Beneath his deference and humbleness was hid the most inquisitorial maliciousness. No one knew better than he how to sneak up and take a bite at a leg, or slip into the larder or steal a muzhik's chicken. More than once they had nearly broken his hind-legs, twice he had been hung up, every week he was nearly flogged to death, but he always recovered.

At this moment, for certain, Vanka's grandfather must be standing at the gate, blinking his eyes at the bright red windows of the village church, stamping his feet in their high felt boots, and jesting with the people in the yard; his cudgel will be hanging from his belt, he will be hugging himself with cold, giving a little dry, old man's cough, and at times pinching a servant-girl or a cook.

"Won't we take some snuff?" he asks, holding out his snuff-box to the women. The women take a pinch of snuff, and sneeze.

The old man goes into indescribable ecstasies, breaks into loud laughter, and cries:

"Off with it, it will freeze to your nose!"

He gives his snuff to the dogs, too. Kashtanka sneezes, twitches her nose, and walks away offended. Viun deferentially refuses to sniff and wags his tail. It is glorious weather, not a breath of wind, clear, and frosty; it is a dark night, but the whole village, its white roofs and streaks of smoke from the chimneys, the trees silvered with hoarfrost, and the snowdrifts, you can see it all. The sky scintillates with bright twinkling stars, and the Milky Way stands out so clearly that it looks as if it had been polished and rubbed over with snow for the holidays. . . .

Vanka sighs, dips his pen in the ink, and continues to write:

"Last night I got a thrashing, my master dragged me by my hair into the yard, and belaboured me with a shoemaker's stirrup, because, while I was rocking his brat in its cradle, I unfortunately fell asleep. And during the week, my mistress told me to clean a herring, and I began by its tail, so she took the herring and stuck its snout into my face. The assistants tease me, send me to the tavern for vodka, make me steal the master's cucumbers, and the master beats me with whatever's handy. Food there is none; in the morning it's bread, at dinner gruel, and in the evening bread again. As for tea or sour-cabbage soup, the master and the mistress themselves guzzle that. They make me sleep in the vestibule, and when their brat cries, I don't sleep at all, but have to rock the cradle. Dear Grandpapa, for Heaven's sake, take me away from here, home to our village, I can't bear this any more. . . . I bow to the ground to you, and will pray to God for ever and ever, take me from here or I shall die. . ."

The corners of Vanka's mouth went down, he rubbed his eyes with his dirty fist, and sobbed.

"I'll grate your tobacco for you," he continued, "I'll pray to God for you, and if there is anything wrong, then flog me like the grey goat. And if you really think I shan't find work, then I'll ask the manager, for Christ's sake, to let me clean the boots, or I'll go instead of Fedya as underherdsman. Dear Grandpapa, I can't bear this any more, it'll kill me. . . . I wanted to run away to our village, but I have no boots, and I was afraid of the frost, and when I grow up I'll look after you, no one shall harm you, and when you die I'll pray for the repose of your soul, just like I do for mamma Pelagueva.

"As for Moscow, it is a large town, there are all gentlemen's houses, lots of horses, no sheep, and the dogs are not vicious. The children don't come round at Christmas with a star, no one is allowed to sing in the choir, and once I saw in a shop window hooks on a line and fishing rods, all for sale, and for every kind of fish, awfully convenient. And there was one hook which would catch a sheat-fish weighing a pound. And there are shops with guns, like the master's, and I am sure they must cost 100 rubles each. And in the meat-shops there are woodcocks, partridges, and hares, but who shot them or where they come from, the shopman won't say.

"Dear Grandpapa, and when the masters give a Christmas tree, take a golden walnut and hide it in my green box. Ask the young lady, Olga Ignatyevna, for it, say it's for Vanka."

Vanka sighed convulsively, and again stared at the window. He remembered that his grandfather always went to the forest for the Christmas tree, and took his grandson with him. What happy times! The frost crackled, his grandfather crackled, and as they both did, Vanka did the same. Then before cutting down the Christmas tree his grandfather smoked his pipe, took a long pinch of snuff, and made fun of poor frozen little Vanka. . . . The young fir trees, wrapt in hoar-frost, stood motionless, waiting for which of them would die. Suddenly a hare springing from somewhere would dart over the snowdrift. . . . His grandfather could not help shouting:

"Catch it, catch it, catch it! Ah, short-tailed devil!"

When the tree was down, his grandfather dragged it to the master's house, and there they set about decorating it. The young lady, Olga Ignatyevna, Vanka's great friend, busied herself most about it. When little Vanka's mother, Pelagueya, was still alive, and was servant-woman in the house, Olga Ignatyevna used to stuff him with sugar-candy, and having nothing to do, taught him to read, write, count up to one hundred, and even to dance the quadrille. When Pelagueya died, they placed the orphan Vanka in the kitchen with his grandfather, and from the kitchen he was sent to Moscow to Aliakhin, the shoemaker.

"Come quick, dear Grandpapa," continued Vanka, "I beseech you for Christ's sake take me from here. Have pity on a poor orphan, for here they beat me, and I am frightfully hungry, and so sad that I can't tell you, I cry all the time. The other day the master hit me on the head with a last: I fell to the ground, and only just returned to life. My life is a misfortune, worse than any dog's. . . . I send greetings to Aliona, to one-eyed Tegor, and the coachman, and don't let any one have my mouth-organ. I remain, your grandson, Ivan Zhukov, dear Grandpapa, do come."

Vanka folded his sheet of paper in four, and put it into an envelope purchased the night before for a kopek. He thought a little, dipped the pen into the ink, and wrote the address:

"The village, to my grandfather." He then scratched his head, thought again, and added: "Konstantin Makarych." Pleased at not having been interfered with in his writing, he put on his cap, and, without putting on his sheep-skin coat, ran out in his shirt-sleeves into the street.

The shopman at the poulterer's from whom he had inquired the night before, had told him that letters were to be put into post-boxes, and from there they were conveyed over the whole earth in mail troikas by drunken post-boys and to the sound of bells. Vanka ran to the first post-box and slipped his precious letter into the slit.

An hour afterwards, lulled by hope he was sleeping soundly. In his dreams he saw a stove, by the stove his grandfather sitting with his legs dangling down, barefooted, and reading a letter to the cooks, and Viun walking round the stove wagging his tail.

KATE CHOPIN (1851–1904), whose father was an Irish immigrant who rose to prominence in St. Louis after building a successful business and died when she was a toddler, was raised by her mother and her extended Creole family. She attended the Academy of the Sacred Heart in St. Louis and then married Oscar Chopin, who was also a member of a prominent French-Creole family. The couple moved to Louisiana, where they had six children. After her husband died, Chopin moved back to St. Louis with her children.

Inspired by the work of French writer Guy de Maupassant, Chopin began to write herself, and, at age forty, she published her first novel, *At Fault* (1890). After publishing some short stories in periodicals, she published her first collection, *Bayou Folk*, in 1894. Her next collection of stories, *A Night in Arcadie*, followed in 1897. Many of these stories, with their regional settings and **dialects**, are recognized as part of the **local color** movement. However, Chopin's fiction is perhaps best known for its forthright examination of human sexuality and a woman's place in society and within the institutions of marriage and motherhood. Her frank portrayals of unconventional (or at least unmentionable) female behavior caused many editors to refuse to publish her work.

An avid reader of biology and anthropology, Chopin incorporated these interests into stories that consider the ways in which both society and heredity shape the characters' behaviors. Chopin was particularly interested in an individual's consciousness of self and the psychology of women who pursue independence in mind and/or spirit. Like Mrs. Mallard in "The Story of an Hour" (1894) and Edna Pontellier in Chopin's novel *The Awakening* (1899), many of the characters' journeys to self-consciousness and independence involve significant suffering and sacrifice. Biology, heredity, and society as determinants of behavior are also present in "Desirée's Baby," a story with a powerful anti-racist theme.

Related Works: Steinbeck, "Chrysanthemums"; Mukherjee, "A Wife's Story"; "The Wife's Lament"; Akmatova, "Lot's Wife"; Bogan, "Women"; Levertov, "The Ache of Marriage"; Grimke, "Mona Lisa" and "Slave Auction."

The Story of an Hour

Knowing that Mrs. Mallard was afflicted with a heart trouble, great care was taken to break to her as gently as possible the news of her husband's death.

It was her sister Josephine who told her, in broken sentences; veiled hints that revealed in half concealing. Her husband's friend Richards was there, too, near her. It was he who had been in the newspaper office when intelligence of the railroad disaster was received, with Brently Mallard's name leading the list of "killed." He had only taken the time to assure himself of its truth by a second telegram, and had hastened to forestall any less careful, less tender friend in bearing the sad message.

She did not hear the story as many women have heard the same, with a paralyzed inability to accept its significance. She wept at once, with sudden, wild abandonment, in her sister's arms. When the storm of grief had spent itself she went away to her room alone. She would have no one follow her.

There stood, facing the open window, a comfortable, roomy armchair. Into this she sank, pressed down by a physical exhaustion that haunted her body and seemed to reach into her soul.

She could see in the open square before her house the tops of trees that were all aquiver with the new spring life. The delicious breath of rain was in the air. In the street below a peddler was crying his wares. The notes of a distant song which some one was singing reached her faintly, and countless sparrows were twittering in the eaves.

There were patches of blue sky showing here and there through the clouds that had met and piled one above the other in the west facing her window.

She sat with her head thrown back upon the cushion of the chair, quite motionless, except when a sob came up into her throat and shook her, as a child who has cried itself to sleep continues to sob in its dreams.

She was young, with a fair, calm face, whose lines bespoke repression and even a certain strength. But now there was a dull stare in her eyes, whose gaze was fixed away off yonder on one of those patches of blue sky. It was not a glance of reflection, but rather indicated a suspension of intelligent thought.

There was something coming to her and she was waiting for it, fearfully. What was it? She did not know; it was too subtle and elusive to name. But she felt it, creeping out of the sky, reaching toward her through the sounds, the scents, the color that filled the air.

Now her bosom rose and fell tumultuously. She was beginning to recognize this thing that was approaching to possess her, and she was striving to beat it back with her will—as powerless as her two white slender hands would have been.

When she abandoned herself a little whispered word escaped her slightly parted lips. She said it over and over under her breath: "free, free, free!" The vacant stare and the look of terror that had followed it went from her eyes. They stayed keen and bright. Her pulses beat fast, and the coursing blood warmed and relaxed every inch of her body.

She did not stop to ask if it were or were not a monstrous joy that held her. A clear and exalted perception enabled her to dismiss the suggestion as trivial.

She knew that she would weep again when she saw the kind, tender hands folded in death; the face that had never looked save with love upon her, fixed and gray and dead. But she saw beyond that bitter moment a long procession of years to come that would belong to her absolutely. And she opened and spread her arms out to them in welcome.

There would be no one to live for her during those coming years; she would live for herself. There would be no powerful will bending hers in that blind persistence with which men and women believe they have a right to impose a private will upon a fellow-creature. A kind intention or a cruel intention made the act seem no less a crime as she looked upon it in that brief moment of illumination.

And yet she had loved him—sometimes. Often she had not. What did it matter! What could love, the unsolved mystery, count for in face of this possession of self-assertion which she suddenly recognized as the strongest impulse of her being!

"Free! Body and soul free!" she kept whispering.

Josephine was kneeling before the closed door with her lips to the keyhole, imploring for admission. "Louise, open the door! I beg; open the door—you will make yourself ill. What are you doing, Louise? For heaven's sake open the door."

"Go away, I am not making myself ill." No; she was drinking in a very elixir of life through that open window.

Her fancy was running riot along those days ahead of her. Spring days, and summer days, and all sorts of days that would be her own. She breathed a quick prayer that life might be long. It was only yesterday she had thought with a shudder that life might be long.

She arose at length and opened the door to her sister's importunities. There was a feverish triumph in her eyes, and she carried herself unwittingly like a goddess of Victory. She clasped her sister's waist, and together they descended the stairs. Richards stood waiting for them at the bottom.

Some one was opening the front door with a latchkey. It was Brently Mallard who entered, a little travel-stained, composedly carrying his grip-sack and umbrella. He had been far from the scene of accident, and did not even know there had been one. He stood amazed at Josephine's piercing cry; at Richards' quick motion to screen him from the view of his wife.

But Richards was too late.

When the doctors came they said she had died of heart disease—of joy that kills.

KATE CHOPIN

Désirée's Baby

As the day was pleasant Madame Valmondé drove over to L'Abri to see Désirée and the baby.

It made her laugh to think of Désirée with a baby. Why, it seemed but yesterday that Désirée was little more than a baby herself; when Monsieur in riding through the gateway of Valmondé had found her lying asleep in the shadow of the big stone pillar.

The little one awoke in his arms and began to cry for "Dada." That was as much as she could do or say. Some people thought she might have strayed there of her own accord, for she was of the toddling age. The prevailing belief was that she had been purposely left by a party of Texans, whose canvas-covered wagon, late in the day, had crossed the ferry that Coton Maïs kept, just below the plantation. In time Madame Valmondé abandoned every speculation but the one that Désirée had been sent to her by a beneficent Providence to be the child of her affection, seeing that she was without child of the flesh. For the girl grew to be beautiful and gentle, affectionate and sincere—the idol of Valmondé.

It was no wonder, when she stood one day against the stone pillar in whose shadow she had lain asleep, eighteen years before, that Armand Aubigny riding by and seeing her there, had fallen in love with her. That was the way all the Aubignys fell in love, as if struck by a pistol shot. The wonder was that he had not loved her before; for he had known her since his father brought him home from Paris, a boy of eight, after his mother died there. The passion that awoke in him that day, when he saw her at the gate, swept along like an avalanche, or like a prairie fire, or like anything that drives headlong over all obstacles.

Monsieur Valmondé grew practical and wanted things well considered: that is, the girl's obscure origin. Armand looked into her eyes and did not care. He was reminded that she was nameless. What did it matter about a name when he could give her one of the oldest and proudest in Louisiana? He ordered the *corbeille** from Paris, and contained himself with what patience he could until it arrived; then they were married.

Madame Valmondé had not seen Désirée and the baby for four weeks. When she reached L'Abri she shuddered at the first sight of it, as she always did. It was a sad looking place, which for many years had not known the gentle presence of a mistress, old Monsieur Aubigny having married and buried his wife in France, and she having loved her own land too well ever to leave it. The roof came down steep and black like a cowl, reaching out beyond the wide galleries that encircled the yellow stuccoed house. Big, solemn oaks grew close to it, and their thick-leaved, far-reaching branches shadowed it like a pall. Young Aubigny's rule was a strict one, too, and under it his negroes had forgotten how to be gay, as they had been during the old master's easy-going and indulgent lifetime.

The young mother was recovering slowly, and lay full length, in her soft white muslins and laces, upon a couch. The baby was beside her, upon her arm, where he had fallen asleep, at her breast. The yellow nurse woman sat beside a window fanning herself.

Madame Valmondé bent her portly figure over Désirée and kissed her, holding her an instant tenderly in her arms. Then she turned to the child.

"This is not the baby!" she exclaimed, in startled tones. French was the language spoken at Valmondé in those days.

"I knew you would be astonished," laughed Désirée, "at the way he has grown. The little *cochon de lait*.† Look at his legs, mamma, and his hands and fingernails—real fingernails. Zandrine had to cut them this morning. Isn't it true, Zandrine?"

The woman bowed her turbaned head majestically, "Mais si,‡ Madame."

"And the way he cries," went on Désirée, "is deafening. Armand heard him the other day as far away as La Blanche's cabin."

Madame Valmondé had never removed her eyes from the child. She lifted it and walked with it over to the window that was lightest. She scanned the baby narrowly, then looked as searchingly at Zandrine, whose face was turned to gaze across the fields.

"Yes, the child has grown, has changed," said Madame Valmondé, slowly, as she replaced it beside its mother, "What does Armand say?"

Désirée's face became suffused with a glow that was happiness itself.

"Oh, Armand is the proudest father in the parish, I believe, chiefly because it is a boy, to bear his name; though he says not—that he would have loved a girl as well. But I know it isn't true. I know he says that to please me. And mamma," she added, drawing Madame Valmondé's head down to her, and speaking in a whisper, "he hasn't punished one of them—not one of them—since baby is born. Even Négrillon, who

---

**corbeille* wedding gifts from the groom to the bride.

†*cochon de lait* suckling pig (French)

‡*Mais si* certainly (French).

pretended to have burnt his leg that he might rest from work—he only laughed, and said Négrillon was a great scamp. Oh, mamma, I'm so happy; it frightens me."

What Désirée said was true. Marriage, and later the birth of his son had softened Armand Aubigny's imperious and exacting nature greatly. This was what made the gentle Désirée so happy, for she loved him desperately. When he frowned she trembled, but loved him. When he smiled, she asked no greater blessing of God. But Armand's dark, handsome face had not often been disfigured by frowns since the day he fell in love with her.

When the baby was about three months old, Désirée awoke one day to the conviction that there was something in the air menacing her peace. It was at first too subtle to grasp. It had only been a disquieting suggestion, an air of mystery among the blacks; unexpected visits from far-off neighbors who could hardly account for their coming. Then a strange, an awful change in her husband's manner, which she dared not ask him to explain. When he spoke to her, it was with averted eyes, from which the old love-light seemed to have gone out. He absented himself from home; and when there, avoided her presence and that of her child, without excuse. And the very spirit of Satan seemed suddenly to take hold of him in his dealings with the slaves. Désirée was miserable enough to die.

She sat in her room, one hot afternoon, in her *peignoir*, listlessly drawing through her fingers the strands of her long, silky brown hair that hung about her shoulders. The baby, half naked, lay asleep upon her own great mahogany bed, that was like a sumptuous throne, with its satin-lined half-canopy. One of La Blanche's little quadroon boys—half naked too—stood fanning the child slowly with a fan of peacock feathers. Désirée's eyes had been fixed absently and sadly upon the baby, while she was striving to penetrate the threatening mist that she felt closing about her. She looked from her child to the boy who stood beside him, and back again; over and over. "Ah!" It was a cry that she could not help; which she was not conscious of having uttered. The blood turned like ice in her veins, and a clammy moisture gathered upon her face.

She tried to speak to the little quadroon boy; but no sound would come, at first. When he heard his name uttered, he looked up, and his mistress was pointing to the door. He laid aside the great, soft fan, and obediently stole away, over the polished floor, on his bare tiptoes.

She stayed motionless, with gaze riveted upon her child, and her face the picture of fright.

Presently her husband entered the room, and without noticing her, went to a table and began to search among some papers which covered it.

"Armand," she called to him, in a voice which must have stabbed him, if he was human. But he did not notice. "Armand," she said again. Then she rose and tottered towards him. "Armand," she panted once more, clutching his arm, "look at our child. What does it mean? tell me."

He coldly but gently loosened her fingers from about his arm and thrust the hand away from him. "Tell me what it means!" she cried despairingly.

"It means," he answered lightly, "that the child is not white, it means that you are not white."

A quick conception of all that this accusation meant for her nerved her with unwonted courage to deny it. "It is a lie; it is not true. I am white! Look at my hair, it is brown; and my eyes are gray, Armand, you know they are gray. And my skin is fair," seizing his wrist. "Look at my hand; whiter than yours, Armand," she laughed hysterically.

"As white as La Blanche's," he returned cruelly; and went away leaving her alone with their child.

When she could hold a pen in her hand, she sent a despairing letter to Madame Valmondé.

"My mother, they tell me I am not white. Armand has told me I am not white. For God's sake tell them it is not true. You must know it is not true. I shall die. I must die. I cannot be so unhappy, and live."

The answer that came was as brief.

"My own Désirée: Come home to Valmondé, back to your mother who loves you. Come with your child."

When the letter reached Désirée she went with it to her husband's study, and laid it open upon the desk before which he sat. She was like a stone image; silent, white, motionless after she placed it there.

In silence he ran his cold eyes over the written words. He said nothing. "Shall I go, Armand?" she asked in tones sharp with agonized suspense.

"Yes, go."

"Do you want me to go?"

"Yes, I want you to go."

He thought Almighty God had dealt cruelly and unjustly with him; and felt, somehow, that he was paying Him back in kind when he stabbed thus into his wife's soul. Moreover he no longer loved her, because of the unconscious injury she had brought upon his home and his name.

She turned away like one stunned by a blow, and walked slowly towards the door, hoping he would call her back.

"Good-by, Armand," she moaned.

He did not answer her. That was his last blow at fate.

Désirée went in search of her child. Zandrine was pacing the sombre gallery with it. She took the little one from the nurse's arms with no word of explanation, and descending the steps, walked away, under the live-oak branches.

It was an October afternoon; the sun was just sinking. Out in the still fields the negroes were picking cotton.

Désirée had not changed the thin white garment nor the slippers which she wore. Her hair was uncovered and the sun's rays brought a golden gleam from its brown meshes. She did not take the broad, beaten road which led to the far-off plantation of Valmondé. She walked across a deserted field, where the stubble bruised her tender feet, so delicately shod, and tore her thin gown to shreds.

She disappeared among the reeds and willows that grew thick along the banks of the deep, sluggish bayou, and she did not come back again.

Some weeks later there was a curious scene enacted at L'Abri. In the centre of the smoothly swept back yard was a great bonfire. Armand Aubigny sat in the wide hallway that commanded a view of the spectacle, and it was he who dealt out to a half dozen negroes the material which kept this fire ablaze.

A graceful cradle of willow, with all its dainty furbishings, was laid upon the pyre, which had already been fed with the richness of a priceless *layette*. Then there were silk gowns, and velvet and satin ones added to these; laces, too, and embroideries, bonnets and gloves, for the *corbeille* had been of rare quality.

The last thing to go was a tiny bundle of letters; innocent little scribblings that Désirée had sent to him during the days of their espousal. There was the remnant of one back in the drawer from which he took them. But it was not Désirée's; it was part of an old letter from his mother to his father. He read it. She was thanking God for the blessing of her husband's love:—

> "But, above all," she wrote, "night and day, I thank the good God for having so arranged our lives that our dear Armand will never know that his mother, who adores him, belongs to the race that is cursed with the brand of slavery."

JAMES JOYCE (1882–1941) was the eldest of ten children. He was raised in a borough of Dublin and went to Jesuit boarding school and day school. A consistently good student, he was able to continue his education at University College, Dublin. Following his graduation in 1902, Joyce traveled to continental Europe before returning to Dublin for an extended stay when his mother became ill. After his mother's death, however, Joyce's self-exile on the continent became permanent.

In Europe, Joyce struggled to support himself by teaching English at a Berlitz school while he worked laboriously on the short stories and the semi-autobiographical novel that eventually became *Dubliners* (1914) and *A Portrait of the Artist as a Young Man* (1916). These books and the early sections of Joyce's masterpiece, *Ulysses* (1922), caught the attention of Ezra Pound, who became Joyce's strongest supporter and brought his work to the notice of other expatriate writers in Europe such as T. S. Eliot and Ernest Hemingway.

Joyce's frank treatment of previously taboo subjects such as sex and religion made his writing controversial and difficult to publish. *Ulysses*, his masterpiece, was published in Paris in 1922, but for years remained banned in the United States and Britain. Joyce's final novel, *Finnegans Wake* (1939), pushed the boundaries of language and narrative as it explored nearly every area of human knowledge through the elaborate use of **myths, symbols**, and dreams. In both of these novels, Joyce employs a variety of the experimental styles and techniques that helped define **modernism**, most notably **stream of consciousness**.

Joyce's short stories are less experimental than his novels though they also develop sophisticated symbolic patterns. The stories build toward an **epiphany**, a moment of clear understanding that occurs as the result of a sudden, unexpected insight. "Araby" (1914) provides one of the finest examples of this technique in telling the coming of age story (or **bildungsroman**) of a naïve young boy in the Dublin of Joyce's youth.

Related Works: Chekhov, "Vanka"; Faulkner, "A Rose for Emily"; Ellison, "Battle Royal"; Updike, "A&P"; Bambara, "The Lesson"; Cofer, "Arturo's Flight."

Araby

North Richmond Street, being blind, was a quiet street except at the hour when the Christian Brothers' School set the boys free. An uninhabited house of two storeys stood at the blind end, detached from its neighbours in a square ground.

The other houses of the street, conscious of decent lives within them, gazed at one another with brown imperturbable faces.

The former tenant of our house, a priest, had died in the back drawing-room. Air, musty from having been long enclosed, hung in all the rooms, and the waste room behind the kitchen was littered with old useless papers. Among these I found a few paper-covered books, the pages of which were curled and damp: *The Abbot*, by Walter Scott, *The Devout Communicant* and *The Memoirs of Vidocq*. I liked the last best because its leaves were yellow. The wild garden behind the house contained a central apple-tree and a few straggling bushes under one of which I found the late tenant's rusty bicycle-pump. He had been a very charitable priest; in his will he had left all his money to institutions and the furniture of his house to his sister.

When the short days of winter came dusk fell before we had well eaten our dinners. When we met in the street the houses had grown sombre. The space of sky above us was the colour of ever-changing violet and towards it the lamps of the street lifted their feeble lanterns. The cold air stung us and we played till our bodies glowed. Our shouts echoed in the silent street. The career of our play brought us through the dark muddy lanes behind the houses where we ran the gauntlet of the rough tribes from the cottages, to the back doors of the dark dripping gardens where odours arose from the ashpits, to the dark odorous stables where a coachman smoothed and combed the horse or shook music from the buckled harness. When we returned to the street, light from the kitchen windows had filled the areas. If my uncle was seen turning the corner we hid in the shadow until we had seen him safely housed. Or if Mangan's sister came out on the doorstep to call her brother in to his tea we watched her from our shadow peer up and down the street. We waited to see whether she would remain or go in and, if she remained, we left our shadow and walked up to Mangan's steps resignedly. She was waiting for us, her figure defined by the light from the half-opened door. Her brother always teased her before he obeyed and I stood by the railings looking at her. Her dress swung as she moved her body and the soft rope of her hair tossed from side to side.

Every morning I lay on the floor in the front parlour watching her door. The blind was pulled down to within an inch of the sash so that I could not be seen. When she came out on the doorstep my heart leaped. I ran to the hall, seized my books and followed her. I kept her brown figure always in my eye and, when we came near the point at which our ways diverged, I quickened my pace and passed her. This happened morning after morning. I had never spoken to her, except for a few casual words, and yet her name was like a summons to all my foolish blood.

Her image accompanied me even in places the most hostile to romance. On Saturday evenings when my aunt went marketing I had to go to carry some of the parcels. We walked through the flaring streets, jostled by drunken men and bargaining women, amid the curses of labourers, the shrill litanies of shop-boys who stood on guard by the barrels of pigs' cheeks, the nasal chanting of street-singers, who sang a *come-all-you* about O'Donovan Rossa, or a ballad about the troubles in our native land. These noises converged in a single sensation of life for me: I imagined that I bore my chalice safely through a throng of foes. Her name sprang to my lips at moments in strange prayers and praises which I myself did not understand. My eyes were often full of tears (I could not tell why) and at times a flood from my heart seemed to pour itself out into my bosom. I thought little of the future. I did not know whether I would ever speak to her or not or, if I spoke to her, how I could tell her of my confused adoration. But my body was like a harp and her words and gestures were like fingers running upon the wires.

One evening I went into the back drawing-room in which the priest had died. It was a dark rainy evening and there was no sound in the house. Through one of the broken panes I heard the rain impinge upon the earth, the fine incessant needles of water playing in the sodden beds. Some distant lamp or lighted window gleamed below me. I was thankful that I could see so little. All my senses seemed to desire to veil themselves and, feeling that I was about to slip from them, I pressed the palms of my hands together until they trembled, murmuring: "*O love! O love!*" many times.

At last she spoke to me. When she addressed the first words to me I was so confused that I did not know what to answer. She asked me was I going to *Araby*. I forgot whether I answered yes or no. It would be a splendid bazaar, she said she would love to go.

"And why can't you?" I asked.

While she spoke she turned a silver bracelet round and round her wrist. She could not go, she said, because there would be a retreat that week in her convent. Her brother and two other boys were fighting for their caps and I was alone at the railings. She held one of the spikes, bowing her head towards me. The light from the lamp opposite our door caught the white curve of her neck, lit up her hair that rested there and, falling, lit up the hand upon the railing. It fell over one side of her dress and caught the white border of a petticoat, just visible as she stood at ease.

"It's well for you," she said.

"If I go," I said, "I will bring you something."

What innumerable follies laid waste my waking and sleeping thoughts after that evening! I wished to annihilate the tedious intervening days. I chafed against the work of school. At night in my bedroom and by day in the classroom her image came between me and the page I strove to read. The syllables of the word *Araby* were called to me through the silence in which my soul luxuriated and cast an Eastern enchantment over me. I asked for leave to go to the bazaar on Saturday night. My aunt was surprised and hoped it was not some Freemason affair. I answered few questions in class. I watched my master's face pass from amiability to sternness; he hoped I was not beginning to idle. I could not call my wandering thoughts together. I had hardly any patience with the serious work of life which, now that it stood between me and my desire, seemed to me child's play, ugly monotonous child's play.

On Saturday morning I reminded my uncle that I wished to go to the bazaar in the evening. He was fussing at the hallstand, looking for the hat-brush, and answered me curtly:

"Yes, boy, I know."

As he was in the hall I could not go into the front parlour and lie at the window. I left the house in bad humour and walked slowly towards the school. The air was pitilessly raw and already my heart misgave me.

When I came home to dinner my uncle had not yet been home. Still it was early. I sat staring at the clock for some time and, when its ticking began to irritate me, I left the room. I mounted the staircase and gained the upper part of the house. The high cold empty gloomy rooms liberated me and I went from room to room singing. From the front window I saw my companions playing below in the street. Their cries reached me weakened and indistinct and, leaning my forehead against the cool glass, I looked over at the dark house where she lived. I may have stood there for an hour, seeing nothing but the brown-clad figure cast by my imagination, touched discreetly by the lamplight at the curved neck, at the hand upon the railings and at the border below the dress.

When I came downstairs again I found Mrs. Mercer sitting at the fire. She was an old garrulous woman, a pawnbroker's widow, who collected used stamps for some pious purpose. I had to endure the gossip of the tea-table. The meal was prolonged beyond an hour and still my uncle did not come. Mrs. Mercer stood up to go: she was sorry she couldn't wait any longer, but it was after eight o'clock and she did not like to be out late, as the night air was bad for her. When she had gone I began to walk up and down the room, clenching my fists. My aunt said:

"I'm afraid you may put off your bazaar for this night of Our Lord."

At nine o'clock I heard my uncle's latchkey in the halldoor. I heard him talking to himself and heard the hallstand rocking when it had received the weight of his overcoat. I could interpret these signs. When he was midway through his dinner I asked him to give me the money to go to the bazaar. He had forgotten.

"The people are in bed and after their first sleep now," he said.

I did not smile. My aunt said to him energetically:

"Can't you give him the money and let him go? You've kept him late enough as it is."

My uncle said he was very sorry he had forgotten. He said he believed in the old saying; "All work and no play makes Jack a dull boy." He asked me where I was going and, when I had told him a second time he asked me did I know *The Arab's Farewell to his Steed*. When I left the kitchen he was about to recite the opening lines of the piece to my aunt.

I held a florin tightly in my hand as I strode down Buckingham Street towards the station. The sight of the streets thronged with buyers and glaring with gas recalled to me the purpose of my journey. I took my seat in a third-class carriage of a deserted train. After an intolerable delay the train moved out of the station slowly. It crept onward among ruinous houses and over the twinkling river. At Westland Row Station a crowd of people pressed to the carriage doors; but the porters moved them back, saying that it was a special train for the bazaar. I remained alone in the bare carriage. In a few minutes the train drew up beside an improvised wooden platform. I passed out on to the road and saw by the lighted dial of a clock that it was ten minutes to ten. In front of me was a large building which displayed the magical name.

I could not find any sixpenny entrance and, fearing that the bazaar would be closed, I passed in quickly through a turnstile, handing a shilling to a weary-looking man. I found myself in a big hall girdled at half its height by a gallery. Nearly all the stalls were closed and the greater part of the hall was in darkness. I recognised a silence like that which pervades a church after a service. I walked into the centre of the bazaar timidly. A few people were gathered about the stalls which were still open. Before a curtain, over which the words *Café Chantant* were written in coloured lamps, two men were counting money on a salver. I listened to the fall of the coins.

Remembering with difficulty why I had come I went over to one of the stalls and examined porcelain vases and flowered tea-sets. At the door of the stall a young lady was talking and laughing with two young gentlemen. I remarked their English accents and listened vaguely to their conversation.

"O, I never said such a thing!"

"O, but you did!"

"O, but I didn't!"

"Didn't she say that?"

"Yes. I heard her."

"O, there's a . . . fib!"

Observing me the young lady came over and asked me did I wish to buy anything. The tone of her voice was not encouraging; she seemed to have spoken to me out of a sense of duty. I looked humbly at the great jars that stood like eastern guards at either side of the dark entrance to the stall and murmured:

"No, thank you."

The young lady changed the position of one of the vases and went back to the two young men. They began to talk of the same subject. Once or twice the young lady glanced at me over her shoulder.

I lingered before her stall, though I knew my stay was useless, to make my interest in her wares seem the more real. Then I turned away slowly and walked down the middle of the bazaar. I allowed the two pennies to fall against the sixpence in my pocket. I heard a voice call from one end of the gallery that the light was out. The upper part of the hall was now completely dark.

Gazing up into the darkness I saw myself as a creature driven and derided by vanity; and my eyes burned with anguish and anger.

Franz Kafka (1883–1924) was the only son born to Jewish parents in Prague. His father was a strict authoritarian with whom Kafka had an extremely strained relationship. Kafka attended a German-speaking university in Prague and received his doctorate in law. He worked for a time at an insurance firm and began publishing fiction in literary magazines in Munich. He was involved in several romances, but never married. His first collection of stories was published as *Meditation* in 1912. He published five more short story collections in the years following, but his novels, including *The Trial* (1925), were not published until after his death.

Not surprisingly, much of Kafka's fiction focuses on estranged relationships between people and the anxiety and alienation individuals feel as they try to survive amid the instability and cruelty of the world around them. Kafka's own despondency with the conditions of his life haunts his fiction, yet gives his characters universal appeal as they try to overcome their distress and guilt in an indifferent world.

"The Metamorphosis" (1915) is a **surreal** tale in which Gregor Samsa is literally transformed by his anxiety and shame. The story is **episodic**; it occurs in three "acts," one for each moment Gregor emerges from his room.

Related Works: Marquez, "Handsomest Drowned Man in the World"; Cofer, "Tales Told under the Mango Tree"; Erdrich, "The Red Convertible"; Strand, "Eating Poetry"; Norman, *'Night Mother*.

FRANZ KAFKA

The Metamorphosis

I

As Gregor Samsa awoke one morning from uneasy dreams he found himself transformed in his bed into a gigantic insect. He was lying on his hard, as it were armor-plated, back and when he lifted his head a little he could see his dome-like brown belly divided into stiff arched segments on top of which the bed quilt could hardly keep in position and was about to slide off completely. His numerous legs, which were pitifully thin compared to the rest of his bulk, waved helplessly before his eyes.

What has happened to me? he thought. It was no dream. His room, a regular human bedroom, only rather too small, lay quiet between the four familiar walls. Above the table on which a collection of cloth samples was unpacked and spread out—Samsa was a commercial traveler—hung the picture which he had recently cut out of an illustrated magazine and put into a pretty gilt frame. It showed a lady, with a fur cap on and a fur stole, sitting upright and holding out to the spectator a huge fur muff into which the whole of her forearm had vanished!

Gregor's eyes turned next to the window, and the overcast sky—one could hear rain drops beating on the window gutter—made him quite melancholy. What about sleeping a little longer and forgetting all this nonsense, he thought, but it could not be done, for he was accustomed to sleep on his right side and in his present condition he could not turn himself over. However violently he forced himself towards his right side he always rolled on to his back again. He tried it at least a hundred times, shutting his eyes to keep from seeing his struggling legs, and only desisted when he began to feel in his side a faint dull ache he had never experienced before.

Oh God, he thought, what an exhausting job I've picked on! Traveling about day in, day out. It's much more irritating work than doing the actual business in the office, and on top of that there's the trouble of constant traveling, of worrying about train connections, the bed and irregular meals, casual acquaintances that are always new and never become intimate friends. The devil take it all! He felt a slight itching up on his belly; slowly pushed himself on his back nearer to the top of the bed so that he could lift his head more easily; identified the itching place which was surrounded by many small white spots the nature of which he could not understand and made to touch it with a leg, but drew the leg back immediately, for the contact made a cold shiver run through him.

He slid down again into his former position. This getting up early, he thought, makes one quite stupid. A man needs his sleep. Other commercials live like harem women. For instance, when I come back to the hotel of a morning to write up the orders I've got, these others are only sitting down to breakfast. Let me just try that with my chief; I'd be sacked on the spot. Anyhow, that might be quite a good thing for me, who can tell? If I didn't have to hold my hand because of my parents I'd have given notice long ago, I'd have gone to the chief and told him exactly what I think of him. That would knock him endways from his desk! It's a queer way of doing, too, this sitting on high at a desk and talking down to employees, especially when they have to come quite near because the chief is hard of hearing. Well, there's still hope; once I've saved enough money to pay back my parents' debts to him—that should take another five or six years—I'll do it without fail. I'll cut myself completely loose then. For the moment, though, I'd better get up, since my train goes at five.

He looked at the alarm clock ticking on the chest. Heavenly Father! he thought. It was half-past six o'clock and the hands were quietly moving on, it was even past the half-hour, it was getting on toward a quarter to seven. Had the alarm clock not gone off? From the bed one could see that it had been properly set for four o'clock; of course it must have gone off. Yes, but was it possible to sleep quietly through that ear-splitting noise? Well, he had not slept quietly, yet apparently all the more soundly for that. But what was he to do now? The next train went at seven o'clock; to catch that he would need to hurry like mad and his samples weren't even packed up, and he himself wasn't feeling particularly fresh and active. And even if he did catch the train he wouldn't avoid a row with the chief, since the firm's porter would have been waiting for the five o'clock train and would have long since reported his failure to turn up. The porter was a creature of the chief's, spineless and stupid. Well, supposing he were to say he was sick? But that would be most unpleasant and would look suspicious, since during his five years' employment he had not been ill once. The chief himself would be sure to come with the sick-insurance doctor, would reproach his parents with their son's laziness and would cut all excuses short by referring to the insurance doctor, who of course regarded all mankind as perfectly healthy malingerers. And would he be so far wrong on this occasion? Gregor really felt quite well, apart from a drowsiness that was utterly superfluous after such a long sleep, and he was even unusually hungry.

As all this was running through his mind at top speed without his being able to decide to leave his bed—the alarm clock had just struck a quarter to seven—there came a cautious tap at the door behind the head of his bed. "Gregor," said a voice—it was his mother's—"it's a quarter to seven. Hadn't you a train to catch?" That gentle voice! Gregor had a shock as he heard his own voice answering hers, unmistakably his own voice, it was true, but with a persistent horrible twittering squeak behind it like an undertone, that left the words in their clear shape only for the first moment and then rose up reverberating round them to destroy their sense, so that one could not be sure one had heard them rightly. Gregor wanted to answer at length and explain everything, but in the circumstances he confined himself to saying: "Yes, yes, thank you, Mother, I'm getting up now." The wooden door between them must have kept the change in his voice from being noticeable outside, for his mother contented herself with this statement and shuffled away. Yet this brief exchange of words had made the other members of the family aware that Gregor was still in the house, as they had not expected, and at one of the side doors his father was already knocking, gently, yet with his fist. "Gregor, Gregor," he called, "what's the matter with you?" And after a little while he called again in a deeper voice: "Gregor! Gregor!" At the other side door his sister was saying in a low, plaintive tone: "Gregor? Aren't you well? Are you needing anything?" He answered them both at once: "I'm just ready," and did his best to make his voice sound as normal as possible by enunciating the words very clearly and leaving long pauses between them. So his father went back to his breakfast, but his sister whispered: "Gregor, open the door, do." However, he was not thinking of opening the door, and felt thankful for the prudent habit he had acquired in traveling of locking all doors during the night, even at home.

His immediate intention was to get up quietly without being disturbed, to put on his clothes and above all eat his breakfast, and only then to consider what else was to be done, since in bed, he was well aware, his meditations would come to no sensible conclusion. He remembered that often enough in bed he had felt small aches and pains, probably caused by awkward postures, which had proved purely imaginary once he got up, and he looked forward eagerly to seeing this morning's delusions gradually fall away. That the change in his voice was nothing but the precursor of a severe chill, a standing ailment of commercial travelers, he had not the least possible doubt.

To get rid of the quilt was quite easy; he had only to inflate himself a little and it fell off by itself. But the next move was difficult, especially because he was so uncommonly broad. He would have needed arms and hands to hoist himself up; instead he had only the numerous little legs which never stopped waving in all directions and which he could not control in the least. When he tried to bend one of them it was the first to stretch itself straight; and did he succeed at last in making it do what he wanted, all the other legs meanwhile waved the more wildly in a high degree of unpleasant agitation. "But what's the use of lying idle in bed," said Gregor to himself.

He thought that he might get out of bed with the lower part of his body first, but this lower part, which he had not yet seen and of which he could form no clear conception, proved too difficult to move; it shifted so slowly; and when finally, almost wild with annoyance, he gathered his forces together and thrust out recklessly, he had miscalculated the direction and bumped heavily against the lower end of the bed, and the stinging pain he felt informed him that precisely this lower part of his body was at the moment probably the most sensitive.

So he tried to get the top part of himself out first, and cautiously moved his head towards the edge of the bed. That proved easy enough, and despite its breadth and mass the bulk of his body at last slowly followed the movement of his head. Still, when he finally got his head free over the edge of the bed he felt too scared to go on advancing, for after all if he let himself fall in this way it would take a miracle to keep his head from being injured. And at all costs he must not lose consciousness now, precisely now; he would rather stay in bed.

But when after a repetition of the same efforts he lay in his former position again, sighing, and watched his little legs struggling against each other more wildly than ever, if that were possible, and saw no way of bringing any order into this arbitrary confusion, he told himself again that it was impossible to stay in bed and that the most sensible course was to risk everything for the smallest hope of getting away from it. At the same time he did not forget meanwhile to remind himself that cool reflection, the coolest possible, was much better than desperate resolves. In such moments he focused his eyes as sharply as possible on the window, but, unfortunately, the prospect of the morning fog, which muffled even the other side of the narrow street, brought him little encouragement and comfort. "Seven o'clock already," he said to himself when the alarm clock chimed again, "seven o'clock already and still such a thick fog." And for a little while he lay quiet, breathing lightly, as if perhaps expecting such complete repose to restore all things to their real and normal condition.

But then he said to himself: "Before it strikes a quarter past seven I must be quite out of this bed, without fail. Anyhow, by that time someone will have come from the office to ask for me, since it opens before seven." And he set himself to rocking his whole body at once in a regular rhythm, with the idea of swinging it out of the bed. If he tipped himself out in that way he could keep his head from injury by lifting it at an acute angle when he fell. His back seemed to be hard and was not likely to suffer from a fall on the carpet. His biggest worry was the loud crash he would not be able to help making, which would probably cause anxiety, if not terror, behind all the doors. Still, he must take the risk.

When he was already half out of the bed—the new method was more a game than an effort, for he needed only to hitch himself across by rocking to and fro—it struck him how simple it would be if he could get help. Two strong people—he thought of his father and the servant girl—would be amply sufficient; they would only have to thrust their arms under his convex back, lever him out of the bed, bend down with their burden and then be patient enough to let him turn himself right over on to the floor, where it was to be hoped his legs would then find their proper function. Well, ignoring the fact that the doors were all locked, ought he really to call for help? In spite of his misery he could not suppress a smile at the very idea of it.

He had got so far that he could barely keep his equilibrium when he rocked himself strongly, and he would have to nerve himself very soon for the final decision since in five minutes' time it would be a quarter past seven—when the front door bell rang. "That's someone from the office," he said to himself, and grew almost rigid, while his little legs only jigged about all the faster. For a moment everything stayed quiet. "They're not going to open the door," said Gregor to himself, catching at some kind of irrational hope. But then of course the servant girl went as usual to the door with her heavy tread and opened it. Gregor needed only to hear the first good morning of the visitor to know immediately who it was—the chief clerk himself. What a fate, to be condemned to work for a firm where the smallest omission at once gave rise to the gravest suspicion! Were all employees in a body nothing but scoundrels, was there not among them one single loyal devoted man who, had he wasted only an hour or so of the firm's time in a morning, was so tormented by conscience as to be driven out of his mind and actually incapable of leaving his bed? Wouldn't it really have been sufficient to send an apprentice to inquire—if any inquiry were necessary at all—did the chief clerk himself have to come and thus indicate to the entire family, an innocent family, that this suspicious circumstance could be investigated by no one less versed in affairs than himself? And more through the agitation caused by these reflections than through any act of will Gregor swung himself out of bed with all his strength. There was a loud thump, but it was not really a crash. His fall was broken to some extent by the carpet, his back, too, was less stiff than he thought, and so there was merely a dull thud, not so very startling. Only he had not lifted his head carefully enough and had hit it; he turned it and rubbed it on the carpet in pain and irritation.

"That was something falling down in there," said the chief clerk in the next room to the left. Gregor tried to suppose to himself that something like what had happened to him today might some day happen to the chief clerk; one really could not deny that it was possible. But as if in brusque reply to this supposition the chief clerk took a couple of firm steps in the next-door room and his patent leather boots creaked. From the right-hand room his sister was whispering to inform him of the situation: "Gregor, the chief clerk's here." "I know," muttered Gregor to himself; but he didn't dare to make his voice loud enough for his sister to hear it.

"Gregor," said his father now from the left-hand room, "the chief clerk has come and wants to know why you didn't catch the early train. We don't know what to say to him. Besides, he wants to talk to you in person. So open the door, please. He will be good enough to excuse the untidiness of your room." "Good morning, Mr. Samsa," the chief clerk was calling amiably meanwhile. "He's not well," said his mother to the visitor, while his father was still speaking through the door, "he's not well, sir, believe me. What else would make him miss a train! The boy thinks about nothing but his work. It makes me almost cross the way he never goes out in the evenings; he's been here the last eight days and has stayed at home every single evening. He just sits there quietly at the table reading a newspaper or looking through railway timetables. The only amusement he gets is doing fretwork. For instance, he spent two or three evenings cutting out a little picture frame; you would be surprised to see how pretty it is; it's hanging in his room; you'll see it in a minute when Gregor opens the door. I must say I'm glad you've come, sir; we should never have got him to unlock the door by ourselves; he's so obstinate; and I'm sure he's unwell, though he wouldn't have it to be so this morning." "I'm just coming," said Gregor slowly and carefully, not moving an inch for fear of losing one word of the conversation. "I can't think of any other explanation, madam," said the chief clerk, "I hope it's nothing serious. Although on the other hand I must say that we men of business—fortunately or unfortunately—very often simply have to ignore any slight indisposition, since business must be attended to." "Well, can the chief clerk come in now?" asked Gregor's father impatiently, again knocking on the door. "No," said Gregor. In the left-hand room a painful silence followed this refusal, in the right-hand room his sister began to sob.

Why didn't his sister join the others? She was probably newly out of bed and hadn't even begun to put on her clothes yet. Well, why was she crying? Because he wouldn't get up and let the chief clerk in, because he was in danger of losing his job, and because the chief would begin dunning his parents again for the old debts? Surely these were things one didn't need to worry about for the present. Gregor was still at home and not in the least thinking of deserting the family. At the moment, true, he was lying on the carpet and no one who knew the condition he was in could seriously expect him to admit the chief clerk. But for such a small discourtesy, which could plausibly be explained away somehow later on, Gregor could hardly be dismissed on the spot. And it seemed to Gregor that it would be much more sensible to leave him in peace for the present than to trouble him with tears and entreaties. Still, of course, their uncertainty bewildered them all and excused their behavior.

"Mr. Samsa," the chief clerk called now in a louder voice, "what's the matter with you? Here you are, barricading yourself in your room, giving only 'yes' and 'no' for answers, causing your parents a lot of unnecessary trouble and neglecting—I mention this only in passing—neglecting your business duties in an incredible fashion. I am speaking here in the name of your parents and of your chief, and I beg you quite seriously to give me an immediate and precise explanation. You amaze me, you amaze me. I thought you were a quiet, dependable person, and now all at once you seem bent on making a disgraceful exhibition of yourself. The chief did hint to me early this morning a possible explanation for your disappearance—with reference to the cash payments that were entrusted to you recently—but I almost pledged my solemn word of honor that this could not be so. But now that I see how incredibly obstinate you are, I no longer have the slightest desire to take your part at all. And your position in the firm is not so unassailable. I came with the intention of telling you all this in private, but since you are wasting my time so needlessly I don't see why your parents shouldn't hear it too. For some time past your work has been most unsatisfactory; this is not the season of the year for a business boom, of course, we admit that, but a season of the year for doing no business at all, that does not exist, Mr. Samsa, must not exist."

"But, sir," cried Gregor, beside himself and in his agitation forgetting everything else, "I'm just going to open the door this very minute. A slight illness, an attack of giddiness, has kept me from getting up. I'm still lying in bed. But I feel all right again. I'm getting out of bed now. Just give me a moment or two longer! I'm not quite so well as I thought. But I'm all right, really. How a thing like that can suddenly strike one down! Only last night I was quite well, my parents can tell you, or rather I did have a slight presentiment, I must have showed some sign of it. Why didn't I report it at the office! But one always thinks that an indisposition can be got over without staying in the house. Oh sir, do spare my parents! All that you're reproaching me with now has no foundation; no one has ever said a word to me about it. Perhaps you haven't looked at the last orders I sent in. Anyhow, I can still catch the eight o'clock train, I'm much the better for my few hours' rest. Don't let me detain you here, sir; I'll be attending to business very soon, and do be good enough to tell the chief so and to make my excuses to him!"

And while all this was tumbling out pell-mell and Gregor hardly knew what he was saying, he had reached the chest quite easily, perhaps because of the practice he had had in bed, and was now trying to lever himself upright by means of it. He meant actually to open the door, actually to show himself and speak to the chief clerk; he was eager to find out what the others, after all their insistence, would say at the sight of him. If they were horrified then the responsibility was no longer his and he could stay quiet. But if they took it calmly, then he had no reason either to be upset, and could really get to the station for the eight o'clock train if he hurried. At first he slipped down a few times from the polished surface of the chest, but at length with a last heave he stood upright; he paid no more attention to the pains in the lower part of his body, however they smarted. Then he let himself fall against the back of a near-by chair, and clung with his little legs to the edges of it. That brought him into control of himself again and he stopped speaking, for now he could listen to what the chief clerk was saying.

"Did you understand a word of it?" the chief clerk was asking; "surely he can't be trying to make fools of us?" "Oh dear," cried his mother, in tears, "perhaps he's terribly ill and we're tormenting him. Grete! Grete!" she called out then. "Yes Mother?" called his sister from the other side. They were calling to each other across Gregor's room. "You must go this minute for the doctor. Gregor is ill. Go for the doctor, quick. Did you hear how he was speaking?" "That was no human voice," said the chief clerk in a voice noticeably low beside the shrillness of the mother's. "Anna! Anna!" his father was calling through the hall to the kitchen, clapping his hands, "get a locksmith at once!" And the two girls were already running through the hall with a swish of skirts—how could his sister have got dressed so quickly?—and were tearing the front door open. There was no sound of its closing again; they had evidently left it open, as one does in houses where some great misfortune has happened.

But Gregor was now much calmer. The words he uttered were no longer understandable, apparently, although they seemed clear enough to him, even clearer than before, perhaps because his ear had grown accustomed to the sound of them. Yet at any rate people now believed that something was wrong with him, and were ready to help him. The positive certainty with which these first measures had been taken comforted him. He felt himself drawn once more into the human circle and hoped for great and remarkable results from both the doctor and the locksmith, without really distinguishing precisely between them. To make his voice as clear as possible for the decisive conversation that was now imminent he coughed a little, as quietly as he could, of course, since this noise too might not sound like a human cough for all he was able to judge. In the next room meanwhile there was complete silence. Perhaps his parents were sitting at the table with the chief clerk, whispering, perhaps they were all leaning against the door and listening.

Slowly Gregor pushed the chair towards the door, then let go of it, caught hold of the door for support—the soles at the end of his little legs were somewhat sticky—and rested against it for a moment after his efforts. Then he set himself to turning the key in the lock with his mouth. It seemed, unhappily, that he hadn't really any teeth—what could he grip the key with?—but on the other hand his jaws were certainly very strong; with their help he did manage to set the key in motion, heedless of the fact that he was undoubtedly damaging them somewhere, since a brown fluid issued from his mouth, flowed over the key and dripped on the floor. "Just listen to that," said the chief clerk next door; "he's turning the key." That was a great encouragement to Gregor; but they should all have shouted encouragement to him, his father and mother too: "Go on, Gregor," they should have called out, "keep going, hold on to that key!" And in the belief that they were all following his efforts intently, he clenched his jaws recklessly on the key with all the force at his command. As the turning of the key progressed he circled round the lock, holding on now only with his mouth, pushing on the key, as required, or pulling it down again with all the weight of his body. The louder click of the finally yielding lock literally quickened Gregor. With a deep breath of relief he said to himself: "So I didn't need the locksmith," and laid his head on the handle to open the door wide.

Since he had to pull the door towards him, he was still invisible when it was really wide open. He had to edge himself slowly round the near half of the double door, and to do it very carefully if he was not to fall plump upon his back just on the threshold. He was still carrying out this difficult manoeuvre, with no time to observe anything else, when he heard the chief clerk utter a loud "Oh!"—it sounded like a gust of wind—and now he could see the man, standing as he was nearest to the door, clapping one hand before his open mouth and slowly backing away as if driven by some invisible steady pressure. His mother—in spite of the chief clerk's being there her hair was still undone and sticking up in all directions—first clasped her hands and looked at his father, then took two steps towards Gregor and fell on the floor among her outspread skirts, her face quite hidden on her breast. His father knotted his fist with a fierce expression on his face as if he meant to knock Gregor back into his room, then looked uncertainly round the living room, covered his eyes with his hands and wept till his great cheat heaved.

Gregor did not go now into the living room, but leaned against the inside of the firmly shut wing of the door, so that only half his body was visible and his head above it bending sideways to look at the others. The light had meanwhile strengthened; on the other side of the street one could see clearly a section of the endlessly long, dark gray building opposite—it was a hospital—abruptly punctuated by its row of regular windows; the rain was still falling, but only in large singly discernible and literally singly splashing drops. The breakfast dishes were set out on the table lavishly, for breakfast was the most important meal of the day to Gregor's father, who lingered it out for hours over various newspapers. Right opposite Gregor on the wall hung a photograph of himself on military service, as a lieutenant, hand on sword, a carefree smile on his face, inviting one to respect his uniform and military bearing. The door leading to the hall was open, and one could see that the front door stood open too, showing the landing beyond and the beginning of the stairs going down.

"Well," said Gregor, knowing perfectly that he was the only one who had retained any composure, "I'll put my clothes on at once, pack up my samples and start off. Will you only let me go? You see, sir, I'm not obstinate, and I'm willing to work; traveling is a hard life, but I couldn't live without it. Where are you going, sir? To the office? Yes? Will you give a true account of all this? One can be temporarily incapacitated, but that's just the moment for remembering former services and bearing in mind that later on, when the incapacity has been got over, one will certainly work with all the more industry and concentration. I'm loyally bound to serve the chief, you know that very well. Besides, I have to provide for my parents and my sister. I'm in great difficulties, but I'll get out of them again. Don't make things any worse for me than they are. Stand up for me in the firm. Travelers are not popular there, I know. People think they earn sacks of money and just have a good time. A prejudice there's no particular reason for revising. But you, sir, have a more comprehensive view of affairs than the rest of the staff, yes, let me tell you in confidence, a more comprehensive view than the chief himself, who, being the owner, lets his judgment easily be swayed against one of his employees. And you know very well that the traveler, who is never seen in the office almost the whole year round, can so easily fall a victim to gossip and ill luck and unfounded complaints, which he mostly knows nothing about, except when he comes back exhausted from his rounds, and only then suffers in person from their evil consequences, which he can no longer trace back to the original causes. Sir, sir, don't go away without a word to me to show that you think me in the right at least to some extent!"

But at Gregor's very first words the chief clerk had already backed away and only stared at him with parted lips over one twitching shoulder. And while Gregor was speaking he did not stand still one moment but stole away towards the door, without taking his eyes off Gregor, yet only an inch at a time, as if obeying some secret injunction to leave the room. He was already at the hall, and the suddenness with which he took his last step out of the living room would have made one believe he had burned the sole of his foot. Once in the hall he stretched his right arm before him towards the staircase, as if some supernatural power were waiting there to deliver him.

Gregor perceived that the chief clerk must on no account be allowed to go away in this frame of mind if his position in the firm were not to be endangered to the utmost. His parents did not understand this so well; they had convinced themselves in the course of years that Gregor was settled for life in this firm, and besides they were so preoccupied with their immediate troubles that all foresight had forsaken them. Yet Gregor had this foresight. The chief clerk must be detained, soothed, persuaded and finally won over; the whole future of Gregor and his family depended on it! If only his sister had been there! She was intelligent; she had begun to cry while Gregor was still lying quietly on his back. And no doubt the chief clerk, so partial to ladies, would have been guided by her; she would have shut the door of the flat and in the hall talked him out of his horror. But she was not there, and Gregor would have to handle the situation himself. And without remembering that he was still unaware what powers of movement he possessed, without even remembering that his words in all possibility, indeed in all likelihood, would again be unintelligible, he let go the wing of the door, pushed himself through the opening, started to walk towards the chief clerk, who was already ridiculously clinging with both hands to the railing on the landing; but immediately, as he was feeling for a support, he fell down with a little cry upon all his numerous legs. Hardly was he down when he experienced for the first time this morning a sense of physical comfort; his legs had firm ground under them; they were completely obedient, as he noted with joy; they even strove to carry him forward in whatever direction he chose; and he was inclined to believe that a final relief from all his sufferings was at hand. But in the same moment as he found himself on the floor, rocking with suppressed eagerness to move, not far from his mother, indeed just in front of her, she, who had seemed so completely crushed, sprang all at once to her feet, her arms and fingers outspread, cried: "Help, for God's sake, help!" bent her head down as if to see Gregor better, yet on the contrary kept backing senselessly away; had quite forgotten that the laden table stood behind her; sat upon it hastily, as if in absence of mind, when she bumped into it; and seemed altogether unaware that the big coffee pot beside her was upset and pouring coffee in a flood over the carpet.

"Mother, Mother," said Gregor in a low voice, and looked up at her. The chief clerk, for the moment, had quite slipped from his mind; instead, he could not resist snapping his jaws together at the sight of the streaming coffee. That made his mother scream again, she fled from the table and fell into the arms of his father, who hastened to catch her. But Gregor had now no time to spare for his parents; the chief clerk was already on the stairs; with his chin on the banisters he was taking one last backward look. Gregor made a spring, to be as sure as possible of overtaking him; the chief clerk must have divined his intention, for he leaped down several steps and vanished; he was still yelling "Ugh!" and it echoed through the whole staircase.

Unfortunately, the flight of the chief clerk seemed completely to upset Gregor's father, who had remained relatively calm until now, for instead of running after the man himself, or at least not hindering Gregor in his pursuit, he seized in his right hand the walking stick which the chief clerk had left behind on a chair, together with a hat and greatcoat, snatched in his left hand a large newspaper from the table and began stamping his feet and flourishing the stick and the newspaper to drive Gregor back into his room. No entreaty of Gregor's availed, indeed no entreaty was even understood, however humbly he bent his head his father only stamped on the floor the more loudly. Behind his father his mother had torn open a window, despite the cold weather, and was leaning far out of it with her face in her hands. A strong draught set in from the street to the staircase, the window curtains blew in, the newspapers on the table fluttered, stray pages whisked over the floor. Pitilessly Gregor's father drove him back, hissing and crying "Shoo!" like a savage. But Gregor was quite unpracticed in walking backwards, it really was a slow business. If he only had a chance to turn round he could get back to his room at once, but he was afraid of exasperating his father by the slowness of such a rotation and at any moment the stick in his father's hand might hit him a fatal blow on the back or on the head. In the end, however, nothing else was left for him to do since to his horror he observed that in moving backwards he could not even control the direction he took; and so, keeping an anxious eye on his father all the time over his shoulder, he began to turn round as quickly as he could, which was in reality very slowly. Perhaps his father noted his good intentions, for he did not interfere except every now and then to help him in the manoeuvre from a distance with the point of the stick. If only he would have stopped making that unbearable hissing noise! It made Gregor quite lose his head. He had turned almost completely round when the hissing noise so distracted him that he even turned a little the wrong way again. But when at last his head was fortunately right in front of the doorway, it appeared that his body was too broad simply to get through the opening. His father, of course, in his present mood was far from thinking of such a thing as opening the other half of the door, to let Gregor have enough space. He had merely the fixed idea of driving Gregor back into his room as quickly as possible. He would never have suffered Gregor to make the circumstantial preparations for standing up on end and perhaps slipping his way through the door. Maybe he was now making more noise than ever to urge Gregor forward, as if no obstacle impeded him; to Gregor, anyhow, the noise in his rear sounded no longer like the voice of one single father; this was really no joke, and Gregor thrust himself—come what might—into the doorway. One side of his body rose up, he was tilted at an angle in the doorway, his flank was quite bruised, horrid blotches stained the white door, soon he was stuck fast and, left to himself, could not have moved at all, his legs on one side fluttered trembling in the air, those on the other were crushed painfully to the floor—when from behind his father gave him a strong push which was literally a deliverance and he flew far into the room, bleeding freely. The door was slammed behind him with the stick, and then at last there was silence.

II

Not until it was twilight did Gregor awake out of a deep sleep, more like a swoon than a sleep. He would certainly have waked up of his own accord not much later, for he felt himself sufficiently rested and well-slept, but it seemed to him as if a fleeting step and a cautious shutting of the door leading into the hall had aroused him. The electric lights in the street cast a pale sheen here and there on the ceiling and the upper surfaces of the furniture, but down below, where he lay, it was dark. Slowly, awkwardly trying out his feelers, which he now first learned to appreciate, he pushed his way to the door to see what had been happening there. His left side felt like one single long, unpleasantly tense scar, and he had actually to limp on his two rows of legs. One little leg, moreover, had been severely damaged in the course of that morning's events—it was almost a miracle that only one had been damaged—and trailed uselessly behind him.

He had reached the door before he discovered what had really drawn him to it: the smell of food. For there stood a basin filled with fresh milk in which floated little sops of white bread. He could almost have laughed with joy, since he was now still hungrier than in the morning, and he dipped his head almost over the eyes straight into the milk. But soon in disappointment he withdrew it again; not only did he find it difficult to feed because of his tender left side—and he could only feed with the palpitating collaboration of his whole body—he did not like the milk either, although milk had been his favorite drink and that was certainly why his sister had set it there for him, indeed it was almost with repulsion that he turned away from the basin and crawled back to the middle of the room.

He could see through the crack of the door that the gas was turned on in the living room, but while usually at this time his father made a habit of reading the afternoon newspaper in a loud voice to his mother and occasionally to his sister as well, not a sound was now to be heard. Well, perhaps his father had recently given up this habit of reading aloud, which his sister had mentioned so often in conversation and in her letters. But there was the same silence all around, although the flat was certainly not empty of occupants. "What a quiet life our family has been leading," said Gregor to himself, and as he sat there motionless staring into the darkness be felt great pride in the fact that he had been able to provide such a life for his parents and sister in such a fine flat. But what if all the quiet, the comfort, the contentment were now to end in horror? To keep himself from being lost in such thoughts Gregor took refuge in movement and crawled up and down the room.

Once during the long evening one of the side doors was opened a little and quickly shut again, later the other side door too; someone had apparently wanted to come in and then thought better of it. Gregor now stationed himself immediately before the living room door, determined to persuade any hesitating visitor to come in or at least to discover who it might be; but the door was not opened again and he waited in vain. In the early morning, when the doors were locked, they had all wanted to come in; now that he had opened one door and the other had apparently been opened during the day, no one came in and even the keys were on the other side of the doors.

It was late at night before the gas went out in the living room, and Gregor could easily tell that his parents and his sister had all stayed awake until then, for he could clearly hear the three of them stealing away on tiptoe. No one was likely to visit him, not until the morning, that was certain; so he had plenty of time to meditate at his leisure on how he was to arrange his life afresh. But the lofty, empty room in which he had to lie flat on the floor filled him with an apprehension he could not account for, since it had been his very own room for the past five years—and with a half-unconscious action, not without a slight feeling of shame, he scuttled under the sofa, where he felt comfortable at once, although his back was a little cramped and he could not lift his head up, and his only regret was that his body was too broad to get the whole of it under the sofa.

He stayed there all night, spending the time partly in a light slumber, from which his hunger kept waking him up with a start, and partly in worrying and sketching vague hopes, which all led to the same conclusion, that he must lie low for the present and, by exercising patience and the utmost consideration, help the family to bear the inconvenience he was bound to cause them in his present condition.

Very early in the morning, it was still almost night, Gregor had the chance to test the strength of his new resolutions, for his sister, nearly fully dressed, opened the door from the hall and peered in. She did not see him at once, yet when she caught sight of him under the sofa—well, he had to be somewhere, he couldn't have flown away, could he?—she was so startled that without being able to help it she slammed the door shut again. But as if regretting her behavior she opened the door again immediately and came in on tiptoe, as if she were visiting an invalid or even a stranger. Gregor had pushed his head forward to the very edge of the sofa and watched her. Would she notice that he had left the milk standing, and not for lack of hunger, and would she bring in some other kind of food more to his taste? If she did not do it of her own accord, he would rather starve than draw her attention to the fact, although he felt a wild impulse to dart out from under the sofa, throw himself at her feet and beg her for something to eat. But his sister at once noticed, with surprise, that the basin was still full, except for a little milk that had been spilt all around it, she lifted it immediately, not with her bare hands, true, but with a cloth and carried it away. Gregor was wildly curious to know what she would bring instead, and made various speculations about it. Yet what she actually did next, in the goodness of her heart, he could never have guessed at. To find out what he liked she brought him a whole selection of food, all set out on an old newspaper. There were old, half-decayed vegetables, bones from last night's supper covered with a white sauce that had thickened; some raisins and almonds; a piece of cheese that Gregor would have called uneatable two days ago; a dry roll of bread, a buttered roll, and a roll both buttered and salted. Besides all that, she set down again the same basin, into which she had poured some water, and which was apparently to be reserved for his exclusive use. And with fine tact, knowing that Gregor would not eat in her presence, she withdrew quickly and even turned the key, to let him understand that he could take his ease as much as he liked. Gregor's legs all whizzed towards the food. His wounds must have healed completely, moreover, for he felt no disability, which amazed him and made him reflect how more than a month ago he had cut one finger a little with a knife and had still suffered pain from the wound only the day before yesterday. Am I less sensitive now? he thought, and sucked greedily at the cheese, which above all the other edibles attracted him at once and strongly. One after another and with tears of satisfaction in his eyes he quickly devoured the cheese, the vegetables and the sauce; the fresh food, on the other hand, had no charms for him, he could not even stand the smell of it and actually dragged away to some little distance the things he could eat. He had long finished his meal and was only lying lazily on the same spot when his sister turned the key slowly as a sign for him to retreat. That roused him at once, although he was nearly asleep, and he hurried under the sofa again. But it took considerable self-control for him to stay under the sofa, even for the short time his sister was in the room, since the large meal had swollen his body somewhat and he was so cramped he could hardly breathe. Slight attacks of breathlessness afflicted him and his eyes were starting a little out of his head as he watched his unsuspecting sister sweeping together with a broom not only the remains of what he had eaten but even the things he had not touched, as if these were now of no use to anyone, and hastily shoveling it all into a bucket, which she covered with a wooden lid and carried away. Hardly had she turned her back when Gregor came from under the sofa and stretched and puffed himself out.

In this manner Gregor was fed, once in the early morning while his parents and the servant girl were still asleep, and a second time after they had all had their midday dinner, for then his parents took a short nap and the servant girl could be sent out on some errand or other by his sister. Not that they would have wanted him to starve, of course, but perhaps they could not have borne to know more about his feeding than from hearsay, perhaps too his sister wanted to spare them such little anxieties wherever possible, since they had quite enough to bear as it was.

Under what pretext the doctor and the locksmith had been got rid of on that first morning Gregor could not discover, for since what he said was not understood by the others it never struck any of them, not even his sister, that he could understand what they said, and so whenever his sister came into his room he had to content himself with hearing her utter only a sigh now and then and an occasional appeal to the saints. Later on, when she had got a little used to the situation—of course she could never get completely used to it—she sometimes threw out a remark which was kindly meant or could be so interpreted. "Well, he liked his dinner today," she would say when Gregor had made a good clearance of his food; and when he had not eaten, which gradually happened more and more often, she would say almost sadly: "Everything's been left standing again."

But although Gregor could get no news directly, he overheard a lot from the neighboring rooms, and as soon as voices were audible, he would run to the door of the room concerned and press his whole body against it. In the first few days especially there was no conversation that did not refer to him somehow, even if only indirectly. For two whole days there were family consultations at every mealtime about what should be done; but also between meals the same subject was discussed, for there were always at least two members of the family at home, since no one wanted to be alone in the flat and to leave it quite empty was unthinkable. And on the very first of these days the household cook—it was not quite clear what and how much she knew of the situation—went down on her knees to his mother and begged leave to go, and when she departed, a quarter of an hour later, gave thanks for her dismissal with tears in her eyes as if for the greatest benefit that could have been conferred on her, and without any prompting swore a solemn oath that she would never say a single word to anyone about what had happened.

Now Gregor's sister had to cook too, helping her mother; true, the cooking did not amount to much, for they ate scarcely anything. Gregor was always hearing one of the family vainly urging another to eat and getting no answer but: "Thanks, I've had all I want," or something similar. Perhaps they drank nothing either. Time and again his sister kept asking his father if he wouldn't like some beer and offered kindly to go and fetch it herself, and when he made no answer suggested that she could ask the concierge to fetch it, so that he need feel no sense of obligation, but then a round "No" came from his father and no more was said about it.

In the course of that very first day Gregor's father explained the family's financial position and prospects to both his mother and his sister. Now and then he rose from the table to get some voucher or memorandum out of the small safe he had rescued from the collapse of his business five years earlier. One could hear him opening the complicated lock and rustling papers out and shutting it again. This statement made by his father was the first cheerful information Gregor had heard since his imprisonment. He had been of the opinion that nothing at all was left over from his father's business, at least his father had never said anything to the contrary, and of course he had not asked him directly. At that time Gregor's sole desire was to do his utmost to help the family to forget as soon as possible the catastrophe which had overwhelmed the business and thrown them all into a state of complete despair. And so he had set to work with unusual ardor and almost overnight had become a commercial traveler instead of a little clerk, with of course much greater chances of earning money, and his success was immediately translated into good round coin which he could lay on the table for his amazed and happy family. These had been fine times, and they had never recurred, at least not with the same sense of glory, although later on Gregor had earned so much money that he was able to meet the expenses of the whole household and did so. They had simply got used to it, both the family and Gregor; the money was gratefully accepted and gladly given, but there was no special uprush of warm feeling. With his sister alone had he remained intimate, and it was a secret plan of his that she, who loved music, unlike himself, and could play movingly on the violin, should be sent next year to study at the Conservatorium, despite the great expense that would entail, which must be made up in some other way. During his brief visits home the Conservatorium was often mentioned in the talks he had with his sister, but always merely as a beautiful dream which could never come true, and his parents discouraged even these innocent references to it; yet Gregor had made up his mind firmly about it and meant to announce the fact with due solemnity on Christmas Day.

Such were the thoughts, completely futile in his present condition, that went through his head as he stood clinging upright to the door and listening. Sometimes out of sheer weariness he had to give up listening and let his head fall negligently against the door, but he always had to pull himself together again at once, for even the slight sound his head made was audible next door and brought all conversation to a stop. "What can he be doing now?" his father would say after a while, obviously turning towards the door, and only then would the interrupted conversation gradually be set going again.

Gregor was now informed as amply as he could wish—for his father tended to repeat himself in his explanations, partly because it was a long time since he had handled such matters and partly because his mother could not always grasp things at once—that a certain amount of investments, a very small amount it was true, had survived the wreck of their fortunes and had even increased a little because the dividends had not been touched meanwhile. And besides that, the money Gregor brought home every month—he had kept only a few dollars for himself—had never been quite used up and now amounted to a small capital sum. Behind the door Gregor nodded his head eagerly, rejoiced at this evidence of unexpected thrift and foresight. True, he could really have paid off some more of his father's debts to the chief with this extra money, and so brought much nearer the day on which he could quit his job, but doubtless it was better the way his father had arranged it.

Yet this capital was by no means sufficient to let the family live on the interest of it; for one year, perhaps, or at the most two, they could live on the principal, that was all. It was simply a sum that ought not to be touched and should be kept for a rainy day; money for living expenses would have to be earned. Now his father was still hale enough but an old man, and he had done no work for the past five years and could not be expected to do much; during these five years, the first years of leisure in his laborious though unsuccessful life, he had grown rather fat and become sluggish. And Gregor's old mother, how was she to earn a living with her asthma, which troubled her even when she walked through the flat and kept her lying on a sofa every other day panting for breath beside an open window? And was his sister to earn her bread, she who was still a child of seventeen and whose life hitherto had been so pleasant, consisting as it did in dressing herself nicely, sleeping long, helping in the housekeeping, going out to a few modest entertainments and above all playing the violin? At first whenever the need for earning money was mentioned Gregor let go his hold on the door and threw himself down on the cool leather sofa beside it, he felt so hot with shame and grief.

Often he just lay there the long nights through without sleeping at all, scrabbling for hours on the leather. Or he nerved himself to the great effort of pushing an armchair to the window, then crawled up over the window sill and, braced against the chair, leaned against the window panes, obviously in some recollection of the sense of freedom that looking out of a window always used to give him. For in reality day by day things that were even a little way off were growing dimmer to his sight; the hospital across the street, which he used to execrate for being all too often before his eyes, was now quite beyond his range of vision, and if he had not known that he lived in Charlotte Street, a quiet street but still a city street, he might have believed that his window gave on a desert waste where gray sky and gray land blended indistinguishably into each other. His quick-witted sister only needed to observe twice that the armchair stood by the window; after that whenever she had tidied the room she always pushed the chair back to the same place at the window and even left the inner casements open.

If he could have spoken to her and thanked her for all she had to do for him, he could have borne her ministrations better; as it was, they oppressed him. She certainly tried to make as light as possible of whatever was disagreeable in her task, and as time went on she succeeded, of course, more and more, but time brought more enlightenment to Gregor too. The very way she came in distressed him. Hardly was she in the room when she rushed to the window, without even taking time to shut the door, careful as she was usually to shield the sight of Gregor's room from the others, and as if she were almost suffocating tore the casements open with hasty fingers, standing then in the open draught for a while even in the bitterest cold and drawing deep breaths. This noisy scurry of hers upset Gregor twice a day; he would crouch trembling under the sofa all the time, knowing quite well that she would certainly have spared him such a disturbance had she found it at all possible to stay in his presence without opening the window.

On one occasion, about a month after Gregor's metamorphosis, when there was surely no reason for her to be still startled at his appearance, she came a little earlier than usual and found him gazing out of the window, quite motionless, and thus well placed to look like a bogey. Gregor would not have been surprised had she not come in at all, for she could not immediately open the window while he was there, but not only did she retreat, she jumped back as if in alarm and banged the door shut; a stranger might well have thought that he had been lying in wait for her there meaning to bite her. Of course he hid himself under the sofa at once, but he had to wait until midday before she came again, and she seemed more ill at ease than usual. This made him realize how repulsive the sight of him still was to her, and that it was bound to go on being repulsive, and what an effort it must cost her not to run away even from the sight of the small portion of his body that stuck out from under the sofa. In order to spare her that, therefore, one day he carried a sheet on his back to the sofa—it cost him four hours' labor—and arranged it there in such a way as to hide him completely, so that even if she were to bend down she could not see him. Had she considered the sheet unneccessary, she would certainly have stripped it off the sofa again, for it was clear enough that this curtaining and confining of himself was not likely to conduce to Gregor's comfort, but she left it where it was, and Gregor even fancied that he caught a thankful glance from her eye when he lifted the sheet carefully a very little with his head to see how she was taking the new arrangement.

For the first fortnight his parents could not bring themselves to the point of entering his room, and he often heard them expressing their appreciation of his sister's activities, whereas formerly they had frequently scolded her for being as they thought a somewhat useless daughter. But now, both of them often waited outside the door, his father and his mother, while his sister tidied his room, and as soon as she came out she had to tell them exactly how things were in the room, what Gregor had eaten, how he had conducted himself this time and whether there was not perhaps some slight improvement in his condition. His mother, moreover, began relatively soon to want to visit him, but his father and sister dissuaded her at first with arguments which Gregor listened to very attentively and altogether approved. Later, however, she had to be held back by main force, and when she cried out: "Do let me in to Gregor, he is my unfortunate son! Can't you understand that I must go to him?" Gregor thought that it might be well to have her come in, not every day, of course, but perhaps once a week; she understood things, after all, much better than his sister, who was only a child despite the efforts she was making and had perhaps taken on so difficult a task merely out of childish thoughtlessness.

Gregor's desire to see his mother was soon fulfilled. During the daytime he did not want to show himself at the window, out of consideration for his parents, but he could not crawl very far around the few square yards of floor space he had, nor could he bear lying quietly at rest all during the night, while he was fast losing any interest he had ever taken in food, so that for mere recreation he had formed the habit of crawling crisscross over the walls and ceiling. He especially enjoyed hanging suspended from the ceiling; it was much better than lying on the floor; one could breathe more freely; one's body swung and rocked lightly; and in the almost blissful absorption induced by this suspension it could happen to his own surprise that he let go and fell plump on the floor. Yet he now had his body much better under control than formerly, and even such a big fall did him no harm. His sister at once remarked the new distraction Gregor had found for himself—he left traces behind him of the sticky stuff on his soles wherever he crawled—and she got the idea in her head of giving him as wide a field as possible to crawl in and of removing the pieces of furniture that hindered him, above all the chest of drawers and the writing desk. But that was more than she could manage all by herself; she did not dare ask her father to help her; and as for the servant girl, a young creature of sixteen who had had the courage to stay on after the cook's departure, she could not be asked to help, for she had begged as an especial favor that she might keep the kitchen door locked and open it only on a definite summons; so there was nothing left but to apply to her mother at an hour when her father was out. And the old lady did come, with exclamations of joyful eagerness, which, however, died away at the door of Gregor's room. Gregor's sister, of course, went in first, to see that everything was in order before letting his mother enter. In great haste Gregor pulled the sheet lower and rucked it more in folds so that it really looked as if it had been thrown accidentally over the sofa. And this time he did not peer out from under it; he renounced the pleasure of seeing his mother on this occasion and was only glad that she had come at all. "Come in, he's out of sight," said his sister, obviously leading her mother in by the hand. Gregor could now hear the two women struggling to shift the heavy old chest from its place, and his sister claiming the greater part of the labor for herself, without listening to the admonitions of her mother who feared she might overstrain herself. It took a long time. After at least a quarter of an hour's tugging his mother objected that the chest had better be left where it was, for in the first place it was too heavy and could never be got out before his father came home, and standing in the middle of the room like that it would only hamper Gregor's movements, while in the second place it was not at all certain that removing the furniture would be doing a service to Gregor. She was inclined to think to the contrary; the sight of the naked walls made her own heart heavy, and why shouldn't Gregor have the same feeling, considering that he had been used to his furniture for so long and might feel forlorn without it. "And doesn't it look," she concluded in a low voice—in fact she had been almost whispering all the time as if to avoid letting Gregor, whose exact whereabouts she did not know, hear even the tones of her voice, for she was convinced that he could not understand her words—"doesn't it look as if we were showing him, by taking away his furniture, that we have given up hope of his ever getting better and are just leaving him coldly to himself? I think it would be best to keep his room exactly as it has always been, so that when he comes back to us he will find everything unchanged and be able all the more easily to forget what has happened in between."

On hearing these words from his mother Gregor realized that the lack of all direct human speech for the past two months together with the monotony of family life must have confused his mind, otherwise he could not account for the fact that he had quite earnestly looked forward to having his room emptied of furnishing. Did he really want his warm room, so comfortably fitted with old family furniture, to be turned into a naked den in which he would certainly be able to crawl unhampered in all directions but at the price of shedding simultaneously all recollection of his human background? He had indeed been so near the brink of forgetfulness that only the voice of his mother, which he had not heard for so long, had drawn him back from it. Nothing should be taken out of his room; everything must stay as it was; he could not dispense with the good influence of the furniture on his state of mind; and even if the furniture did hamper him in his senseless crawling round and round, that was no drawback but a great advantage.

Unfortunately his sister was of the contrary opinion; she had grown accustomed, and not without reason, to consider herself an expert in Gregor's affairs as against her parents, and so her mother's advice was now enough to make her determined on the removal not only of the chest and the writing desk, which had been her first intention, but of all the furniture except the indispensable sofa. This determination was not, of course, merely the outcome of childish recalcitrance and of the self-confidence she had recently developed so unexpectedly and at such cost; she had in fact perceived that Gregor needed a lot of space to crawl about in, while on the other hand he never used the furniture at all, so far as could be seen. Another factor might have been also the enthusiastic temperament of an adolescent girl, which seeks to indulge itself on every opportunity and which now tempted Grete to exaggerate the horror of her brother's circumstances in order that she might do all the more for him. In a room where Gregor lorded it all alone over empty walls no one save herself was likely ever to set foot.

And so she was not to be moved from her resolve by her mother, who seemed moreover to be ill at ease in Gregor's room and therefore unsure of herself, was soon reduced to silence and helped her daughter as best she could to push the chest outside. Now, Gregor could do without the chest, if need be, but the writing desk he must retain. As soon as the two women had got the chest out of his room, groaning as they pushed it, Gregor stuck his head out from under the sofa to see how he might intervene as kindly and cautiously as possible. But as bad luck would have it, his mother was the first to return, leaving Grete clasping the chest in the room next door where she was trying to shift it all by herself, without of course moving it from the spot. His mother however was not accustomed to the sight of him, it might sicken her and so in alarm Gregor backed quickly to the other end of the sofa, yet could not prevent the sheet from swaying a little in front. That was enough to put her on the alert. She paused, stood still for a moment and then went back to Grete.

Although Gregor kept reassuring himself that nothing out of the way was happening, but only a few bits of furniture were being changed round, he soon had to admit that all this trotting to and fro of the two women, their little ejaculations and the scraping of furniture along the floor affected him like a vast disturbance coming from all sides at once, and however much he tucked in his head and legs and cowered to the very floor he was bound to confess that he would not be able to stand it for long. They were clearing his room out; taking away everything he loved; the chest in which he kept his fret saw and other tools was already dragged off; they were now loosening the writing desk which had almost sunk into the floor, the desk at which he had done all his homework when he was at the commercial academy, at the grammar school before that, and, yes, even at the primary school—he had no more time to waste in weighing the good intentions of the two women, whose existence he had by now almost forgotten, for they were so exhausted that they were laboring in silence and nothing could be heard but the heavy scuffling of their feet.

And so he rushed out—the women were just leaning against the writing desk in the next room to give themselves a breather—and four times changed his direction, since he really did not know what to rescue first, then on the wall opposite, which was already otherwise cleared, he was struck by the picture of the lady muffled in so much fur and quickly crawled up to it and pressed himself to the glass, which was a good surface to hold on to and comforted his hot belly. This picture at least, which was entirely hidden beneath him, was going to be removed by nobody. He turned his head towards the door of the living room so as to observe the women when they came back.

They had not allowed themselves much of a rest and were already coming; Grete had twined her arm round her mother and was almost supporting her. "Well, what shall we take now?" said Grete, looking round. Her eyes met Gregor's from the wall. She kept her composure, presumably because of her mother, bent her head down to her mother, to keep her from looking up, and said, although in a fluttering, unpremeditated voice: "Come, hadn't we better go back to the living room for a moment?" Her intentions were clear enough to Gregor, she wanted to bestow her mother in safety and then chase him down from the wall. Well, just let her try it! He clung to his picture and would not give it up. He would rather fly in Grete's face.

But Grete's words had succeeded in disquieting her mother, who took a step to one side, caught sight of the huge brown mass on the flowered wallpaper, and before she was really conscious that what she saw was Gregor screamed in a loud, hoarse voice: "Oh God, oh God!" fell with outspread arms over the sofa as if giving up and did not move. "Gregor!" cried his sister, shaking her fist and glaring at him. This was the first time she had directly addressed him since his metamorphosis. She ran into the next room for some aromatic essence with which to rouse her mother from her fainting fit. Gregor wanted to help too—there was still time to rescue the picture—but he was stuck fast to the glass and had to tear himself loose; he then ran after his sister into the next room as if he could advise her, as he used to do; but then had to stand helplessly behind her; she meanwhile searched among various small bottles and when she turned round started in alarm at the sight of him; one bottle fell on the floor and broke; a splinter of glass cut Gregor's face and some kind of corrosive medicine splashed him; without pausing a moment longer Grete gathered up all the bottles she could carry and ran to her mother with them; she banged the door shut with her foot. Gregor was now cut off from his mother, who was perhaps nearly dying because of him; he dared not open the door for fear of frightening away his sister, who had to stay with her mother; there was nothing he could do but wait; and harassed by self-reproach and worry he began now to crawl to and fro, over everything, walls, furniture and ceiling, and finally in his despair, when the whole room seemed to be reeling round him, fell down on to the middle of the big table.

A little while elapsed, Gregor was still lying there feebly and all around was quiet, perhaps that was a good omen. Then the doorbell rang. The servant girl was of course locked in her kitchen, and Grete would have to open the door. It was his father. "What's been happening?" were his first words; Grete's face must have told him everything. Grete answered in a muffled voice, apparently hiding her head on his breast: "Mother has been fainting, but she's better now. Gregor's broken loose." "Just what I expected," said his father, "just what I've been telling you, but you women would never listen." It was clear to Gregor that his father had taken the worst interpretation of Grete's all too brief statement and was assuming that Gregor had been guilty of some violent act. Therefore Gregor must now try to propitiate his father, since he had neither time nor means for an explanation. And so he fled to the door of his own room and crouched against it, to let his father see as soon as he came in from the hall that his son had the good intention of getting back into his room immediately and that it was not necessary to drive him there, but that if only the door were opened he would disappear at once.

Yet his father was not in the mood to perceive such fine distinctions. "Ah!" he cried as soon as he appeared, in a tone which sounded at once angry and exultant. Gregor drew his head back from the door and lifted it to look at his father. Truly, this was not the father he had imagined to himself; admittedly he had been too absorbed of late in his new recreation of crawling over the ceiling to take the same interest as before in what was happening elsewhere in the flat, and he ought really to be prepared for some changes. And yet, and yet, could that be his father? The man who used to lie wearily sunk in bed whenever Gregor set out on a business journey; who welcomed him back of an evening lying in a long chair in a dressing gown; who could not really rise to his feet but only lifted his arms in greeting, and on the rare occasions when he did go out with his family, on one or two Sundays a year and on high holidays, walked between Gregor and his mother, who were slow walkers anyhow, even more slowly than they did, muffled in his old greatcoat, shuffling laboriously forward with the help of his crook-handled stick which he set down most cautiously at every step and, whenever he wanted to say anything, nearly always came to a full stop and gathered his escort around him? Now he was standing there in fine shape; dressed in a smart blue uniform with gold buttons, such as bank messengers wear; his strong double chin bulged over the stiff high collar of his jacket; from under his bushy eyebrows his black eyes darted fresh and penetrating glances; his onetime tangled white hair had been combed flat on either side of a shining and carefully exact parting. He pitched his cap, which bore a gold monogram, probably the badge of some bank, in a wide sweep across the whole room on to a sofa and with the tailends of his jacket thrown back, his hands in his trouser pockets, advanced with a grim visage towards Gregor. Likely enough he did not himself know what he meant to do; at any rate he lifted his feet uncommonly high, and Gregor was dumbfounded at the enormous size of his shoe soles. But Gregor could not risk standing up to him, aware as he had been from the very first day of his new life that his father believed only the severest measures suitable for dealing with him. And so he ran before his father, stopping when he stopped and scuttling forward again when his father made any kind of move. In this way they circled the room several times without anything decisive happening, indeed the whole operation did not even look like a pursuit because it was carried out so slowly. And so Gregor did not leave the floor, for he feared that his father might take as a piece of peculiar wickedness any excursion of his over the walls or the ceiling. All the same, he could not stay this course much longer, for while his father took one step he had to carry out a whole series of movements. He was already beginning to feel breathless, just as in his former life his lungs had not been very dependable. As he was staggering along, trying to concentrate his energy on running, hardly keeping his eyes open; in his dazed state never even thinking of any other escape than simply going forward; and having almost forgotten that the walls were free to him, which in this room were well provided with finely carved pieces of furniture full of knobs and crevices—suddenly something lightly flung landed close behind him and rolled before him. It was an apple; a second apple followed immediately; Gregor came to a stop in alarm; there was no point in running on, for his father was determined to bombard him. He had filled his pockets with fruit from the dish on the sideboard and was now shying apple after apple, without taking particularly good aim for the moment. The small red apples rolled about the floor as if magnetized and cannoned into each other. An apple thrown without much force grazed Gregor's back and glanced off harmlessly. But another following immediately landed right on his back and sank in; Gregor wanted to drag himself forward, as if this startling, incredible pain could be left behind him; but he felt as if nailed to the spot and flattened himself out in a complete derangement of all his senses. With his last conscious look he saw the door of his room being torn open and his mother rushing out ahead of his screaming sister, in her underbodice, for her daughter had loosened her clothing to let her breathe more freely and recover from her swoon; he saw his mother rushing towards his father, leaving one after another behind her on the floor her loosened petticoats, stumbling over her petticoats straight to his father and embracing him, in complete union with him—but here Gregor's sight began to fail—with her hands clasped round his father's neck as she begged for her son's life.

III

The serious injury done to Gregor, which disabled him for more than a month—the apple went on sticking in his body as a visible reminder, since no one ventured to remove it—seemed to have made even his father recollect that Gregor was a member of the family, despite his present unfortunate and repulsive shape, and ought not to be treated as an enemy, that, on the contrary, family duty required the suppression of disgust and the exercise of patience, nothing but patience.

And although his injury had impaired, probably forever, his powers of movement, and for the time being it took him long, long minutes to creep across his room like an old invalid—there was no question now of crawling up the wall—yet in his own opinion he was sufficiently compensated for this worsening of his condition by the fact that towards evening the living-room door, which he used to watch intently for an hour or two beforehand, was always thrown open, so that lying in the darkness of his room, invisible to the family, he could see them all at the lamp-lit table and listen to their talk, by general consent as it were, very different from his earlier eavesdropping.

True, their intercourse lacked the lively character of former times, which he had always called to mind with a certain wistfulness in the small hotel bedrooms where he had been wont to throw himself down, tired out, on damp bedding. They were now mostly very silent. Soon after supper his father would fall asleep in his armchair; his mother and sister would admonish each other to be silent; his mother, bending low over the lamp, stitched at fine sewing for an underwear firm; his sister, who had taken a job as a salesgirl, was learning shorthand and French in the evenings on the chance of bettering herself. Sometimes his father woke up, and as if quite unaware that he had been sleeping said to his mother: "What a lot of sewing you're doing today!" and at once fell asleep again, while the two women exchanged a tired smile.

With a kind of mulishness his father persisted in keeping his uniform on even in the house; his dressing gown hung uselessly on its peg and he slept fully dressed where he sat, as if he were ready for service at any moment and even here only at the beck and call of his superior. As a result, his uniform, which was not brand new to start with, began to look dirty, despite all the loving care of the mother and sister to keep it clean, and Gregor often spent whole evenings gazing at the many greasy spots on the garment, gleaming with gold buttons always in a high state of polish, in which the old man sat sleeping in extreme discomfort and yet quite peacefully.

As soon as the clock struck ten his mother tried to rouse his father with gentle words and to persuade him after that to get into bed, for sitting there he could not have a proper sleep and that was what he needed most, since he had to go on duty at six. But with the mulishness that had obsessed him since he became a bank messenger he always insisted on staying longer at the table, although he regularly fell asleep again and in the end only with the greatest trouble could be got out of his armchair and into his bed. However insistently Gregor's mother and sister kept urging him with gentle reminders, he would go on slowly shaking his head for a quarter of an hour, keeping his eyes shut, and refuse to get to his feet. The mother plucked at his sleeve, whispering endearments in his ear, the sister left her lessons to come to her mother's help, but Gregor's father was not to be caught. He would only sink down deeper in his chair. Not until the two women hoisted him up by the armpits did he open his eyes and look at them both, one after the other, usually with the remark: "This is a life. This is the peace and quiet of my old age." And leaning on the two of them he would heave himself up, with difficulty, as if he were a great burden to himself, suffer them to lead him as far as the door and then wave them off and go on alone, while the mother abandoned her needlework and the sister her pen in order to run after him and help him farther.

Who could find time, in this overworked and tired-out family, to bother about Gregor more than was absolutely needful? The household was reduced more and more; the servant girl was turned off; a gigantic bony charwoman with white hair flying round her head came in morning and evening to do the rough work; everything else was done by Gregor's mother, as well as great piles of sewing. Even various family ornaments, which his mother and sister used to wear with pride at parties and celebrations, had to be sold, as Gregor discovered of an evening from hearing them all discuss the prices obtained. But what they lamented most was the fact that they could not leave the flat which was much too big for their present circumstances, because they could not think of any way to shift Gregor. Yet Gregor saw well enough that consideration for him was not the main difficulty preventing the removal, for they could have easily shifted him in some suitable box with a few air holes in it; what really kept them from moving into another flat was rather their own complete hopelessness and the belief that they had been singled out for a misfortune such as had never happened to any of their relations or acquaintances. They fulfilled to the uttermost all that the world demands of poor people, the father fetched breakfast for the small clerks in the bank, the mother devoted her energy to making underwear for strangers, the sister trotted to and fro behind the counter at the behest of customers, but more than this they had not the strength to do. And the wound in Gregor's back began to nag at him afresh when his mother and sister, after getting his father into bed, came back again, left their work lying, drew close to each other and sat cheek by cheek; then his mother, pointing towards his room, said: "Shut that door now, Grete," and he was left again in darkness, while next door the women mingled their tears or perhaps sat dry-eyed staring at the table.

Gregor hardly slept at all by night or by day. He was often haunted by the idea that next time the door opened he would take the family's affairs in hand again just as he used to do; once more, after this long interval, there appeared in his thoughts the figures of the chief and the chief clerk, the commercial travelers and the apprentices, the porter who was so dull-witted, two or three friends in other firms, a chambermaid in one of the rural hotels, a sweet and fleeting memory, a cashier in a milliner's shop, whom he had wooed earnestly but too slowly—they all appeared, together with strangers or people he had quite forgotten, but instead of helping him and his family they were one and all unapproachable and he was glad when they vanished. At other times he would not be in the mood to bother about his family, he was only filled with rage at the way they were neglecting him, and although he had no clear idea of what he might care to eat he would make plans for getting into the larder to take the food that was after all his due, even if he were not hungry. His sister no longer took thought to bring him what might especially please him, but in the morning and at noon before she went to business hurriedly pushed into his room with her foot any food that was available, and in the evening cleared it out again with one sweep of the broom, heedless of whether it had been merely tasted, or—as most frequently happened—left untouched. The cleaning of his room, which she now did always in the evenings, could not have been more hastily done. Streaks of dirt stretched along the walls, here and there lay balls of dust and filth. At first Gregor used to station himself in some particularly filthy corner when his sister arrived, in order to reproach her with it, so to speak. But he could have sat there for weeks without getting her to make any improvement; she could see the dirt as well as he did, but she had simply made up her mind to leave it alone. And yet, with a touchiness that was new to her, which seemed anyhow to have infected the whole family, she jealously guarded her claim to be the sole caretaker of Gregor's room. His mother once subjected his room to a thorough cleaning, which was achieved only by means of several buckets of water—all this dampness of course upset Gregor too and he lay widespread, sulky and motionless on the sofa—but she was well punished for it. Hardly had his sister noticed the changed aspect of his room that evening than she rushed in high dudgeon into the living room and, despite the imploringly raised hands of her mother, burst into a storm of weeping, while her parents—her father had of course been startled out of his chair—looked on at first in helpless amazement; then they too began to go into action; the father reproached the mother on his right for not having left the cleaning of Gregor's room to his sister; shrieked at the sister on his left that never again was she to be allowed to clean Gregor's room; while the mother tried to pull the father into his bedroom, since he was beyond himself with agitation; the sister, shaken with sobs, then beat upon the table with her small fists; and Gregor hissed loudly with rage because not one of them thought of shutting the door to spare him such a spectacle and so much noise.

Still, even if the sister, exhausted by her daily work, had grown tired of looking after Gregor as she did formerly, there was no need for his mother's intervention or for Gregor's being neglected at all. The charwoman was there. This old widow, whose strong bony frame had enabled her to survive the worst a long life could offer, by no means recoiled from Gregor. Without being in the least curious she had once by chance opened the door of his room and at the sight of Gregor, who, taken by surprise, began to rush to and fro although no one was chasing him, merely stood there with her arms folded. From that time she never failed to open his door a little for a moment, morning and evening, to have a look at him. At first she even used to call him to her, with words which apparently she took to be friendly, such as: "Come along, then, you old dung beetle!" or "Look at the old dung beetle, then!" To such allocutions Gregor made no answer, but stayed motionless where he was, as if the door had never been opened. Instead of being allowed to disturb him so senselessly whenever the whim took her, she should rather have been ordered to clean out his room daily, that charwoman! Once, early in the morning—heavy rain was lashing on the windowpanes, perhaps a sign that spring was on the way—Gregor was so exasperated when she began addressing him again that he ran at her, as if to attack her, although slowly and feebly enough.

But the charwoman instead of showing fright merely lifted high a chair that happened to be beside the door, and as she stood there with her mouth wide open it was clear that she meant to shut it only when she brought the chair down on Gregor's back. "So you're not coming any nearer?" she asked, as Gregor turned away again, and quietly put the chair back into the corner.

Gregor was now eating hardly anything. Only when he happened to pass the food laid out for him did he take a bit of something in his mouth as a pastime, kept it there for an hour at a time and usually spat it out again. At first he thought it was chagrin over the state of his room that prevented him from eating, yet he soon got used to the various changes in his room. It had become a habit in the family to push into his room things there was no room for elsewhere, and there were plenty of these now, since one of the rooms had been let to three lodgers. These serious gentlemen—all three of them with full beards, as Gregor once observed through a crack in the door—had a passion for order, not only in their own room but, since they were now members of the household, in all its arrangements, especially in the kitchen. Superfluous, not to say dirty, objects they could not bear. Besides, they had brought with them most of the furnishings they needed. For this reason many things could be dispensed with that it was no use trying to sell but that should not be thrown away either. All of them found their way into Gregor's room. The ash can likewise and the kitchen garbage can. Anything that was not needed for the moment was simply flung into Gregor's room by the charwoman, who did everything in a hurry; fortunately Gregor usually saw only the object, whatever it was, and the hand that held it. Perhaps she intended to take the things away again as time and opportunity offered, or to collect them until she could throw them all out in a heap, but in fact they just lay wherever she happened to throw them, except when Gregor pushed his way through the junk heap and shifted it somewhat, at first out of necessity, because he had not room enough to crawl, but later with increasing enjoyment, although after such excursions, being sad and weary to death, he would lie motionless for hours. And since the lodgers often ate their supper at home in the common living room, the living-room door stayed shut many an evening, yet Gregor reconciled himself quite easily to the shutting of the door, for often enough on evenings when it was opened he had disregarded it entirely and lain in the darkest corner of his room, quite unnoticed by the family. But on one occasion the charwoman left the door open a little and it stayed ajar even when the lodgers came in for supper and the lamp was lit. They set themselves at the top end of the table where formerly Gregor and his father and mother had eaten their meals, unfolded their napkins and took knife and fork in hand. At once his mother appeared in the other doorway with a dish of meat and close behind her his sister with a dish of potatoes piled high. The food steamed with a thick vapor. The lodgers bent over the food set before them as if to scrutinize it before eating, in fact the man in the middle, who seemed to pass for an authority with the other two, cut a piece of meat as it lay on the dish, obviously to discover if it were tender or should be sent back to the kitchen. He showed satisfaction, and Gregor's mother and sister, who had been watching anxiously, breathed freely and began to smile.

The family itself took its meals in the kitchen. None the less, Gregor's father came into the living room before going into the kitchen and with one prolonged bow, cap in hand, made a round of the table. The lodgers all stood up and murmured something in their beards. When they were alone again they ate their food in almost complete silence. It seemed remarkable to Gregor that among the various noises coming from the table he could always distinguish the sound of their masticating teeth, as if this were a sign to Gregor that one needed teeth in order to eat, and that with toothless jaws even of the finest make one could do nothing. "I'm hungry enough," said Gregor sadly to himself, "but not for that kind of food. How these lodgers are stuffing themselves, and here am I dying of starvation!"

On that very evening—during the whole of his time there Gregor could not remember ever having heard the violin—the sound of violin-playing came from the kitchen. The lodgers had already finished their supper, the one in the middle had brought out a newspaper and given the other two a page apiece, and now they were leaning back at ease reading and smoking. When the violin began to play they pricked up their ears, got to their feet, and went on tiptoe to the hall door where they stood huddled together. Their movements must have been heard in the kitchen, for Gregor's father called out: "Is the violin-playing disturbing you, gentlemen? It can be stopped at once." "On the contrary," said the middle lodger, "could not Fräulein Samsa come and play in this room, beside us, where it is much more convenient and comfortable?" "Oh certainly," cried Gregor's father, as if he were the violin-player. The lodgers came back into the living room and waited. Presently Gregor's father arrived with the music stand, his mother carrying the music and his sister with the violin. His sister quietly made everything ready to start playing; his parents, who had never let rooms before and so had an exaggerated idea of the courtesy due to lodgers, did not venture to sit down on their own chairs; his father leaned against the door, the right hand thrust between two buttons of his livery coat, which was formally buttoned up; but his mother was offered a chair by one of the lodgers and, since she left the chair just where he had happened to put it, sat down in a corner to one side.

Gregor's sister began to play; the father and mother, from either side, intently watched the movements of her hands. Gregor, attracted by the playing, ventured to move forward a little until his head was actually inside the living room. He felt hardly any surprise at his growing lack of consideration for the others; there had been a time when he prided himself on being considerate. And yet just on this occasion he had more reason than ever to hide himself, since owing to the amount of dust which lay thick in his room and rose into the air at the slightest movement, he too was covered with dust; fluff and hair and remnants of food trailed with him, caught on his back and along his sides; his indifference to everything was much too great for him to turn on his back and scrape himself clean on the carpet, as once he had done several times a day. And in spite of his condition, no shame deterred him from advancing a little over the spotless floor of the living room.

To be sure, no one was aware of him. The family was entirely absorbed in the violin-playing; the lodgers, however, who first of all had stationed themselves, hands in pockets, much too close behind the music stand so that they could all have read the music, which must have bothered his sister, had soon retreated to the window, half-whispering with downbent heads, and stayed there while his father turned an anxious eye on them. Indeed, they were making it more than obvious that they had been disappointed in their expectation of hearing good or enjoyable violin-playing, that they had had more than enough of the performance and only out of courtesy suffered a continued disturbance of their peace. From the way they all kept blowing the smoke of their cigars high in the air through nose and mouth one could divine their irritation. And yet Gregor's sister was playing so beautifully. Her face leaned sideways, intently and sadly her eyes followed the notes of music. Gregor crawled a little farther forward and lowered his head to the ground so that it might be possible for his eyes to meet hers. Was he an animal, that music had such an effect upon him? He felt as if the way were opening before him to the unknown nourishment he craved. He was determined to push forward till he reached his sister, to pull at her skirt and so let her know that she was to come into his room with her violin, for no one here appreciated her playing as he would appreciate it. He would never let her out of his room, at least, not so long as he lived; his frightful appearance would become, for the first time, useful to him; he would watch all the doors of his room at once and spit at intruders; but his sister should need no constraint, she should stay with him of her own free will; she should sit beside him on the sofa, bend down her ear to him and hear him confide that he had had the firm intention of sending her to the Conservatorium, and that, but for his mishap, last Christmas—surely Christmas was long past?—he would have announced it to everybody without allowing a single objection. After this confession his sister would be so touched that she would burst into tears, and Gregor would then raise himself to her shoulder and kiss her on the neck, which, now that she went to business, she kept free of any ribbon or collar.

"Mr. Samsa!" cried the middle lodger, to Gregor's father, and pointed, without wasting any more words, at Gregor, now working himself slowly forwards. The violin fell silent, the middle lodger first smiled to his friends with a shake of the head and then looked at Gregor again. Instead of driving Gregor out, his father seemed to think it more needful to begin by soothing down the lodgers, although they were not at all agitated and apparently found Gregor more entertaining than the violin-playing. He hurried towards them and, spreading out his arms, tried to urge them back into their own room and at the same time to block their view of Gregor. They now began to be really a little angry, one could not tell whether because of the old man's behavior or because it had just dawned on them that all unwittingly they had such a neighbor as Gregor next door. They demanded explanations of his father, they waved their arms like him, tugged uneasily at their beards, and only with reluctance backed towards their room. Meanwhile Gregor's sister, who stood there as if lost when her playing was so abruptly broken off, came to life again, pulled herself together all at once after standing for a while holding violin and bow in nervelessly hanging hands and staring at her music, pushed her violin into the lap of her mother, who was still sitting in her chair fighting asthmatically for breath, and ran into the lodgers' room to which they were now being shepherded by her father rather more quickly than before. One could see the pillows and blankets on the beds flying under her accustomed fingers and being laid in order. Before the lodgers had actually reached their room she had finished making the beds and slipped out.

The old man seemed once more to be so possessed by his mulish self-assertiveness that he was forgetting all the respect he should show to his lodgers. He kept driving them on and driving them on until in the very door of the bedroom the middle lodger stamped his foot loudly on the floor and so brought him to a halt. "I beg to announce," said the lodger, lifting one hand and looking also at Gregor's mother and sister, "that because of the disgusting conditions prevailing in this household and family"—here he spat on the floor with emphatic brevity—"I give you notice on the spot. Naturally I won't pay you a penny for the days I have lived here, on the contrary I shall consider bringing an action for damages against you, based on claims—believe me—that will be easily susceptible of proof." He ceased and stared straight in front of him, as if he expected something. In fact his two friends at once rushed into the breach with these words: "And we too give notice on the spot." On that he seized the door-handle and shut the door with a slam.

Gregor's father, groping with his hands, staggered forward and fell into his chair; it looked as if he were stretching himself there for his ordinary evening nap, but the marked jerkings of his head, which was as if uncontrollable, showed that he was far from asleep. Gregor had simply stayed quietly all the time on the spot where the lodgers had espied him. Disappointment at the failure of his plan, perhaps also the weakness arising from extreme hunger, made it impossible for him to move. He feared, with a fair degree of certainty, that at any moment the general tension would discharge itself in a combined attack upon him, and he lay waiting. He did not react even to the noise made by the violin as it fell off his mother's lap from under her trembling fingers and gave out a resonant note.

"My dear parents," said his sister, slapping her hand on the table by way of introduction, "things can't go on like this. Perhaps you don't realize that, but I do. I won't utter my brother's name in the presence of this creature, and so all I say is: we must try to get rid of it. We've tried to look after it and to put up with it as far as is humanly possible, and I don't think anyone could reproach us in the slightest."

"She is more than right," said Gregor's father to himself. His mother, who was still choking for lack of breath, began to cough hollowly into her hand with a wild look in her eyes.

His sister rushed over to her and held her forehead. His father's thoughts seemed to have lost their vagueness at Grete's words, he sat more upright, fingering his service cap that lay among the plates still lying on the table from the lodgers' supper, and from time to time looked at the still form of Gregor.

"We must try to get rid of it," his sister now said explicitly to her father, since her mother was coughing too much to hear a word, "it will be the death of both of you, I can see that coming. When one has to work as hard as we do, all of us, one can't stand this continual torment at home on top of it. At least I can't stand it any longer." And she burst into such a passion of sobbing that her tears dropped on her mother's face, where she wiped them off mechanically.

"My dear," said the old man sympathetically, and with evident understanding, "but what can we do?"

Gregor's sister merely shrugged her shoulders to indicate the feeling of helplessness that had now overmastered her during her weeping fit, in contrast to her former confidence.

"If he could understand us," said her father, half questioningly; Grete, still sobbing, vehemently waved a hand to show how unthinkable that was.

"If he could understand us," repeated the old man, shutting his eyes to consider his daughter's conviction that understanding was impossible, "then perhaps we might come to some agreement with him. But as it is——"

"He must go," cried Gregor's sister, "that's the only solution, Father. You must just try to get rid of the idea that this is Gregor. The fact that we've believed it for so long is the root of all our trouble. But how can it be Gregor? If this were Gregor, he would have realized long ago that human beings can't live with such a creature, and he'd have gone away on his own accord. Then we wouldn't have any brother, but we'd be able to go on living and keep his memory in honor. As it is, this creature persecutes us, drives away our lodgers, obviously wants the whole apartment to himself and would have us all sleep in the gutter. Just look, Father," she shrieked all at once, "he's at it again!" And in an access of panic that was quite incomprehensible to Gregor she even quitted her mother, literally thrusting the chair from her as if she would rather sacrifice her mother than stay so near to Gregor, and rushed behind her father, who also rose up, being simply upset by her agitation, and half-spread his arms out as if to protect her.

Yet Gregor had not the slightest intention of frightening anyone, far less his sister. He had only begun to turn round in order to crawl back to his room, but it was certainly a startling operation to watch, since because of his disabled condition he could not execute the difficult turning movements except by lifting his head and then bracing it against the floor over and over again. He paused and looked round. His good intentions seemed to have been recognized; the alarm had only been momentary. Now they were all watching him in melancholy silence. His mother lay in her chair, her legs stiffly outstretched and pressed together, her eyes almost closing for sheer weariness; his father and his sister were sitting beside each other, his sister's arm around the old man's neck.

Perhaps I can go on turning round now, thought Gregor, and began his labors again. He could not stop himself from panting with the effort, and had to pause now and then to take breath. Nor did anyone harass him, he was left entirely to himself. When he had completed the turn-round he began at once to crawl straight back. He was amazed at the distance separating him from his room and could not understand how in his weak state he had managed to accomplish the same journey so recently, almost without remarking it. Intent on crawling as fast as possible, he barely noticed that not a single word, not an ejaculation from his family, interfered with his progress. Only when he was already in the doorway did he turn his head round, not completely, for his neck muscles were getting stiff, but enough to see that nothing had changed behind him except that his sister had risen to her feet. His last glance fell on his mother, who was not quite overcome by sleep.

Hardly was he well inside his room when the door was hastily pushed shut, bolted and locked. The sudden noise in his rear startled him so much that his little legs gave beneath him. It was his sister who had shown such haste. She had been standing ready waiting and had made a light spring forward, Gregor had not even heard her coming, and she cried "At last!" to her parents as she turned the key in the lock.

"And what now?" said Gregor to himself, looking round in the darkness. Soon he made the discovery that he was now unable to stir a limb. This did not surprise him, rather it seemed unnatural that he should ever actually have been able to move on these feeble little legs. Otherwise he felt relatively comfortable. True, his whole body was aching, but it seemed that the pain was gradually growing less and would finally pass away. The rotting apple in his back and the inflamed area around it, all covered with soft dust, already hardly troubled him. He thought of his family with tenderness and love. The decision that he must disappear was one that he held to even more strongly than his sister, if that were possible. In this state of vacant and peaceful meditation he remained until the tower clock struck three in the morning. The first broadening of light in the world outside the window entered his consciousness once more. Then his head sank to the floor of its own accord and from his nostrils came the last faint flicker of his breath.

When the charwoman arrived early in the morning—what between her strength and her impatience she slammed all the doors so loudly, never mind how often she had been begged not to do so, that no one in the whole apartment could enjoy any quiet sleep after her arrival—she noticed nothing unusual as she took her customary peep into Gregor's room. She thought he was lying motionless on purpose, pretending to be in the sulks; she credited him with every kind of intelligence. Since she happened to have the long-handled broom in her hand she tried to tickle him up with it from the doorway. When that too produced no reaction she felt provoked and poked at him a little harder, and only when she had pushed him along the floor without meeting any resistance was her attention aroused. It did not take her long to establish the truth of the matter, and her eyes widened, she let out a whistle, yet did not waste much time over it but tore open the door of the Samsas' bedroom and yelled into the darkness at the top of her voice: "Just look at this, it's dead; it's lying here dead and done for!"

Mr. and Mrs. Samsa started up in their double bed and before they realized the nature of the charwoman's announcement had some difficulty in overcoming the shock of it. But then they got out of bed quickly, one on either side, Mr. Samsa throwing a blanket over his shoulders, Mrs. Samsa in nothing but her nightgown; in this array they entered Gregor's room. Meanwhile the door of the living room opened, too, where Grete had been sleeping since the advent of the lodgers; she was completely dressed as if she had not been to bed, which seemed to be confirmed also by the paleness of her face. "Dead?" said Mrs. Samsa, looking questioningly at the charwoman, although she could have investigated for herself, and the fact was obvious enough without investigation. "I should say so," said the charwoman, proving her words by pushing Gregor's corpse a long way to one side with her broomstick. Mrs. Samsa made a movement as if to stop her, but checked it. "Well," said Mr. Samsa, "now thanks be to God." He crossed himself, and the three women followed his example. Grete, whose eyes never left the corpse, said: "Just see how thin he was. It's such a long time since he's eaten anything. The food came out again just as it went in." Indeed, Gregor's body was completely flat and dry, as could only now be seen when it was no longer supported by the legs and nothing prevented one from looking closely at it.

"Come in beside us, Grete, for a little while," said Mrs. Samsa with a tremulous smile, and Grete, not without looking back at the corpse, followed her parents into their bedroom. The charwoman shut the door and opened the window wide. Although it was so early in the morning a certain softness was perceptible in the fresh air. After all, it was already the end of March.

The three lodgers emerged from their room and were surprised to see no breakfast; they had been forgotten. "Where's our breakfast?" said the middle lodger peevishly to the charwoman. But she put her finger to her lips and hastily, without a word, indicated by gestures that they should go into Gregor's room. They did so and stood, their hands in the pockets of their somewhat shabby coats, around Gregor's corpse in the room where it was now fully light.

At that the door of the Samsas' bedroom opened and Mr. Samsa appeared in his uniform, his wife on one arm, his daughter on the other. They all looked a little as if they had been crying; from time to time Grete hid her face on her father's arm.

"Leave my house at once!" said Mr. Samsa, and pointed to the door without disengaging himself from the women. "What do you mean by that?" said the middle lodger, taken somewhat aback, with a feeble smile. The two others put their hands behind them and kept rubbing them together, as if in gleeful expectation of a fine set-to in which they were bound to come off the winners. "I mean just what

I say," answered Mr. Samsa, and advanced in a straight line with his two companions towards the lodger. He stood his ground at first quietly, looking at the floor as if his thoughts were taking a new pattern in his head. "Then let us go, by all means," he said, and looked up at Mr. Samsa as if in a sudden access of humility he were expecting some renewed sanction for this decision. Mr. Samsa merely nodded briefly once or twice with meaning eyes. Upon that the lodger really did go with long strides into the hall, his two friends had been listening and had quite stopped rubbing their hands for some moments and now went scuttling after him as if afraid that Mr. Samsa might get into the hall before them and cut them off from their leader. In the hall they all three took their hats from the rack, their sticks from the umbrella stand, bowed in silence and quitted the apartment. With a suspiciousness which proved quite unfounded Mr. Samsa and the two women followed them out to the landing; leaning over the banister they watched the three figures slowly but surely going down the long stairs, vanishing from sight at a certain turn of the staircase on every floor and coming into view again after a moment or so; the more they dwindled, the more the Samsa family's interest in them dwindled, and when a butcher's boy met them and passed them on the stairs coming up proudly with a tray on his head, Mr. Samsa and the two women soon left the landing and as if a burden had been lifted from them went back into their apartment.

They decided to spend this day in resting and going for a stroll; they had not only deserved such a respite from work, but absolutely needed it. And so they sat down at the table and wrote three notes of excuse, Mr. Samsa to his board of management, Mrs. Samsa to her employer and Grete to the head of her firm. While they were writing, the charwoman came in to say that she was going now, since her morning's work was finished. At first they only nodded without looking up, but as she kept hovering there they eyed her irritably. "Well?" said Mr. Samsa. The charwoman stood grinning in the doorway as if she had good news to impart to the family but meant not to say a word unless properly questioned. The small ostrich feather standing upright on her hat, which had annoyed Mr. Samsa ever since she was engaged, was waving gaily in all directions. "Well, what is it then?" asked Mrs. Samsa, who obtained more respect from the charwoman than the others. "Oh," said the charwoman, giggling so amiably that she could not at once continue, "just this, you don't need to bother about how to get rid of the thing next door. It's been seen to already." Mrs. Samsa and Grete bent over their letters again, as if preoccupied; Mr. Samsa, who perceived that she was eager to begin describing it all in detail, stopped her with a decisive hand. But since she was not allowed to tell her story, she remembered the great hurry she was in, being obviously deeply huffed: "Bye, everybody," she said, whirling off violently, and departed with a frightful slamming of doors.

"She'll be given notice tonight," said Mr. Samsa, but neither from his wife nor his daughter did he get any answer, for the charwoman seemed to have shattered again the composure they had barely achieved. They rose, went to the window and stayed there, clasping each other tight. Mr. Samsa turned in his chair to look at them and quietly observed them for a little. Then he called out: "Come along, now, do. Let bygones be bygones. And you might have some consideration for me." The two of them complied at once, hastened to him, caressed him and quickly finished their letters.

Then they all three left the apartment together, which was more than they had done for months, and went by tram into the open country outside the town. The tram, in which they were the only passengers, was filled with warm sunshine. Leaning comfortably back in their seats they canvassed their prospects for the future, and it appeared on closer inspection that these were not at all bad, for the jobs they had got, which so far they had never really discussed with each other, were all three admirable and likely to lead to better things later on. The greatest immediate improvement in their condition would of course arise from moving to another house; they wanted to take a smaller and cheaper but also better situated and more easily run apartment than the one they had, which Gregor had selected. While they were thus conversing, it struck both Mr. and Mrs. Samsa, almost at the same moment, as they became aware of their daughter's increasing vivacity, that in spite of all the sorrow of recent times, which had made her cheeks pale, she had bloomed into a pretty girl with a good figure. They grew quieter and half unconsciously exchanged glances of complete agreement, having come to the conclusion that it would soon be time to find a good husband for her. And it was like a confirmation of their new dreams and excellent intentions that at the end of their journey their daughter sprang to her feet first and stretched her young body.

ERNEST HEMINGWAY (1899–1961), the most famous writer of his generation, was born into a large, well-to-do family outside of Chicago. Throughout his youth, Hemingway's family spent summers in northern Michigan, where he developed an interest in the outdoors that remained with him his entire life. After graduating from high school, Hemingway worked briefly as a reporter before volunteering to serve as an ambulance driver in World War I. He was soon wounded and returned to the United States, decorated for his service but also disillusioned by his experiences. After the war, Hemingway returned to Europe and continued to work as a reporter as he began to write short stories. The circle of friends and mentors that Hemingway developed in Paris, including Ezra Pound, Gertrude Stein, and F. Scott Fitzgerald, proved instrumental to his development as a writer.

Hemingway's adventurous experiences provided much of the material for his short stories, novels, and **creative nonfiction**. His early short stories draw heavily on his youth, and his novel *The Sun Also Rises* (1926) incorporates his interest in bullfighting. *A Farewell to Arms* (1929) depicts a romance loosely modeled on his own experiences in Italy during the war. *For Whom the Bell Tolls* (1939) is set during the Spanish Civil War, which Hemingway covered as a reporter, and *The Old Man and the Sea* (1952) builds on the many years Hemingway spent deep-sea fishing in the waters around Cuba. This novel, the last published during Hemingway's lifetime, helped him win the Nobel Prize for Literature in 1954.

Hemingway's work is more than adventure writing, however, as "A Clean, Well-Lighted Place" (1926) demonstrates. This simple, uneventful story demonstrates Hemingway's sensitive portrayal of the despair and disillusionment associated with the "Lost Generation" of the post–World War I era. In addition, the story provides a good example of the straightforward, minimalist style that characterized Hemingway's work and made him, along with William Faulkner, one of the two most important American **modernist** writers. Hemingway compared this style to an iceberg, explaining to an interviewer, "There is seven-eighths of it under water for every part that shows."

Related Works: O'Brien, "Stockings"; Arnold, "Dover Beach"; Auden, "The Unknown Citizen"; Rios, "The Vietnam Wall"; Jarrell, "Death of the Ball Turret Gunner."

Blurry chairs of an outdoor cafe beneath luminous lights at twilight

A Clean, Well-Lighted Place

It was late and every one had left the café except an old man who sat in the shadow the leaves of the tree made against the electric light. In the day time the street was dusty, but at night the dew settled the dust and the old man liked to sit late because he was deaf and now at night it was quiet and he felt the difference. The two waiters inside the café knew that the old man was a little drunk, and while he was a good client they knew that if he became too drunk he would leave without paying, so they kept watch on him.

"Last week he tried to commit suicide," one waiter said.

"Why?"

"He was in despair."

"What about?"

"Nothing."

"How do you know it was nothing?"

"He has plenty of money."

They sat together at a table that was close against the wall near the door of the café and looked at the terrace where the tables were all empty except where the old man sat in the shadow of the leaves of the tree that moved slightly in the wind. A girl and a soldier went by in the street. The street light shone on the brass number on his collar. The girl wore no head covering and hurried beside him.

"The guard will pick him up," one waiter said.

"What does it matter if he gets what he's after?"

"He had better get off the street now. The guard will get him. They went by five minutes ago."

The old man sitting in the shadow rapped on his saucer with his glass. The younger waiter went over to him.

"What do you want?"

The old man looked at him. "Another brandy," he said.

"You'll be drunk," the waiter said. The old man looked at him. The waiter went away.

"He'll stay all night," he said to his colleague. "I'm sleepy now. I never get into bed before three o'clock. He should have killed himself last week."

The waiter took the brandy bottle and another saucer from the counter inside the café and marched out to the old man's table. He put down the saucer and poured the glass full of brandy.

"You should have killed yourself last week," he said to the deaf man. The old man motioned with his finger. "A little more," he said. The waiter poured on into the glass so that the brandy slopped over and ran down the stem into the top saucer of the pile. "Thank you," the old man said. The waiter took the bottle back inside the café. He sat down at the table with his colleague again.

"He's drunk now," he said.

"He's drunk every night."

"What did he want to kill himself for?"

"How should I know."

"How did he do it?"

"He hung himself with a rope."

"Who cut him down?"

"His niece."

"Why did they do it?"

"Fear for his soul."

"How much money has he got?"

"He's got plenty."

"He must be eighty years old."

"Anyway I should say he was eighty."

"I wish he would go home. I never get to bed before three o'clock. What kind of hour is that to go to bed?"

"He stays up because he likes it."

"He's lonely. I'm not lonely. I have a wife waiting in bed for me."

"He had a wife once too."

"A wife would be no good to him now."

"You can't tell. He might be better with a wife."

"His niece looks after him. You said she cut him down."

"I know."

"I wouldn't want to be that old. An old man is a nasty thing."

"Not always. This old man is clean. He drinks without spilling. Even now, drunk. Look at him."

"I don't want to look at him. I wish he would go home. He has no regard for those who must work."

The old man looked from his glass across the square, then over at the waiters.

"Another brandy," he said, pointing to his glass. The waiter who was in a hurry came over.

"Finished," he said, speaking with that omission of syntax stupid people employ when talking to drunken people or foreigners. "No more tonight. Close now."

"Another," said the old man.

"No. Finished." The waiter wiped the edge of the table with a towel and shook his head.

The old man stood up, slowly counted the saucers, took a leather coin purse from his pocket and paid for the drinks, leaving half a peseta tip.

The waiter watched him go down the street, a very old man walking unsteadily but with dignity.

"Why didn't you let him stay and drink?" the unhurried waiter asked. They were putting up the shutters. "It is not half-past two."

"I want to go home to bed."

"What is an hour?"

"More to me than to him."

"An hour is the same."

"You talk like an old man yourself. He can buy a bottle and drink at home."

"It's not the same."

"No, it is not," agreed the waiter with a wife. He did not wish to be unjust. He was only in a hurry.

"And you? You have no fear of going home before your usual hour?"

"Are you trying to insult me?"

"No, *hombre*, only to make a joke."

"No," the waiter who was in a hurry said, rising from pulling down the metal shutters. "I have confidence. I am all confidence."

"You have youth, confidence, and a job," the older waiter said. "You have everything."

"And what do you lack?"

"Everything but work."

"You have everything I have."

"No. I have never had confidence and I am not young."

"Come on. Stop talking nonsense and lock up."

"I am of those who like to stay late at the café," the older waiter said. "With all those who do not want to go to bed. With all those who need a light for the night."

"I want to go home and into bed."

"We are of two different kinds," the older waiter said. He was now dressed to go home. "It is not only a question of youth and confidence although those things are very beautiful. Each night I am reluctant to close up because there may be some one who needs the café."

"*Hombre*, there are *bodegas* open all night long."

"You do not understand. This is a clean and pleasant café. It is well lighted. The light is very good and also, now, there are shadows of the leaves."

"Good night," said the younger waiter.

"Good night," the other said. Turning off the electric light he continued the conversation with himself. It is the light of course but it is necessary that the place be clean and pleasant. You do not want music. Certainly you do not want music. Nor can you stand before a bar with dignity although that is all that is provided for these hours. What did he fear? It was not fear or dread. It was a nothing that he knew too well. It was all a nothing and a man was nothing too. It was only that and light was all it needed and a certain cleanness and order. Some lived in it and never felt it but he knew it all was *nada y pues nada y nada y pues nada*. Our *nada* who art in *nada, nada* be thy name thy kingdom *nada* thy will be *nada* in *nada* as it is in *nada*. Give us this *nada* our daily *nada* and *nada* us our *nada* as we *nada* our *nadas* and *nada* us not into *nada* but deliver us from *nada; pues nada*. Hail nothing full of nothing, nothing is with thee. He smiled and stood before a bar with a shining steam pressure coffee machine.

"What's yours?" asked the barman.

"*Nada*."

"*Otro loco más*," said the barman and turned away.

"A little cup," said the waiter.

The barman poured it for him.

"The light is very bright and pleasant but the bar is unpolished," the waiter said.

The barman looked at him but did not answer. It was too late at night for conversation.

"You want another *copita*?" the barman asked.

"No, thank you," said the waiter and went out. He disliked bars and *bodegas*. A clean, well-lighted café was a very different thing. Now, without thinking further, he would go home to his room. He would lie in the bed and finally, with daylight, he would go to sleep. After all, he said to himself, it is probably only insomnia. Many must have it.

KATHERINE ANNE PORTER (1890–1980) was born Callie Russell Porter in a log house on a dirt farm in Texas. Porter's mother died when she was two, and Porter was raised by her paternal grandmother, Catherine Anne Porter. Her grandmother was a domineering woman who maintained control of the household despite the presence of Porter's father. Catherine Porter greatly influenced her granddaughter's attitudes toward the role of women in society. Although she had little formal education, Porter and one of her sisters briefly ran a school of elocution, singing, and drama, and she aspired to become an actress herself. In spite of her career ambitions, Porter married at sixteen and moved to Corpus Christi with her husband, who was a member of a prominent and patriarchal Catholic family. In 1914, Porter left her husband, changed her name, and moved to Chicago to work in a movie studio. After a brief career in the cinema, Porter moved to Louisiana to live with her sister. When she contracted tuberculosis, she was sent back to Texas to recover. While in the hospital, she became inspired by her friendship with a female newspaper editor and, after recovering, wrote for newspapers in Fort Worth and Denver.

Porter began to publish fiction in the 1920s and took several trips to Mexico, where she became friends with artist Diego Rivera, on whom she based her story "The Martyr" (1923). She also established friendships with fellow writers Robert Penn Warren, Hart Crane, and Malcolm Cowley. Her *Collected Stories* (1964) won both a Pulitzer Prize and a National Book Award. Her novel, *Ship of Fools*, was published in 1962.

Like "The Jilting of Granny Weatherall" (1929), much of Porter's fiction contains strong female figures who resist being confined to stereotypical roles imposed by a **patriarchal** society.

Unfortunately, the demeaning patriarchal structures often prove too extensive to overcome, and so the escapes from such socially confined roles often turn out to be only brief respites from the norm.

Related Works: Faulkner, "A Rose for Emily"; Steinbeck, "Chrysanthemums"; Mukherjee, "A Wife's Story"; "The Wife's Lament"; Robert Browning, "My Last Duchess"; Glaspell, *Trifles*; Norman, *'Night Mother.*

The Jilting of Granny Weatherall

She flicked her wrist neatly out of Doctor Harry's pudgy careful fingers and pulled the sheet up to her chin. The brat ought to be in knee breeches. Doctoring around the country with spectacles on his nose! "Get along now, take your schoolbooks and go. There's nothing wrong with me."

Doctor Harry spread a warm paw like a cushion on her forehead where the forked green vein danced and made her eyelids twitch. "Now, now, be a good girl, and we'll have you up in no time."

"That's no way to speak to a woman nearly eighty years old just because she's down. I'd have you respect your elders, young man."

"Well, Missy, excuse me." Doctor Harry patted her cheek. "But I've got to warn you, haven't I? You're a marvel, but you must be careful or you're going to be good and sorry."

"Don't tell me what I'm going to be. I'm on my feet now, morally speaking. It's Cornelia. I had to go to bed to get rid of her."

Her bones felt loose, and floated around in her skin, and Doctor Harry floated like a balloon around the foot of the bed. He floated and pulled down his waistcoat and swung his glasses on a cord, "Well, stay where you are, it certainly can't hurt you."

"Get along and doctor your sick," said Granny Weatherall. "Leave a well woman alone. I'll call for you when I want you. . . . Where were you forty years ago when I pulled through milk-leg and double pneumonia? You weren't even born. Don't let Cornelia lead you on," she shouted, because Doctor Harry appeared to float up to the ceiling and out. "I pay my own bills, and I don't throw my money away on nonsense!"

She meant to wave good-by, but it was too much trouble. Her eyes closed of themselves, it was like a dark curtain drawn around the bed. The pillow rose and floated under her, pleasant as a hammock in a light wind. She listened to the leaves rustling outside the window. No, somebody was swishing newspapers: no, Cornelia and Doctor Harry were whispering together. She leaped broad awake, thinking they whispered in her ear.

"She was never like this, *never* like this!" "Well, what can we expect?" "Yes, eighty years old. . . ."

Well, and what if she was? She still had ears. It was like Cornelia to whisper around doors. She always kept things secret in such a public way. She was always being tactful and kind. Cornelia was dutiful; that was the trouble with her. Dutiful and good: "So good and dutiful," said Granny, "that I'd like to spank her." She saw herself spanking Cornelia and making a fine job of it.

"What'd you say, Mother?"

Granny felt her face tying up in hard knots.

"Can't a body think, I'd like to know?"

"I thought you might want something."

"I do. I want a lot of things. First off, go away and don't whisper."

She lay and drowsed, hoping in her sleep that the children would keep out and let her rest a minute. It had been a long day. Not that she was tired. It was always pleasant to snatch a minute now and then. There was always so much to be done, let me see: tomorrow.

Tomorrow was far away and there was nothing to trouble about. Things were finished somehow when the time came; thank God there was always a little margin over for peace: then a person could spread out the plan of life and tuck in the edges orderly. It was good to have everything clean and folded away, with the hair brushes and tonic bottles sitting straight on the white embroidered linen: the day started without fuss and the pantry shelves laid out with rows of jelly glasses and brown jugs and white stone-china jars with blue whirligigs and words painted on them: coffee, tea, sugar, ginger, cinnamon, allspice: and the bronze clock with the lion on top nicely dusted off. The dust that lion could collect in twenty-four hours! The box in the attic with all those letters tied up, well, she'd have to go through that tomorrow. All those letters—George's letters and John's letters and her letters to them both—lying around for the children to find afterwards made her uneasy. Yes, that would be tomorrow's business. No use to let them know how silly she had been once.

While she was rummaging around she found death in her mind and it felt clammy and unfamiliar. She had spent so much time preparing for death there was no need for bringing it up again. Let it take care of itself now. When she was sixty she had felt very old, finished, and went around making farewell trips to see her children and grandchildren, with a secret in her mind: This is the very last of your mother, children! Then she made her will and came down with a long fever. That was all just a notion like a lot of other things, but it was lucky too, for she had once for all got over the idea of dying for a long time. Now she couldn't be worried. She hoped she had better sense now. Her father had lived to be one hundred and two years old and had drunk a noggin of strong hot toddy on his last birthday. He told the reporters it was his daily habit, and he owed his long life to that. He had made quite a scandal and was very pleased about it. She believed she'd just plague Cornelia a little.

"Cornelia! Cornelia!" No footsteps, but a sudden hand on her check. "Bless you, where have you been?"

"Here, mother."

"Well, Cornelia, I want a noggin of hot toddy."

"Are you cold, darling?"

"I'm chilly, Cornelia. Lying in bed stops the circulation. I must have told you that a thousand times."

Well, she could just hear Cornelia telling her husband that Mother was getting a little childish and they'd have to humor her. The thing that most annoyed her was that Cornelia thought she was deaf, dumb, and blind. Little hasty glances and tiny gestures tossed around her and over her head saying, "Don't cross her, let her have her way, she's eighty years old," and she sitting there as if she lived in a thin glass cage. Sometimes Granny almost made up her mind to pack up and move back to her own house where nobody could remind her every minute that she was old. Wait, wait, Cornelia, till your own children whisper behind your back!

In her day she had kept a better house and had got more work done. She wasn't too old yet for Lydia to be driving eighty miles for advice when one of the children jumped the track, and Jimmy still dropped in and talked things over: "Now, Mammy, you've a good business head, I want to know what you think of this? . . ." Old. Cornelia couldn't change the furniture around without asking. Little things, little things! They had been so sweet when they were little. Granny wished the old days were back again with the children young and everything to be done over. It had been a hard pull, but not too much for her. When she thought of all the food she had cooked, and all the clothes she had cut and sewed, and all the gardens she had made—well, the children showed it. There they were, made out of her, and they couldn't get away from that. Sometimes she wanted to see John again and point to them and say, Well, I didn't do so badly, did I? But that would have to wait. That was for tomorrow. She used to think of him as a man, but now all the children were older than their father, and he would be a child beside her if she saw him now. It seemed strange and there was something wrong in the idea. Why, he couldn't possibly recognize her. She had fenced in a hundred acres once, digging the post holes herself and clamping the wires with just a negro boy to help. That changed a woman. John would be looking for a young woman with the peaked Spanish comb in her hair and the painted fan. Digging post holes changed a woman. Riding country roads in the winter when women had their babies was another thing: sitting up nights with sick horses and sick negroes and sick children and hardly ever losing one. John, I hardly ever lost one of them! John would see that in a minute, that would be something he could understand, she wouldn't have to explain anything!

It made her feel like rolling up her sleeves and putting the whole place to rights again. No matter if Cornelia was determined to be everywhere at once, there were a great many things left undone on this place. She would start tomorrow and do them. It was good to be strong enough for everything, even if all you made melted and changed and slipped under your hands, so that by the time you finished you almost forgot what you were working for. What was it I set out to do? she asked herself intently, but she could not remember. A fog rose over the valley, she saw it marching across the creek swallowing the trees and moving up the hill like an army of ghosts. Soon it would be at the near edge of the orchard, and then it was time to go in and light the lamps. Come in, children, don't stay out in the night air.

Lighting the lamps had been beautiful. The children huddled up to her and breathed like little calves waiting at the bars in the twilight. Their eyes followed the match and watched the flame rise and settle in a blue curve, then they moved away from her. The lamp was lit, they didn't have to be scared and hang on to mother any more. Never, never, never more. God, for all my life I thank Thee. Without Thee, my God, I could never have done it. Hail, Mary, full of grace.

I want you to pick all the fruit this year and see that nothing is wasted. There's always someone who can use it. Don't let good things rot for want of using. You waste life when you waste good food. Don't let things get lost. It's bitter to lose things. Now, don't let me get to thinking, not when I am tired and taking a little nap before supper. . . .

The pillow rose about her shoulders and pressed against her heart and the memory was being squeezed out of it: oh, push down the pillow, somebody: it would smother her if she tried to hold it. Such a fresh breeze blowing and such a green day with no threats in it. But he had not come, just the same. What does a woman do when she has put on the white veil and set out the white cake for a man and he doesn't come? She tried to remember. No, I swear he never harmed me but in that. He never harmed me but in that . . . and what if he did? There was the day, the day, but a whirl of dark smoke rose and covered it, crept up and over into the bright field where everything was planted so carefully in orderly rows. That was hell, she knew hell when she saw it. For sixty years she had prayed against remembering him and against losing her soul in the deep pit of hell, and now the two things were mingled in one and the thought of him was a smoky cloud from hell that moved and crept in her head when she had just got rid of Doctor Harry and was trying to rest a minute. Wounded vanity, Ellen, said a sharp voice in the top of her mind. Don't let your wounded vanity get the upper hand of you. Plenty of girls get jilted. You were jilted, weren't you? Then stand up to it. Her eyelids wavered and let in streamers of blue-gray light like tissue paper over her eyes. She must get up and pull the shades down or she'd never sleep. She was in bed again and the shades were not down. How could that happen? Better turn over, hide from the light, sleeping in the light gave you nightmares. "Mother, how do you feel now?" and a stinging wetness on her forehead. But I don't like having my face washed in cold water!

Hapsy? George? Lydia? Jimmy? No, Cornelia, and her features were swollen and full of little puddles. "They're coming, darling, they'll all be here soon." Go wash your face, child, you look funny.

Instead of obeying, Cornelia knelt down and put her head on the pillow. She seemed to be talking but there was no sound. "Well, are you tongue-tied? Whose birthday is it? Are you going to give a party?"

Cornelia's mouth moved urgently in strange shapes. "Don't do that, you bother me, daughter."

"Oh, no, Mother. Oh, no. . . ."

Nonsense. It was strange about children. They disputed your every word. "No what, Cornelia?"

"Here's Doctor Harry."

"I won't see that boy again. He just left five minutes ago."

"That was this morning, Mother. It's night now. Here's the nurse."

"This is Doctor Harry, Mrs. Weatherall. I never saw you look so young and happy!"

"Ah, I'll never be young again—but I'd be happy if they'd let me lie in peace and get rested."

She thought she spoke up loudly, but no one answered. A warm weight on her forehead, a warm bracelet on her wrist, and a breeze went on whispering, trying to tell her something. A shuffle of leaves in the everlasting hand of God, He blew on them and they danced and rattled. "Mother, don't mind, we're going to give you a little hypodermic." "Look here, daughter, how do ants get in this bed? I saw sugar ants yesterday." Did you send for Hapsy too?

It was Hapsy she really wanted. She had to go a long way back through a great many rooms to find Hapsy standing with a baby on her arm. She seemed to herself to be Hapsy also, and the baby on Hapsy's arm was Hapsy and himself and herself, all at once, and there was no surprise in the meeting. Then Hapsy melted from within and turned flimsy as gray gauze and the baby was a gauzy shadow, and Hapsy came up close and said, "I thought you'd never come," and looked at her very searchingly and said, "You haven't changed a bit!" They leaned forward to kiss, when Cornelia began whispering from a long way off, "Oh, is there anything you want to tell me? Is there anything I can do for you?"

Yes, she had changed her mind after sixty years and she would like to see George. I want you to find George. Find him and be sure to tell him I forgot him. I want him to know I had my husband just the same and my children and my house like any other woman. A good house too and a good husband that I loved and fine children out of him. Better than I hoped for even. Tell him I was given back everything he took away and more. Oh, no, oh, God, no, there was something else besides the house and the man and the children. Oh, surely they were not all? What was it? Something not given back. . . . Her breath crowded down under her ribs and grew into a monstrous frightening shape with cutting edges; it bored up into her head, and the agony was unbelievable: Yes, John, get the Doctor now, no more talk, my time has come.

When this one was born it should be the last. The last. It should have been born first, for it was the one she had truly wanted. Everything came in good time. Nothing left out, left over. She was strong, in three days she would be as well as ever. Better. A woman needed milk in her to have her full health.

"Mother, do you hear me?"

"I've been telling you—"

"Mother, Father Connolly's here."

"I went to Holy Communion only last week. Tell him I'm not so sinful as all that."

"Father just wants to speak to you."

He could speak as much as he pleased. It was like him to drop in and inquire about her soul as if it were a teething baby, and then stay on for a cup of tea and a round of cards and gossip. He always had a funny story of some sort, usually about an Irishman who made his little mistakes and confessed them, and the point lay in some absurd thing he would blurt out in the confessional showing his struggles between native piety and original sin. Granny felt easy about her soul. Cornelia, where are your manners? Give Father Connolly a chair. She had her secret comfortable understanding with a few favorite saints who cleared a straight road to God for her. All as surely signed and sealed as the papers for the new Forty Acres. Forever . . . heirs and assigns forever. Since the day the wedding cake was not cut, but thrown out and wasted. The whole bottom dropped out of the world, and there she was blind and sweating with nothing under her feet and the walls falling away. His hand had caught her under the breast, she had not fallen, there was the freshly polished floor with the green rug on it, just as before. He had cursed like a sailor's parrot and said, "I'll kill him for you." Don't lay a hand on him, for my sake leave something to God. "Now, Ellen, you must believe what I tell you. . . ."

So there was nothing, nothing to worry about any more, except sometimes in the night one of the children screamed in a nightmare, and they both hustled out shaking and hunting for the matches and calling, "There, wait a minute, here we are!" John, get the doctor now, Hapsy's time has come. But there was Hapsy standing by the bed in a white cap. "Cornelia, tell Hapsy to take off her cap. I can't see her plain."

Her eyes opened very wide and the room stood out like a picture she had seen somewhere. Dark colors with the shadows rising towards the ceiling in long angles. The tall black dresser gleamed with nothing on it but John's picture, enlarged from a little one, with John's eyes very black when they should have been blue. You never saw him, so how do you know how he looked? But the man insisted the copy was perfect, it was very rich and handsome. For a picture, yes, but it's not my husband. The table by the bed had a linen cover and a candle and a crucifix. The light was blue from Cornelia's silk lampshades. No sort of light at all, just frippery. You had to live forty years with kerosene lamps to appreciate honest electricity. She felt very strong and she saw Doctor Harry with a rosy nimbus around him.

"You look like a saint, Doctor Harry, and I vow that's as near as you'll ever come to it."

"She's saying something."

"I heard you, Cornelia. What's all this carrying-on?"

"Father Connolly's saying—"

Cornelia's voice staggered and bumped like a cart in a bad road. It rounded corners and turned back again and arrived nowhere. Granny stepped up in the cart very lightly and reached for the reins, but a man sat beside her and she knew him by his hands, driving the cart. She did not look in his face, for she knew without seeing, but looked instead down the road where the trees leaned over and bowed to each other and a thousand birds were singing a Mass. She felt like singing too, but she put her hand in the bosom of her dress and pulled out a rosary, and Father Connolly murmured Latin in a very solemn voice and tickled her feet. My God, will you stop that nonsense? I'm a married woman. What if he did run away and leave me to face the priest by myself? I found another a whole world better. I wouldn't have exchanged my husband for anybody except St. Michael himself, and you may tell him that for me with a thank you in the bargain.

Light flashed on her closed eyelids, and a deep roaring shook her. Cornelia, is that lightning? I hear thunder. There's going to be a storm. Close all the windows. Call the children in. . . . "Mother, here we are, all of us." "Is that you, Hapsy?" "Oh, no, I'm Lydia. We drove as fast as we could." Their faces drifted above her, drifted away. The rosary fell out of her hands and Lydia put it back. Jimmy tried to help, their hands fumbled together, and Granny closed two fingers around Jimmy's thumb. Beads wouldn't do, it must be something alive. She was so amazed her thoughts ran round and round. So, my dear Lord, this is my death and I wasn't even thinking about it. My children have come to see me die. But I can't, it's not time. Oh, I always hated surprises. I wanted to give Cornelia the amethyst set—Cornelia, you're to have the amethyst set, but Hapsy's to wear it when she wants, and, Doctor Harry, do shut up. Nobody sent for you. Oh, my dear Lord, do wait a minute. I meant to do something about the Forty Acres, Jimmy doesn't need it and Lydia will later on, with that worthless husband of hers. I meant to finish the altar cloth and send six bottles of wine to Sister Borgia for her dyspepsia. I want to send six bottles of wine to Sister Borgia, Father Connolly, now don't let me forget.

Cornelia's voice made short turns and tilted over and crashed. "Oh, Mother, oh, Mother, oh, Mother. . . ."

"I'm not going, Cornelia. I'm taken by surprise. I can't go."

You'll see Hapsy again. What about her? "I thought you'd never come." Granny made a long journey outward, looking for Hapsy. What if I don't find her? What then? Her heart sank down and down, there was no bottom to death, she couldn't come to the end of it. The blue light from Cornelia's lampshade drew into a tiny point in the center of her brain, it flickered and winked like an eye, quietly it fluttered and dwindled. Granny lay curled down within herself, amazed and watchful, staring at the point of light that was herself; her body was now only a deeper mass of shadow in an endless darkness and this darkness would curl around the light and swallow it up. God, give a sign!

For the second time there was no sign. Again no bridegroom and the priest in the house. She could not remember any other sorrow because this grief wiped them all away. Oh, no, there's nothing more cruel than this—I'll never forgive it. She stretched herself with a deep breath and blew out the light.

William Faulkner (1897–1962) grew up and spent most of his life in Oxford, Mississippi, the town that provided the model for Jefferson, the seat of his fictional Yoknapatawpha County. The oldest son in a prominent but declining family, Faulkner dropped out of high school in 1915 and later attended the University of Mississippi for a year. More important than formal education was Faulkner's absorption of Southern history, culture, and storytelling, which became central concerns of his writing.

Faulkner drifted from job to job through much of the 1920s, eventually spending time in New Orleans, where he began to publish regularly in journals and newspapers. Here, he also met Sherwood Anderson, who became his mentor. After two early novels, Faulkner turned to his native Mississippi for material. His familiarity with this background enabled Faulkner to develop the most versatile and sophisticated style among the American **modernist** writers. In 1929, he published his first critically acclaimed novel, *The Sound and the Fury*, a complex retelling of the same events from multiple perspectives that makes sophisticated use of **stream of consciousness** narration. This was soon followed by his first short story in a national magazine, "A Rose for Emily" (1930).

Faulkner's artistic success continued throughout the 1930s with the publication of *As I Lay Dying* (1930), *Light in August* (1932), and *Absalom, Absalom!* (1936), among others. The publication of the antiracist *Intruder in the Dust* (1948) brought both economic security and long-lasting critical affirmation when Faulkner was awarded the Nobel Prize for Literature in 1950.

The complicated interconnections between past and present frequently emerge throughout Faulkner's fiction, particularly in "A Rose for Emily." Here, Faulkner fragments the chronology of the story with repeated **flashbacks** as the townspeople attempt to reconstruct an accurate picture of Miss Emily. The climactic revelation exposes the **grotesque** nature of Miss Emily's actions, but Faulkner's linking of past and present, Old South and New South through a gossipy narrator implicates the town and perhaps even the reader in these grotesque events as well.

Related Works: O'Connor, "Good Country People"; Poe, "The Cask of Amontillado"; Porter, "The Jilting of Granny Weatherall"; Lewis, "Limestone Diner."

A Rose for Emily

I

When Miss Emily Grierson died, our whole town went to her funeral: the men through a sort of respectful affection for a fallen monument, the women mostly out of curiosity to see the inside of her house, which no one save an old manservant—a combined gardener and cook—had seen in at least ten years.

It was a big, squarish frame house that had once been white, decorated with cupolas and spires and scrolled balconies in the heavily lightsome style of the seventies, set on what had once been our most select street. But garages and cotton gins had encroached and obliterated even the august names of that neighborhood; only Miss Emily's house was left, lifting its stubborn and coquettish decay above the cotton wagons and the gasoline pumps—an eyesore among eyesores. And now Miss Emily had gone to join the representatives of those august names where they lay in the cedar-bemused cemetery among the ranked and anonymous graves of Union and Confederate soldiers who fell at the battle of Jefferson.

Alive, Miss Emily had been a tradition, a duty, and a care; a sort of hereditary obligation upon the town, dating from that day in 1894 when Colonel Sartoris, the mayor—he who fathered the edict that no Negro woman should appear on the streets without an apron—remitted her taxes, the dispensation dating from the death of her father on into perpetuity. Not that Miss Emily would have accepted charity. Colonel Sartoris invented an involved tale to the effect that Miss Emily's father had loaned money to the town, which the town, as a matter of business, preferred this way of repaying. Only a man of Colonel Sartoris' generation and thought could have invented it, and only a woman could have believed it.

When the next generation, with its more modern ideas, became mayors and aldermen, this arrangement created some little dissatisfaction. On the first of the year they mailed her a tax notice. February came, and there was no reply. They wrote her a formal letter, asking her to call at the sheriff's office at her convenience. A week later the mayor wrote her himself, offering to call or to send his car for her, and received in reply a note on paper of an archaic shape, in a thin, flowing calligraphy in faded ink, to the effect that she no longer went out at all. The tax notice was also enclosed, without comment.

They called a special meeting of the Board of Aldermen. A deputation waited upon her, knocked at the door through which no visitor had passed since she ceased giving china-painting lessons eight or ten years earlier. They were admitted by the old Negro into a dim hall from which a stairway mounted into still more shadow. It smelled of dust and disuse—a close, dank smell. The Negro led them into the parlor. It was furnished in heavy, leather-covered furniture. When the Negro opened the blinds of one window, they could see that the leather was cracked; and when they sat down, a faint dust rose sluggishly about their thighs, spinning with slow motes in the single sun-ray. On a tarnished gilt easel before the fireplace stood a crayon portrait of Miss Emily's father.

They rose when she entered—a small, fat woman in black, with a thin gold chain descending to her waist and vanishing into her belt, leaning on an ebony cane with a tarnished gold head. Her skeleton was small and spare; perhaps that was why what would have been merely plumpness in another was obesity in her. She looked bloated, like a body long submerged in motionless water, and of that pallid hue. Her eyes, lost in the fatty ridges of her face, looked like two small pieces of coal pressed into a lump of dough as they moved from one face to another while the visitors stated their errand.

She did not ask them to sit. She just stood in the door and listened quietly until the spokesman came to a stumbling halt. Then they could hear the invisible watch ticking at the end of the gold chain.

Her voice was dry and cold. "I have no taxes in Jefferson. Colonel Sartoris explained it to me. Perhaps one of you can gain access to the city records and satisfy yourselves."

"But we have. We are the city authorities, Miss Emily. Didn't you get a notice from the sheriff, signed by him?"

"I received a paper, yes," Miss Emily said. "Perhaps he considers himself the sheriff. . . I have no taxes in Jefferson."

"But there is nothing on the books to show that, you see. We must go by the—"

"See Colonel Sartoris. I have no taxes in Jefferson."

"But, Miss Emily—"

"See Colonel Sartoris." (Colonel Sartoris had been dead almost ten years.) "I have no taxes in Jefferson. Tobe!" The Negro appeared. "Show these gentlemen out."

II

So she vanquished them, horse and foot, just as she had vanquished their fathers thirty years before about the smell. That was two years after her father's death and a short time after her sweetheart—the one we believed would marry her—had deserted her. After her father's death she went out very little; after her sweetheart went away, people hardly saw her at all. A few of the ladies had the temerity to call, but were not received, and the only sign of life about the place was the Negro man—a young man then—going in and out with a market basket.

"Just as if a man—any man—could keep a kitchen properly," the ladies said; so they were not surprised when the smell developed. It was another link between the gross, teeming world and the high and mighty Griersons.

A neighbor, a woman, complained to the mayor, Judge Stevens, eighty years old.

"But what will you have me do about it, madam?" he said.

"Why, send her word to stop it," the woman said. "Isn't there a law?"

"I'm sure that won't be necessary," Judge Stevens said. "It's probably just a snake or a rat that nigger of hers killed in the yard. I'll speak to him about it."

The next day he received two more complaints, one from a man who came in diffident deprecation. "We really must do something about it, Judge. I'd be the last one in the world to bother Miss Emily, but we've got to do something." That night the Board of Aldermen met—three graybeards and one younger man, a member of the rising generation.

"It's simple enough," he said. "Send her word to have her place cleaned up. Give her a certain time to do it in, and if she don't. . ."

"Dammit, sir," Judge Stevens said, "will you accuse a lady to her face of smelling bad?"

So the next night, after midnight, four men crossed Miss Emily's lawn and slunk about the house like burglars, sniffing along the base of the brickwork and at the cellar openings while one of them performed a regular sowing motion with his hand out of a sack slung from his shoulder. They broke open the cellar door and sprinkled lime there, and in all the outbuildings. As they recrossed the lawn, a window that had been dark was lighted and Miss Emily sat in it, the light behind her, and her upright torso motionless as that of an idol. They crept quietly across the lawn and into the shadow of the locusts that lined the street. After a week or two the smell went away.

That was when people had begun to feel really sorry for her. People in our town, remembering how old lady Wyatt, her great-aunt, had gone completely crazy at last, believed that the Griersons held themselves a little too high for what they really were. None of the young men were quite good enough to Miss Emily and such. We had long thought of them as a tableau; Miss Emily a slender figure in white in the background, her father a spraddled silhouette in the foreground, his back to her and clutching a horsewhip, the two of them formed by the back-flung front door. So when she got to be thirty and was still single, we were not pleased exactly, but vindicated; even with insanity in the family she wouldn't have turned down all of her chances if they had really materialized.

When her father died, it got about that the house was all that was left to her; and in a way, people were glad. At last they could pity Miss Emily. Being left alone, and a pauper, she had become humanized. Now she too would know the old thrill and the old despair of a penny more or less.

The day after his death all the ladies prepared to call at the house and offer condolence and aid, as is our custom. Miss Emily met them at the door, dressed as usual and with no trace of grief on her face. She told them that her father was not dead. She did that for three days, with the ministers calling on her, and the doctors, trying to persuade her to let them dispose of the body. Just as they were about to resort to law and force, she broke down, and they buried her father quickly.

We did not say she was crazy then. We believed she had to do that. We remembered all the young men her father had driven away, and we knew that with nothing left, she would have to cling to that which had robbed her, as people will.

III

She was sick for a long time. When we saw her again, her hair was cut short, making her look like a girl, with a vague resemblance to those angels in colored church windows—sort of tragic and serene.

The town had just let the contracts for paving the sidewalks, and in the summer after her father's death they began the work. The construction company came with niggers and mules and machinery, and a foreman named Homer Barron, a Yankee—a big, dark, ready man, with a big voice and eyes lighter than his face. The little boys would follow in groups to hear him cuss the niggers, and the niggers singing in time to the rise and fall of picks. Pretty soon he knew everybody in town. Whenever you heard a lot of laughing anywhere about the square, Homer Barron would be in the center of the group. Presently we began to see him and Miss Emily on Sunday afternoons driving in the yellow-wheeled buggy and the matched team of bays from the livery stable.

At first we were glad that Miss Emily would have an interest, because the ladies all said, "Of course a Grierson would not think seriously of a Northerner, a day laborer." But there were still others, older people, who said that even grief could not cause a real lady to forget *noblesse oblige*—without calling it *noblesse oblige*. They just said, "Poor Emily. Her kinsfolk should come to her." She had some kin in Alabama; but years ago her father had fallen out with them over the estate of old lady Wyatt, the crazy woman, and there was no communication between the two families. They had not even been represented at the funeral.

And as soon as the old people said, "Poor Emily," the whispering began. "Do you suppose it's really so?" they said to one another. "Of course it is. What else could . . ." This behind their hands; rustling of craned silk and satin behind jalousies closed upon the sun of Sunday afternoon as the thin, swift clop-clop-clop of the matched team passed: "Poor Emily."

She carried her head high enough—even when we believed that she was fallen. It was as if she demanded more than ever the recognition of her dignity as the last Grierson; as if it had wanted that touch of earthiness to reaffirm her imperviousness. Like when she bought the rat poison, the arsenic. That was over a year after they had begun to say "Poor Emily," and while the two female cousins were visiting her.

"I want some poison," she said to the druggist. She was over thirty then, still a slight woman, though thinner than usual, with cold, haughty black eyes in a face the flesh of which was strained across the temples and about the eye-sockets as you imagine a lighthouse-keeper's face ought to look. "I want some poison," she said.

"Yes, Miss Emily. What kind? For rats and such? I'd recom—"

"I want the best you have. I don't care what kind."

The druggist named several. "They'll kill anything up to an elephant. But what you want is—"

"Arsenic," Miss Emily said. "Is that a good one?"

"Is . . . arsenic? Yes, ma'am. But what you want—"

"I want arsenic."

The druggist looked down at her. She looked back at him, erect, her face like a strained flag. "Why, of course," the druggist said. "If that's what you want. But the law requires you to tell what you are going to use it for."

Miss Emily just stared at him, her head tilted back in order to look him eye for eye, until he looked away and went and got the arsenic and wrapped it up. The Negro delivery boy brought her the package; the druggist didn't come back. When she opened the package at home there was written on the box, under the skull and bones: "For rats."

IV

So the next day we all said, "She will kill herself"; and we said it would be the best thing. When she had first begun to be seen with Homer Barron, we had said, "She will marry him." Then we said, "She will persuade him yet," because Homer himself had remarked—he liked men, and it was known that he drank with the younger men in the Elks' Club—that he was not a marrying man. Later we said, "Poor Emily" behind the jalousies as they passed on Sunday afternoon in the glittering buggy, Miss Emily with her head high and Homer Barron with his hat cocked and a cigar in his teeth, reins and whip in a yellow glove.

Then some of the ladies began to say that it was a disgrace to the town and a bad example to the young people. The men did not want to interfere, but at last the ladies forced the Baptist minister—Miss Emily's people were Episcopal—to call upon her. He would never divulge what happened during that interview, but he refused to go back again. The next Sunday they again drove about the streets, and the following day the minister's wife wrote to Miss Emily's relations in Alabama.

So she had blood-kin under her roof again and we sat back to watch developments. At first nothing happened. Then we were sure that they were to be married. We learned that Miss Emily had been to the jeweler's and ordered a man's toilet set in silver, with the letters H. B. on each piece. Two days later we learned that she had bought a complete outfit of men's clothing, including a nightshirt, and we said, "They are married." We were really glad. We were glad because the two female cousins were even more Grierson than Miss Emily had ever been.

So we were not surprised when Homer Barron—the streets had been finished some time since—was gone. We were a little disappointed that there was not a public blowing-off, but we believed that he had gone on to prepare for Miss Emily's coming, or to give her a chance to get rid of the cousins. (By that time it was a cabal, and we were all Miss Emily's allies to help circumvent the cousins.) Sure enough, after another week they departed. And, as we had expected all along, within three days Homer Barron was back in town. A neighbor saw the Negro man admit him at the kitchen door at dusk one evening.

And that was the last we saw of Homer Barron. And of Miss Emily for some time. The Negro man went in and out with the market basket, but the front door remained closed. Now and then we would see her at a window for a moment, as the men did that night when they sprinkled the lime, but for almost six months she did not appear on the streets. Then we knew that this was to be expected too; as if that quality of her father which had thwarted her woman's life so many times had been too virulent and too furious to die.

When we next saw Miss Emily, she had grown fat and her hair was turning gray. During the next few years it grew grayer and grayer until it attained an even pepper-and-salt iron-gray, when it ceased turning. Up to the day of her death at seventy-four it was still that vigorous iron-gray, like the hair of an active man.

From that time on her front door remained closed, save for a period of six or seven years, when she was about forty, during which she gave lessons in china-painting. She fitted up a studio in one of the downstairs rooms, where the daughters and granddaughters of Colonel Sartoris' contemporaries were sent to her with the same regularity and in the same spirit that they were sent to church on Sundays with a twenty-five cent piece for the collection plate. Meanwhile her taxes had been remitted.

Then the newer generation became the backbone and the spirit of the town, and the painting pupils grew up and fell away and did not send their children to her with boxes of color and tedious brushes and pictures cut from the ladies' magazines. The front door closed upon the last one and remained closed for good. When the town got free postal delivery, Miss Emily alone refused to let them fasten the metal numbers above her door and attach a mailbox to it. She would not listen to them.

Daily, monthly, yearly we watched the Negro grow grayer and more stooped, going in and out with the market basket. Each December we sent her a tax notice, which would be returned by the post office a week later, unclaimed. Now and then we would see her in one of the downstairs windows—she had evidently shut up the top floor of the house—like the carven torso of an idol in a niche, looking or not looking at us, we could never tell which. Thus she passed from generation to generation—dear, inescapable, impervious, tranquil, and perverse.

And so she died. Fell ill in the house filled with dust and shadows, with only a doddering Negro man to wait on her. We did not even know she was sick; we had long since given up trying to get any information from the Negro. He talked to no one, probably not even to her, for his voice had grown harsh and rusty, as if from disuse.

She died in one of the downstairs rooms, in a heavy walnut bed with a curtain, her gray head propped on a pillow yellow and moldy with age and lack of sunlight.

V

The Negro met the first of the ladies at the front door and let them in, with their hushed, sibilant voices and their quick, curious glances, and then he disappeared. He walked right through the house and out the back and was not seen again.

The two female cousins came at once. They held the funeral on the second day, with the town coming to look at Miss Emily beneath a mass of bought flowers, with the crayon face of her father musing profoundly above the bier and the ladies sibilant and macabre; and the very old men—some in their brushed Confederate uniforms—on the porch and the lawn, talking of Miss Emily as if she had been a contemporary of theirs, believing that they had danced with her and courted her perhaps, confusing time with its mathematical progression, as the old do, to whom all the past is not a diminishing road but, instead, a huge meadow which no winter ever quite touches, divided from them now by the narrow bottle-neck of the most recent decade of years.

Already we knew that there was one room in that region above stairs which no one had seen in forty years, and which would have to be forced. They waited until Miss Emily was decently in the ground before they opened it.

The violence of breaking down the door seemed to fill this room with pervading dust. A thin, acrid pall as of the tomb seemed to lie everywhere upon this room decked and furnished as for a bridal: upon the valence curtains of faded rose color, upon the rose-shaded lights, upon the dressing table, upon the delicate array of crystal and the man's toilet things backed with tarnished silver, silver so tarnished that the monogram was obscured. Among them lay a collar and tie, as if they had just been removed, which, lifted, left upon the surface a pale crescent in the dust. Upon a chair hung the suit, carefully folded; beneath it the two mute shoes and the discarded socks.

The man himself lay in the bed.

For a long while we just stood there, looking down at the profound and fleshless grin. The body had apparently once lain in the attitude of an embrace, but now the long sleep that outlasts love, that conquers even the grimace of love, had cuckolded him. What was left of him, rotted beneath what was left of the nightshirt, had become inextricable from the bed in which he lay; and upon him and upon the pillow beside him lay that even coating of the patient and biding dust.

Then we noticed that in the second pillow was the indentation of a head. One of us lifted something from it, and leaning forward, that faint and invisible dust dry and acrid in the nostrils, we saw a long strand of iron-gray hair.

JOHN STEINBECK (1902–1968) was born in Salinas, California, an agricultural area along the Pacific coast. His writing talents were recognized in high school, and when he graduated he enrolled at Stanford as an English major. To earn money to stay in school, Steinbeck hired himself out as a laborer on ranches and farms, although he continued to write. His first collection of stories, *The Pastures of Heaven*, was published in 1932. In 1939 he won the Pulitzer Prize for his novel *The Grapes of Wrath*, and in 1962 he was awarded the Nobel Prize for Literature.

Although he recognized the hardships and struggles of living, Steinbeck had an optimistic view of humanity and the American dream, and he believed in human compassion and kindness despite the continued decline in morality and the increase of materialism. He trusted in the infinite adaptability of humans and the virtues of everyday living despite the hardships. Many of Steinbeck's characters belong to the working class—those laborers whom he acutely observed during his own time as a hired hand—and his stories can be seen as social protests or commentaries on the conditions of their lives.

"The Chrysanthemums" (1938) features a ranch in the Salinas Valley and a woman with a deep connection to the earth and to her prize flowers, a woman struggling to find an outlet for her strength and creativity in a world that restricts women's roles. Because Steinbeck firmly believed that nature—like Elisa's chrysanthemums, the surrounding fields, and the steers Henry raises and sells—is an inescapable part of humankind's survival and a necessary influence on our behaviors, he is often considered to be a **nature writer** as well.

Related Works: Chopin, "Story of an Hour"; Mukherjee, "A Wife's Story"; Cofer, "Tales Told under the Mango Tree"; Donne, "The Flea"; Berry, "The Peace of Wild Things"; Bishop, "The Fish"; Gioia, "California Hills in August."

The Chrysanthemums

The high grey-flannel fog of winter closed off the Salinas Valley from the sky and from all the rest of the world. On every side it sat like a lid on the mountains and made of the great valley a closed pot. On the broad, level land floor the gang plows bit deep and left the black earth shining like metal where the shares had cut. On the foothill ranches across the Salinas River, the yellow stubble fields seemed to be bathed in pale cold sunshine, but there was no sunshine in the valley now in December. The thick willow scrub along the river flamed with sharp and positive yellow leaves.

It was a time of quiet and of waiting. The air was cold and tender. A light wind blew up from the southwest so that the farmers were mildly hopeful of a good rain before long; but fog and rain do not go together.

Across the river, on Henry Allen's foothill ranch there was little work to be done, for the hay was cut and stored and the orchards were plowed up to receive the rain deeply when it should come. The cattle on the higher slopes were becoming shaggy and rough-coated.

Elisa Allen, working in her flower garden, looked down across the yard and saw Henry, her husband, talking to two men in business suits. The three of them stood by the tractor shed, each man with one foot on the side of the little Fordson. They smoked cigarettes and studied the machine as they talked.

Elisa watched them for a moment and then went back to her work. She was thirty-five. Her face was lean and strong and her eyes were as clear as water. Her figure looked blocked and heavy in her gardening costume, a man's black hat pulled low down over her eyes, clod-hopper shoes, a figured print dress almost completely covered by a big corduroy apron with four big pockets to hold the snips, the trowel and scratcher, the seeds and the knife she worked with. She wore heavy leather gloves to protect her hands while she worked.

She was cutting down the old year's chrysanthemum stalks with a pair of short and powerful scissors. She looked down toward the men by the tractor shed now and then. Her face was eager and mature and handsome; even her work with the scissors was over-eager, over-powerful. The chrysanthemum stems seemed too small and easy for her energy.

She brushed a cloud of hair out of her eyes with the back of her glove, and left a smudge of earth on her cheek in doing it. Behind her stood the neat white farm house with red geraniums close-banked around it as high as the windows. It was a hard-swept looking little house, with hard-polished windows, and a clean mud-mat on the front steps.

Elisa cast another glance toward the tractor shed. The strangers were getting into their Ford coupe. She took off a glove and put her strong fingers down into the forest of new green chrysanthemum sprouts that were growing around the old roots. She spread the leaves and looked down among the close-growing stems. No aphids were there, no sowbugs or snails or cutworms. Her terrier fingers destroyed such pests before they could get started.

Elisa started at the sound of her husband's voice. He had come near quietly, and he leaned over the wire fence that protected her flower garden from cattle and dogs and chickens.

"At it again," he said. "You've got a strong new crop coming."

Elisa straightened her back and pulled on the gardening glove again. "Yes. They'll be strong this coming year." In her tone and on her face there was a little smugness.

"You've got a gift with things," Henry observed. "Some of those yellow chrysanthemums you had this year were ten inches across. I wish you'd work out in the orchard and raise some apples that big."

Her eyes sharpened. "Maybe I could do it, too. I've a gift with things, all right. My mother had it. She could stick anything in the ground and make it grow. She said it was having planters' hands that knew how to do it."

"Well, it sure works with flowers," he said.

"Henry, who were those men you were talking to?"

"Why, sure, that's what I came to tell you. They were from the Western Meat Company. I sold those thirty head of three-year-old steers. Got nearly my own price, too."

"Good," she said. "Good for you."

"And I thought," he continued, "I thought how it's Saturday afternoon, and we might go into Salinas for dinner at a restaurant, and then to a picture show—to celebrate, you see."

"Good," she repeated. "Oh, yes. That will be good."

Henry put on his joking tone. "There's fights tonight. How'd you like to go to the fights?"

"Oh, no," she said breathlessly. "No, I wouldn't like fights."

"Just fooling, Elisa. We'll go to a movie. Let's see. It's two now. I'm going to take Scotty and bring down those steers from the hill. It'll take us maybe two hours. We'll go in town about five and have dinner at the Cominos Hotel. Like that?"

"Of course I'll like it. It's good to eat away from home."

"All right, then. I'll go get up a couple of horses."

She said, "I'll have plenty of time to transplant some of these sets, I guess."

She heard her husband calling Scotty down by the barn. And a little later she saw the two men ride up the pale yellow hillside in search of the steers.

There was a little square sandy bed kept for rooting the chrysanthemums. With her trowel she turned the soil over and over, and smoothed it and patted it firm. Then she dug ten parallel trenches to receive the sets. Back at the chrysanthemum bed she pulled out the little crisp shoots, trimmed off the leaves of each one with her scissors and laid it on a small orderly pile.

A squeak of wheels and plod of hoofs came from the road. Elisa looked up. The country road ran along the dense bank of willows and cottonwoods that bordered the river, and up this road came a curious vehicle, curiously drawn. It was an old spring-wagon, with a round canvas top on it like the cover of a prairie schooner. It was drawn by an old bay horse and a little grey-and-white burro. A big stubble-bearded man sat between the cover flaps and drove the crawling team. Underneath the wagon, between the hind wheels, a lean and rangy mongrel dog walked sedately. Words were painted on the canvas, in clumsy, crooked letters. "Pots, pans, knives, sisors, lawn mores, Fixed." Two rows of articles, and the triumphantly definitive "Fixed" below. The black paint had run down in little sharp points beneath each letter.

Elisa, squatting on the ground, watched to see the crazy, loose-jointed wagon pass by. But it didn't pass. It turned into the farm road in front of her house, crooked old wheels skirling and squeaking. The rangy dog darted from between the wheels and ran ahead. Instantly the two ranch shepherds flew out at him. Then all three stopped, and with stiff and quivering tails, with taut straight legs, with ambassadorial dignity, they slowly circled, sniffing daintily. The caravan pulled up to Elisa's wire fence and stopped. Now the newcomer dog, feeling out-numbered, lowered his tail and retired under the wagon with raised hackles and bared teeth.

The man on the wagon seat called out, "That's a bad dog in a fight when he gets started."

Elisa laughed. "I see he is. How soon does he generally get started?"

The man caught up her laughter and echoed it heartily. "Sometimes not for weeks and weeks," he said. He climbed stiffly down, over the wheel. The horse and the donkey drooped like unwatered flowers.

Elisa saw that he was a very big man. Although his hair and beard were greying, he did not look old. His worn black suit was wrinkled and spotted with grease. The laughter had disappeared from his face and eyes the moment his laughing voice ceased. His eyes were dark, and they were full of the brooding that gets in the eyes of teamsters and of sailors. The calloused hands he rested on the wire fence were cracked, and every crack was a black line. He took off his battered hat.

"I'm off my general road, ma'am," he said. "Does this dirt road cut over across the river to the Los Angeles highway?"

Elisa stood up and shoved the thick scissors in her apron pocket. "Well, yes, it does, but it winds around and then fords the river. I don't think your team could pull through the sand."

He replied with some asperity, "It might surprise you what them beasts can pull through."

"When they get started?" she asked.

He smiled for a second. "Yes. When they get started."

"Well," said Elisa, "I think you'll save time if you go back to the Salinas road and pick up the highway there."

He drew a big finger down the chicken wire and made it sing. "I ain't in any hurry, ma'am. I go from Seattle to San Diego and back every year. Takes all my time. About six months each way. I aim to follow nice weather."

Elisa took off her gloves and stuffed them in the apron pocket with the scissors. She touched the under edge of her man's hat, searching for fugitive hairs. "That sounds like a nice kind of a way to live," she said.

He leaned confidentially over the fence. "Maybe you noticed the writing on my wagon. I mend pots and sharpen knives and scissors. You got any of them things to do?"

"Oh, no," she said quickly. "Nothing like that." Her eyes hardened with resistance.

"Scissors is the worst thing," he explained. "Most people just ruin scissors trying to sharpen 'em, but I know how. I got a special tool. It's a little bobbit kind of thing, and patented. But it sure does the trick."

"No. My scissors are all sharp."

"All right, then. Take a pot," he continued earnestly, "a bent pot, or a pot with a hole. I can make it like new so you don't have to buy no new ones. That's a saving for you."

"No," she said shortly. "I tell you I have nothing like that for you to do."

His face fell to an exaggerated sadness. His voice took on a whining undertone. "I ain't had a thing to do today. Maybe I won't have no supper tonight. You see I'm off my regular road. I know folks on the highway clear from Seattle to San Diego. They save their things for me to sharpen up because they know I do it so good and save them money."

"I'm sorry," Elisa said irritably. "I haven't anything for you to do."

His eyes left her face and fell to searching the ground. They roamed about until they came to the chrysanthemum bed where she had been working. "What's them plants, ma'am?"

The irritation and resistance melted from Elisa's face. "Oh, those are chrysanthemums, giant whites and yellows. I raise them every year, bigger than anybody around here."

"Kind of a long-stemmed flower? Looks like a quick puff of colored smoke?" he asked.

"That's it. What a nice way to describe them."

"They smell kind of nasty till you get used to them," he said.

"It's a good bitter smell," she retorted, "not nasty at all."

He changed his tone quickly. "I like the smell myself."

"I had ten-inch blooms this year," she said.

The man leaned farther over the fence. "Look. I know a lady down the road a piece, has got the nicest garden you ever seen. Got nearly every kind of flower but no chrysantheums. Last time I was mending a copper-bottom washtub for her (that's a hard job but I do it good), she said to me, 'If you ever run acrost some nice chrysantheums I wish you'd try to get me a few seeds.' That's what she told me."

Elisa's eyes grew alert and eager. "She couldn't have known much about chrysanthemums. You can raise them from seed, but it's much easier to root the little sprouts you see there."

"Oh," he said, "I s'pose I can't take none to her, then."

"Why yes you can," Elisa cried. "I can put some in damp sand, and you can carry them right along with you. They'll take root in the pot if you keep them damp. And then she can transplant them."

"She'd sure like to have some, ma'am. You say they're nice ones?"

"Beautiful," she said. "Oh, beautiful." Her eyes shone. She tore off the battered hat and shook out her dark pretty hair. "I'll put them in a flower pot, and you can take them right with you. Come into the yard."

While the man came through the picket gate Elisa ran excitedly along the geranium-bordered path to the back of the house. And she returned carrying a big red flower pot. The gloves were forgotten now. She kneeled on the ground by the starting bed and dug up the sandy soil with her fingers and scooped it into the bright new flower pot. Then she picked up the little pile of shoots she had prepared. With her strong fingers she pressed them into the sand and tamped around them with her knuckles. The man stood over her. "I'll tell you what to do," she said. "You remember so you can tell the lady."

"Yes, I'll try to remember."

"Well, look. These will take root in about a month. Then she must set them out, about a foot apart in good rich earth like this, see?" She lifted a handful of dark soil for him to look at. "They'll grow fast and tall. Now remember this: In July tell her to cut them down, about eight inches from the ground."

"Before they bloom?" he asked.

"Yes, before they bloom." Her face was tight with eagerness. "They'll grow right up again. About the last of September the buds will start."

She stopped and seemed perplexed. "It's the budding that takes the most care," she said hesitantly. "I don't know how to tell you." She looked deep into his eyes, searchingly. Her mouth opened a little, and she seemed to be listening. "I'll try to tell you," she said. "Did you ever hear of planting hands?"

"Can't say I have, ma'am."

"Well, I can only tell you what it feels like. It's when you're picking off the buds you don't want. Everything goes right down into your fingertips. You watch your fingers work. They do it themselves. You can feel how it is. They pick and pick the buds. They never make a mistake. They're with the plant. Do you see? Your fingers and the plant. You can feel that, right up your arm. They know. They never make a mistake. You can feel it. When you're like that you can't do anything wrong. Do you see that? Can you understand that?"

She was kneeling on the ground looking up at him. Her breast swelled passionately.

The man's eyes narrowed. He looked away self-consciously. "Maybe I know," he said. "Sometimes in the night in the wagon there———"

Elisa's voice grew husky. She broke in on him, "I've never lived as you do, but I know what you mean. When the night is dark—why, the stars are sharp-pointed, and there's quiet. Why, you rise up and up! Every pointed star gets driven into your body. It's like that. Hot and sharp and—lovely."

Kneeling there, her hand went out toward his legs in the greasy black trousers. Her hesitant fingers almost touched the cloth. Then her hand dropped to the ground. She crouched low like a fawning dog.

He said, "It's nice, just like you say. Only when you don't have no dinner, it ain't."

She stood up then, very straight, and her face was ashamed. She held the flower pot out to him and placed it gently in his arms. "Here. Put it in your wagon, on the seat, where you can watch it. Maybe I can find something for you to do."

At the back of the house she dug in the can pile and found two old and battered aluminum saucepans. She carried them back and gave them to him. "Here, maybe you can fix these."

His manner changed. He became professional. "Good as new I can fix them." At the back of his wagon he set a little anvil, and out of an oily tool box dug a small machine hammer. Elisa came through the gate to watch him while he pounded out the dents in the kettles. His mouth grew sure and knowing. At a difficult part of the work he sucked his under-lip.

"You sleep right in the wagon?" Elisa asked.

"Right in the wagon, ma'am. Rain or shine I'm dry as a cow in there."

"It must be nice," she said. "It must be very nice. I wish women could do such things."

"It ain't the right kind of a life for a woman."

Her upper lip raised a little, showing her teeth. "How do you know? How can you tell?" she said.

"I don't know, ma'am," he protested. "Of course I don't know. Now here's your kettles, done. You don't have to buy no new ones."

"How much?"

"Oh, fifty cents'll do. I keep my prices down and my work good. That's why I have all them satisfied customers up and down the highway."

Elisa brought him a fifty-cent piece from the house and dropped it in his hand. "You might be surprised to have a rival some time. I can sharpen scissors, too. And I can beat the dents out of little pots. I could show you what a woman might do."

He put his hammer back in the oily box and shoved the little anvil out of sight. "It would be a lonely life for a woman, ma'am, and a scarey life, too, with animals creeping under the wagon all night." He climbed over the singletree, steadying himself with a hand on the burro's white rump. He settled himself in the seat, picked up the lines. "Thank you kindly, ma'am," he said. "I'll do like you told me; I'll go back and catch the Salinas road."

"Mind," she called, "if you're long in getting there, keep the sand damp."

"Sand, ma'am?. . . Sand? Oh, sure. You mean around the chrysantheums. Sure I will." He clucked his tongue. The beasts leaned luxuriously into their collars. The mongrel dog took his place between the back wheels. The wagon turned and crawled out the entrance road and back the way it had come, along the river.

Elisa stood in front of her wire fence watching the slow progress of the caravan. Her shoulders were straight, her head thrown back, her eyes half-closed, so that the scene came vaguely into them. Her lips moved silently, forming the words "Goodbye—good-bye." Then she whispered, "That's a bright direction. There's a glowing there." The sound of her whisper startled her. She shook herself free and looked about to see whether anyone had been listening. Only the dogs had heard. They lifted their heads toward her from their sleeping in the dust, and then stretched out their chins and settled asleep again. Elisa turned and ran hurriedly into the house.

In the kitchen she reached behind the stove and felt the water tank. It was full of hot water from the noonday cooking. In the bathroom she tore off her soiled clothes and flung them into the corner. And then she scrubbed herself with a little block of pumice, legs and thighs, loins and chest and arms, until her skin was scratched and red. When she had dried herself she stood in front of a mirror in her bedroom and looked at her body. She tightened her stomach and threw out her chest. She turned and looked over her shoulder at her back.

After a while she began to dress, slowly. She put on her newest underclothing and her nicest stockings and the dress which was the symbol of her prettiness. She worked carefully on her hair, penciled her eyebrows and rouged her lips.

Before she was finished she heard the little thunder of hoofs and the shouts of Henry and his helper as they drove the red steers into the corral. She heard the gate bang shut and set herself for Henry's arrival.

His step sounded on the porch. He entered the house calling, "Elisa, where are you?"

"In my room, dressing. I'm not ready. There's hot water for your bath. Hurry up. It's getting late."

When she heard him splashing in the tub, Elisa laid his dark suit on the bed, and shirt and socks and tie beside it. She stood his polished shoes on the floor beside the bed. Then she went to the porch and sat primly and stiffly down. She looked toward the river road where the willow-line was still yellow with frosted leaves so that under the high grey fog they seemed a thin band of sunshine. This was the only color in the grey afternoon. She sat unmoving for a long time. Her eyes blinked rarely.

Henry came banging out of the door, shoving his tie inside his vest as he came. Elisa stiffened and her face grew tight. Henry stopped short and looked at her. "Why—why, Elisa. You look so nice!"

"Nice? You think I look nice? What do you mean by 'nice'?"

Henry blundered on. "I don't know. I mean you look different, strong and happy."

"I am strong? Yes, strong. What do you mean 'strong'?"

He looked bewildered. "You're playing some kind of a game," he said helplessly. "It's a kind of a play. You look strong enough to break a calf over your knee, happy enough to eat it like a watermelon."

For a second she lost her rigidity. "Henry! Don't talk like that. You didn't know what you said." She grew complete again. "I'm strong," she boasted. "I never knew before how strong."

Henry looked down toward the tractor shed, and where he brought his eyes back to her, they were his own again. "I'll get out the car. You can put on your coat while I'm starting."

Elisa went into the house. She heard him drive to the gate and idle down his motor, and then she took a long time to put on her hat. She pulled it here and pressed it there. When Henry turned the motor off she slipped into her coat and went out.

The little roadster bounced along on the dirt road by the river, raising the birds and driving the rabbits into the brush. Two cranes flapped heavily over the willow-line and dropped into the river-bed.

Far ahead on the road Elisa saw a dark speck. She knew.

She tried not to look as they passed it, but her eyes would not obey. She whispered to herself sadly, "He might have thrown them off the road. That wouldn't have been much trouble, not very much. But he kept the pot," she explained. "He had to keep the pot. That's why he couldn't get them off the road."

The roadster turned a bend and she saw the caravan ahead. She swung full around toward her husband so she could not see the little covered wagon and the mismatched team as the car passed them.

In a moment it was over. The thing was done. She did not look back.

She said loudly, to be heard above the motor, "It will be good, tonight, a good dinner."

"Now you're changed again," Henry complained. He took one hand from the wheel and patted her knee. "I ought to take you in to dinner oftener. It would be good for both of us. We get so heavy out on the ranch."

"Henry," she asked, "could we have wine at dinner?"

"Sure we could. Say! That will be fine."

She was silent for a while; then she said, "Henry, at those prize fights, do the men hurt each other very much?"

"Sometimes a little, not often. Why?"

"Well, I've read how they break noses, and blood runs down their chests. I've read how the fighting gloves get heavy and soggy with blood."

He looked around at her. "What's the matter, Elisa? I didn't know you read things like that." He brought the car to a stop, then turned to the right over the Salinas River bridge.

"Do any women ever go to the fights?" she asked.

"Oh, sure, some. What's the matter, Elisa? Do you want to go? I don't think you'd like it, but I'll take you if you really want to go."

She relaxed limply in the seat. "Oh, no. No. I don't want to go. I'm sure I don't." Her face was turned away from him. "It will be enough if we can have wine. It will be plenty." She turned up her coat collar so he could not see that she was crying weakly—like an old woman.

RALPH ELLISON (1914–1994) published only a single novel in his lifetime, but that novel, *Invisible Man* (1952), became one of the most widely acclaimed American novels of the twentieth century. Ellison grew up in Oklahoma City and won a scholarship to attend the Tuskegee Institute, where he studied music. Following his junior year, he moved to New York City to pursue his interests in music and sculpture. More importantly, however, he became acquainted with two important **Harlem Renaissance** writers, Alain Locke and Langston Hughes, and through them met Richard Wright, who would become his friend and mentor. Under Wright's direction, Ellison began writing book reviews and stories. Wright's leftist politics also strongly influenced Ellison, although both writers later distanced themselves from Communism. *Invisible Man*, in particular, harshly criticizes the radical political organizations that Ellison felt betrayed the interests of the African Americans they claimed to support.

Winner of the National Book Award, *Invisible Man* (1952) offers an unapologetic portrayal of the effects of racism on a young black man coming of age in the late 1930s. Ellison's unnamed African American narrator takes a **picaresque** journey from south to north and through all levels of society in an effort to understand his metaphorical invisibility as a black man in America. The novel is encyclopedic in its breadth and draws extensively on African American **folklore**, the Western canon, American history, Freudian psychology, and contemporary culture. Amidst all of these elements, the narrator painfully struggles to discover his own authentic identity. "Battle Royal," the first chapter of *Invisible Man*, depicts the narrator at the beginning of his journey, determined to do what is expected of him in order to succeed but simultaneously rebelling against these racist expectations.

Following the publication of *Invisible Man*, Ellison published numerous essays and short stories while working for several decades on his second novel. This book remained unfinished at his death; portions of it were published posthumously as *Juneteenth* (1999).

Related Works: Chekhov, "Vanka"; Joyce, "Araby"; Bambara, "The Lesson"; Kincaid, "Girl"; Cofer, "Arturo's Flight"; Wideman, "What We Cannot Speak About We Must Pass Over in Silence"; Dunbar, "We Wear the Mask"; Cullen, "From the Dark Tower"; Langston Hughes, "Harlem" and "Theme for English B"; Young, "Nineteen Seventy Five."

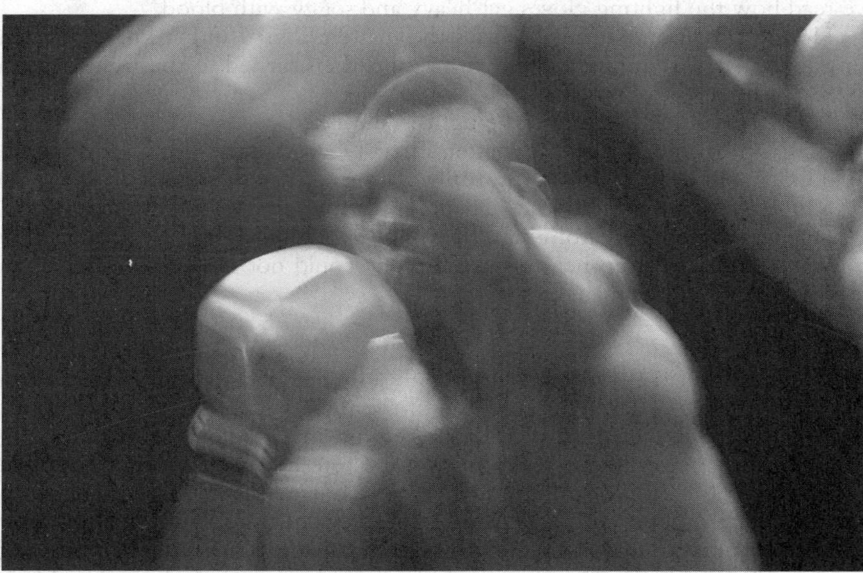

Boxer

Battle Royal

It goes a long way back, some twenty years. All my life I had been looking for something, and everywhere I turned someone tried to tell me what it was. I accepted their answers too, though they were often in contradiction and even self-contradictory. I was naïve. I was looking for myself and asking everyone except myself questions which I, and only I, could answer. It took me a long time and much painful boomeranging of my expectations to achieve a realization everyone else appears to have been born with: That I am nobody but myself. But first I had to discover that I am an invisible man!

And yet I am no freak of nature, nor of history. I was in the cards, other things having been equal (or unequal) eighty-five years ago. I am not ashamed of my grandparents for having been slaves. I am only ashamed of myself for having at one time been ashamed. About eighty-five years ago they were told that they were free, united with others of our country in everything pertaining to the common good, and, in everything social, separate like the fingers of the hand. And they believed it. They exulted in it. They stayed in their place, worked hard, and brought up my father to do the same. But my grandfather is the one. He was an odd old guy, my grandfather, and I am told I take after him. It was he who caused the trouble. On his deathbed he called my father to him and said, "Son, after I'm gone I want you to keep up the good fight. I never told you, but our life is a war and I have been a traitor all my born days, a spy in the enemy's country ever since I give up my gun back in the Reconstruction. Live with your head in the lion's mouth. I want you to overcome 'em with yeses, undermine 'em with grins, agree 'em to death and destruction, let 'em swoller you till they vomit or bust wide open." They thought the old man had gone out of his mind. He had been the meekest of men. The younger children were rushed from the room, the shades drawn and the flame of the lamp turned so low that it sputtered on the wick like the old man's breathing. "Learn it to the younguns," he whispered fiercely; then he died.

But my folks were more alarmed over his last words than over his dying. It was as though he had not died at all, his words caused so much anxiety. I was warned emphatically to forget what he had said and, indeed, this is the first time it has been mentioned outside the family circle. It had a tremendous effect upon me, however. I could never be sure of what he meant. Grandfather had been a quiet old man who never made any trouble, yet on his deathbed he had called himself a traitor and a spy, and he had spoken of his meekness as a dangerous activity. It became a constant puzzle which lay unanswered in the back of my mind. And whenever things went well for me I remembered my grandfather and felt guilty and uncomfortable. It was as though I was carrying out his advice in spite of myself. And to make it worse, everyone loved me for it. I was praised by the most lily-white men of the town. I was considered an example of desirable conduct—just as my grandfather had been. And what puzzled me was that the old man had defined it as *treachery*. When I was praised for my conduct I felt a guilt that in some way I was doing something that was really against the wishes of the white folks, that if they had understood they would have desired me to act just the opposite, that I should have been sulky and mean, and that that really would have been what they wanted, even though they were fooled and thought they wanted me to act as I did. It made me afraid that some day they would look upon me as a traitor and I would be lost. Still I was more afraid to act any other way because they didn't like that at all. The old man's words were like a curse. On my graduation day I delivered an oration in which I showed that humility was the secret, indeed, the very essence of progress. (Not that I believed this—how could I, remembering my grandfather?—I only believed that it worked.) It was a great success. Everyone praised me and I was invited to give the speech at a gathering of the town's leading white citizens. It was a triumph for our whole community.

It was in the main ballroom of the leading hotel. When I got there I discovered that it was on the occasion of a smoker, and I was told that since I was to be there anyway I might as well take part in the battle royal to be fought by some of my schoolmates as part of the entertainment. The battle royal came first.

All of the town's big shots were there in their tuxedoes, wolfing down the buffet foods, drinking beer and whiskey and smoking black cigars. It was a large room with a high ceiling. Chairs were arranged in neat rows around three sides of a portable boxing ring. The fourth side was clear, revealing a gleaming space of polished floor. I had some misgivings over the battle royal, by the way. Not from a distaste for fighting, but because I didn't care too much for the other fellows who were to take part. They were tough guys who seemed to have no grandfather's curse worrying their minds. No one could mistake their toughness. And besides, I suspected that fighting a battle royal might detract from the dignity of my speech. In those pre-invisible days I visualized myself as a potential Booker T. Washington. But the other fellows didn't care too much for me either, and there were nine of them. I felt superior to them in my way, and I didn't like the manner in which we were all crowded together into the servants' elevator. Nor did they like my being there. In fact, as the warmly lighted floors flashed past the elevator we had words over the fact that I, by taking part in the fight, had knocked one of their friends out of a night's work.

We were led out of the elevator through a rococo hall into an anteroom and told to get into our fighting togs. Each of us was issued a pair of boxing gloves and ushered out into the big mirrored hall, which we entered looking cautiously about us and whispering, lest we might accidentally be heard above the noise of the room. It was foggy with cigar smoke. And already the whiskey was taking effect. I was shocked to see some of the most important men of the town quite tipsy. They were all there—bankers, lawyers, judges, doctors, fire chiefs, teachers, merchants. Even one of the more fashionable pastors. Something we could not see was going on up front. A clarinet was vibrating sensuously and the men were standing up and moving eagerly forward. We were a small tight group, clustered together, our bare upper bodies touching and shining with anticipatory sweat; while up front the big shots were becoming increasingly excited over something we still could not see. Suddenly I heard the school superintendent, who had told me to come, yell, "Bring up the shines, gentlemen! Bring up the little shines!"

We were rushed up to the front of the ballroom, where it smelled even more strongly of tobacco and whiskey. Then we were pushed into place. I almost wet my pants. A sea of faces, some hostile, some amused, ringed around us, and in the center, facing us, stood a magnificent blonde—stark naked. There was dead silence. I felt a blast of cold air chill me. I tried to back away, but they were behind me and around me. Some of the boys stood with lowered heads, trembling. I felt a wave of irrational guilt and fear. My teeth chattered, my skin turned to goose flesh, my knees knocked. Yet I was strongly attracted and looked in spite of myself. Had the price of looking been blindness, I would have looked. The hair was yellow like that of a circus kewpie doll, the face heavily powdered and rouged, as though to form an abstract mask, the eyes hollow and smeared a cool blue, the color of a baboon's butt. I felt a desire to spit upon her as my eyes brushed slowly over her body. Her breasts were firm and round as the domes of East Indian temples, and I stood so close as to see the fine skin texture and beads of pearly perspiration glistening like dew around the pink and erected buds of her nipples. I wanted at one and the same time to run from the room, to sink through the floor, or go to her and cover her from my eyes and the eyes of the others with my body; to feel the soft thighs, to caress her and destroy her, to love her and murder her, to hide from her, and yet to stroke where below the small American flag tattooed upon her belly her thighs formed a capital V. I had a notion that of all in the room she saw only me with her impersonal eyes.

And then she began to dance, a slow sensuous movement; the smoke of a hundred cigars clinging to her like the thinnest of veils. She seemed like a fair bird-girl girdled in veils calling to me from the angry surface of some gray and threatening sea. I was transported. Then I became aware of the clarinet playing and the big shots yelling at us. Some threatened us if we looked and others if we did not. On my right I saw one boy faint. And now a man grabbed a silver pitcher from a table and stepped close as he dashed ice water upon him and stood him up and forced two of us to support him as his head hung and moans issued from his thick bluish lips. Another boy began to plead to go home. He was the largest of the group, wearing dark red fighting trunks much too small to conceal the erection which projected from him as though in answer to the insinuating low-registered moaning of the clarinet. He tried to hide himself with his boxing gloves.

And all the while the blonde continued dancing, smiling faintly at the big shots who watched her with fascination, and faintly smiling at our fear. I noticed a certain merchant who followed her hungrily, his lips loose and drooling. He was a large man who wore diamond studs in a shirtfront which swelled with the ample paunch underneath, and each time the blonde swayed her undulating hips he ran his hand through the thin hair of his bald head and, with his arms upheld, his posture clumsy like that of an intoxicated panda, wound his belly in a slow and obscene grind. This creature was completely hypnotized. The music had quickened. As the dancer flung herself about with a detached expression on her face, the men began reaching out to touch her. I could see their beefy fingers sink into the soft flesh. Some of the others tried to stop them and she began to move around the floor in graceful circles, as they gave chase, slipping and sliding over the polished floor. It was mad. Chairs went crashing, drinks were spilt, as they ran laughing and howling after her. They caught her just as she reached a door, raised her from the floor, and tossed her as college boys are tossed at a hazing, and above her red, fixed-smiling lips I saw the terror and disgust in her eyes, almost like my own terror and that which I saw in some of the other boys. As I watched, they tossed her twice and her soft breasts seemed to flatten against the air and her legs flung wildly as she spun. Some of the more sober ones helped her to escape. And I started off the floor, heading for the anteroom with the rest of the boys.

Some were still crying and in hysteria. But as we tried to leave we were stopped and ordered to get into the ring. There was nothing to do but what we were told. All ten of us climbed under the ropes and allowed ourselves to be blindfolded with broad bands of white cloth. One of the men seemed to feel a bit sympathetic and tried to cheer us up as we stood with our backs against the ropes. Some of us tried to grin. "See that boy over there?" one of the men said. "I want you to run across at the bell and give it to him right in the belly. If you don't get him, I'm going to get you. I don't like his looks." Each of us was told the same. The blindfolds were put on. Yet even then I had been going over my speech. In my mind each word was as bright as flame. I felt the cloth pressed into place, and frowned so that it would be loosened when I relaxed.

But now I felt a sudden fit of blind terror. I was unused to darkness. It was as though I had suddenly found myself in a dark room filled with poisonous cottonmouths. I could hear the bleary voices yelling insistently for the battle royal to begin.

"Get going in there!"

"Let me at that big nigger!"

I strained to pick up the school superintendent's voice, as though to squeeze some security out of that slightly more familiar sound.

"Let me at those black sonsabitches!" someone yelled.

"No, Jackson, no!" another voice yelled. "Here, somebody, help me hold Jack."

"I want to get at that ginger-colored nigger. Tear him limb from limb," the first voice yelled.

I stood against the ropes trembling. For in those days I was what they called ginger-colored, and he sounded as though he might crunch me between his teeth like a crisp ginger cookie.

Quite a struggle was going on. Chairs were being kicked about and I could hear voices grunting as with a terrific effort. I wanted to see, to see more desperately than ever before. But the blindfold was tight as a thick skin-puckering scab and when I raised my gloved hands to push the layers of white aside a voice yelled, "Oh, no you don't, black bastard! Leave that alone!"

"Ring the bell before Jackson kills him a coon!" someone boomed in the sudden silence. And I heard the bell clang and the sound of the feet scuffling forward.

A glove smacked against my head. I pivoted, striking out stiffly as someone went past, and felt the jar ripple along the length of my arm to my shoulder. Then it seemed as though all nine of the boys had turned upon me at once. Blows pounded me from all sides while I struck out as best I could. So many blows landed upon me that I wondered if I were not the only blindfolded fighter in the ring, or if the man called Jackson hadn't succeeded in getting me after all.

Blindfolded, I could no longer control my motions. I had no dignity. I stumbled about like a baby or a drunken man. The smoke had become thicker and with each new blow it seemed to sear and further restrict my lungs. My saliva became like hot bitter glue. A glove connected with my head, filling my mouth with warm blood. It was everywhere. I could not tell if the moisture I felt upon my body was sweat or blood. A blow landed hard against the nape of my neck. I felt myself going over, my head hitting the floor. Streaks of blue light filled the black world behind the blindfold. I lay prone, pretending that I was knocked out, but felt myself seized by hands and yanked to my feet. "Get going, black boy! Mix it up!" My arms were like lead, my head smarting from blows. I managed to feel my way to the ropes and held on, trying to catch my breath. A glove landed in my mid-section and I went over again, feeling as though the smoke had become a knife jabbed into my guts. Pushed this way and that by the legs milling around me, I finally pulled erect and discovered that I could see the black, sweat-washed forms weaving in the smoky-blue atmosphere like drunken dancers weaving to the rapid drum-like thuds of blows.

Everyone fought hysterically. It was complete anarchy. Everybody fought everybody else. No group fought together for long. Two, three, four, fought one, then turned to fight each other, were themselves attacked. Blows landed below the belt and in the kidney, with the gloves open as well as closed, and with my eye partly opened now there was not so much terror. I moved carefully, avoiding blows, although not too many to attract attention, fighting from group to group. The boys groped about like blind, cautious crabs crouching to protect their mid-sections, their heads pulled in short against their shoulders, their arms stretched nervously before them, with their fists testing the smoke-filled air like the knobbed feelers of hypersensitive snails. In one corner I glimpsed a boy violently punching the air and heard him scream in pain as he smashed his hand against a ring post. For a second I saw him bent over holding his hand, then going down as a blow caught his unprotected head. I played one group against the other, slipping in and throwing a punch then stepping out of range while pushing the others into the melee to take the blows blindly aimed at me. The smoke was agonizing and there were no rounds, no bells at three minute intervals to relieve our exhaustion. The room spun round me, a swirl of lights, smoke, sweating bodies surrounded by tense white faces. I bled from both nose and mouth, the blood spattering upon my chest.

The men kept yelling, "Slug him, black boy! Knock his guts out!"

"Uppercut him! Kill him! Kill that big boy!"

Taking a fake fall, I saw a boy going down heavily beside me as though we were felled by a single blow, saw a sneaker-clad foot shoot into his groin as the two who had knocked him down stumbled upon him. I rolled out of range, feeling a twinge of nausea.

The harder we fought the more threatening the men became. And yet, I had begun to worry about my speech again. How would it go? Would they recognize my ability? What would they give me?

I was fighting automatically when suddenly I noticed that one after another of the boys was leaving the ring. I was surprised, filled with panic, as though I had been left alone with an unknown danger. Then I understood. The boys had arranged it among themselves. It was the custom for the two men left in the ring to slug it out for the winner's prize. I discovered this too late. When the bell sounded two men in tuxedoes leaped into the ring and removed the blindfold. I found myself facing Tatlock, the biggest of the gang. I felt sick at my stomach. Hardly had the bell stopped ringing in my ears than it clanged again and I saw him moving swiftly toward me. Thinking of nothing else to do I hit him smash on the nose. He kept coming, bringing the rank sharp violence of stale sweat. His face was a black blank of a face, only his eyes alive—with hate of me and aglow with a feverish terror from what had happened to us all. I became anxious. I wanted to deliver my speech and he came at me as though he meant to beat it out of me. I smashed him again and again, taking his blows as they came. Then on a sudden impulse I struck him lightly and as we clinched, I whispered, "Fake like I knocked you out, you can have the prize."

"I'll break your behind," he whispered hoarsely.

"For *them*?"

"For *me*, sonofabitch!"

They were yelling for us to break it up and Tatlock spun me half around with a blow, and as a joggled camera sweeps in a reeling scene, I saw the howling red faces crouching tense beneath the cloud of blue-gray smoke. For a moment the world wavered, unraveled, flowed, then my head cleared and Tatlock bounced before me. That fluttering shadow before my eyes was his jabbing left hand. Then falling forward, my head against his damp shoulder, I whispered,

"I'll make it five dollars more."

"Go to hell!"

But his muscles relaxed a trifle beneath my pressure and I breathed, "Seven?"

"Give it to your ma," he said, ripping me beneath the heart.

And while I still held him I butted him and moved away. I felt myself bombarded with punches. I fought back with hopeless desperation. I wanted to deliver my speech more than anything else in the world, because I felt that only these men could judge truly my ability, and now this stupid clown was ruining my chances. I began fighting carefully now, moving in to punch him and out again with my greater speed. A lucky blow to his chin and I had him going too—until I heard a loud voice yell, "I got my money on the big boy."

Hearing this, I almost dropped my guard. I was confused: Should I try to win against the voice out there? Would not this go against my speech, and was not this a moment for humility, for nonresistance? A blow to my head as I danced about sent my right eye popping like a jack-in-the-box and settled my dilemma. The room went red as I fell. It was a dream fall, my body languid and fastidious as to where to land, until the floor became impatient and smashed up to meet me. A moment later I came to. An hypnotic voice said FIVE emphatically. And I lay there, hazily watching a dark red spot of my own blood shaping itself into a butterfly, glistening and soaking into the soiled gray world of the canvas.

When the voice drawled TEN I was lifted up and dragged to a chair. I sat dazed. My eye pained and swelled with each throb of my pounding heart and I wondered if now I would be allowed to speak. I was wringing wet, my mouth still bleeding. We were grouped along the wall now. The other boys ignored me as they congratulated Tatlock and speculated as to how much they would be paid. One boy whimpered over his smashed hand. Looking up front, I saw attendants in white jackets rolling the portable ring away and placing a small square rug in the vacant space surrounded by chairs. Perhaps, I thought, I will stand on the rug to deliver my speech.

Then the M.C. called to us, "Come on up here boys and get your money."

We ran forward to where the men laughed and talked in their chairs, waiting. Everyone seemed friendly now.

"There it is on the rug," the man said. I saw the rug covered with coins of all dimensions and a few crumpled bills. But what excited me, scattered here and there, were the gold pieces.

"Boys, it's all yours," the man said. "You get all you grab."

"That's right, Sambo," a blond man said, winking at me confidentially.

I trembled with excitement, forgetting my pain. I would get the gold and the bills, I thought. I would use both hands. I would throw my body against the boys nearest me to block them from the gold.

"Get down around the rug now," the man commanded, "and don't anyone touch it until I give the signal."

"This ought to be good," I heard.

As told, we got around the square rug on our knees. Slowly the man raised his freckled hand as we followed it upward with our eyes.

I heard, "These niggers look like they're about to pray!"

Then, "Ready," the man said. "Go!"

I lunged for a yellow coin lying on the blue design of the carpet, touching it and sending a surprised shriek to join those rising around me. I tried frantically to remove my hand but could not let go. A hot, violent force tore through my body, shaking me like a wet rat. The rug was electrified. The hair bristled up on my head as I shook myself free. My muscles jumped, my nerves jangled, writhed. But I saw that this was not stopping the other boys. Laughing in fear and embarrassment, some were holding back and scooping up the coins knocked off by the painful contortions of the others. The men roared above us as we struggled.

"Pick it up, goddamnit, pick it up!" someone called like a bass-voiced parrot. "Go on, get it!"

I crawled rapidly around the floor, picking up the coins, trying to avoid the coppers and to get greenbacks and the gold. Ignoring the shock by laughing, as I brushed the coins off quickly, I discovered that I could contain the electricity—a contradiction, but it works. Then the men began to push us onto the rug. Laughing embarrassedly, we struggled out of their hands and kept after the coins. We were all wet and slippery and hard to hold. Suddenly I saw a boy lifted into the air, glistening with sweat like a circus seal, and dropped, his wet back landing flush upon the charged rug, heard him yell and saw him literally dance upon his back, his elbows beating a frenzied tattoo upon the floor, his muscles twitching like the flesh of a horse stung by many flies. When he finally rolled off, his face was gray and no one stopped him when he ran from the floor amid booming laughter.

"Get the money," the M.C. called. "That's good hard American cash!"

And we snatched and grabbed, snatched and grabbed. I was careful not to come too close to the rug now, and when I felt the hot whiskey breath descend upon me like a cloud of foul air I reached out and grabbed the leg of a chair. It was occupied and I held on desperately.

"Leggo, nigger! Leggo!"

The huge face wavered down to mine as he tried to push me free. But my body was slippery and he was too drunk. It was Mr. Colcord, who owned a chain of movie houses and "entertainment palaces." Each time he grabbed me I slipped out of his hands. It became a real struggle. I feared the rug more than I did the drunk, so I held on, surprising myself for a moment by trying to topple *him* upon the rug. It was such an enormous idea that I found myself actually carrying it out. I tried not to be obvious, yet when I grabbed his leg, trying to tumble him out of the chair, he raised up roaring with laughter, and, looking at me with soberness dead in the eye, kicked me viciously in the chest. The chair leg flew out of my hand and I felt myself going and rolled. It was as though I had rolled through a bed of hot coals. It seemed a whole century would pass before I would roll free, a century in which I was seared through the deepest levels of my body to the fearful breath within me and the breath seared and heated to the point of explosion. It'll all be over in a flash, I thought as I rolled clear. It'll all be over in a flash.

But not yet, the men on the other side were waiting, red faces swollen as though from apoplexy as they bent forward in their chairs. Seeing their fingers coming toward me I rolled away as a fumbled football rolls off the receiver's fingertips, back into the coals. That time I luckily sent the rug sliding out of place and heard the coins ringing against the floor and the boys scuffling to pick them up and the M.C. calling, "All right, boys, that's all. Go get dressed and get your money."

I was limp as a dish rag. My back felt as though it had been beaten with wires.

When we had dressed the M.C. came in and gave us each five dollars, except Tatlock, who got ten for being last in the ring. Then he told us to leave. I was not to get a chance to deliver my speech, I thought. I was going out into the dim alley in despair when I was stopped and told to go back. I returned to the ballroom, where the men were pushing back their chairs and gathering in groups to talk.

The M.C. knocked on a table for quiet. "Gentlemen," he said, "we almost forgot an important part of the program. A most serious part, gentlemen. This boy was brought here to deliver a speech which he made at his graduation yesterday . . . ."

"Bravo!"

"I'm told that he is the smartest boy we've got out there in Greenwood. I'm told that he knows more big words than a pocket-sized dictionary."

Much applause and laughter.

"So now, gentlemen, I want you to give him your attention."

There was still laughter as I faced them, my mouth dry, my eye throbbing. I began slowly, but evidently my throat was tense, because they began shouting, "Louder! Louder!"

"We of the younger generation extol the wisdom of that great leader and educator," I shouted, "who first spoke these flaming words of wisdom: 'A ship lost at sea for many days suddenly sighted a friendly vessel. From the mast of the unfortunate vessel was seen a signal: "Water, water; we die of thirst!" The answer from the friendly vessel came back: "Cast down your bucket where you are." The captain of the distressed vessel, at last heeding the injunction, cast down his bucket, and it came up full of fresh sparkling water from the mouth of the Amazon River.' And like him I say, and in his words, 'To those of my race who depend upon bettering their condition in a foreign land, or who underestimate the importance of cultivating friendly relations with the Southern white man, who is his next-door neighbor, I would say: "Cast down your bucket where you are"—cast it down in making friends in every manly way of the people of all races by whom we are surrounded . . ."

I spoke automatically and with such fervor that I did not realize that the men were still talking and laughing until my dry mouth, filling up with blood from the cut, almost strangled me. I coughed, wanting to stop and go to one of the tall brass, sand-filled spittoons to relieve myself, but a few of the men, especially the superintendent, were listening and I was afraid. So I gulped it down, blood, saliva and all, and continued. (What powers of endurance I had during those days! What enthusiasm! What a belief in the rightness of things!) I spoke even louder in spite of the pain. But still they talked and still they laughed, as though deaf with cotton in dirty ears. So I spoke with greater emotional emphasis. I closed my ears and swallowed blood until I was nauseated. The speech seemed a hundred times as long as before, but I could not leave out a single word. All had to be said, each memorized nuance considered, rendered. Nor was that all. Whenever I uttered a word of three or more syllables a group of voices would yell for me to repeat it. I used the phrase "social responsibility" and they yelled:

"What's that word you say, boy?"

"Social responsibility," I said.

"What?"

"Social . . ."

"Louder."

". . . responsibility."

"More!"

"Respon—"

"Repeat!"

"—sibility."

The room filled with the uproar of laughter until, no doubt, distracted by having to gulp down my blood, I made a mistake and yelled a phrase I had often seen denounced in newspaper editorials, heard debated in private.

"Social . . ."

"What?" they yelled.

". . . equality—"

The laughter hung smokelike in the sudden stillness. I opened my eyes, puzzled. Sounds of displeasure filled the room. The M.C. rushed forward. They shouted hostile phrases at me. But I did not understand.

A small dry mustached man in the front row blared out, "Say that slowly, son!"

"What, sir?"

"What you just said!"

"Social responsibility, sir," I said.

"You weren't being smart, were you, boy?" he said, not unkindly.

"No, sir!"

"You sure that about 'equality' was a mistake?"

"Oh, yes, sir," I said. "I was swallowing blood."

"Well, you had better speak more slowly so we can understand. We mean to do right by you, but you've got to know your place at all times. All right, now, go on with your speech."

I was afraid. I wanted to leave but I wanted also to speak and I was afraid they'd snatch me down.

"Thank you, sir," I said, beginning where I had left off, and having them ignore me as before.

Yet when I finished there was a thunderous applause. I was surprised to see the superintendent come forth with a package wrapped in white tissue paper, and, gesturing for quiet, address the men.

"Gentlemen, you see that I did not overpraise this boy. He makes a good speech and some day he'll lead his people in the proper paths. And I don't have to tell you that that is important in these days and times. This is a good, smart boy, and so to encourage him in the right direction, in the name of the Board of Education I wish to present him a prize in the form of this . . ."

He paused, removing the tissue paper and revealing a gleaming calfskin brief case.

". . . in the form of this first-class article from Shad Whitmore's shop."

"Boy," he said, addressing me, "take this prize and keep it well. Consider it a badge of office. Prize it. Keep developing as you are and some day it will be filled with important papers that will help shape the destiny of your people."

I was so moved that I could hardly express my thanks. A rope of bloody saliva forming a shape like an undiscovered continent drooled upon the leather and I wiped it quickly away. I felt an importance that I had never dreamed.

"Open it and see what's inside," I was told.

My fingers a-tremble, I complied, smelling the fresh leather and finding an official-looking document inside. It was a scholarship to the state college for Negroes. My eyes filled with tears and I ran awkwardly off the floor.

I was overjoyed; I did not even mind when I discovered that the gold pieces I had scrambled for were brass pocket tokens advertising a certain make of automobile.

When I reached home everyone was excited. Next day the neighbors came to congratulate me. I even felt safe from grandfather, whose deathbed curse usually spoiled my triumphs. I stood beneath his photograph with my brief case in hand and smiled triumphantly into his stolid black peasant's face. It was a face that fascinated me. The eyes seemed to follow everywhere I went.

That night I dreamed I was at a circus with him and that he refused to laugh at the clowns no matter what they did. Then later he told me to open my brief case and read what was inside and I did, finding an official envelope stamped with the state seal; and inside the envelope I found another and another, endlessly, and I thought I would fall of weariness. "Them's years," he said, "Now open that one." And I did and in it I found an engraved document containing a short message in letters of gold. "Read it," my grandfather said. "Out loud!"

"To Whom It May Concern," I intoned. "Keep This Nigger-Boy Running."

I awoke with the old man's laughter ringing in my ears.

(It was a dream I was to remember and dream again for many years after. But at that time I had no insight into its meaning. First I had to attend college.)

ISAAC BASHEVIS SINGER (1904–1991) was born in a small, rural Jewish village (a *shtetl*) not far from Warsaw. Both of his parents were from highly religious (though conflicting) backgrounds, and the rituals and traditions of Judaism colored every aspect of the family's life. When Singer was about four, the family moved to Warsaw, where Singer was educated in the rabbinical tradition. He was also interested in Western culture, however, and read works by Shakespeare, Darwin, Poe, Dostoevsky, and others on his own. Both of his parents were natural storytellers, and Singer's older brother Israel would go on to publish essays, short stories, and a novel. Singer followed in his brother's footsteps and became part of the Warsaw Yiddish Writer's Club. In 1927, Singer's first stories "In Old Age" and "Women" were published. In 1935, Singer moved to America, but he continued to write in Yiddish because he felt that the language reflected the uniqueness of his characters.

Singer gained recognition in America after a Saul Bellow translation appeared in *Partisan Review* in 1953. His collection *Gimpel the Fool and Other Stories* was translated by Bellows and others in 1957. Another of his short story collections, *A Crown of Feathers* (1974), won the National Book Award, and in 1978 Singer won the Nobel Prize for Literature. Singer's novels include *Satan in Goray* (1935 trans. 1955), *The Manor* (trans. 1967), and *Enemies, a Love Story* (1972).

Many of Singer's characters struggle to deal with a modern society that is antithetical to their traditions. His characters encounter crises of belief and suffer in their estrangement from their God and their communities. However, redemption is possible and available through human compassion and suffering.

The title character of "Gimpel the Fool" (trans. 1953) suffers mockery and cruelty at the hands of his fellow villagers and the wife he has been deceived into marrying, yet he maintains his faith and lives a long life. Gimpel's narration of his life and his continuity of faith despite numerous hardships can be read as a **parable**, as it provides its readers with a moral lesson that conveys the benefits of spiritual certainty.

Related Works: Hawthorne, "Young Goodman Brown"; Chekhov, "Vanka"; Hecht, "The Book of Yolek"; Garcia, "Why I Left the Church"; Longfellow, "The Jewish Cemetery at Newport."

Gimpel the Fool

(*Translated by Saul Bellow*)

I am Gimpel the Fool. I don't think myself a fool. On the contrary. But that's what folks call me. They gave me the name while I was still in school. I had seven names in all: imbecile, donkey, flax-head, dope, glump, ninny, and fool. The last name stuck. What did my foolishness consist of? I was easy to take in. They said, "Gimpel, you know the rabbi's wife has been brought to childbed?" So I skipped school. Well, it turned out to be a lie. How was I supposed to know? She hadn't had a big belly. But I never looked at her belly. Was that really so foolish? The gang laughed and hee-hawed, stomped and danced and chanted a good-night prayer. And instead of the raisins they give when a woman's lying in, they stuffed my hand full of goat turds. I was no weakling. If I slapped someone he'd see all the way to Cracow. But I'm really not a slugger by nature. I think of myself: Let it pass. So they take advantage of me.

I was coming home from school and heard a dog barking. I'm not afraid of dogs, but of course I never want to start up with them. One of them may be mad, and if he bites there's not a Tartar in the world who can help you. So I made tracks. Then I looked around and saw the whole market place wild with laughter. It was no dog at all but Wolf-Leib the Thief. How was I supposed to know it was he? It sounded like a howling bitch.

When the pranksters and leg-pullers found that I was easy to fool, every one of them tried his luck with me. "Gimpel, the Czar is coming to Frampol; Gimpel, the moon fell down in Turbeen; Gimpel, little Hodel Furpiece found a treasure behind the bathhouse." And I like a golem believed everyone. In the first place, everything is possible, as it is written in the Wisdom of the Fathers, I've forgotten just how. Second, I had to believe when the whole town came down on me! If I ever dared to say, "Ah, you're kidding!" there was trouble. People got angry. "What do you mean! You want to call everyone a liar?" What was I to do? I believed them, and I hope at least that did them some good.

I was an orphan. My grandfather who brought me up was already bent toward the grave. So they turned me over to a baker, and what a time they gave me there! Every woman or girl who came to bake a batch of noodles had to fool me at least once. "Gimpel, there's a fair in heaven; Gimpel, the rabbi gave birth to a calf in the seventh month; Gimpel, a cow flew over the roof and laid brass eggs." A student from the yeshiva came once to buy a roll, and he said, "You, Gimpel, while you stand here scraping with your baker's shovel the Messiah has come. The dead have arisen." "What do you mean?" I said, "I heard no one blowing the ram's horn!" He said, "Are you deaf?" And all began to cry, "We heard it, we heard!" Then in came Rietze the Candle-dipper and called out in her hoarse voice, "Gimpel, your father and mother have stood up from the grave. They're looking for you."

To tell the truth, I knew very well that nothing of the sort had happened, but all the same, as folks were talking, I threw on my wool vest and went out. Maybe something had happened. What did I stand to lose by looking? Well, what a cat music went up! And then I took a vow to believe nothing more. But that was no go either. They confused me so that I didn't know the big end from the small.

I went to the rabbi to get some advice. He said, "It is written, better to be a fool all your days than for one hour to be evil. You are not a fool. They are the fools. For he who causes his neighbor to feel shame loses Paradise himself." Nevertheless the rabbi's daughter took me in. As I left the rabbinical court she said, "Have you kissed the wall yet?" I said, "No; what for?" She answered, "It's the law; you've got to do it after every visit." Well, there didn't seem to be any harm in it. And she burst out laughing. It was a fine trick. She put one over on me, all right.

I wanted to go off to another town, but then everyone got busy matchmaking, and they were after me so they nearly tore my coat tails off. They talked at me and talked until I got water on the ear. She was no chaste maiden, but they told me she was virgin pure. She had a limp, and they said it was deliberate, from coyness. She had a bastard, and they told me the child was her little brother. I cried, "You're wasting your time. I'll never marry that whore." But they said indignantly, "What a way to talk! Aren't you ashamed of yourself? We can take you to the rabbi and have you fined for giving her a bad name." I saw then that I wouldn't escape them so easily and I thought: They're set on making me their butt. But when you're married the husband's the master, and if that's all right with her it's agreeable to me too. Besides, you can't pass through life unscathed, nor expect to.

I went to her clay house, which was built on the sand, and the whole gang, hollering and chorusing, came after me. They acted like bear-baiters. When we came to the well they stopped all the same. They were afraid to start anything with Elka. Her mouth would open as if it were on a hinge, and she had a fierce tongue. I entered the house. Lines were strung from wall to wall and clothes were drying. Barefoot she stood by the tub, doing the wash. She was dressed in a worn hand-me-down gown of plush. She had her hair put up in braids and pinned across her head. It took my breath away, almost, the reek of it all.

Evidently she knew who I was. She took a look at me and said, "Look who's here! He's come, the drip. Grab a seat."

I told her all; I denied nothing. "Tell me the truth," I said, "are you really a virgin, and is that mischievous Yechiel actually your little brother? Don't be deceitful with me, for I'm an orphan."

"I'm an orphan myself," she answered, "and whoever tries to twist you up, may the end of his nose take a twist. But don't let them think they can take advantage of me. I want a dowry of fifty guilders, and let them take up a collection besides. Otherwise they can kiss my you-know-what." She was very plainspoken. I said, "It's the bride and not the groom who gives a dowry." Then she said, "Don't bargain with me. Either a flat 'yes' or a flat 'no'—Go back where you came from."

I thought: No bread will ever be baked from *this* dough. But ours is not a poor town. They consented to everything and proceeded with the wedding. It so happened that there was a dysentery epidemic at the time. The ceremony was held at the cemetery gates, near the little corpse-washing hut. The fellows got drunk. While the marriage contract was being drawn up I heard the most pious high rabbi ask, "Is the bride a widow or a divorced woman?" And the sexton's wife answered for her, "Both a widow and divorced." It was a black moment for me. But what was I to do, run away from under the marriage canopy?

There was singing and dancing. An old granny danced opposite me, hugging a braided white *chalah*. The master of revels made a "God 'a mercy" in memory of the bride's parents. The schoolboys threw burrs, as on Tishe b'Av fast day. There were a lot of gifts after the sermon: a noodle board, a kneading trough, a bucket, brooms, ladles, household articles galore. Then I took a look and saw two strapping young men carrying a crib. "What do we need this for?" I asked. So they said, "Don't rack your brains about it. It's all right, it'll come in handy." I realized I was going to be rooked. Take it another way though, what did I stand to lose? I reflected: I'll see what comes of it. A whole town can't go altogether crazy.

II

At night I came where my wife lay, but she wouldn't let me in. "Say, look here, is this what they married us for?" I said. And she said, "My monthly has come." "But yesterday they took you to the ritual bath, and that's afterward, isn't it supposed to be?" "Today isn't yesterday," said she, "and yesterday's not today. You can beat it if you don't like it." In short, I waited.

Not four months later she was in childbed. The townsfolk hid their laughter with their knuckles. But what could I do? She suffered intolerable pains and clawed at the walls. "Gimpel," she cried, "I'm going. Forgive me!" The house filled with women. They were boiling pans of water. The screams rose to the welkin.

The thing to do was to go to the House of Prayer to repeat Psalms, and that was what I did.

The townsfolk liked that, all right. I stood in a corner saying Psalms and prayers, and they shook their heads at me. "Pray, pray!" they told me. "Prayer never made any woman pregnant." One of the congregation put a straw to my mouth and said, "Hay for the cows." There was something to that too, by God!

She gave birth to a boy. Friday at the synagogue the sexton stood up before the Ark, pounded on the reading table, and announced, "The wealthy Reb Gimpel invites the congregation to a feast in honor of the birth of a son." The whole House of Prayer rang with laughter. My face was flaming. But there was nothing I could do. After all, I *was* the one responsible for the circumcision honors and rituals.

Half the town came running. You couldn't wedge another soul in. Women brought peppered chick-peas, and there was a keg of beer from the tavern. I ate and drank as much as anyone, and they all congratulated me. Then there was a circumcision, and I named the boy after my father, may he rest in peace. When all were gone and I was left with my wife alone, she thrust her head through the bed-curtain and called me to her.

"Gimpel," said she, "why are you silent? Has your ship gone and sunk?"

"What shall I say?" I answered. "A fine thing you've done to me! If my mother had known of it she'd have died a second time."

She said, "Are you crazy, or what?"

"How can you make such a fool," I said, "of one who should be the lord and master?"

"What's the matter with you?" she said. "What have you taken it into your head to imagine?"

I saw that I must speak bluntly and openly. "Do you think this is the way to use an orphan?" I said. "You have borne a bastard."

She answered, "Drive this foolishness out of your head. The child is yours."

"How can he be mine?" I argued. "He was born seventeen weeks after the wedding."

She told me then that he was premature. I said, "Isn't he a little too premature?" She said, she had had a grandmother who carried just as short a time and she resembled this grandmother of hers as one drop of water does another. She swore to it with such oaths that you would have believed a peasant at the fair if he had used them. To tell the plain truth, I didn't believe her; but when I talked it over next day with the schoolmaster he told me that the very same thing had happened to Adam and Eve. Two they went up to bed, and four they descended.

"There isn't a woman in the world who is not the granddaughter of Eve," he said.

That was how it was; they argued me dumb. But then, who really knows how such things are?

I began to forget my sorrow. I loved the child madly, and he loved me too. As soon as he saw me he'd wave his little hands and want me to pick him up, and when he was colicky I was the only one who could pacify him. I bought him a little bone teething ring and a little gilded cap. He was forever catching the evil eye from someone, and then I had to run to get one of those abracadabras for him that would get him out of it. I worked like an ox. You know how expenses go up when there's an infant in the house. I don't want to lie about it; I didn't dislike Elka either, for that matter. She swore at me and cursed, and I couldn't get enough of her. What strength she had! One of her looks could rob you of the power of speech. And her orations! Pitch and sulphur, that's what they were full of, and yet somehow also full of charm. I adored her every word. She gave me bloody wounds though.

In the evening I brought her a white loaf as well as a dark one, and also poppyseed rolls I baked myself. I thieved because of her and swiped everything I could lay hands on: macaroons, raisins, almonds, cakes. I hope I may be forgiven for stealing from the Saturday pots the women left to warm in the baker's oven. I would take out scraps of meat, a chunk of pudding, a chicken leg or head, a piece of tripe, whatever I could nip quickly. She ate and became fat and handsome.

I had to sleep away from home all during the week, at the bakery. On Friday nights when I got home she always made an excuse of some sort. Either she had heartburn, or a stitch in the side, or hiccups, or headaches. You know what women's excuses are. I had a bitter time of it. It was rough. To add to it, this little brother of hers, the bastard, was growing bigger. He'd put lumps on me, and when I wanted to hit back she'd open her mouth and curse so powerfully I saw a green haze floating before my eyes. Ten times a day she threatened to divorce me.

Another man in my place would have taken French leave and disappeared. But I'm the type that bears it and says nothing. What's one to do? Shoulders are from God, and burdens too.

One night there was a calamity in the bakery; the oven burst, and we almost had a fire. There was nothing to do but go home, so I went home. Let me, I thought, also taste the joy of sleeping in bed in mid-week. I didn't want to wake the sleeping mite and tiptoed into the house. Coming in, it seemed to me that I heard not the snoring of one but, as it were, a double snore, one a thin enough snore and the other like the snoring of a slaughtered ox. Oh, I didn't like that! I didn't like it at all. I went up to the bed, and things suddenly turned black. Next to Elka lay a man's form. Another in my place would have made an uproar, and enough noise to rouse the whole town, but the thought occurred to me that I might wake the child. A little thing like that—why frighten a little swallow, I thought. All right then, I went back to the bakery and stretched out on a sack of flour and till morning I never shut an eye. I shivered as if I had had malaria. "Enough of being a donkey," I said to myself. "Gimpel isn't going to be a sucker all his life. There's a limit even to the foolishness of a fool like Gimpel."

In the morning I went to the rabbi to get advice, and it made a great commotion in the town. They sent the beadle for Elka right away. She came, carrying the child. And what do you think she did? She denied it, denied everything, bone and stone! "He's out of his head," she said. "I know nothing of dreams or divinations." They yelled at her, warned her, hammered on the table, but she stuck to her guns: it was a false accusation, she said.

The butchers and the horse-traders took her part. One of the lads from the slaughterhouse came by and said to me, "We've got our eye on you, you're a marked man." Meanwhile the child started to bear down and soiled itself. In the rabbinical court there was an Ark of the Covenant, and they couldn't allow that, so they sent Elka away.

I said to the rabbi, "What shall I do?"

"You must divorce her at once," said he.

"And what if she refuses?" I asked.

He said, "You must serve the divorce. That's all you'll have to do."

I said, "Well, all right, Rabbi. Let me think about it."

"There's nothing to think about," said he. "You mustn't remain under the same roof with her."

"And if I want to see the child?" I asked.

"Let her go, the harlot," said he, "and her brood of bastards with her."

The verdict he gave was that I mustn't even cross her threshold—never again, as long as I should live.

During the day it didn't bother me so much. I thought: It was bound to happen, the abscess had to burst. But at night when I stretched out upon the sacks I felt it all very bitterly. A longing took me, for her and for the child. I wanted to be angry, but that's my misfortune exactly, I don't have it in me to be really angry. In the first place—this was how my thoughts went—there's bound to be a slip sometimes. You can't live without errors. Probably that lad who was with her led her on and gave her presents and what not, and women are often long on hair and short on sense, and so he got around her. And then since she denies it so, maybe I was only seeing things? Hallucinations do happen. You see a figure or a mannikin or something, but when you come up closer it's nothing, there's not a thing there.

And if that's so, I'm doing her an injustice. And when I got so far in my thoughts I started to weep. I sobbed so that I wet the flour where I lay. In the morning I went to the rabbi and told him that I had made a mistake. The rabbi wrote on with his quill, and he said that if that were so he would have to reconsider the whole case. Until he had finished I wasn't to go near my wife, but I might send her bread and money by messenger.

III

Nine months passed before all the rabbis could come to an agreement. Letters went back and forth. I hadn't realized that there could be so much erudition about a matter like this.

Meanwhile Elka gave birth to still another child, a girl this time. On the Sabbath I went to the synagogue and invoked a blessing on her. They called me up to the Torah, and I named the child for my mother-in-law—may she rest in peace. The louts and loudmouths of the town who came into the bakery gave me a going over. All Frampol refreshed its spirits because of my trouble and grief. However, I resolved that I would always believe what I was told. What's the good of *not* believing? Today it's your wife you don't believe; tomorrow it's God Himself you won't take stock in.

By an apprentice who was her neighbor I sent her daily a corn or a wheat loaf, or a piece of pastry, rolls or bagels, or, when I got the chance, a slab of pudding, a slice of honeycake, or wedding strudel—whatever came my way. The apprentice was a goodhearted lad, and more than once he added something on his own. He had formerly annoyed me a lot, plucking my nose and digging me in the ribs, but when he started to be a visitor to my house he became kind and friendly. "Hey, you, Gimpel," he said to me, "you have a very decent little wife and two fine kids. You don't deserve them."

"But the things people say about her," I said.

"Well, they have long tongues," he said, "and nothing to do with them but babble. Ignore it as you ignore the cold of last winter."

One day the rabbi sent for me and said, "Are you certain, Gimpel, that you were wrong about your wife?"

I said, "I'm certain."

"Why, but look here! You yourself saw it."

"It must have been a shadow," I said.

"The shadow of what?"

"Just of one of the beams, I think."

"You can go home then. You owe thanks to the Yanover rabbi. He found an obscure reference in Maimonides that favored you."

I seized the rabbi's hand and kissed it.

I wanted to run home immediately. It's no small thing to be separated for so long a time from wife and child. Then I reflected: I'd better go back to work now, and go home in the evening. I said nothing to anyone, although as far as my heart was concerned it was like one of the Holy Days. The women teased and twitted me as they did every day, but my thought was: Go on, with your loose talk. The truth is out, like the oil upon the water. Maimonides says it's right, and therefore it is right!

At night, when I had covered the dough to let it rise, I took my share of bread and a little sack of flour and started homeward. The moon was full and the stars were glistening, something to terrify the soul. I hurried onward, and before me darted a long shadow. It was winter, and a fresh snow had fallen. I had a mind to sing, but it was growing late and I didn't want to wake the householders. Then I felt like whistling, but I remembered that you don't whistle at night because it brings the demons out. So I was silent and walked as fast as I could.

Dogs in the Christian yards barked at me when I passed, but I thought: Bark your teeth out! What are you but mere dogs? Whereas I am a man, the husband of a fine wife, the father of promising children.

As I approached the house my heart started to pound as though it were the heart of a criminal. I felt no fear, but my heart went thump! thump! Well, no drawing back. I quietly lifted the latch and went in. Elka was asleep. I looked at the infant's cradle. The shutter was closed, but the moon forced its way through the cracks. I saw the newborn child's face and loved it as soon as I saw it—immediately—each tiny bone.

Then I came nearer to the bed. And what did I see but the apprentice lying there beside Elka. The moon went out all at once. It was utterly black, and I trembled. My teeth chattered. The bread fell from my hands, and my wife waked and said, "Who is that, ah?"

I muttered, "It's me."

"Gimpel?" she asked. "How come you're here? I thought it was forbidden."

"The rabbi said," I answered and shook as with a fever.

"Listen to me, Gimpel," she said, "go out to the shed and see if the goat's all right. It seems she's been sick." I have forgotten to say that we had a goat. When I heard she was unwell I went into the yard. The nannygoat was a good little creature. I had a nearly human feeling for her.

With hesitant steps I went up to the shed and opened the door. The goat stood there on her four feet. I felt her everywhere, drew her by the horns, examined her udders, and found nothing wrong. She had probably eaten too much bark. "Good night, little goat," I said. "Keep well." And the little beast answered with a "Maa" as though to thank me for the good will.

I went back. The apprentice had vanished.

"Where," I asked, "is the lad?"

"What lad?" my wife answered.

"What do you mean?" I said. "The apprentice. You were sleeping with him."

"The things I have dreamed this night and the night before," she said, "may they come true and lay you low, body and soul! An evil spirit has taken root in you and dazzles your sight." She screamed out, "You hateful creature! You moon calf! You spook! You uncouth man! Get out, or I'll scream all Frampol out of bed!"

Before I could move, her brother sprang out from behind the oven and struck me a blow on the back of the head. I thought he had broken my neck. I felt that something about me was deeply wrong, and I said, "Don't make a scandal. All that's needed now is that people should accuse me of raising spooks and *dybbuks*." For that was what she had meant. "No one will touch bread of my baking."

In short, I somehow calmed her.

"Well," she said, "that's enough. Lie down, and be shattered by wheels."

Next morning I called the apprentice aside. "Listen here, brother!" I said. And so on and so forth. "What do you say?" He stared at me as though I had dropped from the roof or something.

"I swear," he said, "you'd better go to an herb doctor or some healer. I'm afraid you have a screw loose, but I'll hush it up for you." And that's how the thing stood.

To make a long story short, I lived twenty years with my wife. She bore me six children, four daughters and two sons. All kinds of things happened, but I neither saw nor heard. I believed, and that's all. The rabbi recently said to me, "Belief in itself is beneficial. It is written that a good man lives by his faith."

Suddenly my wife took sick. It began with a trifle, a little growth upon the breast. But she evidently was not destined to live long; she had no years. I spent a fortune on her. I have forgotten to say that by this time I had a bakery of my own and in Frampol was considered to be something of a rich man. Daily the healer came, and every witch doctor in the neighborhood was brought. They decided to use leeches, and after that to try cupping. They even called a doctor from Lublin, but it was too late. Before she died she called me to her bed and said, "Forgive me, Gimpel."

I said, "What is there to forgive? You have been a good and faithful wife."

"Woe, Gimpel!" she said. "It was ugly how I deceived you all these years. I want to go clean to my Maker, and so I have to tell you that the children are not yours."

If I had been clouted on the head with a piece of wood it couldn't have bewildered me more.

"Whose are they?" I asked.

"I don't know," she said. "There are a lot . . . but they're not yours." And as she spoke she tossed her head to the side, her eyes turned glassy, and it was all up with Elka. On her whitened lips there remained a smile.

I imagined that, dead as she was, she was saying, "I deceived Gimpel. That was the meaning of my brief life."

IV

One night, when the period of mourning was done, as I lay dreaming on the flour sacks, there came the Spirit of Evil himself and said to me, "Gimpel, why do you sleep?"

I said, "What should I be doing? Eating *kreplach*?"

"The whole world deceives you," he said, "and you ought to deceive the world in your turn."

"How can I deceive all the world?" I asked him.

He answered, "You might accumulate a bucket of urine every day and at night pour it into the dough. Let the sages of Frampol eat filth."

"What about the judgment in the world to come," I said.

"There is no world to come," he said. "They've sold you a bill of goods and talked you into believing you carried a cat in your belly. What nonsense!"

"Well then," I said, "and is there a God?"

He answered, "There is no God either."

"What," I said, "*is* there, then?"

"A thick mire."

He stood before my eyes with a goatish beard and horn, long-toothed, and with a tail. Hearing such words, I wanted to snatch him by the tail, but I tumbled from the flour sacks and nearly broke a rib. Then it happened that I had to answer the call of nature, and, passing, I saw the risen dough, which seemed to say to me, "Do it!" In brief, I let myself be persuaded.

At dawn the apprentice came. We kneaded the bread, scattered caraway seeds on it, and set it to bake. Then the apprentice went away, and I was left sitting in the little trench by the oven, on a pile of rags. Well, Gimpel, I thought, you've revenged yourself on them for all the shame they've put on you. Outside the frost glittered, but it was warm beside the oven. The flames heated my face. I bent my head and fell into a doze.

I saw in a dream, at once, Elka in her shroud. She called to me, "What have you done, Gimpel?"

I said to her, "It's all your fault," and started to cry.

"You fool!" she said. "You fool! Because I was false is everything false too? I never deceived anyone but myself. I'm paying for it all, Gimpel. They spare you nothing here."

I looked at her face. It was black; I was startled and waked, and remained sitting dumb. I sensed that everything hung in the balance. A false step now and I'd lose Eternal Life. But God gave me His help. I seized the long shovel and took out the loaves, carried them into the yard, and started to dig a hole in the frozen earth.

My apprentice came back as I was doing it. "What are you doing boss?" he said, and grew pale as a corpse.

"I know what I'm doing," I said, and I buried it all before his very eyes.

Then I went home, took my hoard from its hiding place, and divided it among the children. "I saw your mother tonight," I said. "She's turning black, poor thing."

They were so astounded they couldn't speak a word.

"Be well," I said, "and forget that such a one as Gimpel ever existed." I put on my short coat, a pair of boots, took the bag that held my prayer shawl in one hand, my stick in the other, and kissed the *mezzuzah*. When people saw me in the street they were greatly surprised.

"Where are you going?" they said.

I answered, "Into the world." And so I departed from Frampol.

I wandered over the land, and good people did not neglect me. After many years I became old and white; I heard a great deal, many lies and falsehoods, but the longer I lived the more I understood that there were really no lies. Whatever doesn't really happen is dreamed at night. It happens to one if it doesn't happen to another, tomorrow if not today, or a century hence if not next year. What difference can it make? Often I heard tales of which I said, "Now this is a thing that cannot happen." But before a year had elapsed I heard that it actually had come to pass somewhere.

Going from place to place, eating at strange tables, it often happens that I spin yarns—improbable things that could never have happened—about devils, magicians, windmills, and the like. The children run after me, calling, "Grandfather, tell us a story." Sometimes they ask for particular stories, and I try to please them. A fat young boy once said to me, "Grandfather, it's the same story you told us before." The little rogue, he was right.

So it is with dreams too. It is many years since I left Frampol, but as soon as I shut my eyes I am there again. And whom do you think I see? Elka. She is standing by the washtub, as at our first encounter, but her face is shining and her eyes are as radiant as the eyes of a saint, and she speaks outlandish words to me, strange things. When I wake I have forgotten it all. But while the dream lasts I am comforted. She answers all my queries, and what comes out is that all is right. I weep and implore, "Let me be with you." And she consoles me and tells me to be patient. The time is nearer than it is far. Sometimes she strokes and kisses me and weeps upon my face. When I awaken I feel her lips and taste the salt of her tears.

No doubt the world is entirely an imaginary world, but it is only once removed from the true world. At the door of the hovel where I lie, there stands the plank on which the dead are taken away. The gravedigger Jew has his spade ready. The grave waits and the worms are hungry; the shrouds are prepared—I carry them in my beggar's sack. Another *shnorrer* is waiting to inherit my bed of straw. When the time comes I will go joyfully. Whatever may be there, it will be real, without complication, without ridicule, without deception. God be praised: there even Gimpel cannot be deceived.

FLANNERY O'CONNOR (1925–1964) was the only child of Roman Catholic parents. Born in cosmopolitan Savannah, Georgia, she moved to rural Milledgeville when she was thirteen. Her father was a real estate broker who encouraged her to write. As a student at Georgia State College for Women (now Georgia College and State University), O'Connor wrote stories and was the art editor of the school newspaper and the editor of the campus literary magazine. She received a fellowship to the Iowa Writers' Workshop, where she earned her M.F.A. After being diagnosed with lupus in 1950, O'Connor moved back to Milledgeville to live with her mother and continued to write.

Her first collection of short stories, *A Good Man is Hard to Find and Other Stories* (1955), was published three years after her first novel, *Wise Blood* (1952). Another novel, *The Violent Bear it Away*, was published in 1960, and her second collection of short stories, *Everything That Rises Must Converge*, was published posthumously in 1965.

Like that of Nathaniel Hawthorne, O'Connor's work addresses issues of religion and the inherent corruptness of a world tainted by sin and imperfection. Many of her characters are estranged from God and are unaware of their need for redemption. To jolt her characters and her readers into this awareness, O'Connor often incorporated unexpected elements of the **grotesque** and violence as "shock treatments" to illuminate repugnant behaviors and attitudes that might otherwise seem natural and acceptable.

Like many of O'Connor's characters, the protagonist of "Good Country People" (1955), Hulga, who claims to believe in "nothing," is guilty of the sin of pride and in need of a chance for salvation. "Good Country People" also includes some of O'Connor's characteristically **ironic** elements (such as the scene in which Hulga's wooden leg is removed by the Bible salesman).

Related Works: Hawthorne, "Young Goodman Brown"; Faulkner, "A Rose for Emily"; Blake, "The Lamb" and "The Tiger"; Garcia, "Why I Left the Church."

Good Country People

Besides the neutral expression that she wore when she was alone, Mrs. Freeman had two others, forward and reverse, that she used for all her human dealings. Her forward expression was steady and driving like the advance of a heavy truck.

Her eyes never swerved to left or right but turned as the story turned as if they followed a yellow line down the center of it. She seldom used the other expression because it was not often necessary for her to retract a statement, but when she did, her face came to a complete stop, there was an almost imperceptible movement of her black eyes, during which they seemed to be receding, and then the observer would see that Mrs. Freeman, though she might stand there as real as several grain sacks thrown on top of each other, was no longer there in spirit. As for getting anything across to her when this was the case, Mrs. Hopewell had given it up. She might talk her head off. Mrs. Freeman could never be brought to admit herself wrong on any point. She would stand there and if she could be brought to say anything, it was something like, "Well, I wouldn't of said it was and I wouldn't of said it wasn't," or letting her gaze range over the top kitchen shelf where there was an assortment of dusty bottles, she might remark, "I see you ain't ate many of them figs you put up last summer."

They carried on their most important business in the kitchen at breakfast. Every morning Mrs. Hopewell got up at seven o'clock and lit her gas heater and Joy's. Joy was her daughter, a large blonde girl who had an artificial leg. Mrs. Hopewell thought of her as a child though she was thirty-two years old and highly educated. Joy would get up while her mother was eating and lumber into the bathroom and slam the door, and before long, Mrs. Freeman would arrive at the back door. Joy would hear her mother call, "Come on in," and then they would talk for a while in low voices that were indistinguishable in the bathroom. By the time Joy came in, they had usually finished the weather report and were on one or the other of Mrs. Freeman's daughters, Glynese or Carramae. Joy called them Glycerin and Caramel. Glynese, a redhead, was eighteen and had many admirers; Carramae, a blonde, was only fifteen but already married and pregnant. She could not keep anything on her stomach. Every morning Mrs. Freeman told Mrs. Hopewell how many times she had vomited since the last report.

Mrs. Hopewell liked to tell people that Glynese and Carramae were two of the finest girls she knew and that Mrs. Freeman was a *lady* and that she was never ashamed to take her anywhere or introduce her to anybody they might meet. Then she would tell how she had happened to hire the Freemans in the first place and how they were a godsend to her and how she had had them four years. The reason for her keeping them so long was that they were not trash. They were good country people. She had telephoned the man whose name they had given as a reference and he had told her that Mr. Freeman was a good farmer but that his wife was the nosiest woman ever to walk the earth. "She's got to be into everything," the man said. "If she don't get there before the dust settles, you can bet she's dead, that's all. She'll want to know all your business. I can stand him real good," he had said, "but me nor my wife neither could have stood that woman one more minute on this place." That had put Mrs. Hopewell off for a few days.

She had hired them in the end because there were no other applicants but she had made up her mind beforehand exactly how she would handle the woman. Since she was the type who had to be into everything, then, Mrs. Hopewell had decided, she would not only let her be into everything, she would *see to it* that she was into everything—she would give her the responsibility of everything, she would put her in charge. Mrs. Hopewell had no bad qualities of her own but she was able to use other people's in such a constructive way that she never felt the lack. She had hired the Freemans and she had kept them four years.

Nothing is perfect. This was one of Mrs. Hopewell's favorite sayings. Another was: that is life! And still another, the most important, was: well, other people have their opinions too. She would make these statements, usually at the table, in a tone of gentle insistence as if no one held them but her, and the large hulking Joy, whose constant outrage had obliterated every expression from her face, would stare just a little to the side of her, her eyes icy blue, with the look of someone who has achieved blindness by an act of will and means to keep it.

When Mrs. Hopewell said to Mrs. Freeman that life was like that, Mrs. Freeman would say, "I always said so myself." Nothing had been arrived at by anyone that had not first been arrived at by her. She was quicker than Mr. Freeman. When Mrs. Hopewell said to her after they had been on the place a while, "You know, you're the wheel behind the wheel," and winked, Mrs. Freeman had said, "I know it. I've always been quick. It's some that are quicker than others."

"Everybody is different," Mrs. Hopewell said.

"Yes, most people is," Mrs. Freeman said.

"It takes all kinds to make the world."

"I always said it did myself."

The girl was used to this kind of dialogue for breakfast and more of it for dinner; sometimes they had it for supper too. When they had no guest they ate in the kitchen because that was easier. Mrs. Freeman always managed to arrive at some point during the meal and to watch them finish it. She would stand in the doorway if it were summer but in the winter she would stand with one elbow on top of the refrigerator and look down on them, or she would stand by the gas heater, lifting the back of her skirt slightly. Occasionally she would stand against the wall and roll her head from side to side. At no time was she in any hurry to leave. All this was very trying on Mrs. Hopewell but she was a woman of great patience. She realized that nothing is perfect and that in the Freemans she had good country people and that if, in this day and age, you get good country people, you had better hang onto them.

She had had plenty of experience with trash. Before the Freemans she had averaged one tenant family a year. The wives of these farmers were not the kind you would want to be around you for very long. Mrs. Hopewell, who had divorced her husband long ago, needed someone to walk over the fields with her; and when Joy had to be impressed for these services, her remarks were usually so ugly and her face so glum that Mrs. Hopewell would say, "If you can't come pleasantly, I don't want you at all," to which the girl, standing square and rigid-shouldered with her neck thrust slightly forward, would reply, "If you want me, here I am—LIKE I AM."

Mrs. Hopewell excused this attitude because of the leg (which had been shot off in a hunting accident when Joy was ten). It was hard for Mrs. Hopewell to realize that her child was thirty-two now and that for more than twenty years she had had only one leg. She thought of her still as a child because it tore her heart to think instead of the poor stout girl in her thirties who had never danced a step or had any *normal* good times. Her name was really Joy but as soon as she was twenty-one and away from home, she had had it legally changed. Mrs. Hopewell was certain that she had thought and thought until she had hit upon the ugliest name in any language. Then she had gone and had the beautiful name, Joy, changed without telling her mother until after she had done it. Her legal name was Hulga.

When Mrs. Hopewell thought the name, Hulga, she thought of the broad blank hull of a battleship. She would not use it. She continued to call her Joy to which the girl responded but in a purely mechanical way.

Hulga had learned to tolerate Mrs. Freeman who saved her from taking walks with her mother. Even Glynese and Carramae were useful when they occupied attention that might otherwise have been directed at her. At first she had thought she could not stand Mrs. Freeman for she had found that it was not possible to be rude to her. Mrs. Freeman would take on strange resentments and for days together she would be sullen but the source of her displeasure was always obscure; a direct attack, a positive leer, blatant ugliness to her face—these never touched her. And without warning one day, she began calling her Hulga.

She did not call her that in front of Mrs. Hopewell who would have been incensed but when she and the girl happened to be out of the house together, she would say something and add the name Hulga to the end of it, and the big spectacled Joy-Hulga would scowl and redden as if her privacy had been intruded upon. She considered the name her personal affair. She had arrived at it first purely on the basis of its ugly sound and then the full genius of its fitness had struck her. She had a vision of the name working like the ugly sweating Vulcan who stayed in the furnace and to whom, presumably, the goddess had to come when called. She saw it as the name of her highest creative act. One of her major triumphs was that her mother had not been able to turn her dust into Joy, but the greater one was that she had been able to turn it herself into Hulga. However, Mrs. Freeman's relish for using the name only irritated her. It was as if Mrs. Freeman's beady steel-pointed eyes had penetrated far enough behind her face to reach some secret fact. Something about her seemed to fascinate Mrs. Freeman and then one day Hulga realized that it was the artificial leg. Mrs. Freeman had a special fondness for the details of secret infections, hidden deformities, assaults upon children. Of diseases, she preferred the lingering or incurable. Hulga had heard Mrs. Hopewell give her the details of the hunting accident, how the leg had been literally blasted off, how she had never lost consciousness. Mrs. Freeman could listen to it any time as if it had happened an hour ago.

When Hulga stumped into the kitchen in the morning (she could walk without making the awful noise but she made it—Mrs. Hopewell was certain—because it was ugly-sounding), she glanced at them and did not speak. Mrs. Hopewell would be in her red kimono with her hair tied around her head in rags. She would be sitting at the table, finishing her breakfast and Mrs. Freeman would be hanging by her elbow outward from the refrigerator, looking down at the table. Hulga always put her eggs on the stove to boil and then stood over them with her arms folded, and Mrs. Hopewell would look at her—a kind of indirect gaze divided between her and Mrs. Freeman—and would think that if she would only keep herself up a little, she wouldn't be so bad looking. There was nothing wrong with her face that a pleasant expression wouldn't help. Mrs. Hopewell said that people who looked on the bright side of things would be beautiful even if they were not.

Whenever she looked at Joy this way, she could not help but feel that it would have been better if the child had not taken the Ph.D. It had certainly not brought her out any and now that she had it, there was no more excuse for her to go to school again. Mrs. Hopewell thought it was nice for girls to go to school to have a good time but Joy had "gone through." Anyhow, she would not have been strong enough to go again. The doctors had told Mrs. Hopewell that with the best of care, Joy might see forty-five. She had a weak heart. Joy had made it plain that if it had not been for this condition, she would be far from these red hills and good country people. She would be in a university lecturing to people who knew what she was talking about. And Mrs. Hopewell could very well picture her there, looking like a scarecrow and lecturing to more of the same. Here she went about all day in a six-year-old skirt and a yellow sweat shirt with a faded cowboy on a horse embossed on it. She thought this was funny; Mrs. Hopewell thought it was idiotic and showed simply that she was still a child. She was brilliant but she didn't have a grain of sense. It seemed to Mrs. Hopewell that every year she grew less like other people and more like herself—bloated, rude, and squint-eyed. And she said such strange things! To her own mother she had said—without warning, without excuse, standing up in the middle of a meal with her face purple and her mouth half full—"Woman! do you ever look inside? Do you ever look inside and see what you are *not*? God!" she had cried sinking down again and staring at her plate, "Malebranche was right: we are not our own light. We are not our own light!" Mrs. Hopewell had no idea to this day what brought that on. She had only made the remark, hoping Joy would take it in, that a smile never hurt anyone.

The girl had taken the Ph.D. in philosophy and this left Mrs. Hopewell at a complete loss. You could say, "My daughter is a nurse," or "My daughter is a school teacher," or even, "My daughter is a chemical engineer." You could not say, "My daughter is a philosopher." That was something that had ended with the Greeks and Romans. All day Joy sat on her neck in a deep chair, reading. Sometimes she went for walks but she didn't like dogs or cats or birds or flowers or nature or nice young men. She looked at nice young men as if she could smell their stupidity.

One day Mrs. Hopewell had picked up one of the books the girl had just put down and opening it at random, she read, "Science, on the other hand, has to assert its soberness and seriousness afresh and declare that it is concerned solely with what-is. Nothing—how can it be for science anything but a horror and a phantasm? If science is right, then one thing stands firm; science wishes to know nothing of nothing. Such is after all the strictly scientific approach to Nothing. We know it by wishing to know nothing of Nothing." These words had been underlined with a blue pencil and they worked on Mrs. Hopewell like some evil incantation in gibberish. She shut the book quickly and went out of the room as if she were having a chill.

This morning when the girl came in, Mrs. Freeman was on Carramae. "She thrown up four times after supper," she said, "and was up twict in the night after three o'clock. Yesterday she didn't do nothing but ramble in the bureau drawer. All she did. Stand up there and see what she could run up on."

"She's got to eat," Mrs. Hopewell muttered, sipping her coffee, while she watched Joy's back at the stove. She was wondering what the child had said to the Bible salesman. She could not imagine what kind of a conversation she could possibly have had with him.

He was a tall gaunt hatless youth who had called yesterday to sell them a Bible. He had appeared at the door, carrying a large black suitcase that weighted him so heavily on one side that he had to brace himself against the door facing. He seemed on the point of collapse but he said in a cheerful voice, "Good morning, Mrs. Cedars!" and set the suitcase down on the mat. He was not a bad-looking young man though he had on a bright blue suit and yellow socks that were not pulled up far enough. He had prominent face bones and a streak of sticky-looking brown hair falling across his forehead.

"I'm Mrs. Hopewell," she said.

"Oh!" he said, pretending to look puzzled but with his eyes sparkling, "I saw it said 'The Cedars,' on the mailbox so I thought you was Mrs. Cedars!" and he burst out in a pleasant laugh. He picked up the satchel and under cover of a pant, he fell forward into her hall. It was rather as if the suitcase had moved first, jerking him after it. "Mrs. Hopewell!" he said and grabbed her hand. "I hope you are well!" and he laughed again and then all at once his face sobered completely. He paused and gave her a straight earnest look and said, "Lady, I've come to speak of serious things."

"Well, come in," she muttered, none too pleased because her dinner was almost ready. He came into the parlor and sat down on the edge of a straight chair and put the suitcase between his feet and glanced around the room as if he were sizing her up by it. Her silver gleamed on the two sideboards; she decided he had never been in a room as elegant as this.

"Mrs. Hopewell," he began, using her name in a way that sounded almost intimate, "I know you believe in Chrustian service."

"Well yes," she murmured.

"I know," he said and paused, looking very wise with his head cocked on one side, "that you're a good woman. Friends have told me."

Mrs. Hopewell never liked to be taken for a fool. "What are you selling?" she asked.

"Bibles," the young man said and his eye raced around the room before he added, "I see you have no family Bible in your parlor, I see that is the one lack you got!"

Mrs. Hopewell could not say, "My daughter is an atheist and won't let me keep the Bible in the parlor." She said, stiffening slightly, "I keep my Bible by my bedside." This was not the truth. It was in the attic somewhere.

"Lady," he said, "the word of God ought to be in the parlor."

"Well, I think that's a matter of taste," she began. "I think . . ."

"Lady," he said, "for a Chrustian, the word of God ought to be in every room in the house besides in his heart. I know you're a Chrustian because I can see it in every line of your face."

She stood up and said, "Well, young man, I don't want to buy a Bible and I smell my dinner burning."

He didn't get up. He began to twist his hands and looking down at them, he said softly, "Well lady, I'll tell you the truth—not many people want to buy one nowadays and besides, I know I'm real simple. I don't know how to say a thing but to say it. I'm just a country boy." He glanced up into her unfriendly face. "People like you don't like to fool with country people like me!"

"Why!" she cried, "good country people are the salt of the earth! Besides, we all have different ways of doing, it takes all kinds to make the world go 'round. That's life!"

"You said a mouthful," he said.

"Why, I think there aren't enough good country people in the world!" she said, stirred. "I think that's what's wrong with it!"

His face had brightened. "I didn't inraduce myself," he said. "I'm Manley Pointer from out in the country around Willohobie, not even from a place, just from near a place."

"You wait a minute," she said. "I have to see about my dinner." She went out to the kitchen and found Joy standing near the door where she had been listening.

"Get rid of the salt of the earth," she said, "and let's eat."

Mrs. Hopewell gave her a pained look and turned the heat down under the vegetables. "*I* can't be rude to anybody," she murmured and went back into the parlor.

He had opened the suitcase and was sitting with a Bible on each knee.

"You might as well put those up," she told him. "I don't want one."

"I appreciate your honesty," he said. "You don't see any more real honest people unless you go way out in the country."

"I know," she said, "real genuine folks!" Through the crack in the door she heard a groan.

"I guess a lot of boys come telling you they're working their way through college," he said, "but I'm not going to tell you that. Somehow," he said, "I don't want to go to college. I want to devote my life to Chrustian service. See," he said, lowering his voice, "I got this heart condition. I may not live long. When you know it's something wrong with you and you may not live long, well then, lady . . ." He paused, with his mouth open, and stared at her.

He and Joy had the same condition! She knew that her eyes were filling with tears but she collected herself quickly and murmured, "Won't you stay for dinner? We'd love to have you!" and was sorry the instant she heard herself say it.

"Yes mam," he said in an abashed voice, "I would sher love to do that!"

Joy had given him one look on being introduced to him and then throughout the meal had not glanced at him again. He had addressed several remarks to her, which she had pretended not to hear. Mrs. Hopewell could not understand deliberate rudeness, although she lived with it, and she felt she had always to overflow with hospitality to make up for Joy's lack of courtesy. She urged him to talk about himself and he did. He said he was the seventh child of twelve and that his father had been crushed under a tree when he himself was eight year old. He had been crushed very badly, in fact, almost cut in two and was practically not recognizable. His mother had got along the best she could by hard working and she had always seen that her children went to Sunday School and that they read the Bible every evening. He was now nineteen years old and he had been selling Bibles for four months. In that time he had sold seventy-seven Bibles and had the promise of two more sales. He wanted to become a missionary because he thought that was the way you could do most for people. "He who losest his life shall find it," he said simply and he was so sincere, so genuine and earnest that Mrs. Hopewell would not for the world have smiled. He prevented his peas from sliding onto the table by blocking them with a piece of bread which he later cleaned his plate with. She could see Joy observing sidewise how he handled his knife and fork and she saw too that every few minutes, the boy would dart a keen appraising glance at the girl as if he were trying to attract her attention.

After dinner Joy cleared the dishes off the table and disappeared and Mrs. Hopewell was left to talk with him. He told her again about his childhood and his father's accident and about various things that had happened to him. Every five minutes or so she would stifle a yawn. He sat for two hours until finally she told him she must go because she had an appointment in town. He packed his Bibles and thanked her and prepared to leave, but in the doorway he stopped and wrung her hand and said that not on any of his trips had he met a lady as nice as her and he asked if he could come again. She had said she would always be happy to see him.

Joy had been standing in the road, apparently looking at something in the distance, when he came down the steps toward her, bent to the side with his heavy valise. He stopped where she was standing and confronted her directly. Mrs. Hopewell could not hear what he said but she trembled to think what Joy would say to him. She could see that after a minute Joy said something and that then the boy began to speak again, making an excited gesture with his free hand. After a minute Joy said something else at which the boy began to speak once more. Then to her amazement, Mrs. Hopewell saw the two of them walk off together, toward the gate. Joy had walked all the way to the gate with him and Mrs. Hopewell could not imagine what they had said to each other, and she had not yet dared to ask.

Mrs. Freeman was insisting upon her attention. She had moved from the refrigerator to the heater so that Mrs. Hopewell had to turn and face her in order to seem to be listening. "Glynese gone out with Harvey Hill again last night," she said. "She had this sty."

"Hill," Mrs. Hopewell said absently, "is that the one who works in the garage?"

"Nome, he's the one that goes to chiropracter school," Mrs. Freeman said. "She had this sty. Been had it two days. So she says when he brought her in the other night he says, 'Lemme get rid of that sty for you,' and she says. 'How?' and he says, 'You just lay yourself down acrost the seat of that car and I'll show you.' So she done it and he popped her neck. Kept on a popping it several times until she made him quit. This morning," Mrs. Freeman said, "she ain't got no sty. She ain't got no traces of a sty."

"I never heard of that before," Mrs. Hopewell said.

"He ast her to marry him before the Ordinary," Mrs. Freeman went on, "and she told him she wasn't going to be married in no *office*."

"Well, Glynese is a fine girl," Mrs. Hopewell said. "Glynese and Carramae are both fine girls."

"Carramae said when her and Lyman was married Lyman said it sure felt sacred to him. She said he said he wouldn't take five hundred dollars for being married by a preacher."

"How much would he take?" the girl asked from the stove.

"He said he wouldn't take five hundred dollars," Mrs. Freeman repeated.

"Well we all have work to do," Mrs. Hopewell said.

"Lyman said it just felt more sacred to him," Mrs. Freeman said. "The doctor wants Carramae to eat prunes. Says instead of medicine. Says them cramps is coming from pressure. You know where I think it is?"

"She'll be better in a few weeks," Mrs. Hopewell said.

"In the tube," Mrs. Freeman said. "Else she wouldn't be as sick as she is."

Hulga had cracked her two eggs into a saucer and was bringing them to the table along with a cup of coffee that she had filled too full. She sat down carefully and began to eat, meaning to keep Mrs. Freeman there by questions if for any reason she showed an inclination to leave. She could perceive her mother's eye on her. The first round-about question would be about the Bible salesman and she did not wish to bring it on. "How did he pop her neck?" she asked.

Mrs. Freeman went into a description of how he had popped her neck. She said he owned a '55 Mercury but that Glynese said she would rather marry a man with only a '36 Plymouth who would be married by a preacher. The girl asked what if he had a '32 Plymouth and Mrs. Freeman said what Glynese had said was a '36 Plymouth.

Mrs. Hopewell said there were not many girls with Glynese's common sense. She said what she admired in those girls was their common sense. She said that reminded her that they had had a nice visitor yesterday, a young man selling Bibles. "Lord," she said, "he bored me to death but he was so sincere and genuine I couldn't be rude to him. He was just good country people, you know," she said, "—just the salt of the earth."

"I seen him walk up," Mrs. Freeman said, "and then later—I seen him walk off," and Hulga could feel the slight shift in her voice, the slight insinuation, that he had not walked off alone, had he? Her face remained expressionless but the color rose into her neck and she seemed to swallow it down with the next spoonful of egg. Mrs. Freeman was looking at her as if they had a secret together.

"Well, it takes all kinds of people to make the world go 'round," Mrs. Hopewell said. "It's very good we aren't all alike."

"Some people are more alike than others," Mrs. Freeman said.

Hulga got up and stumped, with about twice the noise that was necessary, into her room and locked the door. She was to meet the Bible salesman at ten o'clock at the gate.

She had thought about it half the night. She had started thinking of it as a great joke and then she had begun to see profound implications in it. She had lain in bed imagining dialogues for them that were insane on the surface but that reached below to depths that no Bible salesman would be aware of. Their conversation yesterday had been of this kind.

He had stopped in front of her and had simply stood there. His face was bony and sweaty and bright, with a little pointed nose in the center of it, and his look was different from what it had been at the dinner table. He was gazing at her with open curiosity, with fascination, like a child watching a new fantastic animal at the zoo, and he was breathing as if he had run a great distance to reach her. His gaze seemed somehow familiar but she could not think where she had been regarded with it before. For almost a minute he didn't say anything. Then on what seemed an insuck of breath, he whispered, "You ever ate a chicken that was two days old?"

The girl looked at him stonily. He might have just put this question up for consideration at the meeting of a philosophical association. "Yes," she presently replied as if she had considered it from all angles.

"It must have been mighty small!" he said triumphantly and shook all over with little nervous giggles, getting very red in the face, and subsiding finally into his gaze of complete admiration, while the girl's expression remained exactly the same.

"How old are you?" he asked softly.

She waited some time before she answered. Then in a flat voice she said, "Seventeen."

His smiles came in succession like waves breaking on the surface of a little lake. "I see you got a wooden leg," he said. "I think you're real brave. I think you're real sweet."

The girl stood blank and solid and silent.

"Walk to the gate with me," he said, "You're a brave sweet little thing and I liked you the minute I seen you walk in the door."

Hulga began to move forward.

"What's your name?" he asked, smiling down on the top of her head.

"Hulga," she said.

"Hulga," he murmured, "Hulga. Hulga. I never heard of anybody name Hulga before. You're shy, aren't you, Hulga?" he asked.

She nodded, watching his large red hand on the handle of the giant valise.

"I like girls that wear glasses," he said. "I think a lot. I'm not like these people that a serious thought don't ever enter their heads. It's because I may die."

"I may die too," she said suddenly and looked up at him. His eyes were very small and brown, glittering feverishly.

"Listen," he said, "don't you think some people was meant to meet on account of what all they got in common and all? Like they both think serious thoughts and all?" He shifted the valise to his other hand so that the hand nearest her was free. He caught hold of her elbow and shook it a little. "I don't work on Saturday," he said. "I like to walk in the woods and see what Mother Nature is wearing. O'er the hills and far away. Picnics and things. Couldn't we go on a picnic tomorrow? Say yes, Hulga," he said and gave her a dying look as if he felt his insides about to drop out of him. He had even seemed to sway slightly toward her.

During the night she had imagined that she seduced him. She imagined that the two of them walked on the place until they came to the storage barn beyond the two back fields and there, she imagined, that things came to such a pass that she very easily seduced him and that then, of course, she had to reckon with his remorse. True genius can get an idea across even to an inferior mind. She imagined that she took his remorse in hand and changed it into a deeper understanding of life. She took all his shame away and turned it into something useful.

She set off for the gate at exactly ten o'clock, escaping without drawing Mrs. Hopewell's attention. She didn't take anything to eat, forgetting that food is usually taken on a picnic. She wore a pair of slacks and a dirty white shirt, and as an afterthought, she had put some Vapex on the collar of it since she did not own any perfume. When she reached the gate no one was there.

She looked up and down the empty highway and had the furious feeling that she had been tricked, that he had only meant to make her walk to the gate after the idea of him. Then suddenly he stood up, very tall, from behind a bush on the opposite embankment. Smiling, he lifted his hat which was new and wide-brimmed. He had not worn it yesterday and she wondered if he had bought it for the occasion. It was toast-colored with a red and white band around it and was slightly too large for him. He stepped from behind the bush still carrying the black valise. He had on the same suit and the same yellow socks sucked down in his shoes from walking. He crossed the highway and said, "I knew you'd come!"

The girl wondered acidly how he had known this. She pointed to the valise and asked, "Why did you bring your Bibles?"

He took her elbow, smiling down on her as if he could not stop. "You can never tell when you'll need the word of God, Hulga," he said. She had a moment in which she doubted that this was actually happening and then they began to climb the embankment. They went down into the pasture toward the woods. The boy walked lightly by her side, bouncing on his toes. The valise did not seem to be heavy today; he even swung it. They crossed half the pasture without saying anything and then, putting his hand easily on the small of her back, he asked softly, "Where does your wooden leg join on?"

She turned an ugly red and glared at him and for an instant the boy looked abashed. "I didn't mean you no harm," he said. "I only meant you're so brave and all. I guess God takes care of you."

"No," she said, looking forward and walking fast, "I don't even believe in God."

At this he stopped and whistled. "No!" he exclaimed as if he were too astonished to say anything else.

She walked on and in a second he was bouncing at her side, fanning with his hat. "That's very unusual for a girl," he remarked, watching her out of the corner of his eye. When they reached the edge of the wood, he put his hand on her back again and drew her against him without a word and kissed her heavily.

The kiss, which had more pressure than feeling behind it, produced that extra surge of adrenalin in the girl that enables one to carry a packed trunk out of a burning house, but in her, the power went at once to the brain. Even before he released her, her mind, clear and detached and ironic anyway, was regarding him from a great distance, with amusement but with pity. She had never been kissed before and she was pleased to discover that it was an unexceptional experience and all a matter of the mind's control. Some people might enjoy drain water if they were told it was vodka. When the boy, looking expectant but uncertain, pushed her gently away, she turned and walked on, saying nothing as if such business, for her, were common enough.

He came along panting at her side, trying to help her when he saw a root that she might trip over. He caught and held back the long swaying blades of thorn vine until she had passed beyond them. She led the way and he came breathing heavily behind her. Then they came out on a sunlit hillside, sloping softly into another one a little smaller. Beyond, they could see the rusted top of the old barn where the extra hay was stored.

The hill was sprinkled with small pink weeds. "Then you ain't saved?" he asked suddenly, stopping.

The girl smiled. It was the first time she had smiled at him at all. "In my economy," she said, "I'm saved and you are damned but I told you I didn't believe in God."

Nothing seemed to destroy the boy's look of admiration. He gazed at her now as if the fantastic animal at the zoo had put its paw through the bars and given him a loving poke. She thought he looked as if he wanted to kiss her again and she walked on before he had the chance.

"Ain't there somewheres we can sit down sometime?" he murmured, his voice softening toward the end of the sentence.

"In that barn," she said.

They made for it rapidly as if it might slide away like a train. It was a large two-story barn, cool and dark inside. The boy pointed up the ladder that led into the loft and said, "It's too bad we can't go up there."

"Why can't we?" she asked.

"Yer leg," he said reverently.

The girl gave him a contemptuous look and putting both hands on the ladder, she climbed it while he stood below, apparently awestruck. She pulled herself expertly through the opening and then looked down at him and said, "Well, come on if you're coming," and he began to climb the ladder, awkwardly bringing the suitcase with him.

"We won't need the Bible," she observed.

"You never can tell," he said, panting. After he had got into the loft, he was a few seconds catching his breath. She had sat down in a pile of straw. A wide sheath of sunlight, filled with dust particles, slanted over her. She lay back against a bale, her face turned away, looking out the front opening of the barn where hay was thrown from a wagon into the loft. The two pink-speckled hillsides lay back against a dark ridge of woods. The sky was cloudless and cold blue. The boy dropped down by her side and put one arm under her and the other over her and began methodically kissing her face, making little noises like a fish. He did not remove his hat but it was pushed far enough back not to interfere. When her glasses got in his way, he took them off of her and slipped them into his pocket.

The girl at first did not return any of the kisses but presently she began to and after she had put several on his cheek, she reached his lips and remained there, kissing him again and again as if she were trying to draw all the breath out of him. His breath was clear and sweet like a child's and the kisses were sticky like a child's. He mumbled about loving her and about knowing when he first seen her that he loved her, but the mumbling was like the sleepy fretting of a child being put to sleep by his mother. Her mind, throughout this, never stopped or lost itself for a second to her feelings. "You ain't said you loved me none," he whispered finally, pulling back from her. "You got to say that."

She looked away from him off into the hollow sky and then down at a black ridge and then down farther into what appeared to be two green swelling lakes. She didn't realize he had taken her glasses but this landscape could not seem exceptional to her for she seldom paid any close attention to her surroundings.

"You got to say it," he repeated. "You got to say you love me."

She was always careful how she committed herself. "In a sense," she began, "if you use the word loosely, you might say that. But it's not a word I use. I don't have illusions. I'm one of those people who see *through* to nothing."

The boy was frowning. "You got to say it. I said it and you got to say it," he said.

The girl looked at him almost tenderly. "You poor baby," she murmured. "It's just as well you don't understand," and she pulled him by the neck, face-down, against her. "We are all damned," she said, "but some of us have taken off our blindfolds and see that there's nothing to see. It's a kind of salvation."

The boy's astonished eyes looked blankly through the ends of her hair. "Okay," he almost whined, "but do you love me or don'tcher?"

"Yes," she said and added, "in a sense. But I must tell you something. There mustn't be anything dishonest between us." She lifted his head and looked him in the eye. "I am thirty years old," she said. "I have a number of degrees."

The boy's look was irritated but dogged. "I don't care," he said. "I don't care a thing about what all you done. I just want to know if you love me or don'tcher?" and he caught her to him and wildly planted her face with kisses until she said, "Yes, yes."

"Okay then," he said, letting her go. "Prove it."

She smiled, looking dreamily out on the shifty landscape. She had seduced him without even making up her mind to try. "How?" she asked, feeling that he should be delayed a little.

He leaned over and put his lips to her ear. "Show me where your wooden leg joins on," he whispered.

The girl uttered a sharp little cry and her face instantly drained of color. The obscenity of the suggestion was not what shocked her. As a child she had sometimes been subject to feelings of shame but education had removed the last traces of that as a good surgeon scrapes for cancer; she would no more have felt it over what he was asking than she would have believed in his Bible. But she was as sensitive about the artificial leg as a peacock about his tail. No one ever touched it but her. She took care of it as someone else would his soul, in private and almost with her own eyes turned away. "No," she said.

"I known it," he muttered, sitting up. "You're just playing me for a sucker."

"Oh no no!" she cried. "It joins on at the knee. Only at the knee. Why do you want to see it?"

The boy gave her a long penetrating look. "Because," he said, "it's what makes you different. You ain't like anybody else."

She sat staring at him. There was nothing about her face or her round freezing-blue eyes to indicate that this had moved her; but she felt as if her heart had stopped and left her mind to pump her blood. She decided that for the first time in her life she was face to face with real innocence. This boy, with an instinct that came from beyond wisdom, had touched the truth about her. When after a minute, she said in a hoarse high voice, "All right," it was like surrendering to him completely. It was like losing her own life and finding it again, miraculously, in his.

Very gently he began to roll the slack leg up. The artificial limb, in a white sock and brown flat shoe, was bound in a heavy material like canvas and ended in an ugly jointure where it was attached to the stump. The boy's face and his voice were entirely reverent as he uncovered it and said, "Now show me how to take it off and on."

She took it off for him and put it back on again and then he took it off himself, handling it as tenderly as if it were a real one. "See!" he said with a delighted child's face. "Now I can do it myself!"

"Put it back on," she said. She was thinking that she would run away with him and that every night he would take the leg off and every morning put it back on again. "Put it back on," she said.

"Not yet," he murmured, setting it on its foot out of her reach. "Leave it off for a while. You got me instead."

She gave a little cry of alarm but he pushed her down and began to kiss her again. Without the leg she felt entirely dependent on him. Her brain seemed to have stopped thinking altogether and to be about some other function that it was not very good at. Different expressions raced back and forth over her face. Every now and then the boy, his eyes like two steel spikes, would glance behind him where the leg stood. Finally she pushed him off and said, "Put it back on me now."

"Wait," he said. He leaned the other way and pulled the valise toward him and opened it. It had a pale blue spotted lining and there were only two Bibles in it. He took one of these out and opened the cover of it. It was hollow and contained a pocket flask of whiskey, a pack of cards, and a small blue box with printing on it. He laid these out in front of her one at a time in an evenly-spaced row, like one presenting offerings at the shrine of a goddess. He put the blue box in her hand. THIS PRODUCT TO BE USED ONLY FOR THE PREVENTION OF DISEASE, she read, and dropped it. The boy was unscrewing the top of the flask. He stopped and pointed, with a smile, to the deck of cards. It was not an ordinary deck but one with an obscene picture on the back of each card. "Take a swig," he said, offering her the bottle first. He held it in front of her, but like one mesmerized, she did not move.

Her voice when she spoke had an almost pleading sound. "Aren't you," she murmured, "aren't you just good country people?"

The boy cocked his head. He looked as if he were just beginning to understand that she might be trying to insult him. "Yeah," he said, curling his lip slightly, "but it ain't held me back none. I'm as good as you any day in the week."

"Give me my leg," she said.

He pushed it farther away with his foot. "Come on now, let's begin to have us a good time," he said coaxingly. "We ain't got to know one another good yet."

"Give me my leg!" she screamed and tried to lunge for it but he pushed her down easily.

"What's the matter with you all of a sudden?" he asked, frowning as he screwed the top on the flask and put it quickly back inside the Bible. "You just a while ago said you didn't believe in nothing. I thought you was some girl!"

Her face was almost purple. "You're a Christian!" she hissed. "You're a fine Christian! You're just like them all—say one thing and do another. You're a perfect Christian, you're . . ."

The boy's mouth was set angrily. "I hope you don't think," he said in a lofty indignant tone, "that I believe in that crap! I may sell Bibles but I know which end is up and I wasn't born yesterday and I know where I'm going!"

"Give me my leg!" she screeched. He jumped up so quickly that she barely saw him sweep the cards and the blue box back into the Bible and throw the Bible into the valise. She saw him grab the leg and then she saw it for an instant slanted forlornly across the inside of the suitcase with a Bible at either side of its opposite ends. He slammed the lid shut and snatched up the valise and swung it down the hole and then stepped through himself.

When all of him had passed but his head, he turned and regarded her with a look that no longer had any admiration in it. "I've gotten a lot of interesting things," he said. "One time I got a woman's glass eye this way. And you needn't to think you'll catch me because Pointer ain't really my name. I use a different name at every house I call at and don't stay nowhere long. And I'll tell you another thing, Hulga," he said, using the name as if he didn't think much of it, "you ain't so smart. I been believing in nothing ever since I was born!" and then the toast-colored hat disappeared down the hole and the girl was left, sitting on the straw in the dusty sunlight. When she turned her churning face toward the opening, she saw his blue figure struggling successfully over the green speckled lake.

Mrs. Hopewell and Mrs. Freeman, who were in the back pasture, digging up onions, saw him emerge a little later from the woods and head across the meadow toward the highway. "Why, that looks like that nice dull young man that tried to sell me a Bible yesterday," Mrs. Hopewell said, squinting. "He must have been selling them to the Negroes back in there. He was so simple," she said, "but I guess the world would be better off if we were all that simple."

Mrs. Freeman's gaze drove forward and just touched him before he disappeared under the hill. Then she returned her attention to the evil-smelling onion shoot she was lifting from the ground. "Some can't be that simple," she said. "I know I never could."

CHINUA ACHEBE (b. 1930) was born in a small village in eastern Nigeria. He had a Christian upbringing and attended a mission school, where he learned sufficient

English to attend first Government College at Umuahia in West Africa and later University College, Ibadan, where he studied English literature. He worked for many years as a producer for the Nigerian Broadcasting Company.

Achebe's best-known work may be his novel *Things Fall Apart* (1958). Other novels include *No Longer at Ease* (1960), *Arrow of God* (1964), *A Man of the People* (1966), and *Anthills of the Savannah* (1987). His short story collection, *The Sacrificial Egg and Other Short Stories*, was published in 1962, and in 1971 he published a collection of poems, *Beware, Soul Brother, and Other Poems*.

Like other **postcolonial** writers such as Jamaica Kincaid and Bharati Mukherjee, Achebe's fiction addresses the conflict between traditional and modern cultural values. Achebe grew up in colonial Africa and lived to see the shift to independence; his fiction seeks to portray the merits of precolonial Nigeria and to overturn the characterization of the local customs as inferior or of little value when compared to the occupier's culture. He also attempts to invalidate the literary depictions of Africans made by Western authors such as Joseph Conrad and Joyce Cary.

The **folktale** of "Why the Tortoise's Shell Is Not Smooth," which is told by an African mother to her daughter, functions both as a **myth** explaining why tortoises have bumpy shells and as a **fable** with a straightforward moral.

Related Works: Cofer, "Tales Told under the Mango Tree"; Marquez, "Handsomest Drowned Man in the World"; Silko, "Prayer to the Pacific"; Alexie, "Reservation Love Song"; Wilson, *The Piano Lesson*.

Why the Tortoise's Shell Is Not Smooth

Ekwefi and her daughter, Ezinma, sat on a mat on the floor. It was Ekwefi's turn to tell a story.

'Once upon a time,' she began, 'all the birds were invited to a feast in the sky. They were very happy and began to prepare themselves for the great day. They painted their bodies with red cam wood and drew beautiful patterns on them with *uli*.

'Tortoise saw all these preparations and soon discovered what it all meant. Nothing that happened in the world of the animals ever escaped his notice; he was full of cunning. As soon as he heard of the great feast in the sky his throat began to itch at the very thought. There was a famine in those days and Tortoise had not eaten a good meal for two moons. His body rattled like a piece of dry stick in his empty shell. So he began to plan how he would go to the sky.'

'But he had no wings,' said Ezinma.

'Be patient,' replied her mother. 'That is the story. Tortoise had no wings, but he went to the birds and asked to be allowed to go with them.

'"We know you too well," said the birds when they had heard him. "You are full of cunning and you are ungrateful. If we allow you to come with us you will soon begin your mischief."

'"You do not know me," said Tortoise. "I am a changed man. I have learned that a man who makes trouble for others is also making it for himself."

'Tortoise had a sweet tongue, and within a short time all the birds agreed that he was a changed man, and they each gave him a feather, with which he made two wings.

'At last the great day came and Tortoise was the first to arrive at the meeting place. When all the birds had gathered together, they set off in a body. Tortoise was very happy and voluble as he flew among the birds, and he was soon chosen as the man to speak for the party because he was a great orator.

'"There is one important thing which we must not forget," he said as they flew on their way. "When people are invited to a great feast like this, they take new names for the occasion. Our hosts in the sky will expect us to honor this age-old custom."

'None of the birds had heard of this custom but they knew that Tortoise, in spite of his failings in other directions, was a widely-traveled man who knew the customs of different peoples. And so they each took a new name. When they had all taken, Tortoise also took one. He was to be called *All of you*.

'At last the party arrived in the sky and their hosts were very happy to see them. Tortoise stood up in his many-colored plumage and thanked them for their invitation. His speech was so eloquent that all the birds were glad they had brought him, and nodded their heads in approval of all he said. Their hosts took him as the king of the birds, especially as he looked somewhat different from the others.

'After kola nuts had been presented and eaten, the people of the sky set before their guests the most delectable dishes Tortoise had ever seen or dreamed of. The soup was brought out hot from the fire and in the very pot in which it had been cooked. It was full of meat and fish. Tortoise began to sniff aloud. There was pounded yam and also yam pottage cooked with palm-oil and fresh fish. There were also pots of palm-wine. When everything had been set before the guests, one of the people of the sky came forward and tasted a little from each pot. He then invited the birds to eat. But Tortoise jumped to his feet and asked: "For whom have you prepared this feast?"

'"For all of you," replied the man.

'Tortoise turned to the birds and said: "You remember that my name is *All of you*. The custom here is to serve the spokesman first and the others later. They will serve you when I have eaten."

'He began to eat and the birds grumbled angrily. The people of the sky thought it must be their custom to leave all the food for their king. And so Tortoise ate the best part of the food and then drank two pots of palm-wine, so that he was full of food and drink and his body filled out in his shell.

'The birds gathered round to eat what was left and to peck at the bones he had thrown all about the floor. Some of them were too angry to eat. They chose to fly home on an empty stomach. But before they left each took back the feather he had lent to Tortoise. And there he stood in his hard shell full of food and wine but without any wings to fly home. He asked the birds to take a message for his wife, but they all refused. In the end Parrot, who had felt more angry than the others, suddenly changed his mind and agreed to take the message.

'"Tell my wife," said Tortoise, "to bring out all the soft things in my house and cover the compound with them so that I can jump down from the sky without very great danger."

'Parrot promised to deliver the message, and then flew away. But when he reached Tortoise's house he told his wife to bring out all the hard things in the house. And so she brought out her husband's hoes, machetes, spears, guns and even his cannon. Tortoise looked down from the sky and saw his wife bringing things out, but it was too far to see what they were. When all seemed ready he let himself go. He fell and fell and fell until he began to fear that he would never stop falling. And then like the sound of his cannon he crashed on the compound.'

'Did he die?' asked Ezinma.

'No,' replied Ekwefi. 'His shell broke into pieces. But there was a great medicine man in the neighborhood. Tortoise's wife sent for him and he gathered all the bits of shell and stuck them together. That is why Tortoise's shell is not smooth.'

JOHN UPDIKE (b. 1932) was the only child of a father who taught and a mother who wrote. After graduating from high school in Pennsylvania with straight As, Updike went to Harvard on scholarship, where he edited the *Harvard Lampoon* and graduated with honors in English. Seemingly destined to be a success, he sold his first short story to *The New Yorker* and became a roving reporter for the magazine.

An amazingly prolific writer, Updike has published at least one book a year since publishing a volume of poetry entitled *The Carpentered Hen and Other Tame Creatures* in 1958. His first collection of short stories, *The Same Door*, was published in 1959, and his other story collections include *Pigeon Feathers* (1962). *Museums and Women* (1972), and *Philadelphia and Other Stories* (1995). He earned a National Book Award for *The Centaur* (1963) and Pulitzer Prizes for *Rabbit Is Rich* (1981) and *Rabbit at Rest* (1990), the final books in the series about Harry "Rabbit" Angstrom, which includes *Rabbit, Run* (1960) and *Rabbit Redux* (1971). At 32, Updike was the youngest person ever elected to the National Institute of Arts and Letters.

Updike writes **realistic** stories about the everyday existence of middle-class Americans. His accurate portrayals of the restricted lives of his characters and his talent for finding significance in the seemingly mundane are hallmarks of his writing. As his characters go about their daily routines, they confront their discontents and try to surmount the pettiness of their existence.

In "A&P" (1963), the daily "cat-and-dog-food-breakfast-cereal-macaroni-rice-raisins-seasonings-spreads-spaghetti-soft-drinks-crackers-and-cookies aisle" routine of a checkout clerk at a local market is disrupted by the entrance of "three girls in nothing but bathing suits."

Related Works: Joyce, "Araby"; Ellison, "Battle Royal"; Housman, "To an Athlete Dying Young"; Eliot, "The Love Song of J. Alfred Prufrock."

A & P

In walks these three girls in nothing but bathing suits. I'm in the third checkout slot, with my back to the door, so I don't see them until they're over by the bread. The one that caught my eye first was the one in the plaid green two-piece. She was a chunky kid, with a good tan and a sweet broad soft-looking can with those two crescents of white just under it, where the sun never seems to hit, at the top of the backs of her legs. I stood there with my hand on a box of HiHo crackers trying to remember if I rang it up or not. I ring it up again and the customer starts giving me hell. She's one of these cash-register-watchers, a witch about fifty with rouge on her cheekbones and no eyebrows, and I know it made her day to trip me up. She'd been watching cash registers for fifty years and probably never seen a mistake before.

By the time I got her feathers smoothed and her goodies into a bag—she gives me a little snort in passing, if she'd been born at the right time they would have burned her over in Salem—by the time I get her on her way the girls had circled around the bread and were coming back, without a pushcart, back my way along the counters, in the aisle between the checkouts and the Special bins. They didn't even have shoes on. There was this chunky one, with the two-piece—it was bright green and the seams on the bra were still sharp and her belly was still pretty pale so I guessed she just got it (the suit)—there was this one, with one of those chubby berry-faces, the lips all bunched together under her nose, this one, and a tall one, with black hair that hadn't quite frizzed right, and one of these sunburns right across under the eyes, and a chin that was too long—you know, the kind of girl other girls think is very "striking" and "attractive" but never quite makes it, as they very well know, which is why they like her so much—and then the third one, that wasn't quite so tall. She was the queen. She kind of led them, the other two peeking around and making their shoulders round. She didn't look around, not this queen, she just walked straight on slowly, on these long white prima-donna legs. She came down a little hard on her heels, as if she didn't walk in her bare feet that much, putting down her heels and then letting the weight move along to her toes as if she was testing the floor with every step, putting a little deliberate extra action into it. You never know for sure how girls' minds work (do you really think it's a mind in there or just a little buzz like a bee in a glass jar?) but you got the idea she had talked the other two into coming in here with her, and now she was showing them how to do it, walk slow and hold yourself straight.

She had on a kind of dirty-pink—beige maybe, I don't know—bathing suit with a little nubble all over it and, what got me, the straps were down. They were off her shoulders looped loose around the cool tops of her arms, and I guess as a result the suit had slipped a little on her, so all around the top of the cloth there was this shining rim. If it hadn't been there you wouldn't have known there could have been anything whiter than those shoulders. With the straps pushed off, there was nothing between the top of the suit and the top of her head except just *her*, this clean bare plane of the top of her chest down from the shoulder bones like a dented sheet of metal tilted in the light. I mean, it was more than pretty.

She had sort of oaky hair that the sun and salt had bleached, done up in a bun that was unravelling, and a kind of prim face. Walking into the A & P with your straps down, I suppose it's the only kind of face you *can* have. She held her head so high her neck, coming up out of those white shoulders, looked kind of stretched, but I didn't mind. The longer her neck was, the more of her there was.

She must have felt in the corner of her eye me and over my shoulder Stokesie in the second slot watching, but she didn't tip. Not this queen. She kept her eyes moving across the racks, and stopped, and turned so slow it made my stomach rub the inside of my apron, and buzzed to the other two, who kind of huddled against her for relief, and then they all three of them went up the cat-and-dog-food-breakfast-cereal-macaroni-rice-raisins-seasonings-spreads-spaghetti-soft-drinks-crackers-and-cookies aisle. From the third slot I look straight up this aisle to the meat counter, and I watched them all the way. The fat one with the tan sort of fumbled with the cookies, but on second thought she put the package back. The sheep pushing their carts down the aisle—the girls were walking against the usual traffic (not that we have one-way signs or anything)—were pretty hilarious. You could see them, when Queenie's white shoulders dawned on them, kind of jerk, or hop, or hiccup, but their eyes snapped back to their own baskets and on they pushed. I bet you could set off dynamite in an A & P and the people would by and large keep reaching and checking oatmeal off their lists and muttering "Let me see, there was a third thing, began with A, asparagus, no, ah; yes, applesauce!" or whatever it is they do mutter. But there was no doubt, this jiggled them. A few houseslaves in pin curlers even looked around after pushing their carts past to make sure what they had seen was correct.

You know, it's one thing to have a girl in a bathing suit down on the beach, where what with the glare nobody can look at each other much anyway, and another thing in the cool of the A & P, under the fluorescent lights, against all those stacked packages, with her feet paddling along naked over our checkerboard green-and-cream rubber-tile floor.

"Oh Daddy," Stokesie said beside me. "I feel so faint."

"Darling," I said. "Hold me tight." Stokesie's married, with two babies chalked up on his fuselage already, but as far as I can tell that's the only difference. He's twenty-two, and I was nineteen this April.

"Is it done?" he asks, the responsible married man finding his voice. I forgot to say he thinks he's going to be manager some sunny day, maybe in 1990 when it's called the Great Alexandroy and Petrooshki Tea Company or something.

What he meant was, our town is five miles from a beach, with a big summer colony out on the Point, but we're right in the middle of town, and the women generally put on a shirt or shorts or something before they get out of the car into the street. And anyway these are usually women with six children and varicose veins mapping their legs and nobody, including them, could care less. As I say, we're right in the middle of town, and if you stand at our front doors you can see two banks and the Congregational church and the newspaper store and three real-estate offices and about twenty-seven old freeloaders tearing up Central Street because the sewer broke again. It's not as if we're on the Cape; we're north of Boston and there's people in this town haven't seen the ocean for twenty years.

The girls had reached the meat counter and were asking McMahon something. He pointed, they pointed, and they shuffled out of sight behind a pyramid of Diet Delight peaches. All that was left for us to see was old McMahon patting his mouth and looking after them sizing up their joints. Poor kids, I began to feel sorry for them, they couldn't help it.

• • •

Now here comes the sad part of the story, at least my family says it's sad, but I don't think it's so sad myself. The store's pretty empty, it being Thursday afternoon, so there was nothing much to do except lean on the register and wait for the girls to show up again. The whole store was like a pinball machine and I didn't know which tunnel they'd come out of. After a while they come around out of the far aisle, around the light bulbs, records at discount of the Caribbean Six or Tony Martin Sings or some such gunk you wonder they waste the wax on, sixpacks of candy bars, and plastic toys done up in cellophane that fall apart when a kid looks at them anyway. Around they come, Queenie still leading the way, and holding a little gray jar in her hand. Slots Three through Seven are unmanned and I could see her wondering between Stokes and me, but Stokesie with his usual luck draws an old party in baggy gray pants who stumbles up with four giant cans of pineapple juice (what do these bums *do* with all that pineapple juice? I've often asked myself) so the girls come to me. Queenie puts down the jar and I take it into my fingers icy cold, Kingfish Fancy Herring Snacks in Pure Sour Cream: 49¢. Now her hands are empty, not a ring or a bracelet, bare as God made them, and I wonder where the money's coming from. Still with that prim look she lifts a folded dollar bill out of the hollow at the center of her nubbled pink top. The jar went heavy in my hand. Really, I thought that was so cute.

Then everybody's luck begins to run out. Lengel comes in from haggling with a truck full of cabbages on the lot and is about to scuttle into that door marked MANAGER behind which he hides all day when the girls touch his eye. Lengel's pretty dreary, teaches Sunday school and the rest, but he doesn't miss that much. He comes over and says, "Girls, this isn't the beach."

Queenie blushes, though maybe it's just a brush of sunburn I was noticing for the first time, now that she was so close. "My mother asked me to pick up a jar of herring snacks." Her voice kind of startled me, the way voices do when you see the people first, coming out so flat and dumb yet kind of tony, too, the way it ticked over "pick up" and "snacks." All of a sudden I slid right down her voice into her living room. Her father and the other men were standing around in ice-cream coats and bow ties and the women were in sandals picking up herring snacks on toothpicks off a big glass plate and they were all holding drinks the color of water with olives and sprigs of mint in them. When my parents have somebody over they get lemonade and if it's a real racy affair Schlitz in tall glasses with "They'll Do It Every Time" cartoons stencilled on.

"That's all right," Lengel said, "But this isn't the beach." His repeating this struck me as funny, as if it had just occurred to him, and he had been thinking all these years the A & P was a great big dune and he was the head lifeguard. He didn't like my smiling—as I say he doesn't miss much—but he concentrates on giving the girls that sad Sunday-school-superintendent stare.

Queenie's blush is no sunburn now, and the plump one in plaid, that I liked better from the back—a really sweet can—pipes up. "We weren't doing any shopping. We just came in for the one thing."

"That makes no difference," Lengel tells her, and I could see from the way his eyes went that he hadn't noticed she was wearing a two-piece before. "We want you decently dressed when you come in here."

"We *are* decent," Queenie says suddenly, her lower lip pushing, getting sore now that she remembers her place, a place from which the crowd that runs the A & P must look pretty crummy. Fancy Herring Snacks flashed in her very blue eyes.

"Girls, I don't want to argue with you. After this come in here with your shoulders covered. It's our policy." He turns his back. That's policy for you. Policy is what the kingpins want. What the others want is juvenile delinquency.

All this while, the customers had been showing up with their carts but, you know, sheep, seeing a scene, they had all bunched up on Stokesie, who shook open a paper bag as gently as peeling a peach, not wanting to miss a word. I could feel in the silence everybody getting nervous, most of all Lengel, who asks me, "Sammy, have you rung up their purchase?"

I thought and said "No" but it wasn't about that I was thinking. I go through the punches, 4, 9, GROC, TOT—it's more complicated than you think, and after you do it often enough, it begins to make a little song, that you hear words to, in my case "Hello (*bing*) there, you (*gung*) hap-py *pee*-pul (*splat*)!"—the *splat* being the drawer flying out. I uncrease the bill, tenderly as you may imagine, it just having come from between the two smoothest scoops of vanilla I had ever known were there, and pass a half and a penny into her narrow pink palm, and nestle the herrings in a bag and twist its neck and hand it over, all the time thinking.

The girls, and who'd blame them, are in a hurry to get out, so I say "I quit" to Lengel quick enough for them to hear, hoping they'll stop and watch me, their unsuspected hero. They keep right on going, into the electric eye; the door flies open and they flicker across the lot to their car, Queenie and Plaid and Big Tall Goony-Goony (not that as raw material she was so bad), leaving me with Lengel and a kink in his eyebrow.

"Did you say something, Sammy?"

"I said I quit."

"I thought you did."

"You didn't have to embarrass them."

"It was they who were embarrassing us."

I started to say something that came out "Fiddle-de-doo." It's a saying of my grandmother's, and I know she would have been pleased.

"I don't think you know what you're saying," Lengel said.

"I know you don't," I said. "But I do." I pull the bow at the back of my apron and start shrugging it off my shoulders. A couple customers that had been heading for my slot begin to knock against each other, like scared pigs in a chute.

Lengel sighs and begins to look very patient and old and gray. He's been a friend of my parents for years. "Sammy, you don't want to do this to your Mom and Dad," he tells me. It's true, I don't. But it seems to me that once you begin a gesture it's fatal not to go through with it. I fold the apron, "Sammy" stitched in red on the pocket, and put it on the counter, and drop the bow tie on top of it. The bow tie is theirs, if you've ever wondered. "You'll feel this for the rest of your life," Lengel says, and I know that's true, too, but remembering how he made that pretty girl blush makes me so scrunchy inside I punch the No Sale tab and the machine whirs "pee-pul" and the drawer splats out. One advantage to this scene taking place in summer, I can follow this up with a clean exit, there's no fumbling around getting your coat and galoshes, I just saunter into the electric eye in my white shirt that my mother ironed the night before, and the door heaves itself open, and outside the sunshine is skating around on the asphalt.

I look around for my girls, but they're gone, of course. There wasn't anybody but some young married screaming with her children about some candy they didn't get by the door of a powder-blue Falcon station wagon. Looking back in the big windows, over the bags of peat moss and aluminum lawn furniture stacked on the pavement, I could see Lengel in my place in the slot, checking the sheep through. His face was dark gray and his back stiff, as if he'd just had an injection of iron, and my stomach kind of fell as I felt how hard the world was going to be to me hereafter.

Gabriel García Márquez (b. 1928) is a Columbian who was raised by his maternal grandmother and grandfather, a colonel, in his early years. He attended a high school near Bogotá on scholarship and enrolled in law school at the Universidad Nacional, but had to transfer to the Universidad de Cartegena due to the closure of his first university following political unrest. He never graduated from law school, but worked for some time as a journalist before relocating to New York City in 1961.

Márquez's works center primarily on Latin American history and politics, and he blends facts and fiction together into elaborate nonlinear narratives. He is sometimes compared to William Faulkner (whom he credits as his "master") because he revisits characters and settings in his novels and short stories. His short story collection *No One Writes to the Colonel and Other Stories* was published in 1961 and translated into English in 1968. In 1970, his novel *One Hundred Years of Solitude* (1968) was translated, followed by *The Autumn of the Patriarch* (1975) in 1976, *Chronicle of a Death Foretold* (1981) in 1982, and *Love in the Time of Cholera* (1985) in 1988. In 1982 Márquez was awarded the Nobel Prize for Literature. His work has become so popular that, in order to thwart bootleggers, he changed the last chapter of his most recent novel, *Memories of My Melancholy Whore* (2004) right before shipping it to distributors in Latin America.

Along with his story "A Very Old Man with Enormous Wings" (trans. 1978), "The Handsomest Drowned Man in the World" (trans. 1978) was designated as a "tale for children." In this story of **magic realism**, an extraordinary person enters a rural village briefly and leaves it transformed.

Like many of Márquez's other stories, the moral of the tale is unclear, but the fantastic event clearly has the potential for good.

Related Works: Kafka, "The Metamorphosis"; Cofer, "Tales Told Under the Mango Tree."

The Handsomest Drowned Man in the World

A Tale for Children

The first children who saw the dark and slinky bulge approaching through the sea let themselves think it was an enemy ship. Then they saw it had no flags or masts and they thought it was a whale. But when it was washed up on the beach, they removed the clumps of seaweed, the jellyfish tentacles, and the remains of fish and flotsam, and only then did they see that it was a drowned man.

They had been playing with him all afternoon, burying him in the sand and digging him up again, when someone chanced to see them and spread the alarm in the village. The men who carried him to the nearest house noticed that he weighed more than any dead man they had ever known, almost as much as a horse, and they said to each other that maybe he'd been floating too long and the water had got into his bones. When they laid him on the floor they said he'd been taller than all other men because there was barely enough room for him in the house, but they thought that maybe the ability to keep on growing after death was part of the nature of certain drowned men. He had the smell of the sea about him and only his shape gave one to suppose that it was the corpse of a human being, because the skin was covered with a crust of mud and scales.

They did not even have to clean off his face to know that the dead man was a stranger. The village was made up of only twenty-odd wooden houses that had stone courtyards with no flowers and which were spread about on the end of a desertlike cape. There was so little land that mothers always went about with the fear that the wind would carry off their children and the few dead that the years had caused among them had to be thrown off the cliffs. But the sea was calm and bountiful and all the men fit into seven boats. So when they found the drowned man they simply had to look at one another to see that they were all there.

That night they did not go out to work at sea. While the men went to find out if anyone was missing in neighboring villages, the women stayed behind to care for the drowned man. They took the mud off with grass swabs, they removed the underwater stones entangled in his hair, and they scraped the crust off with tools used for scaling fish. As they were doing that they noticed that the vegetation on him came from faraway oceans and deep water and that his clothes were in tatters, as if he had sailed through labyrinths of coral. They noticed too that he bore his death with pride, for he did not have the lonely look of other drowned men who came out of the sea or that haggard, needy look of men who drowned in rivers. But only when they finished cleaning him off did they become aware of the kind of man he was and it left them breathless. Not only was he the tallest, strongest, most virile, and best built man they had ever seen, but even though they were looking at him there was no room for him in their imagination.

They could not find a bed in the village large enough to lay him on nor was there a table solid enough to use for his wake. The tallest men's holiday pants would not fit him, not the fattest ones' Sunday shirts, nor the shoes of the one with the biggest feet. Fascinated by his huge size and his beauty, the women then decided to make him some pants from a large piece of sail and a shirt from some bridal brabant linen so that he could continue through his death with dignity. As they sewed, sitting in a circle and gazing at the corpse between stitches, it seemed to them that the wind had never been so steady nor the sea so restless as on that night and they supposed that the change had something to do with the dead man. They thought that if that magnificent man had lived in the village, his house would have had the widest doors, the highest ceiling, and the strongest floor, his bedstead would have been made from a midship frame held together by iron bolts, and his wife would have been the happiest woman. They thought that he would have had so much authority that he could have drawn fish out of the sea simply by calling their names and that he would have put so much work into his land that springs would have burst forth from among the rocks so that he would have been able to plant flowers on the cliffs. They secretly compared him to their own men, thinking that for all their lives theirs were incapable of doing what he could do in one night, and they ended up dismissing them deep in their hearts as the weakest, meanest, and most useless creatures on earth. They were wandering through that maze of fantasy when the oldest woman, who as the oldest had looked upon the drowned man with more compassion than passion, sighed:

"He has the face of someone called Esteban."

It was true. Most of them had only to take another look at him to see that he could not have any other name. The more stubborn among them, who were the youngest, still lived for a few hours with the illusion that when they put his clothes on and he lay among the flowers in patent leather shoes his name might be Lautaro. But it was a vain illusion. There had not been enough canvas, the poorly cut and worse sewn pants were too tight, and the hidden strength of his heart popped the buttons on his shirt. After midnight the whistling of the wind died down and the sea fell into its Wednesday drowsiness. The silence put an end to any last doubts: he was Esteban. The women who had dressed him, who had combed his hair, had cut his nails and shaved him were unable to hold back a shudder of pity when they had to resign themselves to his being dragged along the ground. It was then that they understood how unhappy he must have been with that huge body since it bothered him even after death. They could see him in life, condemned to going through doors sideways, cracking his head on crossbeams, remaining on his feet during visits, not knowing what to do with his soft, pink, sea lion hands while the lady of the house looked for her most resistant chair and begged him, frightened to death, sit here, Esteban, please, and he, leaning against the wall, smiling, don't bother, ma'am, I'm fine where I am, his heels raw and his back roasted from having done the same thing so many times whenever he paid a visit, don't bother, ma'am, I'm fine where I am, just to avoid the embarrassment of breaking up the chair, and never knowing perhaps that the ones who said don't go, Esteban, at least wait till the coffee's ready, were the ones who later on would whisper the big boob finally left, how nice, the handsome fool has gone. That was what the women were thinking beside the body a little before dawn. Later, when they covered his face with a handkerchief so that the light would not bother him, he looked so forever dead, so defenseless, so much like their men that the first furrows of tears opened in their hearts. It was one of the younger ones who began the weeping. The others, coming to, went from sighs to wails, and the more they sobbed the more they felt like weeping, because the drowned man was becoming all the more Esteban for them, and so they wept so much, for he was the most destitute, most peaceful, and most obliging man on earth, poor Esteban. So when the men returned with the news that the drowned man was not from the neighboring villages either, the women felt an opening of jubilation in the midst of their tears.

"Praise the Lord," they sighed, "he's ours!"

The men thought the fuss was only womanish frivolity. Fatigued because of the difficult nighttime inquiries, all they wanted was to get rid of the bother of the newcomer once and for all before the sun grew strong on that arid, windless day. They improvised a litter with the remains of foremasts and gaffs, tying it together with rigging so that it would bear the weight of the body until they reached the cliffs. They wanted to tie the anchor from a cargo ship to him so that he would sink easily into the deepest waves, where fish are blind and divers die of nostalgia, and bad currents would not bring him back to shore, as had happened with other bodies. But the more they hurried, the more the women thought of ways to waste time. They walked about like startled hens, pecking with the sea charms on their breasts, some interfering on one side to put a scapular of the good wind on the drowned man, some on the other side to put a wrist compass on him, and after a great deal of *get away from there, woman, stay out of the way, look, you almost made me fall on top of the dead man,* the men began to feel mistrust in their livers and started grumbling about why so many main-altar decorations for a stranger, because no matter how many nails and holy-water jars he had on him, the sharks would chew him all the same, but the women kept piling on their junk relics, running back and forth, stumbling, while they released in sighs what they did not in tears, so that the men finally exploded with *since when has there ever been such a fuss over a drifting corpse, a drowned nobody, a piece of cold Wednesday meat.* One of the women, mortified by so much lack of care, then removed the handkerchief from the dead man's face and the men were left breathless too.

He was Esteban. It was not necessary to repeat it for them to recognize him. If they had been told Sir Walter Raleigh, even they might have been impressed with his gringo accent, the macaw on his shoulder, his cannibal-killing blunderbuss, but there could be only one Esteban in the world and there he was, stretched out like a sperm whale, shoeless, wearing the pants of an undersized child, and with those stony nails that had to be cut with a knife. They only had to take the handkerchief off his face to see that he was ashamed, that it was not his fault that he was so big or so heavy or so handsome, and if he had known that this was going to happen, he would have looked for a more discreet place to drown in, seriously, I even would have tied the anchor off a galleon around my neck and staggered off a cliff like someone who doesn't like things in order not to be upsetting people now with this Wednesday dead body, as you people say, in order not to be bothering anyone with this filthy piece of cold meat that doesn't have anything to do with me. There was so much truth in his manner that even the most mistrustful men, the ones who felt the bitterness of endless nights at sea fearing that their women would tire of dreaming about them and begin to dream of drowned men, even they and others who were harder still shuddered in the marrow of their bones at Esteban's sincerity.

That was how they came to hold the most splendid funeral they could conceive of for an abandoned drowned man. Some women who had gone to get flowers in the neighboring villages returned with other women who could not believe what they had been told, and those women went back for more flowers when they saw the dead man, and they brought more and more until there were so many flowers and so many people that it was hard to walk about. At the final moment it pained them to return him to the waters as an orphan and they chose a father and mother from among the best people, and aunts and uncles and cousins, so that through him all the inhabitants of the village became kinsmen. Some sailors who heard the weeping from a distance went off course and people heard of one who had himself tied to the mainmast, remembering ancient fables about sirens. While they fought for the privilege of carrying him on their shoulders along the steep escarpment by the cliffs, men and women became aware for the first time of the desolation of their streets, the dryness of their courtyards, the narrowness of their dreams as they faced the splendor and beauty of their drowned man. They let him go without an anchor so that he could come back if he wished and whenever he wished, and they all held their breath for the fraction of centuries the body took to fall into the abyss. They did not need to look at one another to realize that they were no longer all present, that they would never be. But they also knew that everything would be different from then on, that their houses would have wider doors, higher ceilings, and stronger floors so that Esteban's memory could go everywhere without bumping into beams and so that no one in the future would dare whisper the big boob finally died, too bad, the handsome fool has finally died, because they were going to paint their house fronts gay colors to make Esteban's memory eternal and they were going to break their backs digging for springs among the stones and planting flowers on the cliffs so that in future years at dawn the passengers on great liners would awaken, suffocated by the smell of gardens on the high seas, and the captain would have to come down from the bridge in his dress uniform, with his astrolabe, his pole star, and his row of war medals and, pointing to the promontory of roses on the horizon, he would say in fourteen languages, look there, where the wind is so peaceful now that it's gone to sleep beneath the beds, over there, where the sun's so bright that the sunflowers don't know which way to turn, yes, over there, that's Esteban's village.

(1968)

TONI CADE BAMBARA (1939–1995) was born Miltona Mirkin Cade in Harlem. Bambara's early life was marked by trips to the Apollo Theater with her father and afternoons at Speakers Corner with her mother, where she listened to members of her community debate politics and current events. She received her B.A. in theater arts and English literature from Queens College and her M.A. in American literature from the City College of New York. After attaining her degrees, she continued to take classes both at home and abroad, and she spent some time as a social worker. She also established relationships with other important African American women writers, including Toni Morrison, Audre Lorde, and Alice Childress.

In 1972, Bambara published her first collection of short stories, *Gorilla, My Love*. Her other books include *Tales and Stories for Black Folks* (1971) and *The Sea Birds Are Still Alive: Collected Stories* (1977). Bambara also wrote two novels, *The Salt Eaters* (1980) and *If Blessing Comes* (1987). A compilation of her fiction, essays, and interviews was published posthumously as *Deep Sightings and Rescue Missions* in 1996.

Bambara hoped that her writing would empower members of her community. Consequently, her fiction actively resists racist stereotypes even as it uses the **dialect** of urban African Americans to assess the social, political, and economic circumstances of the black community and to reveal the inequities of the prevailing systems. Like Miss Moore in "The Lesson" (1972), Bambara wished to expose members of her community to the grim realities of a world dominated by wealthy whites and to lead others to try to resist entrenched behaviors and to be forces of change.

Related Works: Kincaid, "Girl"; Wideman, "What We Cannot Speak About We Must Pass Over in Silence"; Ellison, "Battle Royal"; Joyce, "Araby"; Dunbar, "We Wear the Mask"; Cullen, "From the Dark Tower"; Langston Hughes, "Theme for English B"; Young, "Nineteen Seventy-Five."

The Lesson

Back in the days when everyone was old and stupid or young and foolish and me and Sugar were the only ones just right, this lady moved on our block with nappy hair and proper speech and no makeup. And quite naturally we laughed at her, laughed the way we did at the junk man who went about his business like he was some big-time president and his sorry-ass horse his secretary. And we kinda hated her too, hated the way we did the winos who cluttered up our parks and pissed on our handball walls and stank up our hallways and stairs so you couldn't halfway play hide-and-seek without a goddamn gas mask. Miss Moore was her name. The only woman on the block with no first name. And she was black as hell, cept for her feet, which were fish-white and spooky. And she was always planning these boring-ass things for us to do, us being my cousin, mostly, who lived on the block cause we all moved North the same time and to the same apartment then spread out gradual to breathe. And our parents would yank our heads into some kinda shape and crisp up our clothes so we'd be presentable for travel with Miss Moore, who always looked like she was going to church, though she never did. Which is just one of things the grownups talked about when they talked behind her back like a dog. But when she came calling with some sachet she'd sewed up or some gingerbread she'd made or some book, why then they'd all be too embarrassed to turn her down and we'd get handed over all spruced up. She'd been to college and said it was only right that she should take responsibility for the young ones' education, and she not even related by marriage or blood. So they'd go for it. Specially Aunt Gretchen. She was the main gofer in the family. You got some ole dumb shit foolishness you want somebody to go for, you send for Aunt Gretchen. She been screwed into the go-along for so long, it's a blood-deep natural thing with her. Which is how she got saddled with me and Sugar and Junior in the first place while our mothers were in a la-de-da apartment up the block having a good ole time.

So this one day Miss Moore rounds us all up at the mailbox and it's puredee hot and she's knockin herself out about arithmetic. And school suppose to let up in summer I heard, but she don't never let up. And the starch in my pinafore scratching the shit outta me and I'm really hating this nappy-head bitch and her goddamn college degree. I'd much rather go to the pool or to the show where it's cool. So me and Sugar leaning on the mailbox being surly, which is a Miss Moore word. And Flyboy checking out what everybody brought for lunch. And Fat Butt already wasting his peanut-butter-and-jelly sandwich like the pig he is. And Junebug punchin on Q.T.'s arm for potato chips. And Rosie Giraffe shifting from one hip to the other waiting for somebody to step on her foot or ask her if she from Georgia so she can kick ass, preferably Mercedes'. And Miss Moore asking us do we know what money is, like we a bunch of retards. I mean real money, she say, like it's only poker chips or monopoly papers we lay on the grocer. So right away I'm tired of this and say so. And would much rather snatch Sugar and go to the Sunset and terrorize the West Indian kids and take their hair ribbons and their money too. And Miss Moore files that remark away for next week's lesson on brotherhood, I can tell. And finally I say we oughta get to the subway cause it's cooler and besides we might meet some cute boys. Sugar done swiped her mama's lipstick, so we ready.

So we heading down the street and she's boring us silly about what things cost and what our parents make and how much goes for rent and how money ain't divided up right in this country. And then she gets to the part about we all poor and live in the slums, which I don't feature. And I'm ready to speak on that, but she steps out in the street and hails two cabs just like that. Then she hustles half the crew in with her and hands me a five-dollar bill and tells me to calculate 10 percent tip for the driver. And we're off. Me and Sugar and Junebug and Flyboy hangin out the window and hollering to everybody, putting lipstick on each other cause Flyboy a faggot anyway, and making farts with our sweaty armpits. But I'm mostly trying to figure how to spend this money. But they all fascinated with the meter ticking and Junebug starts laying bets as to how much it'll read when Flyboy can't hold his breath no more. Then Sugar lays bets as to how much it'll be when we get there. So I'm stuck. Don't nobody want to go for my plan, which is to jump out at the next light and run off to the first bar-b-que we can find. Then the driver tells us to get the hell out cause we there already. And the meter reads eighty-five cents. And I'm stalling to figure out the tip and Sugar say give him a dime. And I decide he don't need it bad as I do, so later for him. But then he tries to take off with Junebug foot still in the door so we talk about his mama something ferocious. Then we check out that we on Fifth Avenue and everybody dressed up in stockings. One lady in a fur coat, hot as it is. White folks crazy.

"This is the place," Miss Moore say, presenting it to us in the voice she uses at the museum, "Let's look in the windows before we go in."

"Can we steal?" Sugar asks very serious like she's getting the ground rules squared away before she plays. "I beg your pardon," say Miss Moore, and we fall out. So she leads us around the windows of the toy store and me and Sugar screamin, "This is mine, that's mine, I gotta have that, that was made for me, I was born for that," till Big Butt drowns us out.

"Hey, I'm goin to buy that there."

"That there? You don't even know what it is, stupid."

"I do so," he say punchin on Rosie Giraffe. "It's a microscope."

"Whatcha gonna do with a microscope, fool?"

"Look at things."

"Like what, Ronald?" ask Miss Moore. And Big Butt ain't got the first notion. So here go Miss Moore gabbing about the thousands of bacteria in a drop of water and the somethinorother in a speck of blood and the million and one living things in the air around us is invisible to the naked eye. And what she say that for? Junebug go to town on that "naked" and we rolling. Then Miss Moore ask what it cost. So we all jam into the window smudgin it up and the price tag say $300. So then she ask how long'd take for Big Butt and Junebug to save up their allowances. "Too long," I say. "Yeh," adds Sugar, "outgrown it by that time." And Miss Moore say no, you never outgrow learning instruments. "Why, even medical students and interns and," blah, blah, blah. And we ready to choke Big Butt for bringing it up in the first damn place.

"This here costs four hundred eighty dollars," say Rosie Giraffe. So we pile up all over her to see what she pointin out. My eyes tell me it's a chunk of glass cracked with something heavy, and different-color inks dripped into the splits, then the whole thing put into a oven or something. But for $480 it don't make sense.

"That's a paperweight made of semi-precious stones fused together under tremendous pressure," she explains slowly, with her hands doing the mining and all the factory work.

"So what's a paperweight?" asks Rosie Giraffe.

"To weigh paper with, dumbbell," say Flyboy, the wise man from the East.

"Not exactly," say Miss Moore, which is what she say when you warm or way off too. "It's to weigh paper down so it won't scatter and make your desk untidy." So right away me and Sugar curtsy to each other and then to Mercedes who is more the tidy type.

"We don't keep paper on top of the desk in my class," say Junebug, figuring Miss Moore crazy or lyin one.

"At home, then," she say. "Don't you have a calendar and a pencil case and a blotter and a letter-opener on your desk at home where you do your homework?" And she know damn well what our homes look like cause she nosys around in them every chance she gets.

"I don't even have a desk," say Junebug. "Do we?"

"No. And I don't get no homework neither," say Big Butt.

"And I don't even have a home," say Flyboy like he do at school to keep the white folks off his back and sorry for him. Send this poor kid to camp posters, is his specialty.

"I do," says Mercedes. "I have a box of stationery on my desk and a picture of my cat. My godmother bought the stationery and the desk. There's a big rose on each sheet and the envelopes smell like roses."

"Who wants to know about your smelly-ass stationery," say Rosie Giraffe fore I can get my two cents in.

"It's important to have a work area all your own so that . . ."

"Will you look at this sailboat, please," say Flyboy, cuttin her off and pointin to the thing like it was his. So once again we tumble all over each other to gaze at this magnificent thing in the toy store which is just big enough to maybe sail two kittens across the pond if you strap them to the posts tight. We all start reciting the price tag like we in assembly. "Handcrafted sailboat of fiberglass at one thousand one hundred ninety-five dollars."

"Unbelievable," I hear myself say and am really stunned. I read it again for myself just in case the group recitation put me in a trance. Same thing. For some reason this pisses me off. We look at Miss Moore and she lookin at us, waiting for I dunno what.

Who'd pay all that when you can buy a sailboat set for a quarter at Pop's, a tube of glue for a dime, and a ball of string for eight cents? "It must have a motor and a whole lot else besides," I say. "My sailboat cost me about fifty cents."

"But will it take water?" say Mercedes with her smart ass.

"Took mine to Alley Pond Park once," say Flyboy. "String broke. Lost it. Pity."

"Sailed mine in Central Park and it keeled over and sank. Had to ask my father for another dollar."

"And you got the strap," laugh Big Butt. "The jerk didn't even have a string on it. My old man wailed on his behind."

Little Q.T. was staring hard at the sailboat and you could see he wanted it bad. But he too little and somebody'd just take it from him. So what the hell. "This boat for kids, Miss Moore?"

"Parents silly to buy something like that just to get all broke up," say Rosie Giraffe.

"That much money it should last forever," I figure.

"My father'd buy it for me if I wanted it."

"Your father, my ass," say Rosie Giraffe getting a chance to finally push Mercedes.

"Must be rich people shop here," say Q.T.

"You are a very bright boy," say Flyboy. "What was your first clue?" And he rap him on the head with the back of his knuckles, since Q.T. the only one he could get away with. Though Q.T. liable to come up behind you years later and get his licks in when you half expect it.

"What I want to know is," I says to Miss Moore though I never talk to her, I wouldn't give the bitch that satisfaction, "is how much a real boat costs? I figure a thousand'd get you a yacht any day."

"Why don't you check that out," she says, "and report back to the group?" Which really pains my ass. If you gonna mess up a perfectly good swim day least you could do is have some answers. "Let's go in," she say like she got something up her sleeve. Only she don't lead the way. So me and Sugar turn the corner to where the entrance is, but when we get there I kinda hang back. Not that I'm scared, what's there to be afraid of, just a toy store. But I feel funny, shame. But what I got to be shamed about? Got as much right to go in as anybody. But somehow I can't seem to get hold of the door, so I step away for Sugar to lead. But she hangs back too. And I look at her and she looks at me and this is ridiculous. I mean, damn, I have never ever been shy about doing nothing or going nowhere. But then Mercedes steps up and then Rosie Giraffe and Big Butt crowd in behind and shove, and next thing we all stuffed into the doorway with only Mercedes squeezing past us, smoothing out her jumper and walking right down the aisle. Then the rest of us tumble in like a glued-together jigsaw done all wrong. And people lookin at us. And it's like the time me and Sugar crashed into the Catholic church on a dare. But once we got in there and everything so hushed and holy and the candles and the bowin and the handkerchiefs on all the drooping heads, I just couldn't go through with the plan. Which was for me to run up to the altar and do a tap dance while Sugar played the nose flute and messed around in the holy water. And Sugar kept givin me the elbow. Then later teased me so bad I tied her up in the shower and turned it on and locked her in. And she'd be there till this day if Aunt Gretchen hadn't finally figured I was lyin about the boarder takin a shower.

Same thing in the store. We all walkin on tiptoe and hardly touchin the games and puzzles and things. And I watched Miss Moore who is steady watchin us like she waitin for a sign. Like Mama Drewery watches the sky and sniffs the air and takes note of just how much slant is in the bird formation. Then me and Sugar bump smack into each other, so busy gazing at the toys, 'specially the sailboat. But we don't laugh and go into our fat-lady bump-stomach routine. We just stare at that price tag. Then Sugar run a finger over the whole boat. And I'm jealous and want to hit her. Maybe not her, but I sure want to punch somebody in the mouth.

"Watcha bring us here for, Miss Moore?"

"You sound angry, Sylvia. Are you mad about something?" Givin me one of them grins like she tellin a grown-up joke that never turns out to be funny. And she's lookin very closely at me like maybe she plannin to do my portrait from memory. I'm mad, but I won't give her that satisfaction. So I slouch around the store bein very bored and say, "Let's go."

Me and Sugar at the back of the train watchin the tracks whizzin by large then small then gettin gobbled up in the dark. I'm thinkin about this tricky toy I saw in the store. A clown that somersaults on a bar then does chin-ups just cause you yank lightly at his leg. Cost $35. I could see me askin my mother for a $35 birthday clown. "You wanna who that costs what?" she'd say, cocking her head to the side to get a better view of the hole in my head. Thirty-five dollars could buy new bunk beds for Junior and Gretchen's boy. Thirty-five dollars and the whole household could go visit Granddaddy Nelson in the country. Thirty-five dollars would pay for the rent and the piano bill too. Who are these people that spend that much for performing clowns and $1,000 for toy sailboats? What kinda work they do and how they live and how come we ain't in on it? Where we are is who we are, Miss Moore always pointin out. But it don't necessarily have to be that way, she always adds then waits for somebody to say that poor people have to wake up and demand their share of the pie and don't none of us know what kind of pie she talkin about in the first damn place. But she ain't so smart cause I still got her four dollars from the taxi and she sure ain't gettin it. Messin up my day with this shit. Sugar nudges me in my pocket and winks.

Miss Moore lines us up in front of the mailbox where we started from, seem like years ago, and I got a headache for thinkin so hard. And we lean all over each other so we can hold up under the draggy-ass lecture she always finishes us off with at the end before we thank her for borin us to tears. But she just looks at us like she readin tea leaves. Finally she say, "Well, what did you think of F.A.O. Schwartz?"

Rosie Giraffe mumbles, "White folks crazy."

"I'd like to go there again when I get my birthday money," says Mercedes, and we shove her out the pack so she has to lean on the mailbox by herself.

"I'd like a shower. Tiring day," say Flyboy.

Then Sugar surprises me by sayin, "You know, Miss Moore, I don't think all of us here put together eat in a year what that sailboat costs." And Miss Moore lights up like somebody goosed her. "And?" she say, urging Sugar on. Only I'm standin on her foot so she don't continue.

"Imagine for a minute what kind of society it is in which some people can spend on a toy what it would cost to feed a family of six or seven. What do you think?"

"I think," say Sugar pushing me off her feet like she never done before, cause I whip her ass in a minute, "that this is not much of a democracy if you ask me. Equal chance to pursue happiness means an equal crack at the dough, don't it?" Miss Moore is besides herself and I am disgusted with Sugar's treachery. So I stand on her foot one more time to see if she'll shove me. She shuts up, and Miss Moore looks at me, sorrowfully I'm thinkin. And somethin weird is goin on, I can feel it in my chest.

"Anybody else learn anything today?" lookin dead at me. I walk away and Sugar has to run to catch up and don't even seem to notice when I shrug her arm off my shoulder.

"Well, we got four dollars anyway," she says.

"Uh hunh."

"We could go to Hascombs and get half a chocolate layer and then go to the Sunset and still have plenty money for potato chips and ice-cream sodas."

"Uh hunh."

"Race you to Hascombs," she say.

We start down the block and she gets ahead which is O.K. by me cause I'm goin to the West End and then over to the Drive to think this day through. She can run if she want to and even run faster. But ain't nobody gonna beat me at nuthin.

ALICE WALKER (b. 1944) was born and raised in Eatonton, Georgia. Her childhood was marred by an estranged relationship with her sharecropper father and an accident with a BB gun that left her scarred and blinded in one eye. Although Walker was infuriated by her father's inability to provide adequate support (including access to health care) for his family, she was inspired by her mother's strength and resolve despite the family's poverty. With her mother's guidance and care, Walker graduated from her high school as the valedictorian and earned a scholarship to Spelman College in Atlanta, which she attended for two years. She transferred to Sarah Lawrence College in New York and then moved to Mississippi to work as a teacher and civil rights activist. When she married a Jewish civil rights attorney in 1967, they were the first legally married interracial couple to reside in Jackson, Mississippi.

Walker published her first book of poetry, *Once*, in 1968. Other poetry collections include *Goodnight, Willie Lee, I'll See You in the Morning* (1979) and *Her Blue Body Everything We Know: Earthling Poems 1965–1990* (1991). She has collected her short stories in *In Love and Trouble: Stories of Black Women* (1973) and *You Can't Keep a Good Woman Down* (1981). Walker is perhaps best known for her novel *The Color Purple* (1982), which won an American Book Award and a Pulitzer Prize and was adapted into a major motion picture. Other novels include *Meridian* (1976), *Possessing the Secret of Joy* (1992), and *Now Is the Time to Open Your Heart* (2004).

Often considered a black **feminist** due to her advocacy of civil rights and women's rights. Walker preferred instead a term she coined herself, *womanist*—one who appreciates women's culture, emotions, and character. Like the **symbol** of the quilt that plays so prominently in "Everyday Use" (1973) and appears again in *The Color Purple*, Walker's characters rely on black sisterhood to stitch and transform the scraps of their lives into a dignified and beautiful whole, despite daily hardships and oppressions.

Related Works: Steinbeck, "The Chrysanthemums"; Plath, "Metaphors"; Cofer, "More Room"; Rich, "Diving into the Wreck."

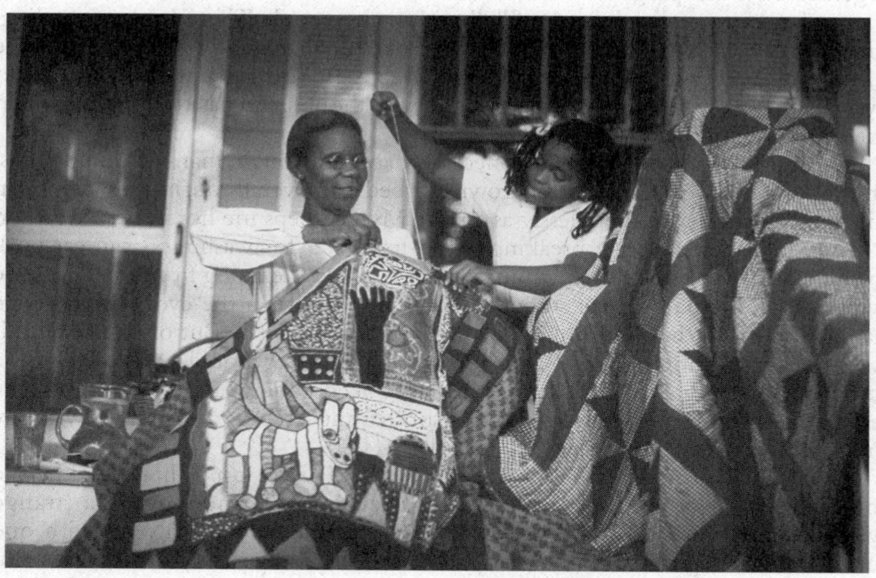

Quilt

Everyday Use

For Your Grandmama

I will wait for her in the yard that Maggie and I made so clean and wavy yesterday afternoon. A yard like this is more comfortable than most people know. It is not just a yard. It is like an extended living room. When the hard clay is swept clean as a floor and the fine sand around the edges lined with tiny, irregular grooves, anyone can come and sit and look up into the elm tree and wait for the breezes that never come inside the house.

Maggie will be nervous until after her sister goes: she will stand hopelessly in corners, homely and ashamed of the burn scars down her arms and legs, eying her sister with a mixture of envy and awe. She thinks her sister has held life always in the palm of one hand, that "no" is a word the world never learned to say to her.

You've no doubt seen those TV shows where the child who has "made it" is confronted, as a surprise, by her own mother and father, tottering in weakly from backstage. (A pleasant surprise, of course: What would they do if parent and child came on the show only to curse out and insult each other?) On TV mother and child embrace and smile into each other's faces. Sometimes the mother and father weep, the child wraps them in her arms and leans across the table to tell how she would not have made it without their help. I have seen these programs.

Sometimes I dream a dream in which Dee and I are suddenly brought together on a TV program of this sort. Out of a dark and soft-seated limousine I am ushered into a bright room filled with many people. There I meet a smiling, gray, sporty man like Johnny Carson who shakes my hand and tells me what a fine girl I have. Then we are on the stage and Dee is embracing me with tears in her eyes. She pins on my dress a large orchid, even though she has told me once that she thinks orchids are tacky flowers.

In real life I am a large, big-boned woman with rough, man-working hands. In the winter I wear flannel nightgowns to bed and overalls during the day. I can kill and clean a hog as mercilessly as a man. My fat keeps me hot in zero weather. I can work outside all day, breaking ice to get water for washing; I can eat pork liver cooked over the open fire minutes after it comes steaming from the hog. One winter I knocked a bull calf straight in the brain between the eyes with a sledge hammer and had the meat hung up to chill before nightfall. But of course all this does not show on television. I am the way my daughter would want me to be: a hundred pounds lighter, my skin like an uncooked barley pancake. My hair glistens in the hot bright lights. Johnny Carson has much to do to keep up with my quick and witty tongue.

But that is a mistake. I know even before I wake up. Who ever knew a Johnson with a quick tongue? Who can even imagine me looking a strange white man in the eye? It seems to me I have talked to them always with one foot raised in flight, with my head turned in whichever way is farthest from them. Dee, though. She would always look anyone in the eye. Hesitation was no part of her nature.

"How do I look, Mama?" Maggie says, showing just enough of her thin body enveloped in pink skirt and red blouse for me to know she's there, almost hidden by the door.

"Come out into the yard," I say.

Have you ever seen a lame animal, perhaps a dog run over by some careless person rich enough to own a car, sidle up to someone who is ignorant enough to be kind to him? That is the way my Maggie walks. She has been like this, chin on chest, eyes on ground, feet in shuffle, ever since the fire that burned the other house to the ground.

Dee is lighter than Maggie, with nicer hair and a fuller figure. She's a woman now, though sometimes I forget. How long ago was it that the other house burned? Ten, twelve years? Sometimes I can still hear the flames and feel Maggie's arms sticking to me, her hair smoking and her dress falling off her in little black papery flakes. Her eyes seemed stretched open, blazed open by the flames reflected in them. And Dee. I see her standing off under the sweet gum tree she used to dig gum out of; a look of concentration on her face as she watched the last dingy gray board of the house fall in toward the red-hot brick chimney. Why don't you do a dance around the ashes? I'd wanted to ask her. She had hated the house that much.

I used to think she hated Maggie, too. But that was before we raised the money, the church and me, to send her to Augusta to school. She used to read to us without pity; forcing words, lies, other folks' habits, whole lives upon us two, sitting trapped and ignorant underneath her voice. She washed us in a river of make-believe, burned us with a lot of knowledge we didn't necessarily need to know. Pressed us to her with the serious way she read, to shove us away at just the moment, like dimwits, we seemed about to understand.

Dee wanted nice things. A yellow organdy dress to wear to her graduation from high school; black pumps to match a green suit she'd made from an old suit somebody gave me. She was determined to stare down any disaster in her efforts. Her eyelids would not flicker for minutes at a time. Often I fought off the temptation to shake her. At sixteen she had a style of her own: and knew what style was.

I never had an education myself. After second grade the school was closed down. Don't ask my why: in 1927 colored asked fewer questions than they do now. Sometimes Maggie reads to me. She stumbles along good-naturedly but can't see well. She knows she is not bright. Like good looks and money, quickness passed her by. She will marry John Thomas (who has mossy teeth in an earnest face) and then I'll be free to sit here and I guess just sing church songs to myself. Although I never was a good singer. Never could carry a tune. I was always better at a man's job. I used to love to milk till I was hooked in the side in '49. Cows are soothing and slow and don't bother you, unless you try to milk them the wrong way.

I have deliberately turned my back on the house. It is three rooms, just like the one that burned, except the roof is tin; they don't make shingle roofs any more. There are no real windows, just some holes cut in the sides, like the portholes in a ship, but not round and not square, with rawhide holding the shutters up on the outside. This house is in a pasture, too, like the other one. No doubt when Dee sees it she will want to tear it down. She wrote me once that no matter where we "choose" to live, she will manage to come see us. But she will never bring her friends. Maggie and I thought about this and Maggie asked me, "Mama, when did Dee ever *have* any friends?"

She had a few. Furtive boys in pink shirts hanging about on washday after school. Nervous girls who never laughed. Impressed with her they worshiped the well-turned phrase, the cute shape, the scalding humor that erupted like bubbles in lye. She read to them.

When she was courting Jimmy T she didn't have much time to pay to us, but turned all her faultfinding power on him. He *flew* to marry a cheap city girl from a family of ignorant flashy people. She hardly had time to recompose herself.

When she comes I will meet—but there they are!

Maggie attempts to make a dash for the house, in her shuffling way, but I stay her with my hand. "Come back here," I say. And she stops and tries to dig a well in the sand with her toe.

It is hard to see them clearly through the strong sun. But even the first glimpse of leg out of the car tells me it is Dee. Her feet were always neat-looking, as if God himself had shaped them with a certain style. From the other side of the car comes a short, stocky man. Hair is all over his head a foot long and hanging from his chin like a kinky mule tail. I hear Maggie suck in her breath. "Uhnnnh," is what it sounds like. Like when you see the wriggling end of a snake just in front of your foot on the road. "Uhnnnh."

Dee next. A dress down to the ground, in this hot weather. A dress so loud it hurts my eyes. There are yellows and oranges enough to throw back the light of the sun. I feel my whole face warming from the heat waves it throws out. Earrings gold, too, and hanging down to her shoulders. Bracelets dangling and making noises when she moves her arm up to shake the folds of the dress out of her armpits. The dress is loose and flows, and as she walks closer, I like it. I hear Maggie go "Uhnnnh" again. It is her sister's hair. It stands straight up like the wool on a sheep. It is black as night and around the edges are two long pigtails that rope about like small lizards disappearing behind her ears.

"Wa-su-zo-Tean-o!" she says, coming on in that gliding way the dress makes her move. The short stocky fellow with the hair to his navel is all grinning and he follows up with "Asalamalakim, my mother and sister!" He moves to hug Maggie but she falls back, right up against the back of my chair. I feel her trembling there and when I look up I see the perspiration falling off her chin.

"Don't get up," says Dee. Since I am stout it takes something of a push. You can see me trying to move a second or two before I make it. She turns, showing white heels through her sandals, and goes back to the car. Out she peeks next with a Polaroid. She stoops down quickly and lines up picture after picture of me sitting there in front of the house with Maggie cowering behind me. She never takes a shot without making sure the house is included. When a cow comes nibbling around the edge of the yard she snaps it and me and Maggie *and* the house. Then she puts the Polaroid in the back seat of the car, and comes up and kisses me on the forehead.

Meanwhile Asalamalakim is going through motions with Maggie's hand. Maggie's hand is as limp as a fish, and probably as cold, despite the sweat, and she keeps trying to pull it back. It looks like Asalamalakim wants to shake hands but wants to do it fancy. Or maybe he don't know how people shake hands. Anyhow, he soon gives up on Maggie.

"Well," I say. "Dee."

"No, Mama," she says. "Not 'Dee,' Wangero Leewanika Kemanjo!"

"What happened to 'Dee'?" I wanted to know.

"She's dead," Wangero said. "I couldn't bear it any longer, being named after the people who oppress me."

"You know as well as me you was named after your aunt Dicie," I said. Dicie is my sister. She named Dee. We called her "Big Dee" after Dee was born.

"But who was *she* named after?" asked Wangero.

"I guess after Grandma Dee," I said.

"And who was she named after?" asked Wangero.

"Her mother," I said, and saw Wangero was getting tired. "That's about as far back as I can trace it," I said. Though, in fact, I probably could have carried it back beyond the Civil War through the branches.

"Well," said Asalamalakim, "there you are."

"Uhnnnh," I heard Maggie say.

"There I was not," I said, "before 'Dicie' cropped up in our family, so why should I try to trace it that far back?"

He just stood there grinning, looking down on me like somebody inspecting a Model A car. Every once in a while he and Wangero sent eye signals over my head.

"How do you pronounce this name?" I asked.

"You don't have to call me by it if you don't want to," said Wangero.

"Why shouldn't I?" I asked. "If that's what you want us to call you, we'll call you."

"I know it might sound awkward at first," said Wangero.

"I'll get used to it," I said. "Ream it out again."

Well, soon we got the name out of the way. Asalamalakim had a name twice as long and three times as hard. After I tripped over it two or three times he told me to just call him Hakim-a-barber. I wanted to ask him was he a barber, but I didn't really think he was, so I didn't ask.

"You must belong to those beef-cattle peoples down the road," I said. They said "Asalamalakim" when they met you, too, but they didn't shake hands. Always too busy: feeding the cattle, fixing the fences, putting up salt-lick shelters, throwing down hay. When the white folks poisoned some of the herd the men stayed up all night with rifles in their hands. I walked a mile and a half just to see the sight.

Hakim-a-barber said, "I accept some of their doctrines, but farming and raising cattle is not my style." (They didn't tell me, and I didn't ask, whether Wangero (Dee) had really gone and married him.)

We sat down to eat and right away he said he didn't eat collards and pork was unclean. Wangero, though, went on through the chitlins and corn bread, the greens and everything else. She talked a blue streak over the sweet potatoes. Everything delighted her. Even the fact that we still used the benches her daddy made for the table when we couldn't afford to buy chairs.

"Oh, Mama!" she cried. Then turned to Hakim-a-barber. "I never knew how lovely these benches are. You can feel the rump prints," she said, running her hands underneath her and along the bench. Then she gave a sigh and her hand closed over Grandma Dee's butter dish. "That's it!" she said. "I knew there was something I wanted to ask you if I could have." She jumped up from the table and went over in the corner where the churn stood, the milk in it clabber by now. She looked at the churn and looked at it.

"This churn top is what I need," she said. "Didn't Uncle Buddy whittle it out of a tree you all used to have?"

"Yes," I said.

"Uh huh," she said happily. "And I want the dasher, too."

"Uncle Buddy whittle that, too?" asked the barber.

Dee (Wangero) looked up at me.

"Aunt Dee's first husband whittled the dash," said Maggie so low you almost couldn't hear her. "His name was Henry, but they called him Stash."

"Maggie's brain is like an elephant's," Wangero said, laughing. "I can use the churn top as a centerpiece for the alcove table," she said, sliding a plate over the churn, "and I'll think of something artistic to do with the dasher."

When she finished wrapping the dasher the handle stuck out. I took it for a moment in my hands. You didn't even have to look close to see where hands pushing the dasher up and down to make butter had left a kind of sink in the wood. In fact, there were a lot of small sinks; you could see where thumbs and fingers had sunk into the wood. It was beautiful light yellow wood, from a tree that grew in the yard where Big Dee and Stash had lived.

After dinner Dee (Wangero) went to the trunk at the foot of my bed and started rifling through it. Maggie hung back in the kitchen over the dishpan. Out came Wangero with two quilts. They had been pieced by Grandma Dee and then Big Dee and me had hung them on the quilt frames on the front porch and quilted them. One was in the Lone Star pattern. The other was Walk Around the Mountain. In both of them were scraps of dresses Grandma Dee had worn fifty and more years ago. Bits and pieces of Grandpa Jarrell's Paisley shirts. And one teeny faded blue piece, about the size of a penny matchbox, that was from Great Grandpa Ezra's uniform that he wore in the Civil War.

"Mama," Wangero said sweet as a bird. "Can I have these old quilts?"

I heard something fall in the kitchen, and a minute later the kitchen door slammed.

"Why don't you take one or two of the others?" I asked. "These old things was just done by me and Big Dee from some tops your grandma pieced before she died."

"No," said Wangero. "I don't want those. They are stitched around the borders by machine."

"That'll make them last better," I said.

"That's not the point," said Wangero. "These are all pieces of dresses Grandma used to wear. She did all this stitching by hand. Imagine!" She held the quilts securely in her arms, stroking them.

"Some of the pieces, like those lavender ones, come from old clothes her mother handed down to her," I said, moving up to touch the quilts. Dee (Wangero) moved back just enough so that I couldn't reach the quilts. They already belonged to her.

"Imagine!" she breathed again, clutching them closely to her bosom.

"The truth is," I said, "I promised to give them quilts to Maggie, for when she marries John Thomas."

She gasped like a bee had stung her.

"Maggie can't appreciate these quilts!" she said. "She'd probably be backward enough to put them to everyday use."

"I reckon she would," I said. "God knows I been saving 'em for long enough with nobody using 'em. I hope she will!" I didn't want to bring up how I had offered Dee (Wangero) a quilt when she went away to college. Then she had told me they were old-fashioned, out of style.

"But they're *priceless!*" she was saying now, furiously; for she has a temper. "Maggie would put them on the bed and in five years they'd be in rags. Less than that!"

"She can always make some more," I said. "Maggie knows how to quilt."

Dee (Wangero) looked at me with hatred. "You just will not understand. The point is these quilts, *these* quilts!"

"Well," I said, stumped. "What would *you* do with them?"

"Hang them," she said. As if that was the only thing you *could* do with quilts.

Maggie by now was standing in the door. I could almost hear the sound her feet made as they scraped over each other.

"She can have them, Mama," she said, like somebody used to never winning anything, or having anything reserved for her. "I can 'member Grandma Dee without the quilts."

I looked at her hard. She had filled her bottom lip with checkerberry snuff and it gave her face a kind of dopey, hangdog look. It was Grandma Dee and Big Dee who taught her how to quilt herself. She stood there with her scarred hands hidden in the folds of her skirt. She looked at her sister with something like fear but she wasn't mad at her. This was Maggie's portion. This was the way she knew God to work.

When I looked at her like that something hit me in the top of my head and ran down to the soles of my feet. Just like when I'm in church and the spirit of God touches me and I get happy and shout I did something I never had done before: hugged Maggie to me, then dragged her on into the room, snatched the quilts out of Miss Wangero's hands and dumped them into Maggie's lap. Maggie just sat there on my bed with her mouth open.

"Take one or two of the others," I said to Dee.

But she turned without a word and went out to Hakim-a-barber.

"You just don't understand," she said, as Maggie and I came out to the car.

"What don't I understand?" I wanted to know.

"Your heritage," she said. And then she turned to Maggie, kissed her, and said, "You ought to try to make something of yourself, too, Maggie. It's really a new day for us. But from the way you and Mama still live you'd never know it."

She put on some sunglasses that hid everything above the tip of her nose and her chin.

Maggie smiled; maybe at the sunglasses. But a real smile, not scared. After we watched the car dust settle I asked Maggie to bring me a dip of snuff. And then the two of us sat there just enjoying, until it was time to go in the house and go to bed.

JAMAICA KINCAID (b. 1949), like Chinua Achebe and Bharati Mukherjee, was raised in a colonized nation and received a British education. Born Elaine Potter Richardson in Antigua in the British West Indies, Kincaid grew up intrigued by the **myths** of the British homeland and its culture, but, eventually, as an adult, she began to see the powerful impact of European imperialism and to sense the loss and devaluation of native customs and independence as a result of the colonial legacy.

Sent to the United States to work as a nanny, Kincaid began writing and submitting her works to periodicals such as *Rolling Stone* and *The New Yorker*, where she became a writer for "Talk of the Town" and, in 1979, married her editor's son. She published her first book, *At the Bottom of the River*, a collection of stories, in 1983. Her other two story collections, *Annie John* (1985) and *Lucy* (1990), are made up of interrelated stories. In addition to writing a novel, *A Small Place* (1988), Kincaid has published the nonfiction works *The Autobiography of My Mother* (1996) and *My Brother* (1997).

"Girl" (1978) was Kincaid's first published fiction. This one-sentence story can be considered **postmodern** in its unconventional and incoherent list/argument about the codes of a woman's social role and a woman's limitations in a male-dominated world.

Related Works: Bambara, "The Lesson"; Mukherjee, "A Wife's Story"; Cofer, "Tales Told Under the Mango Tree"; Ellison, "Battle Royal"; Atwood, "Gertrude Talks Back."

Girl

Wash the white clothes on Monday and put them on the stone heap; wash the color clothes on Tuesday and put them on the clothes-line to dry; don't walk barehead in the hot sun; cook pumpkin fritters in very hot sweet oil; soak your little cloths right after you take them off; when buying cotton to make yourself a nice blouse, be sure that it doesn't have gum on it, because that way it won't hold up well after a wash; soak salt fish overnight before you cook it; is it true that you sing benna* in Sunday school?; always eat your food in such a way that it won't turn someone else's stomach; on Sundays try to walk like a lady and not like the slut you are so bent on becoming; don't sing benna in Sunday school; you mustn't speak to wharf-rat boys, not even to give directions; don't eat fruits on the street—flies will follow you; *but I don't sing benna on Sundays at all and never in Sunday school*; this is how to sew on a button; this is how to make a buttonhole for the button you have just sewed on; this is how to hem a dress when you see the hem coming down and so to prevent yourself from looking like the slut I know you are so bent on becoming; this is how you iron your father's khaki shirt so that it doesn't have a crease; this is how you iron your father's khaki pants so that they don't have a crease; this is how you grow okra—far from the house, because okra tree harbors red ants; when you are growing dasheen, make sure it gets plenty of water or else it makes your throat itch when you are eating it; this is how you sweep a corner; this is how you sweep a whole house; this is how you sweep a yard; this is how you smile to someone you don't like too much; this is how you smile to someone you don't like at all; this is how you smile to someone you like completely; this is how you set a table for tea; this is how you set a table for dinner; this is how you set a table for dinner with an important guest; this is how you set a table for lunch; this is how you set a table for breakfast; this is how to behave in the presence of men who don't know you very well, and this

---

**benna:* Kincaid defined this word, for two editors who inquired, as meaning "songs of the sort your parents didn't want you to sing, at first calypso and later rock and roll" (quoted by Sylvan Barnet and Marcia Stubbes, *The Little Brown Reader,* 2nd ed. [Boston: Little, 1980] 74).

way they won't recognize immediately the slut I have warned you against becoming; be sure to wash every day, even if it is with your own spit; don't squat down to play marbles—you are not a boy, you know; don't pick people's flowers—you might catch something; don't throw stones at blackbirds, because it might not be a blackbird at all; this is how to make a bread pudding; this is how to make doukona; this is how to make pepper pot; this is how to make a good medicine for a cold; this is how to make a good medicine to throw away a child before it even becomes a child; this is how to catch a fish; this is how to throw back a fish you don't like, and that way something bad won't fall on you; this is how to bully a man; this is how a man bullies you; this is how to love a man, and if this doesn't work there are other ways, and if they don't work don't feel too bad about giving up; this is how to spit up in the air if you feel like it, and this is how to move quick so that it doesn't fall on you; this is how to make ends meet; always squeeze bread to make sure it's fresh; *but what if the baker won't let me feel the bread?*; you mean to say that after all you are really going to be the kind of woman who the baker won't let near the bread?

MARGARET ATWOOD (b. 1939). "Gertrude Talks Back" (1983) is a **monologue** in which Hamlet's mother besmirches her former husband's image and chides Hamlet to be kinder to his stepfather/uncle Claudius, to loosen up by having "a nice roll in the hay," and to rid himself of the thought that Claudius killed his father. In this imaginative rewriting of Shakespeare's characters, Atwood provides Gertrude a chance to speak her mind in a way that wasn't possible in the original play. For more details on Atwood's life, see the head note preceding her poetry. For ideas about how you can creatively rewrite and respond to existing texts, see the section on "Creative Responses" in Chapter 6 and in Chapter 8.

Related Works: Kincaid, "Girl"; Browning, "My Last Duchess"; Shakespeare, *Hamlet.*

Gertrude Talks Back

I always thought it was a mistake, calling you Hamlet. I mean, what kind of a name is that for a young boy? It was your father's idea. Nothing would do but that you had to be called after him. Selfish. The other kids at school used to tease the life out of you. The nicknames! And those terrible jokes about pork.

I wanted to call you George.

I am *not* wringing my hands. I'm drying my nails.

Darling, please stop fidgeting with my mirror. That'll be the third one you've broken.

Yes, I've seen those pictures, thank you very much.

I *know* your father was handsomer than Claudius. High brow, aquiline nose and so on, looked great in uniform. But handsome isn't everything, especially in a man, and far be it from me to speak ill of the dead, but I think it's about time I pointed out to you that your dad just wasn't a whole lot of fun. Noble, sure,

I grant you. But Claudius, well, he likes a drink now and then. He appreciates a decent meal. He enjoys a laugh, know what I mean? You don't always have to be tiptoeing around because of some holier-than-thou principle or something.

By the way, darling, I wish you wouldn't call your stepdad *the bloat king*. He does have a slight weight problem, and it hurts his feelings.

The rank sweat of a *what*? My bed is certainly not *enseamed*, whatever that might be! A nasty sty, indeed! Not that it's any of your business, but I change those sheets twice a week, which is more than you do, judging from that student slum pigpen in Wittenberg. I'll certainly never visit you *there* again without prior warning! I see that laundry of yours when you bring it home, and not often enough either, by a long shot! Only when you run out of black socks.

And let me tell you, everyone sweats at a time like that, as you'd find out very soon if you ever gave it a try. A real girlfriend would do you a heap of good. Not like that pasty-faced what's-her-name, all trussed up like a prize turkey in those touch-me-not corsets of hers. If you ask me, there's something off about that girl. Borderline. Any little shock could push her right over the edge.

Go get yourself someone more down-to-earth. Have a nice roll in the hay. Then you can talk to me about nasty sties.

No, darling, I am not *mad* at you. But I must say you're an awful prig sometimes. Just like your Dad. *The Flesh*, he'd say. You'd think it was dog dirt. You can excuse that in a young person, they are always so intolerant, but in someone his age it was getting, well, very hard to live with, and that's the understatement of the year.

Some days I think it would have been better for both of us if you hadn't been an only child. But you realize who you have to thank for *that*. You have no idea what I used to put up with. And every time I felt like a little, you know, just to warm up my aging bones, it was like I'd suggested murder.

Oh! You think *what*? You think Claudius murdered your Dad? Well, no wonder you've been so rude to him at the dinner table!

If I'd known *that*, I could have put you straight in no time flat.

It wasn't Claudius, darling.

It was me.

LOUISE ERDRICH (b. 1954) was the first of seven children born to a Chippewa mother and a German American father who worked together at the Bureau of Indian Affairs boarding school in Wahpeton, North Dakota. Her rural childhood was populated by the family's many storytellers, including her maternal grandfather, who had been tribal chairman of the Turtle Mountain Reservation. Erdrich's novels usually take the form of **short story cycles** and reflect the atmosphere of communal storytelling in which she was raised. In addition to short stories and novels, Erdrich has published memoirs, children's books, and several volumes of poetry.

In 1972, Erdrich entered Dartmouth College as a member of the first coeducational class. There she met Michael Dorris, a professor of anthropology, who later became her husband and collaborator. Following graduation, Erdrich supported herself through various odd jobs before completing her M.A. in creative writing at Johns Hopkins. In 1981, she returned to Dartmouth as writer-in-residence, married Dorris, and began writing the stories that would make up her first novel, *Love Medicine* (1984; rev. 1993). This novel focuses on the interconnections between a group of Native American families on a North Dakota reservation over the course of a half-century. Like William Faulkner's works, her later novels return to many of the same characters, exploring life on the reservation as well as among the descendants of German immigrants in the nearby town of Argus. Each successive novel broadens and deepens Erdrich's canvas, filling gaps and offering alternative perspectives on the events and characters that make up her fictional cosmos.

"The Red Convertible," from *Love Medicine*, depicts Lyman Lamartine's attempts to reconnect with and heal his brother Henry, who has suffered severe psychological trauma after serving in Vietnam and being held as a prisoner of war. Erdrich explores the ways in which the violence of the war is internalized by the participants and the particularly destructive effects this can have on marginalized members of society.

Related Works: Lewis, "Limestone Diner"; Wideman, "What We Cannot Speak About We Must Pass Over in Silence"; Rios, "The Vietnam Wall"; Jarrell, "Death of the Ball Turret Gunner."

The Red Convertible

(1974)

Lyman Lamartine

I was the first one to drive a convertible on my reservation. And of course it was red, a red Olds. I owned that car along with my brother Henry Junior. We owned it together until his boots filled with water on a windy night and he bought out my share. Now Henry owns the whole car, and his younger brother Lyman (that's myself), Lyman walks everywhere he goes.

How did I earn enough money to buy my share in the first place? My one talent was I could always make money. I had a touch for it, unusual in a Chippewa. From the first I was different that way, and everyone recognized it. I was the only kid they let in the American Legion Hall to shine shoes, for example, and one Christmas I sold spiritual bouquets for the mission door to door. The nuns let me keep a percentage. Once I started, it seemed the more money I made the easier the money came. Everyone encouraged it. When I was fifteen I got a job washing dishes at the Joliet Café, and that was where my first big break happened.

It wasn't long before I was promoted to bussing tables, and then the short-order cook quit and I was hired to take her place. No sooner than you know it I was managing the Joliet. The rest is history. I went on managing. I soon become part owner, and of course there was no stopping me then. It wasn't long before the whole thing was mine.

After I'd owned the Joliet for one year, it blew over in the worst tornado ever seen around here. The whole operation was smashed to bits. A total loss. The fryalator was up in a tree, the grill torn in half like it was paper. I was only sixteen.

I had it all in my mother's name, and I lost it quick, but before I lost it I had every one of my relatives, and their relatives, to dinner, and I also bought that red Olds I mentioned, along with Henry.

The first time we saw it! I'll tell you when we first saw it. We had gotten a ride up to Winnipeg, and both of us had money. Don't ask me why, because we never mentioned a car or anything, we just had all our money. Mine was cash, a big bankroll from the Joliet's insurance. Henry had two checks—a week's extra pay for being laid off, and his regular check from the Jewel Bearing Plant.

We were walking down Portage anyway, seeing the sights, when we saw it. There it was, parked, large as life. Really as *if* it was alive. I thought of the word *repose*, because the car wasn't simply stopped, parked, or whatever. That car reposed, cairn and gleaming, a FOR SALE sign in its left front window. Then, before we had thought it over at all, the car belonged to us and our pockets were empty. We had just enough money for gas back home.

We went places in that car, me and Henry. We took off driving all one whole summer. We started off toward the Little Knife River and Mandaree in Fort Berthold and then we found ourselves down in Wakpala somehow, and then suddenly we were over in Montana on the Rocky Boys, and yet the summer was not even half over. Some people hang on to details when they travel, but we didn't let them bother us and just lived our everyday lives here to there.

I do remember this one place with willows. I remember I laid under those trees and it was comfortable. So comfortable. The branches bent down all around me like a tent or a stable. And quiet, it was quiet, even though there was a powwow close enough so I could see it going on. The air was not too still, not too windy either. When the dust rises up and hangs in the air around the dancers like that, I feel good. Henry was asleep with his arms thrown wide. Later on, he woke up and we started driving again. We were somewhere in Montana, or maybe on the Blood Reserve—it could have been anywhere. Anyway it was where we met the girl.

All her hair was in buns around her ears, that's the first thing I noticed about her. She was posed alongside the road with her arm out, so we stopped. That girl was short, so short her lumber shirt looked comical on her, like a nightgown. She had jeans on and fancy moccasins and she carried a little suitcase.

"Hop on in," says Henry. So she climbs in between us.

"We'll take you home," I says. "Where do you live?"

"Chicken," she says.

"Where the hell's that?" I ask her.

"Alaska."

"Okay," says Henry, and we drive.

We got up there and never wanted to leave. The sun doesn't truly set there in summer, and the night is more a soft dusk. You might doze off, sometimes, but before you know it you're up again, like an animal in nature. You never feel like you have to sleep hard or put away the world. And things would grow up there. One day just dirt or moss, the next day flowers and long grass. The girl's name was Susy. Her family really took to us. They fed us and put us up. We had our own tent to live in by their house, and the kids would be in and out of there all day and night. They couldn't get over me and Henry being brothers, we looked so different. We told them we knew we had the same mother, anyway.

One night Susy came in to visit us. We sat around in the tent talking of this thing and that. The season was changing. It was getting darker by that time, and the cold was even getting just a little mean. I told her it was time for us to go. She stood up on a chair.

"You never seen my hair," Susy said.

That was true. She was standing on a chair, but still, when she unclipped her buns the hair reached all the way to the ground. Our eyes opened. You couldn't tell how much hair she had when it was rolled up so neatly. Then my brother Henry did something funny. He went up to the chair and said, "Jump on my shoulders." So she did that, and her hair reached down past his waist, and he started twirling, this way and that, so her hair was flung out from side to side.

"I always wondered what it was like to have long pretty hair," Henry says. Well we laughed. It was a funny sight, the way he did it. The next morning we got up and took leave of those people.

On to greener pastures, as they say. It was down through Spokane and across Idaho then Montana and very soon we were racing the weather right along under the Canadian border through Columbus, Des Lacs, and then we were in Bottineau County and soon home. We'd made most of the trip, that summer, without putting up the car hood at all. We got home just in time, it turned out, for the army to remember Henry had signed up to join it.

I don't wonder that the army was so glad to get my brother that they turned him into a Marine. He was built like a brick outhouse anyway. We liked to tease him that they really wanted him for his Indian nose. He had a nose big and sharp as a hatchet, like the nose on Red Tomahawk, the Indian who killed Sitting Bull, whose profile is on signs all along the North Dakota highways. Henry went off to training camp, came home once during Christmas, then the next thing you know we got an overseas letter from him. It was 1970, and he said he was stationed up in the northern hill country. Whereabouts I did not know. He wasn't such a hot letter writer, and only got off two before the enemy caught him. I could never keep it straight, which direction those good Vietnam soldiers were from.

I wrote him back several times, even though I didn't know if those letters would get through. I kept him informed all about the car. Most of the time I had it up on blocks in the yard or half taken apart, because that long trip did a hard job on it under the hood.

I always had good luck with numbers, and never worried about the draft myself. I never even had to think about what my number was. But Henry was never lucky in the same way as me. It was at least three years before Henry came home. By then I guess the whole war was solved in the government's mind, but for him it would keep on going. In those years I'd put his car into almost perfect shape. I always thought of it as his car while he was gone, even though when he left he said, "Now it's yours," and threw me his key.

"Thanks for the extra key," I'd said. "I'll put it up in your drawer just in case I need it." He laughed.

When he came home, though, Henry was very different, and I'll say this: the change was no good. You could hardly expect him to change for the better, I know. But he was quiet, so quiet, and never comfortable sitting still anywhere but always up and moving around. I thought back to times we'd sat still for whole afternoons, never moving a muscle, just shifting our weight along the ground, talking to whoever sat with us, watching things. He'd always had a joke, then, too, and now you couldn't get him to laugh, or when he did it was more the sound of a man choking, a sound that stopped up the throats of other people around him. They got to leaving him alone most of the time, and I didn't blame them. It was a fact: Henry was jumpy and mean.

I'd bought a color TV set for my mom and the rest of us while Henry was away. Money still came very easy. I was sorry I'd ever bought it though, because of Henry. I was also sorry I'd bought color, because with black-and-white the pictures seem older and farther away. But what are you going to do? He sat in front of it, watching it, and that was the only time he was completely still. But it was the kind of stillness that you see in a rabbit when it freezes and before it will bolt. He was not easy. He sat in his chair gripping the armrests with all his might, as if the chair itself was moving at a high speed and if he let go at all he would rocket forward and maybe crash right through the set.

Once I was in the room watching TV with Henry and I heard his teeth click at something. I looked over, and he'd bitten through his lip. Blood was going down his chin. I tell you right then I wanted to smash that tube to pieces. I went over to it but Henry must have known what I was up to. He rushed from his chair and shoved me out of the way, against the wall. I told myself he didn't know what he was doing.

My mom came in, turned the set off real quiet, and told us she had made something for supper. So we went and sat down. There was still blood going down Henry's chin, but he didn't notice it and no one said anything, even though every time he took a bite of his bread his blood fell onto it until he was eating his own blood mixed in with the food.

While Henry was not around we talked about what was going to happen to him. There were no Indian doctors on the reservation, and my mom was afraid of trusting Old Man Pillager because he courted her long ago and was jealous of her husbands. He might take revenge through her son. We were afraid that if we brought Henry to a regular hospital they would keep him.

"They don't fix them in those places," Mom said; "they just give them drugs."

"We wouldn't get him there in the first place," I agreed, "so let's just forget about it."

Then I thought about the car.

Henry had not even looked at the car since he'd gotten home, though like I said, it was in tip-top condition and ready to drive. I thought the car might bring the old Henry back somehow. So I bided my time and waited for my chance to interest him in the vehicle.

One night Henry was off somewhere. I took myself a hammer. I went out to that car and I did a number on its underside. Whacked it up. Bent the tail pipe double. Ripped the muffler loose. By the time I was done with the car it looked worse than any typical Indian car that has been driven all its life on reservation roads, which they always say are like government promises—full of holes. It just about hurt me, I'll tell you that! I threw dirt in the carburetor and I ripped all the electric tape off the seats. I made it look just as beat up as I could. Then I sat back and waited for Henry to find it.

Still, it took him over a month. That was all right, because it was just getting warm enough, not melting, but warm enough to work outside.

"Lyman," he says, walking in one day, "that red car looks like shit."

"Well it's old," I says. "You got to expect that."

"No way!" says Henry. "That car's a classic! But you went and ran the piss right out of it, Lyman, and you know it don't deserve that. I kept that car in A-one shape. You don't remember. You're too young. But when I left, that car was running like a watch. Now I don't even know if I can get it to start again, let alone get it anywhere near its old condition."

"Well you try," I said, like I was getting mad, "but I say it's a piece of junk."

Then I walked out before he could realize I knew he'd strung together more than six words at once.

After that I thought he'd freeze himself to death working on that car. He was out there all day, and at night he rigged up a little lamp, ran a cord out the window, and had himself some light to see by while he worked. He was better than he had been before, but that's still not saying much. It was easier for him to do the things the rest of us did. He ate more slowly and didn't jump up and down during the meal to get this or that or look out the window. I put my hand in the back of the TV set, I admit, and fiddled around with it good, so that it was almost impossible now to get a clear picture. He didn't look at it very often anyway. He was always out with that car or going off to get parts for it. By the time it was really melting outside, he had it fixed.

I had been feeling down in the dumps about Henry around this time. We had always been together before. Henry and Lyman. But he was such a loner now that I didn't know how to take it. So I jumped at the chance one day when Henry seemed friendly. It's not that he smiled or anything. He just said, "Let's take that old shitbox for a spin." Just the way he said it made me think he could be coming around.

We went out to the car. It was spring. The sun was shining very bright. My only sister, Bonita, who was just eleven years old, came out and made us stand together for a picture. Henry leaned his elbow on the red car's windshield, and he took his other arm and put it over my shoulder, very carefully, as though it was heavy for him to lift and he didn't want to bring the weight down all at once.

"Smile," Bonita said, and he did.

That picture. I never look at it anymore. A few months ago, I don't know why, I got his picture out and tacked it on the wall. I felt good about Henry at the time, close to him. I felt good having his picture on the wall, until one night when I was looking at television. I was a little drunk and stoned. I looked up at the wall and Henry was staring at me. I don't know what it was, but his smile had changed, or maybe it was gone. All I know is I couldn't stay in the same room with that picture. I was shaking. I got up, closed the door, and went into the kitchen. A little later my friend Ray came over and we both went back into that room. We put the picture in a brown bag, folded the bag over and over tightly, then put it way back in a closet.

I still see that picture now, as if it tugs at me, whenever I pass that closet door. The picture is very clear in my mind. It was so sunny that day Henry had to squint against the glare. Or maybe the camera Bonita held flashed like a mirror, blinding him, before she snapped the picture. My face is right out in the sun, big and round. But he might have drawn back, because the shadows on his face are deep as holes. There are two shadows curved like little hooks around the ends of his smile, as if to frame it and try to keep it there—that one, first smile that looked like it might have hurt his face. He has his field jacket on and the worn-in clothes he'd come back in and kept wearing ever since. After Bonita took the picture, she went into the house and we got into the car. There was a full cooler in the trunk. We started off, east, toward Pembina and the Red River because Henry said he wanted to see the high water.

The trip over there was beautiful. When everything starts changing, drying up, clearing off, you feel like your whole life is starting. Henry felt it, too. The top was down and the car hummed like a top. He'd really put it back in shape, even the tape on the seats was very carefully put down and glued back in layers. It's not that he smiled again or even joked, but his face looked to me as if it was clear, more peaceful. It looked as though he wasn't thinking of anything in particular except the bare fields and windbreaks and houses we were passing.

The river was high and full of winter trash when we got there. The sun was still out, but it was colder by the river. There were still little clumps of dirty snow here and there on the banks. The water hadn't gone over the banks yet, but it would, you could tell. It was just at its limit, hard swollen, glossy like an old gray scar. We made ourselves a fire, and we sat down and watched the current go. As I watched it I felt something squeezing inside me and tightening and trying to let go all at the same time. I knew I was not just feeling it myself; I knew I was feeling what Henry was going through at that moment. Except that I couldn't stand it, the closing and opening. I jumped to my feet. I took Henry by the shoulders and I started shaking him. "Wake up," I says, "wake up, wake up, wake up!" I didn't know what had come over me. I sat down beside him again.

His face was totally white and hard. Then it broke, like stones break all of a sudden when water boils up inside them.

"I know it," he says. "I know it. I can't help it. It's no use."

We start talking. He said he knew what I'd done with the car. It was obvious it had been whacked out of shape and not just neglected. He said he wanted to give the car to me for good now, it was no use. He said he'd fixed it just to give it back and I should take it.

"No way," I says, "I don't want it."

"That's okay," he says, "you take it."

"I don't want it, though," I says back to him, and then to emphasize, just to emphasize, you understand, I touch his shoulder. He slaps my hand off.

"Take that car," he says.

"No," I say, "make me," I say, and then he grabs my jacket and rips the arm loose. That jacket is a class act, suede with tags and zippers. I push Henry backwards, off the log. He jumps up and bowls me over. We go down in a clinch and come up swinging hard, for all we're worth, with our fists. He socks my jaw so hard I feel like it swings loose. Then I'm at his ribcage and land a good one under his chin so his head snaps back. He's dazzled. He looks at me and I look at him and then his eyes are full of tears and blood and at first I think he's crying. But no, he's laughing. "Ha! Ha!" he says. "Ha! Ha! Take good care of it."

"Okay," I says, "okay, no problem. Ha! Ha!"

I can't help it, and I start laughing, too. My face feels fat and strange, and after a while I get a beer from the cooler in the trunk, and when I hand it to Henry he takes his shirt and wipes my germs off. "Hoof-and-mouth disease," he says. For some reason this cracks me up, and so we're really laughing for a while, and then we drink all the rest of the beers one by one and throw them in the river and see how far, how fast, the current takes them before they fill up and sink.

"You want to go on back?" I ask after a while. "Maybe we could snag a couple nice Kashpaw girls."

He says nothing. But I can tell his mood is turning again.

"They're all crazy, the girls up here, every damn one of them."

"You're crazy too," I say, to jolly him up. "Crazy Lamartine boys!"

He looks as though he will take this wrong at first. His face twists, then clears, and he jumps up on his feet. "That's right!" he says. "Crazier 'n hell. Crazy Indians!"

I think it's the old Henry again. He throws off his jacket and starts swinging his legs out from the knees like a fancy dancer. He's down doing something between a grouse dance and a bunny hop, no kind of dance I ever saw before, but neither has anyone else on all this green growing earth. He's wild. He wants to pitch whoopee! He's up and at me and all over. All this time I'm laughing so hard, so hard my belly is getting tied up in a knot.

"Got to cool me off!" he shouts all of a sudden. Then he runs over to the river and jumps in.

There's boards and other things in the current. It's so high. No sound comes from the river after the splash he makes, so I run right over. I look around. It's getting dark. I see he's halfway across the water already, and I know he didn't swim there but the current took him. It's far. I hear his voice, though, very clearly across it.

"My boots are filling," he says.

He says this in a normal voice, like he just noticed and he doesn't know what to think of it. Then he's gone. A branch comes by. Another branch. And I go in.

By the time I get out of the river, off the snag I pulled myself onto, the sun is down. I walk back to the car, turn on the high beams, and drive it up the bank. I put it in first gear and then I take my foot off the clutch. I get out, close the door, and watch it plow softly into the water. The headlights reach in as they go down, searching, still lighted even after the water swirls over the back end. I wait. The wires short out. It is all finally dark. And then there is only the water, the sound of it going and running and going and running and running.

BHARATI MUKHERJEE (b. 1940) was born in Calcutta, India. Her father and mother were both Bengali Brahmins, the highest Hindu caste. She received her early schooling at a British missionary school and went on to receive a B.A. in English at the University of Calcutta, an M.A. in English and ancient Indian culture from the University of Baroda, an M.F.A. from the Iowa Writers' Workshop, and a Ph.D. from the University of Iowa. Although she married a Canadian novelist and lived for a time in Canada, she has found the United States to be a less hostile environment for Indian immigrants.

In her fiction, Mukherjee delves into the experiences of Third World immigrants to North America, including interracial biases, cultural clashes, and conflicting ideas about what it means to be an "American." Her writing promotes a view of America as a diverse nation that can no longer overlook the fact that its strength lies in its population's variety, not its homogeny.

Mukherjee's novels include *The Tiger's Daughter* (1972), *Wife* (1975), and *Jasmine* (1989). Her short stories are collected in *Darkness* (1985) and *The Middleman and Other Stories* (1988).

The main characters in "A Wife's Story" (1988), like many of Mukherjee's characters, are immigrants from a **postcolonial** country who are trying to adapt to a new culture in which they are confronted by "Patel" jokes and other xenophobic sentiments of "traditional" Americans, a culture in which the "American Dream" is explored through "pizzas, burgers, McNuggets," the items on the grocery shelves, shopping at sales on Broadway, and New York City—"the richest city in the richest country in the world." Amidst it all, a woman tries to discover a new sense of her self.

Related Works: Chopin, "The Story of an Hour"; Cofer, "Arturo's Flight"; Steinbeck, "The Chrysanthemums"; Ibsen, *A Dollhouse.*

A Wife's Story

Imre says forget it, but I'm going to write David Mamet. So Patels are hard to sell real estate to. You buy them a beer, whisper Glengarry Glen Ross, and they smell swamp instead of sun and surf. They work hard, eat cheap, live ten to a room, stash their savings under futons in Queens, and before you know it they own half of Hoboken. You say, where's the sweet gullibility that made this nation great?

Polish jokes, Patel jokes: that's not why I want to write Mamet.

Seen their women?

Everybody laughs. Imre laughs. The dozing fat man with the Barnes & Noble sack between his legs, the woman next to him, the usher, everybody. The theater isn't so dark that they can't see me. In my red silk sari I'm conspicuous. Plump, gold paisleys sparkle on my chest.

The actor is just warming up. *Seen their women*? He plays a salesman, he's had a bad day and now he's in a Chinese restaurant trying to loosen up. His face is pink. His wool-blend slacks are creased at the crotch. We bought our tickets at half-price, we're sitting in the front row, but at the edge, and we see things we shouldn't be seeing. At least I do, or think I do. Spittle, actors goosing each other, little winks, streaks of makeup.

Maybe they're improvising dialogue too. Maybe Mamet's provided them with insult kits, Thursdays for Chinese, Wednesdays for Hispanics, today for Indians. Maybe they get together before curtain time, see an Indian woman settling in the front row off to the side, and say to each other: "Hey, forget Friday. Let's get *her* today. See if she cries. See if she walks out." Maybe, like the salesmen they play, they have a little bet on.

Maybe I shouldn't feel betrayed.

Their women, he goes again. *They look like they've just been fucked by a dead cat.*

The fat man hoots so hard he nudges my elbow off our shared armrest.

"Imre. I'm going home." But Imre's hunched so far forward he doesn't hear. English isn't his best language. A refugee from Budapest, he has to listen hard. "I didn't pay eighteen dollars to be insulted."

I don't hate Mamet. It's the tyranny of the American dream that scares me. First, you don't exist. Then you're invisible. Then you're funny. Then you're disgusting. Insult, my American friends will tell me, is a kind of acceptance. No instant dignity here. A play like this, back home, would cause riots. Communal, racist, and antisocial. The actors wouldn't make it off stage. This play, and all these awful feelings, would be safely locked up.

I long, at times, for clear-cut answers. Offer me instant dignity, today, and I'll take it.

"What?" Imre moves toward me without taking his eyes off the actor. "Come again?"

Tears come. I want to stand, scream, make an awful scene. I long for ugly, nasty rage.

The actor is ranting, flinging spittle. *Give me a chance. I'm not finished, I can get back on the board. I tell that asshole, give me a real lead. And what does that asshole give me? Patels. Nothing but Patels.*

This time Imre works an arm around my shoulders. "Panna, what is Patel? Why are you taking it all so personally?"

I shrink from his touch, but I don't walk out. Expensive girls' schools in Lausanne and Bombay have trained me to behave well. My manners are exquisite, my feelings are delicate, my gestures refined, my moods undetectable. They have seen me through riots, uprootings, separation, my son's death.

"I'm not taking it personally."

The fat man looks at us. The woman looks too, and shushes.

I stare back at the two of them. Then I stare, mean and cool, at the man's elbow. Under the bright blue polyester Hawaiian shirt sleeve, the elbow looks soft and runny. "Excuse me," I say. My voice has the effortless meanness of well-bred displaced Third World women, though my rhetoric has been learned elsewhere. "You're exploiting my space."

Startled, the man snatches his arm away from me. He cradles it against his breast. By the time he's ready with comebacks, I've turned my back on him. I've probably ruined the first act for him. I know I've ruined it for Imre.

It's not my fault; it's the *situation.* Old colonies wear down. Patels—the new pioneers—have to be suspicious. Idi Amin's lesson is permanent. AT&T wires move good advice from continent to continent. Keep all assets liquid. Get into 7–11s, get out of condos and motels. I know how both sides feel, that's the trouble. The Patel sniffing out scams, the sad salesmen on the stage: postcolonialism has made me their referee. It's hate I long for; simple, brutish, partisan hate.

After the show Imre and I make our way toward Broadway. Sometimes he holds my hand; it doesn't mean anything more than that crazies and drunks are crouched in doorways. Imre's been here over two years, but he's stayed very old-world, very courtly, openly protective of women. I met him in a seminar on special ed. last semester. His wife is a nurse somewhere in the Hungarian countryside. There are two sons, and miles of petitions for their emigration. My husband manages a mill two hundred miles north of Bombay. There are no children.

"You make things tough on yourself," Imre says. He assumed Patel was a Jewish name or maybe Hispanic; everything makes equal sense to him. He found the play tasteless, he worried about the effect of vulgar language on my sensitive ears. "You have to let go a bit." And as though to show me how to let go, he breaks away from me, bounds ahead with his head ducked tight, then dances on amazingly jerky legs. He's a Magyar, he often tells me, and deep down, he's an Asian too. I catch glimpses of it, knife-blade Attila cheekbones, despite the blondish hair. In his faded jeans and leather jacket, he's a rock video star. I watch MTV for hours in the apartment when Charity's working the evening shift at Macy's. I listen to WPLJ on Charity's earphones. Why should I be ashamed? Television in India is so uplifting.

Imre stops as suddenly as he'd started. People walk around us. The summer sidewalk is full of theatergoers in seersucker suits; Imre's year-round jacket is out of place. European. Cops in twos and threes huddle, lightly tap their thighs with night sticks and smile at me with benevolence. I want to wink at them, get us all in trouble, tell them the crazy dancing man is from the Warsaw Pact. I'm too shy to break into dance on Broadway. So I hug Imre instead.

The hug takes him by surprise. He wants me to let go, but he doesn't really expect me to let go. He staggers, though I weigh no more than 104 pounds, and with him, I pitch forward slightly. Then he catches me, and we walk arm in arm to the bus stop. My husband would never dance or hug a woman on Broadway. Nor would my brothers. They aren't stuffy people, but they went to Anglican boarding schools and they have a well-developed sense of what's silly.

"Imre." I squeeze his big, rough hand. "I'm sorry I ruined the evening for you."

"You did nothing of the kind." He sounds tired. "Let's not wait for the bus. Let's splurge and take a cab instead."

Imre always has unexpected funds. The Network, he calls it, Class of '56.

In the back of the cab, without even trying, I feel light, almost free. Memories of Indian destitutes mix with the hordes of New York street people, and they float free, like astronauts, inside my head. I've made it. I'm making something of my life. I've left home, my husband, to get a Ph.D. in special ed. I have a multiple-entry visa and a small scholarship for two years. After that, we'll see. My mother was beaten by her mother-in-law, my grandmother, when she'd registered for French lessons at the Alliance Française. My grandmother, the eldest daughter of a rich zamindar, was illiterate.

Imre and the cabdriver talk away in Russian. I keep my eyes closed. That way I can feel the floaters better. I'll write Mamet tonight. I feel strong, reckless. Maybe I'll write Steven Spielberg too; tell him that Indians don't eat monkey brains.

We've made it. Patels must have made it. Mamet, Spielberg: they're not condescending to us. Maybe they're a little bit afraid.

Charity Chin, my roommate, is sitting on the floor drinking Chablis out of a plastic wineglass. She is five foot six, three inches taller than me, but weighs a kilo and a half less than I do. She is a "hands" model. Orientals are supposed to have a monopoly in the hands-modelling business, she says. She had her eyes fixed eight or nine months ago and out of gratitude sleeps with her plastic surgeon every third Wednesday.

"Oh, good," Charity says. "I'm glad you're back early. I need to talk."

She's been writing checks. MCI, Con Ed, Bonwit Teller. Envelopes, already stamped and sealed, form a pyramid between her shapely, knee-socked legs. The checkbook's cover is brown plastic, grained to look like cowhide. Each time Charity flips back the cover, white geese fly over sky-colored checks. She makes good money, but she's extravagant. The difference adds up to this shared, rent-controlled Chelsea one-bedroom.

"All right. Talk."

When I first moved in, she was seeing an analyst. Now she sees a nutritionist.

"Eric called. From Oregon."

"What did he want?"

"He wants me to pay half the rent on his loft for last spring. He asked me to move back, remember? He *begged* me."

Eric is Charity's estranged husband.

"What does your nutritionist say?" Eric now wears a red jumpsuit and tills the soil in Rajneeshpuram.

"You think Phil's a creep too, don't you? What else can he be when creeps are all I attract?"

Phil is a flutist with thinning hair. He's very touchy on the subject of *flautists* versus *flutists*. He's touchy on every subject, from music to books to foods to clothes. He teaches at a small college upstate, and Charity bought a used blue Datsun ("Nissan," Phil insists) last month so she could spend weekends with him. She returns every Sunday night, exhausted and exasperated. Phil and I don't have much to say to each other—he's the only musician I know; the men in my family are lawyers, engineers, or in business—but I like him. Around me, he loosens up. When he visits, he bakes us loaves of pumpernickel bread. He waxes our kitchen floor. Like many men in this country, he seems to me a displaced child, or even a woman, looking for something that passed him by, or for something that he can never have. If he thinks I'm not looking, he sneaks his hands under Charity's sweater, but there isn't too much there. Here, she's a model with high ambitions. In India, she'd be a flat-chested old maid.

I'm shy in front of the lovers. A darkness comes over me when I see them horsing around.

"It isn't the money," Charity says. Oh? I think. "He says he still loves me. Then he turns around and asks me for five hundred."

What's so strange about that, I want to ask. She still loves Eric, and Eric, red jump suit and all, is smart enough to know it. Love is a commodity, hoarded like any other. Mamet knows. But I say, "I'm not the person to ask about love." Charity knows that mine was a traditional Hindu marriage. My parents, with the help of a marriage broker, who was my mother's cousin, picked out a groom. All I had to do was get to know his taste in food.

It'll be a long evening, I'm afraid. Charity likes to confess. I unpleat my silk sari—it no longer looks too showy—wrap it in muslin cloth and put it away in a dresser drawer. Saris are hard to have laundered in Manhattan, though there's a good man in Jackson Heights. My next step will be to brew us a pot of chrysanthemum tea. It's a very special tea from the mainland. Charity's uncle gave it to us. I like him. He's a humpbacked, awkward, terrified man. He runs a gift store on Mott Street, and though he doesn't speak much English, he seems to have done well. Once upon a time he worked for the railways in Chengdu, Szechwan Province, and during the Wuchang Uprising, he was shot at. When I'm down, when I'm lonely for my husband, when I think of our son, or when I need to be held, I think of Charity's uncle. If I hadn't left home, I'd never have heard of the Wuchang Uprising. I've broadened my horizons.

Very late that night my husband calls me from Ahmadabad, a town of textile mills north of Bombay. My husband is a vice president at Lakshmi Cotton Mills.

Lakshmi is the goddess of wealth, but LCM (Priv.), Ltd., is doing poorly. Lockouts, strikes, rock-throwings. My husband lives on digitalis, which he calls the food for our *yuga* of discontent.

"We had a bad mishap at the mill today." Then he says nothing for seconds.

The operator comes on. "Do you have the right party, sir? We're trying to reach Mrs. Butt."

"Bhatt," I insist. "*B* for Bombay, *H* for Haryana, *A* for Ahmadabad, double *T* for Tamil Nadu." It's a litany. "This is she."

"One of our lorries was firebombed today. Resulting in three deaths. The driver, old Karamchand, and his two children."

I know how my husband's eyes look this minute, how the eye rims sag and the yellow corneas shine and bulge with pain. He is not an emotional man—the Ahmadabad Institute of Management has trained him to cut losses, to look on the bright side of economic catastrophes—but tonight he's feeling low. I try to remember a driver named Karamchand, but can't. That part of my life is over, the way *trucks* have replaced *lorries* in my vocabulary, the way Charity Chin and her lurid love life have replaced inherited notions of marital duty. Tomorrow he'll come out of it. Soon he'll be eating again. He'll sleep like a baby. He's been trained to believe in turnovers. Every morning he rubs his scalp with cantharidine oil so his hair will grow back again.

"It could be your car next." Affection, love. Who can tell the difference in a traditional marriage in which a wife still doesn't call her husband by his first name?

"No. They know I'm a flunky, just like them. Well paid, maybe. No need for undue anxiety, please."

Then his voice breaks. He says he needs me, he misses me, he wants me to come to him damp from my evening shower, smelling of sandalwood soap, my braid decorated with jasmines.

"I need you too."

"Not to worry, please," he says. "I am coming in a fortnight's time. I have already made arrangements."

Outside my window, fire trucks whine, up Eighth Avenue. I wonder if he can hear them, what he thinks of a life like mine, led amid disorder.

"I am thinking it'll be like a honeymoon. More or less."

When I was in college, waiting to be married, I imagined honeymoons were only for the more fashionable girls, the girls who came from slightly racy families, smoked Sobranies in the dorm lavatories and put up posters of Kabir Bedi, who was supposed to have made it as a big star in the West. My husband wants us to go to Niagara. I'm not to worry about foreign exchange. He's arranged for extra dollars through the Gujarati Network, with a cousin in San Jose. And he's bought four hundred more on the black market. "Tell me you need me. Panna, please tell me again."

I change out of the cotton pants and shirt I've been wearing all day and put on a sari to meet my husband at JFK. I don't forget the jewelry; the marriage necklace of *mangalsutra*, gold drop earrings, heavy gold bangles. I don't wear them every day. In this borough of vice and greed, who knows when, or whom, desire will overwhelm.

My husband spots me in the crowd and waves. He has lost weight, and changed his glasses. The arm, uplifted in a cheery wave, is bony, frail, almost opalescent.

In the Carey Coach, we hold hands. He strokes my fingers one by one. "How come you aren't wearing my mother's ring?"

"Because muggers know about Indian women," I say. They know with us it's 24-karat. His mother's ring is showy, in ghastly taste anywhere but India: a blood-red Burma ruby set in a gold frame of floral sprays. My mother-in-law got her guru to bless the ring before I left for the States.

He looks disconcerted. He's used to a different role. He's the knowing, suspicious one in the family. He seems to be sulking, and finally he comes out with it. "You've said nothing about my new glasses." I compliment him on the glasses, how chic and Western-executive they make him look. But I can't help the other things, necessities until he learns the ropes. I handle the money, buy the tickets. I don't know if this makes me unhappy.

Charity drives her Nissan upstate, so for two weeks we are to have the apartment to ourselves. This is more privacy than we ever had in India. No parents, no servants, to keep us modest. We play at housekeeping. Imre has lent us a hibachi, and I grill saffron chicken breasts. My husband marvels at the size of the Perdue hens. "They're big like peacocks, no? These Americans, they're really something!" He tries out pizzas, burgers, McNuggets. He chews. He explores. He judges. He loves it all, fears nothing, feels at home in the summer odors, the clutter of Manhattan streets. Since he thinks that the American palate is bland, he carries a bottle of red peppers in his pocket. I wheel a shopping cart down the aisles of the neighborhood Grand Union, and he follows, swiftly, greedily. He picks up hair rinses and high-protein diet powders. There's so much I already take for granted.

One night, Imre stops by. He wants us to go with him to a movie. In his work shirt and red leather tie, he looks arty or strung out. It's only been a week, but I feel as though I am really seeing him for the first time. The yellow hair worn very short at the sides, the wide, narrow lips. He's a good-looking man, but self-conscious, almost arrogant. He's picked the movie we should see. He always tells me what to see, what to read. He buys the *Voice*. He's a natural avant-gardist. For tonight he's chosen *Numéro Deux*.

"Is it a musical?" my husband asks. The Radio City Music Hall is on his list of sights to see. He's read up on the history of the Rockettes. He doesn't catch Imre's sympathetic wink.

Guilt, shame, loyalty. I long to be ungracious, not ingratiate myself with both men.

That night my husband calculates in rupees the money we've wasted on Godard. "That refugee fellow, Nagy, must have a screw loose in his head. I paid very steep price for dollars on the black market."

Some afternoons we go shopping. Back home we hated shopping, but now it is a lovers' project. My husband's shopping list startles me. I feel I am just getting to know him. Maybe, like Imre, freed from the dignities of old-world culture, he too could get drunk and squirt Cheez Whiz on a guest. I watch him dart into stores in his gleaming leather shoes. Jockey shorts on sale in outdoor bins on Broadway entrance him. White tube socks with different bands of color delight him. He looks for microcassettes, for anything small and electronic and smuggleable. He needs a garment bag. He calls it a "wardrobe," and I have to translate.

"All of New York is having sales, no?"

My heart speeds watching him this happy. It's the third week in August, almost the end of summer, and the city smells ripe, it cannot bear more heat, more money, more energy.

"This is so smashing! The prices are so excellent!" Recklessly, my prudent husband signs away traveller's checks. How he intends to smuggle it all back I don't dare ask. With a microwave, he calculates, we could get rid of our cook.

This has to be love, I think. Charity, Eric, Phil: they may be experts on sex. My husband doesn't chase me around the sofa, but he pushes me down on Charity's battered cushions, and the man who has never entered the kitchen of our Ahmadabad house now comes toward me with a dish tub of steamy water to massage away the pavement heat.

Ten days into his vacation my husband checks out brochures for sightseeing tours. Shortline, Grayline, Crossroads: his new vinyl briefcase is full of schedules and pamphlets. While I make pancakes out of a mix, he comparison-shops. Tour number one costs $10.95 and will give us the World Trade Center, Chinatown, and the United Nations. Tour number three would take us both uptown *and* downtown for $14.95, but my husband is absolutely sure he doesn't want to see Harlem. We settle for tour number four: Downtown and the Dame. It's offered by a new tour company with a small, dirty office at Eighth and Forty-eighth.

The sidewalk outside the office is colorful with tourists. My husband sends me in to buy the tickets because he has come to feel Americans don't understand his accent.

The dark man, Lebanese probably, behind the counter comes on too friendly. "Come on, doll, make my day!" He won't say which tour is his, "Number four? Honey, no! Look, you've wrecked me! Say you'll change your mind." He takes two twenties and gives back change. He holds the tickets, forcing me to pull. He leans closer. "I'm off after lunch."

My husband must have been watching me from the sidewalk. "What was the chap saying?" he demands. "I told you not to wear pants. He thinks you are Puerto Rican. He thinks he can treat you with disrespect."

The bus is crowded and we have to sit across the aisle from each other. The tour guide begins his patter on Forty-sixth. He looks like an actor, his hair bleached and blow-dried. Up close he must look middle-aged, but from where I sit his skin is smooth and his cheeks faintly red.

"Welcome to the Big Apple, folks." The guide uses a microphone. "Big Apple. That's what we native Manhattan degenerates call our city. Today we have guests from fifteen foreign countries and six states from this U.S. of A. That makes the Tourist Bureau real happy. And let me assure you that while we may be the richest city in the richest country in the world, it's okay to tip your charming and talented attendant." He laughs. Then he swings his hip out into the aisle and sings a song.

"And it's mighty fancy on old Delancey Street, you know. . . ."

My husband looks irritable. The guide is, as expected, a good singer. "The bloody man should be giving us histories of buildings we are passing, no?" I pat his hand, the mood passes. He cranes his neck. Our window seats have both gone to Japanese. It's the tour of his life. Next to this, the quick business trips to Manchester and Glasgow pale.

"And tell me what street compares to Mott Street, in July. . . ."

The guide wants applause. He manages a derisive laugh from the Americans up front. He's working the aisles now. "I coulda been somebody, right? I coulda been a star!" Two or three of us smile, those of us who recognize the parody. He catches my smile. The sun is on his harsh, bleached hair. "Right, your highness? Look, we gotta maharani with us! Couldn't I have been a star?"

"Right!" I say, my voice coming out a squeal. I've been trained to adapt; what else can I say?

We drive through traffic past landmark office buildings and churches. The guide flips his hands. "Art deco," he keeps saying. I hear him confide to one of the Americans: "Beats me. I went to a cheap guide's school." My husband wants to know more about this Art Deco, but the guide sings another song.

"We made a foolish choice," my husband grumbles. "We are sitting in the bus only. We're not going into famous buildings." He scrutinizes the pamphlets in his jacket pocket. I think, at least it's air-conditioned in here. I could sit here in the cool shadows of the city forever.

Only five of us appear to have opted for the "Downtown and the Dame" tour. The others will ride back uptown past the United Nations after we've been dropped off at the pier for the ferry to the Statue of Liberty.

An elderly European pulls a camera out of his wife's designer tote bag. He takes pictures of the boats in the harbor, the Japanese in kimonos eating popcorn, scavenging pigeons, me. Then, pushing his wife ahead of him, he climbs back on the bus and waves to us. For a second I feel terribly lost. I wish we were on the bus going back to the apartment. I know I'll not be able to describe any of this to Charity, or to Imre. I'm too proud to admit I went on a guided tour.

The view of the city from the Circle Line ferry is seductive, unreal. The skyline wavers out of reach, but never quite vanishes. The summer sun pushes through fluffy clouds and dapples the glass of office towers. My husband looks thrilled, even more than he had on the shopping trips down Broadway. Tourists and dreamers, we have spent our life's savings to see this skyline, this statue.

"Quick, take a picture of me!" my husband yells as he moves toward a gap of railings. A Japanese matron has given up her position in order to change film. "Before the Twin Towers disappear!"

I focus, I wait for a large Oriental family to walk out of my range. My husband holds his pose tight against the railing. He wants to look relaxed, an international businessman at home in all the financial markets.

A bearded man slides across the bench toward me. "Like this," he says and helps me get my husband in focus. "You want me to take the photo for you?" His name, he says, is Goran. He is Goran from Yugoslavia, as though that were enough for tracking him down. Imre from Hungary. Panna from India. He pulls the old Leica out of my hand, signaling the Orientals to beat it, and clicks away. "I'm a photographer," he says. He could have been a camera thief. That's what my husband would have assumed. Somehow, I trusted. "Get you a beer?" he asks.

"I don't. Drink, I mean. Thank you very much." I say those last words very loud, for everyone's benefit. The odd bottles of Soave with Imre don't count.

"Too bad." Goran gives back the camera.

"Take one more!" my husband shouts from the railing. "Just to be sure!"

The island itself disappoints. The Lady has brutal scaffolding holding her in. The museum is closed. The snack bar is dirty and expensive. My husband reads out the prices to me. He orders two french fries and two Cokes. We sit at picnic tables and wait for the ferry to take us back.

"What was that hippie chap saying?"

As if I could say. A day-care center has brought its kids, at least forty of them, to the island for the day. The kids, all wearing name tags, run around us. I can't help noticing how many are Indian. Even a Patel, probably a Bhatt if I looked hard enough. They toss hamburger bits at pigeons. They kick styrofoam cups. The pigeons are slow, greedy, persistent. I have to shoo one off the table top. I don't think my husband thinks about our son.

"What hippie?"

"The one on the boat. With the beard and the hair."

My husband doesn't look at me. He shakes out his paper napkin and tries to protect his french fries from pigeon feathers.

"Oh, him. He said he was from Dubrovnik." It isn't true, but I don't want trouble.

"What did he say about Dubrovnik?"

I know enough about Dubrovnik to get by. Imre's told me about it. And about Mostar and Zagreb. In Mostar white Muslims sing the call to prayer. I would like to see that before I die: white Muslims. Whole peoples have moved before me; they've adapted. The night Imre told me about Mostar was also the night I saw my first snow in Manhattan. We'd walked down to Chelsea from Columbia. We'd walked and talked and I hadn't felt tired at all.

"You're too innocent," my husband says. He reaches for my hand. "Panna," he cries with pain in his voice, and I am brought back from perfect, floating memories of snow, "I've come to take you back. I have seen how men watch you."

"What?"

"Come back, now. I have tickets. We have all the things we will ever need. I can't live without you."

A little girl with wiry braids kicks a bottle cap at his shoes. The pigeons wheel and scuttle around us. My husband covers his fries with spread-out fingers. "No kicking," he tells the girl. Her name, Beulah, is printed in green ink on a heart-shaped name tag. He forces a smile, and Beulah smiles back. Then she starts to flap her arms. She flaps, she hops. The pigeons go crazy for fries and scraps.

"Special ed. course is two years," I remind him. "I can't go back."

My husband picks up our trays and throws them into the garbage before I can stop him. He's carried disposability a little too far. "We've been taken," he says, moving toward the dock, though the ferry will not arrive for another twenty minutes. "The ferry costs only two dollars round-trip per person. We should have chosen tour number one for $10.95 instead of tour number four for $14.95."

With my Lebanese friend, I think. "But this way we don't have to worry about cabs. The bus will pick us up at the pier and take us back to midtown. Then we can walk home."

"New York is full of cheats and whatnot. Just like Bombay." He is not accusing me of infidelity. I feel dread all the same.

That night, after we've gone to bed, the phone rings. My husband listens, then hands the phone to me. "What is this woman saying?" He turns on the pink Macy's lamp by the bed. "I am not understanding these Negro people's accents."

The operator repeats the message. It's a cable from one of the directors of Lakshmi Cotton Mills. "Massive violent labor confrontation anticipated. Stop. Return posthaste. Stop. Cable flight details. Signed Kantilal Shah."

"It's not your factory," I say. "You're supposed to be on vacation."

"So, you are worrying about me? Yes? You reject my heartfelt wishes but you worry about me?" He pulls me close, slips the straps of my nightdress off my shoulder. "Wait a minute."

I wait, unclothed, for my husband to come back to me. The water is running in the bathroom. In the ten days he has been here he has learned American rites: deodorants, fragrances. Tomorrow morning he'll call Air India; tomorrow evening he'll be on his way back to Bombay. Tonight I should make up to him for my years away, the gutted trucks, the degree I'll never use in India. I want to pretend with him that nothing has changed.

In the mirror that hangs on the bathroom door, I watch my naked body turn, the breasts, the thighs glow. The body's beauty amazes. I stand here shameless, in ways he has never seen me. I am free, afloat, watching somebody else.

TIM O'BRIEN (b. 1946) was born in Minnesota and graduated summa cum laude from Macalester College in St. Paul with a degree in political science. He was drafted into the Army in 1968, although he had contemplated going to either Canada or jail to avoid it. He spent two years as an infantryman in Vietnam and received a Purple Heart. After returning from his tour of duty, he received a Ph.D. in government from Harvard and worked for a time as a sports writer and journalist, but it was his experiences in Vietnam that would shape his career as a fiction writer most significantly.

O'Brien published his **memoir**, *If I Die in a Combat Zone, Box Me Up and Ship Me Home*, in 1973. This was followed in 1978 by his novel *Going After Cacciato*, which won a National Book Award. His other novels include *The Nuclear Age* (1985) and *In the Lake of the Woods* (1994). His book *The Things They Carried* (1990) is a collection of short stories.

O'Brien took to heart Ernest Hemingway's advice in *Men at War* that fiction ought to "produce a truer account than anything factual can be." His fictional **memoirs** of the Vietnam War, such as "Stockings" (1990), do just that as they confront myths of soldierly courage and honor and investigate how an individual weighted down by physical and psychological burdens can attempt to retain his personal integrity and his faith in something while participating in utterly baffling and inherently horrific events.

Related Works: Kincaid, "Girl"; Cofer, "Tales Told Under the Mango Tree"; Erdrich, "The Red Convertible"; Hemingway, "A Clean, Well-Lighted Place"; Reed, "The Naming of Parts"; Rios, "The Vietnam Wall"; Forché, "The Colonel"; Arnold, "Dover Beach."

Stockings

Henry Dobbins was a good man, and a superb soldier, but sophistication was not his strong suit. The ironies went beyond him. In many ways he was like America itself, big and strong, full of good intentions, a roll of fat jiggling at his belly, slow of foot but always plodding along, always there when you needed him, a believer in the virtues of simplicity and directness and hard labor. Like his country, too, Dobbins was drawn toward sentimentality.

Even now, twenty years later, I can see him wrapping his girlfriend's pantyhose around his neck before heading out on ambush.

It was his one eccentricity. The pantyhose, he said, had the properties of a good-luck charm. He liked putting his nose into the nylon and breathing in the scent of his girlfriend's body; he liked the memories this inspired; he sometimes slept with the stockings up against his face, the way an infant sleeps with a flannel blanket, secure and peaceful. More than anything, though, the stockings were a talisman for him. They kept him safe. They gave access to a spiritual world, where things were soft and intimate, a place where he might someday take his girlfriend to live. Like many of us in Vietnam, Dobbins felt the pull of superstition, and he believed firmly and absolutely in the protective power of the stockings. They were like body armor, he thought. Whenever we saddled up for a late-night ambush, putting on our helmets and flak jackets, Henry Dobbins would make a ritual out of arranging the nylons around his neck, carefully tying a knot, draping the two leg sections over his left shoulder. There were some jokes, of course, but we came to appreciate the mystery of it all. Dobbins was invulnerable. Never wounded, never a scratch. In August, he tripped a Bouncing Betty, which failed to detonate. And a week later he got caught in the open during a fierce little firefight, no cover at all, but he just slipped the pantyhose over his nose and breathed deep and let the magic do its work.

It turned us into a platoon of believers. You don't dispute facts.

But then, near the end of October, his girlfriend dumped him. It was a hard blow. Dobbins went quiet for a while, staring down at her letter, then after a time he took out the stockings and tied them around his neck as a comforter.

"No sweat," he said. "The magic doesn't go away."

JUDITH ORTIZ COFER (b. 1952) was born in Puerto Rico, but spent her childhood journeying between her *casa* on that island and an apartment in Paterson, New Jersey, where her family moved after her father, a sailor in the U.S. Navy, was stationed in the Brooklyn shipyard. For more details on Cofer's life, see the head note preceding her poetry.

"Tales Told Under the Mango Tree" (1990) begins with a Puerto Rican grandmother relating the story of the wise trickster María Sabida to the children gathered around her under the giant mango tree. After her grandmother's story is over, the author reflects on the adjustments she and her brother have to make upon returning to the island from the mainland and upon the memories she has of her island relatives. The narrative ends with the author reciting her own, new tale of María Sabida, a signal that she is becoming comfortable with her native heritage and culture.

The protagonist of "Arturo's Flight" (1995) is a young Puerto Rican boy living in the tenements of Paterson, New Jersey. Arturo also recites fiction, but instead of telling a **mythical** tale from his home culture to a gathering of his family members, he is made to recite the seventeenth-century English poet John Donne's poem "The Flea" in front of his literature class at school. Unfortunately for Arturo, "the guys of the barrio" consider reading poetry to be "an unnatural act" and *liking* poetry to be even worse, so Arturo's adventures begin when he trashes Shakespeare's sonnets and tries to escape his current situation.

In the **creative nonfiction** story "More Room" (1990), the narrator remembers her grandmother's house in Puerto Rico, *la casa de Mamá*, the way in which a new room was added by her grandfather after each of her grandparents' children was born, how Mamá's own room served as the "heart of the house," and how, finally, after the birth of eight children, Mamá used physical space to assert control over her body.

Related Works: "Tales Told Under the Mango Tree"; Marquez, "The Handsomest Drowned Man in the World"; O'Brien, "Stockings"; Achebe, "Why the Tortoise's Shell Is Not Smooth"; Silko, "Prayer to the Pacific."

"Arturo's Flight": Ellison, "Battle Royal"; Joyce, "Araby"; Donne, "The Flea"; Shakespeare, *Hamlet*.

"More Room": Rios, "Nani"; Walker, "Everyday Use."

Green mango tree

Tales Told Under the Mango Tree

María Sabida

Once upon a time there lived a girl who was so smart that she was known throughout Puerto Rico as María Sabida. María Sabida came into the world with her eyes open. They say that at the moment of her birth she spoke to the attending midwife and told her what herbs to use to make a special *guarapo*, a tea that would put her mother back on her feet immediately. They say that the two women would have thought the infant was possessed if María Sabida had not convinced them with her descriptions of life in heaven that she was touched by God and not spawned by the Devil.

María Sabida grew up in the days when the King of Spain owned Puerto Rico, but had forgotten to send law and justice to this little island lost on the map of the world. And so thieves and murderers roamed the land terrorizing the poor people. By the time María Sabida was of marriageable age, one such *ladrón* had taken over the district where she lived.

For years people had been subjected to abuse from this evil man and his henchmen. He robbed them of their cattle and then made them buy their own cows back from him. He would take their best chickens and produce when he came into town on Saturday afternoons riding with his men through the stalls set up by farmers. Overturning their tables, he would yell, "Put it on my account." But of course he never paid for anything he took. One year several little children disappeared while walking to the river, and although the townspeople searched and searched, no trace of them was ever found. That is when María Sabida entered the picture. She was fifteen then, and a beautiful girl with the courage of a man, they say.

She watched the chief *ladrón* the next time he rampaged through the pueblo. She saw that he was a young man: red-skinned, and tough as leather. *Cuero y sangre, nada más*, she said to herself, a man of flesh and blood. And so she prepared herself either to conquer or to kill this man.

María Sabida followed the horses' trail deep into the woods. Though she left the town far behind she never felt afraid or lost. María Sabida could read the sun, the moon, and the stars for direction. When she got hungry, she knew which fruits were good to eat, which roots and leaves were poisonous, and how to follow the footprints of animals to a waterhole. At nightfall, María Sabida came to the edge of a clearing where a large house, almost like a fortress, stood in the forest.

"No woman has ever set foot in that house," she thought, "no *casa* is this, but a man-place." It was a house built for violence, with no windows on the ground level, but there were turrets on the roof where men could stand guard with guns. She waited until it was nearly dark and approached the house through the kitchen side. She found it by smell.

In the kitchen which she knew would have to have a door or window for ventilation, she saw an old man stirring a huge pot. Out of the pot stuck little arms and legs. Angered by the sight, María Sabida entered the kitchen, pushed the old man aside, and picking up the pot threw its horrible contents out of the window.

"Witch, witch, what have you done with my master's stew!" yelled the old man. "He will kill us both when he gets home and finds his dinner spoiled."

"Get, you filthy *viejo*." María Sabida grabbed the old man's beard and pulled him to his feet. "Your master will have the best dinner of his life if you follow my instructions."

María Sabida then proceeded to make the most delicious *asopao* the old man had ever tasted, but she would answer no questions about herself, except to say that she was his master's fiancée.

When the meal was done, María Sabida stretched and yawned and said that she would go upstairs and rest until her *prometido* came home. Then she went upstairs and waited.

The men came home and ate ravenously of the food María Sabida had cooked. When the chief *ladrón* had praised the old man for a fine meal, the cook admitted that it had been *la prometida* who had made the tasty chicken stew.

"My what?" the leader roared, "I have no *prometida*." And he and his men ran upstairs. But there were many floors, and by the time they were halfway to the room where María Sabida waited, many of the men had dropped down unconscious and the others had slowed down to a crawl until they too were overcome with irresistible sleepiness. Only the chief *ladrón* made it to where María Sabida awaited him holding a paddle that she had found among his weapons. Fighting to keep his eyes open, he asked her, "Who are you, and why have you poisoned me?"

"I am your future wife, María Sabida, and you are not poisoned, I added a special sleeping powder that tastes like oregano to your *asopao*. You will not die."

"Witch!" yelled the chief *ladrón*, "I will kill you. Don't you know who I am?" And reaching for her, he fell on his knees, whereupon María Sabida beat him with the paddle until he lay curled like a child on the floor. Each time he tried to attack her, she beat him some more. When she was satisfied that he was vanquished, María Sabida left the house and went back to town.

A week later, the chief *ladrón* rode into town with his men again. By then everyone knew what María Sabida had done and they were afraid of what these evil men would do in retribution. "Why did you not just kill him when you had a chance, *muchacha*?" many of the townswomen had asked María Sabida. But she had just answered mysteriously, "It is better to conquer than to kill." The townspeople then barricaded themselves behind closed doors when they heard the pounding of the thieves' horses approaching. But the gang did not stop until they arrived at María Sabida's house. There the men, instead of guns, brought out musical instruments: a *cuatro*, a *güiro*, *maracas*, and a harmonica. Then they played a lovely melody.

"María Sabida, María Sabida, my strong and wise María," called out the leader, sitting tall on his horse under María Sabida's window, "come out and listen to a song I've written for you—I call it *The Ballad of María Sabida*."

María Sabida then appeared on her balcony wearing a wedding dress. The chief *ladrón* sang his song to her: a lively tune about a woman who had the courage of a man and the wisdom of a judge, and who had conquered the heart of the best bandido on the island of Puerto Rico. He had a strong voice and all the people cowering in their locked houses heard his tribute to María Sabida and crossed themselves at the miracle she had wrought.

One by one they all came out and soon María Sabida's front yard was full of people singing and dancing. The *ladrones* had come prepared with casks of wine, bottles of rum, and a wedding cake made by the old cook from the tender meat of coconuts. The leader of the thieves and María Sabida were married on that day.

But all had not yet been settled between them. That evening, as she rode behind him on his horse, she felt the dagger concealed beneath his clothes. She knew then that she had not fully won the battle for this man's heart.

On her wedding night María Sabida suspected that her husband wanted to kill her. After their dinner, which the man had insisted on cooking himself, they went upstairs. María Sabida asked for a little time alone to prepare herself. He said he would take a walk but would return very soon. When she heard him leave the house, María Sabida went down to the kitchen and took several gallons of honey from the pantry. She went back to the bedroom and there she fashioned a life-sized doll out of her clothes and poured the honey into it. She then blew out the candle, covered the figure with a sheet and hid herself under the bed.

After a short time, she heard her husband climbing the stairs. He tip-toed into the dark room thinking her asleep in their marriage bed. Peeking out from under the bed, María Sabida saw the glint of the knife her husband pulled out from inside his shirt. Like a fierce panther he leapt onto the bed and stabbed the doll's body over and over with his dagger. Honey splattered his face and fell on his lips. Shocked, the man jumped off the bed and licked his lips.

"How sweet is my wife's blood. How sweet is María Sabida in death—how sour in life and how sweet in death. If I had known she was so sweet, I would not have murdered her." And so declaring, he kneeled down on the floor beside the bed and prayed to María Sabida's soul for forgiveness.

At that moment María Sabida came out of her hiding place. "Husband, I have tricked you once more, I am not dead." In his joy, the man threw down his knife and embraced María Sabida, swearing that he would never kill or steal again. And he kept his word, becoming in later years an honest farmer. Many years later he was elected mayor of the same town he had once terrorized with his gang of *ladrones*.

María Sabida made a real *casa* out of his thieves' den, and they had many children together, all of whom could speak at birth. But, they say, María Sabida always slept with one eye open, and that is why she lived to be one hundred years old and wiser than any other woman on the Island of Puerto Rico, and her name was known even in Spain.

"Colorín, colorado este cuento se ha acabado." Mamá would slap her knees with open palms and say this little rhyme to indicate to the children sitting around her under the giant mango tree that the story was finished. It was time for us to go play and leave the women alone to embroider in the shade of the tree and to talk about serious things.

I remember that tree as a natural wonder. It was large, with a trunk that took four or five children holding hands to reach across. Its leaves were so thick that the shade it cast made a cool room where we took refuge from the hot sun. When an unexpected shower caught us there, the women had time to gather their embroidery materials before drops came through the leaves. But the most amazing thing about that tree was the throne it had made for Mamá. On the trunk there was a smooth seat-like projection. It was perfect for a storyteller. She would take her place on the throne and lean back. The other women—my mother and her sisters—would bring towels to sit on; the children sat anywhere. Sometimes we would climb to a thick branch we called "the ship," to the right of the throne, and listen there. "The ship" was a thick limb that hung all the way down to the ground. Up to three small children could straddle this branch while the others bounced on the end that sat near the ground making it sway like a ship. When Mamá told her stories, we sat quietly on our crow's nest because if anyone interrupted her narrative she should stop talking and no amount of begging would persuade her to finish the story that day.

The first time my mother took my brother and me back to Puerto Rico, we were stunned by the heat and confused by a houseful of relatives. Mamá's *casa* was filled to capacity with grandchildren, because two of the married daughters had come to stay there until their husbands sent for them: my mother and the two of us and her oldest sister with her five children. Mamá still had three of her own children at home, ranging in age from a teenage daughter to my favorite uncle who was six months older than me.

Our solitary life in New Jersey, where we spent our days inside a small dark apartment watching television and waiting for our father to come home on leave from the navy, had not prepared us for life in Mamá's house or for the multitude of cousins, aunts and uncles pulling us into their loud conversations and rough games. For the first few days my little brother kept his head firmly buried in my mother's neck, while I stayed relatively close to her; but being nearly six, and able to speak as loudly as anyone, I soon joined Mamá's tribe.

In the last few weeks before the beginning of school, when it was too hot for cooking until it was almost dark and when mothers would not even let their boys go to the playgrounds and parks for fear of sunstroke, Mamá would lead us to the mango tree, there to spin the web of her *cuentos* over us, making us forget the heat, the mosquitos, our past in a foreign country, and even the threat of the first day of school looming just ahead.

It was under that mango tree that I first began to feel the power of words. I cannot claim to have always understood the point of the stories I heard there. Some of these tales were based on ancient folklore brought to the colonies by Spaniards from their own versions of even older myths of Greek and Roman origins—which, as I later discovered through my insatiable reading—had been modified in clever ways to fit changing times. María Sabida became the model Mamá used for the "prevailing woman"—the woman who "slept with one eye open"—whose wisdom was gleaned through the senses: from the natural world and from ordinary experiences. Her main virtue was that she was always alert and never a victim. She was by implication contrasted to María La Loca, that poor girl who gave it all up for love, becoming a victim of her own foolish heart.

The mango tree was located at the top of a hill, on land that belonged to "The American," or at least to the sugar refinery that he managed. *La Central*, as it was called, employed the majority of the pueblo's men. Its tall chimney stacks loomed over the town like sentinels, spewing plumes of grey smoke that filled the air during cane season with the syrupy thick aroma of burnt sugar.

In my childhood the sugarcane fields bordered both sides of the main road, which was like a part on a head of spiky, green hair. As we approached the pueblo on our way coming home, I remember how my mother sat up in the back seat of the *carro público*, the taxi, we had taken from the airport in San Juan. Although she was pointing out the bell tower of the famous church of La Monserrate, I was distracted by the hypnotizing motion of men swinging machetes in the fields. They were shirtless, and sweat poured in streams down their backs. Bathed in light reflected by their blades, these laborers moved as on a ballet stage. I wondered whether they practiced like dancers to perfect their synchronicity. It did not occur to me that theirs was "survival choreography"—merely a safety measure—for wild swinging could lead to lost fingers and limbs. Or, as I heard one of the women say once, "there are enough body parts in the cane fields to put one whole man together."

And although trucks were already being used in most *centrales*, in our town, much of the cane harvest was still transported from the fields to the mill in oxen-drawn carts which were piled so high with the stalks, that, when you followed one of them you could see neither the cart driver nor the beasts in front: It was a moving haystack.

To car drivers they were a headache and a menace on the road. A good wind could blow the cane off the top of the cart and smash a windshield. But what most drivers hated was getting stuck behind one that would take up the whole road traveling at five miles per hour and ignore the horn, the mad hand waving and the red-faced man shouting invectives. In later years this vehicle would be almost totally replaced by the open-bed trucks that were also loaded to the limit, traveling the roads of the Island at sixty or seventy miles per hour, granting no other vehicle (except police cars) right-of-way. The driver would keep his hand on the horn and that was all the warning a passenger car received. Pulling over as if for an emergency vehicle was usually the best plan to follow.

We sucked on little pieces of sugar cane Mamá had cut for us under the mango tree. Below us a pasture rolled down to the road and the cane fields could be seen at a distance; the men in their perpetual motion were tiny black ants to our eyes. You looked up to see the red roof of the American's house. It was a big white house with a large porch completely enclosed by mosquito screens (on the Island at that time this was such a rarity that all houses designed in that way were known as "American"). At Mamá's house we slept cozily under mosquito nets, but during the day we fought the stinging, buzzing insects with bare hands and, when we lost a battle, we soothed our scratched raw skin with calamine lotion.

During the first few weeks of our visits both my brother and I, because we were fresh, tender meat, had skin like a pink target, dotted with red spots where the insects had scored bulls-eyes. Amazingly, either we built up a natural resistance, or the mosquitoes gave up, but it happened every time: a period of embarrassment as pink "turistas," followed by brown skin and immunity. Living behind screens, the American couple would never develop the tough skin needed for Island survival.

When Mamá told stories about kings and queens and castles, she would point to the big house on the hill. We were not supposed to go near the place. In fact, we were trespassing when we went to the mango tree. Mamá's backyard ended at the barbed-wire fence that led to the American's pasture. The tree stood just on the other side. She had at some point before my time, placed a strong stick under the barbed wire to make an entrance; but it could only be pulled up so much, so that even the children had to crawl through. Mamá seemed to relish the difficulty of getting to our special place. For us children it was fun to watch our mothers get their hair and clothes caught on the wire and to listen to them curse.

The pasture was a magical realm of treasures and secret places to discover. It even had a forbidden castle we could look at from a distance.

While the women embroidered, my girl-cousins and I would gather leaves and thorns off a lemon tree and do some imaginative stitch work of our own. The boys would be in the "jungle" gathering banana leaves they built tepees with.

Imitating the grownups who were never without a cigarette hanging from their mouths, we would pick the tightly wrapped buds of the hibiscus flowers, which, with their red tips, looked to us like lighted cigarettes. We glued wild flower petals to our fingernails and, although they did not stay on for long, for a little while our hands, busy puncturing the leaves into patterns with lemon tree thorns, looked like our mother's with their red nail polish, pushing needle and thread through white linen, creating improbable landscapes of trailing vines and flowers, decorating the sheets and pillowcases we would sleep on.

We picked ripe guavas in their season and dumped them on Mamá's capacious lap for her to inspect for worms before we ate them. The sweetness of a ripe guava cannot be compared to anything else: its pink, gooey inside can be held on the tongue and savored like a caramel.

During mango season we threw rocks at the branches of our tree, hanging low with fruit. Later in the season, a boy would climb to the highest branches for the best fruit—something I always yearned to do, but was not allowed to: too dangerous.

On days when Mamá felt truly festive she would send us to the store with three dollars for ten bottles of Old Colony pop and the change in assorted candies: Mary Janes, Bazooka gum, lollypops, tiny two-piece boxes of Chicklets, coconut candy wrapped in wax paper, and more—all kept in big glass jars and sold two for one penny. We would have our reckless feast under the mango tree and then listen to a story. Afterwards, we would take turns on the swing that touched the sky.

My grandfather had made a strong swing from a plank of heavy wood and a thick length of rope. Under Mamá's supervision he had hung it from a sturdy lower branch of the mango tree that reached over the swell of the hill. In other words, you boarded the swing on level ground, but since the tree rose out of the summit, one push and you took off for the sky. It was almost like flying. From the highest point I ever reached, I could see the big house, as a bird would see it, to my left; the church tower from above the trees to my right; and far in the distance, below me, my family in a circle under the tree, receding, growing smaller; then, as I came back down to earth, looming larger, my mother's eyes glued to me, reflecting the fear for my safety that she would not voice in her mother's presence and thus risk overriding the other's authority. My mother's greatest fear was that my brother or I would hurt ourselves while at Mamá's, and that she would be held accountable by my excessively protective father when he returned from his tour of duty in Europe. And one day, because fear invites accident, I did fall from a ride up to the clouds.

I had been catapulting myself higher and higher, when out of the corner of my eye I saw my big cousin, Javier, running at top speed after his little brother, swinging a stick in front as if to strike the younger boy. This happened fast. The little boy, Roberto, ran towards Mamá, who at that moment, was leaning towards my mother in conversation. Trying to get to his brother before he reached safe haven, Javier struck, accidentally hitting my mother square on the face. I saw it happening. I saw it as if in slow motion. I saw my mother's broken glasses fly off her face, and the blood begin to flow. Dazed, I let go of the swing ropes and flew down from the clouds and the treetops and onto the soft cushion of pasture grass and just rolled and rolled. Then I lay there stunned, tasting grass and dirt until Mamá's strong arms lifted me up. She carried me through the fence and down to her house where my mother was calling hysterically for me. Her glasses had protected her from serious injury. The bump on her forehead was minor. The nosebleed had already been contained by the age-old method of placing a copper penny on the bridge, between the eyes. Her tears upset me, but not as much as the way she made me stand before her, in front of everyone, while she examined my entire body for bruises, scratches, and broken bones. "What will your father say," she kept repeating, until Mamá pulled me away. "Nothing," she said to my mother, "if you don't tell him." And, leaving her grown daughters to comfort each other, she called the children out to the yard where she had me organize a game of hide-and-seek that she supervised, catching cheaters right and left.

When it rained, the children were made to take naps or play quietly in the bedroom. I asked for Mamá's monumental poster bed, and, when my turn came, I got it. There I lay four or five feet above ground inhaling her particular smells of coconut oil, (which she used to condition her thick black hair) and Palmolive soap. I would luxuriate in her soft pillows and her mattress which was covered with gorgeously embroidered bed linens. I would get sleepy listening to the drone of the women's conversation out of the parlor.

Beyond the double doors of her peacock blue bedroom, I could hear Mamá and her older daughters talking about things that, at my age, would not have interested me: They read letters received from my father traveling with the navy in Europe, or letters from any of the many relatives making their way in the barrios of New York and New Jersey, working in factories and dreaming of returning "in style" to Puerto Rico.

The women would discuss the new school year, and plan a shopping trip to the nearest city, Mayagüez, for materials to make school uniforms for the children, who by September had to be outfitted in brown and white and marched off to the public school looking like Mussolini's troops in our dull uniforms. Their talk would take on more meaning for me as I got older, but that first year back on the Island I was under María Sabida's spell. To entertain myself, I would make up stories about the smartest girl in all of Puerto Rico.

When María Sabida was only six years old, I began, she saved her little brother's life. He was dying of a broken heart, you see, for he desperately wanted some sweet guavas that grew at the top of a steep, rocky hill near the lair of a fierce dragon. No one had ever dared to climb that hill, though everyone could see the huge guava tree and the fruit, as big as pears, hanging from its branches. María Sabida's little brother had stared at the tree until he had made himself sick from yearning for the forbidden fruit.

Everyone knew that the only way to save the boy was to give him one of the guavas. María Sabida's parents were frantic with worry. The little boy was fading fast. The father tried climbing the treacherous hill to the guava tree, but the rocks were loose and for every step forward he took, he slipped back three. He returned home. The mother spent her days cooking delicious meals with which to tempt her little son to eat, but he just turned his sad eyes to the window in his room from where he could see the guava tree loaded with the only food he wanted. The doctor came to examine the boy and pronounced him as good as gone. The priest came and told the women they should start making their black dresses. All hope seemed lost when María Sabida, whose existence everyone seemed to have forgotten, came up with an idea to save her brother one day while she was washing her hair in the special way her grandmother had taught her.

Her mamá had shown her how to collect rainwater—water from the sky—into a barrel, and then, when it was time to wash her hair, how to take a fresh coconut and draw the oil from its white insides. You then took a bowl of clear rainwater and added the coconut oil, using the mixture to rinse your hair. Her mamá had shown her how the rainwater, coming as it did from the sky, had little bits of starshine in it. This starstuff was what made your hair glossy, the oil was to make it stick.

It was while María Sabida was mixing the starshine that she had the brilliant idea which saved her brother. She ran to her father who was in the stable feeding the mule and asked if she could borrow the animal that night. The man, startled by his daughter's wild look (her hair was streaming wet and she still held the coconut scraps in her hands) at first just ordered his daughter into the house, thinking that she had gone crazy with grief over her brother's imminent death. But María Sabida could be stubborn, and she refused to move until her parents heard what she had to say. The man called his wife to the stable, and when María Sabida had finished telling them her plan, he still thought she had lost her mind. He agreed with his desperate wife that at this point anything was worth trying. They let María Sabida have the mule to use that night.

María Sabida then waited until it was pitch black. She knew there would be no moon that night. Then she drew water from her rainbarrel and mixed it with plenty of coconut oil and plastered her mule's hoofs with it. She led the animal to the bottom of the rocky hill where the thick, sweet smell of ripe guavas was irresistible. María Sabida felt herself caught in the spell. Her mouth watered and she felt drawn to the guava tree. The mule must have felt the same thing because it started walking ahead of the girl with quick, sure steps. Though rocks came tumbling down, the animal found footing, and in so doing, left a shiny path with the bits of starshine that María Sabida had glued to its hoofs. María Sabida kept her eyes on the bright trail because it was a dark, dark night.

As she approached the guava tree, the sweet aroma was like a liquid that she drank through her nose. She could see the fruit within arms-reach when the old mule stretched her neck to eat one and a horrible scaly arm reached out and yanked the animal off the path. María Sabida quickly grabbed three guavas and ran down the golden trail all the way back to her house.

When she came into her little brother's room, the women had already gathered around the bed with their flowers and their rosaries, and because María Sabida was a little girl herself and could not see past the crowd, she thought for one terrible minute that she was too late. Luckily, her brother smelled the guavas from just this side of death and he sat up in bed. María Sabida pushed her way through the crowd and gave him one to eat. Within minutes the color returned to his cheeks. Everyone rejoiced remembering other wonderful things that she had done, and why her middle name was "Sabida."

And, yes, María Sabida ate one of the enchanted guavas herself and was never sick a day in her long life. The third guava was made into a jelly that could cure every childhood illness imaginable, from a toothache to the chicken pox.

"Colorín, colorado . . ." I must have said to myself, "Colorín colorado . . ." as I embroidered my own fable, listening all the while to that inner voice which, when I was very young, sounded just like Mamá's when she told her stories in the parlor or under the mango tree. And later, as I gained more confidence in my own ability, the voice telling the story became my own.

JUDITH ORTIZ COFER

Arturo's Flight

Sometimes I just have to get out and walk. It's a real need with me. I guess it's one of the things that make me odd in everyone's opinion. Almost everyone's. My parents worry about me, but they think I'm God's gift. All of them are wrong about me. What I am is impatient. Sometimes I feel trapped, trapped in a school that's like an insane asylum, a trapped rat in this city that's a maze—no matter how long and how far you walk, you always end up in the same place, at least it all looks the same: old apartment buildings with too many people squeezed in, bars with sad-looking people staring into their cups, and stores so bright with lights that they hurt my eyes.

The only place that doesn't give me a headache is that old church my mother still goes to, where I made my first communion: St. Joseph's. An old guy that I know cleans it at night, and he lets me in. At that hour there is only the red security light on, and the candles that the people at the evening service have lit. Johann, the old guy, says that they have to be left alone. They can't be blown out because they're prayers and requests people have made. He acts like he's the keeper of the Olympic torch or something. But I understand what he means. It would be wrong to blow out a candle someone lit for a special reason—like stealing a wish.

I met Johann one night when he found me sitting on the steps outside. I had decided to leave Paterson, and I was making my plans. I think I frightened him with my punk look. That was during my purple hair and leather period. It was a way of making a statement to the people at school. But it backfired and really hurt my mother and the old man. Anyway, that night I was sitting on those steps looking pretty scary, I guess, with my purple spiked hair, black leather jacket, and all. I guess I was looking kind of miserable too because there was this old guy just standing there looking at me with, you know, that good-Samaritan expression on his face. We both stared at each other for a good long time. I was considering taking off when he spoke in a thick accent, in a strange old-fashioned way: "Young man, are you seeking asylum?" It made me smile. That was a line right out of a movie. "No, man, I'm not looking for an asylum, but I know where one is if you need one." I felt like ribbing the old guy a little. But he didn't seem to get my joke.

"Are you hungry?" he asked, lowering his wrinkled old face to look at me. He was wearing glasses so thick that his eyeballs looked like two blue fish swimming in a bowl.

"I'm not hungry, just cold." Then I noticed I really *was* cold. Freezing, in fact. I had been walking the streets for a couple of hours by then. The old man extended his hand to me. I shook it, and it felt like a dry leaf. "My name is Johann. I am the caretaker of the church." He took some heavy-looking keys out of his coat pocket and unlocked the huge wooden front door of the church. "Please follow me," he said, sounding just like a butler in an old black-and-white horror movie. "Walk this way," I said like Igor in the Frankenstein movie, dragging my left foot. I was still trying to be funny. But he didn't seem to get it.

"Are you in pain?" he asked, looking into my eyes again. This time I didn't answer him because the question made me think. Was I?

The church at night is like no other place I've been in. As I followed old Johann, I felt like I was in a dream. It all had a misty quality to it. Like that book we read in English, *Jane Eyre*, or something, where you imagine everything takes place on a foggy night in a spooky old house.

The old man showed me to a pew in the front.

"You may rest here," he said, patting my back as I slid in, for God's sake. The guy was a relic. "Do you need anything?" I shook my head. How the hell was I supposed to tell this guy what I needed? So I sat there and decided I was just going to act like this was the movies or a theater and this old guy was going to put on a play or something for me. Hell, I didn't have anything better to do. I wasn't going to go home. I had one hundred and nineteen dollars and eighty-four cents in my wallet, money I made carrying grocery bags for the old women of El Building, my place of residence, choice tenement for the PRs of Paterson, until my outstanding hair and black leather jacket got to them, that is. The worst one, Doña Monina, ambushed Clara, my mother, after Spanish mass right here in St. Joe's, and told her that I looked like *un bum*. Don Manuel asked me to dress better for work, and no purple spiked hair. But I was in no mood to take orders from anybody at the time. That night I told my mother about getting fired, and the look she gave me made me want to scream. She looked betrayed, for God's sake. Am I an angel or am I Judas? Somebody ought to tell me. My father's got a bad heart, and that worries me a little. I mean, he's been getting so upset lately that the next thing that's going to happen is that he'll drop dead and then I'll be a murderer. Patricide, that's what my English teacher called it when we read about that old Greek guy who killed his old man and married his mother. Very nice. Some kind of example we get in school.

Right about then I started to worry about being locked up in an empty church with the old guy. He'd been gone a long time. The old midnight madness was taking over my mind. I thought maybe I'd get hacked to death and nobody would know it until the *viejas* from El Building dragged in for the 6:00 A.M. mass and found my corpse in the aisle. You never know these days. An ax murderer can look like a nice batty old guy with an accent. Need asylum? Come into my lair, young man, let me feel your purple spiky hair. I can make anything rhyme in two languages.

I have to admit, I'm good at this poetry biz. Not a talent that'll get you very far in the barrio. I've always done real good in English class. The grammar bores me, but the lit-te-ra-turrr, like Miss Rathbone says it, is easy. I can get into those stories.

But it was a poem that started the mess. It was when Rathbone asked me, no, *ordered* me in her marine-drill-sergeant voice, to recite, not just say, but *recite*, a part of John Donne's poem "The Flea." Jesus, I could feel myself burning up. I sweated right through my jeans and flannel shirt. I tried to fake not knowing it, but she knew I did because I had been stupid enough to tell her, *I had thought*, in confidence, after she had told us to find a poem in our book that we could *relate to*. Man, she's like in a time warp. Relate to. Who says that anymore? So I had flipped through the book and opened it to any page, and there it was, "The Flea." Considering the other titles in the index, like "Intimations of Immortality," and "An Essay on Man," this one sounded like something I could "relate to." And it was so weird. This guy, who was a priest or something, writes to his girlfriend to say that he wishes—this is good—that the same flea that bit him and sucked his blood would bite her! I mean, that's kind of sick. But he rhymes it so it sounds like a poem. Still, as Miss Wrathbone would say, "I do not expect that the young lady would relate to this particular declaration of love."

Like I said, I liked the screwy poem. And I stay after class to show off a little: "Mark but this flea," say I in my best imitation English-snob accent, "and mark in this, How little that which thou deniest me is; Me it sucked first, and now sucks thee. And in this flea, our two bloods mingled be." Sick. Old John Donne was a pervert. But if he could make it sound good, maybe he still got the girl. Anyway, I thought that Rathbone liked me. I mean she puts *Good! You have a gift!* and crap like that all over my essay papers. So I thought I'd give her a thrill by memorizing a couple of lines from the poem. And what does the Miss Brutus-You-Too do? She announces it to the whole class the next day. "Arthur, as in King Arthur," she says, for God's sake, "has a surprise for us today." If I didn't wet my pants then, I never will. I mean, I know I had a minor stroke or something. I felt the blood crashing against my eyeballs. Behind me Kenny Matoa said, "King Arthur will now rethite for uth." I knew my life was over then. See, for the guys of the barrio, reading poetry is like an unnatural act. *Liking* poetry makes you suspicious as to your sexual preference. Unless you're a girl. It's so stupid I can't even explain it to myself. It's just words. Poetry is like the words of a song, and these guys would kill to write songs and be rock stars.

Two weeks later it was still hell for me on my street. Someone had spray-painted, "The Flea" on my locker, and that's what they called me. "Suck my blood," signed "The Flea," was scrawled on my notebook when I came back from the bathroom one day. Kenny, a guy I've known and hated since third grade, was leading the campaign against me. Most of the people in my school are also my neighbors in El Building or the barrio, so there was no escaping it. And I admit I didn't know how to fight it. Then last weekend I went crazy and dyed my hair purple. I just wanted everyone to call me something else. Crazy, maybe. But I wanted to shock them into seeing me a different way.

All that happened was that my mother, Clara, screamed when she saw me. And my father took one of his pills and told me that we had to talk. I got fired at the bodega. They started calling me "the *Purple* Flea" at school. I finally made my decision to get out of town for good when Clara looked like she was ready to have a serious talk: a fate worse than death. I walked in. She said, "You gotta grow up, *hijo*." And before she could start another sentence, I went into my room and dragged my book where I kept my money out from under my bed. Shakespeare's sonnets. I took the bills out and threw Willy's poems into the Dumpster down on the street. I can hit it from my window. Very convenient, except at 5:00 A.M. when the truck comes, sounding like a herd of stampeding elephants.

Then I started out for the Greyhound bus station. Destination unknown. I walked for a while, then sat down to rest on the church steps for *un minuto*.

That's when St. Johann of the Broom invited me into his asylum, where he kept me waiting half the night. I didn't know what I was waiting for. I heard him dragging things around in the sacristy. I considered giving him a hand. I changed my mind, since I was thinking about some things. It was like the place made you want to do that. I remembered something important. The next day Kenny was getting to *recite* from Shakespeare. Turns out everybody had to do it. When Miss R. surprises herself with a new idea, she goes nuts. Anyway, since Kenny couldn't find a poem that he could "relate to," Miss R. had chosen one for him, Shakespeare's sonnet number CXII. She had written it on the chalkboard. Is that a hundred and twelve?

I learned those Roman numerals in elementary school and haven't had much use for them since then. I had started to wonder in an obsessive way what the poem was about. But Shakespeare was in the Dumpster, and it was midnight already.

Finally old Johann came in dragging his pail, mop, and broom. I had started walking out, since I figured he had lost his marbles in the back and was trying to find them. I stopped to look around one last time. At that spooky hour, with the candles moving everything around on the walls and the ceiling, the nave looked like the inside of a ship. The names of everything came back to me from catechism class: sacristy, sanctuary, altar, holy of holies, and all that. Clara had walked me here every Saturday afternoon for one year when I was six years old to take first-communion lessons. Then, when I was twelve, I was "confirmed" in the church. That's when the bishop slaps your face (a little tap with his soft hand is all it is) to test your faith. Then you're a real Catholic, whatever that means. I stopped coming to mass with my parents when I started high school this year. I was having doubts of all kinds by then, not just about religion, but about everything. Including myself. Like why was I so different from Matoa, Garcia, Correa, and the other guys? I didn't like to hang with them anymore. I was bored by their stupid talk about gangs, girls, drinking, and stuff. And—this really worried me—I was actually enjoying some of my classes at school.

The old guy came toward me with the mop over one shoulder. He was bent at the spine from an old war injury, he later told me. But that night I thought he was daring me to see him as Jesus Christ. I looked down at his shadow and my hair stood on end. I sat down in the hard pew, letting my frozen hands and feet come back to life, and watched him mop the wooden floor so slowly it drove me crazy. I wanted to take that mop from his shaky old hands and just do it myself. But he seemed happy to be doing it. In a sort of trance. I was getting dizzy myself watching him move down the middle aisle, genuflect at the altar, pull himself up with the mop handle like it was one of those shepherd's staffs you see in Nativity scenes, then go up the sides of the church, moving his lips at every station of the cross, praying maybe. I considered the fact that I might be sitting in an empty church with a crazy man who might hit me over the head with his mop and leave me there to bleed to death in the very clean house of God.

But what happened was that when I sat back down, I started to relax in that church like I hadn't anywhere since I was a little kid. I breathed better. The way the air smelled like incense and candles cleared my head, and the old wood and leather all around made me feel kind of safe, like in a library. And the shape of the place gave me a weightless sensation; it was a cave with plenty of room to move around and breathe. Or maybe I was just spacing out.

After a while I fell into a sort of dream where I could make myself float up to the ceiling and say hello to God up there. His face changed as I stared at it. It looked like old Johann at first, then like my father, then like Miss Rathbone (that surprised me a lot), and even like Kenny Matoa. I shook myself out of it and tried to get back to earth.

I was dozing off when I heard the old guy sort of creak and crack into the pew next to me. Everything smelled good, like lemon or pine or something. It was really late, but I could tell old Johann had things on his mind. I waited awhile, trying to stay awake. I mean, by that time I was wiped out. I asked him why he worked these late hours, being old and all; he should be in bed. Besides, the streets of Paterson aren't safe even at noon! He said he liked being alone, and that's why he cleaned the church late at night.

I started to feel funny after a while because he just sat there with a patient, sort of saintly look on his face, waiting for me to say something, I guessed.

"Johann, when did you come to Paterson?" I said, trying to sound like Johnny Carson interviewing a guest. I mean, we had to get this over with, right?

He folded his hands on his lap and stared at the candles still burning in front of the cross where Jesus hung, then he started talking. In the empty, quiet church, his low voice with its thick accent sounded like it came from far away. I stared at the candles too, making them be a sort of movie screen where I tried to picture what Johann was saying. It was like he had been waiting for me to show up at St. Joe's so he could tell me this story.

He said that he had once lived on a farm in Germany with his wife and his son. Then Hitler took over. For several years they suffered many hardships (he used these words like he had looked them up in a dictionary). But the real problems had begun when troops had come through the village, forcing—conscripting he called it—young men to fight. His son had been made to go with them at gunpoint. When he and his wife had protested, Johann had been beaten with the butt of a gun. That—he smiled in a weird way when he said this—was the "war injury" that had left him minus a couple of ribs and permanently in pain. Though he and his wife survived the war, they had never heard how their son had died, only that he was dead. In the last days of the war, nobody had bothered to keep records. He and his wife had applied for visas in the early fifties and had finally been allowed to come to America during President Kennedy's time in the sixties. His wife's heart had failed during bypass surgery three years ago. He had been alone since then.

"Why Paterson?" I was really curious about how Johann had come to be in this city, of all places in the United States.

"The Church. The Catholic Church sometimes sponsors people. This parish of St. Joseph's used to be mainly Polish, Irish, and German immigrants. Now it has many Puerto Ricans too. I was given a job here."

"You live around here?" Suddenly I wanted to know everything about Johann. His story was sort of like the tragedies we read in class. No happy ending like the ones in grammar school. No good fairy godmothers bringing the lost boy back to his parents. This was more like the ones where somebody pulls their eyes out of their heads because things are so bad they might as well get even worse so they can get better. Old Johann told me he had a room in a private house on Market Street. He also said that Father Capanella had already told him that the Church was making plans to retire him. That meant that he would be going to a Catholic retirement home away from Paterson.

"Do you want to do that?" I couldn't believe how he seemed to just accept the Church's "retiring him." Putting him out to pasture was more like it.

"It does not matter where I go, Arturo. I can always find peace in myself."

"You mean God? Religion?" I was listening very carefully to Johann, but I didn't intend to sit through a sermon. I had made my own decision about religion.

"No, my boy. Not religion in the way most people speak of it. I am religious. I go to mass, I say my prayers. But peace does not come from doing these things. For me, it meant finding my place in this world. My God is in my thoughts, and when I am alone and thinking, I am conversing with Him."

We sat there together for a while longer. Then I left him to watch his candles and went home. I was in no mood anymore to run away. Old Johann's story had made me feel like a crybaby for thinking my troubles were that bad. I don't ever want to be as alone as he is, with only his thoughts for company. That doesn't mean I won't get on that bus another time. But I had something to do first. It was almost three. I still had time to rescue Willy's poems from the jaws of the dump truck. I just had to know what Kenny Matoa was going to have to *recite* in front of our class that day.

So I did what I had to do.

I climbed up on the green monster that smelled of the garbage of humanity, of vomit, rotting meat, the urine of bums who slept in the alley, of everything that people use and abuse and then throw out. I balanced my foot on one of the handles the truck hooks onto and I reached for the top. I pulled myself halfway into the pit of hell and nearly ralphed. Man, ten thousand outhouses could not compete with that stink. But I saw the book right away. It was on top of a ton of trash; nobody had thrown a dead cat on it, or last night's *arroz con pollo*. It took me a couple of minutes to fish it out, but I got it, right before I started to sort of pass out from the stench and all.

I may never tell anyone except old Johann, who can listen to a weird tale if he can tell one, what I felt like leaning on a Dumpster like a strung-out junkie or worse, holding a book of Shakespeare's sonnets to my chest. For God's sake, I must be "The Flea." I must be old Donne's bloodsucking Purple Flea to be climbing a Dumpster at three o'clock in the morning for a stupid book. I could have started bawling like a baby right then, except I remembered why I had gone though all that trouble. The book was a little on the tacky side, so I had to kind of peel the pages apart. Under the lamppost I finally got to CXII. I had to sound out the words, since William wrote in very weird English. "Your love and pity doth the impression fill . . ." I didn't get that, but with Shakespeare you gotta give it a little time before it starts making sense. "Which vulgar scandal stamp'd upon my brow; For what care I who calls me well or ill, So you o'er-green my bad, my good allow?" I decided to give him two more lines to get his message across, or back into the mouth of hell it would doth be tossed. I said the lines out loud; sometimes that helps. "You are my all-the-world, and I must strive," I yelled in the direction of my window two floors up. I saw a light come on. "To know my shames and praises from your tongue . . ."

Right then I saw in my mind Kenny saying these lines and the whole class staring at him. *He* wouldn't have a clue what the poem meant, but I knew what the message was for me: whose opinion did I really care about anyway? *And* I'd get to hear Kenny recite a poem *for me*, even if he didn't know it. Mrs. R. had done it. Revenge, Shakespearian-style. Anon, anon, and all that.

Clara had come to the window and saw me down there orating Shakespeare by the Dumpster.

"Arturo, hijo. Is that you?" There is no better tragic hero than a Puerto Rican mother, I swear. She put so much pain into those few words. Ay, bendito! I was in a sorry state by then, and almost anything would have made me cry. That's what staying up all night listening to sad stories does to you.

"Do you know what time it is?" It was the witch Doña Monina sticking her scrawny neck out of her apartment window on four.

"*¿Saben qué hora es?*" was what she really said.

I yelled back, "*Son las tres, son las tres.*" Because it rhymed with what she had said. Even when I'm not trying, I'm good at this, I can't help myself.

"Arturo, please come in. It's cold." Clara opened her arms out to me as if I could spread my *angelito* wings and fly up to her, for God's sake.

But she was right. I needed to go in. I had never been so cold in all my life. I heard the rumble of the dump truck going down another street, crunching up the garbage of humanity and swallowing it. Soon it would come down my street. Before going home to take the longest shower of my life, I wiped a greasy stain off the cover of my book and put it in the inside pocket of my leather jacket. I thought maybe old Johann might like to borrow it. But first I was going to read along with Kenny Matoa, moving my lips silently right along when he *recited* CXII that day. "For what care I who calls me well or ill." Really. This was going to be good.

JUDITH ORTIZ COFER

More Room

My grandmother's house is like a chambered nautilus; it has many rooms, yet it is not a mansion. Its proportions are small and its design simple. It is a house that has grown organically, according to the needs of its inhabitants. To all of us in the family it is known as *la casa de Mamá*. It is the place of our origin; the stage for our memories and dreams of Island life.

I remember how in my childhood it sat on stilts; this was before it had a downstairs. It rested on its perch like a great blue bird, not a flying sort of bird, more like a nesting hen, but with spread wings. Grandfather had built it soon after their marriage. He was a painter and housebuilder by trade, a poet and meditative man by nature. As each of their eight children were born, new rooms were added. After a few years, the paint did not exactly match, nor the materials, so that there was a chronology to it, like the rings of a tree, and Mamá could tell you the history of each room in her *casa*, and thus the genealogy of the family along with it.

Her room is the heart of the house. Though I have seen it recently, and both woman and room have diminished in size, changed by the new perspective of my eyes, now capable of looking over countertops and tall beds, it is not this picture I carry in my memory of Mamá's *casa*. Instead, I see her room as a queen's chamber where a small woman loomed large, a throne-room with a massive four-poster bed in its center which stood taller than a child's head. It was on this bed where her own children had been born that the smallest grandchildren were allowed to take naps in the afternoons; here too was where Mamá secluded herself to dispense private advice to her daughters, sitting on the edge of the bed, looking down at whoever sat on the rocker where generations of babies had been sung to sleep. To me she looked like a wise empress right out of the fairy tales I was addicted to reading.

Though the room was dominated by the mahogany four-poster, it also contained all of Mamá's symbols of power. On her dresser instead of cosmetics there were jars filled with herbs: *yerba buena, yerba mala,* the making of purgatives and teas to which we were all subjected during childhood crises. She had a steaming cup for anyone who could not, or would not, get up to face life on any given day.

If the acrid aftertaste of her cures for malingering did not get you out of bed, then it was time to call *el doctor*.

And there was the monstrous chifforobe she kept locked with a little golden key she did not hide. This was a test of her dominion over us; though my cousins and I wanted a look inside that massive wardrobe more than anything, we never reached for that little key lying on top of her Bible on the dresser. This was also where she placed her earrings and rosary at night. God's word was her security system. This chifforobe was the place where I imagined she kept jewels, satin slippers, and elegant sequined, silk gowns of heartbreaking fineness. I lusted after those imaginary costumes. I had heard that Mamá had been a great beauty in her youth, and the belle of many balls. My cousins had other ideas as to what she kept in that wooden vault: its secret could be money (Mamá did not hand cash to strangers, banks were out of the question, so there were stories that her mattress was stuffed with dollar bills, and that she buried coins in jars in her garden under rosebushes, or kept them in her inviolate chifforobe); there might be that legendary gun salvaged from the Spanish-American conflict over the Island. We went wild over suspected treasures that we made up simply because children have to fill locked trunks with something wonderful.

On the wall above the bed hung a heavy silver crucifix. Christ's agonized head hung directly over Mamá's pillow. I avoided looking at this weapon suspended over where her head would lay; and on the rare occasions when I was allowed to sleep on that bed, I scooted down to the safe middle of the mattress, where her body's impression took me in like a mother's lap. Having taken care of the obligatory religious decoration with a crucifix, Mamá covered the other walls with objects sent to her over the years by her children in the States. *Los Nueva Yores* were represented by, among other things, a postcard of Niagara Falls from her son Hernán, postmarked, Buffalo, N.Y. In a conspicuous gold frame hung a large color photograph of her daughter Nena, her husband and their five children at the entrance to Disneyland in California. From us she had gotten a black lace fan. Father had brought it to her from a tour of duty with the Navy in Europe (on Sundays she would remove it from its hook on the wall to fan herself at mass). Each year more items were added as the family grew and dispersed, and every object in the room had a story attached to it, a *cuento* which Mamá would bestow on anyone who received the privilege of a day alone with her. It was almost worth pretending to be sick, though the bitter herb purgatives of the body were a big price to pay for the spirit revivals of her story-telling.

Mamá slept alone on her large bed, except for the times when a sick grandchild warranted the privilege, or when a heartbroken daughter came home in need of more than herbal teas. In the family there is a story about how this came to be.

When one of the daughters, my mother or one of her sisters, tells the *cuento* of how Mamá came to own her nights, it is usually preceded by the qualifications that Papá's exile from his wife's room was not a result of animosity between the couple, but that the act had been Mamá's famous bloodless coup for her personal freedom. Papá was the benevolent dictator of her body and her life who had had to be banished from her bed so that Mamá could better serve her family. Before the telling, we had to agree that the old man was not to blame. We all recognized that in the family Papá was as an *alma de Dios*, a saintly, soft-spoken presence whose main pleasures in life, such as writing poetry and reading the

Spanish large-type editions of *Reader's Digest*, always took place outside the vortex of Mamá's crowded realm. It was not his fault, after all, that every year or so he planted a baby-seed in Mamá's fertile body, keeping her from leading the active life she needed and desired. He loved her and the babies. Papá composed odes and lyrics to celebrate births and anniversaries and hired musicians to accompany him in singing them to his family and friends at extravagant pig-roasts he threw yearly. Mamá and the oldest girls worked for days preparing the food. Papá sat for hours in his painter's shed, also his study and library, composing the songs. At these celebrations he was also known to give long speeches in praise of God, his fecund wife, and his beloved island. As a middle child, my mother remembers these occasions as a time when the women sat in the kitchen and lamented their burdens, while the men feasted out in the patio, their rum-thickened voices rising in song and praise for each other, *compañeros* all.

It was after the birth of her eighth child, after she had lost three at birth or in infancy, that Mamá made her decision. They say that Mamá had had a special way of letting her husband know that they were expecting, one that had begun when, at the beginning of their marriage, he had built her a house too confining for her taste. So, when she discovered her first pregnancy, she supposedly drew plans for another room, which he dutifully executed. Every time a child was due, she would demand, *more space, more space*. Papá acceded to her wishes, child after child, since he had learned early that Mamá's renowned temper was a thing that grew like a monster along with a new belly. In this way Mamá got the house that she wanted, but with each child she lost in heart and energy. She had knowledge of her body and perceived that if she had any more children, her dreams and her plans would have to be permanently forgotten, because she would be a chronically ill woman, like Flora with her twelve children: asthma, no teeth, in bed more than on her feet.

And so, after my youngest uncle was born, she asked Papá to build a large room at the back of the house. He did so in joyful anticipation. Mamá had asked him special things this time: shelves on the walls, a private entrance. He thought that she meant this room to be a nursery where several children could sleep. He thought it was a wonderful idea. He painted it his favorite color, sky blue, and made large windows looking out over a green hill and the church spires beyond. But nothing happened. Mamá's belly did not grow, yet she seemed in a frenzy of activity over the house. Finally, an anxious Papá approached his wife to tell her that the new room was finished and ready to be occupied. And Mamá, they say, replied: "Good, it's for *you*."

And so it was that Mamá discovered the only means of birth control available to a Catholic woman of her time: sacrifice. She gave up the comfort of Papá's sexual love for something she deemed greater: the right to own and control her body, so that she might live to meet her grandchildren—me among them—so that she could give more of herself to the ones already there, so that she could be more than a channel for other lives, so that even now that time has robbed her of the elasticity of her body and of her amazing reservoir of energy, she still emanates the kind of joy that can only be achieved by living according to the dictates of one's own heart.

TRUDY LEWIS (b. 1961). Although sometimes anthologized as a Southern writer, Lewis was born in Oklahoma, raised in Nebraska, and earned her bachelor's degree at the University of Tulsa and her Ph.D. from the University of Illinois at Chicago; therefore, she categorizes herself as a Midwesterner. She does have ties to the South, however; she received her M.A. at Vanderbilt and her M.F.A. at the University of North Carolina at Greensboro, and she currently resides in Missouri.

Lewis's novel *Private Correspondence* won the William Goyen Prize for Fiction in 1994, and several of her short stories have been listed on the Distinguished List of Best American Short Stories, including "Vincristine" (1986) and "Half Measures" (1987). Her collection of stories, *The Bones of Garbo*, was published in 2003.

Lewis is a **feminist** writer who was influenced by a father who was active in politics; Lewis's fiction often focuses on rural, working-class characters and women who might not otherwise have their voices heard.

"Limestone Diner" (2003) was selected for the collection *Best American Short Stories 2004*. A tribute to Alice Munro's short story "Circle of Prayer," "Limestone Diner" tells the tale of a grandmother who tries to piece together and reconcile the events of a tragedy in her own past as she investigates the scattered remains of a devastating accident in the present.

Related Works: Chekhov, "Vanka"; Erdrich, "The Red Convertible"; Faulkner, "A Rose for Emily."

Limestone Diner

From Meridian

The morning after her granddaughter's frantic phone call, Lorraine skipped her usual coffee session at the Limestone Diner and drove out to the accident scene instead. Of course, no one had bothered to clean up yet; there were mysterious pieces from deep in the engine scattered all over the road and the green field nearby was covered with smashed yellow cupcakes. Lorraine, still agile at sixty-eight, set her travel mug on a fence post, lifted the barbed wire, and climbed on through. The field belonged to the Graysons, she supposed. They still grazed a few cattle, despite the fact that their income came almost exclusively from the axle factory two towns over. Here and there, a cupcake had survived whole, its yellow face still decorated with two black eyes and a thin slice of smile. How did it happen? She remembered the wildflowers that seemed to blossom in her mama's lawn all in the same day, remembered Sharee tumbling out of the car in that checked blue playsuit, the one Lorraine had cut and wrangled out of a scrap of white-sale bedsheet. Sharee must've been seven at the time, her cheeks spotted with excitement, one of her long red-brown curls caught in a button and stretched out nearly straight, as she declared that Easter had come early this year, there was candy poking out all over the yard. How did some fail and some survive and how did He pick and choose between them?

Lorraine located a likely stick and scraped off a stray streak of frosting that had stuck to her shoe. It was suspiciously spreadable—probably the cheap kind made with shortening instead of real butter, if she knew Kris's mom. She pictured the wiry bleached-blond pot smoker working late in the cramped kitchen of her trailer frosting cupcakes for the Lady Rangers' bake sale, then sending poor Kris out at the last minute like that to drop them off at the high school while the gym door was still unlocked for the track team.

And just as others had blamed her, she blamed the mother—who else was there to blame? In the twenty-nine years since Sharee's accident, Lorraine had tried every other possible angle. She blamed her husband for teaching the girl to drive before she was fifteen. She blamed her remaining children—Sally and Trev—for their good health and sound instincts. She blamed her sister's girl for naming her baby daughter after Sharee before a proper generation had passed, thereby stirring up bad luck for Lorraine's youngest. She blamed the WPA workers who had built the road, the French trappers and traders who had settled the county, the glaciers that had formed the ridge. She got as far back as God, and then she blamed the Rock of Ages too—a dirty old man with clay-stained fingers and halitosis, who didn't let anyone know the breath of life stank like rotted egg salad at the end of a late summer family reunion in the sun.

Still, in the end, it was always the mother who paid. Lorraine squatted down for a closer look and felt the arthritis pinch her knee, as if death was feeling her up in preparation for his next big move. Ha, she told him, you'll have to do better than that. The earth was still damp from this weekend's rain. She dug idly with her stick until she came to the place where the clay gave back its resistance and the smell of iron clogged her nose, then thought of Kris pawing the ground, Kris winding up for a fast ball, Kris raising the dust. The girl was only the relief pitcher, but that was due to inconsistency and a moody temperament. As far as talent went, she could outpitch Daisy Wycliff on three days out of four. On the fourth, however, Kris would shout obscenities at the ref, jam her finger, walk two batters in a row, then sit down on the bench and argue with her spinster coach while inking up the bottom of her shoe, as the other girls, Lorraine's granddaughter Reenie among them, floundered out on the field without her. It was Kris who had gotten them to the Kansas City tournament in the first place, and now she wouldn't be there to pitch them through. Lorraine picked up a cupcake and brought it up to her face, tasted the icing to confirm her suspicions, then buried it in the hole she'd made, sugar still burning on her gums.

Over the rise of the hill, through the white-hot glare of the early morning sun, she saw a woman coming toward her. Old woman, she thought, by the drab loose clothes and the sorrowful walk, or rather a woman just coming into the suspicion of her old age. Lorraine stood up and shaded her eyes, the glare parted, and she saw her daughter Sally, a wry silver blonde sliding toward fifty, in the gray-green work shirt and cargo pants she wore for her job at the State Park Service. Her face still pretty but dry and rough; the wrinkles clawed in next to the eyes and over the forehead like she'd gotten careless with a feral cat. Every time Lorraine saw those marks, she wanted to lift her hand and wipe them away, as she had wiped away the pudding and jam, the dirt and the gravy, for the first ten years of Sally's life.

Sally glanced down at the cupcakes on the ground, then looked at Lorraine with a tentative squint. "Trev called me this morning. He said it was probably over as soon as she hit the ground. They excused the teammates from school, you know, so poor little Reenie's home just sitting in her room and playing that awful music over and over."

"That girl was something else. She had the whole crew blasting them Donnas, when all they ever wanted before was their Shania Twains and their Britney Spears."

"Well, all I'm saying is, they could probably use you over there."

"Let an old woman have her meditation, sister."

Sally's lip pinched inward: Lorraine could always tell when the girl's patience was coming to an end by the way she bit at one corner of her lip until she'd practically sucked the whole side of her face in. Giving rise to even more wrinkles, no doubt. "Really, Ma, why'd I know that you'd be out here? Can't you ever let anything alone? You're like some horrible old turkey hawk. People see you coming, they know some kind of destruction's up and roaming the land."

"Now, don't go having a hot flash on me. I told you, I'm contemplating. I'll get moving here in a St. Louis minute."

How would Sally know? She'd never had kids of her own, and now it was too late. She'd taken up with one fellow after another, finally settled in with a widower who ran the concession up at the Park. The two of them seemed to get along, grew a garden that kept the whole family in squash and tomatoes, ran their matching chocolate Labs through the woods, threw big bonfire parties whenever there was a controlled burn in the forest. To tell the truth, Trev, with his three kids, his furniture dealership, and his twenty-five-year marriage, didn't seem half as happy. But Lorraine could never get used to the fact that Sally had just meandered along from bud to seed without ever coming into a satisfying bloom.

She had to admit that it was a comfort to have someone look up on her, though, to call every evening in the quiet spell between the jays and the whip-poorwills, to help with the lawn work now that Earl had lost interest, to go out to the movies and the mall. Would Sharee have done the same if she'd lived? Sharee with that fine brown woman-down on her calves since before she even started school, the long bony nose with the diamond-cut nostrils that made her seem constantly mad about something, the strawberry-rhubarb smell of sharp sweat on a sweet temperament, the thrill the girl took in packing a suitcase or a picnic, the embroidered denim jacket with its clumsy knots of red and blue and yellow silk hanging out the other side.

Not knowing, Lorraine gave up, speared another cupcake, and let Sally lead her back to the car.

Sharee lives in Kansas City now, far enough from home that her relatives don't include her in their Sunday plans, close enough that she can drive back for the holidays on a single tank of gas and a large thermos of overly sweetened coffee. She is connected to the sticky web of her extended family only by her inherited name and her mother's viscous commentary over the phone line: Cousin Amy got divorced from that drunken auto repairman, Aunt Erma finally quit her job at the Limestone Diner at seventy-three, Cel got him another HUD house and toted it back to the farm on a trailer, Paul Dee knocked up his junior high girlfriend and had to drop out of school to get married and start in full-time at Nolan's Filling and Towing, Aunt Lorraine has pretty much taken over as den mother and mascot of her granddaughter's softball team. As much as she loves her mom, a modernized woman who wears sweater sets half buttoned over her plump plummy breasts, gets Dad to cook burgers or pork chops on his own one night a week, reads mysteries with snappy female detectives and has a euphemistic word for everyone. Sharee wants nothing to do with that backward lot of hillbillies. When she graduated high school, she insisted on going out of state to KU for college, even though it meant taking out extra loans for tuition and working twenty hours a week in a local T-shirt shop. Lawrence, with its import stores and microbreweries, its hordes of unattached singles, amazed her; here, she could finally become herself, separate from the rest of the family and their soap opera plots.

Something about crossing that state line changed Sharee. In Missouri, she couldn't see anything for the caves and creeks and sinkholes, the limestone cliffs, the broken-backed Ozarks, the vine-covered trees, and the clapboard billboards by the highway advertising fetal life and walnut bowls. In Kansas, the horizon is straight like the edge of a place mat; the sky comes at you honestly, every streak of pink visible as the lines in your palm. This plainness Sharee finds appealing because it mirrors Sharee herself; the straight whole-wheat hair, the long nose, the pale unmarked body with its modest round breasts and solid hips. She bought a dress at a thrift store during that first year of college and not another soul in her family would have worn it; it had no shape, no color, it did not do a thing to accentuate her form. It had a huge white Puritan collar; boxy straight seams down the sides, a tiny blue pinstripe on white cotton, a pencil-sized kick pleat at the calf. Only in this dress did Sharee begin to become who she was; in this dress she ate her first tamale baked in a genuine cornhusk, instead of just a paper wrapper from Burrito Bell. In this dress she attended her first live theater—even if it was just a few of her classmates wearing bustles and top hats and stumbling over their *fin-de-siècle* lines. In this dress she felt the pangs that would lead her to surrender her long-contested virginity to a boy all the way from Chicago, who stroked her pale flawless cheek, her long smooth buttocks, and told her she was the "pride of the prairie" even though she feared in her heart she was really only a broke-back belle.

By the time Sally got Lorraine over to Trev's house, the whole team was there, eating doughnuts and drinking milk, their legs and elbows taking over the dining table, the breakfast nook, and the bar. Something about the sight of these big girls comforted Lorraine; they were so healthy and strong, inches taller than she and her five sisters—even some of her brothers—had been at that age, and more thickly muscled, despite the lack of discipline and farm work. All that milk, she thought, all that meat. Nothing like the steady diet of grease-soaked beans and greens and fried eggs she remembered from her own childhood and which still made her give in and splurge on packaged snacks and out-of-season fruit at the grocery store. Close up, the girls smelled mostly of the junk food they downed in great boy-sized portions, of coconut suntan lotion and citrus perfumes that went acid in the sunshine, mango lip-gloss, and cinnamon chewing gum.

Lorraine knew, she had been attending nearly every practice, even touring with them when they went to tournaments, or rather following along behind the schoolbus in the tin-can mobile home she and Earl had bought to celebrate her retirement from her secretarial job at Boonslick High. At every stop, Lorraine held a concession in the parking lot, serving up sweet fizzy sodas in tall lemonade glasses printed with flamingos and sunflowers, filling milky marbled candy bowls with the salty snacks she remembered from her own kids' adolescence. She listened to the shortstop's complaints about her mother's boyfriends, the third baseman's love troubles, and Kris the relief pitcher's blow-by-blow accounts of her arguments with Hettie Barnes, the spinster coach who made them keep their nails short and their grades high. Meanwhile, Lorraine let the girls play their music—Britney Spears, Christina Aguilera, Shania Twain—on the new CD player she bought with her Green Stamps, even through she still preferred the country tunes she grew up with: Louvin Brothers, Hank Williams, Woody Guthrie, Patsy Cline. But the music Kris liked was even worse. She had a boyfriend at the state university who sent her tapes of howls and yelps and curses trussed up as regular tunes. Kris's favorite was the Donnas, an all-girl group who sang about nothing but drinking and boy-hopping. On the CD cover, four pretty brunettes in evening clothes sat drinking at a table covered with empty shot glasses. All of them were named Donna, supposedly, and you couldn't really tell them apart, except for the fact that each had her hair parted and her body pierced in a slightly different location.

In Trev's kitchen, the girls rippled in the speckled sunlight, constantly shifting their long limbs and playing with their hair, while Trev sat as still as a scarecrow among them, his overstuffed shirt exploding with graying chest hair above and expanding love handles below as he tried to maintain control of his *USA Today*. Without ever hearing her daughter go, Lorraine was aware that Sally had disappeared behind her, off for another day of poking and puttering in the park.

"Still, I can't believe it." Irene Mason was saying. "I mean, she was with me yesterday afternoon at the car wash at Burrito Bell, spraying guys' shorts when they walked by. 'How else are you going to know?' she said. I was kind of mortified. But the guys seemed to be into it."

"Like that time she made us all strip in Kirksville and do that Spanish dance."

"Donna A., Donna C., Donna F. She never called anybody by their name anymore. She just yelled for more Donnas to get up and get down."

"'Forty Boys in Forty Nights,' that was her favorite tune," Lorraine said. "She was always telling folks we were on tour with the band."

Some of the girls nodded, as seriously as if they were listening to a teacher talk on about Shakespeare, and Trev dropped the money section of his paper, surprised by his mother's voice and annoyed, no doubt, by her familiarity with the flimflam that seemed to him beneath the attention of a grown-up person, although she could assure him he'd had plenty to say about the Stones and Eagles and Led Zeppelin when he was sixteen. Reenie, the sweet girl with the chin dimple and a single cherry-wood braid, got up to greet her old gran and hand off a cup of coffee. She gave Lorraine a wordless hug, then absent-mindedly rubbed Trev's bald head on the way back to her seat.

"Hmm, needs more polish," she said. "Someone pass the Lemon Pledge."

A second girl—Daisy Wycliff—mimicked passing a bottle, and Reenie proceeded to bring the blood back to her father's scalp. As she did, her boat-necked T-shirt took a dip, and Lorraine spotted the butterfly tattoo that sat folded, as still as a resting swallowtail, on the leeward side of Reenie's left breast.

Due to National Softball Association regulations, the girls couldn't wear jewelry in the game, so they settled for ornamental tattoos instead: bracelets of doodles around their upper arms, tiny hearts and daisies inside the inner slopes of the cleavage where the charm of a necklace might hang, diamonds dotting the vertebrae of their lower backs, so that a row of jeweled peaks emerged from the bottom of the gray Lady Rangers uniform shirt whenever a player swooped down to retrieve a ball. The girls all seemed to have the same color hair too, as if this were part of the team uniform—streaks of blond and brown like caramel and chocolate in a candy bar, the healthy good looks that would bleach out into ordinary unvarnished pine after they'd sat too long in the sun. Reenie was the best of them, a girl with her mother's height and her father's flat-faced determination. She'd slimmed down considerably since she started playing the game: she'd made a whole new level of friends with these teammates who'd known one another all their lives, but who somehow never connected until they picked up a bat and ball.

"Did you know that she actually made out with that security guard in Sedalia?" a girl offered. "He must've been twenty-five at least, and he got bothered enough to pull out a lubricated bad boy before she told him she was engaged."

"Engaged? I didn't know she was engaged."

"Engaged to get pre-engaged, is more like. Besides, the guy's practically her cousin."

"Wait," said Trev. "Just let a dad finish his breakfast here. And Mama Lorraine, could you possibly please get a hold of yourself, show some respect for the—for the family and all?"

Trev's wife came in, red eyes and raw lips, her hands rummaging up the sleeves of her robe as if she were cold on this warm May morning, and the room went still. Lorraine couldn't face her, not without an extra spot of coffee at least. She got up and poured another half cup, touched the poor woman on the small of her back, corralled her into an embrace, and let her go again without ever looking her in the face. But, even so, Lorraine still smelled the dread that she couldn't afford to remember, the turpentine bile of empty insides after hours of vomiting or fasting, the fish-entrails scent of insomnia. It was as if Trev's Catherine were the grieving mother, not Lorraine.

Something about the woman's defenselessness made Lorraine angry, despite her best intentions. The trouble with this middle generation was that they operated without a foundation: they didn't believe in God, they didn't believe in the devil, they didn't believe in the almanac or the Democratic party or the rod. You could hardly get them excited over anything. No use waiting for Trev and Catherine to serve as examples for these young people. It was obviously up to Lorraine to set the tone. "The main thing is, girls, we can't let Kris down now. She'd expect us to go ahead and play this KC tournament best as we can."

"You really think we should try and play?" Daisy said. "Wouldn't that be disrespecting her?" A tear stood in the corner of her chicory blue eye, enhanced, Lorraine knew, by a costly contact lens that had had to be replaced more than once in the course of her brief pitching career.

"Not if you do it in the right spirit. That's just the way things are in this evil world. You never know who's at the wheel of some black chariot waiting to mow your sister down. But you gotta get up and get right back on the business seat anyway. Otherwise, it's just the same as inviting the devil to your shivaree. The sin against the Holy Spirit, girls."

"Sin against the Holy Spirit—what's that?"

"Doing it with a Catholic, according to my mom." Elaine Michaels smirked.

"No—it's overrunning third with one out to go and the bases loaded."

"Peeing on your granny's grave," Reenie said. "Then wiping yourself with the pinky finger of her Sunday gloves."

Today, Sharee is making chicken and dumplings for her husband, the same Chicago native who scored her virginity with a sly Midwestern compliment and a few well-executed sexual maneuvers eleven years back. Usually, it's Matt who makes dinner for her—pierogi, kielbasa, cheesy potatoes, and grilled steak—but Sharee's on an extended leave from her administrative job at Ozark Airlines and she feels she ought to do something, at least, to justify her existence.

Something besides peeing in a cup, that is, giving herself a shot in the hip, taking a blood test to determine the level of her hormones, reading through moms-in-waiting magazines as she sips herbal tea to relieve the symptoms of her long-awaited pregnancy. Four weeks ago, in her second attempt at in vitro, Sharee had five of her own fertilized eggs transferred into her uterus; this afternoon, her pregnancy has been confirmed by ultrasound. Where for years her uterine walls had remained bare and unadorned, there were now four viable embryos clinging to the lush endometrial lining, perhaps too many for her body to accommodate. Maybe she concentrated too hard, she thinks, when she was lying there on the examining table with her legs in the air, the nurse coordinator leading her through a guided meditation and Matt stroking her belly for good luck.

She rolls out the dough for the dumplings and smells the yeasty scent, good as a microbrewery any day. She marvels at her own fertility, her body's ability to double and triple itself. For years, she has been angry at her body's failures, the good round breasts without a reason, the intricate internal pockets and tubes like a malfunctioning pinball game, the childbearing hips with nothing to hold. It poisoned sex for her, that anger, made her just want to roll over and grow old when Matt pressed against her hip or teased her nipple at a futile point in the cycle. She cuts the dough into strips, remembering her own violence, the punishments she wanted to inflict upon herself. "Visualize a beautiful nursery," the nurse had told her at the moment of the transfer. "Pink, blue, farm animals, jungle theme, anything you like. Now look at the wallpaper. Feel the flocking. It's got to be thick, it's got to be sticky, all plumped out with blood and nutrients. These little eggs are counting on it. They're getting ready to climb your wall." But the idea of fertilized eggs didn't necessarily appeal to Sharee, who's just rural enough to remember encountering a fertilized chicken egg with an offending spot of blood on the Melmac platter at her grandma's breakfast table. The fertilized eggs were the ones you wanted to avoid, the old ones, the ruined ones, with possible chicken parts gelling in their soggy centers. So Sharee had envisioned regular hard-boiled eggs instead. Easter eggs with a little purple dye clinging to the meat, deviled eggs topped with fluffy yolk filling and chives, over-boiled eggs with green rings emanating from the yolks. They all climbed the walls with their little suction feet, but then began dripping, wet and formless again, down the fresh zoo-scape wallpaper.

Sharee drops the dumplings, one by one, into the boiling pot and thinks about how she'll pose the problem to her husband, who has possibly reached the end of what he's able to process, in terms of complications. The dumplings puff out quickly, rising to the surface of the boiling water and chicken fat, and as they do Sharee feels the nausea curdle in her abdomen like the fibroid tumors that brought her to this juncture in the first place.

At 5:20, she's lying on the couch in her sea-horse pajamas when she hears Matt's car in the driveway. She notices how he switches off the engine and leaves the radio playing the end of a rock anthem. Smashing Pumpkins, it sounds like. Matt doesn't even like the Pumpkins, despite their Chicago origins. He's just delaying having to hear the good or bad news, which he pointedly resisted having delivered over the phone. The car door opens, closes, opens again. He forgot his sunglasses, he's checking the mileage, he's getting something out of the glove compartment. Once he finally enters the house, she sees that he's brought her flowers—a neutral bouquet of purple blazing stars and yellow daisies, congratulations if it's a go and consolation if it's just another wash. Which, she wonders, is finally more appropriate?

Three days after Kris's death, Lorraine was at her usual table in the Limestone Diner, working out a batting order for the Kansas City tournament. This was Hettie Barnes's job, she knew, but Hettie hadn't been herself, had been out of school with a migraine, and who knew when she'd get around to it. Lorraine, on the contrary, felt energized by the state of emergency. What was this strange excitement, like a fresh redeye gravy lubricating her old bones? She'd been up since 4:30 dusting her living room and waiting for the diner to open. At 5:45, when Earl shuffled into the room in his railroad-striped overalls to turn on the TV, she slipped on her loafers and reached for her pocketbook, which her husband then grabbed out of her grasp with surprising speed, given his age and the hour of day.

"What's your hurry, woman? You think the gossip will be all dried up before you get there?"

Earl didn't appear to be affected by the accident, seemed, in fact, oblivious to the parallels between this death and their own daughter's. Lorraine often doubted that he remembered Sharee at all, despite the photos in the albums and on the walls, the little altar covered with scraps of dresses and award ribbons in the back bedroom where he never went. When the children were coming up, each night after they went to sleep and the parents finally had a minute to themselves, Lorraine and Earl would tally up the day's gains and losses, his run-ins at the garage, her adventures at the high school. Then the conversation would turn, like a dusty road winding into a hidden spring, onto the subject of their children. What about Sally tying a leash on that box turtle? What about the mouth on that Trev? One night a few weeks after the accident, Lorraine tried to slip Sharee's name back into their nightly talk and Earl's face went blank, as if someone had smoothed it over with a trowel. He grasped the coffee table in front of him, then stood up very straight, walked out of the room, out of the house, started the engine of the new pickup the insurance had paid for, and didn't return for over an hour. After that Sharee was a closed subject. Lorraine guessed she understood, although she could never truly forgive him. Only a male god could turn his back on his dying child; only a man would cut off a daughter just because she defied him by going and getting herself killed.

At the diner, Lorraine accepted another half cup and ripped open a sugar packet with her teeth, trying to determine whether to put Elaine Michaels, with her large biceps and uneven motor development, before or after the delicate but precise Daisy Wycliff. She watched as the old-timers filed in to sit at the counter in their caps and overalls, making competitive claims about the heat, and the granny women gathered at a table under a local artist's rendering of a stand of dogwood in the shadow of a rugged cross, a magnified thorn in the right-hand corner beading up with a single drop of dew. A bit later, you'd see the people in the prime of life dragging in, flaunting their soft underbellies and undeveloped wrinkles, full of trouble about their baby's colic or their teenager's boyfriend or their boss's new policy. Relax, she wanted to tell them, you better pace yourself, because you haven't seen the hind end of trouble yet. She stirred in a creamer and began to focus in on the granny women, skin cracked like gray mud dried in the sunshine, bright eyes and crooked fingers, false white teeth that they constantly clicked and readjusted in their mouths. Those three were always looking for something evil to relish, they could never get enough brine to suit their pickled old taste buds. Today they were gumming and jawing on about one of the granddaughters who'd gone and gotten herself tattooed.

"Not a pretty little doodad, mind you, but this big bloody heart with a dead girl's name trailed across it. Right on the thigh, to where you could see it in a pair of decent-length shorts. All the girls on the team are getting them. Boy, is my daughter-in-law up in arms. Some of the moms are gonna pay a visit to the coach and give her a good talking-to."

Lorraine stiffened like a beaten egg white. Why hadn't they told her, at least consulted with her first? The green marbled tabletop swirled beneath her; the deer horns by the door shifted and repositioned themselves as if they were getting ready to spar with Satan; the jam in the jelly jar crystallized before her eyes. She could have talked them out of it, or at least gone with them to supervise the ink. She imagined a tattoo on her own thigh, where the green and blue veins converged to form a map of her complaints; she imagined Earl whooping and taunting her, she imagined Trev's rude grunt of dismay.

She got up, walked over to the granny women, and spit a half-chewed wad of jelly toast on their table.

"That's for backbiting, you old horny toads," she said. Then she spat again, her own clear juices this time, smelling of coffee and cough drops. "And that's for poisoning the chew."

Clearing her head out by the accident scene, she thought of what she could do to raise morale and protect poor Hettie Barnes, whose only crime was to fall in love with a Gulf War hero who then picked up and headed off to Pensacola on his own, leaving his jilted sweetheart to squander all her affection on a shifting squad of ungrateful high school softball players. Hettie had huge squash-shaped bosoms and straight boyish hips, so many reddish freckles she resembled a hunting hound, and a supple apple butter voice that turned just a bit too sugary when she felt a migraine coming on. Her exaggerated arm motions and brisk manner undercut the effect of those monumental breasts, as if she'd had to keep her body in check all her life. That's what made her such an excellent tonic for the girls. But something in her was sad, incomplete, making Lorraine want to lighten old Hettie's sorrow sack whenever she could.

Lorraine walked over the field again, tracing out a circle in the grass. The day was so blue it shaded into purple, and the morning primroses were starting to come into bloom. But no one had bothered to pick up the cupcakes, which were now soggy with dew and spotted with gnats and flies. Kris's funeral was this afternoon, and the tournament was two days after. Lorraine couldn't let anything get in the way of the trip, which more and more seemed like the last dab of pleasure on her horizon. She'd buy Reenie a new outfit, she'd go to the yarn store and pick up a supply for Christmas sweaters, she'd get in a visit with her great-niece, who must be over thirty by now, just to see if the old girl was living up to her name.

In the meantime, someone had to give the girls a pep talk and warn Hettie about the town gossip. As Lorraine was heading back to her vehicle, she saw the truck with the state park emblem; a coneflower, a deer, a flying trout on a disk of green.

"Patrolling the area, ma'am?" It was Sally, her hair pulled back into a ponytail and a fast-food biscuit crumbled in a paper wrapper on her lap.

"I suppose you think you're the police now, just because you got a uniform on your back."

"I suppose you think you're family, just because you tipped a couple of colas with the girl. Now how about you go home and see if Daddy's taken his pill?"

Sharee's mother is on the phone again, relaying the latest in the long saga of death, inbreeding, and destruction in Boonslick, Missouri. This week, a young girl, barely sixteen, had been passing a slow-moving vehicle on Highway 63 when she got into a head-on collision with an oncoming SUV and was killed on the spot. "Those things are a menace. Out-of state tourists speeding along with their cell phones in their armored cars. And the girl's poor family lives in a trailer, doesn't have any kind of insurance to speak of. Your aunt Lorraine is real upset because Kris was on Cousin Reenie's softball team. And you know, it's got to bring up bad memories for her."

Sharee, high on hormones like a chemically treated turkey, is already weeping before her mother even reaches the punch line; after all, she knows some disaster or another is on its way. In these stories it always is, looming over the next hill of purple coneflowers, lurking in a hidden sinkhole, keeping fresh and cool in a devil's icebox of a cave. She tries to focus on the flowers Matt bought for her, still blooming tall and handsome on their slender stalks, the golden apple wallpaper of the kitchen, her own short fingernails in their barely there beige polish. Her nose tickles as if she is about to sneeze, and she feels the physical pleasure of giving in to her grief. All day, on and off, she has been crying over Matt's reaction, which was basically no reaction, to her news. "It's your body after all, the decision's up to you." The truth is, he's too terrified of her emotional state to offer an opinion. He keeps coming up the periphery of her personal space and then standing there with a plate of crackers or a newspaper or a glass of milk, hoping she'll rise to take the bait. A single brutal pimple has appeared on the side of her face, hard to the touch, as painful as a bruise, and she feels like a teenager again, countering her body's rebellions on her own.

"That's terrible, Ma, if there's anything I can do, you just let me know."

"Come to think of it, the girls are going up there for a tournament next week; your aunt's been saying how she'd love to see you." Ma's tried this kind of setup before, with the cousin taking a graduation trip to the big city, the local band teacher in town for a music convention, the divorced trucker uncle with heavy conscience and a cross-country load. Sharee has seen them all, tried to make conversation in parks and diners and hamburger joints, even over her own blue-tiled table, where more than one hillbilly has tasted pierogi or chutney for the first time, and where she has done her best to find some common point of genetic connection. But she's never understood the compulsion to intersect with one's own kin.

Of course, if she told her mother about her current situation, she'd have an excuse not to see her aunt. But she and Matt have agreed to keep the pregnancy a secret until she reaches the end of the dangerous first trimester, which is also the deadline for selectively terminating one or more of the fetuses. Meaning, of course, she thinks bitterly, that she'll never have the opportunity to discuss her decision with anyone until it's already been made.

Sharee has another reason for wanting to avoid Aunt Lorraine; that creepy story that comes attached to her like a bloody shroud or placenta. Twenty-nine years ago, Sharee's mom named her first daughter after a teenage cousin with red hair and iron calves, the star kick-the-can player in the family and the favorite among the scrappy brood Ma had babysat as a teenager herself. That Sharee, Sharee the first, was killed in a car accident a few weeks after Sharee the second was born. The girl was driving her father's truck to the next town, not even sixteen yet and flooring the gas pedal into the next world when she lost control and crashed into the limestone bluff at the side of the road. And then, three days after she buried her daughter, Aunt Lorraine was over to her niece's house with a lawyer, trying to get Ma to legally change Sharee's name. "For the good of both of them," she said. "It's just unlucky, having two girls with the same name in a single generation, it's like having a double or a twin. This little angel's what, all of a month old? She'll never remember that she was once lifted by some other handle. Anyway, we got loads of freed-up names in the family from those who have passed before: Caroline, Mariah, Josephine."

The lawyer, of course, wasn't a legitimate professional contact, but just another relative, an in-law who'd gotten his degree that spring and wasn't yet gainfully employed. He sat on the porch drinking beer with Sharee's dad while the women wrangled inside. Daddy still claims he could see the house moving, the porch swing rocking, the glass shaking in the window frames. "Looked like the earthquake of New Madrid all over again. Thought we was going to have to call an exorcist in on the thing."

Sharee, for one, wishes that her mother had given in to Lorraine's demands and named her something with fewer strings attached. The choices were all old-fashioned, it was true, but they could have been easily transformed into something modern like Cara or Jo. She's been told that her name means "beloved friend" in French, and maybe that was good enough for Sharee the first. But Sharee the second, who's actually been to college and studied a language or two, knows that Cherie also means "too expensive," and that's just what these connections always turn out to be.

At the funeral, Lorraine convinced the usher, a former class president at Boonslick High, to squeeze her in next to her granddaughter, even though the pew was practically full. Earl was left to sit in the row behind, staring at the nearly identical heads of a dozen teenage girls with beer-colored braids and buns and ponytails trussed up in what looked to be black glitter shoestrings.

"Is it true?" Lorraine whispered. "When did you have it done?" Reenie just pulled up her skirt and revealed the silver-dollar-sized tattoo, fuzzy under the nylons, which were, after the local fashion, at least three shades darker than her skin. Lorraine shook her head at the sight and all down the row, girls shifted their thighs to lift the right side of their skirts and display their newly illustrated skin. One of them, Doris McClam, was fresh enough to go without nylons, even in church, and the reds and greens and blues of her tattoo stood out as clear as Sunday morning on her muscled thigh. A pumping anatomical heart. A short brutal dagger. A menstrual drip of blood. But the ribbon across the palpitating organ didn't say "Kris"—there were too many letters for that. Lorraine took her reading glasses out of her pocketbook and read: "Donnas 4-ever, '01."

"That's what Kris would've wanted," Reenie whispered, and Lorraine couldn't tell if there was any sass in it or not.

At the front of the church, Kris sat propped up in a white and silver coffin, purchased, in part, by the Baptist church and Boonslick High. Even the Lady Rangers, urged by Hettie Barnes, had contributed a healthy percentage of their tournament fund. Despite all the comments to the contrary, Kris looked entirely unlike herself, wearing a white dress with tiny black polka dots whose folds nearly drowned out the insistent softball breasts that had always posed a substantial challenge to a sports bra. The dress's puffed sleeves weren't quite long enough to cover the barbed-wire tattoo around her muscular upper arm, and the silver crosses in her ears seemed sadly blasphemous under the holes that ran up the entire length of each lobe like empty pouches in an ammunition belt. Kris's short spiky haircut had obviously frustrated the beautician, who'd tried to soften it into a matronly cowl, but missed one lone cowlick, which now flicked up out of the part in a Pentecostal tongue of flame.

Lorraine stood to lead her team past the coffin and felt her feet moving over the familiar path, each corn and bunion singing its separate strand of harmony. How many times would she tread this road before she got to sit inside the chariot for herself? She stood close and peeked into the driver's seat anyway. Underneath the makeup, Kris looked determined to get off the bench for good. Her right dimple vibrated like the mark of a pebble in a still pond; her pale brown eyebrows were raised as if in anticipation of a good piece of gossip or a dirty joke. In her pitching hand, she gripped a bouquet of prairie dock, coneflowers, and blazing stars like she'd pulled them up by the roots herself. Lorraine reached in to press the girl's hand and felt the sweat in her palm, her own pulse beating in the wrist.

At least Kris's mother, wearing a black leotard with a flowered skirt and twisting her Kleenex in the front row, had the satisfaction of seeing her daughter look as respectable as anybody else's dead. They'd had to bury Sharee in a closed casket, depriving her mother of the pleasure of dressing her for public one last time. Lorraine had done her best anyway with the bruised and mangled body. She brought out the pink trimmed bra and underpants Sharee had gotten as a gift for her fifteenth birthday, she washed the soft purple dress with its lotus flowers and pagodas, she restrung the favorite necklace of purple and green glass beads which had been cut from around Sharee's neck in the hospital. But of the bitterness when the dress had to be ripped to accommodate the swollen waist, the misaligned arm, when the ragged red hair had to be shorn. The sorrow in the barely recognizable purple face. Lorraine remembered the rich ripe skin of babies and very young children, how a cut or bruise would disappear on them overnight, and she couldn't believe that Sharee's wounds would never heal, and that they'd sit there on the beautiful body forever, scarring the best thing she'd ever made.

Lorraine pressed Kris's hand until she felt the blood drain from her own fingertips. Would she bring the girl back if she could? When there had been nothing anyone could do for Sharee? The longer she held onto that hand with its smooth palm and strong bones, the more it seemed like a living thing, a fish or a tree limb, that, caught, killed, or broken, would lead her back to the secret location of her own mistake. She lifted the arm in its barbed-wire bracelet. She kissed the knuckle in its blue birthstone ring. Then she felt an arm on her back, soothing the spot where her bra strap had dug into her for all these years.

Sally took her hand and somehow found the way to unlock it from Kris's fingers, placing the arm back in the casket as the congregation gasped. For a minute, Lorraine believed that she had actually done it. Then she looked back and saw what was really going on.

Behind her, the girls had dropped to their knees in front of the coffin and, one by one, they were lifting their skirts, displaying their tattoos, twisting off their black garters, and dropping them into the coffin. As they enacted this sad backward cancan, they sang a song by the Donnas, one of the rare numbers without underwear or drug references. But between their hoarse voices and swollen sobs, it came out sounding more like a Catholic chant: gloomy, mumbled, and off-key. "Stop Driving Thru My Heart," they pleaded, and Lorraine cringed, remembering the drift of the lyrics. Halfway through, the ramshackle tune broke down entirely, and the girls gathered round the coffin, surrounding it as if it were a cradle. Then they held hands and began to sway, saying Kris's name over and over.

The congregation breathed normally again, and some wise woman toward the back dipped into the first bar of "Shall we Gather at the River" gliding on alone in her shaky soprano until the rest of the group followed her down to the shore. Then, as Lorraine broke the girls' circle to get a good strong grip on her granddaughter's hand, she could swear she saw the corpse take its pinky finger and flick a black garter away from its wildflower bouquet.

Outside, the mica in the concrete steps gave off a glare that caught Lorraine by surprise, and she saw Earl actually applying a handkerchief to the region of his eyelids. Hettie Barnes, in her white blouse and black culottes, stood draped in girls, blotting mascara and handing out Kleenexes. Over by the marquee, the granny women loomed: a navy print dress, a gray fedora, a brown sweater set, blocking out the Scripture, darkening the sun. Lorraine stepped in between them and the team.

"Now you have your satisfaction, gals, you might as well go back to the diner and chew on the cud."

"I hope you been practicing your fastball, hon, because you ain't going to get many permission slips for your tournament after a display such as that."

"Lucky it's a sacred occasion," Lorraine said. "Otherwise, I might be tempted to give you a jagged piece of my mind. But as it is, I just recommend you to the blue-plate special. Go and get it while it's hot." Then she handed them a few extra memorial programs and escorted them out to their cars.

Sharee is throwing up for the seventh time today, and Matt is standing outside the bathroom door, holding the phone. Every time he tries to hand it over, she feels another surge and has to backtrack to the toilet to disgorge one more mouthful of the water, which is the only nourishment she's been able to take in since last night. Each of the four fetuses seems to be emitting its own high-pitched scream inside her hollow head. How will she stay alive to keep her wallpaper up and blooming? How will she ever regain enough consciousness to make a choice? She looks at the yellow tiles on the floor and finds a single chip to hold her focus as she gathers her energy for the next upheaval.

On top of all this, her aunt Lorraine has been calling every few hours with news of the softball tournament. The Lady Rangers, despite the loss of their pitcher, have been knocking them out of the ballpark today, defeating teams from all over the state. Lorraine was supposed to drop by at 11:00, after the morning game, then called to delay until 1:00, then 3:30, and now 7:00 as her team keeps advancing through the finals. Sharee's changed shirts three times, wondering what her aunt will see in her, whether she will live up to the image of the cousin she has never known. Now she just wonders if she'll manage to stay awake. For the millionth time, Matt tells her she should go ahead and cancel, tell her aunt she has the flu, this is getting ridiculous, and given the softball schedule, he doubts the old lady will ever make it over anyway. But Sharee doesn't want to give up yet; she feels a physical craving for her relatives—the jagged jarring accent, the deep-fried fat and suffering, the long brittle family nose—just when it seems as if she has to fight against every cell in her body to make a connection.

She tells Matt to arrange the details with her aunt, then stumbles back to her bed with its scattered body pillows and sticky blankets. Her legs ache as if she has walked every mile from Boonslick, Missouri, to this haven on the open plains. When she rolls over onto her side, she falls into a deep sinkhole of sleep, where she is thirteen again and attending a slumber party. One of the girls has an idea: they should hold a dumb supper, like their mothers used to do, where you all make dinner in complete silence, moving backward, and set a plate by each girl. When the wind blows and the house quakes, then you'll see your future husband sitting there next to you at the table in all his glory, but in complete silence, eating a dumb supper from the provided plate. Sharee is willing to give it a try. But when her turn comes, she sees a woman instead, or a girl, really, sitting turned away from the dinner of sliced tomatoes and macaroni and cheese, and crying into a cell phone. The girl's auburn hair covers her face, her arm is beaded with long jeweled scabs, her knee pumps up and down with the rhythm of her sobs, and one flowered sandal moves back and forth on her heel, the other dangling empty from the table leg at her feet. Sharee is terrified of what she'll see if the girl shows her face, so she tries to concentrate on her own meal instead: the dark yellow cheese paste sticking to the noodles like pollen, the sugar-sprinkled homegrown tomatoes as veined and luminous as panes of stained glass. Her stomach buckles inside her, she's too sick to eat, and in the end she has to face her vision just because there's nowhere else to turn. The girl takes a deep breath, digs her fingernails into her widow's peak, and drags the hair out of her eyes, to reveal a flawless face Sharee has seen only in photographs. Sharee remembers all the individual traits—the high freckled forehead, the heart-shaped jaw that looks romantic or stubborn depending on the angle, the steep, nearly perpendicular nose—but she never realized how they fit together before. Now she can't believe she hasn't always known.

In the end, it was no problem to get the girls' parents to agree to Kansas City. Most of them felt the commotion at the funeral had been innocent, and that the girls could definitely use a change of scene. And for the hard cases, Lorraine just gave in and did her grieving-mother routine. She had lived so long, her story had been dragged through the county so many years it had become a dirty joke, and still she wasn't through with it. She took it out and polished it up again like an old toenail: the blue and gold day, the winding road, the redheaded girl with a scab on her elbow and a green bikini top knotted at her neck. Sharee hadn't spoken to her mother for two days; she'd gotten the idea she wanted to go out to see a boy, an older boy, a German boy, who worked at the quarry in Augustin. He'd invited her for a swim, she said, he was packing the picnic, and all she needed was a ride. Lorraine had flat-out refused, and Earl, Earl couldn't deny her anything, not until he saw the boy for himself and drove the fifteen miles back to Boonslick with Sharee screaming obscenities at him from the passenger seat. Even now, Lorraine couldn't help but feel the satisfaction of that moment, Sharee safe in her bedroom, angry at her father for once, Earl making a ruckus in the garage rather than coming in and admitting that Lorraine had been right. When she went to survey the damage, she found Sharee tearing apart her pillow with a pair of nail scissors, the real goose feathers floating around her and clinging to her swimsuit and her hair. "I just wanted to have a day," she said. "Just one day when I could feel like my life was going somewhere. I could sit in this town until my teeth fall out. You'd like that, wouldn't you? I could sit here and get as old as you and never do anything but marry some cross-eyed loser, then have a bunch of ugly kids I could blame."

Lorraine went from warm to overheated in a single surge of energy; twisting the scissors out of Sharee's sweaty hand, she grasped the girl's head down as if to baptize her, then cut off a swatch of hair from the back of her penny-colored head. "You can say all you want against me, sister," she said. "But don't you ever mock my work."

And all the while, Sally was lying there doing her senior history homework on her bed. Her long ash blond hair covered her face; only once, when she heard the squawk of the scissor, did she shift on her elbow and turn a page, then lift her hand to push her hair behind her pink and blushing ear. Half an hour later, when Lorraine was in the basement doing laundry and Earl had settled into his Sunday nap, Sharee took the spare car keys out of the Green Stamp drawer, got in her father's pickup, and drove off on her own.

"And that's why I go with them now," Lorraine would always say. "Instead of letting them go on alone. Take up your cross and follow me, the Lord tells us. I have my cross by the highway. I have my fork in the road. But I got to keep moving to preserve the faith." She wasn't even certain she believed it anymore, as she stood at the ballpark concession stand with its smells of cotton candy, hot dogs, and warm pee, picked up the receiver of the pay phone, and dialed her great-niece's number, which she had memorized through the long day of victories and reversals. The Lord was one hard character; he didn't have the time to read a softball schedule or watch a baby die. Behind her, she heard a bat crack; she turned and strained to make out the play, another score for the Lady Rangers. Each time the ball connected with the bat, she felt the impact in her own body; the road, the bluff, the ground, the rock, the dirt, the clay. Looking at the girls lined up by the dugout, every one of them a piece of work, she wondered who would be the next to go under. Daisy turning up the cuff of her shorts to check on her tan. Elaine positioning her foot in its tattooed ankle bracelet and striking at a phantom ball. Knock on wood, not Reenie, leaning back on the bench with her pretty braided head resting on Hettie Barnes's bare freckled shoulder.

On the other end of the phone line, Sharee's husband said he'd see if his wife could take the call. But before Lorraine could get an answer out of him, she saw Sally, who'd taken the day off work to help her mother with the drive, striding up from the field on her long legs, a few electric white hairs bristling over the limp blond pageboy, her breasts swinging as if they were tied around her neck on a string, and her neck itself wreathed in a row of dusty wrinkles, making Lorraine relive the frustration of trying to keep the dirt out of all those rolls of baby fat under her children's chins.

"I've got to talk with you, Ma . . . Reenie wanted me to ask . . . well some of the girls think it's a little disturbing, the story you've been telling around, and they wondered how long you plan on repeating it."

"Just a minute. Just keep your uniform pants on," Lorraine warned, lifting the stiff metal phone cord and turning her face away from the worn face in front of her so she could say her daughter's name.

JOHN EDGAR WIDEMAN (b. 1941) was born in Washington, D.C., but spent his early childhood in a poor, predominantly African American neighborhood in Pittsburgh. When he was twelve, his family moved to a predominantly white neighborhood, and Wideman graduated from one of the best high schools in Pittsburgh. Having learned how to have his race ignored by his white peers and how to achieve success in the white world, he went on to study at the University of Pennsylvania, and he received his B.Ph. from Oxford in eighteenth-century British literature. He returned to the University of Pennsylvania, where he helped create the African American Studies program.

Wideman's novels include *A Glance Away* (1967), *Hurry Home* (1969), *The Lynchers* (1973), *Hiding Place* (1981), and *Philadelphia Fire* (1990). In 1975, Wideman's brother was arrested and convicted of murder; he has written about this incident and its repercussions in a nonfiction work entitled *Brothers and Keepers* (1984). His collections of short stories were published as *Damballah* (1981), *Fever* (1989), and *All Stories Are True* (1993). He received a P.E.N./Faulkner Award in 1984 and 1991.

In his fiction, Wideman examines the lives of black families in contemporary urban America, especially the effects of violence and criminal behavior on the male members of the African American community. In "What We Cannot Speak About We Must Pass Over in Silence" (2003), which was collected in the *Best American Short Stories 2004*, a man searches for the son of a dead acquaintance, a son who resides in a prison in Arizona. As he searches, he speculates about the nature of friendships, the nature of parenthood, and the nature of guilt. Portions of the story are an **epistolary** exchange between the narrator and the prisoner.

Related Works: Bambara, "The Lesson"; Erdrich, "The Red Convertible"; Ellison, "Battle Royal"; Young, "Nineteen Seventy-Five"; Plath, "Daddy"; Sophocles, *Antigone.*

Prison Cell

What We Cannot Speak About We Must Pass Over in Silence

I have a friend with a son in prison. About once a year he visits his son. Since the prison is in Arizona and my friend lives here on the East Coast, visiting isn't easy. He's told me the planning, the expense, the long day spent flying there and longer day flying back are the least of it. The moment that's not easy, that's impossible, he said, is after three days six hours each of visiting are over and he passes through the sliding gate of the steel-fenced outdoor holding pen between the prison-visitation compound and visitors' parking lot and steps onto the asphalt that squirms beneath your feet, oozing hot like it just might burn through your shoe soles before you reach the rental car and fling open its doors and blast the air conditioner so the car's interior won't fry your skin, it's then, he said, taking his first steps away from the prison, first steps back into the world, when he almost comes apart, almost loses it completely out there in the desert, emptiness stretching as far as the eye can see, very far usually, ahead to a horizon ironed flat by the weight of blue sky, zigzag mountain peaks to the right and left, marking the edges of the earth, nothing moving but hot air wiggling above the highway, the scrub brush and sand, then, for an unending instant, it's very hard to be alive, he says, and he thinks he doesn't want to live a minute longer and would not make it to the car, the airport, back to this city, if he didn't pause and remind himself it's worse, far worse for the son behind him still trapped inside the prison, so for the son's sake he manages a first step away, then another and another. In these faltering moments he must prepare himself for the turnaround, the jarring transition into a world where he has no access to his son except for rare ten-minute phone calls, a blighted world he must make sense of again, beginning with the first step away and back through the boiling cauldron of parking lot, first step of the trip that will return him in a year to the desert prison.

Now he won't have it to worry about anymore. When I learned of the friend's death, I'd just finished fixing a peanut-butter sandwich. Living alone means you tend to let yourself run out of things. Milk, dishwasher detergent, napkins, toothpaste—staples you must regularly replace. At least it happens to me. In this late bachelorhood with no live-in partner who shares responsibility for remembering to stock up on needful things. Peanut butter probably my only choice that evening so I'd fixed one sandwich, or two, more likely, since they'd be serving as dinner. In the mail I'd ignored till I sat down to my sorry-assed meal, a letter from a lawyer announcing the death of the friend with a son in prison, and inside the legal-sized manila envelope, a sealed white envelope the friend had addressed to me.

I was surprised on numerous counts. First, to learn the friend was gone. Second, to find he'd considered me significant enough to have me informed of his passing. Third, the personal note. Fourth, and now it's time to stop numbering, no point since you could say every event following the lawyer's letter both a surprise and no surprise, so numbering them as arbitrary as including the sluggish detail of peanut-butter sandwiches, "sluggish" because I'd become intrigued by the contents of the manila envelope and stopped masticating the wad in my jaw until

I recalled the friend's description of exiting prison, and the sludge became a mouthful of scalding tar.

What's surprising about death anyway, except how doggedly we insist on being surprised by what we know very well's inevitable, and of course, after a while, this insistence itself unsurprising. So I was (a) surprised and (b) not surprised by the death of a friend who wasn't much of a friend, after all, more acquaintance than intimate cut-buddy, a guy I'd met somewhere through someone and weeks later we'd recognized each other in a line at a movie or a bank and nodded and then run into each other again one morning in a busy coffee shop, and since I'm partial to the coffee there, I did something I never do, asked if it was okay to share his table, and he smiled and said sure so we became in this sense friends. I never knew very much about him and hadn't known him very long. He never visited my apartment nor I his. A couple years of casual bump-ins, tables shared for coffee while we read our newspapers, a meal, a movie or two, a play-off game in a bar once, two middle-aged men who live alone and inhabit a small, self-sufficient corner of a large city and take time-outs here and there from living alone so being alone at this stage in our careers doesn't feel too depressingly like loneliness. He was the kind of person you could see occasionally, enjoy his company more or less, and walk away with no further expectations, no plan to meet again. Like the occasional woman who consents to share my bed. If he'd moved to another city, months might have passed before I'd notice him missing. If we'd lost contact for good, I'm sure I wouldn't have regretted not seeing him again. A smidgen of curiosity perhaps. Perhaps a slight bit of vexation, like when I discover I haven't restocked paper towels or Tabasco sauce. Less, since his absence wouldn't leave a gap I'd be obliged to fill. My usual flat response at this stage in my life to losing things I have no power to hold on to. Most of the world fits into this category now, so what I'm trying to say is something about the manila envelope and its contents bothered me more than I'm used to allowing things to bother me, though I'm not sure why. Was it the son in prison. The friend had told me no one else visited. The son's mother dead of cancer. Her people, like the friend's, like mine, old, scattered, gone. Another son, whereabouts unknown, who'd disowned his father and half-brother, started a new life somewhere else. I wondered if the lawyer who wrote me had been instructed to inform the son in prison of his father's passing. How were such matters handled. A phone call. A registered letter. Maybe a visit from the prison chaplain. I hoped my friend had arranged things to run smoothly, with as little distress as possible for the son. Any alternatives I imagined seemed cruel. Cruel for different reasons, but all equally difficult for the son. Was he even now opening his manila envelope, a second envelope tucked inside with its personal message. I guess I do know why I was upset—the death of the man who'd been my acquaintance for nearly two years moved me not a bit, but I grieved to the point of tears for a son I'd never seen, never spoken to, who probably wasn't aware of my grief or my existence.

I could barely recall the dead friend's face. Once I twisted on the light over the mirror above the bathroom sink, thinking I might milk his features from mine. Hadn't we been vaguely similar in age and color. If I studied hard, maybe the absence in my face of some distinctive trait the friend possessed would trigger my memory, or a trait I bore would recall its absence in the friend's features and *bingo* his whole face would appear.

Seeing a stranger in the mirror, I was afraid I might be suffering from the odd neurological deficit that prevents some people from recognizing faces. Who in God's name was this person staring at me. Who'd been punished with those cracks, blemishes, the mottled complexion, eyes sunken in deep hollows, frightened eyes crying out for acknowledgment, for help, then receding, surrendering, staring blankly, bewildered and exhausted, asking me the same questions I was asking them.

How long had I been losing track of myself. Not really looking when I brushed my teeth or combed my hair, letting the image in the mirror soften and blur, become familiar and invisible as faces on money. Easier to imagine the son than deal with how the father had turned out, the splotched, puffy flesh, lines incised in forehead and cheeks, strings dragging down the corners of the mouth. I switched off the light, let the merciful hood drop over the prisoner's face.

Empathy with the son not surprising, even logical, under the circumstances, you might say. Why worry about the father. He's gone. No more tiptoeing across burning coals. Why not sympathize with a young man suddenly severed from his last living contact with the world this side of prison bars. Did he know his father wouldn't be visiting. Had he phoned. Listened to the ring-ring-ring and ring. How would the son find out. How would he bear the news.

No doubt a bit of self-pity colored my response. On the other hand I'm not a brooder. I quickly become bored when a mood's too intense or lasts too long. Luckily, I have the capacity to step back, step away, escape into a book, a movie, a vigorous walk, and if these distractions don't do the trick, then very soon I discover I'm smiling, perhaps even quietly chuckling at the ridiculous antics of the person who's lost control, who's taking himself and his commonplace dilemmas far too seriously.

> Dear Attorney Koppleman,
>
> I was a friend of the late Mr. Donald Whittaker. You wrote to inform me of Mr. Whittaker's death. Thank you. I'm trying to reach Mr. Whittaker's imprisoned son to offer my belated condolences. If you possess the son's mailing address, could you pass it on to me, please. I appreciate in advance your attention to this matter.

> In response to your inquiry of 6/24/99: This office did execute Mr. Donald K. Whittaker's will. The relevant documents have been filed in Probate Court and, as such are part of the public record you may consult at your convenience.
>
> (P. S.) Wish I could be more helpful, but in our very limited dealings with Mr. Whittaker he never mentioned a son in or out of prison.

I learned there are many prisons in Arizona. Large and small. Local, state, federal. Jails for short stays, penitentiaries for lifers. Perhaps it's the hot, dry climate. Perhaps space is cheap. Perhaps a desert state's economy, with limited employment opportunities for its citizens, relies on prisons. Perhaps corporate-friendly deals make prisons lucrative businesses. Whatever the reasons, the prison industry seems to flourish in Arizona. Many people also end up in Arizona retirement communities. Do the skills accumulated in managing senior citizens who come to the state to die readily translate to prison administration. Or vice versa.

Fortunately, the state employs people to keep track of prisoners. I'm not referring to uniformed guards charged with hands-on monitoring of the inmates' flesh and blood. I mean computer people who know how to punch in and retrieve information. Are they one of the resources attracting prisons to Arizona. Vast emptiness plus a vast legion of specialists adept at processing a steady stream of bodies across borders, orchestrating the dance of dead and living so vacancies are filled and fees collected promptly. Was it the dead friend who told me the downtown streets of Phoenix are eerily vacant during heatstroke daylight hours. People who do the counting must be sequestered in air-conditioned towers or busy as bees underground in offices honeycombed beneath the asphalt, their terminals regulating traffic in and out of hospices, prisons, old folks' homes, juvenile-detention centers, cemeteries, their screens displaying Arizona's archipelago of incarceral facilities, diagrams of individual gulags where a single speck with its unique, identifying tag can be pinpointed at any moment of the day. Thanks to such a highly organized system, after much digging I located the son.

Why did I search. While I searched, I never asked why. Most likely because I possessed no answer. Still don't. Won't fake one now except to suggest (a) curiosity and (b) anger. Curiosity since I had no particular agenda beyond maybe sending a card or note. The curiosity that killed the cat till satisfaction brought it back. My search pure in this sense, an experiment, driven by the simple urge to know. Anger because I learned how perversely the system functions, how slim your chances of winning if you challenge it.

Anger because the system's insatiable clockwork innards had the information I sought and refused to divulge it. Refused fiercely, mindlessly, as only a mindless machine created to do a single, repetitive, mindless task can mindlessly refuse. The prison system assumes an adversarial stance the instant an inquiry attempts to sidestep the prerecorded labyrinth of logical menus that protect its irrational core. When and if you ever reach a human voice, its hostile tone insinuates you've done something stupid or morally suspect by pursuing it to its lair. As punishment for your trespass, the voice will do its best to mimic the tone and manner of the recorded messages you've been compelled to suffer in order to reach it.

Anger because I couldn't help taking the hassle personally. Hated bland bureaucratic sympathy or disdain or deafness or defensiveness or raw, aggressive antagonism, the multiplicity of attitudes and accents live and recorded transmitting exactly the same bottom-line message; yes, what you want we have, but we're not parting with it easily.

I won't bore you or myself by reciting how many times I was put on hold or switched or switched back or the line went dead after hours of Muzak or I weathered various catch-22 routines. I'll just say I didn't let it get the best of me. Swallowed my anger, and with the help of a friend persevered, till one day—accidentally I'm sure—the information I'd been trying to pry from the system's grip collapsed like an escaping hostage into my arms.

Some mornings when I awaken I look out my window and pretend to understand. I reside in a building in the bottom of somebody's pocket. Sunlight never touches its bricks. Any drawer or cabinet or closet shut tight for a day will exude a gust of moldy funk when you open it. The building's neither run-down nor cheap. Just dark, dank, and drab. Drab as the grown-ups children are browbeaten into accepting as their masters. The building, my seventh-floor apartment, languish in the shadow of something fallen, leaning down, leaning over. Water, when you turn on a faucet first thing in the morning, gags on itself, spits, then gushes like a bloody jailbreak from the pipes. In a certain compartment of my heart compassion's supposed to lodge, but there's never enough space in cramped urban dwellings so I store niggling self-pity there too, try to find room for all the millions of poor souls who have less than I have, who would howl for joy if they could occupy as their own one corner of my dreary little flat. I pack them into the compartment for a visit, pack till it's full far beyond capacity and weep with them, share with them my scanty bit of good fortune, tell them I care, tell them be patient, tell them I'm on their side, tell them an old acquaintance of mine who happens to be a poet recently hit the lottery big time, a cool million, and wish them similar luck, wish them clear sailing and swift, painless deaths, tell them it's good to be alive, whatever, good to have been living as long as I've managed and still eating every day, fucking now and then, finding a roof over my head in the morning after finding a bed to lie in at night, grateful to live on even though the pocket's deep and black and a hand may dig in any moment and crush me.

> I'm writing to express my condolences sympathies upon the death of your father
> at the death of your father your father's passing though I was barely acquainted
> only superficially I'm writing to you because I was a friend of your father by now
> prison officials must have informed you of his death his demise the bad news
> I assume I don't want to intrude on your grief sorrow privacy if in fact hadn't
> known your sorrow and the circumstances of our lives known him very long
> only a few years permitted allowed only limited opportunities to become
> acquainted and the circumstances of our lives I considered your father a friend I
> can't claim to know him your father well but our paths crossed often frequently
> I considered him a good valuable friend fine man I was very sorry to hear learn
> of his death spoke often of you on many occasions his words much good love
> affection admiration I feel almost as if I you know you though I'm a complete
> stranger his moving words heart-felt about son compelled me to write this note
> if I can be helpful in any fashion manner if I can be of assistance in this matter
> at this difficult time place don't hesitate to let me know please don't
>
> I was sorry to hear of your father's death. We were friends. Please accept my heart-felt regrets on this sad occasion.
>
> Sir,
>
> Some man must have fucked my mother. All I knew about him until your note said he's dead. Thanks.

It could have ended there. A case of mistaken identity. Or a lie. Or numerous lies. Or a hallucination. Or fabrication. Had I been duped. By whom. Father, son, both. Did they know each other or not. What did I know for sure about either one. What stake did I have in either man's story. If I connected the dots, would a picture emerge. One man dead, the other good as dead locked up two thousand miles away in an Arizona prison. Was any of it my business. Anybody's business.

I dress lightly, relying upon the pretty weather lady's promises.

A woman greets me and introduces herself as Suh Jung, Attorney Koppleman's paralegal assistant. She's a tiny, pleasant Asian woman with jet-black hair brutally cropped above her ears, a helmet, she'll explain later, necessary to protect herself from the cliché of submissiveness, the china-doll stereotype people immediately had applied when they saw a thick rope of hair hanging past her waist, hair that her father insisted must be uncut and worn twisted into a single braid in public, her mother combing, brushing, oiling her hair endlessly till shiny pounds of it lopped off the day the father died, and then, strangely, she'd wanted to save the hair she had hated, wanted to glue it back together strand by strand and drape it over one of those pedestalled heads you see in beauty shops so she and her mother could continue forever the grooming rituals that had been one of the few ways they could relate in a household her father relentlessly, meticulously hammered into an exquisitely lifelike, flawless representation of his will, like those sailing ships in bottles or glass butterflies in the museum, so close to the real thing you stare and stare waiting for them to flutter away, a household the father shattered in a fit of pique or rage or boredom the day she opened the garage door after school and found him barefoot, shitty-pantsed, dangling from a rafter, beside the green family Buick.

In the lawyer's office she listened to my story about father and son, took notes carefully it seemed, though her eyes were cool, a somewhere else distracted cool while she performed her legal-assistant duties. Black, distant eyes framed in round, metal-rimmed old-lady spectacles belying the youthful freshness of her skin. Later when she'd talk about her dead father, I noticed the coolness of the first day, and was left to form my own impression of him since she volunteered few details, spoke instead about being a quiet, terrified girl trying to swim through shark-infested water without making waves. I guessed she had wanted to imitate the father's impenetrable gaze, practicing, practicing till she believed she'd gotten it right, but she didn't get it right, probably because she never understood the father's coldness, never made her peace with the blankness behind his eyes where she yearned to see her image take shape, where it never did, never would. Gradually I came to pity her, her unsuccessful theft of her father's eyes, her transparent attempt to conceal her timidity behind the father's stare, timidity I despised because it reminded me of mine, my inadequacies and half-measures and compromises, begging and fearing to be seen, my lack of directness, decisiveness, my deficiency of enterprise and imagination, manifested in her case by the theatrical gesture of chopping off her hair when confronted by the grand truth of her father's suicide. Timidity dooming her to cliché—staring off inscrutably into space.

Behind a desk almost comically dwarfing her (seeing it now, its acres of polished, blond wood should have alerted me to the limits, the impropriety of any intimacy we'd establish) she had listened politely, eventually dissuaded me from what I'd anticipated as the object of my visit—talking to Attorney Koppleman. She affirmed her postscript: no one in the office knew anything about a son in prison. I thanked her, accepted the card she offered that substantiated her willingness to help in any way she could.

Would you like me to call around out in Arizona. At least save you some time, get you started in the right direction.

Thanks. That's very kind of you. But I probably need to do some more thinking on this. And then I realized how stupidly wishy-washy I must have sounded. It galled me because I work hard to give just the opposite impression—appear as a man sure of himself. So perhaps that's why I flirted. Not flirting exactly, but asserting myself in the only way I could think of at the moment, by plainly, abruptly letting her see I was interested. In her. The woman part of her. A decisive act, yet suspect from the beginning, since it sprang from no particular spark of attraction. Still, a much more decisive move than I'm usually capable of making—true or false. Hitting on her, so to speak, straight up, hard, asking for the home number she hastily scribbled on the back of her card, hurrying as if she suddenly remembered a lineup of urgent tasks awaiting our interview's termination. Her way of attending to a slightly embarrassing necessity. The way some women

I've met treat sex. Jotting down the number, she was as out of character as I was, but we pulled it off.

The world is full of remarkable things. Amiri Baraka penned those words when he was still LeRoi Jones writing his way back to Newark and a new name after a lengthy sojourn among artsy, crazy white folks in the Village. One of my favorite lines from one of my favorite writers. Back in the day when I still pretended books were worth talking about, people were surprised to discover Baraka a favorite of mine, as quietly integrated and nonconfrontational a specimen as I seemed to be of America's longest, most violently reviled minority. It wasn't so much a matter of the quality of what Jones/Baraka had written as it was the chances he'd taken, chances in his art, in his life. Sacrifices of mind and body he endured so I could vicariously participate, safely holed up in my corner. Same lair where I sat out Vietnam, a college boy while my cousin and most guys from my high school were drafted, shot at, jailed, murdered, became drug addicts in wars raging here and abroad.

Remarkable things. With Suh Jung I smoked my first joint in years. At fifty-seven learned to bathe a woman and, what was harder, learned to relax in a tub while a woman bathed me. Contacting the son in prison not exactly on hold while she and I experienced low-order, remarkable things. I knew which Arizona prison held him and had received from the warden's office the information I'd requested about visiting. Completing my business with this woman, a necessary step in the process of preparing myself for whatever I decided to do next. Steaming water, her soapy hands scrubbing my shoulders, cleansed me, fortified me. I shed old skins. When the son in prison set his eyes on me, I wanted to glow. If he saw me at my best, wouldn't he understand everything.

One night I imagined the son here, his cell transformed to this room, the son imprisoned here with Suh Jung, sweet smoke settling in his lungs, mellowing him out after all the icy years. Me locked up in the black Arizona night fantasizing a woman. Would it be the same woman in both places at once or different limbs, eyes, wetnesses, scents, like those tigers whirling about Sambo, tigers no longer tigers as they chase each other faster and faster, overwhelming poor little Sambo's senses, his Sambo black brain as he tosses and turns in waking-sleep, a mixed-up colored boy, the coins his mother gave him clutched in a sweaty fist, trying once more to complete a simple errand and reach home in one piece.

The city bumps past, cut up through the bus windows. Suh Jung and I had headed for the back. Seats on the rear bench facing the driver meant fewer passengers stepping over, around, on you during the long ride uptown to the museum. Fewer people leaning over you. Sneezing. Coughing. Eavesdropping. Fewer strangers boxing you in, saying stuff you don't want to hear but you find yourself listening to anyway, the way you had watched in spite of yourself, the TV set in your mother's living room she never turned off. I notice blood pooled in one of the back benches' butt-molded blue seats. A fresh, silver-dollar-size glob. Fortunately, neither of us had splashed down in it. I check one more time the seats we're poised above, looking for blood, expecting blood, like blood's a constant danger, though I've never seen blood before on a bus bumping from uptown to downtown, downtown to uptown, in all the years of riding until this very day.

The Giacometti closes next weekend. We almost missed it.

Right on time, then. I'm away next week.

So you are going to Arizona.

I've been letting other things get in the way. Unless I set a hard date, the visit won't happen. You know. Like we kept putting off Giacometti.

You booked a flight.

Not yet.

But you're going for sure. Next week. *I think so think so think so think so think so.*

I loved Giacometti's slinky dog. He was so . . . so . . . you know . . . *dog.* An alley-cat dog like the ones always upsetting garbage cans behind my father's store. Stringy and scrawny like them. Swaybacked. Always hunkered down like they're hiding or something's after them. Scruffy barbedwire fur. Those floppy, flat dog feet like bedroom slippers.

To tell the truth, I missed her dog. I was overwhelmed by the crowd, the crowd of objects. Two floors, numerous galleries, still it was like fighting for a handhold on a subway pole. Spent most of my time reading captions. What I did see made me wonder why Giacometti didn't go insane. Maybe he did. He caught the strangeness and menace in everything. Said art always fails. Said art lied. Everybody's eyes lied. If he glanced away from a model to the image of it he was making, he said, when he looked back, the model would be different.

He understood that we go through life trying to remember what's right in front of our eyes. Experiments have demonstrated conclusively how unobservant the average person is, and, worse, how complacent, how unfazed by blindness. A man with a full beard gets paid to remove it and then goes about his usual day. The following day a researcher asks those who encountered the man, his co-workers for example, if he had a beard when they saw him the previous day. Most can't remember one way or the other, but assume he did. A few say the beard was missing. A few admit they'd never noticed a beard. A few insist vehemently they saw the invisible beard. I seem to recall the dead friend sporting a beard at one time or another during the period we were acquainted. Since I can't swear yes or no, I number myself, just as Giacometti numbered himself, among the blind.

I'd written again and the son had responded again. *Why not. My social calendar not full* . . . A smiling leopard in a cage. Step closer if you dare. A visiting form folded and tucked inside the flimsy prison envelope. Of course I couldn't help recalling the letter within a letter I'd received from the lawyer, Koppleman. The son instructed me to check the box for family and write *father* on the line following it. To cut red tape and speed up the process, I assumed, but I let the form sit a day or two, concerned some official would notice my name didn't match the son's, then realized lots of inmates wouldn't use (or know) their father's name, so I checked the family box, printed *father* in the space provided.

An official notice from the warden's office authorizing my visit took more than a month to reach me, and I began to regret lying on a form that had warned me, under penalty of law, not to perjure myself. My misgivings soured into mild paranoia. Had I compromised myself, broken a law that might send me too packing off to jail. Who reads the applications. How carefully do prison officials check alleged facts. What punishments could be levied against a person who falsifies information. The form a perfunctory measure, I had guessed, a form, properly executed and stamped, destined to gather dust in a file, retrievable just in case some official needed to cover her or his ass. Justify his or her existence. The existence of the state. Of teeming prisons in the middle of the desert.

I finally calmed down after I figured out that (a) without a DNA test no one could prove I wasn't the prisoner's father and (b) it wasn't a crime to believe I was. If what the son had written in his first letter was true, the prison would possess no record of his father. The dead friend past proclaiming his paternity. And even if he rose from the dead to argue his case, why would his claim, sans DNA confirmation, be more valid in the eyes of the law than mine. So what if he had visited. So what if he'd married the prisoner's mother. So what if he sincerely believed his belief of paternity. Mama's baby, Daddy's maybe.

Psychologists say there's a stage when a child doubts the adults raising it are its real family. How can parents prove otherwise. And why would a kid want to trade in the glamorous fairy tales he dreams up about his origins for a pair of ordinary, bumbling adults who impose stupid rules, stifling routines. Who needs their hostile world full of horrors and hate.

With Suh Jung's aid—why not use her, wasn't it always about finding uses for the people in your life, why would they be in your life if you had no use for them, and if you're using them, didn't that lend purpose to their lives, you're actually doing them a trickle-down favor, aren't you, allowing them to use you to feel themselves useful, and that's something, isn't it, better than nothing anyway, than being useless or used up—I gathered more information about the son in prison. Accumulated a file, biography, character sketch, rap sheet a.k.a. his criminal career.

Here's what the papers said: He's done lots of bad things, the worst kinds of things, and if we could kill him, we would, but we can't, so we'll never, never let him go.

Are you surprised, she'd asked.

I didn't know what to expect, I had replied. Not traveling out west to forgive him or bust him out or bring him back alive. Just visit. Just fill in for the dead father. Once. One time enough and it's finished.

You're going to wear out the words, she jokes as she glances over at me sitting beside her in her bed that occupies the same room with a pullman fridge and stove. Her jibe less joke than complaint: I'm sick and tired of your obsessive poring over a few dog-eared scraps of paper extracted from Arizona's bottomless pit of records is what she's saying with a slight curl of one side of her thin mouth, a grimace that could be construed as the beginning of a smirk she decides is not worth carrying full term.

I keep on reading. Avoid the disappointment a peek at her naked body would trigger. The eroticism between us had dulled rather too quickly it seemed. An older man's childishness partly at fault. Why else would I be impatient after a few weeks because her hips didn't round and spread, the negligible mounds beneath her nipples swell. Her boyish look not a stage, it was what I was going to get, period, even if the business between us survives longer than I have any reason to expect. No, things aren't going to get better, and I'm wasting precious time. Given my age, how many more chances could I expect.

No matter how many times you read them, she says, the words won't change. Why read the same ugly facts over and over.

(A) Because my willing, skilled accomplice gathered them for me. (B) Curiosity.

This whole visiting business way over the top, you admit it yourself, so I don't pretend I can put myself in your shoes, but still, his crimes would affect any sane person's decision to go or not.

Is he guilty. How can you be certain based on a few sheets of paper.

Too much in the record for a case of mistaken identity. Huh-uh. Plus or minus a few felonies, the man's been busy. A real bad actor.

Are you casting the first stone.

A whole building's been dumped on the poor guy. And he's thrown his share of bricks at other folks. I'd hate to bump into him in a dark alley.

Maybe you already have, my friend. Maybe you have and maybe you've enjoyed it.

You're more than a little weird about this, you know. What the hell are you talking about.

Just that people wind up in situations there's no accounting for. Situations when innocence or guilt are extremely beside the point. Situations when nothing's for sure except some of us are on one side of the bars, some on the other side, and nobody knows which side is which.

Right. But I know I haven't robbed or kidnapped or murdered anyone. Have you.

Have I. Do you really want to know. Everyone has crimes to answer for, don't they. Even you. Suppose I said my crimes are more terrible than his. A string of victims. Many, many murders. Would you believe me. Is your heart beating a little faster.

(A) No. And (B) you're not scaring me. Put those damned papers away, and turn off the light, please. I have work tomorrow.

I will, if you listen to my confession. It might sound better in the dark.

Enough already. I'm tired. I need sleep. Stop acting stupidly because you can't make up your mind about Arizona.

My mind's made up. The prison said yes. I'm on my way.

I'll be fucking glad when it's over and done.

And me back in the arms of my love. Will you be faithful while your sweet, aging serial killer's away.

She tries to snatch the papers but misses. I drop them over the side of the pullout bed. Like the bed she is small and light. Easy to fold up and subdue even for an older fellow. When I wrap myself around her, my body's so much larger than hers, she almost vanishes. When we fuck, or now capturing her, punishing her, I see very little of her flesh. I'm aware of my size, my strength towering over her squirming, her thrashing, her gasps for breath. I am her father's stare, the steel gate dropping over the tiger pit in which she's trapped, naked, begging for food and water. Air. Light.

I arrive on Sunday. Two days late for reasons I can't explain to myself. I flew over mountains, then desert flatness that seemed to go on forever. It must have been Ohio, Illinois, Iowa, Nebraska, not actual desert but the nation's breadbasket, so they say, fruited plains, amber waves of grain, fields irrigated by giant machines day after day spreading water in the same pattern to create circles, squares, rectangles, below. Arable soil gradually giving way to sandy grit as the plane drones westward, through clouds, over another rugged seam of mountains, and then as I peer down at the undramatic nothingness beyond the far edge of wrinkled terrain, the surface of the earth flips over like a pancake. What's above ground buried, what's below ground suddenly exposed. Upside-down mountains are hollow shells, deep, deep gouges in the stony waste, their invisible peaks underground, pointing to hell.

A bit of confusion, bureaucratic stuttering and sputtering when confronted by my tardy arrival, a private calling his sergeant, sergeant phoning officer in charge of visitation, each searching for verification, for duplication, for assurance certified in black and white that she or he is off the hook, not guilty of disrupting the checks and balances of prison routine. I present myself hat in hand, remorseful, apologetic, *please, please, give me another chance please*, forgive me for missing day one and two of the scheduled three-day visit, for checking in the morning of day three instead of day one. Am I still eligible or will I be shooed away like a starving beggar from the rich man's table.

I overhear two guards discussing a coyote whose scavenging brought it down out of the slightly elevated wilderness of rock and brush beginning a few miles or so from the prison's steel-fenced perimeter. I learn how patiently guards in the tower spied on the coyote's cautious trespass, a blip at first, up and back along the horizon, then a discernible shape—skinny legs, long pointed ears, bushy tail—a scraggly critter drawn by easy prey or coyote curiosity closer and closer to the prison until it's within rifle range and the guards take turns profiling it through their sharpshooting sniper scopes, a sad-faced, cartoon coyote they christen whatever guards would christen a creature they will kill one day, a spook, a mirage, so quick on its feet, bolder as it's allowed to approach nearer without being challenged, does it believe it can't be seen, flitting from shadow to shadow, camouflaged by hovering darkness, by mottled fur, a shadow itself, instantly freezing, sniffing the air, then trotting again back and forth along the skyline, skittish through coverless space, up and back, parry, thrust, and retreat, ears pricked to attention when the rare service vehicle enters or leaves the prison parking lot before dawn, murky predawn the coyote's time, the darkness divulging it, a drop from a leaky pipe, a phantom prowling nearer and nearer as if the electrified steel fence is one boundary of its cage, an easy shot now the guards forbear taking, too easy, or perhaps it's more fun to observe their mascot play, watch it pounce on a mouse and pummel it in swift paws bat-bat-bat before its jaws snap the rodent's neck, or maybe the name they named it a kind of protection for a while till somebody comes on duty one morning or pre-morning really when the first shift after the night shift has to haul itself out of bed, out of prefab homes lining the road to the prison entrance, shitty box houses, a few with bright patches of something growing in boxes beside the front steps, boxes you can't see at that black hour from your pickup, eyes locked in the tunnel your headlights carve, a bad-head, bad-attitude morning, thinking about quitting this stinking job, getting the fuck out before you're caught Kilroying or cuckolded in the town's one swinging joint, cussed out, serving pussy probation till further notice, cancer eating his mamma, daddy long gone, kids sick or fighting or crazy on pot or dead or in prison so he draws a bead and *Pow*, blood seeps into the sand, the coyote buzzard bait by the time. I eavesdrop on two guards badmouthing their assassin colleague, laughing at him at the coyote's surprise, the dead animal still serving time as a conversation piece, recycled in this desert sparseness, desert of extremes, of keepers and kept, silence and screams, cold and hot, thirst and drunkenness, no time, too much time.

A spiffy, spit-and-polished platinum-blonde guard whose name tag I read and promptly forget, *Lieutenant*, another guard addresses her, Lieutenant, each breast under her white blouse as large as poor Suh Jung's head, smiles up at me from the counter where she's installed, hands me the document she's stamped, slides me a tray for unloading everything in my pockets, stores it when I'm finished. Now that wasn't so bad, was it, sir. Gives me a receipt and a green ticket with matching numbers. Points me toward a metal detector standing stark and foursquare as a guillotine whose eye I must pass through before I'm allowed to enter the prison.

Beyond the detector one more locked door I must be buzzed through and I'm outside again, in an open-air, tunnel-like enclosure of cyclone fencing bristling on sides and top with razor wire, a corridor or chute or funnel or maze I must negotiate while someone somewhere at a machine measures and records my every step, false move, heartbeat, scream, drop of sweat, of blood when my hands tear at the razor wire.

I pass all the way through the tunnel to a last checkpoint, a small cinderblock hut squatting beside the final sliding gate guarding the visiting yard. Thirty yards away, across the yard, at an identical gated entranceway facing this one, guards are mustering inmates dressed in orange jumpsuits.

In a slot at the bottom of the hut's window you must surrender your numbered green ticket to receive a red one. Two groups of women and children ahead of me in line require a few minutes each for this procedure. Then I hold up the works. Feel on my back the helplessness and irritation of visits stalled. Five, ten minutes in the wire bullpen beside the hut, long enough to register a miraculous change in temperature. Less than an hour before, crossing the parking lot, I'd wondered if I'd dressed warmly enough. Now Arizona sun bakes my neck. I'm wishing for shade, for the sunglasses not permitted inside. My throat's parched. Will I be able to speak if spoken to. Through the hut's thick glass, bulletproof I'm guessing, I watch two officers talking. One steps away to a wall phone. The other plops down at a shelflike mini-desk, shuffles papers, punches buttons on a console. A dumb show since I couldn't hear a thing through the slab of greenish glass.

Did I stand in the cage five minutes or ten or twenty. What I recall is mounting heat, sweat spiders crawling inside my clothes, my eyes blinking, losing track of time, not caring about time, shakiness, numbness, mumbling to myself, stiffening rage, morphing combinations of all the above, yet overriding each sensation, the urge to flee, to be elsewhere, anywhere other than stalled at that gate, waiting to be snatched inside or driven away or, worse, pinned there forever. I dream of coolness, far, far away where I could bury my throbbing head, coolness miles deep below the sand, so deep you can hear the subterranean chortle of rivers on the opposite face of the planet.

At last someone exits the concrete hut from a door I hadn't noticed, addressing me, I think.

Sorry, sir. Computer says your visit's canceled. Try the warden's office after 9 A.M. Monday. Sorry about the mix-up. Now stand back please.

CHAPTER 6

Reading and Writing about Poetry

When power leads man towards arrogance, poetry reminds him of his limitations. When power narrows the area of man's concern, poetry reminds him of the richness and diversity of existence. When power corrupts, poetry cleanses.

—John F. Kennedy

You campaign in poetry. You govern in prose.

—Mario Cuomo

At the touch of love everyone becomes a poet.

—Plato

INTRODUCTION

You have been "studying" poetry ever since you were born. While your early lessons may have been unconscious, all the nursery rhymes, preschool songs, riddles, limericks, jump rope ditties, Dr. Seuss books, and advertising jingles of your youth made a home in your memory and a place for poetry. Humans are universally attracted to the sounds, textures, and layered meanings of poetry and poetic language. In this chapter, you will be introduced to some of the basic approaches experienced readers use to read poems and to a few satisfying ways to start writing about poetry.

WHAT IS POETRY?

Poetry and poetic language surround us. It's important to remember that no sharp distinction exists between poetry and prose; we look, instead, at a continuum, with poetry on one end, prose on the other. In *Analyzing Prose*, Richard Lanham, a well-known scholar of rhetoric and language, distinguishes between poetic and prosaic language by noting that we "look at" the words in poetry—Lanham calls poetry "opaque" language. When we read poetry, we slow down and take time to enjoy the intrinsic pleasure in the look, sound, and feel of the words and phrasing. When we read prose, on the other hand, Lanham observes that we usually want to look "through" it; we want the writer to be "clear"—to use what Lanham calls "transparent language" (199–225). With prose, we hope to be able to understand the content of a statement without paying much attention to the words. To get a sense of the difference between poetry and prose, compare the following descriptions of everyday events:

```
There is a crowd at the metro station.
```

In a Station of the Metro

The apparition of these faces in the crowd;
Petals on a wet, black bough.

(EZRA POUND, 1913)

Here's another example of the way in which poetry differs from prose:

Prose:

```
I ate those plums you left in the fridge. Hope you weren't
saving them for breakfast—they were great! Thanks!
```

Poem:

This Is Just to Say

I have eaten
the plums
that were in
the icebox
and which
you were probably
saving
for breakfast

Forgive me
they were delicious
so sweet
and so cold

(WILLIAM CARLOS WILLIAMS, 1934)

If the samples above were not identified for you, would you be able to recognize the poems as poems and the prose samples as prose? How? What makes you "look at" the poems? How do you "look through" the prose? If something is "opaque," you can't see through it—something gets in the way or stops you from seeing beyond it. What "stops" you in the poems? To begin with, the attribution of a poet's name and a title; for another, typography, or the ways words are laid out on the page. As you go through this chapter, you will be introduced to additional ways in which you may "look at" poems critically and to understand how and why they function as poems rather than just as statements of fact.

In some ways, it is confusing to think of poetry as opaque language; didn't your English teachers always try to get you to "see more deeply" into poems? If a bottle or a window is opaque, we see mostly the surface; deeper views are masked and shadowy. Likewise, if a poem is written in "opaque" language, we see mostly the surface, and the depths are obscured. The poet seems to want us to stop on the surface of the words and linger there. So the question is: Why do poets tend to use "opaque" language that masks or obscures "meaning"? Why not try to state their points clearly, in transparent, straightforward language? As students have perennially complained, "well if that's what he meant, *why* didn't he just say so!?"

That question has at least two interesting answers. First, a technical, biological, or perhaps more accurately, a neurological reason: when words are joined or used in certain ways, they are easier to remember. In fact, some words and phrases are almost impossible to forget, a fact of which poets (and advertisers) take full advantage. James Gorman makes some interesting observations about the relationship between our brains, words, and music in a humorous essay about "earworms"—that is, tunes that stick in one's head. He wonders "can a word be an earworm?," concluding that some words are just as likely to stick in one's head as a musical number (Gorman).[1] Distinctive features of poetry—**rhyme**, repetition, **assonance**, and **alliteration**—aid memory by making words "stick in your head." Because poetry was originally chanted or recited orally, aids to memory, or **mnemonic** devices, had to be built in if a poet wanted to be "unforgettable" to a wide audience.

Poets also use opaque language for cultural reasons. In every language, words accrue layered meanings and associations. Because of their sounds, **denotations**, and **connotations**, many words evoke complex psychological, intellectual, and emotional responses. Simply repeating the word *home* can make some people cry; think of Dorothy, at the end of *The Wizard of Oz* ("And all the time I just kept saying that I wanted to go home," "There's no place like home"), E. T. trying to "phone home," or the Persian cat, Sassy, in Disney's *Homeward Bound* chanting "home, home, home," as violins swell during the final reunion scene. Syntactic patterns can also reinforce poetry's emotional effect. Winston Churchill's famous and stirring call to the British people in World War II—"We will fight them on the beaches, we will fight them in the hills; we will never surrender"—was memorable and effective because he uses a series of short, parallel clauses. As you will learn later in this chapter, beginning each sentence with the same word (*we*)—a rhetorical device known as **anaphora**—emphasizes the determination and solidarity of the British in the face of foreign aggression.

Chidiock Tichborne, an untutored guildsman in the 1500s, gives his only known poem its exceptional simplicity, **pathos**, and gravity by using constructions similar to those of Churchill. Tichborne's poem is an untitled **elegy** on his own life, written the night before his execution for treason in 1586:

My prime of youth is but a frost of cares,
My feast of joy is but a dish of pain,
My crop of corn is but a field of tares,
And all my good is but vain hope of gain.
The day is gone and yet I saw no sun,
And now I live, and now my life is done.

The spring is past, and yet it hath not sprung,
The fruit is dead, and yet the leaves are green,

My youth is gone, and yet I am but young,
I saw the world, and yet I was not seen,
My thread is cut, and yet it was not spun,
And now I live, and now my life is done.

I sought my death and found it in my womb,
I lookt for life and saw it was a shade,
I trode the earth and knew it was my tomb,
And now I die, and now I am but made.
The glass is full, and now the glass is run,
And now I live, and now my life is done.

(CHIDIOCK TICHBORNE, 1586)

In the case of Tichborne's poem, **parallelism** and repetition emphasize both the lack of causal connection between one event and another ("And now I live, and now my life is done") and the depressing **paradox** that life leads inevitably to death ("I sought my death and found it in my womb" or "The fruit is dead, and yet the leaves are green"). **Anaphora** and repetition also work together, evoking the pathos of dying too young with a relentless iteration of the words *I* and *my*.

Throughout this chapter, you will be viewing and reviewing the techniques poets employ to capture and magnify both the mnemonic resonance of their verses and the depth of meaning in their words. These two elements—sound and meaning—combine to provide much of the power that drives poetry and that drives the human response to and pleasure in poetic forms.

ELEMENTS OF POETRY

Most of the elements of drama and short fiction—**plot, setting, character, tone, conflict**, and **dialogue**—can be applied when reading poetry. However, other elements are peculiar to or exaggerated in poetry. For instance, a poem's voice, or its **persona**, can reveal a poem's point of view in unique ways, and poems, in general, tend to make greater use of figurative language than stories and plays. In addition, word order and diction in poems should be attended to with special care. Finally, there are some elements particular to poetry, such as **rhythm** and **meter**, and special poetic forms and types such as the **ballad**, the **haiku**, the **ode**, or the **sonnet**. Below are brief introductions to a few of the most important elements involved in the study of poetry; refer to the Glossary of Literary Terms for a more extensive list and specific definitions of terms.

Persona

We tend to equate the voice of the poem with the voice of the poet. The **persona** (plural: personae), however, is literally, in Latin, the poet's "mask." Although a skilled science writer tries to construct a credible, intelligent **ethos** in order to be believed by her colleagues, a novelist or short story writer creates a fictional narrator whose voice will control a story's point of view. Similarly, a poet constructs a voice and tone—a persona—that is best able to convey a poem's ideas and themes. In "The Ruined Maid," for example, Thomas Hardy adopts the personae of two different women to satirize the superficial gentility of "ladies" in English society. Robert Browning speaks through the persona of the cruel, yet cavalier, Duke in "My Last Duchess," who unknowingly reveals the dark nature of his past in a strange, rambling **dramatic monologue**. When writing about poetry, we refer to the persona, not the author, as the actual speaker of the poem, for even with **confessional poetry** we can never know how closely the two are in fact aligned.

Diction and Syntax

To get a full picture of a poem's construction, you need to pay close attention to its **diction** (choice of words) and its **syntax** (word order). A study of a poem's diction requires familiarizing yourself with both the **denotation** (dictionary definitions) and the **connotations** (underlying or unique associations) of the words in the poem. You should also note the level of formality in the diction. Does the poet use formal diction, including **archaic**, elaborate, or foreign word choices, or does she use informal diction, relying on ordinary language, and, in some cases, slang, dialect, or regional expressions? You might also evaluate the diction with regard to concreteness and specificity. Does the poet choose many words that are abstract, such as *idea, love, freedom, reason*, and *time*, or does she use many concrete words that connect with our senses, such as *flame, icicle, grass*, and *balloons*? Does she generalize about people, places, and things (e.g., streets, farms, women, or cowboys), or does she specify them (e.g., "North Carolina," "walnut grove plantation," "my mama," "Buffalo Bill")?

To study a poem's syntax, or word order, you need to examine its punctuation and note where the poem departs from the typical English word order of subject-verb-object. In addition, you can examine the way the poet matches her sentences to her lines, her rhythm, and her meter. If thought and rhythm stop at the end of a line, the line is **end-stopped**; if they run over the ends of lines, the lines are **enjambed**. Finally, any full consideration of diction and syntax includes checking for the presence of figures of speech, which are discussed in the next section.

Figurative Language: Tropes and Schemes

When a writer's or speaker's language purposefully departs from its ordinary meaning or presentation, he is using one of the two classes of **figures of speech: tropes** or **schemes**. A **trope** (which means "turn") is a figure that changes, or "turns" a word from its usual, literal meaning. Some of the more common poetic tropes include: **metaphor, simile, personification, hyperbole, irony**, and **pun**. **Schemes** are figures that involve changing the normal word order or style of a group of words to create a particular effect. Some of the most common schemes used in poetry include: **anaphora, antithesis, alliteration, ellipsis, parallelism, rhetorical question**, and **chiasmus**.

Remember that the figures are rarely mutually exclusive; readers can often peel back many layers of figures in even a short poem. Take for a familiar example, J. R. R. Tolkien's short set of verses that identify the "One Ring":

One ring to rule them all,
One ring to find them,
One ring to bring them all,
And in the darkness bind them.

We see first simple repetition, and the repetition creates both **consonance** (repeated consonant sounds) and **assonance** (repeated vowel sounds). We could also call these sound repetitions **alliteration**. Because the first three clauses are nearly identical, ("One ring to . . ."), we can also identify **anaphora** (repeated opening words) or, more generally, **parallelism** (any paralleled grammatical units). The One Ring, as presented in the *Lord of the Rings* trilogy, represents, metaphorically, the evil Sauron; that is, the Ring stands in for Sauron himself. These verses extend the **metaphor** so that the Ring itself, as if it were an animated being, can "rule," "find," "bring," and "bind." These verses, therefore, also **personify** the Ring. By identifying figures in poems, you can sometimes discover a poem's otherwise unnoticed themes or ironies.

Rhythm

Poetic rhythms are divided into two main groups:

- **Accentual meter** or rhythms, found in Old English poetry (such as Caedmon's Hymn) and modern **free verse** (such as that found in Williams's "This Is Just to Say") are created by combining informal patterns of words and phrases with various kinds of repetition to create an underlying rhythm. The subtle rhythms of free verse are created through rising and falling emphasis, stress, or accent among the words and syllables in each line.
- Closed-form rhythms are created by controlling the number of lines, stanzas, and (in some cases) the number and type of rhymes in a poem. When we **scan** poetry, we name and count the **metrical feet** (i.e., stressed and unstressed syllables) in each of the poem's lines. Scanning a poem is, essentially, reading the rhythm, the music of the poem. (For more on this subject, see the entry on **meter** in the Glossary of Literary Terms.)

Formal Patterns and Traditional Topics

All poetry is patterned, and many poetic patterns, while rarely followed without some hint of idiosyncrasy, have names. Poetry presents us with two general types of poetic patterns: patterns of form (the metrical shape of a poem, which is determined by scanning the rhyme and meter of a poem) and patterns of content (the traditional poetic occasions and topics such as **elegies** and **odes**).

The most highly patterned, or "closed," forms of poetry are often traditional, such as the **haiku, limerick**, and **sonnet**. Each of these traditional closed poetic forms has an accompanying set of rules. For example, the **Petrarchan sonnet** (a form named for the Italian poet Petrarch) must have fourteen lines, divided between two stanzas: the first stanza has eight lines (an **octave**), which must rhyme *abbaabba* (each letter represents a line's end rhyme), and the second stanza has six lines (a **sestet**), which often will rhyme *cdecde*.

English poets adapted the Petrarchan sonnet rules to better suit English rhythms and developed another traditional form, the **Shakespearean** or **English sonnet**. See a comparison of these two forms below and notice how Wyatt adapted the sestet's rhyme scheme to suit English vocabulary.

William Shakespeare, Sonnet 130

My mistress' eyes are nothing like
the sun; (a)
Coral is far more red than her lips'
red; (b)
If snow be white, why then her breasts
are dun; (a)
If hairs be wires, black wires grow
on her head; (b)
I have seen roses damask'd, red
and white, (c)
But no such roses see I in her cheeks; (d)
And in some perfumes is there more
delight (c)
Than in the breath that from my
mistress reeks. (d)
I love to hear her speak, yet well
I know (e)
That music hath a far more pleasing
sound; (f)
I grant I never saw a goddess go, (e)
My mistress when she walks treads
on the ground. (f)
And yet, by heaven, I think my love
as rare (g)
As any she belied with false
compare. (g)

Sir Thomas Wyatt, "My galley, charged with forgetfulness"

My galley, chargèd with forgetfulness (a)
Thorough sharps seas and winter
nights doth pass (b)
'Tween rock and rock; and eke mine
en'my, alas, (b)
That is my lord, steereth with
cruelness; (a)
And every owre a thought
in readiness, (a)
As though that death were light
in such a case. (b)
An endless wind doth tear the sail
apace (b)
Of forced sighs and trusty
fearfulness. (a)
A rain of tears, a cloud of dark
disdain, (c)
Hath done the wearied cords great
hindrance; (d)
Wreathèd with error and eke with
ignorance (d)
The stars be hid that led me to this
pain; (c)
Drownèd is Reason that should me
comfort, (e)
And I remain despairing of the port. (e)

At the other end of the spectrum of poetic pattern is open-form poetry or **free verse**, which may have any number of lines, syllables, or accents. If not for some additional cues, such as typographical positioning on a page, a title, or use of poetic diction, open-form poetry is often indistinguishable from prose. Two good examples of modern open-form poetry are the poems by Ezra Pound and William Carlos Williams that were used to open this chapter.

In addition to conventional forms, poetry also exhibits traditional topics: themes, situations, styles, and occasions that are so typical to poetry that they have been given distinct names such as elegy, ode, lyric, ballad, or parody. **Elegies** mourn and meditate; **odes** praise and reflect; **parodies** mimic; **lyrics** (which can encompass elegies, odes, serenades, and other types of poems) speak with a personal voice on a variety of topics as, figuratively speaking, "songs." **Ballads** tell stories and are often, literally, sung. **Serenades** praise the evening; **aubades** love the morning; **epithalamia** extol marriages; **reverdies** enjoy the springtime; **pastoral** celebrate the natural life; and **complaints**, of course, complain.

STRATEGIES FOR READING POETRY

Poems, because they are constructed with such highly condensed and patterned language, call for much more active participation and closer attention than do either short stories or plays (unless you are an actor!). In these next sections, you will find several specific ways to read poetry actively.

Reading Aloud

Reading a poem aloud is surely the simplest, yet one of the most effective, ways to approach any poetic work. Reading a poem aloud tests your understanding of a poetic text in a way that looking at the text, reading silently, cannot. Actors soon learn that reading lines without understanding produces a flat, unintelligible character. Conversely, well-read lines, spoken with emphasis, emotion, and close attention to the author's signals—punctuation, capitalization, and rhymes—can convey complex, layered meanings that are hidden when a text is engaged silently. Furthermore, when you want to avoid the painstaking marking of the poem that goes along with **scansion**, reading the passage aloud often helps you find the **rhythm** and **rhyme** naturally.

As you begin to study the poems in this text, try reading the short poems, or short sections of the longer poems, aloud or have a willing friend read them to you. Typically, you will recognize at once those places where the reading loses the thread of meaning or the rhythm. Mark "unreadable" places for further study, and read the poem aloud again after you have tried some of the strategies—such as marking up, paraphrasing, and using a good dictionary—that follow.

Another technique that you might try is reading "against" your perceived notion of the **tone** and **persona** of the poem. For example, try reading Allan Ginsberg's **ranting** poem "Howl" in a despairing whisper; then try a sardonic growl, or a pathetic whine. Varying your emotional pitch, your volume, or your tone as you read can open up a poem to new interpretations. Reading against tone is especially important when you study a poem that has, perhaps, become overly familiar to you, such as Robert Frost's "Stopping by Woods on a Snowy Evening." Finally, the Internet may provide another means of hearing a poem that you are studying. Many Web sites devoted to poetry and to particular poets now include audio files, sometimes including a variety of readers presenting varying interpretations of a single poem.

Transcription

Another simple yet effective way to "read" a poem is to make a transcription, which is perhaps the closest "close reading" that you can do. The instructions are simple: copy the poem out by hand or type it into your word processor. For this exercise, it is important not to "cut and paste" or to use a copy machine. Faithfully copy by hand or type each letter of each word (including variant or old-fashioned spellings), each mark of punctuation, and each capital letter. Try to imitate the length and page positioning of each line. In completing this careful transcription, you are doing your best to see, accurately, all the details that the poet originally recorded. Noticing these details is the literary equivalent of lively and empathetic listening. You take the time to see exactly what details the poet labored to include. (At the same time, you should also remember that some details of typography or even word choice reflect an editor's intervention.) The practice of transcription seems so simple that you may be surprised at the details you notice in transcribing that you overlooked in simply reading through the poem.

Marking Up

Marking up a poem is a variant of transcription and is especially useful when you are working with longer poems. Marking up helps you see the underlying grammar (and thus meanings) that the poetic form often obscures. To mark up a poem, read slowly through the poem, circle the verbs and link them to their respective subjects; put a vertical line at the beginning and end of each sentence, and note which words are modified by any adjectives, adverbs, phrases, or clauses. (To be really thorough, you would note the part of speech and function of every word in the poem, but few of us are patient enough to complete this traditional medieval "grammar" school exercise.) Finally, look up the correct definitions and pronunciation of unfamiliar words and write brief reminders in the margin or above the word. Marking up a poem is a good first step when you are preparing to read a poem aloud to a group, to write a paraphrase, or to write an explication or analysis.

Marginal Annotations or Marginalia

As with short stories, another method of "seeing" a poem is to use your margins to "write back" to the poet. **Marginalia** are simply the comments you write in the margins as you read. Many of you have become accustomed to doing this while you study and need no specific instructions. However, you may want to refer to the section on "Annotating the Text" in Chapter 4 (under "Strategies for Reading Short Stories") to get some tips on how to go about creating marginal annotations.

Writing marginalia keeps your attention focused just as it does when reading a history text, but, more importantly, writing your comments as they occur to you helps you interact with the poem itself. Active marginal commenting can feel like a conversation with the poet, and it provides a record of your changes in understanding over time. (And as you will see in Chapter 11, literary authors themselves often engage in dialogue with or "write back" to one another; this phenomenon is called **intertextuality**.)

Some marginal commentary has become a body of literature in its own right, such as the collected biblical commentary of the Catholic patriarchs. These volumes, collectively entitled *Patria Logia,* originally often appeared as intralinear or marginal translation and commentary in biblical texts. Other, less formal marginalia, collected from a wide variety of medieval manuscripts, give us a window into life in the Middle Ages. Medieval monks and scribes not only commented on the texts they were copying, but, like you, they doodled and complained about things, such as the cold weather and their cramped fingers. We have the Old English version of the first English poem, Caedmon's Hymn, only because a few eighth-century readers of the Venerable Bede's version of the poem took a moment to write out an English translation in the margins of their Latin manuscripts.

Memorizing Poetry

The final strategy for reading poetry is memorization, or learning your favorite lines "by heart." In Aristotle's day, memorization was a major instructional technique for students and teachers of rhetoric, but we can offer you little advice other than repetition and recitation. You should also remember that poetry's rhythms and repetitions act as built-in **mnemonic** aids. If you are struggling with memorization, pick a poem with plenty of rhyme. As you study poetry, taking the time to memorize a few favorite passages is an excellent way to enjoy poetry that may give you just the right words at some important moment in the future.

STRATEGIES FOR WRITING ABOUT POEMS

The strategies suggested below are meant to help you start writing about poetry in a relaxed and relatively informal way. You might try several of them as warm-ups for longer writing assignments such as essays or research papers. You also might want to include some of these short studies in an anthology (see "Ways of Writing about Poems"). If your teacher assigns freewrites or journals as homework without specifying a topic, any of these short writing projects may help you get started.

Paraphrasing

A basic strategy when working with shorter poems is to write a paraphrase; in a paraphrase, you rewrite the poem in your own words. Your intention is to *match the poet's thought as closely as possible* in plain, modern English prose, while filling in missing subjects and verbs, clearing up any pronoun confusion, and tying together as thoughtfully as possible any loose modifiers with their most likely objects. If your paraphrase begins to interpret and explain the poem, your paraphrase will become an explication or an analysis, or in some cases, a parody of the poem. On the other hand, if you do not at least rephrase the poem into complete prose sentences, you will be writing something more like a transcription.

Parodying

Most students are familiar with the parodies of Weird Al Yankovic, who mocks both the lyrics and the styles of popular singers and their songs by imitating the rhythm, meter, rhyme, style, and tone of the original, but adding a satiric twist. Parodies are fun and instructive, but not easy to write! You may prefer to pick a poem you are not particularly fond of to parody. For an example of an excellent parody, see Anthony Hecht's "Dover Bitch," which parodies Matthew Arnold's "Dover Beach."

Creative Responses

A creative response to a poem can be another poem, a short story, a song, a painting, a collage, a sculpture, a photograph, a video, a dance, and so on. Study a poem and then respond to it by producing a creative work that represents something about your reaction to, feeling for, or understanding of a poem. Walter Ralegh's poem "The Nymph's Reply" is a response to another poem, "The Passionate Shepherd to His Love." Some poems are creative responses to other art forms; for instance, W. H. Auden's poem, "Musée des Beaux Arts" reflects on a painting by Pieter Brueghel, "Landscape with the Fall of Icarus."

Personal Responses

A personal response to a poem could certainly include creative responses, but in this case, the strategy is meant to allow you to explore your associative connections to a poem. This strategy is another good one to use if your teacher assigns a freewrite or a nonspecific journal entry. Read the poem on which you plan to write a response, and then write a paragraph or two describing any personal associations that the poem evoked as you read. Maybe a poem such as e. e. cummings's "Buffalo Bill's" will evoke a memory about watching Westerns on television when you were a kid, or John Keats's "Ode on a Grecian Urn" will call up thoughts about how much you hate museums. The point in this exercise is *not* to analyze or even think much about the poem; in a personal response you are, instead, exploring yourself, using the images and thoughts that the poem's words bring to mind.

Head Notes and Annotations

Researching and writing about a poem's historical and critical context is another useful strategy for working with a poem. You might examine an author's life in relationship to a particular poem, you could research the historical events that occurred during a poem's publication or composition, or you could examine the critical response to a particular poetic work. In any case, as preparation for a substantial writing project such as a research paper, you can use the research you gather to write **head notes** or to **annotate** a poem. If you compose the poetry anthology discussed in the section below, you may want to include head notes or annotations for each selection or for groups of selections.

A head note is typically a brief paragraph or two introducing an author and her poem. Because a head note is just a brief introduction, you will need to choose your details carefully and write concisely. Be sure to use several reliable sources and put the information you find into your own words (see Chapter 10, "Literary Research and Documentation"). If you are writing several head notes for a collection, be sure to provide similar details about each author and to make the entries of similar length.

Annotations can be added to the text of a poem as marginal notes, footnotes, or endnotes. The notes that you decide to add will reflect your knowledge and particular interests with regard to the poem you are annotating. Your annotations should explain or discuss particular words, phrases, or references in a poem and should help another reader understand and appreciate the poem in some way. You might annotate to add definitions, provide historical information, explain allusions, note critical responses to a brief passage, or comment on unusual variations in the poem's rhyme and meter. Your annotations should be extremely concise and should provide source references when applicable.

A Word Study Using the OED

To use this strategy, you will need access to the Oxford English Dictionary (OED), an encyclopedic dictionary that traces the roots (etymologies) of English words back to the sixth century. You can find a word's date of entry into the English language, its linguistic heritage, and example sentences showing the word's meaning from its earliest to its most recent use. Most libraries keep a copy of the OED in their Reference areas, and many college and university libraries pay for a subscription to the Internet version of the OED. Spend some time familiarizing yourself with the OED, then choose a word that interests you from a poem you have been studying. Check the poem's composition or publication date, then look up your chosen word in the OED and trace its linguistic roots and the history of its use in English. Write a paragraph describing your findings and noting any interesting changes in the meaning of the word that occurred before or after the word was used in the poem you are studying.

WAYS OF WRITING ABOUT POEMS

Although you can write any of the typical types of essays detailed in Chapter 3 (analysis, comparison and contrast, definition, etc.) when discussing poems, some written projects lend themselves particularly well to the study of poetry. Some of the suggestions below are specific, or nearly specific, to poetry (commonplace books, anthologies, and explications), whereas others suggest ways to focus an assignment with special regard for poetic texts (contexts, comparison/contrast, or critical stances).

Commonplace Books and Anthologies

Making a collection of poems is one satisfying way to study and write about poetry. The writing involved can be fairly minimal or can be quite extensive, depending on the type of collection you are assigned or that you decide to make.

A commonplace book is made up of a personal collection of memorable lines, verses, or texts; it is, more or less, a scrapbook for text. In fact, historically, people used the term *commonplacing* the way we use the word *scrapbooking*. Commonplace books have been kept since classical times, but they became especially prevalent during the Renaissance and continued to be popular right through the nineteenth century. Students kept their commonplace books at hand, copying down witty remarks, definitions, and short quotes or passages as they came across them in books, lectures, and conversations with friends. Items were often indexed so that categories could be cross referenced and added to easily. You can adapt the commonplace book to suit your own design, keeping a handwritten book or an electronic one, collecting any kind of text or just snippets of poetry.

A poetry anthology, on the other hand, is a collection of complete poems. You might want to include head notes or annotations (described in "Strategies for Writing about Poems") with each entry. You can also write a variety of responses to the poems you include in your anthology—creative responses, personal responses, parodies, and paraphrases. These types of responses are described above in "Strategies for Writing about Poems." Whatever types of writing (head notes, annotations, responses) you choose to accompany the poems you've selected, the most important part of an anthology, aside from the poems themselves, is an Introduction to the collection. The Introduction should describe the theme or coherent overriding idea that brings the poems together. What was your plan for the anthology, and how did these selections fit that plan? Explain your rationale and describe how each of the poems fits within its scope.

Writing an Explication

An explication is a "close reading" of a poem or a short passage of a poem; it is literally an "unfolding" of the poem (Latin *ex* = out + *plicare* = to fold or pleat). Because your intention is to observe the poem or passage as completely as possible, it is best to choose a relatively short selection of no more than twenty-five or thirty lines. Before you begin writing an explication, you should take an inventory of the poem's elements ("Elements of Poetry") and write a clear paraphrase ("Strategies for Writing about Poems"). Armed with this information, you can begin the explication itself. The explication's introductory paragraph should provide a summary account of the central features of the poem: Who is speaking the poem (**persona**) and why? Where and when is the "action" taking place? And most important, what is the central problem or conflict in the poem and how is it resolved? Your answer to these last questions should lead to the **thesis** of your explication.

After you have introduced the poem, you can follow the poem line by line, sentence by sentence, or stanza by stanza, depending on which strategy seems most manageable. In each unit, focus your discussion on the features of rhythm, formal patterns, diction, syntax, and figures of speech (listed above as "Elements of Poetry") that contribute most heavily to the unfolding of the poem's central conflict or issue as you have defined it. Typically, your paragraphs will mirror sections of the poem (i.e., a paragraph for each stanza, or, in some cases, a paragraph for each line.) Explications reach a conclusion when you finish making your observations about the final lines of the poem. In your conclusion, as you make your last observations, you should explain how the poem's main issue, tension, problem, or conflict has been explored and left open, or brought to a point of **resolution**.

Writing about Poetry with Research

The biggest challenge you will face when writing about a poem's context—its author, period, sources, or critical reception—is limiting the field of research. After all, in the broadest view, a poem's "context" is the entire universe before, during, and after the poem was written. By getting a clear, focused reading of the poem itself, you may find an interesting complication, a particular idea, a certain image, or a recurring **motif** that will help you frame your research question about the sources, author, period, or reception of the poem. Before you begin research on a poem's context, therefore, you should spend some time inventorying the poem's elements ("Elements of Poetry") and writing a paraphrase ("Strategies for Writing about Poems"). After you know your poem well, you are ready to begin your research.

When writing about context, the broad research question is always the same: What people, places, events, and ideas had an impact on the way this poem was composed and received? To start narrowing this question, begin your research by answering a few basic questions about the poem's context and author:

- Who wrote the poem (birth and death, class, race, gender, culture, health, and friends)?
- When and where was the poem written (date of composition, date of publication, age and location of the poet at composition and publication; type of environment or geography, government, current events, religion, and culture at the time the poem was written)?
- Why was the poem written (was it attached to a particular occasion or event? Was it dedicated to a particular person)?

Write up your answers as a head note or as annotations of the poem (see "Strategies for Writing about Poems"). Keep careful notes on your sources. Now that you know some basic information about the poem's context, you can choose a few limited areas that interest you for further research and compose two or three working research questions. At this point, you should ask for your teacher's input. She may be able to help you sharpen the focus of your question or suggest research sources.

The structure of a researched paper on poetry is determined by your initial question. Your introduction should include your question and should explain why or how answering this question will benefit your audience. The body of your paper will include the information you discovered in your research and should explain how each piece of information contributes to answering your research question. Your conclusion may state your answer to the original research question, indicate how your research brought you closer to answering the question, or suggest why the exploration was beneficial in some other way. You may also want to point out other research suggested by your findings that could be undertaken to begin resolving your question.

A word of caution: choosing to write about a **canonical** (i.e., well-known or very famous) poem or poet increases both the difficulty of formulating unanswered questions and the amount of background reading you will need to do. On the other hand, choosing to write about a little-known work may require original research. Consult your teacher as you begin your research.

Writing a Comparison-and-Contrast Essay

To write a short comparison-and-contrast paper, begin by choosing two or three poems or passages that you want to compare with one another. Explore the poems or passages as thoroughly as you can by completing inventories of their poetic elements, writing paraphrases for each of them, and answering some basic contextual questions as you would for a head note or annotations. Again, the next step, choosing a thesis that compares certain elements of the two poems or passages, is your most critical challenge.

Your paper's introduction will introduce the poems you intend to compare, explain what element or elements you will be comparing, suggest how your comparison resolves some "problem" or tension between the two texts, and may reveal why the comparison interested you in the first place. The body of your paper will present the details of the comparison, providing specific examples from the poems themselves. Your conclusion should draw attention to the way you have resolved some tension or have been able to highlight some feature of one or both poems by comparing them.

CONCLUSION

After reading this chapter, you should have the basic tools you will need to begin exploring the great variety of poetic themes, styles, and voices you will encounter in the next chapter. As you read and write your way through some of the poems in Chapter 7, "An Anthology of Poetry," we would like to recommend that you keep a simple list of titles or first lines on a loose page of notebook paper and keep it tucked inside this book. Which poems "attract" you? Which poems seem gross, repulsive, silly? Which poems bore you or amuse you? Which poems just stick in your head? Notice the way poems make you *feel* as well as what they make you think. Look back over your list at the end of the semester and remember that poems can tell you a good deal about who you are and who you want to be.

NOTE

1. Gorman is particularly taken with the word *amygdala.*

WORKS CITED

Gorman, James. "Ob-La-Di, Ob-La-Da, Amygdala: Word as Earworm." *New York Times,* 11 Jan. 2005. GALILEO. 11 Jan. 2005 <http://www.galileo.usg.edu>.

Lanham, Richard A. "Opaque and Transparent Styles." *Analyzing Prose*. New York: Scribner, 1983. 199–225.

CHAPTER 7

An Anthology of Poetry

CAEDMON (b. 658 CE). In Book 4, Chapter 24 of *The Ecclesiastical History of the English People* (ca. 730 CE), the Venerable Bede (673–735 CE) recounts the story of Caedmon, an illiterate cowherd, who, humiliated by his inability to sing during meadhall fellowship, retreats to sleep in a cowshed and has a miraculous dream. In the dream, an angel gives Caedmon the ability to turn words of scripture into "poetic language adorned with the greatest sweetness and inspiration and well-made in the English language." "Caedmon's Hymn" is the cowherd's first "song" and is the first recorded English poem. "Caedmon's Hymn," like other Old English poetry, was composed orally and was intended to be "sung" or chanted aloud. Composed before the influence of the continental poets, who used rhyme as the foundation of their **meter**. "Caedmon's Hymn," like all early English poetry, depends instead on patterned **alliteration** for its poetic value. Caedmon also follows the tradition of "inspired" poetry, whether the inspiration comes from a **muse**, an angel, or some other miraculous source.

Related Works: Achebe, "Why the Tortoise's Shell Is Not Smooth"; Eliot, "The Love Song of J. Alfred Prufrock"; Whitman, "Oh Captain! my Captain!"; Milton, *Lycidas*; Ginsberg, "Howl."

CAEDMON

Caedmon's Hymn

Nu sculon herigean hefonfrices weard,	It is right that we worship the Warden of heaven,
Meotodes meahte and his modgeþane,	The might of the Maker, His firmness of mind,
Weore wuldorfæder swa he wundra gehwæs,	The Glory-Father's work when of all His wonders,
Ece drihten, or onstealde.	Eternal God made a beginning.
He ærest sceop eorðan bearnum	He earliest established for earth's children
Heofon to hrofe, halig scyppend;	Heaven for a roof, the Holy Shaper;
þa middangeard moneynnes weard,	The mankind's Warden created the world

Leningrad Bede, fol. 1071 Latin text, with Caedmon's Hymn in Latin, transcribed into Old English at the bottom of the mss. leaf.

Ece drihten, æfter teode	Eternal Monarch, making for men
Firum foldan, frea ælmihtig	Land to live on, Almighty Lord!

THE HUSBAND'S MESSAGE and THE WIFE'S LAMENT are both found in the *Exeter Book* Manuscript (ca. 940). These two untitled, anonymous Old English **elegies** are closely akin to the riddles found in the same manuscript. In their **elliptical** references to the circumstances surrounding a wife who laments her husband's absence and a husband who urges his wife to join him—"speaking" through a carved staff and a **runic signature**—the reader must struggle to understand the riddles presented by their situations. Nevertheless, the tone of **elegiac** sadness—even in translation from the original Old English—is clear.

Related Works: Hawthorne, "Young Goodman Brown"; Old English Riddles; Hardy, "The Ruined Maid"; Burns, "A Red, Red Rose"; Akmatova, "Lot's Wife"; Cofer, "The Woman Who Was Left at the Altar"; Levertov, "The Ache of Marriage"; Shakespeare, *The Taming of the Shrew*.

The Husband's Message

Now shall I unseal myself to yourself alone
. . . the wood kind, waxed from saplinghood;
on me . . .   must in foreign lands
set . . .
saltstreams.
            In the beak of ships
I have often been
where my lord . . .   me
among high houses; and here am come now
on board a ship.
                You shall directly
know how you may think of the thorough love
my lord feels for you. I have no fear in promising
you shall find him heart-whole, honour bright.

Hwaet!
    The carver of this token entreats a lady
clad in clear stones to call to mind
and hold in her wit words pledged
often between the two in earlier days:
then he would hand you through hall and yard
lord of his lands, and you might live together
forge your love. A feud drove him
from his war-proud people.
                        That prince, glad now,
gave me this word for you: when you shall hear
in the copse at the cliff's edge the cuckoo pitch
his melancholy cry, come over sea.

You will have listened long: leave then with no notice,
let no man alive delay your going:
into the boat and out to sea,
seagull's range; southward from here
over the paths in the foam you shall find your man,
make landfall where your lord is waiting.

He does not conceive, he said to me,
that a greater happiness could be his in this world
than that all-wielding God should grant you both
days when together you may give out rings
among followers and fellows, free-handed deal
the nailed armbands. Of which he has enough,
of inlaid gold . . .

There lands are his, a hearth among strangers,
estate . . .
            . . . of men,

although my lord here . . .
when the need grew strait, steered his boat out
through steep breakers, and had singlehanded
to run the deep ways, dared escape,
mingled saltstreams. The man has now
laid his sorrows, lacks no gladdeners;
he has a hoard and horses and hall-carousing
and would have everything within an earl's having
had he my lady with him: if my lady will come:
if she will hold to what was sworn and sealed in your youths.

So I set together, S and R twinned,
E A, W, D. The oath is named
whereby he undertakes until the end of his life
to keep the covenants of companionship
that, long ago, you delighted to repeat.

The Wife's Lament

I draw these words from my deep sadness,
my sorrowful lot. I can say that,
since I grew up, I have not suffered
such hardships as now, old or new.
I am tortured by the anguish of exile.

First my lord forsook his family
for the tossing waves; I fretted at dawn
as to where in the world my lord might be.
In my sorrow I set out then,
a friendless wanderer, to search for my man.
But that man's kinsmen laid secret plans
to part us, so that we should live
most wretchedly, far from each other
in this wide world; I was seized with longings.

My lord asked me to live with him here;
I had few loved ones, loyal friends
in this country; that is reason for grief.
Then I found my own husband was ill-starred,
sad at heart, pretending, plotting
murder behind a smiling face. How often
we swore that nothing but death should ever
divide us; that is all changed now;
our friendship is as if it had never been.
Early and late, I must undergo hardship

because of the feud of my own dearest loved one.
Men forced me to live in a forest grove,
under an oak tree in the earth-cave.
This cavern is age-old; I am choked with longings.
Gloomy are the valleys, too high the hills,
harsh strongholds overgrown with briars:
a joyless abode. The journey of my lord so often
cruelly seizes me. There are lovers on earth,
lovers alive who lie in bed,
when I pass through this earth-cave alone
and out under the oak tree at dawn;
there I must sit through the long summer's day
and there I mourn my miseries,
my many hardships; for I am never able
to quiet the cares of my sorrowful mind,
all the longings that are my life's lot.

Young men must always be serious in mind
and stout-hearted; they must hide
their heartaches, that host of constant sorrows,
behind a smiling face.
Whether he is master
of his own fate or is exiled in a far-off land—
sitting under rocky storm-cliffs, chilled
with hoar-frost, weary in mind,
surrounded by the sea in some sad place—
my husband is caught in the clutches of anguish;
over and again he recalls a happier home.
Grief goes side by side with those
who suffer longing for a loved one.

OLD ENGLISH RIDDLES. In the *Rhetoric* (3:11), Aristotle points out that riddles are effective in arguments for the same reason that metaphors are; they make an old idea or word seem new, and audiences like the surprise. Along with charms, spells, and gnomic verses (or maxims), Old English **riddles** form an important category of Old English "wisdom poetry." Very much like the riddles exchanged by Bilbo, Gollum, and other fictional characters in J. R. R. Tolkien's Middle-earth (which are imitations of the Old English originals), real eighth-century Old English riddles use **alliteration** and **accentual meter** to create the **mnemonic** effect of verse. Riddles are meant to defamiliarize the ordinary things of everyday life—onions, swords, fish, and keys. The riddle maker forces the listener to adopt an outsider's perspective—to become for a time an alien within his or her own language—in a way similar to some of the best modern poetry. The riddles preserved for us today go back to a single, anonymous collection found in a unique manuscript, the *Codex Exoniensis* or the *Exeter Book*, a tenth-century Old English "anthology" preserved by the Exeter Cathedral Chapter library in England.

Related Works: Donne, "The Flea"; Blake, "The Tiger"; Atwood, "You fit into me"; Lee, "Persimmons"; Nash, "Very Like a Whale"; Pound, "In a Station of the Metro."

Five Old English Riddles

XIV Horn

I was weaponed warrior. Now proud, young,
a warrior covers me with silver and gold,
with curved wire-bows. Sometimes men kiss me;
sometimes I summon pleasant companions
to war with my voice. Sometimes steed bears me
over the marchland; sometimes a mere-steed
bears over oceans me brightly adorned.
Sometimes a maiden fills ring-adorned bosom;
sometimes on tables, on hard boards,
headless I lie, despoiled by the warriors.
Sometimes I hang with jewels adorned
where men drink, fair on the wall,
noble war-trapping: sometimes folk-warriors
on steed carry me—then must I wind
swallow, wealth-marked, from somebody's bosom.
Sometimes with calls I warriors invite,
proud ones to wine; sometimes from cruel ones
with voice I restore booty, from raiders,
make fiend-scathers flee. Guess me!

XVI Anchor

Oft must I with wave strive and with wind fight,
together against them contend, when I depart seeking
wave-covered earth; foreign is land to me,
I am strong for that strife if I become still;
if I fail of that, they are stronger than I,
wish to carry away the thing I protect.
I withstand that if my tail holds out
and stout stones can hold me
fast against them. Guess what I'm called.

XXVI Book

Some fiend deprived me of life,
took away world-strength, wet me afterward,
dipped me in water, did so again,
set me in sun, where I soon lost
hairs that I had. Hard edge of knife
afterward cut me, scraped me clean.
Fingers folded me, and me fowl's joy
throughout with good drops made tracks enough,
over bright border, swallowed the beam-dye,
travelled swart-tracked. One clothed me after
with boards for protection, covered with hide,

decked me with gold; then on me glistened
rare smith's work, surrounded with wire.

Now those ornaments and that red dye
and those glories widely proclaim
helm of multitudes, not foolish pains.
If sons of men wish to enjoy me,
they are the safer, by that more victorious,
in heart the braver, and blither of thought;
wiser in spirit, they have friends the more,
dearer and nearer, more honest and good,
better and truer. Then their fame and happiness
increase they with favors, and cover themselves
with kindness and grace, and with love's embrace
they clasp themselves fast. Learn what I'm called,
advantage to men. My name is great,
useful to men, and myself holy.

XLVII Bookworm

Moth ate words. It seemed to me
a curious chance, when that wonder I learned,
that the worm forswallowed some man's song,
thief in darkness the glorious speech
and its foundation. Thievish guest was
no whit the wiser for swallowing words.

LX Reed

I was by sound, near seawall
at seashore: securely I dwelt
in my first place. Few of mankind
beheld there my dwelling alone,
but each dawn the dark wave
in sea's embrace closed me. Little I thought
that I, ere or since, ever should
over mead-bench mouthless speak,
weave words. A wondrous lot,
in mind amazing to uncunning one,
how knife's point and right hand,
man's thought together with point,
purposely cut me, so that I with thee
for us two alone errand-speech
should boldly announce, so that no more of men
the words of us two more widely might tell.

GEOFFREY CHAUCER (ca. 1340–1400), best known as the author of the *Canterbury Tales*, was born in London to a middle-class vintner during the reign of King Edward III; he died just after King Richard II, the last of the Plantagenet kings.

For the son of a merchant, Chaucer's career was impressively aristocratic. Records indicate that Chaucer participated in the military, bureaucratic, and diplomatic arms of English government and must have completed his considerable literary efforts alongside an active court life. Chaucer's poetry is represented here by the humorous **complaint** poem, "Complaint to His Purse" (c. 1399), which includes three stanzas, each with a **refrain**, followed by a final unique **stanza** of dedication, the **envoy**. Chaucer also wrote a romance (*Troilus and Criseyde*, 1385), an **elegy** on the death of Edward the Black Prince's wife, Blanche (*The Book of the Duchess*, 1370), debate poetry, scientific essays, and translations.

Related Works: Singer, "Gimpel the Fool"; Old English Riddles; Medieval Lyrics; Ginsberg, "Howl"; Shakespeare, Sonnet 73; Swift, "A Description of the Morning"; Wyatt, "They flee from me"; Behn, "Song"; Randall, "The Ballad of Birmingham."

GEOFFREY CHAUCER

Complaint to His Purse

(Spelling modernized and glosses added by Deborah Miller)

To you, my purse, and to none other wight° — *person*
Complain I, for ye be my lady dear!
I am so sorry, now that ye be light;
For certes, but° ye make me heavy chere,° — *unless, grave face or full weight*
Me were as leef° be laid upon my bere;° — *I would prefer, funeral bier*
For which unto your mercy thus I cry:
Be heavy again, or else must I die!

Now vouch safe° this day, ere it be night, — *vow*
That I of you the blissful sound may hear,
Or see your colour like the sun bright,
That of yellownesse had never peer.
Ye be my life, ye be mine heart's stere,° — *guide*
Queen of comfort and of good company:
Be heavy again, or else must I die!

Ye purse, that been to me my life's light
And saviour, as in this world down here,
Out of this tonne° help me through your might, — *dark area*
Sith that ye will not be my treasurer;
For I am shave as nye° as any frere.° — *close, friar*
But yet I pray unto your courtesy:
Be heavy again, or else must I die!

Envoy of Chaucer to Henry IV

O conqueror of Brutes Albyon
Which that by line° and free election — *inheritance*

Been very° king, this song to you I send; *true*
And ye, that may all our harms amend,
Have mind° upon my supplication! *put your mind to*

MEDIEVAL LYRIC POETRY (1300–1600), composed primarily in the fifteenth and sixteenth centuries, differs from modern **lyric** poetry in that, for the most part, medieval lyrics were actually meant to be sung and accompanied by musical instruments. Many of these lyrics still contain choruses and repetitions. Most English medieval lyrics were adapted from the songs of traveling French troubadours and German Golliards, and these cross-cultural adaptations probably aided in the English transition to continental poetic forms. One of the two main categories of medieval lyrics, the secular lyrics, dealt with romantic love within a seasonal—often springtime (**reverdie**)—setting ("Between March and April," "Fowls in the Frith," "The Cuckoo Song"). The religious lyrics, on the other hand, focused on sacred topics, often the life of Christ or the singer's adoration of Mary, known collectively as the Marian lyrics ("I sing of a maiden that is matchless").

Related Works: Donne, Holy Sonnet 14; Brooks, "The mother"; Williams, "Spring and All"; cummings, "In Just—"; Lord Byron, "She walks in beauty"; Burns, "John Barleycorn: A Ballad"; Wordsworth, "I wandered lonely as a cloud."

Medieval Lyrics

Sumer is ycomen in (Middle English)

Sumer is ycomen in,
Loude sing cuckou!
Groweth seed and bloweth meed,
And springth the wode now.
Sing cuckou!

Ewe bleteth after lamb,
Loweth after calve cow,
Bulloc sterteth, bucke verteth,
Merye sing cuckou!

Cuckou, cuckou,
Wel singest thou cuckou:
Ne swik thou never now!
Cuckou, cuckou.

Summer is i-comin' in

Summer is i-comin' in
Loud sing cuckoo
Growing seed and blowing meadow
And the woods spring up now
Sing cuckoo!

The ewe bleats after the lamb
The cow lows after the calf
The bullock jumps, and the buck farts,
Merry sing cuckoo!

Cuckoo, cuckoo
You sing well, cuckoo!
Don't ever cease, now!
Cuckoo, cuckoo.

Medieval Lyrics

Bitweene Merch and Averil (Middle English)

Bitweene Merch and Averil,
When spray biginneth to springe,
The litel fowl hath hire wil
On hire leod to singe.
Ich libbe in love-longinge
For semlokest of alle thinge.
Heo may me blisse bringe:
Ich am in hire baundoun.
An hendy hap ich habbe yhent,
Ichoot from hevene it is me sent:
From alle wommen my love is lent,
And light on Alisoun.

On hew hire heer is fair ynough,
Hire browe browne, hire yën blake;
With lossum cheere heo on me lough;
With middel smal and wel ymake.
But heo me wolle to hire take
For to been hire owen make,
Longe to liven ichulle forsake,
And feye fallen adown.
An hendy hap, etc.

Nightes when I wende and wake,
Forthy mine wonges waxeth wan:
Levedy, al for thine sake
Longinge is ylent me on.
In world nis noon so witer man
That al hire bountee telle can;
Hire swire is whittere than the swan,
And fairest may in town.
An hendy, etc.

Ich am for wowing al forwake,
Wery so water in wore.
Lest any reve me my make
Ich habbe y-yerned yore.
Bettere is tholien
    while sore
Than mournen evermore.

Between March and April

Between March and April,
When the branches begin to sprout,
And the little fowl has a will
To sing in her language.
I live in love-longing
For the seemliest of all things.
She may bring me bliss:
I am in her power.
A gracious chance, I have received,
I believe from heaven it is sent:
From all women my love is taken,
And lights on Alisoun.

In hue her hair is fair enough,
Her brows are brown, her eyes are black;
With a lovely face she smiled on me;
With a small and well made middle.
Unless she will take me to her
To be her own mate,
I will forsake the longing to live
And fall down and die
A gracious chance, etc.

At nights I toss and wake,
And therefore my cheeks grow pale:
Lady, all for your sake
Longing has overcome me.
In this world there is no clever man
That could tell all her bounty;
Here neck is whiter than the swan,
And the fairest maid in town.
A gracious chance, etc.

I am all worn out from wooing,
Weary as water in a pool.
Lest any steal from me my mate
I have yearned for for so long.
It is better to suffer deeply
    for a long time
Than to mourn for evermore.

Geinest under gore,
Herkne to my roun:
An hendy, etc.

Kindest under the skirts,
Harken to my song:
A gracious chance, etc.

Medieval Lyrics

I Sing of a Maiden (Middle English)

I sing of a maiden
That is makelees:
King of alle kinges
To her sone she chees.

He cam also stille
Ther his moder was
As dewe in Aprille
That falleth on the gras.

He cam also stille
To his modres bowr
As dewe in Aprille
That falleth on the flowr.

He cam also stille
Ther his moder lay
As dewe in Aprille
That falleth on the spray.

Moder and maiden
Was nevere noon but she:
Wel may swich a lady
Godes moder be.

I sing of a maiden that is matchless

I sing of a maiden
That is matchless:
The King of all kings
She chose for her son.

He came so still
To where his mother was
As dew in April
That falls on the grass.

He came so still
To his mother's bower
As dew in April
That falls on the flower.

He came so still
To where his mother lay
As dew in April
That falls on the branch.

Mother and maiden
There was never such a one as she:
Well may such a lady
Gods mother be.

Medieval Lyrics

Fowles in the Frith (Middle English)

Fowles in the frith,
The fishes in the flood,

Fowls in the Frith

Fowls in the woods
The fishes in the flood,

And I mon waxe wood	And I must wax mad
Much sorwe I walke with	Much sorrow I walk with
For beste of boon and blood	For beast of bone and blood

ANONYMOUS BALLADS (ca. 1300–1600). The folk ballads of the late Middle Ages and early Renaissance were sung to dance music and were widely known long before they were written down. As a result, we often have many versions of some **ballads**. In the 1800s, scholars developed an interest in the ballad form, and collectors like F. J. Child (*English and Scottish Popular Ballads*, 5 vols., 1882–98) collected and indexed hundreds of ballads. Most English and Scottish ballads are still referenced by their "Child" catalog number, as are the following three ballads. Ballads traditionally deal with supernatural characters, tragic love, or legendary folk heroes such as Robin Hood. Ballads must relate a story, have a "dance-like" rhythm, and include some active dialogue, but otherwise have few formal features, requiring only **stanzas** with **refrains** and a few stock **epithets** identifying characters and settings.

Related Works: Poe, "The Tell-Tale Heart"; Randall, "Ballad of Birmingham"; Keats, "La Belle Dame sans Merci"; Coleridge, "The Rime of the Ancient Mariner"; Frost, "The Death of the Hired Man"; Wilson, *The Piano Lesson.*

Bonny Barbara Allan

It was in and about the Martinmas time.
When the green leaves were a-fallin';
That Sir John Graeme in the West Country
Fell in love with Barbara Allan.

He sent his man down through the town
To the place where she was dwellin';
"O haste and come to my master dear,
Gin ye be Barbara Allan."

O hooly, hooly rase she up,
To the place where he was lyin';
And when she drew the curtain by;
"Young man, I think you're dyin'."

"O it's I'm sick, and very, very sick,
And 'tis a' for Barbara Allan."
"O the better for me ye sal never be,
Though your heart's blood were a-spillin'."

"O dinna ye mind, young man," said she,
"When ye the cups were fillin'.

That ye made the healths gae round and round,
  And slighted Barbara Allan?"

He turned his face unto the wall,
  And death with him was dealin';
"Adieu, adieu, my dear friends all,
  And be kind to Barbara Allan."

And slowly, slowly, rase she up,
  And slowly, slowly left him;
And sighing said she could not stay,
  Since death of life had reft him.

She had not gane a mile but twa,
  When she heard the dead-bell knellin',
And every jow that the dead-bell ga'ed
  It cried, "Woe to Barbara Allan."

"O mother, mother, make my bed.
  O make it soft and narrow:
Since my love died for me today,
  I'll die for him tomorrow."

Sir Patrick Spens

The king sits in Dumferline town,
  Drinking the blude-reid wine:
"O whar will I get a guid sailor
  To sail this ship of mine?"

Up and spak an eldern knicht,
  Sat at the king's richt knee:
"Sir Patrick Spens is the best sailor
  That sails upon the sea."

The king has written a braid letter
  And signed it wi' his hand,
And sent it to Sir Patrick Spens,
  Was walking on the sand.

The first line that Sir Patrick read,
  A loud lauch lauched he;
The next line that Sir Patrick read,
  The tear blinded his ee.

"O wha' is this has done this deed,
  This ill deed done to me,

To send me out this time o' the year.
  To sail upon the sea?

"Make haste, make haste, my mirry men all,
  Our guid ship sails the morn."
"O say na sae, my master dear,
  For I fear a deadly storm.

"Late late yestre'en I saw the new moon
  Wi' the auld moon in her arm,
And I fear, I fear, my dear master,
  That we will come to harm."

O our Scots nobles were richt laith
  To weet their cork-heeled shoon,
But lang owre a' the play were played
  Their hats they swam aboon.

O lang, lang may their ladies sit,
  Wi' their fans into their hand,
Or e'er they see Sir Patrick Spens
  Come sailing to the land.

O lang, lang may the ladies stand,
  Wi' their gold kembs in their hair,
Waiting for their ain dear lords,
  For they'll see thame na mair.

Half o'er, half o'er to Aberdour
  It's fifty fadom deep,
And there lies guid Sir Patrick Spens,
  Wi' the Scots lords at his feet.

Lord Randall

"Oh where ha'e ye been, Lord Randall my son?
O where ha'e ye been, my handsome young man?"
  "I ha'e been to the wild wood: mother, make my bed soon,
  For I'm weary wi' hunting, and fain wald lie down."

"Where gat ye your dinner, Lord Randall my son?
Where gat ye your dinner, my handsome young man?"
  "I dined wi' my true love: mother, make my bed soon,
  For I'm weary wi' hunting, and fain wald lie down."

"What gat ye to your dinner, Lord Randall my son?
What gat ye to your dinner, my handsome young man?"
  "I gat eels boiled in broo: mother, make my bed soon,
  For I'm weary wi' hunting and fain wald lie down."

"What became of your bloodhounds, Lord Randall my son?
What became of your bloodhounds, my handsome young man?"
  "O they swelled and they died: mother, make my bed soon,
  For I'm weary wi' hunting and fain wald lie down."

"O I fear ye are poisoned, Lord Randall my son!
O I fear ye are poisoned, my handsome young man!"
  "Oh yes, I am poisoned: mother, make my bed soon,
  For I'm sick at the heart, and I fain wald lie down."

APHRA BEHN (1640–1689) is often described as the first English woman to become a professional writer. Most famous for her plays, including a popular, swashbuckler adventure drama, *The Rover* (1677–81), Behn also wrote an important early novel decrying slavery (*Oroonoko, or The History of the Royal Slave*, 1688) and a collection of poetry (*Miscellany*, 1685). After the early death of her first husband, Behn attracted a strong circle of aristocrats and men of letters as friends and admirers, traveled as a spy for Charles II, and led an unusually independent life for a woman of her time. In both poems included here, "Song" (1677) and "On Her Loving Two Equally" (1684), Behn reverses the gender of the **persona** speaking the typical love **complaint**.

Related Works: Updike, "A&P"; Drayton, Sonnet 61; Wyatt, "They flee from me"; Shakespeare, Sonnets 73 and 116; Keats, "La Belle Dame sans Merci"; Hardy, "The Ruined Maid"; H.D., "Helen"; Shakespeare, *The Taming of the Shrew*.

APHRA BEHN

On Her Loving Two Equally

How strongly does my passion flow,
Divided equally 'twixt two?
Damon had ne'er subdued my heart,
Had not Alexis took his part;
Nor could Alexis powerful prove,
Without my Damon's aid, to gain my love.

When my Alexis present is,
Then I for Damon sigh and mourn;
But when Alexis I do miss,
Damon gains nothing but my scorn.
But if it chance they both are by,
For both alike I languish, sigh, and die.

Cure then, thou mighty winged god,
This restless fever in my blood;

One golden-pointed dart take back:
But which, O Cupid, wilt thou take?
If Damon's, all my hopes are crossed;
Or that of my Alexis, I am lost.

APHRA BEHN

Song

Love in fantastic triumph sate
   Whilst bleeding hearts around him flow'd,
For whom fresh pains he did create
   And strange tyrannic power he show'd;
From thy bright eyes he took his fires,
   Which round about in sport he hurl'd;
But 'twas from mine he took desires
   Enough t' undo the amorous world.

From me he took his sighs and tears,
   From thee his pride and cruelty;
From me his languishments and fears,
   And every killing dart from thee.
Thus thou and I the god have arm'd
   And set him up a deity;
But my poor heart alone is harm'd,
   Whilst thine the victor is, and free!

ANNE (DUDLEY) BRADSTREET (ca. 1612–1672) was raised in England in a privileged, well-educated family. In 1630, shortly after she married and as part of the Puritan "Great Migration," she immigrated to the Massachusetts Bay Colonies with her husband, Simon Bradstreet, and her parents. Among the wealthiest of the colonists, both her father and her husband eventually became colony governors. Bradstreet continued developing her craft in America through the birth of eight children. Her first publication in 1650 (*The Tenth Muse Lately Sprung Up in America*) includes poetic discourses on the four ages of man, the four humors, the four seasons, and the four elements. In her later writing, such as "To My Dear and Loving Husband" (1678), Bradstreet deals with increasingly personal material such as her husband, her children, and the circumstances of life in seventeenth-century New England. In "To My Dear and Loving Husband," she develops a **metaphysical conceit** based on debt and payment.

Related Works: Hawthorne, "Young Goodman Brown"; "The Husband's Message"; "The Wife's Lament"; Donne, "The Flea"; Clifton, "my mama moved among the days"; Barrett Browning, Sonnet 43; Glaspell, *Trifles*.

ANNE BRADSTREET

To My Dear and Loving Husband

If ever two were one, then surely we.
If ever man were lov'd by wife, then thee.
If ever wife was happy in a man,
Compare with me, ye women, if you can.
I prize thy love more than whole Mines of gold
Or all the riches that the East doth hold.
My love is such that Rivers cannot quench,
Nor ought but love from thee give recompetence.
Thy love is such I can no way repay.
The heavens reward thee manifold, I pray.
Then while we live, in love let's so persever
That when we live no more, we may live ever.

ANNE BRADSTREET

The Author to Her Book

Thou ill-formed offspring of my feeble brain,
Who after birth did'st by my side remain,
Till snatched from thence by friends, less wise than true,
Who thee abroad exposed to public view;
Made thee in rags, halting, to the press to trudge,
Where errors were not lessened, all may judge.
At thy return my blushing was not small,
My rambling brat (in print) should mother call;
I cast thee by as one unfit for light,
Thy visage was so irksome in my sight;
Yet being mine own, at length affection would
Thy blemishes amend, if so I could:
I washed thy face, but more defects I saw,
And rubbing off a spot, still made a flaw.
I stretched thy joints to make thee even feet,
Yet still thou run'st more hobbling than is meet;
In better dress to trim thee was my mind,
But nought save homespun cloth in the house I find.
In this array, 'mongst vulgars may'st thou roam;
In critics' hands beware thou dost not come;
And take thy way where yet thou are not known.
If for thy Father asked, say thou had'st none;

And for thy Mother, she alas is poor,
Which caused her thus to send thee out of door.

JOHN DONNE (1572–1631), raised a Catholic in a period marked by Protestant upheaval, was denied university degrees and lost a brother due to his family's Catholic heritage. Donne renounced Catholicism in the early 1590s, became a soldier-adventurer, and secretly married his benefactor's niece in 1601. The scandalous marriage resulted in not only twelve children in little more than fifteen years and the early death of his wife, but also a period of deep poverty and dependence for Donne. After his official adoption of Anglicanism, his fortunes improved, and he became a priest, then dean of St. Paul's Cathedral in London, and eventually one of the most celebrated preachers of the time. His sermons and his poetry were collected and published posthumously, but many of his writings were already well-known among his peers, as they were circulated privately in manuscript form. Donne's dense verse, often in **sonnet** form, makes use of highly intellectual extended metaphors or **conceits**, which mark his departure from the traditional metaphors of the early Renaissance sonneteers.

Related Works: Shakespeare, Sonnet 18; Wyatt, "They flee from me"; Barrett Browning, Sonnet 14; Levertov, "O Taste and See."

JOHN DONNE

A Valediction Forbidding Mourning

As virtuous men pass mildly away,
And whisper to their souls to go,
Whilst some of their sad friends do say,
"Now his breath goes," and some say, "No."

So let us melt, and make no noise,
No tear-floods, nor sigh-tempests move;
'Twere profanation of our joys
To tell the laity our love.

Moving of th' earth brings harms and fears;
Men reckon what it did, and meant;
But trepidation of the spheres,
Though greater far, is innocent.

Dull sublunary lovers' love
—Whose soul is sense—cannot admit
Of absence, 'cause it doth remove
The thing which elemented it.

But we by a love so much refined,
That ourselves know not what it is,

Inter-assured of the mind,
  Care less, eyes, lips and hands to miss.

Our two souls therefore, which are one,
  Though I must go, endure not yet
A breach, but an expansion,
  Like gold to aery thinness beat.

If they be two, they are two so
  As stiff twin compasses are two;
Thy soul, the fix'd foot, makes no show
  To move, but doth, if th' other do.

And though it in the centre sit,
  Yet, when the other far doth roam,
It leans, and hearkens after it,
  And grows erect, as that comes home.

Such wilt thou be to me, who must,
  Like th' other foot, obliquely run;
Thy firmness makes my circle just,
  And makes me end where I begun.

JOHN DONNE

The Flea

Mark but this flea, and mark in this,
How little that which thou deniest me is;
It suck'd me first, and now sucks thee,
And in this flea our two bloods mingled be.
Thou know'st that this cannot be said
A sin, nor shame, nor loss of maidenhead;
  Yet this enjoys before it woo,
  And pamper'd swells with one blood made of two;
  And this, alas! is more than we would do.

O stay, three lives in one flea spare,
Where we almost, yea, more than married are.
This flea is you and I, and this
Our marriage bed, and marriage temple is.
Though parents grudge, and you, we're met,
And cloister'd in these living walls of jet.
  Though use make you apt to kill me,
  Let not to that self-murder added be,
  And sacrilege, three sins in killing three.

Cruel and sudden, hast thou since
Purpled thy nail in blood of innocence?
Wherein could this flea guilty be,
Except in that drop which it suck'd from thee?
Yet thou triumph'st, and say'st that thou
Find'st not thyself nor me the weaker now.
'Tis true; then learn how false fears be;
Just so much honour, when thou yield'st to me,
Will waste, as this flea's death took life from thee.

JOHN DONNE

The Apparition

When by thy scorn, O murderess, I am dead,
And that thou thinkst thee free
From all solicitation from me,
Then shall my ghost come to thy bed,
And thee, feigned vestal, in worse arms shall see;
Then thy sick taper will begin to wink,
And he whose thou art then, being tired before,
Will, if thou stir, or pinch to wake him, think
        Thou call'st for more,
And in false sleep will from thee shrink,
And then, poor aspen wretch, neglected thou
Bathed in a cold quicksilver sweat wilt lie
        A verier ghost than I;
What I will say, I will not tell thee now,
Lest that preserve thee; and since my love is spent,
I had rather thou shouldst painfully repent,
Than by my threatenings rest still innocent.

JOHN DONNE

Holy Sonnets

XIV

Batter my heart, three-person'd God; for you
As yet but knock; breathe, shine and seek to mend;

That I may rise, and stand, o'erthrow me,
and bend
Your force, to break, blow, burn, and make
me new.
I, like an usurp'd town, to another due,
Labour to admit you, but O, to no end.
Reason, your viceroy in me, me should defend,
But is captived, and proves weak or untrue.
Yet dearly I love you, and would be loved fain,
But am betroth'd unto your enemy;
Divorce me, untie, or break that knot again,
Take me to you, imprison me, for I,
Except you enthrall me, never shall be free,
Nor ever chaste, except you ravish me.

JOHN DONNE

10

Death, be not proud, though some have called thee
Mighty and dreadful, for thou art not so;
For those whom thou think'st thou dost overthrow
Die not, poor Death, nor yet canst thou kill me.
From rest and sleep, which but thy pictures be,
Much pleasure; then from thee much more must flow,
And soonest our best men with thee do go,
Rest of their bones, and soul's delivery.
Thou art slave to fate, chance, kings, and desperate men,
And dost with poison, war, and sickness dwell,
And poppy or charms can make us sleep as well
And better than thy stroke; why swell'st thou then?
One short sleep past, we wake eternally
And death shall be no more; Death, thou shalt die.

MICHAEL DRAYTON (1563–1631). Living and writing during William Shakespeare's life, Drayton was a prolific creator of **sonnets, pastorals, odes, satires**, philosophic poems, and historical-geographic poems. Very little is known about his life. Drayton's favorite work, a 30,000 line **epic** tribute to the English landscape, *Poly-Olbion*, is less often read than his **sonnets**, many of which he directs to his patroness and "lady" Anne Goodyere, the Lady Rainsford. Sonnet 61 from *Ideas Mirrour: Amours in Quatorzains* (1601 and 1619) is one of these. Drayton **personifies** Lady Rainsford as "Idea."

Related Works: Shakespeare, Sonnets 18, 73, 116, and 130; Millay, Sonnet 42; Donne, "The Flea"; Barrett Browning, Sonnets 14 and 43.

MICHAEL DRAYTON

From
Idea

LXI

Since there's no help, come, let us kiss and part,
Nay, I have done: you get no more of me,
And I am glad, yea, glad with all my heart,
That thus so cleanly, I myself can free.
Shake hands for ever, cancel all our vows,
And when we meet at any time again
Be it not seen in either of our brows
That we one jot of former love retain.
Now at the last gasp of Love's latest breath,
When, his pulse failing, Passion speechless lies,
When Faith is kneeling by his bed of death,
And Innocence is closing up his eyes.
  Now, if thou wouldst, when all have given him over,
  From death to life thou might'st him yet recover.

GEORGE HERBERT (1593–1633), the fifth son in a wealthy and influential family, began writing poetry in his early adolescence as a student at Westminster and Cambridge. Despite a prestigious career in academia and, briefly, as a representative to Parliament, Herbert retired from public life in his early thirties and became rector to a rural parish. He then married, adopted two children, and continued to write until he died, just before turning forty. The majority of his poetry was collected shortly after his death and published as *The Temple* in 1633. His poems were much admired by Puritans and Anglicans alike for their piety, and the collection went through thirteen editions over the next forty years. Aside from his striking use of religious themes, Herbert was also one of the first to adopt visual-thematic resonances in his poetry, creating a **pattern poem** in "Easter Wings" (1633).

Related Works: Donne, Holy Sonnet 14; Milton, "When I consider how my light is spent"; Hopkins, "Pied Beauty"; Garcia, "Why I Left the Church"; cummings, "since feeling is first"; Atwood, "You fit into me."

GEORGE HERBERT

Easter Wings

Lord, Who createdst man in wealth and store,
Though foolishly he lost the same,
Decaying more and more,
Till he became
Most poore:

With Thee
O let me rise,
As larks, harmoniously,
And sing this day Thy victories;
Then shall the fall further the flight in me.

My tender age in sorrow did beginne;
And still with sicknesses and shame
Thou didst so punish sinne,
That I became
Most thinne.

With Thee
Let me combine,
And feel this day Thy victorie;
For, if I imp my wing on Thine,
Affliction shall advance the flight in me.

GEORGE HERBERT

The Collar

I struck the board, and cry'd, No more;
I will abroad.
What? shall I ever sigh and pine?
My lines and life are free; free as the rode,
Loose as the winde, as large as store.
Shall I be still in suit?
Have I no harvest but a thorn
To let me bloud, and not restore
What I have lost with cordiall fruit?
Sure there was wine,

Before my sighs did drie it: there was corn
Before my tears did drown it.
Is the yeare onely lost to me?
Have I no bayes to crown it?
No flowers, no garlands gay? all blasted?
All wasted?
Not so, my heart: but there is fruit,
And thou hast hands.
Recover all thy sigh-blown age
On double pleasures: leave thy cold dispute
Of what is fit, and not forsake thy cage,
Thy rope of sands,
Which pettie thoughts have made, and made to thee
Good cable, to enforce and draw,
And be thy law,
While thou didst wink and wouldst not see.
Away; take heed:
I will abroad.
Call in thy deaths head there: tie up thy fears.
He that forbears
To suit and serve his need,
Deserves his load.
But as I rav'd and grew more fierce and wilde,
At every word,
Methought I heard one calling, *Childe:*
And I reply'd, *My Lord.*

GEORGE HERBERT

The Pulley

When God at first made man,
Having a glass of blessings standing by,
"Let us," said he, "pour on him all we can:
Let the world's riches, which dispersed lie,
Contract into a span."

So strength first made a way;
Then beauty flowed, then wisdom, honor, pleasure.
When almost all was out, God made a stay,
Perceiving that, alone of all his treasure,
Rest in the bottom lay.

"For if I should," said he,
"Bestow this jewel also on my creature,
He would adore my gifts instead of me,

And rest in Nature, not the God of Nature;
So both should losers be.

"Yet let him keep the rest,
But keep them with repining restlessness:
Let him be rich and weary, that at least,
If goodness lead him not, yet weariness
May toss him to my breast."

ROBERT HERRICK (1591–1674). As a great admirer of Ben Jonson, a lively member of London's sophisticated literary circle, and an enthusiastic participant in the pleasures of taverns and women, it seems ironic that Herrick spent much of his long adult life as a reluctant parish priest in Devonshire. His poems, all published in a single volume with two titles, *Hesperides* and *Nobel Numbers* (1648), were split into two groups, one with secular, one with sacred themes. His poems often have the quality of song lyrics and dwell on classical pagan and nature themes. "To the Virgins" (1648), with its central ***carpe diem*** message, is typical of Herrick's worldview.

Related Works: Chopin, "The Story of an Hour"; Erdrich, "The Red Convertible"; Medieval Lyrics, "Summer is i-comin' in"; Donne, "The Flea"; Drayton, Sonnet 61; Marlowe, "The Passionate Shepherd to His Love"; Ralegh, "The Nymph's Reply to the Shepherd"; Marvell, "To His Coy Mistress"; Millay, "What lips my lips have kissed"; *Everyman*.

ROBERT HERRICK

To the Virgins, to Make Much of Time

Gather ye rosebuds while ye may,
Old time is still a-flying:
And this same flower that smiles to-day
To-morrow will be dying.

The glorious lamp of heaven, the sun,
The higher he's a-getting,
The sooner will his race be run,
And nearer he's to setting.

That age is best which is the first,
When youth and blood are warmer;
But being spent, the worse, and worst
Times still succeed the former.

Then be not coy, but use your time,
And while ye may go marry:
For having lost but once your prime
You may for ever tarry.

BEN JONSON (1572–1637) was Shakespeare's contemporary. As a fellow actor, playwright, and poet, Ben Jonson's popularity and notoriety during his life greatly exceeded Shakespeare's. He attracted a brilliant literary circle, and his younger admirers, the "Sons of Ben," formed the core of the **Cavalier poets**. Aside from his literary career, Jonson was equally (if not more) famous as the soldier who fought in single combat in Flanders, as the duelist who killed a fellow actor and barely escaped hanging, and as a suspect in the notorious Gunpowder Plot. After great popular success with his brilliantly conceived plays, *Volpone* (1605–1606) and *Every Man in His Humour* (1598), Jonson was awarded a comfortable stipend by James I in 1616 and began producing court masques while continuing to write ceremonial poems, such as "To Penshurst" (1616). He also wrote **elegies** directed to both famous (Shakespeare and Donne) and familiar persons (his son and daughter). He is generally believed to be the first English writer to legitimize and dignify a purely literary career.

Related Works: Tichborne, "My prime of youth is but a frost of cares"; Coleridge, "Frost at Midnight"; Whitman, "When lilacs last in the dooryard bloom'd"; Bishop, "Sestina"; Thomas, "Do Not Go Gentle Into that Good Night"; Shakespeare, *Hamlet.*

BEN JONSON

On My First Son

Farewell, thou child of my right hand, and joy;
  My sin was too much hope of thee, lov'd boy.
Seven years thou wert lent to me, and I thee pay,
  Exacted by thy fate, on the just day.
Oh, could I lose all father now! For why
  Will man lament the state he should envy?
To have so soon 'scaped world's and flesh's rage,
  And if no other misery, yet age!
Rest in soft peace, and, asked, say, Here doth lie
  Ben Jonson his best piece of poetry.
For whose sake henceforth all his vows be such
  As what he loves may never like too much.

BEN JONSON

On My First Daughter

Here lies, to each her parents' ruth,
Mary, the daughter of their youth;
Yet all heaven's gifts being heaven's due,

It makes the father less to rue.
At six months' end, she parted hence
With safety of her innocence;
Whose soul heaven's queen, whose name she bears,
In comfort of her mother's tears,
Hath placed amongst her virgin-train:
Where, while that severed doth remain,
This grave partakes the fleshly birth;
Which cover lightly, gentle earth!

CHRISTOPHER MARLOWE'S (1564–1593) life was short, violent, and brilliant. After six years at Cambridge between the ages of 16 and 22, Marlowe was granted his degree only after the direct intervention of Queen Elizabeth, who hinted that he may have been working for her as a spy. He left Cambridge having already written two plays, *Tamburlaine* (1587) and *Dido Queen of Carthage* (1594). *Tamburlaine,* the story of a fourteenth-century shepherd who sets out to conquer the world, revolutionized dramatic poetry by introducing **blank verse** to the stage—called later, "Marlowe's Mighty Line." His other important plays, *The Jew of Malta* (1592) and *Dr. Faustus* (1604), were not published until after his death. Marlowe's erotic, comic, and mythic poetic treatment of Ovid's *Hero and Leander* (1593) also demonstrates his poetic facility, as does "The Passionate Shepherd to His Love" (1599), a short, **pastoral** "song." Marlowe was in serious jeopardy for brawling in 1589, again in 1591, and was killed during a knife fight at an inn in 1593.

Related Works: Anonymous Ballads; "The Husband's Message"; Bradstreet, "To My Dear and Loving Husband"; Herrick, "To the Virgins"; Ralegh, "The Nymph's Reply to the Shepherd"; Marvell, "To His Coy Mistress"; Housman, "To an Athlete Dying Young."

MARLOWE

The Passionate Shepherd to His Love

Come live with me and be my Love,
And we will all the pleasures prove
That hills and valleys, dale and field,
And all the craggy mountains yield.

There will we sit upon the rocks
And see the shepherds feed their flocks,
By shallow rivers, to whose falls
Melodious birds sing madrigals.

There will I make thee beds of roses
And a thousand fragrant posies,

A cap of flowers, and a kirtle
Embroider'd all with leaves of myrtle.

A gown made of the finest wool
Which from our pretty lambs we pull,
Fair lined slippers for the cold,
With buckles of the purest gold.

A belt of straw and ivy buds
With coral clasps and amber studs:
And if these pleasures may thee move,
Come live with me and be my Love.

Thy silver dishes for thy meat
As precious as the gods do eat,
Shall on an ivory table be
Prepared each day for thee and me.

The shepherd swains shall dance and sing
For thy delight each May-morning:
If these delights thy mind may move,
Then live with me and be my Love.

SIR WALTER RALEGH (1552–1618), a great court favorite of Elizabeth I until he seduced and married one of her ladies-in-waiting, is best known as a traveler, adventurer, and soldier, although he wrote a substantial *History of the World* (1614) and a good deal of poetry. His voyages to South America and other parts of the New World were legendary. Ralegh spent the greater part of his final fifteen years with his wife and children as a prisoner of James I, locked in the Tower of London. He was executed for treason in October of 1618. The poem included here, of uncertain date, is a reply to Marlowe's "The Passionate Shepherd to His Love." In it, Ralegh adopts the **persona** of a surprisingly level-headed nymph.

Related Works: Atwood, "Gertrude Talks Back"; Marlowe, "The Passionate Shepherd to His Love"; Herrick, "To the Virgins"; Donne, "The Flea"; Medieval Lyrical Poetry, "I sing of a maiden that is matchless" and "Summer is i-comin' in"; Behn, "On Her Loving Two Equally"; Parker, "One Perfect Rose"; Shakespeare, *Taming of the Shrew*; Glaspell, *Trifles*.

SIR WALTER RALEGH

The Nymph's Reply to the Shepherd

If all the world and love were young,
And truth in every shepherd's tongue,

These pretty pleasures might me move
To live with thee and be thy love.

Time drives the flocks from field to fold
When rivers rage and rocks grow cold,
And Philomel becometh dumb;
The rest complains of cares to come.

The flowers do fade, and wanton fields
To wayward winter reckoning yields;
A honey tongue, a heart of gall,
Is fancy's spring, but sorrow's fall.

Thy gowns, thy shoes, thy beds of roses,
Thy cap, thy kirtle, and thy posies
Soon break, soon wither, soon forgotten—
In folly ripe, in reason rotten.

Thy belt of straw and ivy buds,
Thy coral clasps and amber studs,
All these in me no means can move
To come to thee and be thy love.

But could youth last and love still breed,
Had joys no date nor age no need,
Then these delights my mind might move
To live with thee and be thy love.

ANDREW MARVELL (1621–1678), in his day, was widely appreciated as a member of the British Parliament, a diplomat, a pamphleteer, a satirist, and a tutor to the children of England's most powerful families. Marvell's poetry, however, was virtually unknown during his lifetime; *Miscellaneous Poems*, a single collection of all his known work, was published posthumously in 1681. Marvell worked as John Milton's secretary during the later years of the Puritan Commonwealth government and is often credited with saving Milton's life through his Royalist friendships during the Restoration of Charles II. Marvell's poetry was "rediscovered" late in the nineteenth and early twentieth centuries, and, since that time, the reputation of his work has continued to grow. Marvell's clever take on the ***carpe diem*** theme in "To His Coy Mistress" (1681) uses particularly vivid imagery. His use of **irony** within conventional forms makes him perhaps the most fascinating of all the **metaphysical** poets.

Related Works: Herrick, "To the Virgins"; Ralegh, "The Nymph's Reply to the Shepherd"; Marlowe, "The Passionate Shepherd to His Love"; Shakespeare, Sonnets 18 and 130; Hardy, "'Ah, are you digging on my grave?'"; Dickinson, "Because I could not stop for Death"; Ibsen, *A Doll House.*

ANDREW MARVELL

To His Coy Mistress

Had we but world enough, and time,
This coyness, Lady, were no crime
We would sit down and think which way
To walk and pass our long love's day.
Thou by the Indian Ganges' side
Shouldst rubies find: I by the tide
Of Humber would complain. I would
Love you ten years before the Flood,
And you should, if you please, refuse
Till the conversion of the Jews.
My vegetable love should grow
Vaster than empires, and more slow;
An hundred years should go to praise
Thine eyes and on thy forehead gaze;
Two hundred to adore each breast,
But thirty thousand to the rest;
An age at least to every part,
And the last age should show your heart.
For, Lady, you deserve this state,
Nor would I love at lower rate.
  But at my back I always hear
Time's wingèd chariot hurrying near;
And yonder all before us lie
Deserts of vast eternity.
Thy beauty shall no more be found,
Nor, in thy marble vault, shall sound
My echoing song: then worms shall try
That long preserved virginity,
And your quaint honour turn to dust,
And into ashes all my lust:
The grave's a fine and private place,
But none, I think, do there embrace.
  Now therefore, while the youthful hue
Sits on thy skin like morning dew,
And while thy willing soul transpires
At every pore with instant fires,
Now let us sport us while we may,
And now, like amorous birds of prey,
Rather at once our time devour
Than languish in his slow-chapt power.
Let us roll all our strength and all

Our sweetness up into one ball,
And tear our pleasures with rough strife
Thorough the iron gates of life:
Thus, though we cannot make our sun
Stand still, yet we will make him run.

ANDREW MARVELL

The Mower Against Gardens

Luxurious man, to bring his vice in use,
  Did after him the world seduce,
And from the fields the flowers and plants allure,
  Where Nature was most plain and pure.
He first enclosed within the garden's square
  A dead and standing pool of air,
And a more luscious earth for them did knead,
  Which stupefied them while it fed.
The pink grew then as double as his mind;
  The nutriment did change the kind.
With strange perfumes he did the roses taint;
  And flowers themselves were taught to paint.
The tulip white did for complexion seek,
  And learned to interline its cheek;
Its onion root they then so high did hold,
  That one was for a meadow sold;
Another world was searched through oceans new,
  To find the marvel of Peru;
And yet these rarities might be allowed
  To man, that sovereign thing and proud.
Had he not dealt between the bark and tree,
  Forbidden mixtures there to see.
No plant now knew the stock from which it came;
  He grafts upon the wild the tame,
That the uncertain and adult'rate fruit
  Might put the palate in dispute.
His green seraglio has its eunuchs too,
  Lest any tyrant him outdo;
And in the cherry he does Nature vex,
  To procreate without a sex.
'Tis all enforced, the fountain and the grot,
  While the sweet fields do lie forgot,
Where willing Nature does to all dispense
  A wild and fragrant innocence;

And fauns and fairies do the meadows till
    More by their presence than their skill.
Their statues polished by some ancient hand
    May to adorn the gardens stand;
But, howsoe'er the figures do excel,
    The gods themselves with us do dwell.

JOHN MILTON (1608–1674) is most famous as the author of the **epic** poem *Paradise Lost* (1667), written in the last years of his life. Milton began composing **odes** and **epitaphs**, however, as a young student at Cambridge. Supported by an indulgent father long after his graduation, Milton continued his studies independently into his early thirties. Two **elegies** remembering college friends, published in 1637 (*Lycidas*) and 1639 (*Epitaphium Damonis*), seem to conclude Milton's exclusively scholarly years. Soon afterwards, Milton became actively involved as an ardent Puritan, contributing important tracts to the public debate on divorce (*The Doctrine and Discipline of Divorce*, 1643), freedom of the press (*Areopagitica*, 1644), and the role of the state Church (*Of Reformation in England*, 1641). Shortly after their marriage in 1642, Milton's seventeen-year-old Royalist wife, Mary, left to visit her family and did not return until 1645. In the five years after her return, Mary bore four children: three daughters, Anne, Deborah, and Mary, and a son, John, who died in infancy in 1651. It is not clear when Milton began to be aware that he was going blind, but it was probably during this period. Most historians agree that Milton was completely blind by 1651. "When I consider how my light is spent," which was composed between 1652 and 1655 (published in 1673 in *Poems*), is on one level Milton's commentary on his own blindness. Lines 3–6 contain an **allusion** to the Parable of the Talents (Matthew 25).

Related Works: Bradstreet, "To My Dear and Loving Husband"; Donne, Holy Sonnet 14; Drayton, Sonnet 61; Dickinson, "Because I could not stop for Death"; Glück, "Gratitude"; *Everyman*.

JOHN MILTON

When I Consider How My Light is Spent

19

When I consider how my light is spent
  Ere half my days in this dark world and wide,
  And that one talent which is death to hide
  Lodg'd with me useless, though my soul more bent

To serve therewith my Maker, and present
My true account, lest he returning chide,
"Doth God exact day-labour, light denied?"
I fondly ask. But Patience, to prevent
That murmur, soon replies: "God doth not need
Either man's work or his own gifts: who best
Bear his mild yoke, they serve him best. His state
Is kingly; thousands at his bidding speed
And post o'er land and ocean without rest:
They also serve who only stand and wait."

JOHN MILTON

Lycidas

Yet once more, O ye laurels, and once more
Ye myrtles brown, with ivy never sere,
I come to pluck your berries harsh and crude,
And with forc'd fingers rude
Shatter your leaves before the mellowing year,
Bitter constraint and sad occasion dear
Compels me to disturb your season due;
For Lycidas is dead, dead ere his prime,
Young Lycidas, and hath not left his peer.
Who would not sing for Lycidas? he knew
Himself to sing, and build the lofty rhyme.
He must not float upon his wat'ry bier
Unwept, and welter to the parching wind,
Without the meed of some melodious tear.

Begin then, Sisters of the sacred well
That from beneath the seat of Jove doth spring;
Begin, and somewhat loudly sweep the string.
Hence with denial vain and coy excuse!
So may some gentle muse
With lucky words favour my destin'd urn,
And as he passes turn
And bid fair peace be to my sable shroud!
For we were nurs'd upon the self-same hill,

Fed the same flock, by fountain, shade, and rill;
Together both, ere the high lawns appear'd
Under the opening eyelids of the morn,
We drove afield, and both together heard
What time the gray-fly winds her sultry horn,
Batt'ning our flocks with the fresh dews of night,

Oft till the star that rose at ev'ning bright
Toward heav'n's descent had slop'd his westering wheel.
Meanwhile the rural ditties were not mute.
Temper'd to th'oaten flute;
Rough Satyrs danc'd, and Fauns with clov'n heel,
From the glad sound would not be absent long;
And old Damætas lov'd to hear our song.

But O the heavy change now thou art gone,
Now thou art gone, and never must return!
Thee, Shepherd, thee the woods and desert caves,
With wild thyme and the gadding vine o'ergrown,
And all their echoes mourn.
The willows and the hazel copses green
Shall now no more be seen
Fanning their joyous leaves to thy soft lays.
As killing as the canker to the rose,
Or taint-worm to the weanling herds that graze,
Or frost to flowers that their gay wardrobe wear
When first the white thorn blows:
Such, Lycidas, thy loss to shepherd's ear.

Where were ye, Nymphs, when the remorseless deep
Clos'd o'er the head of your lov'd Lycidas?
For neither were ye playing on the steep
Where your old bards, the famous Druids, lie,
Nor on the shaggy top of Mona high,
Nor yet where Deva spreads her wizard stream.
Ay me! I fondly dream
Had ye been there—for what could that have done?
What could the Muse herself that Orpheus bore,
The Muse herself, for her enchanting son,
Whom universal nature did lament,
When by the rout that made the hideous roar
His gory visage down the stream was sent,
Down the swift Hebrus to the Lesbian shore?

Alas! what boots it with incessant care
To tend the homely, slighted shepherd's trade,
And strictly meditate the thankless Muse?
Were it not better done, as others use,
To sport with Amaryllis in the shade,
Or with the tangles of Neæra's hair?
Fame is the spur that the clear spirit doth raise
(That last infirmity of noble mind)
To scorn delights and live laborious days;
But the fair guerdon when we hope to find,
And think to burst out into sudden blaze,
Comes the blind Fury with th'abhorred shears,
And slits the thin-spun life. "But not the praise,"
Phoebus replied, and touch'd my trembling ears;

"Fame is no plant that grows on mortal soil,
Nor in the glistering foil
Set off to th'world, nor in broad rumour lies,
But lives and spreads aloft by those pure eyes
And perfect witness of all-judging Jove;
As he pronounces lastly on each deed,
Of so much fame in Heav'n expect thy meed."

O fountain Arethuse, and thou honour'd flood,
Smooth-sliding Mincius, crown'd with vocal reeds,
That strain I heard was of a higher mood.
But now my oat proceeds,
And listens to the Herald of the Sea,
That came in Neptune's plea.
He ask'd the waves, and ask'd the felon winds,
"What hard mishap hath doom'd this gentle swain?"
And question'd every gust of rugged wings
That blows from off each beaked promontory.
They knew not of his story;
And sage Hippotades their answer brings,
That not a blast was from his dungeon stray'd;
The air was calm, and on the level brine
Sleek Panope with all her sisters play'd.
It was that fatal and perfidious bark,
Built in th'eclipse, and rigg'd with curses dark,
That sunk so low that sacred head of thine.

Next Camus, reverend sire, went footing slow,
His mantle hairy, and his bonnet sedge,
Inwrought with figures dim, and on the edge
Like to that sanguine flower inscrib'd with woe.
"Ah! who hath reft," quoth he, "my dearest pledge?"
Last came, and last did go,
The Pilot of the Galilean lake;
Two massy keys he bore of metals twain
(The golden opes, the iron shuts amain),
He shook his mitred locks, and stern bespake:
"How well could I have spar'd for thee, young swain,
Enow of such as for their bellies' sake
Creep and intrude, and climb into the fold?
Of other care they little reck'ning make
Than how to scramble at the shearers' feast
And shove away the worthy bidden guest.
Blind mouths! that scarce themselves know how to hold
A sheep-hook, or have learn'd aught else the least
That to the faithful herdman's art belongs!
What recks it them? What need they? They are sped;
And when they list their lean and flashy songs
Grate on their scrannel pipes of wretched straw,
The hungry sheep look up, and are not fed,

But, swoll'n with wind and the rank mist they draw,
Rot inwardly, and foul contagion spread;
Besides what the grim wolf with privy paw
Daily devours apace, and nothing said,
But that two-handed engine at the door
Stands ready to smite once, and smite no more."

Return, Alpheus: the dread voice is past
That shrunk thy streams; return, Sicilian Muse,
And call the vales and bid them hither cast
Their bells and flow'rets of a thousand hues.
Ye valleys low, where the mild whispers use
Of shades and wanton winds, and gushing brooks,
On whose fresh lap the swart star sparely looks,
Throw hither all your quaint enamel'd eyes,
That on the green turf suck the honied showers
And purple all the ground with vernal flowers,
Bring the rathe primrose that forsaken dies,
The tufted crow-toe, and pale jessamine,
The white pink, and the pansy freak'd with jet,
The glowing violet,
The musk-rose, and the well attir'd woodbine,
With cowslips wan that hang the pensive head,
And every flower that sad embroidery wears;
Bid amaranthus all his beauty shed,
And daffadillies fill their cups with tears,
To strew the laureate hearse where Lycid lies.
For so to interpose a little ease,
Let our frail thoughts dally with false surmise.
Ay me! Whilst thee the shores and sounding seas
Wash far away, where'er thy bones are hurl'd;
Whether beyond the stormy Hebrides,
Where thou perhaps under the whelming tide
Visit'st the bottom of the monstrous world,
Or whether thou, to our moist vows denied,
Sleep'st by the fable of Bellerus old,
Where the great vision of the guarded mount
Looks toward Namancos and Bayona's hold:
Look homeward Angel now, and melt with ruth;
And, O ye dolphins, waft the hapless youth.

Weep no more, woeful shepherds, weep no more,
For Lycidas, your sorrow, is not dead,
Sunk though he be beneath the wat'ry floor;
So sinks the day-star in the ocean bed,
And yet anon repairs his drooping head,
And tricks his beams, and with new spangled ore
Flames in the forehead of the morning sky:
So Lycidas sunk low, but mounted high
Through the dear might of him that walk'd the waves;

Where, other groves and other streams along,
With nectar pure his oozy locks he laves,
And hears the unexpressive nuptial song,
In the blest kingdoms meek of joy and love.
There entertain him all the Saints above,
In solemn troops, and sweet societies,
That sing, and singing in their glory move,
And wipe the tears for ever from his eyes.
Now, Lycidas, the shepherds weep no more:
Henceforth thou art the Genius of the shore,
In thy large recompense, and shalt be good
To all that wander in that perilous flood.

Thus sang the uncouth swain to th'oaks and rills,
While the still morn went out with sandals gray;
He touch'd the tender stops of various quills,
With eager thought warbling his Doric lay;
And now the sun had stretch'd out all the hills,
And now was dropp'd into the western bay;
At last he rose, and twitch'd his mantle blue:
To-morrow to fresh woods, and pastures new.

WILLIAM SHAKESPEARE (1564–1616). The sonnets below are from a collection of 154 sonnets attributed to William Shakespeare. The collection, published in 1609 by Thomas Thorpe, also included a poem called "The Lover's Complaint." Like other **sonnet** sequences of the time, the sonnets in this collection seem to trace out the various ups and downs of one or more love affairs, but unlike the traditional sequence, which amounted to a stylized adoration or castigation of an equally stylized lover, the sonnets in this sequence strike a much more realistic position. Shakespeare typically creates dramatic effects by comparing and contrasting **motifs** and **themes** between the **quatrains**. The final **couplet** often summarizes or comments on the quatrains above it and sometimes exhibits a shift in the voice of the poetic **persona**. For more details on Shakespeare's life, see the head note preceding his drama.

Related Works: Joyce, "Araby"; Updike, "A&P"; Old English Riddles; Donne, "The Flea"; Barrett Browning, Sonnets 14 and 43; Millay, "What lips my lips have kissed"; Shakespeare, *Hamlet* and *The Taming of the Shrew.*

WILLIAM SHAKESPEARE

18

Shall I compare thee to a summer's day?
Thou art more lovely and more temperate.
Rough winds do shake the darling buds of May,

And summer's lease hath all too short a date.
Sometimes too hot the eye of heaven shines,
And often is his gold complexion dimmed;
And every fair from fair sometimes declines,
By chance or nature's changing course untrimmed.
But thy eternal summer shall not fade
Nor lose possession of that fair thou ow'st;
Nor shall Death brag thou wanderest in his shade,
When in eternal lines to time thou grow'st.
So long as men can breathe or eyes can see,
So long lives this, and this gives life to thee.

WILLIAM SHAKESPEARE

73

That time of year thou mayst in me behold
When yellow leaves, or none, or few, do hang
Upon those boughs which shake against the cold,
Bare ruined choirs where late the sweet birds sang.
In me thou seest the twilight of such day
As after sunset fadeth in the west,
Which by and by black night doth take away,
Death's second self, that seals up all in rest.
In me thou seest the glowing of such fire
That on the ashes of his youth doth lie
As the deathbed whereon it must expire,
Consumed with that which it was nourished by.
This thou perceiv'st, which makes thy love more strong,
To love that well which thou must leave ere long.

WILLIAM SHAKESPEARE

116

Let me not to the marriage of true minds
Admit impediments. Love is not love
Which alters when it alteration finds,
Or bends with the remover to remove.
O, no, it is an ever-fixed mark
That looks on tempests and is never shaken;
It is the star to every wandering bark,

Whose worth's unknown, although his height be taken.
Love's not Time's fool, though rosy lips and cheeks
Within his bending sickle's compass come;
Love alters not with his brief hours and weeks,
But bears it out even to the edge of doom.
    If this be error and upon me proved,
    I never writ, nor no man ever loved.

WILLIAM SHAKESPEARE

130

My mistress' eyes are nothing like the sun;
Coral is far more red than her lips' red;
If snow be white, why then her breasts are dun;
If hairs be wires, black wires grow on her head.
I have seen roses damasked, red and white,
But no such roses see I in her cheeks;
And in some perfumes is there more delight
Than in the breath that from my mistress reeks,
I love to hear her speak, yet well I know
That music hath a far more pleasing sound.
I grant I never saw a goddess go;
My mistress, when she walks, treads on the ground.
    And yet, by heaven, I think my love as rare
    As any she belied with false compare.

CHIDIOCK TICHBORNE (ca. 1558–1586), raised in England as a Catholic during a time of religious instability, was convicted of treason for plotting to murder Anglican queen Elizabeth I and replace her with a Catholic, Mary Queen of Scots. He was imprisoned in the Tower of London and, before being hanged from the gallows, was disemboweled alive. On the night before his execution, he wrote to his wife, enclosing the following **elegiac** stanzas that describe his dark mood and, in plain language, the waste of his own young life. The poem, Tichborne's only known work, was famous in the period.

Related Works: O'Brien, "Stockings"; Jonson, "On My First Son"; Milton, "When I consider how my light is spent"; Blake, "The Lamb"; Housman, "To an Athlete Dying Young"; Heaney, "Punishment"; Jarrell, "The Death of the Ball Turret Gunner"; Sophocles, *Antigone*.

Chidiock Tichborne's Elegy

written with his own hand in the Tower before his execution

My prime of youth is but a frost of cares,
My feast of joy is but a dish of pain,
My crop of corn is but a field of tares,
And all my good is but vain hope of gain.
The day is past, and yet I saw no sun,
And now I live, and now my life is done.

My tale was heard and yet it was not told,
My fruit is fallen and yet my leaves are green;
My youth is spent and yet I am not old,
I saw the world and yet I was not seen.
My thread is cut and yet it is not spun,
And now I live, and now my life is done.

I sought my death and found it in my womb,
I looked for life and saw it was a shade:
I trod the earth and knew it was my tomb,
And now I die, and now I was but made.
My glass is full, and now my glass is run,
And now I live, and now my life is done.

PHILLIS WHEATLEY (1753/54–1784). Kidnapped in West Africa and sold as a slave in Boston in 1761, when she was around seven years old, Wheatley became the first black American author. She was given her Christian name and surname by her owners John and Susanna Wheatley, who also discovered the child's talent for language—she could read, speak, and write fluently in English within two years of her arrival. By 1765, Phillis Wheatley was composing and publishing verse, and in 1770, she achieved wide celebrity with her **elegy** to a well-known clergyman, George Whitefield. Her first and only collection (*Poems on Various Subjects*) was published in England in 1773, the same year that the Wheatleys granted Phillis her freedom. After both John and Susanna Wheatley died, Phillis married John Peters, a free black man, by whom she bore three children. Peters left her, and all three children died, the last just before Phillis herself died in hardship and poverty. Wheatley's poetry primarily addresses classical themes in **heroic couplets** and shows the influence of John Milton, Alexander Pope, and perhaps Anne Bradstreet.

Related Works: Walker, "Everyday Use"; Bradstreet, "The Author to Her Book"; Jonson, "On My First Son"; Milton, "When I Consider How My Light is Spent"; Grimké, "The Black Finger"; Harper, "The Slave Auction" and "The Burial of Moses"; Clifton, "my mama moved among the days"; Wilson, *The Piano Lesson*; Glaspell, *Trifles*.

PHILLIS WHEATLEY

A Funeral Poem on the Death of C. E. an Infant of Twelve Months

Through airy roads he wings his instant flight
To purer regions of celestial light;
Enlarg'd he sees unnumber'd systems roll,
Beneath him sees the universal whole,
Planets on planets run their destin'd round,
And circling wonders fill the vast profound.
Th' ethereal now, and now th' empyreal skies
With growing splendors strike his wond'ring eyes;
The angels view him with delight unknown,
Press his soft hand, and seat him on his throne;
Then smiling thus: "To this divine abode,
"The seat of saints, of seraphs, and of God,
"Thrice welcome thou." The raptur'd babe replies,
"Thanks to my God, who snatch'd me to the skies,
"E'er vice triumphant had possess'd my heart,
"E'er yet the tempter had beguil'd my heart,
"E'er yet on sin's base actions I was bent,
"E'er yet I knew temptation's dire intent;
"E'er yet the lash for horrid crimes I felt,
"E'er vanity had led my way to guilt,
"But, soon arriv'd at my celestial goal,
"Full glories rush on my expanding soul."
Joyful he spoke: exulting cherubs round
Clapt their glad wings, the heav'nly vaults resound.

Say, parents, why this unavailing moan?
Why heave your pensive bosoms with the groan?
To *Charles*, the happy subject of my song,
A brighter world, and nobler strains belong.
Say would you tear him from the realms above
By thoughtless wishes, and prepost'rous love?
Doth his felicity increase your pain?
Or could you welcome to this world again
The heir of bliss? with a superior air
Methinks he answers with a smile severe,
"Thrones and dominions cannot tempt me there."
But still you cry, "Can we the sigh forbear,
"And still and still must we not pour the tear?
"Our only hope, more dear than vital breath,
"Twelve moons revolv'd, becomes the prey of death;
"Delightful infant, nightly visions give

"Thee to our arms, and we with joy receive,
"We fain would clasp the *Phantom* to our breast,
"The *Phantom* flies, and leaves the soul unblest."

To yon bright regions let your faith ascend,
Prepare to join your dearest infant friend
In pleasures without measure, without end.

To a Lady on Her Remarkable Preservation in an Hurricane in North-Carolina

Though thou did'st hear the tempest from afar,
And felt'st the horrors of the wat'ry war,
To me unknown, yet on this peaceful shore
Methinks I hear the storm tumultuous roar,
And how stern *Boreas* with impetuous hand
Compell'd the *Nereids* to usurp the land.
Reluctant rose the daughters of the main,
And slow ascending glided o'er the plain,
Till *Æolus* in his rapid chariot drove
In gloomy grandeur from the vault above:
Furious he comes. His winged sons obey
Their frantic sire, and madden all the sea.
The billows rave, the wind's fierce tyrant roars,
And with his thund'ring terrors shakes the shores:
Broken by waves the vessel's frame is rent,
And strows with planks the wat'ry element.

But thee, *Maria*, a kind *Nereid's* shield
Preserv'd from sinking, and thy form upheld:
And sure some heav'nly oracle design'd
At that dread crisis to instruct thy mind
Things of eternal consequence to weigh,
And to thine heart just feelings to convey
Of things above, and of the future doom,
And what the births of the dread world to come.

From tossing seas I welcome thee to land.
"Resign her, *Nereid*," 'twas thy God's command.
Thy spouse late buried, as thy fears conceiv'd,
Again returns, thy fears are all reliev'd:
Thy daughter blooming with superior grace
Again thou see'st, again thine arms embrace;
O come, and joyful show thy spouse his heir,
And what the blessings of maternal care!

LADY MARY WROTH (ca. 1587–1651) was the daughter, niece, cousin, friend, and lover of some of the most wealthy and powerful people in her time. Her ten-year arranged marriage to Robert Wroth, by many accounts a drunk and a womanizer, left Lady Mary seriously in debt after his death in 1614. Wroth herself had a long affair with a first cousin and had two illegitimate children by him. Her longest work, the prose romance *The Countess of Montgomery's Urania* (1621), with its thinly veiled accounts of contemporary scandals, included a **sonnet** sequence, *Pamphilia to Amphilanthus*, a cycle of 103 **Petrarchan sonnets** in which the female narrator, Pamphilia, adopts the traditional male role as the lover and instructs Amphilanthus in standards of fidelity and responsibility.

Related Works: Atwood, "Gertrude Talks Back"; "The Husband's Message" and "The Wife's Lament"; "Bonny Barbara Allan" (Child Ballad #84); Marlowe, "The Passionate Shepherd to His Love"; Ralegh, "The Nymph's Reply to the Shepherd"; Marvell, "To His Coy Mistress"; Shakespeare, Sonnet 18, Sonnet 73, and Sonnet 116; Barrett Browning, Sonnets 14 and 43; Glaspell, *Trifles*.

LADY MARY WROTH

"In This Strange Labyrinth"

In this strange Labyrinth how shall I turn,
Ways are on all sides while the way I miss:
If to the right hand, there, in love I burn,
Let me go forward, therein danger is.
If to the left, suspicion hinders bliss;
Let me turn back, shame cries I ought return:
Nor faint, though crosses my fortunes kiss,
Stand still is harder, although sure to mourn.
Thus let me take the right, or left-hand way,
Go forward, or stand still, or back retire:
I must these doubts endure without allay
Or help, but travel finde for my best hire.
Yet that which most my troubled sense doth move,
Is to leave all, and take the thread of Love.

LADY MARY WROTH

From *Pamphilia to Amphilanthus*

When night's black mantle could most darkness prove,
　And sleep, death's image, did my senses hire
　From knowledge of myself, then thoughts did move
　Swifter than those most swiftness need require.
In sleep, a chariot drawn by winged desire

I saw, where sat bright Venus, Queene of Love,
And at her feet, her son, still adding fire
To burning hearts, which she did hold above.
But one heart flaming more than all the rest
The goddess held, and put it to my breast.
"Dear son, now shut," said she: "thus must we win."
He her obeyed, and martyred my poor heart.
I, waking, hoped as dreams it would depart:
Yet since, O me, a lover I have been.

SIR THOMAS WYATT (ca. 1503–1542) introduced English poets to the fourteen-line **Italian sonnet** form (also known as the **Petrarchan sonnet**) after traveling to Italy a number of times on diplomatic missions and having translated Italian sonnets by Petrarch and others. Wyatt was an important member of Henry VIII's dangerous court and was imprisoned several times as a result of court intrigues and quarrels. During this period, courtiers circulated handwritten manuscripts of their work among friends; the work was rarely, if ever published. Several versions of the poem on the next page have survived; this one is from a private manuscript, the Edgerton Manuscript. Although **sonnet** form influences the rhythm of "They flee from me" (1536), it is a more loosely structured poem. The poem seems to reverse the common **motif** of the male predator chasing a helpless female victim.

Related Works: Joyce, "Araby"; Chopin, "The Story of an Hour"; Updike, "A&P"; Drayton, Sonnet 61; Herrick, "To the Virgins"; Shakespeare, Sonnet 18, Sonnet 73, Sonnet 116, Sonnet 130, and *The Taming of the Shrew.*

SIR THOMAS WYATT

They Flee from Me That Sometime Did Me Seek

They flee from me that sometime did me seek
With naked foot, stalking in my chamber.
I have seen them gentle, tame, and meek,
That now are wild and do not remember
That sometime they put themself in danger
To take bread at my hand; and now they range,
Busily seeking with a continual change.

Thanked be fortune it hath been otherwise
Twenty times better; but once in special,
In thin array after a pleasant guise,
When her loose gown from her shoulders did fall,
And she me caught in her arms long and small;

Therewithall sweetly did me kiss
And softly said, "dear heart, how like you this?"

It was no dream: I lay broad waking.
But all is turned thorough my gentleness
Into a strange fashion of forsaking;
And I have leave to go of her goodness,
And she also, to use newfangleness.
But since that I so kindly am served
I would fain know what she hath deserved.

JONATHAN SWIFT'S (1667–1745) vast and complex writing career was marked throughout by an energetic, social, and political sensibility, and a sharp, satirical voice. Despite his self-characterization as a misanthrope, Swift had a wide circle of friends among all classes, spent much of his income on charity, and was beloved as the voice of the Irish resistance. His most famous work, *Gulliver's Travels*, along with the widely anthologized essay "A Modest Proposal," are representative of his style. In "A Description of the Morning" (1709), Swift uses **heroic couplets**, a form often associated with romance and epic adventure (hence "heroic"), to describe a low street scene.

Swift wrote many poems to "Stella" or Esther Johnson, whom he had met in 1689, when she was eight and he was twenty-two years old. Stella was not only young and beautiful but interested in education, and Swift served as her friend and mentor for her entire life. She, in return, had a profound impact on Swift's thought and life, and he went into a depression after her death. The **ironic** wit of Swift's series of poems on Stella's various birthdays compliment their recipient by addressing her as a sensible and witty person in her own right. "Phyllis, or The Progress of Love" is typical of Swift's **satire**, and his riddles, although inspired by a French literary fashion, can be compared to the Old English Riddles in this anthology.

Related Works: Nash, "Very Like a Whale"; Wordsworth, "Composed upon Westminster Bridge, September 3, 1802"; Chaucer, "Complaint to His Purse"; Donne, "The Apparition"; Shakespeare, Sonnet 130; Hardy, "The Ruined Maid"; Old English Riddles.

JONATHAN SWIFT

A Description of the Morning

Now hardly here and there a hackney-coach
Appearing, show'd the ruddy morn's approach.
Now Betty from her master's bed had flown,
And softly stole to discompose her own.
The slip-shod 'prentice from his master's door
Had par'd the dirt, and sprinkled round the floor.
Now Moll had whirl'd her mop with dext'rous airs,

Prepar'd to scrub the entry and the stairs.
 The youth with broomy stumps began to trace
The kennel-edge, where wheels had worn the place.
The small-coal man was heard with cadence deep;
Till drown'd in shriller notes of "chimney-sweep."
Duns at his lordship's gate began to meet;
 And brickdust Moll had scream'd through half a street.
The turnkey now his flock returning sees,
 Duly let out a-nights to steal for fees.
The watchful bailiffs take their silent stands;
And schoolboys lag with satchels in their hands.

JONATHAN SWIFT

Stella's Birth-Day, 1724–25

As, when a beauteous nymph decays,
We say, she's past her dancing days;
So poets lose their feet by time,
And can no longer dance in rhyme.
Your annual bard had rather chose
To celebrate your birth in prose:
Yet merry folks, who want by chance
A pair to make a country dance,
Call the old housekeeper, and get her
To fill a place for want of better:
While Sheridan is off the hooks,
And friend Delany at his books,
That Stella may avoid disgrace,
Once more the Dean supplies their place.
 Beauty and wit, too sad a truth!
Have always been confined to youth;
The god of wit and beauty's queen,
He twenty-one and she fifteen,
No poet ever sweetly sung,
Unless he were, like Phœbus, young;
Nor ever nymph inspired to rhyme,
Unless, like Venus, in her prime,
At fifty-six, if this be true,
Am I a poet fit for you?
Or, at the age of forty-three,
Are you a subject fit for me?

Adieu! bright wit, and radiant eyes!
You must be grave and I be wise,
Our fate in vain we would oppose:

But I'll be still your friend in prose:
Esteem and friendship to express,
Will not require poetic dress;
And if the Muse deny her aid
To have them sung, they may be said.
  But, Stella, say, what evil tongue
Reports you are no longer young;
That Time sits with his scythe to mow
Where erst sat Cupid with his bow;
That half your locks are turn'd to gray?
I'll ne'er believe a word they say,
'Tis true, but let it not be known,
My eyes are somewhat dimmish grown;
For nature, always in the right,
To your decays adapts my sight;
And wrinkles undistinguish'd pass,
For I'm ashamed to use a glass:
And till I see them with these eyes,
Whoever says you have them, lies.
  No length of time can make you quit
Honour and virtue, sense and wit;
Thus you may still be young to me,
While I can better hear than see,
O ne'er may Fortune show her spite,
To make me deaf, and mend my sight!

JONATHAN SWIFT

Phyllis

Or, the Progress of Love, 1716

Desponding Phyllis was endued
With every talent of a prude:
She trembled when a man drew near;
Salute her, and she turn'd her ear:
If o'er against her you were placed,
She durst not look above your waist:
She'd rather take you to her bed,
Than let you see her dress her head;
In church you hear her, through the crowd,
Repeat the absolution loud:
In church, secure behind her fan,
She durst behold that monster man:
There practised how to place her head,
And bite her lips to make them red;

Or, on the mat devoutly kneeling,
Would lift her eyes up to the ceiling.
And heave her bosom unaware,
For neighbouring beaux to see it bare.
 At length a lucky lover came,
And found admittance to the dame.
Suppose all parties now agreed,
The writings drawn, the lawyer feed,
The vicar and the ring bespoke:
Guess, how could such a match be broke?
See then what mortals place their bliss in!

Next morn betimes the bride was missing:
The mother scream'd, the father chid;
Where can this idle wench be hid?
No news of Phyl! the bridegroom came,
And thought his bride had skulk'd for shame;
Because her father used to say,
The girl had such a bashful way!
 Now John the butler must be sent
To learn the road that Phyllis went:
The groom was wish'd to saddle Crop;
For John must neither light nor stop,
But find her wheresoe'er she fled,
And bring her back alive or dead.
 See here again the devil to do!
For truly John was missing too:
The horse and pillion both were gone!
Phyllis, it seems, was fled with John.
 Old Madam, who went up to find
What papers Phyl had left behind,
A letter on the toilet sees,
"To my much honour'd father—these—"
('Tis always done, romances tell us,
When daughters run away with fellows,)
Fill'd with the choicest common-places,
By others used in the like cases,
"That long ago a fortune-teller
Exactly said what now befell her;
And in a glass had made her see
A serving-man of low degree.
It was her fate, must be forgiven;
For marriages were made in Heaven:
His pardon begg'd: but, to be plain,
She'd do't if 'twere to do again:
Thank'd God, 'twas neither shame nor sin;
For John was come of honest kin.
Love never thinks of rich and poor;
She'd beg with John from door to door.

Forgive her, if it be a crime;
She'll never do't another time.
She ne'er before in all her life
Once disobey'd him, maid nor wife."
One argument she summ'd up all in,
"The thing was done and past recalling;
And therefore hoped she should recover
His favour when his passion's over,
She valued not what others thought her,
And was—his most obedient daughter."
Fair maidens all, attend the Muse,
Who now the wandering pair pursues:
Away they rode in homely sort,
Their journey long, their money short;
The loving couple well bemired;
The horse and both the riders tired:
Their victuals bad, their lodgings worse;
Phyl cried! and John began to curse:
Phyl wish'd that she had strain'd a limb,
When first she ventured out with him;
John wish'd that he had broke a leg,
When first for her he quitted Peg.
    But what adventures more befell them,
The Muse has now no time to tell them;
How Johnny wheedled, threaten'd, fawn'd,
Till Phyllis all her trinkets pawn'd:
How oft she broke her marriage vows,
In kindness to maintain her spouse,
Till swains unwholesome spoil'd the trade;
For now the surgeons must be paid,
To whom those perquisites are gone,
In Christian justice due to John.
    When food and raiment now grew scarce,
Fate put a period to the farce,
And with exact poetic justice;
For John was landlord, Phyllis hostess;
They keep, at Stains, the Old Blue Boar,
Are cat and dog, and rogue and whore.

JONATHAN SWIFT

On the Vowels

We are little airy creatures,
All of different voice and features;
One of us in glass is set,

One of us you'll find in jet.
T'other you may see in tin,
And the fourth a box within,
If the fifth you should pursue,
It can never fly from you.

JONATHAN SWIFT

On a Pair of Dice

We are little brethren twain,
Arbiters of loss and gain,
Many to our counters run,
Some are made, and some undone:
But men find it to their cost,
Few are made, but numbers lost,
Though we play them tricks for ever,
Yet they always hope our favour.

JONATHAN SWIFT

On Ink

I am jet black, as you may see,
 The son of pitch and gloomy night:
Yet all that know me will agree,
 I'm dead except I live in light.

Sometimes in panegyric high,
 Like lofty Pindar, I can soar;
And raise a virgin to the sky,
 Or sink her to a pocky whore.

My blood this day is very sweet,
 To-morrow of a bitter juice;
Like milk, 'tis cried about the street,
 And so applied to different use.

Most wondrous is my magic power:
 For with one colour I can paint;
I'll make the devil a saint this hour,
 Next make a devil of a saint.

Through distant regions I can fly,
Provide me but with paper wings;
And fairly show a reason why
There should be quarrels among kings

And, after all, you'll think it odd,
When learned doctors will dispute,
That I should point the word of God,
And show where they can best confute.

Let lawyers bawl and strain their throats:
'Tis I that must the lands convey,
And strip their clients to their coats;
Nay, give their very souls away.

WILLIAM BLAKE (1757–1827), son of a craftsman and an artisan who was apprenticed to an engraver at fourteen, is one of the most enigmatic and distinctive of the English Romantic poets. Almost wholly self-educated but widely read, Blake developed a mythic vision with an entirely new cosmology that is revealed throughout his many engravings, drawings, poems, prose pieces, and etchings. "Infant Joy" and "The Lamb" are included in Blake's collection *Songs of Innocence* (1789), whereas "The Tiger" (intended to contrast with "The Lamb") and "London" make up part of a later volume *Songs of Experience* (1794). In the contrasting pair of poems, Blake uses simple images and a series of **rhetorical questions** to frame divergent images of God, as the creator of both tiger and lamb. In "London," Blake's chanting repetition and **alliteration** create the sound of a threatening drumbeat.

Related Works: Hawthorne, "Young Goodman Brown"; Singer, "Gimpel the Fool"; Old English Riddles; Tichborne, "My prime of youth is but a frost of cares"; Browning, "Childe Roland to the Dark Tower Came"; Swift, "A Description of the Morning"; Whitman, "When lilacs last in the dooryard bloom'd"; Wordsworth, "I wandered lonely as a cloud" and "Composed upon Westminster Bridge, September 3, 1802"; *Everyman*.

WILLIAM BLAKE

Infant Joy

"I have no name.
I am but two days old."
What shall I call thee?
"I happy am,
Joy is my name."
Sweet joy befall thee!

Pretty joy!
Sweet joy but two days old,
Sweet joy I call thee;
Thou dost smile,
I sing the while—
Sweet joy befall thee.

WILLIAM BLAKE

The Lamb

    Little Lamb, who made thee?
    Dost thou know who made thee?
Gave thee life, and bid thee feed

William Blake, "The Lamb," from *Songs of Innocence*

By the stream and o'er the mead;
Gave thee clothing of delight;
Softest clothing, wooly, bright;
Gave thee such a tender voice,
Making all the vales rejoice?
  Little Lamb, who made thee?
  Dost thou know who made thee?

  Little Lamb, I'll tell thee,
  Little Lamb, I'll tell thee:
He is called by thy name,
For he calls himself a Lamb.
He is meek, and he is mild;
He became a little child.
I a child, and thou a lamb,
We are called by His name.
    Little Lamb, God bless thee!
    Little Lamb, God bless thee!

WILLIAM BLAKE

The Tiger

Tiger, tiger, burning bright
In the forests of the night,
What immortal hand or eye
Could frame thy fearful symmetry?

In what distant deeps or skies
Burnt the fire of thine eyes?
On what wings dare he aspire?
What the hand dare seize the fire?

And what shoulder and what art
Could twist the sinews of thy heart?
And when thy heart began to beat,
What dread hand and what dread feet?

What the hammer? what the chain?
In what furnace was thy brain?
What the anvil? What dread grasp
Dare its deadly terrors clasp?

When the stars threw down their spears,
And water'd heaven with their tears,
Did He smile His work to see?
Did He who made the lamb make thee?

William Blake, "The Tiger," from *Songs of Experience*

Tiger, tiger, burning bright
In the forests of the night,
What immortal hand or eye
Dare frame thy fearful symmetry?

WILLIAM BLAKE

London

I wander thro' each charter'd street
Near where the charter'd Thames does flow,
And mark in every face I meet
Marks of weakness, marks of woe.

In every cry of every Man,
In every Infant's cry of fear,
In every voice: in every ban,
The mind-forg'd manacles I hear.

How the Chimney-sweepers cry
Every blackning Church appalls,
And the hapless Soldier's sigh
Runs in blood down Palace walls.

But most thro' midnight streets I hear
How the youthful Harlot's curse
Blasts the new-born Infant's tear
And blights with plagues the Marriage-hearse.

ELIZABETH BARRETT BROWNING (1806–1861) was forty when she escaped from both chronic poor health and her father's tyranny to marry a fellow poet and live in Italy. In addition to raising her eleven siblings after her mother's death, by the time she eloped with Robert Browning from England, she had written three major collections of poetry and completed a translation of the Greek *Prometheus Bound*. Browning, six years younger than Elizabeth, began corresponding with her when she was thirty-eight, and they exchanged hundreds of letters over the next two years. Secretly, during this time Elizabeth began composing the **sonnets** included in *Sonnets from the Portuguese* (1850); the two sonnets on the next page are from this group. The *Sonnets from the Portuguese* form a narrative, describing the evolution of Elizabeth and Robert's love and their relationship. Elizabeth bore a child in Florence and continued writing until her early death (1861), completing at least three major additional works, including her verse novel *Aurora Leigh* (1857).

Related Works: Chopin, "The Story of an Hour"; Faulkner, "A Rose for Emily"; Bradstreet, "To My Dear and Loving Husband"; Browning, "My Last Duchess" and "Childe Rolande to the Dark Tower Came"; Byron, "She walks in beauty"; Levertov, "The Ache of Marriage"; Ibsen, *A Dollhouse*.

ELIZABETH BARRETT BROWNING

Sonnets from the Portuguese

XIV

If thou must love me, let it be for nought
Except for love's sake only. Do not say
"I love her for her smile—her look—her way
Of speaking gently,—for a trick of thought

That falls in well with mine, and certes brought
A sense of pleasant ease on such a day"–
For these things in themselves, Beloved, may
Be changed, or change for thee,—and love, so wrought,
May be unwrought so. Neither love me for
Thine own dear pity's wiping my cheeks dry,-
A creature might forget to weep, who bore
Thy comfort long, and lose thy love thereby!
But love me for love's sake, that evermore
Thou may'st love on, through love's eternity.

ELIZABETH BARRETT BROWNING

Sonnets from the Portuguese

XLIII

How do I love thee? Let me count the ways.
I love thee to the depth and breadth and height
My soul can reach, when feeling out of sight
For the ends of Being and ideal Grace.
I love thee to the level of everyday's
Most quiet need, by sun and candlelight.
I love thee freely, as men strive for Right;
I love thee purely, as they turn from Praise.
I love thee with the passion put to use
In my old griefs, and with my childhood's faith.
I love thee with a love I seemed to lose
With my lost saints,—I love thee with the breath,
Smiles, tears, of all my life!—and, if God choose,
I shall but love thee better after death.

ROBERT BROWNING (1812–1889), despite the fact that he was a productive poet and playwright in his own right, was, for most of his life, chiefly famous as Elizabeth Barrett's husband. After their marriage, Robert dedicated an excellent, but little regarded collection of poems, *Men and Women* (1855), to Elizabeth. Although not successful in his time, his **dramatic monologues**, like the three below—"Porphyria's Lover" (1836), "My Last Duchess" (1842), and "Childe Roland to the Dark Tower Came" (1855)—influenced later poets significantly. As a playwright, Browning developed a fine ear for each character's individual pacing and diction, and these two poems reflect this talent.

Related Works: Poe, "The Tell-Tale Heart" and "The Raven"; Atwood, "Gertrude Talks Back"; Wideman, "What We Cannot Speak About We Must Pass Over in Silence"; Arnold, "Dover Beach"; Ginsberg, "Howl"; Frost, "The Death of the Hired Man"; Shakespeare, *Hamlet*; Miller, *Death of a Salesman*.

ROBERT BROWNING

Porphyria's Lover

The rain set early in tonight,
    The sullen wind was soon awake,
It tore the elm-tops down for spite,
    And did its worst to vex the lake:
    I listened with heart fit to break.
When glided in Porphyria; straight
    She shut the cold out and the storm,
And kneeled and made the cheerless grate
    Blaze up, and all the cottage warm;
    Which done, she rose, and from her form
Withdrew the dripping cloak and shawl,
    And laid her soiled gloves by, untied
Her hat and let the damp hair-fall,
    And, last, she sat down by my side
    And called me. When no voice replied,
She put my arm about her waist,
    And made her smooth white shoulder bare,
And all her yellow hair displaced,
    And, stooping, made my cheek lie there,
    And spread, o'er all, her yellow hair.
Murmuring how she loved me—she
    Too weak, for all her heart's endeavor,
To set its struggling passion free
    From pride, and vainer ties dissever,
    And give herself to me forever.
But passion sometimes would prevail,
    Nor could tonight's gay feast restrain
A sudden thought of one so pale
    For love of her, and all in vain:-
    So, she was come through wind and rain.
Be sure I looked up at her eyes
    Happy and proud; at last I knew

Porphyria worshiped me: surprise
    Made my heart swell, and still it grew
    While I debated what to do.
That moment she was mine, mine, fair,
    Perfectly pure and good: I found
A thing to do, and all her hair
    In one long yellow string I wound
    Three times her little throat around.
And strangled her. No pain felt she;
    I am quite sure she felt no pain.
As a shut bud that holds a bee,
    I warily oped her lids; again
    Laughed the blue eyes without a stain.
And I untightened next the tress
    About her neck; her cheek once more
Blushed bright beneath my burning kiss:
    I propped her head up as before,
    Only this time my shoulder bore
Her head, which droops upon it still;
    The smiling rosy little head,
So glad it has its utmost will,
    That all it scorned at once is fled,
    And I, its love, am gained instead!
Porphyria's love; she guessed not how
    Her darling one wish would be heard.
And thus we sit together now,
    And all night long we have not stirred,
    And yet God has not said a word!

ROBERT BROWNING

My Last Duchess

Ferrara

That's my last Duchess painted on the wall,
Looking as if she were alive. I call
That piece a wonder, now: Frà Pandolf's hands
Worked busily a day, and there she stands.
Will't please you sit and look at her? I said
"Frà Pandolf" by design, for never read
Strangers like you that pictured countenance,
The depth and passion of its earnest glance,

But to myself they turned (since none puts by
The curtain I have drawn for you, but I)
And seemed as they would ask me, if they durst,
How such a glance came there; so, not the first
Are you to turn and ask thus. Sir, 'twas not
Her husband's presence only, called that spot
Of joy into the Duchess' cheek: perhaps
Frà Pandolf chanced to say, "Her mantle laps
Over my Lady's wrist too much," or "Paint
Must never hope to reproduce the faint
Half-flush that dies along her throat"; such stuff
Was courtesy, she thought, and cause enough
For calling up that spot of joy. She had
A heart . . . how shall I say? . . . too soon made glad,
Too easily impressed; she liked whate'er
She looked on, and her looks went everywhere.
Sir, 'twas all one! My favour at her breast,
The dropping of the daylight in the West,
The bough of cherries some officious fool
Broke in the orchard for her, the white mule
She rode with round the terrace—all and each
Would draw from her alike the approving speech,
Or blush, at least. She thanked men,—good; but thanked
Somehow . . . I know not how . . . as if she ranked
My gift of a nine-hundred-years-old name
With anybody's gift. Who'd stoop to blame
This sort of trifling? Even had you skill
In speech—(which I have not)—to make your will
Quite clear to such an one, and say, "Just this
Or that in you disgusts me; here you miss,
Or there exceed the mark"—and if she let
Herself be lessoned so, nor plainly set
Her wits to yours, forsooth, and made excuse,
—E'en then would be some stooping; and I chuse
Never to stoop. Oh, sir, she smiled, no doubt,
Whene'er I passed her; but who passed without
Much the same smile? This grew; I gave commands;
Then all smiles stopped together. There she stands
As if alive. Will't please you rise? We'll meet
The company below, then. I repeat,
The Count your Master's known munificence
Is ample warrant that no just pretence
Of mine for dowry will be disallowed;
Though his fair daughter's self, as I avowed
At starting, is my object. Nay, we'll go
Together down, Sir! Notice Neptune, though,
Taming a sea-horse, thought a rarity,
Which Claus of Innsbruck cast in bronze for me.

ROBERT BROWNING

Childe Roland to the Dark Tower Came

(*See Edgar's Song in "Lear"*)

I

My first thought was, he lied in every word,
That hoary cripple, with malicious eye
Askance to watch the working of his lie
On mine, and mouth scarce able to afford
Suppression of the glee, that pursed and scored
Its edge, at one more victim gained thereby.

II

What else should he be set for, with his staff?
What, save to waylay with his lies, ensnare
All travellers who might find him posted there,
And ask the road? I guessed what skull-like laugh
Would break, what crutch 'gin write my epitaph
For pastime in the dusty thoroughfare,

III

If at his counsel I should turn aside
Into that ominous tract which, all agree,
Hides the Dark Tower. Yet acquiescingly
I did turn as he pointed: neither pride
Nor hope rekindling at the end descried,
So much as gladness that some end might be.

IV

For, what with my whole world-wide wandering,
What with my search drawn out thro' years, my hope
Dwindled into a ghost not fit to cope
With that obstreperous joy success would bring,—
I hardly tried now to rebuke the spring
My heart made, finding failure in its scope.

V

As when a sick man very near to death
Seems dead indeed, and feels begin and end
The tears and takes the farewell of each friend,
And hears one bid the other go, draw breath
Freelier outside, ("since all is o'er," he saith,
"And the blow fallen no grieving can amend;")

VI

While some discuss if near the other graves
  Be room enough for this, and when a day
  Suits best for carrying the corpse away,
With care about the banners, scarves and staves:
And still the man hears all, and only craves
  He may not shame such tender love and stay.

VII

Thus, I had so long suffered in this quest,
  Heard failure prophesied so oft, been writ
  So many times among "The Band"—to wit,
The knights who to the Dark Tower's search addressed
Their steps—that just to fail as they, seemed best,
  And all the doubt was now—should I be fit?

VIII

So, quiet as despair, I turned from him,
  That hateful cripple, out of his highway
  Into the path he pointed. All the day
Had been a dreary one at best, and dim
Was settling to its close, yet shot one grim
  Red leer to see the plain catch its estray.

IX

For mark! no sooner was I fairly found
  Pledged to the plain, after a pace or two,
  Than, pausing to throw backward a last view
O'er the safe road, 'twas gone; grey plain all - round:
Nothing but plain to the horizon's bound.
  I might go on; nought else remained to do.

X

So, on I went. I think I never saw
  Such starved ignoble nature; nothing throve:
  For flowers—as well expect a cedar grove!
But cockle, spurge, according to their law
Might propagate their kind, with none to awe,
  You'd think; a burr had been a treasure-trove.

XI

No! penury, inertness and grimace,
  In some strange sort, were the land's portion.
      "See
  "Or shut your eyes," said Nature peevishly,
"It nothing skills: I cannot help my case:
" 'Tis the Last Judgment's fire must cure this place,
  "Calcine its clods and set my prisoners free."

XII

If there pushed any ragged thistle-stalk
  Above its mates, the head was chopped; the bents
  Were jealous else. What made those holes and rents
In the dock's harsh swarth leaves, bruised as to baulk
All hope of greenness? 't is a brute must walk
  Pashing their life out, with a brute's intents.

XIII

As for the grass, it grew as scant as hair
  In leprosy; thin dry blades pricked the mud
  Which underneath looked kneaded up with blood.
One stiff blind horse, his every bone a-stare,
Stood stupefied, however he came there:
  Thrust out past service from the devil's stud!

XIV

Alive? he might be dead for aught I know,
  With that red gaunt and colloped neck a-strain,
  And shut eyes underneath the rusty mane;
Seldom went such grotesqueness with such woe;
I never saw a brute I hated so;
  He must be wicked to deserve such pain.

XV

I shut my eyes and turned them on my heart.
  As a man calls for wine before he fights,
  I asked one draught of earlier, happier sights,
Ere fitly I could hope to play my part.
Think first, fight afterwards—the soldier's art:
  One taste of the old time sets all to rights.

XVI

Not it! I fancied Cuthbert's reddening face
  Beneath its garniture of curly gold,
  Dear fellow, till I almost felt him fold
An arm in mine to fix me to the place,
That way he used. Alas, one night's disgrace!
  Out went my heart's new fire and left it cold.

XVII

Giles then, the soul of honour—there he stands
  Frank as ten years ago when knighted first.
  What honest man should dare (he said) he durst,
Good—but the scene shifts—faugh! what hangman hands
'in to his breast a parchment? His own bands
  Read it. Poor traitor, spit upon and curst!

XVIII

Better this present than a past like that;
Back therefore to my darkening path again!
No sound, no sight as far as eye could strain.
Will the night send a howlet or a bat?
I asked: when something on the dismal flat
Came to arrest my thoughts and change their train.

XIX

A sudden little river crossed my path
As unexpected as a serpent comes.
No sluggish tide congenial to the glooms;
This, as it frothed by, might have been a bath
For the fiend's glowing hoof—to see the wrath
Of its black eddy bespate with flakes and spumes.

XX

So petty yet so spiteful! All along,
Low scrubby alders kneeled down over it;
Drenched willows flung them headlong in a fit
Of mute despair, a suicidal throng:
The river which had done them all the wrong,
Whate'er that was, rolled by, deterred no whit.

XXI

Which, while I forded,—good saints, how I feared
To set my foot upon a dead man's cheek,
Each step, or feel the spear I thrust to seek
For hollows, tangled in his hair or beard!
—It may have been a water-rat I speared,
But, ugh! it sounded like a baby's shriek.

XXII

Glad was I when I reached the other bank.
Now for a better country. Vain presage
Who were the strugglers, what war did they wage,
Whose savage trample thus could pad the dank
Soil to a plash? Toads in a poisoned tank,
Or wild cats in a red-hot iron cage—

XXIII

The fight must so have seemed in that fell cirque.
What penned them there, with all the plain to choose?
No foot-print leading to that horrid mews,
None out of it. Mad brewage set to work

Their brains, no doubt, like galley-slaves the Turk
  Pits for his pastime, Christians against Jews.

XXIV

And more than that—a furlong on—why, there!
  What bad use was that engine for, that wheel,
  Or brake, not wheel—that harrow fit to reel
Men's bodies out like silk? with all the air
Of Tophet's tool, on earth left unaware,
  Or brought to sharpen its rusty teeth of steel.

XXV

Then came a bit of stubbed ground, once a wood,
  Next a marsh, it would seem, and now mere earth
  Desperate and done with; (so a fool finds mirth,
Makes a thing and then mars it, till his mood
Changes and off he goes!) within a rood—
  Bog, clay and rubble, sand and stark black dearth.

XXVI

Now blotches rankling, coloured gay and grim,
  Now patches where some leanness of the soil's
  Broke into moss or substances like boils;
Then came some palsied oak, a cleft in him
Like a distorted mouth that splits its rim
  Gaping at death, and dies while it recoils.

XXVII

And just as far as ever from the end!
  Nought in the distance but the evening, nought
  To point my footstep further! At the thought,
A great black bird, Apollyon's bosom-friend,
Sailed past, nor beat his wide wing dragon-penned
  That brushed my cap—perchance the guide I sought.

XXVIII

For, looking up, aware I somehow grew,
  'Spite of the dusk, the plain had given place
  All round to mountains—with such name to grace
Mere ugly heights and heaps now stolen in view.
How thus they had surprised me,—solve it, you!
  How to get from them was no clearer case.

XXIX

Yet half I seemed to recognize some trick
  Of mischief happened to me, God knows when—

In a bad dream perhaps. Here ended, then,
Progress this way. When, in the very nick
Of giving up, one time more, came a click
As when a trap shuts—you're inside the den!

XXX

Burningly it came on me all at once,
This was the place! those two hills on the right,
Crouched like two bulls locked horn in horn in fight;
While to the left, a tall scalped mountain . . . Dunce,
Dotard, a-dozing at the very nonce,
After a life spent training for the sight!

XXXI

What in the midst lay but the Tower itself?
The round squat turret, blind as the fool's heart,
Built of brown stone, without a counterpart
In the whole world. The tempest's mocking elf
Points to the shipman thus the unseen shelf
He strikes on, only when the timbers start.

XXXII

Not see? because of night perhaps?—why, day
Came back again for that! before it left,
The dying sunset kindled through a cleft:
The hills, like giants at a hunting, lay,
Chin upon hand, to see the game at bay,—
"Now stab and end the creature—to the heft!

XXXIII

Not hear? when noise was everywhere! it tolled
Increasing like a bell. Names in my ears
Of all the lost adventurers my peers,—
How such a one was strong, and such was bold,
And such was fortunate, yet each of old
Lost, lost! one moment knelled the woe of years.

XXXIV

There they stood, ranged along the hill-sides, met
To view the last of me, a living frame
For one more picture! in a sheet of flame
I saw them and I knew them all. And yet
Dauntless the slug-horn to my lips I set,
And blew "*Childe Roland to the Dark Tower came.*"

ROBERT BURNS (1759–1796), perhaps most famous for his lyrics, "Auld Lang Syne" and "Coming Thru the Rye," was the eldest son in a large farming family in Scotland. Largely self-educated, he began writing songs and lyrics in 1781, but his verse was first published in the collection *Poems, Chiefly in the Scottish Dialect* (1786). The two poems included here, like most of Burns's poems, were meant to be sung. Burns's songs achieved extraordinary popularity not only in Scotland, but throughout England and America—see collections of his songs in George Thomson's *Select Collection of Original Scottish Airs for the Voice* (6 vols., 1793–1811) and James Johnson's *Scots Musical Museum* (5 vols., 1787–1803). Burns wrote in Scottish **dialect**, describing with humor and accuracy the traits of traditional Scottish rural life. Notice the **riddle**-like quality of Burns's description of malting and distilling whiskey in "John Barleycorn: A Ballad" (1782). In "A Red, Red Rose" (1796) Burns brings the vitality of his local dialect to these traditional **similes**.

Related Works: Old English Riddles; Anonymous Ballads; Hardy, "Ah, are you digging on my grave?" and "The Ruined Maid"; Robinson, "Richard Cory"; Randall, "Ballad of Birmingham."

ROBERT BURNS

A Red, Red Rose

O my Luve's like a red, red rose.
  That's newly sprung in June;
O my Luve's like the melodie
  That's sweetly played in tune.

As fair art thou, my bonie lass,
  So deep in luve am I;
And I will love thee still, my Dear,
  Till a' the seas gang dry.

Till a' the seas gang dry, my Dear,
  And the rocks melt wi' the sun:
O I will love thee still, my Dear,
  While the sands o' life shall run.

And fare thee weel, my only Luve!
  And fare thee weel, a while!
And I will come again, my Luve,
  Tho' it were ten thousand mile!

ROBERT BURNS

John Barleycorn

A Ballad

I

There was three kings into the east,
   Three kings both great and high,
And they hae sworn a solemn oath
   John Barleycorn should die.

II

They took a plough and plough'd him down,
   Put clods upon his head,
And they hae sworn a solemn oath
   John Barleycorn was dead.

III

But the cheerful Spring came kindly on,
   And show'rs began to fall;
John Barleycorn got up again,
   And sore surpris'd them all.

IV

The sultry suns of Summer came,
   And he grew thick and strong:
His head weel arm'd wi' pointed spears,
   That no one should him wrong.

V

The sober Autumn enter'd mild,
   When he grew wan and pale;
His bending joints and drooping head
   Show'd he began to fail.

VI

His colour sicken'd more and more,
   He faded into age;
And then his enemies began
   To show their deadly rage.

VII

They've taen a weapon long and sharp,
And cut him by the knee;
Then ty'd him fast upon a cart,
Like a rogue for forgerie.

VIII

They laid him down upon his back,
And cudgell'd him full sore.
They hung him up before the storm,
And turn'd him o'er and o'er.

IX

They fillèd up a darksome pit
With water to the brim,
They heavèd in John Barleycorn—
There, let him sink or swim!

X

They laid him out upon the floor,
To work him farther woe;
And still, as signs of life appear'd,
They toss'd him to and fro.

XI

They wasted o'er a scorching flame
The marrow of his bones;
But a miller us'd him worst of all,
For he crushed him between two stones.

XII

And they hae taen his very heart's blood,
And drank it round and round;
And still the more and more they drank,
Their joy did more abound.

XIII

John Barleycorn was a hero bold,
Of noble enterprise;
For if you do but taste his blood,
'Twill make your courage rise.

XIV

'Twill make a man forget his woe;
'Twill heighten all his joy:
'Twill make the widow's heart to sing,
Tho' the tear were in her eye.

XV

Then let us toast John Barleycorn,
Each man a glass in hand;
And may his great posterity
Ne'er fail in old Scotlànd!

GEORGE GORDON, LORD BYRON (1788–1824), like the hero of his most important work, *Don Juan* (1819–1833), gave the world the fiction, if not the reality, of the Byronic Hero—moody, dark, fascinating, and erotically charged. His liaisons with both women and men were legendary and scandalous. In his time, he was considered the epitome of a Romantic period poet, although most of his poetry—satirical, **epigrammatic**, and witty—has much more in common with the Neoclassical poets, Pope (1688–1744) and Swift (1667–1745), than with his fellow Romantic poets Wordsworth (1770–1850), Keats (1795–1821), Coleridge (1772–1834), and Shelley (1792–1822). The poem below "She walks in beauty" (1815), a lyric meant to accompany a traditional Jewish tune, recalls an even earlier tradition, the **Cavalier poets** (ca. 1650); notice the gallant and elaborate compliment to a specific lady, in this case Mrs. Robert John Wilmot, a cousin by marriage, who wears a black mourning gown.

Related Works: Medieval Lyrical Poetry; Anonymous Ballads; Barrett Browning, Sonnets 14 and 43; Marlowe, "The Passionate Shepherd to His Love"; Ralegh, "The Nymph's Reply to the Shepherd"; Marvell, "To His Coy Mistress"; Browning, "Childe Roland to the Dark Tower Came"; Keats, "La Belle Dame sans Merci"; Millay, "What lips my lips have kissed"; Ibsen, *A Doll House*.

LORD BYRON

She Walks in Beauty

1.

She walks in beauty, like the night
Of cloudless climes and starry skies;
And all that's best of dark and bright
Meet in her aspect and her eyes:

Thus mellow'd to that tender light
  Which heaven to gaudy day denies.

2.

One shade the more, one ray the less,
  Had half impair'd the nameless grace
Which waves in every raven tress,
  Or softly lightens o'er her face;
Where thoughts serenely sweet express
  How pure, how dear their dwelling place.

3.

And on that cheek, and o'er that brow,
  So soft, so calm, yet eloquent,
The smiles that win, the tints that glow,
  But tell of days in goodness spent,
A mind at peace with all below,
  A heart whose love is innocent!

SAMUEL TAYLOR COLERIDGE (1772–1834). When Coleridge published *Lyrical Ballads* in 1798 with fellow poet and writer William Wordsworth, the two Englishmen revolutionized poetry and introduced the **Romantic movement**. "The Rime of the Ancient Mariner," perhaps Coleridge's most famous poem, appeared in *Lyrical Ballads* and includes the elements of mysticism and/or magic, passion, and lyricism that characterize much Romantic poetry. Coleridge also made important strides in literary theory and criticism in his long digressive volume the *Biographia Literaria* (1817), wherein he developed some early observations on the nature of consciousness, reason, and imagination. "Frost at Midnight" is one of his most lyrical works, written in 1798 during one of the happiest periods of Coleridge's often unhappy life.

Related Works: Poe, "The Tell-Tale Heart"; Faulkner, "A Rose for Emily"; Medieval Lyrics; Keats, "La Belle Dame sans Merci" and "Ode on a Grecian Urn"; Shelley, "Ozymandias"; Wordsworth, "I wandered lonely as a cloud" and "Composed upon Westminster Bridge, September 3, 1802"; Williams, *The Glass Menagerie*.

SAMUEL TAYLOR COLERIDGE

Frost at Midnight

The frost performs its secret ministry,
Unhelped by any wind. The owlet's cry
Came loud—and hark, again! loud as before.

The inmates of my cottage, all at rest,
Have left me to that solitude, which suits
Abstruser musings: save that at my side
My cradled infant slumbers peacefully.
'Tis calm indeed! so calm, that it disturbs
And vexes meditation with its strange
And extreme silentness. Sea, hill, and wood,
This populous village! Sea, and hill, and wood,
With all the numberless goings on of life,
Inaudible as dreams! the thin blue flame
Lies on my low burnt fire, and quivers not;
Only that film, which fluttered on the grate,
Still flutters there, the sole unquiet thing.
Methinks, its motion in this hush of nature
Gives it dim sympathies with me who live,
Making it a companionable form,
Whose puny flaps and freaks the idling Spirit
By its own moods interprets, every where
Echo or mirror seeking of itself,
And makes a toy of Thought.

But O! how oft,
How oft, at school, with most believing mind,
Presageful, have I gazed upon the bars,
To watch that fluttering stranger! and as oft
With unclosed lids, already had I dreamt
Of my sweet birth-place, and the old church-tower,
Whose bells, the poor man's only music, rang
From morn to evening, all the hot Fair-day,
So sweetly, that they stirred and haunted me
With a wild pleasure, falling on mine ear
Most like articulate sounds of things to come!
So gazed I, till the soothing things I dreamt
Lulled me to sleep, and sleep prolonged my dreams!
And so I brooded all the following morn,
Awed by the stern preceptor's face, mine eye
Fixed with mock study on my swimming book:
Save if the door half opened, and I snatched
A hasty glance, and still my heart leaped up,
For still I hoped to see the stranger's face,
Townsman, or aunt, or sister more beloved,
My play-mate when we both were clothed alike!

Dear Babe, that sleepest cradled by my side,
Whose gentle breathings, heard in this deep calm,
Fill up the interspersèd vacancies
And momentary pauses of the thought!
My babe so beautiful! it thrills my heart
With tender gladness, thus to look at thee,
And think that thou shalt learn far other lore

And in far other scenes! For I was reared
In the great city, pent 'mid cloisters dim,
And saw nought lovely but the sky and stars.
But thou, my babe! shalt wander like a breeze
By lakes and sandy shores, beneath the crags
Of ancient mountain, and beneath the clouds,
Which image in their bulk both lakes and shores
And mountain crags: so shalt thou see and hear
The lovely shapes and sounds intelligible
Of that eternal language, which thy God
Utters, who from eternity doth teach
Himself in all, and all things in himself.
Great universal Teacher! he shall mould
Thy spirit, and by giving make it ask.

Therefore all seasons shall be sweet to thee,
Whether the summer clothe the general earth
With greenness, or the redbreast sit and sing
Betwixt the tufts of snow on the bare branch
Of mossy apple-tree, while the night thatch
Smokes in the sun-thaw; whether the eve-drops fall
Heard only in the trances of the blast,
Or if the secret ministry of frost
Shall hang them up in silent icicles,
Quietly shining to the quiet Moon.

SAMUEL TAYLOR COLERIDGE

The Rime of the Ancyent Marinere

In Seven Parts

Part I

It is an ancyent Marinere,
   And he stoppeth one of three:
'By thy long grey beard and thy glittering eye
   Now wherefore stoppest me?

The Bridegroom's doors are open'd wide
   And I am next of kin;
The Guests are met, the Feast is set,—
   May'st hear the merry din.'

But still he holds the wedding-guest—
   There was a Ship, quoth he—

'Nay, if thou'st got a laughsome tale,
  Marinere! come with me.'

He holds him with his skinny hand,
  Quoth he, there was a Ship—
'Now get thee hence, thou grey-beard Loon!
  Or my Staff shall make thee skip.'

He holds him with his glittering eye—
  The wedding-guest stood still
And listens like a three year's child;
  The Marinere hath his will.

The wedding-guest sate on a stone,
  He cannot chuse but hear:
And thus spake on that ancyent man,
  The bright-eyed Marinere.

The Ship was cheer'd, the Harbour clear'd—
  Merrily did we drop
Below the Kirk, below the Hill,
  Below the Light-house top.

The Sun came up upon the left,
  Out of the Sea came he:
And he shone bright, and on the right
  Went down into the Sea.

Higher and higher every day,
  Till over the mast at noon—
The wedding-guest here beat his breast,
  For he heard the loud bassoon.

The Bride hath pac'd into the Hall,
  Red as a rose is she;
Nodding their heads before her goes
  The merry Minstralsy.

The wedding-guest he beat his breast,
  Yet he cannot chuse but hear:
And thus spake on that ancyent Man,
  The bright-eyed Marinere.

Listen, Stranger! Storm and Wind,
  A Wind and Tempest strong!
For days and weeks it play'd us freaks—
  Like Chaff we drove along.

Listen, Stranger! Mist and Snow,
  And it grew wond'rous cauld:
And Ice mast-high came floating by
  As green as Emerauld.

And thro' the drifts the snowy clifts
  Did send a dismal sheen;
Ne shapes of men ne beasts we ken—
  The Ice was all between.

The Ice was here, the Ice was there,
  The Ice was all around
It crack'd and growl'd, and roar'd and howl'd—
  Like noises of a swound.

At length did cross an Albatross,
  Thorough the Fog it came;
And an it were a Christian Soul,
  We hail'd it in God's name.

The Marineres gave it biscuit-worms,
  And round and round it flew;
The Ice did split with a Thunder-fit;
  The Helmsman steer'd us thro'.

And a good south wind sprung up behind,
  The Albatross did follow;
And every day for food or play
  Came to the Marinere's hollo!

In mist or cloud on mast or shroud
  It perch'd for vespers nine,
Whiles all the night thro' fog smoke-white
  Glimmer'd the white moon-shine.

'God save thee, ancyent Marinere!
  From the fiends that plague thee thus—
Why look'st thou so?'—with my cross bow
  I shot the Albatross.

Part II

The Sun came up upon the right,
  Out of the Sea came he;
And broad as a weft upon the left
  Went down into the Sea.

And the good south wind still blew behind,
  But no sweet Bird did follow
Ne any day for food or play
  Came to the Marinere's hollo!

And I had done an hellish thing
  And it would work 'em woe;
For all averr'd, I had kill'd the Bird
  That made the Breeze to blow.

Ne dim ne red, like God's own head,
  The glorious Sun uprist:

Then all averr'd, I had kill'd the Bird
   That brought the fog and mist.
'Twas right, said they, such birds to slay
   That bring the fog and mist.

The breezes blew, the white foam flew,
   The furrow follow'd free:
We were the first that ever burst
   Into that silent Sea.

Down dropt the breeze, the Sails dropt down,
   'Twas sad as sad could be
And we did speak only to break
   The silence of the Sea.

All in a hot and copper sky
   The bloody sun at noon,
Right up above the mast did stand,
   No bigger than the moon.

Day after day, day after day,
   We stuck, ne breath ne motion,
As idle as a painted Ship
   Upon a painted Ocean.

Water, water, every where
   And all the boards did shrink;
Water, water every where,
   Ne any drop to drink.

The very deeps did rot: O Christ!
   That ever this should be!
Yea, slimly things did crawl with legs
   Upon the slimy Sea.

About, about, in reel and rout
   The Death-fires danc'd at night;
The water, like a witch's oils,
   Burnt green and blue and white.

And some in dreams assured were
   Of the Spirit that plagued us so:
Nine fathom deep he had follow'd us
   From the Land of Mist and Snow.

And every tongue thro' utter drouth
   Was wither'd at the root;
We could not speak no more than if
   We had been choked with soot.

Ah wel-a-day! what evil looks
   Had I from old and young;
Instead of the Cross the Albatross
   About my neck was hung.

Part III

I saw a something in the Sky
No bigger than my fist;
At first it seem'd a little speck
And then it seem'd a mist:
It mov'd and mov'd, and took at last
A certain shape, I wist.

A speck, a mist, a shape, I wist!
And still it ner'd and ner'd;
And, an it dodg'd a water-sprite,
It plung'd and tack'd and veer'd.

With throat unslack'd, with black lips bak'd
Ne could we laugh, ne wail:
Then while thro' drouth all dumb they stood
I bit my arm and suck'd the blood
And cry'd, A sail! a sail!

With throat unslack'd, with black lips bak'd
Agape they hear'd me call:
Gramercy! they for joy did grin
And all at once their breath drew in
As they were drinking all.

She doth not tack from side to side—
Hither to work us weal
Withouten wind, withouten tide
She steddies with upright keel.

The western wave was all a flame,
The day was well nigh done!
Almost upon the western wave
Rested the broad bright Sun;
When that strange shape drove suddenly
Betwixt us and the Sun.

And strait the Sun was fleck'd with bars
(Heaven's mother send us grace)
As if thro' a dungeon grate he peer'd
With broad and burning face.

Alas! (thought I, and my heart beat loud)
How fast she neres and neres!
Are those *her* Sails that glance in the Sun
Like restless gossameres?

Are those *her* naked ribs, which fleck'd
The sun that did behind them peer?
And are those two all, all the crew,
That woman and her fleshless Pheere?

His bones were black with many a crack,
All black and bare, I ween;
Jet-black and bare, save where with rust
Of mouldy damps and charnel crust
They're patch'd with purple and green.

Her lips are red, *her* looks are free,
Her locks are yellow as gold:
Her skin is as white as leprosy,
And she is far liker Death than he;
Her flesh makes the still air cold.

The naked Hulk alongside came
And the Twain were playing dice;
'The Game is done! I've won, I've won!'
Quoth she, and whistled thrice.

A gust of wind sterte up behind
And whistled thro' his bones;
Thro' the holes of his eyes and the hole of his mouth
Half-whistles and half-groans.

With never a whisper in the Sea
Oft darts the Spectre-ship;
While clombe above the Eastern bar
The hornèd Moon, with one bright Star
Almost atween the tips.

One after one by the hornèd Moon
(Listen, O Stranger! to me)
Each turn'd his face with a ghastly pang
And curs'd me with his ee.

Four times fifty living men,
With never a sigh or groan.
With heavy thump, a lifeless lump
They dropp'd down one by one.

Their souls did from their bodies fly,—
They fled to bliss or woe;
And every soul it pass'd me by,
Like the whiz of my Cross-bow.

Part IV

'I fear thee, ancyent Marinere!
I fear thy skinny hand;
And thou art long and lank and brown
As is the ribb'd Sea-sand.

I fear thee and thy glittering eye
And thy skinny hand so brown—
Fear not, fear not, thou wedding-guest!
This body dropt not down.

Alone, alone, all all alone
   Alone on the wide wide Sea;
And Christ would take no pity on
   My soul in agony.

The many men so beautiful,
   And they all dead did lie!
And a million million slimy things
   Liv'd on—and so did I.

I look'd upon the rotting Sea,
   And drew my eyes away;
I look'd upon the eldritch deck,
   And there the dead men lay.

I look'd to Heaven, and try'd to pray;
   But or ever a prayer had gusht,
A wicked whisper came and made
   My heart as dry as dust.

I clos'd my lids and kept them close,
   Till the balls like pulses beat;
For the sky and the sea, and the sea and the sky
Lay like a load on my weary eye,
   And the dead were at my feet.

The cold sweat melted from their limbs,
   Ne rot, ne reek did they;
The look with which they look'd on me,
   Had never pass'd away.

An orphan's curse would drag to Hell
   A spirit from on high:
But O! more horrible than that
   Is the curse in a dead man's eye!
Seven days, seven nights I saw that curse,
   And yet I could not die.

The moving Moon went up the sky
   And no where did abide:
Softly she was going up
   And a star or two beside—

Her beams bemock'd the sultry main
   Like morning frosts yspread;
But where the ship's huge shadow lay,
The charmèd water burnt alway
   A still and awful red.

Beyond the shadow of the ship
   I watch'd the water-snakes:
They mov'd in tracks of shining white;
And when they rear'd, the elfish light
   Fell off in hoary flakes.

Within the shadow of the ship
   I watch'd their rich attire:
Blue, glossy green, and velvet black
They coil'd and swam; and every track
   Was a flash of golden fire.

O happy living things! no tongue
   Their beauty might declare:
A spring of love gusht from my heart,
   And I bless'd them unaware!
Sure my kind saint took pity on me,
   And I bless'd them unaware.

The self-same moment I could pray;
   And from my neck so free
The Albatross fell off, and sank
   Like lead into the sea.

Part V

O sleep, it is a gentle thing
   Belov'd from pole to pole!
To Mary-queen the praise be yeven
She sent the gentle sleep from heaven
   That slid into my soul.

The silly buckets on the deck
   That had so long remain'd,
I dreamt that they were fill'd with dew
   And when I awoke it rain'd.

My lips were wet, my throat was cold,
   My garments all were dank;
Sure I had drunken in my dreams
   And still my body drank.

I mov'd and could not feel my limbs,
   I was so light, almost
I thought that I had died in sleep,
   And was a blessed Ghost.

The roaring wind! it roar'd far off,
   It did not come anear;
But with its sound it shook the sails
   That were so thin and sere.

The upper air bursts into life,
   And a hundred fire-flags sheen
To and fro they are hurried about;
And to and fro, and in and out
   The stars dance on between.

The coming wind doth roar more loud;
   The sails do sigh, like sedge:

The rain pours down from one black cloud
  And the Moon is at its edge.

Hark! hark! the thick black cloud is cleft,
  And the Moon is at its side:
Like waters shot from some high crag,
The lightning falls with never a jag
  A river steep and wide.

The strong wind reach'd the ship: it roar'd
  And dropp'd down, like a stone!
Beneath the lightning and the moon
  The dead men gave a groan.

They groan'd, they stirr'd, they all uprose,
  Ne spake, ne mov'd their eyes:
It had been strange, even in a dream
  To have seen those dead men rise.

The helmsman steerd, the ship mov'd on;
  Yet never a breeze up-blew;
The Marineres all 'gan work the ropes,
  Where they were wont to do:
They rais'd their limbs like lifeless tools—
  We were a ghastly crew.

The body of my brother's son
  Stood by me knee to knee:
The body and I pull'd at one rope,
  But he said nought to me—
And I quak'd to think of my own voice
  How frightful it would be!

The day-light dawn'd—they dropp'd their arms,
  And cluster'd round the mast:
Sweet sounds rose slowly thro' their mouths
  And from their bodies pass'd.

Around, around, flew each sweet sound,
  Then darted to the sun:
Slowly the sounds came back again
  Now mix'd, now one by one.

Sometimes a dropping from the sky
  I heard the Lavrock sing;
Sometimes all little birds that are
How they seem'd to fill the sea and air
  With their sweet jargoning.

And now 'twas like all instruments,
  Now like a lonely flute;
And now it is an angel's song
  That makes the heavens be mute.

It ceas'd: yet still the sails made on
 A pleasant noise till noon,
A noise like of a hidden brook
 In the leafy month of June,
That to the sleeping woods all night
 Singeth a quiet tune.

Listen, O listen, thou Wedding-guest!
 'Marinere! thou hast thy will:
For that, which comes out of thine eye, doth make
 My body and soul to be still.'

Never sadder tale was told
 To a man of woman born:
Sadder and wiser thou wedding-guest!
 Thou'lt rise to-morrow morn.

Never sadder tale was heard
 By a man of woman born:
The Marineres all return'd to work
 As silent as before.

The Marineres all 'gan pull the ropes,
 But look at me they n'old:
Thought I, I am as thin as air—
 They cannot me behold.

Till noon we silently sail'd on
 Yet never a breeze did breathe:
Slowly and smoothly went the ship
 Mov'd onward from beneath.

Under the keel nine fathom deep
 From the land of mist and snow
The spirit slid: and it was He
 That made the Ship to go.
The sails at noon left off their tune
 And the Ship stood still also.

The sun right up above the mast
 Had fix'd her to the ocean:
But in a minute she 'gan stir
 With a short uneasy motion—
Backwards and forwards half her length
 With a short uneasy motion.

Then, like a pawing horse let go,
 She made a sudden bound:
It flung the blood into my head,
 And I fell into a swound.

How long in that same fit I lay,
 I have not to declare;

But ere my living life return'd,
I heard and in my soul discern'd
  Two voices in the air,

'Is it he?' quoth one, 'Is this the man?'
  By him who died on cross,
With his cruel bow he lay'd full low
  The harmless Albatross.

'The spirit who 'bideth by himself
  In the land of mist and snow,
He lov'd the bird that lov'd the man
  Who shot him with his bow.'

The other was a softer voice,
  As soft as honey-dew:
Quoth he the man hath penance done,
  And penance more will do.

Part VI

First voice
'But tell me, tell me! speak again,
  Thy soft response renewing—
What makes that ship drive on so fast?
  What is the Ocean doing?'

Second voice
'Still as a Slave before his Lord,
  The Ocean hath no blast:
His great bright eye most silently
  Up to the moon is cast—

'If he may know which way to go,
  For she guides him smooth or grim.
See, brother, see! how graciously
  She looketh down on him.'

First voice
'But why drives on that ship so fast
  Withouten wave or wind?'

Second voice
'The air is cut away before,
  And closes from behind.

Fly, brother, fly! more high, more high,
  Or we shall be belated.
For slow and slow that ship will go,
  When the Marinere's trance is abated.'

I woke, and we were sailing on
  As in a gentle weather:
'Twas night, calm night, the moon was high;
  The dead men stood together.

All stood together on the deck,
   For a charnel-dungeon fitter:
All fix'd on me their stony eyes
   That in the moon did glitter.

The pang, the curse, with which they died,
   Had never pass'd away:
I could not draw my een from theirs
   Ne turn them up to pray.

And in its time the spell was snapt,
   And I could move my een:
I look'd far-forth, but little saw
   Of what might else be seen.

Like one, that on a lonely road
   Doth walk in fear and dread,
And having once turn'd round, walks on
   And turns no more his head:
Because he knows, a frightful fiend
   Doth close behind him tread.

But soon there breath'd a wind on me,
   Ne sound ne motion made:
Its path was not upon the sea
   In ripple or in shade.

It rais'd my hair, it fann'd my cheek,
   Like a meadow-gale of spring—
It mingled strangely with my fears,
   Yet it felt like a welcoming.

Swiftly, swiftly flew the ship,
   Yet she sail'd softly too:
Sweetly, sweetly blew the breeze—
   On me alone it blew.

O dream of joy! is this indeed
   The light-house top I see?
Is this the Hill? Is this the Kirk?
   Is this mine own countrèe?

We drifted o'er the Harbour-bar,
   And I with sobs did pray—
'O let me be awake, my God!
   Or let me sleep alway!'

The harbour-bay was clear as glass,
   So smoothly it was strewn!
And on the bay the moonlight lay,
   And the shadow of the moon.

The moonlight bay was white all o'er,
   Till rising from the same,

Full many shapes, that shadows were,
  Like as of torches came.

A little distance from the prow
  Those dark-red shadows were;
But soon I saw that my own flesh
  Was red as in a glare.

I turn'd my head in fear and dread,
  And by the holy rood,
The bodies had advanc'd, and now
  Before the mast they stood.

They lifted up their stiff right arms,
  They held them strait and tight;
And each right-arm burnt like a torch,
  A torch that's borne upright.
Their stony eye-balls glitter'd on
  In the red and smoky light.

I pray'd and turn'd my head away
  Forth looking as before.
There was no breeze upon the bay,
  No wave against the shore.

The rock shone bright, the kirk no less
  That stands above the rock:
The moonlight steep'd in silentness
  The steady weathercock.

And the bay was white with silent light,
  Till rising from the same
Full many shapes, that shadows were,
  In crimson colours came.

A little distance from the prow
  Those crimson shadows were:
I turn'd my eyes upon the deck—
  O Christ! what saw I there?

Each corse lay flat, lifeless and flat;
  And by the Holy rood
A man all light, a seraph-man,
  On every corse there stood.

This seraph-band, each wav'd his hand:
  It was a heavenly sight:
They stood as signals to the land,
  Each one a lovely light:

This seraph-band, each wav'd his hand,
  No voice did they impart—
No voice; but O! the silence sank,
  Like music on my heart.

Eftsones I heard the dash of oars,
   I heard the pilot's cheer:
My head was turn'd perforce away
   And I saw a boat appear.

Then vanish'd all the lovely lights;
   The bodies rose anew:
With silent pace, each to his place,
   Came back the ghastly crew.
The wind, that shade nor motion made,
   On me alone it blew.

The pilot, and the pilot's boy
   I heard them coming fast:
Dear Lord in Heaven! it was a joy,
   The dead men could not blast.

I saw a third—I heard his voice:
   It is the Hermit good!
He singeth loud his godly hymns
   That he makes in the wood.
He'll shrieve my soul, he'll wash away
   The Albatross's blood.

Part VII

This Hermit good lives in that wood
   Which slopes down to the Sea.
How loudly his sweet voice he rears!
He loves to talk with Marineres
   That come from a far Contrèe.

He kneels at morn and noon and eve—
   He hath a cushion plump:
It is the moss, that wholly hides
   The rotted old Oak-stump.

The Skiff-boat ne'rd: I heard them talk,
   'Why, this is strange, I trow!
Where are those lights so many and fair
   That signal made but now?'

'Strange, by my faith!' the Hermit said—
   'And they answer'd not our cheer.'
The planks look warp'd, and see those sails
   How thin they are and sere!
I never saw aught like to them
   Unless perchance it were

'The skeletons of leaves that lag
   My forest brook along:

When the Ivy-tod is heavy with snow,
And the Owlet whoops to the wolf below
That eats the she-wolf's young.'

'Dear Lord! it has a fiendish look—'
(The Pilot made reply)
'I am a-fear'd.'—'Push on, push on!'
Said the Hermit cheerily.

The Boat came closer to the Ship,
But I ne spake ne stirr'd!
The Boat came close beneath the Ship,
And strait a sound was heard!

Under the water it rumbled on,
Still louder and more dread:
It reach'd the Ship, it split the bay;
The Ship went down like lead.

Stunn'd by that loud and dreadful sound,
Which sky and ocean smote:
Like one that hath been seven days drown'd
My body lay afloat:
But, swift as dreams, myself I found
Within the Pilot's boat.

Upon the whirl, where sank the Ship,
The boat spun round and round:
And all was still, save that the hill
Was telling of the sound.

I mov'd my lips: the Pilot shriek'd
And fell down in a fit.
The Holy Hermit rais'd his eyes
And pray'd where he did sit.

Since then at an uncertain hour,
Now oftimes and now fewer,
That anguish comes and makes me tell
My ghastly aventure.

I pass, like night, from land to land;
I have strange power of speech;
The moment that his face I see
I know the man that must hear me;
To him my tale I teach.

What loud uproar bursts from that door!
The Wedding-guests are there;
But in the Garden-bower the Bride
And Bride-maids singing are:
And hark the little Vesper-bell
Which biddeth me to prayer.

O Wedding-guest! this soul hath been
Alone on a wide wide sea:
So lonely 'twas, that God himself
Scarce seemed there to be.

O sweeter than the Marriage-feast,
'Tis sweeter far to me
To walk together to the Kirk
With a goodly company.

To walk together to the Kirk
And all together pray,
While each to his great father bends,
Old men, and babes, and loving friends,
And Youths, and Maidens gay.

Farewell, farewell! but this I tell
To thee, thou wedding-guest!
He prayeth well who loveth well,
Both man and bird and beast.

He prayeth best who loveth best,
All things both great and small:
For the dear God, who loveth us,
He made and loveth all.

I took the oars: the Pilot's boy,
Who now doth crazy go,
Laugh'd loud and long, and all the while
His eyes went to and fro,
'Ha! ha!' quoth he—'full plain I see,
The devil knows how to row.'

And now all in mine own Countrèe
I stood on the firm land!
The Hermit stepp'd forth from the boat,
And scarcely he could stand.

'O shrieve me, shrieve me, holy Man!'
The Hermit cross'd his brow—
'Say quick,' quoth he, 'I bid thee say
What manner man art thou?'

Forthwith this frame of mine was wrench'd
With a woeful agony,
Which forc'd me to begin my tale
And then it left me free.

The Marinere, whose eye is bright,
Whose beard with age is hoar,
Is gone; and now the wedding-guest
Turn'd from the bridegroom's door.

He went, like one that hath been stunn'd
    And is of sense forlorn:
A sadder and a wiser man
    He rose the morrow morn.

SAMUEL TAYLOR COLERIDGE

Kubla Khan

In Xanadu did Kubla Khan
A stately pleasure-dome decree:
Where Alph, the sacred river, ran
Through caverns measureless to man
    Down to a sunless sea.
So twice five miles of fertile ground
With walls and towers were girdled round:
And there were gardens bright with sinuous rills
Where blossomed many an incense-bearing tree;
And here were forests ancient as the hills,
Enfolding sunny spots of greenery.

But oh! that deep romantic chasm which slanted
Down the green hill athwart a cedarn cover!
A savage place! as holy and enchanted
As e'er beneath a waning moon was haunted
By woman wailing for her demon-lover!
And from this chasm, with ceaseless turmoil seething,
As if this earth in fast thick pants were breathing,
A mighty fountain momently was forced:
Amid whose swift half-intermitted burst
Huge fragments vaulted like rebounding hail,
Or chaffy grain beneath the thresher's flail:
And 'mid these dancing rocks at once and ever
It flung up momently the sacred river.
Five miles meandering with a mazy motion
Through wood and dale the sacred river ran,
Then reached the caverns measureless to man,
And sank in tumult to a lifeless ocean:
And 'mid this tumult Kubla heard from far
Ancestral voices prophesying war!

    The shadow of the dome of pleasure
    Floated midway on the waves;
    Where was heard the mingled measure
    From the fountain and the caves.

It was a miracle of rare device,
A sunny pleasure-dome with caves of ice!
  A damsel with a dulcimer
  In a vision once I saw:
  It was an Abyssinian maid,
  And on her dulcimer she played,
  Singing of Mount Abora.
  Could I revive within me
  Her symphony and song,
  To such a deep delight 'twould win me.
That with music loud and long,
I would build that dome in air,
That sunny dome! those caves of ice!
And all who heard should see them there,
And all should cry, Beware! Beware!
His flashing eyes, his floating hair!
Weave a circle round him thrice,
And close your eyes with holy dread,
For he on honey-dew hath fed,
And drunk the milk of Paradise.

JOHN KEATS (1795–1821), the oldest of four children in a closely knit, but decidedly lower-middle-class family, was educated to be a surgeon and practiced for a few years as an intern. He began writing poetry in 1814, and in 1817 published his first volume, *Poems*; contemporary critics dismissed it as the work of an amateur from the "Cockney School." Another volume of poems, *Lamia, Isabella, The Eve of St. Agnes, and Other Poems*, published just before his death from tuberculosis at age twenty-five, met with critical success. Considered one of the premier **Romantic** poets, Keats infuses his romantic-erotic poetic narratives of classical and medieval legend and myth with an underlying melancholy and fascination with the transitory nature of life, love, and beauty. The concluding **epigram** in "Ode on a Grecian Urn" (1819) sums up a basic Romantic creed.

Related Works: Updike, "A&P"; Joyce, "Araby"; Medieval Lyrical Poetry; Old English Riddles; Anonymous Ballads; Burns, "A Red, Red Rose"; Coleridge, "Frost at Midnight" and "The Rime of the Ancient Mariner"; Wordsworth, "Composed upon Westminster Bridge, September 3, 1802"; Shelley, "Ozymandias"; Byron, "She walks in beauty"; Williams, *The Glass Menagerie.*

JOHN KEATS

La Belle Dame sans Merci

Ah, what can ail thee, wretched wight,
  Alone and palely loitering;

The sedge is wither'd from the lake,
  And no birds sing.

Ah, what can ail thee, wretched wight,
  So haggard and so woe-begone?
The squirrel's granary is full,
  And the harvest's done.

I see a lily on thy brow,
  With anguish moist and fever dew;
And on thy cheek a fading rose
  Fast withereth too.

I met a lady in the meads
  Full beautiful, a faery's child;
Her hair was long, her foot was light,
  And her eyes were wild.

I set her on my pacing steed,
  And nothing else saw all day long;
For sideways would she lean, and sing
  A faery's song.

I made a garland for her head,
  And bracelets too, and fragrant zone;
She look'd at me as she did love,
  And made sweet moan.

She found me roots of relish sweet,
  And honey wild, and manna dew;
And sure in language strange she said,
  I love thee true.

She took me to her elfin grot,
  And there she gaz'd and sighed deep,
And there I shut her wild sad eyes—
  So kiss'd to sleep.

And there we slumber'd on the moss,
  And there I dream'd, ah woe betide,
The latest dream I ever dream'd
  On the cold hill side.

I saw pale kings, and princes too,
  Pale warriors, death-pale were they all;
Who cry'd—"La belle Dame sans merci
  Hath thee in thrall!"

I saw their starv'd lips in the gloam
  With horrid warning gaped wide,
And I awoke, and found me here
  On the cold hill side.

And this is why I sojourn here
  Alone and palely loitering,
Though the sedge is wither'd from the lake,
  And no birds sing.

JOHN KEATS

Ode on a Grecian Urn

Thou still unravish'd bride of quietness,
  Thou foster-child of silence and slow time,
Sylvan historian, who canst thus express
  A flowery tale more sweetly than our rhyme:
What leaf-fring'd legend haunts about thy shape
  Of deities or mortals, or of both,
    In Tempe or the dales of Arcady?
  What men or gods are these? What maidens loth?
What mad pursuit? What struggle to escape?
    What pipes and timbrels? What wild ecstasy?

Heard melodies are sweet, but those unheard
  Are sweeter; therefore, ye soft pipes, play on;
Not to the sensual ear, but, more endear'd,
  Pipe to the spirit ditties of no tone:
Fair youth, beneath the trees, thou canst not leave
  Thy song, nor ever can those trees be bare;
    Bold Lover, never, never canst thou kiss,
Though winning near the goal yet, do not grieve;
  She cannot fade, though thou hast not thy bliss,
    For ever wilt thou love, and she be fair!

Ah, happy, happy boughs! that cannot shed
  Your leaves, nor ever bid the Spring adieu;
And, happy melodist, unwearied,
  For ever piping songs for ever new;
More happy love! more happy, happy love!
  For ever warm and still to be enjoy'd,
    For ever panting, and for ever young;
All breathing human passion far above,
  That leaves a heart high-sorrowful and cloy'd,
    A burning forehead, and a parching tongue.

Who are these coming to the sacrifice?
  To what green altar, O mysterious priest,
Lead'st thou that heifer lowing at the skies,
  And all her silken flanks with garlands drest?

What little town by river or sea shore,
Or mountain-built with peaceful citadel,
Is emptied of this folk, this pious morn?
And, little town, thy streets for evermore
Will silent be; and not a soul to tell
Why thou art desolate, can e'er return.

O Attic shape! Fair attitude! with brede
Of marble men and maidens overwrought,
With forest branches and the trodden weed;
Thou, silent form, dost tease us out of thought
As doth eternity: Cold Pastoral!
When old age shall this generation waste,
Thou shalt remain, in midst of other woe
Than ours, a friend to man, to whom thou say'st,
"Beauty is truth, truth beauty,—that is all
Ye know on earth, and all ye need to know."

PERCY BYSSHE SHELLEY (1792–1822), perhaps the most privileged and aristocratic of the **Romantic** poets, broke with his father when he was dismissed from Oxford for publishing a tract on atheism. He lost most of his inheritance when, at eighteen, he married a tavern owner's sixteen-year-old daughter, Harriet. An early adherent of "free love," Shelley lost friends and reputation when he began living with Mary Godwin (daughter of feminist Mary Wollstonecraft) while offering to let Harriet remain with the couple as a "sister." He married Mary shortly after Harriet's suicide and moved to Italy, where most of his greatest works were composed, including the **sonnet** "Ozymandias." "Ozymandias" is the Greek form of the name of Ramses II, and the poem, published in 1818, refers to an inscription found on a statue of the Egyptian pharaoh. The Anglo-Saxon ***ubi sunt*** ("Where are they now?") theme is echoed throughout the **sonnet**, but Shelley adds an ironically triumphant twist to the typical **elegiac** tone.

Related Works: Marquez, "The Handsomest Drowned Man in the World"; Shakespeare, Sonnet 130; Barrett Browning, Sonnets 14 and 43; Drayton, Sonnet 61; Frost, "Acquainted with the Night"; Millay, "What lips my lips have kissed."

PERCY BYSSHE SHELLEY

Ozymandias

I met a traveller from an antique land,
Who said—"Two vast and trunkless legs of stone
Stand in the desart. . . . Near them, on the sand,
Half sunk a shattered visage lies, whose frown,
And wrinkled lip, and sneer of cold command,
Tell that its sculptor well those passions read

Which yet survive, stamped on these lifeless things.
The hand that mocked them, and the heart that fed;
And on the pedestal, these words appear:
My name is Ozymandias, King of Kings.
Look on my Works, ye Mighty, and despair!
Nothing beside remains. Round the decay
Of that colossal Wreck, boundless and bare
The lone and level sands stretch far away."

WILLIAM WORDSWORTH (1770–1850), collaborating with Samuel Taylor Coleridge, published the **Romantic** movement's manifesto, *Lyrical Ballads*, in 1798. The most domestic and sane of the Romantic poets by most accounts, Wordsworth eventually settled comfortably with his wife, Mary Hutchinson, and his beloved but ailing sister, Dorothy. He was made Poet Laureate of England in 1843. His early work is usually considered his best, especially *The Prelude*, which was completed in 1805 and *Poems, In Two Volumes*, which appeared in 1807. Both of the poems included here were published in the 1807 volume and seem to epitomize Wordsworth's claim, in the Preface to the *Lyrical Ballads*, that "poetry is the spontaneous overflow of powerful feelings: it takes it origin from emotion recollected in tranquility."

Related Works: Blake, "London"; Byron, "She walks in beauty"; Coleridge, "Frost at Midnight" and "The Rime of the Ancient Mariner"; Keats, "La Belle Dame sans Merci" and "Ode on a Grecian Urn"; Shelley, "Ozymandias"; Barrett Browning, Sonnet 14; Browning, "Childe Roland to the Dark Tower Came."

WILLIAM WORDSWORTH

I Wandered Lonely as a Cloud

I wandered lonely as a cloud
That floats on high o'er vales and hills,
When all at once I saw a crowd,
A host, of golden daffodils;
Beside the lake, beneath the trees,
Fluttering and dancing in the breeze.

Continuous as the stars that shine
And twinkle on the milky way,
They stretched in never-ending line
Along the margin of a bay:
Ten thousand saw I at a glance,
Tossing their heads in sprightly dance.

The waves beside them danced; but they
Out-did the sparkling waves in glee:
A poet could not but be gay,
In such a jocund company:
I gazed—and gazed—but little thought
What wealth the show to me had brought:

For oft, when on my couch I lie
In vacant or in pensive mood,
They flash upon that inward eye
Which is the bliss of solitude;
And then my heart with pleasure fills,
And dances with the daffodils.

WILLIAM WORDSWORTH

Composed upon Westminster Bridge, September 3, 1802

Earth has not anything to show more fair:
Dull would he be of soul who could pass by
A sight so touching in its majesty:
This City now doth, like a garment, wear
The beauty of the morning; silent, bare,
Ships, towers, domes, theatres, and temples lie
Open unto the fields, and to the sky;
All bright and glittering in the smokeless air.
Never did sun more beautifully steep
In his first splendour, valley, rock, or hill;
Ne'er saw I, never felt, a calm so deep!
The river glideth at his own sweet will:
Dear God! the very houses seem asleep;
And all that mighty heart is lying still!

MATTHEW ARNOLD (1822–1888), a Victorian poet and a school inspector, is still admired as one of the first serious literary critics. He was also famous for his passion to bring "culture" to the British middle class in such critical works as *Culture and Anarchy* (1882). "Dover Beach" is a **dramatic monologue** published in *New Poems* (1867); like much of Arnold's poetry, this poem comments symbolically on faith, human love, and knowledge set in the context of classical history.

Related Works: Milton, "When I consider how my light is spent"; Owen, "Dulce et Decorum Est"; Auden, "The Unknown Citizen"; MacNeice, "Snow"; Reed,

"Naming of Parts"; Hecht, "Dover Bitch"; Shakespeare, *Hamlet*; Miller, *Death of a Salesman*.

MATTHEW ARNOLD

Dover Beach

THE sea is calm to-night.
The tide is full, the moon lies fair
Upon the straits;—on the French coast the light
Gleams and is gone; the cliffs of England stand,
Glimmering and vast, out in the tranquil bay.
Come to the window, sweet is the night-air!
Only, from the long line of spray
Where the sea meets the moon-blanch'd land,
Listen! you hear the grating roar
Of pebbles which the waves draw back, and fling,
At their return, up the high strand,
Begin, and cease, and then again begin,
With tremulous cadence slow, and bring
The eternal note of sadness in.

Sophocles long ago
Heard it on the Ægæan, and it brought
Into his mind the turbid ebb and flow
Of human misery; we
Find also in the sound a thought,
Hearing it by this distant northern sea.

The sea of faith
Was once, too, at the full, and round earth's shore
Lay like the folds of a bright girdle furl'd.
But now I only hear
Its melancholy, long, withdrawing roar,
Retreating to the breath
Of the night-wind down the vast edges drear
And naked shingles of the world.

Ah, love, let us be true
To one another! for the world, which seems
To lie before us like a land of dreams,
So various, so beautiful, so new,
Hath really neither joy, nor love, nor light,
Nor certitude, nor peace, nor help for pain;
And we are here as on a darkling plain
Swept with confused alarms of struggle and flight.
Where ignorant armies clash by night.

MATTHEW ARNOLD
Shakspeare

OTHERS abide our question. Thou art free.
We ask and ask: Thou smilest and art still,
Out-topping knowledge. For the loftiest hill
That to the stars uncrowns his majesty,
Planting his stedfast footsteps in the sea,
Making the Heaven of Heavens his dwelling-place,
Spares but the cloudy border of his base
To the foil'd searching of mortality:
And thou, who didst the stars and sunbeams know,
Self-school'd, self-scann'd, self-honour'd, self-secure,
Didst walk on Earth unguess'd at. Better so!
All pains the immortal spirit must endure,
All weakness that impairs, all griefs that bow,
Find their sole voice in that victorious brow.

LEWIS CARROLL (1832–1898) is famous as the author of *Alice's Adventures in Wonderland* (1866). The poem below, "Jabberwocky," is included in the sequel, *Through the Looking-Glass and What Alice Found There* (1871). Alice reads the first stanza of the poem by holding it up to a mirror and discusses its meaning with literary "critic" Humpty Dumpty:

> "You seem very clever at explaining words, Sir," said Alice. "Would you kindly tell me the meaning of the poem called 'Jabberwocky'?"
>
> "Let's hear it," said Humpty Dumpty. "I can explain all the poems that ever were invented—and a good many that haven't been invented just yet."
>
> [Alice reads the first stanza of Jabberwocky.]
>
> "That's enough to begin with," Humpty Dumpty interrupted; "there are plenty of hard words there. '*Brillig*' means four o'clock in the afternoon—the time when you begin *broiling* things for dinner."
>
> "That'll do very well," said Alice; "and '*slithy*'?"
>
> "Well, '*slithy*' means 'lithe and slimy.' 'Lithe' is the same as 'active.' You see it's like a portmanteau—there are two meanings packed up into one word."
>
> "I see it now," Alice remarked thoughtfully: "and what are '*toves*'?"
>
> "Well, '*toves*' are something like badgers—they're something like lizards—and they're something like corkscrews."
>
> (Lewis Carroll, *Through the Looking-Glass, and What Alice Found There* [London: Macmillan and Co., 1872], 21–24)

Related Works: Achebe, "Why the Tortoise's Shell Is Not Smooth"; Old English Riddles; Anonymous Ballads; Poe, "The Raven"; cummings, "since feeling is first"; Mayers, "All-American Sestina"; Nash, "The Hunter," "Celery," and "Very Like a Whale"; Parker, "One Perfect Rose" and "Solace."

LEWIS CARROLL

Jabberwocky

'Twas brillig, and the slithy toves
Did gyre and gimble in the wabe;
All mimsy were the borogoves,
And the mome raths outgrabe.

'Beware the Jabberwock, my son!
The jaws that bite, the claws that catch!
Beware the Jubjub bird, and shun
The frumious Bandersnatch!'

He took his vorpal sword in hand:
Long time the manxome foe he sought—
So rested he by the Tumtum tree,
And stood awhile in thought.

And as in uffish thought he stood,
The Jabberwock, with eyes of flame,
Came whiffling through the tulgey wood,
And burbled as it came!

One, two! One, two! And through and through
The vorpal blade went snicker-snack!
He left it dead, and with its head
He went galumphing back.

'And hast thou slain the Jabberwock?
Come to my arms, my beamish boy!
O frabjous day! Callooh! Callay!'
He chortled in his joy.

'Twas brillig, and the slithy toves
Did gyre and gimble in the wabe;
All mimsy were the borogoves,
And the mome raths outgrabe.

EMILY DICKINSON (1830–1886), a contemporary of that other most innovative American poet, Walt Whitman, was the second daughter in a prominent Amherst, Massachusetts, family. After attending Mount Holyoke Female Seminary, she spent her entire adult life in seclusion in her father's home. Her friendships were conducted largely by mail. Of her nearly 2,000 poems, she published only seven during her lifetime, although three volumes of her poetry were published less than a decade after her death (1890, 1891, and 1896). Dickinson's untitled poems were handwritten on various scraps of paper, then bound in hand-sewn packets. Her characteristic and idiosyncratic punctuation—full of dashes, capital letters, and periods—along with her variants on **rhymes** sometimes obscure her musical **rhythms**, which are based solidly on the meters of English hymns. Pay attention to the **persona** of each poem, Dickinson's distinctive **metaphors**, and her unique use of words in uncharacteristic parts of speech.

Related Works: Hawthorne, "Young Goodman Brown"; Bradstreet, "To My Dear and Loving Husband"; cummings, "In Just—"; Whitman, "O Captain! my Captain!" and "When lilacs last in the dooryard bloom'd"; Williams, "The Red Wheelbarrow."

EMILY DICKINSON

712

Because I could not stop for Death—
He kindly stopped for me—
The Carriage held but just Ourselves—
And Immortality.

We slowly drove—He knew no haste
And I had put away
My labor and my leisure too,
For His Civility—

We passed the School, where Children strove
At Recess—in the Ring—
We passed the Fields of Gazing Grain—
We passed the Setting Sun—

Or rather—He passed Us—
The Dews drew quivering and chill—
For only Gossamer, my Gown—
My Tippet—only Tulle—

We paused before a House that seemed
A Swelling of the Ground—
The Roof was scarcely visible—
The Cornice—in the Ground—

Since then—'tis Centuries—and yet
Feels shorter than the Day
I first surmised the Horses' Heads
Were toward Eternity—

EMILY DICKINSON

254

"Hope" is the thing with feathers—
That perches in the soul—
And sings the tune without the words—
And never stops—at all—

And sweetest—in the Gale—is heard—
And sore must be the storm—
That could abash the little Bird
That kept so many warm—

I've heard it in the chillest land—
And on the strangest Sea—
Yet, never, in Extremity,
It asked a crumb—of Me.

EMILY DICKINSON

465

I heard a Fly buzz—when I died—
The Stillness in the Room
Was like the Stillness in the Air—
Between the Heaves of Storm—

The Eyes around—had wrung them dry—
And Breaths were gathering firm
For that last Onset—when the King
Be witnessed—in the Room—

I willed my Keepsakes—Signed away
What portion of me be
Assignable—and then it was
There interposed a Fly—

With Blue—uncertain stumbling Buzz—
Between the light—and me—
And then the Windows failed—and then
I could not see to see—

W. E. B. (WILLIAM EDWARD BURGHARDT) DU BOIS (1868–1963) was the first African American to complete a Ph.D. at Harvard University (1896), and his dissertation, "The Suppression of the Slave Trade to the United States of America, 1638–1870," became the first volume in the prestigious Harvard Historical Series.

A controversial figure all his life, Du Bois published more than thirty books during his long, active, and distinguished academic career based at Atlanta University (now Clark Atlanta University). Although he was chiefly a sociologist and historian, his publications range from history and sociology to romance and poetry. Du Bois's 1903 book, *The Souls of Black Folk*, is credited with sparking the Harlem Renaissance. In 1909, he founded the National Association for the Advancement of Colored People (NAACP) and for many years edited its journal, *Crisis*. In 1933, he left the NAACP, eventually joining the Communist Party in 1961 and living out his last years as a citizen of Ghana. In "The Song of the Smoke" (published in *The Horizon*, 1907), Du Bois redirects negative **images** of black/darkness through the central **metaphor** of smoke. Note also the use of **repetition** and **rhyme**.

Related Works: Walker, "Everyday Use"; Wheatley, "A Funeral Poem on the Death of C. E. an Infant of Twelve Months"; Grimké, "The Black Finger"; Harper, "The Slave Auction" and "The Burial of Moses"; Clifton, "my mama moved among the days"; McKay, "In Bondage"; Hughes, "Harlem"; Wilson, *The Piano Lesson*.

W.E.B. DU BOIS

The Song of the Smoke

I am the Smoke King
I am black!
I am swinging in the sky,
I am wringing worlds awry;
I am the thought of the throbbing mills,
I am the soul of the soul-toil kills,
Wraith of the ripple of trading rills;
Up I'm curling from the sod,
I am whirling home to God;
I am the Smoke King
I am black.

I am the Smoke King,
I am black!
I am wreathing broken hearts,
I am sheathing love's light darts;
Inspiration of iron times
Wedding the toil of toiling climes,
Shedding the blood of bloodless crimes—
Lurid lowering 'mid the blue,
Torrid towering toward the true,
I am the Smoke King,
I am black.

I am the Smoke King,
I am black!
I am darkening with song,
I am hearkening to wrong!
I will be black as blackness can—
The blacker the mantle, the mightier the man!
For blackness was ancient ere whiteness began.
I am daubing God in night,
I am swabbing Hell in white:
I am the Smoke King
I am black.

I am the Smoke King
I am black!
I am cursing ruddy morn,
I am hearsing hearts unborn:
Souls unto me are as stars in a night,
I whiten my black men—I blacken my white!
What's the hue of a hide to a man in his might?
Hail! great, gritty, grimy hands—
Sweet Christ, pity toiling lands!
I am the Smoke King
I am black.

PAUL LAURENCE DUNBAR (1872–1906), the son of ex-slaves, was the first African American poet to receive national attention. He was not able to attend college, but nevertheless published his first book of poetry, *Oak and Ivy*, in 1893. He married in 1898 and, until 1902, lived in Washington D.C., where he was able to support himself through stories, essays, and lectures. He returned to Dayton, Ohio, when his marriage foundered and lived with his mother until his death at age thirty-three. He published at least five other important volumes of poetry in his lifetime, *Majors and Minors* (1895), *Lyrics of Lowly Life* (1896), *Lyrics of the Hearthside* and *Poems of Cabin and Field* (1899), and *Lyrics of Sunshine and Shadow* (1905), as well as short stories, a play, and five novels. His distinctive use of black **dialect** is not shown in the two poems included here. "We wear the mask" (1895) may act as an apologia (or justification) for the minstrel quality of some of his dialect poems. The central **metaphor** of the "caged bird" in "Sympathy" (1899) is often read as a direct reference to slavery and racial stereotyping, but Dunbar's wife believed the image was suggested by "the iron grating of the book stacks in the Library of Congress," where Dunbar worked.

Related Works: Old English Riddles; Tichborne, "My prime of youth is but a frost of cares"; Alexie, "Reservation Love Song"; Angelou, "Still I Rise"; Brooks, "The Pool Players: Seven at the Golden Shovel"; Cullen, "From the Dark Tower"; Hughes, "Harlem"; McKay, "America" and "In Bondage"; Wilson, *The Piano Lesson*.

PAUL LAURENCE DUNBAR

We Wear the Mask

We wear the mask that grins and lies,
It hides our cheeks and shades our eyes,—
This debt we pay to human guile;
With torn and bleeding hearts we smile,
And mouth with myriad subtleties.

Why should the world be over-wise,
In counting all our tears and sighs?
Nay, let them only see us, while
  We wear the mask.

We smile, but, O great Christ, our cries
To thee from tortured souls arise.
We sing, but oh the clay is vile
Beneath our feet, and long the mile;
But let the world dream otherwise,
  We wear the mask!

PAUL LAURENCE DUNBAR

Sympathy

I know what the caged bird feels, alas!
  When the sun is bright on the upland slopes;
When the wind stirs soft through the springing grass,
And the river flows like a stream of glass;
  When the first bird sings and the first bud opes,
And the faint perfume from its chalice steals—
I know what the caged bird feels!

I know why the caged bird beats his wing
  Till its blood is red on the cruel bars;
For he must fly back to his perch and cling
When he fain would be on the bough a-swing;
  And a pain still throbs in the old, old scars
And they pulse again with a keener sting—
I know why he beats his wing!

I know why the caged bird sings, ah me,
  When his wing is bruised and his bosom sore,—

When he beats his bars and he would be free;
It is not a carol of joy or glee,
    But a prayer that he sends from his heart's deep core,
But a plea, that upward to Heaven he flings—
I know why the caged bird sings!

MICHAEL FIELD is the pen name adopted by collaborative poets Katherine Bradley (1846–1914) and Edith Cooper (1862–1913). Aunt and niece, the pair lived together for forty-eight years, as lovers for much of that time, and published more than thirty plays, eleven collections of poetry, and thirty collaborative journal volumes. As part of the Victorian period's "New Woman" movement, they joined in an extensive, self-directed program of classical education and were active in promoting women's suffrage. Praised by contemporary poet Robert Browning (and later by William Butler Yeats), their work was read by a small, appreciative audience at the turn of the century and then "rediscovered" late in the twentieth century. Classical and **mythical themes** and **motifs** complement Field's complex **rhymes**, which are typically focused on equivalency and identification between seemingly unequal entities, such as those found in "A Pen-Drawing of Leda" (1892) and "The Mummy Invokes His Soul" (1908).

Related Works: Chopin, "The Story of an Hour"; Behn, "Song"; Barrett Browning, Sonnet 14; Browning, "Porphyria's Lover"; Keats, "La Belle Dame sans Merci"; Atwood, "Siren Song"; Glück, "Circe's Power"; Yeats, "Leda and the Swan"; Wilde, *The Importance of Being Earnest.*

MICHAEL FIELD

A Pen-Drawing of Leda

Sodoma

The Grand Duke's Palace at Weimar

'Tis Leda lovely, wild and free,
    Drawing her gracious Swan down through the grass to see
    Certain round eggs without a speck;
One hand plunged in the reeds and one dinting the downy neck,
    Although his hectoring bill
    Gapes toward her tresses,
She draws the fondled creature to her will.

She joys to bend in the live light
Her glistening body toward her love, how much more bright!
Though on her breast the sunshine lies
And spreads its affluence on the wide curves of her waist and thighs,
To her meek, smitten gaze
Where her hand presses
The Swan's white neck sink Heaven's concentred rays.

MICHAEL FIELD

The Mummy Invokes His Soul

Down to me quickly, down! I am such dust,
Baked, pressed together; let my flesh be fanned
With thy fresh breath; come from thy reedy land
Voiceful with birds; divert me, for I lust
To break, to crumble—prick with pores this crust!—
And fall apart, delicious, loosening sand.
Oh, joy, I feel thy breath, I feel thy hand
That searches for my heart, and trembles just
Where once it beat. How light thy touch, thy frame!
Surely thou perchest on the summer trees . . .
And the garden that we loved? Soul take thine ease,
I am content, so thou enjoy the same
Sweet terraces and founts, content, for thee,
To burn in this immense torpidity.

ANGELINA WELD GRIMKÉ (1880–1958) was the only child of Archibald Grimké, a nationally known African American lawyer from Boston, and his wife, Sarah. When Angelina was seven, Sarah left her daughter and husband to return to her prominent white family. As a highly educated, upper-middle class, biracial, closeted lesbian living in turn-of-the-century America, Grimké was often isolated; this isolation is reflected in much of her poetry, which deals typically with themes of love, death, and grief. Her play *Rachel*, published in 1920 and produced in Washington D.C. with an all-black cast for the newly established NAACP, takes on racial issues directly, chronicling the life of a black woman who, in response to her violent and racist world, refuses to bear children.

In the majority of her 173 extant poems, Grimké's narrative **persona**e are white and male. However, the narrators in the three poems included here possess no distinct gender and address, more or less directly, the racial issues ("The Black Finger," 1923, and "Tenebris," 1927) and sexual issues ("A Mona Lisa," ca.1925) that Grimké faced. Notice the contrasting uses of color **imagery** in all three poems.

Related Works: Kafka, "Metamorphosis"; Bambara, "The Lesson"; Kincaid, "Girl"; Behn, "On Her Loving Two Equally"; Wheatley, "To a Lady on Her Remarkable Preservation in an Hurricane in North Carolina"; Du Bois, "The Song of the Smoke"; Harper, "The Slave Mother"; Dunbar, "We wear the mask"; Brooks, "The mother"; Cullen, "From the Dark Tower"; Hughes, "I, Too, Sing America"; McKay, "America"; Sophocles, *Antigone.*

ANGELINA WELD GRIMKÉ

The Black Finger

I have just seen a most beautiful thing
Slim and still
Against a gold, gold sky,

A straight black cypress,
Sensitive,
Exquisite,
A black finger
Pointing upwards.
Why, beautiful still finger, are you black?
And why are you pointing upwards?

ANGELINA WELD GRIMKÉ

Tenebris

There is a tree, by day,
That, at night,
Has a shadow,
A hand huge and black,
With fingers long and black.
All through the dark,
Against the white man's house,
In the little wind,
The black hand plucks and plucks
At the bricks.

The bricks are the color of blood and very small.
  Is it a black hand,
  Or is it a shadow?

ANGELINA WELD GRIMKÉ

A Mona Lisa

I should like to creep
Through the long brown grasses
    That are your lashes;
I should like to poise
    On the very brink
Of the leaf-brown pools
    That are your shadowed eyes;
I should like to cleave
    Without sound,
Their glimmering waters,
    Their unrippled waters,
I should like to sink down
    And down
        And down . . . . .
            And deeply drown.

Would I be more than a bubble breaking?
    Or an ever-widening circle
    Ceasing at the marge?
Would my white bones
    Be the only white bones
Wavering back and forth, back and forth
    In their depths?

THOMAS HARDY (1840–1928), whose father was a mason, apprenticed as an architect and worked in that profession before he gained fame as a novelist. His novels include *Far From the Madding Crowd* (1874), *The Return of the Native* (1878), *The Mayor of Casterbridge* (1886), *Tess of the D'urbervilles* (1891), and *Jude the Obscure* (1895). Hardy had written poetry throughout his life, however, and began to write poetry exclusively in his late fifties after the open sexual relationships portrayed in his novels continued to scandalize Victorian era readers. "The Convergence of the Twain" reflects on the Titanic disaster of 1912 by **personifying** both the Titanic and her "mate," the iceberg, as pawns of an "Immanent Will." Hardy **satirizes** both Victorian sentimentality and Romantic idealism in the two poems, "'Ah, are you digging on my grave?'" (1914) and "The Ruined Maid" (1902).

Related Works: Kafka, "The Metamorphosis"; O'Connor, "Good Country People"; Chaucer, "Complaint to His Purse"; "Sir Patrick Spens" (Child Ballad #58); "Lord Randall" (Child Ballad #12); Lord Byron, "She walks in beauty"; Keats, "La Belle Dame sans Merci"; Shelley, "Ozymandias"; Pound, "The River Merchant's Wife"; Miller, *Death of a Salesman.*

THOMAS HARDY

The Convergence of the Twain

(Lines on the loss of the "Titanic")

I

In a solitude of the sea
Deep from human vanity,
And the Pride of Life that planned her, stilly couches she.

II

Steel chambers, late the pyres
Of her salamandrine fires,
Cold currents thrid, and turn to rhythmic tidal lyres.

III

Over the mirrors meant
To glass the opulent
The sea-worm crawls—grotesque, slimed, dumb, indifferent.

IV

Jewels in joy designed
To ravish the sensuous mind
Lie lightless, all their sparkles bleared and black and blind.

V

Dim moon-eyed fishes near
Gaze at the gilded gear
And query: "What does this vaingloriousness down here?". . .

VI

Well: while was fashioning
This creature of cleaving wing,
The Immanent Will that stirs and urges everything

VII

Prepared a sinister mate
For her—so gaily great—
A shape of Ice, for the time far and dissociate.

VIII

And as the smart ship grew
In stature, grace, and hue,
In shadowy silent distance grew the Iceberg too.

IX

Alien they seemed to be;
No mortal eye could see
The intimate welding of their later history.

X

Or sign that they were bent
By paths coincident
On being anon twin halves of one august event.

XI

Till the Spinner of the Years
Said "Now!" And each one hears,
And consummation comes, and jars two hemispheres.

THOMAS HARDY

"*Ah, Are You Digging on My Grave?*"

"Ah, are you digging on my grave,
My loved one?—planting rue?"
—'No: yesterday he went to wed
One of the brightest wealth has bred.
'It cannot hurt her now,' he said,
"That I should not be true.'"

"Then who is digging on my grave?
My nearest dearest kin?"
—"Ah, no: they sit and think, 'What use!
What good will planting flowers produce?
No tendance of her mound can loose
Her spirit from Death's gin.'"

"But some one digs upon my grave?
My enemy?—prodding sly?"
—"Nay: when she heard you had passed the Gate
That shuts on all flesh soon or late,
She thought you no more worth her hate,
And cares not where you lie."

"Then, who is digging on my grave?
Say—since I have not guessed!"

—"O it is I, my mistress dear,
Your little dog, who still lives near,
And much I hope my movements here
Have not disturbed your rest?"

"Ah, yes! *You* dig upon my grave. . . .
Why flashed it not on me
That one true heart was left behind!
What feeling do we ever find
To equal among human kind
A dog's fidelity!"

THOMAS HARDY

The Ruined Maid

"O 'melia, my dear, this does everything crown!
Who could have supposed I should meet you in Town?
And whence such fair garments, such prosperi-ty?"—
"O didn't you know I'd been ruined?" said she.

—"You left us in tatters, without shoes or socks,
Tired of digging potatoes, and spudding up docks;
And now you've gay bracelets and bright feathers three!"—
"Yes: that's how we dress when we're ruined," said she.

—"At home in the barton you said 'thee' and 'thou,'
And 'thik oon', and 'theäs oon', and 't'other'; but now
Your talking quite fits 'ee for high compa-ny!"—
"Some polish is gained with one's ruin," said she.

—"Your hands were like paws then, your face blue and bleak
But now I'm bewitched by your delicate cheek,
And your little gloves fit as on any la-dy!"—
"We never do work when we're ruined," said she.

—"You used to call home-life a hag-ridden dream,
And you'd sigh, and you'd sock; but at present you seem
To know not of megrims or melancho-ly!"—
"True. One's pretty lively when ruined," said she.

—"I wish I had feathers, a fine sweeping grown,
And a delicate face, and could strut about Town!"—
"My dear—a raw country girl, such as you be,
Cannot quite expect that. You ain't ruined," said she.

FRANCES ELLEN WATKINS HARPER (1825–1911). Harper's long, dynamic career as an abolitionist and lecturer was matched by her prolific career as a writer of poetry and prose. Often cited as the first African American woman to publish both a novel and a short story, her letters, essays, and poetry make up the greater part of her published writing. After being born free and educated in Maryland, Harper left her home because slave laws introduced with the Fugitive Slave Act put her in constant danger of enforced slavery. She spent most of her adult life in the Northeast lecturing against slavery, working for the Underground Railroad, and promoting temperance, women's rights, and peace efforts. Her poems such as "The Slave Auction" (1854) and "The Slave Mother" (1874) articulate her political stance through sympathetic human narratives within easily remembered, four-line rhymed **stanzas**. Harper based "The Slave Mother" on the 1856 case of Margaret Garner, a runaway slave in Ohio who killed her three-year-old daughter rather than allow her to be returned to slavery, a case which Toni Morrison also featured in her novel, *Beloved*. In "The Burial of Moses" (1856), Harper dramatizes a biblical **narrative**, which speaks **metaphorically** to the displacement of Harper and other African Americans both within the Union and from their African homeland.

Related Works: Ellison, "Battle Royal"; Walker, "Everyday Use"; Wheatley, "A Funeral Poem on the Death of C. E. an Infant of Twelve Months"; Du Bois, "The Song of the Smoke"; Grimké, "The Black Finger"; Dunbar, "Sympathy"; Angelou, "Still I Rise"; McKay, "America"; Wilson, *The Piano Lesson*.

FRANCES E. W. HARPER

The Slave Mother

A Tale of the Ohio

I have but four, the treasures of my soul,
They lay like doves around my heart;
I tremble lest some cruel hand
Should tear my household wreaths apart.

My baby girl, with childish glance,
Looks curious in my anxious eye,
She little knows that for her sake
Deep shadows round my spirit lie.

My playful boys could I forget,
My home might seem a joyous spot,
But with their sunshine mirth I blend
The darkness of their future lot.

And thou my babe, my darling one.
My last, my loved, my precious child,
Oh! when I think upon thy doom
My heart grows faint and then throbs wild.

The Ohio's bridged and spanned with ice,
The northern star is shining bright,

I'll take the nestlings of my heart
  And search for freedom by its light.

★ ★ ★

Winter and night were on the earth,
  And feebly moaned the shivering trees,
A sigh of winter seemed to run
  Through every murmur of the breeze.

She fled, and with her children all,
  She reached the stream and crossed it o'er,
Bright visions of deliverance came
  Like dreams of plenty to the poor.

Dreams! vain dreams, heroic mother,
  Give all thy hopes and struggles o'er,
The pursuer is on thy track,
  And the hunter at thy door.

Judea's refuge cities had power
  To shelter, shield and save,
E'en Rome had altars: 'neath whose shade
  Might crouch the wan and weary slave.

But Ohio had no sacred fane,
  To human rights so consecrate,
Where thou may'st shield thy hapless ones
  From their darkly gathering fate.

Then, said the mournful mother,
  If Ohio cannot save,
I will do a deed for freedom,
  She shall find each child a grave.

I will save my precious children
  From their darkly threatened doom,
I will hew their path to freedom
  Through the portals of the tomb.

A moment in the sunlight,
  She held a glimmering knife,
The next moment she had bathed it
  In the crimson fount of life.

They snatched away the fatal knife,
  Her boys shrieked wild with dread;
The baby girl was pale and cold,
  They raised it up, the child was dead.

Sends this deed of fearful daring
  Through my country's heart no thrill,
Do the icy hands of slavery
  Every pure emotion chill?

Oh! if there is any honor,
 Truth or justice in the land,
Will ye not, as men and Christians,
 On the side of freedom stand?

FRANCES E. W. HARPER

The Slave Auction

The sale began—young girls were there,
 Defenceless in their wretchedness,
Whose stifled sobs of deep despair
 Revealed their anguish and distress.

And mothers stood with streaming eyes,
 And saw their dearest children sold;
Unheeded rose their bitter cries,
 While tyrants bartered them for gold.

And woman, with her love and truth—
 For these in sable forms may dwell—
Gaz'd on the husband of her youth,
 With anguish none may paint or tell.

And men, whose sole crime was their hue,
 The impress of their Marker's hand,
And frail and shrinking children, too,
 Were gathered in that mournful band.

Ye who have laid your love to rest,
 And wept above their lifeless clay,
Know not the anguish of that breast,
 Whose lov'd are rudely torn away.

Ye may not know how desolate
 Are bosoms rudely forced to part,
And how a dull and heavy weight
 Will press the life-drops from the heart.

FRANCES E. W. HARPER

The Burial of Moses

And He buried him in a valley in the land of Moab,
over against Bethpeor; but no man knoweth of his
sepulchre unto this day.

DEUT. 34: 6.

By Nebo a lonely mountain,
  On this side Jordan's wave,
In a vale in the land of Moab
  There lies a lonely grave.
And no man dug that sepulchre,
  And no man saw it e'er;
For the angels of God upturned the sod,
  And laid the dead man there.

That was the grandest funeral
  That ever passed on earth,
But no man heard the trampling
  Or saw the train go forth.
Noiselessly as the daylight
  Comes when the night is done,
And the crimson streak on ocean's cheek
  Grows into the great sun.

Noiselessly as the springtime
  Her crown of verdure weaves,
And all the trees on all the hills
  Open their thousand leaves:
So, without sound of music,
  Or voice of them that wept,
Silently down from the mountain's crown
  The great procession swept.

Perchance the bald old eagle,
  On grey Bethpeor's height,
Out of his rocky eirie
  Looked on the wondrous sight.
Perchance the lion stalking
  Still shuns that hallow'd spot:
For best [sic] and birds have seen and heard
  That which man knoweth not.

But when the warrior dieth,
  His comrades in the war,
With arms reversed and muffled drum,
  Follow the funeral car.
They show the banners taken,
  They tell his battles won,
And after him lead his masterless steed,
  While peals the minute gun.

Amid the noblest of the land
  Men lay the sage to rest,
And give the bard an honour'd place
  With costly marble drest

In the great minster transept,
  Where lights like glories fall,
And the sweet choir sings, and the organ rings
  Along the emblazoned wall.

This was the bravest warrior
  That ever buckled sword;
This the most gifted Poet
  That ever breath'd a word;
And never earth's philosopher
  Traced with his golden pen
On the deathless page truths half so sage
  As he wrote down for men.

And had he not high honour?
  The hill-side for his pall,
To lie in state while angels wait
  With stars for tapers tall,
And the dark rock pines like tossing plumes
  Over his bier to wave,
And God's own hand in that lonely land
  To lay him in the grave.

In that deep grave without a name,
  Whence his uncoffin'd clay
Shall break again, most wondrous thought
  Before the Judgment Day;
And stand with glory wrapped around
  On the hills he never trod,
And speak of the strife that won our life
  With th' Incarnate Son of God.

O lonely tomb in Moab's land,
  O dark Bethpeor' hill,
Speak to these curious hearts of ours,
  And teach them to be still.
God hath his mysteries of grace,
  Ways that we cannot tell;
He hides them deep like the secret sleep
  Of him He loved so well.

GERARD MANLEY HOPKINS (1844–1889) converted to Catholicism during his university years at Oxford, eventually becoming a Jesuit priest and a professor at University College in Dublin. His verse was collected by a friend and published posthumously in 1918. Hopkins's most important contribution to English poetry was his adoption of some of the older metrical structures found in traditional Old English poetry, which Hopkins called **sprung rhythm**, as opposed to "running rhythm." Hopkins's sprung rhythm escapes some of the constraints of the French-style rhymed verse by using different numbers of syllables within **metrical feet** and stressing the first syllable in each foot. He also makes heavy use of **alliteration**, as can be seen in "Pied Beauty" (1918) below.

Related Works: "The Husband's Message" and "The Wife's Lament"; Old English Riddles; Medieval Lyrical Poetry; Anonymous Ballads; Burns, "John Barleycorn: A Ballad"; Donne, Holy Sonnet 14; Herbert, "The Collar"; Eliot, "The Love Song of J. Alfred Prufrock"; cummings, "Buffalo Bill's"; Levertov, "Oh Taste and See"; *Everyman*.

GERARD MANLEY HOPKINS

Pied Beauty

Glory be to God for dappled things—
For skies of couple-colour as a brinded cow;
For rose-moles all in stipple upon trout that swim;
Fresh-firecoal chestnut-falls; finches' wings;
Landscape plotted & pieced—fold, fallow, & plough;
And all trades, their gear & tackle & trim.

All things counter, original, spare, strange;
Whatever is fickle, freckled, (who knows how?)
With swift, slow; sweet, sour; adazzle, dim;
He fathers-forth whose beauty is pást change:
Práise him.

GERARD MANLEY HOPKINS

"The Child is Father to the Man"

(Wordsworth)

"The child is father to the man"
How can he be? The words are wild.
Suck any sense from that who can:
"The child is father to the man."
No; what the poet did write ran,
"The man is father to the child."
"The child is father to the man!"
How *can* he be? The words are wild.

GERARD MANLEY HOPKINS

God's Grandeur

The world is charged with the grandeur of God.
It will flame out, like shining from shook foil;
It gathers to a greatness, like the ooze of oil
Crushed. Why do men then now not reck his rod?
Generations have trod, have trod, have trod;
And all is seared with trade; bleared, smeared with toil;
And wears man's smudge and shares man's smell: the soil
Is bare now, nor can foot feel, being shod.

And for all this, nature is never spent;
There lives the dearest freshness deep down things;
And though the last lights off the black West went
Oh, morning, at the brown brink eastward, springs—
Because the Holy Ghost over the bent
World broods with warm breast and with ah! bright wings.

ALFRED EDWARD (A. E.) HOUSMAN (1859–1936) published two collections of poetry during his lifetime: *A Shropshire Lad* (1896)—sixty-three poems adapting traditional Classical **lyric** and English **ballad** forms, dealing mainly with the themes of failed love, death, and a romanticized vision of military life—and *Last Poems* (1922). A third collection, *More Poems* (1936), was published posthumously by his brother. Housman was famous as a bitterly sharp literary critic, Latin scholar, and academic writer. An early unrequited and unreturned homosexual love haunted him throughout his life. In "To an Athlete Dying Young" (1920) and "Terence, this is stupid stuff" (1896), Housman makes an ironic departure from the ***carpe diem*** motif.

Related Works: Lewis, "The Limestone Diner"; Burns, "John Barleycorn: A Ballad"; Anonymous Ballads; Herrick, "To the Virgins"; Marvell, "To His Coy Mistress"; Cofer, "Cold as Heaven"; Shakespeare, *Hamlet.*

A. E. HOUSMAN

To an Athlete Dying Young

The time you won your town the race
We chaired you through the market-place;
Man and boy stood cheering by,
And home we brought you shoulder-high.

To-day, the road all runners come,
Shoulder-high we bring you home,
And set you at your threshold down,
Townsman of a stiller town.

Smart lad, to slip betimes away
From fields where glory does not stay
And early though the laurel grows
It withers quicker than the rose.

Eyes the shady night has shut
Cannot see the record cut,
And silence sounds no worse than cheers
After earth has stopped the ears:

Now you will not swell the rout
Of lads that wore their honours out,
Runners whom renown outran
And the name died before the man.

So set, before its echoes fade,
The fleet foot on the sill of shade,
And hold to the low lintel up
The still-defended challenge-cup.

And round that early-laurelled head
Will flock to gaze the strengthless dead,
And find unwithered on its curls
The garland briefer than a girl's.

A. E. HOUSMAN

Terence, This is Stupid Stuff

"Terence, this is stupid stuff:
You eat your victuals fast enough;
There can't be much amiss, 'tis clear,
To see the rate you drink your beer.
But oh, good Lord, the verse you make,
It gives a chap the belly-ache.
The cow, the old cow, she is dead;
It sleeps well, the horned head:
We poor lads, 'tis our turn now
To hear such tunes as killed the cow.
Pretty friendship 'tis to rhyme
Your friends to death before their time
Moping melancholy mad:
Come, pipe a tune to dance to, lad."

Why, if 'tis dancing you would be,
There's brisker pipes than poetry,
Say, for what were hop-yards meant,
Or why was Burton built on Trent?
Oh many a peer of England brews
Livelier liquor than the Muse,
And malt does more than Milton can
To justify God's ways to man.
Ale, man, ale's the stuff to drink
For fellows whom it hurts to think:
Look into the pewter pot
To see the world as the world's not.
And faith, 'tis pleasant till 'tis past:
The mischief is that 'twill not last.
Oh I have been to Ludlow fair
And left my necktie God knows where,
And carried half way home, or near,
Pints and quarts of Ludlow beer:
Then the world seemed none so bad,
And I myself a sterling lad;
And down in lovely muck I've lain,
Happy till I woke again.
Then I saw the morning sky:
Heigho, the tale was all a lie;
The world, it was the old world yet,
I was I, my things were wet,
And nothing now remained to do
But begin the game anew.

Therefore, since the world has still
Much good, but much less good than ill,
And while the sun and moon endure
Luck's a chance, but trouble's sure,
I'd face it as a wise man would,
And train for ill and not for good.
'Tis true, the stuff I bring for sale
Is not so brisk a brew as ale:
Out of a stem that scored the hand
I wrung it in a weary land.
But take it: if the smack is sour,
The better for the embittered hour;
It should do good to heart and head
When your soul is in my soul's stead;
And I will friend you, if I may,
In the dark and cloudy day.

There was a king reigned in the east:
There, when kings will sit to feast,
They get their fill before they think

With poisoned meat and poisoned drink.
He gathered all that springs to birth
From the many-venomed earth;
First a little, thence to more,
He sampled all her killing store;
And easy, smiling, seasoned sound,
Sate the king when healths went round.
They put arsenic in his meat
And stared aghast to watch him eat;
They poured strychnine in his cup
And shook to see him drink it up:
They shook, they stared as white's their shirt:
Them it was their poison hurt.
—I tell the tale that I heard told.
Mithridates, he died old.

RUDYARD KIPLING (1865–1936), the first Englishman to receive the Nobel Prize for Literature (1907), is best known for his young people's books *The Jungle Book* (1894), *Captains Courageous* (1897), *Kim* (1901), and the *Just So Stories* (1902). Kipling was born in Bombay but educated largely in England. As a journalist, he returned to India, where he published a collection of stories (*The Phantom Rickshaw*, 1888). Later, back in London, he published more stories in *Life's Handicap* (1891) and two volumes of poems, *Barrack-Room Ballads* (1892) and *Departmental Ditties* (1886). Kipling glorified the British Empire and racial stereotypes in his poem "The White Man's Burden" (1899). In "If" (1910), Kipling idealizes the role of Dr. Leander Starr Jameson, who led the so-called Jameson Raid in South Africa. Although the raid failed and may have led to the Boer War, Kipling sees the raid as a triumph and Jameson as a hero. "Danny Deever" offers an altogether darker view of military reality.

Related Works: Ellison, "Battle Royal"; O'Brien, "Stockings"; "Sir Patrick Spens" (Child Ballad #58); "Lord Randall" (Child Ballad #12); Tichborne, "My prime of youth is but a frost of cares"; Longfellow, "The Jewish Cemetery at Newport"; Owen, "Dulce et Decorum Est"; Tennyson, "Ulysses"; Whitman, "O Captain! my Captain!"; Wilson, *The Piano Lesson*.

RUDYARD KIPLING

If—

If you can keep your head when all about you
  Are losing theirs and blaming it on you,
If you can trust yourself when all men doubt you,
  But make allowance for their doubting too;

If you can wait and not be tired by waiting,
 Or being lied about, don't deal in lies,
Or being hated, don't give way to hating,
 And yet don't look too good, nor talk too wise:

If you can dream—and not make dreams your master;
 If you can think—and not make thoughts your aim;
If you can meet with Triumph and Disaster
 And treat those two impostors just the same;
If you can bear to hear the truth you've spoken
 Twisted by knaves to make a trap for fools,
Or watch the things you gave your life to, broken,
 And stoop and build 'em up with worn-out tools:

If you can make one heap of all your winnings
 And risk it on one turn of pitch-and-toss,
And lose, and start again at your beginnings
 And never breathe a word about your loss;
If you can force your heart and nerve and sinew
 To serve your turn long after they are gone,
And so hold on when there is nothing in you
 Except the Will which says to them: "Hold on!"

If you can talk with crowds and keep your virtue,
 Or walk with Kings—nor lose the common touch,
If neither foes nor loving friends can hurt you,
 If all men count with you, but none too much;
If you can fill the unforgiving minute
 With sixty seconds' worth of distance run,
Yours is the Earth and everything that's in it,
 And—which is more—you'll be a Man, my son!

RUDYARD KIPLING

Danny Deever

"What are the bugles blowin' for?" said Files-on-Parade.
"To turn you out, to turn you out," the Color-Sergeant said.
"What makes you look so white, so white?" said Files-on-Parade.
"I'm dreadin' what I've got to watch," the Color-Sergeant said.
  For they're hangin' Danny Deever, you can hear the Dead March play.
  The regiment's in 'ollow square—they're hangin' him today:
  They've taken of his buttons off an' cut his stripes away,
  An they're hangin' Danny Deever in the mornin'.

"What makes the near rank breathe so 'ard?" said Files-on-Parade.
"It's bitter cold, it's bitter cold," the Color-Sergeant said.
"What makes that front-rank man fall down?" said Files-on-Parade.

"A touch o' sun, a touch o' sun," the Color-Sergeant said.
    They are hangin' Danny Deever, they are marchin' of 'im round,
    They 'ave 'alted Danny Deever by 'is coffin on the ground;
    An' 'e'll swing in 'arf a minute for a sneakin' shootin' hound—
    O they're hangin' Danny Deever in the mornin'!

" 'Is cot was right- 'and cot to mine," said Files-on-Parade.
" 'E's sleepin' out an' far tonight," the Color-Sergeant said.
"I've drunk 'is beer a score o' times," said Files-on-Parade.
" 'E's drinkin bitter beer alone," the Color-Sergeant said.
    They are hangin' Danny Deever, you must mark 'im to 'is place.
    For 'e shot a comrade sleepin'—you must look 'im in the face;
    Nine 'undred of 'is county an' the Regiment's disgrace,
    While they're hangin' Danny Deever in the mornin'.

"What's that so black agin the sun?" said Files-on-Parade.
"It's Danny fightin' 'ard for life," the Color-Sergeant said.
"What's that that whimpers over'ead?" said Files-on-Parade.
"It's Danny's soul that's passin' now," the Color-Sergeant said.
    For they're done with Danny Deever, you can 'ear the quickstep play,
    The regiment's in column, an they're marchin us away:
    Ho! the young recruits are shakin', an' they'll want their beer today.
    After hangin' Danny Deever in the mornin'.

HENRY WADSWORTH LONGFELLOW (1807–1882), the first truly celebrated American poet, was born and educated in Maine and, from 1836 to 1854, taught modern languages at Harvard, after which he retired to write poetry exclusively. His most famous poems, long narrative **ballads** such as *Evangeline* (1847), *The Song of Hiawatha* (1855), *The Courtship of Miles Standish* (1858), and *Tales of a Wayside Inn* (1863), which included "Paul Revere's Ride" and his shorter poems such as "The Village Blacksmith," "Excelsior," "The Wreck of the Hesperus," "A Psalm of Life," and "A Cross of Snow" were composed in an unforgettable (and easily **parodied**) rhythm and rhyme. The poem included here, "The Jewish Cemetery at Newport" (1854), reveals the naïve cultural stereotyping that has undermined Longfellow's reputation with modern literary critics.

Related Works: Anonymous Ballads; Kipling, "If"; Poe, "The Raven"; Tennyson, "Ulysses"; Frost, "The Death of the Hired Man"; Randall, "The Ballad of Birmingham."

HENRY WADSWORTH LONGFELLOW

The Jewish Cemetery at Newport

How strange it seems! These Hebrews in their graves,
    Close by the street of this fair seaport town,
Silent beside the never-silent waves,
    At rest in all this moving up and down!

The trees are white with dust, that o'er their sleep
  Wave their broad curtains in the south-wind's breath,
While underneath these leafy tents they keep
  The long, mysterious Exodus of Death.

And these sepulchral stones, so old and brown,
  That pave with level flags their burial-place,
Seem like the tablets of the Law, thrown down
  And broken by Moses at the mountain's base.

The very names recorded here are strange,
  Of foreign accent, and of different climes;
Alvares and Rivera interchange
  With Abraham and Jacob of old times.

"Blessed be God, for he created Death!"
  The mourners said, "and Death is rest and peace;"
Then added, in the certainty of faith,
  "And giveth Life that nevermore shall cease."

Closed are the portals of their Synagogue,
  No Psalms of David now the silence break,
No Rabbi reads the ancient Decalogue
  In the grand dialect the Prophets spake.

Gone are the living, but the dead remain,
  And not neglected, for a hand unseen,
Scattering its bounty, like a summer rain,
  Still keeps their graves and their remembrance green.

How came they here? What burst of Christian hate,
  What persecution, merciless and blind,
Drove o'er the sea—that desert desolate—
  These Ishmaels and Hagars of mankind?

They lived in narrow streets and lanes obscure,
  Ghetto and Judenstrass, in mirk and mire;
Taught in the school of patience to endure
  The life of anguish and the death of fire.

All their lives long, with the unleavened bread
  And bitter herbs of exile and its fears,
The wasting famine of the heart they fed,
  And slaked its thirst with marah of their tears.

Anathema maranatha! was the cry
  That rang from town to town, from street to street
At every gate the accursed Mordecai
  Was mocked and jeered, and spurned by Christian feet.

Pride and humiliation hand in hand
  Walked with them through the world where'er they went;
Trampled and beaten were they as the sand,
  And yet unshaken as the continent.

For in the background figures vague and vast
  Of patriarchs and of prophets rose sublime.
And all the great traditions of the Past
  They saw reflected in the coming time.

And thus forever with reverted look
  The mystic volume of the world they read,
Spelling it backward, like a Hebrew book,
  Till life became a Legend of the Dead.

But ah! what once has been shall be no more!
  The groaning earth in travail and in pain
Brings forth its races, but does not restore,
  And the dead nations never rise again.

WILFRED OWEN (1893–1918), a soldier who was killed in France one week before the World War I armistice, used traditional **meters** and **diction** to develop his theme that war is a horror to be avoided at all costs. The poetry he wrote before World War I showed little evidence of his later antiwar beliefs. Owen's poetry was collected and published posthumously by friend and mentor Siegfried Sassoon as *Poems by Wilfred Owen with an Introduction by Siegfried Sassoon* in 1921.

Related Works: Ellison, "Battle Royal"; Erdrich, "The Red Convertible"; O'Brien, "Stockings"; Tichborne, "My prime of youth is but a frost of cares"; Arnold, "Dover Beach"; Forché, "The Colonel"; Jarrell, "The Death of the Ball Turret Gunner"; Reed, "Naming of Parts"; Rios, "The Vietnam Wall"; Sophocles, *Antigone*.

WILFRED OWEN

Dulce et Decorum Est

Bent double, like old beggars under sacks,
Knock-kneed, coughing like hags, we cursed through sludge,
Till on the haunting flares we turned our backs
And towards our distant rest began to trudge.
Men marched asleep. Many had lost their boots
But limped on, blood-shod. All went lame; all blind;
Drunk with fatigue; deaf even to the hoots
Of gas shells dropping softly behind.

Gas! Gas! Quick, boys!—An ecstasy of fumbling,
Fitting the clumsy helmets just in time;
But someone still was yelling out and stumbling,

And flound'ring like a man in fire or lime . . .
Dim, through the misty panes and thick green light,
As under a green sea, I saw him drowning.

In all my dreams, before my helpless sight,
He plunges at me, guttering, choking, drowning.

If in some smothering dreams you too could pace
Behind the wagon that we flung him in,
And watch the white eyes writhing in his face,
His hanging face, like a devil's sick of sin;
If you could hear, at every jolt, the blood
Come gargling from the froth-corrupted lungs,
Bitter as the cud
Of vile, incurable sores on innocent tongues,—
My friend, you would not tell with such high zest
To children ardent for some desperate glory,
The old Lie: Dulce et decorum est
Pro patria mori.

EDGAR ALLAN POE (1809–1849) was an American writer most famous for his macabre short stories. Poe's poetry often has variant texts; he was known to rewrite poems numerous times after publication. Students of his poetry will want to consult authoritative critical editions and facsimile versions of his early publications to compare the way Poe continually reenvisioned the darkly **lyrical,** narrative **ballads** included here. For more details on Poe's life, see the head note preceding his short fiction.

Related Works: Hawthorne, "Young Goodman Brown"; Faulkner, "A Rose for Emily"; Anonymous Ballads; Browning, "My Last Duchess"; Randall, "Ballad of Birmingham"; Wilson, *The Piano Lesson.*

EDGAR ALLAN POE

Annabel Lee

It was many and many a year ago,
In a kingdom by the sea,
That a maiden there lived who you may know
By the name of Annabel Lee;
And this maiden she lived with no other thought
Than to love and be loved by me.

I was a child and she was a child.
In this kingdom by the sea;

But we loved with a love that was more
than love—
I and my Annabel Lee;
With a love that the winged seraphs of heaven
Coveted her and me.

And this was the reason that, long ago,
In this kingdom by the sea,
A wind blew out of a cloud, chilling
My beautiful Annabel Lee;
So that her highborn kinsman came
And bore her away from me,
To shut her up in a sepulchre
In this kingdom by the sea.

The angels, not half so happy in heaven,
Went envying her and me—
Yes!—that was the reason (as all men know,
In this kingdom by the sea)
That the wind came out of the cloud by night,
Chilling and killing my Annabel Lee.

But our love it was stronger by far than the love
Of those who were older than we—
Of many far wiser than we—
And neither the angels in Heaven above,
Nor the demons down under the sea,
Can ever dissever my soul from the soul
Of the beautiful Annabel Lee.

For the moon never beams without
bringing me dreams
Of the beautiful Annabel Lee;
And the stars never rise but I feel the bright eyes
Of the beautiful Annabel Lee;
And so, all the night-tide, I lie down by the side
Of my darling—my darling—my life and my bride,
In the sepulchre there by the sea,
In her tomb by the side of the sea.

EDGAR ALLAN POE

The Haunted Palace

In the greenest of our valleys
By good angels tenanted,
Once a fair and stately palace—

Radiant palace—reared its head.
In the monarch Thought's dominion,
It stood there;
Never seraph spread a pinion
Over fabric half so fair.

Banners yellow, glorious, golden,
On its roof did float and flow
(This—all this—was in the olden
Time long ago),
And every gentle air that dallied,
In that sweet day,
Along the ramparts plumed and pallid,
A wingèd odor went away.

Wanderers in that happy valley
Through two luminous windows saw
Spirits moving musically,
To a lute's well-tunèd law,
Round about a throne where, sitting,
Porphyrogene,
In state his glory well befitting,
The ruler of the realm was seen.

And all with pearl and ruby glowing
Was the fair palace door,
Through which came flowing, flowing,
flowing,
And sparkling evermore,
A troop of Echoes, whose sweet duty
Was but to sing,
In voices of surpassing beauty,
The wit and wisdom of their king.

But evil things, in robes of sorrow,
Assailed the monarch's high estate;
(Ah, let us mourn, for never morrow
Shall dawn upon him desolate!)
And round about his home the glory
That blushed and bloomed,
Is but a dim-remembered story
Of the old time entombed.

And travellers now within that valley
Through the red-litten windows see
Vast forms that move fantastically
To a discordant melody;
While, like a ghastly rapid river,
Through the pale door
A hideous throng rush out forever,
And laugh—but smile no more.

EDGAR ALLAN POE

The Raven

Once upon a midnight dreary, while I pondered weak and weary,
Over many a quaint and curious volume of forgotten lore,
While I nodded, nearly napping, suddenly there came a tapping,
As of some one gently rapping, rapping at my chamber door.
"'Tis some visitor," I muttered, "tapping at my chamber door—
Only this, and nothing more."

Ah, distinctly I remember it was in the bleak December,
And each separate dying ember wrought its ghost upon the floor.
Eagerly I wished the morrow;—vainly I had sought to borrow
From my books surcease of sorrow—sorrow for the lost Lenore—
For the rare and radiant maiden whom the angels named Lenore—
Nameless here for evermore.

And the silken sad uncertain rustling of each purple curtain
Thrilled me—filled me with fantastic terrors never felt before;
So that now, to still the beating of my heart, I stood repeating
"'Tis some visitor entreating entrance at my chamber door—
Some late visitor entreating entrance at my chamber door;—
This it is, and nothing more."

Presently my heart grew stronger; hesitating then no longer,
"Sir," said I, "or Madam, truly your forgiveness I implore;
But the fact is I was napping, and so gently you came rapping,
And so faintly you came tapping, tapping at my chamber door,
That I scarce was sure I heard you"—here I opened wide the door;—
Darkness there, and nothing more.

Deep into that darkness peering, long I stood there wondering, fearing,
Doubting, dreaming dreams no mortal ever dared to dream before;
But the silence was unbroken, and the darkness gave no token,
And the only word there spoken was the whispered word, "Lenore!"
This I whispered, and an echo murmured back the word "Lenore!"
Merely this and nothing more.

Back into the chamber turning, all my soul within me burning,
Soon again I heard a tapping somewhat louder than before.
"Surely," said I, "surely that is, something at my window lattice;
Let me see then, what thereat is, and this mystery explore—
Let my heart be still a moment and this mystery explore;—
'Tis the wind and nothing more!"

Open here I flung the shutter, when, with many a flirt and flutter,
In there stepped a stately raven of the saintly days of yore.
Not the least obeisance made he; not an instant stopped or stayed he;
But, with mien of lord or lady, perched above my chamber door—

Perched upon a bust of Pallas just above my chamber door—
Perched, and sat, and nothing more.

Then this ebony bird beguiling my sad fancy into smiling,
By the grave and stern decorum of the countenance it wore,
"Though thy crest be shorn and shaven, thou," I said, "art sure no craven.
Ghastly grim and ancient raven wandering from the Nightly shore—
Tell me what thy lonely name is on the Night's Plutonian shore!"
Quoth the raven, "Nevermore."

Much I marvelled this ungainly fowl to hear discourse so plainly,
Though its answer little meaning—little relevancy bore;
For we cannot help agreeing that no living human being
Ever yet was blessed with seeing bird above his chamber door—
Bird or beast above the sculptured bust above his chamber door,
With such name as "Nevermore."

But the raven, sitting lonely on the placid bust, spoke only
That one word, as if his soul in that one word he did outpour.
Nothing further then he uttered—not a feather then he fluttered—
Till I scarcely more than muttered "Other friends have flown before—
On the morrow will he leave me, as my hopes have flown before."
Then the bird said, "Nevermore."

Startled at the stillness broken by reply so aptly spoken,
"Doubtless," said I, "what it utters is its only stock and store,
Caught from some unhappy master whom unmerciful Disaster
Followed fast and followed faster till his songs one burden bore—
Till the dirges of his Hope that melancholy burden bore
Of 'Never-nevermore.'"

But the Raven still beguiling all my sad soul into smiling,
Straight I wheeled a cushioned seat in front of bird and bust and door;
Then, upon the velvet sinking, I betook myself to linking
Fancy unto fancy, thinking what this ominous bird of yore—
What this grim, ungainly, gaunt, and ominous bird of yore
Meant in croaking "Nevermore."

This I sat engaged in guessing, but no syllable expressing
To the fowl whose fiery eyes now burned into my bosom's core;
This and more I sat divining, with my head at ease reclining
On the cushion's velvet violet lining that the lamp-light gloated o'er,
But whose velvet violet lining with the lamp-light gloated o'er,
She shall press, ah, nevermore!

Then, methought the air grew denser, perfumed from an unseen censer
Swung by angels whose faint foot-falls tinkled on the tufted floor.
"Wretch," I cried, "thy God hath lent thee—by these angels he has sent thee
Respite—respite and nepenthe from the memories of Lenore!
Quaff, oh quaff this kind nepenthe, and forget this lost Lenore!"
Quoth the raven, "Nevermore."

"Prophet!" said I, "thing of evil!—prophet still, if bird or devil!—
Whether Tempter sent, or whether tempest tossed thee here ashore,
Desolate yet all undaunted, on this desert land enchanted—
On this home by Horror haunted—tell me truly, I implore—
Is there—is there balm in Gilead?—tell me—tell me, I implore!"
Quoth the raven, "Nevermore."

"Prophet!" said I, "thing of evil!—prophet still, if bird or devil!
By that Heaven that bends above us—by that God we both adore—
Tell this soul with sorrow laden if, within the distant Aidenn,
It shall clasp a sainted maiden whom the angels named Lenore—
Clasp a rare and radiant maiden, whom the angels named Lenore?"
Quoth the raven, "Nevermore."

"Be that word our sign of parting, bird or fiend!" I shrieked upstarting—
"Get thee back into the tempest and the Night's Plutonian shore!
Leave no black plume as a token of that lie thy soul hath spoken!
Leave my loneliness unbroken!—quit the bust above my door!
Take thy beak from out my heart, and take thy form from off my door!"
Quoth the raven, "Nevermore."

And the raven, never flitting, still is sitting, still is sitting
On the pallid bust of Pallas just above my chamber door;
And his eyes have all the seeming of a demon's that is dreaming,
And the lamp-light o'er his streaming throws his shadow on the floor;
And my soul from out that shadow that lies floating on the floor
Shall be lifted—nevermore.

EDGAR ALLAN POE

To Helen

I saw thee once—once only—years ago:
I must not say how many—but not many.
It was a July midnight; and from out
A full-orbed moon, that, like thine own soul, soaring,
Sought a precipitate pathway up through heaven.
There fell a silvery-silken veil of light,
With quietude, and sultriness, and slumber,
Upon the upturned faces of a thousand
Roses that grew in an enchanted garden,
Where no wind dared to stir, unless on tiptoe-
Fell on the upturn'd faces of these roses
That gave out, in return for the love-light,
Their odorous souls in an ecstatic death-
Fell on the upturn'd faces of these roses
That smiled and died in this parterre, enchanted
By thee, and by the poetry of thy presence.

Clad all in white, upon a violet bank
I saw thee half reclining; while the moon
Fell on the upturn'd faces of the roses.
And on thine own, upturn'd—alas, in sorrow!

Was it not Fate, that, on this July midnight-
Was it not Fate, (whose name is also Sorrow,)
That bade me pause before that garden-gate,
To breathe the incense of those slumbering roses?
No footstep stirred: the hated world an slept,
Save only thee and me. (Oh, Heaven!—oh, God!
How my heart beats in coupling those two words!)
Save only thee and me. I paused—I looked-
And in an instant all things disappeared.
(Ah, bear in mind this garden was enchanted!)

The pearly lustre of the moon went out:
The mossy banks and the meandering paths,
The happy flowers and the repining trees,
Were seen no more: the very roses' odors
Died in the arms of the adoring airs.
All—all expired save thee—save less than thou:
Save only the divine light in thine eyes.
Save but the soul in thine uplifted eyes.
I saw but them—they were the world to me!
I saw but them—saw only them for hours,
Saw only them until the moon went down.
What wild heart-histories seemed to be enwritten
Upon those crystalline, celestial spheres!
How dark a woe, yet how sublime a hope!
How silently serene a sea of pride!
How daring an ambition; yet how deep-
How fathomless a capacity for love!

But now, at length, dear Dian sank from sight,
Into a western couch of thunder-cloud;
And thou, a ghost, amid the entombing trees
Didst glide away. Only thine eyes remained;
They would not go—they never yet have gone;
Lighting my lonely pathway home that night,
They have not left me (as my hopes have) since;
They follow me—they lead me through the years.
They are my ministers—yet I their slave.
Their office is to illumine and enkindle-
My duty, to be saved by their bright light,
And purified in their electric fire,
And sanctified in their elysian fire.
They fill my soul with Beauty (which is Hope),
And are far up in Heaven—the stars I kneel to
In the sad, silent watches of my night;
While even in the meridian glare of day

I see them still—two sweetly scintillant
Venuses, unextinguished by the sun!

EDWIN ARLINGTON ROBINSON (1869–1935) was born in Maine and attended Harvard for a brief time. Robinson spent most of his early career as a customs officer in New York City. After winning the Pulitzer Prize for *Collected Poems* (1921), which included "Richard Cory" (1897), he was awarded an honorary doctorate from Yale and the Pulitzer Prize for Literature twice more for *The Man Who Died Twice* (1924) and *Tristram* (1927). Robinson combined formulaic Renaissance verse styles with realistic, modern, and personal subject matter, a combination that distinguished his poetry from both the open verse style of Whitman and the idealistic subject matter of other poetry of his time.

Related Works: Hawthorne, "Young Goodman Brown"; Wideman, "What We Cannot Speak About We Must Pass Over in Silence"; Anonymous Ballads; Dunbar, "We wear the mask"; Auden, "The Unknown Citizen"; Miller, *Death of a Salesman.*

EDWIN ARLINGTON ROBINSON

Richard Cory

Whenever Richard Cory went down town,
We people on the pavement looked at him:
He was a gentleman from sole to crown,
Clean favored, and imperially slim.

And he was always quietly arrayed,
And he was always human when he talked;
But still he fluttered pulses when he said,
"Good-morning," and he glittered when he walked.

And he was rich—yes, richer than a king—
And admirably schooled in every grace:
In fine, we thought that he was everything
To make us wish that we were in his place.

So on we worked, and waited for the light,
And went without the meat, and cursed the bread;
And Richard Cory, one calm summer night,
Went home and put a bullet through his head.

CHRISTINA ROSSETTI (1830–1894), the youngest of four children in the highly educated and creative Gabriel and Francis Rossetti family, began writing poetry as a young teenager. With her brothers, William Michael and Dante Gabriel, she shared in the artistic and aesthetic values of the Pre-Raphaelite movement. With her sister, Maria Francesca—an Anglican nun—she shared a deep involvement with religion and ritual. Rossetti never married, ending two serious relationships because of her suitors' religious beliefs. Rossetti's *Goblin Market and Other Poems* (1862), which was illustrated by her brother Dante Gabriel, was both her most important and her most popular work. The narrative poem "Goblin Market" weaves together elements of the **Romantic** and **Gothic** traditions (magic, sensuality, darkness) with a later Victorian emphasis on morality and sentiment. Readers and critics often compare "Goblin Market" to Samuel Coleridge's "The Rime of the Ancient Mariner" because both poems construct a dark, fantasy world featuring embedded tales of moral failure and redemption. The differences between the two poems, however, are crucial; note, especially, in each poem the different causes of failure, as well as the values implicit in each means of redemption. "Goblin Market" is especially notable for its recurring **images, symbols**, and literary (especially biblical) **allusions**. In this poem, too, you can observe Rossetti's method of framing her characters with a rich variety of **metaphors**.

Related Works: Hawthorne, "The Birthmark"; Faulkner, "A Rose for Emily"; Medieval Lyric Poetry, "I Sing of a Maiden that is Matchless"; Anonymous Ballads, "Bonny Barbara Allan" and "Lord Randall"; Coleridge, "The Rime of the Ancient Mariner"; Keats, "La Belle Dame sans Merci"; Atwood, "Siren Song"; *Everyman*; Sophocles, *Antigone*.

CHRISTINA ROSSETTI

Goblin Market

Morning and evening
Maids heard the goblins cry:
"Come buy our orchard fruits.
Come buy, come buy:
Apples and quinces,
Lemons and oranges,
Plump unpecked cherries,
Melons and raspberries,
Bloom-down-cheeked peaches,
Swart-beaded mulberries,
Wild free-born cranberries,
Crab-apples, dewberries,
Pine-apples, blackberries,
Apricots, strawberries;—
All ripe together
In summer weather,—
Morns that pass by,
Fair eves that fly;
Come buy, come buy:
Our grapes fresh from the vine,
Pomegranates full and fine,
Dates and sharp bullaces,

Rare pears and greengages,
Damsons and bilberries,
Taste them and try:
Currants and gooseberries,
Bright-fire-like barberries,
Figs to fill your mouth,
Citrons from the South,
Sweet to tongue and sound to eye:
Come buy, come buy."

Evening by evening
Among the brookside rushes,
Laura bowed her head to hear,
Lizzie veiled her blushes:
Crouching close together
In the cooling weather,
With clasping arms and cautioning lips,
With tingling cheeks and finger tips.
"Lie close," Laura said,
Pricking up her golden head:
"We must not look at goblin men,
We must not buy their fruits:
Who knows upon what soil they fed
Their hungry thirsty roots:"
"Come buy," call the goblins
Hobbling down the glen.
"Oh," cried Lizzie. "Laura, Laura,
You should not peep at goblin men."
Lizzie covered up her eyes,
Covered close lest they should look:
Laura reared her glossy head,
And whispered like the restless brook:
"Look, Lizzie, look, Lizzie,
Down the glen tramp little men.
One hauls a basket,
One bears a plate,
One lugs a golden dish
Of many pounds weight.
How fair the vine must grow
Whose grapes are so luscious;
How warm the wind must blow
Thro' those fruit bushes."
"No," said Lizzie: "No, no, no,
Their offers should not charm us,
Their evil gifts would harm us."
She thrust a dimpled finger
In each ear, shut eyes and ran:
Curious Laura chose to linger

Wondering at each merchant man.
One had a cat's face,
One whisked a tail,
One tramped at a rat's pace,
One crawled like a snail,
One like a wombat prowled obtuse and furry,
One like a ratel tumbled hurry skurry.
She heard a voice like voice of doves
Cooing all together:
They sounded kind and full of loves
In the pleasant weather.

Laura stretched her gleaming neck
Like a rush-imbedded swan,
Like a lily from the beck,
Like a moonlit poplar branch,
Like a vessel at the launch
When its last restraint is gone.

Backwards up the mossy glen
Turned and trooped the goblin men,
With their shrill repeated cry,
"Come buy, come buy."
When they reached where Laura was
They stood stock still upon the moss.
Leering at each other,
Brother with queer brother;
Signalling each other,
Brother with sly brother.
One set his basket down,
One reared his plate;
One began to weave a crown
Of tendrils, leaves and rough nuts brown
(Men sell not such in any town);
One heaved the golden weight
Of dish and fruit to offer her:
"Come buy, come buy," was still their cry.
Laura stared but did not stir,
Longed but had no money;
The whisk-tailed merchant bade her taste
In tones as smooth as honey,
The cat-faced purr'd,
The rat-paced spoke a word
Of welcome, and the snail-paced even was heard;
One parrot-voiced and jolly
Cried "Pretty Goblin" still for "Pretty Polly:"—
One whistled like a bird.

But sweet-tooth Laura spoke in haste:
"Good folk, I have no coin;

To take were to purloin:
I have no copper in my purse,
I have no silver either,
And all my gold is on the furze
That shakes in windy weather
Above the rusty heather."
"You have much gold upon your head,"
They answered all together:
"Buy from us with a golden curl."
She clipped a precious golden lock,
She dropped a tear more rare than pearl,
Then sucked their fruit globes fair or red:
Sweeter than honey from the rock.
Stronger than man-rejoicing wine,
Clearer than water flowed that juice;
She never tasted such before,
How should it cloy with length of use?
She sucked and sucked and sucked the more
Fruits which that unknown orchard bore;
She sucked until her lips were sore;
Then flung the emptied rinds away
But gathered up one kernel-stone,
And knew not was it night or day
As she turned home alone.

Lizzie met her at the gate
Full of wise upbraidings:
"Dear, you should not stay so late,
Twilight is not good for maidens:
Should not loiter in the glen
In the haunts of goblin men.
Do you not remember Jeanie,
How she met them in the moonlight,
Took their gifts both choice and many,
Ate their fruits and wore their flowers
Plucked from bowers
Where summer ripens at all hours?
But ever in the noonlight
She pined and pined away:
Sought them by night and day,
Found them no more but dwindled and grew grey;
Then fell with the first snow,
While to this day no grass will grow
Where she lies low:
I planted daisies there a year ago
That never blow,
You should not loiter so."
"Nay, hush," said Laura:
"Nay, hush, my sister:

I ate and ate my fill,
Yet my mouth waters still:
Tomorrow night I will
Buy more:" and kissed her:
"Have done with sorrow;
I'll bring you plums tomorrow
Fresh on their mother twigs,
Cherries worth getting;
You cannot think what figs
My teeth have met in,
What melons icy-cold
Piled on a dish of gold
Too huge for me to hold,
What peaches with a velvet nap,
Pellucid grapes without one seed:
Odorous indeed must be the mead
Whereon they grow, and pure the wave they drink
With lilies at the brink,
And sugar-sweet their sap."

Golden head by golden head,
Like two pigeons in one nest
Folded in each other's wings,
They lay down in their curtained bed:
Like two blossoms on one stem,
Like two flakes of new-fall 'n snow,
Like two wands of ivory
Tipped with gold for awful kings,
Moon and stars gazed in at them,
Wind sang to them lullaby,
Lumbering owls forbore to fly,
Not a bat flapped to and fro
Round their rest:
Cheek to cheek and breast to breast
Locked together in one nest.

Early in the morning
When the first cock crowed his warning,
Neat like bees, as sweet and busy,
Laura rose with Lizzie:
Fetched in honey, milked the cows,
Aired and set to rights the house,
Kneaded cakes of whitest wheat,
Cakes for dainty mouths to eat,
Next churned butter, whipped up cream,
Fed their poultry, sat and sewed;
Talked as modest maidens should:
Lizzie with an open heart,
Laura in an absent dream,

One content, one sick in part;
One warbling for the mere bright day's delight,
One longing for the night.

At length slow evening came:
They went with pitchers to the reedy brook;
Lizzie most placid in her look,
Laura most like a leaping flame.
They drew the gurgling water from its deep;
Lizzie plucked purple and rich golden flags,
Then turning homewards said: "The sunset flushes
Those furthest loftiest crags;
Come, Laura, not another maiden lags,
No wilful squirrel wags,
The beasts and birds are fast asleep."
But Laura loitered still among the rushes
And said the bank was steep.

And said the hour was early still,
The dew not fall'n, the wind not chill:
Listening ever, but not catching
The customary cry,
"Come buy, come buy,"
With its iterated jingle
Of sugar-baited words:
Not for all her watching
Once discerning even one goblin
Racing, whisking, tumbling, hobbling;
Let alone the herds
That used to tramp along the glen,
In groups or single,
Of brisk fruit-merchant men,
Till Lizzie urged, "O Laura, come;
I hear the fruit-call but I dare not look:
You should not loiter longer at this brook:
Come with me home.
The stars rise, the moon bends her arc,
Each glowworm winks her spark,
Let us get home before the night grows dark:
For clouds may gather
Tho' this is summer weather,
Put out the lights and drench us thro';
Then if we lost our way what should we do?"

Laura turned cold as stone
To find her sister heard that cry alone,
That goblin cry,
"Come buy our fruits, come buy."
Must she then buy no more such dainty fruit?

Must she no more such succous pasture find,
Gone deaf and blind?
Her tree of life drooped from the root:
She said not one word in her heart's sore ache;
But peering thro' the dimness, nought discerning,
Trudged home, her pitcher dripping all the way;
So crept to bed, and lay
Silent till Lizzie slept;
Then sat up in a passionate yearning,
And gnashed her teeth for baulked desire, and wept
As if her heart would break.

Day after day, night after night,
Laura kept watch in vain
In sullen silence of exceeding pain.
She never caught again the goblin cry:
"Come buy, come buy:"—
She never spied the goblin men
Hawking their fruits along the glen;
But when the noon waxed bright
Her hair grew thin and gray:
She dwindled, as the fair full moon doth turn
To swift decay and burn
Her fire away.

One day remembering her kernel-stone
She set it by a wall that faced the south:
Dewed it with tears, hoped for a root,
Watched for a waxing shoot,
But there came none;
It never saw the sun,
It never felt the trickling moisture run:
While with sunk eyes and faded mouth
She dreamed of melons, as a traveller sees
False waves in desert drouth
With shade of leaf-crowned trees,
And burns the thirstier in the sandful breeze.

She no more swept the house,
Tended the fowls or cows,
Fetched honey, kneaded cakes of wheat,
Brought water from the brook:
But sat down listless in the chimney-nook
And would not eat.

Tender Lizzie could not bear
To watch her sister's cankerous care
Yet not to share.
She night and morning
Caught the goblins' cry:

"Come buy our orchard fruits,
Come buy, come buy:"—
Beside the brook, along the glen,
She heard the tramp of goblin men,
The voice and stir
Poor Laura could not hear;
Longed to buy fruit to comfort her,
But feared to pay too dear.
She thought of Jeanie in her grave,
Who should have been a bride;
But who for joys brides hope to have
Fell sick and died
In her gay prime,
In earliest Winter time,
With the first glazing rime,
With the first snow-fall of crisp Winter time.

Till Laura dwindling
Seemed knocking at Death's door:
Then Lizzie weighed no more
Better and worse;
But put a silver penny in her purse,
Kissed Laura, crossed the heath with clumps of furze
At twilight, halted by the brook:
And for the first time in her life
Began to listen and look.

Laughed every goblin
When they spied her peeping:
Came towards her hobbling,
Flying, running, leaping,
Puffing and blowing,
Chuckling, clapping, crowing,
Clucking and gobbling,
Mopping and mowing,
Full of airs and graces,
Pulling wry faces,
Demure grimaces,
Cat-like and rat-like,
Ratel- and wombat-like,
Snail-paced in a hurry,
Parrot-voiced and whistler,
Helter skelter, hurry skurry,
Chattering like magpies,
Fluttering like pigeons,
Gliding like fishes,—
Hugged her and kissed her,
Squeezed and caressed her:
Stretched up their dishes,
Panniers, and plates:

"Look at our apples
Russet and dun,
Bob at our cherries,
Bite at our peaches,
Citrons and dates,
Grapes for the asking,
Pears red with basking
Out in the sun,
Plums on their twigs;
Pluck them and suck them,
Pomegranates, figs,"—

"Good folk," said Lizzie,
Mindful of Jeanie:
"Give me much and many:"—
Held out her apron,
Tossed them her penny.
"Nay, take a seat with us,
Honour and eat with us,"
They answered grinning:
"Our feast is but beginning.
Night yet is early,
Warm and dew-pearly,
Wakeful and starry:
Such fruits as these
No man can carry;
Half their bloom would fly,
Half their dew would dry,
Half their flavour would pass by.
Sit down and feast with us,
Be welcome guest with us,
Cheer you and rest with us,"—
"Thank you," said Lizzie: "But one waits
At home alone for me:
So without further parleying,
If you will not sell me any
Of your fruits tho' much and many,
Give me back my silver penny
I tossed you for a fee."—
They began to scratch their pates.
No longer wagging, purring,
But visibly demurring.
Grunting and snarling.
One called her proud,
Cross-grained, uncivil;
Their tones waved loud,
Their looks were evil.
Lashing their tails
They trod and hustled her,

Elbowed and jostled her,
Clawed with their nails,
Barking, mewing, hissing, mocking,
Tore her gown and soiled her stocking,
Twitched her hair out by the roots,
Stamped upon her tender feet,
Held her hands and squeezed their fruits
Against her mouth to make her eat.

White and golden Lizzie stood,
Like a lily in a flood,—
Like a rock of blue-veined stone
Lashed by tides obstreperously,—
Like a beacon left alone
In a hoary roaring sea,
Sending up a golden fire,—
Like a fruit-crowned orange-tree
White with blossoms honey-sweet
Sore beset by wasp and bee,—
Like a royal virgin town
Topped with gilded dome and spire
Close beleaguerred by a fleet
Mad to tug her standard down.

One may lead a horse to water,
Twenty cannot make him drink.
Tho' the goblins cuffed and caught her,
Coaxed and fought her,
Bullied and besought her,
Scratched her, pinched her black as ink,
Kicked and knocked her,
Mauled and mocked her,
Lizzie uttered not a word;
Would not open lip from lip
Lest they should cram a mouthful in:
But laughed in heart to feel the drip
Of juice that syruped all her face,
And lodged in dimples of her chin.
And streaked her neck which quaked like curd.
At last the evil people
Worn out by her resistance
Flung back her penny, kicked their fruit
Along whichever road they took,
Not leaving root or stone or shoot;
Some writhed into the ground,
Some dived into the brook
With ring and ripple,
Some scudded on the gale without a sound,
Some vanished in the distance.

In a smart, ache, tingle,
Lizzie went her way;
Knew not was it night or day;
Sprang up the bank, tore thro' the furze,
Threaded copse and dingle,
And heard her penny jingle
Bouncing in her purse,
Its bounce was music to her ear.
She ran and ran
As if she feared some goblin man
Dogged her with gibe or curse
Or something worse:
But not one goblin skurried after,
Nor was she pricked by fear;
The kind heart made her windy-paced
That urged her home quite out of breath with haste
And inward laughter.

She cried "Laura," up the garden,
"Did you miss me?
Come and kiss me.
Never mind my bruises,
Hug me, kiss me, suck my juices
Squeezed from goblin fruits for you,
Goblin pulp and goblin dew.
Eat me, drink me, love me;
Laura, make much of me:
For your sake I have braved the glen
And had to do with goblin merchant men."

Laura started from her chair,
Flung her arms up in the air.
Clutched her hair:
"Lizzie, Lizzie, have you tasted
For my sake the fruit forbidden?
Must your light like mine be hidden,
Your young life like mine be wasted,
Undone in mine undoing
And ruined in my ruin,
Thirsty, cankered, goblin-ridden?"—
She clung about her sister,
Kissed and kissed and kissed her:
Tears once again
Refreshed her shrunken eyes,
Dropping like rain
After long sultry drouth;
Shaking with aguish fear, and pain,
She kissed and kissed her with a hungry mouth.

Her lips began to scorch,
That juice was wormwood to her tongue,
She loathed the feast:
Writhing as one possessed she leaped and sung,
Rent all her robe, and wrung
Her hands in lamentable haste,
And beat her breast,
Her locks streamed like the torch
Borne by a racer at full speed,
Or like the mane of horses in their flight,
Or like an eagle when she stems the light
Straight toward the sun,
Or like a caged thing freed,
Or like a flying flag when armies run.

Swift fire spread thro' her veins, knocked at her heart,
Met the fire smouldering there
And overbore its lesser flame;
She gorged on bitterness without a name:
Ah! fool, to choose such part
Of soul-consuming care!
Sense failed in the mortal strife:
Like the watch-tower of a town
Which an earthquake shatters down,
Like a lightning-stricken mast.
Like a wind-uprooted tree
Spun about,
Like a foam-topped waterspout
Cast down headlong in the sea,
She fell at last:
Pleasure past and anguish past,
Is it death or is it life?

Life out of death.
That night long Lizzie watched by her,
Counted her pulse's flagging stir,
Felt for her breath,
Held water to her lips, and cooled her face
With tears and fanning leaves:
But when the first birds chirped about their eaves,
And early reapers plodded to the place
Of golden sheaves,
And dew-wet grass
Bowed in the morning winds so brisk to pass.
And new buds with new day
Opened of cup-like lilies on the stream,
Laura awoke as from a dream,
Laughed in the innocent old way,
Hugged Lizzie but not twice or thrice;
Her gleaming locks showed not one thread of grey,

Her breath was sweet as May
And light danced in her eyes.

Days, weeks, months, years
Afterwards, when both were wives
With children of their own;
Their mother-hearts beset with fears,
Their lives bound up in tender lives;
Laura would call the little ones
And tell them of her early prime,
Those pleasant days long gone
Of not-returning time:
Would talk about the haunted glen,
The wicked, quaint fruit-merchant men,
Their fruits like honey to the throat
But poison in the blood;
(Men sell not such in any town:)
Would tell them how her sister stood
In deadly peril to do her good,
And win the fiery antidote:
Then joining hands to little hands
Would bid them cling together,
"For there is no friend like a sister
In calm or stormy weather;
To cheer one on the tedious way,
To fetch one if one goes astray,
To lift one if one totters down,
To strengthen whilst one stands."

ALFRED, LORD TENNYSON (1809–1892) was appointed England's Poet Laureate in 1850, succeeding William Wordsworth. Additionally, he became a baron and was given the title "Lord" by Queen Victoria in 1884, firmly establishing him as the most celebrated poet of the Victorian era. The first poem included here, "Ulysses," first published in *Poems* (1842) and written in **blank verse**, was written soon after Tennyson's dearest friend, who was engaged to Tennyson's sister, died suddenly at the age of twenty-two. Famously, Tennyson wrote that he felt this poem "gave my feeling about the need of going forward, and braving the struggle of life," a sentiment that some critics feel is belied by the difficulty of identifying the audience for Ulysses' monologue. "The Charge of the Light Brigade" (1854) commemorates the fall of British soldiers in an episode during the Crimean War, imitating the men's relentless movement forward to their death through the poem's unusual **dactylic meter**.

Related Works: Joyce, "Araby"; Browning, "My Last Duchess"; Arnold, "Dover Beach"; Kipling, "If"; Eliot, "The Love Song of J. Alfred Prufrock"; Frost, "The Death of the Hired Man"; Yeats, "Sailing to Byzantium"; Jarrell, "The Death of the Ball Turret Guner"; Owen, "Dulce et Decorum Est"; Rios, "The Vietnam Wall."

ALFRED, LORD TENNYSON

Ulysses

It little profits that an idle king,
By this still hearth, among these barren crags,
Match'd with an aged wife, I mete and dole
Unequal laws unto a savage race,
That hoard, and sleep, and feed, and know not me.
I cannot rest from travel: I will drink
Life to the lees: All times I have enjoy'd
Greatly, have suffer'd greatly, both with those
That loved me, and alone, on shore, and when
Thro' scudding drifts the rainy Hyades
Vext the dim sea: I am become a name;
For always roaming with a hungry heart
Much have I seen and known; cities of men
And manners, climates, councils, governments,
Myself not least, but honour'd of them all;
And drunk delight of battle with my peers,
Far on the ringing plains of windy Troy,
I am a part of all that I have met;
Yet all experience is an arch wherethro'
Gleams that untravell'd world whose margin fades
For ever and forever when I move.
How dull it is to pause, to make an end,
To rust unburnish'd, not to shine in use!
As tho' to breathe were life! Life piled on life
Were all too little, and of one to me
Little remains; but every hour is saved
From that eternal silence, something more,
A bringer of new things; and vile it were
For some three suns to store and hoard myself,
And this gray spirit yearning in desire
To follow knowledge like a sinking star,
Beyond the utmost bound of human thought.

This is my son, mine own Telemachus.
To whom I leave the sceptre and the isle,—
Well-loved of me, discerning to fulfil
This labour, by slow prudence to make mild
A rugged people, and thro' soft degrees
Subdue them to the useful and the good.
Most blameless is he, centred in the sphere
Of common duties, decent not to fail
In offices of tenderness, and pay

Meet adoration to my household gods,
When I am gone. He works his work, I mine.

There lies the port; the vessel puffs her sail:
There gloom the dark, broad seas. My mariners,
Souls that have toil'd, and wrought, and thought with me—
That ever with a frolic welcome took
The thunder and the sunshine, and opposed
Free hearts, free foreheads—you and I are old;
Old age hath yet his honour and his toil;
Death closes all; but something ere the end.
Some work of noble note, may yet be done,
Not unbecoming men that strove with Gods.
The lights begin to twinkle from the rocks:
The long day wanes; the slow moon climbs; the deep
Moans round with many voices. Come, my friends,
'Tis not too late to seek a newer world,
Push off, and sitting well in order smite
The sounding furrows; for my purpose holds
To sail beyond the sunset, and the baths
Of all the western stars, until I die,
It may be that the gulfs will wash us down:
It may be we shall touch the Happy Isles,
And see the great Achilles, whom we knew.
Tho' much is taken, much abides; and tho'
We are not now that strength which in old days
Moved earth and heaven, that which we are, we are;
One equal temper of heroic hearts,
Made weak by time and fate, but strong in will
To strive, to seek, to find, and not to yield.

ALFRED, LORD TENNYSON

The Charge of the Light Brigade

1

Half a league, half a league,
Half a league onward,
All in the valley of Death
Rode the six hundred.
"Forward the Light Brigade!
Charge for the guns!" he said,
Into the valley of Death
Rode the six hundred.

2

"Forward, the Light Brigade!"
Was there a man dismayed?
Not though the soldier knew
  Someone had blundered.
Theirs not to make reply,
Theirs not to reason why,
Theirs but to do and die.
Into the valley of Death
  Rode the six hundred.

3

Cannon to right of them,
Cannon to left of them,
Cannon in front of them
  Volleyed and thundered:
Stormed at with shot and shell,
Boldly they rode and well,
Into the jaws of Death,
Into the mouth of hell
  Rode the six hundred.

4

Flashed all their sabers bare,
Flashed as they turned in air
Sab'ring the gunners there,
Charging an army, while
  All the world wondered.
Plunged in the battery smoke
Right through the line they broke;
Cossack and Russian
Reeled from the saber stroke
  Shattered and sundered.
Then they rode back, but not,
  Not the six hundred.

5

Cannon to right of them,
Cannon to left of them,
Cannon behind them
  Volleyed and thundered;
Stormed at with shot and shell,
While horse and hero fell,
They that had fought so well
Came through the jaws of Death,
Back from the mouth of hell,
All that was left of them,
  Left of six hundred.

6

When can their glory fade?
O the wild charge they made!
   All the world wondered,
Honor the charge they made!
Honor the Light Brigade,
   Noble six hundred!

WALT WHITMAN (1819–1892). After years as an itinerant journalist, school teacher, newspaper editor, and carpenter, Whitman self-published the first edition of *Leaves of Grass* in 1855 and, with it, revolutionized American and, later, European poetry. Whitman's simple style primarily relies on images and the use of phrase-length or longer units rather than syllables to create its rhythm; this kind of rhythm is called **cadence**, and Whitman's loose style came to be known as **free verse**. Whitman's main theme is freedom—political, sexual, and religious—and because of this theme and the importance of Whitman's innovations in *Leaves of Grass*, many critics consider him the most important American poet. His Civil War poetry, first published in *Drum Taps* (1865), includes the **elegies** on the death of Abraham Lincoln, "Oh Captain! my Captain!" and "When lilacs last in the dooryard bloom'd."

Related Works: Steinbeck, "The Chrysanthemums"; Wideman, "What We Cannot Speak About We Must Pass Over in Silence"; "The Wife's Lament"; Jonson, "On My First Son"; Milton, *Lycidas*; Arnold, "Dover Beach"; Thomas, "A Refusal to Mourn the Death, by Fire, of a Child of London"; Stevens, "Thirteen Ways of Looking at a Blackbird"; Ortiz, "Speaking."

WALT WHITMAN

O Captain! My Captain!

O Captain! my Captain! our fearful trip is done,
The ship has weather'd every rack, the prize we sought is won,
The port is near, the bells I hear, the people all exulting,
While follow eyes the steady keel, the vessel grim and daring;
      But O heart! heart! heart!
         O the bleeding drops of red,
            Where on the deck my Captain lies,
               Fallen cold and dead.

O Captain! my Captain! rise up and hear the bells;
Rise up—for you the flag is flung—for you the bugle trills,
For you bouquets and ribbon'd wreaths—for you the shores a-crowding,
For you they call, the swaying mass, their eager faces turning;
      Here Captain! dear father!
         This arm beneath your head!

It is some dream that on the deck,
You've fallen cold and dead.

My Captain does not answer, his lips are pale and still,
My father does not feel my arm, he has no pulse nor will,
The ship is anchor'd safe and sound, its voyage closed and done,
From fearful trip the victor ship comes in with object won;
Exult O shores, and ring O bells!
But I with mournful tread,
Walk the deck my Captain lies,
Fallen cold and dead.

WALT WHITMAN

When Lilacs Last in the Dooryard Bloom'd

1

When lilacs last in the dooryard bloom'd,
And the great star early droop'd in the western sky in the night,
I mourn'd and yet shall mourn with ever-returning spring.

Ever-returning spring, trinity sure to me you bring,
Lilac blooming perennial and drooping star in the west,
And thought of him I love.

2

O powerful western fallen star!
O shades of night—O moody, tearful night!
O great star disappear'd—O the black murk that hides the star!
O cruel hands that hold me powerless—O helpless soul of me!
O harsh surrounding cloud that will not free my soul.

3

In the dooryard fronting an old farm-house near the white-wash'd palings,
Stands the lilac-bush tall-growing with heart-shaped leaves of rich green,
With many a pointed blossom rising delicate, with the perfume strong I love,
With every leaf a miracle—and from this bush in the dooryard,
With delicate-color'd blossoms and heart-shaped leaves of rich green,
A sprig with its flower I break.

4

In the swamp in secluded recesses,
A shy and hidden bird is warbling a song.

Solitary the thrush,
The hermit withdrawn to himself, avoiding the settlements,
Sings by himself a song.

Song of the bleeding throat,
Death's outlet song of life, (for well dear brother I know,
If thou wast not granted to sing thou would'st surely die.)

5

Over the breast of the spring, the land, amid cities,
Amid lanes and through old woods, where lately the violets peep'd from the
ground, spotting the gray debris.
Amid the grass in the fields each side of the lanes, passing the endless grass,
Passing the yellow-spear'd wheat, every grain from its shroud in the dark-brown
fields uprisen,
Passing the apple-tree blows of white and pink in the orchards,
Carrying a corpse to where it shall rest in the grave,
Night and day journeys a coffin.

6

Coffin that passes through lanes and streets,
Through day and night with the great cloud darkening the land,
With the pomp of the inloop'd flags with the cities draped in black,
With the show of the States themselves as of crape-veil'd women standing,
With processions long and winding and the flambeaus of the night,
With the countless torches lit, with the silent sea of faces and the unbared heads,
With the waiting depot, the arriving coffin, and the sombre faces,
With dirges through the night, with the thousand voices rising strong and solemn,
With all the mournful voices of the dirges pour'd around the coffin,
The dim-lit churches and the shuddering organs—where amid these you journey,
With the tolling tolling bells' perpetual clang,
Here, coffin that slowly passes,
I give you my sprig of lilac.

7

(Nor for you, for one alone,
Blossoms and branches green to coffins all I bring,
For fresh as the morning, thus would I chant a song for you O sane and sacred death.

All over bouquets of roses,
O death, I cover you over with roses and early lilies,
But mostly and now the lilac that blooms the first,
Copious I break, I break the sprigs from the bushes,
With loaded arms I come, pouring for you,
For you and the coffins all of you O death.)

8

O western orb sailing the heaven,
Now I know what you must have meant as a month since I walk'd,
As I walk'd in silence the transparent shadowy night,
As I saw you had something to tell as you bent to me night after night,
As you droop'd from the sky low down as if to my side, (while the other stars
all look'd on,)

As we wander'd together the solemn night, (for something I know not what kept
me from sleep,)
As the night advanced, and I saw on the rim of the west how full you were of woe,
As I stood on the rising ground in the breeze in the cool transparent night,
As I watch'd where you pass'd and was lost in the netherward black of the night,
As my soul in its trouble dissatisfied sank, as where you sad orb,
Concluded, dropt in the night, and was gone.

9

Sing on there in the swamp,
O singer bashful and tender, I hear your notes, I hear your call,
I hear, I come presently, I understand you,
But a moment I linger, for the lustrous star has detain'd me,
The star my departing comrade holds and detains me.

10

O how shall I warble myself for the dead one there I loved?
And how shall I deck my song for the large sweet soul that has gone?
And what shall my perfume be for the grave of him I love?
Sea-winds blown from east and west,
Blown from the Eastern sea and blown from the Western sea, till there on the
prairies meeting,
These and with these and the breath of my chant,
I'll perfume the grave of him I love.

11

O what shall I hang on the chamber walls?
And what shall the pictures be that I hang on the walls,
To adorn the burial-house of him I love?

Pictures of growing spring and farms and homes,
With the Fourth-month eve at sundown, and the gray smoke lucid and bright,
With floods of the yellow gold of the gorgeous, indolent, sinking sun, burning,
expanding the air,
With the fresh sweet herbage under foot, and the pale green leaves of the trees
prolific,
In the distance the flowing glaze, the breast of the river, with a wind-dapple here
and there,
With ranging hills on the banks, with many a line against the sky, and shadows,
And the city at hand with dwellings so dense, and stacks of chimneys,
And all the scenes of life and the workshops, and the workmen homeward returning.

12

Lo, body and soul—this land,
My own Manhattan with spires, and the sparkling and hurrying tides, and the ships,
The varied and ample land, the South and the North in the light, Ohio's shores
and flashing Missouri,
And ever the far-spreading prairies cover'd with grass and corn.

Lo, the most excellent sun so calm and haughty,
The violet and purple morn with just-felt breezes,
The gentle soft-born measureless light,
The miracle spreading bathing all, the fulfill'd noon,
The coming eve delicious, the welcome night and the stars,
Over my cities shining all, enveloping man and land.

13

Sing on, sing on you gray-brown bird,
Sing from the swamps, the recesses, pour your chant from the bushes,
Limitless out of the dusk, out of the cedars and pines.

Sing on dearest brother, warble your reedy song,
Loud human song, with voice of uttermost woe.

O liquid and free and tender!
O wild and loose to my soul—O wondrous singer!
You only I hear—yet the star holds me, (but will soon depart,)
Yet the lilac with mastering odor holds me.

14

Now while I sat in the day and look'd forth,
In the close of the day with its light and the fields of spring, and the farmers
preparing their crops,
In the large unconscious scenery of my land with its lakes and forests,
In the heavenly aerial beauty, (after the perturb'd winds and the storms,)
Under the arching heavens of the afternoon swift passing, and the voices
of children and women,
The many-moving sea-tides, and I saw the ships how they sail'd,
And the summer approaching with richness, and the fields all busy with labor,
And the infinite separate houses, how they all went on, each with its meals and
minutia of daily usages,
And the streets how their throbbings throbb'd, and the cities pent—lo, then and there,
Falling upon them all and among them all, enveloping me with the rest,
Appear'd the cloud, appear'd the long black trail,
And I knew death, its thought and the sacred knowledge of death.

Then with the knowledge of death as walking one side of me,
And the thought of death close-walking the other side of me,
And I in the middle as with companions, and as holding the hands of companions,
I fled forth to the hiding receiving night that talks not,
Down to the shores of the water, the path by the swamp in the dimness,
To the solemn shadowy cedars and ghostly pines so still.

And the singer so shy to the rest receiv'd me,
The gray-brown bird I know receiv'd us comrades three,
And he sang the carol of death, and a verse for him I love.

From deep secluded recesses,
From the fragrant cedars and the ghostly pines so still,
Came the carol of the bird.

And the charm of the carol rapt me,
As I held as if by their hands my comrades in the night,
And the voice of my spirit tallied the song of the bird.

Come lovely and soothing death,
Undulate round the world, serenely arriving, arriving,
In the day, in the night, to all, to each,
Sooner or later delicate death.

Prais'd be the fathomless universe,
For life and joy, and for objects and knowledge curious,
And for love, sweet love—but praise! praise! praise!
For the sure-enwinding arms of cool-enfolding death.

Dark mother always gliding near with soft feet,
Have none chanted for thee a chant of fullest welcome?
Then I chant it for thee, I glorify thee above all,
I bring thee a song that when thou must indeed come, come unfalteringly.

Approach strong deliveress,
When it is so, when thou hast taken them I joyously sing the dead,
Lost in the loving floating ocean of thee,
Laved in the flood of thy bliss O death.

From me to thee glad serenades,
Dances for thee I propose saluting thee, adornments and feastings for thee,
And the sights of the open landscape and the high-spread sky are fitting,
And life and the fields, and the huge and thoughtful night.

The night in silence under many a star,
The ocean shore and the husky whispering wave whose voice I know
And the soul turning to thee O vast and well-veil'd death,
And the body gratefully nestling close to thee.

Over the tree-tops I float thee a song,
Over the rising and sinking waves, over the myriad fields and the prairies wide,
Over the dense-pack'd cities all and the teeming wharves and ways,
I float this carol with joy, with joy to thee O death.

15

To the tally of my soul,
Loud and strong kept up the gray-brown bird,
With pure deliberate notes spreading filling the night.

Loud in the pines and cedars dim,
Clear in the freshness moist and the swamp-perfume,
And I with my comrades there in the night.

While my sight that was bound in my eyes unclosed,
As to long panoramas of visions.

And I saw askant the armies,
I saw as in noiseless dreams hundreds of battle-flags,
Borne through the smoke of the battles and pierc'd with missiles I saw them,

And carried hither and yon through the smoke, and torn and bloody,
And at last but a few shreds left on the staffs, (and all in silence,)
And the staffs all splinter'd and broken.
I saw battle-corpses, myriads of them,
And the white skeletons of young men, I saw them,
I saw the debris and debris of all the slain soldiers of the war,
But I saw they were not as was thought,
They themselves were fully at rest, they suffer'd not,
The living remain'd and suffer'd, the mother suffer'd,
And the wife and the child and the musing comrade suffer'd,
And the armies that remain'd suffer'd.

16

Passing the visions, passing the night,
Passing, unloosing the hold of my comrades' hands,
Passing the song of the hermit bird and the tallying song of my soul,
Victorious song, death's outlet song, yet varying ever-altering song,
As low and wailing, yet clear the notes, rising and falling, flooding the night,
Sadly sinking and fainting, as warning and warning, and yet again bursting with joy,
Covering the earth and filling the spread of the heaven,
As that powerful psalm in the night I heard from recesses,
Passing, I leave thee lilac with heart-shaped leaves,
I leave thee there in the door-yard, blooming, returning with spring.

I cease from my song for thee,
From my gaze on thee in the west, fronting the west, communing with thee,
O comrade lustrous with silver face in the night.

Yet each to keep and all, retrievements out of the night,
The song, the wondrous chant of the gray-brown bird,
And the tallying chant, the echo arous'd in my soul,
With the lustrous and drooping star with the countenance full of woe.
With the holders holding my hand nearing the call of the bird,
Comrades mine and I in the midst, and their memory ever to keep, for the dead
 I loved so well,
For the sweetest, wisest soul of all my days and lands—and this for his dear sake,
Lilac and star and bird twined with the chant of my soul,
There in the fragrant pines and the cedars dusk and dim.

WALT WHITMAN

A Noiseless Patient Spider

A noiseless patient spider,
I mark'd where on a little promontory it stood isolated,
Mark'd how to explore the vacant vast surrounding,
It launch'd forth filament, filament, filament, out of itself,

Ever unreeling them, ever tirelessly speeding them.
And you O my soul where you stand,
Surrounded, detached, in measureless oceans of space,
Ceaselessly musing, venturing, throwing, seeking the spheres to connect them,
Till the bridge you will need be form'd, till the ductile anchor hold,
Till the gossamer thread you fling catch somewhere, O my soul.

OSCAR WILDE (1854–1900) was born in Dublin, Ireland, and died in Paris, France. In 1894, Wilde was accused of being a "sodomite" by the father of his aristocratic lover. Wilde sued for libel, but eventually found himself convicted and sentenced to two years at hard labor, serving the full two-year sentence at Reading Gaol. In prison, Wilde endured hard conditions, being in solitary confinement for all but one hour a day, but was allowed to read and write. He sought to bring the horror of England's prison conditions to public notice. After his release, Wilde produced "The Ballad of Reading Gaol," which proved to be his last completed work. It was published in 1898. For more information, see the head note to Oscar Wilde, *The Importance of Being Earnest*, in Chapter 9, "An Anthology of Drama."

Related Works: Forché, "The Colonel"; Hardy, "'Ah, are you digging on my grave?'" and "Lord Randall"; Poe, "The Raven"; Tichborne, "My prime of youth is but a frost of cares"; Kipling, "Danny Deever."

OSCAR WILDE

The Ballad of Reading Gaol

In Memoriam
C.T.W.
Sometime Trooper of the Royal Horse Guards.
Obiit HM Prison, Reading, Berkshire,
July 7th, 1896.

I

He did not wear his scarlet coat,
  For blood and wine are red,
And blood and wine were on his hands
  When they found him with the dead,
The poor dead woman whom he loved,
  And murdered in her bed.

He walked amongst the Trial Men
  In a suit of shabby gray;
A cricket cap was on his head,
  And his step seemed light and gay;
But I never saw a man who looked
  So wistfully at the day.

I never saw a man who looked
With such a wistful eye
Upon that little tent of blue
Which prisoners call the sky,
And at every drifting cloud that went
With sails of silver by.

I walked, with other souls in pain,
Within another ring,
And was wondering if the man had done
A great or little thing,
When a voice behind me whispered low,
'*That fellow's got to swing.*'

Dear Christ! the very prison walls
Suddenly seemed to reel,
And the sky above my head became
Like a casque of scorching steel;
And, though I was a soul in pain,
My pain I could not feel.

I only knew what hunted thought
Quickened his steps, and why
He looked upon the garish day
With such a wistful eye;
The man had killed the thing he loved,
And so he had to die.

⋆

Yet each man kills the thing he loves,
By each let this be heard,
Some do it with a bitter look,
Some with a flattering word,
The coward does it with a kiss,
The brave man with a sword!

Some kill their love when they are young,
And some when they are old;
Some strangle with the hands of Lust,
Some with the hands of Gold:
The kindest use a knife, because
The dead so soon grow cold.

Some love too little, some too long,
Some sell, and others buy;
Some do the deed with many tears,
And some without a sigh:
For each man kills the thing he loves,
Yet each man does not die.

⋆

He does not die a death of shame
On a day of dark disgrace,

Nor have a noose about his neck,
   Nor a cloth upon his face,
Nor drop feet foremost through the floor
   Into an empty space.

He does not sit with silent men
   Who watch him night and day;
Who watch him when he tries to weep,
   And when he tries to pray;
Who watch him lest himself should rob
   The prison of its prey.

He does not wake at dawn to see
   Dread figures throng his room,
The shivering Chaplain robed in white,
   The Sheriff stern with gloom,
And the Governor all in shiny black,
   With the yellow face of Doom.

He does not rise in piteous haste
   To put on convict-clothes,
While some coarse-mouthed Doctor gloats, and notes
   Each new and nerve-twitched pose,
Fingering a watch whose little ticks
   Are like horrible hammer-blows.

He does not know that sickening thirst
   That sands one's throat, before
The hangman with his gardener's gloves
   Slips through the padded door,
And binds one with three leathern thongs,
   That the throat may thirst no more.

He does not bend his head to hear
   The Burial Office read,
Nor, while the terror of his soul
   Tells him he is not dead,
Cross his own coffin, as he moves
   Into the hideous shed.

He does not stare upon the air
   Through a little roof of glass:
He does not pray with lips of clay
   For his agony to pass;
Nor feel upon his shuddering cheek
   The kiss of Caiaphas.

II

Six weeks our guardsman walked the yard,
   In the suit of shabby gray:
His cricket cap was on his head,
   And his step seemed light and gay,

But I never saw a man who looked
  So wistfully at the day.

I never saw a man who looked
  With such a wistful eye
Upon that little tent of blue
  Which prisoners call the sky,
And at every wandering cloud that trailed
  Its ravelled fleeces by.

He did not wring his hands, as do
  Those witless men who dare
To try to rear the changeling Hope
  In the cave of black Despair:
He only looked upon the sun,
  And drank the morning air.

He did not wring his hands nor weep,
  Nor did he peek or pine,
But he drank the air as though it held
  Some healthful anodyne;
With open mouth he drank the sun
  As though it had been wine!

And I and all the souls in pain,
  Who tramped the other ring,
Forgot if we ourselves had done
  A great or little thing,
And watched with gaze of dull amaze
  The man who had to swing.

And strange it was to see him pass
  With a step so light and gay,
And strange it was to see him look
  So wistfully at the day,
And strange it was to think that he
  Had such a debt to pay.

⋆

For oak and elm have pleasant leaves
  That in the spring-time shoot:
But grim to see is the gallows-tree,
  With its adder-bitten root,
And, green or dry, a man must die
  Before it bears its fruit!

The loftiest place is that seat of grace
  For which all worldlings try:
But who would stand in hempen band
  Upon a scaffold high,
And through a murderer's collar take
  His last look at the sky?

It is sweet to dance to violins
    When Love and Life are fair:
To dance to flutes, to dance to lutes
    Is delicate and rare:
But it is not sweet with nimble feet
    To dance upon the air!

So with curious eyes and sick surmise
    We watched him day by day,
And wondered if each one of us
    Would end the self-same way,
For none can tell to what red Hell
    His sightless soul may stray.

★

At last the dead man walked no more
    Amongst the Trial Men,
And I knew that he was standing up
    In the black dock's dreadful pen,
And that never would I see his face
    In God's sweet world again.

Like two doomed ships that pass in storm
    We had crossed each other's way:
But we made no sign, we said no word,
    We had no word to say;
For we did not meet in the holy night,
    But in the shameful day.

A prison wall was round us both,
    Two outcast men we were:
The world had thrust us from its heart,
    And God from out His care:
And the iron gin that waits for Sin
    Had caught us in its snare.

III

In Debtor's Yard the stones are hard,
    And the dripping wall is high,
So it was there he took the air
    Beneath the leaden sky,
And by each side a Warder walked,
    For fear the man might die.

Or else he sat with those who watched
    His anguish night and day;
Who watched him when he rose to weep,
    And when he crouched to pray;
Who watched him lest himself should rob
    Their scaffold of its prey.

The Governor was strong upon
  The Regulations Act:
The Doctor said that Death was but
  A scientific fact:
And twice a day the Chaplain called,
  And left a little tract.

And twice a day he smoked his pipe,
  And drank his quart of beer:
His soul was resolute, and held
  No hiding-place for fear;
He often said that he was glad
  The hangman's hands were near.

But why he said so strange a thing
  No Warder dared to ask:
For he to whom a watcher's doom
  Is given as his task,
Must set a lock upon his lips,
  And make his face a mask.

Or else he might be moved, and try
  To comfort or console:
And what should Human Pity do
  Pent up in Murderers' Hole?
What word of grace in such a place
  Could help a brother's soul?

*

With slouch and swing around the ring
  We trod the Fools' Parade!
We did not care: we knew we were
  The Devil's Own Brigade:
And shaven head and feet of lead
  Make a merry masquerade.

We tore the tarry rope to shreds
  With blunt and bleeding nails;
We rubbed the doors, and scrubbed the floors,
  And cleaned the shining rails:
And, rank by rank, we soaped the plank,
  And clattered with the pails.

We sewed the sacks, we broke the stones,
  We turned the dusty drill:
We banged the tins, and bawled the hymns,
  And sweated on the mill:
But in the heart of every man
  Terror was lying still.

So still it lay that every day
  Crawled like a weed-clogged waved:

And we forgot the bitter lot
  That waits for fool and knave,
Till once, as we tramped in from work,
  We passed an open grave.

With yawning mouth the yellow hole
  Gaped for a living thing;
The very mud cried out for blood
  To the thirsty asphalte ring:
And we knew that ere one dawn grew fair
  Some prisoner had to swing.

Right in we went, with soul intent
  On Death and Dread and Doom:
The hangman, with his little bag,
  Went shuffling through the gloom:
And each man trembled as he crept
  Into his numbered tomb.

That night the empty corridors
  Were full of forms of Fear,
And up and down the iron town
  Stole feet we could not hear,
And through the bars that hide the stars
  White faces seemed to peer.

He lay as one who lies and dreams
  In a pleasant meadow-land,
The watchers watched him as he slept,
  And could not understand
How one could sleep so sweet a sleep
  With a hangman close at hand.

But there is no sleep when men must weep
  Who never yet have wept:
So we—the fool, the fraud, the knave—
  That endless vigil kept,
And through each brain on hands of pain
  Another's terror crept.

★

Alas! it is a fearful thing
  To feel another's guilt!
For, right within, the sword of Sin
  Pierced to its poisoned hilt,
And as molten lead were the tears we shed
  For the blood we had not spilt.

The Warders with their shoes of felt
  Crept by each padlocked door,
And peeped and saw, with eyes of awe,
  Gray figures on the floor,

And wondered why men knelt to pray
  Who never prayed before.

All through the night we knelt and prayed,
  Mad mourners of a corse!
The troubled plumes of midnight were
  The plumes upon a hearse:
And bitter wine upon a sponge
  Was the savour of Remorse.

⋆

The gray cock crew, the red cock crew,
  But never came the day:
And crooked shapes of Terror crouched,
  In the corners where we lay:
And each evil sprite that walks by night
  Before us seemed to play.

They glided past, they glided fast,
  Like travellers through a mist:
They mocked the moon in a rigadoon
  Of delicate turn and twist,
And with formal pace and loathsome grace
  The phantoms kept their tryst.

With mop and mow, we saw them go,
  Slim shadows hand in hand:
About, about, in ghostly rout
  They trod a saraband:
And the damned grotesques made arabesques,
  Like the wind upon the sand!

With the pirouettes of marionettes,
  They tripped on pointed tread:
But with flutes of Fear they filled the ear,
  As their grisly masque they led,
And loud they sang, and long they sang,
  For they sang to wake the dead.

"Oho!" they cried, *"The world is wide,*
  But fettered limbs go lame!
And once, or twice, to throw the dice
  Is a gentlemanly game,
But he does not win who plays with Sin
  In the secret House of Shame."

⋆

No things of air these antics were,
  That frolicked with such glee:
To men whose lives were held in gyves,
  And whose feet might not go free,
Ah! wounds of Christ! they were living things,
  Most terrible to see.

Around, around, they waltzed and wound;
Some wheeled in smirking pairs;
With the mincing step of a demirep
Some sidled up the stairs:
And with subtle sneer, and fawning leer,
Each helped us at our prayers.

★

The morning wind began to moan,
But still the night went on:
Through its giant loom the web of gloom
Crept till each thread was spun:
And, as we prayed, we grew afraid
Of the Justice of the Sun.

The moaning wind went wandering round
The weeping prison-wall:
Till like a wheel of turning steel
We felt the minutes crawl:
O moaning wind! what had we done
To have such a seneschal?

At last I saw the shadowed bars,
Like a lattice wrought in lead,
Move right across the whitewashed wall
That faced my three-plank bed,
And I knew that somewhere in the world
God's dreadful dawn was red.

★

At six o'clock we cleaned our cells,
At seven all was still,
But the sough and swing of a mighty wing
The prison seemed to fill,
For the Lord of Death with icy breath
Had entered in to kill.

He did not pass in purple pomp,
Nor ride a moon-white steed.
Three yards of cord and a sliding board
Are all the gallows' need:
So with rope of shame the Herald came
To do the secret deed.

★

We were as men who through a fen
Of filthy darkness grope:
We did not dare to breathe a prayer,
Or to give our anguish scope:
Something was dead in each of us,
And what was dead was Hope.

For Man's grim Justice goes its way,
   And will not swerve aside:
It slays the weak, it slays the strong,
   It has a deadly stride:
With iron heel it slays the strong,
   The monstrous parricide!

⋆

We waited for the stroke of eight:
   Each tongue was thick with thirst:
For the stroke of eight is the stroke of Fate
   That makes a man accursed,
And Fate will use a running noose
   For the best man and the worst.

We had no other thing to do,
   Save to wait for the sign to come:
So, like things of stone in a valley lone,
   Quiet we sat and dumb:
But each man's heart beat thick and quick,
   Like a madman on a drum!

⋆

With sudden shock the prison-clock
   Smote on the shivering air,
And from all the gaol rose up a wail
   Of impotent despair,
Like the sound that frightened marshes hear
   From some leper in his lair.

And as one sees most fearful things
   In the crystal of a dream,
We saw the greasy hempen rope
   Hooked to the blackened beam,
And heard the prayer the hangman's snare
   Strangled into a scream.

And all the woe that moved him so
   That he gave that bitter cry,
And the wild regrets, and the bloody sweats,
   None knew so well as I:
For he who lives more lives than one
   More deaths than one must die.

IV

There is no chapel on the day
   On which they hang a man:
The Chaplain's heart is far too sick,
   Or his face is far too wan,
Or there is that written in his eyes
   Which none should look upon.

So they kept us close till nigh on noon,
  And then they rang the bell,
And the Warders with their jingling keys
  Opened each listening cell,
And down the iron stair we tramped,
  Each from his separate Hell.

Out into God's sweet air we went,
  But not in wonted way,
For this man's face was white with fear,
  And that man's face was gray,
And I never saw sad men who looked
  So wistfully at the day.

I never saw sad men who looked
  With such a wistful eye
Upon that little tent of blue
  We prisoners called the sky,
And at every careless cloud that passed
  In happy freedom by.

But there were those amongst us all
  Who walked with downcast head,
And knew that, had each got his due,
  They should have died instead;
He had but killed a thing that lived,
  Whilst they had killed the dead.

For he who sins a second time
  Wakes a dead soul to pain,
And draws it from its spotted shroud,
  And makes it bleed again,
And makes it bleed great gouts of blood,
  And makes it bleed in vain!

⋆

Like ape or clown, in monstrous garb
  With crooked arrows starred,
Silently we went round and round
  The slippery asphalte yard;
Silently we went round and round,
  And no man spoke a word.

Silently we went round and round,
  And through each hollow mind
The Memory of dreadful things
  Rushed like a dreadful wind,
And Horror stalked before each man,
  And Terror crept behind.

⋆

The Warders strutted up and down,
  And kept their herd of brutes,
Their uniforms were spick and span,
  And they wore their Sunday suits,
But we knew the work they had been at,
  By the quicklime on their boots.

For where a grave had opened wide,
  There was no grave at all:
Only a stretch of mud and sand
  By the hideous prison-wall,
And a little heap of burning lime,
  That the man should have his pall.

For he has a pall, this wretched man,
  Such as few men can claim:
Deep down below a prison-yard,
  Naked for greater shame,
He lies, with fetters on each foot,
  Wrapt in a sheet of flame!

And all the while the burning lime
  Eats flesh and bone away,
It eats the brittle bone by night,
  And the soft flesh by day,
It eats the flesh and bone by turns,
  But it eats the heart alway.

⋆

For three long years they will not sow
  Or root or seedling there:
For three long years the unblessed spot
  Will sterile be and bare,
And look upon the wondering sky
  With unreproachful stare.

They think a murderer's heart would taint
  Each simple seed they sow.
It is not true! God's kindly earth
  Is kindlier than men know,
And the red rose would but blow more red,
  The white rose whiter blow.

Out of his mouth a red, red rose!
  Out of his heart a white!
For who can say by what strange way,
  Christ brings His will to light,
Since the barren staff the pilgrim bore
  Bloomed in the great Pope's sight?

⋆

But neither milk-white rose nor red
May bloom in prison air;
The shard, the pebble, and the flint,
Are what they give us there:
For flowers have been known to heal
A common man's despair.

So never will wine-red rose or white,
Petal by petal, fall
On that stretch of mud and sand that lies
By the hideous prison-wall,
To tell the men who tramp the yard
That God's Son died for all.

*

Yet though the hideous prison-wall
Still hems him round and round,
And a spirit may not walk by night
That is with fetters bound,
And a spirit may but weep that lies
In such unholy ground.

He is at peace—this wretched man—
At peace, or will be soon:
There is no thing to make him mad,
Nor does Terror walk at noon,
For the lampless Earth in which he lies
Has neither Sun nor Moon.

*

They hanged him as a beast is hanged:
They did not even toll
A requiem that might have brought
Rest to his startled soul,
But hurriedly they took him out,
And hid him in a hole.

They stripped him of his canvas clothes,
And gave him to the flies:
They mocked the swollen purple throat,
And the stark and staring eyes:
And with laughter loud they heaped the shroud
In which their convict lies.

The Chaplain would not kneel to pray
By his dishonoured grave:
Nor mark it with that blessed Cross
That Christ for sinners gave,
Because the man was one of those
Whom Christ came down to save.

Yet all is well; he has but passed
To Life's appointed bourne:

And alien tears will fill for him
  Pity's long-broken urn,
For his mourners will be outcast men,
  And outcasts always mourn.

V

I know not whether Laws be right,
  Or whether Laws be wrong;
All that we know who lie in gaol
  Is that the wall is strong;
And that each day is like a year,
  A year whose days are long.

But this I know, that every Law
  That men have made for Man,
Since first Man took his brother's life,
  And the sad world began,
But straws the wheat and saves the chaff
  With a most evil fan.

This too I know—and wise it were
  If each could know the same—
That every prison that men build
  Is built with bricks of shame,
And bound with bars lest Christ should see
  How men their brothers maim.

With bars they blur the gracious moon,
  And blind the goodly sun:
And they do well to hide their Hell,
  For in it things are done
That Son of God nor son of Man
  Ever should look upon!

⋆

The vilest deeds like poison weeds
  Bloom well in prison-air:
It is only what is good in Man
  That wastes and withers there:
Pale Anguish keeps the heavy gate,
  And the Warder is Despair.

For they starve the little frightened child
  Till it weeps both night and day:
And they scourge the weak, and flog the fool,
  And gibe the old and gray,
And some grow mad, and all grow bad,
  And none a word may say.

Each narrow cell in which we dwell
  Is a foul and dark latrine,

And the fetid breath of living Death
Chokes up each grated screen,
And all, but Lust, is turned to dust
In Humanity's machine.

The brackish water that we drink
Creeps with a loathsome slime,
And the bitter bread they weigh in scales
Is full of chalk and lime,
And Sleep will not lie down, but walks
Wild-eyed, and cries to Time.

⋆

But though lean Hunger and green Thirst
Like asp with adder fight,
We have little care of prison fare,
For what chills and kills outright
Is that every stone one lifts by day
Becomes one's heart by night.

With midnight always in one's heart,
And twilight in one's cell,
We turn the crank, or tear the rope,
Each in his separate Hell,
And the silence is more awful far
Than the sound of a brazen bell.

And never a human voice comes near
To speak a gentle word:
And the eye that watches through the door
Is pitiless and hard:
And by all forgot, we rot and rot,
With soul and body marred.

And thus we rust Life's iron chain
Degraded and alone:
And some men curse, and some men weep,
And some men make no moan:
But God's eternal Laws are kind
And break the heart of stone.

⋆

And every human heart that breaks,
In prison-cell or yard,
Is as that broken box that gave
Its treasure to the Lord,
And filled the unclean leper's house
With the scent of costliest nard.

Ah! happy they whose hearts can break
And peace of pardon win!

How else may man make straight his plan
  And cleanse his soul from Sin?
How else but through a broken heart
  May Lord Christ enter in?

⋆

And he of the swollen purple throat,
  And the stark and staring eyes,
Waits for the holy hands that took
  The Thief to Paradise;
And a broken and a contrite heart
  The Lord will not despise.

The man in red who reads the Law
  Gave him three weeks of life,
Three little weeks in which to heal
  His soul of his soul's strife,
And cleanse from every blot of blood
  The hand that held the knife.

And with tears of blood he cleansed the hand,
  The hand that held the steel:
For only blood can wipe out blood,
  And only tears can heal:
And the crimson stain that was of Cain
  Became Christ's snow-white seal.

VI

In Reading gaol by Reading town
  There is a pit of shame,
And in it lies a wretched man
  Eaten by teeth of flame,
In a burning winding-sheet he lies,
  And his grave has got no name.

And there, till Christ call forth the dead,
  In silence let him lie:
No need to waste the foolish tear,
  Or heave the windy sigh:
The man had killed the thing he loved,
  And so he had to die.

And all men kill the thing they love,
  By all let this be heard,
Some do it with a bitter look,
  Some with a flattering word,
The coward does it with a kiss,
  The brave man with a sword!

ANNA AKHMATOVA (1889–1966). A Russian poet and translator, Anna Andreevna Gorenko grew up as a privileged aristocrat. As part of the bohemian, intellectual scene in St. Petersburg before World War I, she had many lovers and was married at least three times. In her long life, she survived serious deprivation under both Lenin and Stalin. Known for her "tragic beauty," she took the name Akhmatova as a pen name. Her poetry is noted for its **elliptical** and **concrete** style and the suggestion of conflicted emotions. This translation of her poem, "Lot's Wife" (ca. 1915), was published in *Poems of Anna Akhmatova* in 1973. In it she adopts the perspective of Lot's wife from the biblical story in Genesis 19.

Related Works: Chopin, "The Story of an Hour"; Steinbeck, "The Chrysanthemums"; Atwood, "Siren's Song"; Yeats, "Leda and the Swan"; Auden, "Musée des Beaux Arts"; Sophocles, *Antigone*; Ibsen, *A Dollhouse*.

ANNA AKHMATOVA

Lot's Wife

And the just man trailed God's shining agent,
over a black mountain, in his giant track,
while a restless voice kept harrying his woman:
"It's not too late, you can still look back

at the red towers of your native Sodom,
the square where once you sang, the spinning-shed,
at the empty windows set in the tall house
where sons and daughters blessed your marriage-bed."

A single glance: a sudden dart of pain
stitching her eyes before she made a sound . . .
Her body flaked into transparent salt,
and her swift legs rooted to the ground.

Who will grieve for this woman? Does she not seem
too insignificant for our concern?
Yet in my heart I never will deny her,
Who suffered death because she chose to turn.

SHERMAN ALEXIE (b. 1966) is a Native American (Spokane and Coeur d'Alene) poet, novelist, short story writer, and essayist. He also collaborated on the film *Smoke Signals*, which was derived from one of his stories, *The Lone Ranger and Tonto Fistfight in Heaven*, which was published in *Atlantic Monthly* in 1993. "Reservation Love Song" appears in the collection *The Business of Fancydancing: Stories and Poems* (1992). Alexie's stories and poems often serve to debunk stereotypes of Native Americans.

Related Works: Mukherjee, "A Wife's Story"; Cofer, "Arturo's Flight"; McKay, "America"; Forché, "The Colonel"; Erdrich, "A Love Medicine," "Family Reunion," and "Windigo"; Komunyakaa, "My Father's Love Letters"; Garcia, "Why I Left the Church."

SHERMAN ALEXIE

Reservation Love Song

I can meet you
in Springdale buy you beer
& take you home
in my one-eyed Ford

I can pay your rent
on HUD house get you free
food from the BIA
get your teeth fixed at IHS

I can buy you alcohol
& not drink it all
while you're away I won't fuck
any of your cousins

if I don't get too drunk
I can bring old blankets
to sleep with in winter
they smell like grandmother

hands digging up roots
they have powerful magic
we can sleep good
we can sleep warm

MAYA ANGELOU (b. 1928) grew up in Missouri and Arkansas. She is perhaps best known for her autobiographical novel *I Know Why the Caged Bird Sings* (1969), but she has directed films, published several volumes of poetry, worked nearly a decade as a journalist in Africa, and acted and sung on stage. She currently holds a Chair at Wake Forest University. The poem "Still I Rise," from the collection *And Still I Rise* (1978), makes use of **rhyme**, repetition, and her distinctive **persona**.

Related Works: Akhmatova, "Lot's Wife"; Brooks, "The mother"; Bishop, "The Fish"; Rich, "Diving into the Wreck"; Lorde, "Hanging Fire"; Whitman, "Oh Captain! my Captain!"; Behn, "On Her Loving Two Equally."

MAYA ANGELOU

Still I Rise

You may write me down in history
With your bitter, twisted lies,
You may trod me in the very dirt
But still, like dust, I'll rise.

Does my sassiness upset you?
Why are you beset with gloom?
'Cause I walk like I've got oil wells
Pumping in my living room.

Just like moons and like suns,
With the certainty of tides,
Just like hopes springing high,
Still I'll rise.

Did you want to see me broken?
Bowed head and lowered eyes?
Shoulders falling down like teardrops,
Weakened by my soulful cries.

Does my haughtiness offend you?
Don't you take it awful hard
'Cause I laugh like I've got gold mines
Diggin' in my own back yard.

You may shoot me with your words,
You may cut me with your eyes,
You may kill me with your hatefulness,
But still, like air, I'll rise.

Does my sexiness upset you?
Does it come as a surprise
That I dance like I've got diamonds
At the meeting of my thighs?

Out of the huts of history's shame
I rise
Up from a past that's rooted in pain
I rise
I'm a black ocean, leaping and wide,
Welling and swelling I bear in the tide.

Leaving behind nights of terror and fear
I rise
Into a daybreak that's wondrously clear

I rise
Bringing the gifts that my ancestors gave,
I am the dream and the hope of the slave.
I rise
I rise
I rise.

GLORIA ANZALDÚA (1942–2004) described herself as a "chicana dyke-feminist, tejana patlache poet, writer, and cultural theorist." She grew up as a migrant worker in South Texas and Arkansas but eventually attended college, going on to complete an M.A. at the University of Texas and to teach writing. Her two major collections, *This Bridge Called My Back* (1981) and *Borderlands: La Frontera / The New Mestiza* (1987), are written in combinations of several English and Spanish **dialects** and deal often with the literary, spiritual, and cultural gaps and spaces between bordering groups. She coined the term *nepantlera* to describe people of vision who inhabit the borders between cultural worlds and who are able to use this position to transform people on both sides of the border. In the preface to the 1983 edition of *This Bridge Called My Back*, she writes, "Caminante, no hay puentes, se hace puentes al andar. *Voyager, there are no bridges, one builds them as one walks.*"

Related Works: Alexie, "Reservation Love Song"; Dunbar, "We wear the mask"; Longfellow, "The Jewish Cemetery at Newport."

GLORIA ANZALDÚA

horse

(para la gente de *Hargill, Texas)*

Great horse running in the fields
come thundering toward
the outstretched hands
nostrils flaring at the corn
only it was knives in the hidden hands
can a horse smell tempered steel?

Anoche some kids cut up a horse
it was night and the *pueblo* slept
the Mexicans mutter among themselves:
they hobbled the two front legs
the two hind legs, kids aged sixteen
but they're *gringos*
and the sheriff won't do a thing

he'd just say boys will be boys
just following their instincts.

But it's the mind that kills
the animal the *mexicanos* murmur
killing it would have been a mercy
black horse running in the dark
came thundering toward
the outstretched hands
nostrils flaring at the smell
only it was knives in the hidden hands
did it pray all night for morning?

It was the owner came running
30-30 in his hand
put the *caballo* out of its pain
the Chicanos shake their heads
turn away some rich father
fished out his wallet
held out the folds of green
as if green could staunch red
pools dripping from the ribbons
on the horse's flanks
could cast up testicles
grow back the ears on the horse's head
no ears of corn but sheaths
hiding blades of steel
earth drinking blood sun rusting it
in that small Texas town
the *mexicanos* shuffle their feet
shut their faces stare at the ground.

Dead horse neighing in the night
come thundering toward the open faces
hooves iron-shod hurling lightning

only it is red red in the moonlight
in their sleep the *gringos* cry out
the *mexicanos* mumble if you're Mexican
you are born old.

JOHN ASHBERY (b. 1927), a native of upstate New York, has authored over twenty books of poetry, a collection of plays, a novel, and a great deal of art criticism. He lived and worked as an art critic in Paris for many years and, by most accounts, his poetry reflects the motifs of modern cubist and **surrealist** art. In "Paradoxes and Oxymorons" (1981), he pursues a favorite question—do you speak language or does it speak you?

Related Works: Dickinson, "Hope is the thing with feathers"; Bishop, "One Art" and "The Fish"; cummings, "since feeling is first"; Graham, "Reading Plato."

JOHN ASHBERY

Paradoxes and Oxymorons

This poem is concerned with language on a very plain level.
Look at it talking to you. You look out a window
Or pretend to fidget. You have it but you don't have it.
You miss it, it misses you. You miss each other.

The poem is sad because it wants to be yours, and cannot.
What's a plain level? It is that and other things,
Bringing a system of them into play. Play?
Well, actually, yes, but I consider play to be

A deeper outside thing, a dreamed role-pattern,
As in the division of grace these long August days
Without proof. Open-ended. And before you know
It gets lost in the steam and chatter of typewriters.

It has been played once more. I think you exist only
To tease me into doing it, on your level, and then you aren't there
Or have adopted a different attitude. And the poem
Has set me softly down beside you. The poem is you.

MARGARET ATWOOD (b. 1939), a Canadian poet, completed degrees at University of Toronto and at Radcliff, but left Harvard before finishing her Ph.D. She self-published her first collection of poetry (*Double Persephone*, 1961) when she was nineteen, and since then, has produced over seventy texts, including novels, poetry collections, and works of cultural and literary criticism. Atwood addresses feminist themes in most of her work, using treatments that combine fantasy, myth, magic, and realism. In both "You fit into me" (1971), which makes a startling use of **simile**, and "Siren Song" (1976), in which Atwood adopts the **persona** of a mythical siren, Atwood comments pointedly on gender inequalities.

Related Works: Chopin, "The Story of an Hour"; Behn, "On Her Loving Two Equally"; Glück, "Circe's Power"; Levertov, "O Taste and See"; Parker, "One Perfect Rose"; Piercy, "Barbie Doll"; Norman, *'Night Mother*; Ibsen, *A Dollhouse.*

MARGARET ATWOOD

You Fit into Me

you fit into me
like a hook into an eye

a fish hook
an open eye

MARGARET ATWOOD

Siren Song

This is the one song everyone
would like to learn: the song
that is irresistible:

the song that forces men
to leap overboard in squadrons
even though they see the beached skulls

the song nobody knows
because anyone who has heard it
is dead, and the others can't remember.

Shall I tell you the secret
and if I do, will you get me
out of this bird suit?

I don't enjoy it here
squatting on this island
looking picturesque and mythical

with these two feathery maniacs,
I don't enjoy singing
this trio, fatal and valuable.

I will tell the secret to you,
to you, only to you.
Come closer. This song

is a cry for help: Help me!
Only you, only you can,
you are unique

at last. Alas
it is a boring song
but it works every time.

W. H. (WYSTAN HUGH) AUDEN (1907–1973), often ranked as one of the greatest and most prolific twentieth-century poets, grew up as part of a comfortably upper middle-class doctor's family in England. After graduating from Oxford, he taught school and continued to write. In 1939, he moved to the United States. Both of the poems included here, "The Unknown Citizen" and "Musée des Beaux Arts," were published in 1940 in *Another Time*, which by all accounts includes some of his greatest poetry. Each of the poems presented here shows Auden's unusual combination of seriousness and playful **satire** and each addresses Auden's favorite themes—loss, exile, detachment, and society's apathy. A master of many traditional

Pieter Brueghel, "Landscape with the Fall of Icarus"

forms, including **ballads, odes, elegies**, the **epithalamium, villanelles**, and **sonnets**, Auden experimented throughout his career.

Related Works: Anonymous Ballads; Herrick, "To the Virgins"; Swift, "A Description of the Morning"; Owen, "Dulce et Decorum Est"; Robinson, "Richard Cory"; MacNeice, "Snow"; Eliot, "The Love Song of J. Alfred Prufrock"; Miller, *Death of a Salesman.*

W. H. AUDEN

Musée des Beaux Arts

About suffering they were never wrong,
The Old Masters: how well they understood
Its human position: how it takes place
While someone else is eating or opening a window or just walking dully along;
How, when the aged are reverently, passionately waiting
For the miraculous birth, there always must be
Children who did not specially want it to happen, skating
On a pond at the edge of the wood:
They never forgot
That even the dreadful martyrdom must run its course
Anyhow in a corner, some untidy spot
Where the dogs go on with their doggy life and the torturer's horse

Scratches its innocent behind on a tree.
In Brueghel's *Icarus*, for instance: how everything turns away
Quite leisurely from the disaster; the ploughman may
Have heard the splash, the forsaken cry,
But for him it was not an important failure; the sun shone
As it had to on the white legs disappearing into the green
Water; and the expensive delicate ship that must have seen
Something amazing, a boy falling out of the sky,
Had somewhere to get to and sailed calmly on.

W. H. AUDEN

The Unknown Citizen

To JS/07/M/378
This Marble Monument is Erected by the State

He was found by the Bureau of Statistics to be
One against whom there was no official complaint,
And all the reports on his conduct agree
That, in the modern sense of an old-fashioned word, he was a saint,
For in everything he did he served the Greater Community.
Except for the War till the day he retired
He worked in a factory and never got fired,
But satisfied his employers, Fudge Motors Inc.
Yet he wasn't a scab or odd in his views,
For his Union reports that he paid his dues,
(Our report on his Union shows it was sound)
And our Social Psychology workers found
That he was popular with his mates and liked a drink.
The Press are convinced that he bought a paper every day
And that his reactions to advertisements were normal in every way.
Policies taken out in his name prove that he was fully insured,
And his Health-card shows he was once in hospital but left it cured.
Both Producers Research and High-Grade Living declare
He was fully sensible to the advantages of the Installment Plan
And had everything necessary to the Modern Man,
A gramophone, a radio, a car and a frigidaire.
Our researchers into Public Opinion are content
That he held the proper opinions for the time of year;
When there was peace, he was for peace; when there was war, he went.
He was married and added five children to the population,
Which our Eugenist says was the right number for a parent of his generation,
And our teachers report that he never interfered with their education.
Was he free? Was he happy? The question is absurd:
Had anything been wrong, we should certainly have heard.

WENDELL BERRY (b. 1934), primarily known for his environmental essays and interest in alternative agriculture, lives with his family on a farm in Kentucky. He received both his B.A. and M.A. in English at the University of Kentucky and then spent a year at Stanford University on a fellowship. Following a brief stint at New York University, Berry returned to the University of Kentucky as a faculty member. In 1977, as part of his commitment to personal action and responsibility, he left his professorship to work full time as a writer and farmer. Berry has published novels, short story collections, fourteen books of poems, and sixteen volumes of essays. He currently works for Rodale Press on the magazine *Organic Gardening*. The brief **lyric** poems "The Peace of Wild Things" and "Another Descent" (*Collected Poems*, 1985) focus on human relationships within nature.

Related Works: Medieval Lyrical Poetry; Blake, "The Lamb"; Wordsworth, "I wandered lonely as a cloud"; Frost, "Birches"; Ginsberg, "Howl."

WENDELL BERRY

Another Descent

Through the weeks of deep snow
we walked above the ground
on fallen sky, as though we did
not come of root and leaf, as though
we had only air and weather
for our difficult home.
But now
as March warms, and the rivulets
run like birdsong on the slopes,
and the branches of light sing in the hills,
slowly we return to earth.

WENDELL BERRY

The Peace of Wild Things

When despair for the world grows in me
and I wake in the night at the least sound
in fear of what my life and my children's lives may be,
I go and lie down where the wood drake
rests in his beauty on the water, and the great heron feeds.
I come into the peace of wild things
who do not tax their lives with forethought
of grief. I come into the presence of still water.
And I feel above me the day-blind stars

waiting with their light. For a time
I rest in the grace of the world, and am free.

ELIZABETH BISHOP (1911–1979) lost her father before she was one, and her mother was committed to a mental institution before she was five. Eventually, she was taken in by her father's parents, who were quite wealthy, and she attended excellent private schools and graduated from Vassar in 1934. She traveled widely and lived in Brazil and then Key West for many years. In her poetry, Bishop sought out and used nearly every possible form—from **prose poems** to **free verse** to **sonnets, sestinas**, and **villanelles**. Despite some of her poems' formal complexity, as in the following sestina, Bishop's craft tends to efface rather than emphasize the formal elements. "One Art," a villanelle, responds to the death of her lover and partner.

Related Works: Porter, "The Jilting of Granny Weatherall"; Bambara, "The Lesson"; Kincaid, "Girl"; Herbert, "Easter Wings"; Dickinson, "I heard a fly buzz"; Stevens, "Thirteen Ways of Looking at a Blackbird"; Rios, "Nani"; Mayers, "All-American Sestina"; Hacker, "Villanelle for D.G.B."; Yau, "Chinese Villanelle."

ELIZABETH BISHOP

The Fish

I caught a tremendous fish
and held him beside the boat
half out of water, with my hook
fast in a corner of his mouth.
He didn't fight.
He hadn't fought at all.
He hung a grunting weight,
battered and venerable
and homely. Here and there
his brown skin hung in strips
like ancient wall-paper,
and its pattern of darker brown
was like wall-paper:
shapes like full-blown roses
stained and lost through age.
He was speckled with barnacles,
fine rosettes of lime,
and infested
with tiny white sea-lice,
and underneath two or three
rags of green weed hung down.
While his gills were breathing in
the terrible oxygen
—the frightening gills,

fresh and crisp with blood,
that can cut so badly—
I thought of the coarse white flesh
packed in like feathers,
the big bones and the little bones,
the dramatic reds and blacks
of his shiny entrails,
and the pink swim-bladder
like a big peony.
I looked into his eyes
which were far larger than mine
but shallower, and yellowed,
the irises backed and packed
with tarnished tinfoil
seen through the lenses
of old scratched isinglass.
They shifted a little, but not
to return my stare.
—It was more like the tipping
of an object toward the light.
I admired his sullen face,
the mechanism of his jaw,
and then I saw
that from his lower lip
—if you could call it a lip—
grim, wet, and weapon-like,
hung five old pieces of fish-line,
or four and a wire leader
with the swivel still attached,
with all their five big hooks
grown firmly in his mouth.
A green line, frayed at the end
where he broke it, two heavier lines.
and a fine black thread
still crimped from the strain and snap
when it broke and he got away.
Like medals with their ribbons
frayed and wavering,
a five-haired beard of wisdom
trailing from his aching jaw.
I stared and stared
and victory filled up
the little rented boat,
from the pool of bilge
where oil had spread a rainbow
around the rusted engine
to the bailer rusted orange,
the sun-cracked thwarts,
the oarlocks on their strings,

the gunnels—until everything
was rainbow, rainbow, rainbow!
And I let the fish go.

ELIZABETH BISHOP

One Art

The art of losing isn't hard to master:
so many things seem filled with the intent
to be lost that their loss is no disaster.

Lose something every day. Accept the fluster
of lost door keys, the hour badly spent.
The art of losing isn't hard to master.

Then practice losing farther, losing faster:
places, and names, and where it was you meant
to travel. None of these will bring disaster.

I lost my mother's watch. And look! my last, or
next-to-last, of three loved houses went.
The art of losing isn't hard to master.

I lost two cities, lovely ones. And, vaster,
some realms I owned, two rivers, a continent.
I miss them, but it wasn't a disaster.

—Even losing you (the joking voice, a gesture
I love) I shan't have lied. It's evident
the art of losing's not too hard to master
though it may look like (*Write* it!) like disaster.

ELIZABETH BISHOP

Sestina

September rain falls on the house.
In the failing light, the old grandmother
sits in the kitchen with the child
beside the Little Marvel Stove,
reading the jokes from the almanac,
laughing and talking to hide her tears.

She thinks that her equinoctial tears
and the rain that beats on the roof of the house
were both foretold by the almanac,

but only known to a grandmother.
The iron kettle sings on the stove.
She cuts some bread and says to the child,

It's time for tea now; but the child
is watching the teakettle's small hard tears
dance like mad on the hot black stove,
the way the rain must dance on the house.
Tidying up, the old grandmother
hangs up the clever almanac

on its string. Birdlike, the almanac
hovers half open above the child,
hovers above the old grandmother
and her teacup full of dark brown tears.
She shivers and says she thinks the house
feels chilly, and puts more wood in the stove.

It was to be, says the Marvel Stove.
I know what I know, says the almanac.
With crayons the child draws a rigid house
and a winding pathway. Then the child
puts in a man with buttons like tears
and shows it proudly to the grandmother.

But secretly, while the grandmother
busies herself about the stove,
the little moons fall down like tears
from between the pages of the almanac
into the flower bed the child
has carefully placed in the front of the house.

Time to plant tears, says the almanac.
The grandmother sings to the marvelous stove
and the child draws another inscrutable house.

LOUISE BOGAN (1897–1970) was born in Maine and briefly attended Boston University before marrying and having a child. Her unhappy marriage ended with her husband's death in 1922; shortly afterward, her child was taken in by her parents when Bogan suffered repeated bouts of depression. In 1931, she was hired by *The New Yorker* as its poetry editor, which provided her with economic support for the next thirty-eight years. She would eventually publish four more collections of poetry and a major critical work, *Achievement in American Poetry, 1900–1950* (1951), among other translations and critical essays. The poem, "Women," was published in her first collection of poetry, *Body of This Death: Poems* (1923); "The Dream" was published in 1968 in her last collection, *The Blue Estuaries: Poems, 1923–1968*. Bogan's use of traditional **lyric** forms and impersonal, metaphysical **personae** set her apart from the experimental, **confessional** trends in the poetry of her time.

Related Works: Donne, Holy Sonnet 14; Dickinson, "Hope is the thing with feathers"; Dunbar, "We wear the mask"; Rich, "Diving into the Wreck"; Levertov, "O Taste and See"; Roethke, "The Waking."

LOUISE BOGAN

Women

Women have no wilderness in them,
They are provident instead.
Content in the tight hot cell of their hearts
To eat dusty bread.

They do not see cattle cropping red winter grass,
They do not hear
Snow water going down under culverts
Shallow and clear.

They wait, when they should turn to journeys,
They stiffen, when they should bend.
They use against themselves that benevolence
To which no man is friend.

They cannot think of so many crops to a field
Or of clean wood cleft by an axe.
Their love is an eager meaninglessness
Too tense, or too lax.

They hear in every whisper that speaks to them
A shout and a cry.
As like as not, when they take life over their door-sills
They should let it go by.

LOUISE BOGAN

The Dream

O God, in the dream the terrible horse began
To paw at the air, and make for me with his blows.
Fear kept for thirty-five years poured through his mane,
And retribution equally old, or nearly, breathed through his nose.

Coward complete, I lay and wept on the ground
When some strong creature appeared, and leapt for the rein.
Another woman, as I lay half in a swound,
Leapt in the air, and clutched at the leather and chain.

Give him, she said, something of yours as a charm.
Throw him, she said, some poor thing you alone claim.
No, no, I cried, he hates me; he's out for harm,
And whether I yield or not, it is all the same.

But, like a lion in a legend, when I flung the glove
Pulled from my sweating, my cold right hand,
The terrible beast, that no one may understand,
Came to my side, and put down his head in love.

GWENDOLYN BROOKS (1917–2000), who lived most of her life in Chicago, published over twenty volumes of poetry. Her **dramatic monologue**, "The mother," appeared in her first volume, *A Street in Bronzeville* (1945). In 1949, her collection, *Annie Allen*, earned her the 1950 Pulitzer Prize, the first awarded to an African American. "The Bean Eaters" and "The Pool Players: Seven at the Golden Shovel" both appeared in *The Bean Eaters* (1960), a collection published just after the death of her beloved father that moves her poetic focus from race to class issues. In much of her poetry, Brooks merges the daily life of Chicago's poor, black Southside with traditional **ballad, sonnet**, and even **epic** forms.

Related Works: O'Connor, "Good Country People"; Bambara, "The Lesson"; Blake, "London"; Swift, "A Description of the Morning"; Dunbar, "Sympathy"; Auden, "The Unknown Citizen"; Lorde, "Hanging Fire."

GWENDOLYN BROOKS

The Pool Players Seven at the Golden Shovel

We real cool. We
Left school. We

Lurk late. We
Strike straight. We

Sing sin. We
Thin gin. We

Jazz June. We
Die soon.

GWENDOLYN BROOKS

The Bean Eaters

They eat beans mostly, this old yellow pair.
Dinner is a casual affair.
Plain chipware on a plain and creaking wood,
Tin flatware.

Two who are Mostly Good.
Two who have lived their day,
But keep on putting on their clothes
And putting things away.

And remembering . . .
Remembering, with twinklings and twinges,
As they lean over the beans in their rented back room that
 is full of beads and receipts and dolls and cloths,
 tobacco crumbs, vases and fringes.

GWENDOLYN BROOKS

The mother

Abortions will not let you forget.
You remember the children you got that you did not get,
The damp small pulps with a little or with no hair,
The singers and workers that never handled the air.
You will never neglect or beat
Them, or silence or buy with a sweet,
You will never wind up the sucking-thumb
Or scuttle off ghosts that come.
You will never leave them, controlling your luscious sigh,
Return for a snack of them, with gobbling mother-eye.

I have heard in the voices of the wind the voices of my dim killed children,
I have contracted. I have eased
My dim dears at the breasts they could never suck.
I have said, Sweets, if I sinned, if I seized
Your luck
And your lives from your unfinished reach,
If I stole your births and your names,
Your straight baby tears and your games,
Your stilted or lovely loves, your tumults, your marriages, aches, and your deaths,
If I poisoned the beginnings of your breaths,
Believe that even in my deliberateness I was not deliberate.
Though why should I whine,
Whine that the crime was other than mine?—
Since anyhow you are dead.
Or rather, or instead,
You were never made.
But that too, I am afraid,
Is faulty: oh, what shall I say, how is the truth to be said?
You were born, you had body, you died.
It is just that you never giggled or planned or cried.

Believe me, I loved you all.
Believe me, I knew you, though faintly, and I loved, I loved you
All.

HAYDEN CARRUTH (b. 1921) was born in Connecticut and educated at the University of North Carolina at Chapel Hill and the University of Chicago. He has since lived in Vermont and upstate New York, working as a professor of Creative Writing and acting as poetry editor for *Poetry, Harpers*, and the *Hudson Review*. He has published twenty-nine volumes of poetry, a novel, and numerous critical articles. Carruth's major themes include rural life and rural poverty, undergirded by his finely tuned sense of social and cultural responsibility. Carruth often experiments with traditional forms, and in "An Apology for Using the Word 'Heart' in Too Many Poems" (*Collected Shorter Poems 1946–1991*) he presents us with a series of **rhymed couplets** commenting on the word that he avoids using.

Related Works: Jonson, "On My First Son"; Herrick, "To the Virgins"; Frost, "Acquainted with the Night"; Wilbur, "Junk."

HAYDEN CARRUTH

An Apology for Using the Word "Heart" in Too Many Poems

What does it mean? Lord knows; least of all I.
   Faced with it, schoolboys are shy,
And grown-ups speak it at moments of excess
   Which later seem more or less
Unfeasible. It is equivocal, sentimental,
   Debatable, really a sort of lentil—
Neither pea nor bean. Sometimes it's a muscle,
   Sometimes courage or at least hustle,
Sometimes a core or center, but mostly it's
   A sound that slushily fits
The meters of popular songwriters without
   Meaning anything. It is stout,
Leonine, chicken, great, hot, warm, cold,
   Broken, whole, tender, bold,
Stony, soft, green, blue, red, white,
   Faint, true, heavy, light,

Open, down, shallow, etc. No wonder
   Our superiors thunder
Against it. And yet in spite of a million abuses
   The word survives; its uses

Are such that it remains virtually indispensable
    And, I think, defensible.
The Freudian terminology is awkward or worse,
    And suggests so many perverse
Etiologies that it is useless; but "heart" covers
    The whole business, lovers
To monks, i.e., the capacity to love in the fullest
    Sense. Not even the dullest
Reader misapprehends it, although locating
    It is a matter awaiting
Someone more ingenious than I. But given
    This definition, driven
Though it is out of a poet's necessity, isn't
    The word needed at present
As much as ever, if it is well written and said,
    With the heart and the head?

MARILYN CHIN (b. 1955), born in Hong Kong, completed a B.A. at Amherst and an M.F.A. at the University of Iowa. In addition to translations, anthologies, and a play, Chin has published three collections of her poetry: *Dwarf Bamboo* (1987), *The Phoenix Gone, The Terrace Empty* (1994), and *Rhapsody in Plain Yellow* (2002). The poems included here, both from *The Phoenix Gone, The Terrace Empty*, deal with problematic aspects of cultural assimilation through extended, sometimes enigmatic, **metaphors**.

Related Works: Anzaldúa, "horse"; Alexie, "Reservation Love Song"; Erdrich, "A Love Medicine"; Lee, "Persimmons"; Song, "Girl Powdering Her Neck"; Norman, *'Night Mother.*

MARILYN CHIN

Turtle Soup

You go home one evening tired from work,
and your mother boils you turtle soup.
Twelve hours hunched over the hearth
(who knows what else is in that cauldron).

You say, "Ma, you've poached the symbol of long life;
that turtle lived four thousand years, swam
the Wet, up the Yellow, over the Yangtze.
Witnessed the Bronze Age, the High Tang,
grazed on splendid sericulture."
(So, she boils the life out of him.)

"All our ancestors have been fools.
Remember Uncle Wu who rode ten thousand miles

to kill a famous Manchu and ended up
with his head on a pole? Eat, child,
its liver will make you strong."

"Sometimes you're the life, sometimes the sacrifice."
Her sobbing is inconsolable.
So, you spread that gentle napkin
over your lap in decorous Pasadena.

Baby, some high priestess has got it wrong.
The golden decal on the green underbelly
says "Made in Hong Kong."

Is there nothing left but the shell
and humanity's strange inscriptions,
the songs, the rites, the oracles?

MARILYN CHIN

Autumn Leaves

The dead piled up, thick, fragrant, on the fire escape.
My mother ordered me again, and again, to sweep it clean.
All that blooms must fall. I learned this not from the Tao,
    but from high school biology.

Oh, the contradictions of having a broom and not a dustpan!
I swept the leaves down, down through the iron grille
and let the dead rain over the Wong family's patio.

And it was Achilles Wong who completed the task.
  We called her:
The-one-who-cleared-away-another-family's-autumn.
She blossomed, tall, benevolent, notwithstanding.

LUCILLE (SAYLES) CLIFTON'S (b. 1936) father worked in the steel mills and her mother took in laundry outside of Buffalo, New York, but both parents emphasized education. Clifton entered Howard University at sixteen and began friendships with intellectuals Chloe Wofford (a.k.a., Toni Morrison), A. B. Spellman, Sterling A. Brown, and Fred Clifton, whom she married in 1958. Clifton completed her college years at Fredonia State Teachers College in 1955. In 1969, while raising six children, Clifton published her first book, *Good Times*. Other major collections include: *Good News About the Earth* (1972), *An Ordinary Woman* (1974), *Next: New Poems* (1987), which includes "my mama moved among the days," *Quilting: Poems 1987–1990* (1991), which includes "at the cemetery, walnut grove plantation, South Carolina, 1989." Clifton is also well known for her many children's books. She has been a writer-in-residence and faculty member at universities around the country, and since 1991 she has been Distinguished Professor of Humanities at St. Mary's College of Maryland. Her poems celebrate African American heritage and resilience, while highlighting injustices. Simple diction, some use of **dialect**, and reliance on repetition characterize her poetic style.

Related Works: Angelou, "Still I Rise"; Bogan, "Women"; Dunbar, "We wear the mask" and "Sympathy"; Heaney, "Punishment"; Lorde, "Hanging Fire"; Bambara, "The Lesson"; Walker, "Everyday Use."

LUCILLE CLIFTON

at the cemetery, walnut grove plantation, South Carolina, 1989

among the rocks
at walnut grove
your silence drumming
in my bones,
tell me your names.

nobody mentioned slaves
and yet the curious tools
shine with your fingerprints.
nobody mentioned slaves
but somebody did this work
who had no guide, no stone,
who moulders under rock.

tell me your names,
tell me your bashful names
and i will testify.

the inventory lists ten slaves
but only the men were recognized.
among the rocks
at walnut grove
some of these honored dead
were dark
some of the dark
were slaves
some of these slaves
were women
some of them did this
honored work.
tell me your names
foremothers, brothers,
tell me your dishonored names.

here lies
here lies
here lies
here lies
hear

LUCILLE CLIFTON

my mama moved among the days
like a dreamwalker in a field;
seemed like what she touched was hers
seemed like what touched her couldn't hold,
she got us almost through the high grass
then seemed like she turned around and ran
right back in
right back on in

JUDITH ORTIZ COFER (b. 1952) was born in Puerto Rico; Ortiz Cofer has maintained roots there throughout her life, as she was shuttled between the island and her father's naval base in New Jersey. Her family spoke Spanish at home, but, attending schools in the United States for all but the first years of her education, Ortiz Cofer spoke English during the greater part of each day. She finished a Master's degree in English at Florida Atlantic University in 1977, and, during the completion of her thesis, she began to write stories and poems. Since then, Ortiz Cofer has published over a dozen novels, plays, poetry collections, and **memoirs**. She has won many awards and fellowships, including a grant from the National Endowment for the Arts (1989), a Pulitzer Prize nomination (1989) for her novel *The Line of the Sun*, the Pushcart Prize (1990), and the O. Henry Prize (1994). Ortiz Cofer's writing seems to dwell easily in the space between her two primary languages, and she often uses both in a single piece. Thematically, she focuses on the transformative and reconciliatory properties of memory and language. She is currently the Regents Professor of English and Creative Writing at the University of Georgia.

Related Works: Behn, "Song"; Barrett Browning, Sonnets 14 and 43; Anzaldúa, "horse"; Angelou, "Still I Rise"; Erdrich, "Family Reunion"; Chin, "Turtle Soup"; Clifton, "my mama moved among the days"; Piercy, "Barbie Doll"; Shakespeare, *Taming of the Shrew*; Marquez, "The Handsomest Drowned Man in the World."

JUDITH ORTIZ COFER

Cold as Heaven

Before there is a breeze again
before the cooling days of Lent, she may be gone.

My grandmother asks me to tell her
again about the snow.
We sit on her white bed
in this white room, while outside
the Caribbean sun winds up the world
like an old alarm clock. I tell her
about the enveloping blizzard I lived through
that made everything and everyone the same;
how we lost ourselves in drifts so tall
we fell through our own footprints;
how wrapped like mummies in layers of wool
that almost immobilized us, we could only
take hesitant steps like toddlers
toward food, warmth, shelter.
I talk winter real for her,
as she would once conjure for me to dream
at sweltering siesta time,
cool stone castles in lands far north.
Her eyes wander to the window,
to the teeming scene of children
pouring out of a yellow bus, then to the bottle
dripping minutes through a tube
into her veins. When her eyes return to me,
I can see she's waiting to hear more
about the purifying nature of ice,
how snow makes way for a body,
how you can make yourself an angel
by just lying down and waving your arms
as you do when you say
good-bye.

JUDITH ORTIZ COFER

Claims

Last time I saw her, Grandmother
had grown seamed as a Bedouin tent.
She had claimed the right
to sleep alone, to own
her nights, to never bear
the weight of sex again nor to accept
its gift of comfort, for the luxury
of stretching her bones.
She'd carried eight children,
three had sunk in her belly, *náufragos*
she called them, shipwrecked babies

drowned in her black waters.
Children are made in the night and
steal your days
for the rest of your life, amen. She said this
to each of her daughters in turn. Once she had made a pact
with man and nature and kept it. Now like the sea,
she is claiming back her territory.

JUDITH ORTIZ COFER

The Other

A sloe-eyed dark woman shadows me.
In the morning she sings
Spanish love songs in a high falsetto,
filling my shower stall
with echoes.
She is by my side
in front of the mirror as I slip
into my tailored skirt and she
into her red cotton dress.
She shakes out her black mane as I
run a comb through my closely cropped cap.
Her mouth is like a red bull's eye
daring me.
Everywhere I go I must
make room for her; she crowds me
in elevators where others wonder
at all the space I need.
At night her weight tips my bed, and
it is her wild dreams that run rampant
through my head exhausting me. Her heartbeats,
like dozens of spiders carrying the poison
of her restlessness,
drag their countless legs
over my bare flesh.

JUDITH ORTIZ COFER

Learning to Walk Alone

Today I followed my servant, Hestia, down the dusty path
that leads away from the sea. Trudging towards
the barren hills that separate my house from her world,

her stiff back told me
that a woman walking home after a day of laboring
over someone else's hearth
had nothing to share with a fortunate fool
strolling in the heat of late afternoon
for pleasure.
As we approached the last clump of trees
huddled together like beggars at the edge of the village,
I gave up the contest of wills. I followed Hestia's brown form
with my eyes, as she descended into a marketplace
filled with hagglers, stray dogs, and flies, until
she became part of the crowd.
I stood there with my arms around a thin old tree
for a long time, listening to the sounds of words
I could not decipher, the empty cadences of far-away voices
rising and falling.
Without you, Odysseus,
I have come to hate living on this island—the constant whine
of the sea licking its own wounds. If I could, I would follow
the vagrant gulls to crowded places and feast on crumbs,
I would wait with the winning patience of birds
for someone to extend an open hand.

JUDITH ORTIZ COFER

The Names of the Dead: An Essay on the Phrase

The functions of the human body are phrased this way:
the heart beats and rests; the lungs fill and subside; muscles
demand rest from effort, as sustained tension results quickly
in exhaustion.

FROM *THE ART OF MAKING DANCES* BY DORIS HUMPHREY

We live by the phrase. We long for the order of declaration and pause. The functions of the human body are phrased this way: the heart beats and rests; the lungs fill and subside. Outside of the body, in the general world of matter, tension and relaxation also operate as a law; this counterpoint of energy and loss is inescapable as a pattern. *Scenes of chaos and destruction evocative of the nightmare world of Hieronymus Bosch*, reported the New York Times, *with smoke and debris blotting out the sun. But the real carnage was concealed by the twisted, smoking, ash-choked carcasses of the structures. There were hundreds of people on the street waiting for the names of the dead. There is nothing anybody can do*, a firefighter replied, *nothing anybody can do*. In long stretches of unphrased movement, the kinesthetic link of our bodies with an event is sometimes lost. This counterpoint of energy and loss.

Outside of the body. *Scenes of chaos and destruction.* In the general world of matter. *There is nothing anybody can do.* Confronted with the loss. The heart beats and rests. *With smoke and debris blotting out the sun.* The lungs fill and subside. *Concealed by the twisted, smoking, ash-choked carcasses of the structures.* Muscles of the heart demand rest from continued effort. *But the real carnage was concealed. Nothing anybody can do.* We long for the order of declaration and pause. Inescapable as a pattern. This counterpoint of energy and loss. *The names of the dead.*

• • •

In long stretches of unphrased movement, the kinesthetic link of our bodies with an event is sometimes lost. Confronted with the loss, the heart beats and rests; the lungs fill and subside. According to the Times, *Washington struggled to regain a sense of equilibrium; with warplanes crossing overhead, national security officials discussed the possibility of a declaration of war.* Long sentences leave us breathless and tired. Sustained tension results quickly in exhaustion. The heart beats and rests; the lungs fill and subside. *The possibility of a declaration of war. There is nothing anybody can do.* And the very short statement is also unsatisfactory: *The search is under way for those behind these evil acts,* the President said, *The resolve of our great nation is being tested.* Here the rests are too frequent; the breath is too short and therefore unfulfilling. *This is a difficult time for America,* he said. The heart beats and rests, beats and rests. *Nothing anybody can do.* The lungs fill and subside, fill and subside, *With warplanes crossing overhead. The search is under way. Nothing anybody can do. The names of the dead.*

• • •

Outside of the body, in the general world of matter, tension and relaxation also operate as a law; this counterpoint of energy and loss is inescapable as a pattern. *There were refugees everywhere,* said the Times. *A memorial was set up. Long sheets of brown paper taped to the ground. Repeated on almost every one the single word, why? There were hundreds of pieces of paper in the air. A woman grabbed my hand,* said a passerby. *She was saying the Lord's Prayer. It was late in the afternoon. Hundreds of people on the street watching the stubs of the buildings burn. Hundreds of people on the street. Paper in the air. Late in the afternoon. Waiting for the names of the dead. A single word, repeated.*

Outside of the body. *Nothing anybody can do. Scenes of chaos and destruction. Late in the afternoon.* In the general world of matter. *The real carnage was concealed. A woman grabbed my hand. With warplanes overhead. Smoke and debris blotting out the sun.* The kinesthetic link. *She was saying the Lord's Prayer. Long sheets of brown paper.* Long stretches of unphrased movement. Long sentences. The inescapable pattern. *Late in the afternoon. A single word, repeated. The nightmare world of Hieronymus Bosch. Nothing anybody can do.* This counterpoint of energy and loss. *The evil acts. The resolve. A difficult time. Nothing anybody can do. America.* The names of the dead.

JUDITH ORTIZ COFER

The Woman Who Was Left at the Altar

She calls her shadow Juan,
looking back often as she walks.

She has grown fat, her breasts huge
as reservoirs. She once opened her blouse
in church to show the silent town
what a plentiful mother she could be.
Since her old mother died, buried in black,
she lives alone.
Out of the lace she made curtains for her room,
doilies out of the veil. They are now
yellow as malaria.
She hangs live chickens from her waist to sell,
walks to town swinging her skirts of flesh.
She doesn't speak to anyone. Dogs follow
the scent of blood to be shed. In their hungry,
yellow eyes she sees his face. She takes him
to the knife time after time.

COUNTEE CULLEN (1903–1946). Not as well-known currently as his contemporaries Langston Hughes and Zora Neale Hurston, Cullen was the most celebrated poet of the **Harlem Renaissance** of the late 1920s and early 1930s. He was secretive about his earliest years, but Cullen began his rise to fame when he was unofficially adopted by the Methodist minister Frederick Asbury Cullen in 1917. Cullen proved to be an outstanding scholar, attending Dewitt Clinton High School for Boys in Manhattan and completing a Master's degree at Harvard in 1926. *Color,* Cullen's first poetry collection, was published in 1925. Cullen dealt with issues of race, but he wrote in traditional forms—**sonnets, quatrains, ballads**—after the British **Romantics**; he especially admired Keats.

Related Works: Browning, "Childe Roland to the Dark Tower Came"; Keats, "Ode on a Grecian Urn"; Barrett Browning, Sonnet 14; Dunbar, "Sympathy"; cummings, "Next to of course god America I"; Brooks, "The mother"; Hughes, "Harlem" and "Theme for English B"; Wilson, *The Piano Lesson*; Ellison, "Battle Royal."

COUNTEE CULLEN

From the Dark Tower

We shall not always plant while others reap
The golden increment of bursting fruit,
Not always countenance, abject and mute,
That lesser men should hold their brothers cheap;
Not everlastingly while others sleep
Shall we beguile their limbs with mellow flute,
Not always bend to some more subtle brute;
We were not made to eternally weep.

The night whose sable breast relieves the stark,
White stars is no less lovely being dark.
And there are buds that cannot bloom at all
In light, but crumple, piteous, and fall;
So in the dark we hide the heart that bleeds,
And wait, and tend our agonizing seeds.

e. e. (EDWARD ESTLIN) CUMMINGS (1894–1962) grew up in Cambridge, Massachusetts, the son of a Harvard professor. He attended Harvard, receiving both B.A. and M.A. degrees there, before joining an ambulance corps in France during World War I. Following the war, he wrote, painted, and traveled. His first collection of poems, *Tulips and Chimneys* (1923), and his account of his experience in a French detention camp, *The Enormous Room* (1924), established his reputation as an ***avant-garde*** poet. Popular reception of cummings has always been favorable, but critical reception of cummings's work has varied; nevertheless, critics agree that by abandoning traditional constraints on form, punctuation, diction, and syntax, cummings was able to rehabilitate the traditional topics of verse—romance, flowers, sexual and spiritual love, springtime, and joy—releasing them from sentimental ruts and contemporary disdain. Jenny Penberthy, in the *Dictionary of Literary Biography*, calls cummings an "unabashed *lyricist*, a modern ***cavalier*** *love poet*." Note the play on the ***carpe diem*** theme in "since feeling is first" (1926) and his take on the **sonnet** in "next to of course god america I" (1926).

Related Works: Medieval Lyrical Poetry; Drayton, Sonnet 61; Donne, Holy Sonnet 14; Herbert, "Easter Wings"; Herrick, "To the Virgins"; Marlowe, "The Passionate Shepherd to His Love"; Marvell, "To His Coy Mistress"; Wordsworth, "I wandered lonely as a cloud"; Updike. "A&P."

---

e. e. cummings

since feeling is first

since feeling is first
who pays any attention
to the syntax of things
will never wholly kiss you;
wholly to be a fool
while Spring is in the world
my blood approves,
and kisses are a better fate
than wisdom
lady i swear by all flowers. Don't cry
—the best gesture of my brain is less than
your eyelids' flutter which says
we are for each other: then
laugh leaning back in my arms

for life's not a paragraph
And death i think is no parenthesis

---

e.e. cummings

in Just—

in Just—
spring   when the world is mud-
luscious the little lame balloonman

whistles   far   and wee

and eddyandbill come
running from marbles and
piracies and it's
spring

when the world is puddle-wonderful

the queer
old balloonman whistles
far   and   wee
and bettyandisbel come dancing

from hop-scotch and jump-rope and

it's
spring
and
the
goat-footed

balloonMan   whistles
far
and
wee

---

e.e. cummings

Buffalo Bill's

Buffalo Bill's
defunct
    who used to
    ride a watersmooth-silver
        stallion

and break onetwothreefourfive pigeonsjustlikethat
            Jesus

he was a handsome man
            and what i want to know is
how do you like your blueeyed boy
Mister Death

---

e.e. cummings

next to of course god america i

"next to of course god america i
love you land of the pilgrims' and so forth oh
say can you see by the dawn's early my
country 'tis of centuries come and go
and are no more what of it we should worry
in every language even deafanddumb
thy sons acclaim your glorious name by gorry
by jingo by gee by gosh by gum
why talk of beauty what could be more beautiful than these heroic happy dead
who rushed like lions to the roaring slaughter
they did not stop to think they died instead
then shall the voice of liberty be mute?"

He spoke. And drank rapidly a glass of water

JAMES DICKEY (1923–1997), born and raised in Atlanta, left a promising college football career at Clemson to join the Army Air Corps in World War II. During his stint in the South Pacific, he developed a passion for writing. After returning from the war, he completed a B.A. and M.A. at Vanderbilt and began his academic career teaching at Rice University in Texas. Later, at the University of Florida, his poetry proved controversial, and he left academics for several years to work in advertising. After receiving a Guggenheim award following the publication of *Into the Stone and Other Poems* in 1960, he spent a year with his family in Europe, and upon his return, accepted a chaired professorship at the University of South Carolina, where he remained until his death. He published over twenty volumes of poetry, among other work, including his novel *Deliverance*, which was made into a film. Dickey's poetry is a favorite of veterans and often shocks its readers with juxtapositions or **antitheses** of the beauty and violence of war. In "The Heaven of Animals," Dickey considers the antithesis between animals and humans, another kind of war.

Related Works: Shakespeare, *Hamlet*; Berry, "The Peace of Wild Things."

JAMES DICKEY

The Heaven of Animals

Here they are. The soft eyes open.
If they have lived in a wood
It is a wood.
If they have lived on plains
It is grass rolling
Under their feet forever.

Having no souls, they have come,
Anyway, beyond their knowing.
Their instincts wholly bloom
And they rise.
The soft eyes open.

To match them, the landscape flowers,
Outdoing, desperately
Outdoing what is required;
The richest wood,
The deepest field.

For some of these,
It could not be the place
It is, without blood.
These hunt, as they have done
But with claws and teeth grown perfect,

More deadly than they can believe.
They stalk more silently,
And crouch on the limbs of trees.
And their descent
Upon the bright backs of their prey

May take years
In a sovereign floating of joy.
And those that are hunted
Know this as their life,
Their reward: to walk

Under such trees in full knowledge
Of what is in glory above them,
And to feel no fear,
But acceptance, compliance.
Fulfilling themselves without pain

At the cycle's center,
They tremble, they walk
Under the tree,

They fall, they are torn,
They rise, they walk again.

Bart Edelman (b. 1951) grew up in New Jersey, earning undergraduate and graduate degrees from Hofstra University. He has published four collections of poetry, including *Crossing the Hackensack* (1993), *Under Damaris' Dress* (1996), and *The Alphabet of Love* (1999). "Chemistry Experiment" appears in his fourth collection, *The Gentle Man* (2001). Thematically, Edelman's poetry focuses on small moments of love and loss and particularly the complexity of men's roles in society and in relationships.

Related Works: Singer, "Gimpel the Fool"; cummings, "since feeling is first"; Carruth, "An Apology for Using the Word 'Heart' in Too Many Poems"; Shakespeare, *Hamlet.*

BART EDELMAN

Chemistry Experiment

We listened intently to the professor,
Followed each one of her instructions,
Read through the textbook twice,
Wore lab coats and safety goggles,
Mixed the perfect chemical combinations
In the proper amounts and order.
It was all progressing smoothly;
We thought we were a complete success.
And then the flash of light,
The loud, perplexing explosion,
The black rope of smoke,
Rising freely above our singed hair.
Someone in another lab down the hallway
Phoned the local fire department
Which arrived lickety-split
With the hazardous waste crew,
And they assessed the accident,
Deciding we were out of danger.
It was the talk of the campus
For many weeks afterwards.
We, however, became so disillusioned
That we immediately dropped the course
And slowly retreated from each other.
The very idea we could have done
More damage than we actually did—
Blown up ourselves and the building
From the base of its foundation—

Shook us, like nothing had before.
And even now, years later,
When anyone still asks about you,
I get this sick feeling in my stomach
And wonder what really happened
To all that elementary matter.

T. S. (THOMAS STEARNS) ELIOT (1888–1965) is considered by many scholars to be the most influential poet of the twentieth century. His intellectual, highly allusive poetry uses strong **rhythms** to blend formal and informal verse, **dialogue**, and vivid **metaphors**. "The Love Song of J. Alfred Prufrock" (1917), a lyrical, **dramatic monologue**, continues to intrigue scholars with classical and biblical **allusions**, complex **ironies**, and **symbols**. Born in St. Louis, Missouri, to a distinguished, traditional, New England family, Eliot entered Harvard in 1906, completing his B.A. and M.A. by 1910. He spent the next six years in Europe at the Sorbonne, Oxford, and Marburg, and then returned to Harvard to complete his dissertation in philosophy. After completing his dissertation, he went to England and rarely returned to America; in 1927 he became an English citizen. Between 1916 and 1917, he married an English woman, took a job in a London bank, and published *Prufrock and Other Observations* with the help of Ezra Pound. A breakdown, resulting in a lengthy stay in a Swiss sanatorium, was followed by the publication of *The Waste Land* in 1922 and the start of Eliot's literary magazine, *Criterion*. In addition to his early poetry, Eliot published influential lectures on literary criticism, plays (*The Cocktail Party* and *Murder in the Cathedral*), and his last major poetic work, *The Four Quartets*. "The Naming of Cats" (1939) is from *Old Possum's Book of Practical Cats*, a playful exercise in variation which was eventually made into a Broadway musical.

Related Works: Shakespeare, *Hamlet*; Tennyson, "Ulysses"; Yeats, "Leda and the Swan" and "Sailing to Byzantium"; Stevens, "Thirteen Ways of Looking at a Blackbird"; Hawthorne, "Young Goodman Brown"; Faulkner, "A Rose for Emily."

T. S. ELIOT

The Love Song of J. Alfred Prufrock

S'io credesse che mia risposta fosse a persona che mai tornasse al
mondo, questa fiamma staria senza più scosse. Ma per cio cche
giammai di questo fondo non torno vivo alcun, s'i'odo il vero,
senza tema d'infamia ti rispondo.

Let us go then, you and I,
When the evening is spread out against the sky
Like a patient etherised upon a table;

Let us go, through certain half-deserted streets,
The muttering retreats
Of restless nights in one-night cheap hotels
And sawdust restaurants with oyster shells:
Streets that follow like a tedious argument
Of insidious intent
To lead you to an overwhelming question . . .
Oh, do not ask, 'What is it?'
Let us go and make our visit.

In the room the women come and go
Talking of Michelangelo.

The yellow fog that rubs its back upon the window-panes,
The yellow smoke that rubs its muzzle on the window-panes
Licked its tongue into the corners of the evening,
Lingered upon the pools that stand in drains,
Let fall upon its back the soot that falls from chimneys,
Slipped by the terrace, made a sudden leap,
And seeing that it was a soft October night,
Curled once about the house, and fell asleep.

And indeed there will be time
For the yellow smoke that slides along the street,
Rubbing its back upon the window-panes:
There will be time, there will be time
To prepare a face to meet the faces that you meet;
There will be time to murder and create,
And time for all the works and days of hands
That lift and drop a question on your plate;
Time for you and time for me,
And time yet for a hundred indecisions,
And for a hundred visions and revisions,
Before the taking of a toast and tea.

In the room the women come and go
Talking of Michelangelo.

And indeed there will be time
To wonder, "Do I dare?" and, "Do I dare?"
Time to turn back and descend the stair.
With a bald spot in the middle of my hair—
(They will say: "How his hair is growing thin!")
My morning coat, my collar mounting firmly to the chin,
My necktie rich and modest, but asserted by a simple pin—
(They will say: "But how his arms and legs are thin!")
Do I dare
Disturb the universe?
In a minute there is time
For decisions and revisions which a minute will reverse.

For I have known them all already, known them all—
Have known the evenings, mornings, afternoons,
I have measured out my life with coffee spoons;
I know the voices dying with a dying fall
Beneath the music from a farther room.
So how should I presume?

And I have known the eyes already, known them all—
The eyes that fix you in a formulated phrase,
And when I am formulated, sprawling on a pin,
When I am pinned and wriggling on the wall,
Then how should I begin
To spit out all the butt-ends of my days and ways?
And how should I presume?

And I have known the arms already, known them all—
Arms that are braceleted and white and bare
(But in the lamplight, downed with light brown hair!)
Is it perfume from a dress
That makes me so digress?
Arms that lie along a table, or wrap about a shawl.
And should I then presume?
And how should I begin?

• • •

Shall I say, I have gone at dusk through narrow streets
And watched the smoke that rises from the pipes
Of lonely men in shirt-sleeves, leaning out of windows? . . .

I should have been a pair of ragged claws
Scuttling across the floors of silent seas.

• • •

And the afternoon, the evening, sleeps so peacefully!
Smoothed by long fingers,
Asleep . . . tired . . . or it malingers,
Stretched on the floor, here beside you and me.
Should I, after tea and cakes and ices,
Have the strength to force the moment to its crisis?
But though I have wept and fasted, wept and prayed,
Though I have seen my head (grown slightly bald) brought
in upon a platter,
I am no prophet—and here's no great matter;
I have seen the moment of my greatness flicker,
And I have seen the eternal Footman hold my coat, and snicker,
And in short, I was afraid.

And would it have been worth it, after all,
After the cups, the marmalade, the tea,
Among the porcelain, among some talk
of you and me,

Would it have been worth while,
To have bitten off the matter with a smile,
To have squeezed the universe into a ball
To roll it toward some overwhelming question,
To say: "I am Lazarus, come from the dead,
Come back to tell you all, I shall tell you all"—
If one, settling a pillow by her head,
Should say: "That is not what I meant at all.
That is not it, at all"

• • •

And would it have been worth it, after all,
Would it have been worth while,
After the sunsets and the dooryards and the sprinkled streets,
After the novels, after the teacups, after the skirts that trail
along the floor—
And this, and so much more?—
It is impossible to say just what I mean!
But as if a magic lantern threw the nerves in patterns
on a screen:
Would it have been worth while
If one, settling a pillow or throwing off a shawl,
And turning toward the window, should say:
'That is not it at all,
That is not what I meant, at all.'

No! I am not Prince Hamlet, nor was meant to be;
Am an attendant lord, one that will do
To swell a progress, start a scene or two,
Advise the prince; no doubt, an easy tool,
Deferential, glad to be of use,
Politic, cautious, and meticulous;
Full of high sentence, but a bit obtuse;
At times, indeed, almost ridiculous—
Almost, at times, the Fool.

I grow old . . . I grow old . . .
I shall wear the bottoms of my trousers rolled.

Shall I part my hair behind? Do I dare to eat a peach?
I shall wear white flannel trousers, and walk upon the beach.
I have heard the mermaids singing, each to each.

I do not think that they will sing to me.

I have seen them riding seaward on the waves
Combing the white hair of the waves blown back
When the wind blows the water white and black.

We have lingered in the chambers of the sea
By sea-girls wreathed with seaweed red and brown
Till human voices wake us, and we drown.

T. S. ELIOT

The Naming of Cats

The Naming of Cats is a difficult matter,
    It isn't just one of your holiday games;
You may think at first I'm as mad as a hatter
When I tell you, a cat must have THREE DIFFERENT NAMES.
First of all, there's the name that the family use daily,
    Such as Peter, Augustus, Alonzo or James,
Such as Victor or Jonathan, George or Bill Bailey—
    All of them sensible everyday names.
There are fancier names if you think they sound sweeter,
    Some for the gentlemen, some for the dames:
Such as Plato, Admetus, Electra, Demeter—
    But all of them sensible everyday names.
But I tell you, a cat needs a name that's particular,
    A name that's peculiar, and more dignified,
Else how can he keep up his tail perpendicular,
    Or spread out his whiskers, or cherish his pride?
Of names of this kind, I can give you a quorum,
    Such as Munkustrap, Quaxo, or Coricopat,
Such as Bombalurina, or else Jellylorum—
    Names that never belong to more than one cat.
But above and beyond there's still one name left over,
    And that is the name that you never will guess;
The name that no human research can discover—
    But THE CAT HIMSELF KNOWS, and will never confess.
When you notice a cat in profound meditation,
    The reason, I tell you, is always the same:
His mind is engaged in a rapt contemplation
    Of the thought, of the thought, of the thought of his name:
        His ineffable effable
        Effanineffable
Deep and inscrutable singular Name.

LOUISE ERDRICH (b. 1954) is best known for her six novels, beginning with *Love Medicine* (1984), detailing the history of a fictional Native American clan, but she is also an accomplished poet. "Family Reunion," a **dramatic monologue**, draws a **symbolic** link between an abusive uncle and a turtle he once killed. "A Love Medicine" (1984) dramatizes the bonds of sisterhood, and "Windigo" (1984) draws on Native American mythic tradition. For more details on Erdrich's life, see the head note preceding her short fiction.

Related Works: Faulkner, "A Rose for Emily"; O'Connor, "Good Country People"; Old English Riddles; Anonymous Ballads; Dickinson, "I heard a fly buzz"; Alexie, "Reservation Love Song"; Chin, "Turtle Soup"; Forché, "The Colonel"; Sophocles, *Antigone*; Shakespeare, *The Taming of the Shrew*.

LOUISE ERDRICH

A Love Medicine

Still it is raining lightly
in Wahpeton. The pickup trucks
sizzle beneath the blue neon
bug traps of the dairy bar.

Theresa goes out in green halter and chains
that glitter at her throat.
This dragonfly, my sister,
she belongs more than I
to this night of rising water.

The Red River swells to take the bridge.
She laughs and leaves her man in his Dodge.
He shoves off to search her out.
He wears a long rut in the fog.

And later, at the crest of the flood,
when the pilings are jarred from their sockets
and pitch into the current,
she steps against the fistwork of a man.
She goes down in wet grass
and his boot plants its grin
among the arches of her face.

Now she feels her way home in the dark.
The white-violet bulbs of the streetlamps
are seething with insects,
and the trees lean down aching and empty.
The river slaps at the dike works, insistent.

I find her curled up in the roots of a cottonwood.
I find her stretched out in the park, where all night
the animals are turning in their cages.
I find her in a burnt-over ditch, in a field
that is gagging on rain,
sheets of rain sweep up down
to the river held tight against the bridge.

We see that now the moon is leavened and the water,
as deep as it will go,
stops rising. Where we wait for the night to take us

the rain ceases. *Sister, there is nothing*
I would not do.

LOUISE ERDRICH

Family Reunion

Ray's third new car in half as many years.
Full cooler in the trunk, Ray sogging the beer
as I solemnly chauffeur us through the bush
and up the backroads, hardly cowpaths and hub-deep in mud.
All day the sky lowers, clears, lowers again.
Somewhere in the bush near Saint John
there are uncles, a family, one mysterious brother
who stayed on the land when Ray left for the cities.
One week Ray is crocked. We've been through this before.
Even, as a little girl, hands in my dress,
Ah punka, you's my Debby, come and ki me.

Then the road ends in a yard full of dogs.
Them's Indian dogs, Ray says, lookit how they know me.
And they do seem to know him, like I do. His odor—
rank beef of fierce turtle pulled dripping from Metagoshe,
and the inflammable mansmell: hair tonic, ashes, alcohol.
Ray dances an old woman up in his arms.
Fiddles reel in the phonograph and I sink apart
in a corner, start knocking the Blue Ribbons down.
Four generations of people live here.
No one remembers Raymond Twobears.

So what. The walls shiver, the old house caulked with mud
sails back into the middle of Metagoshe.
A three-foot-long snapper is hooked on a troutline,
so mean that we do not dare wrestle him in
but tow him to shore, heavy as an old engine.
Then somehow Ray pries the beak open and shoves
down a cherry bomb. Lights the string tongue.

Headless and clenched in its armor, the snapper
is lugged home in the trunk for tomorrow's soup.
Ray rolls it beneath a bush in the backyard and goes in
to sleep his own head off. Tomorrow I find
that the animal has dragged itself someplace.
I follow torn tracks up a slight hill and over
into a small stream that deepens and widens into a marsh.

Ray finds his way back through the room into his arms.
When the phonograph stops, he slumps hard in his hands
and the boys and their old man fold him into the car
where he curls around his bad heart, hearing how it knocks
and rattles at the bars of his ribs to break out.

Somehow we find our way back. Uncle Ray
sings an old song to the body that pulls him
toward home. The gray fins that his hands have become
screw their bones in the dashboard. His face
has the odd, calm patience of a child who has always
let bad wounds alone, or a creature that has lived
for a long time underwater. And the angels come
lowering their slings and litters.

LOUISE ERDRICH

Windigo

The Windigo is a flesh-eating, wintry demon with a man buried deep inside of it. In some Chippewa stories, a young girl vanquishes this monster by forcing boiling lard down its throat, thereby releasing the human at the core of ice.

You knew I was coming for you, little one,
when the kettle jumped into the fire.
Towels flapped on the hooks,
and the dog crept off, groaning,
to the deepest part of the woods.

In the hackles of dry brush a thin laughter started up.
Mother scolded the food warm and smooth in the pot
and called you to eat.
But I spoke in the cold trees:
New one, I have come for you, child hide and lie still.

The sumac pushed sour red cones through the air.
Copper burned in the raw wood.
You saw me drag toward you.
Oh touch me, I murmured, and licked the soles of your feet.
You dug your hands into my pale, melting fur.

I stole you off, a huge thing in my bristling armor.
Steam rolled from my wintry arms, each leaf shivered
from the bushes we passed
until they stood, naked, spread like the cleaned spines of fish.

Then your warm hands hummed over and shoveled themselves full
of the ice and the snow. I would darken and spill

all night running, until at last morning broke the cold earth
and I carried you home,
a river shaking in the sun.

CAROLYN FORCHÉ (b. 1950). Forché's first poetry collection, *Gathering the Tribes* (1976), won the Yale series of Younger Poets Award. Between 1978 and 1980, Forché traveled through El Salvador, and upon her return in 1982 published *The Country Between Us* as "witness" poetry. She has since continued her activism in South Africa and Lebanon, completed several translations, written text to accompany *El Salvador: Work of Thirty Photographers* (1983), and published two additional collections of her poetry: *Against Forgetting: Twentieth Century Poetry of Witness* (1993) and *The Angel of History* (1994). "The Colonel" (1978) is notable for its form—a **prose poem**—and for its complex narrative **persona**.

Related Works: O'Brien, "Stockings"; Poe, "The Cask of Amontillado"; "Lord Randall" (Child Ballad #12); Dickey, "The Heaven of Animals"; Plath, "Daddy."

CAROLYN FORCHE

The Colonel

What you have heard is true. I was in his house. His wife carried a tray of coffee and sugar. His daughter filed her nails, his son went out for the night. There were daily papers, pet dogs, a pistol on the cushion beside him. The moon swung bare on its black cord over the house. On the television was a cop show. It was in English. Broken bottles were embedded in the walls around the house to scoop the kneecaps from a man's legs or cut his hands to lace. On the windows there were gratings like those in liquor stores. We had dinner, rack of lamb, good wine, a gold bell was on the table for calling the maid. The maid brought green mangoes, salt, a type of bread. I was asked how I enjoyed the country. There was a brief commercial in Spanish. His wife took everything away. There was some talk of how difficult it had become to govern. The parrot said hello on the terrace. The colonel told it to shut up, and pushed himself from the table. My friend said to me with his eyes: say nothing. The colonel returned with a sack used to bring groceries home. He spilled many human ears on the table. They were like dried peach halves. There is no other way to say this. He took one of them in his hands, shook it in our faces, dropped it into a water glass. It came alive there. I am tired of fooling around he said. As for the rights of anyone, tell your people they can go fuck themselves. He swept the ears to the floor with his arm and held the last of his wine in the air. Something for your poetry, no? he said. Some of the ears on the floor caught this scrap of his voice. Some of the ears on the floor were pressed to the ground.

RUTH FORMAN (b. 1968), an African American poet, has written two collections of poetry, *We Are the Young Magicians* (1993) and *Renaissance* (1998), celebrating the **Harlem Renaissance** poets. Often cited for her use of **dialect** and "street" language, Forman also keenly observes concrete and specific details. In "Cancer" (1998) we see **allusions** to the biblical texts *Romans* and *Corinthians*.

Related Works: Kincaid, "Girl"; Donne, "A Valediction: Forbidding Mourning"; Dunbar, "We wear the mask" and "Sympathy"; Brooks, "The Pool Players: Seven at the Golden Shovel" and "The Bean Eaters"; Clifton, "my mama moved among the days"; Cullen, "From the Dark Tower"; Williams, *The Glass Menagerie*.

RUTH FORMAN

Cancer

The end is coming
can see it on every plateau of breath inhaled
Johanna your eldest daughter/a deer
bends for water
at your palm

you Margaret
looking for your peace song
angels writing it
the chorus the first part finished
your son your sister brother mother father
    they all singing
you the solo
the chorus the first part
the harmony done
the melody they write
pens in hand
Margaret the peace song is in your
    tongue
dry from open mouth calling in breath
drinking air like kisses
holding time like a big hand

our eyes red
skin pale from being inside
I watch you search for your song
woman on water
looking for the next stone
i witness the growing marks on your cheeks
    from the rub of oxygen tubes

the brows come together like praying hands
the mouth not knowing the right words to say
the direction home or what time
there are hands of a child holding yours

somehow the air tells me not to break this spell
    not to leave this room at 10:15
silver hair mother from apple vinegar rinse
wrinkle wrists from blood stolen by I.V.s those
    thirsty worms
the feeding tube hangs from the I.V. stand a suitor

your coughs
scraps of sandpaper
we have to wait for you to find your voice

I've had to get used to so many things in its absence
the whir of fans
the grumbling of the oxygen machine
your slow morphine nod growing slower
to tapes of Romans and Corinthians

how fortunate i am to write this while your breath
    blesses this room
I catch it in my hands
like shallow water

ROBERT FROST (1874–1963) was born in San Francisco, the son of a journalist and a school teacher. After his father's death, Frost's mother moved the family back East, and Frost, then eleven, finished high school in Massachusetts, where he was co-valedictorian of his class with his future wife, Elinor White. Elinor finished her degree at St. Lawrence College while Frost started school at Dartmouth, dropped out, then attended Harvard for two years before withdrawing. His grandfather set him up with a small New Hampshire farm in 1899, and seven years later, with five children to support, he took a teaching position. Frost was successful as a teacher and, at this time, wrote many of the poems that would later appear in his first book. Frost sold his farm and moved his family to England in 1911. There he was able to make connections with W. B. Yeats, Ezra Pound, and other important English poets and, with their support, published *A Boy's Will* (1913) and *North of Boston* (1914). When he returned to the United States, Frost found ready publishers for his work, and many colleges and universities offered him professorships or positions as poet-in-residence. Despite his relative economic security from this time forward, Frost's personal life was difficult; his wife died in 1938, in 1940 a son committed suicide, and his sister was long institutionalized as insane. Frost worked hard to make his poetry reflect his New England setting, using **dialect, dramatic dialogue, monologue**, and a decidedly rural vocabulary to create the colloquial effect so at odds with his strict formal **rhythms** and **rhymes**. He creates a deceptively open, plain-spoken surface, but, in one of his few essays, Frost reminds us that poets work in "parables and in hints and in indirections."[1]

NOTE

1. Robert Frost, "Education by Poetry," in *Selected Prose*, ed. Hyde Cox and Edward Connery Lathem (New York: Holt, Rinehart and Winston, 1956), 36–37.

Related Works: Joyce, "Araby"; Browning, "My Last Duchess"; Hardy, "The Convergence of the Twain"; Whitman, "When lilacs last in the dooryard bloom'd"; Yeats, "Sailing to Byzantium"; Williams, "Spring and All"; Stevens, "The Emperor of Ice Cream"; Glaspell, *Trifles*.

ROBERT FROST

"Out, Out—"

The buzz-saw snarled and rattled in the yard
And made dust and dropped stove-length sticks of wood,
Sweet-scented stuff when the breeze drew across it.
And from there those that lifted eyes could count
Five mountain ranges one behind the other
Under the sunset far into Vermont.
And the saw snarled and rattled, snarled and rattled,
As it ran light, or had to bear a load.
And nothing happened: day was all but done.
Call it a day, I wish they might have said
To please the boy by giving him the half hour
That a boy counts so much when saved from work.
His sister stood beside them in her apron
To tell them "Supper." At the word, the saw,
As if to prove saws knew what supper meant,
Leaped out at the boy's hand, or seemed to leap—
He must have given the hand. However it was,
Neither refused the meeting. But the hand!
The boy's first outcry was a rueful laugh,
As he swung toward them holding up the hand
Half in appeal, but half as if to keep
The life from spilling. Then the boy saw all—
Since he was old enough to know, big boy
Doing a man's work, though a child at heart—
He saw all spoiled. "Don't let him cut my hand off—
The doctor, when he comes. Don't let him, sister!"
So. But the hand was gone already.
The doctor put him in the dark of ether.
He lay and puffed his lips out with his breath.

And then—the watcher at his pulse took fright.
No one believed. They listened at his heart.
Little—less—nothing!—and that ended it.
No more to build on there. And they, since they
Were not the one dead, turned to their affairs.

ROBERT FROST

Birches

When I see birches bend to left and right
Across the lines of straighter darker trees,
I like to think some boy's been swinging them.
But swinging doesn't bend them down to stay.
Ice-storms do that. Often you must have seen them
Loaded with ice a sunny winter morning
After a rain. They click upon themselves
As the breeze rises, and turn many-colored
As the stir cracks and crazes their enamel.
Soon the sun's warmth makes them shed crystal shells
Shattering and avalanching on the snow-crust—
Such heaps of broken glass to sweep away
You'd think the inner dome of heaven had fallen.
They are dragged to the withered bracken by the load,
And they seem not to break; though once they are bowed
So low for long, they never right themselves:
You may see their trunks arching in the woods
Years afterwards, trailing their leaves on the ground
Like girls on hands and knees that throw their hair
Before them over their heads to dry in the sun.
But I was going to say when Truth broke in
With all her matter-of-fact about the ice-storm
(Now am I free to be poetical?)
I should prefer to have some boy bend them
As he went out and in to fetch the cows—
Some boy too far from town to learn baseball,
Whose only play was what he found himself,
Summer or winter, and could play alone.
One by one he subdued his father's trees
By riding them down over and over again
Until he took the stiffness out of them,
And not one but hung limp, not one was left
For him to conquer. He learned all there was
To learn about not launching out too soon
And so not carrying the tree away

Clear to the ground. He always kept his poise
To the top branches, climbing carefully
With the same pains you use to fill a cup
Up to the brim, and even above the brim.
Then he flung outward, feet first, with a swish,
Kicking his way down through the air
to the ground.
So was I once myself a swinger of birches.
And so I dream of going back to be.
It's when I'm weary of considerations,
And life is too much like a pathless wood
Where your face burns and tickles with the cobwebs
Broken across it, and one eye is weeping
From a twig's having lashed across it open.
I'd like to get away from earth awhile
And then come back to it and begin over.
May no fate willfully misunderstand me
And half grant what I wish and snatch me away
Not to return. Earth's the right place for love:
I don't know where it's likely to go better.
I'd like to go by climbing a birch tree,
And climb black branches up a snow-white trunk
Toward heaven, till the tree could bear no more,
But dipped its top and set me down again.
That would be good both going and coming back.
One could do worse than be a swinger of birches.

ROBERT FROST

Design

I found a dimpled spider, fat and white,
On a white heal-all, holding up a moth
Like a white piece of rigid satin cloth—
Assorted characters of death and blight
Mixed ready to begin the morning right,
Like the ingredients of a witches' broth—
A snow-drop spider, a flower like a froth,
And dead wings carried like a paper kite.

What had that flower to do with being white,
The wayside blue and innocent heal-all?
What brought the kindred spider to that height,
Then steered the white moth thither in the night?
What but design of darkness to appall?—
If design govern in a thing so small.

ROBERT FROST

Mending Wall

Something there is that doesn't love a wall,
That sends the frozen-ground-swell under it,
And spills the upper boulders in the sun;
And makes gaps even two can pass abreast.
The work of hunters is another thing:
I have come after them and made repair
Where they have left not one stone on a stone,
But they would have the rabbit out of hiding,
To please the yelping dogs. The gaps I mean,
No one has seen them made or heard them made,
But at spring mending-time we find them there.
I let my neighbour know beyond the hill;
And on a day we meet to walk the line
And set the wall between us once again.
We keep the wall between us as we go.
To each the boulders that have fallen to each.
And some are loaves and some so nearly balls
We have to use a spell to make them balance:
"Stay where you are until our backs are turned!"
We wear our fingers rough with handling them.
Oh, just another kind of out-door game,
One on a side. It comes to little more:
There where it is we do not need the wall:
He is all pine and I am apple orchard.
My apple trees will never get across
And eat the cones under his pines, I tell him.
He only says, "Good fences make good neighbours."
Spring is the mischief in me, and I wonder
If I could put a notion in his head:
"*Why* do they make good neighbours? Isn't it
Where there are cows? But here there are no cows.
Before I built a wall I'd ask to know
What I was walling in or walling out,
And to whom I was like to give offence.
Something there is that doesn't love a wall,
That wants it down." I could say "Elves" to him,
But it's not elves exactly, and I'd rather
He said it for himself. I see him there
Bringing a stone grasped firmly by the top
In each hand, like an old-stone savage armed.
He moves in darkness as it seems to me,
Not of woods only and the shade of trees.

He will not go behind his father's saying,
And he likes having thought of it so well
He says again, "Good fences make good neighbours."

ROBERT FROST

The Death of the Hired Man

Mary sat musing on the lamp-flame at the table
Waiting for Warren. When she heard his step,
She ran on tip-toe down the darkened passage
To meet him in the doorway with the news
And put him on his guard. "Silas is back."
She pushed him outward with her through the door
And shut it after her. "Be kind," she said.
She took the market things from Warren's arms
And set them on the porch, then drew him down
To sit beside her on the wooden steps.

"When was I ever anything but kind to him?
But I'll not have the fellow back," he said.
"I told him so last haying, didn't I?
'If he left then,' I said 'that ended it.'
What good is he? Who else will harbour him
At his age for the little he can do?
What help he is there's no depending on.
Off he goes always when I need him most.
'He thinks he ought to earn a little pay,
Enough at least to buy tobacco with,
So he won't have to beg and be beholden.'
'All right,' I say, 'I can't afford to pay
Any fixed wages, though I wish I could.'
'Someone else can.' 'Then someone else will have to.'
I shouldn't mind his bettering himself
If that was what it was. You can be certain,
When he begins like that, there's someone at him
Trying to coax him off with pocket-money,—
In haying time, when any help is scarce.
In winter he comes back to us. I'm done."

"Sh! not so loud: he'll hear you," Mary said.

"I want him to: he'll have to soon or late."

"He's worn out. He's asleep beside the stove.
When I came up from Rowe's I found him here,
Huddled against the barn-door fast asleep,
A miserable sight, and frightening, too—

You needn't smile—I didn't recognise him—
I wasn't looking for him—and he's changed.
Wait till you see."

"Where did you say he'd been?"

"He didn't say. I dragged him to the house,
And gave him tea and tried to make him smoke.
I tried to make him talk about his travels.
Nothing would do: he just kept nodding off."

"What did he say? Did he say anything?"

"But little."

"Anything? Mary, confess
He said he'd come to ditch the meadow for me."

"Warren!"

"But did he? I just want to know."

"Of course he did. What would you have him say?
Surely you wouldn't grudge the poor old man
Some humble way to save his self-respect.
He added, if you really care to know,
He meant to clear the upper pasture, too.
That sounds like something you have heard before?
Warren, I wish you could have heard the way
He jumbled everything. I stopped to look
Two or three times—he made me feel so queer—
To see if he was talking in his sleep.
He ran on Harold Wilson—you remember—
The boy you had in haying four years since.
He's finished school, and teaching in his college.
Silas declares you'll have to get him back.
He says they two will make a team for work:
Between them they will lay this farm as smooth!
The way he mixed that in with other things.
He thinks young Wilson a likely lad, though daft
On education—you know how they fought
All through July under the blazing sun,
Silas up on the cart to build the load,
Harold along beside to pitch it on."

"Yes, I took care to keep well out of earshot."

"Well, those days trouble Silas like a dream.
You wouldn't think they would. How some things linger!
Harold's young college boy's assurance piqued him.
After so many years he still keeps finding
Good arguments he sees he might have used.
I sympathise. I know just how it feels
To think of the right thing to say too late,

Harold's associated in his mind with Latin.
He asked me what I thought of Harold's saying
He studied Latin like the violin
Because he liked it—that an argument!
He said he couldn't make the boy believe
He could find water with a hazel prong—
Which showed how much good school had
ever done him.
He wanted to go over that. But most of all
He thinks if he could have another chance
To teach him how to build a load of hay——"

"I know, that's Silas' one accomplishment.
He bundles every forkful in its place,
And tags and numbers it for future reference,
So he can find and easily dislodge it
In the unloading. Silas does that well.
He takes it out in bunches like big birds' nests.
You never see him standing on the hay
He's trying to lift, straining to lift himself."
"He thinks if he could teach him that, he'd be
Some good perhaps to someone in the world.
He hates to see a boy the fool of books.
Poor Silas, so concerned for other folk,
And nothing to look backward to with pride,
And nothing to look forward to with hope,
So now and never any different."

Part of a moon was falling down the west,
Dragging the whole sky with it to the hills.
Its light poured softly in her lap. She saw
And spread her apron to it. She put out her hand
Among the harp-like morning-glory strings,
Taut with the dew from garden bed to eaves,
As if she played unheard the tenderness
That wrought on him beside her in the night.
"Warren," she said, "he has come home to die:
You needn't be afraid he'll leave you this time."

"Home," he mocked gently.

"Yes, what else but home?
It all depends on what you mean by home.
Of course he's nothing to us, any more
Than was the hound that came a stranger to us
Out of the woods, worn out upon the trail."

"Home is the place where, when you have to go there,
They have to take you in."

"I should have called it
Something you somehow haven't to deserve."

Warren leaned out and took a step or two,
Picked up a little stick, and brought it back
And broke it in his hand and tossed it by.
"Silas has better claim on us you think
Than on his brother? Thirteen little miles
As the road winds would bring him to his door.
Silas has walked that far no doubt to-day.
Why didn't he go there? His brother's rich,
A somebody—director in the bank."

"He never told us that."

"We know it though."

"I think his brother ought to help, of course.
I'll see to that if there is need. He ought of right
To take him in, and might be willing to—
He may be better than appearances.
But have some pity on Silas. Do you think
If he'd had any pride in claiming kin
Or anything he looked for from his brother,
He'd keep so still about him all this time?"

"I wonder what's between them."

"I can tell you.

Silas is what he is—we wouldn't mind him—
But just the kind that kinsfolk can't abide.
He never did a thing so very bad.
He don't know why he isn't quite as good
As anyone. He won't be made ashamed
To please his brother, worthless though he is."

"*I* can't think Si ever hurt anyone."

"No, but he hurt my heart the way he lay
And rolled his old head on that sharp-edged
chair-back.
He wouldn't let me put him on the lounge.
You must go in and see what you can do.
I made the bed up for him there to-night.
You'll be surprised at him—how much he's broken.
His working days are done; I'm sure of it."

"I'd not be in a hurry to say that."

"I haven't been. Go, look, see for yourself.
But, Warren, please remember how it is:
He's come to help you ditch the meadow.
He has a plan. You mustn't laugh at him.
He may not speak of it, and then he may.
I'll sit and see if that small sailing cloud
Will hit or miss the moon."

It hit the moon.
Then there were three there, making a dim row,
The moon, the little silver cloud, and she.

Warren returned—too soon, it seemed to her,
Slipped to her side, caught up her hand and waited.

"Warren," she questioned.

"Dead," was all he answered.

ROBERT FROST

The Silken Tent

She is as in a field a silken tent
At midday when the sunny summer breeze
Has dried the dew and all its ropes relent,
So that in guys it gently sways at ease,
And its supporting central cedar pole,
That is its pinnacle to heavenward
And signifies the sureness of the soul,
Seems to owe naught to any single cord,
But strictly held by none, is loosely bound
By countless silken ties of love and thought
To everything on earth the compass round,
And only by one's going slightly taut
In the capriciousness of summer air
Is of the slightest bondage made aware.

ROBERT FROST

Acquainted with the Night

I have been one acquainted with the night.
I have walked out in rain—and back in rain.
I have outwalked the furthest city light.

I have looked down the saddest city lane.
I have passed by the watchman on his beat
And dropped my eyes, unwilling to explain.

I have stood still and stopped the sound of feet
When far away an interrupted cry
Came over houses from another street,

But not to call me back or say good-bye;
And further still at an unearthly height
One luminary clock against the sky

Proclaimed the time was neither wrong nor right.
I have been one acquainted with the night.

ROBERT FROST

After Apple Picking

My long two-pointed ladder's sticking through a tree
Toward heaven still,
And there's a barrel that I didn't fill
Beside it, and there may be two or three
Apples I didn't pick upon some bough.
But I am done with apple-picking now.
Essence of winter sleep is on the night,
The scent of apples: I am drowsing off.
I cannot rub the strangeness from my sight
I got from looking through a pane of glass
I skimmed this morning from the drinking trough
And held against the world of hoary grass.
It melted, and I let it fall and break.
But I was well
Upon my way to sleep before it fell,
And I could tell
What form my dreaming was about to take.
Magnified apples appear and disappear,
Stem end and blossom end,
And every fleck of russet showing clear.
My instep arch not only keeps the ache,
It keeps the pressure of a ladder-round.
I feel the ladder sway as the boughs bend.
And I keep hearing from the cellar bin
The rumbling sound
Of load on load of apples coming in.
For I have had too much
Of apple-picking: I am overtired
Of the great harvest I myself desired.
There were ten thousand thousand fruit to touch,
Cherish in hand, lift down, and not let fall.
For all
That struck the earth,
No matter if not bruised or spiked with stubble,
Went surely to the cider-apple heap
As of no worth.

One can see what will trouble
This sleep of mine, whatever sleep it is.
Were he not gone,
 The woodchuck could say whether it's like his
Long sleep, as I describe its coming on.
Or just some human sleep.

RICHARD GARCIA (b. 1941) grew up in and near San Francisco as a first-generation American in a half-Mexican, half-Puerto Rican household. He began writing poetry in high school and published his first collection, *Selected Poems*, in 1972. This first collection, though successful with critics, was not popular within Garcia's Chicano poetic community, and Garcia stopped writing for over a decade. "Why I Left the Church" appeared in his second collection, *The Flying Garcias* (1993). His most recent collection is *Rancho Notorious* (2001). Garcia has joked that in his childhood home they only had one book, on dream interpretation; many critics have taken note of the dreamlike images in his poetry.

Related Works: Marquez, "The Handsomest Drowned Man in the World"; Cofer, "Arturo's Flight"; Donne, "The Flea"; Stevens, "Of Mere Being"; Williams, *The Glass Menagerie*.

RICHARD GARCIA

Why I Left the Church

Maybe it was
because the only time
I hit a baseball
it smashed the neon cross
on the church across
the street. Even
twenty-five years later
when I saw Father Harris
I would wonder
if he knew it was me.
Maybe it was the demon-stoked
rotisseries of purgatory
where we would roast
hundreds of years
for the smallest of sins.
Or was it the day
I wore my space helmet
to catechism? Clear plastic
with a red and white
inflatable rim.

Sister Mary Bernadette
pointed toward the door
and said, "Out! Come back
when you're ready."
I rose from my chair
and kept rising
toward the ceiling
while the children
screamed and Sister
kept crossing herself.
The last she saw of me
was my shoes disappearing
through cracked plaster.
I rose into the sky and beyond.
It is a good thing
I am wearing my helmet,
I thought as I floated
and turned in the blackness
and brightness of outer space.
My body cold on one side and hot
on the other. It would
have been very quiet
if my blood had not been
rumbling in my ears so loud.
I remember thinking,
Maybe I will come back
when I'm ready.
But I won't tell
the other children
what it was like.
I'll have to make something up.

ALLEN GINSBERG (1926–1997) grew up in New Jersey with his mother, a Russian immigrant and member of the Communist Party who was troubled throughout her life by mental illness, and his father, a poet and teacher. Ginsberg attended Columbia University and, while there, befriended Jack Kerouac (*On the Road*) and William Burroughs (*Naked Lunch*). Together they formed the core of the **Beat Movement**, a counterculture group of poets and artists who eventually became involved with the peace and environmental movements and drug cultures of the 1960s and 1970s. In 1954, Ginsberg relocated to San Francisco, where he met Lawrence Ferlinghetti, another important Beat poet, whose small press, City Lights, published Ginsberg's first and most famous collection of poetry *Howl and Other Poems* (1956). Ginsberg's public reading of "Howl" led to a landmark obscenity trial, great notoriety, and the introduction of the **rant** as a semi-legitimate poetic form. Part 1 of "Howl" is reproduced here.

Related Works: Kafka, "Metamorphosis"; Caedmon's Hymn; Blake, "The Tiger," "The Lamb," and "London"; Swift, "A Description of the Morning"; Wordsworth,

"I wandered lonely as a cloud"; Whitman, "O Captain! my Captain!" and "When lilacs last in the dooryard bloom'd"; Forché, "The Colonel"; Norman, *'Night Mother.*

ALLEN GINSBERG

Howl, Part I

For Carl Solomon

I saw the best minds of my generation destroyed by madness, starving hysterical
  naked,
dragging themselves through the negro streets at dawn looking for an angry fix,
angelheaded hipsters burning for the ancient heavenly connection to the starry
  dynamo in the machinery of night,
who poverty and tatters and hollow-eyed and high sat up smoking in the
  supernatural darkness of cold-water flats floating across the tops of cities
  contemplating jazz,
who bared their brains to Heaven under the El and saw Mohammedan angels
  staggering on tenement roofs illuminated,
who passed through universities with radiant cool eyes hallucinating Arkansas
  and Blake-light tragedy among the scholars of war,
who were expelled from the academies for crazy & publishing obscene odes
  on the windows of the skull,
who cowered in unshaven rooms in underwear, burning their money in
  wastebaskets and listening to the Terror through the wall,
who got busted in their pubic beards returning through Laredo with a belt
  of marijuana for New York,
who ate fire in paint hotels or drank turpentine in Paradise Alley, death, or
  purgatoried their torsos night after night
with dreams, with drugs, with waking nightmares, alcohol and cock and
  endless balls,
incomparable blind streets of shuddering cloud and lightning in the mind
  leaping toward poles of Canada & Paterson, illuminating all the motionless
  world of Time between,
Peyote solidities of halls, backyard green tree cemetery dawns, wine drunkenness
  over the rooftops, storefront boroughs of teahead joyride neon blinking traffic
  light, sun and moon and tree vibrations in the roaring winter dusks of
  Brooklyn, ashcan rantings and kind king light of mind,
who chained themselves to subways for the endless ride from Battery to holy
  Bronx on benzedrine until the noise of wheels and children brought them
  down shuddering mouth-wracked and battered bleak of brain all drained of
  brilliance in the drear light of Zoo,
who sank all night in submarine light of Bickford's floated out and sat through
  the stale beer afternoon in desolate Fugazzi's, listening to the crack of doom
  on the hydrogen jukebox,

who talked continuously seventy hours from park to pad to bar to Bellevue
to museum to the Brooklyn Bridge,
a lost battalion of platonic conversationalists jumping down the stoops off fire
escapes off windowsills of Empire State out of the moon,
yacketayakking screaming vomiting whispering facts and memories and
anecdotes and eyeball kicks and shocks of hospitals and jails and wars,
whole intellects disgorged in total recall for seven days and nights with brilliant
eyes, meat for the Synagogue cast on the pavement,
who vanished into nowhere Zen New Jersey leaving a trail of ambiguous picture
postcards of Atlantic City Hall,
suffering Eastern sweats and Tangerian bone-grindings and migraines of china
under junk-withdrawal in Newark's bleak furnished room,
who wandered around and around at midnight in the railroad yard wondering
where to go, and went, leaving no broken hearts,
who lit cigarettes in boxcars boxcars boxcars racketing through snow toward
lonesome farms in grandfather night,
who studied Plotinus Poe St. John of the Cross telepathy and bop kabbalah
because the cosmos instinctively vibrated at their feet in Kansas,
who loned it through the streets of Idaho seeking visionary indian angels who
were visionary indian angels,
who thought they were only mad when Baltimore gleamed in supernatural ecstasy,
who jumped in limousines with the Chinaman of Oklahoma on the impulse of
winter midnight streetlight smalltown rain,
who lounged hungry and lonesome through Houston seeking jazz or sex or
soup, and followed the brilliant Spaniard to converse about America and
Eternity, a hopeless task, and so took ship to Africa,
who disappeared into the volcanoes of Mexico leaving behind nothing but the
shadow of dungarees and the lava and ash of poetry scattered in fireplace
Chicago,
who reappeared on the West Coast investigating the FBI in beards and shorts
with big pacifist eyes sexy in their dark skin passing out incomprehensible
leaflets,
who burned cigarette holes in their arms protesting the narcotic tobacco haze
of Capitalism,
who distributed Supercommunist pamphlets in Union Square weeping and
undressing while the sirens of Los Alamos wailed them down, and wailed
down Wall, and the Staten Island ferry also wailed,
who broke down crying in white gymnasiums naked and trembling before the
machinery of other skeletons,
who bit detectives in the neck and shrieked with delight in policecars for
committing no crime but their own wild cooking pederasty and intoxication,
who howled on their knees in the subway and were dragged off the roof waving
genitals and manuscripts,
who let themselves be fucked in the ass by saintly motorcyclists, and screamed
with joy,
who blew and were blown by those human seraphim, the sailors, caresses of
Atlantic and Caribbean love,
who balled in the morning in the evenings in rosegardens and the grass of public
parks and cemeteries scattering their semen freely to whomever come who may,

who hiccuped endlessly trying to giggle but wound up with a sob behind a
partition in a Turkish Bath when the blond & naked angel came to pierce
them with a sword,
who lost their loveboys to the three old shrews of fate the one eyed shrew of the
heterosexual dollar the one eyed shrew that winks out of the womb and the
one eyed shrew that does nothing but sit on her ass and snip the intellectual
golden threads of the craftsman's loom,
who copulated ecstatic and insatiate with a bottle of beer a sweetheart a package
of cigarettes a candle and fell off the bed, and continued along the floor and
down the hall and ended fainting on the wall with a vision of ultimate cunt
and come eluding the last gyzym of consciousness,
who sweetened the snatches of a million girls trembling in the sunset, and were
red eyed in the morning but prepared to sweeten the snatch of the sunrise,
flashing buttocks under barns and naked in the lake,
who went out whoring through Colorado in myriad stolen night-cars, N.C.,
secret hero of these poems, cocksman and Adonis of Denver—joy to the
memory of his innumerable lays of girls in empty lots & diner backyards,
moviehouses' rickety rows, on mountaintops in caves or with gaunt waitresses
in familiar roadside lonely petticoat upliftings & especially secret gas-station
solipsisms of johns, & hometown alleys too,
who faded out in vast sordid movies, were shifted in dreams, woke on a sudden
Manhattan, and picked themselves up out of basements hungover with
heartless Tokay and horrors of Third Avenue iron dreams & stumbled to
unemployment offices,
who walked all night with their shoes full of blood on the snowbank docks waiting
for a door in the East River to open to a room full of steam-heat and opium,
who created great suicidal dramas on the apartment cliff-banks of the Hudson
under the wartime blue floodlight of the moon & their heads shall be
crowned with laurel in oblivion,
who ate the lamb stew of the imagination or digested the crab at the muddy
bottom of the rivers of Bowery,
who wept at the romance of the streets with their pushcarts full of onions and
bad music,
who sat in boxes breathing in the darkness under the bridge, and rose up to build
harpsichords in their lofts,
who coughed on the sixth floor of Harlem crowned with flame under the
tubercular sky surrounded by orange crates of theology,
who scribbled all night rocking and rolling over lofty incantations which in the
yellow morning were stanzas of gibberish,
who cooked rotten animals lung heart feet tail borsht & tortillas dreaming of the
pure vegetable kingdom,
who plunged themselves under meat trucks looking for an egg,
who threw their watches off the roof to cast their ballot for Eternity outside
of Time, & alarm clocks fell on their heads every day for the next decade,
who cut their wrists three times successively unsuccessfully, gave up and were
forced to open antique stores where they thought they were growing old
and cried,
who were burned alive in their innocent flannel suits on Madison Avenue
amid blasts of leaden verse & the tanked-up clatter of the iron regiments of

fashion & the nitroglycerine shrieks of the fairies of advertising & the mustard gas of sinister intelligent editors, or were run down by the drunken taxicabs of Absolute Reality,
who jumped off the Brooklyn Bridge this actually happened and walked away unknown and forgotten into the ghostly daze of Chinatown soup alleyways & firetrucks, not even one free beer,
who sang out of their windows in despair, fell out of the subway window, jumped in the filthy Passaic, leaped on negroes, cried all over the street, danced on broken wineglasses barefoot smashed phonograph records of nostalgic European 1930s German jazz finished the whiskey and threw up groaning into the bloody toilet, moans in their ears and the blast of colossal steamwhistles,
who barreled down the highways of the past journeying to the each other's hotrod-Golgotha jail-solitude watch or Birmingham jazz incarnation,
who drove crosscountry seventytwo hours to find out if I had a vision or you had a vision or he had a vision to find out Eternity,
who journeyed to Denver, who died in Denver, who came back to Denver & waited in vain, who watched over Denver & brooded & loned in Denver and finally went away to find out the Time, & now Denver is lonesome for her heroes,
who fell on their knees in hopeless cathedrals praying for each other's salvation and light and breasts, until the soul illuminated its hair for a second,
who crashed through their minds in jail waiting for impossible criminals with golden heads and the charm of reality in their hearts who sang sweet blues to Alcatraz,
who retired to Mexico to cultivate a habit, or Rocky Mount to tender Buddha or Tangiers to boys or Southern Pacific to the black locomotive or Harvard to Narcissus to Woodlawn to the daisychain or grave,
who demanded sanity trials accusing the radio of hypnotism & were left with their insanity & their hands & a hung jury,
who threw potato salad at CCNY lecturers on Dadaism and subsequently presented themselves on the granite steps of the madhouse with shaven heads and harlequin speech of suicide, demanding instantaneous lobotomy,
and who were given instead the concrete void of insulin Metrazol electricity hydrotherapy psychotherapy occupational therapy pingpong & amnesia,
who in humorless protest overturned only one symbolic pingpong table, resting briefly in catatonia,
returning years later truly bald except for a wig of blood, and tears and fingers, to the visible madman doom of the wards of the madtowns of the East,
Pilgrim State's Rockland's and Greystone's foetid halls, bickering with the echoes of the soul, rocking and rolling in the midnight solitude-bench dolmen-realms of love, dream of life a nightmare, bodies turned to stone as heavy as the moon,
with mother finally ******, and the last fantastic book flung out of the tenement window, and the last door closed at 4 a.m. and the last telephone slammed at the wall in reply and the last furnished room emptied down to the last piece of mental furniture, a yellow paper rose twisted on a wire hanger in the closet, and even that imaginary, nothing but a hopeful little bit of hallucination—
ah, Carl, while you are not safe I am not safe, and now you're really in the total animal soup of time—

and who therefore ran through the icy streets obsessed with a sudden flash of the
   alchemy of the use of the ellipse the catalog the meter & the vibrating plane,
who dreamt and made incarnate gaps in Time & Space through images
   juxtaposed, and trapped the archangel of the soul between 2 visual images and
   joined the elemental verbs and set the noun and dash of consciousness
   together jumping with sensation of Pater Omnipotens Aeterna Deus
to recreate the syntax and measure of poor human prose and stand before you
   speechless and intelligent and shaking with shame, rejected yet confessing out
   the soul to conform to the rhythm of thought in his naked and endless head,
the madman bum and angel beat in Time, unknown, yet putting down here
   what might be left to say in time come after death,
and rose reincarnate in the ghostly clothes of jazz in the goldhorn shadow of the
   band and blew the suffering of America's naked mind for love into an eli eli
   lamma lamma sabacthani saxophone cry that shivered the cities down
   to the last radio
with the absolute heart of the poem of life butchered out of their own bodies
   good to eat a thousand years.

DANA GIOIA (b. 1950), born in Los Angeles of Italian and Mexican heritage, earned a B.A. and M.B.A. from Stanford University and an M.A. in Comparative Literature from Harvard. Between 1977 and 1992, he worked as a business executive in New York, becoming vice president of General Foods. In 1992, Gioia left business to be a writer, and, in 1996, returned to California. He is author of three books of poetry: *Daily Horoscope* (1986), *The Gods of Winter* (1991), and *Interrogations at Noon* (2001), which won the American Book Award. He also publishes criticism (e.g., *Can Poetry Matter?* 1992) and has written the libretto for *Nosferatu*, an opera with music by Alva Henderson. In 1993, Dana Gioia was appointed by President Bush to be chairman of the National Endowment of the Arts. Gioia employs both **free verse** and traditional poetic forms. "California Hills in August" (1986) combines irregular or **accentual meter** with a regular stanza pattern, while "Unsaid" (2001) promises, then frustrates the desire for a regular **rhyme** scheme within the brief space of a single **sestet** stanza. Dana Gioia is a spokesperson for the poetic movement known as the **New Formalism**.

Related Works: Wordsworth, "I wandered lonely as a cloud"; Frost, "Birches"; Lowell, "Skunk Hour"; Thomas, "Fern Hill" and "Do Not Go Gentle into that Good Night"; Bishop, "One Art"; Norman, *'Night, Mother*; Tichborne, "My prime of youth is but a frost of cares."

DANA GIOIA

California Hills in August

I can imagine someone who found
these fields unbearable, who climbed

the hillside in the heat, cursing the dust,
cracking the brittle weeds underfoot,
wishing a few more trees for shade.

An Easterner especially, who would scorn
the meagerness of summer, the dry
twisted shapes of black elm,
scrub oak, and chaparral, a landscape
August has already drained of green.

One who would hurry over the clinging
thistle, foxtail, golden poppy,
knowing everything was just a weed,
unable to conceive that these trees
and sparse brown bushes were alive.

And hate the bright stillness of the noon
without wind, without motion,
the only other living thing
a hawk, hungry for prey, suspended
in the blinding, sunlit blue.

And yet how gentle it seems to someone
raised in a landscape short of rain—
the skyline of a hill broken by no more
trees than one can count, the grass,
the empty sky, the wish for water.

DANA GIOIA

Unsaid

So much of what we live goes on inside—
The diaries of grief, the tongue-tied aches
Of unacknowledged love are no less real
For having passed unsaid. What we conceal
Is always more than what we dare confide.
Think of the letters that we write our dead.

LOUISE GLÜCK (b. 1943) was born in New York City and grew up on Long Island. She had a privileged family education, becoming familiar with classical mythology by the age of three, and studied at Sarah Lawrence College and then Columbia University. Louise Glück has won many prizes for her poetry, including the Pulitzer Prize and the Poetry Society of America's William Carlos Williams Award for *The Wild Iris* (1992) and the National Book Critics Circle Award for *The Triumph of Achilles* (1985). She was elected as a chancellor of the Academy of American Poets in 1999, and in 2003–2004 served as U.S. Poet Laureate Consultant in Poetry at the Library of Congress. Glück currently teaches at Williams College.

For Glück, as for T. S. Eliot, poetry is a spiritual quest. Her compressed style connects her to Emily Dickinson, her interest in classical myth to H.D. (Hilda Doolittle). Like Dickinson's poetry, "School Children" (1975) and "Gratitude" (1975) work through **metaphor** and **personification** to link domestic life with **myth**.

In *Meadowlands* (1996), the long-suffering Penelope and wandering Odysseus from Homer's *Odyssey* are recast as a contemporary couple in a disintegrating marriage. The story line is carried by **monologues** from characters from Homer's *Odyssey* who find themselves embroiled in this marital drama: one of the most insightful and funny is the sorceress Circe. These poems show Glück's interest in **paradox** and **riddles** and exhibit what has been called her "aesthetics of renunciation," in which speakers struggle to establish the boundaries of the self and find a voice by separating themselves from others.

Related Works: Bradstreet, "To My Dear and Loving Husband"; Dickinson, "Hope is the thing with feathers"; Drayton, Sonnet 61; H.D., "Helen"; "The Husband's Message" and "The Wife's Lament"; Ibsen, *A Dollhouse*; Levertov, "The Ache of Marriage"; Old English Riddles.

LOUISE GLÜCK

The School Children

The children go forward with their little satchels.
And all morning the mothers have labored
to gather the late apples, red and gold,
like words of another language.

And on the other shore
are those who wait behind great desks
to receive these offerings.

How orderly they are—the nails
on which the children hang
their overcoats of blue or yellow wool.

And the teachers shall instruct them in silence
and the mothers shall scour the orchards for
    a way out,
drawing to themselves the gray limbs of the fruit trees
bearing so little ammunition.

LOUISE GLÜCK

Gratitude

Do not think I am not grateful for your small
kindness to me.
I like small kindnesses.
In fact I actually prefer them to the more
substantial kindness, that is always eying you,
like a large animal on a rug,
until your whole life reduces
to nothing but waking up morning after morning
cramped, and the bright sun shining on its tusks.

LOUISE GLÜCK

Circe's Power

I never turned anyone into a pig.
Some people are pigs; I make them
look like pigs.

I'm sick of your world
that lets the outside disguise the inside.

Your men weren't bad men;
undisciplined life
did that to them. As pigs,

under the care of
me and my ladies, they
sweetened right up.

Then I reversed the spell,
showing you my goodness
as well as my power. I saw

we could be happy here,
as men and women are
when their needs are simple. In the same breath,

I foresaw your departure,
your men with my help braving
the crying and pounding sea. You think

a few tears upset me? My friend,
every sorceress is

a pragmatist at heart; nobody
sees essence who can't
face limitation. If I wanted only to hold you

I could hold you prisoner.

JORIE GRAHAM (b. 1951) was born in New York City to Curtis Bill (a scholar of religion) and Beverly Stoll Pepper (an artist). Raised in Italy, she also studied at the Sorbonne. Graham earned her B.A. from New York University and an M.F.A. from the University of Iowa's Writers Workshop. She has written nine books of poetry and won the 1996 Pulitzer Prize for *The Dream of a Unified Field*, which contains "Reading Plato." Graham is currently Boyleston Professor of Rhetoric and Oratory at Harvard University.

"Reading Plato," as the title suggests, concerns itself with the relation between the natural and ideal worlds; this tension is reflected in Graham's use of a regular **sestina** stanza combined with irregular **meter**, unrhymed line endings, and a striking disjunction between the poetic line and **syntax**. At the same time, her use of the fishing fly as an overarching **metaphor** recalls T. S. Eliot; her analogy between the seasons and the span of man's life suggests Shakespeare's use of the same metaphor, and her interest in religious experience can be traced to John Milton.

Related Works: Atwood, "You fit into me"; Eliot, "The Love Song of J. Alfred Prufrock"; Milton, "When I consider how my light is spent"; Plath, "Metaphors"; Shakespeare, Sonnet 73.

JORIE GRAHAM

Reading Plato

This is the story
    of a beautiful
lie, what slips
    through my fingers,
your fingers. It's winter,
    it's far

in the lifespan
    of man.
Bareheaded, in a soiled
    shirt,
speechless, my friend
    is making

lures, his hobby. Flies
    so small
he works with tweezers and
    a magnifying glass.

They must be
so believable

they're true—feelers,
antennae,
quick and frantic
as something
drowning. His heart
beats wildly

in his hands. It is
blinding
and who will forgive him
in his tiny
garden? He makes them
out of hair,

deer hair, because it's hollow
and floats.
Past death, past sight,
this is
his good idea, what drives
the silly days

together. Better than memory. Better
than love.
Then they are done, a hook
under each pair
of wings, and it's Spring,
and the men

wade out into the riverbed
at dawn. Above,
the stars still connect-up
their hungry animals.
Soon they'll be satisfied
and go. Meanwhile

upriver, downriver, imagine, quick
in the air,
in flesh, in a blue
swarm of
flies, our knowledge of
the graceful

deer skips easily across
the surface.
Dismembered, remembered,
it's finally
alive. Imagine
the body

they were all once
      a part of,
these men along the lush
      green banks
trying to slip in
      and pass

for the natural world.

ROBERT GRAVES (1895–1985) was born in Wimbledon, near London. His father, a Gaelic scholar and Irish poet, was an inspector of schools. Together, the father and mother raised ten children from two different families. In his youth, Graves enjoyed life in his large family, which made summer excursions to visit his mother's extended family in Germany. Graves disliked public school (the British equivalent of American private schools), but began to write poetry seriously there. During World War I, Graves saw action in France; he was injured and witnessed such destruction that he nearly suffered a breakdown. During his first marriage, Graves met American author Laura Riding, who became his partner, critic, and "muse." Graves was a prolific writer of both prose and poetry; most notably, he is the author of *I, Claudius* (1934) and *The White Goddess* (1948), a matriarchal grammar of poetic myth that informs Graves's later poetry and has been widely influential. Graves won many prizes, including a bronze medal for poetry at the 1924 Olympics and a gold medal at the 1968 Olympics. He died in Majorca, Spain.

Related Works: Swift, "A Description of the Morning"; Hopkins, "Pied Beauty"; Carruth, "An Apology for Using the Word 'Heart' in Too Many Poems"; cummings, "since feeling is first"; Reed, "Naming of Parts"; Stevens, "Thirteen Ways of Looking at a Blackbird."

ROBERT GRAVES

The Naked and the Nude

For me, the naked and the nude
(By lexicographers construed
As synonyms that should express
The same deficiency of dress
Or shelter) stand as wide apart
As love from lies, or truth from art.

Lovers without reproach will gaze
On bodies naked and ablaze;
The Hippocratic eye will see
In nakedness, anatomy;
And naked shines the Goddess when
She mounts her lion among men.

The nude are bold, the nude are sly
To hold each treasonable eye.
While draping by a showman's trick
Their dishabille in rhetoric,
They grin a mock-religious grin
Of scorn at those of naked skin.

The naked, therefore, who compete
Against the nude may know defeat;
Yet when they both together tread
The briary pastures of the dead,
By Gorgons with long whips pursued,
How naked go the sometime nude!

H.D. (HILDA DOLITTLE) (1886–1961) was born in Pennsylvania and attended private schools and, briefly, Bryn Mawr. She spent most of the rest of her life in England and Switzerland. Ezra Pound, Marianne Moore, and other **Modernists** influenced her early poetry. Her work through the 1930s was generally minimalist. Although still focused on mysticism, myth, and classical themes, after World War II Doolittle's poetry became increasingly experimental. Her own bisexuality was a complex theme that H.D. explored through the metaphor of the palimpsest, a manuscript leaf or page that has been erased and then reinscribed.

Related Works: Behn, "On Her Loving Two Equally"; Dickinson, "Because I could not stop for Death"; Bishop, "One Art"; Glück "Circe's Power"; Pound, "The River Merchant's Wife"; Eliot, "The Love Song of J. Alfred Prufrock"; Sophocles, *Antigone.*

H.D.

Helen

All Greece hates
the still eyes in the white face,
the lustre of the olives
where she stands,
and the white hands.

All Greece reviles
the wan face when she smiles,
hating it deeper still
when it grows wan and white,
remembering past enchantments
and past ills.

Greece sees unmoved,
God's daughter, born of love,
the beauty of cool feet

and slenderest knees,
could love indeed the maid,
only if she were laid,
white ash amid funeral cypresses.

Marilyn Hacker (b. 1942) has published more than a dozen collections of poetry. From 1990 to 1994, Hacker edited *The Kenyon Review*. She was awarded the Bernard F. Conners Prize from the *Paris Review*, the John Masefield Memorial Award of the Poetry Society of America, and fellowships from the Guggenheim Foundation and the Ingram Merrill Foundation. Much of her work follows strict and complex traditional forms such as the **villanelle** included below.

Related Works: Bishop, "One Art" and "Sestina"; Roethke, "The Waking"; Thomas, "Do Not Go Gentle into that Good Night"; Yau, "Chinese Villanelle"; Norman, *'Night, Mother.*

MARILYN HACKER

Villanelle for D. G. B.

Every day our bodies separate,
exploded torn and dazed.
Not understanding what we celebrate

we grope through languages and hesitate
and touch each other, speechless and amazed;
and every day our bodies separate

us further from our planned, deliberate
ironic lives. I am afraid, disphased,
not understanding what we celebrate

when our fused limbs and lips communicate
the unlettered power we have raised.
Every day our bodies' separate

routines are harder to perpetuate.
In wordless darkness we learn wordless praise,
not understanding what we celebrate;

wake to ourselves, exhausted, in the late
morning as the wind tears off the haze,
not understanding how we celebrate
our bodies. Every day we separate.

Joy Harjo (b. 1951) attended the University of New Mexico (B.A. 1976) and the University of Iowa (M.F.A. 1978). A full professor at the University of New Mexico since 1991, she is an enrolled member of the Muskogee Tribe. Her collections of poetry include *What Moon Drove Me to This*? (1979), *She Had Some Horses* (1983), *Secrets from the Center of the World* (1989), *In Mad Love and War* (1990), and *The Woman Who Fell from the Sky* (1994). In the two poems included here, readers should attend to Harjo's **persona** and the use of repetition, an important link to musical adaptations of her poetry.

Related Works: Erdrich, "The Red Convertible"; Alexie, "Reservation Love Song"; Anzaldúa, "horse"; Brooks, "The mother."

JOY HARJO

She had some horses.

She had horses who were bodies of sand.
She had horses who were maps drawn of blood.
She had horses who were skins of ocean water.
She had horses who were the blue air of sky.
She had horses who were fur and teeth.
She had horses who were clay and would break.
She had horses who were splintered red cliff.

She had some horses.

She had horses with eyes of trains,
She had horses with full brown thighs.
She had horses who laughed too much.
She had horses who threw rocks at glass houses.
She had horses who licked razor blades.

She had some horses.

She had horses who danced in their mother's arms.
She had horses who thought they were the sun and
their bodies shone and burned like stars.
She had horses who waltzed nightly on the moon.
She had horses who were much too shy, and kept quiet
in stalls of their own making.

She had some horses.

She had horses who liked Creek Stomp Dance songs.
She had horses who cried in their beer.
She had horses who spit at male queens who made
them afraid of themselves.
She had horses who said they weren't afraid.
She had horses who lied.
She had horses who told the truth, who were stripped
bare of their tongues.

She had some horses.

She had horses who called themselves "horse."
She had horses who called themselves "spirit,"
and kept their voices secret and to themselves.
She had horses who had no names.
She had horses who had books of names.

She had some horses.

She had horses who whispered in the dark, who were afraid to speak.
She had horses who screamed out of fear of the silence,
who carried knives to protect themselves from ghosts.
She had horses who waited for destruction.
She had horses who waited for resurrection.

She had some horses.

She had horses who got down on their knees for any savior.
She had horses who thought their high price had saved them.
She had horses who tried to save her,
who climbed in her bed at night and prayed as they raped her.

She had some horses.

She had some horses she loved.
She had some horses she hated.

They were the same horses.

JOY HARJO

The Woman Hanging from the Thirteenth Floor Window

She is the woman hanging from the 13th floor
window. Her hands are pressed white against the
concrete molding of the tenement building. She
hangs from the 13th floor window in east Chicago.
with a swirl of birds over her head. They could
be a halo, or a storm of glass waiting to crush her.

She thinks she will be set free.

The woman hanging from the 13th floor window
on the east side of Chicago is not alone.
She is a woman of children, of the baby, Carlos,
and of Margaret, and of Jimmy who is the oldest.
She is her mother's daughter and her father's son.
She is several pieces between the two husbands

she has had. She is all the women of the apartment
building who stand watching her, watching themselves.

When she was young she ate wild rice on scraped down
plates in warm wood rooms. It was in the farther
north and she was a baby then. They rocked her.

She sees Lake Michigan lapping at the shores of
herself. It is a dizzy hole of water and the rich
live in tall glass houses at the edge of it. In some
places Lake Michigan speaks softly, here, it just sputters
and butts itself against the asphalt. She sees
other buildings just like hers. She sees other
women hanging from many-floored windows
counting their lives in the palms of their hands
and in the palms of their children's hands.

She is the woman hanging from the 13th floor window
on the Indian side of town. Her belly is soft from
her children's births, her worn levis swing down below
her waist, and then her feet, and then her heart.
She is dangling.

The woman hanging from the 13th floor hears voices.
They come to her in the night when the lights have gone
dim. Sometimes they are little cats mewing and scratching
at the door, sometimes they are her grandmother's voice,
and sometimes they are gigantic men of light whispering
to her to get up, to get up, to get up. That's when she wants
to have another child to hold onto in the night, to be able to fall back into dreams.

And the woman hanging from the 13th floor window
hears other voices. Some of them scream out from below
for her to jump, they would push her over. Others cry softly
from the sidewalks, pull their children up like flowers and gather
them into their arms. They would help her, like themselves.

But she is the woman hanging from the 13th floor window,
and she knows she is hanging by her own fingers, her
own skin, her own thread of indecision.

She thinks of Carlos, of Margaret, of Jimmy.
She thinks of her father and of her mother.
She thinks of all the women she has been, of all
the men. She thinks of the color of her skin, and
of the Chicago streets, and of waterfalls and pines.
She thinks of moonlight nights, and of cool spring storms.
Her mind chatters like neon and northside bars.
She thinks of the 4 a.m. lonelinesses that have folded
her up like death, discordant, without logical and
beautiful conclusion. Her teeth break off at the edges.
She would speak.

The woman hangs from the thirteenth floor window crying for
the lost beauty of her own life. She sees the
sun falling west over the gray plane of Chicago.
She think she remembers listening to her own life
break loose, as she falls from the 13th floor
window on the east side of Chicago, or as she
climbs back up to claim herself again.

ROBERT HAYDEN (1913–1980) grew up in Detroit and was raised largely as a foster child in the home of neighbors. He graduated from high school in 1932 and attended Detroit City College (Wayne State University) on scholarship. W. H. Auden mentored Hayden during graduate school at Michigan State University. While Hayden explored many of his concerns about American history, race, and politics in his poetry, his Baha'i faith is often credited as the source of his compassionate, transcendental vision. In "Those Winter Sundays" (1962), Hayden juxtaposes images of cold and warmth to emphasize the difficult **ironies** of love in a cold and angry household.

Related Works: Roethke, "My Papa's Waltz"; Plath, "Daddy"; Rankine, "Him."

ROBERT HAYDEN

Those Winter Sundays

Sundays too my father got up early
and put his clothes on in the blueblack cold,
then with cracked hands that ached
from labor in the weekday weather made
banked fires blaze. No one ever thanked him.

I'd wake and hear the cold splintering, breaking.
When the rooms were warm, he'd call,
and slowly I would rise and dress,
fearing the chronic angers of that house,

Speaking indifferently to him,
who had driven out the cold
and polished my good shoes as well.
What did I know, what did I know
of love's austere and lonely offices?

SEAMUS HEANEY (b. 1939), the eldest of nine children from a rural Irish family, grew up in County Derry; and although he has since lived in urban environments in Ireland, England, and America, Heaney believes that County Derry is still his "country of the mind" and the foundation of his poetry. Along with a dozen collections of poetry, Heaney has published a translation of *Beowulf* and seven important critical volumes. His first poetry collection, *Death of a Naturalist*, published in 1966, showed his inclination towards darkly **pastoral** themes. His style favors Gaelic derivatives and simple, colloquial diction.

Related Works: Old English Riddles; Berry, "Another Descent" and "The Peace of Wild Things"; Frost, "Mending Wall" and "The Silken Tent"; Hayden, "Those Winter Sundays"; Kinnell, "The Bear"; Sandberg, "Chicago"; Stafford, "Traveling Through the Dark"; Yeats, "Sailing to Byzantium"; Glaspell, *Trifles*.

SEAMUS HEANEY

Digging

Between my finger and my thumb
The squat pen rests; as snug as a gun.

Under my window a clean rasping sound
When the spade sinks into gravelly ground:
My father, digging. I look down

Till his straining rump among the flowerbeds
Bends low, comes up twenty years away
Stooping in rhythm through potato drills
Where he was digging.

The coarse boot nestled on the lug, the shaft
Against the inside knee was levered firmly.
He rooted out tall tops, buried the bright edge deep
To scatter new potatoes that we picked
Loving their cool hardness in our hands.

By God, the old man could handle a spade.
Just like his old man.

My grandfather could cut more turf in a day
Than any other man on Toner's bog.
Once I carried him milk in a bottle
Corked sloppily with paper. He straightened up
To drink it, then fell to right away
Nicking and slicing neatly, heaving sods
Over his shoulder, digging down and down
For the good turf. Digging.

The cold smell of potato mold, the squelch and slap
Of soggy peat, the curt cuts of an edge
Through living roots awaken in my head.
But I've no spade to follow men like them.

Between my finger and my thumb
The squat pen rests.
I'll dig with it.

SEAMUS HEANEY

Punishment

I can feel the tug
of the halter at the nape
of her neck, the wind
on her naked front.

It blows her nipples
to amber beads,
it shakes the frail rigging
of her ribs.

I can see her drowned
body in the bog,
the weighing stone,
the floating rods and boughs.

Under which at first
she was a barked sapling
that is dug up
oak-bone, brain-firkin:

her shaved head
like a stubble of black corn,
her blindfold a soiled bandage,
her noose a ring

to store
the memories of love.
Little adulteress,
before they punished you

you were flaxen-haired,
undernourished, and your
tar-black face was beautiful.
My poor scapegoat,

I almost love you
but would have cast, I know,
the stones of silence.
I am the artful voyeur

of your brain's exposed
and darkening combs,

your muscles' webbing
and all your numbered bones:

I who have stood dumb
when your betraying sisters,
cauled in tar,
wept by the railings,

who would connive
in civilised outrage
yet understand the exact
and tribal, intimate revenge.

ANTHONY HECHT (1923–2004), an American poet, has published eight collections of poetry, including *The Hard Hours* (1967), which won the Pulitzer Prize. Hecht's volumes of literary criticism and translations from the Greek indicate his interest in formal artistry. Both Hecht's sense of humor and his sharp critical eye are in evidence in "The Dover Bitch" (1967), a **parody** of Matthew Arnold's "Dover Beach." In another vein entirely, "The Book of Yolek" (1990), a **sestina** reflecting on Hecht's participation in the liberation of Holocaust victims as a member of the 97th U.S. Infantry Division during World War II, carries a deceptively subtle accusation.

Related Works: Chekov, "Vanka"; Wideman, "What We Cannot Speak About We Must Pass Over in Silence"; Donne, "A Valediction: Forbidding Mourning"; Arnold, "Dover Beach"; Bishop, "Sestina"; Wilbur, "Junk"; Sophocles, *Antigone*.

ANTHONY HECHT

The Dover Bitch

A Criticism of Life: for Andrews Wanning

So there stood Matthew Arnold and this girl
With the cliffs of England crumbling away behind them,
And he said to her, "Try to be true to me,
And I'll do the same for you, for things are bad
All over, etc., etc.'"
Well now, I knew this girl. It's true she had read
Sophocles in a fairly good translation
And caught that bitter allusion to the sea,
But all the time he was talking she had in mind
The notion of what his whiskers would feel like
On the back of her neck. She told me later on
That after a while she got to looking out
At the lights across the channel, and really felt sad,
Thinking of all the wine and enormous beds
And blandishments in French and the perfumes.

And then she got really angry. To have been brought
All the way down from London, and then be addressed
As a sort of mournful cosmic last resort
Is really tough on a girl, and she was pretty.
Anyway, she watched him pace the room
And finger his watch-chain and seem to sweat a bit,
And then she said one or two unprintable things.
But you mustn't judge her by that. What I mean to say is,
She's really all right. I still see her once in a while
And she always treats me right. We have a drink
And I give her a good time, and perhaps it's a year
Before I see her again, but there she is,
Running to fat, but dependable as they come.
And sometimes I bring her a bottle of *Nuit d'Amour.*

ANTHONY HECHT

The Book of Yolek

Wir Haben ein Gesetz,
*Und nach dem Gesetz soll er sterben.**

The dowsed coals fume and hiss after your meal
Of grilled brook trout, and you saunter off for a walk
Down the fern trail. It doesn't matter where to,
Just so you're weeks and worlds away from home,
And among midsummer hills have set up camp
In the deep bronze glories of declining day.

You remember, peacefully, an earlier day
In childhood, remember a quite specific meal:
A corn roast and bonfire in summer camp.
That summer you got lost on a Nature Walk;
More than you dared admit, you thought of home:
No one else knows where the mind wanders to.

The fifth of August, 1942.
It was the morning and very hot. It was the day
They came at dawn with rifles to The Home
For Jewish Children, cutting short the meal
Of bread and soup, lining them up to walk
In close formation off to a special camp.

How often you have thought about that camp,
As though in some strange way you were driven to,
And about the children, and how they were made to walk,

---

*We have a law, and according to the law he must die.

Yolek who had bad lungs, who wasn't a day
Over five years old, commanded to leave his meal
And shamble between armed guards to his long home.

We're approaching August again. It will drive home
The regulation torments of that camp
Yolek was sent to, his small, unfinished meal,
The electric fences, the numeral tattoo,
The quite extraordinary heat of the day
They all were forced to take that terrible walk.

Whether on a silent, solitary walk
Or among crowds, far off or safe at home,
You will remember, helplessly, that day,
And the smell of smoke, and the loudspeakers of the camp.
Wherever you are, Yolek will be there, too.
His unuttered name will interrupt your meal.

Prepare to receive him in your home some day.
Though they killed him in the camp they sent him to,
He will walk in as you're sitting down to a meal.

BRIAN HENRY (b. 1972) grew up outside Richmond, Virginia. He received his B.A. in English from the College of William and Mary in 1994 and an M.F.A. in poetry from the University of Massachusetts at Amherst in 1997. A Fulbright Scholar in Australia in 1997–1998, Henry has written five books of poetry. *Astronaut* (2000), in which "Garage Sale" appears, was published in England, the United States, and Slovenia and made the short list for the 2000 Forward Prize in England. Henry is the editor of *Verse* and contributing editor for several magazines and presses and teaches at the University of Richmond.

Critics of Henry's poetry note his stylistic virtuosity and playful approach to form. "Garage Sale," which could be considered a **dramatic monologue** or a list poem, has an open-ended form and consists of a series of **epithets** (not unlike Caedmon's Hymn) that is transformed into poetry through **accentual meter** (three beats per line) and an insistent rhyming pattern on the syllable "er." **Feminine endings** on most lines keep the parade of social types moving. For best enjoyment, this poem needs to be read out loud!

Related Works: Caedmon's Hymn; Eliot, "The Love Song of J. Alfred Prufrock"; Stevens, "Thirteen Ways of Looking at a Blackbird."

BRIAN HENRY

Garage Sale

They all came by today.
Passersby, browsers, neck-craners.

Big Wheel riders, circus goers. Small time hustlers,
phone tappers, cheque bouncers, rear enders.
Tattle talers, crank callers, nose pickers.
Water bearers, moped wreckers, trash compactors,
furniture refinishers. Stroller pushers, leaf rakers,
windshield wipers, trash talkers, diaper changers.
Backstabbers, manure shovellers, gem inspectors,
toy breakers. Left-turn-on-red takers.
Baby killers, fortune tellers, right wingers,
bumper stickerers. Neck wringers, forgotten drifters.
Seat belt fasteners, shape shifters. Dizzy spinners,
plain clothes snoopers, house sitters, baby sitters,
couch sitters. They came by. Reckless drivers,
ancient mariners, natural fooders, kindergarten teachers.
Lounge singers, artificial colourers, dog trainers,
spaghetti strainers. Marriage counsellors, bargain shoppers.
Lottery losers, hair receders, hair croppers.
Loot stashers, wave riders, wishbone breakers,
wish makers. Drink downers, bet takers,
fat watchers, purse snatchers. Pork barrellers,
farewellers, racetrack gawkers, foreskin snippers.
Butt pinchers, crotch grabbers. They all came by.
Door knockers, shot blockers, mailbox bashers,
fulsome praisers. Nostalgia waxers, coke snorters,
streetwalkers, penny pinchers, orgasm fakers.
Movers and shakers. Cussers, chain smokers,
court jesters. Paddy wagon passengers.
Raggedy Ann clutchers. Belly button pokers,
pipe dreamers. Car bombers, cat nappers,
gun toters, bong hitters. Sword wielders,
sword swallowers, dirty dancers, last chancers.
Dixie whistlers, middle finger givers. Allegiance pledgers,
carpet deodorizers, crap shooters, paper shredders.
Natural selectors, conversation makers. Bread bakers,
contagious yawners, butt kissers, baby kissers,
tree huggers, tree climbers. All of them,
they all came by: so much paint flaking
 from these walls.

LANGSTON HUGHES (1902–1967) achieved fame during the **Harlem Renaissance** with his first volume of poetry, *The Weary Blues*, which appeared in 1926. From that time forward, Hughes was able to earn a living as a writer. In the decades after his Harlem period, he was extraordinarily prolific, writing novels, essays, newspaper columns, song lyrics, histories, anthologies, and plays while nurturing and influencing other African American writers, such as Zora Neale Hurston, Alice Walker, and Maya Angelou. His world travels gave Hughes a broad perspective and material for his columns as well as temporary reprieves from

American racism. His poetry is often noted for its blues and jazz **rhythms** as well as its distinctive **images** and **metaphors**.

Related Works: Ellison, "Battle Royal"; Dunbar, "We wear the mask" and "Sympathy"; Angelou, "Still I Rise"; Brooks, "The Bean Eaters"; Lorde, "Hanging Fire"; Young, "Langston Hughes"; Wilson, *The Piano Lesson.*

LANGSTON HUGHES

Theme for English B

The instructor said,

Go home and write
a page tonight.

And let that page come out of you—
Then, it will be true.

I wonder if it's that simple?
I am twenty-two, colored, born in Winston-Salem.
I went to school there, then Durham, then here
to this college on the hill above Harlem.
I am the only colored student in my class.
The steps from the hill lead down into Harlem,
through a park, then I cross St. Nicholas,
Eighth Avenue, Seventh, and I come to the Y,
the Harlem Branch Y, where I take the elevator
up to my room, sit down, and write this page:

It's not easy to know what is true for you or me
at twenty-two, my age. But I guess I'm what
I feel and see and hear, Harlem. I hear you:
hear you, hear me—we two—you, me, talk on this page.
(I hear New York, too.) Me—who?
Well, I like to eat, sleep, drink, and be in love.
I like to work, read, learn, and understand life.
I like a pipe for a Christmas present,
or records—Bessie, bop, or Bach.
I guess being colored doesn't make me *not* like
the same things other folks like who are other races.
So will my page be colored that I write?

Being me, it will not be white.
But it will be
a part of you, instructor.
You are white—
yet a part of me, as I am a part of you.
That's American.

Sometimes perhaps you don't want to be a part of me.
Nor do I often want to be a part of you.
But we are, that's true!
As I learn from you,
I guess you learn from me—
although you're older—and white—
and somewhat more free.

This is my page for English B.

LANGSTON HUGHES

Harlem

What happens to a dream deferred?
Does it dry up
Like a raisin in the sun?
Or fester like a sore—
And then run?
Does it stink like rotten meat?
Or crust and sugar over—
Like a syrupy sweet?

Maybe it just sags
Like a heavy load.

Or does it explode?

LANGSTON HUGHES

I, Too, Sing America

I, too, sing America.

I am the darker brother.
They send me to eat in the kitchen
When company comes,
But I laugh,
And eat well,
And grow strong.

Tomorrow,
I'll be at the table
When company comes.
Nobody'll dare

Say to me,
"Eat in the kitchen,"
Then.

Besides,
They'll see how beautiful I am
And be ashamed—

I, too, am America.

Randall Jarrell (1914–1965), American poet and essayist, joined the Army Air Corps in 1942. When he returned from the war, the publication of *Little Friend, Little Friend* (1945) established his reputation as a poet. "The Ball Turret Gunner," with its paradoxical imagery of birth and death and its **elegiac** tone is, perhaps, his most frequently anthologized poem. His sharp critical voice mellowed as Jarrell matured, and his critical volume, *Poetry and the Age* (1953), includes thoughtful, readable essays on, among others, Robert Frost, Walt Whitman, Marianne Moore, Wallace Stevens, and William Carlos Williams.

Related Works: O'Brien, "Stockings"; Auden, "The Unknown Citizen"; Frost, "The Hired Man"; Hecht, "The Book of Yolek"; Stafford, "At the Bomb Testing Site"; Sophocles, *Antigone.*

RANDALL JARRELL

The Death of the Ball Turret Gunner

From my mother's sleep I fell into the State,
And I hunched in its belly till my wet fur froze.
Six miles from earth, loosed from its dream of life,
I woke to black flak and the nightmare fighters.
When I died they washed me out of the turret with a hose.

Galway Kinnell (b. 1927) published *Selected Poems* in 1980, for which he received both the Pulitzer Prize and the National Book Award; he now divides his time between Vermont and New York City, where he is the Erich Maria Remarque Professor of Creative Writing at New York University. Kinnell's short lines, coupled with strong **rhythms** and repetition, tend to recreate the sound of a spell or charm. Because his subjects often circle around the foundational human experiences (e.g., birth, sex, death), his poetry tends to have a ritual quality.

Related Works: Hemingway, "A Clean, Well-Lighted Place"; Steinbeck, "The Chrysanthemums"; Whitman, "O Captain! my Captain!"; Bishop, "The Fish"; Brooks, "The mother"; Dickey, "The Heaven of Animals"; Frost, "Out, Out—"; Heaney, "Punishment."

GALWAY KINNELL

The Bear

1

In late winter
I sometimes glimpse bits of steam
coming up from
some fault in the old snow
and bend close and see it is lung-colored
and put down my nose
and know
the chilly, enduring odor of bear.

2

I take a wolf's rib and whittle
it sharp at both ends
and coil it up
and freeze it in blubber and place it out
on the fairway of the bears.

And when it has vanished
I move out on the bear tracks,
roaming in circles
until I come to the first, tentative, dark
splash on the earth.

And I set out
running, following the splashes
of blood wandering over the world.
At the cut, gashed resting places
I stop and rest,
at the crawl-marks
where he lay out on his belly
to overpass some stretch of bauchy ice
I lie out
dragging myself forward with bear-knives in my fists.

3

On the third day I begin to starve,
at nightfall I bend down as I knew I would
at a turd sopped in blood,
and hesitate, and pick it up.
and thrust it in my mouth, and gnash it down,
and rise
and go on running.

4

On the seventh day,
living by now on bear blood alone,
I can see his upturned carcass far out ahead, a scraggled,
steamy hulk,
the heavy fur riffling in the wind.
I come up to him
and stare at the narrow-spaced, petty eyes,
the dismayed
face laid back on the shoulder, the nostrils
flared, catching
perhaps the first taint of me as he
died.

I hack
a ravine in his thigh, and eat and drink,
and tear him down his whole length
and open him and climb in
and close him up after me, against the wind,
and sleep.

5

And dream
of lumbering flatfooted
over the tundra,
stabbed twice from within,
splattering a trail behind me,
splattering it out no matter which way I lurch,
no matter which parabola of bear-transcendence,
which dance of solitude I attempt,
which gravity-clutched leap,
which trudge, which groan.

6

Until one day I totter and fall—
fall on this
stomach that has tried so hard to keep up,
to digest the blood as it leaked in,
to break up
and digest the bone itself: and now the breeze
blows over me, blows off
the hideous belches of ill-digested bear blood
and rotted stomach
and the ordinary, wretched odor of bear,

blows across
my sore, lolled tongue a song
or screech, until I think I must rise up
and dance. And I lie still.

7

I awaken I think. Marshlights
reappear, geese
come trailing again up the flyway.
In her ravine under old snow the dam-bear
lies, licking
lumps of smeared fur
and drizzly eyes into shapes
with her tongue. And one
hairy-soled trudge stuck out before me,
the next groaned out,
the next,
the next,
the rest of my days I spend
wandering: wondering
what, anyway,
  was that sticky infusion, that rank flavor of blood, that
  poetry, by which I lived?

GALWAY KINNELL

Wait

Wait, for now.

Distrust everything, if you have to.
But trust the hours. Haven't they
carried you everywhere, up to now?
Personal events will become interesting again.
Hair will become interesting.
Pain will become interesting.
Buds that open out of season will become lovely again.
Second-hand gloves will become lovely again,
their memories are what give them
the need for other hands. And the desolation
of lovers is the same: that enormous emptiness
carved out of such tiny beings as we are
asks to be filled; the need
for the new love is faithfulness to the old.

Wait.
Don't go too early.
You're tired. But everyone's tired.
But no one is tired enough.
Only wait a while and listen.
Music of hair,

Music of pain,
music of looms weaving all our loves again.
Be there to hear it, it will be the only time.
most of all to hear,
the flute of your whole existence,
rehearsed by the sorrows, play itself into total exhaustion.

YUSEF KOMUNYAKAA (b. 1947), an American poet born in Louisiana, won the Pulitzer Prize and a $50,000 Kingsley Tufts Poetry Award in 1994 for *Neon Vernacular: New and Selected Poems*. He has published over a dozen collections of poetry and contributed to anthologies of jazz poetry. His work is noted for short **vernacular** lines that are used to express complex views about war, nature, and art as well as his interest in jazz poetry and **concrete** poetry. He served in Vietnam from 1965 to 1967 and is currently a professor of creative writing at Emory University.

Related Works: O'Brien, "Stockings"; Owen, "Dulce et Decorum Est"; Auden, "The Unknown Citizen"; Hayden, "Those Winter Sundays"; McKay, "America"; Rios, "The Vietnam Wall."

YUSEF KOMUNYAKAA

Facing It

My black face fades,
hiding inside the black granite.
I said I wouldn't,
dammit: No tears.
I'm stone. I'm flesh.
My clouded reflection eyes me
like a bird of prey, the profile of night
slanted against morning. I turn
this way—the stone lets me go.
I turn that way—I'm inside
the Vietnam Veterans Memorial
again, depending on the light
to make a difference.
I go down the 58,022 names,
half-expecting to find
my own in letters like smoke.
I touch the name Andrew Johnson;
I see the booby trap's white flash.
Names shimmer on a woman's blouse
but when she walks away
the names stay on the wall.

Brushstrokes flash, a red bird's
wings cutting across my stare.
The sky. A plane in the sky.
A white vet's image floats
closer to me, then his pale eyes
look through mine. I'm a window.
He's lost his right arm
inside the stone. In the black mirror
a woman's trying to erase names:
No, she's brushing a boy's hair.

YUSEF KOMUNYAKAA

My Father's Love Letters

On Fridays he'd open a can of Jax
After coming home from the mill,
& ask me to write a letter to my mother
Who sent postcards of desert flowers
Taller than men. He would beg,
Promising to never beat her
Again. Somehow I was happy
She had gone, & sometimes wanted
To slip in a reminder, how Mary Lou
Williams' "Polka Dots & Moonbeams"
Never made the swelling go down.
His carpenter's apron always bulged
With old nails, a claw hammer
Looped at his side & extension cords
Coiled around his feet.
Words rolled from under the pressure
Of my ballpoint: Love,
Baby, Honey, Please.
We sat in the quiet brutality
Of voltage meters & pipe threaders,
Lost between sentences . . .
The gleam of a five-pound wedge
On the concrete floor
Pulled a sunset
Through the doorway of his toolshed.
I wondered if she laughed
& held them over a gas burner.
My father could only sign
His name, but he'd look at blueprints
& say how many bricks
Formed each wall. This man,

Who stole roses & hyacinth
For his yard, would stand there
With eyes closed & fists balled,
Laboring over a simple word, almost
Redeemed by what he tried to say.

YUSEF KOMUNYAKAA

Starlight Scope Myopia

Gray-blue shadows lift
shadows onto an oxcart.

Making night work for us,
the starlight scope brings
men into killing range.

The river under Vi Bridge
takes the heart away

like the Water God
riding his dragon.
Smoke-colored

Viet Cong
move under our eyelids,

lords over loneliness
winding like coral vine through
sandalwood & lotus,

inside our lowered heads
years after this scene

ends. The brain closes
down. What looks like
one step into the trees,

they're lifting crates of ammo
& sacks of rice, swaying

under their shared weight.
Caught in the infrared,
what are they saying?

Are they talking about women
or calling the Americans

beaucoup dien cai dau?
One of them is laughing.
You want to place a finger

to his lips & say "shhhh."
You try reading ghost talk

on their lips. They say
"up-up we go," lifting as one.
This one, old, bowlegged,

you feel you could reach out
& take him into your arms. You

peer down the sights of your M-16,
seeing the full moon
loaded on an oxcart.

LI-YOUNG LEE (b. 1957) was born in Indonesia, but his family spent the next seven years as political refugees in Hong Kong, Macau, and Japan. The family eventually settled in Pennsylvania, where Lee declared American citizenship and then attended college in Pittsburgh, at the University of Arizona, and at the State University of New York at Brockport. Lee's first collection of poetry, *Rose* (1986), established him as an important new poet. Lee has since published two more volumes of poetry and an autobiographical work, *The Winged Seed* (1995). Many of Lee's poems deal with family relationships, especially with his father. His **open form**, lyric poems are noted for their precision and tenderness; they frequently present a central **metaphor** that carries **symbolic** overtones, as with the splinter in "The Gift" (1986) and the persimmons in "Persimmons" (1986).

Related Works: Keats, "Ode on a Grecian Urn"; Chin, "Turtle Soup" and "Autumn Leaves"; Yau, "Chinese Villanelle"; Song, "Girl Powdering Her Neck."

LI-YOUNG LEE

Persimmons

In sixth grade Mrs. Walker
slapped the back of my head
and made me stand in the corner
for not knowing the difference
between *persimmon* and *precision*.
How to choose

persimmons. This is precision.
Ripe ones are soft and brown-spotted.
Sniff the bottoms. The sweet one
will be fragrant. How to eat:
put the knife away, lay down newspaper.

Peel the skin tenderly, not to tear the meat.
Chew on the skin, suck it,
and swallow. Now, eat
the meat of the fruit,
so sweet
all of it, to the heart.

Dona undresses, her stomach is white.
In the yard, dewy and shivering
with crickets, we lie naked,
face-up, face-down.
I teach her Chinese. Crickets: *chiu chiu*. Dew: I've forgotten.
Naked: I've forgotten.
Ni, wo: you and me.
I part her legs,
remember to tell her
she is beautiful as the moon.

Other words
that got me into trouble were
fight and *fright, wren* and *yarn*.
Fight was what I did when I was frightened,
fright was what I felt when I was fighting.
Wrens are small, plain birds,
yarn is what one knits with.
Wrens are soft as yarn.
My mother made birds out of yarn.
I loved to watch her tie the stuff;
a bird, a rabbit, a wee man.

Mrs. Walker brought a persimmon to class
and cut it up
so everyone could taste
a *Chinese apple*. Knowing
it wasn't ripe or sweet, I didn't eat
but watched the other faces.

My mother said every persimmon has a sun
inside, something golden, glowing,
warm as my face.

Once, in the cellar, I found two wrapped in newspaper
forgotten and not yet ripe.
I took them and set them both on my
        bedroom windowsill,
where each morning a cardinal
sang. *The sun, the sun.*

Finally understanding
he was going blind,
my father would stay up all one night
waiting for a song, a ghost.

I gave him the persimmons,
swelled, heavy as sadness,
and sweet as love.

This year, in the muddy lighting
of my parents' cellar, I rummage, looking
for something I lost.
My father sits on the tired, wooden stairs,
black cane between his knees,
hand over hand, gripping the handle.

He's so happy that I've come home.
I ask how his eyes are, a stupid question.
All gone, he answers.

Under some blankets, I find a box.
Inside the box I find three scrolls.
I sit beside him and untie
three paintings by my father:
Hibiscus leaf and a white flower.
Two cats preening.
Two persimmons, so full they want to drop from the cloth.

He raises both hands to touch the cloth,
asks, *Which is this?*

This is persimmons, Father.

Oh, the feel of the wolftail on the silk,
the strength, the tense
precision in the wrist.
I painted them hundreds of times
eyes closed. These I painted blind.
Some things never leave a person:
scent of the hair of one you love,
the texture of persimmons,
in your palm, the ripe weight.

LI-YOUNG LEE

The Gift

To pull the metal splinter from my palm
my father recited a story in a low voice.
I watched his lovely face and not the blade.
Before the story ended, he'd removed
the iron sliver I thought I'd die from.

I can't remember the tale,
but hear his voice still, a well

of dark water, a prayer.
And I recall his hands,

two measures of tenderness
he laid against my face,
the flames of discipline
he raised above my head.

Had you entered that afternoon
you would have thought you saw a man
planting something in a boy's palm.
a silver tear, a tiny flame.
Had you followed that boy
you would have arrived here,
where I bend over my wife's right hand.

Look how I shave her thumbnail down
so carefully she feels no pain.
Watch as I lift the splinter out.
I was seven when my father
took my hand like this,
and I did not hold that shard
between my fingers and think,
Metal that will bury me.
christen it Little Assassin,
Ore Going Deep for My Heart.
And I did not lift up my wound and cry.
Death visited here!
I did what a child does
when he's given something to keep.
I kissed my father.

URSULA LE GUIN (b. 1929) grew up in Berkeley, California, the fourth child and only daughter of an anthropologist and a writer. After graduating from Radcliffe College and Columbia University, she met and married historian Charles Le Guin and wrote while raising three children. Most famous for her science fiction and fantasy novels, especially the *Earthsea* series, Le Guin has also published several collections of poetry. Like her fiction, her poems often include dreams or dreamlike **images**.

Related Works: Kafka, "The Metamorphosis"; Atwood, "Siren Song"; Erdrich, "Windigo"; Yeats, "Leda and the Swan."

URSULA K. LE GUIN

The Old Falling Down

In the old falling-down
house of my childhood

I go down-
stairs to sleep out-
side on the porch
under stars and dream
of trying to go up-
stairs but there are no
stairs so I climb
hand over hand clambering
scared and when I get there
to my high room, find
no bed, no chair, bare floor.

DENISE LEVERTOV (1923–1997) was born in England, where her family had immigrated after her father, a Russian Jew, became an Anglican priest. She worked in England as a nurse during World War II, then met Mitchell Goodman, a writer, and moved with him to the United States when she was twenty-five. Ranging across feminist and religious themes, Levertov's poetry is perhaps best remembered for her poems concerning the Vietnam War. As a political activist, Levertov founded the Writers and Artists Protest against the War in Vietnam. Her **lyric** poetry is filled with **allusion, symbol**, and **metaphor**. The Vietnam poem included here, "What Were They Like?" (1966), **parodies** a journalistic style and strategy.

Related Works: O'Brien, "Stockings"; Wordsworth, "Composed upon Westminster Bridge, September 3, 1802"; Forché, "The Colonel"; Olds, "I Go Back to May 1937"; Williams, "Spring and All"; Glaspell, *Trifles*; Sophocles, *Antigone*.

DENISE LEVERTOV

The Ache of Marriage

The ache of marriage:

thigh and tongue, beloved,
are heavy with it,
it throbs in the teeth

We look for communion
and are turned away, beloved,
each and each

It is leviathan and we
in its belly
looking for joy, some joy
not to be known outside it

two by two in the ark of
the ache of it.

DENISE LEVERTOV

What Were They Like?

Did the people of Vietnam
use lanterns of stone?
Did they hold ceremonies
to reverence the opening of buds?
Were they inclined to quiet laughter?
Did they use bone and ivory,
jade and silver, for ornament?
Had they an epic poem?
Did they distinguish between speech and singing?

Sir, their light hearts turned to stone.
It is not remembered whether in gardens
stone lanterns illumined pleasant ways.
Perhaps they gathered once to delight in blossom,
but after the children were killed
there were no more buds.
Sir, laughter is bitter to the burned mouth.
A dream ago, perhaps. Ornament is for joy.
All the bones were charred.
It is not remembered. Remember,
most were peasants; their life
was in rice and bamboo.
When peaceful clouds were reflected in the paddies
and the water buffalo stepped surely along terraces,
maybe fathers told their sons old tales.
When bombs smashed those mirrors
there was time only to scream.

There is an echo yet
of their speech which was like a song.
It was reported their singing resembled
the flight of moths in moonlight.
Who can say? It is silent now.

DENISE LEVERTOV

O Taste and See

The world is
not with us enough.
O taste and see

the subway Bible poster said,
meaning The Lord, meaning
if anything all that lives
to the imagination's tongue,

grief, mercy, language,
tangerine, weather, to
breathe them, bite,
savor, chew, swallow, transform
into our flesh our
deaths, crossing the street, plum, quince,
living in the orchard and being

hungry, and plucking
the fruit.

AUDRE LORDE (1934–1992) was born in New York to West Indian parents. She attended Catholic schools and, later, Hunter College. She married, had two children, earned a library science degree, and, eventually, worked as a librarian in Mount Vernon and New York City. In 1968, she left her job to pursue radical feminist, racial, and gay activism, along with creative writing, full time. She published many volumes of poetry and was a distinguished essayist. In some of her later poetry, she began to include African **symbols** and **mythologies**, but earlier works, such as "Hanging Fire" (1978), evoke images from her own life. "Hanging Fire" may be read as the **hyperbolic** thinking of an overly dramatic teenager, or as the voice of someone truly in distress.

Related Works: Walker, "Everyday Use"; Dunbar, "We wear the mask"; Roethke, "My Papa's Waltz"; Hayden, "Those Winter Sundays"; Anzaldúa, "horse"; Angelou, "Still I Rise"; Shakespeare, *Taming of the Shrew.*

AUDRE LORDE

Hanging Fire

I am fourteen
and my skin has betrayed me
the boy I cannot live without
still sucks his thumb
in secret
how come my knees are
always so ashy
what if I die
before morning
and momma's in the bedroom
with the door closed.

I have to learn how to dance
in time for the next party

my room is too small for me
suppose I die before graduation
they will sing sad melodies
but finally
tell the truth about me
There is nothing I want to do
and too much
that has to be done
and momma's in the bedroom
with the door closed.

Nobody even stops to think
about my side of it
I should have been on Math Team
my marks were better than his
why do I have to be
the one
wearing braces
I have nothing to wear tomorrow.

ROBERT LOWELL (1917–1977) was born into an old, prominent Boston family. He split with his family after two years at Harvard, completing his education at Kenyon College and Louisiana State. He spent a year in jail as a conscientious objector during World War II and became active in the antiwar movement during the Vietnam War. *Lord Weary's Castle* (for which he received a Pulitzer Prize in 1946) is representative of his formal and highly wrought early poetry. In 1959, under the influence of the **Beat** poets, Lowell turned to open form, personal, **confessional** poetry, and his collection *Life Studies* (1959), which includes "Skunk Hour," is considered a watershed volume in American poetry. In his final years, Lowell moved to England, continuing to publish until his death in 1977. One of his last volumes, *The Dolphin*, was awarded the 1974 Pulitzer Prize.

Related Works: Hawthorne, "Young Goodman Brown"; Milton, *Lycidas*; Bishop, "One Art" and "The Fish"; Eliot, "The Love Song of J. Alfred Prufrock"; Ginsberg, "Howl"; Williams, *The Glass Menagerie*.

ROBERT LOWELL

Skunk Hour

[For Elizabeth Bishop]

Nautilus Island's hermit
heiress still lives through winter in her Spartan cottage;

her sheep still graze above the sea.
Her son's a bishop. Her farmer
is first selectman in our village,
she's in her dotage.

Thirsting for
the hierarchic privacy
of Queen Victoria's century,
she buys up all
the eyesores facing her shore,
and lets them fall.

The season's ill—
we've lost our summer millionaire,
who seemed to leap from an L. L. Bean
catalogue. His nine-knot yawl
was auctioned off to lobstermen.
A red fox stain covers Blue Hill.

And now our fairy
decorator brightens his shop for fall,
his fishnet's filled with orange cork,
orange, his cobbler's bench and awl,
there is no money in his work,
he'd rather marry.

One dark night,
my Tudor Ford climbed the hill's skull,
I watched for love-cars. Lights
        turned down,
they lay together, hull to hull,
where the graveyard shelves on the town. . . .
My mind's not right.

A car radio bleats,
"Love, O careless Love . . . ." I hear
my ill-spirit sob in each blood cell,
as if my hand were at its throat . . . .
I myself am hell,
nobody's here—

only skunks, that search
in the moonlight for a bite to eat.
They march on their soles up Main Street:
white stripes, moonstruck eyes' red fire
under the chalk-dry and spar spire
of the Trinitarian Church.

I stand on top
of our back steps and breathe the rich air—a
a mother skunk with her column of kittens swills the garbage pail.
She jabs her wedge-head in a cup

of sour cream, drops her ostrich tail,
and will not scare.

LOUIS MACNEICE (1907–1963) was born in Ireland, but completed his education as a classical scholar in England. He was part of a small group of radical poets in the 1930s led by W. H. Auden; however, MacNeice's poetry, although sometimes political, retains a much more **colloquial** and informal expression and a more dispassionate, if not cynical, view of life than that of his fellow radicals. Like "Snow" (1935), many of his poems are deeply sensory—visual and tactile. He published more than twenty volumes of poetry. Then, in the 1940s, MacNeice wrote and produced a series of stage, radio, and television plays, including his allegorical quest, *The Dark Tower.*

Related Works: Joyce, "Araby"; Burns, "A Red, Red Rose"; Auden, "Musée des Beaux Arts"; Heaney, "Digging"; Thomas, "Fern Hill."

LOUIS MACNEICE

Snow

The room was suddenly rich and the great bay-window was
Spawning snow and pink roses against it
Soundlessly collateral and incompatible:
World is suddener than we fancy it.

World is crazier and more of it than we think,
Incorrigibly plural. I peel and portion
A tangerine and spit the pips and feel
The drunkenness of things being various.

And the fire flames with a bubbling sound for world
Is more spiteful and gay than one supposes—
On the tongue on the eyes on the ears in the palms of one's hands—
There is more than glass between the snow and the huge roses.

FLORENCE CASSEN MAYERS (b. 1940) is known primarily for her children's counting and alphabet books; her unusually sophisticated presentations for children take on subjects as varied as the National Basketball Association, an "alef-bet" tour (via the Hebrew alphabet) through the Israel museum in Jerusalem and New York's Museum of Modern Art. Her poem "All-American Sestina" (1996) first appeared in the *Atlantic Monthly* and tinkers with the highly structured, numerically controlled **sestina** form.

Related Works: Old English Riddles; Bishop, "Sestina"; Forché, "The Colonel."

FLORENCE CASSEN MAYERS

All-American Sestina

One nation, indivisible
two-car garage
three strikes you're out
four-minute mile
five-cent cigar
six-string guitar

six-pack Bud
one-day sale
five-year warranty
two-way street
fourscore and seven years ago
three cheers

three-star restaurant
sixty-
four dollar question
one-night stand
two-pound lobster
five-star general

five-course meal
three sheets to the wind
two bits
six-shooter
one-armed bandit
four-poster

four-wheel drive
five-and-dime
hole in one
three-alarm fire
sweet sixteen
two-wheeler

two-ton Chevy
four rms, hi flr, w/vu
six-footer
high five
three-ring circus
one-room schoolhouse

two thumbs up, five-karat diamond
Fourth of July, three-piece suit
six feet under, one-horse town

CLAUDE MCKAY (1889–1948) was born in rural Jamaica and educated at home by his older brother and an English neighbor who introduced him to the British classics and taught him classical forms—see the **sonnets** "America" (1922) and "In Bondage," below. McKay wrote his first volumes of poetry in Jamaica, using the vernacular **dialect** to extol black rural life and condemn the racism that he found in Kingston. In his twenties, he moved to the United States. Despite the fact that he lived in Harlem only intermittently, spending years traveling in Europe and Africa, McKay's volumes of poetry, essays, short stories, and novels set the tenor for the **Harlem Renaissance** and inspired other black writers such as Langston Hughes.

Related Works: Ellison, "Battle Royal"; Achebe, "Why the Tortoise Shell Is Not Smooth"; Dunbar, "Sympathy"; Brooks, "The Bean Eaters"; Cullen, "From the Dark Tower"; Hughes, "Harlem"; Randall, "Ballad of Birmingham"; Wilson, *The Piano Lesson.*

CLAUDE MCKAY

America

Although she feeds me bread of bitterness,
And sinks into my throat her tiger's tooth,
Stealing my breath of life, I will confess
I love this cultured hell that tests my youth!
Her vigor flows like tides into my blood,
Giving me strength erect against her hate.
Her bigness sweeps my being like a flood.
Yet as a rebel fronts a king in state,
I stand within her walls with not a shred
Of terror, malice, not a word of jeer.
Darkly I gaze into the days ahead.
And see her might and granite wonders there,
Beneath the touch of Time's unerring hand,
Like priceless treasures sinking in the sand.

CLAUDE MCKAY

In Bondage

I would be wandering in distant fields
Where man, and bird, and beast, lives leisurely,
And the old earth is kind, and ever yields
Her goodly gifts to all her children free;
Where life is fairer, lighter, less demanding,

And boys and girls have time and space for play
Before they come to years of understanding—
Somewhere I would be singing, far away.
For life is greater than the thousand wars
Men wage for it in their insatiate lust.
And will remain like the eternal stars,
When all that shines to-day is drift and dust
But I am bound with you in your mean graves.
O black men, simple slaves of ruthless slaves.

CLAUDE MCKAY

Harlem Shadows

I hear the halting footsteps of a lass
  In Negro Harlem when the night lets fall
Its veil. I see the shapes of girls who pass
  To bend and barter at desire's call.
Ah, little dark girls who in slippered feet
Go prowling through the night from street to street!
Through the long night until the silver break
  Of day the little gray feet know no rest;
Through the lone night until the last snow-flake
  Has dropped from heaven upon the earth's white breast,
The dusky, half-clad girls of tired feet
Are trudging, thinly shod, from street to street.
Ah, stern harsh world, that in the wretched way
  Of poverty, dishonor and disgrace,
Has pushed the timid little feet of clay,
  The sacred brown feet of my fallen race!
Ah, heart of me, the weary, weary feet
In Harlem wandering from street to street.

EDNA ST. VINCENT MILLAY (1892–1950), a poet and playwright, was born in Maine. She published her first poem "Renascence" in 1912, which led to a Vassar scholarship. After college, Millay moved to Greenwich Village in New York City and adopted a bohemian and openly bisexual lifestyle. In 1923, her fourth volume of poems, *The Harp Weaver*, won a Pulitzer Prize. In the same year, Millay married a widower, Eugen Boissevain, who became her manager and publicist for the next twenty-six years. Millay's romantic and passionate verse was most often framed in traditional forms, as in the following **sonnet**.

Related Works: Porter, "The Jilting of Granny Weatherall"; Shakespeare, Sonnet 18; Dickinson, "Because I could not stop for Death"; Rich, "Diving into the Wreck"; Plath, "Daddy"; Glaspell, *Trifles*.

EDNA ST. VINCENT MILLAY

What lips my lips have kissed, and where, and why (Sonnet 43)

What lips my lips have kissed, and where, and why,
I have forgotten, and what arms have lain
Under my head till morning; but the rain
Is full of ghosts tonight, that tap and sigh
Upon the glass and listen for reply,
And in my heart there stirs a quiet pain
For unremembered lads that not again
Will turn to me at midnight with a cry.
Thus in winter stands the lonely tree,
Nor knows what birds have vanished one by one,
Yet knows its boughs more silent than before:
I cannot say what loves have come and gone,
I only know that summer sang in me
A little while, that in me sings no more.

JUDITH MINTY (b. 1937), a Midwestern poet, was born and raised in Detroit, Michigan, where she spent her summers in the northern woods around Lake Michigan. Although she lived and taught for many years at Humboldt State University in California, she maintained a retreat in Michigan, moving home permanently in the early 1990s. Michigan's Upper Peninsula provides the landscape for much of her poetry, which often explores the relationship between civilized and natural consciousness.

Related Works: Shakespeare, Sonnet 116; MacNeice, "Snow"; Marquez, "The Handsomest Drowned Man in the World"; Cofer, "Tales Told Under the Mango Tree"; Medieval Lyrics; Blake, "The Lamb" and "The Tiger"; Kinnell, "The Bear"; Lowell, "Skunk Hour."

JUDITH MINTY

Conjoined

a marriage poem

The onion in my cupboard, a monster, actually
two joined under one transparent skin:

each half-round, then flat and deformed
where it pressed and grew against the other.

An accident, like the two-headed calf rooted
in one body, fighting to suck at its mother's teats;
or like those other freaks, Chang and Eng, twins
joined at the chest by skin and muscle, doomed
to live, even make love, together for sixty years.

Do you feel the skin that binds us
together as we move, heavy in this house?
To sever the muscle could free one,
but might kill the other. Ah, but men
don't slice onions in the kitchen, seldom see
what is invisible. We cannot escape each other.

OGDEN NASH (1902–1971), prolific writer of light, witty, and highly memorable verse, worked as a teacher, salesman, advertising copywriter, lyricist, and editor at the *New Yorker* while developing his unique poetic voice. A devoted family man, Nash published *Hard Lines*, his first volume of characteristic light verse, in 1931. Nash's unpretentious comedic wit and clever **satires** drew a huge American audience throughout the 1940s and 1950s, during which time Nash was a frequent guest on radio and television shows and a popular lecturer and reader. His tightly structured verses echo the turns of the eighteenth-century **epigram** and the clever quasi-journalistic humor of Mark Twain, as well as the linguistic virtuosity of Lewis Carroll.

Related Works: Swift, "A Description of the Morning"; Carroll, "Jabberwocky"; Hardy, "Ah, are you digging on my grave?"; Auden, "The Unknown Citizen"; Stevens, "The Emperor of Ice Cream"; Parker, "One Perfect Rose" and "Solace"; Twain, "The Celebrated Jumping Frog of Calaveras County."

OGDEN NASH

The Hunter

The hunter crouches in his blind
'Neath camouflage of every kind
And conjures up a quacking noise
To lend allure to his decoys
This grown-up man, with pluck and luck
is hoping to outwit a duck.

OGDEN NASH

Celery

Celery, raw
Develops the jaw,
But celery, stewed,
Is more quietly chewed

OGDEN NASH

Very Like a Whale

One thing that literature would be greatly the better for
Would be a more restricted employment by the authors of simile and metaphor.
Authors of all races, be they Greeks, Romans, Teutons or Celts,
Can't seem just to say that anything is the thing it is but have to go out of their way to say that it is like something else.
What does it mean when we are told
That that Assyrian came down like a wolf on the fold?
In the first place, George Gordon Byron had enough experience
To know that it probably wasn't just one Assyrian, it was a lot of Assyrians.
However, as too many arguments are apt to induce apoplexy and thus hinder longevity.
We'll let it pass as one Assyrian for the sake of brevity.
Now then, this particular Assyrian, the one whose cohorts were gleaming in purple and gold,
Just what does the poet mean when he says he came down like a wolf on the fold?
In heaven and earth more than is dreamed of in our philosophy there are great many things.
But I don't imagine that among them there is a wolf with purple and gold cohorts or purple and gold anythings.
No, no, Lord Byron, before I'll believe that this Assyrian was actually like a wolf I must have some kind of proof;
Did he run on all fours and did he have a hairy tail and a big red mouth and big white teeth and did he say Woof Woof?
Frankly I think it is very unlikely, and all you were entitled to say, at the very most,
Was that the Assyrian cohorts came down like a lot of Assyrian cohorts about to destroy the Hebrew host.
But that wasn't fancy enough for Lord Byron, oh dear me no, he had to invent a lot of figures of speech and then interpolate them,

With the result that whenever you mention Old Testament soldiers to people
they say Oh yes, they're the ones that a lot of wolves dressed up in gold
and purple ate them.
That's the kind of thing that's being done all the time by poets, from
Homer to Tennyson;
They're always comparing ladies to lilies and veal to venison,
And they always say things like that the snow is a white blanket after a
winter storm.
Oh it is, is it, all right then, you sleep under a six-inch blanket of snow and I'll
sleep under a half-inch blanket of unpoetical blanket material and we'll see
which one keeps warm,
And after that maybe you'll begin to comprehend dimly
What I mean by too much metaphor and simile.

JOYCE CAROL OATES (b. 1938) is, perhaps, the most remarkably prolific writer working today. Best known for her novels (she has written thirty-seven to date, not including a series of suspense novels written under a pseudonym), Oates has also published twenty-three volumes of short stories, seven volumes of poetry, four volumes of plays, and articles about everything from boxing to Emily Dickinson. Born and raised in upstate New York, Oates attended Syracuse University on scholarship, graduating as Valedictorian in 1960, and completed her M.A. at the University of Wisconsin the following year. Oates works in the violent, black comic, **American Gothic** tradition of Edgar Allen Poe, William Faulkner, and Flannery O'Connor.

Related Works: Hawthorne, "Young Goodman Brown"; Poe, "The Purloined Letter"; O'Connor, "Good Country People"; "Bonny Barbara Allan" (Child Ballad #84); "Sir Patrick Spens" (Child Ballad #58); "Lord Randall" (Child Ballad #12); Atwood, "Siren Song"; Levertov, "What They Were Like" and "O Taste and See"; Parker, "One Perfect Rose" and "Solace"; Piercy, "Barbie Doll"; Miller, *Death of a Salesman.*

JOYCE CAROL OATES

Loving

A balloon of gauze around us,
sheerest gauze: it is a balloon of skin
around us, fine light-riddled skin,
invisible.

If we reach out to pinch its walls it floats from us—
it eludes us wetly, this sac.

It is warmed by a network of veins
fine as hairs and invisible.
The veins pulsate and expand to the width

of eyelashes.
In them blood floats weightless as color.
The warm walls sink upon us when we love
each other, and are blinded by the heavier skin
that closes over our eyes.

We are in here together.
Outside, people are walking in a landscape—
it is a city landscape, it is theirs.
Their shouts and laughter come to us in broken sounds.
Their strides take them everywhere in daylight.
If they turn suddenly toward us we draw back—
the skin shudders wetly, finely—
will we be torn into two people?

The balloon will grow up around us again
as if breathed out of us, moist and sticky and light
as skin, more perfect than our own skin,
invisible.

SHARON OLDS (b. 1942), often described as a **confessional poet**, grew up in San Francisco, graduated from Stanford, and earned a Ph.D. at Columbia University. Her career as a poet came late in life; her first volume, *Satan Says*, was published in 1980 when she was thirty-seven. In vivid language and concrete and highly visual **images**, she deals with intensely physical and personal topics ranging from sexual passion to childbirth to the death of her alcoholic father.

Related Works: Atwood, "Gertrude Talks Back"; Cofer, "Tales Told Under the Mango Tree"; Plath, "Daddy" and "Metaphors"; Sexton, "To a Friend Whose Work Has Come to Triumph"; Lorde, "Hanging Fire"; Levertov, "The Ache of Marriage"; Oates, "Loving"; Norman, *'Night Mother.*

SHARON OLDS

I Go Back to May 1937

I see them standing at the formal gates of their colleges,
I see my father strolling out
under the ochre sandstone arch, the
red tiles glinting like bent
plates of blood behind his head, I
see my mother with a few light books at her hip
standing at the pillar made of tiny bricks with the
wrought-iron gate still open behind her, its
sword-tips black in the May air,
they are about to graduate, they are about to get married,

they are kids, they are dumb, all they know is they are
innocent, they would never hurt anybody.
I want to go up to them and say Stop,
don't do it—she's the wrong woman,
he's the wrong man, you are going to do things
you cannot imagine you would ever do,
you are going to do bad things to children,
you are going to suffer in ways you never heard of,
you are going to want to die. I want to go
up to them there in the late May sunlight and say it,
her hungry pretty blank face turning to me,
her pitiful beautiful untouched body,
his arrogant handsome blind face turning to me,
his pitiful beautiful untouched body,
but I don't do it. I want to live. I
take them up like the male and female
paper dolls and bang them together
at the hips like chips of flint as if to
strike sparks from them, I say
Do what you are going to do, and I will tell about it.

SIMON ORTIZ (b. 1941) was born into the Acoma Pueblo in New Mexico to an Acoma-speaking family. He continued to use his native language and his Native American name privately while attending English-only U.S. government schools; eventually Ortiz spent three years in the Armed Services and later graduated from University of Iowa with an M.F.A. He has since taught at many universities, including several in the Southwest and now in Toronto, Canada. He has authored more than a dozen books of poems and stories, as well as edited collections of stories and Native American poetry. In the poem below, "Speaking" (1977), some readers identify a poetic **frame**: that is, the poem's first three and last three lines "frame" the middle portion of the poem.

Related Works: Bambara, "The Lesson"; Erdrich, "The Red Convertible"; Whitman, "O Captain! my Captain!"; Silko, "Prayer to the Pacific"; Alexie, "Reservation Love Song"; Anzaldúa, "horse"; Harjo, "She had some horses"; Sophocles, *Antigone*.

SIMON J. ORTIZ

Speaking

I take him outside
under the trees,
have him stand on the ground.
We listen to the crickets,

cicadas, million years old sound.
Ants come by us.
I tell them,
"This is he, my son.

This boy is looking at you.
I am speaking for him."

The crickets, cicadas,
the ants, the millions of years
are watching us,
hearing us.
My son murmurs infant words,
speaking, small laughter
bubbles from him.
Tree leaves tremble.
They listen to this boy
speaking for me.

DOROTHY PARKER (1893–1967), a writer of short stories, screenplays, and poetry, was most famous for her acerbic remarks and her critical essays in *Vogue*, *Vanity Fair*, and the *New Yorker* (where she wrote under the pen name "Constant Reader"). Parker grew up in an old and wealthy New England family (she was a Rothschild) and had a finishing school education. Her poetry takes a **satirical**, if not cynical, stance, often **parodying** the traditional poetic subjects—love, flowers, and spring—and using tight **rhythms**, repetition, and a sharp turn in the final lines.

Related Works: Updike, "A&P"; Herrick, "To the Virgins"; Marvell, "To His Coy Mistress"; Hardy, "The Ruined Maid"; Robinson, "Richard Cory"; Nash, "Very Like a Whale."

DOROTHY PARKER

One Perfect Rose

A single flow'r he sent me, since we met,
All tenderly his messenger he chose;
Deep-hearted, pure, with scented dew still wet—
One perfect rose.

I knew the language of the floweret:
"My fragile leaves," it said, "his heart enclose."
Love long has taken for his amulet
One perfect rose.

Why is it no one sent me yet
One perfect limousine, do you suppose?

Ah no, it's always just my luck to get
One perfect rose.

DOROTHY PARKER

Solace

There was a rose that faded young;
I saw its shattered beauty hung
    Upon a broken stem.

I heard them say, "What need to care
With roses budding everywhere?"
    I did not answer them.

There was a bird, brought down to die:
They said, "A hundred fill the sky—
    What reason to be sad?"
There was a girl, whose lover fled;
I did not wait, the while they said:
    "There's many another lad."

MARGE PIERCY (b. 1936), poet, novelist, feminist, and political activist, was born and raised in Detroit. She completed degrees at the University of Michigan (A.B. 1957) and Northwestern University (M.A. 1958) on scholarship and was the first member of her family to attend college. She has published plays and essay collections, as well as more than a dozen collections of poetry and fifteen novels. In her poetry, she relies on simple **diction**, repetition, and **antithesis** to carry her thoughts on sexism and the difficulties it poses for women and men.

Related Works: Chopin, "The Story of an Hour"; Atwood, "Gertrude Talks Back," "You fit into me," and "Siren Song"; "The Husband's Message" and "The Wife's Lament"; Keats, "La Belle Dame sans Merci"; Akhmatova, "Lot's Wife"; Olds, "I Go Back to May 1937"; Levertov, "The Ache of Marriage"; Shakespeare, *The Taming of the Shrew.*

MARGE PIERCY

Barbie Doll

This girlchild was born as usual
and presented dolls that did pee-pee
and miniature GE stoves and irons

and wee lipsticks the color of cherry candy.
Then in the magic of puberty, a classmate said:
You have a great big nose and fat legs.

She was healthy, tested intelligent,
possessed strong arms and back,
abundant sexual drive and manual dexterity.
She went to and fro apologizing,
Everyone saw a fat nose on thick legs.

She was advised to play coy,
exhorted to come on hearty,
exercise, diet, smile and wheedle.
Her good nature wore out
like a fan belt.
So she cut off her nose and her legs
and offered them up.

In the casket displayed on satin she lay
with the undertaker's cosmetics painted on,
a turned-up putty nose,
dressed in a pink and white nightie.
Doesn't she look pretty? everyone said,
Consummation at last,
To every woman a happy ending.

SYLVIA PLATH (1932–1963) was born in Boston, where she was raised largely by her single working mother. Her father died after suffering from a long illness when she was eight years old. After graduating summa cum laude in 1955 from Smith College, she attended Cambridge on a Fulbright scholarship, and, while in England, she met and married fellow poet Ted Hughes. She returned to America in 1957 to teach at Smith, but went back to England and Hughes in 1959. She had two children before she committed suicide in 1963. Her volumes of poetry include *The Colossus* (1960), *Crossing the Water* (1960), and *Ariel* (1963). Her autobiographical novel, *The Bell Jar*, in which she gives an account of her ongoing clinical depression, was published in 1963.

Although her father was a German immigrant, Plath claimed that the eponymous father figure in "Daddy" (1962) was not a portrait of her own father. In this rancorous poem, Plath uses techniques of repetition, **assonance**, and **alliteration** to drive the poem forward, as in the seventh stanza, where the repetition of "An engine, an engine" is followed by the repeated ending of "Jew, Jew, Jew." The image of a train on which "there's no getting off" appears once again in "Metaphors" (1960), a poem in the form of a **riddle**.

Related Works: Roethke, "My Papa's Waltz"; Wideman, "What We Cannot Speak About We Must Pass Over in Silence"; Thomas, "Do Not Go Gentle into that Good Night"; Hayden, "Those Winter Sundays"; Old English Riddles; Levertov, "The Ache of Marriage"; Dickinson, "Hope is the thing with feathers."

SYLVIA PLATH

Daddy

You do not do, you do not do
Anymore, black shoe
In which I have lived like a foot
For thirty years, poor and white,
Barely daring to breathe or Achoo.

Daddy, I have had to kill you.
You died before I had time—
Marble-heavy, a bag full of God,
Ghastly statue with one gray toe
Big as a Frisco seal

And a head in the freakish Atlantic
Where it pours bean green over blue
In the waters off beautiful Nauset.
I used to pray to recover you.
Ach, du.

In the German tongue, in the Polish Town
Scraped flat by the roller
Of wars, wars, wars.
But the name of the town is common.
My Polack friend

Says there are a dozen or two.
So I never could tell where you
Put your foot, your root,
I never could talk to you.
The tongue stuck in my jaw.

It stuck in a barb wire snare.
Ich, ich, ich, ich,
I could hardly speak.
I thought every German was you.
And the language obscene

An engine, an engine
Chuffing me off like a Jew.
A Jew to Dachau, Auschwitz, Belsen.
I began to talk like a Jew.
I think I may well be a Jew.

The snows of the Tyrol, the clear beer of Vienna
Are not very pure or true.

With my gypsy-ancestress and my weird luck
And my Taroc pack and my Taroc pack
I may be a bit of a Jew.

I have always been scared of *you*,
With your Luftwaffe, your gobbledygoo.
And your neat mustache
And your Aryan eye, bright blue.
Panzer-man, panzer-man, O You—

Not God but a swastika
So black no sky could squeak through.
Every woman adores a Fascist,
The boot in the face, the brute
Brute heart of a brute like you.

You stand at the blackboard, daddy,
In the picture I have of you,
A cleft in your chin instead of your foot
But no less a devil for that, no not
Any less the black man who

Bit my pretty red heart in two.
I was ten when they buried you.
At twenty I tried to die
And get back, back, back to you.
I thought even the bones would do.

But they pulled me out of the sack,
And they stuck me together with glue.
And then I knew what to do.
I made a model of you,
A man in black with a Meinkampf look

And a love of the rack and the screw.
And I said I do, I do.
So daddy, I'm finally through.
The black telephone's off at the root,
The voices just can't worm through.

If I've killed one man I've killed two—
The vampire who said he was you
And drank my blood for a year,
Seven years, if you want to know.
Daddy, you can lie back now.

There's a stake in your fat black heart
And the villagers never liked you.
They are dancing and stamping on you.
They always *knew* it was you.
Daddy, daddy, you bastard, I'm through.

SYLVIA PLATH

Metaphors

I'm a riddle in nine syllables,
An elephant, a ponderous house,
A melon strolling on two tendrils.
O red fruit, ivory, fine timbers!
This loaf's big with its yeasty rising.
Money's new-minted in this fat purse.
I'm a means, a stage, a cow in calf.
I've eaten a bag of green apples,
Boarded the train there's no getting off.

EZRA POUND (1885–1972) was born in Idaho, but spent much of his adult life abroad. A well-regarded poet in his own right, Pound is also considered to have been the greatest influence on other poets of the twentieth century. He urged his contemporaries, including T. S. Eliot, William Carlos Williams, H. D., William Butler Yeats, and others, to break away from the metaphorical diction and strict forms of traditional verse and to strive for greater directness and simplicity in their poetry. His new principles of poetry were labeled **imagist**. His poetry volumes include *A Lume Spento* (1908), *Lustra and Other Poems* (1917), and the encyclopedic **epic** poem *The Cantos*, which was published as a complete volume in 1972.

"In a Station of the Metro" (1916) is a crowning achievement of the simplicity and brevity of imagist poetry. It has no superfluous words; it treats the subject directly; and it focuses on a single image. Pound attributed this "technical breakthrough" to his study of Japanese **haiku**. "The River-Merchant's Wife" (1915) is Pound's translation of a Chinese poem. In this poem, Pound demonstrates that the emotions of an eighth-century Chinese woman decrying the absence of her husband can still resonate in the twentieth-century West.

Related Works: Williams, "The Red Wheelbarrow"; Sandburg, "Fog"; "The Wife's Lament"; Bradstreet, "To My Dear and Loving Husband"; Akhmatova, "Lot's Wife"; Levertov, "The Ache of Marriage"; Song, "Girl Powdering Her Neck"; Yau, "Chinese Villanelle."

EZRA POUND

In a Station of the Metro

The apparition of these faces in the crowd:
Petals on a wet, black bough.

EZRA POUND

The River-Merchant's Wife: A Letter

(after Ribaku)

While my hair was still cut straight across my forehead
I played about the front gate, pulling flowers.
You came by on bamboo stilts, playing horse,
You walked about my seat, playing with blue plums.
And we went on living in the village of Chokan:
Two small people, without dislike or suspicion.

At fourteen I married My Lord you.
I never laughed, being bashful.
Lowering my head, I looked at the wall.
Called to, a thousand times, I never looked back.

At fifteen I stopped scowling,
I desired my dust to be mingled with yours
For ever and for ever and for ever.
Why should I climb the look out?

At sixteen you departed,
You went into far Ku-to-yen, by the river of swirling eddies,
And you have been gone five months.
The monkeys make sorrowful noise overhead.

You dragged your feet when you went out,
By the gate now, the moss is grown, the different mosses,
Too deep to clear them away!
The leaves fall early this autumn, in wind.
The paired butterflies are already yellow with August
Over the grass in the West garden;
They hurt me. I grow older
If you are coming down through the narrows of the river Kiang,
Please let me know beforehand,
And I will come out to meet you
    As far as Cho-fu-Sa.

DUDLEY RANDALL (1914–2000) served in the military and spent many years working in a foundry and as a post office clerk in Detroit while completing degrees in English and library science. Randall founded Broadside Press in 1965 for the sole purpose of publishing the "Ballad of Birmingham," a poem written in response to the 1963 bombing of an African American church, in which four girls were killed. Randall went on to publish more than a dozen collections of poetry, many of which experimented with a variety of forms. The Broadside Press provided an important venue and established a political platform for many African American poets and writers during the civil rights movement of the 1960s and 1970s.

Related Works: Tichborne, "My prime of youth is but a frost of cares"; "Sir Patrick Spens"; "Bonny Barbara Allan"; "Lord Randall"; Dunbar, "We wear the mask"; Cullen, "From the Dark Tower"; Hughes, "Theme for English B" and "Harlem"; Wilson, *The Piano Lesson.*

DUDLEY RANDALL

Ballad of Birmingham

(On the bombing of a church in Birmingham, Alabama, 1963)

"Mother dear, may I go downtown
Instead of out to play,
And march the streets of Birmingham
In a Freedom March today?"

"No, baby, no, you may not go,
For the dogs are fierce and wild,
And clubs and hoses, guns and jails
Aren't good for a little child."

"But, mother, I won't be alone.
Other children will go with me,
And march the streets of Birmingham
To make our country free."

"No, baby, no, you may not go,
For I fear those guns will fire.
But you may go to church instead
And sing in the children's choir."

She has combed and brushed her night-dark hair,
And bathed rose petal sweet,
And drawn white gloves on her small brown hands,
And white shoes on her feet.

The mother smiled to know her child
Was in the sacred place,
But that smile was the last smile
To come upon her face.

For when she heard the explosion,
Her eyes grew wet and wild.

She raced through the streets of Birmingham
Calling for her child.

She clawed through bits of glass and brick,
Then lifted out a shoe
"Oh, here's the shoe my baby wore,
But, baby, where are you?"

CLAUDIA RANKINE (b. 1963) was born in Jamaica. She received her B.A. from Williams College and her M.F.A. from Columbia University. Her poetry collections include *Nothing in Nature Is Private* (1995), *The End of the Alphabet* (1998), *Plot* (2001), and *Don't Let Me Be Lonely* (2004).

Like other foreign-born American authors, Rankine's poems, including "Him" (1995), often incorporate the **vernacular** of her homeland and address the difficulties immigrants face when reconciling their current lives in America with their former lives elsewhere as well as chronicling their struggles to fit in.

Related Works: Mukherjee, "A Wife's Story"; Cofer, "Arturo's Flight"; Plath, "Daddy."

CLAUDIA RANKINE

Him

West Indian, him left like de rest,
to sail for New York, to plant and pot
whatever fi root in de new soil,
dasheen, callaloo, fevergrass.
From somewhere him find chickens
for de rented backyard as him wait—
Lord, how him wait—for him Alien
Registration card. And when it come,
him toast himself: *Immigrant! American
immigrant!* So him talk and laugh
with him lips quick parting, *Who
feel dem can bad mouth America
don't know a damn thing!* But
soon him voice quiet (*Yes, Sir.*) Him
newness slipping clean into de past.
Holding two, sometime three job,
(steward, carpenter, cook) him give up
a few things (sleep, Red Stripe,

dominoes) for him waan believe, pursue,
dream de dream though something
put shadow pon him. (*Boy*) Glasses pon
de table. Head in him hand. Please.
Please. Him break him back, and for
what? (*Boy*) A promise no nothing.
So then, American women, nuff new
woman, him go through dem like
butter: Ackee and saltfish. Cassava.
Stuffed breadfruit. Oxtail . . . till
one Sunday him wake, and as sun full
him yard, him kneel ina grass and begin
weed him garden. Him little one see him
and ask, *What's his name?* And de
bigger child answer, *He's our father.*

HENRY REED (1914–1986), British poet, radio dramatist, and broadcaster, worked in the British Foreign Office as a journalist during World War II. Reed graduated from Birmingham University and established himself in the circle of W. H. Auden and Louis MacNeice in the years just prior to the war. He eventually wrote or co-wrote over three dozen radio plays or adaptations, three collections of poetry, and was a frequent contributor to literary magazines. In "Naming of Parts" (1946), he blends the voices of more than one speaker and weaves together the **jargon** of the military with a traditional poetic ***reverdie***.

Related Works: Medieval Lyrics; Owen, "Dulce et Decorum Est"; Auden, "The Unknown Citizen"; MacNeice, "Snow"; Rich, "Diving into the Wreck"; Strand, "Eating Poetry."

HENRY REED

Naming of Parts

To-day we have naming of parts. Yesterday,
We had daily cleaning. And to-morrow morning,
We shall have what to do after firing. But to-day,
To-day we have naming of parts. Japonica
Glistens like coral in all of the neighboring gardens,
   And to-day we have naming of parts.

This is the lower sling swivel. And this
Is the upper sling swivel, whose use you will see,

When you are given your slings. And this is the piling swivel,
Which in your case you have not got. The branches
Hold in the gardens their silent, eloquent gestures,
    Which in our case we have not got.

This is the safety-catch, which is always released
With an easy flick of the thumb. And please do not let me
See anyone using his finger. You can do it quite easy
If you have any strength in your thumb. The blossoms
Are fragile and motionless, never letting anyone see
    Any of them using their finger.

And this you can see is the bolt. The purpose of this
Is to open the breech, as you see. We can slide it
Rapidly backwards and forwards: we call this
Easing the spring. And rapidly backwards and forwards
The early bees are assaulting and fumbling the flowers:
    They call it easing the Spring.

They call it easing the Spring: it is perfectly easy
If you have any strength in your thumb: like the bolt,
And the breech, and the cocking-piece, and the point of balance,
Which in our case we have not got; and the almond-blossom
Silent in all of the gardens and the bees going backwards and forwards.
    For to-day we have naming of parts.

ADRIENNE RICH (b. 1929) spent her childhood in Baltimore, Maryland, where she was encouraged to write by her father, a physician. In 1951, she not only graduated with honors from Radcliffe College, but also published her first volume of poems, *A Change of World*. She has since published numerous volumes of poetry, including *The Diamond Cutters and Other Poems* (1955), *Necessities of Life* (1966), *Leaflets* (1972), *Diving into the Wreck* (1973), and *Dark Fields of the Republic* (1995). She won the National Book Award for Poetry in 1974.

Rich's poetry is notable for its attentiveness to women's issues. Like many feminists, she strives to give voice to other women who cannot be heard. "Aunt Jennifer's Tigers" (1951) is one of Rich's earlier poems in which she explores women's engagement with arts and crafts as a potential coping strategy against the struggles of modern life. "Diving into the Wreck" (1973) is a later poem that shrugs off the defense mechanisms and, with the controlling **metaphor** of the dive, more directly confronts the necessity for women to strive for self-realization and to cast off former selves.

Related Works: Walker, "Everyday Use"; Chopin, "The Story of an Hour"; Steinbeck, "The Chrysanthemums"; Mukherjee, "A Wife's Story"; Angelou, "Still I Rise"; Yeats, "Leda and the Swan"; Hardy, "The Ruined Maid"; Browning, "My Last Duchess."

ADRIENNE RICH

Diving into the Wreck

First having read the book of myths,
and loaded the camera,
and checked the edge of the knife-blade,
I put on
the body-armor of black rubber
the absurd flippers
the grave and awkward mask.
I am having to do this
not like Cousteau with his
assiduous team
aboard the sun-flooded schooner
but here alone.

There is a ladder.
The ladder is always there
hanging innocently
close to the side of the schooner.
We know what it is for,
we who have used it.
Otherwise
it's a piece of maritime floss
some sundry equipment.

I go down.
Rung after rung and still
the oxygen immerses me
the blue light
the clear atoms
of our human air.
I go down.
My flippers cripple me,
I crawl like an insect down the ladder
and there is no one
to tell me when the ocean
will begin.

First the air is blue and then
it is bluer and then green and then
black I am blacking out and yet
my mask is powerful
it pumps my blood with power
the sea is another story
the sea is not a question of power

I have to learn alone
to turn my body without force
in the deep element.

And now: it is easy to forget
what I came for
among so many who have always
lived here
swaying their crenellated fans
between the reefs
and besides
you breathe differently down here.

I came to explore the wreck.
The words are purposes.
The words are maps.
I came to see the damage that was done
and the treasures that prevail.
I stroke the beam of my lamp
slowly along the flank
of something more permanent
than fish or weed

the thing I came for:
the wreck and not the story of the wreck
the thing itself and not the myth
the drowned face always staring
toward the sun
the evidence of damage
worn by salt and sway into this threadbare beauty
the ribs of the disaster
curving their assertion
among the tentative haunters.

This is the place.
And I am here, the mermaid whose dark hair
streams black, the merman in his armored body
We circle silently
about the wreck
we dive into the hold.
I am she: I am he

whose drowned face sleeps with open eyes
whose breasts still bear the stress
whose silver, copper, vermeil cargo lies
obscurely inside barrels
half-wedged and left to rot
we are the half-destroyed instruments
that once held to a course

the water-eaten log
the fouled compass

We are, I am, you are
by cowardice or courage
the one who find our way
back to this scene
carrying a knife, a camera
a book of myths
in which
our names do not appear.

ADRIENNE RICH

Aunt Jennifer's Tigers

Aunt Jennifer's tigers prance across a screen,
Bright topaz denizens of a world of green.
They do not fear the men beneath the tree;
They pace in sleek chivalric certainty.

Aunt Jennifer's fingers fluttering through her wool
Find even the ivory needle hard to pull.
The massive weight of Uncle's wedding band
Sits heavily upon Aunt Jennifer's hand.

When Aunt is dead, her terrified hands will lie
Still ringed with ordeals she was mastered by.
The tigers in the panel that she made
Will go on prancing, proud and unafraid.

ALBERTO RÍOS (b. 1952) was born in Nogales, an Arizona border town, to a Mexican father and a British mother. He received two B.A.s—one in English and one in psychology—and an M.F.A. from the University of Arizona. His collections of poetry include *Whispering to Fool the Wind* (1982), *Five Indiscretions* (1985), *The Lime Orchard Women* (1989), and *Teodora Luna's Two Kisses* (1990). He is also a short story author.

In his poetry, Ríos draws on the oral tradition of the stories told to him by his paternal grandparents, his *nani* (grandmother) and *abuelo* (grandfather). His work also exhibits features of the **magic realism** characteristic of Latin American authors. "Nani" (1981) is a **sestina** about a grandmother and the stories she carries all about her, even when she is not speaking. "The Vietnam Wall" (1988) is a realistic poem about a first encounter with the memorial in Washington, D.C.

Related Works: Cofer, "More Room"; Rich, "Aunt Jennifer's Tigers"; Chekhov, "Vanka"; Keats, "Ode on a Grecian Urn"; Wordsworth, "Composed upon Westminster Bridge, September 3, 1802"; O'Brien, "Stockings"; Arnold, "Dover Beach"; Auden, "The Unknown Citizen."

ALBERTO RÍOS

Nani

Sitting at her table, she serves
the sopa de arroz to me
instinctively, and I watch her,
the absolute *mamá*, and eat words
I might have had to say more
out of embarrassment. To speak,
now-foreign words I used to speak,
too, dribble down her mouth as she serves
me albondigas. No more
than a third are easy to me.
By the stove she does something with words
and looks at me only with her
back. I am full. I tell her
I taste the mint, and watch her speak
smiles at the stove. All my words
make her smile. Nani never serves
herself, she only watches me
with her skin, her hair. I ask for more.

I watch the *mamá* warming more
tortillas for me. I watch her
fingers in the flame for me.
Near her mouth, I see a wrinkle speak
of a man whose body serves
the ants like she serves me, then more words
from more wrinkles about children, words
about this and that, flowing more
easily from these other mouths. Each serves
as a tremendous string around her,
holding her together. They speak
nani was this and that to me
and I wonder just how much of me

ALBERTO RÍOS

The Vietnam Wall

I
Have seen it
And I like it: The magic,
The way like cutting onions

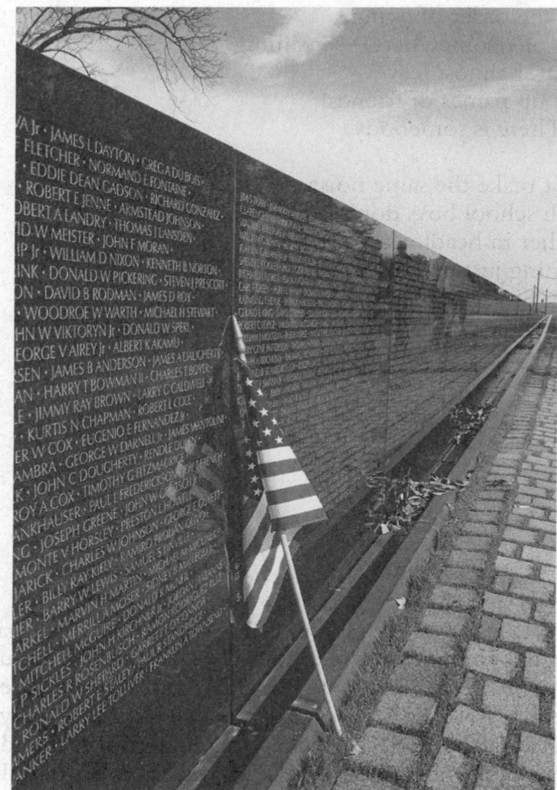

The Vietnam Memorial, Washington, D.C.

It brings water out of nowhere.
Invisible from one side, a scar
Into the skin of the ground
From the other, a black winding
Appendix line.
    A dig.
    An archaeologist can explain.
The walk is slow at first
Easy, a little black marble wall
Of a dollhouse,
A smoothness, a shine
The boys in the street want to give.
One name. And then more
Names, long lines, lines of names until
They are the shape of the U.N. building
Taller than I am: I have walked
Into a grave.
And everything I expect has been taken away, like that, quick:
    The names are not alphabetized.

They are in the order of dying,
An alphabet of—somewhere—screaming.
I start to walk out. I almost leave
But stop to look up names of friends,
My own name. There is somebody
Severiano Ríos.
Little kids do not make the same noise
Here, junior high school boys don't run
Or hold each other in headlocks.
No rules, something just persists
Like pinching on St. Patrick's Day
Every year for no green.
No one knows why.
Flowers are forced
Into the cracks
Between sections.
Men have cried
At this wall.
I have
Seen them.

THEODORE ROETHKE (1908–1963) was born in Saginaw, Michigan. His father, a German immigrant, managed a greenhouse, so Roethke grew up with a close connection to nature. After receiving his B.A. and M.A. at the University of Michigan, Roethke held several teaching positions, but finally settled at the University of Washington in Seattle, where he enjoyed the abundance of natural settings in the Pacific Northwest. Although his total number of published works is relatively small, the books he did publish were highly acclaimed. His awards include a Pulitzer Prize for *The Waking* (1954) and National Book Awards for *Words for the Wind* (1957) and *The Far Field* (1964).

The **rhythmic** pattern of "My Papa's Waltz" (1948) accentuates both the cadence of the waltz steps (and missteps) and the excessive liveliness of the father. The energetic force that draws the father into dancing also pervades the field and wood of "The Waking" (1953), a **villanelle** in which even the stones sing.

Related Works: Plath, "Daddy"; Hayden, "Those Winter Sundays"; Thomas, "Do Not Go Gentle into That Good Night"; Tichborne, "My prime of youth is but a frost of cares"; Williams, "Spring and All"; Chin, "Autumn Leaves"; Angelou, "Still I Rise"; Wordsworth, "I wandered lonely as a cloud"; Berry, "The Peace of Wild Things"; Gioia, "California Hills in August"; Thomas, "Fern Hill."

THEODORE ROETHKE

My Papa's Waltz

The whiskey on your breath
Could make a small boy dizzy;

But I hung on like death:
Such waltzing was not easy.

We romped until the pans
Slid from the kitchen shelf;
My mother's countenance
Could not unfrown itself.

The hand that held my wrist
Was battered on one knuckle;
At every step you missed
My right ear scraped a buckle.

You beat time on my head
With a palm caked hard by dirt,
Then waltzed me off to bed
Still clinging to your shirt.

THEODORE ROETHKE

The Waking

I strolled across
An open field;
The sun was out;
Heat was happy.

This way! This way!
The wren's throat shimmered,
Either to other,
The blossoms sang.

The stones sang,
The little ones did,
And flowers jumped
Like small goats.

A ragged fringe
Of daisies waved;
I wasn't alone
In a grove of apples.

Far in the wood
A nestling sighed;
The dew loosened
Its morning smells.

I came where the river
Ran over stones:
My ears knew
An early joy.

And all the waters

Of all the streams
Sang in my veins
That summer day.

CARL SANDBURG (1878–1967) was born in Galesburg, Illinois. He had a poor childhood and dropped out of school at thirteen to help support his family. He spent some time "riding the rails" as a hobo and served in Puerto Rico during the Spanish American War. After the war, he enrolled in Lombard College; although he never completed a degree, as a student there he did write and begin publishing his poetry. He spent some time as a journalist and as a member of the Social Democrat party in Wisconsin, but eventually ended up in Chicago, where he earned a reputation as a member of the Chicago literary renaissance, along with other writers such as Theodore Dreiser and Sherwood Anderson. He won the Pulitzer Prize for his *Complete Poems* in 1950.

Sandburg's poetry celebrates the life of common Americans and the settings of his homeland. His **free verse** style, his inclusion of the **vernacular**, and his praise of blue-collar workers serve to demonstrate that poetry and art are not reserved for the upper classes. "Chicago" (1916) **personifies** the city, turns its **epithets** into proud monikers, and praises the work of the butchers and tool makers and railroad workers who build and rebuild the city where they toil. "Grass" (1918), an unsentimental war poem, also praises the rejuvenating power of work—nature's work. However, the fog that is personified in the poem of the same name, "Fog" (1916), seems unimpressed by human architecture.

Related Works: Blake, "London"; Hughes, "Harlem"; Stafford, "At the Bomb Testing Site"; Rios, "The Vietnam Wall"; Arnold, "Dover Beach"; Wordsworth, "Composed upon Westminster Bridge, September 3, 1802"; Pound, "In a Station of the Metro."

CARL SANDBURG

Fog

The fog comes
on little cat feet.
It sits looking
over harbor and city
on silent haunches
and then moves on.

CARL SANDBURG

Chicago

Hog Butcher for the World,
Tool Maker, Stacker of Wheat,
Player with Railroads and the Nation's Freight Handler;

Stormy, husky, brawling,
City of the Big Shoulders:

They tell me you are wicked and I believe them, for I have seen your painted women under the gas lamps luring the farm boys.
And they tell me you are crooked and I answer: Yes, it is true I have seen the gunman kill and go free to kill again.
And they tell me you are brutal and my reply is: On the faces of women and children I have seen the marks of wanton hunger.
And having answered so I turn once more to those who sneer at this my city, and I give them back the sneer and say to them:
Come and show me another city with lifted head singing so proud to be alive and coarse and strong and cunning.
Flinging magnetic curses amid the toil of piling job on job, here is a tall bold slugger set vivid against the little soft cities;
Fierce as a dog with tongue lapping for action, cunning as a savage pitted against the wilderness,
Bareheaded,
Shoveling,
Wrecking,
Planning,
Building, breaking, rebuilding,
Under the smoke, dust all over his mouth, laughing with white teeth,
Under the terrible burden of destiny laughing as a young man laughs,
Laughing even as an ignorant fighter laughs who has never lost a battle,
Bragging and laughing that under his wrist is the pulse, and under his ribs the heart of the people,
Laughing!
Laughing the stormy, husky, brawling laughter of Youth, half-naked, sweating, proud to be Hog Butcher, Tool Maker, Stacker of Wheat, Player with Railroads and Freight Handler to the Nation.

CARL SANDBURG

Grass

Pile the bodies high at Austerlitz and Waterloo.
Shovel them under and let me work—
I am the grass; I cover all.

And pile them high at Gettysburg
And pile them high at Ypres and Verdun.
Shovel them under and let me work.
Two years, ten years, and passengers ask the conductor:
What place is this?
Where are we now?

I am the grass.
Let me work.

ANNE SEXTON (1928–1974) was born in Newton, Massachusetts. She married young after receiving a junior college degree. After the birth of her first child, she was diagnosed with depression and was encouraged to use her writing to help stave off her unhappiness. Eventually, she began taking poetry workshops, including those led by Robert Lowell, where she met and befriended fellow poet Sylvia Plath. Like Plath, she took her own life at a relatively early age. Her volumes of poetry include *To Bedlam and Partway Back* (1960), *All My Pretty Ones* (1962), *Live or Die* (1966), for which she was awarded the Pulitzer Prize, and *The Death Notebooks* (1974).

Because Sexton's poetry is subjective and unafraid to expose emotional suffering and pain, she is categorized as a **confessional** poet. Sexton wrote "To a Friend Whose Work Has Come to Triumph" (1962) for her mentor William Snodgrass, and in it she honors the imprudent but glorious trajectory of Icarus' brief flight.

Related Works: Auden, "Musée des Beaux Arts"; Young, "Langston Hughes."

ANNE SEXTON

To a Friend Whose Work Has Come to Triumph

Consider Icarus, pasting those sticky wings on,
testing that strange little tug at his shoulder blade,
and think of that first flawless moment over the lawn
of the labyrinth. Think of the difference it made!
There below are the trees, as awkward as camels;
and here are the shocked starlings pumping past
and think of innocent Icarus who is doing quite well:
larger than a sail, over the fog and the blast
of the plushy ocean, he goes. Admire his wings!
Feel the fire at his neck and see how casually
he glances up and is caught, wondrously tunneling
into that hot eye. Who cares that he fell back to the sea?
See him acclaiming the sun and come plunging down
while his sensible daddy goes straight into town.

LESLIE MARMON SILKO (b. 1948) was born in Albuquerque, New Mexico, but spent much of her childhood in the Laguna Indian pueblo. She has a mixed heritage of Native American, Mexican, and Caucasian, but is most often regarded as a Native American author. She received her bachelor's degree from the University of New Mexico, and her first novel, *Ceremony* (1977), was one of the first to be published by a Native American woman. In addition to writing novels and short stories, she has published volumes of poetry, including *Laguna Women Poems* (1974) and *Storyteller* (1981).

Although the **setting** for much of her poetry and fiction is her native Southwest, "Prayer to the Pacific" (1975) is a poem of a journey "distant" from the "southwest land of sandrock" and a tribute to the **myth** of her people's origin and arrival from the sea. The use of indentation and separation in the poem's form emphasize the distance the speaker has traveled, her separation from her place of origin, and the lengthy journey and separation her ancestors made from their origins.

Related Works: Achebe, "Why the Tortoise's Shell is not Smooth"; Alexie, "Reservation Love Song."

LESLIE MARMON SILKO

Prayer to the Pacific

I traveled to the ocean
distant
from my southwest land of sandrock
to the moving blue water
Big as the myth of origin.

Pale
pale water in the yellow-white light of
sun floating west
to China
where ocean herself was born.
Clouds that blow across the sand are wet.

Squat in the wet sand and speak to the Ocean:
I return to you turquoise the red coral you sent us,
sister spirit of Earth.
Four round stones in my pocket I carry back the ocean
to suck and to taste.

Thirty thousand years ago
Indians came riding across the ocean
carried by giant sea turtles.

Waves were high that day
great sea turtles waded slowly out
from the gray sundown sea.
Grandfather Turtle rolled in the sand four times
and disappeared
swimming into the sun.

And so from that time
immemorial,
as the old people say,

rain clouds drift from the west
gift from the ocean.

Green leaves in the wind
Wet earth on my feet
swallowing raindrops
clear from China.

CHARLES SIMIC (b. 1938) was born in Belgrade, Yugoslavia, but moved to the United States when he was still a boy. Although he does not disavow his birthplace, he is insistent about his status as an American poet. He has published more than sixty books and received a Pulitzer Prize for *The World Doesn't End: Prose Poems* in 1989. He was elected to the American Academy of Arts and Letters in 1995 and a chancellor to the American Academy of Poets in 2000.

Simic is often considered to be a **mythical** and **folkloristic** poet, and he often incorporates images from a Freudian unconscious or dreamscapes in his **surrealistic** poems. In "Old Couple," a neighbor watches the eponymous pair across the way and imagines what is going through their minds and what motivates their actions.

Related Works: Stanton, "Childhood"; Kafka, "The Metamorphosis"; Strand, "Eating Poetry."

CHARLES SIMIC

Old Couple

They're waiting to be murdered,
Or evicted. Soon
They expect to have nothing to eat.
In the meantime, they sit.

A violent pain is coming, they think,
It will start in the heart
And climb into the mouth.
They'll be carried off in stretchers, howling.

Tonight they watch the window
Without exchanging a word.
It has rained, and now it looks
Like it's going to snow a little.

I see him get up to lower the shades.
If their window stays dark,
I know his hand has reached hers
Just as she was about to turn on the lights.

Cathy Song (b. 1955) is an Asian American author who was born in Honolulu and grew up on the island of Hawaii. She left the island for the mainland when she transferred from the University of Hawaii at Manoa to Wellesley College, where she received her B.A. She remained on the mainland to earn her M.A. in creative writing at Boston University, but eventually returned to Hawaii, where she has remained since. She is generally regarded as the first Hawaiian-born author to achieve national acclaim for her work when she won the Yale Younger Poets Award for her first volume of poetry, *Picture Bride* (1983). She has been a strong advocate of other Hawaiian authors through her work as the editor of the Bamboo Ridge Press.

"Girl Powdering Her Neck" (1983), an **ekphrastic** poem which was inspired by a ukiyo-e print by Kitagawa Utamaro, captures a particular moment in a young girl's life as she prepares herself to be seen by others. As she does so, her actions recollect the traditional actions of countless other women through the ages.

Related Works: Auden, "Musée des Beaux Arts"; Pound, "The River Merchant's Wife"; Yau, "Chinese Villanelle"; Dunbar, "We wear the mask."

CATHY SONG

Girl Powdering Her Neck

from a ukiyo-e print by Utamaro

The light is the inside
sheen of an oyster shell,
sponged with talc and vapor,
moisture from a bath.

A pair of slippers
are placed outside
the rice-paper doors.
She kneels at a low table
in the room,
her legs folded beneath her
as she sits on a buckwheat pillow.

Her hair is black
with hints of red,
the color of seaweed
spread over rocks.

Morning begins the ritual
wheel of the body,
the application of translucent skins.
She practices pleasure:
the pressure of three fingertips
applying powder.
Fingerprints of pollen
some other hand will trace.

Kitagawa Utamaro (1753–1806) "Woman Powdering Her Neck"

The peach-dyed kimono
patterned with maple leaves
drifting across the silk,
falls from right to left
in a diagonal, revealing
the nape of her neck
and the curve of a shoulder
like the slope of a hill
set deep in snow in a country
of huge white solemn birds.
Her face appears in the mirror,
a reflection in a winter pond,
rising to meet itself.

She dips a corner of her sleeve
like a brush into water
to wipe the mirror;
she is about to paint herself.

The eyes narrow
in a moment of self-scrutiny.
The mouth parts
as if desiring to disturb
the placid plum face;
break the symmetry of silence.
But the berry-stained lips,
stenciled into the mask of beauty,
do not speak.

Two chrysanthemums
touch in the middle of the lake
and drift apart.

WILLIAM STAFFORD (1914–1993) was born in Hutchinson, Kansas. He received both his B.A. and M.A. at the University of Kansas and his Ph.D. from the University of Iowa. He spent most of his academic career as a professor at Lewis and Clark College in Portland, Oregon, and he is often regarded as a regionalist writer since many of his poems conjure up scenes and animals from the American West. Stafford's volumes of poetry include *Traveling Through the Dark* (1962), which won a National Book Award, *The Rescued Year* (1966), and *Stories That Could Be True: New and Collected Poems* (1977). He also wrote a **memoir** of his experience as a conscientious objector during World War II, *Down My Heart* (1947), and a volume on his writing process, *Writing the Australian Crawl: Views on the Writer's Vocation* (1978).

Poetry, as Stafford describes it in *Writing the Australian Crawl*, "is the kind of thing you have to see from the corner of your eye. You can be too well prepared for poetry . . . . It's like a very faint star. If you look straight at it you can't see it, but if you look a little to one side it is there." "Traveling Through the Dark" (1960) is a poem in which the speaker encounters an event for which he's not prepared, and makes a decision that, when looked at straight on may seem odd, but, when looked at from the side, begins to make sense. "Traveling Through the Dark" is a **voice poem** in which the speaker speaks normally, as if he's having a conversation. Like "Traveling Through the Dark," "At the Bomb Testing Site" (1966) is another poem that addresses the confrontation between human technology and nature.

Related Works: Bishop, "The Fish"; Kinnell, "The Bear," Lowell, "Skunk Hour"; Sandburg, "Grass"; Berry, "The Peace of Wild Things"; Arnold, "Dover Beach," Ríos, "The Vietnam Wall."

WILLIAM STAFFORD

Traveling Through the Dark

Traveling through the dark I found a deer
dead on the edge of the Wilson River road.

It is usually best to roll them into the canyon:
that road is narrow; to swerve might make more dead.

By glow of the tail-light I stumbled back of the car
and stood by the heap, a doe, a recent killing;
she had stiffened already, almost cold.
I dragged her off; she was large in the belly.

My fingers touching her side brought me the reason—
her side was warm; her fawn lay there waiting,
alive, still, never to be born.
Beside that mountain road I hesitated.

The car aimed ahead its lowered parking lights;
under the hood purred the steady engine.
I stood in the glare of the warm exhaust turning red;
around our group I could hear the wilderness listen.

I thought hard for us all—my only swerving—,
then pushed her over the edge into the river.

WILLIAM STAFFORD

At the Bomb Testing Site

At noon in the desert a panting lizard
waited for history, its elbows tense,
watching the curve of a particular road
as if something might happen.

It was looking at something farther off
than people could see, an important scene
acted in stone for little selves
at the flute end of consequences.

There was just a continent without much on it
under a sky that never cared less.
Ready for a change, the elbows waited.
The hands gripped hard on the desert.

MAURA STANTON (b. 1946) was born in Evanston, Illinois. She received her B.A. from the University of Minnesota and her M.F.A. from the University of Iowa. She published her first book of poetry, *Snow on Snow*, in 1975 as part of the Yale Younger Poets series. Her other volumes of poetry include: *Cries of Swimmers* (1984), *Tales of the Supernatural* (1988), *Life Among the Trolls* (1994), and *Glacier Wine* (2001). She has also published a novel, *Molly Companion* (1977), and several collections of short stories, including *The Country I Come From* (1988), *Do Not Forsake Me, Oh My Darling* (2002), and *Cities in the Sea* (2003).

"Childhood" (1984), which is written in **free verse** and evokes **surrealistic** images, is characteristic of Stanton's other poetry. In this poem, Stanton uses both **end-stopped** lines and **enjambed** lines to reinforce the speaker's alternating vision of the disarrayed real house and the "perfect floorplan" of her new house on the ceiling.

Related Works: Kafka, "The Metamorphosis"; Simic, "Old Couple"; Strand, "Eating Poetry."

MAURA STANTON

Childhood

I used to lie on my back, imagining
A reverse house on the ceiling of my house
Where I could walk around in empty rooms
All by myself. There was no furniture
Up there, only a glass globe in the floor,
And knee-high barriers at every door.
The low silled windows opened on blue air.
Nothing hung in the closet; even the kitchen
Seemed immaculate, a place for thought.
I liked to walk across the swirling plaster
Into the parts of the house I couldn't see.
The hum from the other house, now my ceiling,
Reached me only faintly. I'd look up
To find my brothers watching old cartoons,
Or my mother vacuuming the ugly carpet.
I'd stare amazed at unmade beds, the clutter,
Shoes, half-dressed dolls, the telephone,
Then return dizzily to my perfect floorplan
Where I never spoke or listened to anyone.

I must have turned down the wrong hall,
Or opened a door that locked shut behind me,
For I live on the ceiling now, not the floor.
This is my house, room after empty room.
How do I ever get back to the real house
Where my sisters spill milk, my father calls,
And I am at the table, eating cereal?
I fill my white rooms with furniture,
Hang curtains over the piercing blue outside.
I lie on my back. I strive to look down.
This ceiling is higher than it used to be,
The floor so far away I can't determine
Which room I'm in, which year, which life.

WALLACE STEVENS (1879–1955) was born in Reading, Pennsylvania, where he had a comfortable middle-class childhood. Both of his parents were educated and encouraged him to read and to listen to the orchestra and the opera on the radio as a boy. He attended Harvard as an undergraduate, and, after working for some time as a reporter, went on to obtain a law degree from New York University Law School. He spent his career as a lawyer working in the insurance industry and continued to write his poetry in his free time. His volumes of poetry include *Harmonium* (1923), *Ideas of Order* (1935), *The Man with the Blue Guitar and Other Poems* (1937), *Notes Toward a Supreme Fiction* (1942), *Thirteen Ways of Looking at a Blackbird* (1954), and *Collected Poems* (1954), the first volume for which he received widespread recognition. Stevens also wrote *The Necessary Angel: Essays on Reality and the Imagination* (1951), a collection of essays on the theory of poetry. For Stevens, an agnostic, fiction was "supreme" because, as he wrote in a collection of his notes published after his death, *Opus Posthumous* (1957), "in the absence of a belief in God, the mind turns to its own creations and examines them, not alone from the aesthetic point of view, but for what they reveal, for what they validate and invalidate, for the support they give."

"Thirteen Ways of Looking at a Blackbird" (1923) is a poem of perspectives, and its **haiku**-like stanzas demonstrate Stevens's familiarity, like his contemporary Ezra Pound, with Chinese literature. Like "Thirteen Ways of Looking at a Blackbird," "The Emperor of Ice-Cream" (1923) investigates the differences between "seeming" and "being" and draws the conclusion that "be" ought to be the "finale of seem." Variations on the verb "to be" appear again in "Of Mere Being," which employs **anagogic metaphor** in its wordplay.

Related Works: Stanton, "Childhood"; Simic, "Old Couple"; Strand, "Eating Poetry"; Kafka, "The Metamorphosis"; Williams, "The Red Wheelbarrow"; Reed, "Naming of Parts"; Nash, "Very Like a Whale"; Marquez, "The Handsomest Drowned Man in the World"; Yeats, "Sailing to Byzantium"; Dickinson, "Because I could not stop for Death"; Shelley, "Ozymandias."

WALLACE STEVENS

The Emperor of Ice-Cream

Call the roller of big cigars,
The muscular one, and bid him whip
In kitchen cups concupiscent curds.
Let the wenches dawdle in such dress
As they are used to wear, and let the boys
Bring flowers in last month's newspapers.
Let be be finale of seem.
The only emperor is the emperor of ice-cream.

Take from the dresser of deal,
Lacking the three glass knobs, that sheet
On which she embroidered fantails once
And spread it so as to cover her face.
If her horny feet protrude, they come
To show how cold she is, and dumb.

Let the lamp affix its beam.
The only emperor is the emperor of ice-cream.

WALLACE STEVENS

Thirteen Ways of Looking at a Blackbird

1

Among twenty snowy mountains,
The only moving thing
Was the eye of the blackbird.

2

I was of three minds,
Like a tree
In which there are three blackbirds.

3

The blackbird whirled in the autumn winds.
It was a small part of the pantomime.

4

A man and a woman
Are one.
A man and a woman and a blackbird
Are one.

5

I do not know which to prefer,
The beauty of inflections
Or the beauty of innuendoes,
The blackbird whistling
Or just after.

6

Icicles filled the long window
With barbaric glass.
The shadow of the blackbird
Crossed it, to and fro.
The mood
Traced in the shadow
An indecipherable cause.

7

O thin men of Haddam,
Why do you imagine golden birds?

Do you not see how the blackbird
Walks around the feet
Of the women about you?

8

I know noble accents
And lucid, inescapable rhythms;
But I know, too,
That the blackbird is involved
In what I know.

9

When the blackbird flew out of sight,
It marked the edge
Of one of many circles.

10

At the sight of blackbirds
Flying in a green light,
Even the bawds of euphony
Would cry out sharply.

11

He rode over Connecticut
In a glass coach.
Once, a fear pierced him,
In that he mistook
The shadow of his equipage
For blackbirds.

12

The river is moving.
The blackbird must be flying.

13

It was evening all afternoon.
It was snowing
And it was going to snow.
The blackbird sat
In the cedar-limbs.

WALLACE STEVENS

Of Mere Being

The palm at the end of the mind,
Beyond the last thought, rises
In the bronze decor,

A gold-feathered bird
Sings in the palm, without human meaning,
Without human feeling, a foreign song.

You know then that it is not the reason
That makes us happy or unhappy.
The bird sings. Its feathers shine.

The palm stands on the edge of space.
The wind moves slowly in the branches.
The bird's fire-fangled feathers dangle down.

MARK STRAND (b. 1934) was born on Prince Edward Island in Canada, but was raised primarily in the United States and South America. He received his B.A. at Antioch College in Ohio, his B.F.A. at Harvard, and his M.A. at the University of Iowa. He has traveled widely as a lecturer and professor. His books of poetry include *Sleeping with One Eye Open* (1964), *Darker* (1970), *Blizzard of One* (1998), which won the Pulitzer Prize, and *Dark Harbor* (1993).

In his introductory essay to *The Making of a Poem* (2000), which he co-wrote with Eavan Boland, Strand describes a poem as "a place where the conditions of beyondness and withinness are made palpable, where to imagine is to feel what it is like to be. It allows us to have the life we are denied because we are too busy living." Indeed, much of Strand's own poetry is **ontological** in nature and investigates the relationship between various selves and ways of being. In "Eating Poetry" (1968), the speaker is literally transformed by the power of poetry after he ingests it.

Related Works: Kafka, "The Metamorphosis"; Stanton, "Childhood"; Stevens, "Of Mere Being."

MARK STRAND

Eating Poetry

Ink runs from the corners of my mouth.
There is no happiness like mine.
I have been eating poetry.

The librarian does not believe what she sees.
Her eyes are sad
and she walks with her hands in her dress.

The poems are gone.
The light is dim.
The dogs are on the basement stairs and coming up.

Their eyeballs roll,
their blond legs burn like brush.
The poor librarian begins to stamp her feet and weep.

She does not understand.
When I get on my knees and lick her hand,
she screams.

I am a new man.
I snarl at her and bark.
I romp with joy in the bookish dark.

DYLAN THOMAS (1914–1953) was born in Wales. Thomas's father was a schoolmaster in English and, although Thomas was not a very good student and eventually dropped out of school at sixteen, he did read extensively from his father's collection of poetry during his childhood. Thomas's first volume of poetry, *Eighteen Poems*, was published when he was twenty and received much critical acclaim. Unlike other poets of the modern era, Thomas did not shun lyric, emotional poetry, and consequently his poetry is often considered to have more in common with the **Romantic** poets than the **Modernist** poets. Dylan was known as a heavy drinker and intense reader, and he did dramatic readings and broadcasts on poets and poetry for BBC (British Broadcasting Corporation) radio. He also made several reading tours in the United States before his early death. His collections of poetry include *Twenty-five Poems* (1936), *The World I Breathe* (1939), *The Map of Love* (1939), *Deaths and Entrances* (1946), and *In Country Sleep and Other Poems* (1952).

"Do Not Go Gentle into That Good Night" (1952) is characteristic of Thomas's **lyric** and emotionally charged poetry. In this **villanelle**, the speaker urges his father to live the remainder of his life to the fullest but also recognizes that death, finally, is inevitable and natural. "Fern Hill" (1946) is a nostalgic **pastoral** poem that recalls the wonder of childlike vision while acknowledging that time can only move in one direction; this forward movement, like death, is a natural phenomenon. "A Refusal to Mourn the Death, by Fire, of a Child in London" (1946) was written by Thomas in response to World War II. Although not ignoring human suffering, the poem recognizes the kind of "majesty" of death, even in "innocence and youth."

Related Works: Herrick, "To the Virgins"; Marvell, "To His Coy Mistress"; Norman, *'Night Mother*, Roethke, "My Papa's Waltz"; Yau, "Chinese Villanelle"; Wordsworth, "I wandered lonely as a cloud"; Berry, "The Peace of Wild Things"; Sandburg, "Chicago"; Jarrell, "Death of the Ball Turret Gunner"; Housman, "To an Athlete Dying Young."

DYLAN THOMAS

Do Not Go Gentle into That Good Night

Do not go gentle into that good night,
Old age should burn and rave at close of day;
Rage, rage against the dying of the light.

Though wise men at their end know dark is right,
Because their words had forked no lightning they
Do not go gentle into that good night.

Good men, the last wave by, crying how bright
Their frail deeds might have danced in a green bay,
Rage, rage against the dying of the light.

Wild men who caught and sang the sun in flight,
And learn, too late, they grieved it on its way,
Do not go gentle into that good night.

Grave men, near death, who see with blinding sight
Blind eyes could blaze like meteors and be gay,
Rage, rage against the dying of the light.

And you, my father, there on the sad height,
Curse, bless, me now with your fierce tears, I pray.
Do not go gentle into that good night.
Rage, rage against the dying of the light.

DYLAN THOMAS

Fern Hill

Now as I was young and easy under the apple boughs
About the lilting house and happy as the grass was green,
 The night above the dingle starry,
  Time let me hail and climb
 Golden in the heydays of his eyes,
And honoured among wagons I was prince of the apple towns
And once below a time I lordly had the trees and leaves
  Trail with daisies and barley
 Down the rivers of the windfall light.

And as I was green and carefree, famous among the barns
About the happy yard and singing as the farm was home,
 In the sun that is young once only,
  Time let me play and be
 Golden in the mercy of his means,
And green and golden I was huntsman and herdsman, the calves
Sang to my horn, the foxes on the hills barked clear and cold,
  And the sabbath rang slowly
 In the pebbles of the holy streams.

All the sun long it was running, it was lovely, the hay
Fields high as the house, the tunes from the chimneys, it was air
 And playing, lovely and watery
  And fire green as grass.
 And nightly under the simple stars
As I rode to sleep the owls were bearing the farm away,
All the moon long I heard, blessed among stables, the nightjars
 Flying with the ricks, and the horses
  Flashing into the dark.

DYLAN THOMAS

A Refusal to Mourn the Death, by Fire, of a Child in London

Never until the mankind making
Bird beast and flower
Fathering and all humbling darkness
Tells with silence the last light breaking
And the still hour
Is come of the sea tumbling in harness

And I must enter again the round
Zion of the water bead
And the synagogue of the ear of corn
Shall I let pray the shadow of a sound
Or sow my salt seed
In the least valley of sackcloth to mourn

The majesty and burning of the child's death.
I shall not murder
The mankind of her going with a grave truth
Nor blaspheme down the stations of the breath
With any further
Elegy of innocence and youth.

Deep with the first dead lies London's daughter,
Robed in the long friends,
The grains beyond age, the dark veins of her mother,
Secret by the unmourning water
Of the riding Thames.
After the first death, there is no other.

And then to awake, and the farm, like a wanderer white
With the dew, come back, the cock on his shoulder: it was all
Shining, it was Adam and maiden,
The sky gathered again
And the sun grew round that very day.
So it must have been after the birth of the simple light
In the first, spinning place, the spellbound horses walking warm
Out of the whinnying green stable
On to the fields of praise.

And honoured among foxes and pheasants by the gay house
Under the new made clouds and happy as the heart was long,
In the sun born over and over,
I ran my heedless ways,
My wishes raced through the house high hay

And nothing I cared, at my sky blue trades, that time allows
In all his tuneful turning so few and such morning songs
    Before the children green and golden
        Follow him out of grace,

Nothing I cared, in the lamb white days, that time would take me
Up to the swallow thronged loft by the shadow of my hand,
    In the moon that is always rising,
        Nor that riding to sleep
    I should hear him fly with the high fields
And wake to the farm forever fled from the childless land.
Oh as I was young and easy in the mercy of his means,
        Time held me green and dying
    Though I sang in my chains like the sea.

RICHARD WILBUR (b. 1921) was born in New York City but grew up in more rural surroundings in neighboring New Jersey. His father was a painter and his mother came from a family of journalists, so Wilbur was introduced to art and writing at an early age. He wrote for school newspapers in high school and at Amherst College, but he did not begin writing his own poetry until he was called to active duty in Italy and Germany during World War II as, he said later in a 1964 interview with *The Amherst Literary Magazine*, a "momentary stay against confusion." Upon returning from the war, Wilbur earned his M.A. at Harvard and spent some time teaching. He is a highly acclaimed poet. Two of his volumes of poetry, *Things of This World* (1956) and *New and Collected Poems* (1988) have won the Pulitzer Prize, and *Things of This World* was also a National Book Award winner. He has been a Poet Laureate and is a chancellor emeritus of the Academy of American Poets.

Although Wilbur is known to be a defender of strict poetic forms, in "Junk" (1961) he experiments with a different kind of poetic line. This highly **alliterative** poem examines the double nature of things (and through **personification**, the double nature of people as well) and suggests the redemptive value of returning "ordinary" things to the earth.

Related Works: Old English Riddles; Thomas, "A Refusal to Mourn the Death, by Fire, of a Child in London"; Sandburg, "Grass"; Henry, "Garage Sale."

RICHARD WILBUR

Junk

Huru Welandes
                    worc ne geswiceð
monna œnigum
                    ðara ðe Mimming can
heardne gehealdan.

WALDERE

An axe angles
from my neighbor's ashcan;
It is hell's handiwork,
the wood not hickory,
The flow of the grain
not faithfully followed.
The shivered shaft
rises from a shellheap
Of plastic playthings,
paper plates,
And the sheer shards
of shattered tumblers
That were not annealed
for the time needful.
At the same curbside,
a cast-off cabinet
Of wavily-warped
unseasoned wood
Waits to be trundled
in the trash-man's truck.
Haul them off! Hide them!
The heart winces
For junk and gimcrack,
for jerrybuilt things
And the men who make them
for a little money,
Bartering pride
like the bought boxer
Who pulls his punches,
or the paid-off jockey
Who in the home stretch
holds in his horse.
Yet the things themselves
in thoughtless honor
Have kept composure,
like captives who would not
Talk under torture.
Tossed from a tailgate
Where the dump displays
its random dolmens,
Its black barrows
and blazing valleys,
They shall waste in the weather
toward what they were.
The sun shall glory
in the glitter of glass-chips,
Foreseeing the salvage
of the prisoned sand,
And the blistering paint

peel off in patches,
That the good grain
be discovered again.
Then burnt, bulldozed,
they shall all be buried
To the depth of diamonds,
in the making dark
Where halt Hephaestus
keeps his hammer
And Wayland's work
is worn away.

William Carlos Williams (1883–1963) was born in Rutherford, New Jersey, to a British father and Caribbean mother. Although Williams left Rutherford for a time to study in Europe as a young man and again to pursue his medical degree at the University of Pennsylvania (where he also met and befriended fellow poets Ezra Pound and Hilda Doolittle), after finishing his internship in New York City and a pediatric course in Leipzig, Germany, Williams returned permanently to his hometown to practice his duel lifetime careers as a physician and a writer. Although he is known primarily as a poet, Williams was also an accomplished novelist, essayist, and playwright. His volumes of poetry include *Spring and All* (1923), *Pictures from Brueghel and Other Poems* (1962), *Imaginations* (1970), and the five-volume Paterson series, which was published as a complete set, *Paterson Books I–V* (with notes for Book VI) in 1963.

Like other poets of the **imagist** movement, Williams abandoned traditional poetic forms and experimented with new kinds of **meter** and lines. However, unlike his contemporaries Pound and Eliot, he remained much more connected to the American continent and saw himself not as an intellectual, but as an acute observer of the routine experiences and lives of everyday people. "The Red Wheelbarrow" (1923) is a kind of "still life" poem that illuminates the profound in the apparently mundane as well as the restorative power of a rain shower. "Spring and All" (1923) also focuses on an ordinary sight, a roadside, but hints at the power of nature and its constant capacity for rebirth.

Related Works: Sandburg, "Fog"; Stevens, "Thirteen Ways of Looking at a Blackbird"; Pound, "In a Station of the Metro"; Frost, "Birches"; Gioia, "California Hills in August"; Berry, "The Peace of Wild Things"; Chin, "Autumn Leaves."

WILLIAM CARLOS WILLIAMS

The Red Wheelbarrow

so much depends
upon

a red wheel
barrow

glazed with rain
water

beside the white
chickens.

WILLIAM CARLOS WILLIAMS

Spring and All

By the road to the contagious hospital
under the surge of the blue
mottled clouds driven from the
northeast—a cold wind. Beyond, the
waste of broad, muddy fields
brown with dried weeds, standing and fallen

patches of standing water
the scattering of tall trees

All along the road the reddish
purplish, forked, upstanding, twiggy
stuff of bushes and small trees
with dead, brown leaves under them
leafless vines—

Lifeless in appearance, sluggish
dazed spring approaches—

They enter the new world naked,
cold, uncertain of all
save that they enter. All about them
the cold, familiar wind—

Now the grass, tomorrow
the stiff curl of wildcarrot leaf

One by one objects are defined—
It quickens: clarity, outline of leaf

But now the stark dignity of
entrance—Still, the profound change
has come upon them; rooted, they
grip down and begin to awaken

JOHN YAU (b. 1950) was born in Lynn, Massachusetts, soon after his parents fled from Shanghai in 1949 as it fell to the Communists. Yau was confronted with the struggle for identity early in his youth, as his father was half British and half Chinese, whereas his mother came from an influential Shanghai family and never adjusted to her drastic change in status in the United States. Yau obtained his B.A. from Bard College and his M.F.A. from Brooklyn College. In addition to being a poet, he is a fiction writer and an art critic. His volumes of poetry include *Corpse and Mirror* (1983), *Edificio Sayonara* (1992), *Berlin Diptychon* (1995), *Forbidden Entries* (1996), and *Borrowed Love Poems* (2002).

Yau's poems frequently contain overtones of marginality, alienation, and **lyricism**, and many focus on explorations of identity. In "Chinese Villanelle" (1979), the speaker struggles to define himself as he recalls spending time with someone who looked at him but could not describe him.

Related Works: Pound, "The River Merchant's Wife"; Hughes, "Theme for English B"; Song, "Girl Powdering Her Neck"; Lee, "Persimmons"; Dunbar, "We wear the mask"; Wilson, *The Piano Lesson.*

JOHN YAU

Chinese Villanelle

I have been with you, and I have thought of you
Once the air was dry and drenched with light
I was like a lute filling the room with description

We watched glum clouds reject their shape
We dawdled near a fountain, and listened
I have been with you, and I have thought of you

Like a river worthy of its gown
And like a mountain worthy of its insolence
Why am I like a lute? left with only description

How does one cut an axe-handle with an axe?
What shall I do to tell you all my thoughts
When I have been with you, and thought of you

A pelican sits on the dam, while a duck
Folds its wings again; the song does not melt
I remember you looking at me without description

Perhaps a king's business is never finished,
Though "perhaps" implies a different beginning
I have been with you, and I have thought of you
Now I am a lute filled with this wandering description

William Butler Yeats (1865–1939) was born in Dublin, Ireland, where his father was a well-known painter. Although Yeats tried his own hand at painting, he soon discovered his talent lay in writing poetry instead, and he went on to become possibly *the* greatest writer of poetry in English in the twentieth century. Although Yeats was influenced by his contemporary Pound, he never discarded traditional verse forms. He was a strict adherent to **symbolism** and even developed his own symbology, which he described in his book *A Vision* (1925). Yeats was a strong Irish nationalist and served as a senator in the Irish Free State. As part of the Celtic revival in literature, Yeats founded Irish literary societies in London and Dublin and organized an Irish dramatic movement. He drew liberally from Irish **myth** and folklore in his own writing. His collections of poetry include *The Wanderings of Oisin and Other Poems* (1889), *The Celtic Twilight* (1893), *The Wind Among the Reeds* (1899), *In the Seven Woods* (1903), *The Green Helmet and Other Poems* (1910), *The Wild Swans at Coole* (1916), *The Cat and the Moon* (1924), *The Winding Stair and Other Poems* (1933), and *The Collected Poems* (1933). Yeats was also a dramatist and an essayist. He won the Nobel Prize for Literature in 1923.

"Leda and the Swan" (1924) turns not to Irish myth, but to Classical myth for its subject matter. In this sensual and carnal **sonnet**, the poetic persona is a voyeur who observes the violent act with a foreknowledge of the violent acts that will result. "Sailing to Byzantium" (1927), which is written in **ottava rima** stanzas, is another poem in which the poetic persona voyeuristically observes the sensual life and flesh before him and ponders about what is "to come."

Related Works: Rich, "Diving into the Wreck"; Hardy, "The Ruined Maid"; Browning, "My Last Duchess"; Shelley, "Ozymandias"; Stevens, "Of Mere Being"; Tennyson, "Ulysses"; Atwood, "Siren Song"; *Everyman*; Field, "A Pen-Drawing of Leda."

WILLIAM BUTLER YEATS

Leda and the Swan

A sudden blow: the great wings beating still
Above the staggering girl, her thighs caressed
By the dark webs, her nape caught in his bill,
He holds her helpless breast upon his breast.

How can those terrified vague fingers push
The feathered glory from her loosening thighs?
And how can body, laid in that white rush,
But feel the strange heart beating where it lies?

A shudder in the loins engenders there
The broken wall, the burning roof and tower
And Agamemnon dead,
                                        Being so caught up,
So mastered by the brute blood of the air,
Did she put on his knowledge with his power
Before the indifferent beak could let her drop?

WILLIAM BUTLER YEATS

Sailing to Byzantium

1

That is no country for old men. The young
In one another's arms, birds in the trees
—Those dying generations—at their song,
The salmon-falls, the mackerel-crowded seas,
Fish, flesh, or fowl, commend all summer long
Whatever is begotten, born, and dies.
Caught in that sensual music all neglect
Monuments of unageing intellect.

2

An aged man is but a paltry thing,
A tattered coat upon a stick, unless
Soul clap its hands and sing, and louder sing
For every tatter in its mortal dress,
Nor is there singing school but studying
Monuments of its own magnificence;
And therefore I have sailed the seas and come
To the holy city of Byzantium.

3

O sages standing in God's holy fire
As in the gold mosaic of a wall,
Come from the holy fire, perne in a gyre,
And be the singing-masters of my soul.
Consume my heart away: sick with desire
And fastened to a dying animal
It knows not what it is; and gather me
Into the artifice of eternity.

4

Once out of nature I shall never take
My bodily form from any natural thing,
But such a form as Grecian goldsmiths make
Of hammered gold and gold enamelling
To keep a drowsy Emperor awake:
Or set upon a golden bough to sing
To lords and ladies of Byzantium
Of what is past or passing, or to come.

KEVIN YOUNG (b. 1970) was born in Lincoln, Nebraska and earned his B.A. at Harvard and his M.F.A. at Brown University. His first book of poetry, *Most Way*

Home (1995) was selected as a National Poetry Series winner. His other volumes of poetry are *To Repel Ghosts* (2001) and *Jelly Roll: A Blues* (2003). He is also the editor of the collection *Giant Steps: The New Generation of African American Writers* (2000) and an active participant in the conference "Furious Flower: Regenerating the Black Poetic Tradition."

Young's poetry addresses the past and present lives of African Americans and does not shy away from tackling unpleasant subjects such as slavery, racism, and poverty. Young draws on the blues tradition in his 2000 "riff" on Langston Hughes in the poem of the same name, as the speaker asks the famous poet to reveal how he managed to become "a saint." "Nineteen Seventy-Five" examines both the loss of the speaker's hair and the diminishment of the Black Power Movement over the twelve years of his pet dog's life.

Related Works: Langston Hughes, "Theme for English B"; Sexton, "To a Friend Whose Work Has Come to Triumph"; Brooks, "The Pool Players: Seven at the Golden Shovel"; Lorde, "Hanging Fire"; Wideman, "What We Cannot Speak About We Must Pass Over in Silence."

KEVIN YOUNG

Langston Hughes

LANGSTON HUGHES
LANGSTON HUGHES
        O come now
        & sang
them weary blues—

Been tired here
feelin' low down
        Real
        tired here
since you quit town

Our ears no longer trumpets
Our mouths no more bells
        FAMOUS POET©—
        Busboy—Do tell
us of hell—

Mr. Shakespeare in Harlem
Mr. Theme for English B
        Preach on
        kind sir
of death, if it please—

We got no more promise
We only got ain't

Let us in
on how
you 'came a saint

LANGSTON
LANGSTON
LANGSTON HUGHES
Won't you send
all heaven's news

KEVIN YOUNG

Nineteen Seventy-Five

Since there was no better color
or name, we called the dog
Blackie, insurance no one would forget
the obvious. One of the few dark ones
in the bunch, the only male,
he died twelve human years later
standing on a vet's table;
when the news came Mama
Lucille, visiting, gathered us
in a circle of hands, called up
Jesus to the touch, to protect.

But that year when beautiful
still meant Black, when I carried
home my first dog full of whimpers
& sudden dukey, we warmed him
in our basement with a bottle disguised
as his mother, we let his hair grow long
around his feet, just as ours did

around ears, unbent necks. Back
in the day, my mother cut my afro
every few months, bathroom layered
with headlines proclaiming the world's end,
our revolution. I cannot recall
when I first stepped into the reclining
thrones of the barbershop
when I first demanded to go there alone,
motherless, past the spinning white
& red sign left over from days of giving
blood, to ask for my head turned
clean, shorn, for the cold to hold.

I only remember how back then the room
seemed to fill with darkness as she trimmed

my globe of hair, curls falling like an earth
I never thought would be anywhere
but at my feet, how the scissors twanged
by these ears like the raised voice
of a Southern gentleman the moment after
some beautiful boy segregates coffee, no cream,
black, onto his creased & bleached lap.

CHAPTER 8

Reading and Writing about Drama

All the world's a stage,
And all the men and women merely players.
—William Shakespeare

[T]he play's the thing
Wherein I'll catch the conscience of the king.
—William Shakespeare

INTRODUCTION

Although you have been telling stories and learning poetry since the time you could listen and talk, for most of us plays are a form of "high art," requiring a trip to a professional theater, fancy dress, and expensive tickets. But drama is also related to one of humanity's most basic impulses, the desire to play. Drama, for people, begins with child's play, from dress-up to playing school or pretending to be a knight in King Arthur's Court. For adults, the play impulse remains evident in activities ranging from karaoke performance to Civil War reenactments. Holiday venues such as Colonial Williamsburg and Disneyland also tap into the impulse toward make-believe that is exhibited by people of all ages.

"All the world's a stage," a sentiment made famous by William Shakespeare, is in fact a basic metaphor for many cultures. Sociologists have, accordingly, analyzed everyday life as a form of drama (e.g., Berger and Luckmann). Attitudes toward the idea that "life is a play," however, vary. An upbeat article on the uses of blogging to help U.S. elementary-school students find an audience and gain confidence in themselves as writers, for instance, is entitled "All the World's a Stage" (Fallon). In this view, young writers are empowered by finding themselves on the virtual "stage" of the World Wide Web. On the other hand, in Shakespeare's *As You Like It* this same sentiment is expressed by the grumpy, melancholic Jacques; in his version of the "world-as-stage" **metaphor**, we enter life as crying, vomiting babies and exit in second childhood—blind, toothless, and senile. How you interpret the complex metaphor "the world is a stage + men and women are actors" depends on whether you think people are generally headed toward comedy or tragedy. In either case, however, drama remains a powerful symbol of life itself.

WHAT IS DRAMA?

Drama, like poetry, is a very old form of literature. Some scholars argue that in ancient Greece, drama developed directly out of the oral performance of epic poetry, where the bard would take on the identities of different characters and also act as narrator. Over the centuries, Greek drama continued to enact for audiences the story of their culture—at once reinforcing key civic and moral values and encouraging serious examination of these values—through the visual and oral performance of actors. For instance, *Antigone* tells one portion of the history of the House of Thebes. Antigone herself must face the conflict between two important cultural values: respect for the dead and the King's law. Sophocles' play is one part history, one part ethical education, and one part literature. In other words, ancient drama works both to teach and delight.

A very long span of time separates ancient Greek drama from the most recent play contained in *Prentice Hall Literature Portfolio* which is August Wilson's *The Piano Lesson*. To some extent, though, drama retains its **didactic** function; the earliest printed editions of *Everyman*, for instance, describe the work as a moral "treatise." Hoping to trick his uncle into betraying his crime by playing the King's murder before Claudius, Hamlet also expresses faith in drama's ethical impact. In later centuries, playwrights have continued to be motivated by ethical and social concerns. Susan Glaspell and her husband founded a theater company as part of a

Here begynneth a treatyse how ye hye fader of heuen sendeth dethe to somon euery creature to come and gyue a counte of theyr lyues in this worlde/and is in maner of a morall playe.

Everyman: Here Begynneth a Treatyse

utopian community project—aimed at improving society—and Arthur Miller's plays consistently addressed issues of politics and social justice. A **realistic** play, such as Henrik Ibsen's *A Dollhouse*, also can seriously consider social issues of its time. As Marsha Norman puts it, every dramatic character, like Ibsen's Nora, wants *something*—even something so simple as for her husband to stop calling her his "little bird"—and drama's representation of these desires is part of literature's first function: to teach (Norman 141). Even so witty a comedy as Oscar Wilde's *The Importance of Being Earnest* offers social commentary, this time on the hypocrisy of the rich.

In drama, literature's second function—"to delight"—perhaps varies more over time than do its educational goals because the stage itself changes radically from period to period. The stage of the ancient Greeks, for instance, was large enough to accommodate several thousand spectators, who sat in a circle on three sides. Medieval plays often were performed in the great halls of aristocrats, in the streets, or on the steps of cathedrals. Renaissance drama grew out of inn yard performances, but by the time Shakespeare was writing his plays, the Globe and other professional London theaters featured a large proscenium stage that jutted out into the audience, with spectators seated in the round and the famous "groundlings" gathered around

Stage of the Globe Theatre, London, England

the bottom edge of the stage. In the drama of later centuries, the proscenium stage is framed by an arch that turns the stage into a separate reality that is cut off from the world of the theater audience by an invisible "fourth wall."

ELEMENTS OF DRAMA

We might imagine the basic elements of drama—plot, character, setting, language, and theme—as constituting the points of a pentad that interact in continuously changing ways.

Plot

The most famous discussion of drama undoubtedly is found in Aristotle's *Poetics*, which establishes **plot** as the most basic ingredient of drama and the foundation of all other elements. (The *Poetics* is concerned solely with tragedy, but later thinkers often extend its observations to drama in general.) For Aristotle, a tragedy is an imitation of an action; it must be complete, serious, and possess a certain degree of grandeur. The **tragic hero** falls from high estate to low, and the audience experiences pity (because the hero does not deserve such a harsh end) and fear (because they too could suffer the same calamity). The purging of these negative emotions, the **catharsis**, leaves the spectators in a state of satisfaction at the drama's conclusion. Marsha Norman, in an updated view of the dramatist's challenge, also considers plot as crucial to audience engagement. She argues that "a play has to move. It has to go where it says it is going." Norman offers as a metaphor the "dramatic plotline-as-a-ski-lift":

> What you want from a ski lift is to get in, ride to the top of the mountain, get out, look at the view, say "Wow," and go home. What you don't want, in a ski lift or a play, is to stop halfway up the mountain and just hang there. Nor do you want somebody to pull the shades, come on the loudspeaker, and lecture you about the politics of Kansas, or tell you about their Aunt June, to whom nothing really happened, or show you pictures of their very pleasant children. . . . If you have paid your money, you want to see the mountain for yourself. You want the ride. You want to go someplace you've never been and feel how things are there. (Norman 139–40)

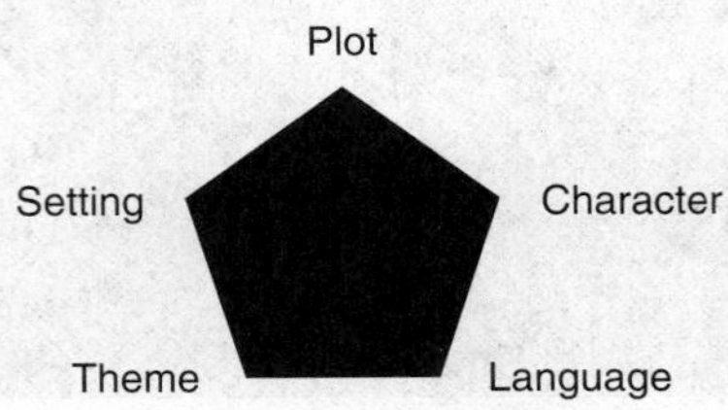

Figure 8.1 The Pentad of Drama

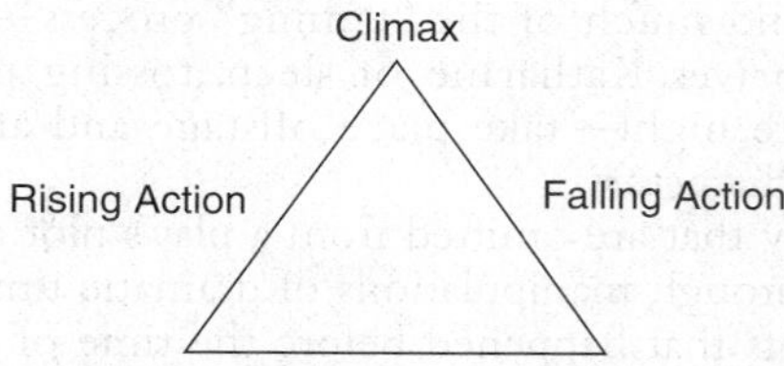

Figure 8.2 Shape of Aristotelian Tragedy

The metaphors may differ, but these two writers, widely separated in time and place, share the feeling that drama needs to have a **plot** representing a significant and attention-getting action.

An Aristotelian plot has triangular symmetry. There is a rising action, **climax** or **peripeteia**, and then falling action.

In *Antigone*, for instance, we might say that the rising action is Antigone's secret burial of her brother Polyneices, in defiance of the king's law. The climax comes when Creon, the king, confronts Antigone with her so-called crime, she defends herself, and Creon sentences Antigone to death. The falling action involves Antigone's mourning of her untimely death, her live burial, the twin suicides of Antigone and her betrothed, Haemon, and the remaining suicides. Other plays are constructed according to different concepts or metaphors. *Everyman*, for instance, is constructed according to the master **metaphor** of life as a journey, with death as the traveler's destination. As a spiritual journey, the play has a strictly linear plot. Because God, or Divine Providence, controls Everyman's destiny, there also can be no true crisis or climax, as in ancient drama.

In some cases, the plot and experience of a play are exactly the same thing. Such plays obey the **dramatic unities**. Aristotle's *Poetics* is usually cited as the source for the idea that a play should have **unity of time** (represent eight hours or a single day), **unity of place** (take place in a single location), and **unity of action** (focus on a single crucial idea). Marsha Norman's *'Night Mother* observes all three unities. The entire action, which involves Jessie Cates's preparation for suicide (unity of action), takes place within the house shared by Jessie and her mother, Thelma (unity of place). The play's action spans eighty-five minutes; Norman stresses that the two women come to an understanding within the short time that it takes the audience to experience a one-act play by displaying prominently multiple stage clocks that are set to 8:15 PM. Except during matinees, the audience and characters experience a **unity of time**.

As in short stories, dramatic **plot** is a selection of events taken from the complete **story** that lies behind it; plot is the sequence of events as we experience them, story the sum total of events necessary for understanding what is happening and why. The events depicted on stage are crucial to dramatic plot, but sometimes missing pieces of the story—events not shown on stage that either are referred to by the characters or inferred by the audience—can be significant. What happened to Oedipus and Jocasta, the parents of Antigone, is crucial to understanding why her two brothers should have been fighting one another in the first place. In *Trifles*, the scene of John Wright's murder remains a powerful absence that both the women characters, as detectives, and the audience must reconstruct imaginatively. In *The Taming of the Shrew*, Kate and Petruchio's unruly marriage ceremony and much of the "taming" process—particularly the part where Petruchio deprives Katharine of sleep, tossing pillows and shouting sermons for the entire night—take place offstage and are reported from the perspective of minor characters.

Events of the story that are omitted from a play's plot can be brought to the audience's attention through manipulations of dramatic time and space. The plot can refer back to events that happened before the time of the plot (**flashbacks**) and can allude less directly to places, persons, or events that have not yet occurred (**foreshadowing**). For instance, that Willy's affair with The Woman is the cause of Biff's anger toward him becomes clear only when their confrontation is replayed as a flashback. Dislocations of place are less common in this anthology. Perhaps the best example is in *Death of a Salesman*, where there is an important contrast between Brooklyn, the center of home and family, and Boston, the land of commerce and marital betrayal. Africa, where Willy's brother Ben made his fortune, and the American West, from which Biff has recently returned, exist offstage only as imaginary, symbolic places.

Character

In drama, the term *character* refers to both the persons who appear on stage and their psychological, moral, and social identity. For Aristotle drama is driven by plot, whereas for Marsha Norman writing a play is a process of becoming familiar with the fictional characters that people her plots until they take on an imaginative existence of their own. According to Norman's own account, she gradually comes to understand her own characters by the way they talk, and once she "knows" them thoroughly, the plot arises out of their "characters": "The plot is nothing more than what the main character does and what the other characters do back. The characters act as they do because they must" (Norman 143). In other words, character drives plot. In performance, we also come to know characters largely through their speech and interactions with others on stage; our sense of character is conditioned by changing relationships among those fictional persons as the plot unfolds. Furthermore, because of drama's live nature, we are always aware of the actor's body beneath the fictional character. Our response to dramatic characters is therefore complex, something more than simple identification with fictional persons.

In Aristotle's view—which influences many, although not all, later understandings of the term—in plays character emerges from action, as it does in life. According to Aristotle's understanding of human nature, people become who they are by their public actions, which through repetition over time become habits and solidify into enduring qualities of **character**, both moral and psychological. That is, we become what we do. Under ordinary circumstances, behavior hardens slowly into character, but in the extraordinary circumstances of tragedy, the tragic hero is destroyed by **hamartia**. This Greek term, often mistranslated as a "tragic flaw," is a "mistake" or wrong choice made by the **tragic hero**. Oedipus, for instance, falls because he kills an unknown man at the crossroads—who turns out to be his own father—and marries a woman who, as it turns out, is his mother. Rather than blaming Oedipus for uncontrollable anger or incestuous passion, from the Aristotelian point of view we should recognize how wrong choices or fatal errors lead to his downfall.

Aristotle's *Poetics* did not influence all playwrights directly; Shakespeare, for instance, probably did not have firsthand knowledge of the *Poetics*. But others take Aristotle as their touchstone and define their own goals against the *Poetics*. During the first run of *Death of a Salesman*, for instance, Arthur Miller wrote an op-ed piece for the *New York Times* defending Willy Loman's stature as a modern tragic hero, even though he is not aristocratic and does not fall from high estate: "I think that the tragic feeling is evoked when we are in the presence of a character who is ready to lay down his life, if need be, to secure one thing—his sense of personal dignity. From Orestes to Hamlet, Medea to Macbeth, the underlying struggle is that of the individual attempting to gain his 'rightful' position in his society" (Miller X1). For Miller, the common man has as much potential for tragic stature as does the noblest member of the House of Thebes.

In short stories, as discussed in Chapter 4, characters tend to be either dynamic (round) or static (flat). To some extent, this categorization also works for drama. In **realistic drama**, such as Henrik Ibsen's *A Dollhouse*, characters are so well-developed that they seem almost detachable from their plots. When Nora leaves her husband and family at the end of *A Dollhouse*, slamming the door behind her, we can readily imagine her achieving some new life beyond that door. Not all drama offers strictly realistic characters, however. The figures that populate *Everyman*, for instance, are **allegorical**; they represent a concept (Knowledge), physical entity (Goods), or set of behaviors (Good Deeds). In *The Glass Menagerie*, the Gentleman Caller, although in actuality a co-worker of Tom, is also a nearly allegorical figure called forth from Amanda's memories of her youth. Another category of dramatic character might be absent characters, persons mentioned in the play but who never make an appearance on stage. The father/husband of *The Glass Menagerie*, represented on stage only by his portrait, is nevertheless a key player in the family dynamics we see in that play.

When analyzing and evaluating dramatic characters, we often measure them against social types that would be familiar to the audience. In *The Taming of the Shrew*, for instance, the old man Gremio, an unsuitable wooer of the lovely Bianca, is the stock figure of the ***senex***, the old man who tries to prevent the young lovers from getting together. **Realistic** and **expressionistic** drama can offer characters who evoke social types, but prove themselves to be more complex. A good example might be Amanda, the mother from Tennessee Williams's *The Glass Menagerie*. She is an archetypal Southern belle, a faded beauty living on old memories of romance and fine manners. But as a mother who truly loves her children and who has been reduced to selling magazines over the telephone to friends who try to evade her, Amanda is a fully realized and sympathetic character. August Wilson's *The Piano Lesson* consistently calls into question the relationship between social types—and especially vicious stereotypes—and full-fledged characters or persons.

The Greeks introduced to the drama one final kind of character that has remained important in the history of drama: the Chorus. In plays like *Antigone*, the Chorus comments on what is happening in the play. The Chorus tends to express mainstream sentiments; it can undergo a change of position or attitude, and can at times be ethically or factually wrong in its judgment. Thus, while the Chorus provides guidance, the audience must approach its statements critically. Very few later plays use an actual Chorus, but there are "guides" who function in a similar way. Most notable among recent plays is the role played by Tom in *The Glass Menagerie*, who steps outside the frame of the dramatic fiction to address the audience directly.

Setting

Although for Aristotelian drama, plot is preeminent and for Norman, the characters take shape first in the playwright's imagination, Susan Glaspell's *Trifles* (1916) has its origins in a particular setting. Perhaps this fact should not surprise us, for Glaspell wrote for a particular company and space, the Wharf Theater in Provincetown, Massachusetts. Glaspell writes that when preparing to write *Trifles*, she

> went out on the wharf, sat alone on one of our wooden benches without a back, and looked a long time at that bare little stage. After a time the stage became a kitchen—a kitchen there all by itself. I saw just where the stove was, the table, and the steps going upstairs. Then the door at the back opened, and people all bundled up came in—two or three men, I wasn't sure which, but sure enough about the two women, who hung back, reluctant to enter that kitchen. (Glaspell 255)

Glaspell's characters enter her mind's eye only after the *location* has taken shape. Setting gives rise to plot and character. But Glaspell had in mind not only the specific theatrical space of the Wharf Theater, but also a real kitchen, that of a woman accused of murder whose case Glaspell had covered as a newspaper reporter in Iowa. Most plays are set in specific places, with absent places often functioning as symbolic opposites. August Wilson's *The Piano Lesson* takes place in the Pittsburgh of Wilson's own youth, and the South from which Lymon and Boy Willie arrive is both a real place with a long, complicated, and sometimes terrible history and a symbolic place from which Sutter's ghost, much like the ghost of Hamlet's father, returns. *The Glass Menagerie* is set precisely in late 1930s America, a time when the Great Depression has receded, but war had already broken out in Spain and America's involvement in World War II loomed in the near future. The play itself is set in St. Louis; fuzzy memories of the Mississippi Delta of Amanda's youth and myths about Mexico, the foreign land to which Tom and Amanda's father has escaped, frame the grim realities of urban life as symbolic alternatives.

Language

At its simplest, drama requires only three things: actors, a space, and language that is either spoken or sung. Diction in drama should not be confused with ordinary speech. If you were to take a tape recorder and capture a random conversation on a bus, you would be surprised at how fragmentary, vague, and inelegant a transcript of that conversation would seem. Even a conversational play such as *Death of a Salesman* can have strongly poetic diction. Try removing from its emotional context Linda's statement that "attention must be paid," and you will see readily that her emotional speech is far from ordinary.

At the same time, some dramatists try to capture as closely as possible the everyday speech of actual people. **Expressionist drama**, represented in this anthology by *The Glass Menagerie*, infuses conversational prose with poetic diction. August Wilson's plays are also known for their powerful combination of poetic and colloquial modes of speech. Finally, the characters of Wilde's *The Importance of Being Earnest* speak almost entirely in witty **epigrams**. In Wilde's play, we might say, the mannered language creates both the play's improbable plot and its volatile characters. Wilde's detractors complained that in *Earnest*, all of the characters talked alike, but the witty language is also what keeps the characters—the greedy Lady Bracknell, for instance—from being truly evil.

Drama relies primarily on **dialogue**, the exchange of ideas and attitudes among two or more fictional persons. Not all speech in a play, however, is a direct exchange between characters. A **monologue** delivered before passive listeners onstage is one obvious exception. So too is the **soliloquy**, an extended speech by one character alone on stage, based on the fiction that the character speaks either to herself or himself—musing aloud—or directly to the audience. In some cases, the line between dialogue and monologue is difficult to draw. *Death of a Salesman*, for instance, is subtitled "Certain Private Conversations in Two Acts" and a "Requiem." Although some of these conversations are conventional exchanges between members of Willy Loman's family, others take place inside Willy's head. In other words, Willy's memories of former conversations with Ben and his fantasized talks with Ben in the present are both dramatized on stage as concrete realities.

Some drama—most notably, ancient Greek drama—relies heavily on elaborate **speeches** and formal exchanges between characters. In *Antigone*, for instance, both the first confrontation between Antigone and Creon and the following conversation between Antigone and her sister, Ismene, take place in short, tense exchanges of lines. (Sometimes the characters speak in one-line sequences that follow rapidly on one another, a device called **stichomythia**.) But once Antigone has been condemned to a live burial in her tomb, she and the Chorus engage in a deeper argument about the merits of Creon's sentence on her that is conducted in more lengthy speeches.

Theme

The pentad of drama with which this chapter opened represents the five basic elements of drama—plot, character, setting, language, and theme—as equal points on the diagram. But dramatic **themes**, like themes in the other literary genres, are in a sense the end result of interaction among the other four elements. A theme is a generalization—almost like the topic around which you would construct a thesis statement—and the play itself provides evidence in support of that thesis. Some authors start with a theme that they want to explore—women's place in society, in the case of Ibsen, or the failure of the American dream, in the case of Arthur Miller. Sometimes viewers, reviewers, readers, and critics have to extract themes from plays on their own. But responding to plays at the level of theme is part of what makes drama capable of communicating and questioning cultural values and beliefs. Theme helps us to read drama "symbol-wise."

One striking theme of drama is the genre's ability to reflect on its own artfulness. **Metadrama** may be defined as those moments when plays call attention to their own artificiality or to their status as fiction. When Hamlet, for instance, tells the traveling players how to deliver their lines, he reminds the audience that "Hamlet" himself is played by an actor who has made choices about how to deliver his lines. In *Antigone*, the Chorus's praise of the god Dionysus would remind the audience that the play was being performed as part of the dramatic festival for that god. Metadramatic moments remind us that although a play is merely fiction, life itself can be like a play. Metadrama is yet one more feature of drama that helps us to read both art and life "symbol-wise."

STRATEGIES FOR READING DRAMA

Short stories and poetry are most often consumed silently by solitary readers, whereas plays are meant to be performed on stage by actors, so that events unroll in real time before the eyes and ears of the spectators. Part of drama's delight is engaging the physical senses along with the minds of audiences. At the same time, any play takes on additional meaning through retrospection, the art of not only remembering, but also **interpreting**, what has been seen and heard. Even students who have seen a play in live or filmed performance need to exercise their memories and imaginations when interpreting that text. Thus, although readers need to compensate for not having seen a play in performance, students of literature must also supplement theatrical experience with close reading of the printed text in order to get the most that they can out of a play.

Watching Plays

To engage fully with drama, it is always preferable to see a live performance. A good amateur production can be as engaging as a Broadway hit; so if your town or college is producing one of the plays you have read or studied, you will enjoy and benefit from seeing a performance. Today, we also have available to us on video and DVD a wide range of filmed productions and film adaptations; although films lack

Harriet Smithson as Ophelia in Shakespeare's *Hamlet*

some of the electricity of live performance, they have the advantage of letting you watch a scene, or even a whole play, several times.

When watching a live or filmed performance, you should be aware that you are responding to a combination of the playwright's directions, the director's interpretation, and the actors' choices. What the set looks like, the way in which lines are spoken, how characters are costumed and wear their hair, and the gestures they make are all arranged to produce a particular effect. Dustin Hoffman, for instance, is a short, slight man, whereas Brian Dennehy has a large, imposing figure and broad shoulders. Their physical differences affected profoundly the two actors' portrayal of Willy Loman in *Death of a Salesman*.

Often, directors and actors are responding to a theatrical tradition. Ophelia in *Hamlet*, according to a long-standing stage tradition, is pale, wears white (as a sign of her innocence) and has long, flowing hair—preferably blond—that spills across her shoulders (as a sign of youth and later of madness). Nineteenth-century actress Harriet Smithson played Ophelia in this vein, and to some extent, later productions have taken as their point of departure this archetypal portrait of a wistful, innocent, beautiful, and doomed Ophelia. In the 1999 film of *Hamlet* directed by

Kate Winslet as Ophelia in Kenneth Branagh's *Hamlet*

Kenneth Branagh, Kate Winslet as Ophelia has gorgeous dark blond ringlets, but she also wears sensuous red lipstick and red clothing at the beginning of the film. The effect is to polarize Ophelia's character, to place her within the traditional paradigm of fragile innocence while hinting at her potential for passion and sexuality. In a Royal Shakespeare Company production of *Hamlet* from 1984, Frances Barber played Ophelia with brown hair, dark clothing, and a brooding manner. When she learned that she would play the role of Ophelia, Barber writes,

> I had a fairly traditional image of Ophelia in my mind. The obedient young girl whose sense of self is defined by the court in which she lives, and hence the men around her, is used as an instrument of political machinations, and ends up hysterical. This invariably took on an image of nightgowns and flowers. (Barber 137)

Ophelia in nightgowns and flowers is precisely the image portrayed by Harriet Smithson. But as the production went into rehearsal, Barber recalls, she came to see Ophelia instead as a strong woman who is destroyed by the social imbalances around her. For the first half of the play, in Barber's interpretation, Ophelia acts forcefully, turning on her father fiercely even as she agrees to return Hamlet's gifts. When she goes mad, furthermore, Barber's Ophelia is dressed not in a white nightgown, but in a formal black mourning dress that links her to the stark reality of death. Hers is, in all respects, a dark character.

Ophelia (Frances Barber) with Laertes (Kenneth Branagh) in the 1984 Royal Shakespeare Company production of *Hamlet*, directed by Ron Daniels and Maria Bjornson

As a student of literature, when watching filmed versions of drama or even stage productions, you should be careful not to be so thoroughly influenced by a particular interpretation that you cannot imagine other possibilities. Many contemporary students are convinced that Hamlet and Ophelia had been intimate previously because Kenneth Branagh provides a **flashback** in which this encounter takes place. The play text, by contrast, is ambiguous on the subject; Hamlet makes sexual innuendos to Ophelia, but we have no proof that he has slept with her. Some ways to expand your understanding of different dramatic interpretations and choices might be to search the Internet for the title of your selected play. There you will find announcements and reviews of productions large and small from many places, sometimes complete with cast pictures. If you search Google's image database, you can also find images of plays and characters in production that will show you how staging and costuming work in different versions of the same play.

Listening to Plays

If you cannot attend a live performance of a play or find a suitable video or DVD, you can always listen to the play on CD or tape. There are available many complete versions of different plays read by actors from well-known theater companies. By listening to rather than watching a play, you can not only familiarize yourself with the text while walking or driving, but also become deeply focused on its language. In some plays, furthermore, sounds and music produced onstage or off exert a strong influence on the overall mood and its changes. According to Arthur Miller's directions, for instance, every appearance on stage by Willy Loman is accompanied by plaintive flute music. The crash of Willy's car offstage, by contrast, is jarring and disturbing. So too is the offstage gunshot that concludes *'Night, Mother*. Some plays use song to enhance dramatic atmosphere and underscore key themes. African American work songs, for instance, figure prominently in August Wilson's *The Piano Lesson*, evoking memories of both Africa and slavery, two cultures that contrast with the white (Southern) culture represented by the piano itself. In *Hamlet*, as well, the distracted Ophelia sings snatches of ballads that the audience would have found familiar. Thinking specifically about the symbolic relation of these songs to what has happened on stage can significantly enhance your **interpretation** of its characters and themes.

Performance and Play Readings

Probably the best way to get to know a play well is to perform in one yourself. Most of us are not gifted actors, and many of us are downright shy, but there are ways to keep the experience manageable and pleasant. For instance, you might work with others to act out a single scene. You can memorize the text or read from a script if that makes you more comfortable. From the experience of staging a scene or portion of a play, you will learn important information about its key elements, such as how the scene might be staged (are all actors on the same plane? are some above or below the others?); how the action is blocked (who stands where and how do the characters interact in that physical space?); and what props are necessary for the plot to make sense.

Another useful activity is the group play reading, which many scholars use to familiarize themselves with lesser-known plays that they may never have the opportunity to see on stage. Readers usually take the part of different characters, switching roles every now and then. The group reading, which can take up to three hours, allows you to experience a play in its entirety, to grasp the plot and characters in a more visceral way than you can when reading silently, and to enjoy intermittently the pleasures of histrionic performance in a low-stress environment. Adding snacks makes the play reading a festive occasion.

Reading Plays Critically

When we talk about reading plays, we mean at once the preparatory act of reading to understand and the later act of close reading, which is necessary if you are to move from experiencing to **interpreting** drama. To read a play actively and critically, you can use any of the techniques outlined in Chapters 3, 4, and 6. Read the text aloud when you are having trouble making sense of it; mark up and annotate your book to indicate important parts (you can also mark those passages your teacher and peers focus on in class); keep a double-entry journal of quotations and comments for any topic or image pattern that you might want to trace through the play.

In contrast to poems and short stories, which are trim and compact, plays can seem big and sprawling and therefore resistant to close reading. For this reason, it is useful to reduce the text to a manageable scheme, through an outline or other method of brainstorming. For instance, you might simply outline the main divisions of the play (generally acts and scenes) and **summarize** what happens in each section; such a memory aid is particularly useful if you will be asked to write an exam or final essay covering an entire semester's work. Plots and characters can fade quickly from memory or become confused with one another!

Printed drama as a genre has particular features that can help you with your reading and interpretation. Among them are descriptions of setting and/or staging, stage directions, lists of characters, and references to props.

Descriptions and Stage Directions

Many older plays embed information about place, gesture, or attitude in the text itself. In *The Taming of the Shrew*, for instance, we know that Lucentio has just arrived in Padua because Tranio *says* so. Likewise, we know that at the Mousetrap play, Hamlet invites Ophelia to lie in his lap because we hear him issue the invitation. How the actress playing Ophelia responds, however, varies from production to production. This stage direction is open to interpretation. In later plays, separate stage directions can give us valuable information to guide our interpretation. Henrik Ibsen, for instance, describes the set of *A Dollhouse* in minute detail at the beginning of the printed play. From this description, we learn not only what objects the staging should include—a sofa, a rocking chair, engravings on the wall, and even a Christmas tree—but also receive information about the play's imaginative setting ("It is winter") and character (the room is "furnished comfortably and tastefully, but not extravagantly").

Stage directions can also provide both actor and reader with clues about how a character should act and even feel. In *A Dollhouse*, Ibsen provides many stage directions that tell the actress playing Nora what to do, actions that range from wiping her mouth to placing her suitcase on a chair. The conclusion to *Death of a*

Salesman, which is conducted in silence, also depends heavily on stage directions. We are told, for instance, that "All stop a moment when Linda, in clothes of mourning, bearing a little bunch of roses, comes through the draped doorway into the kitchen." From this small part of an extended stage direction, we can infer both Linda's feelings and the respect others show towards her.

Character Lists and Props

Sometimes, a printed play will contain brief descriptions of characters within the list of *dramatis personae*, or persons who appear on the stage. These descriptions might identify a character by profession, social and dramatic type, or personality; the character list might also tell you who played the part in the original production. When consulting lists of characters, be aware that sometimes they are provided by the author, sometimes by an editor.

As objects demanded by the text of a play, props are important sources of meaning for students of drama. But because very few plays have lists of props, you need to read the play text closely to recognize their significance. In a play, props may be nothing more than ordinary objects, but they may also be saturated with **symbolism**. In *'Night, Mother*, for instance, Jessie chooses to commit suicide with her father's rather than her husband's gun. The gun, which is featured on stage, is a prominent prop that **foreshadows** the inevitability of Jessie's death, but also symbolizes her choice to align herself with her father. Within the dialogue between Jessie and Mama, to give a second example, the power of food to nurture is a subject of discussion. There is abundant use of food imagery in this play, but the cocoa pan—the source of a treat that ultimately proves unsatisfying—is a physical prop that also comes to symbolize the way in which ordinary objects and everyday existence must support Mama after Jessie's death. Jessie instructs her mother to wash the pan until the police arrive. Collapsing on the floor, Thelma clutches the cocoa pan to her breast. *The Importance of Being Earnest*, by contrast, uses few props, and those called for by the script have no symbolic significance. In the tense tea shared by Gwendolyn and Cecily, however, sugar and tea-cakes are the objects around which Wilde builds a hilarious battle of words.

On spare stages, props can have even greater impact than they do on crowded ones. Arthur Miller, for instance, uses props very economically. Chairs, tables, and the refrigerator are the only kitchen objects referred to and therefore necessary to *Death of a Salesman*; besides the two beds for the boys, the bedroom contains only Biff's oversized athletic trophy. By restricting his props to those essential to the plot, Miller paradoxically charges them with symbolic meaning. Tennessee Williams also relies on props to establish setting, in particular the time frame of *The Glass Menagerie*. Such objects as the Victrola and typewriter help to place the action in the late 1930s. Finally, the lavishly carved piano in August Wilson's *The Piano Lesson* dominates the stage as a prop and also acquires symbolic significance as the characters describe its carvings and complicated history.

Working with Dramatic Language

Not every utterance in a play deserves the kind of close scrutiny you would devote to a poem, but you will want to look particularly hard at statements that stand out, patterns of repetition, and long speeches. As in poetry and sometimes in short stories, through repetition particular words, phrases, or images will "jump out" at you and become significant. Paradoxically, statements that are uttered only once can also carry great weight. Linda Loman's statement that "attention must be paid" to a man like Willy and Tom's statement in *The Glass Menagerie* that America "is matriculating in a school for the blind" are pieces of dialogue that stand out as thematically significant statements.

Long speeches also deserve close attention. Whenever a character delivers a substantial speech, the attention of the audience and usually of the other characters is focused on that character and her words. The very pacing of dramatic experience asks us to give particular weight to such speeches. In some cases, dramatic speeches can be analyzed almost as if they were free-standing poems. In *The Taming of the Shrew*, for instance, much of the comedy takes place in energetic dialogue; but in a few key places—most notably the **soliloquy** that Petruchio delivers to the audience outlining his plan for "taming" his shrew (4.1.) and Kate's long speech directed against the stubborn wives in the final scene (5.2)—we must attend to the long speeches carefully, not only for content, but for poetic devices such as **metaphor** and **symbolism**.

Besides the basic distinction between dialogue and speeches, for some earlier drama we should also pay attention to the distinction between poetry and prose. Ancient drama, as you will remember, is very close to song. A play that is entirely in verse, such as *Everyman*, achieves a sense of calm formality from poetic rhythm and patterning. Shakespearean drama, on the other hand, combines poetry with prose in significant ways. It is a critical commonplace that in Shakespeare, noble characters speak in verse whereas comic or low-born characters speak in prose, but this distinction is by no means absolute. In *Hamlet*, for instance, the grave-digger discusses death and decay in prose, whereas Hamlet's "To be or not to be" soliloquy (2.2) is conducted in iambic poetry. But in the same scene, another of Hamlet's long speeches, which considers "What a piece of work is a man," is spoken in down-to-earth prose (2.2).

Plays that use poetry predominantly or exclusively rely not only on poetic devices, but on the rhythm of poetic lines to convey attitude and emotion. Shakespeare's plays, for instance, are written in **iambic pentameter**. When listening to Hamlet speak, you need to hear not only the ongoing rhythm of iambic pentameter, but also places where that rhythm is disrupted. In Hamlet's very first soliloquy, for instance, we can hear Hamlet's agitation and disgust in the irregular rhythms of its opening lines:

```
/   ˘    ˘    /   /   /    ˘      /     ˘    /

O, that this too too sullied flesh would melt

/      ˘      ˘  /     ˘    /    ˘/˘  /

Thaw and resolve itself into a dew!
```

Attention to rhythm and meter gives both actors and readers of a play insight into the characters who speak those lines. For this reason, it is also instructive to read long speeches aloud, if only in the privacy of your own bedroom.

STRATEGIES FOR WRITING ABOUT DRAMA

Once you have watched, listened to, performed, and read through your play actively and critically, you are ready to start writing about drama. Because drama is a complex form, you will probably want to spend some time prewriting, brainstorming, and exploring the basic elements of drama. Although the final section of this chapter discusses some approaches that are particularly well suited for essays about drama, here we will look at writing as both a way of learning about a play and of analyzing it critically for a formal essay.

Plot and Structure

Outlining and summarizing the plot of a play is a useful technique for helping you understand and remember its action, but most writers and readers would find an essay that rehearses the plot of a play quite boring. In fact, throughout *Prentice Hall Literature Portfolio*, we have encouraged you always to go beyond plot summary. Analyzing dramatic structure, on the other hand, can help you to reach new insights about *why* the events and persons in a play are arranged as they are.

As opposed to the **plot**, which is the sequence of events as they unfold on stage, a diagram of dramatic structure reveals a guiding idea or concept *behind* the organization of events. For instance, scenes or entire plots can mirror one another to alert viewers to a significant connection between them. In *The Taming of the Shrew*, the division of the cast into parallel wooings invites us to compare Kate's marriage to Petruchio with that between Lucentio and Bianca. In *The Glass Menagerie*, the father's abandonment of his family before the start of the play is mirrored by Tom's abandonment of his sister, Laura. Not only is the structural repetition of loss depressing, but the parallelism invites us to think about what constitutes a real family or real love.

Visualizing a play's structure can be rather similar to the clustering exercise discussed in Chapter 3. Figure 8.3, for instance, shows one reader's effort to depict the structure of *Death of a Salesman*. This reader sees the play as structured around a basic contrast between past and present, with Willy Loman at the center.

A diagram such as this one could produce any number of analysis or comparison-and-contrast topics. How do Willy's relations with other people differ in the past and present? How does one relationship, such as that with his wife Linda, change over time? Why, in the diagram, is The Woman paralleled with Howard Wagner? Or even more simply, why is this Willy's play? Why is he, rather than another character, at the heart of our structural diagram?

Another way of analyzing dramatic structure is to examine the relation of parts to wholes. Most of the plays in this anthology are divided into acts and subdivided further into **scenes**. One good way of generating material for an essay is to focus on one scene and analyze its significance to the play as a whole. An example of this exercise might be an analysis of the scene in *Hamlet* where Claudius confesses his murder and attempts to pray (3.3). A successful essay might explore such questions as why Claudius's confession occurs at this particular point in the play; how Hamlet's failure to take his revenge reflects on his character; or more broadly, the thematic distinction between appearance and reality. Another way of asking the same question might be: How would our opinion of Hamlet, Claudius, or the play change if this scene were omitted?

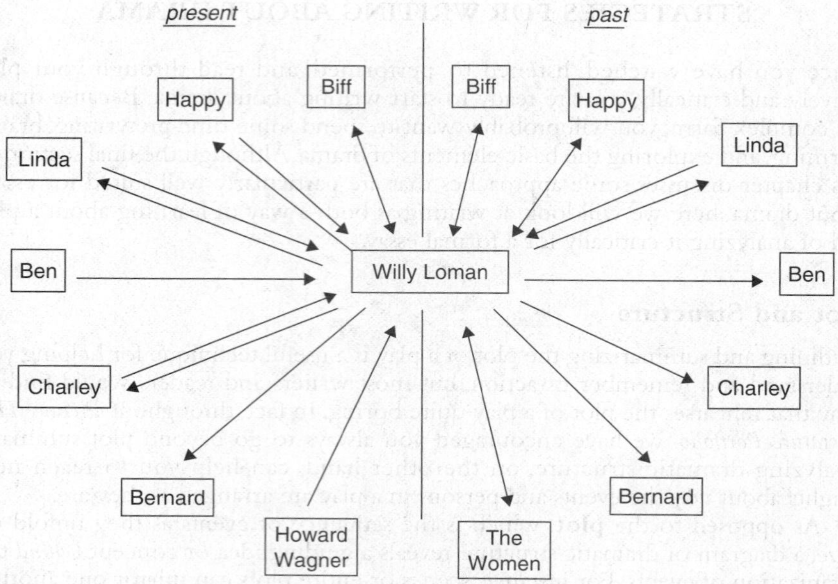

Figure 8.3 Diagram of *Death of a Salesman*'s Structure

In many productions, directors do omit scenes; film versions can also omit scenes, speeches, or other portions of text, reorder scenes, and even add events and characters to the play text. Analyzing the significance of these changes in a particular filmed or live production, either by analyzing the alterations or by comparing and contrasting the two versions, could produce an excellent essay.

Character and Relationships

Character analysis is a long-standing tradition in literary studies, but when analyzing dramatic characters, you will need to attend closely to the other elements in order to understand characters within their dramatic contexts. When analyzing character, you might want to focus on the complexities of a single character, such as Nora from *A Dollhouse* or Berniece from *The Piano Lesson*. Because in drama character is revealed in action, you should also pay attention to relationships between characters. On stage, the principal characters naturally come into conflict with, collaborate with, or interact in other ways with the characters that surround them. Minor characters often act as **foils** to the principal characters. In *The Piano Lesson*, for instance, the shallow and worldly Grace contrasts with Berniece, who brings into her home not merely the symbolic piano, but also the values generated by her family's endurance of slavery. Hamlet's pseudo-friends Rosencrantz and Guildenstern, to give another example, might be contrasted with the faithful Horatio.

One good way to approach character in context is to use the double-entry journal that is described in Chapter 3, "Writing about Literature," to create a "character inventory." In the left column, jot down qualities that you perceive in your chosen character; in the right, write down the evidence for that judgment, derived from the play text or from particular productions. If you are comparing a main character and a foil, use the journal to spell out specific ways in which the characters are similar and different. If your explorations into character develop into a formal essay, you have a choice of forms. If writing about a single character, you will be producing an analytic essay; if writing about a principal character and a foil, you will produce a comparison-and-contrast essay. In either case, you need to provide evidence in support of your thesis.

Finally, when writing about character, you should be alert to associations between particular characters and **symbolic** figures, derived from sources ranging from classical mythology and the Bible to previous monuments of literature. Antigone, as a woman who will die childless, is contrasted with Danae, the mythological lover of Zeus who conceives a child by him in spite of her father's efforts when Zeus comes to her as a shower of gold, but is reduced to ashes by the god's power. (In this case, however, Danae is actually Antigone's ancestor.) In *Hamlet*, the ghost's complaints against Gertrude evoke strongly the Adam and Eve story, and the murderer Claudius identifies himself with the biblical Cain, the first human to murder his own brother. Laura, from *The Glass Menagerie*, is associated with the mythical unicorn through her treasured collection of glass figurines.

Some controversial characters have been the subject of ongoing critical debate, and if you are using outside critical sources or writing from a particular critical stance, you might want to participate in those controversies. Critics have long argued, for instance, about whether Creon or Antigone is the "tragic hero" of Sophocles' play. The question of whether Kate is or is not "tamed" at the end of *The Taming of the Shrew* is another question of this sort. When you write about character controversies, you are writing a complex essay that is part response, part analysis, and sometimes part evaluation.

Setting and Staging

To sharpen your thoughts about setting, you can comb through the text for evidence of time and place, working out your thoughts in a double-entry journal. You can also use visual resources, such as photos and images found on the Web, to see how actual productions translated the play text's evocations of setting into a concrete staging. One useful brainstorming exercise is to create your own stage set through visual means, using magazines and scissors, computer graphics, dolls, or other items. Try to create a set using the minimal number of entrances and exits, items of furniture, and props. Or let your visual imagination run wild. Your exploration of settings and stagings—whether actual or virtual, imagined or realized—can become the basis for formal essays and other writing assignments. Finally, you might analyze a play's symbolic props in the same way that you analyze verbal **symbols, images**, and poetic **figures**. Writing about setting, and particularly about staging, offers many opportunities for combining visual with verbal analysis.

Language

As we have discussed, plays are enacted by actors who speak their lines and use their bodies to communicate meaning to their audiences. Other sounds and music can also contribute to that meaning. Dramatic language, even from plays written in prose, can be studied closely using the same resources that you use to analyze poetry, with a focus on such features as diction, syntax, rhythm, and figurative language. For a brainstorming exercise or even for a formal essay, you might analyze a single speech, compare two speeches, or evaluate the significance of a speech for the play as a whole (see "Strategies for Reading Poetry" in Chapter 6).

You might also make anthologies of important passages from a given play, either as an end in itself or as a brainstorming exercise for an essay on the play's language, setting, structure, or even a particular character. As with poetry, you can follow the tradition of readers stretching back to Shakespeare's time and make your own personal anthology of beautiful or significant passages, with or without accompanying annotations and introduction (see "Ways of Writing about Poems" in Chapter 6).

Another useful assignment involves analyzing *patterns* of words or images. Shakespeare, for instance, often writes his plays so that important pairs of imagery (e.g., black vs. white or old vs. young) or more elaborate patterns (e.g., patterns of disease in *Hamlet* or of animals in *The Taming of the Shrew*) help readers to analyze the action and characters. In some cases, the repetition of single words (e.g., "flesh" or "incest" in *Hamlet*) is significant. In the age of the Internet, it is simple enough to find online texts. Using the "Edit, Find" function in your browser, you can let the computer help you with your word searches. The computer provides a second pair of "eyes," adding to your list of words or image patterns and helping you get some distance from your own responses to the text. Once you have found the passages you want, you can simply cut-and-paste them into a word processor as a basis for your drama anthology.

If you want to write an essay on word patterns or image patterns in a particular play, you can use your anthology of quotations, complete with act-scene-line references, to jump-start your analytic process. Your teacher might even make such a collection of passages part of the assignment. Then you can begin to think about larger questions: For instance, does the word appear only at particular points in the play? Is it associated with a particular character or characters? You may also discover that certain **figures of speech** characterize a play, just as they do certain poems. In *Antigone*, for instance, the tragic conflict might be encapsulated by the single **oxymoron** or **paradox** that characterizes Antigone's choice: her "crime of holy reverence."

Theme

The form of analysis that links drama most directly to texts in other genres is thematic analysis. Although plays may reflect a number of broad themes, the trick is to provide evidence of their existence. Some ways to give credibility to a thematic analysis are to link the theme to a statement or statements made by characters in the play (Hamlet says, for instance, that Denmark's "a prison"); to focus on a particular character or characters (e.g., Nora in *A Dollhouse* for a discussion of Ibsen's position on women's social place); and by reference to language (the imagery of animals in *Taming of the Shrew*) or to setting and staging (the symbolic contrast between kitchen and bedroom as a way of analyzing the theme of feminine values in *Trifles*). In short, when writing about theme you will want to draw your evidence from analysis of other dramatic elements. For this reason, a strong essay about dramatic themes can be the most difficult kind of essay to write.

FURTHER WAYS OF WRITING ABOUT DRAMA

Although you can write many splendid essays simply by focusing on drama's basic elements, there are other kinds of writing, both critical and creative, that can make the plays come alive for you and enhance your interpretation of them.

Writing about Drama in Production

Excellent essays can be written about drama in production. One type of evaluative essay is the performance review. The reviews you read in your local newspaper do not always observe this rule, but a good drama review is more than a collection of observations; it has a unifying thesis and provides specific evidence in support of that thesis. Like any other kind of formal literary essay, the drama review draws its evidence from the five basic dramatic elements of our imaginary pentad.

All of the drama in this anthology has been translated into one or more film or video versions that can be found in university libraries or bought, often for quite reasonable prices. Some, such as *Hamlet* and *Death of a Salesman*, can be seen in two or three versions. There are a number of other kinds of essay that you might want to write about live or filmed productions of the plays in this anthology. You might, for instance, analyze the concrete choices made by directors and actors for any of the dramatic elements—for instance, Kenneth Branagh's selection of Blenheim Palace (outside Oxford, England) as the setting for his *Hamlet*; or the use of modern dress for a production of *Antigone*. You might also write about the ways in which certain poetic **figures** (such as **metaphor** or **oxymoron**) are realized (or not realized) visually in a performance. To give an example, although Hamlet says that "Denmark is a prison," the Franco Zeffirelli version of the play, starring Mel Gibson, places the castle in a lush, rolling green landscape. If Hamlet's environment is not ugly or physically cramped—indeed, it is quite the opposite in this interpretation—then what would make Denmark a prison for him?

If you are working with a play on video or DVD, you should be aware of the distinction between filmed theater performances and films per se, in which cinematic techniques help to shape your viewing of the action and characters. Although you will want to consult with your teacher for in-depth advice on how to learn about cinematography, anyone who watches films on the big screen or at home will recognize the basic ways in which camera angles, lighting, music, and sound can influence your interpretation of a film.

Research

Reading and discussing plays can take up more time, both inside and outside of class, than do the other literary genres represented in this anthology; for this reason, teachers may assign or students may choose to write longer papers on drama, papers that often use outside research.

Drama in Context: Author, Historical Period, Sources, and Reception

Literature is, to some extent, personal, and reflects aspects of its author's life and social situation. Literary critics caution us against committing the "biographical fallacy"—that is, reducing a play to nothing more than a mirror of its author's personal circumstances and concerns—but it is also true that many writers draw heavily on personal and cultural experience for their material. August Wilson, for instance, grew up in Pittsburgh, which is also the setting for *The Piano Lesson*. Henrik Ibsen responded to an ongoing debate about woman's sphere in nineteenth-century Europe. With your teacher's guidance, you can investigate both the authors and social contexts for all of the plays included in *Prentice Hall Literature Portfolio* using reputable sources from both the World Wide Web and your school's library.

When looking for materials about a play's author or context, you might begin with such standard reference sources as *Contemporary Authors* or *Contemporary Literary Criticism*, if your library has these works in print or electronic form. You may find useful sources by just performing a simple author or title search in your library's catalogue. Shakespeare studies, in particular, offers many volumes of background material and criticism about the plays that are directed at students. If the catalogue search produces an overwhelming amount of material, ask your instructor for help in narrowing the field and picking the best sources.

Some plays have a specific historical source. Susan Glaspell's *Trifles* was inspired by a murder trial that Glaspell had covered for the *Des Moines Daily News*, in which Margaret Hossack, from Indianola, was accused of killing her husband with an ax while he was asleep. (Hossack, unlike Minnie Wright, was sentenced to life in prison.) Others, such as *Hamlet*, may have one or more textual sources. *The Piano Lesson*, to give a third example, draws its inspiration from Romare Bearden's collage of the same name (1983), whose central subject may be another Pittsburgh native, jazz pianist Mary Lou Williams. (To this extent, Wilson's play may have both a visual and a historical source.) When dealing with a direct source rather than a broad historical context, writers often find themselves engaged in a direct comparison and contrast between play and source. The more indirect the source, the more tentative that comparison needs to be.

Students are probably less familiar with literary reception, which simply means the study of how a work was understood and appreciated in its own and then in later times. We can learn a great deal about how plays were received by their first audiences from performance reviews in newspapers and other venues. Although there are no reviews for *Everyman* or *The Taming of the Shrew*, for most of the later drama in this anthology reviews do exist. The *New York Times* is a logical place to begin looking for reviews of such plays as *Death of Salesman*, *The Glass Menagerie*, *'Night Mother*, and *The Piano Lesson*. (The *New York Times* is available online at http://www.nytimes.com/.) Many print collections of criticism on specific plays or playwrights will also include early reviews. Conversely, on the Internet you can find reviews of recent stage productions, sometimes complete with production photographs. And although reproducing these images publicly can be a violation of copyright, they do provide valuable information for the student seeking to understand how a particular play has been performed in the past and might be performed in the future.

Sometimes playwrights write commentary on their own works. Arthur Miller not only wrote "Tragedy and the Common Man" for the *New York Times* in order to argue that Willy Loman is a tragic hero, but he also reflected back on his work in the Introduction to his *Collected Plays*. To find authorial commentary, do a catalogue search on the author's name in your college or local library.

Creative Responses: Writing as Re-creation

Studies of human creativity stress that exercising the imagination strengthens your skill at logical analysis; writing activities outside the confines of the traditional, thesis-driven essay therefore can enhance the work you do for more traditional literary essays. As either a writing-to-learn exercise or an assignment in its own right, you might try working with short pieces of a play—a speech or a short stretch of dialogue—and write a translation, imitation, or parody of that piece of text. A translation takes a speech or section of text and reproduces it in another verbal "register." You can translate Shakespearean soliloquies, for instance, into plain modern English as a way of understanding what the characters are saying. You can also translate dramatic speeches into different idioms for an amusing effect. (But be sure not to indulge in social stereotypes; that can be offensive!) To imitate a speech or dialogue, take the form and reproduce it with new, but not inappropriate, content. A serious imitation, for instance, might be a reworking of Hamlet's "To be or not to be" speech—which addresses suicide as a response to life's difficulties—in contemporary terms as an argument for and against physician-assisted suicide of terminally ill patients. Parody, a particularly engaging literary form, involves keeping the form of the original intact but substituting an absurd content for the original content. There are many parodies of "To be or not to be," and you can probably make up more of your own: "To ________ or not to ________; that is the question."

A more freewheeling exercise is the creative revision of a famous speech or scene. In this anthology, Margaret Atwood's very short story, "Gertrude Talks Back," is a reworking and response to *Hamlet*'s closet scene (4.1) from the perspective of Gertrude. The story is part murder mystery (who killed Hamlet's father?) and part a demonstration of gender politics (finally, Gertrude gets a chance to talk without Hamlet's constant interruptions). Take a scene from any of the plays in this anthology and try rewriting it from a silenced character's perspective. On a broader scale, you might write new scenes for a play based on "lost moments." In *The Taming of the Shrew*, for instance, why do Katharina and Bianca have no mother? (This is not a trivial question, for many Shakespeare scholars have wondered why there are many fathers, but very few mothers, in his plays.) In the tradition of the American movie blockbuster, you can also write prequels (what *really* happened on Sutter's farm before the action proper of *The Piano Lesson*?) and sequels (do the young men quit "bunburying" and settle down once they are married in *The Importance of Being Earnest*? What is Nora's life like after she slams that door for the last time?). Use your imagination: many writers before you have enjoyed the same creative exercise!

CONCLUSION

Although drama is a complex art form, it also satisfies our most basic human values and desires. Reading and writing about drama tells us a great deal about who we are, who we once were, and who we might someday become. Drama, perhaps more than any other art form, puts before us the best and worst of the human condition and moves us to take our own place in the drama of life.

WORKS CITED

Barber, Frances. "Ophelia in *Hamlet*." *Players of Shakespeare, 2*. Ed. Russell Jackson and Robert Smallwood. Cambridge: Cambridge UP, 1988. 137–50.

Berger, Peter L., and Thomas Luckmann. *The Social Construction of Reality: A Treatise in the Sociology of Knowledge*. New York: Anchor Books, 1966.

Fallon, Sarah. "All the World's a Stage." *Edutopia* 3 (Feb. 2005). 27 November 2005. <http://www.edutopia.org/magazine/ed1article.php?id=Art_1223&issue=feb_05>.

Glaspell, Susan. *The Road to the Temple*. New York: Frederick A. Stokes Company, 1927.

Miller, Arthur. "Tragedy and the Common Man." *New York Times*, 27 Feb. 1947: X1.

Norman, Marsha. "Highlights." *Sewanee Writers on Writing*. Ed. Wyatt Prunty. Baton Rouge: Louisiana State UP, 2000. 138–44.

CHAPTER 9

An Anthology of Drama

SOPHOCLES (ca. 496–406 BCE) was an Athenian playwright. The son of a wealthy family, he was handsome, talented, and well-educated. Sophocles may have written more than 120 plays, although only seven survive. He is credited with several dramatic innovations, including introducing a third speaking actor, increasing the size of the Chorus from twelve to fifteen, limiting the Chorus's role while increasing the artistic complexity of its responses, and improving costumes and scenery. His innovations resulted in improved dialogue and stronger characters. Sophocles was also active in civic and military affairs. He was a priest of Asclepius, the god of medicine; he was a general during the Peloponnesian War; and, for a while, he managed the Treasury.

Although written before *Oedipus the King*, *Antigone* dramatizes the sequel to that story, which itself was a piece of the ongoing history of the House of Thebes. Laius, married to Jocasta, is King of Thebes. In response to the prophecy that he would be killed by his own son, Laius had caused his only son to have his feet bound together and then be abandoned to his death on a mountaintop. The child, later named Oedipus (or "swollen foot"), was rescued and placed with Polybius, the king of Corinth, and his wife. Learning later about the prophecy, Oedipus leaves Corinth in order to spare the life of the man he thinks is his father. In his journey, he quarrels with and kills some men at a crossroad, one of whom turns out later to be his birth father, King Laius. Having solved the riddle of the Sphinx (who was eating the Thebans), Oedipus becomes King of Thebes and marries Jocasta, who is—unbeknownst to either her or Oedipus—his own mother.

He has four children by Jocasta: Antigone, Ismene, Polynices, and Eteocles. After a plague decimates Thebes, Oedipus seeks the cause from the seer Tiresius, who reveals Oedipus' secret to him. When Oedipus' incest and parricide become known, Jocasta commits suicide, and Oedipus famously puts out his own eyes and is exiled. After Creon, Jocasta's brother, takes over as regent, the sons of Oedipus agree to alternate as rulers of Thebes on an annual basis. But Eteocles, refusing to yield the throne after one year, drives out Polynices, who then returns with a military force to attack the city. During the fighting, Polynices and Eteocles kill one another. At that point, Creon takes the throne and the action represented in *Antigone* unfolds.

Though not all drama is centered on a thematic **conflict**, in this classic Greek play Antigone must choose not between good and evil, but between two social goods, which may be defined as obedience to the law and family piety, family and state, or human and divine law. Critics disagree as to whether Creon or Antigone is the **tragic hero** of this drama. The decision depends in part on which character

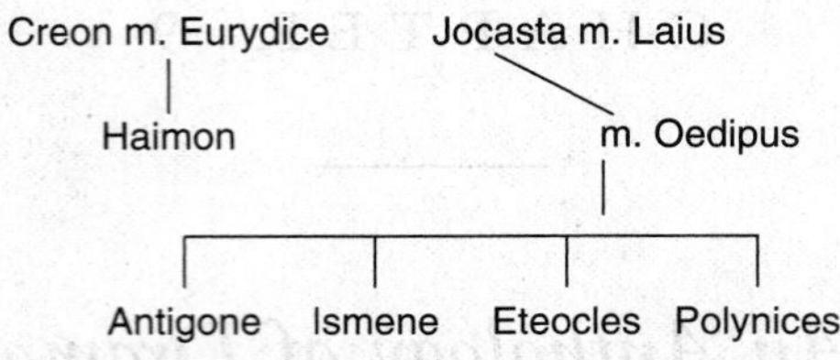

Figure 9.1 The House of Thebes

is identified as committing the tragedy's **hamartia**, or unfortunate choice on which subsequent events depend. (Is it Creon's **hubris** or overconfidence that he can justly implement laws that go against basic respect for human needs and rituals or Antigone's **hubris** in believing that she can be a law unto herself?) The Chorus's partial understanding, moralistic impulse, and changing judgments indicate the complexity of these questions. Finally, the play is full of **dramatic irony**: Creon puts the state before family, and winds up destroying utterly the family and badly damaging the state of Thebes.

Related Works: Cofer, "The Names of the Dead" and "Tales Told Under the Mango Tree"; Ellison, "Battle Royal"; Glaspell, *Trifles*; Hardy, "The Convergence of the Twain"; Hecht, "The Book of Yolek"; Jarrell, "The Death of the Ball Turret Gunner"; Jonson, "On My First Son" and "On My First Daughter"; Miller, *Death of a Salesman*; Milton, *Lycidas*; Old English Riddles; Randall, "Ballad of Birmingham"; Rios, "The Vietnam Wall"; Shakespeare, *Hamlet*; Shelley, "Ozymandias"; Updike, "A&P"; Wideman, "What We Cannot Speak About We Must Pass Over in Silence."

Antigone

Characters

ANTIGONE daughter of Oedipus and Jocasta
ISMENE sister of Antigone
A CHORUS of old Theban citizens and their LEADER
CREON king of Thebes, uncle of Antigone and Ismene
A SENTRY
HAEMON son of Creon and Eurydice
TIRESIAS a blind prophet
A MESSENGER
EURYDICE wife of Creon
Guards, attendants, and a boy

TIME AND SCENE: *The royal house of Thebes. It is still night, and the invading armies of Argos have just been driven from the city. Fighting on opposite sides, the sons of Oedipus, Eteocles and Polynices, have killed each other in combat. Their uncle,* CREON, *is now king of Thebes.*

Enter ANTIGONE, *slipping through the central doors of the palace. She motions to her sister,* ISMENE, *who follows her cautiously toward an altar at the center of the stage.*

ANTIGONE: My own flesh and blood—dear sister, dear Ismene,
how many griefs our father Oedipus handed down!
Do you know one, I ask you, one grief
that Zeus will not perfect for the two of us
while we still live and breathe? There's nothing,
no pain—our lives are pain—no private shame,
no public disgrace, nothing I haven't seen
in your griefs and mine. And now this:
an emergency decree, they say, the Commander
has just declared for all of Thebes.
What, haven't you heard? Don't you see?
The doom reserved for enemies
marches on the ones we love the most.

ISMENE: Not I, I haven't heard a word, Antigone.
Nothing of loved ones,
no joy or pain has come my way, not since
the two of us were robbed of our two brothers,
both gone in a day, a double blow—
not since the armies of Argos vanished,
just this very night. I know nothing more,
whether our luck's improved or ruin's still to come.

ANTIGONE: I thought so. That's why I brought you out here,
past the gates, so you could hear in private.

ISMENE: What's the matter? Trouble, clearly . . .
you sound so dark, so grim.

ANTIGONE: Why not? Our own brothers' burial!
Hasn't Creon graced one with all the rites,
disgraced the other? Eteocles, they say,
has been given full military honors,
rightly so—Creon's laid him in the earth
and he goes with glory down among the dead.
But the body of Polynices, who died miserably—
why, a city-wide proclamation, rumor has it,
forbids anyone to bury him, even mourn him.
He's to be left unwept, unburied, a lovely treasure
for birds that scan the field and feast to their heart's content.

Such, I hear, is the martial law our good Creon
lays down for you and me—yes, me, I tell you—
and he's coming here to alert the uninformed
in no uncertain terms,
and he won't treat the matter lightly. Whoever
disobeys in the least will die, his doom is sealed:
stoning to death inside the city walls!

There you have it. You'll soon show what you are,
worth your breeding, Ismene, or a coward—
for all your royal blood.

ISMENE: My poor sister, if things have come to this,

who am I to make or mend them, tell me,
what good am I to you?
ANTIGONE: Decide.
Will you share the labor, share the work?
ISMENE: What work, what's the risk? What do you mean?
ANTIGONE: *Raising her hands.*
Will you lift up his body with these bare hands
and lower it with me?
ISMENE: What? You'd bury him—
when a law forbids the city?
ANTIGONE: Yes!
He is my brother and—deny it as you will—
your brother too.
No one will ever convict me for a traitor.
ISMENE: So desperate, and Creon has expressly—
ANTIGONE: No,
he has no right to keep me from my own.
ISMENE: Oh my sister, think—
think how our own father died, hated,
his reputation in ruins, driven on
by the crimes he brought to light himself
to gouge out his eyes with his own hands—
then mother. . . his mother and wife, both in one,
mutilating her life in the twisted noose—
and last, our two brothers dead in a single day,
both shedding their own blood, poor suffering boys,
battling out their common destiny hand-to-hand.

Now look at the two of us, left so alone . . .
think what a death we'll die, the worst of all
if we violate the laws and override
the fixed decree of the throne, its power—
we must be sensible. Remember we are women,
we're not born to contend with men. Then too,
we're underlings, ruled by much stronger hands,
so we must submit in this, and things still worse.

I, for one, I'll beg the dead to forgive me—
I'm forced, I have no choice—I must obey
the ones who stand in power. Why rush to extremes?
It's madness, madness.
ANTIGONE: I won't insist,
no, even if you should have a change of heart,
I'd never welcome you in the labor, not with me.
So, do as you like, whatever suits you best—
I will bury him myself.
And even if I die in the act, that death will be a glory.
I will lie with the one I love and loved by him—
an outrage sacred to the gods! I have longer

to please the dead than please the living here:
in the kingdom down below I'll lie forever.
Do as you like, dishonor the laws
the gods hold in honor.

ISMENE: I'd do them no dishonor . . .
but defy the city? I have no strength for that.

ANTIGONE: You have your excuses. I am on my way,
I'll raise a mound for him, for my dear brother.

ISMENE: Oh Antigone, you're so rash—I'm so afraid for you!

ANTIGONE: Don't fear for me. Set your own life in order.

ISMENE: Then don't, at least, blurt this out to anyone.
Keep it a secret. I'll join you in that, I promise.

ANTIGONE: Dear god, shout it from the rooftops. I'll hate you
all the more for silence—tell the world!

ISMENE: So fiery—and it ought to chill your heart.

ANTIGONE: I know I please where I must please the most.

ISMENE: Yes, if you can, but you're in love with impossibility.

ANTIGONE: Very well then, once my strength gives out
I will be done at last.

ISMENE: You're wrong from the start,
you're off on a hopeless quest.

ANTIGONE: If you say so, you will make me hate you,
and the hatred of the dead, by all rights,
will haunt you night and day.
But leave me to my own absurdity, leave me
to suffer this—dreadful thing. I will suffer
nothing as great as death without glory.

Exit to the side.

ISMENE: Then go if you must, but rest assured,
wild, irrational as you are, my sister,
you are truly dear to the ones who love you.

Withdrawing to the palace.
Enter a CHORUS, *the old citizens*
of Thebes, chanting as the sun
begins to rise.

CHORUS: Glory!—great beam of the sun, brightest of all
that ever rose on the seven gates of Thebes,
you burn through night at last!
Great eye of the golden day,
mounting the Dirce's banks you throw him back—
the enemy out of Argos, the white shield, the man of bronze—
he's flying headlong now
the bridle of fate stampeding him with pain!

And he had driven against our borders,
launched by the warring claims of Polynices—
like an eagle screaming, winging havoc
over the land, wings of armor
shielded white as snow,

a huge army massing,
crested helmets bristling for assault.

He hovered above our roofs, his vast maw gaping
closing down around our seven gates,
his spears thirsting for the kill
but now he's gone, look,
before he could glut his jaws with Theban blood
or the god of fire put our crown of towers to the torch.
He grappled the Dragon none can master—Thebes—
the clang of our arms like thunder at his back!

Zeus hates with a vengeance all bravado,
the mighty boasts of men. He watched them
coming on in a rising flood, the pride
of their golden armor ringing shrill—
and brandishing his lightning
blasted the fighter just at the goal,
rushing to shout his triumph from our walls.
Down from the heights he crashed, pounding down on the earth!
And a moment ago, blazing torch in hand—
mad for attack, ecstatic
he breathed his rage, the storm
of his fury hurling at our heads!
But now his high hopes have laid him low
and down the enemy ranks the iron god of war
deals his rewards, his stunning blows—Ares
rapture of battle, our right arm in the crisis.

Seven captains marshaled at seven gates
seven against their equals, gave
their brazen trophies up to Zeus,
god of the breaking rout of battle,
all but two: those blood brothers,
one father, one mother—matched in rage,
spears matched for the twin conquest—
clashed and won the common prize of death.

But now for Victory! Glorious in the morning,
joy in her eyes to meet our joy
she is winging down to Thebes,
our fleets of chariots wheeling in her wake—
Now let us win oblivion from the wars,
thronging the temples of the gods
in singing, dancing choirs through the night!
Lord Dionysus, god of the dance
that shakes the land of Thebes, now lead the way!

Enter CREON *from the palace,*
attended by his guard.

But look, the king of the realm is coming,
Creon, the new man for the new day,
whatever the gods are sending now . . .
what new plan will he launch?
Why this, this special session?
Why this sudden call to the old men
summoned at one command?

CREON: My countrymen,
the ship of state is safe. The gods who rocked her,
after a long, merciless pounding in the storm,
have righted her once more.
Out of the whole city
I have called you here alone. Well I know,
first, your undeviating respect
for the throne and royal power of King Laius.
Next, while Oedipus steered the land of Thebes,
and even after he died, your loyalty was unshakable,
you still stood by their children. Now then,
since the two sons are dead—two blows of fate
in the same day, cut down by each other's hands,
both killers, both brothers stained with blood—
as I am next in kin to the dead,
I now possess the throne and all its powers.

Of course you cannot know a man completely,
his character, his principles, sense of judgment,
not till he's shown his colors, ruling the people,
making laws. Experience, there's the test.
As I see it, whoever assumes the task,
the awesome task of setting the city's course,
and refuses to adopt the soundest policies
but fearing someone, keeps his lips locked tight,
he's utterly worthless. So I rate him now,
I always have. And whoever places a friend
above the good of his own country, he is nothing:
I have no use for him. Zeus my witness,
Zeus who sees all things, always—
I could never stand by silent, watching destruction
march against our city, putting safety to rout,
nor could I ever make that man a friend of mine
who menaces our country. Remember this:
our country *is* our safety.
Only while she voyages true on course
can we establish friendships, truer than blood itself.
Such are my standards. They make our city great.

Closely akin to them I have proclaimed,
just now, the following decree to our people
concerning the two sons of Oedipus.

Eteocles, who died fighting for Thebes,
excelling all in arms: he shall be buried,
crowned with a hero's honors, the cups we pour
to soak the earth and reach the famous dead.

But as for his blood brother, Polynices,
who returned from exile, home to his father-city
and the gods of his race, consumed with one desire—
to burn them roof to roots—who thirsted to drink
his kinsmen's blood and sell the rest to slavery:
that man—a proclamation has forbidden the city
to dignify him with burial, mourn him at all.
No, he must be left unburied, his corpse
carrion for the birds and dogs to tear,
an obscenity for the citizens to behold!

These are my principles. Never at my hands
will the traitor be honored above the patriot.
But whoever proves his loyalty to the state—
I'll prize that man in death as well as life.

LEADER: If this is your pleasure, Creon, treating
our city's enemy and our friend this way . . .
The power is yours, I suppose, to enforce it
with the laws, both for the dead and all of us,
the living.

CREON: Follow my orders closely then,
be on your guard.

LEADER: We're too old.
Lay that burden on younger shoulders.

CREON: No, no,
I don't mean the body—I've posted guards already.

LEADER: What commands for us then? What other service?

CREON: See that you never side with those who break my orders.

LEADER: Never. Only a fool could be in love with death.

CREON: Death is the price—you're right. But all too often
the mere hope of money has ruined many men.

A SENTRY *enters from the side.*

SENTRY: My lord,
I can't say I'm winded from running, or set out
with any spring in my legs either—no sir,
I was lost in thought, and it made me stop, often,
dead in my tracks, wheeling, turning back,
and all the time a voice inside me muttering,
"Idiot, why? You're going straight to your death."
Then muttering, "Stopped again, poor fool?
If somebody gets the news to Creon first,
what's to save your neck?"
And so,

mulling it over, on I trudged, dragging my feet,
you can make a short road take forever . . .
but at last, look, common sense won out,
I'm here, and I'm all yours,
and even though I come empty-handed
I'll tell my story just the same, because
I've come with a good grip on one hope,
what will come will come, whatever fate—

CREON: Come to the point!
What's wrong—why so afraid?

SENTRY: First, myself, I've got to tell you,
I didn't do it, didn't see who did—
Be fair, don't take it out on me.

CREON: You're playing it safe, soldier,
barricading yourself from any trouble.
It's obvious, you've something strange to tell.

SENTRY: Dangerous too, and danger makes you delay
for all you're worth.

CREON: Out with it—then dismiss!

SENTRY: All right, here it comes. The body—
someone's just buried it, then run off. . .
sprinkled some dry dust on the flesh,
given it proper rites.

CREON: What?
What man alive would dare—

SENTRY: I've no idea, I swear it.
There was no mark of a spade, no pickaxe there,
no earth turned up, the ground packed hard and dry,
unbroken, no tracks, no wheelruts, nothing,
the workman left no trace. Just at sunup
the first watch of the day points it out—
it was a wonder! We were stunned . . .
a terrific burden too, for all of us, listen:
you can't see the corpse, not that it's buried,
really, just a light cover of road-dust on it,
as if someone meant to lay the dead to rest
and keep from getting cursed.
Not a sign in sight that dogs or wild beasts
had worried the body, even torn the skin.
But what came next! Rough talk flew thick and fast,
guard grilling guard—we'd have come to blows
at last, nothing to stop it; each man for himself
and each the culprit, no one caught red-handed,
all of us pleading ignorance, dodging the charges,
ready to take up red-hot iron in our fists,
go through fire, swear oaths to the gods—
"I didn't do it, I had no hand in it either,
not in the plotting, not the work itself!"

Finally, after all this wrangling came to nothing,
one man spoke out and made us stare at the ground,
hanging our heads in fear. No way to counter him,
no way to take his advice and come through
safe and sound. Here's what he said:
"Look, we've got to report the facts to Creon,
we can't keep this hidden." Well, that won out,
and the lot fell to me, condemned me,
unlucky as ever, I got the prize. So here I am,
against my will and yours too, well I know—
no one wants the man who brings bad news.

LEADER: My king,
ever since he began I've been debating in my mind,
could this possibly be the work of the gods?

CREON: Stop—
before you make me choke with anger—the gods!
You, you're senile, must you be insane?
You say—why it's intolerable—say the gods
could have the slightest concern for that corpse?
Tell me, was it for meritorious service
they proceeded to bury him, prized him so? The hero
who came to burn their temples ringed with pillars,
their golden treasures—scorch their hallowed earth
and fling their laws to the winds.
Exactly when did you last see the gods
celebrating traitors? Inconceivable!

No, from the first there were certain citizens who
could hardly stand the spirit of my regime, grumbling
against me in the dark, heads together, tossing
wildly, never keeping their necks beneath the yoke,
loyally submitting to their king. These are the
instigators, I'm convinced—they've perverted
my own guard, bribed them to do their work.
Money! Nothing worse
in our lives, so current, rampant, so corrupting.
Money—you demolish cities, root men from their homes,
you train and twist good minds and set them on
to the most atrocious schemes. No limit,
you make them adept at every kind of outrage,
every godless crime—money!
Everyone—
the whole crew bribed to commit this crime,
they've made one thing sure at least:
sooner or later they will pay the price.

Wheeling on the SENTRY.

You—
I swear to Zeus as I still believe in Zeus,

if you don't find the man who buried that corpse,
the very man, and produce him before my eyes,
simple death won't be enough for you,
not till we string you up alive
and wring the immorality out of you.
Then you can steal the rest of your days,
better informed about where to make a killing.
You'll have learned, at last, it doesn't pay
to itch for rewards from every hand that beckons.
Filthy profits wreck most men, you'll see—
they'll never save your life.

SENTRY: Please,
may I say a word or two, or just turn and go?

CREON: Can't you tell? Everything you say offends me.

SENTRY: Where does it hurt you, in the ears or in the heart?

CREON: And who are you to pinpoint my displeasure?

SENTRY: The culprit grates on your feelings,
I just annoy your ears.

CREON: Still talking?
You talk too much! A born nuisance—

SENTRY: Maybe so,
but I never did this thing, so help me!

CREON: Yes you did—
what's more, you squandered your life for silver!

SENTRY: Oh it's terrible when the one who does the judging
judges things all wrong.

CREON: Well now,
you just be clever about your judgments—
if you fail to produce the criminals for me,
you'll swear your dirty money brought you pain.

Turning sharply, reentering the palace.

SENTRY: I hope he's found. Best thing by far.
But caught or not, that's in the lap of fortune:
I'll never come back, you've seen the last of me.
I'm saved, even now, and I never thought,
I never hoped—
dear gods, I owe you all my thanks!

Rushing out.

CHORUS: Numberless wonders
terrible wonders walk the world but none the match for man—
that great wonder crossing the heaving gray sea,
driven on by the blasts of winter
on through breakers crashing left and right,
holds his steady course
and the oldest of the gods he wears away—
the Earth, the immortal, the inexhaustible—

as his plows go back and forth, year in, year out
with the breed of stallions turning up the furrows.

And the blithe, lightheaded race of birds he snares,
the tribes of savage beasts, the life that swarms the depths—
with one fling of his nets
woven and coiled tight, he takes them all,
man the skilled, the brilliant!
He conquers all, taming with his techniques
the prey that roams the cliffs and wild lairs,
training the stallion, clamping the yoke across
his shaggy neck, and the tireless mountain bull.
And speech and thought, quick as the wind
and the mood and mind for law that rules the city—
all these he has taught himself
and shelter from the arrows of the frost
when there's rough lodging under the cold clear sky
and the shafts of lashing rain—
ready, resourceful man!
Never without resources
never an impasse as he marches on the future—
only Death, from Death alone he will find no rescue
but from desperate plagues he has plotted his escapes.

Man the master, ingenious past all measure
past all dreams, the skills within his grasp—
he forges on, now to destruction
now again to greatness. When he weaves in
the laws of the land, and the justice of the gods
that binds his oaths together
he and his city rise high—
but the city casts out
that man who weds himself to inhumanity
thanks to reckless daring. Never share my hearth
never think my thoughts, whoever does such things.

Enter ANTIGONE *from the side, accompanied by the* SENTRY.

Here is a dark sign from the gods—
what to make of this? I know her,
how can I deny it? That young girl's Antigone!
Wretched, child of a wretched father,
Oedipus. Look, is it possible?
They bring you in like a prisoner—
why? did you break the king's laws?
Did they take you in some act of mad defiance?

SENTRY: She's the one, she did it single-handed—
we caught her burying the body. Where's Creon?

Enter CREON *from the palace.*

LEADER: Back again, just in time when you need him.

CREON: In time for what? What is it?
SENTRY: My king,
there's nothing you can swear you'll never do—
second thoughts make liars of us all.
I could have sworn I wouldn't hurry back
(what with your threats, the buffeting I just took),
but a stroke of luck beyond our wildest hopes,
what a joy, there's nothing like it. So,
back I've come, breaking my oath, who cares?
I'm bringing in our prisoner—this young girl—
we took her giving the dead the last rites.
But no casting lots this time; this is *my* luck,
my prize, no one else's.
Now, my lord,
here she is. Take her, question her,
cross-examine her to your heart's content.
But set me free, it's only right—
I'm rid of this dreadful business once for all.
CREON: Prisoner! Her? You took her—where, doing what?
SENTRY: Burying the man. That's the whole story.
CREON: What?
You mean what you say, you're telling me the truth?
SENTRY: She's the one. With my own eyes I saw her
bury the body, just what you've forbidden.
There. Is that plain and clear?
CREON: What did you see? Did you catch her in the act?
SENTRY: Here's what happened. We went back to our post,
those threats of yours breathing down our necks—
we brushed the corpse clean of the dust that covered it,
stripped it bare . . . it was slimy, going soft,
and we took to high ground, backs to the wind
so the stink of him couldn't hit us;
jostling, baiting each other to keep awake,
shouting back and forth—no napping on the job,
not this time. And so the hours dragged by
until the sun stood dead above our heads,
a huge white ball in the noon sky, beating,
blazing down, and then it happened—
suddenly, a whirlwind!
Twisting a great dust-storm up from the earth,
a black plague of the heavens, filling the plain,
ripping the leaves off every tree in sight,
choking the air and sky. We squinted hard
and took our whipping from the gods.

And after the storm passed—it seemed endless—
there, we saw the girl!
And she cried out a sharp, piercing cry,
like a bird come back to an empty nest,

peering into its bed, and all the babies gone . . .
Just so, when she sees the corpse bare
she bursts into a long, shattering wail
and calls down withering curses on the heads
of all who did the work. And she scoops up dry dust,
handfuls, quickly, and lifting a fine bronze urn,
lifting it high and pouring, she crowns the dead
with three full libations.
Soon as we saw
we rushed her, closed on the kill like hunters,
and she, she didn't flinch. We interrogated her,
charging her with offenses past and present—
she stood up to it all, denied nothing. I tell you,
it made me ache and laugh in the same breath.
It's pure joy to escape the worst yourself,
it hurts a man to bring down his friends.
But all that, I'm afraid, means less to me
than my own skin. That's the way I'm made.

CREON: *Wheeling on* ANTIGONE.
You,
with your eyes fixed on the ground—speak up.
Do you deny you did this, yes or no?

ANTIGONE: I did it. I don't deny a thing.

CREON: *To the* SENTRY.
You, get out, wherever you please—
you're clear of a very heavy charge.

He leaves; CREON *turns back to* ANTIGONE.

You, tell me briefly, no long speeches—
were you aware a decree had forbidden this?

ANTIGONE: Well aware. How could I avoid it? It was public.

CREON: And still you had the gall to break this law?

ANTIGONE: Of course I did. It wasn't Zeus, not in the least,
who made this proclamation—not to me.
Nor did that Justice, dwelling with the gods
beneath the earth, ordain such laws for men.
Nor did I think your edict had such force
that you, a mere mortal, could override the gods,
the great unwritten, unshakable traditions.
They are alive, not just today or yesterday:
they live forever, from the first of time,
and no one knows when they first saw the light.

These laws—I was not about to break them,
not out of fear of some man's wounded pride,
and face the retribution of the gods.
Die I must, I've known it all my life—
how could I keep from knowing?—even without
your death-sentence ringing in my ears.

And if I am to die before my time
I consider that a gain. Who on earth,
alive in the midst of so much grief as I,
could fail to find his death a rich reward?
So for me, at least, to meet this doom of yours
is precious little pain. But if I had allowed
my own mother's son to rot, an unburied corpse—
that would have been an agony! This is nothing.
And if my present actions strike you as foolish,
let's just say I've been accused of folly
by a fool.
LEADER: Like father like daughter,
passionate, wild . . .
she hasn't learned to bend before adversity.
CREON: No? Believe me, the stiffest stubborn wills
fall the hardest; the toughest iron,
tempered strong in the white-hot fire,
you'll see it crack and shatter first of all.
And I've known spirited horses you can break
with a light bit—proud, rebellious horses.
There's no room for pride, not in a slave,
not with the lord and master standing by.

This girl was an old hand at insolence
when she overrode the edicts we made public.
But once she'd done it—the insolence,
twice over—to glory in it, laughing,
mocking us to our face with what she'd done.
I am not the man, not now: she is the man
if this victory goes to her and she goes free.

Never! Sister's child or closer in blood
than all my family clustered at my altar
worshiping Guardian Zeus—she'll never escape,
she and her blood sister, the most barbaric death.
Yes, I accuse her sister of an equal part
in scheming this, this burial.

To his attendants.

Bring her here!
I just saw her inside, hysterical, gone to pieces.
It never fails: the mind convicts itself
in advance, when scoundrels are up to no good,
plotting in the dark. Oh but I hate it more
when a traitor, caught red-handed,
tries to glorify his crimes.
ANTIGONE: Creon, what more do you want
than my arrest and execution?
CREON: Nothing. Then I have it all.
ANTIGONE: Then why delay? Your moralizing repels me,

every word you say—pray god it always will.
So naturally all I say repels you too.
Enough.
Give me glory! What greater glory could I win
than to give my own brother decent burial?
These citizens here would all agree,

To the CHORUS.

they'd praise me too
if their lips weren't locked in fear.

Pointing to CREON.

Lucky tyrants—the perquisites of power!
Ruthless power to do and say whatever pleases *them*.
CREON: You alone, of all the people in Thebes,
see things that way.
ANTIGONE: They see it just that way
but defer to you and keep their tongues in leash.
CREON: And you, aren't you ashamed to differ so from them?
So disloyal!
ANTIGONE: Not ashamed for a moment,
not to honor my brother, my own flesh and blood.
CREON: Wasn't Eteocles a brother too—cut down, facing him?
ANTIGONE: Brother, yes, by the same mother, the same father.
CREON: Then how can you render his enemy such honors,
such impieties in his eyes?
ANTIGONE: He'll never testify to that,
Eteocles dead and buried.
CREON: He will—
if you honor the traitor just as much as him.
ANTIGONE: But it was his brother, not some slave that died—
CREON: Ravaging our country!—
but Eteocles died fighting in our behalf.
ANTIGONE: No matter—Death longs for the same rites for all.
CREON: Never the same for the patriot and the traitor.
ANTIGONE: Who, Creon, who on earth can say the ones below
don't find this pure and uncorrupt?
CREON: Never. Once an enemy, never a friend,
not even after death.
ANTIGONE: I was born to join in love, not hate—
that is my nature.
CREON: Go down below and love,
if love you must—love the dead! While I'm alive,
no woman is going to lord it over me.

Enter ISMENE *from the palace, under guard*.

CHORUS: Look,
Ismene's coming, weeping a sister's tears,
loving sister, under a cloud . . .
her face is flushed, her cheeks streaming.
Sorrow puts her lovely radiance in the dark.

CREON: You—
in my own house, you viper, slinking undetected,
sucking my life-blood! I never knew
I was breeding twin disasters, the two of you
rising up against my throne. Come, tell me,
will you confess your part in the crime or not?
Answer me. Swear to me.

ISMENE: I did it, yes—
if only she consents—I share the guilt,
the consequences too.

ANTIGONE: No,
Justice will never suffer that—not you,
you were unwilling. I never brought you in.

ISMENE: But now you face such dangers . . . I'm not ashamed
to sail through trouble with you,
make your troubles mine.

ANTIGONE: Who did the work?
Let the dead and the god of death bear witness!
I have no love for a friend who loves in words alone.

ISMENE: Oh no, my sister, don't reject me, please,
let me die beside you, consecrating
the dead together.

ANTIGONE: Never share my dying,
don't lay claim to what you never touched.
My death will be enough.

ISMENE: What do I care for life, cut off from you?

ANTIGONE: Ask Creon. Your concern is all for him.

ISMENE: Why abuse me so? It doesn't help you now.

ANTIGONE: You're right—
if I mock you, I get no pleasure from it,
only pain.

ISMENE: Tell me, dear one,
what can I do to help you, even now?

ANTIGONE: Save yourself. I don't grudge you your survival.

ISMENE: Oh no, no, denied my portion in your death?

ANTIGONE: You chose to live, I chose to die.

ISMENE: Not, at least,
without every kind of caution I could voice.

ANTIGONE: Your wisdom appealed to one world—mine, another.

ISMENE: But look, we're both guilty, both condemned to death.

ANTIGONE: Courage! Live your life. I gave myself to death,
long ago, so I might serve the dead.

CREON: They're both mad, I tell you, the two of them.
One's just shown it, the other's been that way
since she was born.

ISMENE: True, my king,
the sense we were born with cannot last forever . . .
commit cruelty on a person long enough
and the mind begins to go.

CREON: Yours did,
when you chose to commit your crimes with her.
ISMENE: How can I live alone, without her?
CREON: Her?
Don't even mention her—she no longer exists.
ISMENE: What? You'd kill your own son's bride?
CREON: Absolutely:
there are other fields for him to plow.
ISMENE: Perhaps,
but never as true, as close a bond as theirs.
CREON: A worthless woman for my son? It repels me.
ISMENE: Dearest Haemon, your father wrongs you so!
CREON: Enough, enough—you and your talk of marriage!
ISMENE: Creon—you're really going to rob your son of Antigone?
CREON: Death will do it for me—break their marriage off.
LEADER: So, it's settled then? Antigone must die?
CREON: Settled, yes—we both know that.

To the guards.

Stop wasting time. Take them in.
From now on they'll act like women.
Tie them up, no more running loose;
even the bravest will cut and run,
once they see Death coming for their lives.

The guards escort ANTIGONE *and* ISMENE *into the palace.* CREON *remains while the old citizens form their* CHORUS.

CHORUS: Blest, they are the truly blest who all their lives
have never tasted devastation. For others, once
the gods have rocked a house to its foundations
the ruin will never cease, cresting on and on
from one generation on throughout the race—
like a great mounting tide
driven on by savage northern gales,
surging over the dead black depths
roiling up from the bottom dark heaves of sand
and the headlands, taking the storm's onslaught full-force,
roar, and the low moaning
echoes on and on
and now
as in ancient times I see the sorrows of the house,
the living heirs of the old ancestral kings,
piling on the sorrows of the dead
and one generation cannot free the next—
some god will bring them crashing down,
the race finds no release.
And now the light, the hope
springing up from the late last root
in the house of Oedipus, that hope's cut down in turn

by the long, bloody knife swung by the gods of death
by a senseless word
by fury at the heart.
Zeus,
yours is the power, Zeus, what man on earth
can override it, who can hold it back?
Power that neither Sleep, the all-ensnaring
no, nor the tireless months of heaven
can ever overmaster—young through all time,
mighty lord of power, you hold fast
the dazzling crystal mansions of Olympus.
And throughout the future, late and soon
as through the past, your law prevails:
no towering form of greatness
enters into the lives of mortals
free and clear of ruin.
True,
our dreams, our high hopes voyaging far and wide
bring sheer delight to many, to many others
delusion, blithe, mindless lusts
and the fraud steals on one slowly . . . unaware
till he trips and puts his foot into the fire.
He was a wise old man who coined
the famous saying: "Sooner or later
foul is fair, fair is foul
to the man the gods will ruin"—
He goes his way for a moment only
free of blinding ruin.

Enter HAEMON *from the palace.*

Here's Haemon now, the last of all your sons.
Does he come in tears for his bride,
his doomed bride, Antigone—
bitter at being cheated of their marriage?

CREON: We'll soon know, better than seers could tell us.

Turning to HAEMON.

Son, you've heard the final verdict on your bride?
Are you coming now, raving against your father?
Or do you love me, no matter what I do?

HAEMON: Father, I'm your *son* . . . you in your wisdom
set my bearings for me—I obey you.
No marriage could ever mean more to me than you,
whatever good direction you may offer.

CREON: Fine, Haemon.
That's how you ought to feel within your heart,
subordinate to your father's will in every way.
That's what a man prays for: to produce good sons—
households full of them, dutiful and attentive,
so they can pay his enemy back with interest
and match the respect their father shows his friend.

But the man who rears a brood of useless children,
what has he brought into the world, I ask you?
Nothing but trouble for himself, and mockery
from his enemies laughing in his face.
Oh Haemon,
never lose your sense of judgment over a woman.
The warmth, the rush of pleasure, it all goes cold
in your arms, I warn you . . . a worthless woman
in your house, a misery in your bed.
What wound cuts deeper than a loved one
turned against you? Spit her out,
like a mortal enemy—let the girl go.
Let her find a husband down among the dead.
Imagine it: I caught her in naked rebellion,
the traitor, the only one in the whole city.
I'm not about to prove myself a liar,
not to my people, no, I'm going to kill her!
That's right—so let her cry for mercy, sing her hymns
to Zeus who defends all bonds of kindred blood.
Why, if I bring up my own kin to be rebels,
think what I'd suffer from the world at large.
Show me the man who rules his household well:
I'll show you someone fit to rule the state.
That good man, my son,
I have every confidence he and he alone
can give commands and take them too. Staunch
in the storm of spears he'll stand his ground,
a loyal, unflinching comrade at your side.

But whoever steps out of line, violates the laws
or presumes to hand out orders to his superiors,
he'll win no praise from me. But that man
the city places in authority, his orders
must be obeyed, large and small,
right and wrong.
Anarchy—
show me a greater crime in all the earth!
She, she destroys cities, rips up houses,
breaks the ranks of spearmen into headlong rout.
But the ones who last it out, the great mass of them
owe their lives to discipline. Therefore
we must defend the men who live by law,
never let some woman triumph over us.
Better to fall from power, if fall we must,
at the hands of a man—never be rated
inferior to a woman, never.

LEADER: To us,
unless old age has robbed us of our wits,
you seem to say what you have to say with sense.

HAEMON: Father, only the gods endow a man with reason,
the finest of all their gifts, a treasure.
Far be it from me—I haven't the skill,
and certainly no desire, to tell you when,
if ever, you make a slip in speech . . . though
someone else might have a good suggestion.

Of course it's not for you,
in the normal run of things, to watch
whatever men say or do, or find to criticize.
The man in the street, you know, dreads your glance,
he'd never say anything displeasing to your face.
But it's for me to catch the murmurs in the dark,
the way the city mourns for this young girl.
"No woman," they say, "ever deserved death less,
and such a brutal death for such a glorious action.
She, with her own dear brother lying in his blood—
she couldn't bear to leave him dead, unburied,
food for the wild dogs or wheeling vultures.
Death? She deserves a glowing crown of gold!"
So they say, and the rumor spreads in secret,
darkly . . .
I rejoice in your success, father—
nothing more precious to me in the world.
What medal of honor brighter to his children
than a father's growing glory? Or a child's
to his proud father? Now don't, please,
be quite so single-minded, self-involved,
or assume the world is wrong and you are right.
Whoever thinks that he alone possesses intelligence,
the gift of eloquence, he and no one else,
and character too . . . such men, I tell you,
spread them open—you will find them empty.
No,
it's no disgrace for a man, even a wise man,
to learn many things and not to be too rigid.
You've seen trees by a raging winter torrent,
how many sway with the flood and salvage every twig,
but not the stubborn—they're ripped out, roots and all.
Bend or break. The same when a man is sailing:
haul your sheets too taut, never give an inch,
you'll capsize, and go the rest of the voyage
keel up and the rowing-benches under.

Oh give way. Relax your anger—change!
I'm young, I know, but let me offer this:
it would be best by far, I admit,
if a man were born infallible, right by nature.
If not—and things don't often go that way,
it's best to learn from those with good advice.

Leader: You'd do well, my lord, if he's speaking to the point,
to learn from him,
Turning to Haemon.
and you, my boy, from him.
You both are talking sense.
Creon: So,
men our age, we're to be lectured, are we?—
schooled by a boy his age?
Haemon: Only in what is right. But if I seem young,
look less to my years and more to what I do.
Creon: Do? Is admiring rebels an achievement?
Haemon: I'd never suggest that you admire treason.
Creon: Oh?—
isn't that just the sickness that's attacked her?
Haemon: The whole city of Thebes denies it, to a man.
Creon: And is Thebes about to tell me how to rule?
Haemon: Now, you see? Who's talking like a child?
Creon: Am I to rule this land for others—or myself?
Haemon: It's no city at all, owned by one man alone.
Creon: What? The city *is* the king's—that's the law!
Haemon: What a splendid king you'd make of a desert island—
you and you alone.
Creon: *To the* Chorus.
This boy, I do believe,
is fighting on her side, the woman's side.
Haemon: If you are a woman, yes—
my concern is all for you.
Creon: Why, you degenerate—bandying accusations,
threatening me with justice, your own father!
Haemon: I see my father offending justice—wrong.
Creon: Wrong?
To protect my royal rights?
Haemon: Protect your rights?
When you trample down the honors of the gods?
Creon: You, you soul of corruption, rotten through—
woman's accomplice!
Haemon: That may be,
but you'll never find me accomplice to a criminal.
Creon: That's what *she* is,
and every word you say is a blatant appeal for her—
Haemon: And you, and me, and the gods beneath the earth.
Creon: You will never marry her, not while she's alive.
Haemon: Then she'll die . . . but her death will kill another.
Creon: What, brazen threats? You go too far!
Haemon: What threat?
Combating your empty, mindless judgments with a word?
Creon: You'll suffer for your sermons, you and your empty wisdom!
Haemon: If you weren't my father, I'd say you were insane.
Creon: Don't flatter me with Father—you woman's slave!

HAEMON: You really expect to fling abuse at me
and not receive the same?
CREON: Is that so!
Now, by heaven, I promise you, you'll pay—
taunting, insulting me! Bring her out,
that hateful—she'll die now, here,
in front of his eyes, beside her groom!
HAEMON: No, no, she will never die beside me—
don't delude yourself. And you will never
see me, never set eyes on my face again.
Rage your heart out, rage with friends
who can stand the sight of you.

Rushing out.

LEADER: Gone, my king, in a burst of anger.
A temper young as his . . . hurt him once,
he may do something violent.
CREON: Let him do—
dream up something desperate, past all human limit!
Good riddance. Rest assured,
he'll never save those two young girls from death.
LEADER: Both of them, you really intend to kill them both?
CREON: No, not her, the one whose hands are clean—
you're quite right.
LEADER: But Antigone—
what sort of death do you have in mind for her?
CREON: I'll take her down some wild, desolate path
never trod by men, and wall her up alive
in a rocky vault, and set out short rations,
just a gesture of piety
to keep the entire city free of defilement.
There let her pray to the one god she worships:
Death—who knows?—may just reprieve her from death.
Or she may learn at last, better late than never,
what a waste of breath it is to worship Death.

Exit to the palace.

CHORUS: Love, never conquered in battle
Love the plunderer laying waste the rich!
Love standing the night-watch
guarding a girl's soft cheek,
you range the seas, the shepherds' steadings
off in the wilds—
not even the deathless gods can flee your onset,
nothing human born for a day—
whoever feels your grip is driven mad.
Love!—
you wrench the minds of the righteous into outrage,
swerve them to their ruin—you have ignited this,
this kindred strife, father and son at war
and Love alone the victor—

warm glance of the bride triumphant, burning with desire!
Throned in power, side-by-side with the mighty laws!
Irresistible Aphrodite, never conquered—
Love, you mock us for your sport.

ANTIGONE *is brought from the palace under guard.*

But now, even I'd rebel against the king,
I'd break all bounds when I see this—
I fill with tears, can't hold them back,
not any more . . . I see Antigone make her way
to the bridal vault where all are laid to rest.

ANTIGONE: Look at me, men of my fatherland,
setting out on the last road
looking into the last light of day
the last I'll ever see . . .
the god of death who puts us all to bed
takes me down to the banks of Acheron alive—
denied my part in the wedding-songs,
no wedding-song in the dusk has crowned my marriage—
I go to wed the lord of the dark waters.

CHORUS: Not crowned with glory, crowned with a dirge,
you leave for the deep pit of the dead.
No withering illness laid you low,
no strokes of the sword—a law to yourself,
alone, no mortal like you, ever, you go down
to the halls of Death alive and breathing.

ANTIGONE: But think of Niobe—well I know her story—
think what a living death she died,
Tantalus' daughter, stranger queen from the east:
there on the mountain heights, growing stone
binding as ivy, slowly walled her round
and the rains will never cease, the legends say
the snows will never leave her . . .
wasting away, under her brows the tears
showering down her breasting ridge and slopes—
a rocky death like hers puts me to sleep.

CHORUS: But she was a god, born of gods,
and we are only mortals born to die.
And yet, of course, it's a great thing
for a dying girl to hear, just hear
she shares a destiny equal to the gods,
during life and later, once she's dead.

ANTIGONE: O you mock me!
Why, in the name of all my fathers' gods
why can't you wait till I am gone—
must you abuse me to my face?
O my city, all your fine rich sons!
And you, you springs of the Dirce,
holy grove of Thebes where the chariots gather,

you at least, you'll bear me witness, look,
unmourned by friends and forced by such crude laws
I go to my rockbound prison, strange new tomb—
always a stranger, O dear god,
I have no home on earth and none below,
not with the living, not with the breathless dead.

CHORUS: You went too far, the last limits of daring—
smashing against the high throne of Justice!
Your life's in ruins, child—I wonder . . .
do you pay for your father's terrible ordeal?

ANTIGONE: There—at last you've touched it, the worst pain
the worst anguish! Raking up the grief for father
three times over, for all the doom
that's struck us down, the brilliant house of Laius.
O mother, your marriage-bed
the coiling horrors, the coupling there—
you with your own son, my father—doomstruck mother!
Such, such were my parents, and I their wretched child.
I go to them now, cursed, unwed, to share their home—
I am a stranger! O dear brother, doomed
in your marriage—your marriage murders mine,
your dying drags me down to death alive!

Enter Creon.

CHORUS: Reverence asks some reverence in return—
but attacks on power never go unchecked,
not by the man who holds the reins of power.
Your own blind will, your passion has destroyed you.

ANTIGONE: No one to weep for me, my friends,
no wedding-song—they take me away
in all my pain . . . the road lies open, waiting.
Never again, the law forbids me to see
the sacred eye of day. I am agony!
No tears for the destiny that's mine,
no loved one mourns my death.

CREON: Can't you see?
If a man could wail his own dirge *before* he dies,
he'd never finish.

To the guards.

Take her away, quickly!
Wall her up in the tomb, you have your orders.
Abandon her there, alone, and let her choose—
death or a buried life with a good roof for shelter.
As for myself, my hands are clean. This young girl—
dead or alive, she will be stripped of her rights,
her stranger's rights, here in the world above.

ANTIGONE: O tomb, my bridal-bed—my house, my prison
cut in the hollow rock, my everlasting watch!
I'll soon be there, soon embrace my own,
the great growing family of our dead

Persephone has received among her ghosts.
I,
the last of them all, the most reviled by far,
go down before my destined time's run out.
But still I go, cherishing one good hope:
my arrival may be dear to father,
dear to you, my mother,
dear to you, my loving brother, Eteocles—
When you died I washed you with my hands,
I dressed you all, I poured the cups
across your tombs. But now, Polynices,
because I laid your body out as well,
this, this is my reward. Nevertheless
I honored you—the decent will admit it—
well and wisely too.
Never, I tell you.
if I had been the mother of children
or if my husband died, exposed and rotting—
I'd never have taken this ordeal upon myself,
never defied our people's will. What law,
you ask, do I satisfy with what I say?
A husband dead, there might have been another.
A child by another too, if I had lost the first.
But mother and father both lost in the halls of Death,
no brother could ever spring to light again.
For this law alone I held you first in honor.
For this, Creon, the king, judges me a criminal
guilty of dreadful outrage, my dear brother!
And now he leads me off, a captive in his hands,
with no part in the bridal-song, the bridal-bed,
denied all joy of marriage, raising children—
deserted so by loved ones, struck by fate,
I descend alive to the caverns of the dead.

What law of the mighty gods have I transgressed?
Why look to the heavens any more, tormented as I am?
Whom to call, what comrades now? Just think,
my reverence only brands me for irreverence!
Very well: if this is the pleasure of the gods,
once I suffer I will know that I was wrong.
But if these men are wrong, let them suffer
nothing worse than they mete out to me—
these masters of injustice!

LEADER: Still the same rough winds, the wild passion
raging through the girl.

CREON: *To the guards.*
Take her away.
You're wasting time—you'll pay for it too,

ANTIGONE: Oh god, the voice of death. It's come, it's here.

CREON: True. Not a word of hope—your doom is sealed.
ANTIGONE: Land of Thebes, city of all my fathers—
O you gods, the first gods of the race!
They drag me away, now, no more delay.
Look on me, you noble sons of Thebes—
the last of a great line of kings,
I alone, see what I suffer now
at the hands of what breed of men—
all for reverence, my reverence for the gods!

She leaves under guard:
the CHORUS *gathers.*

CHORUS: Danaë, Danaë—
even she endured a fate like yours,
in all her lovely strength she traded
the light of day for the bolted brazen vault—
buried within her tomb, her bridal-chamber,
wed to the yoke and broken.
But she was of glorious birth
my child, my child
and treasured the seed of Zeus within her womb,
the cloudburst streaming gold!
The power of fate is a wonder,
dark, terrible wonder—
neither wealth nor armies
towered walls nor ships
black hulls lashed by the salt
can save us from that force.

The yoke tamed him too
young Lycurgus flaming in anger
king of Edonia, all for his mad taunts
Dionysus clamped him down, encased
in the chain-mail of rock
and there his rage
his terrible flowering rage burst—
sobbing, dying away . . . at last that madman
came to know his god—
the power he mocked, the power
he taunted in all his frenzy
trying to stamp out
the women strong with the god—
the torch, the raving sacred cries—
enraging the Muses who adore the flute.
And far north where the Black Rocks
cut the sea in half
and murderous straits
split the coast of Thrace
a forbidding city stands
where once, hard by the walls

the savage Ares thrilled to watch
a king's new queen, a Fury rearing in rage
against his two royal sons—
her bloody hands, her dagger-shuttle
stabbing out their eyes—cursed, blinding wounds—
their eyes blind sockets screaming for revenge!

They wailed in agony, cries echoing cries
the princes doomed at birth . . .
and their mother doomed to chains,
walled off in a tomb of stone—
but she traced her own birth back
to a proud Athenian line and the high gods
and off in caverns half the world away,
born of the wild North Wind
she sprang on her father's gales,
racing stallions up the leaping cliffs—
child of the heavens. But even on her the Fates
the gray everlasting Fates rode hard
my child, my child.

Enter Tiresias, *the blind prophet, led by a boy.*

Tiresias: Lords of Thebes,
I and the boy have come together,
hand in hand. Two see with the eyes of one . . .
so the blind must go, with a guide to lead the way.
Creon: What is it, old Tiresias? What news now?
Tiresias: I will teach you. And you obey the seer.
Creon: I will,
I've never wavered from your advice before.
Tiresias: And so you kept the city straight on course.
Creon: I owe you a great deal, I swear to that.
Tiresias. Then reflect, my son: you are poised,
once more, on the razor-edge of fate.
Creon: What is it? I shudder to hear you.
Tiresias: You will learn
when you listen to the warnings of my craft.
As I sat on the ancient seat of augury,
in the sanctuary where every bird I know
will hover at my hands—suddenly I heard it,
a strange voice in the wingbeats, unintelligible,
barbaric, a mad scream! Talons flashing, ripping,
they were killing each other—that much I knew—
the murderous fury whirring in those wings
made that much clear!
I was afraid,
I turned quickly, tested the burnt-sacrifice,
ignited the altar at all points—but no fire,
the god in the fire never blazed.

Not from those offerings . . . over the embers
slid a heavy ooze from the long thighbones,
smoking, sputtering out, and the bladder
puffed and burst—spraying gall into the air—
and the fat wrapping the bones slithered off
and left them glistening white. No fire!
The rites failed that might have blazed the future
with a sign. So I learned from the boy here:
he is my guide, as I am guide to others.
And it's you—
your high resolve that sets this plague on Thebes.
The public altars and sacred hearths are fouled,
one and all, by the birds and dogs with carrion
torn from the corpse, the doomstruck son of Oedipus!
And so the gods are deaf to our prayers, they spurn
the offerings in our hands, the flame of holy flesh.
No birds cry out an omen clear and true—
they're gorged with the murdered victim's blood and fat.
Take these things to heart, my son, I warn you.
All men make mistakes, it is only human.
But once the wrong is done, a man
can turn his back on folly, misfortune too,
if he tries to make amends, however low he's fallen,
and stops his bullnecked ways. Stubbornness
brands you for stupidity—pride is a crime.
No, yield to the dead!
Never stab the fighter when he's down.
Where's the glory, killing the dead twice over?

I mean you well. I give you sound advice.
It's best to learn from a good adviser
when he speaks for your own good:
it's pure gain.

CREON: Old man—all of you! So,
you shoot your arrows at my head like archers at the target—
I even have *him* loosed on me, this fortune-teller.
Oh his ilk has tried to sell me short
and ship me off for years. Well,
drive your bargains, traffic—much as you like—
in the gold of India, silver-gold of Sardis.
You'll never bury that body in the grave,
not even if Zeus's eagles rip the corpse
and wing their rotten pickings off to the throne of god!
Never, not even in fear of such defilement
will I tolerate his burial, that traitor.
Well I know, we can't defile the gods—
no mortal has the power.
No,
reverend old Tiresias, all men fall,

it's only human, but the wisest fall obscenely
when they glorify obscene advice with rhetoric—
all for their own gain.
TIRESIAS: Oh god, is there a man alive
who knows, who actually believes . . .
CREON: What now?
What earth-shattering truth are you about to utter?
TIRESIAS: . . . just how much a sense of judgment, wisdom
is the greatest gift we have?
CREON: Just as much, I'd say,
as a twisted mind is the worst affliction going.
TIRESIAS: You are the one who's sick, Creon, sick to death.
CREON: I am in no mood to trade insults with a seer.
TIRESIAS: You have already, calling my prophecies a lie.
CREON: Why not?
You and the whole breed of seers are mad for money!
TIRESIAS: And the whole race of tyrants lusts to rake it in.
CREON: This slander of yours—
are you aware you're speaking to the king?
TIRESIAS: Well aware. Who helped you save the city?
CREON: You—
you have your skills, old seer, but you lust for injustice!
TIRESIAS: You will drive me to utter the dreadful secret in my heart.
CREON: Spit it out! Just don't speak it out for profit.
TIRESIAS: Profit? No, not a bit of profit, not for you.
CREON: Know full well, you'll never buy off my resolve.
TIRESIAS: Then know this too, learn this by heart!
The chariot of the sun will not race through
so many circuits more, before you have surrendered
one born of your own loins, your own flesh and blood,
a corpse for corpses given in return, since you have thrust
to the world below a child sprung for the world above,
ruthlessly lodged a living soul within the grave—
then you've robbed the gods below the earth,
keeping a dead body here in the bright air,
unburied, unsung, unhallowed by the rites.

You, you have no business with the dead,
nor do the gods above—this is violence
you have forced upon the heavens.
And so the avengers, the dark destroyers late
but true to the mark, now lie in wait for you,
the Furies sent by the gods and the god of death
to strike you down with the pains that you perfected!

There. Reflect on that, tell me I've been bribed.
The day comes soon, no long test of time, not now,
that wakes the wails for men and women in your halls.
Great hatred rises against you—

cities in tumult, all whose mutilated sons
the dogs have graced with burial, or the wild beasts
or a wheeling crow that wings the ungodly stench of carrion
back to each city, each warrior's hearth and home.

These arrows for your heart! Since you've raked me
I loose them like an archer in my anger,
arrows deadly true. You'll never escape
their burning, searing force.

Motioning to his escort.

Come, boy, take me home.
So he can vent his rage on younger men,
and learn to keep a gentler tongue in his head
and better sense than what he carries now.

Exit to the side.

LEADER: The old man's gone, my king—
terrible prophecies. Well I know,
since the hair on this old head went gray,
he's never lied to Thebes.
CREON: I know it myself—I'm shaken, torn.
It's a dreadful thing to yield . . . but resist now?
Lay my pride bare to the blows of ruin?
That's dreadful too.
LEADER: But good advice,
Creon, take it now, you must.
CREON: What should I do? Tell me . . . I'll obey.
LEADER: Go! Free the girl from the rocky vault
and raise a mound for the body you exposed.
CREON: That's your advice? You think I should give in?
LEADER: Yes, my king, quickly. Disasters sent by the gods
cut short our follies in a flash.
CREON: Oh it's hard,
giving up the heart's desire . . . but I will do it—
no more fighting a losing battle with necessity.
LEADER: Do it now, go, don't leave it to others.
CREON: Now—I'm on my way! Come, each of you,
take up axes, make for the high ground,
over there, quickly! I and my better judgment
have come round to this—I shackled her,
I'll set her free myself. I am afraid . . .
it's best to keep the established laws
to the very day we die.

Rushing out, followed by his entourage. The CHORUS *clusters around the altar.*

CHORUS: God of a hundred names!
Great Dionysus—
Son and glory of Semele! Pride of Thebes—
Child of Zeus whose thunder rocks the clouds—

Lord of the famous lands of evening—
King of the Mysteries!
King of Eleusis, Demeter's plain
her breasting hills that welcome in the world—
Great Dionysus!
Bacchus, living in Thebes
the mother-city of all your frenzied women—
Bacchus
living along the Ismenus' rippling waters
standing over the field sown with the Dragon's teeth!

You—we have seen you through the flaring smoky fires,
your torches blazing over the twin peaks
where nymphs of the hallowed cave climb onward
fired with you, your sacred rage—
we have seen you at Castalia's running spring
and down from the heights of Nysa crowned with ivy
the greening shore rioting vines and grapes
down you come in your storm of wild women
ecstatic, mystic cries—
Dionysus—
down to watch and ward the roads of Thebes!
First of all cities, Thebes you honor first
you and your mother, bride of the lightning—
come, Dionysus! now your people lie
in the iron grip of plague,
come in your racing, healing stride
down Parnassus' slopes
or across the moaning straits.
Lord of the dancing—
dance, dance the constellations breathing fire!
Great master of the voices of the night!
Child of Zeus, God's offspring, come, come forth!
Lord, king, dance with your nymphs, swirling, raving
arm-in-arm in frenzy through the night
they dance you, Iacchus—
Dance, Dionysus
giver of all good things!

Enter a MESSENGER *from the side.*

MESSENGER: Neighbors,
friends of the house of Cadmus and the kings,
there's not a thing in this mortal life of ours
I'd praise or blame as settled once for all.
Fortune lifts and Fortune fells the lucky
and unlucky every day. No prophet on earth
can tell a man his fate. Take Creon:
there was a man to rouse your envy once,
as I see it. He saved the realm from enemies,
taking power, he alone, the lord of the fatherland,

he set us true on course—he flourished like a tree
with the noble line of sons he bred and reared . . .
and now it's lost, all gone.
Believe me,
when a man has squandered his true joys,
he's good as dead, I tell you, a living corpse.
Pile up riches in your house, as much as you like—
live like a king with a huge show of pomp,
but if real delight is missing from the lot,
I wouldn't give you a wisp of smoke for it,
not compared with joy.

LEADER: What now?
What new grief do you bring the house of kings?

MESSENGER: Dead, dead—and the living are guilty of their death!

LEADER: Who's the murderer? Who is dead? Tell us.

MESSENGER: Haemon's gone, his blood spilled by the very hand—

LEADER: His father's or his own?

MESSENGER: His own . . .
raging mad with his father for the death—

LEADER: Oh great seer,
you saw it all, you brought your word to birth!

MESSENGER: Those are the facts. Deal with them as you will.

As he turns to go, EURYDICE
enters from the palace.

LEADER: Look, Eurydice. Poor woman, Creon's wife,
so close at hand. By chance perhaps,
unless she's heard the news about her son.

EURYDICE: My countrymen,
all of you—I caught the sound of your words
as I was leaving to do my part,
to appeal to queen Athena with my prayers.
I was just loosing the bolts, opening the doors,
when a voice filled with sorrow, family sorrow,
struck my ears, and I fell back, terrified,
into the women's arms—everything went black.
Tell me the news, again, whatever it is . . .
sorrow and I are hardly strangers.
I can bear the worst.

MESSENGER: I—dear lady,
I'll speak as an eye-witness. I was there.
And I won't pass over one word of the truth.
Why should I try to soothe you with a story,
only to prove a liar in a moment?
Truth is always best.
So,
I escorted your lord, I guided him
to the edge of the plain where the body lay,
Polynices, torn by the dogs and still unmourned.
And saying a prayer to Hecate of the Crossroads,

Pluto too, to hold their anger and be kind,
we washed the dead in a bath of holy water
and plucking some fresh branches, gathering . . .
what was left of him, we burned them all together
and raised a high mound of native earth, and then
we turned and made for that rocky vault of hers,
the hollow, empty bed of the bride of Death.
And far off, one of us heard a voice,
a long wail rising, echoing
out of that unhallowed wedding-chamber,
he ran to alert the master and Creon pressed on,
closer—the strange, inscrutable cry came sharper,
throbbing around him now, and he let loose
a cry of his own, enough to wrench the heart,
"Oh god, am I the prophet now? going down
the darkest road I've ever gone? My son—
it's *his* dear voice, he greets me! Go, men,
closer, quickly! Go through the gap,
the rocks are dragged back—
right to the tomb's very mouth—and look,
see if it's Haemon's voice I think I hear,
or the gods have robbed me of my senses."

The king was shattered. We took his orders,
went and searched, and there in the deepest,
dark recesses of the tomb we found her . . .
hanged by the neck in a fine linen noose,
strangled in her veils—and the boy,
his arms flung around her waist,
clinging to her, wailing for his bride,
dead and down below, for his father's crimes
and the bed of his marriage blighted by misfortune.
When Creon saw him, he gave a deep sob,
he ran in, shouting, crying out to him,
"Oh my child—what have you done? what seized you,
what insanity? what disaster drove you mad?
Come out, my son! I beg you on my knees!"
But the boy gave him a wild burning glance,
spat in his face, not a word in reply,
he drew his sword—his father rushed out,
running as Haemon lunged and missed!—
and then, doomed, desperate with himself,
suddenly leaning his full weight on the blade,
he buried it in his body, halfway to the hilt.
And still in his senses, pouring his arms around her,
he embraced the girl and breathing hard,
released a quick rush of blood,
bright red on her cheek glistening white.
And there he lies, body enfolding body . . .

he has won his bride at last, poor boy,
not here but in the houses of the dead.

Creon shows the world that of all the ills
afflicting men the worst is lack of judgment.

EURYDICE turns and reenters the palace.

LEADER: What do you make of that? The lady's gone,
without a word, good or bad.

MESSENGER: I'm alarmed too
but here's my hope—faced with her son's death
she finds it unbecoming to mourn in public.
Inside, under her roof, she'll set her women
to the task and wail the sorrow of the house.
She's too discreet. She won't do something rash.

LEADER: I'm not so sure. To me, at least,
a long heavy silence promises danger,
just as much as a lot of empty outcries.

MESSENGER: We'll see if she's holding something back,
hiding some passion in her heart.
I'm going in. You may be right—who knows?
Even too much silence has its dangers.

Exit to the palace. Enter CREON from the side, escorted by attendants carrying HAEMON's body on a bier.

LEADER: The king himself! Coming toward us,
look, holding the boy's head in his hands.
Clear, damning proof, if it's right to say so—
proof of his own madness, no one else's,
no, his own blind wrongs.

CREON: Ohhh,
so senseless, so insane . . . my crimes,
my stubborn, deadly—
Look at us, the killer, the killed,
father and son, the same blood—the misery!
My plans, my mad fanatic heart,
my son, cut off so young!
Ai, dead, lost to the world,
not through your stupidity, no, my own.

LEADER: Too late,
too late, you see what justice means.

CREON: Oh I've learned
through blood and tears! Then, it was then,
when the god came down and struck me—a great weight
shattering, driving me down that wild savage path,
ruining, trampling down my joy. Oh the agony,
the heartbreaking agonies of our lives.

Enter the MESSENGER from the palace.

MESSENGER: Master,
what a hoard of grief you have, and you'll have more.
The grief that lies to hand you've brought yourself—
Pointing to HAEMON*'s body.*
the rest, in the house, you'll see it all too soon.
CREON: What now? What's worse than this?
MESSENGER: The queen is dead.
The mother of this dead boy . . . mother to the end—
poor thing, her wounds are fresh.
CREON: No, no,
harbor of Death, so choked, so hard to cleanse!—
why me? why are you killing me?
Herald of pain, more words, more grief?
I died once, you kill me again and again!
What's the report, boy . . . some news for me?
My wife dead? O dear god!
Slaughter heaped on slaughter?
The doors open; the body of
EURYDICE *is brought out on her bier.*
MESSENGER: See for yourself:
now they bring her body from the palace.
CREON: Oh no,
another, a second loss to break the heart.
What next, what fate still waits for me?
I just held my son in my arms and now,
look, a new corpse rising before my eyes—
wretched, helpless mother—O my son!
MESSENGER: She stabbed herself at the altar,
then her eyes went dark, after she'd raised
a cry for the noble fate of Megareus, the hero
killed in the first assault, then for Haemon,
then with her dying breath she called down
torments on your head—you killed her sons.
CREON: Oh the dread,
I shudder with dread! Why not kill me too?—
run me through with a good sharp sword?
Oh god, the misery, anguish—
I, I'm churning with it, going under.
MESSENGER: Yes, and the dead, the woman lying there,
piles the guilt of all their deaths on you.
CREON: How did she end her life, what bloody stroke?
MESSENGER: She drove home to the heart with her own hand,
once she learned her son was dead . . . that agony.
CREON: And the guilt is all mine—
can never be fixed on another man,
no escape for me. I killed you,
I, god help me, I admit it all!
To his attendants.

Take me away, quickly, out of sight.
I don't even exist—I'm no one. Nothing.

LEADER: Good advice, if there's any good in suffering.
Quickest is best when troubles block the way.

CREON: *Kneeling in prayer.*
Come, let it come!—that best of fates for me
that brings the final day, best fate of all.
Oh quickly, now—
so I never have to see another sunrise.

LEADER: That will come when it comes;
we must deal with all that lies before us.
The future rests with the ones who tend the future.

CREON: That prayer—I poured my heart into that prayer!

LEADER: No more prayers now. For mortal men
there is no escape from the doom we must endure.

CREON: Take me away, I beg you, out of sight.
A rash, indiscriminate fool!
I murdered you, my son, against my will—
you too, my wife . . .
Wailing wreck of a man,
whom to look to? where to lean for support?
Desperately turning from HAEMON *to* EURYDICE *on their biers.*
Whatever I touch goes wrong—once more
a crushing fate's come down upon my head!
The MESSENGER *and attendants lead* CREON *into the palace.*

CHORUS: Wisdom is by far the greatest part of joy,
and reverence toward the gods must be safeguarded.
The mighty words of the proud are paid in full
with mighty blows of fate, and at long last
those blows will teach us wisdom.
The old citizens exit to the side.

EVERYMAN (late 1400s), an anonymous **morality play**, was performed in England from the time of Geoffrey Chaucer through the youth of William Shakespeare. Although many medieval plays were played on moveable pageant wagons, others were produced inside or near important religious and secular buildings. A morality play such as *Everyman* examines in analytic detail some difficult facets of moral and spiritual experience. The plot is **allegorical**; that is, characters and events in the narrative have both a primary (literal) and secondary (symbolic or allegorical) meaning. Enacted by abstract characters such as "Knowledge," "Kindred," and "Everyman" himself, the plot of *Everyman* unfolds a complex idea through a sequence of events that the main character experiences. (Even though characters can be simple, an allegorical plot is often complicated and so demands close attention to the sequence of actions.) Like a sermon or moral treatise, a morality play aims to be both educational (teaching us how to prepare for important life events) and admonitory (warning us against spiritual challenges to religious salvation).

The specific subject of *Everyman* is life's journey, or the difficulty of understanding and preparing for death; but the play's emphasis on how Everyman has misused his worldly Goods and neglected his Good Deeds also makes it a guide for living well in the world. Although not biblical in its subject matter, *Everyman* alludes to the Parable of the Talents from the New Testament or Christian Bible (Matthew 25). The term *talent*, a biblical measure of money, creates a pun in English, suggesting that Everyman's misuse of his Goods is symptomatic of his general approach to life. Whether seen in public performance or read in privacy, a morality play such as *Everyman* invites audience members to identify emotionally with the main character, but also appeals to their intellectual understanding of issues raised by **allegory**.

Related Works: Dickinson, "Because I could not stop for Death"; Hawthorne, "Young Goodman Brown"; Kafka, "The Metamorphosis"; Miller, *Death of a Salesman*; Norman, *'Night, Mother*; Porter, "The Jilting of Granny Weatherall."

Characters

GOD

MESSENGER
DEATH
EVERYMAN
FELLOWSHIP
KINDRED
COUSIN
GOODS
GOOD DEEDS

KNOWLEDGE
CONFESSION
BEAUTY
STRENGTH
DISCRETION
FIVE WITS
ANGEL
DOCTOR

Everyman

Here beginneth a treatise how the high father of heaven sendeth death to summon every creature to come and give account of their lives in this world, and is in manner of a moral play.

MESSENGER: I pray you all give your audience,
And hear this matter with reverence,
By figure a moral play: *in form*
The *Summoning of Everyman* called it is,
That of our lives and ending shows
How transitory we be all day. *always*
This matter is wondrous precious,
But the intent of it is more gracious,
And sweet to bear away.
The story saith: Man, in the beginning
Look well, and take good heed to the ending,
Be you never so gay!

---

8 But the purpose of it is more devout.

Ye think sin in the beginning full sweet,
Which in the end causeth the soul to weep,
When the body lieth in clay.
Here shall you see how Fellowship and Jollity,
Both Strength, Pleasure, and Beauty,
Will fade from thee as flower in May;
For ye shall hear how our Heaven King
Calleth Everyman to a general reckoning:
Give audience, and hear what he doth say. [*Exit.*

God speaketh:

GOD: I perceive, here in my majesty,
How that all creatures be to me unkind, *ungrateful*
Living without dread in worldly prosperity:
Of ghostly sight the people be so blind,
Drowned in sin, they know me not for their God;
In worldly riches is all their mind,
They fear not my righteousness, the sharp rod.
My law that I showed, when I for them died,
They forget clean, and shedding of my blood red;
I hanged between two, it cannot be denied;
To get them life I suffered to be dead;
I healed their feet, with thorns hurt was my head.
I could do no more than I did, truly;
And now I see the people do clean forsake me:
They use the seven deadly sins damnable,
As pride, covetise, wrath, and lechery *covetousness*
Now in the world be made commendable;
And thus they leave of angels the heavenly company.
Every man liveth so after his own pleasure,
And yet of their life they be nothing sure:
I see the more that I them forbear
The worse they be from year to year.
All that liveth appaireth fast; *degenerates*
Therefore I will, in all the haste,
Have a reckoning of every man's person;
For, and I leave the people thus alone *if*
In their life and wicked tempests, *tumults*
Verily they will become much worse than beasts;
For now one would by envy another up eat;
Charity they do all clean forget.
I hoped well that every man
In my glory should make his mansion,
And thereto I had them all elect;
But now I see, like traitors deject, *abject*

---

25 In spiritual vision.
32 I consented to die.
41 And yet their lives are by no means secure.

They thank me not for the pleasure that I to them meant, *for*
Nor yet for their being that I them have lent.
I proffered the people great multitude of mercy,
And few there be that asketh it heartily. *earnestly*
They be so cumbered with wordly riches
That needs on them I must do justice,
On every man living without fear.
Where art thou, Death, thou mighty messenger?

[*Enter Death*]

DEATH: Almighty God, I am here at your will,
Your commandment to fulfil.

GOD: Go thou to Everyman,
And show him, in my name,
A pilgrimage he must on him take,
Which he in no wise may escape;
And that he bring with him a sure reckoning
Without delay or any tarrying. [*God withdraws.*

DEATH: Lord, I will in the world go run overall, *everywhere*
And cruelly outsearch both great and small;
Every man will I beset that liveth beastly
Out of God's laws, and dreadeth not folly.
He that loveth riches I will strike with my dart,
His sight to blind, and from heaven to depart— *separate*
Except that alms be his good friend—
In hell for to dwell, world without end.
Lo, yonder I see Everyman walking.
Full little he thinketh on my coming;
His mind is on fleshly lusts and his treasure,
And great pain it shall cause him to endure
Before the Lord, Heaven King.

[*Enter Everyman*]

Everyman, stand still! Whither art thou going
Thus gaily? Hast thou thy Maker forget?

EVERYMAN: Why askest thou?
Wouldest thou wit? *know*

DEATH: Yea, sir; I will show you:
In great haste I am sent to thee
From God out of his majesty.

EVERYMAN: What, sent to me?

DEATH: Yea, certainly.
Though thou have forget him here,
He thinketh on thee in the heavenly sphere,
As, ere we depart, thou shalt know.

EVERYMAN: What desireth God of me?

DEATH: That shall I show thee:
A reckoning he will needs have
Without any longer respite.

EVERYMAN: To give a reckoning longer leisure I crave;
This blind matter troubleth my wit. *obscure*

DEATH: On thee thou must take a long journey;
Therefore thy book of count with thee thou bring, *accounts*
For turn again thou cannot by no way. *return*
And look thou be sure of thy reckoning,
For before God thou shalt answer, and show
Thy many bad deeds, and good but a few;
How thou hast spent thy life, and in what wise,
Before the chief Lord of paradise.
Have ado that we were in that way,
For, wit thou well, thou shalt make none attorney.
EVERYMAN: Full unready I am such reckoning to give.
I know thee not. What messenger art thou?
DEATH: I am Death, that no man dreadeth,
For every man I rest, and no man spareth; *arrest*
For it is God's commandment
That all to me should be obedient.
EVERYMAN: O Death, thou comest when I had thee least in mind!
In thy power it lieth me to save;
Yet of my good will I give thee, if thou will be kind— *goods*
Yea, a thousand pound shalt thou have—
And defer this matter till another day.
DEATH: Everyman, it may not be, by no way.
I set not by gold, silver, not riches, *set no store by*
Ne by pope, emperor, king, duke, ne princes;
For, and I would receive gifts great, *if*
All the world I might get;
But my custom is clean contrary.
I give thee no respite. Come hence, and not tarry.
EVERYMAN: Alas, shall I have no longer respite?
I may say Death giveth no warning!
To think on thee, it maketh my heart sick,
For all unready is my book of reckoning.
But twelve year and I might have abiding,
My counting-book I would make so clear
That my reckoning I should not need to fear.
Wherefore, Death, I pray thee, for God's mercy,
Spare me till I be provided of remedy.
DEATH: Thee availeth not to cry, weep, and pray;
But haste thee lightly that thou were gone that journey,
And prove thy friends if thou can;
For, wit thou well, the tide abideth no man, *time*
And in the world each living creature
For Adam's sin must die of nature.

111 i.e., let's see about making that journey.
112 No one [your] advocate.
115 Who fears no man.
135 If I could stay for just twelve years more.
141 But set off quickly on that journey.
145 In the course of nature.

EVERYMAN: Death, if I should this pilgrimage take,
And my reckoning surely make,
Show me, for saint charity,
Should I not come again shortly?
DEATH: No, Everyman; and thou be once there,
Thou mayst never more come here,
Trust me verily.
EVERYMAN: O gracious God in the high seat celestial,
Have mercy on me in this most need!
Shall I have no company from this vale terrestrial
Of mine acquaintance, that way me to lead?
DEATH: Yea, if any be so hardy
That would go with thee and bear thee company.
Hie thee that thou were gone to God's magnificence,
Thy reckoning to give before his presence.
What, weenest thou thy life is given thee, *suppose*
And thy worldly goods also?
EVERYMAN: I had wend so, verily. *supposed*
DEATH: Nay, nay; it was but lent thee;
For as soon as thou art go, *gone*
Another a while shall have it, and then go therefro, *from it*
Even as thou hast done.
Everyman, thou art mad! Thou hast thy wits five,
And here on earth will not amend thy life;
For suddenly I do come.
EVERYMAN: O wretched caitiff, whither shall I flee,
That I might scape this endless sorrow?
Now, gentle Death, spare me till to-morrow,
That I may amend me
With good advisement. *due consideration*
DEATH: Nay, thereto I will not consent,
Nor no man will I respite;
But to the heart suddenly I shall smite
Without any advisement.
And now out of thy sight I will me hie;
See thou make thee ready shortly,
For thou mayst say this is the day
That no man living may scape away.
[*Exit Death.*

EVERYMAN: Alas, I may well weep with sighs deep!
Now have I no manner of company
To help me in my journey, and me to keep; *guard*
And also my writing is full unready.
How shall I do now for to excuse me?

---

148 In the name of holy charity.
159 Hurry up and go.
187 *writing*, i.e. the writing of Everyman's accounts.

I would to God I had never be get! *been born*
To my soul a full great profit it had be;
For now I fear pains huge and great.
The time passeth. Lord, help, that all wrought!
For though I mourn it availeth nought.
The day passeth, and is almost ago; *gone*
I wot not well what for to do.
To whom were I best my complaint to make?
What and I to Fellowship thereof spake, *if*
And showed him of this sudden chance?
For in him is all mine affiance; *trust*
We have in the world so many a day
Be good friends in sport and play.
I see him yonder, certainly.
I trust that he will bear me company;
Therefore to him will I speak to ease my sorrow.
Well met, good Fellowship, and good morrow!

Fellowship speaketh:

FELLOWSHIP: Everyman, good morrow, by this day!
Sir, why lookest thou so piteously?
If any thing be amiss, I pray thee me say,
That I may help to remedy.
EVERYMAN: Yea, good Fellowship, yea;
I am in great jeopardy.
FELLOWSHIP: My true friend, show to me your mind;
I will not forsake thee to my life's end,
In the way of good company.
EVERYMAN: That was well spoken, and lovingly.
FELLOWSHIP: Sir, I must needs know your heaviness; *sorrow*
I have pity to see you in any distress.
If any have you wronged, ye shall revenged be,
Though I on the ground be slain for thee—
Though that I know before that I should die.
EVERYMAN: Verily, Fellowship, gramercy.
FELLOWSHIP: Tush! by thy thanks I set not a straw.
Show me your grief, and say no more.
EVERYMAN: If I my heart should to you break, *open*
And then you to turn your mind from me,
And would not me comfort when ye hear me speak,
Then should I ten times sorrier be.
FELLOWSHIP: Sir, I say as I will do indeed.
EVERYMAN: Then be you a good friend at need:
I have found you true herebefore.
FELLOWSHIP: And so ye shall evermore;
For, in faith, and thou go to hell,
I will not forsake thee by the way.

---

206 *by this day*, an asseveration.

EVERYMAN: Ye speak like a good friend; I believe you well.
I shall deserve it, and I may. *repay*
FELLOWSHIP: I speak of no deserving, by this day!
For he that will say, and nothing do,
Is not worthy with good company to go;
Therefore show me the grief of your mind,
As to your friend most loving and kind.
EVERYMAN: I shall show you how it is:
Commanded I am to go a journey,
A long way, hard and dangerous,
And give a strait count, without delay, *strict account*
Before the high Judge, Adonai.
Wherefore, I pray you, bear me company,
As ye have promised, in this journey.
FELLOWSHIP: That is matter indeed. Promise is duty;
But, and I should take such a voyage on me,
I know it well, it should be to my pain;
Also it maketh me afeard, certain.
But let us take counsel here as well as we can,
For your words would fear a strong man. *frighten*
EVERYMAN: Why, ye said if I had need
Ye would me never forsake, quick ne dead,
Though it were to hell, truly.
FELLOWSHIP: So I said, certainly,
But such pleasures be set aside, the sooth to say;
And also, if we took such a journey,
When should we come again?
EVERYMAN: Nay, never again, till the day of doom.
FELLOWSHIP: In faith, then will not I come there!
Who hath you these tidings brought?
EVERYMAN: Indeed, Death was with me here.
FELLOWSHIP: Now, by God that all hath bought, *redeemed*
If Death were the messenger,
For no man that is living to-day
I will not go that loath journey— *loathsome*
Not for the father that begat me!
EVERYMAN: Ye promised otherwise, pardie. *by God*
FELLOWSHIP: I wot well I said so, truly;
And yet if thou wilt eat, and drink, and make good cheer,
Or haunt to women the lusty company,
I would not forsake you while the day is clear,
Trust me verily.
EVERYMAN: Yea, thereto ye would be ready!
To go to mirth, solace, and play,

245 *Adonai*, a Hebrew name for God.
248 That's a serious matter indeed.
273 Or frequent the pleasant company of women.
274 Until daybreak.

Your mind will sooner apply, *attend*
Than to bear me company in my long journey.
FELLOWSHIP: Now, in good faith, I will not that way.
But and thou will murder, or any man kill,
In that I will help thee with a good will.
EVERYMAN: O, that is a simple advice indeed.
Gentle fellow, help me in my necessity!
We have loved long, and now I need;
And now, gentle Fellowship, remember me.
FELLOWSHIP: Whether ye have loved me or no,
By Saint John, I will not with thee go.
EVERYMAN: Yet, I pray thee, take the labour, and do so much for me
To bring me forward, for saint charity, *escort me*
And comfort me till I come without the town.
FELLOWSHIP: Nay, and thou would give me a new gown,
I will not a foot with thee go;
But, and thou had tarried, I would not have left thee so.
And as now God speed thee in thy journey,
For from thee I will depart as fast as I may.
EVERYMAN: Whither away, Fellowship? Will thou forsake me?
FELLOWSHIP: Yea, by my fay! To God I betake thee. *faith; commend*
EVERYMAN: Farewell, good Fellowship; for thee my heart is sore.
Adieu for ever! I shall see thee no more.
FELLOWSHIP: In faith, Everyman, farewell now at the ending;
For you I will remember that parting is mourning.
[*Exit Fellowship.*
EVERYMAN: Alack! shall we thus depart indeed— *part*
Ah, Lady, help!—without any more comfort?
Lo, Fellowship forsaketh me in my most need.
For help in this world whither shall I resort?
Fellowship herebefore with me would merry make,
And now little sorrow for me doth he take.
It is said, 'In prosperity men friends may find,
Which in adversity be full unkind.'
Now whither for succour shall I flee,
Sith that Fellowship hath forsaken me? *since*
To my kinsmen I will, truly,
Praying them to help me in my necessity;
I believe that they will do so,
For kind will creep where it may not go.
I will go say, for yonder I see them. *essay, try*
Where be ye now, my friends and kinsmen?
[*Enter Kindred and Cousin*]
KINDRED: Here be we now at your commandment.
Cousin, I pray you show us your intent
In any wise, and do not spare.

---

316 For kinship will creep where it cannot walk, i.e. blood is thicker than water.
321 In any case, and do not hold back.

COUSIN: Yea, Everyman, and to us declare
If ye be disposed to go anywhither; *anywhere*
For, wit you well, we will live and die together.
KINDRED: In wealth and woe we will with you hold, *side*
For over his kin a man may be bold.
EVERYMAN: Gramercy, my friends and kinsmen kind.
Now shall I show you the grief of my mind:
I was commanded by a messenger,
That is a high king's chief officer;
He bade me go a pilgrimage, to my pain,
And I know well I shall never come again;
Also I must give a reckoning strait,
For I have a great enemy that hath me in wait,
Which intendeth me for to hinder.
KINDRED: What account is that which ye must render?
That would I know.
EVERYMAN: Of all my works I must show
How I have lived and my days spent;
Also of ill deeds that I have used *practised*
In my time, sith life was me lent;
And all virtues that I have refused.
Therefore, I pray you, go thither with me
To help to make mine account, for saint charity.
COUSIN: What, to go thither? Is that the matter?
Nay, Everyman, I had liefer fast bread and water
All this five year and more.
EVERYMAN: Alas, that ever I was bore! *born*
For now shall I never be merry,
If that you forsake me.
KINDRED: Ah, sir, what ye be a merry man!
Take good heart to you, and make no moan.
But one thing I warn you, by Saint Anne—
As for me, ye shall go alone.
EVERYMAN: My Cousin, will you not with me go?
COUSIN: No, by our Lady! I have the cramp in my toe.
Trust not to me, for, so God me speed,
I will deceive you in your most need.
KINDRED: It availeth not us to tice.
Ye shall have my maid with all my heart;
She loveth to go to feasts, there to be nice, *wanton*
And to dance, and abroad to start:

---

326 For a man can be sure of his kinsfolk.
334 A great enemy (i.e. the devil) who has me under observation.
346 I had rather fast on bread and water.
351 What a merry man you are!
359 It is no use trying to entice us.
362 And to gad about.

I will give her leave to help you in that journey,
If that you and she may agree.
EVERYMAN: Now show me the very effect of your mind: *tenor*
Will you go with me, or abide behind?
KINDRED: Abide behind? Yea, that will I, and I may!
Therefore farewell till another day. [*Exit Kindred.*
EVERYMAN: How should I be merry or glad?
For fair promises men to me make,
But when I have most need they me forsake.
I am deceived; that maketh me sad.
COUSIN: Cousin Everyman, farewell now,
For verily I will not go with you.
Also of mine own an unready reckoning
I have to account; therefore I make tarrying.
Now God keep thee, for now I go. [*Exit Cousin.*
EVERYMAN: Ah, Jesus, is all come hereto?
Lo, fair words maketh fools fain;
They promise, and nothing will do, certain.
My kinsmen promised me faithfully
For to abide with me steadfastly,
And now fast away do they flee:
Even so Fellowship promised me.
What friend were best me of to provide?
I lose my time here longer to abide.
Yet in my mind a thing there is:
All my life I have loved riches;
If that my Good now help me might, *Goods*
He would make my heart full light.
I will speak to him in this distress—
Where art thou, my Goods and riches?
[*Goods speaks from a corner*]
GOODS: Who calleth me? Everyman? What! hast thou haste?
I lie here in corners, trussed and piled so high,
And in chests I am locked so fast,
Also sacked in bags. Thou mayst see with thine eye
I cannot stir; in packs low I lie.
What would ye have? Lightly me say. *quickly*
EVERYMAN: Come hither, Good, in all the haste thou may,
For of counsel I must desire thee.
GOODS: Sir, and ye in the world have sorrow or adversity,
That can I help you to remedy shortly.
EVERYMAN: It is another disease that grieveth me; *trouble*
In this world it is not, I tell thee so.
I am sent for, another way to go,
To give a strait count general

385 To provide myself with.
400 For I must entreat your advice.

Before the highest Jupiter of all;
And all my life I have had joy and pleasure in thee,
Therefore, I pray thee, go with me;
For, peradventure, thou mayst before God Almighty
My reckoning help to clean and purify;
For it is said ever among
That money maketh all right that is wrong.
GOODS: Nay, Everyman, I sing another song.
I follow no man in such voyages;
For, and I went with thee,
Thou shouldst fare much the worse for me;
For because on me thou did set thy mind,
Thy reckoning I have made blotted and blind, *obscure*
That thine account thou cannot make truly;
And that hast thou for the love of me.
EVERYMAN: That would grieve me full sore.
When I should come to that fearful answer.
Up, let us go thither together.
GOODS: Nay, not so! I am too brittle, I may not endure;
I will follow no man one foot, be ye sure.
EVERYMAN: Alas, I have thee loved, and had great pleasure
All my life-days on good and treasure.
GOODS: That is to thy damnation, without leasing,
For my love is contrary to the love everlasting;
But if thou had me loved moderately during,
As to the poor to give part of me,
Then shouldst thou not in this dolour be, *distress*
Nor in this great sorrow and care.
EVERYMAN: Lo, now was I deceived ere I was ware, *ready*
And all I may wite my spending of time.
GOODS: What, weenest thou that I am thine?
EVERYMAN: I had wend so. *supposed*
GOODS: Nay, Everyman, I say no.
As for a while I was lent thee;
A season thou hast had me in prosperity.
My condition is man's soul to kill; *nature*
If I save one, a thousand I do spill. *ruin*
Weenest thou that I will follow thee?
Nay, not from this world, verily.
EVERYMAN: I had wend otherwise.
GOODS: Therefore to thy soul Good is a thief;
For when thou art dead, this is my guise— *practice*
Another to deceive in this same wise
As I have done thee, and all to his soul's reprief. *shame*

---

412 For it is commonly said.
429 Without a lie, i.e. truly.
431–2 But if you had loved me moderately during your lifetime, so as to give part of me to the poor.
436 And I can blame it all on my waste of time.

Everyman: O false Good, cursed may thou be,
Thou traitor to God, that hast deceived me
And caught me in thy snare!
Goods: Marry, thou brought thyself in care,
Whereof I am glad;
I must needs laugh, I cannot be sad.
Everyman: Ah, Good, thou hast had long my heartly love; *heartfelt*
I gave thee that which should be the Lord's above.
But wilt thou not go with me indeed?
I pray thee truth to say.
Goods: No, so God me speed!
Therefore farewell, and have good day. [*Exit Goods.*
Everyman: O, to whom shall I make my moan
For to go with me in that heavy journey?
First Fellowship said he would with me gone; *go*
His words were very pleasant and gay,
But afterward he left me alone.
Then spake I to my kinsmen, all in despair,
And also they gave me words fair;
They lacked no fair speaking,
But all forsook me in the ending.
Then went I to my Goods, that I loved best,
In hope to have comfort, but there had I least;
For my Goods sharply did me tell
That he bringeth many into hell.
Then of myself I was ashamed,
And so I am worthy to be blamed;
Thus may I well myself hate.
Of whom shall I now counsel take?
I think that I shall never speed
Till that I go to my Good Deed.
But, alas, she is so weak
That she can neither go nor speak; *walk*
Yet will I venture on her now. *make trial of*
My Good Deeds, where be you?
[*Good Deeds speaks from the ground*]
Good Deeds: Here I lie, cold in the ground;
Thy sins hath me sore bound,
That I cannot stir.
Everyman: O Good Deeds, I stand in fear!
I must you pray of counsel,
For help now should come right well.
Good Deeds: Everyman, I have understanding
That ye be summoned account to make
Before Messias, of Jerusalem King;
And you do by me, that journey with you will I take.

491 For help would now be very welcome.
495 If you do as I advise.

EVERYMAN: Therefore I come to you, my moan to make;
I pray you that ye will go with me.
GOOD DEEDS: I would full fain, but I cannot stand, verily.
EVERYMAN: Why, is there anything on you fall? *befallen*
GOOD DEEDS: Yea, sir, I may thank you of all; *for*
If ye had perfectly cheered me,
Your book of count full ready had be.
Look, the books of your works and deeds eke! *also*
Behold how they lie under the feet,
To your soul's heaviness.
EVERYMAN: Our Lord Jesus help me!
For one letter here I cannot see.
GOOD DEEDS: There is a blind reckoning in time of distress.
EVERYMAN: Good Deeds, I pray you help me in this need,
Or else I am for ever damned indeed;
Therefore help me to make reckoning
Before the Redeemer of all thing,
That King is, and was, and ever shall.
GOOD DEEDS: Everyman, I am sorry of your fall,
And fain would I help you, and I were able.
EVERYMAN: Good Deeds, your counsel I pray you give me.
GOOD DEEDS: That shall I do verily;
Though that on my feet I may not go,
I have a sister that shall with you also,
Called Knowledge, which shall with you abide,
To help you to make that dreadful reckoning.
[*Enter Knowledge*]
KNOWLEDGE: Everyman, I will go with thee, and be thy guide,
In thy most need to go by thy side.
EVERYMAN: In good condition I am now in every thing,
And am wholly content with this good thing,
Thanked be God my creator.
GOOD DEEDS: And when she hath brought you there
Where thou shalt heal thee of thy smart, *part*
Then go you with your reckoning and your Good Deeds together,
For to make you joyful at heart
Before the blessed Trinity.
EVERYMAN: My Good Deeds, gramercy!
I am well content, certainly,
With your words sweet.
KNOWLEDGE: Now go we together lovingly
To Confession, that cleansing river.

---

501 If you had encouraged me fully.
508 i.e. a sinful person in his hour of need finds that the account of his good deeds is dimly written and difficult to read.
520 Knowledge represents Everyman's spiritual understanding of the religious doctrine necessary for his salvation.

EVERYMAN: For joy I weep; I would we were there!
But, I pray you, give me cognition *knowledge*
Where dwelleth that holy man, Confession.
KNOWLEDGE: In the house of salvation:
We shall find him in that place,
That shall us comfort, by God's grace.
[*Knowledge takes Everyman to Confession*]
Lo, this is Confession. Kneel down and ask mercy,
For he is in good conceit with God Almighty. *esteem*
EVERYMAN: O glorious fountain, that all uncleanness doth clarify,
Wash from me the spots of vice unclean,
That on me no sin may be seen.
I come with Knowledge for my redemption,
Redempt with heart and full contrition;
For I am commanded a pilgrimage to take,
And great accounts before God to make.
Now I pray you, Shrift, mother of salvation, *confession*
Help my Good Deeds for my piteous exclamation.
CONFESSION: I know your sorrow well, Everyman.
Because with Knowledge ye come to me,
I will you comfort as well as I can,
And a precious jewel I will give thee,
Called penance, voider of adversity; *expeller*
Therewith shall your body chastised be,
With abstinence and perseverance in God's service.
Here shall you receive that scourge of me,
Which is penance strong that ye must endure,
To remember thy Saviour was scourged for thee
With sharp scourges, and suffered it patiently;
So must thou, ere thou scape that painful pilgrimage.
Knowledge, keep him in this voyage,
And by that time Good Deeds will be with thee.
But in any wise be siker of mercy, *sure*
For your time draweth fast; and ye will saved be, *if*
Ask God mercy, and he will grant truly.
When with the scourge of penance man doth him bind, *himself*
The oil of forgiveness then shall he find.
EVERYMAN: Thanked be God for his gracious work!
For now I will my penance begin;
This hath rejoiced and lighted my heart, *lightened*
Though the knots be painful and hard within.

540 i.e. in the church.
549 Redeemed by heartfelt and full contrition.
553 In answer to my piteous cry.
569 Draws quickly to an end.
575–6 This has made my heart joyful and illumined it within, though the knots [of the scourge] be painful and hard.

KNOWLEDGE: Everyman, look your penance that ye fulfil,
What pain that ever it to you be;
And Knowledge shall give you counsel at will
How your account ye shall make clearly.
EVERYMAN: O eternal God, O heavenly figure,
O way of righteousness, O goodly vision,
Which descended down in a virgin pure
Because he would every man redeem,
Which Adam forfeited by his disobedience:
O blessed Godhead, elect and high divine, *divinity*
Forgive my grievous offence;
Here I cry thee mercy in this presence.
O ghostly treasure, O ransomer and redeemer,
Of all the world hope and conductor,
Mirror of joy, and founder of mercy,
Which enlumineth heaven and earth thereby, *by means of it*
Hear my clamorous complaint, though it late be;
Receive my prayers, of thy benignity;
Though I be a sinner most abominable,
Yet let my name be written in Moses' table.
O Mary, pray to the Maker of all thing,
Me for to help at my ending;
And save me from the power of my enemy,
For Death assaileth me strongly.
And, Lady, that I may be mean of thy prayer
Of your Son's glory to be partner,
By the means of his passion, I it crave;
I beseech you help my soul to save,
Knowledge, give me the scourge of penance;
My flesh therewith shall give acquittance:
I will now begin, if God give me grace.
KNOWLEDGE: Everyman, God give you time and space! *opportunity*
Thus I bequeath you in the hands of our Saviour;
Now may you make your reckoning sure.
EVERYMAN: In the name of the Holy Trinity,
My body sore punished shall be:
Take this, body, for the sin of the flesh!
[*Scourges himself.*
Also thou delightest to go gay and fresh, *finely dressed*
And in the way of damnation thou did me bring,

---

588 *in this presence*, i.e. in the presence of Knowledge and Confession.
596 Medieval theologians regarded the two tables given on Sinai as symbols of baptism and penance respectively. Thus Everyman is asking to be numbered among those who have escaped damnation by doing penance for their sins.
599 i.e. from the devil.
601–3 And, Lady, I beg that through the mediation of thy prayer I may share in your Son's glory, in consequence of His passion.
606 *acquittance*, satisfaction (as a part of the sacrament of penance).

Therefore suffer now strokes of punishing.
Now of penance I will wade the water clear,
To save me from purgatory, that sharp fire.
[*Good Deeds rises from the ground*]
GOOD DEEDS: I thank God, now I can walk and go,
And am delivered of my sickness and woe.
Therefore with Everyman I will go, and not spare;
His good works I will help him to declare.
KNOWLEDGE: Now, Everyman, be merry and glad!
Your Good Deeds cometh now; ye may not be sad.
Now is your Good Deeds whole and sound,
Going upright upon the ground.
EVERYMAN: My heart is light, and shall be evermore;
Now will I smite faster than I did before.
GOOD DEEDS: Everyman, pilgrim, my special friend,
Blessed be thou without end;
For thee is preparate the eternal glory. *prepared*
Ye have me made whole and sound,
Therefore I will bide by thee in every stound. *trial*
EVERYMAN: Welcome, my Good Deeds; now I hear thy voice,
I weep for very sweetness of love.
KNOWLEDGE: Be no more sad, but ever rejoice;
God seeth thy living in his throne above.
Put on this garment to thy behoof, *advantage*
Which is wet with your tears,
Or else before God you may it miss,
When ye to your journey's end come shall.
EVERYMAN: Gentle Knowledge, what do ye it call?
KNOWLEDGE: It is a garment of sorrow:
From pain it will you borrow; *protect*
Contrition it is,
That geteth forgiveness;
It pleaseth God passing well. *exceedingly*
GOOD DEEDS: Everyman, will you wear it for your heal? *salvation*
EVERYMAN: Now blessed be Jesu, Mary's Son,
For now have I on true contrition.
And let us go now without tarrying;
Good Deeds, have we clear our reckoning?
GOOD DEEDS: Yea, indeed, I have it here.
EVERYMAN: Then I trust we need not fear;
Now, friends, let us not part in twain.
KNOWLEDGE: Nay, Everyman, that will we not, certain.
GOOD DEEDS: Yet must thou lead with thee
Three persons of great might.
EVERYMAN: Who should they be?
GOOD DEEDS: Discretion and Strength they hight, *are called*
And thy Beauty may not abide behind.
KNOWLEDGE: Also ye must call to mind
Your Five Wits as for your counsellors. *senses*

GOOD DEEDS: You must have them ready at all hours.
EVERYMAN: How shall I get them hither?
KNOWLEDGE: You must call them all together,
And they will hear you incontinent. *immediately*
EVERYMAN: My friends, come hither and be present,
Discretion, Strength, my Five Wits, and Beauty.
[*Enter Beauty, Strength, Discretion, and Five Wits*]
BEAUTY: Here at your will we be all ready.
What will ye that we should do?
GOOD DEEDS: That ye would with Everyman go,
And help him in his pilgrimage.
Advise you, will ye with him or not in that voyage? *consider*
STRENGTH: We will bring him all thither,
To his help and comfort, ye may believe me.
DISCRETION: So will we go with him all together.
EVERYMAN: Almighty God, lofed may thou be! *praised*
I give thee laud that I have hither brought
Strength, Discretion, Beauty, and Five Wits. Lack I nought.
And my Good Deeds, with Knowledge clear,
All be in my company at my will here;
I desire no more to my business. *for*
STRENGTH: And I, Strength, will by you stand in distress,
Though thou would in battle fight on the ground.
FIVE WITS: And though it were through the world round,
We will not depart for sweet ne sour.
BEAUTY: No more will I unto death's hour, *until*
Whatsoever thereof befall.
DISCRETION: Everyman, advise you first of all;
Go with a good advisement and deliberation. *reflection*
We all give you virtuous monition *forewarning*
That all shall be well.
EVERYMAN: My friends, harken what I will tell:
I pray God reward you in his heavenly sphere.
Now harken, all that be here,
For I will make my testament
Here before you all present:
In alms half my good I will give with my hands twain
In the way of charity, with good intent,
And the other half still shall remain
In queth, to be returned there it ought to be. *bequest; where*
This I do in despite of the fiend of hell,
To go quit out of his peril
Ever after and this day.

---

687 i.e. in happiness or adversity.
702 This line probably refers to restitution, i.e. the restoration to its rightful owners of property which has been unjustly acquired.
704–5 To go free out of his power to-day and ever after.

KNOWLEDGE: Everyman, harken what I say:
Go to priesthood, I you advise,
And receive of him in any wise *in any case*
The holy sacrament and ointment together.
Then shortly see ye turn again hither;
We will all abide you here.
FIVE WITS: Yea, Everyman, hie you that ye ready were.
There is no emperor, king, duke, ne baron,
That of God hath commission *authority*
As hath the least priest in the world being; *living*
For of the blessed sacraments pure and benign
He beareth the keys, and thereof hath the cure *charge*
For man's redemption—it is ever sure—
Which God for our soul's medicine
Gave us out of his heart with great pine. *suffering*
Here in this transitory life, for thee and me,
The blessed sacraments seven there be:
Baptism, confirmation, with priesthood good,
And the sacrament of God's precious flesh and blood,
Marriage, the holy extreme unction, and penance;
These seven be good to have in remembrance,
Gracious sacraments of high divinity.
EVERYMAN: Fain would I receive that holy body,
And meekly to my ghostly father I will go. *spiritual*
FIVE WITS: Everyman, that is the best that ye can do.
God will you to salvation bring,
For priesthood exceedeth all other thing:
To us Holy Scripture they do teach,
And converteth man from sin heaven to reach;
God hath to them more power given
Than to any angel that is in heaven.
With five words he may consecrate,
God's body in flesh and blood to make,
And handleth his Maker between his hands.
The priest bindeth and unbindeth all bands,
Both in earth and in heaven.
Thou ministers all the sacraments seven; *administer*
Though we kissed thy feet, thou were worthy;
Thou art surgeon that cureth sin deadly:
No remedy we find under God
But all only priesthood.
Everyman, God gave priests that dignity,

---

712 Hurry and prepare yourself.
728 i.e. the Eucharist.
737 *five words*, i.e. *Hoc est enim corpus meum*.
740 Matt. xvi. 19.
746 Except only from the priesthood.

And setteth them in his stead among us to be;
Thus be they above angels in degree.
[*Everyman goes to the priest to receive the last sacraments*]
KNOWLEDGE: If priests be good, it is so, surely.
But when Jesus hanged on the cross with great smart,
There he gave out of his blessed heart
The same sacrament in great torment:
He sold them not to us, that Lord omnipotent.
Therefore Saint Peter the apostle doth say
That Jesu's curse hath all they
Which God their Saviour do buy or sell,
Or they for any money do take or tell. *pay*
Sinful priests giveth the sinners example bad;
Their children sitteth by other men's fires, I have heard;
And some haunteth women's company
With unclean life, as lusts of lechery:
These be with sin made blind.
FIVE WITS: I trust to God no such may we find;
Therefore let us priesthood honour,
And follow their doctrine for our souls' succour.
We be their sheep, and they shepherds be
By whom we all be kept in surety.
Peace, for yonder I see Everyman come,
Which hath made true satisfaction.
GOOD DEEDS: Methink it is he indeed.
[*Re-enter Everyman*]
EVERYMAN: Now Jesu be your alder speed!
I have received the sacrament for my redemption,
And then mine extreme unction:
Blessed be all they that counselled me to take it!
And now, friends, let us go without longer respite;
I thank God that ye have tarried so long.
Now set each of you on this rood your hand, *cross*
And shortly follow me:
I go before there I would be; God be our guide!
STRENGTH: Everyman, we will not from you go
Till ye have done this voyage long.
DISCRETION: I, Discretion, will bide by you also.
KNOWLEDGE: And though this pilgrimage be never so strong, *harsh*
I will never part you fro. *from you*
STRENGTH: Everyman, I will be as sure by thee
As ever I did by Judas Maccabee.
[*Everyman comes to his grave*]

---

750 *it is so*, i.e. that they are above the angels.
755–8 The reference here is to the sin of simony (Acts viii. 18 ff.)
760 i.e. illegitimate children.
772 Be the helper of you all.
786–7 I will stand by you as steadfastly as ever I did by Judas Maccabeus (I Macc. iii).

EVERYMAN: Alas, I am so faint I may not stand;
My limbs under me doth fold.
Friends, let us not turn again to this land,
Not for all the world's gold;
For into this cave must I creep
And turn to earth, and there to sleep.
BEAUTY: What, into this grave? Alas!
EVERYMAN: Yea, there shall ye consume, more and less.
BEAUTY: And what, should I smother here?
EVERYMAN: Yea, by my faith, and never more appear.
In this world live no more we shall,
But in heaven before the highest Lord of all.
BEAUTY: I cross out all this; adieu, by Saint John!
I take my tap in my lap, and am gone.
EVERYMAN: What, Beauty, whither will ye?
BEAUTY: Peace, I am deaf; I look not behind me,
Not and thou wouldest give me all the gold in thy chest
[*Exit Beauty.*
EVERYMAN: Alas, whereto may I trust?
Beauty goeth fast away from me;
She promised with me to live and die.
STRENGTH: Everyman, I will thee also forsake and deny;
Thy game liketh me not at all. *pleases*
EVERYMAN: Why, then, ye will forsake me all?
Sweet Strength, tarry a little space. *while*
STRENGTH: Nay, sir, by the rood of grace!
I will hie me from thee fast,
Though thou weep till thy heart to-brast. *break*
EVERYMAN: Ye would ever bide by me, ye said.
STRENGTH: Yea, I have you far enough conveyed.
Ye be old enough, I understand,
Your pilgrimage to take on hand;
I repent me that I hither came.
EVERYMAN: Strength, you to displease I am to blame;
Yet promise is debt, this ye well wot.
STRENGTH: In faith, I care not.
Thou art but a fool to complain;
You spend your speech and waste your brain.
Go thrust thee into the ground!
[*Exit Strength.*
EVERYMAN: I had wend surer I should you have found.
He that trusteth in his Strength
She him deceiveth at the length.

---

795 Decay, all of you.
800 I cancel all this, i.e. my promise to stay with you.
801 *I take my tap in my lap*, i.e. I'm going quickly: a proverbial phrase, from the practice of women carrying with them to a neighbour's house a portion of tow or flax (*tap*) for spinning.
820 I am to blame for displeasing you.

Both Strength and Beauty forsaketh me;
Yet they promised me fair and lovingly.
DISCRETION: Everyman, I will after Strength be gone;
As for me, I will leave you alone.
EVERYMAN: Why, Discretion, will ye forsake me?
DISCRETION: Yea, in faith, I will go from thee,
For when Strength goeth before
I follow after evermore.
EVERYMAN: Yet, I pray thee, for the love of the Trinity,
Look in my grave once piteously.
DISCRETION: Nay, so nigh will I not come;
Farewell, every one! [*Exit Discretion.*
EVERYMAN: O, all thing faileth, save God alone—
Beauty, Strength, and Discretion;
For when Death bloweth his blast,
They all run from me full fast.
FIVE WITS: Everyman, my leave now of thee I take;
I will follow the other, for here I thee forsake.
EVERYMAN: Alas, then may I wail and weep,
For I took you for my best friend.
FIVE WITS: I will no longer thee keep;
Now farewell, and there an end. [*Exit Five Wits.*
EVERYMAN: O Jesu, help! All hath forsaken me.
GOOD DEEDS: Nay, Everyman; I will bide with thee.
I will not forsake thee indeed;
Thou shalt find me a good friend at need.
EVERYMAN: Gramercy, Good Deeds! Now may I true friends see.
They have forsaken me, every one;
I loved them better than my Good Deeds alone.
Knowledge, will ye forsake me also?
KNOWLEDGE: Yea, Everyman, when ye to Death shall go;
But not yet, for no manner of danger.
EVERYMAN: Gramercy, Knowledge, with all my heart.
KNOWLEDGE: Nay, yet I will not from hence depart
Till I see where ye shall become.
EVERYMAN: Methink, alas, that I must be gone
To make my reckoning and my debts pay,
For I see my time is nigh spent away.
Take example, all ye that this do hear or see,
How they that I loved best do forsake me,
Except my Good Deeds that bideth truly.
GOOD DEEDS: All earthly things is but vanity:
Beauty, Strength, and Discretion do man forsake,
Foolish friends, and kinsmen, that fair spake—
All fleeth save Good Deeds, and that am I.
EVERYMAN: Have mercy on me, God most mighty;
And stand by me, thou mother and maid, holy Mary.

863 What shall become of you.

GOOD DEEDS: Fear not; I will speak for thee.
EVERYMAN: Here I cry God mercy.
GOOD DEEDS: Short our end, and minish our pain;
Let us go and never come again.
EVERYMAN: Into thy hands, Lord, my soul I commend;
Receive it, Lord, that it be not lost.
As thou me boughtest, so me defend,
And save me from the fiend's boast,
That I may appear with that blessed host
That shall be saved at the day of doom.
In manus tuas, of mights most
For ever, *commendo spiritum meum*.
[*He sinks into his grave.*
KNOWLEDGE: Now hath he suffered that we all shall endure;
The Good Deeds shall make all sure.
Now hath he made ending;
Methinketh that I hear angels sing,
And make great joy and melody
Where Everyman's soul received shall be.
ANGEL: Come, excellent elect spouse, to Jesu!
Hereabove thou shalt go
Because of thy singular virtue.
Now the soul is taken the body fro,
Thy reckoning is crystal-clear.
Now shalt thou into the heavenly sphere,
Unto the which all ye shall come
That liveth well before the day of doom.
[*Enter Doctor*]
DOCTOR: This moral men may have in mind.
Ye hearers, take it of worth, old and young, *value it*
And forsake Pride, for he deceiveth you in the end;
And remember Beauty, Five Wits, Strength, and Discretion,
They all at the last do every man forsake,
Save his Good Deeds there doth he take. *unless*
But beware, for and they be small
Before God, he hath no help at all;
None excuse may be there for every man.
Alas, how shall he do then?
For after death amends may no man make,
For then mercy and pity doth him forsake.
If his reckoning be not clear when he doth cóme,
God will say: '*Ite, maledicti, in ignem eternum*.'
And he that hath his account whole and sound,

---

878 Shorten our end, and diminish our pain.
886–7 Into thy hands, greatest in might for ever, I commend my spirit.
894 Bride of Jesus (a common medieval metaphor to express the idea of the soul's union with God).
915 Depart, ye cursed, into everlasting fire (Matt. xxv. 41).

High in heaven he shall be crowned;
Unto which place God bring us all thither,
That we may live body and soul together.
Thereto help the Trinity!
Amen, say ye, for saint charity.

Thus endeth this moral play of Everyman

WILLIAM SHAKESPEARE (1564–1616) was born in Stratford-upon-Avon to John Shakespeare, a glover or trader in leather goods, and Mary Arden, the daughter of a wealthy farmer. He may have attended the Stratford Free School, where he would have learned to read and write, studied Latin, and read classical authors such as Ovid. In 1582, Shakespeare married Ann Hathaway and in 1583 Susanna, their first child, was born. Twins Hamnet (probably named for a neighbor) and Judith followed. Little is known of Shakespeare's life after this until 1592, when he is referred to satirically by Robert Greene, another London playwright. In the 1590s, Shakespeare became an actor and playwright for the Lord Chamberlain's Men (later the King's Men); he was also a shareholder in the company. Although tradition assigns Shakespeare minor roles such as the ghost in *Hamlet*, he probably devoted more attention to writing plays and is unusual among writers for his attachment to a single company. The leading actor for whom Shakespeare wrote was Richard Burbage, who would have played Hamlet. The company's Clown at this time, Will Kemp, was famous for his impromptu repartee with the audience, a quality that Hamlet discourages in his advice to the Players.

Although we tend to associate all of Shakespeare's plays with the Globe Theatre, *The Taming of the Shrew* (ca. 1592) was probably written a full seven years before the Globe was built (1599). The main action, the wooing of Kate by Petruchio and the antics of other lovers and servants, is preceded by a **dramatic frame**, in which a nobleman and actors persuade the tinker (or pot mender) Christopher Sly that he is himself a nobleman with a lovely wife (played by a boy actor) who has long mourned her husband's loss of his wits.

The play itself can be interpreted as a **farce**, in which the shrew-taming arouses only laughter in audience members. Petruchio apparently imagines himself as playing his part in such a farce in his **soliloquy** at the end of 4.1. The second love plot of Lucentio and Bianca—in which the hero falls in love at first sight and in which aristocrats and servants conspire to hoodwink both lovers' fathers—also reinforces a sense of comic detachment from the main characters.

Nevertheless, both Kate and Petruchio have always aroused interest and strong opinions from the members of Shakespearean audiences. Some readers and playgoers think that the final kiss between the two indicates that Petruchio has acted in both partners' best interest to promote peace and love in their marriage. According to them, he believes in the late Renaissance ideal of a companionate marriage based on respect rather than wealth. Others, however, point out that Petruchio's shrew-taming is cruel. Still others think that Kate learns how to "play" the part of a submissive wife. Whether this means she loses her true self or maneuvers happily within the patriarchal society of Padua is a matter of interpretation.

At the heart of many of these differing interpretations of *Taming* is Kate's long final speech, in which she praises wifely obedience and condemns women's "forwardness" or stubbornness. Does Kate now believe in conservative values? Or has she successfully tricked Petruchio into *thinking* that she has changed? Or do Kate and Petruchio, as a couple, fool the rest of their family, winning praise and money in the process? And finally, does Kate *really* put her hand under Petruchio's foot as a gesture of submission?

Whether as the play's heroine or its scapegoat, Kate is a powerful presence in *The Taming of the Shrew*. In *Hamlet* (1600–1601), by contrast, women become tragic victims of larger metaphysical and political conflicts. Maddened by her father's death and Hamlet's cruelty, Ophelia suffers an ambiguous death by drowning that may be suicide. Gertrude, devastated by Hamlet's accusations and generally violent behavior, finally is killed by poison that her husband had intended for her son. Even leaving aside the generic difference between **comedy** and **tragedy**, Hamlet represents Shakespeare's turn toward darker and more intellectual themes. Hamlet himself fits some, but not all, of the qualities of a **tragic hero**. In past generations, scholars linked Shakespeare's frame of mind to the death of his son, Hamnet (1596). More recently, *Hamlet*'s dark mood has been linked to political anxieties and upheavals, such as the question of who would succeed Elizabeth I on the English throne or the Earl of Essex's abortive rebellion against Elizabeth (1601).

Nineteenth-century readers, and actor-filmmaker Laurence Olivier after them, considered Hamlet to be a "man who could not make up his mind." Hamlet's youth and confusion, family relations and the issue of Gertrude's remarriage, thwarted love for Ophelia, and other psychological pressures have all been noted as possible reasons why Hamlet takes five acts to carry out the ghost's requests.

Other critics locate the problem of whether Hamlet should take revenge in the nature of the world in which the Prince finds himself. On the most basic level, *Hamlet* is a very complicated murder mystery whose clues are difficult to read. Theologically-oriented critics have also noted the "questionable" form and identity of the ghost who announces his own murder. The play's heavily biblical overtones (both the Fall in Eden and Cain's murder of Abel receive overt references), the status of Ophelia's death, and Claudius' concerns about his inability to pray also suggest that religious issues are part of this tragedy. The implicit comparison between Shakespeare's imaginary Denmark and Shakespeare's England indicates that the nature of proper government is still another a topic of consideration. Hamlet asks Horatio to make sure that his story is told accurately, but such a task is an exceedingly difficult one.

Related Works: The Taming of the Shrew: Shakespeare, Sonnet 130; Bogan, "Women"; Cofer, "The Woman Who Was Left at the Altar"; Heaney, "Punishment"; Levertov, "The Ache of Marriage"; Ibsen, *A Dollhouse*; Shakespeare, *Hamlet*.

Hamlet: Hawthorne, "Young Goodman Brown"; Faulkner, "A Rose for Emily"; Atwood, "Gertrude Talks Back"; Cofer, "Arturo's Flight"; "The Husband's Message" and "The Wife's Lament"; "Sir Patrick Spens" (Child Ballad #58); Jonson, "On My First Son"; Shakespeare, Sonnet 116; Dickinson, "Because I could not stop for Death"; Robinson, "Richard Cory"; Bishop, "One Art"; Eliot, "The Love Song of J. Alfred Prufrock"; Nash, "Very Like a Whale"; Shakespeare, *The Taming of the Shrew*; Wilson, *The Piano Lesson*.

Final Scene of William Shakespeare, *The Taming of the Shrew*

The Taming of the Shrew

[The Names of the Actors]

In the induction:

A LORD, later posing as a servant
CHRISTOPHER SLY
BARTHOLOMEW, page to the lord, posing as Sly's wife
A COMPANY OF STROLLING PLAYERS
HUNTSMEN AND SERVANTS TO THE LORD
HOSTESS OF A TAVERN

In the play proper:

BAPTISTA MINOLA, father to Kate and Bianca
VINCENTIO, father to Lucentio
GREMIO, a pantaloon, a suitor to Bianca
LUCENTIO, in love with Bianca, later posing as Cambio
HORTENSIO, suitor to Bianca, later posing as Litio
PETRUCHIO, suitor to Kate
A PEDANT, later posing as Vincentio
TRANIO, servant to Lucentio, later posing as Lucentio
BIONDELLO, page to Lucentio
GRUMIO, servant to Petruchio
CURTIS, servant to Petruchio

A TAILOR
A HABERDASHER
KATHERINE (KATE), the shrew
BIANCA
A WIDOW
SERVANTS to Baptista, Petruchio, Lucentio

SCENE: *Warwickshire; Padua; near Verona*]

★

[INDUCTION]

IND. 1

Enter Beggar (Christophero Sly) and Hostess.

SLY: I'll feeze you, in faith.
HOSTESS: A pair of stocks, you rogue!
SLY: You're a baggage, the Slys are no rogues. Look in the chronicles: we came in with Richard Conqueror. Therefore *pocas palabras*, let the world slide. Sessa!
HOSTESS: You will not pay for the glasses you have burst?
SLY: No, not a denier. Go by, Saint Jeronimy, go to thy cold bed and warm thee.
HOSTESS: I know my remedy: I must go fetch the headborough.

[*Exit.*]

SLY: Third or fourth or fifth borough, I'll answer him by law. I'll not budge an inch, boy; let him come, and kindly.

Falls asleep.
Wind horns. Enter a Lord from hunting, with his train.

LORD: Huntsman, I charge thee, tender well my hounds.
Breathe Merriman, the poor cur is embossed,
And couple Clowder with the deep-mouthed brach.

Induction, scene 1 A country inn, Warwickshire
1 *feeze* fix
2 *A . . . stocks* (she threatens to have him put in the stocks)
4 *Richard Conqueror* (Sly's error for William the Conqueror); *pocas palabras* few words (Spanish)
4–5 *let. . . slide* (proverbial: "forget it")
5 *Sessa* shut up, stop it (perhaps from French *cessez*)
6 *burst* broken
7 *denier* French copper coin of little value; *Go. . . Jeronimy* i.e., forget it (Sly misquotes a famous line from Kyd's *The Spanish Tragedy* "Hieronimo beware, go by, go by." III. 12.30, mistaking the hero of the play for Saint Jerome)
9 *headborough* constable (the alternative term was "thirdborough," hence Sly's reply)
11 *boy* (an interjection, not addressed to anyone); s.d. *Wind* sound
12 *tender* care for
13 *Breathe* rest; *embossed* exhausted
14 *couple* leash together; *deep-mouthed* with a deep bark; *brach* bitch

Saw'st thou not, boy, how Silver made it good
At the hedge corner in the coldest fault?
I would not lose the dog for twenty pound.
First Huntsman: Why Bellman is as good as he, my lord.
He cried upon it at the merest loss
And twice today picked out the dullest scent.
Trust me, I take him for the better dog.
Lord: Thou art a fool. If Echo were as fleet,
I would esteem him worth a dozen such.
But sup them well and look unto them all.
Tomorrow I intend to hunt again.
First Huntsman: I will, my lord.
Lord: What's here? One dead or drunk? See, doth he breathe?
Second Huntsman: He breathes, my lord. Were he not warmed with ale
This were a bed but cold to sleep so soundly.
Lord: O monstrous beast, how like a swine he lies!
Grim death, how foul and loathsome is thine image!
Sirs, I will practice on this drunken man.
What think you, if he were conveyed to bed,
Wrapped in sweet clothes, rings put upon his fingers,
A most delicious banquet by his bed,
And brave attendants near him when he wakes,
Would not the beggar then forget himself?
First Huntsman: Believe me, lord, I think he cannot choose.
Second Huntsman: It would seem strange unto him when he waked.
Lord: Even as a flatt'ring dream or worthless fancy.
Then take him up and manage well the jest.
Carry him gently to my fairest chamber
And hang it round with all my wanton pictures.
Balm his foul head in warm distillèd waters
And burn sweet wood to make the lodging sweet.
Procure me music ready when he wakes
To make a dulcet and a heavenly sound.
And if he chance to speak be ready straight,
And with a low submissive reverence
Say, "What is it your honor will command?"
Let one attend him with a silver basin
Full of rose water and bestrewed with flowers,
Another bear the ewer, the third a diaper,
And say, "Will't please your lordship cool your hands?"

---

16 *in. . . fault* even though the scent was cold
19 *cried. . . loss* barked to show that he had picked up the scent after it had been utterly lost
22 *fleet* swift
32 *practice* play a trick
34 *sweet* perfumed
36 *brave* finely dressed
48 *straight* immediately
53 *diaper* linen towel

Some one be ready with a costly suit
And ask him what apparel he will wear,
Another tell him of his hounds and horse
And that his lady mourns at his disease.
Persuade him that he hath been lunatic,
And when he says he is, say that he dreams, 60
For he is nothing but a mighty lord.
This do, and do it kindly, gentle sirs. 62
It will be pastime passing excellent, 63
If it be husbanded with modesty. 64
FIRST HUNTSMAN: My lord, I warrant you we will play our part,
As he shall think, by our true diligence, 66
He is no less than what we say he is.
LORD: Take him up gently, and to bed with him,
And each one to his office when he wakes.
[Sly is carried out.] Sound trumpets.
Sirrah, go see what trumpet 'tis that sounds. 70
[*Exit Servingman.*]
Belike some noble gentleman that means, 71
Traveling some journey, to repose him here.
Enter Servingman.
How now, who is it?
SERVINGMAN: An't please your honor, players 74
That offer service to your lordship.
Enter Players.
LORD: Bid them come near.—Now, fellows, you are welcome.
PLAYERS We thank your honor.
LORD: Do you intend to stay with me tonight?
A PLAYER: So please your lordship to accept our duty. 79
LORD: With all my heart. This fellow I remember 80
Since once he played a farmer's eldest son.
'Twas where you wooed the gentlewoman so well.
I have forgot your name, but sure that part
Was aptly fitted and naturally performed.
A PLAYER: I think 'twas Soto that your honor means.
LORD: 'Tis very true, thou didst it excellent.
Well, you are come to me in happy time, 87
The rather for I have some sport in hand

---

60 *is* i.e., must be lunatic
62 *kindly* naturally
63 *passing* surpassingly
64 *husbanded* managed; *modesty* moderation
66 *As* so that
70 *Sirrah* (usual form of address to an inferior)
71 *Belike* probably
74 *An't* if it
79 *duty* service
87 *happy* opportune

Wherein your cunning can assist me much. 89
There is a lord will hear you play tonight; 90
But I am doubtful of your modesties, 91
Lest, overeyeing of his odd behavior— 92
For yet his honor never heard a play—
You break into some merry passion 94
And so offend him; for I tell you, sirs,
If you should smile he grows impatient.

A PLAYER: Fear not, my lord, we can contain ourselves
Were he the veriest antic in the world. 98

LORD: Go, sirrah, take them to the buttery 99
And give them friendly welcome every one, 100
Let them want nothing that my house affords.

Exit one with the Players.

Sirrah, go you to Barthol'mew my page 102
And see him dressed in all suits like a lady. 103
That done, conduct him to the drunkard's chamber
And call him madam; do him obeisance.
Tell him from me—as he will win my love.—
He bear himself with honorable action
Such as he hath observed in noble ladies
Unto their lords, by them accomplishèd. 109
Such duty to the drunkard let him do 110
With soft low tongue and lowly courtesy, 111
And say, "What is't your honor will command
Wherein your lady and your humble wife
May show her duty and make known her love?"
And then with kind embracements, tempting kisses,
And with declining head into his bosom,
Bid him shed tears, as being overjoyed
To see her noble lord restored to health
Who for this seven years hath esteemed him 119
No better than a poor and loathsome beggar. 120
And if the boy have not a woman's gift
To rain a shower of commanded tears,
An onion will do well for such a shift, 123

---

89 *cunning* skill
91 *modesties* discretion
92 *overeyeing of* witnessing
94 *merry passion* laughing fit
98 *veriest antic* greatest buffoon
99 *buttery* larder
102 *Barthol'mew* (pronounced "Bartlemy")
103 *suits* respects
109 *accomplishèd* performed
111 *lowly courtesy* humble curtsy
119 *esteemed him* considered himself
123 *shift* purpose

Which in a napkin being close conveyed 124
Shall in despite enforce a watery eye.
See this dispatched with all the haste thou canst:
Anon I'll give thee more instructions. 127
Exit a Servingman.
I know the boy will well usurp the grace, 128
Voice, gait, and action of a gentlewoman.
I long to hear him call the drunkard husband, 130
And how my men will stay themselves from laughter
When they do homage to this simple peasant.
I'll in to counsel them; haply my presence
May well abate their overmerry spleen 134
Which otherwise would grow into extremes. [*Exeunt.*]

★

IND.2

Enter aloft the Drunkard [Sly] with Attendants, some with apparel, basin and ewer, and other appurtenances; and Lord [as a Servant].

SLY: For God's sake, a pot of small ale. 1
FIRST SERVINGMAN: Will't please your lordship drink a cup of sack? 2
SECOND SERVINGMAN: Will't please your honor taste of these conserves? 3
THIRD SERVINGMAN: What raiment will your honor wear today?
SLY: I am Christophero Sly, call not me honor nor lordship. I ne'er drank
sack in my life, and if you give me any conserves, give me conserves 6
of beef. Ne'er ask me what raiment I'll wear, for I have no more
doublets than backs, no more stockings than legs, nor no more shoes 8
than feet; nay, sometime more feet than shoes, or such shoes as my
toes look through the overleather. 10
LORD: Heaven cease this idle humor in your honor! 11
O that a mighty man of such descent,
Of such possessions and so high esteem,
Should be infusèd with so foul a spirit!

---

124 *napkin* handkerchief; *close* secretly
127 *Anon* shortly
128 *usurp* assume
134 *spleen* mood

Induction, scene 2 The lord's manor house s.d. *aloft* i.e., in the tiring-house gallery over the stage (Capell, 1768, supplied a stage direction calling for a bed and other stage properties, but l. 35 makes clear that a bed was not used in the original staging)
1 *small* weak (hence cheap)
2 *sack* sherry (a gentleman's drink)
3 *conserves* candied fruit
6 *conserves of beef* salt beef
8 *doublets* coats
11 *humor* obsession

Sly: What, would you make me mad? Am not I Christopher Sly, old
Sly's son of Burton-heath, by birth a peddler, by education a card- 16
maker, by transmutation a bearherd, and now by present profession a 17
tinker? Ask Marian Hacket, the fat alewife of Wincot, if she know 18
me not. If she say I am not fourteen pence on the score for sheer ale, 19
score me up for the lyingest knave in Christendom. What, I am not 20
bestraught: here's— 21

Third Servingman: O this it is that makes your lady mourn.

Second Servingman: O this it is that makes your servants droop.

Lord: Hence comes it that your kindred shuns your house,
As beaten hence by your strange lunacy.
O noble lord, bethink thee of thy birth,
Call home thy ancient thoughts from banishment 27
And banish hence these abject lowly dreams.
Look how thy servants do attend on thee,
Each in his office ready at thy beck. 30
Wilt thou have music? Hark, Apollo plays, 31
Music.
And twenty cagèd nightingales do sing.
Or wilt thou sleep? We'll have thee to a couch
Softer and sweeter than the lustful bed
On purpose trimmed up for Semiramis.
Say thou wilt walk, we will bestrew the ground. 36
Or wilt thou ride? Thy horses shall be trapped, 37
Their harness studded all with gold and pearl.
Dost thou love hawking? Thou hast hawks will soar
Above the morning lark. Or wilt thou hunt? 40
Thy hounds shall make the welkin answer them 41
And fetch shrill echoes from the hollow earth.

First Servingman: Say thou wilt course, thy greyhounds are as swift 43
As breathèd stags, ay, fleeter than the roe. 44

Second Servingman: Dost thou love pictures? We will fetch thee
straight

---

16 *Burton-heath* Burton-on-the-Heath (a village near Stratford)
16–17 *cardmaker* (a card was a comb used in preparing wool for spinning)
17 *bearherd* keeper of a tame bear; *tinker* itinerant pot mender (proverbially a hard drinker)
18 *Wincot* a hamlet four miles southwest of Stratford (Hackets were living in the parish in 1591)
19 *on the score* chalked up as owing; *sheer* unmixed
20 *score me up for* write me down as
21 *bestraught* distraught, mad
27 *ancient* former
31 *Apollo* god of music
35 *Semiramis* notoriously lustful queen of Assyria
36 *bestrew* spread carpets on
37 *trapped* adorned
41 *welkin* sky
43 *course* hunt hares
44 *breathèd* in good wind; *roe* small deer

Adonis painted by a running brook
And Cytherea all in sedges hid,
Which seem to move and wanton with her breath
Even as the waving sedges play with wind.
LORD: We'll show thee Io as she was a maid
And how she was beguilèd and surprised,
As lively painted as the deed was done.
THIRD SERVINGMAN: Or Daphne roaming through a thorny wood.
Scratching her legs that one shall swear she bleeds,
And at that sight shall sad Apollo weep,
So workmanly the blood and tears are drawn.
LORD: Thou art a lord and nothing but a lord.
Thou hast a lady far more beautiful
Than any woman in this waning age.
FIRST SERVINGMAN: And till the tears that she hath shed for thee
Like envious floods o'errun her lovely face
She was the fairest creature in the world,
And yet she is inferior to none.
SLY: Am I a lord, and have I such a lady?
Or do I dream? Or have I dreamed till now?
I do not sleep: I see, I hear, I speak,
I smell sweet savors and I feel soft things.
Upon my life, I am a lord indeed,
And not a tinker nor Christopher Sly.
Well, bring our lady hither to our sight,
And once again, a pot o' th' smallest ale.
SECOND SERVINGMAN: Will't please your mightiness to wash your hands?
O how we joy to see your wit restored.
O that once more you knew but what you are!
These fifteen years you have been in a dream,
Or when you waked, so waked as if you slept.
SLY: These fifteen years? By my fay, a goodly nap.
But did I never speak of all that time?
FIRST SERVINGMAN: O yes, my lord, but very idle words,
For though you lay here in this goodly chamber,

---

46 *Adonis* (loved by Venus and killed by a wild boar while hunting; cf. Shakespeare's *Venus and Adonis*)
47 *Cytherea* Venus (associated with the island of Cytherea); *sedges* water rushes
48 *wanton* sway seductively
50 *Io* (loved by Jupiter in the shape of a cloud and changed by him into a heifer to deceive the jealous Juno)
52 *lively* energetically
53 *Daphne* (wooed by Apollo and changed into a laurel tree to escape his pursuit)
59 *waning* degenerate
61 *envious* hateful
63 *yet* even now
71 *smallest* weakest
73 *wit* reason
77 *fay* faith

Yet would you say ye were beaten out of door
And rail upon the hostess of the house, 82
And say you would present her at the leet 83
Because she brought stone jugs and no sealed quarts. 84
Sometimes you would call out for Cicely Hacket. 85
SLY: Ay, the woman's maid of the house.
THIRD SERVINGMAN: Why, sir, you know no house not no such maid,
Nor no such men as you have reckoned up, 88
As Stephen Sly, and old John Naps of Greet, 89
And Peter Turph, and Henry Pimpernell, 90
And twenty more such names and men as these,
Which never were nor no man ever saw.
SLY: Now Lord be thanked for my good amends! 93
ALL: Amen.

Enter [the Page as a] Lady, with Attendants.

SLY: I thank thee, thou shalt not lose by it.
PAGE: How fares my noble lord?
SLY: Marry, I fare well, for here is cheer enough. Where is my wife? 97
PAGE: Here, noble lord, what is thy will with her?
SLY: Are you my wife and will not call me husband?
My men should call me lord; I am your goodman. 100
PAGE: My husband and my lord, my lord and husband,
I am your wife in all obedience.
SLY: I know it well. What must I call her?
LORD: Madam.
SLY: Al'ce madam or Joan madam?
LORD: Madam and nothing else, so lords call ladies.
SLY: Madam wife, they say that I have dreamed
And slept above some fifteen year or more.
PAGE: Ay, and the time seems thirty unto me,
Being all this time abandoned from your bed. 110
SLY: 'Tis much, Servants, leave me and her alone.
[*Exeunt Lord and Servants.*]
Madam, undress you and come now to bed.
PAGE: Thrice-noble lord, let me entreat of you
To pardon me yet for a night or two,

---

82 *house* inn

83 *present . . . leet* accuse her before the court held by the lord of the manor (which had authority to punish such minor crimes as selling short weights and measures)

84 *brought . . . quarts* i.e., brought the liquor in open stoneware pottery jugs, in which the quantity was uncertain and variable, rather than in sealed, officially certified, quart bottles

85 *Cicely Hacket* (presumably related to the alewife Marian Hacket of l. 20, and working as a maid at her inn)

88 *reckoned up* named

89 *Greet* a Gloucestershire village near Stratford

93 *amends* recovery

97 *Marry* (a mild interjection, originally an oath invoking the Virgin Mary); *cheer* entertainment

100 *goodman* husband (but the term is appropriate to a peasant, not a lord)

110 *abandoned* banished

Or if not so, until the sun be set.
For your physicians have expressly charged,
In peril to incur your former malady,
That I should yet absent me from your bed.
I hope this reason stands for my excuse.

SLY: Ay, it stands so that I may hardly tarry so long—but I would be loath to fall into my dreams again. I will therefore tarry in despite of the flesh and the blood.

Enter a Messenger.

MESSENGER: Your honor's players, hearing your amendment,
Are come to play a pleasant comedy,
For so your doctors hold it very meet,
Seeing too much sadness hath congealed your blood
And melancholy is the nurse of frenzy.
Therefore they thought it good you hear a play
And frame your mind to mirth and merriment,
Which bars a thousand harms and lengthens life.

SLY: Marry, I will, let them play it. Is not a commonty a Christmas gambol or a tumbling trick?

PAGE: No, my good lord, it is more pleasing stuff.

SLY: What, household stuff?

PAGE: It is a kind of history.

SLY: Well, we'll see't. Come, madam, wife, sit by my side and let the world slip: we shall ne'er be younger.

[*They sit over the stage.*]

⋆

I.1

Flourish. Enter [below] Lucentio and his man Tranio.

LUCENTIO: Tranio, since for the great desire I had
To see fair Padua, nursery of arts,
I am arrived in fruitful Lombardy,
The pleasant garden of great Italy,
And by my father's love and leave am armed
With his good will and thy good company,
My trusty servant, well approved in all,

---

120 *it stands so* (1) as it happens, (2) since I have an erection
122 s.d. *Messenger* (presumably the lord reenters as the messenger)
127 *frenzy* madness
131 *commonty* (Sly's mistake for "comedy")
135 *history* story

1.1 A street in Padua s. d., *man* servant; *Tranio* (name from the *Mozellaria* of Plautus connoting "clarifier, revealer")
2 *Padua* (famous for its university)
3 *Lombardy* northern Italy
7 *approved* i.e., proved dependable

Here let us breathe and haply institute
A course of learning and ingenious studies.
Pisa, renowned for grave citizens,
Gave me my being and my father first,
A merchant of great traffic through the world,
Vincentio, come of the Bentivolii.
Vincentio's son, brought up in Florence,
It shall become to serve all hopes conceived,
To deck his fortune with his virtuous deeds.
And therefore, Tranio, for the time I study
Virtue, and that part of philosophy
Will I apply that treats of happiness
By virtue specially to be achieved.
Tell me thy mind, for I have Pisa left
And am to Padua come, as he that leaves
A shallow plash to plunge him in the deep
And with satiety seeks to quench his thirst.

TRANIO: *Mi perdonato*, gentle master mine.
I am in all affected as yourself,
Glad that you thus continue your resolve
To suck the sweets of sweet philosophy.
Only, good master, while we do admire
This virtue and this moral discipline,
Let's be no stoics nor no stocks, I pray,
Or so devote to Aristotle's checks
As Ovid be an outcast quite abjured.
Balk logic with acquaintance that you have
And practice rhetoric in your common talk.
Music and poesy use to quicken you.
The mathematics and the metaphysics,
Fall to them as you find your stomach serves you.
No profit grows where is no pleasure ta'en.
In brief, sir, study what you most affect.

---

9 *ingenious* intellectual
11 *first* i.e., before me
15 *serve . . . conceived* i.e., fulfill his father's hopes for him
19 *apply* pursue
23 *plash* pool
25 *Mi perdonato* pardon me (Italian)
26 *affected* inclined
31 *stocks* post (i.e., incapable of feeling; punning on *stoics*)
32 *checks* restraints
33 *As . . . abjured* i.e., that we would have to give up everything that Ovid, the Roman love poet, represents (cf. III.1.28–29; IV.2.8)
34 *Balk logic* bandy logical arguments
36 *quicken* enliven
38 *stomach* appetite
40 *affect* like

LUCENTIO: Gramercies, Tranio, well dost thou advise.
If Biondello now were come ashore,
We could at once put us in readiness
And take a lodging fit to entertain
Such friends as time in Padua shall beget.
But stay awhile, what company is this?

TRANIO: Master, some show to welcome us to town.

Enter Baptista with his two daughters Kate and Bianca, Gremio a pantaloon, [and] Hortensio suitor to Bianca. Lucentio [and] Tranio stand by.

BAPTISTA: Gentlemen, importune me no further,
For how I firmly am resolved you know.
That is, not to bestow my youngest daughter
Before I have a husband for the elder.
If either of you both love Katherina,
Because I know you well and love you well,
Leave shall you have to court her at your pleasure.

GREMIO: To cart her rather, she's too rough for me.
There, there, Hortensio, will you any wife?

KATE: I pray you, sir, is it your will
To make a stale of me amongst these mates?

HORTENSIO: "Mates," maid, how mean you that? No mates for you
Unless you were of gentler, milder mold.

KATE: I' faith, sir, you shall never need to fear:
Iwis it is not halfway to her heart.
But if it were, doubt not her care should be
To comb your noddle with a three-legged stool
And paint your face and use you like a fool.

HORTENSIO: From all such devils, good Lord deliver us.

GREMIO: And me too, good Lord.

TRANIO: [*Aside*]
Hush, master, here's some good pastime toward.
That wench is stark mad or wonderful froward.

LUCENTIO: But in the other's silence do I see
Maid's mild behavior and sobriety.
Peace, Tranio!

---

41 *Gramercies* many thanks

42 *come ashore* (like Mantua and Bergarno later, Padua is not, in fact, a seaport, though one could reach it from Venice by river and canal)

47 s.d. *pantaloon* foolish old man (a stock character in the commedia dell'arte)

55 *cart her* i.e., have her driven through the streets in a cart, like a prostitute undergoing punishment

58 *stale* (1) laughingstock, (2) prostitute (suggested by *cart*); *mates* (1) boors, (2) potential husbands (and the conjunction quibbles on "stalemate")

60 *mold* character

62 *Iwis* indeed; *it* i.e., marriage; *her* i.e., Kate's

65 *paint* redden (by drawing blood)

68 *toward* in prospect

69 *wonderful froward* extremely obstinate

TRANIO: Well said, master; mum, and gaze your fill.
BAPTISTA: Gentlemen, that I may soon make good
  What I have said—Bianca, get you in,
  And let it not displease thee, good Bianca,
  For I will love thee ne'er the less, my girl.
KATE: A pretty peat! it is best 78
  Put finger in the eye, an she knew why.
BIANCA: Sister, content you in my discontent. 80
  Sir, to your pleasure humbly I subscribe.
  My books and instruments shall be my company,
  On them to look and practice by myself.
LUCENTIO: [*Aside*]
  Hark, Tranio, thou mayst hear Minerva speak. 84
HORTENSIO: Signor Baptista, will you be so strange? 85
  Sorry am I that our good will effects
  Bianca's grief. 87
GREMIO: Why, will you mew her up,
  Signor Baptista, for this fiend of hell
  And make her bear the penance of her tongue?
BAPTISTA: Gentlemen, content ye, I am resolved. 90
  Go in, Bianca. [*Exit Bianca.*]
  And for I know she taketh most delight 92
  In music, instruments, and poetry,
  Schoolmasters will I keep within my house,
  Fit to instruct her youth. If you, Hortensio,
  Or Signor Gremio, you, know any such,
  Prefer them hither, for to cunning men 97
  I will be very kind, and liberal
  To mine own children in good bringing-up.
  And so, farewell. Katherina, you may stay, 100
  For I have more to commune with Bianca. *Exit.* 101
KATE: Why, and I trust I may go too, may I not? What, shall I be
  appointed hours, as though, belike, I knew not what to take and what 103
  to leave? Ha! *Exit.*
GREMIO: You may go to the devil's dam. Your gifts are so good, here's 105
  none will hold you. Their love is not so great, Hortensio, but we may 106

---

78 *peat* spoiled darling
78–79 *it . . . why* if she knew what she was doing she would have been better off to put on a show of weeping
84 *Minerva* goddess of wisdom and of the arts
85 *strange* unnatural
87 *mew* coop (term for caging a falcon)
92 *for* since
97 *Prefer* recommend; *cunning* well-trained
101 *commune* discuss
103 *belike* presumably
105 *dam* mother
106 *hold* endure; *Their* i.e., women's

blow our nails together and fast it fairly out. Our cake's dough on both sides. Farewell—yet for the love I bear my sweet Bianca, if I can by any means light on a fit man to teach her that wherein she delights, I will wish him to her father.

HORTENSIO: So will I, Signor Gremio. But a word, I pray. Though the nature of our quarrel yet never brooked parley, know now, upon advice it toucheth us both, that we may yet again have access to our fair mistress and be happy rivals in Bianca's love, to labor and effect one thing specially.

GREMIO: What's that, I pray?

HORTENSIO: Marry, sir, to get a husband for her sister.

GREMIO: A husband? A devil.

HORTENSIO: I say, a husband.

GREMIO: I say, a devil. Think'st thou, Hortensio, though her father be very rich, any man is so very a fool to be married to hell?

HORTENSIO: Tush, Gremio, though it pass your patience and mine to endure her loud alarums, why, man, there be good fellows in the world, an a man could light on them, would take her with all her faults, and money enough.

GREMIO: I cannot tell, but I had as lief take her dowry with this condition, to be whipped at the high cross every morning.

HORTENSIO: Faith, as you say, there's small choice in rotten apples. But come, since this bar in law makes us friends, it shall be so far forth friendly maintained, till by helping Baptista's eldest daughter to a husband we set his youngest free for a husband, and then have to't afresh. Sweet Bianca! Happy man be his dole. He that runs fastest gets the ring. How say you, Signor Gremio?

GREMIO: I am agreed, and would I had given him the best horse in Padua to begin his wooing that would thoroughly woo her, wed her, and bed her, and rid the house of her. Come on.

Exeunt ambo. Manent Tranio and Lucentio.

TRANIO: I pray, sir, tell me, is it possible
That love should of a sudden take such hold?

LUCENTIO: O Tranio, till I found it to be true
I never thought it possible or likely.

---

107 *blow . . . together* i.e., be patient; *Our cake's dough* i.e., out expectations are disappointed (proverbial)

110 *wish* recommend

112 *brooked parley* permitted discussion; *advice* reflection

121 *so very a* such a complete

123 *alarums* calls to arms

124 *an* if

127 *high cross* market cross (i.e., the center of town)

129 *bar* obstacle

131 *have to't* let us set to it

132 *Happy . . . dole* happiness be his lot (i.e., his who wins her; proverbial)

133 *ring* prize (playing on "wedding ring")

136 s.d. *ambo* both (Gremio and Hortenssio); *Manent* remain

But see, while idly I stood looking on,
I found the effect of love-in-idleness
And now in plainness do confess to thee,
That art to me as secret and as dear
As Anna to the Queen of Carthage was,
Tranio, I burn, I pine, I perish, Tranio,
If I achieve not this young modest girl.
Counsel me, Tranio, for I know thou canst.
Assist me, Tranio, for I know thou wilt.
TRANIO: Master, it is no time to chide you now.
Affection is not rated from the heart.
If love have touched you, nought remains but so,
"Redime te captum, quam queas minimo."
LUCENTIO: Gramercies, lad. Go forward, this contents;
The rest will comfort, for thy counsel's sound.
TRANIO: Master, you looked so longly on the maid,
Perhaps you marked not what's the pith of all.
LUCENTIO: O yes, I saw sweet beauty in her face,
Such as the daughter of Agenor had,
That made great Jove to humble him to her hand
When with his knees he kissed the Cretan strand.
TRANIO: Saw you no more? Marked you not how her sister
Began to scold and raise up such a storm
That mortal ears might hardly endure the din?
LUCENTIO: Tranio, I saw her coral lips to move,
And with her breath she did perfume the air.
Sacred and sweet was all I saw in her.
TRANIO: Nay, then, 'tis time to stir him from his trance.
I pray, awake, sir. If you love the maid
Bend thoughts and wits to achieve her. Thus it stands:
Her elder sister is so curst and shrewd
That till the father rid his hands of her,
Master, your love must live a maid at home,
And therefore has he closely mewed her up,
Because she will not be annoyed with suitors.

---

142 *love-in-idleness* the pansy (supposed to have magical power in love)
145 *Anna* Dido's sister and confidante
147 *achieve* win
151 *rated* driven out by scolding
153 *Redime . . . minimo* redeem yourself from captivity as cheaply as you can (from the *Eunuchus* of Terence but quoted from Lily's *Latin Grammar*)
156 *longly* longingly
159 *daughter of Agenor* Europa (loved by Jupiter, who in the shape of a bull abducted her)
165, 166 *coral perfume* (hackneyed comparisons of the Petrarchan sonnet tradition; cf. Shakespeare's Sonnet 130)
171 *curst* bad-tempered; *shrewd* shrewish
174 *mewed* cooped
175 *Because* so that

LUCENTIO: Ah, Tranio, what a cruel father's he.
But art thou not advised he took some care 177
To get her cunning schoolmasters to instruct her?
TRANIO: Ay, marry, am I, sir, and now 'tis plotted. 179
LUCENTIO: I have it, Tranio. 180
TRANIO: Master, for my hand,
Both our inventions meet and jump in one. 181
LUCENTIO: Tell me thine first.
TRANIO: You will be schoolmaster
And undertake the teaching of the maid.
That's your device.
LUCENTIO: It is. May it be done?
TRANIO: Not possible, for who shall bear your part
And be in Padua here Vincentio's son,
Keep house and ply his book, welcome his friends,
Visit his countrymen and banquet them?
LUCENTIO: Basta, content thee, for I have it full. 189
We have not yet been seen in any house 190
Nor can we be distinguished by our faces
For man or master. Then it follows thus.
Thou shalt be master, Tranio, in my stead,
Keep house and port and servants as I should. 194
I will some other be, some Florentine,
Some Neapolitan or meaner man of Pisa. 196
'Tis hatched and shall be so. Tranio, at once
Uncase thee, take my colored hat and cloak. 198
When Biondello comes he waits on thee,
But I will charm him first to keep his tongue. 200
TRANIO: So had you need.
[*They exchange cloaks and hats.*]
In brief, sir, sith it your pleasure is 202
And I am tied to be obedient—
For so your father charged me at our parting,
"Be serviceable to my son," quoth he,
Although I think 'twas in another sense—
I am content to be Lucentio
Because so well I love Lucentio.
LUCENTIO: Tranio, be so, because Lucentio loves,

---

177 *advised* aware
179 *'tis plotted* I have a plan
180 *for . . . hand* I'll wager
181 *inventions* plans; *jump* agree
189 *Basta* enough; *have it full* see it clearly
194 *port* style of living
196 *meaner* i.e., of lower than my true rank
198 *Uncase* uncloak
202 *sith* since

And let me be a slave, t' achieve that maid
Whose sudden sight hath thralled my wounded eye.
Enter Biondello.
Here comes the rogue.—Sirrah, where have you been?
BIONDELLO: Where have I been? Nay, how now, where are you?
Master, has my fellow Tranio stol'n your clothes,
Or you stol'n his, or both? Pray, what's the news?
LUCENTIO: Sirrah, come hither. 'Tis no time to jest,
And therefore frame your manners to the time.
Your fellow Tranio, here, to save my life,
Puts my apparel and my count'nance on,
And I for my escape have put on his,
For in a quarrel since I came ashore
I killed a man and fear I was descried.
Wait you on him, I charge you, as becomes,
While I make way from hence to save my life.
You understand me?
BIONDELLO: I, sir? Ne'er a whit.
LUCENTIO: And not a jot of Tranio in your mouth.
Tranio is changed into Lucentio.
BIONDELLO: The better for him, would I were so too.
TRANIO: So could I, faith, boy, to have the next wish after,
That Lucentio indeed had Baptista's youngest daughter.
But, sirrah, not for my sake but your master's, I advise
You use your manners discreetly in all kind of companies.
When I am alone, why then I am Tranio,
But in all places else, your master Lucentio.
LUCENTIO: Tranio, let's go.
One thing more rests, that thyself execute—
To make one among these wooers. If thou ask me why,
Sufficeth my reasons are both good and weighty. *Exeunt.*
The Presenters above speak.
FIRST SERVINGMAN: My lord, you nod, you do not mind the play.
SLY: Yes, by Saint Anne, do I. A good matter, surely. Comes there any more of it?
PAGE: My lord, 'tis but begun.
SLY: 'Tis a very excellent piece of work, madam lady—would 'twere done.
They sit and mark.

★

---

211 *thralled* enslaved
212 *Sirrah* (usual form of address to an inferior)
219 *count'nance* appearance, deportment.
236 *rests* remains; *execute* arrange
238 s.d., *Presenters* choral characters of an induction who "present" the play proper
239 *mind* pay attention to
244 s.d. *They sit and mark* (the presenters are not heard from again; see the Introduction); *mark* watch

I.2

Enter [below] Petruchio and his man Grumio.

PETRUCHIO: Verona, for a while I take my leave
To see my friends in Padua, but of all
My best beloved and approvèd friend
Hortensio; and I trow this is his house. 4
Here, sirrah Grumio, knock, I say.
GRUMIO: Knock, sir? Whom should I knock? Is there any man has
rebused your worship? 7
PETRUCHIO: Villain, I say, knock me here soundly. 8
GRUMIO: Knock you here, sir? Why, sir, what am I, sir, that I should
knock you here, sir? 10
PETRUCHIO: Villain, I say, knock me at this gate, 11
And rap me well or I'll knock your knave's pate.
GRUMIO: My master is grown quarrelsome. I should knock you first,
And then I know after who comes by the worst.
PETRUCHIO: Will it not be?
Faith, sirrah, an you'll not knock, I'll ring it. 16
I'll try how you can sol, fa, and sing it. 17
He wrings him by the ears.
GRUMIO: Help, masters, help! My master is mad. 18
PETRUCHIO: Now, knock when I bid you, sirrah villain.
Enter Hortensio.
HORTENSIO: How now, what's the matter? My old friend Grumio, and 20
my good friend Petruchio! How do you all at Verona?
PETRUCHIO: Signer Hortensio, come you to part the fray?
Con tutto il cuore bentrovato, may I say. 23
HORTENSIO: *Alla nostra casa benvenuto,* 24
Molto honorato signor mio Petruchio.
Rise, Grumio, rise, we will compound this quarrel. 26
GRUMIO: Nay, 'tis no matter, sir, what he 'leges in Latin. If this be not a 27
lawful cause for me to leave his service, look you, sir; he bid me

---

I.2 A street in Padua s.d. *Petruchio* (Shakespeare's phonetic spelling of Petruccio, diminutive of Pietro; pronounced "Petrutchio," not "Petruckio"); *Grumio* (the name, like Tranio, is that of a slave in Plautus's (*Mostellaria*)
4 *trow* believe
7 *rebused* (Grumio's mistake for "abused")
8 *me* i.e., for me (but Grumio, perhaps deliberately, misunderstands)
11 *gate* door
16 *ring* (playing on "wring")
17 *sol, fa* sing the scale
18 *Help, masters* (to the audience)
23 *Con . . . trovato* with all my heart well met (Italian)
24–25 *Alla . . . Petruchio* welcome to our house, my very honorable Signor Petruchio (Italian)
26 *compound* settle
27 *'leges* alleges

knock him and rap him soundly, sir. Well, was it fit for a servant to use his master so, being perhaps, for aught I see, two and thirty, a pip out?
Whom would to God I had well knocked at first,
Then had not Grumio come by the worst.

PETRUCHIO: A senseless villain. Good Hortensio,
I bade the rascal knock upon your gate
And could not get him for my heart to do it.

GRUMIO: Knock at the gate? O heavens! Spake you not these words plain, "Sirrah, knock me here, rap me here, knock me well, and knock me soundly"? And come you now with "knocking at the gate"?

PETRUCHIO: Sirrah, be gone, or talk not, I advise you.

HORTENSIO: Petruchio, patience, I am Grumio's pledge.
Why, this' a heavy chance 'twixt him and you,
Your ancient, trusty, pleasant servant Grumio.
And tell me now, sweet friend, what happy gale
Blows you to Padua here from old Verona?

PETRUCHIO: Such wind as scatters young men through the world
To seek their fortunes farther than at home,
Where small experience grows. But in a few,
Signor Hortensio, thus it stands with me.
Antonio my father is deceased,
And I have thrust myself into this maze,
Happily to wive and thrive as best I may.
Crowns in my purse I have and goods at home,
And so am come abroad to see the world.

HORTENSIO: Petruchio, shall I then come roundly to thee
And wish thee to a shrewd ill-favored wife?
Thou'dst thank me but a little for my counsel.
And yet I'll promise thee she shall be rich,
And very rich—but thou'rt too much my friend
And I'll not wish thee to her.

PETRUCHIO: Signor Hortensio, 'twixt such friends as we
Few words suffice. And therefore if thou know
One rich enough to be Petruchio's wife—
As wealth is burden of my wooing dance—

30–31 *two . . . out* very drunk (a slang expression derived from the card game one-and-thirty, hence a little more drunk than drunk; a *pip* is the mark identifying the suit on a playing card, such as a heart or spade)
43 *this'* this is; *heavy chance* sad event
49 *in a few* i.e., words
53 *Happily* (1) cheerfully, (2) by chance
56 *come roundly* speak plainly
57 *shrewd* shrewish; *ill-favored* ill-natured
65 *burden* bass or undersong

Be she as foul as was Florentius' love,
As old as Sibyl, and as curst and shrewd
As Socrates' Xanthippe, or a worse,
She moves me not, or not removes, at least,
Affection's edge in me, were she as rough
As are the swelling Adriatic seas.
I come to wive it wealthily in Padua—
If wealthily, then happily in Padua.

GRUMIO: Nay, look you, sir, he tells you flatly what his mind is. Why, give him gold enough and marry him to a puppet or an aglet-baby or an old trot with ne'er a tooth in her head, though she have as many diseases as two and fifty horses. Why, nothing comes amiss, so money comes withal.

HORTENSIO: Petruchio, since we are stepped thus far in,
I will continue that I broached in jest.
I can, Petruchio, help thee to a wife
With wealth enough, and young and beauteous,
Brought up as best becomes a gentlewoman.
Her only fault—and that is faults enough—
Is that she is intolerable curst,
And shrewd and froward, so beyond all measure,
That were my state far worser than it is
I would not wed her for a mine of gold.

PETRUCHIO: Hortensio, peace. Thou know'st not gold's effect.
Tell me her father's name, and 'tis enough,
For I will board her though she chide as loud
As thunder when the clouds in autumn crack.

HORTENSIO: Her father is Baptista Minola,
An affable and courteous gentleman.
Her name is Katherina Minola,
Renowned in Padua for her scolding tongue.

PETRUCHIO: I know her father though I know not her,
And he knew my deceased father well.
I will not sleep, Hortensio, till I see her,
And therefore let me be thus bold with you,

---

66 *foul* ugly; *Florentius* (A knight who married an old hag in return for the answer to a riddle—"What do women most desire?"—that would save his life; the answer is to rule their husbands. She then turned into a beautiful maiden, cf. Gower's *Confessio Amantis.* Book I, or Chaucer's Wife of Bath's Tale.)

67 *Sibyl* the Cumaean Sibyl (a prophetess to whom Apollo granted as many years of life as she could hold grains of sand in her hand)

68 *Xanthippe* (the philosopher's wife, reputedly a shrew)

75 *aglet-baby* tiny doll figure (aglet indicating either a spangle or the metal point of a lace)

76 *trot* hag

77 *withal* at the same time

79 *that* that which

85 *froward* obstinate

90 *board* (as in attacking a ship)

To give you over at this first encounter
Unless you will accompany me thither.

GRUMIO: I pray you, sir, let him go while the humor lasts. A my word, an she knew him as well as I do, she would think scolding would do little good upon him. She may perhaps call him half a score knaves or so—why, that's nothing, an he begin once, he'll rail in his rope tricks. I'll tell you what, sir, an she stand him but a little, he will throw a figure in her face and so disfigure her with it that she shall have no more eyes to see withal than a cat. You know him not, sir.

HORTENSIO: Tarry, Petruchio, I must go with thee,
For in Baptista's keep my treasure is.
He hath the jewel of my life in hold,
His youngest daughter, beautiful Bianca,
And her withholds from me and other more,
Suitors to her and rivals in my love,
Supposing it a thing impossible,
For those defects I have before rehearsed,
That ever Katherina will be wooed.
Therefore this order hath Baptista ta'en,
That none shall have access unto Bianca
Till Katherine the curst have got a husband.

GRUMIO: Katherine the curst!
A title for a maid of all titles the worst.

HORTENSIO: Now shall my friend Petruchio do me grace
And offer me, disguised in sober robes,
To old Baptista as a schoolmaster
Well seen in music, to instruct Bianca,
That so I may, by this device, at last
Have leave and leisure to make love to her
And unsuspected court her by herself.

Enter Gremio [with a paper] and Lucentio disguised [as a schoolmaster].

GRUMIO: Here's no knavery! See, to beguile the old folks, how the young folks lay their heads together! Master, master, look about you. Who goes there, ha?

HORTENSIO: Peace, Grumio, it is the rival of my love.
Petruchio, stand by awhile.

---

100 *give you over* leave you
102 *humor* whim; *A* on, by
105–106 *rope tricks* (Grumio's mistake for "rhetoric"—i.e., abusive language, with a glance at tricks punishable by hanging); *stand* withstand
107 *figure* rhetorical figure (i.e., a telling expression)
110 *keep* (1) keeping, (2) fortified tower
111 *hold* confinement
118 *order* measure
123 *grace* a favor
126 *seen* versed

GRUMIO: A proper stripling, and an amorous!
[*They stand aside.*]
GREMIO: O very well, I have perused the note.
Hark you, sir, I'll have them very fairly bound,
All books of love, see that at any hand,
And see you read no other lectures to her.
You understand me. Over and beside
Signor Baptista's liberality,
I'll mend it with a largess. Take your paper too,
And let me have them very well perfumed,
For she is sweeter than perfume itself
To whom they go. What will you read to her?
LUCENTIO: Whate'er I read to her, I'll plead for you,
As for my patron, stand you so assured,
As firmly as yourself were still in place,
Yea and perhaps with more successful words
Than you—unless you were a scholar, sir.
GREMIO: O this learning, what a thing it is!
GRUMIO: [*Aside*]
O this woodcock, what an ass it is!
PETRUCHIO: Peace, sirrah.
HORTENSIO: Grumio, mum! [*Advancing*] God save you, Signor Gremio.
GREMIO: And you are well met, Signor Hortensio.
Trow you whither I am going? To Baptista Minola.
I promised to inquire carefully
About a schoolmaster for the fair Bianca,
And by good fortune I have lighted well
On this young man, for learning and behavior
Fit for her turn, well read in poetry
And other books, good ones, I warrant ye.
HORTENSIO: 'Tis well, and I have met a gentleman
Hath promised me to help me to another,
A fine musician to instruct our mistress.
So shall I no whit be behind in duty
To fair Bianca, so beloved of me.
GREMIO: Beloved of me, and that my deeds shall prove.

---

135 *proper stripling* handsome youth (ironically, of the "pantaloon" Gremio)
136 *note* i.e., a list of books for Bianca
138 *at any hand* in any case
139 *read* teach; *lectures* lessons
142 *mend* increase; *largess* gift of money; *paper* i.e., the *note*
143 *them* i.e., the books
148 *in place* present
152 *woodcock* (bird easily caught, hence proverbially stupid)
156 *Trow* know
161 *turn* need
165 *mistress* beloved

GRUMIO: [*Aside*]
And that his bags shall prove.
HORTENSIO: Gremio, 'tis now no time to vent our love.
Listen to me, and if you speak me fair
I'll tell you news indifferent good for either.
Here is a gentleman whom by chance I met,
Upon agreement from us to his liking,
Will undertake to woo curst Katherine,
Yea and to marry her if her dowry please.
GREMIO: So said, so done, is well.
Hortensio, have you told him all her faults?
PETRUCHIO: I know she is an irksome brawling scold.
If that be all, masters, I hear no harm.
GREMIO: No, sayst me so, friend? What countryman?
PETRUCHIO: Born in Verona, old Antonio's son.
My father dead, my fortune lives for me,
And I do hope good days and long to see.
GREMIO: O sir, such a life, with such a wife, were strange.
But if you have a stomach, to't a God's name,
You shall have me assisting you in all.
But will you woo this wildcat?
PETRUCHIO: Will I live?
GRUMIO: [*Aside*]
Will he woo her? Ay, or he'll hang her.
PETRUCHIO: Why came I hither but to that intent?
Think you a little din can daunt mine ears?
Have I not in my time heard lions roar?
Have I not heard the sea, puffed up with winds,
Rage like an angry boar chafèd with sweat?
Have I not heard great ordnance in the field
And heaven's artillery thunder in the skies?
Have I not in a pitchèd battle heard
Loud 'larums, neighing steeds, and trumpets' clang?
And do you tell me of a woman's tongue,
That gives not half so great a blow to th' ear
As will a chestnut in a farmer's fire?
Tush, tush, fear boys with bugs.

---

169 *bags* moneybags
170 *vent* utter
172 *indifferent* equally
174 *agreement* terms (they will pay his expenses of wooing, l. 213)
175 *Will undertake* i.e., who, upon agreement, will undertake
186 *stomach* appetite; *a* in
188 *Will I live?* i.e., certainly
198 *'larums* calls to arms
202 *fear* frighten; *bugs* bogeymen

GRUMIO: [*Aside*]
For he fears none.
GREMIO: Hortensio, hark.
This gentleman is happily arrived,
My mind presumes, for his own good and ours.
HORTENSIO: I promised we would be contributors,
And bear his charge of wooing whatsoe'er.
GREMIO: And so we will, provided that he win her.
GRUMIO: [*Aside*]
I would I were as sure of a good dinner.
Enter Tranio brave [as Lucentio], and Biondello.
TRANIO: Gentlemen, God save you. If I may be bold,
Tell me, I beseech you, which is the readiest way
To the house of Signor Baptista Minola?
BIONDELLO: He that has the two fair daughters, is't he you mean?
TRANIO: Even he, Biondello.
GREMIO: Hark you, sir; you mean not her to woo?
TRANIO: Perhaps him and her, sir, what have you to do?
PETRUCHIO: Not her that chides, sir, at any hand, I pray.
TRANIO: I love no chiders, sir.—Biondello, let's away.
LUCENTIO: [*Aside*]
Well begun, Tranio.
HORTENSIO: Sir, a word ere you go.
Are you a suitor to the maid you talk of, yea or no?
TRANIO: An if I be, sir, is it any offense?
GREMIO: No, if without more words you will get you hence.
TRANIO: Why, sir, I pray, are not the streets as free
For me as for you?
GREMIO: But so is not she.
TRANIO: For what reason, I beseech you?
GREMIO: For this reason, if you'll know,
That she's the choice love of Signor Gremio.
HORTENSIO: That she's the chosen of Signor Hortensio.
TRANIO: Softly, my masters. If you be gentlemen,
Do me this right, hear me with patience.
Baptista is a noble gentleman,
To whom my father is not all unknown,
And were his daughter fairer than she is
She may more suitors have, and me for one.
Fair Leda's daughter had a thousand wooers,
Then well one more may fair Bianca have.

207 *charge* expenses
209 s.d. *brave* finely dressed
216 *what . . . do* what business is it of yours
234 *Leda's daughter* Helen of Troy (Leda was made love to by Jupiter in the shape of a swan)
235 *one more* i.e., than she now has

And so she shall: Lucentio shall make one,
Though Paris came in hope to speed alone.
GREMIO: What, this gentleman will outtalk us all.
LUCENTIO: Sir, give him head. I know he'll prove a jade.
PETRUCHIO: Hortensio, to what end are all these words?
HORTENSIO: Sir, let me be so bold as to ask you,
Did you yet ever see Baptista's daughter?
TRANIO: No, sir, but I do hear that he hath two,
The one as famous for a scolding tongue
As is the other for beauteous modesty.
PETRUCHIO: Sir, sir, the first's for me, let her go by.
GREMIO: Yea, leave that labor to great Hercules,
And let it be more than Alcides' twelve.
PETRUCHIO: Sir, understand you this of me, in sooth.
The youngest daughter, whom you hearken for,
Her father keeps from all access of suitors
And will not promise her to any man
Until the elder sister first be wed.
The younger then is free, and not before.
TRANIO: If it be so, sir, that you are the man
Must stead us all, and me amongst the rest,
And if you break the ice and do this feat,
Achieve the elder, set the younger free
For our access, whose hap shall be to have her
Will not so graceless be to be ingrate.
HORTENSIO: Sir, you say well, and well you do conceive,
And since you do profess to be a suitor,
You must, as we do, gratify this gentleman,
To whom we all rest generally beholding.
TRANIO: Sir, I shall not be slack, in sign whereof,
Please ye we may contrive this afternoon
And quaff carouses to our mistress' health,

---

237 *Paris* Helen's lover (who took her away from her husband, Menelaus); *came* were to come; *speed* succeed
239 *jade* worthless horse (easily tired)
248 *Alcide* Hercules (so called from his grandfather Alcaeus); *twelve* (Hercules was required to perform twelve labors, or impossible tasks)
249 *sooth* truth
250 *hearken for* ask after
256 *stead* help
258 *Achieve* win
259 *whose hap* he whose luck
261 *well you . . . conceive* you understand the matter well
263 *gratify* reward
264 *beholding* beholden, indebted
266 *contrive* pass the time
267 *quaff carouses* drink toasts

And do as adversaries do in law,
Strive mightily but eat and drink as friends.
GRUMIO, BIONDELLO: O excellent motion! Fellows, let's be gone.
HORTENSIO: The motion's good indeed, and be it so.
Petruchio, I shall be your *benvenuto.* *Exeunt.*

⋆

II.1

Enter Kate and Bianca [with her hands tied].

BIANCA: Good sister, wrong me not, nor wrong yourself,
To make a bondmaid and a slave of me—
That I disdain. But for these other gawds,
Unbind my hands, I'll pull them off myself,
Yea, all my raiment, to my petticoat,
Or what you will command me will I do,
So well I know my duty to my elders.
KATE: Of all thy suitors, here I charge thee, tell
Whom thou lov'st best. See thou dissemble not.
BIANCA: Believe me, sister, of all the men alive
I never yet beheld that special face
Which I could fancy more than any other.
KATE: Minion, thou liest. Is't not Hortensio?
BIANCA: If you affect him, sister, here I swear
I'll plead for you myself but you shall have him.
KATE: O then, belike, you fancy riches more.
You will have Gremio to keep you fair.
BIANCA: Is it for him you do envy me so?
Nay, then you jest, and now I well perceive
You have but jested with me all this while.
I prithee, sister Kate, untie my hands.
KATE: If that be jest then all the rest was so.
Strikes her.
Enter Baptista.
BAPTISTA: Why, how now, dame, whence grows this insolence?
Bianca, stand aside. Poor girl, she weeps.

---

268 *adversaries* lawyers (not their clients)
272 *benvenuto* welcome (Italian)

II.1 Baptista's house
3 *gawds* ornaments
13 *Minion* minx
14 *affect* love
16 *belike* probably
17 *fair* in finery
18 *envy* hate

Go ply thy needle, meddle nor with her.
For shame, thou hilding of a devilish spirit,
Why dost thou wrong her that did ne'er wrong thee?
When did she cross thee with a bitter word?

KATE: Her silence flouts me and I'll be revenged.
Flies after Bianca.

BAPTISTA: What, in my sight? Bianca, get thee in.
Exit [Bianca].

KATE: Will you not suffer me? Nay, now I see
She is your treasure, she must have a husband;
I must dance barefoot on her wedding day,
And for your love to her lead apes in hell.
Talk not to me, I will go sit and weep
Till I can find occasion of revenge. [*Exit.*]

BAPTISTA: Was ever gentleman thus grieved as I?
But who comes here?

Enter Gremio, [with] Lucentio [as a schoolmaster] in the habit of a mean man, Petruchio with [Hortensio as a music master, and] Tranio [as Lucentio] with his boy [Biondello] bearing a lute and books.

GREMIO: Good morrow, neighbor Baptista.

BAPTISTA: Good morrow, neighbor Gremio. God save you, gentlemen.

PETRUCHIO: And you, good sir. Pray, have you not a daughter
Called Katherina, fair and virtuous?

BAPTISTA: I have a daughter, sir, called Katherina.

GREMIO: You are too blunt, go to it orderly.

PETRUCHIO: You wrong me, Signor Gremio, give me leave.
I am a gentleman of Verona, sir,
That, hearing of her beauty and her wit,
Her affability and bashful modesty,
Her wondrous qualities and mild behavior,
Am bold to show myself a forward guest
Within your house, to make mine eye the witness
Of that report which I so oft have heard.
And for an entrance to my entertainment
I do present you with a man of mine,
[*Presenting Hortensio*]
Cunning in music and the mathematics,
To instruct her fully in those sciences,
Whereof I know she is not ignorant.

---

26 *hilding* vicious beast
33 *dance . . . day* (proverbially the fate of an unmarried elder sister)
34 *lead . . . hell* (proverbial fate of old maids)
38 s.d. *habit* garments; *mean* lower-class; *boy* page
44 *orderly* politely
53 *entrance* entrance fee; *entertainment* welcome (as a suitor)

Accept of him or else you do me wrong.
His name is Litio, born in Mantua.

BAPTISTA: You're welcome, sir, and he for your good sake.
But for my daughter Katherine, this I know,
She is not for your turn, the more my grief.

PETRUCHIO: I see you do not mean to part with her,
Or else you like not of my company.

BAPTISTA: Mistake me not, I speak but as I find.
Whence are you, sir? What may I call your name?

PETRUCHIO: Petruchio is my name, Antonio's son,
A man well known throughout all Italy.

BAPTISTA: I know him well, you are welcome for his sake.

GREMIO: Saving your tale, Petruchio, I pray, let us, that are poor petitioners, speak too. Backare, you are marvelous forward.

PETRUCHIO: O pardon me, Signor Gremio, I would fain be doing.

GREMIO: I doubt it not, sir, but you will curse your wooing. Neighbor, this is a gift very grateful, I am sure of it. To express the like kindness, myself, that have been more kindly beholding to you than any, freely give unto you this young scholar, [*Presenting Lucentio*] that hath been long studying at Rheims; as cunning in Greek, Latin, and other languages as the other in music and mathematics. His name is Cambio, pray accept his service.

BAPTISTA: A thousand thanks, Signor Gremio. Welcome, good Cambio. [*To Tranio*] But, gentle sir, methinks you walk like a stranger. May I be so bold to know the cause of your coming?

TRANIO: Pardon me, sir, the boldness is mine own,
That, being a stranger in this city here,
Do make myself a suitor to your daughter,
Unto Bianca, fair and virtuous.
Nor is your firm resolve unknown to me
In the preferment of the eldest sister.
This liberty is all that I request,
That, upon knowledge of my parentage,
I may have welcome 'mongst the rest that woo,
And free access and favor as the rest.
And toward the education of your daughters
I here bestow a simple instrument,
And this small packet of Greek and Latin books.
If you accept them, then their worth is great.

---

59 *Litio* (or Lizio, an old Italian word for garlic; pronounced "Leet-sio")
62 *turn* purpose
69 *know him* i.e., know who he is
70 *Saving* with no disrespect to
71 *Backare* back off (pronounced "back-AR-ay"; mock Latin)
72 *fain* gladly
77 *Rheims* (here pronounced "Reams")
80 *Cambio* (the word means "exchange" in Italian)

BAPTISTA: Lucentio is your name, of whence, I pray? 97
TRANIO: Of Pisa, sir, son to Vincentio.
BAPTISTA: A mighty man of Pisa by report,
I know him well. You are very welcome, sir. 100
[*To Hortensio*]
Take you the lute, [*To Lucentio*] and you the set of books.
You shall go see your pupils presently. 102
Holla, within!
Enter a Servant.
Sirrah, lead these gentlemen
To my daughters, and tell them both
These are their tutors; bid them use them well.
[*Exit Servant with Hortensio,*
Lucentio, and Biondello.]
We will go walk a little in the orchard 107
And then to dinner. You are passing welcome, 108
And so I pray you all to think yourselves.
PETRUCHIO: Signor Baptista, my business asketh haste, 110
And every day I cannot come to woo.
You knew my father well, and in him me,
Left solely heir to all his lands and goods,
Which I have bettered rather than decreased.
Then tell me, if I get your daughter's love
What dowry shall I have with her to wife?
BAPTISTA: After my death the one half of my lands,
And in possession twenty thousand crowns. 118
PETRUCHIO: And for that dowry, I'll assure her of
Her widowhood, be it that she survive me, 120
In all my lands and leases whatsoever.
Let specialties be therefore drawn between us, 122
That covenants may be kept on either hand.
BAPTISTA: Ay, when the special thing is well obtained,
That is, her love, for that is all in all.
PETRUCHIO: Why, that is nothing, for I tell you, father,
I am as peremptory as she proud-minded, 127
And where two raging fires meet together
They do consume the thing that feeds their fury.

---

97 *Lucentio* (Tranio has not mentioned the name yet; does he offer Baptista some identification? Does Baptista find his name in one of the books?)
100 *know him* i.e., know who he is
102 *presently* immediately
107 *orchard* garden
108 *dinner* (the main meal, served at midday); *passing* exceedingly
118 *possession* i.e., immediate possession
120 *widowhood* income if widowed
122 *specialties* contracts
127 *peremptory* determined

Though little fire grows great with little wind,
Yet extreme gusts will blow out fire and all.
So I to her, and so she yields to me,
For I am rough and woo not like a babe.
BAPTISTA: Well mayst thou woo, and happy be thy speed,
But be thou armed for some unhappy words.
PETRUCHIO: Ay, to the proof, as mountains are for winds,
That shakes not though they blow perpetually.
Enter Hortensio [as Litio] with his head broke.
BAPTISTA: How now, my friend, why dost thou look so pale?
HORTENSIO: For fear, I promise you, if I look pale.
BAPTISTA: What, will my daughter prove a good musician?
HORTENSIO: I think she'll sooner prove a soldier.
Iron may hold with her but never lutes.
BAPTISTA: Why, then thou canst not break her to the lute?
HORTENSIO: Why, no, for she hath broke the lute to me.
I did but tell her she mistook her frets
And bowed her hand to teach her fingering,
When, with a most impatient devilish spirit,
"Frets, call you these?" quoth she, "I'll fume with them."
And with that word she struck me on the head,
And through the instrument my pate made way,
And there I stood amazed for a while
As on a pillory, looking through the lute,
While she did call me rascal, fiddler,
And twangling jack, with twenty such vile terms,
As had she studied to misuse me so.
PETRUCHIO: Now, by the world, it is a lusty wench.
I love her ten times more than e'er I did.
O how I long to have some chat with her!
BAPTISTA: [*To Hortensio*]
Well, go with me, and be not so discomfited.
Proceed in practice with my younger daughter.
She's apt to learn and thankful for good turns.
Signor Petruchio, will you go with us
Or shall I send my daughter Kate to you?

---

134 *speed* fortune
136 *to the proof* in tested armor
137 s.d, *broke* i.e., with the skin broken, bleeding
142 *hold with her* (1) suit her, (2) withstand her; *lutes* (playing on "cement made of clay")
143 *break* tame
145 *frets* rings of gut, placed on the fingerboard to regulate the fingering (Kate quibbled on "fret and fume," be indignant)
146 *bowed* bent
154 *Jack* knave
156 *lusty* lively
161 *apt* willing

PETRUCHIO: I pray you do. I will attend her here,

Exit [Baptista with Gremio, Tranio, and Hortensio]. Manet Petruchio.

And woo her with some spirit when she comes.
Say that she rail, why then I'll tell her plain
She sings as sweetly as a nightingale.
Say that she frown, I'll say she looks as clear
As morning roses newly washed with dew.
Say she be mute and will not speak a word,
Then I'll commend her volubility
And say she uttereth piercing eloquence.
If she do bid me pack I'll give her thanks
As though she bid me stay by her a week.
If she deny to wed I'll crave the day
When I shall ask the banns, and when be married.

Enter Kate.

But here she comes, and now, Petruchio, speak.
Good morrow, Kate, for that's your name, I hear.

KATE: Well have you heard, but something hard of hearing.
They call me Katherine that do talk of me.

PETRUCHIO: You lie, in faith, for you are called plain Kate,
And bonny Kate, and sometimes Kate the curst.
But Kate, the prettiest Kate in Christendom,
Kate of Kate Hall, my superdainty Kate,
For dainties are all cates, and therefore, Kate,
Take this of me, Kate of my consolation:
Hearing thy mildness praised in every town,
Thy virtues spoke of, and thy beauty sounded,
Yet not so deeply as to thee belongs,
Myself am moved to woo thee for my wife.

KATE: Moved? In good time: let him that moved you hither
Remove you hence. I knew you at the first,
You were a movable.

PETRUCHIO: Why, what's a movable?

KATE: A joint stool.

PETRUCHIO: Thou hast hit it: come sit on me.

KATE: Asses are made to bear, and so are you.

---

164 *attend* wait for
175 *deny* refuse
176 *ask the banns* announce in church the intent to marry
179 *hard* (playing on *heard*, pronounced similarly)
182 *bonny* strapping
185 *dainties* delicacies; *cates* choice foods (playing, of course, on "Kates")
188 *sounded* proclaimed (with a play, in *deeply* on "plumbed")
191 *In good time* indeed
194 *movable* piece of furniture
195 *joint stool* stool made by a joiner ("I took you for a joint stool" was a standard joke, meaning "you're not worth noticing")

PETRUCHIO: Women are made to bear, and so are you.
KATE: No such jade as you, if me you mean.
PETRUCHIO: Alas, good Kate, I will not burden thee,
  For knowing thee to be but young and light.
KATE: Too light for such a swain as you to catch,
  And yet as heavy as my weight should be.
PETRUCHIO: Should be? should—buzz!
KATE: Well ta'en, and like a buzzard.
PETRUCHIO: O slow-winged turtle! Shall a buzzard take thee?
KATE: Ay, for a turtle, as he takes a buzzard.
PETRUCHIO: Come, come, you wasp, i' faith you are too angry.
KATE: If I be waspish best beware my sting.
PETRUCHIO: My remedy is then to pluck it out.
KATE: Ay, if the fool could find it where it lies.
PETRUCHIO: Who knows not where a wasp does wear his sting?
  In his tail.
KATE: In his tongue.
PETRUCHIO: Whose tongue?
KATE: Yours, if you talk of tales, and so farewell.
PETRUCHIO: What, with my tongue in your tail?
  Nay, come again, good Kate, I am a gentleman.
KATE: That I'll try.
  She strikes him.
PETRUCHIO: I swear I'll cuff you if you strike again.
KATE: So may you lose your arms.
  If you strike me you are no gentleman,
  And if no gentleman, why then no arms.
PETRUCHIO: A herald, Kate? O put me in thy books.
KATE: What is your crest, a coxcomb?
PETRUCHIO: A combless cock, so Kate will be my hen.
KATE: No cock of mine, you crow too like a craven.
PETRUCHIO: Nay, come, Kate, come, you must not look so sour.

---

198 *bear* (1) bear children, (2) bear the weight of men in lovemaking
199 *jade* worthless horse
201 *For knowing* because I know; *light* (1) weak, (2) inconsequential, (3) flirtatious
202 *swain* peasant lover
203 *heavy . . . be* (the image is from coinage; not counterfeit or cut down)
204 *buzz* (exclamation meaning "nonsense," playing on *be[e]*); *buzzard* untrainable type of hawk, hence fool
205 *turtle* turtledove
206 *buzzard* (the term was applied to large moths and beetles, insects that the dove doesn't like: the line means "you're a fool if you think I'm a turtledove")
220 *arms* coat of arms
223 *in thy books* in your heraldic registers (playing on "in your good graces")
224 *crest* armorial device; *coxcomb* cap of a court fool (playing on *crest,* comb; Petruchio then quibbles on "cock's comb")
225 *combless* gentle (with "comb" or crest cut down)
226 *craven* cock that will not fight

KATE: It is my fashion when I see a crab.
PETRUCHIO: Why, here's no crab, and therefore look not sour.
KATE: There is, there is.
PETRUCHIO: Then show it me.
KATE: Had I a glass I would.
PETRUCHIO: What, you mean my face?
KATE: Well aimed of such a young one.
PETRUCHIO: Now, by Saint George, I am too young for you.
KATE: Yet you are withered.
PETRUCHIO: 'Tis with cares.
KATE: I care not.
PETRUCHIO: Nay, hear you, Kate, in sooth you scape not so.
KATE: I chafe you if I tarry; let me go.
PETRUCHIO: No, not a whit. I find you passing gentle.
'Twas told me you were rough and coy and sullen,
And now I find report a very liar,
For thou art pleasant, gamesome, passing courteous,
But slow in speech, yet sweet as springtime flowers,
Thou canst not frown, thou canst not look askance,
Nor bite the lip as angry wenches will,
Nor hast thou pleasure to be cross in talk.
But thou with mildness entertain'st thy wooers,
With gentle conference, soft and affable.
Why does the world report that Kate doth limp?
O sland'rous world! Kate like a hazel twig
Is straight and slender, and as brown in hue
As hazelnuts and sweeter than the kernels,
O let me see thee walk. Thou dost not halt.
KATE: Go, fool, and whom thou keep'st command.
PETRUCHIO: Did ever Dian so become a grove
As Kate this chamber with her princely gait?
O be thou Dian and let her be Kate.
And then let Kate be chaste and Dian sportful.
KATE: Where did you study all this goodly speech?
PETRUCHIO: It is extempore, from my mother wit.
KATE: A witty mother, witless else her son.

---

228 *crab* crab apple (notoriously sour)
231 *glass* looking glass
233 *aimed of* guessed for; *young* inexperienced
236 *sooth* truth
239 *coy* haughty
243 *askance* scornfully
252 *halt* limp
253 *whom thou keep'st* i.e., your servants
254 *Dian* Diana (goddess of virginity and of the hunt)
257 *sportful* amorous
259 *mother wit* native intelligence
260 *witless . . . son* otherwise her son would be witless (his only wit being inherited from her)

KETRUCHIO: Am I not wise?
KATE: Yes, keep you warm.
PETRUCHIO: Marry, so I mean, sweet Katherine, in thy bed.
And therefore, setting all this chat aside,
Thus in plain terms. Your father hath consented
That you shall be my wife, your dowry 'greed upon,
And will you, nill you, I will marry you.
Now, Kate, I am a husband for your turn,
For by this light, whereby I see thy beauty—
Thy beauty that doth make me like thee well—
Thou must be married to no man but me,
Enter Baptista, Gremio, [and] Tranio [as Lucentio].
For I am he am born to tame you. Kate,
And bring you from a wild Kate to a Kate
Conformable as other household Kates.
Here comes your father. Never make denial,
I must and will have Katherine to my wife.
BAPTISTA: Now, Signor Petruchio, how speed you with my daughter?
PETRUCHIO: How but well, sir? How but well?
It were impossible I should speed amiss.
BAPTISTA: Why, how now, daughter Katherine? In your dumps?
KATE: Call you me daughter? Now, I promise you
You have showed a tender fatherly regard
To wish me wed to one half lunatic.
A madcap ruffian and a swearing jack,
That thinks with oaths to face the matter out.
PETRUCHIO: Father, 'tis thus. Yourself and all the world
That talked of her have talked amiss of her.
If she be curst it is for policy,
For she's not froward but modest as the dove.
She is not hot but temperate as the morn.
For patience she will prove a second Grissel,
And Roman Lucrece for her chastity.
And, to conclude, we have 'greed so well together
That upon Sunday is the wedding day,

---

262 *keep you warm* i.e., take care of yourself (to have the wit or wisdom to keep warm being proverbial)
267 *will you, nill you* whether you will or not
268 *for your turn* to suit you
273 *wild Kate* (punning on "wildcat")
277 *speed* succeed
281 *promise* assure
285 *face* brazen
288 *policy* cunning
290 *hot* of angry disposition
291 *Grissel* Griselda (the epitome of wifely patience and obedience; cf. Boccaccio's *Decameron*, X, 10, or Chaucer's Clerk's Tale)
292 *Lucrece* (she killed herself after being raped by Sextus Tarquinius, hence became the epitome of wifely chastity and honor; cf. Shakespeare's *Lucrece*)

KATE: I'll see thee hanged on Sunday first.
GREMIO: Hark, Petruchio, she says she'll see thee hanged first.
TRANIO: Is this your speeding? Nay, then good night our part!
PETRUCHIO: Be patient, gentlemen, I choose her for myself.
If she and I be pleased, what's that to you?
'Tis bargained 'twixt us twain, being alone,
That she shall still be curst in company.
I tell you, 'tis incredible to believe
How much she loves me. O the kindest Kate!
She hung about my neck, and kiss on kiss
She vied so fast, protesting oath on oath,
That in a twink she won me to her love.
O you are novices. 'Tis a world to see
How tame, when men and women are alone,
A meacock wretch can make the curstest shrew.
Give me thy hand, Kate, I will unto Venice
To buy apparel 'gainst the wedding day.
Provide the feast, father, and bid the guests.
I will be sure my Katherine shall be fine,
BAPTISTA: I know not what to say—but give me your hands.
God send you joy! Petruchio, 'tis a match.
GREMIO, TRANIO: Amen, say we, we will be witnesses.
PETRUCHIO: Father, and wife, and gentlemen, adieu.
I will to Venice. Sunday comes apace.
We will have rings and things and fine array,
And kiss me, Kate, [*Sings.*] "We will be married a Sunday."

Exeunt Petruchio and Kate [severally].

GREMIO: Was ever match clapped up so suddenly?
BAPTISTA: Faith, gentlemen, now I play a merchant's part
And venture madly on a desperate mart.
TRANIO: 'Twas a commodity lay fretting by you.
'Twill bring you gain or perish on the seas,
BAPTISTA: The gain I seek is quiet in the match.
GREMIO: No doubt but he hath got a quiet catch.
But now, Baptista, to your younger daughter.
Now is the day we long have looked for.
I am your neighbor and was suitor first.

---

297 *speeding* success; *good . . . part* good-bye to our hopes (of marrying Bianca)
305 *vied* raised the bid (cardplaying term)
307 *world* i.e., worth a world
309 *meacock* cowardly
311 *'gainst* in anticipation of
313 *fine* finely dressed
320 s.d. *severally* at different doors
321 *match* contract (with a play on "mating"); *clapped up* shaken hands on, agreed to
323 *mart* bargain
324 *fretting* (of a stored commodity that decays, as wool "fretted" by moths; with a play on "chafing")

TRANIO: And I am one that love Bianca more
Than words can witness or your thoughts can guess.
GREMIO: Youngling, thou canst not love so dear as I.
TRANIO: Graybeard, thy love doth freeze.
GREMIO: But thine doth fry.
Skipper, stand back, 'tis age that nourisheth.
TRANIO: But youth in ladies' eyes that flourisheth.
BAPTISTA: Content you, gentlemen, I will compound this strife.
'Tis deeds must win the prize, and he of both
That can assure my daughter greatest dower
Shall have Bianca's love.
Say, Signor Gremio, what can you assure her?
GREMIO: First, as you know, my house within the city
Is richly furnished with plate and gold,
Basins and ewers to lave her dainty hands;
My hangings all of Tyrian tapestry;
In ivory coffers I have stuffed my crowns;
In cypress chests my arras counterpoints,
Costly apparel, tents, and canopies,
Fine linen, Turkey cushions bossed with pearl,
Valance of Venice gold in needlework,
Pewter and brass, and all things that belongs
To house or housekeeping. Then at my farm
I have a hundred milk kine to the pail,
Six score fat oxen standing in my stalls,
And all things answerable to this portion.
Myself am struck in years, I must confess,
And if I die tomorrow this is hers,
If whilst I live she will be only mine.
TRANIO: That "only" came well in. Sir, list to me.
I am my father's heir and only son.
If I may have your daughter to my wife
I'll leave her houses three or four as good,
Within rich Pisa walls, as any one

---

335 *Skipper* flighty youth
337 *compound* settle
338 *he of both* whichever of the two (of you)
339 *assure* guarantee; *dower* portion of the husband's estate left to the widow
344 *lave* wash
345 *Tyrian* purple
346 *crowns* money
347 *arras counterpoints* quilted tapestry counterpanes
348 *tents, canopies* (types of bed hangings)
349 *bossed* embroidered
350 *Valance* drapery for the bed canopy
353 *milk kine . . . pail* dairy cows
355 *all . . . portion* all my possessions are equally valuable
356 *struck* advanced

Old Signor Gremio has in Padua,
Besides two thousand ducats by the year
Of fruitful land, all which shall be her jointure.
What, have I pinched you, Signor Gremio?
GREMIO: Two thousand ducats by the year of land!
[*Aside*]
My land amounts not to so much in all.—
That she shall have, besides an argosy
That now is lying in Marseilles' road.
What, have I choked you with an argosy?
TRANIO: Gremio, 'tis known my father hath no less
Than three great argosies, besides two galliasses
And twelve tight galleys. These I will assure her
And twice as much whate'er thou off'rest next.
GREMIO: Nay, I have offered all, I have no more,
And she can have no more than all I have,
If you like me, she shall have me and mine.
TRANIO: Why, then the maid is mine from all the world
By your firm promise. Gremio is outvied.
BAPTISTA: I must confess your offer is the best,
And let your father make her the assurance,
She is your own, else you must pardon me.
If you should die before him, where's her dower?
TRANIO: That's but a cavil. He is old, I young.
GREMIO: And may not young men die as well as old?
BAPTISTA: Well, gentlemen, I am thus resolved.
On Sunday next, you know,
My daughter Katherine is to be married.
Now on the Sunday following shall Bianca
Be bride to you, if you make this assurance.
If not, to Signor Gremio.
And so I take my leave and thank you both. *Exit.*
GREMIO: Adieu, good neighbor. Now I fear thee not.
Sirrah young gamester, your father were a fool
To give thee all and in his waning age
Set foot under thy table. Tut, a toy!
An old Italian fox is not so kind, my boy. *Exit.*

---

365 *ducats* gold coins
366 *Of* i.e., the income from; *jointure* settlement
370 *argosy* large merchant ship
371 *Marseilles'* (pronounced "Marsellus"); *road* harbor
374 *galliasses* large galleys
375 *tight* sound, well caulked
381 *outvied* outbid
383 *assurance* guarantee
396 *Sirrah* (contemptuous to a person of equal rank); *were* would be
398 *Set . . . table* i.e., become your dependent; *a toy* nonsense

TRANIO: A vengeance on your crafty withered hide!
Yet I have faced it with a card of ten.
'Tis in my head to do my master good.
I see no reason but supposed Lucentio
Must get a father, called supposed Vincentio;
And that's a wonder. Fathers commonly
Do get their children, but in this case of wooing
A child shall get a sire if I fail not of my cunning.
Exit.

★

III.1

Enter Lucentio [as Cambio], Hortensio [as Litio], and Bianca.

LUCENTIO: Fiddler, forbear, you grow too forward, sir.
Have you so soon forgot the entertainment
Her sister Katherine welcomed you withal?
HORTENSIO: But, wrangling pedant, this is
The patroness of heavenly harmony.
Then give me leave to have prerogative,
And when in music we have spent an hour
Your lecture shall have leisure for as much.
LUCENTIO: Preposterous ass, that never read so far
To know the cause why music was ordained!
Was it not to refresh the mind of man
After his studies or his usual pain?
Then give me leave to read philosophy,
And while I pause, serve in your harmony.
HORTENSIO: Sirrah, I will not bear these braves of thine.
BIANCA: Why, gentlemen, you do me double wrong
To strive for that which resteth in my choice.
I am no breeching scholar in the schools.
I'll not be tied to hours nor 'pointed times,
But learn my lessons as I please myself.
And, to cut off all strife, here sit we down.

---

401 *faced . . . ten* bluffed successfully with a ten-spot
406 *get* beget

III.1 Baptista's house
5 *patroness* goddess
6 *prerogative* precedence
8 *lecture* lesson
12 *pain* toil
13 *read* teach
15 *braves* insults
18 *breeching scholar* schoolboy liable to whipping

Take you your instrument, play you the whiles;
His lecture will be done ere you have tuned.
HORTENSIO: You'll leave his lecture when I am in tune?
LUCENTIO: That will be never. Tune your instrument.
BIANCA: Where left we last?
LUCENTIO: Here, madam:
[*Reads.*]
"Hic ibat Simois, hic est Sigeia tellus,
Hic steterat Priami regia celsa senis."
BIANCA: Conster them.
LUCENTIO: "Hic ibat," as I told you before; "Simois," I am Lucentio; "hic est," son unto Vincentio of Pisa; "Sigeia tellus," disguised thus to get your love; "Hic steterat," and that Lucentio that comes a-wooing; "Priami," is my man Tranio; "regia," bearing my port; "celsa senis," that we might beguile the old pantaloon.
HORTENSIO: Madam, my instrument's in tune.
BIANCA: Let's hear. [*He plays.*] O fie, the treble jars.
LUCENTIO: Spit in the hole, man, and tune again.
BIANCA: Now let me see if I can conster it.
"Hic ibat Simois," I know you not; "hic est Sigeia tellus," I trust you not; "Hic steterat Priami," take heed he hear us not; "regia," presume not; "celsa senis," despair not.
HORTENSIO: Madam, 'tis now in tune.
LUCENTIO: All but the bass.
HORTENSIO: The bass is right, 'tis the base knave that jars.
[*Aside*]
How fiery and forward our pedant is!
Now, for my life, the knave doth court my love.
Pedascule, I'll watch you better yet.
BIANCA: In time I may believe, yet I mistrust.
LUCENTIO: Mistrust it not, for sure Aeacides
Was Ajax, called so from his grandfather.
BIANCA: I must believe my master, else I promise you,
I should be arguing still upon that doubt.

---

22 *the whiles* meanwhile

28–29 *Hic . . . senis* here flowed the Simois, here lies the Sigeian plain, here stood the lofty palace of old Priam (Ovid, *Epistolae Heroidum*, I, a letter from Penelope to Ulysses)

30 *Conster* construe (translate)

34 *bearing my port* behaving as I would

35 *pantaloon* foolish old man

37 *jars* is discordant

38 *Spit in the hole* (to make the peg hold)

45 *pedant* schoolmaster or tutor

47 *Pedascule* (Latin coinage from *pedant*, contemptuously diminutive; four syllables)

49 *Aeacides* descendant of Aeacus (Lucentio explains a reference in the line of Ovid's epistle that follows immediately after the two lines already quoted)

50 *Ajax* one of the Greek heroes at Troy

But let it rest. Now, Litio, to you.
Good master, take it not unkindly, pray,
That I have been thus pleasant with you both.
HORTENSIO: You may go walk and give me leave a while.
My lessons make no music in three parts. 57
LUCENTIO: Are you so formal, sir? [*Aside*] Well, I must wait 58
And watch withal, for but I be deceived, 59
Our fine musician groweth amorous. 60
HORTENSIO: Madam, before you touch the instrument
To learn the order of my fingering,
I must begin with rudiments of art,
To teach you gamut in a briefer sort, 64
More pleasant, pithy, and effectual
Than hath been taught by any of my trade.
And there it is in writing, fairly drawn.
BIANCA: Why, I am past my gamut long ago.
HORTENSIO: Yet read the gamut of Hortensio. 69
BIANCA: [*Reads.*]
"*Gamut* I am, the ground of all accord, 70
A re, to plead Hortensio's passion;
B mi, Bianca, take him for thy lord,
C fa ut, that loves with all affection; 73
D sol re, one clef, two notes have I;
E la mi, show pity or I die."
Call you this gamut? Tut, I like it not.
Old fashions please me best; I am not so nice 77
To change true rules for odd inventions.
Enter a Messenger.
MESSENGER: Mistress, your father prays you leave your books
And help to dress your sister's chamber up. 80
You know tomorrow is the wedding day.
BIANCA: Farewell, sweet masters both, I must be gone.
[*Exeunt Bianca and Messenger.*]
LUCENTIO: Faith, mistress, then I have no cause to stay.
[*Exit.*]
HORTENSIO: But I have cause to pry into this pedant.
Methinks he looks as though he were in love.
Yet if thy thoughts, Bianca, be so humble

---

57 *in three parts* for three voices
58 *formal* precise
59 *withal* at the same time; *but* unless
64 *gamut* the scale
69 s.d. *Reads* (she intones each line on the appropriate note)
70 *ground* (*gamut* is also the lowest note, or ground, of the scale; also called *ut*, as in l. 73, or, in modern terminology, "do"); *accord* harmony
73–75 *ut, re, mi* (repeated because a second scale starts at C)
77 *nice* capricious

To cast thy wand'ring eyes on every stale.
Seize thee that list. If once I find thee ranging,
Hortensio will be quit with thee by changing. *Exit.*

★

III.2

Enter Baptista, Gremio, Tranio [as Lucentio], Kate, Bianca, [Lucentio as Cambio,] and others (Attendants).

BAPTISTA: [*To Tranio*]
Signor Lucentio, this is the 'pointed day
That Katherine and Petruchio should be married,
And yet we hear not of our son-in-law.
What will be said? What mockery will it be
To want the bridegroom when the priest attends
To speak the ceremonial rites of marriage?
What says Lucentio to this shame of ours?
KATE: No shame but mine. I must, forsooth, be forced
To give my hand opposed against my heart
Unto a mad-brain rudesby, full of spleen,
Who wooed in haste and means to wed at leisure.
I told you, I, he was a frantic fool,
Hiding his bitter jests in blunt behavior.
And to be noted for a merry man,
He'll woo a thousand, 'point the day of marriage,
Make friends, invite, and proclaim the banns,
Yet never means to wed where he hath wooed.
Now must the world point at poor Katherine
And say, "Lo, there is mad Petruchio's wife,
If it would please him come and marry her."
TRANIO: Patience, good Katherine, and Baptista too.
Upon my life, Petruchio means but well,
Whatever fortune stays him from his word.
Though he be blunt, I know him passing wise;
Though he be merry, yet withal he's honest.
KATE: Would Katherine had never seen him though!
Exit weeping.

---

87 *stale* decoy, bait
88 *Seize . . . list* let him take you that pleases; *ranging* straying
89 *be quit* get even; *changing* i.e., to another love

III.2 Before Baptista's house
5 *want* lack
8 *forsooth* indeed
10 *rudesby* boor; *spleen* capriciousness
14 *noted for* known as
25 *withal* at the same time

BAPTISTA: Go, girl, I cannot blame thee now to weep,
For such an injury would vex a very saint,
Much more a shrew of thy impatient humor.

Enter Biondello.

BIONDELLO: Master, master, old news! And such news as you never heard of!

BAPTISTA: Is it new and old too? How may that be?

BIONDELLO: Why, is it not news to hear of Petruchio's coming?

BAPTISTA: Is he come?

BIONDELLO: Why, no, sir.

BAPTISTA: What then?

BIONDELLO: He is coming.

BAPTISTA: When will he be here?

BIONDELLO: When he stands where I am and sees you there.

TRANIO: But say, what to thine old news?

BIONDELLO: Why, Petruchio is coming, in a new hat and an old jerkin; a pair of old breeches thrice turned; a pair of boots that have been candle cases, one buckled, another laced; an old rusty sword ta'en out of the town armory, with a broken hilt and chapeless; with two broken points; his horse hipped—with an old mothy saddle and stirrups of no kindred—besides, possessed with the glanders and like to mose in the chine; troubled with the lampas, infected with the fashions, full of windgalls, sped with spavins, rayed with the yellows, past cure of the fives, stark spoiled with the staggers, begnawn with the bots, swayed in the back, and shoulder-shotten; near-legged before, and with a half-checked bit and a headstall of sheep's leather which, being restrained to keep him from stumbling, hath been often burst and new-repaired with knots; one girth six times pieced, and a

---

29 *humor* disposition
30 *old* great, rare (Baptista misunderstands)
40 *to* about
41 *jerkin* jacket
42–43 *candle cases* (worn-out boots were sometimes hung on the wall to hold candle ends and the like)
44 *chapeless* without the metal plate on the scabbard covering the sword point
45 *points* laces holding up his breeches; *hipped* lamed in the hip
46 *possessed* afflicted; *glanders* horse disease affecting the nose and mouth
46–47 *mose . . . chine* grow weak in the back (chine is the spine, but mose has not been satisfactorily explained)
47 *lampas* infected mouth; *fashions* (or "farcins") equine ulcerations
48 *windgalls* leg tumors; *sped . . . spavins* destroyed by inflammations of the joints; *rayed . . . yellows* streaked with jaundice
49 *fives* (or "avives") swelling of the glands behind the ears; *stark* utterly; *staggers* equine palsy; *begnawn . . . bots* eaten up by intestinal worms
50 *shoulder-shotten* weak in the shoulder; *near-legged before* knock-kneed in front
51 *half-checked bit* bit that is only halfway effective; *headstall* part of the bridle going around the head; *sheep's leather* (inferior to pigskin)
52 *restrained* drawn back
53 *pieced* patched

woman's crupper of velure which hath two letters for her name 54
fairly set down in studs, and here and there pieced with packthread. 55
BAPTISTA: Who comes with him?
BIONDELLO: O sir, his lackey, for all the world caparisoned like the horse:
with a linen stock on one leg and a kersey boothose on the other, 58
gartered with a red and blue list; an old hat and the humor of forty 59
fancies pricked in't for a feather—a monster, a very monster in 60
apparel, and not like a Christian footboy or a gentleman's lackey. 61
TRANIO: 'Tis some odd humor pricks him to this fashion, 62
Yet oftentimes he goes but mean-appareled.
BAPTISTA: I am glad he's come, howsoe'er he comes.
BIONDELLO: Why, sir, he comes not.
BAPTISTA: Didst thou not say he comes?
BIONDELLO: Who? That Petruchio came?
BAPTISTA: Ay, that Petruchio came.
BIONDELLO: No, sir, I say his horse comes, with him on his back.
BAPTISTA: Why, that's all one. 70
BIONDELLO: [*Sings.*]
Nay, by Saint Jamy,
I hold you a penny, 72
A horse and a man
Is more than one
And yet not many.

Enter Petruchio and Grumio.

PETRUCHIO: Come, where be these gallants? Who's at home?
BAPTISTA: You are welcome, sir.
PETRUCHIO: And yet I come not well.
BAPTISTA: And yet you halt not. 78
TRANIO: Not so well appareled as I wish you were.
PETRUCHIO: Were it better, I should rush in thus. 80
But where is Kate? Where is my lovely bride?
How does my father? Gentles, methinks you frown.
And wherefore gaze this goodly company

---

54 *crupper* strap that passes under the horse's tail to keep the saddle in place; *velure* velvet (the crupper would normally be of leather; a velvet one would be largely useless for serious riding); *two letters* (the initials of the woman whose velvet crupper Petruchio is using)
55 *pieced* tied together
58 *stock* stocking; *kersey boothose* coarse woolen overstocking
59 *list* strip of cloth
59–60 *humor . . . fancies* (not satisfactorily explained: presumably a wildly fanciful decoration)
60 *pricked* pinned
61 *footboy* page
62 *humor* whim; *pricks* drives
70 *all one* the same thing
72 *hold* bet
78 *halt* limp (Baptista quibbles on *come* in the sense of "walk")
80 *it* i.e., my apparel

As if they saw some wondrous monument,
Some comet or unusual prodigy?

BAPTISTA: Why, sir, you know this is your wedding day.
First were we sad, fearing you would not come,
Now sadder that you come so unprovided.
Fie, doff this habit, shame to your estate,
An eyesore to our solemn festival.

TRANIO: And tell us what occasion of import
Hath all so long detained you from your wife
And sent you hither so unlike yourself?

PETRUCHIO: Tedious it were to tell and harsh to hear.
Sufficeth I am come to keep my word,
Though in some part enforcèd to digress,
Which at more leisure I will so excuse
As you shall well be satisfied with all.
But where is Kate? I stay too long from her.
The morning wears, 'tis time we were at church.

TRANIO: See not your bride in these unreverent robes.
Go to my chamber; put on clothes of mine.

PETRUCHIO: Not I, believe me. Thus I'll visit her.

BAPTISTA: But thus, I trust, you will not marry her?

PETRUCHIO: Good sooth, even thus. Therefore ha' done with words.
To me she's married, not unto my clothes.
Could I repair what she will wear in me
As I can change these poor accoutrements,
'Twere well for Kate and better for myself.
But what a fool am I to chat with you
When I should bid good morrow to my bride
And seal the title with a lovely kiss. *Exit [with Grumio].*

TRANIO: He hath some meaning in his mad attire.
We will persuade him, be it possible,
To put on better ere he go to church.

BAPTISTA: I'll after him and see the event of this.
Exit [with Bianca, Gremio, and Attendants].

TRANIO: But sir, to love concerneth us to add
Her father's liking, which to bring to pass,
As I before imparted to your worship,

---

85 *prodigy* unnatural phenomenon
88 *unprovided* improperly equipped
89 *habit* clothing; *estate* social position
96 *digress* deviate (from his intention to dress well; see II.1.316)
100 *wears* is passing
105 *Good sooth* indeed
107 *wear* wear out
112 *seal the title* confirm my rights; *lovely* loving
116 *event* outcome
117–18 *to love . . . liking* i.e., to woo Bianca successfully we need her father's approval in addition (the speech appears to begin in the middle of the conversation)

I am to get a man—whate'er he be
It skills not much, we'll fit him to our turn—
And he shall be Vincentio of Pisa,
And make assurance here in Padua
Of greater sums than I have promisèd.
So shall you quietly enjoy your hope
And marry sweet Bianca with consent.
LUCENTIO: Were it not that my fellow schoolmaster
Doth watch Bianca's steps so narrowly,
'Twere good, methinks, to steal our marriage,
Which once performed, let all the world say no,
I'll keep mine own despite of all the world.
TRANIO: That by degrees we mean to look into
And watch our vantage in this business.
We'll overreach the graybeard, Gremio,
The narrow-prying father, Minola,
The quaint musician, amorous Litio—
All for my master's sake, Lucentio.
Enter Gremio.
Signor Gremio, come you from the church?
GREMIO: As willingly as e'er I came from school.
TRANIO: And is the bride and bridegroom coming home?
GREMIO: A bridegroom, say you? 'Tis a groom indeed,
A grumbling groom, and that the girl shall find.
TRANIO: Curster than she? Why, 'tis impossible.
GREMIO: Why, he's a devil, a devil, a very fiend.
TRANIO: Why, she's a devil, a devil, the devil's dam.
GREMIO: Tut, she's a lamb, a dove, a fool to him.
I'll tell you, Sir Lucentio. When the priest
Did ask if Katherine should be his wife,
"Ay, by gog's wouns," quoth he, and swore so loud
That, all amazed, the priest let fall the book,
And as he stooped again to take it up
This mad-brained bridegroom took him such a cuff
That down fell priest and book, and book and priest.
"Now, take them up," quoth he, "if any list."

---

121 *skills* matters; *turn* purpose
123 *make assurance* give guarantees
128 *narrowly* closely
129 *steal . . . marriage* elope
133 *watch our vantage* look out for our opportunity
136 *quaint* crafty
141 *groom* (quibbling on "servant," "boor")
145 *dam* mother
146 *a fool to* an innocent compared with
149 *by gogs wouns* by God's (Christ's) wounds
152 *took* gave
154 *take* pick; *if any list* if anyone pleases

TRANIO: What said the wench when he rose again?
GREMIO: Trembled and shook, for why he stamped and swore, 156
As if the vicar meant to cozen him. 157
But after many ceremonies done
He calls for wine. "A health!" quoth he, as if
He had been aboard, carousing to his mates
After a storm; quaffed off the muscadel 161
And threw the sops all in the sexton's face, 162
Having no other reason
But that his beard grew thin and hungerly 164
And seemed to ask him sops as he was drinking.
This done, he took the bride about the neck
And kissed her lips with such a clamorous smack
That at the parting all the church did echo.
I, seeing this, came thence for very shame,
And after me, I know, the rout is coming.
Such a mad marriage never was before.
Hark, hark, I hear the minstrels play.

Music plays.
Enter Petruchio, Kate, Bianca, Hortensio [as Litio], Baptista [, and Grumio, with Attendants].

PETRUCHIO: Gentlemen and friends, I thank you for your pains.
I know you think to dine with me today
And have prepared great store of wedding cheer,
But so it is, my haste doth call me hence
And therefore here I mean to take my leave.
BAPTISTA: Is't possible you will away tonight?
PETRUCHIO: I must away today, before night come.
Make it no wonder. If you knew my business
You would entreat me rather go than stay.
And, honest company, I thank you all,
That have beheld me give away myself
To this most patient, sweet, and virtuous wife.
Dine with my father, drink a health to me,
For I must hence; and farewell to you all.
TRANIO: Let us entreat you stay till after dinner.
PETRUCHIO: It may not be.

---

156 *for why* because
157 *cozen* cheat (with an invalid ceremony)
161 *muscadel* (or muscatel) a sweet wine (Petruchio should be offering it to the guests, not drinking it himself)
162 *sops* cakes dipped in the wine
164 *hungerly* sparsely
165 *ask him* ask him for
170 *rout* mob
175 *cheer* entertainment
180 *Make* consider

GREMIO: Let me entreat you.
PETRUCHIO: It cannot be.
KATE: Let me entreat you.
PETRUCHIO: I am content.
KATE: Are you content to stay?
PETRUCHIO: I am content you shall entreat me stay,
But yet not stay, entreat me how you can.
KATE: Now if you love me, stay.
PETRUCHIO: Grumio, my horse!
GRUMIO: Ay, sir, they be ready; the oats have eaten the horses.
KATE: Nay then,
Do what thou canst, I will not go today,
No, nor tomorrow nor till I please myself.
The door is open, sir, there lies your way;
You may be jogging whiles your boots are green.
For me, I'll not be gone till I please myself.
'Tis like you'll prove a jolly surly groom,
That take it on you at the first so roundly.
PETRUCHIO: O Kate, content thee; prithee, be not angry.
KATE: I will be angry. What hast thou to do?
Father, be quiet, he shall stay my leisure.
GREMIO: Ay, marry, sir, now it begins to work.
KATE: Gentlemen, forward to the bridal dinner.
I see a woman may be made a fool
If she had not a spirit to resist.
PETRUCHIO: They shall go forward, Kate, at thy command.
Obey the bride, you that attend on her,
Go to the feast, revel and domineer,
Carouse full measure to her maidenhead,
Be mad and merry or go hang yourselves.
But for my bonny Kate, she must with me.
Nay, look not big, nor stamp, nor stare, nor fret;
I will be master of what is mine own.
She is my goods, my chattels; she is my house,
My household stuff, my field, my barn,
My horse, my ox, my ass, my anything;
And here she stands, touch her whoever dare.

---

195 *horse* horses (old plural)
196 *the oats . . . horses* (Grumio gets it backwards)
201 *You may . . . green* (proverbial for getting an early start); *green* i.e., fresh
203 *jolly* arrogant
204 *take it on you* assert yourself; *roundly* unceremoniously
206 *What . . . do* what business is it of yours
214 *domineer* carouse
218 *big* threatening
220–22 *my house . . . ass* (echoing the Tenth Commandment, "Thou shalt not covet thy neighbor's house . . . nor his ox, nor his ass . . .")

I'll bring mine action on the proudest he
That stops my way in Padua. Grumio,
Draw forth thy weapon, we are beset with thieves.
Rescue thy mistress, if thou be a man.
Fear not, sweet wench; they shall not touch thee, Kate.
I'll buckler thee against a million.
Exeunt Petruchio, Kate [, and Grumio].

BAPTISTA: Nay, let them go, a couple of quiet ones.
GREMIO: Went they not quickly, I should die with laughing.
TRANIO: Of all mad matches never was the like.
LUCENTIO: Mistress, what's your opinion of your sister?
BIANCA: That being mad herself, she's madly mated.
GREMIO: I warrant him, Petruchio is Kated.
BAPTISTA: Neighbors and friends, though bride and bridegroom wants
For to supply the places at the table,
You know there wants no junkets at the feast.
Lucentio, you supply the bridegroom's place,
And let Bianca take her sister's room.
TRANIO: Shall sweet Bianca practice how to bride it?
BAPTISTA: She shall, Lucentio. Come, gentlemen, let's go. *Exeunt.*

★

IV.1

Enter Grumio.

GRUMIO: Fie, fie, on all tired jades, on all mad masters, and all foul ways! Was ever man so beaten? Was ever man so rayed? Was ever man so weary? I am sent before to make a fire, and they are coming after to warm them. Now were not I a little pot and soon hot, my very lips might freeze to my teeth, my tongue to the roof of my mouth, my heart in my belly, ere I should come by a fire to thaw me. But I with blowing the fire shall warm myself, for considering the weather, a taller man than I will take cold. Holla, ho! Curtis.

Enter Curtis (a Servant).

CURTIS: Who is that calls so coldly?

---

224 *action* lawsuit
229 *buckler* shield
236 *wants* are missing
238 *junkets* delicacies
240 *room* place

IV.1 Petruchio's country house
1 *jades* worthless horses; *ways* roads
2 *rayed* dirtied
4 *a little . . . hot* (proverbial for a small person easily angered)
8 *taller* better
9 *is that* is it who

GRUMIO: A piece of ice. If thou doubt it, thou mayst slide from my shoulder to my heel with no greater a run but my head and my neck. A fire, good Curtis.

CURTIS: Is my master and his wife coming, Grumio?

GRUMIO: O ay, Curtis, ay, and therefore fire, fire; cast on no water.

CURTIS: Is she so hot a shrew as she's reported?

GRUMIO: She was, good Curtis, before this frost. But thou know'st winter tames man, woman, and beast, for it hath tamed my old master and my new mistress and myself, fellow Curtis.

CURTIS: Away, you three-inch fool! I am no beast.

GRUMIO: Am I but three inches? Why, thy horn is a foot, and so long am I at the least. But wilt thou make a fire or shall I complain on thee to our mistress, whose hand—she being now at hand—thou shalt soon feel, to thy cold comfort, for being slow in thy hot office?

CURTIS: I prithee, good Grumio, tell me, how goes the world?

GRUMIO: A cold world, Curtis, in every office but thine, and therefore fire. Do thy duty, and have thy duty, for my master and mistress are almost frozen to death.

CURTIS: There's fire ready, and therefore, good Grumio, the news.

GRUMIO: Why, [*Sings.*] "Jack boy, ho boy," and as much news as thou wilt.

CURTIS: Come, you are so full of cony-catching.

GRUMIO: Why therefore fire, for I have caught extreme cold. Where's the cook? Is supper ready, the house trimmed, rushes strewed, cobwebs swept, the servingmen in their new fustian and white stockings, and every officer his wedding garment on? Be the jacks fair within, the jills fair without, the carpets laid, and everything in order?

CURTIS: All ready, and therefore, I pray thee, news.

GRUMIO: First, know my horse is tired, my master and mistress fall'n out.

CURTIS: How?

GRUMIO: Out of their saddles into the dirt—and thereby hangs a tale.

CURTIS: Let's ha't, good Grumio.

GRUMIO: Lend thine ear.

CURTIS: Here.

GRUMIO: There.

[*Strikes him.*]

CURTIS: This is to feel a tale, not to hear a tale.

---

14 *fire . . . water* (alluding to the popular round "Scotland's Burning": "Fire, fire! Cast on water!")
19 *three-inch* i.e., very short; *I am no beast* (Grumio having called himself a *beast* and Curtis his *fellow*)
20 *horn* i.e., of a cuckold
23–24 *hot office* task of providing heat
27 *have thy duty* have thy due, reward (proverbial)
31 *cony-catching* trickery (a cony being a rabbit; with a play on *Jack boy, ho boy*, a "catch" or round)
33 *rushes strewed* i.e., on the floor (the normal floor covering)
34 *fustian* coarse cotton cloth
35 *jacks* leather drinking vessels (playing on "fellows," servingmen)
36 *jills* metal measuring cups (playing on "girls," maidservants); *carpets* table covers

GRUMIO: And therefore 'tis called a sensible tale, and this cuff was but to knock at your ear and beseech listening. Now I begin. Imprimis, we came down a foul hill, my master riding behind my mistress—

CURTIS: Both of one horse?

GRUMIO: What's that to thee?

CURTIS: Why, a horse.

GRUMIO: Tell thou the tale—but hadst thou not crossed me thou shouldst have heard how her horse fell, and she under her horse; thou shouldst have heard in how miry a place; how she was bemoiled, how he left her with the horse upon her, how he beat me because her horse stumbled, how she waded through the dirt to pluck him off me; how he swore, how she prayed, that never prayed before; how I cried, how the horses ran away, how her bridle was burst; how I lost my crupper—with many things of worthy memory, which now shall die in oblivion, and thou return unexperienced to thy grave.

CURTIS: By this reck'ning he is more shrew than she.

GRUMIO: Ay, and that thou and the proudest of you all shall find when he comes home. But what talk I of this? Call forth Nathaniel, Joseph, Nicholas, Philip, Walter, Sugarsop, and the rest. Let their heads be sleekly combed, their blue coats brushed, and their garters of an indifferent knit. Let them curtsy with their left legs and not presume to touch a hair of my master's horsetail till they kiss their hands. Are they all ready?

CURTIS: They are.

GRUMIO: Call them forth.

CURTIS: Do you hear, ho! You must meet my master to countenance my mistress.

GRUMIO: Why, she hath a face of her own.

CURTIS: Who knows not that?

GRUMIO: Thou, it seems, that calls for company to countenance her.

CURTIS: I call them forth to credit her.

Enter four or five Servingmen.

GRUMIO: Why, she comes to borrow nothing of them.

NATHANIEL: Welcome home, Grumio!

PHILIP: How now, Grumio?

JOSEPH: What, Grumio!

---

47 *sensible* (playing on "capable of being felt")
48 *Imprimis* first
50 *of* on
53 *crossed* interrupted
55 *bemoiled* bemired
61 *unexperienced* (hence ignorant)
64 *what* why
66 *blue coats* (dark blue was the usual color of a servant's dress)
67 *indifferent* (either not different, matching, or any knit whatever); *curtsy . . . legs* (like kissing their hands, below, absurdly elaborate forms of welcome)
72 *countenance* do honor to (Grumio then quibbles on countenance as *face*)
77 *credit* pay respect to (Grumio then quibbles on the financial sense)

NICHOLAS: Fellow Grumio!
NATHANIEL: How now, old lad!
GRUMIO: Welcome, you; how now, you; what, you; fellow, you; and thus much for greeting. Now, my spruce companions, is all ready and all things neat?
NATHANIEL: All things is ready. How near is our master?
GRUMIO: E'en at hand, alighted by this. And therefore be not—Cock's passion, silence, I hear my master.

Enter Petruchio and Kate.

PETRUCHIO: Where be these knaves? What, no man at door
To hold my stirrup nor to take my horse?
Where is Nathaniel, Gregory, Philip?
ALL SERVINGMEN: Here, here, sir; here, sir.
PETRUCHIO: Here, sir; here, sir; here, sir; here, sir!
You loggerheaded and unpolished grooms!
What, no attendance? No regard? No duty?
Where is the foolish knave I sent before.
GRUMIO: Here, sir, as foolish as I was before.
PETRUCHIO: You peasant swain, you whoreson malt-horse drudge!
Did I not bid thee meet me in the park
And bring along these rascal knaves with thee?
GRUMIO: Nathaniel's coat, sir, was not fully made,
And Gabriel's pumps were all unpinked i' th' heel.
There was no link to color Peter's hat,
And Walter's dagger was not come from sheathing.
There were none fine but Adam, Rafe, and Gregory;
The rest were ragged, old, and beggarly.
Yet, as they are, here are they come to meet you.
PETRUCHIO: Go, rascals, go, and fetch my supper in. *Exeunt Servants.*
[*Sings.*]
"Where is the life that late I led?
Where are those—?"
Sit down, Kate, [*They sit at table.*] and welcome. Food, food, food, food!

Enter Servants with supper.

Why, when, I say?—Nay, good sweet Kate, be merry.
Off with my boots, you rogues! You villains, when?
[*Sings.*]

---

88 *this* this time
88–89 *Cock's passion* God's (Christ's) passion (on the Cross)
95 *loggerheaded* blockheaded
99 *swain* lout; *whoreson* contemptible; *malt-horse drudge* brewer's horse (which ploddingly turns a grain mill)
100 *park* deer park
103 *unpinked* without their ornamental patterns
104 *link* torch (the smoke was used to blacken hats)
106 *fine* well turned out
111 *Where are those* (the ballad continues, "Where are those pleasant days?")

"It was the friar of orders gray,
As he forth walkèd on his way"—
Out, you rogue! You pluck my foot awry.
[*Strikes him.*]
Take that, and mend the plucking off the other. 119
Be merry, Kate. Some water here, what ho! 120
Enter one with water.
Where's my spaniel Troilus? Sirrah, get you hence
And bid my cousin Ferdinand come hither—
[*Exit Servant.*]
One, Kate, that you must kiss and be acquainted with.
Where are my slippers? Shall I have some water?
Come, Kate, and wash, and welcome heartily.
You whoreson villain, will you let it fall?
[*Strikes him.*]

KATE: Patience, I pray you, 'twas a fault unwilling.

PETRUCHIO: A whoreson, beetleheaded, flap-eared knave! 128
Come, Kate, sit down; I know you have a stomach. 129
Will you give thanks, sweet Kate, or else shall I? 130
What's this, mutton?

FIRST SERVANT: Ay. 132

PETRUCHIO: Who brought it?

PETER: I.

PETRUCHIO: 'Tis burnt, and so is all the meat.
What dogs are these! Where is the rascal cook?
How durst you, villains, bring it from the dresser, 137
And serve it thus to me that love it not?
[*He throws it at them.*]
There, take it to you, trenchers, cups, and all. 139
You heedless joltheads and unmannered slaves! 140
What, do you grumble? I'll be with you straight. 141
[*Exeunt Servants.*]

KATE: I pray you, husband, be not so disquiet.
The meat was well if you were so contented.

PETRUCHIO: I tell thee, Kate, 'twas burnt and dried away,
And I expressly am forbid to touch it,
For it engenders choler, planteth anger, 146

---

119 *mend* do better at

128 *beetle-headed* blockheaded, stupid (the "head" of a "beetle," or mallet, being a heavy block of wood)

129 *stomach* appetite (playing on "temper")

130 *give thanks* i.e., say grace

132 *FIRST SERVANT* (Curtis or Peter)

137 *dresser* sideboard

139 *trenchers* wooden plates

141 *with you* even with you

146 *choler* that "humor" (hot and dry) which produces anger (roast meat was to be avoided by persons of such disposition)

And better 'twere that both of us did fast,
Since of ourselves, ourselves are choleric,
Than feed it with such overroasted flesh. 149
Be patient. Tomorrow't shall be mended, 150
And for this night we'll fast in company.
Come, I will bring thee to thy bridal chamber. *Exeunt.* 152
Enter Servants severally.
NATHANIEL: Peter, didst ever see the like?
PETER: He kills her in her own humor. 154
Enter Curtis.
GRUMIO: Where is he?
CURTIS: In her chamber, making a sermon of continency to her,
And rails and swears and rates, that she, poor soul, 157
Knows not which way to stand, to look, to speak,
And sits as one new-risen from a dream.
Away, away, for he is coming hither. [*Exeunt.*] 160
Enter Petruchio.
PETRUCHIO: Thus have I politicly begun my reign, 161
And 'tis my hope to end successfully.
My falcon now is sharp and passing empty, 163
And till she stoop she must not be full-gorged, 164
For then she never looks upon her lure. 165
Another way I have to man my haggard, 166
To make her come and know her keeper's call:
That is, to watch her as we watch these kites 168
That bate and beat and will not be obedient. 169
She ate no meat today, nor none shall eat. 170
Last night she slept not, nor tonight she shall not.
As with the meat, some undeserved fault
I'll find about the making of the bed,
And here I'll fling the pillow, there the bolster, 174
This way the coverlet, another way the sheets.
Ay, and amid this hurly I intend 176
That all is done in reverent care of her.
And in conclusion she shall watch all night,

---

149 *it* i.e., their choler
152 s.d. *severally* at different doors
154 *kills . . . humor* subdues her by acting like her
157 *rates* berates; *that* so that
161 *politicly* cunningly
163 *sharp* starved
164 *stoop* fly to and seize the lure (playing on "bow to authority")
165 *lure* decoy bird used to recall a hawk
166 *man* tame (hawking term, with a quibble); *haggard* wild female hawk
168 *watch* keep awake (as in taming a wild hawk); *kites* inferior hawks
169 *bate and beat* flutter and flap the wings
174 *bolster* long narrow cushion supporting the pillow
176 *intend* pretend

And if she chance to nod I'll rail and brawl
And with the clamor keep her still awake.
This is a way to kill a wife with kindness, 181
And thus I'll curb her mad and headstrong humor. 182
He that knows better how to tame a shrew, 183
Now let him speak: 'tis charity to show. *Exit.*

★

IV.2

Enter Tranio [as Lucentio] and Hortensio [as Litio].

TRANIO: Is't possible, friend Litio, that Mistress Bianca
Doth fancy any other but Lucentio?
I tell you, sir, she bears me fair in hand. 3
HORTENSIO: Sir, to satisfy you in what I have said,
Stand by and mark the manner of his teaching.
[*They stand aside.*]
Enter Bianca [and Lucentio as Cambio].
LUCENTIO: Now mistress, profit you in what you read? 6
BIANCA: What, master, read you? First resolve me that. 7
LUCENTIO: I read that I profess, *The Art to Love.* 8
BIANCA: And may you prove, sir, master of your art. 9
LUCENTIO: While you, sweet dear, prove mistress of my heart.
[*They stand aside.*]
HORTENSIO: [*Advancing with Tranio*]
Quick proceeders, marry! Now tell me, I pray, 11
You that durst swear that your mistress Bianca
Loved none in the world so well as Lucentio—
TRANIO: O despiteful love, unconstant womankind! 14
I tell thee, Litio, this is wonderful. 15
HORTENSIO: Mistake no more: I am not Litio,
Nor a musician, as I seem to be,

---

181 *kill . . . kindness* (ironically, referring to the proverb for spoiling a wife through overindulgence)
182 *humor* disposition
183 *shrew* (pronounced "shrow"; a rhyme with *show*)

IV.2 Before Baptista's house
3 *bears . . . hand* encourages me
6 *read* study
7 *read* (quibbling on "teach"); *resolve* answer
8 *that I profess* what I'm an expert on; *The Art to Love* Ovid's *Ars amatoria*
9 *master . . . art* (quibbling on the "M.A. degree")
11 *proceeders* degree candidates; *marry* indeed (originally an oath on the name of the Virgin Mary)
14 *despiteful* spiteful
15 *wonderful* amazing

But one that scorn to live in this disguise,
For such a one as leaves a gentleman
And makes a god of such a cullion.
Know, sir, that I am called Hortensio.

Tranio: Signor Hortensio, I have often heard
Of your entire affection to Bianca,
And since mine eyes are witness of her lightness
I will, with you, if you be so contented,
Forswear Bianca and her love forever.

Hortensio: See how they kiss and court. Signor Lucentio,
Here is my hand and here I firmly vow
Never to woo her more, but do forswear her,
As one unworthy all the former favors
That I have fondly flattered her withal.

Tranio: And here I take the like unfeigned oath,
Never to marry with her though she would entreat.
Fie on her, see how beastly she doth court him.

Hortensio: Would all the world but he had quite forsworn.
For me, that I may surely keep mine oath,
I will be married to a wealthy widow
Ere three days pass, which hath as long loved me
As I have loved this proud disdainful haggard.
And so farewell, Signor Lucentio.
Kindness in women, not their beauteous looks,
Shall win my love—and so I take my leave,
In resolution as I swore before.

[*Exit.*]

Tranio: Mistress Bianca, bless you with such grace
As 'longeth to a lover's blessed case.
Nay, I have ta'en you napping, gentle love,
And have forsworn you with Hortensio.

Bianca: [*Advancing*]
Tranio, you jest. But have you both forsworn me?

Tranio: Mistress, we have.

Lucentio: Then we are rid of Litio.

Tranio: I' faith, he'll have a lusty widow now,
That shall be wooed and wedded in a day.

Bianca: God give him joy.

Tranio: Ay, and he'll tame her.

Bianca: He says so, Tranio.

---

20 *cullion* scoundrel (the schoolmaster)
24 *lightness* inconstancy
31 *fondly* foolishly
34 *beastly* lasciviously
35 *Would . . . forsworn* i.e., would that he were my only competition
39 *haggard* wild hawk
48 *Tranio* (Lucentio has revealed Tranio's identity to Bianca in III.1.35)
50 *lusty* (1) merry, (2) lustful

TRANIO: Faith, he is gone unto the taming school.
BIANCA: The taming school? What, is there such a place?
TRANIO: Ay, mistress, and Petruchio is the master,
That teacheth tricks eleven and twenty long
To tame a shrew and charm her chattering tongue.
Enter Biondello.
BIONDELLO: O master, master, I have watched so long
That I am dog-weary, but at last I spied
An ancient angel coming down the hill
Will serve the turn.
TRANIO: What is he, Biondello?
BIONDELLO: Master, a mercatante or a pedant,
I know not what; but formal in apparel,
In gait and countenance surely like a father.
LUCENTIO: And what of him, Tranio?
TRANIO: If he be credulous and trust my tale
I'll make him glad to seem Vincentio,
And give assurance to Baptista Minola
As if he were the right Vincentio.
Take in your love and then let me alone.
[*Exeunt Lucentio and Bianca.*]
Enter a Pedant.
PEDANT: God save you, sir.
TRANIO: And you, sir. You are welcome.
Travel you far on, or are you at the farthest?
PEDANT: Sir, at the farthest for a week or two.
But then up farther and as far as Rome,
And so to Tripoli, if God lend me life.
TRANIO: What countryman, I pray?
PEDANT: Of Mantua.
TRANIO: Of Mantua, sir? Marry, God forbid!
And come to Padua, careless of your life?
PEDANT: My life, sir? How, I pray? For that goes hard.
TRANIO: 'Tis death for anyone in Mantua
To come to Padua. Know you not the cause?
Your ships are stayed at Venice, and the duke—
For private quarrel 'twixt your duke and him—

---

57 *eleven . . . long* i.e., a great many (referring to the card game of one-and-thirty)
61 *angel* fellow of the good old stamp (an "angel" being a gold coin)
62 *the turn* our purposes
63 *mercatante* merchant; *pedant* schoolmaster
65 *countenance* appearance
67 *trust my tale* believe what I tell him
73 *far on* farther; *at the farthest* i.e., at your destination
75–76 *up . . . Tripoli* (Padua is "up" from Mantua, but Rome is very far south: Tripoli is either the North African city and state or the city in Syria)
80 *goes hard* is serious
83 *stayed* impounded

Hath published and proclaimed it openly.
'Tis marvel, but that you are newly come,
You might have heard it else proclaimed about.

PEDANT: Alas, sir, it is worse for me than so,
For I have bills for money by exchange
From Florence and must here deliver them.

TRANIO: Well, sir, to do you courtesy,
This will I do and thus I will advise you—
First, tell me, have you ever been at Pisa?

PEDANT: Ay, sir, in Pisa have I often been,
Pisa, renownèd for grave citizens.

TRANIO: Among them, know you one Vincentio?

PEDANT: I know him not but I have heard of him,
A merchant of incomparable wealth.

TRANIO: He is my father, sir, and sooth to say,
In count'nance somewhat doth resemble you.

BIONDELLO: [*Aside*] As much as an apple doth an oyster, and all one.

TRANIO: To save your life in this extremity
This favor will I do you for his sake,
And think it not the worst of all your fortunes
That you are like to Sir Vincentio.
His name and credit shall you undertake,
And in my house you shall be friendly lodged.
Look that you take upon you as you should.
You understand me, sir. So shall you stay
Till you have done your business in the city.
If this be courtesy, sir, accept of it.

PEDANT: O sir, I do, and will repute you ever
The patron of my life and liberty.

TRANIO: Then go with me to make the matter good.
This, by the way, I let you understand.
My father is here looked for every day
To pass assurance of a dower in marriage
'Twixt me and one Baptista's daughter here.
In all these circumstances I'll instruct you.
Go with me to clothe you as becomes you.

Exeunt.

*

86 *but that* except for the fact that
89 *bills . . . exchange* (bills of exchange were money orders due on a certain date)
91 *courtesy* a good turn
101 *all one* no matter
106 *credit* reputation; *undertake* assume
108 *take upon you* play your part
112 *repute* consider
115 *by the way* along the way, as we go
117 *pass* convey (legal term); *assurance* a guarantee

IV.3

Enter Kate and Grumio.

GRUMIO: No, no, forsooth, I dare not for my life.
KATE: The more my wrong, the more his spite appears.
What, did he marry me to famish me?
Beggars that come unto my father's door,
Upon entreaty have a present alms;
If not, elsewhere they meet with charity.
But I, who never knew how to entreat
Nor never needed that I should entreat,
Am starved for meat, giddy for lack of sleep,
With oaths kept waking and with brawling fed.
And that which spites me more than all these wants,
He does it under name of perfect love,
As who should say, if I should sleep or eat
'Twere deadly sickness or else present death.
I prithee go and get me some repast,
I care not what, so it be wholesome food.
GRUMIO: What say you to a neat's foot?
KATE: 'Tis passing good, I prithee let me have it.
GRUMIO: I fear it is too choleric a meat.
How say you to a fat tripe finely broiled?
KATE: I like it well, good Grumio, fetch it me.
GRUMIO: I cannot tell; I fear 'tis choleric.
What say you to a piece of beef and mustard?
KATE: A dish that I do love to feed upon.
GRUMIO: Ay, but the mustard is too hot a little.
KATE: Why then, the beef, and let the mustard rest.
GRUMIO: Nay then, I will not; you shall have the mustard
Or else you get no beef of Grumio.
KATE: Then both or one, or anything thou wilt.
GRUMIO: Why then, the mustard without the beef.
KATE: Go, get thee gone, thou false deluding slave,
Beats him.
That feed'st me with the very name of meat.
Sorrow on thee and all the pack of you

IV.3 Petruchio's house
2 *my wrong* i.e., the wrong done me
5 *a present* immediate
9 *meat* food
13 *As who* as though one
17 *a neat's food* an ox's or a calf's foot
19 *choleric* engendering anger
32 *very* i.e., mere

That triumph thus upon my misery.
Go, get thee gone, I say.

Enter Petruchio and Hortensio with meat.

PETRUCHIO: How fares my Kate? What, sweeting, all amort?
HORTENSIO: Mistress, what cheer?
KATE: Faith, as cold as can be.
PETRUCHIO: Pluck up thy spirits, look cheerfully upon me.
Here, love, thou seest how diligent I am
To dress thy meat myself and bring it thee.
I am sure, sweet Kate, this kindness merits thanks.
What, not a word? Nay then, thou lov'st it not.
And all my pains is sorted to no proof.
Here, take away this dish.
KATE: I pray you, let it stand.
PETRUCHIO: The poorest service is repaid with thanks,
And so shall mine before you touch the meat.
KATE: I thank you, sir.
HORTENSIO: Signor Petruchio, fie, you are to blame.
Come, Mistress Kate, I'll bear you company.

[*They sit at table.*]

PETRUCHIO: [*Aside*]
Eat it up all, Hortensio, if thou lov'st me.
Much good do it unto thy gentle heart.
Kate, eat apace. And now, my honey love,
Will we return unto thy father's house
And revel it as bravely as the best,
With silken coats and caps and golden rings.
With ruffs and cuffs and farthingales and things;
With scarfs and fans and double change of bravery,
With amber bracelets, beads, and all this knavery.
What, hast thou dined? The tailor stays thy leisure,
To deck thy body with his ruffling treasure.

Enter Tailor [with a gown].

Come, tailor, let us see these ornaments.

Enter Haberdasher [with a cap].

Lay forth the gown.—What news with you, sir?
HABERDASHER: Here is the cap your worship did bespeak.

---

36 *sweeting* sweetheart; *all amort* spiritless dejected
40 *dress* prepare
43 *is . . . proof* have resulted in nothing
52 *apace* quickly
54 *bravely* finely dressed
56 *farthingales* hooped petticoats
57 *bravery* finery
60 *ruffling* ornamented with ruffles
63 *bespeak* order

PETRUCHIO: Why, this was molded on a porringer:
A velvet dish. Fie, fie, 'tis lewd and filthy.
Why, 'tis a cockle or a walnut shell,
A knack, a toy, a trick, a baby's cap.
Away with it. Come, let me have a bigger.
KATE: I'll have no bigger, this doth fit the time,
And gentlewomen wear such caps as these.
PETRUCHIO: When you are gentle you shall have one too,
And not till then.
HORTENSIO: That will not be in haste.
KATE: Why, sir, I trust I may have leave to speak,
And speak I will. I am no child, no babe.
Your betters have endured me say my mind,
And if you cannot, best you stop your ears.
My tongue will tell the anger of my heart
Or else my heart, concealing it, will break,
And rather than it shall, I will be free
Even to the uttermost, as I please, in words.
PETRUCHIO: Why, thou sayst true. It is a paltry cap,
A custard coffin, a bauble, a silken pie.
I love thee well in that thou lik'st it not.
KATE: Love me or love me not, I like the cap,
And I will have it or I will have none.
[*Exit Haberdasher.*]
PETRUCHIO: Thy gown? Why, ay—come, tailor, let us see't.
O mercy, God, what masquing stuff is here?
What's this, a sleeve? 'Tis like a demicannon.
What, up and down carved like an apple tart?
Here's snip and nip and cut and slish and slash,
Like to a censer in a barber's shop.
Why, what a devil's name, tailor, call'st thou this?
HORTENSIO: [*Aside*]
I see she's like to have neither cap nor gown.
TAILOR: You bid me make it orderly and well,
According to the fashion and the time.

---

64 *porringer* porridge bowl
65 *lewd* vile
66 *cockle* cockleshell
67 *knack* trinket; *trick* trifle
69 *fit the time* accord with present fashion
75 *say* speaking
82 *custard coffin* crust of a custard pie; *silken pie* pie of silk
87 *masquing stuff* clothing fit for masquerades
88 *demicannon* large cannon
89 *carved . . . tart* (the sleeve has slashes, like the slits in a piecrust, to show the fabric beneath)
91 *censer* incense burner (with perforated cover)

PETRUCHIO: Marry, I did. But if you be remembered,
I did not bid you mar it to the time.
Go, hop me over every kennel home,
For you shall hop without my custom, sir.
I'll none of it. Hence, make your best of it.
KATE: I never saw a better-fashioned gown,
More quaint, more pleasing, nor more commendable.
Belike you mean to make a puppet of me.
PETRUCHIO: Why, true, he means to make a puppet of thee.
TAILOR: She says your worship means to make a puppet of her.
PETRUCHIO: O monstrous arrogance!
Thou liest, thou thread, thou thimble,
Thou yard, three-quarters, half-yard, quarter, nail!
Thou flea, thou nit, thou winter cricket thou!
Braved in mine own house with a skein of thread?
Away, thou rag, thou quantity, thou remnant,
Or I shall so bemete thee with thy yard
As thou shalt think on prating whilst thou liv'st.
I tell thee, I, that thou hast marred her gown.
TAILOR: Your worship is deceived. The gown is made
Just as my master had direction.
Grumio gave order how it should be done.
GRUMIO: I gave him no order, I gave him the stuff.
TAILOR: But how did you desire it should be made?
GRUMIO: Marry, sir, with needle and thread.
TAILOR: But did you not request to have it cut?
GRUMIO: Thou hast faced many things.
TAILOR: I have.
GRUMIO: Face not me. Thou hast braved many men: brave not me. I will neither be faced nor braved. I say unto thee, I bid thy master cut out the gown but I did not bid him cut it to pieces. Ergo, thou liest.
TAILOR: Why, here is the note of the fashion to testify.

---

98 *hop . . . home* you can hop home over every gutter for all I care
102 *quaint* elegant
103 *Belike* it seems; *puppet* (contemptuous term for a woman)
108 *nail* two and a quarter inches (a measure of length for cloth)
109 *nit* louse egg
110 *Braved* defied; *with* by
111 *quantity* fragment
112 *bemete* punish; *yard* yardstick
113 *think on* think before
118 *stuff* cloth
122 *faced* (1) trimmed, (2) faced down
124 *braved* (1) dressed finely, (2) defied
126 *Ergo* therefore (Latin)
127 *to testify* as evidence

PETRUCHIO: Read it.
GRUMIO: The note lies in's throat if he say I said so. 129
TAILOR: [*Reads.*] "Imprimis, a loose-bodied gown—" 130
GRUMIO: Master, if ever I said loose-bodied gown, sew me in the skirts
of it and beat me to death with a bottom of brown thread. I said, a 132
gown.
PETRUCHIO: Proceed.
TAILOR: "With a small compassed cape—" 135
GRUMIO: I confess the cape.
TAILOR: "With a trunk sleeve—" 137
GRUMIO: I confess two sleeves.
TAILOR: "The sleeves curiously cut." 139
PETRUCHIO: Ay, there's the villainy. 140
GRUMIO: Error i' th' bill, sir, error i' th' bill. I commanded the sleeves
should be cut out and sewed up again, and that I'll prove upon thee, 142
though thy little finger be armed in a thimble.
TAILOR: This is true that I say. An I had thee in place where thou shouldst 144
know it.
GRUMIO: I am for thee straight. Take thou the bill, give me thy mete- 146
yard, and spare not me.
HORTENSIO: God-a-mercy, Grumio, then he shall have no odds. 148
PETRUCHIO: Well, sir, in brief, the gown is not for me.
GRUMIO: You are i' th' right, sir, 'tis for my mistress. 150
PETRUCHIO: Go, take it up unto thy master's use. 151
GRUMIO: Villain, not for thy life. Take up my mistress' gown for thy 152
master's use!
PETRUCHIO: Why, sir, what's your conceit in that? 154
GRUMIO: O sir, the conceit is deeper than you think for.
Take up my mistress' gown to his master's use!
O fie, fie, fie!

---

129 *lies . . . throat* (1) is a low (musical) note, (2) is an outrageous lie
130 *Imprimis* first; *loose-bodied gown* (Loose gowns were fashionable; all editors claim that the point is that prostitutes wore them, but they wore them because fashionable ladies wore them. The point is that there is nothing wrong with the dress.)
132 *bottom* skein
135 *compassed* flared
137 *trunk* very full
139 *curiously* elaborately
142 *prove upon thee* maintain by defeating you in combat
144 *An . . . where* if only I had you in the right place
146 *bill* (punning on the weapon: a bill was a halberd)
146–47 *meteyard* yardstick
148 *he . . . odds* he won't have a chance
151 *take . . . use* i.e., return it to your master for whatever use he can make of it
152 *Take . . . gown* i.e., lift up her skirts
154 *conceit* meaning

PETRUCHIO: [*Aside*]
Hortensio, say thou wilt see the tailor paid.
[*To Tailor*]
Go take it hence, be gone and say no more.
HORTENSIO: Tailor, I'll pay thee for thy gown tomorrow.
Take no unkindness of his hasty words.
Away, I say. Commend me to thy master.
Exit Tailor.
PETRUCHIO: Well, come, my Kate; we will unto your father's,
Even in these honest mean habiliments.
Our purses shall be proud, our garments poor,
For 'tis the mind that makes the body rich;
And as the sun breaks through the darkest clouds
So honor peereth in the meanest habit.
What, is the jay more precious than the lark
Because his feathers are more beautiful?
Or is the adder better than the eel
Because his painted skin contents the eye?
O no, good Kate; neither art thou the worse
For this poor furniture and mean array.
If thou account'st it shame, lay it on me.
And therefore frolic; we will hence forthwith
To feast and sport us at thy father's house.
[*To Grumio*]
Go call my men, and let us straight to him;
And bring our horses unto Long Lane end.
There will we mount, and thither walk on foot.
Let's see, I think 'tis now some seven o'clock,
And well we may come there by dinnertime.
KATE: I dare assure you, sir, 'tis almost two,
And 'twill be suppertime ere you come there.
PETRUCHIO: It shall be seven ere I go to horse.
Look what I speak or do or think to do,
You are still crossing it. Sirs, let't alone.
I will not go today, and ere I do,
It shall be what o'clock I say it is.
HORTENSIO: Why, so this gallant will command the sun.
[*Exeunt.*]

★

---

164 *honest . . . habiliments* respectable, plain clothes
168 *peereth in* appears through; *habit* clothing
174 *furniture* clothing
175 *lay it* blame it
176 *hence* i.e., go hence; *forthwith* immediately
182 *dinnertime* about noon
186 *Look what* whatever

IV.4

Enter Tranio [as Lucentio] and the Pedant booted and dressed like Vincentio.

TRANIO: Sir, this is the house. Please it you that I call?
PEDANT: Ay, what else? And but I be deceived, 2
Signor Baptista may remember me, 3
Near twenty years ago, in Genoa,
Where we were lodgers at the Pegasus. 5
TRANIO: 'Tis well, and hold your own in any case
With such austerity as 'longeth to a father, 7
Enter Biondello.
PEDANT: I warrant you. But sir, here comes your boy;
'Twere good he were schooled. 9
TRANIO: Fear you not him. Sirrah Biondello, 10
Now do your duty throughly, I advise you. 11
Imagine 'twere the right Vincentio.
BIONDELLO: Tut, fear not me.
TRANIO: But hast thou done thy errand to Baptista?
BIONDELLO: I told him that your father was at Venice,
And that you looked for him this day in Padua. 16
TRANIO: Thou'rt a tall fellow. Hold thee that to drink. 17
[*Gives money.*]
Here comes Baptista. Set your countenance, sir. 18
Enter Baptista and Lucentio [as Cambio]. Pedant bareheaded.
Signor Baptista, you are happily met.
[*To Pedant*]
Sir, this is the gentleman I told you of. 20
I pray you, stand good father to me now, 21
Give me Bianca for my patrimony.
PEDANT: Soft, son.
Sir, by your leave. Having come to Padua
To gather in some debts, my son Lucentio
Made me acquainted with a weighty cause
Of love between your daughter and himself.
And—for the good report I hear of you,

IV.4 Before Baptista's house s.d. *booted* (as from traveling)
2 *but* unless
3 *may remember me* (the pedant is rehearsing his part)
5 *Pegasus* (name of an inn, after the winged horse of classical myth)
7 *austerity* dignity; *'longeth to* befits
9 *schooled* taught how to play his part
11 *throughly* thoroughly
16 *looked for* expected
17 *tall* fine; *Hold . . . drink* have a drink on me
18 *Set . . . countenance* i.e., look dignified; s.d. *bareheaded* (the pedant doffs his hat to Baptista)
21 *stand* prove to be a

And for the love he beareth to your daughter,
And she to him—to stay him not too long,
I am content, in a good father's care.
To have him matched. And if you please to like
No worse than I, upon some agreement
Me shall you find ready and willing
With one consent to have her so bestowed.
For curious I cannot be with you,
Signor Baptista, of whom I hear so well.

BAPTISTA: Sir, pardon me in what I have to say.
Your plainness and your shortness please me well.
Right true it is, your son Lucentio here
Doth love my daughter, and she loveth him—
Or both dissemble deeply their affections.
And therefore if you say no more than this,
That like a father you will deal with him
And pass my daughter a sufficient dower,
The match is made and all is done:
Your son shall have my daughter with consent.

TRANIO: I thank you, sir. Where then do you know best
We be affied and such assurance ta'en
As shall with either part's agreement stand?

BAPTISTA: Not in my house, Lucentio, for you know
Pitchers have ears, and I have many servants.
Besides, old Gremio is hearkening still,
And happily we might be interrupted.

TRANIO: Then at my lodging, an it like you.
There doth my father lie, and there this night
We'll pass the business privately and well.
Send for your daughter by your servant here.
My boy shall fetch the scrivener presently.
The worst is this, that at so slender warning
You are like to have a thin and slender pittance.

---

30 *stay* delay
32 *like* approve (the match)
35 *With . . . consent* i.e., with the same consent as yours
36 *curious* overparticular, fussy
45 *pass* settle on
49 *affied* formally betrothed
49–50 *such . . . stand* such guarantees be given as shall formalize our agreement
53 *hearkening still* always eavesdropping
54 *happily* perhaps
55 *an . . . you* if you please
56 *lie* lodge
57 *pass* transact
59 *scrivener* notary (a scribe empowered to draw up legal agreements)
61 *pittance* meal

BAPTISTA: It likes me well. Cambio, hie you home
And bid Bianca make her ready straight.
And if you will, tell what hath happened:
Lucentio's father is arrived in Padua,
And how she's like to be Lucentio's wife. *[Exit Lucentio.]*

BIONDELLO: I pray the gods she may with all my heart. *Exit.*

TRANIO: Dally not with the gods, but get thee gone.
Signor Baptista, shall I lead the way?
Welcome, one mess is like to be your cheer.
Come, sir, we will better it in Pisa.

BAPTISTA: I follow you. *Exeunt.*

Enter [severally] Lucentio [as Cambio] and Biondello.

BIONDELLO: Cambio!

LUCENTIO: What sayst thou, Biondello?

BIONDELLO: You saw my master wink and laugh upon you?

LUCENTIO: Biondello, what of that?

BIONDELLO: Faith, nothing, but he's left me here behind to expound the meaning or moral of his signs and tokens.

LUCENTIO: I pray thee, moralize them.

BIONDELLO: Then thus. Baptista is safe, talking with the deceiving father of a deceitful son.

LUCENTIO: And what of him?

BIONDELLO: His daughter is to be brought by you to the supper.

LUCENTIO: And then?

BIONDELLO: The old priest at Saint Luke's church is at your command at all hours.

LUCENTIO: And what of all this?

BIONDELLO: I cannot tell, except they are busied about a counterfeit assurance. Take you assurance of her, "cum privilegio ad imprimendum solum." To th' church with the priest, clerk, and some sufficient honest witnesses. If this be not that you look for, I have no more to say, But bid Bianca farewell forever and a day.

LUCENTIO: Hear'st thou, Biondello—

BIONDELLO: I cannot tarry. I knew a wench married in an afternoon as she went to the garden for parsley to stuff a rabbit, and so may you, sir, and so adieu, sir. My master hath appointed me to go to Saint Luke's, to bid the priest be ready against you come with your appendix. *Exit.*

---

62 *likes me* pleases me
70 *mess* dish; *cheer* entertainment
78 *moral* deep significance
79 *moralize* explain
80 *safe* i.e., safely dealt with
89 *assurance* agreement (the betrothal); *Take . . . assurance* insure yourself (by marrying her)
89–90 *cum . . . solum* with exclusive right to print (Latin; the publisher's copyright formula, analogized to the husband's exclusive right to "imprint himself on" his wife)
97 *against . . . come* in anticipation of your coming; *appendix* appendage (i.e., bride)

LUCENTIO: I may and will, if she be so contented.
She will be pleased, then wherefore should I doubt?
Hap what hap may, I'll roundly go about her.
It shall go hard if Cambio go without her.
Exit.

★

IV.5

Enter Petruchio, Kate, Hortensio [, and Grumio, with Attendants].

PETRUCHIO: Come on, a God's name, once more toward our father's.
Good Lord, how bright and goodly shines the moon!
KATE: The moon? The sun. It is not moonlight now.
PETRUCHIO: I say it is the moon that shines so bright.
KATE: I know it is the sun that shines so bright.
PETRUCHIO: Now by my mother's son, and that's myself,
It shall be moon or star or what I list,
Or e'er I journey to your father's house.
[*To Servants*]
Go on and fetch our horses back again.
Evermore crossed and crossed, nothing but crossed.
HORTENSIO: [*Aside to Kate*]
Say as he says or we shall never go.
KATE: Forward, I pray, since we have come so far,
And be it moon or sun or what you please.
An if you please to call it a rush candle,
Henceforth I vow it shall be so for me.
PETRUCHIO: I say it is the moon.
KATE: I know it is the moon.
PETRUCHIO: Nay, then you lie. It is the blessèd sun.
KATE: Then God be blessed, it is the blessèd sun,
But sun it is not when you say it is not,
And the moon changes even as your mind.
What you will have it named, even that it is,
And so it shall be still for Katherine.
HORTENSIO: Petruchio, go thy ways, the field is won.

---

100 *Hap . . . may* whatever comes of it; *I'll . . . her* I'll go find her immediately
101 *go hard* be hard to bear; *go* return

IV.5 A country road
1 *a* in
7 *list* please
8 *Or* ere, before
14 *rush candle* rush dipped in grease to serve as candle
22 *still* always

PETRUCHIO: Well, forward, forward! Thus the bowl should run,
And not unluckily against the bias.
But soft, what company is coming here?
Enter Vincentio.
[*To Vincentio*]
Good morrow, gentle mistress, where away?
Tell me, sweet Kate, and tell me truly too,
Hast thou beheld a fresher gentlewoman?
Such war of white and red within her cheeks!
What stars do spangle heaven with such beauty
As those two eyes become that heavenly face?
Fair lovely maid, once more good day to thee.
Sweet Kate, embrace her for her beauty's sake.
HORTENSIO: [*Aside*]
A will make the man mad, to make a woman of him.
KATE: Young budding virgin, fair and fresh and sweet,
Whither away, or where is thy abode?
Happy the parents of so fair a child,
Happier the man whom favorable stars
Allots thee for his lovely bedfellow.
PETRUCHIO: Why, how now, Kate, I hope thou art not mad.
This is a man, old, wrinkled, faded, withered,
And not a maiden, as thou sayst he is.
KATE: Pardon, old father, my mistaking eyes
That have been so bedazzled with the sun
That everything I look on seemeth green.
Now I perceive thou art a reverend father.
Pardon, I pray thee, for my mad mistaking.
PETRUCHIO: Do, good old grandsire, and withal make known
Which way thou travelest. If along with us,
We shall be joyful of thy company.
VINCENTIO: Fair sir, and you my merry mistress,
That with your strange encounter much amazed me,
My name is called Vincentio, my dwelling Pisa,
And bound I am to Padua, there to visit
A son of mine, which long I have not seen.
PETRUCHIO: What is his name?
VINCENTIO: Lucentio, gentle sir.

24 *bowl* ball in game of bowls
25 *unluckily* unsuccessfully; *against the bias* contrary to the intended course (the bias being a weight in the side of the bowl that enables the bowler to roll it in a curve)
35 *A* he
44 *father* (respectful term of address to an old man)
46 *green* young
53 *encounter* greeting

PETRUCHIO: Happily met, the happier for thy son.
And now by law, as well as reverend age,
I may entitle thee my loving father.
The sister to my wife, this gentlewoman,
Thy son by this hath married. Wonder not
Nor be not grieved. She is of good esteem,
Her dowry wealthy, and of worthy birth;
Beside, so qualified as may beseem
The spouse of any noble gentleman.
Let me embrace with old Vincentio,
And wander we to see thy honest son,
Who will of thy arrival be full joyous.
VINCENTIO: But is this true, or is it else your pleasure,
Like pleasant travelers, to break a jest
Upon the company you overtake?
HORTENSIO: I do assure thee, father, so it is.
PETRUCHIO: Come, go along, and see the truth hereof,
For our first merriment hath made thee jealous.
Exeunt [all but Hortensio].
HORTENSIO: Well, Petruchio, this has put me in heart.
Have to my widow, and if she be froward,
Then hast thou taught Hortensio to be untoward. *Exit.*

★

V.1

Enter Biondello, Lucentio [as Cambio], and Bianca. Gremio is out before [and stands aside].

BIONDELLO: Softly and swiftly, sir, for the priest is ready.
LUCENTIO: I fly, Biondello—but they may chance to need thee at home; therefore leave us. *Exit [with Bianca].*
BIONDELLO: Nay, faith, I'll see the church a your back, and then come back to my master as soon as I can. [*Exit.*]

---

62 *Thy . . . married* (since Petruchio has been out of town, he should not know this information, and in any case, Lucentio and Bianca are not married yet; moreover, Hortensio has heard the suitor he knows as Lucentio forswear her); *this* this time
63 *esteem* reputation
65 *so qualified* having such qualities
68 *wander we* let's go out of our way
71 *pleasant* merry
71–72 *break . . . /Upon* play a joke on
75 *jealous* suspicious
77 *froward* stubborn
78 *untoward* perverse, difficult (and thereby how to tame her)

V.1 Before Lucentio's house s.d. *out before* onstage before the others (whom he does not "see")
4 *a your back* at your back (i.e., I'll see you enter it)

GREMIO: I marvel Cambio comes not all this while.

Enter Petruchio, Kate, Vincentio, [and] Grumio, with Attendants.

PETRUCHIO: Sir, here's the door, this is Lucentio's house.
My father's bears more toward the marketplace.
Thither must I, and here I leave you, sir.

VINCENTIO: You shall not choose but drink before you go.
I think I shall command your welcome here,
And by all likelihood some cheer is toward.

Knock.

GREMIO: [*Advancing*] They're busy within; you were best knock louder.

Pedant [as Vincentio] looks out of the window.

PEDANT: What's he that knocks as he would beat down the gate?

VINCENTIO: Is Signor Lucentio within, sir?

PEDANT: He's within, sir, but not to be spoken withal.

VINCENTIO: What if a man bring him a hundred pound or two, to make merry withal?

PEDANT: Keep your hundred pounds to yourself. He shall need none so long as I live.

PETRUCHIO: Nay, I told you your son was well beloved in Padua. Do you hear, sir? To leave frivolous circumstances, I pray you tell Signor Lucentio that his father is come from Pisa and is here at the door to speak with him.

PEDANT: Thou liest. His father is come from Pisa and is here looking out at the window.

VINCENTIO: Art thou his father?

PEDANT: Ay sir, so his mother says, if I may believe her.

PETRUCHIO: [*To Vincentio*] Why how now, gentleman! Why this is flat knavery, to take upon you another man's name.

PEDANT: Lay hands on the villain. I believe a means to cozen somebody in this city under my countenance.

Enter Biondello.

BIONDELLO: I have seen them in the church together. God send 'em good shipping! But who is here? Mine old master, Vincentio! Now we are undone and brought to nothing.

VINCENTIO: Come hither, crackhemp.

BIONDELLO: I hope I may choose, sir.

---

8 *bears* lies

13 s.d. *looks . . . window* i.e., appears in the gallery over the stage—are Sly, the lord, and his retinue still there?

14 *What* who

16 *withal* with

29 *flat* downright

31 *cozen* cheat

32 *under my countenance* by posing as me

34 *good shipping* fair sailing

35 *undone* ruined

36 *crackhemp* fellow ripe for hanging

37 *choose* do as I choose

VINCENTIO: Come hither, you rogue. What, have you forgot me?

BIONDELLO: Forgot you? No sir. I could not forget you, for I never saw you before in all my life.

VINCENTIO: What, you notorious villain, didst thou never see thy master's father, Vincentio?

BIONDELLO: What, my worshipful old master? Yes, marry, sir, see where he looks out of the window.

VINCENTIO: Is't so indeed?

He beats Biondello.

BIONDELLO: Help, help, help! Here's a madman will murder me. [*Exit.*]

PEDANT: Help, son! Help, Signor Baptista! [*Exit above.*]

PETRUCHIO: Prithee, Kate, let's stand aside and see the end of this controversy.

[*They stand aside.*]

Enter [below] Pedant [as Vincentio] with Servants, Baptista, [and] Tranio [as Lucentio].

TRANIO: Sir, what are you that offer to beat my servant?

VINCENTIO: What am I, sir? Nay, what are you, sir? O immortal gods! O fine villain! A silken doublet, a velvet hose, a scarlet cloak, and a copatain hat! O I am undone, I am undone! While I play the good husband at home, my son and my servant spend all at the university.

TRANIO: How now, what's the matter?

BAPTISTA What, is the man lunatic?

TRANIO: Sir, you seem a sober ancient gentleman by your habit, but your words show you a madman. Why sir, what 'cerns it you if I wear pearl and gold? I thank my good father, I am able to maintain it.

VINCENTIO: Thy father! O villain, he is a sailmaker in Bergamo.

BAPTISTA: You mistake, sir, you mistake, sir. Pray, what do you think is his name?

VINCENTIO: His name? As if I knew not his name! I have brought him up ever since he was three years old, and his name is Tranio.

PEDANT: Away, away, mad ass! His name is Lucentio. He is mine only son, and heir to the lands of me, Signor Vincentio.

VINCENTIO: Lucentio? O he hath murdered his master! Lay hold on him, I charge you in the duke's name. O my son, my son! Tell me, thou villain, where is my son Lucentio?

TRANIO: [*To a Servant*] Call forth an officer.

[*Enter an Officer.*]

---

50 *what* who
53 *copatain* high-crowned
54 *good husband* careful manager
58 *habit* bearing
59 *'cerns* concerns
62 *Bergamo* (like Mantua and Padua, not a seaport)

Carry this mad knave to the jail. Father Baptista, I charge you see that he be forthcoming.

VINCENTIO: Carry me to the jail!

GREMIO: Stay, officer, he shall not go to prison.

BAPTISTA: Talk not, Signor Gremio. I say he shall go to prison.

GREMIO: Take heed, Signor Baptista, lest you be cony-catched in this business. I dare swear this is the right Vincentio.

PEDANT: Swear, if thou dar'st.

GREMIO: Nay, I dare not swear it.

TRANIO: Then thou wert best say that I am not Lucentio.

GREMIO: Yes, I know thee to be Signor Lucentio.

BAPTISTA: Away with the dotard, to the jail with him!

Enter Biondello, Lucentio, and Bianca.

VINCENTIO: Thus strangers may be halèd and abused. O monstrous villain!

BIONDELLO: O we are spoiled, yonder he is. Deny him, forswear him, or else we are all undone.

Exeunt Biondello, Tranio, and Pedant as fast as may be.

LUCENTIO: Pardon, sweet father.

Kneel.

VINCENTIO: Lives my sweet son?

BIANCA: Pardon, dear father.

BAPTISTA: How hast thou offended? Where is Lucentio?

LUCENTIO: Here's Lucentio, right son to the right Vincentio,
That have by marriage made thy daughter mine
While counterfeit supposes bleared thine eyne.

GREMIO: Here's packing, with a witness, to deceive us all!

VINCENTIO: Where is that damnèd villain Tranio,
That faced and braved me in this matter so?

BAPTISTA: Why, tell me, is not this my Cambio?

BIANCA: Cambio is changed into Lucentio.

LUCENTIO: Love wrought these miracles. Bianca's love
Made me exchange my state with Tranio
While he did bear my countenance in the town,
And happily I have arrived at the last
Unto the wished haven of my bliss.
What Tranio did, myself enforced him to;
Then pardon him, sweet father, for my sake.

---

74 *forthcoming* i.e., to stand trial
78 *cony-catched* duped
82 *wert best* might as well
85 *halèd* hauled about, molested
95 *counterfeit supposes* false assumptions (with an allusion to Gascoigne's play *Supposes*); *eyne* eyes
96 *packing* plotting; *with a witness* with a vengeance
98 *faced and braved* outfaced and defied
103 *bear my countenance* pose as me

VINCENTIO: I'll slit the villain's nose that would have sent me to the jail.

BAPTISTA: [*To Lucentio*] But do you hear, sir? Have you married my daughter without asking my good will?

VINCENTIO: Fear not, Baptista, we will content you, go to. But I will in, to be revenged for this villainy. *Exit.*

BAPTISTA: And I, to sound the depth of this knavery. *Exit.*

LUCENTIO: Look not pale, Bianca, thy father will not frown. *Exeunt [Lucentio and Bianca].*

GREMIO: My cake is dough, but I'll in among the rest,
Out of hope of all but my share of the feast. [*Exit.*]

KATE: [*Advancing*] Husband, let's follow, to see the end of this ado.

PETRUCHIO: First kiss me, Kate, and we will.

KATE: What, in the midst of the street?

PETRUCHIO: What, art thou ashamed of me?

KATE: No sir, God forbid, but ashamed to kiss.

PETRUCHIO: Why, then let's home again.
[*To Grumio*] Come, sirrah, let's away.

KATE: Nay, I will give thee a kiss. Now pray thee, love, stay.

PETRUCHIO: Is not this well? Come, my sweet Kate.
Better once than never, for never's too late. *Exeunt.*

★

V.2

Enter Baptista, Vincentio, Gremio, the Pedant, Lucentio, and Bianca; Tranio, Biondello, [and] Grumio; [Petruchio, Kate, Hortensio,] and Widow; the Servingmen with Tranio bringing in a banquet.

LUCENTIO: At last, though long, our jarring notes agree,
And time it is, when raging war is done,
To smile at scapes and perils overblown.
My fair Bianca, bid my father welcome
While I with selfsame kindness welcome thine.
Brother Petruchio, sister Katherina,
And thou, Hortensio, with thy loving widow,
Feast with the best and welcome to my house.
My banquet is to close our stomachs up
After our great good cheer. Pray you, sit down,
For now we sit to chat as well as eat.
[*They sit at table.*]

---

111 *go to* (expression of impatience)
115 *My cake is dough* i.e., my hopes are dashed (proverbial)
125 *Better . . . late* i.e., better late than never (proverbial); *once* at one time or another

V.2 Lucentio's house s.d. *bringing in* i.e., carrying onstage; *banquet* dessert (sweets, fruit, and wine)
1 *long* after a long time
10 *After . . . cheer* (Lucentio's banquet apparently follows a bridal feast given by Baptista)

PETRUCHIO: Nothing but sit and sit, and eat and eat!
BAPTISTA: Padua affords this kindness, son Petruchio.
PETRUCHIO: Padua affords nothing but what is kind.
HORTENSIO: For both our sakes I would that word were true.
PETRUCHIO: Now, for my life, Hortensio fears his widow. 16
WIDOW: Then never trust me if I be afeard. 17
PETRUCHIO: You are very sensible, and yet you miss my sense: I mean
    Hortensio is afeard of you.
WIDOW: He that is giddy thinks the world turns round. 20
PETRUCHIO: Roundly replied. 21
KATE: Mistress, how mean you that?
WIDOW: Thus I conceive by him. 22
PETRUCHIO: Conceive by me? How likes Hortensio that?
HORTENSIO: My widow says, thus she conceives her tale. 24
PETRUCHIO: Very well mended. Kiss him for that, good widow.
KATE: "He that is giddy thinks the world turns round"—
    I pray you, tell me what you meant by that.
WIDOW: Your husband, being troubled with a shrew, 28
    Measures my husband's sorrow by his woe— 29
    And now you know my meaning. 30
KATE: A very mean meaning. 31
WIDOW: Right, I mean you.
KATE: And I am mean indeed, respecting you. 32
PETRUCHIO: To her, Kate!
HORTENSIO: To her, widow!
PETRUCHIO: A hundred marks, my Kate does put her down. 35
HORTENSIO: That's my office.
PETRUCHIO: Spoke like an officer—ha' to thee, lad. 37
    Drinks to Hortensio.
BAPTISTA: How likes Gremio these quick-witted folks?
GREMIO: Believe me, sir, they butt together well.
BIANCA: Head and butt! An hasty-witted body 40
    Would say your head and butt were head and horn. 41
VINCENTIO: Ay, mistress bride, hath that awakened you?

---

16 *fears* is afraid of (the widow quibbles on "frightens")
17 *afeard* frightened (Petruchio quibbles on "suspicious")
21 *Roundly* straightforwardly
22 *conceive by* am inspired by (Petruchio quibbles on "become pregnant by")
24 *conceives* devises
28, 29 *shrew, woe* (a rhyme, as at IV.1.200–1)
29 *Measures* judges
31 *mean* contemptible (the widow quibbles on have in mind, and Kate then quibbles on "moderate"—i.e., in shrewishness)
32 *respecting* compared with
35 *put her down* defeat her (Hortensio quibbles on "have sex with her")
37 *ha' to* here's to
40 *hasty-witted body* quick-witted person
41 *Would . . . horn* (presumably the usual joke about cuckoldry, but it is not clear why this should be aimed at the unmarried Gremio)

BIANCA: Ay, but not frighted me; therefore I'll sleep again.
PETRUCHIO: Nay, that you shall not; since you have begun.
  Have at you for a better jest or two.
BIANCA: Am I your bird? I mean to shift my bush,
  And then pursue me as you draw your bow.
  You are welcome all.
Exit Bianca [with Kate and Widow].
PETRUCHIO: She hath prevented me. Here, Signor Tranio,
  This bird you aimed at, though you hit her not.
  Therefore a health to all that shot and missed.
TRANIO: O sir, Lucentio slipped me, like his greyhound.
  Which runs himself and catches for his master.
PETRUCHIO: A good swift simile but something currish.
TRANIO: 'Tis well, sir, that you hunted for yourself;
  'Tis thought your deer does hold you at a bay.
BAPTISTA: O ho, Petruchio! Tranio hits you now.
LUCENTIO: I thank thee for that gird, good Tranio.
HORTENSIO: Confess, confess, hath he not hit you here?
PETRUCHIO: A has a little galled me, I confess.
  And as the jest did glance away from me,
  'Tis ten to one it maimed you two outright.
BAPTISTA: Now, in good sadness, son Petruchio,
  I think thou hast the veriest shrew of all.
PETRUCHIO: Well, I say no. And therefore, for assurance,
  Let's each one send unto his wife.
  And he whose wife is most obedient,
  To come at first when he doth send for her,
  Shall win the wager which we will propose.
HORTENSIO: Content. What's the wager?
LUCENTIO: Twenty crowns.
PETRUCHIO: Twenty crowns?
  I'll venture so much of my hawk or hound,
  But twenty times so much upon my wife.
LUCENTIO: A hundred then.
HORTENSIO: Content.
PETRUCHIO: A match, 'tis done.
HORTENSIO: Who shall begin?

---

45 *Have . . . for* get ready for
48 *You . . . all* (Bianca, as the hostess, leads the ladies out)
49 *prevented* forestalled; *Signor* (Petruchio ironically addresses Tranio as a gentleman)
52 *slipped* unleashed
58 *gird* taunt
60 *A* he; *galled* annoyed
63 *sadness* seriousness
64 *veriest* most perfect
65 *assurance* proof
72 *of* on
74 *match* bet

LUCENTIO: That will I.
Go, Biondello, bid your mistress come to me.
BIONDELLO: I go. *Exit.*
BAPTISTA: Son, I'll be your half, Bianca comes.
LUCENTIO: I'll have no halves; I'll bear it all myself.
Enter Biondello.
How now, what news?
BIONDELLO: Sir, my mistress sends you word
That she is busy and she cannot come.
PETRUCHIO: How? "She's busy and she cannot come"?
Is that an answer?
GREMIO: Ay, and a kind one too.
Pray God, sir, your wife send you not a worse.
PETRUCHIO: I hope better.
HORTENSIO: Sirrah Biondello, go and entreat my wife to come to me forthwith. *Exit Biondello.*
PETRUCHIO: O ho, "entreat her"! Nay, then she must needs come.
HORTENSIO: I am afraid, sir, do what you can, yours will not be entreated. (*Enter Biondello.*) Now where's my wife?
BIONDELLO: She says you have some goodly jest in hand.
She will not come. She bids you come to her.
PETRUCHIO: Worse and worse, "she will not come"!
O vile, intolerable, not to be endured!
Sirrah Grumio, go to your mistress,
Say I command her come to me. *Exit [Grumio].*
HORTENSIO: I know her answer.
PETRUCHIO: What?
HORTENSIO: She will not.
PETRUCHIO: The fouler fortune mine, and there an end.
Enter Kate [with Grumio].
BAPTISTA: Now, by my halidom, here comes Katherina!
KATE: What is your will, sir, that you send for me?
PETRUCHIO: Where is your sister and Hortensio's wife?
KATE: They sit conferring by the parlor fire.
PETRUCHIO: Go fetch them hither. If they deny to come,
Swinge me them soundly forth unto their husbands.
Away, I say, and bring them hither straight. [*Exit Kate.*]
LUCENTIO: Here is a wonder, if you talk of a wonder.
HORTENSIO: And so it is. I wonder what it bodes.
PETRUCHIO: Marry, peace it bodes, and love, and quiet life,
An awful rule and right supremacy,
And, to be short, what not that's sweet and happy.

---

79 *be your half* take half your bet that
89 *forthwith* immediately
103 *by my halidom* bless my soul (originally an oath by a sacred relic)
108 *Swinge me them* whip them for me
113 *awful* awe-inspiring; *right* proper
114 *what not* everything

Baptista: Now fair befall thee, good Petruchio.
The wager thou hast won, and I will add
Unto their losses twenty thousand crowns,
Another dowry to another daughter,
For she is changed as she had never been.
Petruchio: Nay, I will win my wager better yet
And show more sign of her obedience,
Her new-built virtue and obedience.
Enter Kate, Bianca, and Widow.
See where she comes and brings your froward wives
As prisoners to her womanly persuasion.
Katherine, that cap of yours becomes you not.
Off with the bauble, throw it under foot.
[*She obeys.*]
Widow: Lord, let me never have a cause to sigh
Till I be brought to such a silly pass.
Bianca: Fie, what a foolish duty call you this?
Lucentio: I would your duty were as foolish too.
The wisdom of your duty, fair Bianca,
Hath cost me a hundred crowns since suppertime.
Bianca: The more fool you for laying on my duty.
Petruchio: Katherine, I charge thee, tell these headstrong women
What duty they do owe their lords and husbands.
Widow: Come, come, you're mocking; we will have no telling.
Petruchio: Come on, I say, and first begin with her.
Widow: She shall not.
Petruchio: I say she shall—and first begin with her.
Kate: Fie, fie, unknit that threat'ning unkind brow
And dart not scornful glances from those eyes
To wound thy lord, thy king, thy governor.
It blots thy beauty as frosts do bite the meads,
Confounds thy fame as whirlwinds shake fair buds,
And in no sense is meet or amiable.
A woman moved is like a fountain troubled,
Muddy, ill-seeming, thick, bereft of beauty,
And while it is so, none so dry or thirsty
Will deign to sip or touch one drop of it.
Thy husband is thy lord, thy life, thy keeper,
Thy head, thy sovereign; one that cares for thee
And for thy maintenance; commits his body

---

128 *pass* predicament
133 *laying* betting
140 *unkind* (1) unfriendly, (2) unnatural
142 *governor* rules
144 *Confounds thy fame* spoils your good name
146 *moved* angry
151 *head* (1) ruler, (2) principle of reason

To painful labor both by sea and land,
To watch the night in storms, the day in cold,
Whilst thou liest warm at home, secure and safe;
And craves no other tribute at thy hands
But love, fair looks, and true obedience—
Too little payment for so great a debt.
Such duty as the subject owes the prince,
Even such a woman oweth to her husband;
And when she is froward, peevish, sullen, sour,
And not obedient to his honest will,
What is she but a foul contending rebel
And graceless traitor to her loving lord?
I am ashamed that women are so simple
To offer war where they should kneel for peace,
Or seek for rule, supremacy, and sway,
When they are bound to serve, love, and obey.
Why are our bodies soft and weak and smooth,
Unapt to toil and trouble in the world,
But that our soft conditions and our hearts
Should well agree with our external parts?
Come, come, you froward and unable worms,
My mind hath been as big as one of yours,
My heart as great, my reason haply more,
To bandy word for word and frown for frown.
But now I see our lances are but straws,
Our strength as weak, our weakness past compare,
That seeming to be most which we indeed least are.
Then vail your stomachs, for it is no boot,
And place your hands below your husband's foot,
In token of which duty, if he please,
My hand is ready, may it do him ease.

PETRUCHIO: Why, there's a wench! Come on and kiss me, Kate!
LUCENTIO: Well, go thy ways, old lad, for thou shalt ha't.
VINCENTIO: 'Tis a good hearing when children are toward.
LUCENTIO: But a harsh hearing when women are froward.
PETRUCHIO: Come, Kate, we'll to bed.

---

159 *prince* monarch
161 *peevish* obstinate
165 *simple* foolish
170 *Unapt to* unsuited for
171 *conditions* qualities
173 *unable* feeble
174 *big* haughty
176 *bandy* exchange (as in hitting a tennis ball back and forth)
180 *vail your stomachs* curb your willfulness; *no boot* no use
183 *may* it if it may
186 a *good hearing* i.e., good news; *toward* docile

We three are married, but you two are sped.
[*To Lucentio*]
'Twas I won the wager, though you hit the white,
And being a winner, God give you good night.
Exit Petruchio [with Kate].

HORTENSIO: Now, go thy ways, thou hast tamed a curst shrew.
LUCENTIO: 'Tis a wonder, by your leave, she will be tamed so. [*Exeunt.*]

The Tragical History of Hamlet Prince of Denmark

[Names of the Actors]

KING CLAUDIUS, of Denmark
HAMLET, son of the late, and nephew of the present, King
POLONIUS, Danish councillor
HORATIO, Hamlet's friend
LAERTES, Polonius's son
VOLTEMAND, CORNELIUS, ROSENCRANTZ, GUILDENSTERN, OSRIC, A GENTLEMAN } courtiers
A PRIEST
MARCELLUS, BARNARDO, FRANCISCO } soldiers
REYNALDO, servant in Polonius's household
PLAYERS, including Player King, Player Queen, Player Lucianus
TWO CLOWNS, one a gravedigger
FORTINBRAS, Prince of Norway
A NORWEGIAN CAPTAIN, in Fortinbras's army
ENGLISH AMBASSADORS
QUEEN GERTRUDE, of Denmark, Hamlet's mother
OPHELIA, Polonius's daughter
GHOST OF HAMLET'S FATHER
LORDS, LADIES, OFFICERS, SOLDIERS, SAILORS, MESSENGERS, ATTENDANTS

SCENE: *Denmark*]

★

---

189 *sped* done for (through having disobedient wives)
190 *white* bull's-eye (playing on "Bianca," white)
192, 193 *shrew, so* (a rhyme)

I.1

Enter Barnardo and Francisco, two sentinels.

BARNARDO: Who's there?
FRANCISCO: Nay, answer me. Stand and unfold yourself.
BARNARDO: Long live the king!
FRANCISCO: Barnardo?
BARNARDO: He.
FRANCISCO: You come most carefully upon your hour.
BARNARDO: 'Tis now struck twelve. Get thee to bed, Francisco.
FRANCISCO: For this relief much thanks. 'Tis bitter cold,
And I am sick at heart.
BARNARDO: Have you had quiet guard?
FRANCISCO: Not a mouse stirring.
BARNARDO: Well, good night.
If you do meet Horatio and Marcellus,
The rivals of my watch, bid them make haste.
Enter Horatio and Marcellus.
FRANCISCO: I think I hear them. Stand, ho! Who is there?
HORATIO: Friends to this ground.
MARCELLUS: And liegemen to the Dane.
FRANCISCO: Give you good night.
MARCELLUS: O, farewell, honest soldier.
Who hath relieved you?
FRANCISCO: Barnardo hath my place.
Give you good night.

Exit Francisco.

MARCELLUS: Holla, Barnardo!
BARNARDO: Say—
What, is Horatio there?
HORATIO: A piece of him.
BARNARDO: Welcome, Horatio. Welcome, good Marcellus.
HORATIO: What, has this thing appeared again tonight?
BARNARDO: I have seen nothing.
MARCELLUS: Horatio says 'tis but our fantasy,
And will not let belief take hold of him
Touching this dreaded sight twice seen of us.
Therefore I have entreated him along
With us to watch the minutes of this night,
That, if again this apparition come,
He may approve our eyes and speak to it.

I.1 Elsinore Castle, Denmark: the battlements
6 *upon your hour* right on time
13 *rivals* sharers
15 *liegemen* sworn followers; *Dane* King of Denmark
23 *fantasy* imagination
29 *approve* confirm

Horatio: Tush, tush, 'twill not appear.
Barnardo: Sit down awhile,
And let us once again assail your ears,
That are so fortified against our story,
What we have two nights seen.
Horatio: Well, sit we down,
And let us hear Barnardo speak of this.
Barnardo: Last night of all,
When yond same star that's westward from the pole
Had made his course t' illume that part of heaven
Where now it burns, Marcellus and myself,
The bell then beating one—
Enter Ghost.
Marcellus: Peace, break thee off. Look where it comes again.
Barnardo: In the same figure like the king that's dead.
Marcellus: Thou art a scholar; speak to it, Horatio.
Barnardo: Looks a not like the king? Mark it, Horatio.
Horatio: Most like. It harrows me with fear and wonder.
Barnardo: It would be spoke to.
Marcellus: Speak to it, Horatio.
Horatio: What art thou that usurp'st this time of night
Together with that fair and warlike form
In which the majesty of buried Denmark
Did sometimes march? By heaven I charge thee, speak.
Marcellus: It is offended.
Barnardo: See, it stalks away.
Horatio: Stay. Speak, speak. I charge thee, speak.
Exit Ghost.
Marcellus: 'Tis gone and will not answer.
Barnardo: How now, Horatio? You tremble and look pale.
Is not this something more than fantasy?
What think you on't?
Horatio: Before my God, I might not this believe
Without the sensible and true avouch
Of mine own eyes.
Marcellus: Is it not like the king?
Horatio: As thou art to thyself.
Such was the very armor he had on
When he the ambitious Norway combated.
So frowned he once when, in an angry parle,

---

36 *pole* polestar
43 *a* he
48 *buried Denmark* the buried King of Denmark (old Hamlet)
49 *sometimes* formerly
57 *avouch* assurance
61 *Norway* King of Norway
62 *parle* parley, negotiation under truce (said ironically)

He smote the sledded Polacks on the ice.
'Tis strange.
MARCELLUS: Thus twice before, and jump at this dead hour, 65
With martial stalk hath he gone by our watch.
HORATIO: In what particular thought to work I know not;
But, in the gross and scope of my opinion, 68
This bodes some strange eruption to our state. 69
MARCELLUS: Good now, sit down, and tell me he that knows, 70
Why this same strict and most observant watch
So nightly toils the subject of the land, 72
And why such daily cast of brazen cannon
And foreign mart for implements of war, 74
Why such impress of shipwrights, whose sore task 75
Does not divide the Sunday from the week.
What might be toward that this sweaty haste 77
Doth make the night joint laborer with the day?
Who is't that can inform me?
HORATIO: That can I.
At least the whisper goes so. Our last king, 80
Whose image even but now appeared to us,
Was as you know by Fortinbras of Norway, 82
Thereto pricked on by a most emulate pride, 83
Dared to the combat; in which our valiant Hamlet
(For so this side of our known world esteemed him)
Did slay this Fortinbras; who, by a sealed compact
Well ratified by law and heraldry, 87
Did forfeit, with his life, all those his lands
Which he stood seized of to the conqueror; 89
Against the which a moiety competent 90
Was gagèd by our king, which had returned 91
To the inheritance of Fortinbras
Had he been vanquisher, as, by the same comart 93
And carriage of the article designed, 94

65 *jump* just, exactly
68 *gross and scope* gross scope, general view
69 *strange eruption* unexpected, destructive change
72 *toils* makes toil; *subject*, subjects
74 *mart* trading
75 *impress* conscription
77 *toward* in preparation, coming on
82 *Fortinbras of Norway* i.e., father of *young Fortinbras* (l. 95)
83 *emulate* jealously rivaling
87 *law and heraldry* law of heralds regulating combat
89 *seized* possessed
90 *moiety competent* sufficient portion
91 *gagèd* engaged, staked
93 *comart* joint bargain
94 *carriage* purport

His fell to Hamlet. Now, sir, young Fortinbras, 95
Of unimprovèd mettle hot and full, 96
Hath in the skirts of Norway here and there
Sharked up a list of lawless resolutes 98
For food and diet to some enterprise
That hath a stomach in't; which is no other, 100
As it doth well appear unto our state,
But to recover of us by strong hand
And terms compulsatory those foresaid lands
So by his father lost; and this, I take it,
Is the main motive of our preparations,
The source of this our watch, and the chief head 106
Of this posthaste and rummage in the land. 107

BARNARDO: I think it be no other but e'en so.
Well may it sort that this portentous figure 109
Comes armèd through our watch so like the king 110
That was and is the question of these wars.

HORATIO: A mote it is to trouble the mind's eye. 112
In the most high and palmy state of Rome, 113
A little ere the mightiest Julius fell,
The graves stood tenantless and the sheeted dead 115
Did squeak and gibber in the Roman streets;
As stars with trains of fire and dews of blood, 117
Disasters in the sun; and the moist star 118
Upon whose influence Neptune's empire stands 119
Was sick almost to doomsday with eclipse. 120
And even the like precurse of feared events, 121
As harbingers preceding still the fates 122
And prologue to the omen coming on, 123
Have heaven and earth together demonstrated

---

95 *His* i.e., old Fortinbras's share, had he won
96 *unimprovèd* unused
98 *Sharked* snatched indiscriminately, press-ganged; *list* roll call; *resolutes* determined people
100 *stomach* promise of danger
106 *head* fountainhead, source
107 *posthaste* bustle, urgency; *rummage* disorder, ransacking
109 *sort* be fitting; *portentous* ominous
112 *mote* speck of dust
113 *palmy* successful, victorious
115 *sheeted* in burial shrouds
117 *As* (this line does not follow grammatically from the preceding one, although it continues to list dangerous portents; some words have probably been omitted accidentally)
118 *Disasters* omens; *moist star* moon
119 *stands* depends
120 *sick almost to doomsday* almost as terrible as the Christian Apocalypse
121 *precurse* foreshadowing
122 *harbingers* forerunners; *still* constantly
123 *omen* calamity

Unto our climatures and countrymen.
Enter Ghost.
But soft, behold, lo where it comes again!
I'll cross it, though it blast me.—Stay, illusion.
[He] spreads his arms.
If thou hast any sound or use of voice,
Speak to me.
If there be any good thing to be done
That may to thee do ease and grace to me,
Speak to me.
If thou art privy to thy country's fate,
Which happily foreknowing may avoid,
O, speak!
Or if thou hast uphoarded in thy life
Extorted treasure in the womb of earth,
For which, they say, your spirits oft walk in death,
The cock crows.
Speak of it. Stay and speak. Stop it, Marcellus.

MARCELLUS: Shall I strike it with my partisan?

HORATIO: Do, if it will not stand.

BARNARDO: 'Tis here.

HORATIO: 'Tis here.

MARCELLUS: 'Tis gone. [*Exit Ghost.*]
We do it wrong, being so majestical,
To offer it the show of violence,
For it is as the air invulnerable,
And our vain blows malicious mockery.

BARNARDO: It was about to speak when the cock crew.

HORATIO: And then it started, like a guilty thing
Upon a fearful summons. I have heard
The cock, that is the trumpet to the morn,
Doth with his lofty and shrill-sounding throat
Awake the god of day, and at his warning,
Whether in sea or fire, in earth or air,
Th' extravagant and erring spirit hies
To his confine; and of the truth herein
This present object made probation.

---

125 *climatures* regions
127 *cross it* cross its path, confront it
134 *happily* haply, perchance
138 *your* (an indefinite usage referring to hearers in general, not a specific interlocutor; F reads "you")
140 *partisan* pike (a spearlike weapon)
141 *stand* stop, stand still
152 *god of day* i.e., sun
154 *extravagant* wandering beyond bounds; *erring* wandering
156 *probation* test

MARCELLUS: It faded on the crowing of the cock.
Some say that ever 'gainst that season comes 158
Wherein our Savior's birth is celebrated,
This bird of dawning singeth all night long, 160
And then, they say, no spirit dare stir abroad,
The nights are wholesome, then no planets strike, 162
No fairy takes, nor witch hath power to charm, 163
So hallowed and so gracious is that time. 164
HORATIO: So have I heard and do in part believe it.
But look, the morn in russet mantle clad 166
Walks o'er the dew of yon high eastward hill.
Break we our watch up, and by my advice
Let us impart what we have seen tonight
Unto young Hamlet, for upon my life 170
This spirit, dumb to us, will speak to him. 171
Do you consent we shall acquaint him with it,
As needful in our loves, fitting our duty?
MARCELLUS: Let's do't, I pray, and I this morning know
Where we shall find him most convenient. 175
Exeunt.

★

I.2

Flourish. Enter Claudius, King of Denmark, Gertrude the Queen, Councillors, Polonius and his son Laertes, Hamlet, cum aliis [including Voltemand and Cornelius].

KING: Though yet of Hamlet our dear brother's death 1
The memory be green, and that it us befitted
To bear our hearts in grief, and our whole kingdom
To be contracted in one brow of woe,
Yet so far hath discretion fought with nature
That we with wisest sorrow think on him
Together with remembrance of ourselves.
Therefore our sometime sister, now our queen, 8

---

158 *'gainst* just before
158–59 *season . . . celebrated* i.e., Christmastime
162 *strike* work evil by influence
163 *takes* bewitches
164 *gracious* full of (divine) grace
166 *russet* reddish brown rough cloth
171 *dumb* silent
175 *convenient* i.e., conveniently (Shakespeare often uses adjectives for adverbs)

I.2 Elsinore s.d. *cum aliis* with others
1 *our* my (the royal plural)
8 *sometime sister* former sister-in-law

Th' imperial jointress to this warlike state,
Have we, as 'twere with a defeated joy,
With an auspicious and a dropping eye,
With mirth in funeral and with dirge in marriage,
In equal scale weighing delight and dole,
Taken to wife. Nor have we herein barred
Your better wisdoms, which have freely gone
With this affair along. For all, our thanks.
Now follows, that you know, young Fortinbras,
Holding a weak supposal of our worth,
Or thinking by our late dear brother's death
Our state to be disjoint and out of frame,
Colleaguèd with this dream of his advantage,
He hath not failed to pester us with message
Importing the surrender of those lands
Lost by his father, with all bands of law,
To our most valiant brother. So much for him.
Now for ourself and for this time of meeting.
Thus much the business is: we have here writ
To Norway, uncle of young Fortinbras—
Who, impotent and bedrid, scarcely hears
Of this his nephew's purpose—to suppress
His further gait herein, in that the levies,
The lists, and full proportions are all made
Out of his subject; and we here dispatch
You, good Cornelius, and you, Voltemand,
For bearers of this greeting to old Norway,
Giving to you no further personal power
To business with the king, more than the scope
Of these delated articles allow.
Farewell, and let your haste commend your duty.

CORNELIUS, VOLTEMAND: In that, and all things, will we show our duty.

KING: We doubt it nothing. Heartily farewell.

[*Exeunt Voltemand and Cornelius.*]

And now, Laertes, what's the news with you?
You told us of some suit. What is't, Laertes?
You cannot speak of reason to the Dane

---

9 *jointress* widow who has a jointure, or joint tenancy, of an estate (with this word and *imperial*, Claudius acknowledges Gertrude as co-sovereign)
14 *barred* excluded
21 *Colleaguèd* united
24 *bands* bonds
31 *gait* going
32 *proportions* amounts of forces and supplies
38 *delated* (1) expressly stated, (2) conveyed
43 *suit* request
44 *Dane* King of Denmark

And lose your voice. What wouldst thou beg, Laertes,
That shall not be my offer, not thy asking?
The head is not more native to the heart,
The hand more instrumental to the mouth,
Than is the throne of Denmark to thy father.
What wouldst thou have, Laertes?

LAERTES: My dread lord,
Your leave and favor to return to France,
From whence though willingly I came to Denmark
To show my duty in your coronation,
Yet now I must confess, that duty done,
My thoughts and wishes bend again toward France
And bow them to your gracious leave and pardon.

KING: Have you your father's leave? What says Polonius?

POLONIUS: He hath, my lord, wrung from me my slow leave
By laborsome petition, and at last
Upon his will I sealed my hard consent.
I do beseech you give him leave to go.

KING: Take thy fair hour, Laertes. Time be thine,
And thy best graces spend it at thy will.
But now, my cousin Hamlet, and my son—

HAMLET: [*Aside*]
A little more than kin, and less than kind!

KING: How is it that the clouds still hang on you?

HAMLET: Not so, my lord. I am too much in the sun.

QUEEN: Good Hamlet, cast thy nighted color off,
And let thine eye look like a friend on Denmark,
Do not for ever with thy vailèd lids
Seek for thy noble father in the dust.
Thou know'st 'tis common. All that lives must die,
Passing through nature to eternity.

HAMLET: Ay, madam, it is common.

QUEEN: If it be,
Why seems it so particular with thee?

HAMLET: Seems, madam? Nay, it is. I know not "seems."
'Tis not alone my inky cloak, good mother,
Nor customary suits of solemn black,
Nor windy suspiration of forced breath,
No, nor the fruitful river in the eye,

---

45 *lose your voice* speak in vain
47 *native* joined by nature
48 *instrumental* serviceable
60 *hard* i.e., hard-won
64 *cousin* kinsman more distant than parent, child, brother, or sister
65 *kin* related as nephew; *kind* (1) natural, (2) kindly, affectionate, (3) related by direct descent, member of the immediate family
67 *sun* sunshine of the king's unwanted favor (with wordplay on "place of a son")
70 *vailèd* downcast

Nor the dejected havior of the visage,
Together with all forms, moods, shapes of grief,
That can denote me truly. These indeed seem,
For they are actions that a man might play,
But I have that within which passes show—
These but the trappings and the suits of woe.

KING: 'Tis sweet and commendable in your nature, Hamlet,
To give these mourning duties to your father,
But you must know your father lost a father,
That father lost, lost his, and the survivor bound
In filial obligation for some term
To do obsequious sorrow. But to persever
In obstinate condolement is a course
Of impious stubbornness. 'Tis unmanly grief.
It shows a will most incorrect to heaven,
A heart unfortified, or mind impatient,
An understanding simple and unschooled.
For what we know must be and is as common
As any the most vulgar thing to sense,
Why should we in our peevish opposition
Take it to heart? Fie, 'tis a fault to heaven,
A fault against the dead, a fault to nature,
To reason most absurd, whose common theme
Is death of fathers, and who still hath cried,
From the first corpse till he that died today,
"This must be so." We pray you throw to earth
This unprevailing woe, and think of us
As of a father, for let the world take note
You are the most immediate to our throne,
And with no less nobility of love
Than that which dearest father bears his son
Do I impart toward you. For your intent
In going back to school in Wittenberg,
It is most retrograde to our desire,
And we beseech you, bend you to remain
Here in the cheer and comfort of our eye,
Our chiefest courtier, cousin, and our son.

QUEEN: Let not thy mother lose her prayers, Hamlet.
I pray thee stay with us, go not to Wittenberg.

HAMLET: I shall in all my best obey you, madam.

KING: Why, 'tis a loving and a fair reply.
Be as ourself in Denmark. Madam, come.

---

81 *havior* behavior, demeanor
84 *play* feign, playact
92 *obsequious* proper to obsequies (funerals); *persever* persevere (accented on the second syllable, as always in Shakespeare)
109 *most immediate to* i.e., next to inherit
114 *retrograde* contrary

This gentle and unforced accord of Hamlet
Sits smiling to my heart, in grace whereof
No jocund health that Denmark drinks today
But the great cannon to the clouds shall tell,
And the king's rouse the heaven shall bruit again, 127
Respeaking earthly thunder. Come away.

Flourish. Exeunt all but Hamlet.

HAMLET: O that this too too sullied flesh would melt, 129
Thaw, and resolve itself into a dew, 130
Or that the Everlasting had not fixed
His canon 'gainst self-slaughter. O God, God, 132
How weary, stale, flat, and unprofitable
Seem to me all the uses of this world!
Fie on't, ah, fie, 'tis an unweeded garden
That grows to seed. Things rank and gross in nature
Possess it merely. That it should come to this, 137
But two months dead, nay, not so much, not two,
So excellent a king, that was to this
Hyperion to a satyr, so loving to my mother 140
That he might not beteem the winds of heaven 141
Visit her face too roughly. Heaven and earth,
Must I remember? Why, she would hang on him
As if increase of appetite had grown
By what it fed on, and yet within a month—
Let me not think on't; frailty, thy name is woman—
A little month, or ere those shoes were old
With which she followed my poor father's body
Like Niobe, all tears, why she— 149
O God, a beast that wants discourse of reason 150
Would have mourned longer—married with my uncle,
My father's brother, but no more like my father
Than I to Hercules. Within a month,
Ere yet the salt of most unrighteous tears
Had left the flushing in her gallèd eyes, 155
She married. O, most wicked speed, to post

---

127 *rouse* toast drunk in wine; *bruit* echo, make noise
129 *sullied* dirtied, discolored
130 *resolve* dissolve
132 *canon* law
137 *merely* completely
140 *Hyperion* the sun god
141 *beteem* allow
149 *Niobe* (in Greek myth, after Niobe boasted she had more children than Leto, Niobe's children were killed by Apollo and Artemis, Leto's children; Zeus transformed the grieving Niobe into a stone that continually dropped tears)
150 *discourse* logical power or process
155 *gallèd* irritated

With such dexterity to incestuous sheets!
It is not nor it cannot come to good.
But break my heart, for I must hold my tongue.
Enter Horatio, Marcellus, and Barnardo.
HORATIO: Hail to your lordship!
HAMLET: I am glad to see you well.
Horatio—or I do forget myself.
HORATIO: The same, my lord, and your poor servant ever.
HAMLET: Sir, my good friend, I'll change that name with you.
And what make you from Wittenberg, Horatio?
Marcellus?
MARCELLUS: My good lord!
HAMLET: I am very glad to see you. [*To Barnardo*] Good even, sir.
But what, in faith, make you from Wittenberg?
HORATIO: A truant disposition, good my lord.
HAMLET: I would not hear your enemy say so,
Nor shall you do my ear that violence
To make it truster of your own report
Against yourself. I know you are no truant.
But what is your affair in Elsinore?
We'll teach you for to drink ere you depart.
HORATIO: My lord, I came to see your father's funeral.
HAMLET: I prithee do not mock me, fellow student.
I think it was to see my mother's wedding.
HORATIO: Indeed, my lord, it followed hard upon.
HAMLET: Thrift, thrift, Horatio. The funeral baked meats
Did coldly furnish forth the marriage tables.
Would I had met my dearest foe in heaven
Or ever I had seen that day, Horatio!
My father—methinks I see my father.
HORATIO: Where, my lord?
HAMLET: In my mind's eye, Horatio.
HORATIO: I saw him once. A was a goodly king.
HAMLET: A was a man, take him for all in all,
I shall not look upon his like again.
HORATIO: My lord, I think I saw him yesternight.
HAMLET: Saw? Who?
HORATIO: My lord, the king your father.
HAMLET: The king my father?

---

159 *But . . . tongue* (Hamlet alludes to a Latin and an English proverb claiming that unspoken griefs crush the heart)
163 *change* exchange
164 *make* do
175 *for to* to (archaic phrase)
182 *dearest* direst, bitterest
186, 187 *A* he

HORATIO: Season your admiration for a while
With an attent ear till I may deliver
Upon the witness of these gentlemen
This marvel to you.
HAMLET: For God's love let me hear!
HORATIO: Two nights together had these gentlemen,
Marcellus and Barnardo, on their watch
In the dead waste and middle of the night
Been thus encountered. A figure like your father,
Armèd at point exactly, cap-à-pie,
Appears before them and with solemn march
Goes slow and stately by them. Thrice he walked
By their oppressed and fear-surprisèd eyes
Within his truncheon's length, whilst they, distilled
Almost to jelly with the act of fear.
Stand dumb and speak not to him. This to me
In dreadful secrecy impart they did,
And I with them the third night kept the watch,
Where, as they had delivered, both in time,
Form of the thing, each word made true and good,
The apparition comes. I knew your father.
These hands are not more like.
HAMLET: But where was this?
MARCELLUS: My lord, upon the platform where we watched.
HAMLET: Did you not speak to it?
HORATIO: My lord, I did,
But answer made it none. Yet once methought
It lifted up it head and did address
Itself to motion like as it would speak.
But even then the morning cock crew loud,
And at the sound it shrunk in haste away
And vanished from our sight.
HAMLET: 'Tis very strange.
HORATIO: As I do live, my honored lord, 'tis true,
And we did think it writ down in our duty
To let you know of it.
HAMLET: Indeed, sirs, but this troubles me.
Hold you the watch tonight?
ALL: We do, my lord.
HAMLET: Armed, say you?

---

192 *Season your admiration* control your wonder
193 *attent* attentive, alert
200 *at point* completely; *cap-à-pie* from head to foot
204 *truncheon* military commander's baton
207 *dreadful* full of dread, fearful
213 *platform* battlement
216 *it* its (archaic, but common in Shakespeare)
216–17 *did address . . . motion* began to move

ALL: Armed, my lord.
HAMLET: From top to toe?
ALL: My lord, from head to foot.
HAMLET: Then saw you not his face?
HORATIO: O, yes, my lord. He wore his beaver up.
HAMLET: What, looked he frowningly?
HORATIO: A countenance more in sorrow than in anger.
HAMLET: Pale or red?
HORATIO: Nay, very pale.
HAMLET: And fixed his eyes upon you?
HORATIO: Most constantly.
HAMLET: I would I had been there.
HORATIO: It would have much amazed you.
HAMLET: Very like. Stayed it long?
HORATIO: While one with moderate haste might tell a hundred.
BOTH: Longer, longer.
HORATIO: Not when I saw't.
HAMLET: His beard was grizzled, no?
HORATIO: It was as I have seen it in his life,
A sable silvered.
HAMLET: I will watch tonight.
Perchance 'twill walk again.
HORATIO: I warr'nt it will.
HAMLET: If it assume my noble father's person,
I'll speak to it though hell itself should gape
And bid me hold my peace. I pray you all,
If you have hitherto concealed this sight,
Let it be tenable in your silence still,
And whatsomever else shall hap tonight,
Give it an understanding but no tongue.
I will requite your loves. So fare you well.
Upon the platform, 'twixt eleven and twelve
I'll visit you.
ALL: Our duty to your honor.
HAMLET: Your loves, as mine to you. Farewell.

Exeunt [all but Hamlet].

My father's spirit—in arms? All is not well.
I doubt some foul play. Would the night were come!
Till then sit still, my soul. Foul deeds will rise
Though all the earth o'erwhelm them to men's eyes. *Exit.*

★

230 *beaver* movable face guard of the helmet
238 *tell* count
240 *grizzled* gray
242 *sable silvered* black mixed with white
248 *tenable* held firmly
256 *doubt* suspect, fear
257–58 *Foul . . . eyes* (proverbially, murder cannot be hidden)

I.3

Enter Laertes and Ophelia, his sister.

LAERTES: My necessaries are embarked. Farewell.
And, sister, as the winds give benefit
And convoy is assistant, do not sleep,
But let me hear from you.
OPHELIA: Do you doubt that?
LAERTES: For Hamlet, and the trifling of his favor,
Hold it a fashion and a toy in blood,
A violet in the youth of primy nature,
Forward, not permanent, sweet, not lasting,
The perfume and suppliance of a minute,
No more.
OPHELIA: No more but so?
LAERTES: Think it no more.
For nature crescent does not grow alone
In thews and bulk, but as this temple waxes
The inward service of the mind and soul
Grows wide withal. Perhaps he loves you now,
And now no soil nor cautel doth besmirch
The virtue of his will, but you must fear,
His greatness weighed, his will is not his own.
He may not, as unvalued persons do,
Carve for himself, for on his choice depends
The safety and health of this whole state,
And therefore must his choice be circumscribed
Unto the voice and yielding of that body
Whereof he is the head. Then if he says he loves you,
It fits your wisdom so far to believe it
As he in his particular act and place
May give his saying deed, which is no further
Than the main voice of Denmark goes withal,
Then weigh what loss your honor may sustain

I.3 Elsinore Castle: Polonius's rooms
3 *convoy* means of transport
6 *toy* passing fancy
7 *of primy* of the springtime
8 *Forward* blooming early
9 *perfume and suppliance* filling sweetness
11 *crescent* growing
12 *this temple* the body
15 *cautel* deceit
16 *virtue* (1) strength, (2) virtuousness; *will* desire
17 *greatness weighed* high position considered
19 *Carve* choose (with romantic or erotic choice implied)
22 *yielding* assent

If with too credent ear you list his songs, 29
Or lose your heart, or your chaste treasure open 30
To his unmastered importunity.
Fear it, Ophelia, fear it, my dear sister,
And keep you in the rear of your affection, 33
Out of the shot and danger of desire.
The chariest maid is prodigal enough 35
If she unmask her beauty to the moon.
Virtue itself scapes not calumnious strokes.
The canker galls the infants of the spring 38
Too oft before their buttons be disclosed, 39
And in the morn and liquid dew of youth 40
Contagious blastments are most imminent. 41
Be wary then; best safety lies in fear.
Youth to itself rebels, though none else near.

OPHELIA: I shall the effect of this good lesson keep
As watchman to my heart, but, good my brother,
Do not as some ungracious pastors do,
Show me the steep and thorny way to heaven,
Whiles like a puffed and reckless libertine
Himself the primrose path of dalliance treads
And recks not his own rede. 50

Enter Polonius.

LAERTES: O, fear me not.
I stay too long. But here my father comes.
A double blessing is a double grace;
Occasion smiles upon a second leave.

POLONIUS: Yet here, Laertes? Aboard, aboard, for shame!
The wind sits in the shoulder of your sail,
And you are stayed for. There—my blessing with thee,
And these few precepts in thy memory
Look thou character. Give thy thoughts no tongue, 58
Nor any unproportioned thought his act. 59
Be thou familiar, but by no means vulgar. 60
Those friends thou hast, and their adoption tried,
Grapple them unto thy soul with hoops of steel,
But do not dull thy palm with entertainment
Of each new-hatched, unfledged courage. Beware 64

---

29 *credent* credulous; *list* listen to
33 *affection* feeling (which rashly lead into dangers)
35 *chariest* most careful
38 *canker* rose worm; *galls* injures
39 *buttons* buds
41 *blastments* blights
50 *recks* regards; *rede* counsel
58 *character* inscribe, write
59 *unproportioned* distorted from what is right
64 *courage* man of spirit, young blood

Of entrance to a quarrel; but being in,
Bear't that th' opposèd may beware of thee.
Give every man thy ear, but few thy voice;
Take each man's censure, but reserve thy judgment.
Costly thy habit as thy purse can buy,
But not expressed in fancy; rich, not gaudy,
For the apparel oft proclaims the man,
And they in France of the best rank and station
Are of a most select and generous chief in that.
Neither a borrower nor a lender be,
For loan oft loses both itself and friend,
And borrowing dulleth edge of husbandry.
This above all, to thine own self be true,
And it must follow as the night the day
Thou canst not then be false to any man.
Farewell, My blessing season this in thee!
LAERTES: Most humbly do I take my leave, my lord.
POLONIUS: The time invites you. Go, your servants tend.
LAERTES: Farewell, Ophelia, and remember well
What I have said to you.
OPHELIA: 'Tis in my memory locked,
And you yourself shall keep the key of it.
LAERTES: Farewell. *Exit Laertes.*
POLONIUS: What is't, Ophelia, he hath said to you?
OPHELIA: So please you, something touching the Lord Hamlet.
POLONIUS: Marry, well bethought.
'Tis told me he hath very oft of late
Given private time to you, and you yourself
Have of your audience been most free and bounteous.
If it be so—as so 'tis put on me,
And that in way of caution—I must tell you
You do not understand yourself so clearly
As it behooves my daughter and your honor.
What is between you? Give me up the truth.
OPHELIA: He hath, my lord, of late made many tenders
Of his affection to me.
POLONIUS: Affection? Pooh! You speak like a green girl,
Unsifted in such perilous circumstance.
Do you believe his tenders, as you call them?

---

68 *censure* judgment
73 *chief* eminence (English prejudice found the French overly fashion-conscious)
76 *husbandry* thriftiness
80 *season* ripen and make fruitful
82 *tend* wait
89 *Marry* by (the Virgin) Mary (a weak oath)
98 *tenders* offers
101 *Unsifted* untested

Ophelia: I do not know, my lord, what I should think.
Polonius: Marry, I will teach you. Think yourself a baby
 That you have ta'en these tenders for true pay
 Which are not sterling. Tender yourself more dearly,
 Or (not to crack the wind of the poor phrase,
 Running it thus) you'll tender me a fool.
Ophelia: My lord, he hath importuned me with love
 In honorable fashion.
Polonius: Ay, fashion you may call it. Go to, go to.
Ophelia: And hath given countenance to his speech, my lord,
 With almost all the holy vows of heaven.
Polonius: Ay, springes to catch woodcocks. I do know,
 When the blood burns, how prodigal the soul
 Lends the tongue vows. These blazes, daughter,
 Giving more light than heat, extinct in both
 Even in their promise, as it is a-making,
 You must not take for fire. From this time
 Be something scanter of your maiden presence.
 Set your entreatments at a higher rate
 Than a command to parley. For Lord Hamlet,
 Believe so much in him that he is young,
 And with a larger tether may he walk
 Than may be given you. In few, Ophelia,
 Do not believe his vows, for they are brokers,
 Not of that dye which their investments show,
 But mere implorators of unholy suits,
 Breathing like sanctified and pious bawds
 The better to beguile. This is for all:
 I would not, in plain terms, from this time forth
 Have you so slander any moment leisure.
 As to give words or talk with the Lord Hamlet.
 Look to't, I charge you. Come your ways.
Ophelia: I shall obey, my lord.

Exeunt.

⋆

105–8 *tenders . . . Tender . . . tender* offers . . . hold in regard . . . present (wordplay runs through these three meanings; the last use of the word yields further complexity with its implication that she will show herself to Polonius as a *fool* [l, 108], will show him to the world as a fool, and may go so far as to present him with a *fool*, an Elizabethan term of endearment especially applied to an infant)
107 *crack . . . of* make wheeze like a horse driven too hard
111 *Go to* go away, go on (an expression of impatience)
114 *springes* snares; *woodcocks* (birds believed to be foolish)
121 *entreatments* military negotiations for surrender
122 *parley* confer with a besieger
126 *brokers* middlemen, panders
127 *investments* clothes
132 *slander* use disgracefully; *moment* momentary

I.4

Enter Hamlet, Horatio, and Marcellus.

HAMLET: The air bites shrewdly; it is very cold. 1
HORATIO: It is a nipping and an eager air. 2
HAMLET: What hour now?
HORATIO: I think it lacks of twelve.
MARCELLUS: No, it is struck.
HORATIO: Indeed? I heard it not. It then draws near the season
Wherein the spirit held his wont to walk. 6
A flourish of trumpets, and two pieces goes off.
What does this mean, my lord?
HAMLET: The king doth wake tonight and takes his rouse, 8
Keeps wassail, and the swaggering upspring reels, 9
And as he drains his draughts of Rhenish down 10
The kettledrum and trumpet thus bray out
The triumph of his pledge. 12
HORATIO: Is it a custom?
HAMLET: Ay, marry, is't,
But to my mind, though I am native here
And to the manner born, it is a custom
More honored in the breach than the observance. 16
This heavy-headed revel east and west
Makes us traduced and taxed of other nations. 18
They clepe us drunkards and with swinish phrase 19
Soil our addition, and indeed it takes 20
From our achievements, though performed at height,
The pith and marrow of our attribute. 22
So oft it chances in particular men
That (for some vicious mole of nature in them, 24
As in their birth, wherein they are not guilty,
Since nature cannot choose his origin) 26

I.4 Elsinore: the battlements
1 *shrewdly* wickedly, bitterly
2 *an eager* a sharp
6 s.d. *pieces* cannon
8 *rouse* carousal
9 *upspring* German dance
10 *draughts* gulps; *Rhenish* Rhine wine
12 *triumph* achievement, feat (in downing a cup of wine at one gulp)
16 *More . . . observance* better broken than observed
18 *taxed of* censured by
19 *clepe* call
20 *addition* reputation, title added as a distinction
22 *attribute* reputation, what is attributed
24 *mole* blemish, flaw
26 *his* its

By the o'ergrowth of some complexion,
Oft breaking down the pales and forts of reason,
Or by some habit that too much o'erleavens
The form of plausive manners—that (these men
Carrying, I say, the stamp of one defect,
Being nature's livery, or fortune's star)
His virtues else, be they as pure as grace,
As infinite as man may undergo,
Shall in the general censure take corruption
From that particular fault. The dram of evil
Doth all the noble substance often dout,
To his own scandal.

Enter Ghost.

HORATIO: Look, my lord, it comes.

HAMLET: Angels and ministers of grace defend us!
Be thou a spirit of health or goblin damned,
Bring with thee airs from heaven or blasts from hell,
Be thy intents wicked or charitable,
Thou com'st in such a questionable shape
That I will speak to thee. I'll call thee Hamlet,
King, father, royal Dane. O, answer me!
Let me not burst in ignorance, but tell
Why thy canonized bones, hearsèd in death,
Have burst their cerements, why the sepulchre
Wherein we saw thee quietly interred
Hath oped his ponderous and marble jaws
To cast thee up again. What may this mean
That thou, dead corpse, again in complete steel,
Revisits thus the glimpses of the moon,
Making night hideous, and we fools of nature
So horridly to shake our disposition
With thoughts beyond the reaches of our souls?
Say, why is this? wherefore? what should we do?

[Ghost] beckons.

HORATIO: It beckons you to go away with it,

---

27 *complexion* part of an individual's human nature
28 *pales* barriers, fences
29 *o'erleavens* works change throughout, as yeast ferments dough
30 *plausive* pleasing
32 *livery* (1) badge or other identifying token, (2) provision, what *nature* gives us; *star* astrologically determined human nature
37 *dout* extinguish, put out
40 *of health* sound, good; *goblin* fiend
47 *canonized* buried with the established rites of the church
48 *cerements* waxed grave cloths
54 *fools of nature* men made conscious of natural limitations by a supernatural manifestation
55 *disposition* mental constitution

As if it some impartment did desire
To you alone.
MARCELLUS: Look with what courteous action
It waves you to a more removèd ground.
But do not go with it.
HORATIO: No, by no means.
HAMLET: It will not speak. Then I will follow it.
HORATIO: Do not, my lord.
HAMLET: Why, what should be the fear?
I do not set my life at a pin's fee,
And for my soul, what can it do to that,
Being a thing immortal as itself?
It waves me forth again. I'll follow it.
HORATIO: What if it tempt you toward the flood, my lord,
Or to the dreadful summit of the cliff
That beetles o'er his base into the sea,
And there assume some other horrible form,
Which might deprive your sovereignty of reason
And draw you into madness? Think of it.
The very place puts toys of desperation,
Without more motive, into every brain
That looks so many fathoms to the sea
And hears it roar beneath.
HAMLET: It waves me still.
Go on. I'll follow thee.
MARCELLUS: You shall not go, my lord.
HAMLET: Hold off your hands.
HORATIO: Be ruled. You shall not go.
HAMLET: My fate cries out
And makes each petty artire in this body
As hardy as the Nemean lion's nerve.
Still am I called. Unhand me, gentlemen.
By heaven, I'll make a ghost of him that lets me!
I say, away! Go on. I'll follow thee.
Exit Ghost and Hamlet.

HORATIO: He waxes desperate with imagination.
MARCELLUS: Let's follow. 'Tis not fit thus to obey him.

---

59 *some impartment* something to impart, to say
61 *removèd* farther away, more remote
65 *a pin's fee* the value of a pin (i.e., very little)
71 *beetles* juts out
73 *deprive* take away; *sovereignty of reason* state of being ruled by reason
75 *toys* fancies
82 *artire* artery
83 *Nemean lion* lion Hercules killed in the first of his twelve labors; *nerve* sinew
85 *lets* hinders

HORATIO: Have after. To what issue will this come?
MARCELLUS: Something is rotten in the state of Denmark.
HORATIO: Heaven will direct it.
MARCELLUS: Nay, let's follow him.
Exeunt.

★

I.5

Enter Ghost and Hamlet.

HAMLET: Whither wilt thou lead me? Speak. I'll go no further.
GHOST: Mark me.
HAMLET: I will.
GHOST: My hour is almost come,
When I to sulph'rous and tormenting flames
Must render up myself.
HAMLET: Alas, poor ghost!
GHOST: Pity me not, but lend thy serious hearing
To what I shall unfold.
HAMLET: Speak. I am bound to hear.
GHOST: So art thou to revenge, when thou shalt hear.
HAMLET: What?
GHOST: I am thy father's spirit,
Doomed for a certain term to walk the night,
And for the day confined to fast in fires,
Till the foul crimes done in my days of nature
Are burnt and purged away. But that I am forbid
To tell the secrets of my prison house,
I could a tale unfold whose lightest word
Would harrow up thy soul, freeze thy young blood,
Make thy two eyes like stars start from their spheres,
Thy knotted and combinèd locks to part,
And each particular hair to stand an end
Like quills upon the fearful porcupine.
But this eternal blazon must not be

---

90 *state* highest position (here, royal status)

I.5 Elsinore the battlements
2 *My hour* daybreak
3 *flames* sufferings in purgatory (not hell)
11 *fast* do penance
17 *spheres* transparent revolving shells in each of which, according to Ptolemaic astronomy, a planet or other heavenly body was placed
19 *an* on
20 *fearful* (1) frightened, (2) frightening
21 *eternal blazon* depiction of eternity

To ears of flesh and blood. List, list, O, list!
If thou didst ever thy dear father love—
HAMLET: O God!
GHOST: Revenge his foul and most unnatural murder.
HAMLET: Murder?
GHOST: Murder most foul, as in the best it is,
But this most foul, strange, and unnatural.
HAMLET: Haste me to know't, that I, with wings as swift
As meditation or the thoughts of love,
May sweep to my revenge.
GHOST: I find thee apt,
And duller shouldst thou be than the fat weed
That roots itself in ease on Lethe wharf,
Wouldst thou not stir in this. Now, Hamlet, hear.
'Tis given out that, sleeping in my orchard,
A serpent stung me. So the whole ear of Denmark
Is by a forgèd process of my death
Rankly abused. But know, thou noble youth,
The serpent that did sting thy father's life
Now wears his crown.
HAMLET: O my prophetic soul!
My uncle?
GHOST: Ay, that incestuous, that adulterate beast,
With witchcraft of his wit, with traitorous gifts—
O wicked wit and gifts, that have the power
So to seduce!—won to his shameful lust
The will of my most seeming-virtuous queen.
O Hamlet, what a falling off was there
From me, whose love was of that dignity
That it went hand in hand even with the vow
I made to her in marriage, and to decline
Upon a wretch whose natural gifts were poor
To those of mine!
But virtue, as it never will be moved,
Though lewdness court it in a shape of heaven,
So lust, though to a radiant angel linked,
Will sate itself in a celestial bed
And prey on garbage.
But soft, methinks I scent the morning air.
Brief let me be. Sleeping within my orchard,
My custom always of the afternoon,

---

30 *meditation* thought
33 *Lethe* a river in Hades (drinking from it produced forgetfulness of one's past life)
37 *forgèd process* fabricated official report
42 *adulterate* adulterous
54 *a shape of heaven* angelic disguise
59 *orchard* garden

Upon my secure hour thy uncle stole 61
With juice of cursed hebona in a vial, 62
And in the porches of my ears did pour
The leperous distillment, whose effect
Holds such an enmity with blood of man
That swift as quicksilver it courses through
The natural gates and alleys of the body
And with a sudden vigor it doth posset 68
And curd, like eager droppings into milk, 69
The thin and wholesome blood. So did it mine, 70
And a most instant tetter barked about 71
Most lazarlike with vile and loathsome crust 72
All my smooth body.
Thus was I sleeping by a brother's hand
Of life, of crown, of queen at once dispatched,
Cut off even in the blossoms of my sin,
Unhouseled, disappointed, unaneled, 77
No reck'ning made, but sent to my account
With all my imperfections on my head.
O, horrible! O, horrible! most horrible! 80
If thou hast nature in thee, bear it not.
Let not the royal bed of Denmark be
A couch for luxury and damnèd incest. 83
But howsomever thou pursues this act,
Taint not thy mind, nor let thy soul contrive
Against thy mother aught. Leave her to heaven
And to those thorns that in her bosom lodge
To prick and sting her. Fare thee well at once.
The glowworm shows the matin to be near 89
And gins to pale his uneffectual fire. 90
Adieu, adieu, adieu. Remember me. [*Exit.*]

HAMLET: O all you host of heaven! O earth! What else?
And shall I couple hell? O fie! Hold, hold, my heart, 93
And you, my sinews, grow not instant old,
But bear me stiffly up. Remember thee?
Ay, thou poor ghost, while memory holds a seat

---

61 *secure* carefree, unsuspecting
62 *hebona* poisonous plant
68 *posset* curdle
69 *eager* sour
71 *tetter* eruption; *barked* covered as with bark
72 *lazarlike* leperlike
77 *Unhouseled* without the Christian Eucharist; *disappointed* unprepared spiritually; *unaneled* without extreme unction (a Christian rite involving holy oil, given at the end of a believer's life)
83 *luxury* lust
89 *matin* morning
93 *couple* join with, marry

In this distracted globe. Remember thee? 97
Yea, from the table of my memory 98
I'll wipe away all trivial fond records, 99
All saws of books, all forms, all pressures past 100
That youth and observation copied there,
And thy commandment all alone shall live
Within the book and volume of my brain,
Unmixed with baser matter. Yes, by heaven!
O most pernicious woman!
O villain, villain, smiling, damnèd villain!
My tables—meet it is I set it down 107
That one may smile, and smile, and be a villain.
At least I am sure it may be so in Denmark.
[*Writes.*]
So, uncle, there you are. Now to my word: 110
It is "Adieu, adieu, remember me."
I have sworn't.

Enter Horatio and Marcellus.

HORATIO: My lord, my lord!
MARCELLUS: Lord Hamlet!
HORATIO: Heavens secure him!
HAMLET: So be it!
MARCELLUS: Illo, ho, ho, my lord! 115
HAMLET: Hillo, ho, ho, boy! Come and come.
MARCELLUS: How is't, my noble lord?
HORATIO: What news, my lord?
HAMLET: O, wonderful! 118
HORATIO: Good my lord, tell it.
HAMLET: No, you will reveal it.
HORATIO: Not I, my lord, by heaven. 120
MARCELLUS: Nor I, my lord.
HAMLET: How say you then? Would heart of man once think it?
But you'll be secret?
BOTH: Ay, by heaven.
HAMLET: There's never a villain dwelling in all Denmark
But he's an arrant knave.
HORATIO: There needs no ghost, my lord, come from the grave
To tell us this.
HAMLET: Why, right, you are in the right,
And so, without more circumstance at all, 127

---

97 *globe* head
98 *table* writing tablet, record book
99 *fond* foolish
100 *saws* wise sayings; *forms* mental images, concepts; *pressures* impressions
107 *meet* appropriate
115 *Illo, ho, ho* (cry of the falconer to summon his hunting bird)
118 *wonderful* full of wonder, amazing
127 *circumstance* ceremony

I hold it fit that we shake hands and part:
You, as your business and desire shall point you,
For every man hath business and desire
Such as it is, and for my own poor part,
I will go pray.
HORATIO: These are but wild and whirling words, my lord.
HAMLET: I am sorry they offend you, heartily;
Yes, faith, heartily.
HORATIO: There's no offense, my lord.
HAMLET: Yes, by Saint Patrick, but there is, Horatio,
And much offense too. Touching this vision here,
It is an honest ghost, that let me tell you.
For your desire to know what is between us,
O'ermaster't as you may. And now, good friends,
As you are friends, scholars, and soldiers,
Give me one poor request.
HORATIO: What is't, my lord? We will.
HAMLET: Never make known what you have seen tonight.
BOTH: My lord, we will not.
HAMLET: Nay, but swear't.
HORATIO: In faith, my lord, not I.
MARCELLUS: Nor I, my lord—in faith.
HAMLET: Upon my sword.
MARCELLUS: We have sworn, my lord, already.
HAMLET: Indeed, upon my sword, indeed.
Ghost cries under the stage.
GHOST: Swear.
HAMLET: Ha, ha, boy, sayst thou so? Art thou there, truepenny?
Come on. You hear this fellow in the cellarage.
Consent to swear.
HORATIO: Propose the oath, my lord.
HAMLET: Never to speak of this that you have seen,
Swear by my sword.
GHOST: [*Beneath*] Swear.
HAMLET: *Hic et ubique?* Then we'll shift our ground.
Come hither, gentlemen,
And lay your hands again upon my sword.
Swear by my sword
Never to speak of this that you have heard.
GHOST: [*Beneath*] Swear by his sword.
HAMLET: Well said, old mole! Canst work i' th' earth so fast?
A worthy pioner! Once more remove, good friends.

---

136 *Saint Patrick* the legendary keeper of purgatory
138 *an honest ghost* a genuine ghost (not a disguised demon)
149 *sword* i.e., upon the cross formed by the sword hilt
153 *truepenny* honest old fellow
159 *Hic et ubique* here and everywhere (Latin)
166 *pioner* pioneer, miner (the archaic spelling is stressed on the first syllable)

HORATIO: O day and night, but this is wondrous strange!
HAMLET: And therefore as a stranger give it welcome.
There are more things in heaven and earth, Horatio,
Than are dreamt of in your philosophy.
But come:
Here as before, never, so help you mercy,
How strange or odd some'er I bear myself
(As I perchance hereafter shall think meet
To put an antic disposition on),
That you, at such times seeing me, never shall,
With arms encumbered thus, or this headshake,
Or by pronouncing of some doubtful phrase,
As "Well, well, we know," or "We could, an if we would,"
Or "If we list to speak," or "There be, an if they might,"
Or such ambiguous giving out, to note
That you know aught of me—this do swear,
So grace and mercy at your most need help you.
GHOST: [*Beneath*] Swear.
[*They swear.*]
HAMLET: Rest, rest, perturbèd spirit! So, gentlemen,
With all my love I do commend me to you,
And what so poor a man as Hamlet is
May do t' express his love and friending to you,
God willing, shall not lack. Let us go in together,
And still your fingers on your lips, I pray.
The time is out of joint. O cursèd spite
That ever I was born to set it right!
Nay, come, let's go together. *Exeunt.*

⋆

II.1

Enter old Polonius, with his man [Reynaldo].

POLONIUS: Give him this money and these notes, Reynaldo.
REYNALDO: I will, my lord.
POLONIUS: You shall do marvelous wisely, good Reynaldo,
Before you visit him, to make inquire
Of his behavior.

---

170 *your philosophy* this philosophizing one hears about
175 *antic* grotesque, mad
177 *encumbered* folded
179 *an if* if
186 *commend* entrust
190 *still* always

II.1 Polonius's rooms in Elsinore

REYNALDO: My lord, I did intend it.
POLONIUS: Marry, well said, very well said. Look you, sir,
Inquire me first what Danskers are in Paris,
And how, and who, what means, and where they keep,
What company, at what expense; and finding
By this encompassment and drift of question
That they do know my son, come you more nearer
Than your particular demands will touch it.
Take you as 'twere some distant knowledge of him,
As thus, "I know his father and his friends,
And in part him"—do you mark this, Reynaldo?
REYNALDO: Ay, very well, my lord.
POLONIUS: "And in part him, but," you may say, "not well,
But if't be he I mean, he's very wild,
Addicted so and so." And there put on him
What forgeries you please; marry, none so rank
As may dishonor him—take heed of that—
But, sir, such wanton, wild, and usual slips
As are companions noted and most known
To youth and liberty.
REYNALDO: As gaming, my lord.
POLONIUS: Ay, or drinking, fencing, swearing, quarreling,
Drabbing. You may go so far.
REYNALDO: My lord, that would dishonor him.
POLONIUS: Faith, as you may season it in the charge.
You must not put another scandal on him,
That he is open to incontinency.
That's not my meaning. But breathe his faults so quaintly
That they may seem the taints of liberty,
The flash and outbreak of a fiery mind,
A savageness in unreclaimèd blood,
Of general assault.
REYNALDO: But, my good lord—
POLONIUS: Wherefore should you do this?
REYNALDO: Ay, my lord,
I would know that.

7 *Danskers* Danes
8 *what means* what their wealth; *keep* dwell
10 *encompassment* roundabout means
12 *particular demands* definite questions
20 *forgeries* invented wrongdoings; *rank* exaggerated, terrible
26 *Drabbing* whoring
28 *Faith* (a mild oath: F reads "Faith, no."); *season* soften
30 *incontinency* extreme promiscuity
31 *quaintly* artfully
34 *unreclaimèd* untamed
35 *Of general assault* assailing all young men

POLONIUS: Marry, sir, here's my drift,
And I believe it is a fetch of wit.
You laying these slight sullies on my son
As 'twere a thing a little soiled with working,
Mark you,
Your party in converse, him you would sound,
Having ever seen in the prenominate crimes
The youth you breathe of guilty, be assured
He closes with you in this consequence:
"Good sir," or so, or "friend," or "gentleman"—
According to the phrase or the addition
Of man and country—

REYNALDO: Very good, my lord.

POLONIUS: And then, sir, does a this—a does—
What was I about to say? By the mass, I was about to say something!
Where did I leave?

REYNALDO: At "closes in the consequence."

POLONIUS: At "closes in the consequence"—Ay, marry!
He closes thus: "I know the gentleman;
I saw him yesterday, or th' other day,
Or then, or then, with such or such, and, as you say,
There was a gaming, there o'ertook in's rouse,
There falling out at tennis"; or perchance,
"I saw him enter such a house of sale,"
Videlicet, a brothel, or so forth.
See you now—
Your bait of falsehood takes this carp of truth,
And thus do we of wisdom and of reach,
With windlasses and with assays of bias,
By indirections find directions out.
So, by my former lecture and advice,
Shall you my son. You have me, have you not?

REYNALDO: My lord, I have.

POLONIUS: God buy ye, fare ye well.

---

38 *fetch of wit* clever trick
43 *Having ever* if he has ever; *prenominate* aforementioned
45 *closes with* agrees with; *consequence* following way
47 *addition* title
49 *a* he
57 *a* he; *o'ertook* overcome with drunkenness; *rouse* carousal
58 *falling out* quarreling
60 *Videlicet* namely (Latin)
63 *reach* far-reaching comprehension
64 *windlasses* roundabout courses; *assays of bias* devious attacks (metaphors from the game of bowls, in which balls are weighted or "biased")
65 *directions* ways of procedure
67 *have me* understand me
68 *God buy ye* God be with you, good-bye

REYNALDO: Good my lord.
POLONIUS: Observe his inclination in yourself.
REYNALDO: I shall, my lord.
POLONIUS: And let him ply his music.
REYNALDO: Well, my lord.
POLONIUS: Farewell.
Exit Reynaldo.
Enter Ophelia.
How now, Ophelia, what's the matter?
OPHELIA: O my lord, my lord, I have been so affrighted!
POLONIUS: With what, i' th' name of God?
OPHELIA: My lord, as I was sewing in my closet,
Lord Hamlet, with his doublet all unbraced,
No hat upon his head, his stockings fouled,
Ungartered, and down-gyvèd to his ankle,
Pale as his shirt, his knees knocking each other,
And with a look so piteous in purport
As if he had been loosèd out of hell
To speak of horrors—he comes before me.
POLONIUS: Mad for thy love?
OPHELIA: My lord, I do not know,
But truly I do fear it.
POLONIUS: What said he?
OPHELIA: He took me by the wrist and held me hard,
Then goes he to the length of all his arm,
And with his other hand thus o'er his brow
He falls to such perusal of my face
As a would draw it. Long stayed he so.
At last, a little shaking of mine arm
And thrice his head thus waving up and down,
He raised a sigh so piteous and profound
As it did seem to shatter all his bulk
And end his being. That done, he lets me go,
And with his head over his shoulder turned
He seemed to find his way without his eyes,
For out o' doors he went without their helps
And to the last bended their light on me.
POLONIUS: Come, go with me. I will go seek the king.
This is the very ecstasy of love,
Whose violent property fordoes itself
And leads the will to desperate undertakings
As oft as any passion under heaven

---

76 *closet* private room
77 *doublet* jacket; *unbraced* unlaced
79 *down-gyvèd* fallen down like gyves (chains) on a prisoner's legs
101 *ecstasy* madness
102 *property* quality; *fordoes* destroys

That does afflict our natures. I am sorry.
What, have you given him any hard words of late?
OPHELIA: No, my good lord; but as you did command
I did repel his letters and denied
His access to me.
POLONIUS: That hath made him mad.
I am sorry that with better heed and judgment 110
I had not quoted him. I feared he did but trifle 111
And meant to wrack thee; but beshrew my jealousy. 112
By heaven, it is as proper to our age
To cast beyond ourselves in our opinions 114
As it is common for the younger sort
To lack discretion. Come, go we to the king.
This must be known, which, being kept close, might move 117
More grief to hide than hate to utter love. 118
Come. *Exeunt.*

★

II.2

Flourish. Enter King and Queen, Rosencrantz, and Guildenstern [with others].

KING: Welcome, dear Rosencrantz and Guildenstern.
Moreover that we much did long to see you, 2
The need we have to use you did provoke
Our hasty sending. Something have you heard
Of Hamlet's transformation—so call it,
Sith nor th' exterior nor the inward man 6
Resembles that it was. What it should be,
More than his father's death, that thus hath put him
So much from th' understanding of himself,
I cannot dream of. I entreat you both 10
That, being of so young days brought up with him,
And sith so neighbored to his youth and havior, 12
That you vouchsafe your rest here in our court 13

---

111 *quoted* observed
112 *wrack* ruin (by sexual seduction); *beshrew* curse
114 *cast beyond ourselves* pay more attention to (or, suppose more significance in) something than we ought to
117 *close* secret; *move* cause
118 *to hide . . . love* i.e., more grief will come from concealing Hamlet's supposed love for Ophelia than hate will come from making that love public

II.2 Elsinore
2 *Moreover* besides; *we* (the royal plural)
6 *Sith* since
10 *dream of* imagine
12 *youth and havior* youthful ways of life ("behavior")
13 *vouchsafe your rest* agree to stay

Some little time, so by your companies
To draw him on to pleasures, and to gather
So much as from occasion you may glean,
Whether aught to us unknown afflicts him thus,
That opened lies within our remedy.

QUEEN: Good gentlemen, he hath much talked of you,
And sure I am two men there is not living
To whom he more adheres. If it will please you
To show us so much gentry and good will
As to expend your time with us a while
For the supply and profit of our hope,
Your visitation shall receive such thanks
As fits a king's remembrance.

ROSENCRANTZ: Both your majesties
Might, by the sovereign power you have of us,
Put your dread pleasures more into command
Than to entreaty.

GUILDENSTERN: But we both obey,
And here give up ourselves in the full bent
To lay our service freely at your feet,
To be commanded.

KING: Thanks, Rosencrantz and gentle Guildenstern.

QUEEN: Thanks, Guildenstern and gentle Rosencrantz.
And I beseech you instantly to visit
My too much changèd son.—Go, some of you,
And bring these gentlemen where Hamlet is.

GUILDENSTERN: Heavens make our presence and our practices
Pleasant and helpful to him!

QUEEN: Ay, amen!

Exeunt Rosencrantz and Guildenstern [with some Attendants].

Enter Polonius.

POLONIUS: Th' ambassadors from Norway, my good lord,
Are joyfully returned.

KING: Thou still hast been the father of good news.

POLONIUS: Have I, my lord? I assure my good liege
I hold my duty as I hold my soul,
Both to my God and to my gracious king,
And I do think—or else this brain of mine
Hunts not the trail of policy so sure
As it hath used to do—that I have found
The very cause of Hamlet's lunacy.

---

18 *opened* revealed
20 *is* (a singular verb with a plural subject is common in Shakespeare's period)
21 *more adheres* is more attached
22 *gentry* courtesy
30 *in the full bent* to full capacity (a metaphor from the *bent* bow)
42 *still* always

KING: O, speak of that! That do I long to hear.
POLONIUS: Give first admittance to th' ambassadors.
My news shall be the fruit to that great feast.
KING: Thyself do grace to them and bring them in. [*Exit Polonius.*]
He tells me, my dear Gertrude, he hath found
The head and source of all your son's distemper.
QUEEN: I doubt it is no other but the main,
His father's death and our o'erhasty marriage.
KING: Well, we shall sift him.
Enter Ambassadors [Voltemand and Cornelius, with Polonius].
Welcome, my good friends.
Say, Voltemand, what from our brother Norway?
VOLTEMAND: Most fair return of greetings and desires.
Upon our first, he sent out to suppress
His nephew's levies, which to him appeared
To be a preparation 'gainst the Polack,
But better looked into, he truly found
It was against your highness, whereat grieved,
That so his sickness, age, and impotence
Was falsely borne in hand, sends out arrests
On Fortinbras, which he in brief obeys,
Receives rebuke from Norway, and in fine
Makes vow before his uncle never more
To give th' assay of arms against your majesty.
Whereon old Norway, overcome with joy,
Gives him threescore thousand crowns in annual fee
And his commission to employ those soldiers,
So levied as before, against the Polack,
With an entreaty, herein further shown,
[*Gives a paper.*]
That it might please you to give quiet pass
Through your dominions for this enterprise,
On such regards of safety and allowance
As therein are set down.
KING: It likes us well;
And at our more considered time we'll read,
Answer, and think upon this business.
Meantime we thank you for your well-took labor.

---

52 *fruit* dessert
53 *grace* honor
56 *doubt* suspect
61 *our first* our first words about the matter
67 *borne in hand* deceived
69 *in fine* in the end
71 *assay* trial, test
74–80 *And his . . . well* (see IV.4)
79 *regards* terms
81 *considered time* convenient time for consideration

Go to your rest; at night we'll feast together.
Most welcome home! *Exeunt Ambassadors.*
POLONIUS: This business is well ended.
My liege and madam, to expostulate
What majesty should be, what duty is,
Why day is day, night night, and time is time,
Were nothing but to waste night, day, and time.
Therefore, since brevity is the soul of wit,
And tediousness the limbs and outward flourishes,
I will be brief. Your noble son is mad.
Mad call I it, for, to define true madness,
What is't but to be nothing else but mad?
But let that go.
QUEEN: More matter, with less art.
POLONIUS: Madam, I swear I use no art at all.
That he's mad, 'tis true: 'tis true 'tis pity,
And pity 'tis 'tis true—a foolish figure.
But farewell it, for I will use no art.
Mad let us grant him then, and now remains
That we find out the cause of this effect—
Or rather say, the cause of this defect,
For this effect defective comes by cause.
Thus it remains, and the remainder thus.
Perpend.
I have a daughter (have while she is mine),
Who in her duty and obedience, mark,
Hath given me this. Now gather and surmise.
[Reads the] letter.
"To the celestial, and my soul's idol, the most beautified Ophelia"—
That's an ill phrase, a vile phrase; "beautified" is a vile phrase. But you shall hear. Thus:
[*Reads.*]
"In her excellent white bosom, these, etc."
QUEEN: Came this from Hamlet to her?
POLONIUS: Good madam, stay a while. I will be faithful.
[*Reads.*]
"Doubt thou the stars are fire;
Doubt that the sun doth move;
Doubt truth to be a liar;
But never doubt I love.

---

86 *expostulate* discuss
90 *wit* understanding
98 *figure* figure of speech
105 *Perpend* consider, think about (this)
112 *etc.* (i.e., other conventional words of greeting: early modern letters often include "etc." for such common, formalized greetings)
114 *faithful* i.e., true to the text
115 *Doubt* suspect

O dear Ophelia, I am ill at these numbers. I have not art to reckon 119
my groans, but that I love thee best, O most best, believe it. Adieu. 120
Thine evermore, most dear lady,
whilst this machine is to him, Hamlet." 122

This in obedience hath my daughter shown me,
And more above hath his solicitings, 124
As they fell out by time, by means, and place, 125
All given to mine ear.

KING: But how hath she
Received his love?

POLONIUS: What do you think of me?

KING: As of a man faithful and honorable.

POLONIUS: I would fain prove so. But what might you think, 129
When I had seen this hot love on the wing 130
(As I perceived it, I must tell you that,
Before my daughter told me), what might you,
Or my dear majesty your queen here, think,
If I had played the desk or table book, 134
Or given my heart a winking, mute and dumb, 135
Or looked upon this love with idle sight?
What might you think? No, I went round to work 137
And my young mistress thus I did bespeak: 138
"Lord Hamlet is a prince, out of thy star. 139
This must not be." And then I prescripts gave her 140
That she should lock herself from his resort,
Admit no messengers, receive no tokens.
Which done, she took the fruits of my advice,
And he, repelled, a short tale to make,
Fell into a sadness, then into a fast,
Thence to a watch, thence into a weakness, 146
Thence to a lightness, and, by this declension, 147
Into the madness wherein now he raves,
And all we mourn for.

KING: Do you think this?

---

119 *numbers* verses
122 *machine* body; *to* attached to
124 *above* besides
125 *fell out* came about
129 *fain* wish to, prefer to
134 *desk or table book* i.e., silent receptacle
135 *winking* closing of the eyes
137 *round* plainly
138 *mistress* i.e., "miss" (a dismissive term for his daughter)
139 *star* status determined by stellar influence
140 *prescripts* instructions
146 *watch* sleepless state
147 *lightness* light-headedness

QUEEN: It may be, very like. 150
POLONIUS: Hath there been such a time—I would fain know that—
That I have positively said "'Tis so,"
When it proved otherwise?
KING: Not that I know.
POLONIUS: Take this from this, if this be otherwise. 154
If circumstances lead me, I will find
Where truth is hid, though it were hid indeed
Within the center. 157
KING: How may we try it further?
POLONIUS: You know sometimes he walks four hours together
Here in the lobby.
QUEEN: So he does indeed.
POLONIUS: At such a time I'll loose my daughter to him. 160
Be you and I behind an arras then. 161
Mark the encounter. If he love her not,
And be not from his reason fallen thereon, 163
Let me be no assistant for a state
But keep a farm and carters.
KING: We will try it.

Enter Hamlet [reading on a book].

QUEEN: But look where sadly the poor wretch comes reading. 166
POLONIUS: Away, I do beseech you both, away.

Exit King and Queen [with Attendants].

I'll board him presently. O, give me leave. 168
How does my good Lord Hamlet?
HAMLET: Well, God-a-mercy. 170
POLONIUS: Do you know me, my lord?
HAMLET: Excellent well. You are a fishmonger. 172
POLONIUS: Not I, my lord.
HAMLET: Then I would you were so honest a man.
POLONIUS: Honest, my lord?
HAMLET: Ay, sir. To be honest, as this world goes, is to be one man picked out of ten thousand.
POLONIUS: That's very true, my lord.

---

154 *Take . . . from this* i.e., behead me (traditionally the actor is directed to gesture to head and neck or shoulder)
157 *center* center of the earth
160 *loose* release (the word refers specifically to the breeding of domesticated animals and hence is coarse when used of humans, much less one's daughter)
161 *an arras* a hanging tapestry
163 *thereon* on that account
166 *sadly* seriously
168 *board* greet; *presently* at once
170 *God-a-mercy* thank you (literally, "God have mercy!")
172 *fishmonger* seller of fish (but also slang for procurer: Ophelia is "bait")

HAMLET: For if the sun breed maggots in a dead dog, being a good kissing carrion—Have you a daughter?

POLONIUS: I have, my lord.

HAMLET: Let her not walk i' th' sun. Conception is a blessing, but as your daughter may conceive, friend, look to't.

POLONIUS: [*Aside*] How say you by that? Still harping on my daughter. Yet he knew me not at first. A said I was a fishmonger. A is far gone. And truly in my youth I suffered much extremity for love, very near this. I'll speak to him again.—What do you read, my lord?

HAMLET: Words, words, words.

POLONIUS: What is the matter, my lord?

HAMLET: Between who?

POLONIUS: I mean the matter that you read, my lord.

HAMLET: Slanders, sir, for the satirical rogue says here that old men have gray beards, that their faces are wrinkled, their eyes purging thick amber and plum-tree gum, and that they have a plentiful lack of wit, together with most weak hams. All which, sir, though I most powerfully and potently believe, yet I hold it not honesty to have it thus set down, for yourself, sir, shall grow old as I am if, like a crab, you could go backward.

POLONIUS: [*Aside*] Though this be madness, yet there is method in't.—Will you walk out of the air, my lord?

HAMLET: Into my grave.

POLONIUS: Indeed, that's out of the air. [*Aside*] How pregnant sometimes his replies are! a happiness that often madness hits on, which reason and sanity could not so prosperously be delivered of. I will leave him [and suddenly contrive the means of meeting between him] and my daughter.—My lord, I will take my leave of you.

HAMLET: You cannot take from me anything that I will not more willingly part withal—except my life, except my life, except my life.

Enter Guildenstern and Rosencrantz.

POLONIUS: Fare you well, my lord.

HAMLET: These tedious old fools!

POLONIUS: You go to seek the Lord Hamlet. There he is.

ROSENCRANTZ: [*To Polonius*] God save you, sir. [*Exit Polonius.*]

GUILDENSTERN: My honored lord!

ROSENCRANTZ: My most dear lord!

HAMLET: My excellent good friends! How dost thou, Guildenstern? Ah, Rosencrantz! Good lads, how do you both?

179–80 *a good kissing carrion* flesh good for kissing
190 *Between who* (Hamlet jokingly misunderstands *matter* as the subject of a quarrel or a lawsuit)
194 *gum* resin (?)
195 *hams* legs
197–98 *shall . . . backward* you will be as old as I am if you could age backward
202 *pregnant* full of meaning
203 *a happiness* an aptness of expression
207 *cannot . . . not* (a common double negative)
208 *withal* with

ROSENCRANTZ: As the indifferent children of the earth.

GUILDENSTERN: Happy in that we are not overhappy on Fortune's cap. We are not the very button.

HAMLET: Nor the soles of her shoe?

ROSENCRANTZ: Neither, my lord.

HAMLET: Then you live about her waist or in the middle of her favors?

GUILDENSTERN: Faith, her privates we.

HAMLET: In the secret parts of Fortune? O, most true; she is a strumpet. What news?

ROSENCRANTZ: None, my lord, but the world's grown honest.

HAMLET: Then is doomsday near. But your news is not true. But in the beaten way of friendship, what make you at Elsinore?

ROSENCRANTZ: To visit you, my lord; no other occasion.

HAMLET: Beggar that I am, I am ever poor in thanks, but I thank you; and sure, dear friends, my thanks are too dear a halfpenny. Were you not sent for? Is it your own inclining? Is it a free visitation? Come, come, deal justly with me. Come, come. Nay, speak.

GUILDENSTERN: What should we say, my lord?

HAMLET: Anything but to th' purpose. You were sent for, and there is a kind of confession in your looks, which your modesties have not craft enough to color. I know the good king and queen have sent for you.

ROSENCRANTZ: To what end, my lord?

HAMLET: That you must teach me. But let, me conjure you by the rights of our fellowship, by the consonancy of our youth, by the obligation of our ever-preserved love, and by what more dear a better proposer can charge you withal, be even and direct with me whether you were sent for or no.

ROSENCRANTZ: [*Aside to Guildenstern*] What say you?

HAMLET: [*Aside*] Nay then, I have an eye of you.—If you love me, hold not off.

GUILDENSTERN: My lord, we were sent for.

HAMLET: I will tell you why. So shall my anticipation prevent your discovery, and your secrecy to the king and queen molt no feather. I have of late—but wherefore I know not—lost all my mirth, forgone all custom of exercises; and indeed, it goes so heavily with my disposition that this goodly frame the earth seems to me a sterile

---

217 *indifferent* average

223 *privates* ordinary men in private, not public, life (with wordplay on "private parts," which Hamlet emphasizes with *secret parts*)

228 *beaten* well-trodden, well-worn; *make* do

231 *a halfpenny* at a halfpenny

237 *color* conceal, cover up with deceptive colorings

241 *consonancy* accord (in sameness of age)

242 *proposer* propounder

243 *withal* with; *even* straight

249 *prevent* forestall

250 *discovery* disclosure; *molt no feather* let fall no feather (i.e., be left whole)

promontory; this most excellent canopy, the air, look you, this brave o'erhanging firmament, this majestical roof fretted with golden fire—why, it appeareth nothing to me but a foul and pestilent congregation of vapors. What piece of work is a man, how noble in reason, how infinite in faculties, in form and moving how express and admirable, in action how like an angel, in apprehension how like a god: the beauty of the world, the paragon of animals! And yet to me what is this quintessence of dust? Man delights not me—nor woman neither, though by your smiling you seem to say so.

ROSENCRANTZ: My lord, there was no such stuff in my thoughts.

HAMLET: Why did ye laugh then, when I said "Man delights not me"?

ROSENCRANTZ: To think, my lord, if you delight not in man, what lenten entertainment the players shall receive from you. We coted them on the way, and hither are they coming to offer you service.

HAMLET: He that plays the king shall be welcome—his majesty shall have tribute of me—, the adventurous knight shall use his foil and target, the lover shall not sigh gratis, the humorous man shall end his part in peace, [the clown shall make those laugh whose lungs are tickle o' th' sere,] and the lady shall say her mind freely, or the blank verse shall halt for't. What players are they?

ROSENCRANTZ: Even those you were wont to take such delight in, the tragedians of the city.

HAMLET: How chances it they travel? Their residence, both in reputation and profit, was better both ways.

ROSENCRANTZ: I think their inhibition comes by the means of the late innovation.

HAMLET: Do they hold the same estimation they did when I was in the city? Are they so followed?

ROSENCRANTZ: No indeed, are they not.

---

255 *firmament* sky; *fretted* decorated with fretwork (it is traditionally supposed that the original actor of Hamlet here gestured toward the roof of the Globe's stage, which was painted with *golden fire*, the zodiac and stars)

258 *express* well-framed

261 *quintessence* fifth (*quint-*) and finest essence (an alchemical term for something superior to the four essences or elements—fire, air, earth, water—that constituted all earthly life); *dust* the earth of which humankind is created according to the Judeo-Christian Scriptures (see V.I.186 ff.)

265 *lenten* scanty (from "Lent," the forty-day period of abstinence and repentance before the Christian Easter)

266 *coted* overtook

269 *foil and target* sword and shield

270 *the humorous man* an eccentric character

271–72 *tickle o' th' sere* hair-triggered for the discharge of laughter (*sere* = part of a gunlock)

273 *halt* go lame (a joke on metrical "feet" in verse)

276 *residence* (for Shakespeare and his audience, this word would evoke the theatrical center, London)

278–79 *late innovation* new fashion (possibly the companies of boy actors who had reappeared circa 1601 as competitors for adult companies such as Shakespeare's; possibly a reference to political upheaval)

281 *city* (as in 1. 298, presumably *city* = London for Shakespeare's original audiences)

HAMLET: It is not very strange, for my uncle is King of Denmark, and those that would make mouths at him while my father lived give twenty, forty, fifty, a hundred ducats apiece for his picture in little. 'Sblood, there is something in this more than natural, if philosophy could find it out.

A flourish.

GUILDENSTERN: There are the players.

HAMLET: Gentlemen, you are welcome to Elsinore. Your hands, come then. Th' appurtenance of welcome is fashion and ceremony. Let me comply with you in this garb, lest my extent to the players (which I tell you must show fairly outwards) should more appear like entertainment than yours. You are welcome. But my uncle-father and aunt-mother are deceived.

GUILDENSTERN: In what, my dear lord?

HAMLET: I am but mad north-northwest. When the wind is southerly I know a hawk from a handsaw.

Enter Polonius.

POLONIUS: Well be with you, gentlemen.

HAMLET: Hark you, Guildenstern—and you too—at each ear a hearer. That great baby you see there is not yet out of his swaddling clouts.

ROSENCRANTZ: Happily he is the second time come to them, for they say an old man is twice a child.

HAMLET: I will prophesy he comes to tell me of the players. Mark it.—You say right, sir; a Monday morning, 'twas then indeed.

POLONIUS: My lord, I have news to tell you.

HAMLET: My lord, I have news to tell you. When Roscius was an actor in Rome—

POLONIUS: The actors are come hither, my lord.

HAMLET: Buzz, buzz.

POLONIUS: Upon my honor—

HAMLET: Then came each actor on his ass—

POLONIUS: The best actors in the world, either for tragedy, comedy, history, pastoral, pastoral-comical, historical-pastoral; scene individable, or poem unlimited. Seneca cannot be too heavy, nor Plautus too light. For the law of writ and the liberty, these are the only men.

---

284 *make mouths at him* make faces at him, ridicule him

285 *his picture in little* a miniature

286 *'Sblood* by God's [i.e., Christ's] blood

291 *garb* manner; *extent* showing, behavior

297 *hawk* mattock or pickax (also called "hack"; here used apparently with a play on *hawk*, the bird); *handsaw* carpenter's tool (apparently with a play on some form of "hernshaw," the heron)

300 *clouts* clothes

301 *Happily* haply, perhaps

306 *Roscius* a legendary Roman comic actor

313 *scene individable* drama observing the unity of place (?)

314 *poem unlimited* drama not observing the unity of place (?); *Seneca* classical Roman writer of tragedies; *heavy* serious; *Plautus* classical Roman writer of comedies; *light* unserious

315 *law of writ* drama written (as Shakespeare's was not) according to classical of neoclassical rules; *liberty* freedom from such rule-based orthodoxy

HAMLET: O Jephthah, judge of Israel, what a treasure hadst thou!
POLONIUS: What a treasure had he, my lord?
HAMLET: Why,
"One fair daughter, and no more,
The which he lovèd passing well."
POLONIUS: [*Aside*] Still on my daughter.
HAMLET: Am I not i' th' right, old Jephthah?
POLONIUS: If you call me Jephthah, my lord, I have a daughter that I love passing well.
HAMLET: Nay, that follows not.
POLONIUS: What follows then, my lord?
HAMLET: Why,
"As by lot, God wot,"
and then, you know,
"It came to pass, as most like it was."
The first row of the pious chanson will show you more, for look where my abridgment comes.
Enter the Players.
You are welcome, masters, welcome, all.—I am glad to see thee well.—Welcome, good friends.—O, old friend, why, thy face is valanced since I saw thee last. Com'st thou to beard me in Denmark?—What, my young lady and mistress? By'r Lady, your ladyship is nearer to heaven than when I saw you last by the altitude of a chopine. Pray God your voice, like a piece of uncurrent gold, be not cracked within the ring.—Masters, you are all welcome. We'll e'en to't like French falconers, fly at anything we see. We'll have a speech straight. Come, give us a taste of your quality. Come, a passionate speech.
PLAYER: What speech, my good lord?
HAMLET: I heard thee speak me a speech once, but it was never acted, or if it was, not above once, for the play, I remember, pleased not the million; 'twas caviar to the general, but it was (as I received it, and others, whose judgments in such matters cried in the top of mine) an

---

316 *Jephthah* biblical father whose rash vow compelled him to sacrifice his beloved daughter (Judges 11:30–40)
320 *passing* surpassingly (the verses are from a surviving ballad on Jephthah)
331 *row* stanza; *chanson* song (French)
332 *my abridgment* something that shortens my talk
335 *valanced* fringed (with a *beard*)
336 *young lady* boy who plays women's parts
338 *chopine* woman's thick-soled shoe; *uncurrent* not legal tender
338–39 *a piece . . . cracked within the ring* i.e., literally, a coin that has had precious metal removed from within the *ring* surrounding the sovereign's image; figuratively, the boy actor's voice, which has *cracked*, making him unsuitable for women's roles; finally there is bawdy wordplay on the *ring* of a woman's (or female character's) vagina, *cracked* by sexual intercourse
346 *general* multitude
347 *in the top of* more authoritatively than

excellent play, well digested in the scenes, set down with as much modesty as cunning. I remember one said there were no sallets in the lines to make the matter savory, nor no matter in the phrase that might indict the author of affection, but called it an honest method, as wholesome as sweet, and by very much more handsome than fine. One speech in't I chiefly loved. 'Twas Aeneas' tale to Dido, and thereabout of it especially when he speaks of Priam's slaughter. If it live in your memory, begin at this line—let me see, let me see:

"The rugged Pyrrhus, like th' Hyrcanian beast—

'Tis not so; it begins with Pyrrhus:

"The rugged Pyrrhus, he whose sable arms,
Black as his purpose, did the night resemble
When he lay couchèd in the ominous horse,
Hath now this dread and black complexion smeared
With heraldry more dismal. Head to foot
Now is he total gules, horridly tricked
With blood of fathers, mothers, daughters, sons,
Baked and impasted with the parching streets,
That lend a tyrannous and a damnèd light
To their lord's murder. Roasted in wrath and fire.
And thus o'ersizèd with coagulate gore,
With eyes like carbuncles, the hellish Pyrrhus
Old grandsire Priam seeks."

So, proceed you.

POLONIUS: 'Fore God, my lord, well spoken, with good accent and good discretion.

PLAYER: "Anon he finds him,
Striking too short at Greeks. His antique sword,
Rebellious to his arm, lies where it falls,
Repugnant to command. Unequal matched,
Pyrrhus at Priam drives, in rage strikes wide,
But with the whiff and wind of his fell sword
Th' unnervèd father falls. [Then senseless Ilium,]

---

349 *sallets* salads (metaphorically: highly seasoned literary passages)
351 *affection* affectation
354 *Priam's slaughter* i.e., at the fall of Troy (Virgil, *Aeneid* II, 506 ff.; *Priam* was King of Troy, *Aeneas* his son-in-law, *Hecuba* his wife; after Troy's fall, Aeneas wandered the Mediterranean Sea and visited Carthage, whose queen was *Dido*)
356 *Hyrcanian beast* tiger (Hyrcania is on the southern shores of the Caspian Sea)
358 *sable* black
360 *ominous* fateful; *horse* wooden horse by which the Greeks gained entrance to Troy
362 *dismal* ill-omened
363 *gules* red (a heraldic term); *tricked* decorated in color (another heraldic term)
365 *parching* drying (i.e., because Troy is burning)
368 *o'ersizèd* covered as with "size," a glutinous material used for filling, for example, pores of plaster or gaps in cloth; *coagulate* clotted
379 *But* even (i.e., with only the sword's movement); *fell* cruel
380 *senseless* without feeling

Seeming to feel this blow, with flaming top
Stoops to his base, and with a hideous crash
Takes prisoner Pyrrhus' ear. For lo! his sword,
Which was declining on the milky head
Of reverend Priam, seemed i' th' air to stick.
So as a painted tyrant Pyrrhus stood,
And like a neutral to his will and matter
Did nothing.
But as we often see, against some storm,
A silence in the heavens, the rack stand still,
The bold winds speechless, and the orb below
As hush as death, anon the dreadful thunder
Doth rend the region, so after Pyrrhus' pause,
Arousèd vengeance sets him new awork,
And never did the Cyclops' hammers fall
On Mars's armor, forged for proof eterne,
With less remorse than Pyrrhus' bleeding sword
Now falls on Priam.
Out, out, thou strumpet Fortune! All you gods,
In general synod take away her power,
Break all the spokes and fellies from her wheel,
And bowl the round nave down the hill of heaven,
As low as to the fiends."

POLONIUS: This is too long.

HAMLET: It shall to the barber's, with your beard,— Prithee say on. He's for a jig or a tale of bawdry, or he sleeps. Say on; come to Hecuba.

PLAYER: "But who (ah woe!) had seen the mobled queen—"

HAMLET: "The mobled queen"?

POLONIUS: That's good.

PLAYER: "Run barefoot up and down, threat'ning the flames
With bisson rheum; a clout upon that head
Where late the diadem stood, and for a robe,

---

382 *his* its
386 *painted* pictured
387 *will and matter* desire and aim (between which he stands *neutral,* motionless)
389 *against* just before
390 *rack* clouds
393 *region* sky
395 *Cyclops* in Greek myth, giant workmen who made armor in Vulcan's forge
396 *proof eterne* eternal protection
397 *remorse* pity, compassion
401 *fellies* segments of the rim of a wheel
402 *nave* hub of a wheel
406 *a jig* comic singing and dancing often performed following a play in the public theaters
407 *mobled* muffled (the archaic word's pronuncation is uncertain, "mobled" or "mobbled," short or long *o*)
411 *bisson rheum* blinding tears; *clout* cloth

About her lank and all o'erteemèd loins, 413
A blanket in the alarm of fear caught up—
Who this had seen, with tongue in venom steeped
'Gainst Fortune's state would treason have pronounced. 416
But if the gods themselves did see her then,
When she saw Pyrrhus make malicious sport
In mincing with his sword her husband's limbs,
The instant burst of clamor that she made 420
(Unless things mortal move them not at all)
Would have made milch the burning eyes of heaven 422
And passion in the gods."

POLONIUS: Look, where he has not turned his color, and has tears in's 424
eyes. Prithee no more.

HAMLET: 'Tis well. I'll have thee speak out the rest of this soon.—Good
my lord, will you see the players well bestowed? Do you hear? Let 427
them be well used, for they are the abstract and brief chronicles of 428
the time. After your death you were better have a bad epitaph than
their ill report while you live. 430

POLONIUS: My lord, I will use them according to their desert.

HAMLET: God's bodkin, man, much better! Use every man after his 432
desert, and who shall scape whipping? Use them after your own honor and dignity. The less they deserve, the more merit is in your bounty. Take them in.

POLONIUS: Come, sirs.

HAMLET: Follow him, friends. We'll hear a play tomorrow. [*Aside to Player*] Dost thou hear me, old friend? Can you play "The Murder of Gonzago"?

PLAYER: Ay, my lord. 440

HAMLET: We'll ha't tomorrow night. You could for a need study a speech 441
of some dozen or sixteen lines which I would set down and insert in't, could you not?

PLAYER: Ay, my lord.

HAMLET: Very well. Follow that lord, and look you mock him not.—My good friends, I'll leave you till night. You are welcome to Elsinore.

Exeunt Polonius and Players.

ROSENCRANTZ: Good my lord.

Exeunt [Rosencrantz and Guildenstern].

HAMLET: Ay, so, God buy to you.—Now I am alone.
O, what a rogue and peasant slave am I!

---

413 *o'erteemèd* exhausted by childbearing
416 *state* government of worldly events
422 *milch* tearful (milk-giving); *eyes* i.e., stars
424 *where* whether
427 *bestowed* lodged
428–29 *they . . . time* i.e., the players tell the stories of our times
432 *God's bodkin* by God's little body (an oath)
441 *for a need* if necessary

Is it not monstrous that this player here,
But in a fiction, in a dream of passion,
Could force his soul so to his own conceit
That from her working all his visage wanned,
Tears in his eyes, distraction in his aspect,
A broken voice, and his whole function suiting
With forms to his conceit? And all for nothing,
For Hecuba!
What's Hecuba to him, or he to her,
That he should weep for her? What would he do
Had he the motive and the cue for passion
That I have? He would drown the stage with tears
And cleave the general ear with horrid speech,
Make mad the guilty and appall the free,
Confound the ignorant, and amaze indeed
The very faculties of eyes and ears.
Yet I,
A dull and muddy-mettled rascal, peak
Like John-a-dreams, unpregnant of my cause,
And can say nothing. No, not for a king,
Upon whose property and most dear life
A damned defeat was made. Am I a coward?
Who calls me villain? breaks my pate across?
Plucks off my beard and blows it in my face?
Tweaks me by the nose? gives me the lie i' th' throat
As deep as to the lungs? Who does me this?
Ha, 'swounds, I should take it, for it cannot be
But I am pigeon-livered and lack gall
To make oppression bitter, or ere this
I should ha' fatted all the region kites
With this slave's offal. Bloody, bawdy villain!
Remorseless, treacherous, lecherous, kindless villain!
Why, what an ass am I! This is most brave,
That I, the son of a dear father murdered,

---

452 *conceit* conception, idea
453 *wanned* paled
455 *function* action of bodily powers
467 *muddy-mettled* dull-spirited; *peak* mope
468 *John-a-dreams* a lazy dawdler; *unpregnant* barren of realization
470 *property* proper (own) person (?)
472 *pate* head
476 *'swounds* by God's (i.e., Christ's) wounds (an oath)
477 *pigeon-livered* unaggressive (pigeons were supposed to lack a *gall* bladder and hence to be meek)
479 *region kites* kites (scavenging birds) of the air
480 *offal* guts
481 *kindless* unnatural (after this line F has, as a single line, "O Vengeance!")

Prompted to my revenge by heaven and hell,
Must like a whore unpack my heart with words
And fall a-cursing like a very drab,
A stallion! Fie upon't, foh! About, my brains.
Hum—
I have heard that guilty creatures sitting at a play
Have by the very cunning of the scene
Been struck so to the soul that presently
They have proclaimed their malefactions.
For murder, though it have no tongue, will speak
With most miraculous organ. I'll have these players
Play something like the murder of my father
Before mine uncle. I'll observe his looks.
I'll tent him to the quick. If a do blench,
I know my course. The spirit that I have seen
May be a devil, and the devil hath power
T' assume a pleasing shape, yea, and perhaps
Out of my weakness and my melancholy,
As he is very potent with such spirits,
Abuses me to damn me. I'll have grounds
More relative than this. The play's the thing
Wherein I'll catch the conscience of the king. *Exit.*

★

III.1

Enter King, Queen, Polonius, Ophelia, Rosencrantz, Guildenstern, Lords.

KING: And can you by no drift of conference
Get from him why he puts on this confusion,
Grating so harshly all his days of quiet
With turbulent and dangerous lunacy?
ROSENCRANTZ: He does confess he feels himself distracted,
But from what cause a will by no means speak.
GUILDENSTERN: Nor do we find him forward to be sounded,
But with a crafty madness keeps aloof

---

487 *stallion* (slang for "prostitute," male or female); *About* get working, get going
489–92 *guilty . . . malefactions* (popular belief held that such incidents occurred)
491 *presently* immediately
497 *tent* probe; *a* he; *blench* flinch
503 *Abuses* deludes
504 *relative* cogent

III.1 Elsinore
1 *drift of conference* course of conversation
6 *a* he
7 *forward . . . sounded* willing to be (thoroughly) understood

When we would bring him on to some confession
Of his true state.
QUEEN: Did he receive you well?
ROSENCRANTZ: Most like a gentleman.
GUILDENSTERN: But with much forcing of his disposition.
ROSENCRANTZ: Niggard of question, but of our demands 13
Most free in his reply. 14
QUEEN: Did you assay him
To any pastime?
ROSENCRANTZ: Madam, it so fell out that certain players
We o'erraught on the way. Of these we told him, 17
And there did seem in him a kind of joy
To hear of it. They are here about the court,
And, as I think, they have already order
This night to play before him.
POLONIUS: 'Tis most true,
And he beseeched me to entreat your majesties
To hear and see the matter.
KING: With all my heart, and it doth much content me
To hear him so inclined.
Good gentlemen, give him a further edge 26
And drive his purpose into these delights.
ROSENCRANTZ: We shall, my lord.

Exeunt Rosencrantz and Guildenstern.

KING: Sweet Gertrude, leave us too,
For we have closely sent for Hamlet hither, 29
That he, as 'twere by accident, may here
Affront Ophelia. 31
Her father and myself, lawful espials, 32
We'll so bestow ourselves that, seeing unseen,
We may of their encounter frankly judge
And gather by him, as he is behaved,
If't be th' affliction of his love or no
That thus he suffers for.
QUEEN: I shall obey you.—
And for your part, Ophelia, I do wish
That your good beauties be the happy cause
Of Hamlet's wildness. So shall I hope your virtues
Will bring him to his wonted way again,
To both your honors.
OPHELIA: Madam, I wish it may. [*Exit Queen.*]

---

13 *Niggard of* chary of, not forthcoming with
14 *assay* try to win
17 *o'erraught* overtook
26 *edge* keen desire
29 *closely* privately
31 *Affront* come face to face with
32 *espials* spies

POLONIUS: Ophelia, walk you here.—Gracious, so please you,
We will bestow ourselves.
[*To Ophelia*] Read on this book,
That show of such an exercise may color
Your loneliness. We are oft to blame in this,
'Tis too much proved, that with devotion's visage
And pious action we do sugar o'er
The devil himself.

KING: [*Aside*] O, 'tis too true.
How smart a lash that speech doth give my conscience!
The harlot's cheek, beautied with plast'ring art,
Is not more ugly to the thing that helps it
Than is my deed to my most painted word.
O heavy burden!

POLONIUS: I hear him coming. Let's withdraw, my lord.
[*Exeunt King and Polonius.*]

Enter Hamlet.

HAMLET: To be, or not to be—that is the question:
Whether 'tis nobler in the mind to suffer
The slings and arrows of outrageous fortune
Or to take arms against a sea of troubles
And by opposing end them. To die, to sleep
No more, and by a sleep to say we end
The heartache, and the thousand natural shocks
That flesh is heir to. 'Tis a consummation
Devoutly to be wished. To die, to sleep,
To sleep—perchance to dream—ay, there's the rub,
For in that sleep of death what dreams may come
When we have shuffled off this mortal coil
Must give us pause. There's the respect
That makes calamity of so long life.
For who would bear the whips and scorns of time,
Th' oppressor's wrong, the proud man's contumely,
The pangs of despised love, the law's delay,
The insolence of office, and the spurns
That patient merit of th' unworthy takes,
When he himself might his quietus make

---

45 *an exercise* a religious exercise (the *book* is apparently a devotional text); *color* give an appearance of naturalness to

46 *loneliness* solitude

48 *sugar o'er* conceal beneath sweetness

52 *to* compared to

65 *rub* obstacle (literally, obstruction encountered by a lawn bowler's ball)

67 *shuffled* cast; *coil* to-do, turmoil

68 *respect* consideration, regard

69 *of so long life* so long-lived (but also, perhaps, *long life* as a *calamity*)

70 *time* the world as we experience it

71 *contumely* rudeness, contempt

75 *quietus* settlement (literally, release, "quit," from debt)

With a bare bodkin? Who would fardels bear, 76
To grunt and sweat under a weary life,
But that the dread of something after death,
The undiscovered country, from whose bourn 79
No traveler returns, puzzles the will,
And makes us rather bear those ills we have
Than fly to others that we know not of?
Thus conscience does make cowards of us all, 83
And thus the native hue of resolution
Is sicklied o'er with the pale cast of thought,
And enterprises of great pitch and moment 86
With this regard their currents turn awry 87
And lose the name of action.—Soft you now, 88
The fair Ophelia!—Nymph, in thy orisons 89
Be all my sins remembered.

OPHELIA: Good my lord,
How does your honor for this many a day?

HAMLET: I humbly thank you, well.

OPHELIA: My lord, I have remembrances of yours
That I have longèd long to redeliver.
I pray you, now receive them.

HAMLET: No, not I,
I never gave you aught.

OPHELIA: My honored lord, you know right well you did,
And with them words of so sweet breath composed
As made the things more rich. Their perfume lost,
Take these again, for to the noble mind
Rich gifts wax poor when givers prove unkind.
There, my lord.

HAMLET: Ha, ha! Are you honest? 103

OPHELIA: My lord?

HAMLET: Are you fair?

OPHELIA: What means your lordship?

HAMLET: That if you be honest and fair, your honesty should admit no discourse to your beauty.

OPHELIA: Could beauty, my lord, have better commerce than with honesty? 109

---

76 *bodkin* short dagger; *fardels* burdens
79 *bourn* region
83 *conscience* (1) inner moral sense, (2) consciousness
86 *pitch* height (of a soaring falcon's flight)
87 *regard* consideration
88 *Soft you now* be quiet, stop talking
89 *orisons* prayers
103 *honest* (1) truthful, (2) chaste
109 *commerce* intercourse

HAMLET: Ay, truly; for the power of beauty will sooner transform honesty from what it is to a bawd than the force of honesty can translate beauty into his likeness. This was sometime a paradox, but now the time gives it proof. I did love you once.

OPHELIA: Indeed, my lord, you made me believe so.

HAMLET: You should not have believed me, for virtue cannot so inoculate our old stock but we shall relish of it. I loved you not.

OPHELIA: I was the more deceived.

HAMLET: Get thee to a nunnery. Why wouldst thou be a breeder of sinners? I am myself indifferent honest, but yet I could accuse me of such things that it were better my mother had not borne me: I am very proud, revengeful, ambitious, with more offenses at my beck than I have thoughts to put them in, imagination to give them shape, or time to act them in. What should such fellows as I do crawling between earth and heaven? We are arrant knaves all; believe none of us. Go thy ways to a nunnery. Where's your father?

OPHELIA: At home, my lord.

HAMLET: Let the doors be shut upon him, that he may play the fool nowhere but in's own house. Farewèll.

OPHELIA: O, help him, you sweet heavens!

HAMLET: If thou dost marry, I'll give thee this plague for thy dowry: be thou as chaste as ice, as pure as snow, thou shalt not escape calumny. Get thee to a nunnery, farewell. Or if thou wilt needs marry, marry a fool, for wise men know well enough what monsters you make of them. To a nunnery, go, and quickly too. Farewell.

OPHELIA: Heavenly powers, restore him!

HAMLET: I have heard of your paintings well enough. God hath given you one face, and you make yourselves another. You jig and amble, and you lisp; you nickname God's creatures and make your wantonness your ignorance. Go to, I'll no more on't; it hath made me mad. I say we will have no more marriage. Those that are married already—all but one—shall live. The rest shall keep as they are. To a nunnery, go. *Exit.*

OPHELIA: O, what a noble mind is here o'erthrown!
The courtier's, soldier's, scholar's, eye, tongue, sword,
Th' expectancy and rose of the fair state,
The glass of fashion and the mold of form,

---

113 *a paradox* an idea contrary to common opinion
117 *inoculate* graft (in horticulture); *relish* have a flavor
119 *nunnery* house of nuns (but also slang, by opposition, for "whorehouse")
120 *indifferent honest* moderately respectable
134 *monsters* cuckolds (?)
139–40 *wantonness* affectation
140 *your ignorance* something you pretend you don't know better than to do
146 *expectancy and rose* fair hope
147 *glass* mirror

Th' observed of all observers, quite, quite down!
And I, of ladies most deject and wretched,
That sucked the honey of his music vows,
Now see that noble and most sovereign reason
Like sweet bells jangled, out of time and harsh,
That unmatched form and feature of blown youth
Blasted with ecstasy. O, woe is me
T' have seen what I have seen, see what I see.

Enter King and Polonius.

KING: Love? his affections do not that way tend,
Nor what he spake, though it lacked form a little,
Was not like madness. There's something in his soul
O'er which his melancholy sits on brood,
And I do doubt the hatch and the disclose
Will be some danger; which for to prevent,
I have in quick determination
Thus set it down: he shall with speed to England
For the demand of our neglected tribute.
Haply the seas, and countries different,
With variable objects, shall expel
This something-settled matter in his heart,
Whereon his brains still beating puts him thus
From fashion of himself. What think you on't?

POLONIUS: It shall do well. But yet do I believe
The origin and commencement of his grief
Sprung from neglected love.—How now, Ophelia?
You need not tell us what Lord Hamlet said.
We heard it all.—My lord, do as you please,
But if you hold it fit, after the play
Let his queen mother all alone entreat him
To show his grief. Let her be round with him,
And I'll be placed, so please you, in the ear
Of all their conference. If she find him not,
To England send him, or confine him where
Your wisdom best shall think.

KING: It shall be so.
Madness in great ones must not unwatched go.

Exeunt.

★

---

153 *blown* in full flower
154 *Blasted* destroyed (as of a decayed flower); *ecstasy* madness
156 *affections* emotions
160 *doubt* fear; *hatch and the disclose* revealing, outcome (as of birds emerging from eggs)
167 *something-settled* somewhat settled
168 *still* constantly
169 *fashion of himself* Hamlet's normal behavior
177 *round* plainspoken

III.2

Enter Hamlet and three of the Players.

HAMLET: Speak the speech, I pray you, as I pronounced it to you, trippingly 1
on the tongue. But if you mouth it, as many of our players do, I had as
lief the town crier spoke my lines. Nor do not saw the air too much
with your hand, thus, but use all gently, for in the very torrent, tempest,
and (as I may say) whirlwind of your passion, you must acquire and
beget a temperance that may give it smoothness. O, it offends me to
the soul to hear a robustious periwig-pated fellow tear a passion to 7
tatters, to very rags, to split the ears of the groundlings, who for the 8
most part are capable of nothing but inexplicable dumb shows and 9
noise. I would have such a fellow whipped for o'erdoing Termagant. 10
It out-Herods Herod. Pray you avoid it. 11

PLAYER: I warrant your honor.

HAMLET: Be not too tame neither, but let your own discretion be your
tutor. Suit the action to the word, the word to the action, with this
special observance, that you o'erstep not the modesty of nature. For
anything so overdone is from the purpose of playing, whose end, 16
both at the first and now, was and is, to hold, as 'twere, the mirror up
to nature, to show virtue her feature, scorn her own image, and the
very age and body of the time his form and pressure. Now this over- 19
done, or come tardy off, though it makes the unskillful laugh, cannot 20
but make the judicious grieve, the censure of the which one must in 21
your allowance o'erweigh a whole theater of others. O, there be
players that I have seen play, and heard others praise, and that highly
(not to speak it profanely), that neither having th' accent of
Christians, nor the gait of Christian, pagan, nor man, have so strutted
and bellowed that I have thought some of Nature's journeymen had 26
made men, and not made them well, they imitated humanity so
abominably.

PLAYER: I hope we have reformed that indifferently with us. 29

III.2 Elsinore
1 *trippingly* easily
7 *robustious* boisterous; *periwig-pated* wig-wearing (as contemporary actors were)
8 *groundlings* spectators who paid least and stood in the yard of the open-air theater
9 *dumb shows* brief pantomimes sketching dramatic matter to follow
10 *Termagant* a Saracen "god" in medieval romance and drama
11 *Herod* a stereotypical tyrant, based on the biblical kings of that name and a common character in pre-Shakespearean religious plays
16 *from* apart from
19 *pressure* impression (as of a stamp in wax or on a coin)
20 *come tardy off* brought off slowly and badly
21 *the censure of the which one* the judgment of even one of whom (note Hamlet's elitist streak)
26 *journeymen* workmen not yet masters of their trade
29 *indifferently* fairly well

HAMLET: O, reform it altogether! And let those that play your clowns speak no more than is set down for them, for there be of them that will themselves laugh, to set on some quantity of barren spectators to laugh too, though in the meantime some necessary question of the play be then to be considered. That's villainous and shows a most pitiful ambition in the fool that uses it. Go make you ready.
[*Exeunt Players.*]
Enter Polonius, Guildenstern, and Rosencrantz.
How now, my lord? Will the king hear this piece of work?
POLONIUS: And the queen too, and that presently.
HAMLET: Bid the players make haste. [*Exit Polonius.*]
Will you two help to hasten them?
ROSENCRANTZ: Ay, my lord. *Exeunt they two.*
HAMLET: What, ho, Horatio!
Enter Horatio.
HORATIO: Here, sweet lord, at your service.
HAMLET: Horatio, thou art e'en as just a man
As e'er my conversation coped withal.
HORATIO: O, my dear lord—
HAMLET: Nay, do not think I flatter.
For what advancement may I hope from thee,
That no revenue hast but thy good spirits
To feed and clothe thee? Why should the poor be flattered?
No, let the candied tongue lick absurd pomp,
And crook the pregnant hinges of the knee
Where thrift may follow fawning. Dost thou hear?
Since my dear soul was mistress of her choice
And could of men distinguish her election,
S' hath sealed thee for herself, for thou hast been
As one in suff'ring all that suffers nothing,
A man that Fortune's buffets and rewards
Hast ta'en with equal thanks; and blessed are those
Whose blood and judgment are so well commeddled
That they are not a pipe for Fortune's finger
To sound what stop she please. Give me that man
That is not passion's slave, and I will wear him
In my heart's core, ay, in my heart of heart,

---

30 *clowns* comic actors
31 *of them* some of them
37 *presently* at once
43 *just* well-balanced
44 *conversation coped withal* dealings (not just talk) with men encountered
50 *pregnant* quick to move
51 *thrift* profit
54 *S' hath sealed* she (the soul) has marked
58 *blood* passion; *commeddled* mingled
59 *a pipe* an instrument like a recorder or flute

As I do thee. Something too much of this—
There is a play tonight before the king.
One scene of it comes near the circumstance
Which I have told thee, of my father's death.
I prithee, when thou seest that act afoot,
Even with the very comment of thy soul 68
Observe my uncle. If his occulted guilt 69
Do not itself unkennel in one speech, 70
It is a damnèd ghost that we have seen, 71
And my imaginations are as foul
As Vulcan's stithy. Give him heedful note, 73
For I mine eyes will rivet to his face,
And after we will both our judgments join
In censure of his seeming. 76

HORATIO: Well, my lord.
If a steal aught the whilst this play is playing, 77
And scape detecting, I will pay the theft.

Enter Trumpets and Kettledrums, King, Queen, Polonius, Ophelia [, Rosencrantz, Guildenstern, and other Lords attendant].

HAMLET: They are coming to the play. I must be idle. Get you a place. 79

KING: How fares our cousin Hamlet? 80

HAMLET: Excellent, i' faith, of the chameleon's dish. I eat the air, promise-crammed. You cannot feed capons so. 81

KING: I have nothing with this answer, Hamlet. These words are not mine. 83

HAMLET: No, nor mine now. [*To Polonius*] My lord, you played once i' th' university, you say?

POLONIUS: That did I, my lord, and was accounted a good actor.

HAMLET: What did you enact?

POLONIUS: I did enact Julius Caesar. I was killed i' th' Capitol; Brutus killed me. 88

HAMLET: It was a brute part of him to kill so capital a calf there. Be the players ready? 90

---

68 *the very . . . soul* thy deepest consideration
69 *occulted* hidden
70 *unkennel* dislodge, come out (literally, *unkennel* = to drive a fox from its hole; *kennel* also means "gutter")
71 *a damnèd ghost* an evil spirit, a devil (as thought of in II.2.537 ff.)
73 *stithy* smithy (hence, "black," "hellish")
76 *censure of* sentence upon
77–78 *If . . . theft* (Horatio analogizes Claudius with the pickpockets who haunted the Elizabethan public theater)
77 *a* he
79 *be idle* be foolish, act like the madman
80 *cousin* nephew
81 *chameleon's dish* i.e., air (which was believed the chameleon's food; Hamlet jokingly misunderstands *fares*)
83 *not mine* not for me as the asker of my question
88 *Capitol* (it was on the summit of the Capitoline hill, overlooking classical Rome's Forum)

ROSENCRANTZ: Ay, my lord. They stay upon your patience. 92
QUEEN: Come hither, my dear Hamlet, sit by me.
HAMLET: No, good mother. Here's metal more attractive.
POLONIUS: [*To the King*] O ho! do you mark that?
HAMLET: Lady, shall I lie in your lap? 96
OPHELIA: No, my lord.
HAMLET: Do you think I meant country matters? 98
OPHELIA: I think nothing, my lord.
HAMLET: That's a fair thought to lie between maids' legs. 100
OPHELIA: What is, my lord?
HAMLET: Nothing.
OPHELIA: You are merry, my lord.
HAMLET: Who, I?
OPHELIA: Ay, my lord.
HAMLET: O God, your only jig-maker! What should a man do but be 106
merry? For look you how cheerfully my mother looks, and my
father died within's two hours.
OPHELIA: Nay, 'tis twice two months, my lord.
HAMLET: So long? Nay then, let the devil wear black, for I'll have a suit 110
of sables. O heavens! die two months ago, and not forgotten yet? 111
Then there's hope a great man's memory may outlive his life half a
year. But, by'r Lady, a must build churches then, or else shall a suffer
not thinking on, with the hobbyhorse, whose epitaph is "For O, for 114
O, the hobbyhorse is forgot!"

The trumpets sounds. Dumb show follows.

Enter a King and a Queen [very lovingly], the Queen embracing him, and he her. [She kneels; and makes show of protestation unto him.] He takes her up, and declines his head upon her neck. He lies him down upon a bank of flowers. She, seeing him asleep, leaves him. Anon come in another man: takes off his crown, kisses it, pours poison in the sleeper's ears, and leaves him. The Queen returns, finds the King dead, makes passionate action. The poisoner, with some three or four, come in again, seem to condole with her. The dead body is carried away. The poisoner woos the Queen with gifts; she seems harsh awhile, but in the end accepts love. [*Exeunt.*]

OPHELIA: What means this, my lord?
HAMLET: Marry, this is miching mallecho; it means mischief. 117
OPHELIA: Belike this show imports the argument of the play. 118

Enter Prologue.

---

92 *stay upon your patience* await your indulgence
96 *lie. . . lap* have sexual intercourse with you
98 *country* rustic (with a bawdy pun on the first syllable: "cunt-try")
106 *jig-maker* writer of jigs (see II.2.440)
111 *sables* black furs (luxurious garb, not for mourning)
114 *hobbyhorse* (an imitation horse worn by a performer in May games and morris dances so the performer appeared to ride the horse suspended from his own shoulders)
117 *miching mallecho* sneaking iniquity
118 *argument* (1) subject, (2) plot outline

HAMLET: We shall know by this fellow. The players cannot keep counsel; they'll tell all.

OPHELIA: Will a tell us what this show meant?

HAMLET: Ay, or any show that you will show him. Be not you ashamed to show, he'll not shame to tell you what it means.

OPHELIA: You are naught, you are naught. I'll mark the play.

PROLOGUE:

For us and for our tragedy,
Here stooping to your clemency,
We beg your hearing patiently. [*Exit.*]

HAMLET: Is this a prologue, or the posy of a ring?

OPHELIA: 'Tis brief, my lord.

HAMLET: As woman's love.

Enter [two Players as] King and Queen.

PLAYER KING: Full thirty times hath Phoebus' cart gone round
Neptune's salt wash and Tellus' orbèd ground,
And thirty dozen moons with borrowed sheen
About the world have times twelve thirties been,
Since love our hearts, and Hymen did our hands,
Unite commutual in most sacred bands.

PLAYER QUEEN: So many journeys may the sun and moon
Make us again count o'er ere love be done!
But woe is me, you are so sick of late,
So far from cheer and from your former state,
That I distrust you. Yet, though I distrust,
Discomfort you, my lord, it nothing must.
For women fear too much, even as they love,
And women's fear and love hold quantity,
In neither aught, or in extremity.
Now what my love is, proof hath made you know,
And as my love is sized, my fear is so.
Where love is great, the littlest doubts are fear;
Where little fears grow great, great love grows there.

PLAYER KING: Faith, I must leave thee, love, and shortly too;
My operant powers their functions leave to do.
And thou shalt live in this fair world behind,

---

124 *naught* indecent, offensive
128 *posy* brief motto in rhyme often engraved inside a *ring*
131 *Phoebus' cart* the sun's chariot
132 *Tellus* Roman goddess of the earth
133 *borrowed* i.e., taken from the sun
134 *twelve thirties* i.e., thirty years
135 *Hymen* the Greek god of marriage
136 *commutual* mutually
141 *distrust you* fear for you
144 *quantity* proportion
151 *operant powers* active bodily forces

Honored, beloved, and haply one as kind
For husband shalt thou—
PLAYER QUEEN: O, confound the rest!
Such love must needs be treason in my breast.
In second husband let me be accurst!
None wed the second but who killed the first.
HAMLET: [*Aside*] That's wormwood.
PLAYER QUEEN: The instances that second marriage move
Are base respects of thrift, but none of love.
A second time I kill my husband dead
When second husband kisses me in bed.
PLAYER KING: I do believe you think what now you speak,
But what we do determine oft we break.
Purpose is but the slave to memory,
Of violent birth, but poor validity,
Which now, the fruit unripe, sticks on the tree,
But fall unshaken when they mellow be.
Most necessary 'tis that we forget
To pay ourselves what to ourselves is debt.
What to ourselves in passion we propose,
The passion ending, doth the purpose lose.
The violence of either grief or joy
Their own enactures with themselves destroy.
Where joy most revels, grief doth most lament;
Grief joys, joy grieves, on slender accident.
This world is not for aye, nor 'tis not strange
That even our loves should with our fortunes change,
For 'tis a question left us yet to prove,
Whether love lead fortune, or else fortune love.
The great man down, you mark his favorite flies,
The poor advanced makes friends of enemies;
And hitherto doth love on fortune tend,
For who not needs shall never lack a friend,
And who in want a hollow friend doth try,
Directly seasons him his enemy.
But, orderly to end where I begun,

---

157 *None . . . first* (a general statement: *None* is plural)
158 *wormwood* a bitter herb
159 *instances* motives
165 *Purpose . . . memory* i.e., fulfilling our intentions depends upon our remembering them, and memory may be faulty (see l. 190–91, 209); *slave to* i.e., dependent on
166 *validity* strength
167–68 *Which . . . be* i.e., as time passes, the *fruit* ripens and falls, just as *purpose* fails when not sustained by *memory*
174 *enactures* fulfillments
179 *prove* test
186 *seasons him* ripens him into

Our wills and fates do so contrary run
That our devices still are overthrown;
Our thoughts are ours, their ends none of our own.
So think thou wilt no second husband wed,
But die thy thoughts when thy first lord is dead.

PLAYER QUEEN: Nor earth to me give food, nor heaven light,
Sport and repose lock from me day and night,
To desperation turn my trust and hope,
An anchor's cheer in prison be my scope,
Each opposite that blanks the face of joy
Meet what I would have well, and it destroy,
Both here and hence pursue me lasting strife,
If, once a widow, ever I be wife!

HAMLET: If she should break it now!

PLAYER KING: 'Tis deeply sworn. Sweet, leave me here a while.
My spirits grow dull, and fain I would beguile
The tedious day with sleep.

PLAYER QUEEN: Sleep rock thy brain, [*He sleeps.*]
And never come mischance between us twain! [*Exit.*]

HAMLET: Madam, how like you this play?

QUEEN: The lady doth protest too much, methinks.

HAMLET: O, but she'll keep her word.

KING: Have you heard the argument? Is there no offense in't?

HAMLET: No, no, they do but jest, poison in jest; no offense i' th' world.

KING: What do you call the play?

HAMLET: "The Mousetrap." Marry, how? Tropically. This play is the image of a murder done in Vienna. Gonzago is the duke's name; his wife, Baptista. You shall see anon. 'Tis a knavish piece of work, but what of that? Your majesty, and we that have free souls, it touches us not. Let the galled jade wince; our withers are unwrung.

Enter [a Player as] Lucianus.

This is one Lucianus, nephew to the king.

OPHELIA: You are as good as a chorus, my lord.

HAMLET: I could interpret between you and your love, if I could see the puppets dallying.

---

188 *wills* desires, intentions
189 *still* always
196 *An anchor's cheer* a hermit's way of life (*anchor* = anchorite—i.e., hermit); *scope* limit, all I may have
197 *blanks* blanches, makes pale
199 *hence* in the next world
209 *argument* (1) subject, (2) plot outline
212 *Tropically* in the way of a "trope" or rhetorical figure (with a play on "trapically"—as in *Mousetrap*)
215 *free* guiltless
216 *galled* sore-backed; *jade* horse; *withers* shoulders (of a horse)
219 *a chorus* one in a play who explains the action
221 *puppets* i.e., you and your lover as in a puppet show

OPHELIA: You are keen, my lord, you are keen. 222
HAMLET: It would cost you a groaning to take off mine edge.
OPHELIA: Still better, and worse.
HAMLET: So you mis-take your husbands.—Begin, murderer. Leave thy damnable faces and begin. Come, the croaking raven doth bellow for revenge.
PLAYER LUCIANUS: Thoughts black, hands apt, drugs fit, and time agreeing,
    Confederate season, else no creature seeing, 229
    Thou mixture rank, of midnight weeds collected, 230
    With Hecate's ban thrice blasted, thrice infected, 231
    Thy natural magic and dire property
    On wholesome life usurps immediately.
        [*Pours the poison in his ears.*]
HAMLET: A poisons him i' th' garden for his estate. His name's Gonzago. 234
The story is extant, and written in very choice Italian. You shall see anon how the murderer gets the love of Gonzago's wife.
OPHELIA: The king rises.
QUEEN: How fares my lord?
POLONIUS: Give o'er the play.
KING: Give me some light. Away! 240
POLONIUS: Lights, lights, lights! *Exeunt all but Hamlet and Horatio.*
HAMLET: Why, let the stricken deer go weep,
        The hart ungallèd play.
    For some must watch, while some must sleep; 244
        Thus runs the world away.
Would not this, sir, and a forest of feathers—if the rest of my fortunes 246
turn Turk with me—with Provincial roses on my razed shoes, get me 247
a fellowship in a cry of players? 248
HORATIO: Half a share.
HAMLET: A whole one, I. 250
    For thou dost know, O Damon dear, 251
        This realm dismantled was
    Of Jove himself; and now reigns here
        A very, very—pajock. 254

222–23 *keen . . . edge* (Hamlet turns *keen* wit into the bite of sexual desire whose gratification might bring *groaning* in sexual pleasure and/or pain in childbirth)
229 *Confederate season* the moment agreeing with my plan
231 *Hecate* the goddess of magic arts; *ban* curse
234 *A* he
244 *watch* stay awake at night
246 *feathers* plumes for actors' costumes
247 *turn Turk* turn renegade, like a Christian turning Muslim; *Provincial roses* rosettes that covered shoelaces in fashionable garb (the Provençal rose is a large-blossomed cabbage rose); *razed* decorated with slashed patterns
248 *fellowship* financial partnership (such as Shakespeare had) in a theatrical company, a *share* (I 274); *cry* pack (of hounds)
251 *Damon* (conventional name for a shepherd-friend in classical Greco-Roman and early modern pastoral literature)
254 *pajock* patchock, disreputable fellow

HORATIO: You might have rhymed.

HAMLET: O good Horatio, I'll take the ghost's word for a thousand pound. Didst perceive?

HORATIO: Very well, my lord.

HAMLET: Upon the talk of the poisoning?

HORATIO: I did very well note him.

HAMLET: Aha! Come, some music! Come, the recorders!
For if the king like not the comedy,
Why then, belike he likes it not, perdy.
Come, some music!

Enter Rosencrantz and Guildenstern.

GUILDENSTERN: Good my lord, vouchsafe me a word with you.

HAMLET: Sir, a whole history.

GUILDENSTERN: The king, sir—

HAMLET: Ay, sir, what of him?

GUILDENSTERN: Is in his retirement marvelous distempered.

HAMLET: With drink, sir?

GUILDENSTERN: No, my lord, with choler.

HAMLET: Your wisdom should show itself more richer to signify this to the doctor, for for me to put him to his purgation would perhaps plunge him into more choler.

GUILDENSTERN: Good my lord, put your discourse into some frame, and start not so wildly from my affair.

HAMLET: I am tame, sir; pronounce.

GUILDENSTERN: The queen, your mother, in most great affliction of spirit hath sent me to you.

HAMLET: You are welcome.

GUILDENSTERN: Nay, good my lord, this courtesy is not of the right breed. If it shall please you to make me a wholesome answer, I will do your mother's commandment. If not, your pardon and my return shall be the end of my business.

HAMLET: Sir, I cannot.

ROSENCRANTZ: What, my lord?

HAMLET: Make you a wholesome answer; my wit's diseased. But, sir, such answer as I can make, you shall command, or rather, as you say, my mother. Therefore no more, but to the matter. My mother, you say—

ROSENCRANTZ: Then thus she says: your behavior hath struck her into amazement and admiration.

---

261 *recorders* wind instruments (cf. l. 69)

262 *comedy* i.e., any drama (Latin: *comoedia*), not just one meant to amuse

263 *perdy* by God (French *pardieu*)

266 *history* lengthy discourse

269 *distempered* out of temper, vexed (twisted by Hamlet into "drunk")

271 *choler* anger

275 *frame* logical order

277 *tame* calm (i.e., quietly awaiting your speech)

282 *wholesome* i.e., rational

291 *admiration* wonder, astonishment (cf. *stonish*, l. 321)

HAMLET: O wonderful son, that can so stonish a mother! But is there no sequel at the heels of this mother's admiration? Impart.

ROSENCRANTZ: She desires to speak with you in her closet ere you go to bed.

HAMLET: We shall obey, were she ten times our mother.
Have you any further trade with us?

ROSENCRANTZ: My lord, you once did love me.

HAMLET: And do still, by these pickers and stealers.

ROSENCRANTZ: Good my lord, what is your cause of distemper? You do surely bar the door upon your own liberty, if you deny your griefs to your friend.

HAMLET: Sir, I lack advancement.

ROSENCRANTZ: How can that be, when you have the voice of the king himself for your succession in Denmark?

HAMLET: Ay, sir, but "while the grass grows"—the proverb is something musty.

Enter the Players with recorders.

O, the recorders. Let me see one. To withdraw with you—why do you go about to recover the wind of me, as if you would drive me into a toil?

GUILDENSTERN: O my lord, if my duty be too bold, my love is too unmannerly.

HAMLET: I do not well understand that. Will you play upon this pipe?

GUILDENSTERN: My lord, I cannot.

HAMLET: I pray you.

GUILDENSTERN: Believe me, I cannot.

HAMLET: I do beseech you.

GUILDENSTERN: I know no touch of it, my lord.

HAMLET: It is as easy as lying. Govern these ventages with your fingers and thumb, give it breath with your mouth, and it will discourse most eloquent music. Look you, these are the stops.

GUILDENSTERN: But these cannot I command to any utterance of harmony. I have not the skill.

HAMLET: Why, look you now, how unworthy a thing you make of me! You would play upon me, you would seem to know my stops, you

---

294 *closet* private room
297 *trade* business
299 *pickers and stealers* i.e., hands (a quotation from the Anglican catechism)
300 *Good my lord* my good lord
304–5 *voice . . . succession* (cf. I.2. 109)
306 *while the grass grows* (a proverb, ending: "the horse starves")
308 *withdraw* step aside
309 *recover the wind* come up to windward (as a hunter might in order to drive game into the *toil*); *toil* snare
310–11 *is too unmannerly* leads me beyond the restraint of good manners
320 *ventages* holes, vents

would pluck out the heart of my mystery, you would sound me from
my lowest note to the top of my compass; and there is much music, 326
excellent voice, in this little organ, yet cannot you make it speak.
'Sblood, do you think I am easier to be played on than a pipe? Call
me what instrument you will, though you can fret me, you cannot 329
play upon me. 330

Enter Polonius.

God bless you, sir!

POLONIUS: My lord, the queen would speak with you, and presently. 332

HAMLET: Do you see yonder cloud that's almost in shape of a camel?

POLONIUS: By th' mass and 'tis, like a camel indeed.

HAMLET: Methinks it is like a weasel.

POLONIUS: It is backed like a weasel.

HAMLET: Or like a whale.

POLONIUS: Very like a whale.

HAMLET: Then I will come to my mother by and by. [*Aside*] They fool 339
me to the top of my bent.—I will come by and by. 340

POLONIUS: I will say so.

[*Exit.*]

HAMLET: "By and by" is easily said. Leave me, friends.

[*Exeunt all but Hamlet.*]

'Tis now the very witching time of night, 343
When churchyards yawn, and hell itself breathes out
Contagion to this world. Now could I drink hot blood
And do such bitter business as the day
Would quake to look on. Soft, now to my mother.
O heart, lose not thy nature; let not ever 348
The soul of Nero enter this firm bosom. 349
Let me be cruel, not unnatural; 350
I will speak daggers to her, but use none.
My tongue and soul in this be hypocrites:
How in my words somever she be shent, 353
To give them seals never, my soul, consent! 354

Exit.

★

326 *compass* range
329 *fret* irritate (with wordplay on the fingering of some stringed musical instruments)
332 *presently* at once
339 *by and by* immediately
340 *bent* (see II.2.30 n.)
343 *witching* i.e., associated with witches
348 *nature* filial love
349 *Nero* Roman emperor and murderer of his mother, Agrippina
353 *shent* reproved
354 *seals* authentications in actions; *never* may never

III.3

Enter King, Rosencrantz, and Guildenstern.

KING: I like him not, nor stands it safe with us
To let his madness range. Therefore prepare you.
I your commission will forthwith dispatch, 3
And he to England shall along with you.
The terms of our estate may not endure 5
Hazard so near's as doth hourly grow
Out of his brows. 7
GUILDENSTERN: We will ourselves provide.
Most holy and religious fear it is
To keep those many many bodies safe
That live and feed upon your majesty. 10
ROSENCRANTZ: The single and peculiar life is bound 11
With all the strength and armor of the mind
To keep itself from noyance, but much more 13
That spirit upon whose weal depends and rests 14
The lives of many. The cess of majesty 15
Dies not alone, but like a gulf doth draw 16
What's near it with it; or it is a massy wheel
Fixed on the summit of the highest mount,
To whose huge spokes ten thousand lesser things
Are mortised and adjoined, which when it falls, 20
Each small annexment, petty consequence,
Attends the boist'rous ruin. Never alone 22
Did the king sigh, but with a general groan.
KING: Arm you, I pray you, to this speedy voyage, 24
For we will fetters put about this fear,
Which now goes too free-footed.
ROSENCRANTZ: We will haste us.
Exeunt Gentlemen.

Enter Polonius.

III.3 Elsinore
3 *commission* written order
5 *terms* circumstances; *estate* royal position
7 *brows* (1) frowns (?), (2) head (i.e., Hamlet's plans) (?)
11 *peculiar* individual
13 *noyance* harm
14 *weal* health
15 *cess* decease, cessation
16 *gulf* whirlpool
22 *Attends* joins in (like a royal attendant)
24 *Arm* prepare; *speedy* immediate

POLONIUS: My lord, he's going to his mother's closet.
Behind the arras I'll convey myself 28
To hear the process. I'll warrant she'll tax him home, 29
And, as you said, and wisely was it said, 30
'Tis meet that some more audience than a mother,
Since nature makes them partial, should o'erhear
The speech, of vantage. Fare you well, my liege. 33
I'll call upon you ere you go to bed
And tell you what I know. 35
KING: Thanks, dear my lord.
Exit [Polonius].

O, my offense is rank, it smells to heaven;
It hath the primal eldest curse upon't, 37
A brother's murder. Pray can I not,
Though inclination be as sharp as will.
My stronger guilt defeats my strong intent, 40
And like a man to double business bound
I stand in pause where I shall first begin,
And both neglect. What if this cursèd hand
Were thicker than itself with brother's blood,
Is there not rain enough in the sweet heavens 45
To wash it white as snow? Whereto serves mercy
But to confront the visage of offense? 47
And what's in prayer but this twofold force,
To be forestallèd ere we come to fall,
Or pardoned being down? Then I'll look up. 50
My fault is past, but, O, what form of prayer
Can serve my turn? "Forgive me my foul murder"?
That cannot be, since I am still possessed
Of those effects for which I did the murder, 54
My crown, mine own ambition, and my queen.
May one be pardoned and retain th' offense? 56
In the corrupted currents of this world
Offense's gilded hand may shove by justice, 58
And oft 'tis seen the wicked prize itself

---

28 *arras* cloth wall hanging
29 *process* proceedings; *tax him home* reprimand him severely
33 *of vantage* from an advantageous position
35 *dear my lord* my dear lord
37 *primal eldest curse* God's curse on the biblical Cain, who also murdered a brother (Genesis 4:11–12)
45 *rain* i.e., heavenly mercy (see Ecclesiasticus 35:20 and *The Merchant of Venice*, IV.1.182–83)
47 *offense* sin
54 *effects* things I acquired
56 *offense* i.e., what Claudius has gained by murdering old Hamlet
58 *gilded* gold-laden

Buys out the law. But 'tis not so above.
There is no shuffling; there the action lies
In his true nature, and we ourselves compelled,
Even to the teeth and forehead of our faults,
To give in evidence. What then? What rests?
Try what repentance can. What can it not?
Yet what can it when one cannot repent?
O wretched state! O bosom black as death!
O limèd soul, that struggling to be free
Art more engaged! Help, angels! Make assay.
Bow, stubborn knees, and, heart with strings of steel,
Be soft as sinews of the newborn babe.
All may be well.
[*He kneels.*]
Enter Hamlet.

HAMLET: Now might I do it pat, now a is a-praying,
And now I'll do't. And so a goes to heaven,
And so am I revenged. That would be scanned.
A villain kills my father, and for that
I, his sole son, do this same villain send
To heaven.
Why, this is [hire and salary,] not revenge.
A took my father grossly, full of bread,
With all his crimes broad blown, as flush as May;
And how his audit stands, who knows save heaven?
But in our circumstance and course of thought,
'Tis heavy with him; and am I then revenged,
To take him in the purging of his soul,
When he is fit and seasoned for his passage?
No.
Up, sword, and know thou a more horrid hent.
When he is drunk asleep, or in his rage,
Or in th' incestuous pleasure of his bed,
At game a-swearing, or about some act
That has no relish of salvation in't—

---

61 *shuffling* cheating; *action* legal proceeding (in heaven's court)
63 *to the teeth and forehead* face-to-face
68 *limèd* caught in birdlime, a gluey material spread as a bird snare
69 *engaged* embedded; *assay* essay, attempt
73 *pat* opportunely
73, 74 *a* he
75 *scanned* studied, thought about
80 *grossly* morally unprepared; *full of bread* i.e., sensually gratified (hence not ready for a purified death)
81 *broad blown* fully blossomed; *flush* vigorous
82 *audit* account
88 *hent* occasion
92 *relish* flavor

Then trip him, that his heels may kick at heaven,
And that his soul may be as damned and black
As hell, whereto it goes. My mother stays.
This physic but prolongs thy sickly days. *Exit.*

KING: [*Rises.*]
My words fly up, my thoughts remain below.
Words without thoughts never to heaven go. *Exit.*

⋆

III.4

Enter [Queen] Gertrude and Polonius.

POLONIUS: A will come straight. Look you lay home to him. 1
Tell him his pranks have been too broad to bear with, 2
And that your grace hath screened and stood between
Much heat and him. I'll silence me even here.
Pray you be round. 5

QUEEN: I'll warrant you; fear me not. Withdraw; I hear him coming.
[*Polonius hides behind the arras.*]
Enter Hamlet.

HAMLET: Now, mother, what's the matter?

QUEEN: Hamlet, thou hast thy father much offended.

HAMLET: Mother, you have my father much offended.

QUEEN: Come, come, you answer with an idle tongue. 10

HAMLET: Go, go, you question with a wicked tongue.

QUEEN: Why, how now, Hamlet? 12

HAMLET: What's the matter now?

QUEEN: Have you forgot me? 13

HAMLET: No, by the rood, not so!
You are the queen, your husband's brother's wife,
And (would it were not so) you are my mother.

QUEEN: Nay, then I'll set those to you that can speak.

HAMLET: Come, come, and sit you down. You shall not budge.
You go not till I set you up a glass 18
Where you may see the inmost part of you.

QUEEN: What wilt thou do? Thou wilt not murder me? 20
Help, ho!

POLONIUS: [*Behind*] What, ho! help! 22

III.4 Elsinore: Gertrude's private rooms
1 *A* he; *lay home to* tax (see III.3.29)
2 *broad* unrestrained
5 *round* plainspoken
10 *an idle* a foolish
12 *matter* subject, point of our discussion
13 *rood* cross
18 *glass* mirror
22 s.d. *Behind* (for the action here, see IV.1.8–12)

Hamlet: [*Draws.*]
How now? a rat? Dead for a ducat, dead!
[*Thrusts through the arras and kills Polonius.*]
Polonius: [*Behind*]
O, I am slain!
Queen: O me, what hast thou done?
Hamlet: Nay, I know not. Is it the king?
Queen: O, what a rash and bloody deed is this!
Hamlet: A bloody deed—almost as bad, good mother,
As kill a king, and marry with his brother.
Queen: As kill a king?
Hamlet: Ay, lady, it was my word.
[*Looks behind the arras and sees Polonius.*]
Thou wretched, rash, intruding fool, farewell!
I took thee for thy better. Take thy fortune.
Thou find'st to be too busy is some danger.—
Leave wringing of your hands. Peace, sit you down
And let me wring your heart, for so I shall
If it be made of penetrable stuff,
If damnèd custom have not brazed it so
That it be proof and bulwark against sense.
Queen: What have I done that thou dar'st wag thy tongue
In noise so rude against me?
Hamlet: Such an act
That blurs the grace and blush of modesty,
Calls virtue hypocrite, takes off the rose
From the fair forehead of an innocent love,
And sets a blister there, makes marriage vows
As false as dicers' oaths. O, such a deed
As from the body of contraction plucks
The very soul, and sweet religion makes
A rhapsody of words! Heaven's face does glow,
O'er this solidity and compound mass,
With heated visage, as against the doom,
Is thought-sick at the act.
Queen: Ay me, what act,
That roars so loud and thunders in the index?

---

36 *custom* habit; *brazed* hardened like brass
37 *proof* armor; *sense* feeling
43 *blister* brand (in the early modern period, convicted prostitutes were sometimes branded on the forehead; see IV.5. 118–19)
45 *contraction* the category, contract-making of which marriage is an instance
46 *religion* i.e., sacred marriage vows
47 *rhapsody* confused heap
48 *compound mass* the earth as compounded of the four elements (see II.2.278 n.)
49 *against* in expectation of; *doom* Day of Judgment
51 *index* table of contents preceding the body of a book, prefatory matter

HAMLET: Look here upon this picture, and on this,
The counterfeit presentment of two brothers.
See what a grace was seated on this brow:
Hyperion's curls, the front of Jove himself,
An eye like Mars, to threaten and command,
A station like the herald Mercury
New lighted on a heaven-kissing hill—
A combination and a form indeed
Where every god did seem to set his seal
To give the world assurance of a man.
This was your husband. Look you now what follows.
Here is your husband, like a mildewed ear
Blasting his wholesome brother. Have you eyes?
Could you on this fair mountain leave to feed,
And batten on this moor? Ha! have you eyes?
You cannot call it love, for at your age
The heyday in the blood is tame, it's humble,
And waits upon the judgment, and what judgment
Would step from this to this? Sense sure you have,
Else could you not have motion, but sure that sense
Is apoplexed, for madness would not err,
Nor sense to ecstasy was ne'er so thralled
But it reserved some quantity of choice
To serve in such a difference. What devil was't
That thus hath cozened you at hoodman-blind?
Eyes without feeling, feeling without sight,
Ears without hands or eyes, smelling sans all,
Or but a sickly part of one true sense
Could not so mope.
O shame, where is thy blush? Rebellious hell,
If thou canst mutine in a matron's bones,
To flaming youth let virtue be as wax
And melt in her own fire. Proclaim no shame

53 *counterfeit presentment* representation in a portrait
55 *Hyperion* the sun god; *front* forehead
57 *station* stance; *herald Mercury* messenger of the Olympian gods, typifying grace
66 *batten* feed greedily
68 *heyday* excitement of passion
69 *waits upon* yields to
70 *Sense* feeling
71 *motion* desire, impulse
72 *apoplexed* paralyzed
73 *ecstasy* madness
75 *serve . . . difference* i.e., make a choice where there is such great difference
76 *cozened* cheated; *hoodman-blind* blindman's buff
78 *sans* without (French)
80 *mope* be in a daze
82 *mutine* mutiny

When the compulsive ardor gives the charge,
Since frost itself as actively doth burn,
And reason panders will.

QUEEN: O Hamlet, speak no more.
Thou turn'st my eyes into my very soul,
And there I see such black and grainèd spots
As will leave there their tinct.

HAMLET: Nay, but to live
In the rank sweat of an enseamèd bed,
Stewed in corruption, honeying and making love
Over the nasty sty—

QUEEN: O, speak to me no more.
These words like daggers enter in my ears.
No more, sweet Hamlet.

HAMLET: A murderer and a villain,
A slave that is not twentieth part the tithe
Of your precedent lord, a vice of kings,
A cutpurse of the empire and the rule,
That from a shelf the precious diadem stole
And put it in his pocket—

QUEEN: No more,

Enter [the] Ghost [in his nightgown].

HAMLET: A king of shreds and patches—
Save me and hover o'er me with your wings,
You heavenly guards! What would your gracious figure?

QUEEN: Alas, he's mad.

HAMLET: Do you not come your tardy son to chide,
That, lapsed in time and passion, lets go by
Th' important acting of your dread command?
O, say!

GHOST: Do not forget. This visitation
Is but to whet thy almost blunted purpose.
But look, amazement on thy mother sits.
O, step between her and her fighting soul!

---

85 *compulsive* compelling; *gives the charge* delivers the attack
87 *panders will* acts as procurer for desire (implied: *reason* should control *will*—desire in general, sexual desire in particular)
89 *grainèd* indelibly dyed ("grain" = dye)
90 *leave there* (F reads "not leave," which amounts to the same thing); *tinct* color
91 *enseamèd* grease-laden ("seam" = grease)
96 *tithe* tenth part
97 *vice* clownish rogue (like the Vice, a staple character of the earlier morality plays)
98 *cutpurse* skulking thief
100 s.d. *nightgown* dressing gown
102–3 *Save . . . guards* (cf. I.4.39)
106 *lapsed . . . passion* having let both the moment and passionate purpose slip
111 *amazement* bewilderment (literally, "in a maze")

Conceit in weakest bodies strongest works. 113
Speak to her, Hamlet.
HAMLET: How is it with you, lady?
QUEEN: Alas, how is't with you,
That you do bend your eye on vacancy,
And with th' incorporal air do hold discourse? 117
Forth at your eyes your spirits wildly peep,
And as the sleeping soldiers in th' alarm 119
Your bedded hair, like life in excrements, 120
Start up and stand an end. O gentle son, 121
Upon the heat and flame of thy distemper 122
Sprinkle cool patience. Whereon do you look?
HAMLET: On him, on him! Look you, how pale he glares!
His form and cause conjoined, preaching to stones,
Would make them capable.—Do not look upon me, 126
Lest with this piteous action you convert
My stern effects. Then what I have to do 128
Will want true color—tears perchance for blood. 129
QUEEN: To whom do you speak this? 130
HAMLET: Do you see nothing there?
QUEEN: Nothing at all; yet all that is I see.
HAMLET: Nor did you nothing hear?
QUEEN: No, nothing but ourselves.
HAMLET: Why, look you there! Look how it steals away!
My father, in his habit as he lived!
Look where he goes even now out at the portal!
Exit Ghost.
QUEEN: This is the very coinage of your brain.
This bodiless creation ecstasy 137
Is very cunning in.
HAMLET: My pulse as yours doth temperately keep time
And makes as healthful music. It is not madness 140
That I have uttered. Bring me to the test,
And I the matter will reword, which madness
Would gambol from. Mother, for love of grace, 143

---

113 *Conceit* imagination
117 *incorporal* bodiless
119 *alarm* call to arms
120 *excrements* outgrowths
121 *an* on
122 *distemper* mental disorder
126 *capable* responsive, able to comprehend
128 *effects* planned actions
129 *want* lack; *color* (1) character, distinguishing quality, (2) tincture (i.e., red *blood* rather than colorless *tears*)
137 *ecstasy* madness
143 *gambol* shy (like a startled horse)

Lay not that flattering unction to your soul,
That not your trespass but my madness speaks.
It will but skin and film the ulcerous place
Whiles rank corruption, mining all within,
Infects unseen. Confess yourself to heaven,
Repent what's past, avoid what is to come,
And do not spread the compost on the weeds
To make them ranker. Forgive me this my virtue.
For in the fatness of these pursy times
Virtue itself of vice must pardon beg,
Yea, curb and woo for leave to do him good.

QUEEN: O Hamlet, thou hast cleft my heart in twain.

HAMLET: O, throw away the worser part of it,
And live the purer with the other half.
Good night—but go not to my uncle's bed.
Assume a virtue, if you have it not.
That monster custom, who all sense doth eat
Of habits evil, is angel yet in this,
That to the use of actions fair and good
He likewise gives a frock or livery
That aptly is put on. Refrain tonight,
And that shall lend a kind of easiness
To the next abstinence; the next more easy;
For use almost can change the stamp of nature,
And either [lodge] the devil, or throw him out
With wondrous potency. Once more, good night,
And when you are desirous to be blessed,
I'll blessing beg of you.—For this same lord,
I do repent; but heaven hath pleased it so,
To punish me with this, and this with me,
That I must be their scourge and minister.
I will bestow him and will answer well
The death I gave him. So again, good night.
I must be cruel only to be kind.
This bad begins, and worse remains behind.
One word more, good lady.

QUEEN: What shall I do?

HAMLET: Not this, by no means, that I bid you do:

---

144 *unction* ointment

147 *mining* undermining

152 *fatness* grossness (physical and moral); *pursy* corpulent (derived from "purse")

154 *curb* bow to

160–62 *custom . . . evil* i.e., long continuance (*custom*) deprives us of knowing that our behavior is *evil* (the next lines explain that we may also become habituated to good behavior)

163 *livery* characteristic dress

167 *use* habit; *stamp* impression, form

175 *bestow* stow, hide; *answer* be responsible for

178 *This* i.e., the killing of Polonius; *behind* to come

Let the bloat king tempt you again to bed,
Pinch wanton on your cheek, call you his mouse,
And let him, for a pair of reechy kisses,
Or paddling in your neck with his damned fingers,
Make you to ravel all this matter out,
That I essentially am not in madness,
But mad in craft. 'Twere good you let him know,
For who that's but a queen, fair, sober, wise,
Would from a paddock, from a bat, a gib,
Such dear concernings hide? Who would do so?
No, in despite of sense and secrecy,
Unpeg the basket on the house's top,
Let the birds fly, and like the famous ape,
To try conclusions, in the basket creep
And break your own neck down.

QUEEN: Be thou assured, if words be made of breath,
And breath of life, I have no life to breathe
What thou hast said to me.

HAMLET: I must to England; you know that?

QUEEN: Alack,
I had forgot. 'Tis so concluded on.

HAMLET: There's letters sealed, and my two schoolfellows,
Whom I will trust as I will adders fanged,
They bear the mandate; they must sweep my way
And marshal me to knavery. Let it work.
For 'tis the sport to have the enginer
Hoist with his own petard, and 't shall go hard
But I will delve one yard below their mines
And blow them at the moon. O, 'tis most sweet
When in one line two crafts directly meet.
This man shall set me packing.
I'll lug the guts into the neighbor room.
Mother, good night. Indeed, this counselor
Is now most still, most secret, and most grave,
Who was in life a foolish prating knave.

---

181 *bloat* flabby
183 *reechy* filthy (i.e., "reeky")
185 *ravel . . . out* disentangle
189 *paddock* road; *gib* tomcat
190 *dear concernings* matters so personally important
193 *famous ape* (the story, if there was one, is now unknown)
194 *conclusions* experiments
203 *mandate* order
204 *marshal* conduct, lead
205 *enginer* maker of military engines (the spelling, from Q2, indicates stress on the first syllable)
206 *Hoist* blown up; *petard* bomb or mine
210 *packing* (1) traveling in a hurry, (2) carrying Polonius's body, (3) plotting, contriving
213 *grave* (a bad pun)

Come, sir, to draw toward an end with you.
Good night, mother.
[*Exit the Queen. Then*] *exit* [*Hamlet, lugging in Polonius*].

★

IV.1

Enter King and Queen, with Rosencrantz and Guildenstern.

KING: There's matter in these sighs. These profound heaves
You must translate; 'tis fit we understand them.
Where is your son?
QUEEN: Bestow this place on us a little while. 4
[*Exeunt Rosencrantz and Guildenstern.*]
Ah, mine own lord, what have I seen tonight!
KING: What, Gertrude? How does Hamlet?
QUEEN: Mad as the sea and wind when both contend
Which is the mightier. In his lawless fit,
Behind the arras hearing something stir,
Whips out his rapier, cries "A rat, a rat!" 10
And in this brainish apprehension kills 11
The unseen good old man.
KING: O heavy deed!
It had been so with us, had we been there. 13
His liberty is full of threats to all,
To you yourself, to us, to every one.
Alas, how shall this bloody deed be answered?
It will be laid to us, whose providence 17
Should have kept short, restrained, and out of haunt 18
This mad young man. But so much was our love
We would not understand what was most fit, 20
But, like the owner of a foul disease,
To keep it from divulging, let it feed 22
Even on the pith of life. Where is he gone?
QUEEN: To draw apart the body he hath killed;
O'er whom his very madness, like some ore 25
Among a mineral of metals base, 26
Shows itself pure. A weeps for what is done. 27

IV.1 Elsinore (the act break here is not in Q2 or F, and Gertrude remains onstage)
4 *Bestow this place on us* give us privacy (a polite formula)
11 *brainish* deluded, crazed
13 *us* me (the royal plural and so throughout the scene)
17 *providence* foresight
18 *short* i.e., on a short leash; *haunt* association with others
22 *divulging* becoming known
25 *some* (the printer's manuscript might have read "fine"); *ore* vein of gold
26 *mineral* mine
27 *A* he

KING: O Gertrude, come away!
The sun no sooner shall the mountains touch
But we will ship him hence, and this vile deed
We must with all our majesty and skill
Both countenance and excuse. Ho, Guildenstern!
Enter Rosencrantz and Guildenstern.
Friends both, go join you with some further aid.
Hamlet in madness hath Polonius slain,
And from his mother's closet hath he dragged him.
Go seek him out; speak fair, and bring the body
Into the chapel. I pray you haste in this.
[*Exeunt Rosencrantz and Guildenstern.*]
Come, Gertrude, we'll call up our wisest friends
And let them know both what we mean to do
And what's untimely done.
Whose whisper o'er the world's diameter,
As level as the cannon to his blank
Transports his poisoned shot, may miss our name
And hit the woundless air. O, come away!
My soul is full of discord and dismay. *Exeunt.*

⋆

IV.2

Enter Hamlet.

HAMLET: Safely stowed. [*Calling within*] But soft, what noise? Who calls on Hamlet? O, here they come.

[Enter] Rosencrantz, [Guildenstern,] and others.

ROSENCRANTZ: What have you done, my lord, with the dead body?

HAMLET: Compounded it with dust, whereto 'tis kin.

ROSENCRANTZ: Tell us where 'tis, that we may take it thence
And bear it to the chapel.

HAMLET: Do not believe it.

ROSENCRANTZ: Believe what?

HAMLET: That I can keep your counsel and not mine own. Besides, to be demanded of a sponge, what replication should be made by the son of a king?

31–32 *majesty . . . excuse* i.e., royal power will *countenance*, make publicly acceptable, and *skill* political savvy, will make palatable

40 *And . . . done* (some words seem to be missing after this partial line; two editorial guesses: "So, haply, slander" [Capell]; "So envious slander" [Jenkins])

42 *As level* with as direct aim; *blank* mark, central white spot on a target

IV.2 Elsinore

1 s.d. *Calling within* (in F, "Gentlemen within" call Hamlet's name after *stowed*)

4 *dust . . . kin* (see Genesis 3:19: ". . . dust thou art, and unto dust shalt thou return")

10 *sponge* i.e., something that absorbs (e.g., *counsel*) and may also be squeezed dry (i.e., by Claudius); *replication* reply (a legal term)

ROSENCRANTZ: Take you me for a sponge, my lord?
HAMLET: Ay, sir, that soaks up the king's countenance, his rewards, his 13
authorities. But such officers do the king best service in the end. He
keeps them, like an ape, in the corner of his jaw, first mouthed, to be
last swallowed. When he needs what you have gleaned, it is but
squeezing you and, sponge, you shall be dry again.
ROSENCRANTZ: I understand you not, my lord.
HAMLET: I am glad of it. A knavish speech sleeps in a foolish ear. 19
ROSENCRANTZ: My lord, you must tell us where the body is and go with 20
us to the king.
HAMLET: The body is with the king, but the king is not with the body.
The king is a thing—
GUILDENSTERN: A thing, my lord?
HAMLET: Of nothing. Bring me to him. *Exeunt.* 25

⋆

IV.3

Enter King, and two or three.

KING: I have sent to seek him and to find the body.
How dangerous is it that this man goes loose!
Yet must not we put the strong law on him;
He's loved of the distracted multitude, 4
Who like not in their judgment, but their eyes,
And where 'tis so, th' offender's scourge is weighed, 6
But never the offense. To bear all smooth and even,
This sudden sending him away must seem
Deliberate pause. Diseases desperate grown 9
By desperate appliance are relieved, 10
Or not at all.
Enter Rosencrantz [, Guildenstern,] and all the rest.
How now? What hath befallen?
ROSENCRANTZ: Where the dead body is bestowed, my lord,
We cannot get from him.
KING: But where is he?
ROSENCRANTZ: Without, my lord; guarded, to know your pleasure.
KING: Bring him before us.

---

13 *countenance* favor
19 *sleeps in* means nothing to
25 *Of nothing* (cf. the Anglican Book of Common Prayer, Psalm 144:4, "Man is like a thing of naught: his time passeth away like a shadow")

IV.3 Elsinore
4 *distracted* confused
6 *scourge* punishment
9 *Deliberate pause* i.e., something thoughtfully deliberated
10 *appliance* treatment

ROSENCRANTZ: Ho! Bring in the lord.

They enter [with Hamlet].

KING: Now, Hamlet, where's Polonius?

HAMLET: At supper.

KING: At supper? Where?

HAMLET: Not where he eats, but where a is eaten. A certain convocation of politic worms are e'en at him. Your worm is your only emperor for diet. We fat all creatures else to fat us, and we fat ourselves for maggots. Your fat king and your lean beggar is but variable service—two dishes, but to one table. That's the end.

KING: Alas, alas!

HAMLET: A man may fish with the worm that hath eat of a king, and eat of the fish that hath fed of that worm.

KING: What dost thou mean by this?

HAMLET: Nothing but to show you how a king may go a progress through the guts of a beggar.

KING: Where is Polonius?

HAMLET: In heaven. Send thither to see. If your messenger find him not there, seek him i' th' other place yourself. But if indeed you find him not within this month, you shall nose him as you go up the stairs into the lobby.

KING: [*To Attendants*] Go seek him there.

HAMLET: A will stay till you come. [*Exeunt Attendants.*]

KING: Hamlet, this deed, for thine especial safety,
Which we do tender as we dearly grieve
For that which thou hast done, must send thee hence
With fiery quickness. Therefore prepare thyself.
The bark is ready and the wind at help,
Th' associates tend, and everything is bent
For England.

HAMLET: For England?

KING: Ay, Hamlet.

HAMLET: Good.

KING: So is it, if thou knew'st our purposes.

HAMLET: I see a cherub that sees them. But come, for England! Farewell, dear mother.

---

19 *a* he

20 *politic worms* craftily scheming worms (just as Polonius was a schemer)

21 *diet* food and drink (perhaps with a play upon a famous *convocation*, the Diet [Council] of Worms opened by Charles V on 28 January 1521, before which the Protestant reformer Martin Luther appeared)

22 *variable service* different servings of one food

25 *eat* (past tense, pronounced "et")

28 *progress* royal journey through the hinterlands

38 *tender* hold dear; *dearly* intensely

41 *bark* ship

42 *tend* wait; *bent* set in readiness (like a bent bow)

45 *cherub* one of the cherubim, second in the nine orders of angels

KING: Thy loving father, Hamlet.
HAMLET: My mother—father and mother is man and wife, man and wife
is one flesh; so, my mother. Come, for England! *Exit.* 49
KING: Follow him at foot; tempt him with speed aboard. 50
Delay it not; I'll have him hence tonight.
Away! for everything is sealed and done
That else leans on th' affair. Pray you make haste. 53
[*Exeunt all but the King.*]
And, England, if my love thou hold'st at aught— 54
As my great power thereof may give thee sense,
Since yet thy cicatrice looks raw and red 56
After the Danish sword, and thy free awe 57
Pays homage to us—thou mayst not coldly set 58
Our sovereign process, which imports at full 59
By letters congruing to that effect 60
The present death of Hamlet. Do it, England, 61
For like the hectic in my blood he rages, 62
And thou must cure me. Till I know 'tis done,
Howe'er my haps, my joys will ne'er begin. *Exit.* 64

*

IV.4

Enter Fortinbras with his Army [including a Norwegian Captain, marching] over the stage.

FORTINBRAS: Go, captain, from me greet the Danish king.
Tell him that by his license Fortinbras
Craves the conveyance of a promised march 3
Over his kingdom. You know the rendezvous.
If that his majesty would aught with us,
We shall express our duty in his eye; 6
And let him know so.

---

49 *one flesh* (many biblical passages endorse this claim; see Genesis 2:24, Matthew 19:5–6, Mark 10:8)
50 *at foot* closely
53 *else* otherwise; *leans on* is connected with
54 *England* King of England; *aught* anything, any value
56 *cicatrice* scar
57 *free awe* voluntary respect
58 *set* esteem
59 *process* formal command
60 *congruing* agreeing
61 *present* instant
62 *the hectic* a continuous fever
64 *haps* fortunes

IV.4 Somewhere in Denmark's territories
3 *conveyance* escort; *promised* i.e., agreed upon by diplomats (see II.2.77–80)
6 *eye* presence

NORWEGIAN CAPTAIN: I will do't, my lord.
FORTINBRAS: Go softly on. [*Exeunt all but the Captain.*] 8
Enter Hamlet, Rosencrantz, [Guildenstern,] and others.
HAMLET: Good sir, whose powers are these? 9
NORWEGIAN CAPTAIN: They are of Norway, sir. 10
HAMLET: How purposed, sir, I pray you?
NORWEGIAN CAPTAIN: Against some part of Poland.
HAMLET: Who commands them, sir?
NORWEGIAN CAPTAIN: The nephew to old Norway, Fortinbras.
HAMLET: Goes it against the main of Poland, sir, 15
Or for some frontier?
NORWEGIAN CAPTAIN: Truly to speak, and with no addition, 17
We go to gain a little patch of ground
That hath in it no profit but the name,
To pay five ducats, five, I would not farm it, 20
Not will it yield to Norway or the Pole
A ranker rate, should it be sold in fee. 22
HAMLET: Why, then the Polack never will defend it.
NORWEGIAN CAPTAIN: Yes, it is already garrisoned. 24
HAMLET: Two thousand souls and twenty thousand ducats
Will not debate the question of this straw.
This is th' imposthume of much wealth and peace, 27
That inward breaks, and shows no cause without
Why the man dies. I humbly thank you, sir.
NORWEGIAN CAPTAIN: God buy you, sir. [*Exit.*] 30
ROSENCRANTZ: Will't please you go, my lord?
HAMLET: I'll be with you straight. Go a little before.
[*Exeunt all but Hamlet.*]

How all occasions do inform against me 32
And spur my dull revenge! What is a man,
If his chief good and market of his time 34
Be but to sleep and feed? A beast, no more.
Sure he that made us with such large discourse, 36
Looking before and after, gave us not
That capability and godlike reason
To fust in us unused. Now, whether it be 39

---

8 *softly* slowly
9 *powers* forces
15 *main* main body
17 *addition* exaggeration
20 *To pay* (i.e., as rent)
22 *ranker* more lavish; *in fee* outright
24 *garrisoned* guarded by soldiers
27 *imposthume* abscess
32 *inform* take shape
34 *market of* compensation for
36 *discourse* power of thought
39 *fust* mold

Bestial oblivion, or some craven scruple
Of thinking too precisely on th' event—
A thought which, quartered, hath but one part wisdom
And ever three parts coward—I do not know
Why yet I live to say "This thing's to do,"
Sith I have cause, and will, and strength, and means
To do't. Examples gross as earth exhort me.
Witness this army of such mass and charge,
Led by a delicate and tender prince,
Whose spirit, with divine ambition puffed,
Makes mouths at the invisible event,
Exposing what is mortal and unsure
To all that fortune, death, and danger dare,
Even for an eggshell. Rightly to be great
Is not to stir without great argument,
But greatly to find quarrel in a straw
When honor's at the stake. How stand I then,
That have a father killed, a mother stained,
Excitements of my reason and my blood,
And let all sleep, while to my shame I see
The imminent death of twenty thousand men
That for a fantasy and trick of fame
Go to their graves like beds, fight for a plot
Whereon the numbers cannot try the cause,
Which is not tomb enough and continent
To hide the slain? O, from this time forth,
My thoughts be bloody, or be nothing worth! *Exit.*

⋆

IV.5

Enter Horatio, [Queen] Gertrude, and a Gentleman.

QUEEN: I will not speak with her.
GENTLEMAN: She is importunate, indeed distract.
Her mood will needs be pitied.

---

40 *oblivion* forgetfulness
41 *event* outcome (see l. 50)
42 *quartered* divided in four (see the many earlier mathematical divisions: e.g., III.4.97)
46 *gross* large and evident
47 *charge* expense
50 *Makes mouths* makes scornful faces
55 *greatly . . . straw* to recognize the *great argument* even in some small matter
61 *fantasy* fanciful image; *trick* something negligible
63 *try the cause* fight to a conclusion the issue in contention

IV.5 Elsinore
2 *distract* insane

QUEEN: What would she have?
GENTLEMAN: She speaks much of her father, says she hears
There's tricks i' th' world, and hems, and beats her heart, 5
Spurns enviously at straws, speaks things in doubt 6
That carry but half sense. Her speech is nothing,
Yet the unshapèd use of it doth move 8
The hearers to collection; they aim at it, 9
And botch the words up fit to their own thoughts, 10
Which, as her winks and nods and gestures yield them,
Indeed would make one think there might be thought,
Though nothing sure, yet much unhappily.
HORATIO: 'Twere good she were spoken with, for she may strew
Dangerous conjectures in ill-breeding minds.
QUEEN: Let her come in. [*Exit Gentleman.*]
[*Aside*]
To my sick soul (as sin's true nature is)
Each toy seems prologue to some great amiss. 18
So full of artless jealousy is guilt 19
It spills itself in fearing to be spilt. 20
Enter Ophelia [distracted].
OPHELIA: Where is the beauteous majesty of Denmark?
QUEEN: How now, Ophelia?
OPHELIA:
She sings.
How should I your truelove know
From another one?
By his cockle hat and staff 25
And his sandal shoon. 26
QUEEN: Alas, sweet lady, what imports this song?
OPHELIA: Say you? Nay, pray you mark.
Song.
He is dead and gone, lady,
He is dead and gone; 30
At his head a grass-green turf,
At his heels a stone.

O, ho!
QUEEN: Nay, but Ophelia—

---

5 *tricks* deceits
6 *Spurns enviously* kicks spitefully, takes offense, *straws* trifles
8 *unshapèd use* disordered manner
9 *collection* attempts at making her *speech* coherent; *aim* guess
10 *botch* patch
18 *toy* trifle; *amiss* misdeed, evil deed
19 *artless* unskillfully managed; *jealousy* suspicion
20 *spills* destroys
25 *cockle hat* hat bearing a cockleshell, worn by a pilgrim who had been to the shrine of Saint James of Compostela in northwestern Spain
26 *shoon* shoes

OPHELIA: Pray you mark.

[*Sings.*]

White his shroud as the mountain snow—

Enter King.

QUEEN: Alas, look here, my lord.

OPHELIA: *Song.*

Larded all with sweet flowers;
Which bewept to the ground did not go
With truelove showers.

KING: How do you, pretty lady?

OPHELIA: Well, good dild you! They say the owl was a baker's daughter. Lord, we know what we are, but know not what we may be. God be at your table!

KING: Conceit upon her father.

OPHELIA: Pray let's have no words of this, but when they ask you what it means, say you this:

Song.

Tomorrow is Saint Valentine's day.
All in the morning betime,
And I a maid at your window,
To be your Valentine.
Then up he rose and donned his clo'es
And dupped the chamber door,
Let in the maid, that out a maid
Never departed more.

KING: Pretty Ophelia!

OPHELIA: Indeed without an oath, I'll make an end on't:

[*Sings.*]

By Gis and by Saint Charity,
Alack, and fie for shame!
Young men will do't if they come to't.
By Cock, they are to blame.
Quoth she, "Before you tumbled me,
You promised me to wed."

He answers:

"So would I 'a' done, by yonder sun,
And thou hadst not come to my bed."

KING: How long hath she been thus?

---

38 *Larded* bedecked

42 *good dild* (a colloquial form of "God yield," or repay); *the owl* (according to a folktale, a baker's daughter was transformed into an owl because she wasn't generous when Christ asked for bread)

45 *Conceit upon* fantasies about

49 *betime* early

53 *dupped* opened

58 *Gis* Jesus; *Saint Charity* (not a recognized saint, but a common saying)

61 *Cock* (1) God (a common verbal corruption), (2) penis (?)

OPHELIA: I hope all will be well. We must be patient, but I cannot choose but weep to think they would lay him i' th' cold ground. My brother shall know of it; and so I thank you for your good counsel. Come, 70
my coach! Good night, ladies, good night. Sweet ladies, good night, good night.

[*Exit*.]

KING: Follow her close; give her good watch, I pray you.

[*Exit Horatio*.]

O, this is the poison of deep grief; it springs
All from her father's death and now behold,
O Gertrude, Gertrude,
When sorrows come, they come not single spies, 77
But in battalions; first, her father slain;
Next, your son gone, and he most violent author
Of his own just remove; the people muddied, 80
Thick and unwholesome in their thoughts and whispers
For good Polonius' death, and we have done but greenly 82
In hugger-mugger to inter him; poor Ophelia 83
Divided from herself and her fair judgment,
Without the which we are pictures or mere beasts; 85
Last, and as much containing as all these,
Her brother is in secret come from France,
Feeds on this wonder, keeps himself in clouds, 88
And wants not buzzers to infect his ear 89
With pestilent speeches of his father's death, 90
Wherein necessity, of matter beggared, 91
Will nothing stick our person to arraign 92
In ear and ear. O my dear Gertrude, this,
Like to a murd'ring piece, in many places 94
Gives me superfluous death. 95
A noise within.
Attend!
Where is my Switzers? Let them guard the door. 96
What is the matter?
Enter a Messenger.

---

77 *spies* scouts (the entire idea is proverbial; cf. IV.7.161–62)
80 *muddied* stirred up and confused
82 *greenly* foolishly
83 *hugger-mugger* secrecy
85 *pictures* soulless images, vacant forms; *mere* solely
88 *clouds* obscurity
89 *wants* lacks; *buzzers* rumor bearers
91 *of matter beggared* unprovided with facts
92 *Will nothing stick* doesn't hesitate; *arraign* accuse
94 *murd'ring piece* cannon loaded with shot meant to scatter
95 *superfluous* (since one *death* would suffice)
96 *Switzers* Swiss mercenaries

MESSENGER: Save yourself, my lord.
The ocean, overpeering of his list, 98
Eats not the flats with more impetuous haste
Than young Laertes, in a riotous head, 100
O'erbears your officers. The rabble call him lord,
And, as the world were now but to begin,
Antiquity forgot, custom not known,
The ratifiers and props of every word, 104
They cry, "Choose we! Laertes shall be king!"
Caps, hands, and tongues applaud it to the clouds,
"Laertes shall be king! Laertes king!"
A noise within.
QUEEN: How cheerfully on the false trail they cry! 108
O, this is counter, you false Danish dogs! 109
KING: The doors are broke. 110
Enter Laertes with others.
LAERTES: Where is this king?—Sirs, stand you all without.
ALL: No, let's come in.
LAERTES: I pray you give me leave.
ALL: We will, we will.
LAERTES: I thank you. Keep the door. [*Exeunt his Followers.*]
O thou vile king,
Give me my father.
QUEEN: Calmly, good Laertes.
LAERTES: That drop of blood that's calm proclaims me bastard,
Cries cuckold to my father, brands the harlot
Even here between the chaste unsmirchèd brow
Of my true mother.
KING: What is the cause, Laertes,
That thy rebellion looks so giantlike? 120
Let him go, Gertrude. Do not fear our person. 121
There's such divinity doth hedge a king 122
That treason can but peep to what it would, 123
Acts little of his will. Tell me, Laertes,
Why thou art thus incensed.—Let him go, Gertrude.—
Speak, man.
LAERTES: Where is my father?

---

98 *overpeering of* rising above; *list* boundary
100 *head* armed force
104 *word* motto, slogan
108 *cry* bellow (i.e., like a pack of hounds)
109 *counter* hunting the scent backward
120 *giantlike* (an allusion to the war the giants made on Olympus: see Ovid; *Metamorphoses* I, and mentions of Pelion and Ossa here at V.1.242 and 273)
121 *fear* fear for
122 *divinity . . . king* (an allusion to the contemporary theory that God appointed and protected earthly monarchs)
123 *peep to* i.e., through the barrier

KING: Dead.
QUEEN: But not by him.
KING: Let him demand his fill.
LAERTES: How came he dead? I'll not be juggled with.
To hell allegiance, vows to the blackest devil,
Conscience and grace to the profoundest pit!
I dare damnation. To this point I stand,
That both the worlds I give to negligence,
Let come what comes, only I'll be revenged
Most throughly for my father.
KING: Who shall stay you?
LAERTES: My will, not all the world's.
And for my means, I'll husband them so well
They shall go far with little.
KING: Good Laertes,
If you desire to know the certainty
Of your dear father, is't writ in your revenge
That sweepstake you will draw both friend and foe,
Winner and loser?
LAERTES: None but his enemies.
KING: Will you know them then?
LAERTES: To his good friends thus wide I'll ope my arms
And like the kind life-rend'ring pelican
Repast them with my blood.
KING: Why, now you speak
Like a good child and a true gentleman.
That I am guiltless of your father's death,
And am most sensibly in grief for it,
It shall as level to your judgment 'pear
As day does to your eye.
A noise within [: "Let her come in"].
LAERTES: How now? What noise is that?
Enter Ophelia.
O heat, dry up my brains; tears seven times salt
Burn out the sense and virtue of mine eye!
By heaven, thy madness shall be paid with weight
Till our scale turn the beam. O rose of May,
Dear maid, kind sister, sweet Ophelia!
O heavens, is't possible a young maid's wits
Should be as mortal as an old man's life?

---

133 *both the worlds* this world and the next; *give to negligence* disregard
135 *throughly* thoroughly
141 *sweepstake* taking all stakes on the gambling table
145 *life-rend'ring* life-yielding (fable held that the mother pelican took blood from her breast to feed her young)
149 *sensibly* feelingly
150 *level* plain
156 *beam* bar of a balance

OPHELIA: *Song.*

They bore him barefaced on the bier
And in his grave rained many a tear—
Fare you well, my dove!

LAERTES: Hadst thou thy wits, and didst persuade revenge,
It could not move thus.

OPHELIA: You must sing "A-down a-down, and you call him a-down-a." O, how the wheel becomes it! It is the false steward, that stole his master's daughter.

LAERTES: This nothing's more than matter.

OPHELIA: There's rosemary, that's for remembrance. Pray you, love, remember. And there is pansies, that's for thoughts.

LAERTES: A document in madness, thoughts and remembrance fitted.

OPHELIA: There's fennel for you, and columbines. There's rue for you, and here's some for me. We may call it herb of grace o' Sundays. You must wear your rue with a difference. There's a daisy. I would give you some violets, but they withered all when my father died. They say a made a good end.

[*Sings.*]

For bonny sweet Robin is all my joy.

LAERTES: Thought and afflictions, passion, hell itself,
She turns to favor and to prettiness.

OPHELIA:

Song.

And will a not come again?
And will a not come again?
No, no, he is dead;
Go to thy deathbed;
He never will come again.
His beard was as white as snow,
Flaxen was his poll.
He is gone, he is gone,
And we cast away moan.
God 'a' mercy on his soul.

And of all Christian souls, God buy you. [*Exit.*]

---

166 *wheel* refrain
168 *more than matter* more meaningful than sane speech
169–72 *rosemary . . . violets* (to whom Ophelia distributes which flowers and herbs is uncertain; perhaps: rosemary and pansies to Laertes, fennel and columbines to Gertrude, rue to Claudius, with daisy kept for herself)
170 *pansies . . . for thoughts* (*pansies* derives from French *pensees*—i.e., *thoughts*)
171 *document* lesson
172 *fennel* (symbol of flattery or deceit); *columbines* (symbol of infidelity); *rue* (symbol of regret)
174 *daisy* (symbol of dissembling [?])
175 *violets* (symbol of faithfulness: see V.1.228–29)
179 *favor* charm
186 *poll* head
190 *of* on

LAERTES: Do you see this, O God?
KING: Laertes, I must commune with your grief,
Or you deny me right. Go but apart,
Make choice of whom your wisest friends you will,
And they shall hear and judge 'twixt you and me.
If by direct or by collateral hand
They find us touched, we will our kingdom give,
Our crown, our life, and all that we call ours,
To you in satisfaction; but if not,
Be you content to lend your patience to us,
And we shall jointly labor with your soul
To give it due content.
LAERTES: Let this be so.
His means of death, his obscure funeral—
No trophy, sword, nor hatchment o'er his bones,
No noble rite nor formal ostentation—
Cry to be heard, as 'twere from heaven to earth,
That I must call't in question.
KING: So you shall;
And where th' offense is, let the great ax fall.
I pray you go with me.

Exeunt.

★

IV.6

Enter Horatio and others.

HORATIO: What are they that would speak with me?
GENTLEMAN: Seafaring men, sir. They say they have letters for you.
HORATIO: Let them come in. [*Exit Attendant.*]
I do not know from what part of the world
I should be greeted, if not from Lord Hamlet.
Enter Sailors.
SAILOR: God bless you, sir.
HORATIO: Let him bless thee too.
SAILOR: A shall, sir, and't please him. There's a letter for you, sir—it came from th' ambassador that was bound for England—if your name be Horatio, as I am let to know it is.

---

196 *collateral* indirect
197 *touched* i.e., with the crime
204 *trophy* memorial; *hatchment* coat of arms (hung up as a memorial)
205 *ostentation* ceremony
207 *That* so that

IV.6 Elsinore
8 *A* he

HORATIO: [*Reads the letter.*] "Horatio, when thou shalt have overlooked 11
this, give these fellows some means to the king. They have letters for 12
him. Ere we were two days old at sea, a pirate of very warlike 13
appointment gave us chase. Finding ourselves too slow of sail, we put 14
on a compelled valor, and in the grapple I boarded them. On the
instant they got clear of our ship; so I alone became their prisoner.
They have dealt with me like thieves of mercy, but they knew what 17
they did: I am to do a turn for them. Let the king have the letters I 18
have sent, and repair thou to me with as much speed as thou wouldest
fly death. I have words to speak in thine ear will make thee dumb; yet 20
are they much too light for the bore of the matter. These good fellows 21
will bring thee where I am. Rosencrantz and Guildenstern hold their
course for England. Of them I have much to tell thee. Farewell.
He that thou knowest thine, Hamlet."

Come, I will give you way for these your letters,
And do't the speedier that you may direct me
To him from whom you brought them. *Exeunt.*

★

IV.7

Enter King and Laertes.

KING: Now must your conscience my acquittance seal,
And you must put me in your heart for friend,
Sith you have heard, and with a knowing ear,
That he which hath your noble father slain
Pursued my life.
LAERTES: It well appears. But tell me
Why you proceeded not against these feats 6
So criminal and so capital in nature, 7
As by your safety, wisdom, all things else,
You mainly were stirred up. 9
KING: O, for two special reasons,
Which may to you perhaps seem much unsinewed, 10

---

11 *overlooked* scanned
12 *means* i.e., of access
13 *pirate* i.e., pirate ship
14 *appointment* equipment
17 *thieves of mercy* merciful thieves
18 *turn* i.e., an act responding to the sailors' (good) act
20 *dumb* silent, dumbstruck
21 *bore* caliber (as of a gun)

IV.7 Elsinore
6 *feats* acts
7 *capital* punishable by death
9 *mainly* powerfully

But yet to me th' are strong. The queen his mother
Lives almost by his looks, and for myself—
My virtue or my plague, be it either which—
She is so conjunctive to my life and soul
That, as the star moves not but in his sphere,
I could not but by her. The other motive
Why to a public count I might not go
Is the great love the general gender bear him,
Who, dipping all his faults in their affection,
Work like the spring that turneth wood to stone,
Convert his gyves to graces; so that my arrows,
Too slightly timbered for so loud a wind,
Would have reverted to my bow again,
But not where I had aimed them.

LAERTES: And so have I a noble father lost,
A sister driven into desp'rate terms,
Whose worth, if praises may go back again,
Stood challenger on mount of all the age
For her perfections. But my revenge will come.

KING: Break not your sleeps for that. You must not think
That we are made of stuff so flat and dull
That we can let our beard be shook with danger,
And think it pastime. You shortly shall hear more.
I loved your father, and we love ourself,
And that, I hope, will teach you to imagine—

Enter a Messenger with letters.

MESSENGER: These to your majesty, this to the queen.

KING: From Hamlet? Who brought them?

MESSENGER: Sailors, my lord, they say; I saw them not.
They were given me by Claudio; he received them
Of him that brought them.

KING: Laertes, you shall hear them.—
Leave us.

[*Exit Messenger.*]

[*Reads.*] "High and mighty, you shall know I am set naked on your kingdom. Tomorrow shall I beg leave to see your kingly eyes; when I shall (first asking your pardon thereunto) recount the occasion of my sudden return."

---

14 *conjunctive* closely united
15 *his* its
17 *count* trial, accounting
18 *general gender* ordinary people
21 *gyves* chains
26 *terms* circumstances
27 *back again* i.e., to her former (sane) self
28 *on mount* on a height
42 *naked* i.e., without a princely entourage (cf. *rest*, l. 47)

What should this mean? Are all the rest come back?
Or is it some abuse, and no such thing?
LAERTES: Know you the hand?
KING: 'Tis Hamlet's character. "Naked"!
And in a postscript here, he says "alone."
Can you devise me?
LAERTES: I am lost in it, my lord. But let him come.
It warms the very sickness in my heart
That I shall live and tell him to his teeth,
"Thus didest thou."
KING: If it be so, Laertes—
As how should it be so? how otherwise?—
Will you be ruled by me?
LAERTES: Ay, my lord,
So you will not o'errule me to a peace.
KING: To thine own peace. If he be now returned,
As checking at his voyage, and that he means
No more to undertake it, I will work him
To an exploit now ripe in my device,
Under the which he shall not choose but fall;
And for his death no wind of blame shall breathe,
But even his mother shall uncharge the practice
And call it accident.
LAERTES: My lord, I will be ruled;
The rather if you could devise it so
That I might be the organ.
KING: It falls right.
You have been talked of since your travel much,
And that in Hamlet's hearing, for a quality
Wherein they say you shine. Your sum of parts
Did not together pluck such envy from him
As did that one, and that, in my regard,
Of the unworthiest siege.
LAERTES: What part is that, my lord?
KING: A very ribbon in the cap of youth,
Yet needful too, for youth no less becomes
The light and careless livery that it wears
Than settled age his sables and his weeds

---

47 *abuse* deception
48 *hand* handwriting; *character* handwriting
50 *devise* explain to
59 *checking* shying
64 *uncharge the practice* acquit the stratagem of being a plot
67 *organ* instrument
73 *siege* status, rank
74 *ribbon* decoration
76 *livery* distinctive attire
77 *sables* richly furred robes; *weeds* garments

Importing health and graveness. Two months since
Here was a gentleman of Normandy.
I have seen myself and served against the French,
And they can well on horseback, but this gallant
Had witchcraft in't. He grew unto his seat,
And to such wondrous doing brought his horse
As had he been incorpsed and deminatured
With the brave beast. So far he topped my thought
That I, in forgery of shapes and tricks,
Come short of what he did.

LAERTES: A Norman was't?
KING: A Norman.
LAERTES: Upon my life, Lamord.
KING: The very same.
LAERTES: I know him well. He is the brooch indeed
And gem of all the nation.
KING: He made confession of you,
And gave you such a masterly report
For art and exercise in your defense
And for your rapier most especial,
That he cried out 'twould be a sight indeed
If one could match you. The scrimers of their nation
He swore had neither motion, guard, nor eye,
If you opposed them. Sir, this report of his
Did Hamlet so envenom with his envy
That he could nothing do but wish and beg
Your sudden coming o'er to play with you.
Now, out of this—
LAERTES: What out of this, my lord?
KING: Laertes, was your father dear to you?
Or are you like the painting of a sorrow,
A face without a heart?
LAERTES: Why ask you this?
KING: Not that I think you did not love your father,
But that I know love is begun by time,

78 *health* prosperity
81 *well* perform well
84 *incorpsed* made one body; *deminatured* made sharer of nature half and half (as man shares with horse in the centaur)
85 *topped* excelled; *thought* imagination of possibilities
86 *forgery* inventions; *shapes and tricks* i.e., various show-stopping exercises
89 *Lamord* i.e., "the death" (French; *la mort*)
90 *brooch* jewel, decorative ornament
92 *made confession of* testified to
97 *scrimers* fencers
105–6 *painting . . . heart* (cf. IV.5.86 and n.)
108–10 *But . . . it* (cf. III.2.178 ff.)

And that I see, in passages of proof,
Time qualifies the spark and fire of it.
There lives within the very flame of love
A kind of wick or snuff that will abate it,
And nothing is at a like goodness still,
For goodness, growing to a plurisy,
Dies in his own too-much. That we would do
We should do when we would, for this "would" changes,
And hath abatements and delays as many
As there are tongues, are hands, are accidents,
And then this "should" is like a spendthrift sigh,
That hurts by easing. But to the quick of th' ulcer—
Hamlet comes back; what would you undertake
To show yourself in deed your father's son
More than in words?

LAERTES: To cut his throat i' th' church!

KING: No place indeed should murder sanctuarize;
Revenge should have no bounds. But, good Laertes,
Will you do this? Keep close within your chamber.
Hamlet returned shall know you are come home.
We'll put on those shall praise your excellence
And set a double varnish on the fame
The Frenchman gave you, bring you in fine together
And wager o'er your heads. He, being remiss,
Most generous, and free from all contriving,
Will not peruse the foils, so that with ease,
Or with a little shuffling, you may choose
A sword unbated, and, in a pass of practice,
Requite him for your father.

LAERTES: I will do't,
And for that purpose I'll anoint my sword.
I bought an unction of a mountebank,
So mortal that, but dip a knife in it,
Where it draws blood no cataplasm so rare,

---

109 *passages of proof* experience
110 *qualifies* weakens
112 *snuff* unconsumed portion of burned *wick*
113 *still* always
114 *a plurisy* an excess
120 *hurts* i.e., shortens life by drawing blood from the heart (as was believed); *quick* sensitive flesh
124 *sanctuarize* protect from punishment
128 *put on* instigate
130 *in fine* at the end (*fine* derives from Latin *finis,* the end; cf. the jokes on *fine* at V. I.100 ff.)
131 *remiss* negligent
133 *peruse* examine
135 *unbated* not blunted; *pass of practice* thrust made effective by trickery
138 *unction* ointment; *mountebank* snake oil salesman, quack
140 *cataplasm* poultice

Collected from all simples that have virtue
Under the moon, can save the thing from death
That is but scratched withal. I'll touch my point
With this contagion, that, if I gall him slightly,
It may be death.

KING: Let's further think of this,
Weigh what convenience both of time and means
May fit us to our shape. If this should fail,
And that our drift look through our bad performance,
'Twere better not assayed. Therefore this project
Should have a back or second, that might hold
If this did blast in proof. Soft, let me see.
We'll make a solemn wager on your cunnings—
I ha't!
When in your motion you are hot and dry—
As make your bouts more violent to that end—
And that he calls for drink, I'll have prepared him
A chalice for the nonce, whereon but sipping,
If he by chance escape your venomed stuck,
Our purpose may hold there.—But stay, what noise?

Enter Queen.

QUEEN: One woe doth tread upon another's heel,
So fast they follow. Your sister's drowned, Laertes.

LAERTES: Drowned! O, where?

QUEEN: There is a willow grows askant the brook,
That shows his hoary leaves in the glassy stream.
Therewith fantastic garlands did she make
Of crowflowers, nettles, daisies, and long purples,
That liberal shepherds give a grosser name,
But our cold maids do dead-men's-fingers call them.
There on the pendent boughs her crownet weeds
Clamb'ring to hang, an envious sliver broke,
When down her weedy trophies and herself
Fell in the weeping brook. Her clothes spread wide,
And mermaidlike awhile they bore her up,

---

141 *simples* herbs
143 *withal* with it
144 *gall* scratch
147 *shape* plan
148 *drift* scheme; *look* be seen
151 *blast in proof* blow up during trial (like a faulty cannon?)
152 *cunnings* respective skills (i.e., how you do and how he does)
157 *nonce* occasion
158 *stuck* thrust
163 *askant* alongside
164 *his* its; *hoary* gray
167 *liberal* free-spoken, licentious
169 *crownet* coronet (a small crown)

Which time she chanted snatches of old lauds,
As one incapable of her own distress,
Or like a creature native and indued
Unto that element. But long it could not be
Till that her garments, heavy with their drink,
Pulled the poor wretch from her melodious lay
To muddy death.

LAERTES: Alas, then she is drowned?

QUEEN: Drowned, drowned.

LAERTES: Too much of water hast thou, poor Ophelia,
And therefore I forbid my tears; but yet
It is our trick; nature her custom holds,
Let shame say what it will. When these are gone,
The woman will be out. Adieu, my lord.
I have a speech o' fire, that fain would blaze
But that this folly drowns it. *Exit.*

KING: Let's follow, Gertrude.
How much I had to do to calm his rage!
Now fear I this will give it start again;
Therefore let's follow. *Exeunt.*

★

V. 1

Enter two Clowns [, one a gravedigger].

CLOWN: Is she to be buried in Christian burial when she willfully seeks her own salvation?

OTHER: I tell thee she is. Therefore make her grave straight. The crowner hath sat on her, and finds it Christian burial.

CLOWN: How can that be, unless she drowned herself in her own defense?

OTHER: Why, 'tis found so.

CLOWN: It must be *se offendendo*; it cannot be else. For here lies the point: if I drown myself wittingly, it argues an act, and an act hath three branches—it is to act, to do, to perform. Argal, she drowned herself wittingly.

---

174 *lauds* hymns
175 *incapable of* insensible to
176 *indued* endowed
184 *trick* (human) way (i.e., to shed tears when sorrowful)

V.1 A churchyard s.d. *Clowns* humble rural folk (the gravedigger probably here carries a spade and pickax; see l. 88)
1 *Christian burial* consecrated ground with the prescribed service of the church (a burial denied to suicides)
3 *straight* straightaway, at once; *crowner* coroner
7 *se offendendo* (a misspeaking of Latin *se defendendo* in "self-defense")
9 *Argal* (a comic [?] mispronunciation of Latin *ergo*, "therefore")

OTHER: Nay, but hear you, Goodman Delver.

CLOWN: Give me leave. Here lies the water—good. Here stands the man—good. If the man go to this water and drown himself, it is, will he nill he, he goes, mark you that. But if the water come to him and drown him, he drowns not himself. Argal, he that is not guilty of his own death shortens not his own life.

OTHER: But is this law?

CLOWN: Ay marry, is't—crowner's quest law.

OTHER: Will you ha' the truth on't? If this had not been a gentlewoman, she should have been buried out o'Christian burial.

CLOWN: Why, there thou sayst. And the more pity that great folk should have countenance in this world to drown or hang themselves more than their even-Christian. Come, my spade. There is no ancient gentlemen but gard'ners, ditchers, and gravemakers. They hold up Adam's profession.

OTHER: Was he a gentleman?

CLOWN: A was the first that ever bore arms. I'll put another question to thee. If thou answerest me not to the purpose, confess thyself—

OTHER: Go to.

CLOWN: What is he that builds stronger than either the mason, the shipwright, or the carpenter?

OTHER: The gallowsmaker, for that frame outlives a thousand tenants.

CLOWN: I like thy wit well, in good faith. The gallows does well. But how does it well? It does well to those that do ill. Now thou dost ill to say the gallows is built stronger than the church. Argal, the gallows may do well to thee. To't again, come.

OTHER: Who builds stronger than a mason, a shipwright, or a carpenter?

CLOWN: Ay, tell me that, and unyoke.

OTHER: Marry, now I can tell.

CLOWN: To't.

OTHER: Mass, I cannot tell.

CLOWN: Cudgel thy brains no more about it, for your dull ass will not mend his pace with beating. And when you are asked this question next, say "a gravemaker." The houses he makes lasts till doomsday. Go, get thee in, and fetch me a stoup of liquor.

[*Exit Other Clown.*]

Enter Hamlet and Horatio [as Clown digs and sings].

---

11 *Delver* Digger (spoken as if the gravedigger's occupation was also his family name)
13–14 *will he nill he* willy-nilly
18 *quest* inquest
21 *thou sayst* you're right
22 *countenance* privilege
23 *even-Christian* fellow Christians
27 *A* he
38 *unyoke* i.e., unharness your powers of thought after a good day's work
41 *Mass by* the mass
45 *stoup* tankard

Song.

In youth when I did love, did love,
Methought it was very sweet
To contract—O—the time for—a—my behove,
O, methought there—a—was nothing—a—meet.

HAMLET: Has this fellow no feeling of his business? A sings in gravemaking.

HORATIO: Custom hath made it in him a property of easiness.

HAMLET: 'Tis e'en so. The hand of little employment hath the daintier sense.

CLOWN: *Song.*

But age with his stealing steps
Hath clawed me in his clutch,
And hath shipped me into the land,
As if I had never been such.

[*Throws up a skull.*]

HAMLET: That skull had a tongue in it, and could sing once. How the knave jowls it to the ground, as if 'twere Cain's jawbone, that did the first murder! This might be the pate of a politician, which this ass now o'erreaches; one that would circumvent God, might it not?

HORATIO: It might, my lord.

HAMLET: Or of a courtier, which could say "Good morrow, sweet lord! How dost thou, sweet lord?" This might be my Lord Such-a-one, that praised my Lord Such-a-one's horse when a meant to beg it, might it not?

HORATIO: Ay, my lord.

HAMLET: Why, e'en so, and now my Lady Worm's, chopless, and knocked about the mazard with a sexton's spade. Here's fine revolution, an we had the trick to see't. Did these bones cost no more the breeding but to play at loggets with them? Mine ache to think on't.

CLOWN: *Song.*

A pickax and a spade, a spade,
For and a shrouding sheet;
O, a pit of clay for to be made
For such a guest is meet.

[*Throws up another skull.*]

---

48 *behove* behoof, advantage
50 *A* he
51 *property of easiness* matter of indifference
52–53 *daintier sense* more delicate feeling (because the *hand* is less callused)
59 *jowls* hurls; *Cain's jawbone* (according to Genesis 4, Cain killed his brother Abel—traditionally, but not biblically, using the jawbone of an ass)
60 *politician* crafty schemer
61 *o'erreaches* gets the better of (with a play on the literal meaning)
65 *a* he
68 *chopless* lacking the lower chop, or jaw
69 *mazard* head (a jocular, slangy word)
71 *loggets* small pieces of wood thrown in a game
73 *For and* and moreover

HAMLET: There's another. Why may not that be the skull of a lawyer? Where be his quiddities now, his quillities, his cases, his tenures, and his tricks? Why does he suffer this mad knave now to knock him about the sconce with a dirty shovel, and will not tell him of his action of battery? Hum! This fellow might be in's time a great buyer of land, with his statutes, his recognizances, his fines, his double vouchers, his recoveries. [Is this the fine of his fines, and the recovery of his recoveries,] to have his fine pate full of fine dirt? Will his vouchers vouch him no more of his purchases, and double ones too, than the length and breadth of a pair of indentures? The very conveyances of his lands will scarcely lie in this box, and must th' inheritor himself have no more, ha?

HORATIO: Not a jot more, my lord.

HAMLET: Is not parchment made of sheepskins?

HORATIO: Ay, my lord, and of calfskins too.

HAMLET: They are sheep and calves which seek out assurance in that. I will speak to this fellow. Whose grave's this, sirrah?

CLOWN: Mine, sir.

[*Sings.*]

O, a pit of clay for to be made—

HAMLET: I think it be thine indeed, for thou liest in't.

CLOWN: You lie out on't, sir, and therefore 'tis not yours.
For my part, I do not lie in't, yet it is mine.

HAMLET: Thou dost lie in't, to be in't and say it is thine.
'Tis for the dead, not for the quick; therefore thou liest.

CLOWN: 'Tis a quick lie, sir; 'twill away again from me to you.

HAMLET: What man dost thou dig it for?

CLOWN: For no man, sir.

HAMLET: What woman then?

CLOWN: For none neither.

HAMLET: Who is to be buried in't?

CLOWN: One that was a woman, sir; but, rest her soul, she's dead.

HAMLET: How absolute the knave is! We must speak by the card, or equivocation will undo us. By the Lord, Horatio, this three years I have took note of it, the age is grown so picked that the toe of the

---

77 *quiddities* subtleties (from medieval scholastic terminology, "quidditas," meaning the distinctive nature of anything); *quillities* nice distinctions (variant of *quiddities*); *tenures* holdings of property
79 *sconce* head (another slang term)
81 *statutes, recognizances* (two forms of legal acknowledgments of debt); *fines, recoveries* (legal ways of converting from a limited to a more absolute form of property ownership); *vouchers* persons called on ("vouched") to warrant a legal title
82 *fine* conclusion, end (the word introduces wordplay punning on four meanings of *fine*)
84–85 *pair of indentures* deed or legal agreement in duplicate
85 *conveyances* deeds
98 *quick* living
106 *How absolute* how strict, what a stickler for accuracy; *by the card* accurately (*card* = mariner's chart?), to the point
107 *equivocation* ambiguity
108 *picked* refined, spruce

peasant comes so near the heel of the courtier he galls his kibe.—How long hast thou been gravemaker?

CLOWN: Of all the days i' th' year, I came to't that day that our last king Hamlet overcame Fortinbras.

HAMLET: How long is that since?

CLOWN: Cannot you tell that? Every fool can tell that. It was that very day that young Hamlet was born—he that is mad, and sent into England.

HAMLET: Ay, marry, why was he sent into England?

CLOWN: Why, because a was mad. A shall recover his wits there; or, if a do not, 'tis no great matter there.

HAMLET: Why?

CLOWN: 'Twill not be seen in him there. There the men are as mad as he.

HAMLET: How came he mad?

CLOWN: Very strangely, they say.

HAMLET: How strangely?

CLOWN: Faith, e'en with losing his wits.

HAMLET: Upon what ground?

CLOWN: Why, here in Denmark. I have been sexton here, man and boy, thirty years.

HAMLET: How long will a man lie i' th' earth ere he rot?

CLOWN: Faith, if a be not rotten before a die (as we have many pocky corpses nowadays that will scarce hold the laying in), a will last you some eight year or nine year. A tanner will last you nine year.

HAMLET: Why he more than another?

CLOWN: Why, sir, his hide is so tanned with his trade that a will keep out water a great while, and your water is a sore decayer of your whoreson dead body. Here's a skull now hath lien you i' th' earth three and twenty years.

HAMLET: Whose was it?

CLOWN: A whoreson mad fellow's it was. Whose do you think it was?

HAMLET: Nay, I know not.

CLOWN: A pestilence on him for a mad rogue! A poured a flagon of Rhenish on my head once. This same skull, sir, was Sir Yorick's skull, the king's jester.

HAMLET: This? [*Takes the skull.*]

CLOWN: E'en that.

HAMLET: Alas, poor Yorick! I knew him, Horatio, a fellow of infinite jest, of most excellent fancy. He hath bore me on his back a thousand times. And now how abhorred in my imagination it is! My gorge

---

109 *galls* chafes; *kibe* chilblain (the analogy means the peasant affects a courtier's garb and hence diminishes the latter's status)

129 *pocky* rotten by pox (syphilis)

130 *laying in* i.e., in the ground

134 *whoreson* (coarse, here jocular, term of familiarity, perhaps of contempt)

141 *Rhenish* Rhine wine; *Sir* (the title is ironic, affectionate, and a common Shakespearean quip; cf. "Lady Worm," l. 83)

rises at it. Here hung those lips that I have kissed I know not how oft. Where be your gibes now? Your gambols, your songs, your flashes of merriment that were wont to set the table on a roar? Not one now to mock your own grinning? Quite chopfallen? Now get you to my lady's table, and tell her, let her paint an inch thick, to this favor she must come. Make her laugh at that. Prithee, Horatio, tell me one thing.

HORATIO: What's that, my lord?

HAMLET: Dost thou think Alexander looked o' this fashion i' th' earth?

HORATIO: E'en so.

HAMLET: And smelt so? Pah!

[*Puts down the skull.*]

HORATIO: E'en so, my lord.

HAMLET: To what base uses we may return, Horatio! Why may not imagination trace the noble dust of Alexander till a find it stopping a bunghole?

HORATIO: 'Twere to consider too curiously, to consider so.

HAMLET: No, faith, not a jot, but to follow him thither with modesty enough, and likelihood to lead it. Alexander died, Alexander was buried, Alexander returneth to dust; the dust is earth; of earth we make loam; and why of that loam whereto he was converted might they not stop a beer barrel?

Imperious Caesar, dead and turned to clay,
Might stop a hole to keep the wind away.
O, that that earth which kept the world in awe
Should patch a wall t' expel the winter's flaw!
But soft, but soft awhile! Here comes the king—

Enter King, Queen, Laertes, and the Corpse [with Lords attendant and a Doctor of Divinity as Priest].

The queen, the courtiers. Who is this they follow?
And with such maimed rites? This doth betoken
The corpse they follow did with desp'rate hand
Fordo it own life. 'Twas of some estate.
Couch we awhile, and mark.

LAERTES: What ceremony else?

---

151 *chopfallen* lacking the lower chop, or jaw (also "down in the mouth," "dejected")
152 *table* (1) piece of furniture, (2) painted portrait; *favor* countenance, aspect
162 *a bunghole* an opening in a barrel (e.g., of wine or beer)
163 *curiously* (1) minutely, (2) ingeniously
164 *modesty* moderation
166 *loam* clay or cement (called "lute" in archaic English) used to seal an opening (in a barrel, l. 194, or a *wall*, l. 206)
169 *Imperious* imperial
172 *flaw* gust of wind
177 *Fordo* destroy; *it* its; *estate* rank
178 *Couch* hide (Hamlet and Horatio are not seen or heard by the other characters until l. 244)

HAMLET: That is Laertes,
A very noble youth. Mark.
LAERTES: What ceremony else?
DOCTOR: Her obsequies have been as far enlarged
As we have warranty. Her death was doubtful,
And, but that great command o'ersways the order,
She should in ground unsanctified have lodged
Till the last trumpet. For charitable prayers,
Flints and pebbles should be thrown on her.
Yet here she is allowed her virgin crants,
Her maiden strewments, and the bringing home
Of bell and burial.
LAERTES: Must there no more be done?
DOCTOR: No more be done.
We should profane the service of the dead
To sing a requiem and such rest to her
As to peace-parted souls.
LAERTES: Lay her i' th' earth,
And from her fair and unpolluted flesh
May violets spring! I tell thee, churlish priest,
A minist'ring angel shall my sister be
When thou liest howling.
HAMLET: What, the fair Ophelia?
QUEEN: Sweets to the sweet! Farewell.
[*Scatters flowers.*]
I hoped thou shouldst have been my Hamlet's wife.
I thought thy bridebed to have decked, sweet maid,
And not have strewed thy grave.
LAERTES: O, treble woe
Fall ten times double on that cursèd head
Whose wicked deed thy most ingenious sense
Deprived thee of! Hold off the earth awhile,
Till I have caught her once more in mine arms,
[*Leaps in the grave.*]
Now pile your dust upon the quick and dead
Till of this flat a mountain you have made
T' o'ertop old Pelion or the skyish head
Of blue Olympus.

---

188 *crants* garlands, chaplets
189 *strewments* strewings of the grave with flowers; *bringing home* laying to rest
198 *howling* i.e., in hell (see Matthew 13:42)
204 *most ingenious* of quickest apprehension
209 *Pelion* (a mountain in Thessaly, as are *Olympus*, l. 244, and *Ossa*. l. 273; when the Titans fought the gods [cf. IV.5.121 n.], the Titans attempted to heap Ossa and Olympus on Pelion, or Pelion and Ossa on Olympus, in order to scale heaven)

HAMLET: What is he whose grief
Bears such an emphasis? whose phrase of sorrow
Conjures the wand'ring stars, and makes them stand
Like wonder-wounded hearers? This is I,
Hamlet the Dane.
LAERTES: The devil take thy soul!
[*Grapples with him.*]
HAMLET: Thou pray'st not well.
I prithee take thy fingers from my throat,
For, though I am not splenitive and rash,
Yet have I in me something dangerous,
Which let thy wisdom fear. Hold off thy hand.
KING: Pluck them asunder.
QUEEN: Hamlet, Hamlet!
ALL: Gentlemen!
HORATIO: Good my lord, be quiet.
HAMLET: Why, I will fight with him upon this theme
Until my eyelids will no longer wag.
QUEEN: O my son, what theme?
HAMLET: I loved Ophelia. Forty thousand brothers
Could not with all their quantity of love
Make up my sum. What wilt thou do for her?
KING: O, he is mad, Laertes.
QUEEN: For love of God, forbear him.
HAMLET: 'Swounds, show me what thou't do.
Woo't weep? woo't fight? woo't fast? woo't tear thyself?
Woo't drink up eisel? eat a crocodile?
I'll do't. Dost come here to whine?
To outface me with leaping in her grave?
Be buried quick with her, and so will I.
And if thou prate of mountains, let them throw
Millions of acres on us, till our ground,
Singeing his pate against the burning zone,

---

211 *an emphasis* violent, exaggerated language
212 *Conjures* charms, puts a spell upon; *wand'ring stars* planets
214 *Hamlet . . . Dane* One of the earliest versions of the play, the first Quarto of 1603, directs Hamlet to join Laertes in the grave following this line, and near-contemporary comment supports a struggle there—perhaps an open trapdoor—but many different stagings have been tried, and precisely what happened in early performances is unknown
217 *splenitive* hot-tempered (the spleen was considered the seat of anger)
226 *quantity* (used here as a contemptuous term: "a small amount")
229 *forbear him* leave him alone
231 *Woo't* wilt (thou)
232 *eisel* vinegar
238 *burning zone* i.e., where the sun is

Make Ossa like a wart! Nay, an thou'lt mouth,
I'll rant as well as thou. 240
QUEEN: This is mere madness;
And thus a while the fit will work on him.
Anon, as patient as the female dove
When that her golden couplets are disclosed, 243
His silence will sit drooping.
HAMLET: Hear you, sir.
What is the reason that you use me thus?
I loved you ever. But it is no matter.
Let Hercules himself do what he may, 247
The cat will mew, and dog will have his day. *Exit.* 248
KING: I pray thee, good Horatio, wait upon him. *Exit Horatio.*
[*To Laertes*]
Strengthen your patience in our last night's speech. 250
We'll put the matter to the present push.— 251
Good Gertrude, set some watch over your son.—
This grave shall have a living monument.
An hour of quiet shortly shall we see;
Till then in patience our proceeding be. *Exeunt.*

*

V.2

Enter Hamlet and Horatio.

HAMLET: So much for this, sir; now shall you see the other.
You do remember all the circumstance?
HORATIO: Remember it, my lord!
HAMLET: Sir, in my heart there was a kind of fighting
That would not let me sleep. Methought I lay
Worse than the mutines in the bilboes. Rashly, 6
And praised be rashness for it—let us know,
Our indiscretion sometime serves us well
When our deep plots do pall, and that should learn us 9

---

240 *mere* absolute
243 *couplets* pair of fledgling birds; *disclosed* hatched
247 *Hercules* (1) a legendary and mighty demigod, (2) literarily famous as a boastful ranter (Hamlet casts Laertes as Hercules)
248 *dog . . . day* (proverbially, even the least creature will have a turn at success and happiness: Hamlet views himself as *cat* and *dog*)
250 *in* in the thought of, by calling to mind
251 *the present push* immediate action

V.2 Elsinore
6 *mutines* mutineers; *bilboes* fetters, chains
9 *pall* fail

There's a divinity that shapes our ends,
Rough-hew them how we will—
HORATIO: That is most certain.
HAMLET: Up from my cabin,
My sea gown scarfed about me, in the dark
Groped I to find out them, had my desire,
Fingered their packet, and in fine withdrew
To mine own room again, making so bold,
My fears forgetting manners, to unseal
Their grand commission; where I found, Horatio—
Ah, royal knavery!—an exact command,
Larded with many several sorts of reasons,
Importing Denmark's health, and England's too,
With, ho! such bugs and goblins in my life,
That on the supervise, no leisure bated,
No, not to stay the grinding of the ax,
My head should be struck off.
HORATIO: Is't possible?
HAMLET: Here's the commission; read it at more leisure.
But wilt thou hear now how I did proceed?
HORATIO: I beseech you.
HAMLET: Being thus benetted round with villainies,
Or I could make a prologue to my brains,
They had begun the play. I sat me down,
Devised a new commission, wrote it fair.
I once did hold it, as our statists do,
A baseness to write fair, and labored much
How to forget that learning, but, sir, now
It did me yeoman's service. Wilt thou know
Th' effect of what I wrote?
HORATIO: Ay, good my lord.
HAMLET: An earnest conjuration from the king,
As England was his faithful tributary,

10 *ends* (1) purposes, (2) outcomes
11 *Rough-hew* shape roughly in trial form
15 *Fingered* filched; *in fine* finally
20 *Larded* garnished (a metaphor from cooking)
21 *Importing* relating to
22 *bugs* bugbears, bogeymen; *in my life* i.e., in my (Hamlet's) being allowed to live
23 *supervise* perusal; *no leisure bated* no time allowed
30 *Or* ere, before
32 *fair* with professional clarity (like a scrivener, not like a gentleman; see l. 34)
33 *statists* statesmen, politicians
36 *yeoman's service* brave service such as yeomen foot soldiers gave as archers
37 *effect* purport
39 *tributary* one who pays tribute

As love between them like the palm might flourish, 40
As peace should still her wheaten garland wear 41
And stand a comma 'tween their amities, 42
And many suchlike as's of great charge, 43
That on the view and knowing of these contents,
Without debatement further, more or less,
He should those bearers put to sudden death,
Not shriving time allowed. 47

HORATIO: How was this sealed?

HAMLET: Why, even in that was heaven ordinant. 48
I had my father's signet in my purse,
Which was the model of that Danish seal, 50
Folded the writ up in the form of th' other, 51
Subscribed it, gave't th' impression, placed it safely, 52
The changeling never known. Now, the next day
Was our sea fight, and what to this was sequent 54
Thou knowest already.

HORATIO: So Guildenstern and Rosencrantz go to't.

HAMLET: They are not near my conscience; their defeat
Does by their own insinuation grow. 58
'Tis dangerous when the baser nature comes
Between the pass and fell incensèd points 60
Of mighty opposites.

HORATIO: Why, what a king is this!

HAMLET: Does it not, think thee, stand me now upon— 62
He that hath killed my king and whored my mother,
Popped in between th' election and my hopes, 64
Thrown out his angle for my proper life, 65
And with such coz'nage—is't not perfect conscience? 66

Enter [Osric,] a courtier.

OSRIC: Your lordship is right welcome back to Denmark.

---

40 *palm . . . flourish* (see Psalm 92:12, "The righteous shall flourish like the palm tree")
41 *wheaten garland* (traditional symbol of peace)
42 *comma* i.e., something small
43 *charge* burden (with a double meaning to fit wordplay that makes *as's* into "asses")
47 *shriving time* time for confession and absolution
48 *ordinant* ordaining
50 *model* likeness
51 *writ* writing
52 *impression* i.e., of the signet (a seal)
54 *sequent* subsequent, following
58 *insinuation* slipping in
60 *pass* sword thrust; *fell* fierce
62 *stand me now upon* an I now obliged (i.e., to do something about these facts)
64 *election* i.e., to the kingship (the Danish kingship was elective, not inherited, as the English and Scottish crowns were in Shakespeare's day)
65 *angle* fishhook; *proper* own
66 *coz'nage* cozenage, trickery

HAMLET: I humbly thank you, sir. [*Aside to Horatio*] Dost know this waterfly?

HORATIO: [*Aside to Hamlet*] No, my good lord.

HAMLET: [*Aside to Horatio*] Thy state is the more gracious, for 'tis a vice to know him. He hath much, land, and fertile. Let a beast be lord of beasts, and his crib shall stand at the king's mess. 'Tis a chough, but, as I say, spacious in the possession of dirt.

OSRIC: Sweet lord, if your lordship were at leisure, I should impart a thing to you from his majesty.

HAMLET: I will receive it, sit, with all diligence of spirit. Your bonnet to his right use. 'Tis for the head.

OSRIC: I thank your lordship, it is very hot.

HAMLET: No, believe me, 'tis very cold; the wind is northerly.

OSRIC: It is indifferent cold, my lord, indeed.

HAMLET: But yet methinks it is very sultry and hot for my complexion.

OSRIC: Exceedingly, my lord; it is very sultry, as 'twere—I cannot tell how. My lord, his majesty bade me signify to you that a has laid a great wager on your head. Sir, this is the matter—

HAMLET: I beseech you remember.

OSRIC: Nay, good my lord; for my ease, in good faith. Sir, here is newly come to court Laertes—believe me, an absolute gentleman, full of most excellent differences, of very soft society and great showing. Indeed, to speak feelingly of him, he is the card or calendar of gentry; for you shall find in him the continent of what part a gentleman would see.

HAMLET: Sir, his definement suffers no perdition in you, though, I know, to divide him inventorially would dozy th' arithmetic of memory, and yet but yaw neither in respect of his quick sail. But, in the verity of extolment, I take him to be a soul of great article, and his infusion of such dearth and rareness as, to make true diction of him, his semblable

---

69 *waterfly* dragonfly (?)—some gaudy insect
73 *mess* table; *chough* jackdaw (a screeching bird), chatterer
74 *as I say* I'd guess; *spacious in . . . dirt* (he) owns a lot of land
81 *indifferent* somewhat
82 *complexion* temperament
84 *a* he
86 *remember* i.e., to put on your hat (see l. 79)
87 *for my ease* i.e., I keep my hat off just for comfort (a conventional polite phrase)
88 *an absolute* a complete, flawless
89 *differences* differentiating qualities; *soft society* refined manners; *great showing* noble appearance
90 *feelingly* appropriately; *card* map; *calendar* guide
91 *gentry* gentlemanliness; *continent* containment (but with wordplay on *card*)
93 *definement* definition; *perdition* loss
94 *dozy* dizzy
95 *yaw* veer like a ship that steers wild; *neither* for all that; *in respect of* in comparison with
96 *article* scope, importance; *infusion* essence
97 *dearth* scarcity; *semblable* likeness

is his mirror, and who else would trace him, his umbrage, nothing more.

OSRIC: Your lordship speaks most infallibly of him.

HAMLET: The concernancy, sir? Why do we wrap the gentleman in our more rawer breath?

OSRIC: Sir?

HORATIO: Is't not possible to understand in another tongue? You will to't, sir, really.

HAMLET: What imports the nomination of this gentleman?

OSRIC: Of Laertes?

HORATIO: [*Aside to Hamlet*] His purse is empty already. All's golden words are spent.

HAMLET: Of him, sir.

OSRIC: I know you are not ignorant—

HAMLET: I would you did, sir; yet, in faith, if you did, it would not much approve me. Well, sir?

OSRIC: You are not ignorant of what excellence Laertes is—

HAMLET: I dare not confess that, lest I should compare with him in excellence; but to know a man well were to know himself.

OSRIC: I mean, sir, for his weapon; but in the imputation laid on him by them, in his meed he's unfellowed.

HAMLET: What's his weapon?

OSRIC: Rapier and dagger.

HAMLET: That's two of his weapons—but well.

OSRIC: The king, sir, hath wagered with him six Barbary horses, against the which he has impawned, as I take it, six French rapiers and poniards, with their assigns, as girdle, hanger, and so. Three of the carriages, in faith, are very dear to fancy, very responsive to the hilts, most delicate carriages, and of very liberal conceit.

HAMLET: What call you the carriages?

HORATIO: [*Aside to Hamlet*] I knew you must be edified by the margent ere you had done.

OSRIC: The carriage, sir, are the hangers.

HAMLET: The phrase would be more germane to the matter if we could carry a cannon by our sides. I would it might be hangers till then.

---

98 *trace* follow (from hunting terminology); *umbrage* shadow
101 *concernancy* relevance
102 *rawer breath* cruder speech
105 *to't* i.e., get to an understanding
106 *nomination* mention
113 *approve* commend
115 *compare* compete
118 *meed* reward
123 *impawned* staked
124 *assigns* appurtenances; *hanger* straps by which the sword hangs from the belt
125 *dear to fancy* finely designed; *responsive* corresponding closely
126 *liberal conceit* tasteful design, refined conception
128 *margent* margin (i.e., explanatory notes printed in the margin of a page)

But on! Six Barbary horses against six French swords, their assigns, and three liberal-conceited carriages—that's the French bet against the Danish. Why is this all impawned, as you call it?

OSRIC: The king, sir, hath laid, sir, that in a dozen passes between yourself and him he shall not exceed you three hits; he hath laid on twelve for nine, and it would come to immediate trial if your lordship would vouchsafe the answer.

HAMLET: How if I answer no?

OSRIC: I mean, my lord, the opposition of your person in trial.

HAMLET: Sir, I will walk here in the hall. If it please his majesty, it is the breathing time of day with me. Let the foils be brought, the gentleman willing, and the king hold his purpose, I will win for him and I can; if not, I will gain nothing but my shame and the odd hits.

OSRIC: Shall I deliver you so?

HAMLET: To this effect, sir, after what flourish your nature will.

OSRIC: I commend my duty to your lordship.

HAMLET: Yours. [*Exit Osric.*] He does well to commend it himself; there are no tongues else for's turn.

HORATIO: This lapwing runs away with the shell on his head.

HAMLET: A did comply with his dug before a sucked it. Thus has he, and many more of the same breed that I know the drossy age dotes on, only got the tune of the time and, out of an habit of encounter, a kind of yeasty collection, which carries them through and through the most [fanned] and [winnowed] opinions; and do but blow them to their trial, the bubbles are out.

Enter a Lord.

LORD: My lord, his majesty commended him to you by young Osric, who brings back to him that you attend him in the hall. He sends to know if your pleasure hold to play with Laertes, or that you will take longer time.

HAMLET: I am constant to my purposes; they follow the king's pleasure. If his fitness speaks, mine is ready; now or whensoever, provided I be so able as now.

LORD: The king and queen and all are coming down.

HAMLET: In happy time.

LORD: The queen desires you to use some gentle entertainment to Laertes before you fall to play.

HAMLET: She well instructs me.

[*Exit Lord.*]

HORATIO: You will lose, my lord.

---

143 *breathing time* exercise hour
144 *and* if
151 *lapwing* (a bird reputed to be so precocious as to run as soon as hatched)
152 *comply* observe formalities of courtesy; *dug* nipple
153 *drossy* frivolous
156 *fanned and winnowed* select and refined
166 *In happy time* I am happy (a polite response)
167 *entertainment* courtesy

HAMLET: I do not think so. Since he went into France I have been in continual practice. I shall win at the odds. Thou wouldst not think how ill all's here about my heart, but it is no matter.

HORATIO: Nay, good my lord—

HAMLET: It is but foolery, but it is such a kind of gaingiving as would perhaps trouble a woman.

HORATIO: If your mind dislike anything, obey it. I will forestall their repair hither and say you are not fit.

HAMLET: Not a whit, we defy augury. There is special providence in the fall of a sparrow. If it be now, 'tis not to come; if it be not to come, it will be now; if it be not now, yet it will come. The readiness is all. Since no man of aught he leaves knows, what is't to leave betimes? Let be.

A table prepared. [Enter] Trumpets, Drums, and Officers with cushions; King, Queen, [Osric,] and all the State, [with] foils, daggers, and Laertes.

KING: Come, Hamlet, come, and take this hand from me.

HAMLET: Give me your pardon, sir. I have done you wrong,
But pardon't, as you are a gentleman.
This presence knows, and you must needs have heard,
How I am punished with a sore distraction.
What I have done
That might your nature, honor, and exception
Roughly awake, I here proclaim was madness.
Was't Hamlet wronged Laertes? Never Hamlet.
If Hamlet from himself be ta'en away,
And when he's not himself does wrong Laertes,
Then Hamlet does it not, Hamlet denies it.
Who does it then? His madness. If't be so,
Hamlet is of the faction that is wronged;
His madness is poor Hamlet's enemy.
[Sir, in this audience,]
Let my disclaiming from a purposed evil
Free me so far in your most generous thoughts
That I have shot my arrow o'er the house
And hurt my brother.

LAERTES: I am satisfied in nature,
Whose motive in this case should stir me most
To my revenge. But in my terms of honor

---

175 *gaingiving* misgiving
181 *all* all that matters
183 s.d. *State* court and courtiers (there must also be props for serving wine)
184 *this hand* i.e., Laertes' hand
187 *presence* assembly
190 *exception* disapproval
197 *faction* political group in opposition to another group
203 *nature* natural feeling
205 *terms of honor* position as a man of honor

I stand aloof, and will no reconcilement
Till by some elder masters of known honor
I have a voice and precedent of peace 208
To keep my name ungored. But till that time 209
I do receive your offered love like love, 210
And will not wrong it. 211
HAMLET: I embrace it freely,
And will this brother's wager frankly play.
Give us the foils.
LAERTES: Come, one for me.
HAMLET: I'll be your foil, Laertes. In mine ignorance 214
Your skill shall, like a star i' th' darkest night,
Stick fiery off indeed. 216
LAERTES: You mock me, sir.
HAMLET: No, by this hand.
KING: Give them the foils, young Osric. Cousin Hamlet.
You know the wager?
HAMLET: Very well, my lord.
Your grace has laid the odds o' th' weaker side. 220
KING: I do not fear it, I have seen you both;
But since he is bettered, we have therefore odds. 222
LAERTES: This is too heavy; let me see another.
HAMLET: This likes me well. These foils have all a length?
[*Prepare to play.*]
OSRIC: Ay, my good lord.
KING: Set me the stoups of wine upon that table.
If Hamlet give the first or second hit,
Or quit in answer of the third exchange, 228
Let all the battlements their ordnance fire.
The king shall drink to Hamlet's better breath, 230
And in the cup an union shall he throw 231
Richer than that which four successive kings
In Denmark's crown have worn. Give me the cups,
And let the kettle to the trumpet speak, 234
The trumpet to the cannoneer without,
The cannons to the heavens, the heaven to earth,
"Now the king drinks to Hamlet." Come, begin.
Trumpets the while.
And you, the judges, bear a wary eye.

---

208 *a voice* an authoritative statement
209 *ungored* uninjured
214 *foil* setting that displays a jewel advantageously (punning on *foil* as a weapon)
216 *Stick fiery off* show off in brilliant relief
222 *bettered* said to be better by public opinion (?)
228 *quit* repay by a hit
231 *an union* a pearl
234 *kettle* kettledrum

HAMLET: Come on, sir.
LAERTES: Come, my lord.
[*They play.*]
HAMLET: One.
LAERTES: No.
HAMLET: Judgment?
OSRIC: A hit, a very palpable hit.
Drum, trumpets, and shot. Flourish; a piece goes off.
LAERTES: Well, again.
KING: Stay, give me drink. Hamlet, this pearl is thine.
Here's to thy health. Give him the cup.
HAMLET: I'll play this bout first; set it by awhile.
Come. [*They play.*] Another hit. What say you?
LAERTES: I do confess't.
KING: Our son shall win.
QUEEN: He's fat, and scant of breath.
Here, Hamlet, take my napkin, rub thy brows.
The queen carouses to thy fortune, Hamlet.
HAMLET: Good madam!
KING: Gertrude, do not drink.
QUEEN: I will, my lord; I pray you pardon me.
[*Drinks.*]
KING: [*Aside*]
It is the poisoned cup; it is too late.
HAMLET: I dare not drink yet, madam—by and by.
QUEEN: Come, let me wipe thy face.
LAERTES: My lord, I'll hit him now.
KING: I do not think't.
LAERTES: [*Aside*]
And yet it is almost against my conscience.
HAMLET: Come for the third, Laertes. You do but dally.
I pray you pass with your best violence;
I am sure you make a wanton of me.
LAERTES: Say you so? Come on.
[*They play.*]
OSRIC: Nothing neither way.
LAERTES: Have at you now!
[*In scuffling they change rapiers.*]
KING: Part them. They are incensed.
HAMLET: Nay, come—again!
[*The Queen falls.*]
OSRIC: Look to the queen there, ho!

---

244 s.d. *piece* cannon
251 *fat* (1) not physically fit (?), (2) sweaty (?)
252 *napkin* handkerchief
253 *carouses* drinks a toast
262 *pass* thrust (with a sword)
263 *wanton* spoiled child

HORATIO: They bleed on both sides. How is it, my lord?
OSRIC: How is't, Laertes?
LAERTES: Why, as a woodcock to mine own springe, Osric.
  I am justly killed with mine own treachery.
HAMLET: How does the queen?
KING: She swoons to see them bleed.
QUEEN: No, no, the drink, the drink! O my dear Hamlet!
  The drink, the drink! I am poisoned.
    [*Dies.*]
HAMLET: O villainy! Ho! let the door be locked.
  Treachery! Seek it out. [*Exit Osric.*]
LAERTES: It is here, Hamlet. Hamlet, thou art slain;
  No med'cine in the world can do thee good.
  In thee there is not half an hour's life.
  The treacherous instrument is in thy hand,
  Unbated and envenomed. The foul practice
  Hath turned itself on me. Lo, here I lie,
  Never to rise again. Thy mother's poisoned.
  I can no more. The king, the king's to blame.
HAMLET: The point envenomed too?
  Then venom, to thy work.
    [*Wounds the King.*]
ALL: Treason! treason!
KING: O, yet defend me, friends. I am but hurt.
HAMLET: Here, thou incestuous, murd'rous, damned Dane,
  Drink off this potion. Is thy union here?
  Follow my mother.
    [*King dies.*]
LAERTES: He is justly served.
  It is a poison tempered by himself.
  Exchange forgiveness with me, noble Hamlet.
  Mine and my father's death come not upon thee,
  Nor thine on me!
    [*Dies.*]
HAMLET: Heaven make thee free of it! I follow thee.
  I am dead, Horatio. Wretched queen, adieu!
  You that look pale and tremble at this chance,
  That are but mutes or audience to this act,
  Had I but time—as this fell sergeant, Death,
  Is strict in his arrest—O, I could tell you—
  But let it be. Horatio, I am dead;

---

270 *woodcock* (a bird reputed to be stupid and easily trapped); *springe* trap
281 *Unbated* unblunted; *practice* trick
290 *union* (1) pearl (cf. l. 250 n.), (2) marriage to Gertrude
292 *tempered* mixed
299 *mutes* actors without speaking parts
300 *sergeant* court officer with power of arrest
301 *strict* (1) just, (2) inescapable

Thou livest; report me and my cause aright
To the unsatisfied.

HORATIO: Never believe it.
I am more an antique Roman than a Dane.
Here's yet some liquor left.

HAMLET: As th' art a man,
Give me the cup. Let go. By heaven, I'll ha't!
O God, Horatio, what a wounded name,
Things standing thus unknown, shall I leave behind me!
If thou didst ever hold me in thy heart,
Absent thee from felicity awhile,
And in this harsh world draw thy breath in pain,
To tell my story.
A march afar off.
What warlike noise is this?
Enter Osric.

OSRIC: Young Fortinbras, with conquest come from Poland,
To the ambassadors of England gives
This warlike volley.

HAMLET: O, I die, Horatio!
The potent poison quite o'ercrows my spirit.
I cannot live to hear the news from England,
But I do prophesy th' election lights
On Fortinbras. He has my dying voice.
So tell him, with th' occurrents, more and less,
Which have solicited—the rest is silence.
[*Dies.*]

HORATIO: Now cracks a noble heart. Good night, sweet prince,
And flights of angels sing thee to thy rest!
[*March within.*]
Why does the drum come hither?
Enter Fortinbras, with the Ambassadors [and Drum, Colors, and Attendants].

FORTINBRAS: Where is this sight?

HORATIO: What is it you would see?
If aught of woe or wonder, cease your search.

FORTINBRAS: This quarry cries on havoc. O proud Death,
What feast is toward in thine eternal cell

---

305 *antique Roman* i.e., someone who prefers suicide to a dishonored life
317 *o'ercrows* triumphs over (as a crow does over its meal? as a cock does in a cockfight?)
319 *election* i.e., for the throne of Denmark (cf. l. 64)
320 *voice* vote
321 *occurrents* occurrences
322 *solicited* incited, provoked
327 *wonder* disaster (an archaic meaning in Shakespeare's day?)
328 *quarry* pile of dead (literally, killed deer gathered after the hunt); *cries on* proclaims loudly; *havoc* indiscriminate killing and destruction
329 *toward* forthcoming, about to occur (i.e., *Death* will feast on *so many princes*)

That thou so many princes at a shot
So bloodily hast struck?
AMBASSADOR: The sight is dismal;
And our affairs from England come too late.
The ears are senseless that should give us hearing
To tell him his commandment is fulfilled,
That Rosencrantz and Guildenstern are dead.
Where should we have our thanks?
HORATIO: Not from his mouth,
Had it th' ability of life to thank you.
He never gave commandment for their death.
But since, so jump upon this bloody question,
You from the Polack wars, and you from England,
Are here arrived, give order that these bodies
High on a stage be placèd to the view,
And let me speak to th' yet unknowing world
How these things came about. So shall you hear
Of carnal, bloody, and unnatural acts,
Of accidental judgments, casual slaughters,
Of deaths put on by cunning and forced cause,
And, in this upshot, purposes mistook
Fall'n on th' inventors' heads. All this can I
Truly deliver.
FORTINBRAS: Let us haste to hear it,
And call the noblest to the audience.
For me, with sorrow I embrace my fortune.
I have some rights of memory in this kingdom,
Which now to claim my vantage doth invite me.
HORATIO: Of that I shall have also cause to speak,
And from his mouth whose voice will draw on more.
But let this same be presently performed,
Even while men's minds are wild, lest more mischance
On plots and errors happen.
FORTINBRAS: Let four captains
Bear Hamlet like a soldier to the stage,
For he was likely, had he been put on,
To have proved most royal; and for his passage

339 *jump* precisely
342 *stage* platform (the meaning for performance or the early modern audience is uncertain)
346 *accidental* i.e., inscrutable to human eyes; *judgments* retributions; *casual* not humanly planned (the word reinforces *accidental*)
347 *put on* instigated; *forced* contrived
353 *of memory* unforgotten
354 *vantage* advantageous opportunity
356 *more* i.e., more voices, or votes, for the kingship
357 *presently* immediately
359 *On* on the basis of
361 *put on* set to perform in office
362 *passage* death

The soldiers' music and the rite of war
Speak loudly for him.
Take up the bodies. Such a sight as this
Becomes the field, but here shows much amiss.
Go, bid the soldiers shoot.

Exeunt [marching; after the which a peal of ordnance is shot off].

SUSAN GLASPELL (1876–1948) was born in Davenport, Iowa, the descendent of pioneers. She graduated from Drake University in 1899, attended the University of Chicago, and worked as a reporter for the *Des Moines Daily News* and *Des Moines Capital*. In Davenport, Glaspell joined the Monist Society, a socialist group, where she met George Cram Cook, a married man and classics scholar turned gentleman farmer, who modeled his life on that of Henry David Thoreau. After his divorce, Glaspell married Cook; they moved to Provincetown, Massachusetts, and founded the Provincetown Players, for whom Glaspell wrote her plays. Other notable members were poet Edna St. Vincent Millay and playwright Eugene O'Neill. In 1931, Glaspell won the Pulitzer Prize for drama for *Alison's House*. Between 1936 and 1938, Glaspell directed the Midwest Play Bureau of the Federal Theater Project, a Works Progress Administration program that was intended to promote American theater. Although she had traveled in Europe and lived in Greece, Glaspell returned to Provincetown for her final years.

Trifles (1916), which was later reworked as the short story "A Jury of Her Peers," is a one-act play, like *'Night Mother*, that observes the **dramatic unities**. Technically a murder mystery, *Trifles* is also a study in women's relationships and of how violence destroys relations between men and women. As in *Hamlet*, the literal facts about the murder become less important than evolving relationships among the characters. Setting is crucially important to *Trifles*, which might be considered a **metadramatic** play: the objects that help solve the mystery—a dirty towel, unwashed pans, badly sewn quilt, dead bird, and damaged birdcage—take on meaning only when the characters interpret them. Like stage **props**, these clues are signs rather than mere objects. Glaspell's dialogue, which like that of Hemingway relies on **irony** created through understatement, packs a great deal of meaning into a small number of words.

Related Works: Atwood, "Gertrude Talks Back"; "Bonny Barbara Allan" (Child Ballad #84); Hemingway, "A Clean, Well-Lighted Place"; Norman, *'Night, Mother*; Poe, "The Purloined Letter" and "The Tell-Tale Heart"; Shakespeare, *Hamlet*.

Trifles

A PLAY IN ONE ACT

SCENE: *The kitchen in the now abandoned farmhouse of* JOHN WRIGHT, *a gloomy kitchen, and left without having been put in order—unwashed pans under the sink, a loaf of bread outside the bread-box, a dish-towel on the table—other signs of incompleted work. At the rear the outer door opens and the* SHERIFF *comes in followed by the* COUNTY ATTORNEY *and* HALE. *The* SHERIFF *and* HALE *are men in middle life, the* COUNTY ATTORNEY *is a young man; all are much bundled up and go at once to the stove. They are followed by the two women—the* SHERIFF'S *wife first; she is a slight wiry woman, a thin nervous face.* MRS. HALE *is larger and would ordinarily be called more comfortable looking, but she is disturbed now and looks fearfully about as she enters. The women have come in slowly, and stand close together near the door.*

COUNTY ATTORNEY: [*Rubbing his hands.*] This feels good. Come up to the fire, ladies.

MRS. PETERS: [*After taking a step forward.*] I'm not—cold.

SHERIFF: [*Unbuttoning his overcoat and stepping away from the stove as if to mark the beginning of official business.*] Now, Mr. Hale, before we move things about, you explain to Mr. Henderson just what you saw when you came here yesterday morning.

COUNTY ATTORNEY: By the way, has anything been moved? Are things just as you left them yesterday?

SHERIFF: [*Looking about.*] It's just the same. When it dropped below zero last night I thought I'd better send Frank out this morning to make a fire for us—no use getting pneumonia with a big case on, but I told him not to touch anything except the stove—and you know Frank.

COUNTY ATTORNEY: Somebody should have been left here yesterday.

SHERIFF: Oh—yesterday. When I had to send Frank to Morris Center for that man who went crazy—I want you to know I had my hands full yesterday. I knew you could get back from Omaha by today and as long as I went over everything here myself—

COUNTY ATTORNEY: Well, Mr. Hale, tell just what happened when you came here yesterday morning.

HALE: Harry and I had started to town with a load of potatoes. We came along the road from my place and as I got here I said, "I'm going to see if I can't get John Wright to go in with me on a party telephone." I spoke to Wright about it once before and he put me off, saying folks talked too much anyway, and all he asked was peace and quiet—I guess you know about how much he talked himself; but I thought maybe if I went to the house and talked about it before his wife, though I said to Harry that I didn't know as what his wife wanted made much difference to John—

COUNTY ATTORNEY: Let's talk about that later, Mr. Hale. I do want to talk about that, but tell now just what happened when you got to the house.

HALE: I didn't hear or see anything; I knocked at the door, and still it was all quiet inside. I knew they must be up, it was past eight o'clock. So I knocked again, and I thought I heard somebody say, "Come in." I wasn't sure, I'm not sure yet, but I opened the door—this door [*indicating the door by which the two women are still standing*] and there in that rocker—[*pointing to it*] sat Mrs. Wright.

[*They all look at the rocker.*

COUNTY ATTORNEY: What—was she doing?

HALE: She was rockin' back and forth. She had her apron in her hand and was kind of—pleating it.

COUNTY ATTORNEY: And how did she—look?

HALE: Well, she looked queer.

COUNTY ATTORNEY: How do you mean—queer?

HALE: Well, as if she didn't know what she was going to do next. And kind of done up.

COUNTY ATTORNEY: How did she seem to feel about your coming?

HALE: Why, I don't think she minded—one way or other. She didn't pay much attention. I said, "How do, Mrs. Wright, it's cold, ain't it?" And she said, "Is it?"—and went on kind of pleating at her apron. Well, I was surprised; she didn't ask me to come up to the stove, or to set down, but just sat there, not even looking at me, so I said. "I want to see John." And then she—laughed. I guess you would call it a laugh. I thought of Harry and the team outside, so I said a little sharp: "Can't I see John?" "No," she says, kind o' dull like. "Ain't he home?" says I. "Yes," says she, "he's home." "Then why can't I see him?" I asked her, out of patience. "'Cause he's dead," says she. "*Dead?*" says I. She just nodded her head, not getting a bit excited, but rockin' back and forth. "Why—where is he?" says I, not knowing what to say. She just pointed upstairs—like that [*himself pointing to the room above*]. I got up, with the idea of going up there. I walked from there to here—then I says, "Why, what did he die of?" "He died of a rope round his neck," says she, and just went on pleatin' at her apron. Well, I went out and called Harry. I thought I might—need help. We went upstairs and there he was lyin'—

COUNTY ATTORNEY: I think I'd rather have you go into that upstairs, where you can point it all out. Just go on now with the rest of the story.

HALE: Well, my first thought was to get that rope off. It looked . . . [*Stops, his face twitches*] . . . but Harry, he went up to him, and he said, "No, he's dead all right, and we'd better not touch anything." So we went back down stairs. She was still sitting that same way. "Has anybody been notified?" I asked. "No," says she, unconcerned. "Who did this, Mrs. Wright?" said Harry. He said it business-like—and she stopped pleatin' of her apron. "I don't know," she says. "You don't *know?*" says Harry. "No," says she. "Weren't you sleepin' in the bed with him?" says Harry. "Yes," says she, "but I was on the inside." "Somebody slipped a rope round his neck and strangled him and you didn't wake up?" says Harry. "I didn't wake up," she said after him. We must 'a looked as if we didn't see how that could be, for after a minute she said, "I sleep sound." Harry was going to ask her more questions but I said maybe we ought to let her tell her story first to the coroner, or the sheriff, so Harry went fast as he could to Rivers' place, where there's a telephone.

COUNTY ATTORNEY: And what did Mrs. Wright do when she knew that you had gone for the coroner?

HALE: She moved from that chair to this one over here [*Pointing to a small chair in the corner*] and just sat there with her hands held together and looking down. I got a feeling that I ought to make some conversation, so I said I had come in to see if John wanted to put in a telephone, and at that she started to laugh, and then she stopped and looked at me—scared. [*The* COUNTY ATTORNEY, *who has had his notebook out, makes a note.*] I dunno, maybe it wasn't scared. I wouldn't like to say it was. Soon Harry got back, and then Dr. Lloyd came, and you, Mr. Peters, and so I guess that's all I know that you don't.

COUNTY ATTORNEY: [*Looking around.*] I guess we'll go upstairs first—and then out to the barn and around there. [*To the* SHERIFF.] You're convinced that there was nothing important here—nothing that would point to any motive.

SHERIFF: Nothing here but kitchen things.

[*The* COUNTY ATTORNEY, *after again looking around the kitchen, opens the door of a cupboard closet. He gets up on a chair and looks on a shelf. Pulls his hand away, sticky.*

COUNTY ATTORNEY: Here's a nice mess.

[*The women draw nearer.*

MRS. PETERS: [*To the other woman.*] Oh, her fruit; it did freeze. [*To the* LAWYER.] She worried about that when it turned so cold. She said the fire'd go out and her jars would break.

SHERIFF: Well, can you beat the women! Held for murder and worryin' about her preserves.

COUNTY ATTORNEY: I guess before we're through she may have something more serious than preserves to worry about.

HALE: Well, women are used to worrying over trifles.

[*The two women move a little closer together.*

COUNTY ATTORNEY: [*With the gallantry of a young politician.*] And yet, for all their worries, what would we do without the ladies? [*The women do not unbend. He goes to the sink, takes a dipperful of water from the pail and pouring it into a basin, washes his hands. Starts to wipe them on the roller-towel, turns it for a cleaner place.*] Dirty towels! [*Kicks his foot against the pans under the sink.*] Not much of a housekeeper, would you say, ladies?

MRS. HALE: [*Stiffly.*] There's a great deal of work to be done on a farm.

COUNTY ATTORNEY: To be sure. And yet [*With a little bow to her*] I know there are some Dickson county farmhouses which do not have such roller towels.

[*He gives it a pull to expose its full length again.*

MRS. HALE: Those towels get dirty awful quick. Men's hands aren't always as clean as they might be.

COUNTY ATTORNEY: Ah, loyal to your sex, I see. But you and Mrs. Wright were neighbors. I suppose you were friends, too.

MRS. HALE: [*Shaking her head.*] I've not seen much of her of late years. I've not been in this house—it's more than a year.

COUNTY ATTORNEY: And why was that? You didn't like her?

MRS. HALE: I liked her all well enough. Farmers' wives have their hands full, Mr. Henderson. And then—

COUNTY ATTORNEY: Yes—?

MRS. HALE: [*Looking about.*] It never seemed a very cheerful place.

COUNTY ATTORNEY: No—it's not cheerful. I shouldn't say she had the home-making instinct.

MRS. HALE: Well, I don't know as Wright had, either.

COUNTY ATTORNEY: You mean that they didn't get on very well?

MRS. HALE: No, I don't mean anything. But I don't think a place'd be any cheerfuller for John Wright's being in it.

COUNTY ATTORNEY: I'd like to talk more of that a little later. I want to get the lay of things upstairs now.

[*He goes to the left, where three steps lead to a stair door.*

SHERIFF: I suppose anything Mrs. Peters does'll be all right. She was to take in some clothes for her, you know, and a few little things. We left in such a hurry yesterday.

County Attorney: Yes, but I would like to see what you take, Mrs. Peters, and keep an eye out for anything that might be of use to us.

Mrs. Peters: Yes, Mr. Henderson.

[*The women listen to the men's steps on the stairs, then look about the kitchen.*

Mrs. Hale: I'd hate to have men coming into my kitchen, snooping around and criticising.

[*She arranges the pans under sink which the* Lawyer *had shoved out of place.*

Mrs. Peters: Of course it's no more than their duty.

Mrs. Hale: Duty's all right, but I guess that deputy sheriff that came out to make the fire might have got a little of this on. [*Gives the roller towel a pull.*] Wish I'd thought of that sooner. Seems mean to talk about her for not having things slicked up when she had to come away in such a hurry.

Mrs. Peters: [*Who has gone to a small table in the left rear corner of the room, and lifted one end of a towel that covers a pan.*] She had bread set.

[*Stands still.*

Mrs. Hale: [*Eyes fixed on a loaf of bread beside the bread-box, which is on a low shelf at the other side of the room. Moves slowly toward it.*] She was going to put this in there. [*Picks up loaf, then abruptly drops it. In a manner of returning to familiar things.*] It's a shame about her fruit. I wonder if it's all gone. [*Gets up on the chair and looks.*] I think there's some here that's all right, Mrs. Peters. Yes—here; [*Holding it toward the window*] this is cherries, too. [*Looking again.*] I declare I believe that's the only one. [*Gets down, bottle in her hand. Goes to the sink and wipes it off on the outside.*] She'll feel awful bad after all her hard work in the hot weather. I remember the afternoon I put up my cherries last summer.

[*She puts the bottle on the big kitchen table, center of the room. With a sigh, is about to sit down in the rocking-chair. Before she is seated realises what chair it is; with a slow look at it, steps back. The chair which she has touched rocks back and forth.*

Mrs. Peters: Well, I must get those things from the front room closet. [*She goes to the door at the right, but after looking into the other room, steps back.*] You coming with me, Mrs. Hale? You could help me carry them.

[*They go in the other room; reappear,* Mrs. Peters *carrying a dress and skirt,* Mrs. Hale *following with a pair of shoes.*

Mrs. Peters: My, it's cold in there.

[*She puts the clothes on the big table, and hurries to the stove.*

Mrs. Hale: [*Examining the skirt.*] Wright was close. I think maybe that's why she kept so much to herself. She didn't even belong to the Ladies Aid. I suppose she felt she couldn't do her part, and then you don't enjoy things when you feel shabby. She used to wear pretty clothes and be lively, when she was Minnie Foster, one of the town girls singing in the choir. But that—oh, that was thirty years ago. This all you was to take in?

Mrs. Peters: She said she wanted an apron. Funny thing to want, for there isn't much to get you dirty in jail, goodness knows. But I suppose just to make her feel more natural. She said they was in the top drawer in this cupboard. Yes, here. And then her little shawl that always hung behind the door. [*Opens stair door and looks.*] Yes, here it is.

[*Quickly shuts door leading upstairs.*

MRS. HALE: [*Abruptly moving toward her.*] Mrs. Peters?

MRS. PETERS: Yes, Mrs. Hale?

MRS. HALE: Do you think she did it?

MRS. PETERS: [*In a frightened voice.*] Oh, I don't know,

MRS. HALE: Well, I don't think she did. Asking for an apron and her little shawl. Worrying about her fruit.

MRS. PETERS: [*Starts to speak, glances up, where footsteps are heard in the room above. In a low voice.*] Mr. Peters says it looks bad for her. Mr. Henderson is awful sarcastic in a speech and he'll make fun of her sayin' she didn't wake up.

MRS. HALE: Well, I guess John Wright didn't wake when they was slipping that rope under his neck.

MRS. PETERS: No, it's strange. It must have been done awful crafty and still. They say it was such a—funny way to kill a man, rigging it all up like that.

MRS. HALE: That's just what Mr. Hale said. There was a gun in the house. He says that's what he can't understand.

MRS. PETERS: Mr. Henderson said coming out that what was needed for the case was a motive; something to show anger, or—sudden feeling.

MRS. HALE: [*Who is standing by the table.*] Well, I don't see any signs of anger around here. [*She puts her hand on the dish towel which lies on the table, stands looking down at table, one half of which is clean, the other half messy.*] It's wiped to here. [*Makes a move as if to finish work, then turns and looks at loaf of bread outside the breadbox. Drops towel. In that voice of coming back to familiar things.*] Wonder how they are finding things upstairs. I hope she had it a little more red-up up there. You know, it seems kind of *sneaking*. Locking her up in town and then coming out here and trying to get her own house to turn against her!

MRS. PETERS: But Mrs. Hale, the law is the law.

MRS. HALE: I s'pose 'tis. [*Unbuttoning her coat.*] Better loosen up your things, Mrs. Peters. You won't feel them when you go out.

[MRS. PETERS *takes off her fur tippel, goes to hang it on hook at back of room, stands looking at the under part of the small corner table.*

MRS. PETERS: She was piecing a quilt.

[*She brings the large sewing basket and they look at the bright pieces.*

MRS. HALE: It's log cabin pattern. Pretty, isn't it? I wonder if she was goin' to quilt it or just knot it?

[*Footsteps have been heard coming down the stairs. The* SHERIFF *enters followed by* HALE *and the* COUNTY ATTORNEY.

SHERIFF: They wonder if she was going to quilt it or just knot it!

[*The men laugh, the women look abashed.*

COUNTY ATTORNEY: [*Rubbing his hands over the stove.*] Frank's fire didn't do much up there, did it? Well, let's go out to the barn and get that cleared up.

[*The men go outside.*

MRS. HALE: [*Resentfully.*] I don't know as there's anything so strange, our takin' up our time with little things while we're waiting for them to get the evidence. [*She sits down at the big table smoothing out a block with decision.*] I don't see as it's anything to laugh about.

MRS. PETERS: [*Apologetically.*] Of course they've got awful important things on their minds.

[*Pulls up a chair and joins* MRS. HALE *at the table.*

MRS. HALE: [*Examining another block.*] Mrs. Peters, look at this one. Here, this is the one she was working on, and look at the sewing! All the rest of it has been so nice and even. And look at this! It's all over the place! Why, it looks as if she didn't know what she was about!

[*After she has said this they look at each other, then start to glance back at the door. After an instant* MRS. HALE *has pulled at a knot and ripped the sewing.*

MRS. PETERS: Oh, what are you doing. Mrs. Hale?

MRS. HALE: [*Mildly.*] Just pulling out a stitch or two that's not sewed very good. [*Threading a needle.*] Bad sewing always made me fidgety.

MRS. PETERS: [*Nervously.*] I don't think we ought to touch things.

MRS. HALE: I'll just finish up this end. [*Suddenly stopping and leaning forward.*] Mrs. Peters?

MRS. PETERS: Yes, Mrs. Hale?

MRS. HALE: What do you suppose she was so nervous about?

MRS. PETERS: Oh—I don't know. I don't know as she was nervous. I sometimes sew awful queer when I'm just tired. [MRS. HALE *starts to say something, looks at* MRS. PETERS, *then goes on sewing.*] Well I must get these things wrapped up. They may be through sooner than we think. [*Putting apron and other things together.*] I wonder where I can find a piece of paper, and string.

MRS. HALE: In that cupboard, maybe.

MRS. PETERS: [*Looking in cupboard.*] Why, here's a bird-cage. [*Holds it up.*] Did she have a bird, Mrs. Hale?

MRS. HALE: Why, I don't know whether she did or not—I've not been here for so long. There was a man around last year selling canaries cheap, but I don't know as she took one; maybe she did. She used to sing real pretty herself.

MRS. PETERS: [*Glancing around.*] Seems funny to think of a bird here. But she must have had one, or why would she have a cage? I wonder what happened to it.

MRS. HALE: I s'pose maybe the cat got it.

MRS. PETERS: No, she didn't have a cat. She's got that feeling some people have about cats—being afraid of them. My cat got in her room and she was real upset and asked me to take it out.

MRS. HALE: My sister Bessie was like that. Queer, ain't it?

MRS. PETERS: [*Examining the cage.*] Why, look at this door. It's broke. One hinge is pulled apart.

MRS. HALE: [*Looking too.*] Looks as if someone must have been rough with it.

MRS. PETERS: Why, yes.

[*She brings the cage forward and puts it on the table.*

MRS. HALE: I wish if they're going to find any evidence they'd be about it. I don't like this place.

MRS. PETERS: But I'm awful glad you came with me, Mrs. Hale. It would be lonesome for me sitting here alone.

MRS. HALE: It would, wouldn't it? [*Dropping her sewing.*] But I tell you what I do wish Mrs. Peters. I wish I had come over sometimes when *she* was here. I—[*Looking around the room*]—wish I had.

MRS. PETERS: But of course you were awful busy, Mrs. Hale—your house and your children.

MRS. HALE: I could've come. I stayed away because it weren't cheerful—and that's why I ought to have come. I—I've never liked this place. Maybe because it's down in a hollow and you don't see the road. I dunno what it is, but it's a lonesome place and always was. I wish I had come over to see Minnie Foster sometimes. I can see now—

[*Shakes her head.*

MRS. PETERS: Well, you mustn't reproach yourself, Mrs. Hale. Somehow we just don't see how it is with other folks until—something comes up.

MRS. HALE: Not having children makes less work—but it makes a quiet house, and Wright out to work all day, and no company when he did come in. Did you know John Wright, Mrs. Peters?

MRS. PETERS: Not to know him; I've seen him in town. They say he was a good man.

MRS. HALE: Yes—good; he didn't drink, and kept his word as well as most, I guess, and paid his debts. But he was a hard man, Mrs. Peters. Just to pass the time of day with him—[*Shivers.*] Like a raw wind that gets to the bone. [*Pauses, her eye falling on the cage.*] I should think she would 'a wanted a bird. But what do you suppose went with it?

MRS. PETERS: I don't know, unless it got sick and died.

[*She reaches over and swings the broken door, swings it again, both women watch it.*

MRS. HALE: You weren't raised round here, were you? [MRS. PETERS *shakes her head.*] You didn't know—her?

MRS. PETERS: Not till they brought her yesterday.

MRS. HALE: She—come to think of it, she was kind of like a bird herself—real sweet and pretty, but kind of timid and—fluttery. How—she—did—change. [*Silence; then as if struck by a happy thought and relieved to get back to every day things.*] Tell you what, Mrs. Peters, why don't you take the quilt in with you? It might take up her mind.

MRS. PETERS: Why, I think that's a real nice idea. Mrs. Hale. There couldn't possibly be any objection to it, could there? Now, just what would I take? I wonder if her patches are in here—and her things.

[*They look in the sewing basket.*

MRS. HALE: Here's some red. I expect this has got sewing things in it. [*Brings out a fancy box.*] What a pretty box. Looks like something somebody would give you. Maybe her scissors are in here. [*Opens box. Suddenly puts her hand to her nose.*] Why—[MRS. PETERS *bends nearer, then turns her face away.*] There's something wrapped up in this piece of silk.

MRS. PETERS: Why, this isn't her scissors.

MRS. HALE: [*Lifting the silk.*] Oh, Mrs. Peters—its—

[MRS. PETERS *bends closer.*

MRS. PETERS: It's the bird.

MRS. HALE: [*Jumping up.*] But, Mrs. Peters—look at it! It's neck! Look at its neck! It's all—other side *to*.

MRS. PETERS: Somebody—wrung—its—neck.

[*Their eyes meet. A look of growing comprehension, of horror. Steps are heard outside.* MRS. HALE *slips box under quilt pieces, and sinks into her chair. Enter* SHERIFF *and* COUNTY ATTORNEY. MRS. PETERS *rises.*

COUNTY ATTORNEY: [*As one turning from serious things to little pleasantries.*] Well, ladies, have you decided whether she was going to quilt it or knot it?

MRS. PETERS: We think she was going to—knot it.

COUNTY ATTORNEY: Well, that's interesting, I'm sure. [*Seeing the birdcage.*] Has the bird flown?

MRS. HALE: [*Putting more quilt pieces over the box.*] We think the—cat got it.

COUNTY ATTORNEY: [*Preoccupied.*] Is there a cat?

[MRS. HALE *glances in a quick covert way at* MRS. PETERS

MRS. PETERS: Well, not *now*. They're superstitious, you know. They leave.

COUNTY ATTORNEY: [*To* SHERIFF PETERS, *continuing an interrupted conversation.*] No sign at all of anyone having come from the outside. Their own rope. Now let's go up again and go over it piece by piece. [*They start upstairs.*] It would have to have been someone who knew just the—

[MRS. PETERS *sits down. The two women sit there not looking at one another, but as if peering into something and at the same time holding back. When they talk now it is in the manner of feeling their way over strange ground, as if afraid of what they are saying, but as if they can not help saying it.*

MRS. HALE: She liked the bird. She was going to bury it in that pretty box.

MRS. PETERS: [*In a whisper.*] When I was a girl—my kitten—there was a boy took a hatchet, and before my eyes—and before I could get there—[*Covers her face an instant.*] If they hadn't held me back I would have—[*Catches herself, looks upstairs where steps are heard, falters weakly*]—hurt him.

MRS. HALE: [*With a slow look around her.*] I wonder how it would seem never to have had any children around. [*Pause.*] No, Wright wouldn't like the bird—a thing that sang. She used to sing. He killed that, too.

MRS. PETERS: [*Moving uneasily.*] We don't know who killed the bird.

MRS. HALE: I knew John Wright.

MRS. PETERS: It was an awful thing was done in this house that night, Mrs. Hale. Killing a man while he slept, slipping a rope around his neck that choked the life out of him.

MRS. HALE: His neck. Choked the life out of him.

[*Her hand goes out and rests on the bird-cage.*

MRS. PETERS: [*With rising voice.*] We don't know who killed him. We don't *know*.

MRS. HALE: [*Her own feeling not interrupted.*] If there'd been years and years of nothing, then a bird to sing to you, it would be awful—still, after the bird was still.

MRS. PETERS: [*Something within her speaking.*] I know what stillness is. When we homesteaded in Dakota, and my first baby died—after he was two years old, and me with no other then—

MRS. HALE: [*Moving.*] How soon do you suppose they'll be through, looking for the evidence?

MRS. PETERS: I know what stillness is. [*Pulling herself back.*] The law has got to punish crime, Mrs. Hale.

MRS. HALE: [*Not as if answering that.*] I wish you'd seen Minnie Foster when she wore a white dress with blue ribbons and stood up there in the choir and sang. [*A look around the room.*] Oh, I *wish* I'd come over here once in a while! That was a crime! That was a crime! Who's going to punish that?

MRS. PETERS: [*Looking upstairs.*] We mustn't—take on.

MRS. HALE: I might have known she needed help! I know how things can be—for women. I tell you, it's queer, Mrs. Peters. We live close together and we live far apart. We all go through the same things—it's all just a different kind of the same thing. [*Brushes her eyes, noticing the bottle of fruit, reaches out for it.*] If I was you I wouldn't tell her her fruit was gone. Tell her it *ain't*. Tell her it's all right. Take this in to prove it to her. She—she may never know whether it was broke or not.

MRS. PETERS: [*Takes the bottle, looks about for something to wrap it in; takes petticoat from the clothes brought from the other room, very nervously begins winding this around the bottle. In a false voice.*] My, it's a good thing the men couldn't hear us. Wouldn't they just laugh! Getting all stirred up over a little thing like a—dead canary. As if that could have anything to do with—with—wouldn't they *laugh*!

[*The men are heard coming down stairs.*

MRS. HALE: [*Under her breath.*] Maybe they would—maybe they wouldn't.

COUNTY ATTORNEY: No, Peters, it's all perfectly clear except a reason for doing it. But you know juries when it comes to women. If there was some definite thing. Something to show—something to make a story about—a thing that would connect up with this strange way of doing it—

[*The women's eyes meet for an instant. Enter* HALE *from outer door.*

HALE: Well, I've got the team around. Pretty cold out there.

COUNTY ATTORNEY: I'm going to stay here a while by myself. [*To the* SHERIFF.] You can send Frank out for me, can't you? I want to go over everything. I'm not satisfied that we can't do better.

SHERIFF: Do you want to see what Mrs. Peters is going to take in?

[*The* LAWYER *goes to the table, picks up the apron, laughs.*

COUNTY ATTORNEY: Oh, I guess they're not very dangerous things the ladies have picked out. [*Moves a few things about, disturbing the quilt pieces which cover the box. Steps back.*] No, Mrs. Peters doesn't need supervising. For that matter, a sheriff's wife is married to the law. Ever think of it that way, Mrs. Peters?

MRS. PETERS: Not—just that way.

SHERIFF: [*Chuckling.*] Married to the law. [*Moves toward the other room.*] I just want you to come in here a minute, George. We ought to take a look at these windows.

COUNTY ATTORNEY: [*Scoffingly.*] Oh, windows!

SHERIFF: We'll be right out, Mr. Hale.

[HALE *goes outside. The* SHERIFF *follows the* COUNTY ATTORNEY *into the other room. Then* MRS. HALE *rises, hands tight together, looking intensely at* MRS. PETERS, *whose eyes make a slow turn, finally meeting* MRS. HALE'S. *A moment* MRS. HALE *holds her, then her own eyes point the way to where the box is concealed. Suddenly* MRS. PETERS *throws back quilt pieces and tries to put the box in the bag she is wearing. It is too big. She opens box, starts to take bird out, cannot touch it, goes to pieces, stands there helpless. Sound of a knob turning in the other room.* MRS. HALE *snatches the box and puts it in the pocket of her big coat. Enter* COUNTY ATTORNEY *and* SHERIFF.

COUNTY ATTORNEY: [*Facetiously.*] Well, Henry, at least we found out that she was not going to quilt it. She was going to—what is it you call it, ladies?

MRS. HALE: [*Her hand against her pocket.*] We call it—knot it, Mr. Henderson.

(CURTAIN)

Original Cast

GEORGE HENDERSON, *County Attorney* . . . . ROBERT ROGERS
HENRY PETERS, *Sheriff* . . . . ROBERT CONVILLE
LEWIS HALE, *A Neighboring Farmer* . . . . GEORGE CRAM COOK
MRS. PETERS . . . . ALICE HALL
MRS. HALE . . . . SUSAN GLASPELL

OSCAR WILDE (1854–1900), was born in Dublin, Ireland, and died in Paris, France. Wilde's father was a prominent surgeon, his mother a supporter of Irish nationalist politics and of women's rights. Wilde was well educated, attending the Portora Royal School, then Trinity College, Dublin, and finally Magdalen College, Oxford. As a scholar, Wilde was interested in the classics, in particular the Hellenistic culture of ancient Greece. At Oxford, he also acquired the exaggerated mannerisms of a dandy, combined with a serious, evolving identity as an aesthete, a philosophical position that values art over life and seeks to make life as much like art as possible. In *The Importance of Being Earnest*, this philosophy is expressed most concisely by Gwendolyn when she says, "In matters of grave importance, style, not sincerity is the vital thing." At Oxford, Wilde was also known for his brilliant conversation.

After a lecture tour of the United States, Wilde lived in Paris, where he met writers such as Victor Hugo and artists such as Edgar Degas and Camille Pisarro and absorbed the aesthetic philosophy and disposition of such decadent writers as Charles Baudelaire. In 1883, he married Constance Lloyd, the sister of a man he had known at Oxford, with whom he had two sons. Wilde also became involved with Lord Alfred Douglas (nicknamed "Bosie").

In 1894, Douglas's father accused Wilde of being a "sodomite." Wilde, with financial help from Bosie himself, sued the father for libel. Although he proved a compelling and witty witness, evidence gathered by private detectives who had been hired by Douglas's father forced Wilde to drop the suit. Wilde now found himself on trial, and he was sentenced to two years at hard labor for "gross indecencies." At Reading Gaol, where he served the full two-year sentence, Wilde endured bleak living conditions, being in solitary confinement for all but one hour a day, but was allowed to read and write, and published a letter on England's dehumanizing prison conditions.

In 1897, Wilde moved to France, where he wrote about the horrors of life in prison. In 1898, "The Ballad of Reading Gaol" was published under the pseudonym of C.3.3, which had been the number of Wilde's cell block. In April 1898,

---

First Performed by the Provincetown Players at the Wharf Theatre, Provincetown, Mass., August 8, 1916.

Wilde's wife, Constance, died. Oscar Wilde lived for two more years, always on the edge of poverty, but sustained by an allowance left to him by Constance and by some money from Douglas.

The Importance of Being Earnest, a "society comedy" deeply indebted to ancient Greek comedy through its interest in mistaken identities, was by far Wilde's most successful drama. This story of two dandies who lead double lives, and of the women who become engaged to them, challenges conventional manners and moralities, although in a most elegant and polite manner. At the same time, the play's witty reversals of common moral sayings and attitudes satirize the hypocrisy of the rich and upper classes. For all its humor, *The Importance of Being Earnest* also offers serious social commentary. The title's **pun** on "earnest" as a proper name and character trait highlights the play's central **irony**, that the most charming and endearing people are also the most artificial and even deceitful. Men and women alike are dandies in this play, yet somehow deserve their happy fates because, paradoxically, they are deceptively good and—well, earnest. *The Importance of Being Earnest*'s hallmark is its brilliant dialogue, which one unsympathetic critic had called Wilde's "**epigram** factory."

Related Works: Hardy, "The Ruined Maid"; Marlowe, "The Passionate Shepherd to His Love"; Marvell, "To His Coy Mistress"; Shakespeare, *The Taming of the Shrew*.

OSCAR WILDE

The Importance of Being Earnest

The Persons of the Play

JOHN WORTHING, J.P.
ALGERNON MONCRIEFF
REV. CANON CHASUBLE, D.D.
MERRIMAN, BUTLER
LANE, MANSERVANT
LADY BRACKNELL
HON. GWENDOLEN FAIRFAX
CECILY CARDEW
MISS PRISM, GOVERNESS

THE SCENES OF THE PLAY

—ACT I, *Algernon Moncrieff's Flat in Half-Moon Street, W.* ACT II, *The Garden at the Manor House, Woolton.* ACT III, *Morning-room at the Manor House, Woolton. Time, The Present.*

FIRST ACT

SCENE—*Morning-room in* ALGERNON'S *flat in Half-Moon Street. The room is luxuriously and artistically furnished. The sound of a piano is heard in the adjoining room.*

[LANE *is arranging afternoon tea on the table, and after the music has ceased,* ALGERNON enters.]

ALGERNON: Did you hear what I was playing, Lane?

LANE: I didn't think it polite to listen, sir.

ALGERNON: I'm sorry for that, for your sake. I don't play accurately—anyone can play accurately—but I play with wonderful expression. As far as the piano is concerned, sentiment is my forte. I keep science for Life.

LANE: Yes, sir.

ALGERNON: And, speaking of the science of Life, have you got the cucumber sandwiches cut for Lady Bracknell?

LANE: Yes, sir. [*Hands them on a salver.*]

ALGERNON: [*Inspects them, takes two, and sits down on the sofa.*] Oh! . . . by the way, Lane, I see from your book that on Thursday night, when Lord Shoreman and Mr. Worthing were dining with me, eight bottles of champagne are entered as having been consumed.

LANE: Yes, sir; eight bottles and a pint.

ALGERNON: Why is it that at a bachelor's establishment the servants invariably drink the champagne? I ask merely for information.

LANE: I attribute it to the superior quality of the wine, sir. I have often observed that in married households the champagne is rarely of a first-rate brand.

ALGERNON: Good Heavens! Is marriage so demoralising as that?

LANE: I believe it *is* a very pleasant state, sir. I have had very little experience of it myself up to the present. I have only been married once. That was in consequence of a misunderstanding between myself and a young person.

ALGERNON: [*Languidly.*] I don't know that I am much interested in your family life, Lane.

LANE: No, sir; it is not a very interesting subject. I never think of it myself.

ALGERNON: Very natural, I am sure. That will do, Lane, thank you.

LANE: Thank you, sir. [LANE *goes out.*]

ALGERNON: Lane's views on marriage seem somewhat lax. Really, if the lower orders don't set us a good example, what on earth is the use of them? They seem, as a class, to have absolutely no sense of moral responsibility.

[*Enter* LANE.]

LANE: Mr. Ernest Worthing.

[*Enter* JACK.] [LANE *goes out.*]

ALGERNON: How are you, my dear Ernest? What brings you up to town?

JACK: Oh, pleasure, pleasure! What else should bring one anywhere? Eating as usual, I see, Algy!

ALGERNON: [*Stiffly.*] I believe it is customary in good society to take some slight refreshment at five o'clock. Where have you been since last Thursday?

JACK: [*Sitting down on the sofa.*] In the country.

ALGERNON: What on earth do you do there?

JACK: [*Pulling off his gloves.*] When one is in town one amuses oneself. When one is in the country one amuses other people. It is excessively boring.

ALGERNON: And who are the people you amuse?

JACK: [*Airily.*] Oh, neighbours, neighbours.

ALGERNON: Got nice neighbours in your part of Shropshire?

JACK: Perfectly horrid! Never speak to one of them.

ALGERNON: How immensely you must amuse them! [*Goes over and takes sandwich.*] By the way, Shropshire is your county, is it not?

JACK: Eh? Shropshire? Yes, of course. Hallo! Why all these cups? Why cucumber sandwiches? Why such reckless extravagance in one so young? Who is coming to tea?

ALGERNON: Oh! merely Aunt Augusta and Gwendolen.

JACK: How perfectly delightful!

ALGERNON: Yes, that is all very well; but I am afraid Aunt Augusta won't quite approve of your being here.

JACK: May I ask why?

ALGERNON: My dear fellow, the way you flirt with Gwendolen is perfectly disgraceful. It is almost as bad as the way Gwendolen flirts with you.

JACK: I am in love with Gwendolen. I have come up to town expressly to propose to her.

ALGERNON: I thought you had come up for pleasure? . . . I call that business.

JACK: How utterly unromantic you are!

ALGERNON: I really don't see anything romantic in proposing. It is very romantic to be in love. But there is nothing romantic about a definite proposal. Why, one may be accepted. One usually is, I believe. Then the excitement is all over. The very essence of romance is uncertainty. If ever I get married, I'll certainly try to forget the fact.

JACK: I have no doubt about that, dear Algy. The Divorce Court was specially invented for people whose memories are so curiously constituted.

ALGERNON: Oh! there is no use speculating on that subject. Divorces are made in Heaven——[JACK *puts out his hand to take a sandwich.* ALGERNON *at once interferes.*] Please don't touch the cucumber sandwiches. They are ordered specially for Aunt Augusta. [*Takes one and eats it.*]

JACK: Well, you have been eating them all the time.

ALGERNON: That is quite a different matter. She is my aunt. [*Takes plate from below.*] Have some bread and butter. The bread and butter is for Gwendolen. Gwendolen is devoted to bread and butter.

JACK: [*Advancing to table and helping himself.*] And very good bread and butter it is too.

ALGERNON: Well, my dear fellow, you need not eat as if you were going to eat it all. You behave as if you were married to her already. You are not married to her already, and I don't think you ever will be.

JACK: Why on earth do you say that?

ALGERNON: Well, in the first place girls never marry the men they flirt with. Girls don't think it right.

JACK: Oh, that is nonsense!

ALGERNON: It isn't. It is a great truth. It accounts for the extraordinary number of bachelors that one sees all over the place. In the second place, I don't give my consent.

JACK: Your consent!

ALGERNON: My dear fellow, Gwendolen is my first cousin. And before I allow you to marry her, you will have to clear up the whole question of Cecily. [*Rings bell.*]

JACK: Cecily! What on earth do you mean? What do you mean, Algy, by Cecily? I don't know anyone of the name of Cecily.

[*Enter* LANE.]

ALGERNON: Bring me that cigarette case Mr. Worthing left in the smoking-room the last time he dined here.

LANE: Yes, sir. [LANE *goes out.*]

JACK: Do you mean to say you have had my cigarette case all this time? I wish to goodness you had let me know. I have been writing frantic letters to Scotland Yard about it. I was very nearly offering a large reward.

ALGERNON: Well, I wish you would offer one. I happen to be more than usually hard up.

JACK: There is no good offering a large reward now that the thing is found.

[*Enter* LANE *with the cigarette case on a salver.* ALGERNON *takes it at once.* LANE *goes out.*]

ALGERNON: I think that is rather mean of you, Ernest, I must say. [*Opens case and examines it.*] However, it makes no matter, for, now that I look at the inscription inside, I find that the thing isn't yours after all.

JACK: Of course it's mine. [*Moving to him.*] You have seen me with it a hundred times, and you have no right whatsoever to read what is written inside. It is a very ungentlemanly thing to read a private cigarette case.

ALGERNON: Oh! it is absurd to have a hard-and-fast rule about what one should read and what one shouldn't. More than half of modern culture depends on what one shouldn't read.

JACK: I am quite aware of the fact, and I don't propose to discuss modern culture. It isn't the sort of thing one should talk of in private. I simply want my cigarette case back.

ALGERNON: Yes; but this isn't your cigarette case. This cigarette case is a present from someone of the name of Cecily, and you said you didn't know anyone of that name.

JACK: Well, if you want to know, Cecily happens to be my aunt.

ALGERNON: Your aunt!

JACK: Yes. Charming old lady she is, too. Lives at Tunbridge Wells. Just give it back to me, Algy.

ALGERNON: [*Retreating to back of sofa.*] But why does she call herself Cecily if she is your aunt and lives at Tunbridge Wells? [*Reading.*] "From little Cecily with her fondest love."

JACK: [*Moving to sofa and kneeling upon it.*] My dear fellow, what on earth is there in that? Some aunts are tall, some aunts are not tall. That is a matter that surely an aunt may be allowed to decide for herself. You seem to think that every aunt should be exactly like your aunt! That is absurd! For Heaven's sake give me back my cigarette case. [*Follows* ALGY *round the room.*]

ALGERNON: Yes. But why does your aunt call you her uncle? "From little Cecily, with her fondest love to her dear Uncle Jack." There is no objection, I admit, to an aunt being a small aunt, but why an aunt, no matter what her size may be, should call her own nephew her uncle, I can't quite make out. Besides, your name isn't Jack at all; it is Ernest.

JACK: It isn't Ernest; it's Jack.

ALGERNON: You have always told me it was Ernest. I have introduced you to everyone as Ernest. You answer to the name of Ernest. You look as if your name was Ernest. You are the most earnest looking person I ever saw in my life. It is perfectly absurd your saying that your name isn't Ernest. It's on your cards. Here is one of them. [*Taking it from case.*] "Mr. Ernest Worthing, B. 4. The

Albany." I'll keep this as a proof that your name is Ernest if ever you attempt to deny it to me or to Gwendolen, or to anyone else. [*Puts the card in his pocket.*]

JACK: Well, my name is Ernest in town and Jack in the country, and the cigarette case was given to me in the country.

ALGERNON: Yes, but that does not account for the fact that your small Aunt Cecily, who lives at Tunbridge Wells, calls you her dear uncle. Come, old boy, you had much better have the thing out at once.

JACK: My dear Algy, you talk exactly as if you were a dentist. It is very vulgar to talk like a dentist when one isn't a dentist. It produces a false impression.

ALGERNON: Well, that is exactly what dentists always do. Now, go on! Tell me the whole thing. I may mention that I have always suspected you of being a confirmed and secret Bunburyist; and I am quite sure of it now.

JACK: Bunburyist! What on earth do you mean by a Bunburyist?

ALGERNON: I'll reveal to you the meaning of that incomparable expression as soon as you are kind enough to inform me why you are Ernest in town and Jack in the country.

JACK: Well, produce my cigarette case first.

ALGERNON: Here it is. [*Hands cigarette case.*] Now produce your explanation, and pray make it improbable. [*Sits on sofa.*]

JACK: My dear fellow, there is nothing improbable about my explanation at all. In fact it's perfectly ordinary. Old Mr. Thomas Cardew, who adopted me when I was a little boy, made me in his will guardian to his grand-daughter, Miss Cecily Cardew. Cecily, who addresses me as her uncle from motives of respect that you could not possibly appreciate, lives at my place in the country under the charge of her admirable governess, Miss Prism.

ALGERNON: Where is that place in the country, by the way?

JACK: That is nothing to you, dear boy. You are not going to be invited. . . . I may tell you candidly that the place is not in Shropshire.

ALGERNON: I suspected that, my dear fellow! I have Bunburyed all over Shropshire on two separate occasions. Now go on. Why are you Ernest in town and Jack in the country?

JACK: My dear Algy. I don't know whether you will be able to understand my real motives. You are hardly serious enough. When one is placed in the position of guardian, one has to adopt a very high moral tone on all subjects. It's one's duty to do so. And as a high moral tone can hardly be said to conduce very much to either one's health or one's happiness, in order to get up to town I have always pretended to have a younger brother of the name of Ernest, who lives in the Albany, and gets into the most dreadful scrapes. That, my dear Algy, is the whole truth pure and simple.

ALGERNON: The truth is rarely pure and never simple. Modern life would be very tedious if it were either, and modern literature a complete impossibility!

JACK: That wouldn't be at all a bad thing.

ALGERNON: Literary criticism is not your forte, my dear fellow. Don't try it. You should leave that to people who haven't been at a University. They do it so well in the daily papers. What you really are is a Bunburyist. I was quite right in saying you were a Bunburyist. You are one of the most advanced Bunburyists I know.

JACK: What on earth do you mean?

ALGERNON: You have invented a very useful young brother called Ernest, in order that you may be able to come up to town as often as you like. I have invented an invaluable permanent invalid called Bunbury, in order that I may be able to go down into the country whenever I choose. Bunbury is perfectly invaluable. If it wasn't for Bunbury's extraordinary bad health, for instance, I wouldn't be able to dine with you at Willis's to-night, for I have been really engaged to Aunt Augusta for more than a week.

JACK: I haven't asked you to dine with me anywhere to-night.

ALGERNON: I know. You are absurdly careless about sending out invitations. It is very foolish of you. Nothing annoys people so much as not receiving invitations.

JACK: You had much better dine with your Aunt Augusta.

ALGERNON: I haven't the smallest intention of doing anything of the kind. To begin with, I dined there on Monday, and once a week is quite enough to dine with one's own relations. In the second place, whenever I do dine there I am always treated as a member of the family, and sent down with either no woman at all, or two. In the third place, I know perfectly well whom she will place me next to, to-night. She will place me next Mary Farquhar, who always flirts with her own husband across the dinner-table. That is not very pleasant. Indeed, it is not even decent . . . and that sort of thing is enormously on the increase. The amount of women in London who flirt with their own husbands is perfectly scandalous. It looks so bad. It is simply washing one's clean linen in public. Besides, now that I know you to be a confirmed Bunburyist, I naturally want to talk to you about Bunburying. I want to tell you the rules.

JACK: I'm not a Bunburyist at all. If Gwendolen accepts me, I am going to kill my brother, indeed I think I'll kill him in any case. Cecily is a little too much interested in him. It is rather a bore. So I am going to get rid of Ernest. And I strongly advise you to do the same with Mr. . . . with your invalid friend who has the absurd name.

ALGERNON: Nothing will induce me to part with Bunbury, and if you ever get married, which seems to me extremely problematic, you will be very glad to know Bunbury. A man who marries without knowing Bunbury has a very tedious time of it.

JACK: That is nonsense. If I marry a charming girl like Gwendolen, and she is the only girl I ever saw in my life that I would marry, I certainly won't want to know Bunbury.

ALGERNON: Then your wife will. You don't seem to realize, that in married life three is company and two is none.

JACK: [*Sententiously.*] That, my dear young friend, is the theory that the corrupt French Drama has been propounding for the last fifty years.

ALGERNON: Yes; and that the happy English home has proved in half the time.

JACK: For heaven's sake, don't try to be cynical. It's perfectly easy to be cynical.

ALGERNON: My dear fellow, it isn't easy to be anything now-a-days. There's such a lot of beastly competition about. [*The sound of an electric bell is heard.*] Ah! that must be Aunt Augusta. Only relatives, or creditors, ever ring in that Wagnerian manner. Now, if I get her out of the way for ten minutes, so that you can have as opportunity for proposing to Gwendolen, may I dine with you to-night at Willis's?

JACK: I suppose so, if you want to.

ALGERNON: Yes, but you must be serious about it. I hate people who are not serious about meals. It is so shallow of them.

[*Enter* LANE.]

LANE: Lady Bracknell and Miss Fairfax.

[ALGERNON *goes forward to meet them. Enter* LADY BRACKNELL *and* GWENDOLEN.]

LADY BRACKNELL: Good afternoon, dear Algernon, I hope you are behaving very well.

ALGERNON: I'm feeling very well, Aunt Augusta.

LADY BRACKNELL: That's not quite the same thing. In fact the two things rarely go together. [*Sees* JACK *and bows to him with icy coldness.*]

ALGERNON: [*To* GWENDOLEN.] Dear me, you are smart!

GWENDOLEN: I am always smart! Aren't I, Mr. Worthing?

JACK: You are quite perfect, Miss Fairfax.

GWENDOLEN: Oh! I hope I am not that. It would leave no room for developments, and I intend to develop in many directions. [GWENDOLEN *and* JACK *sit down together in the corner.*]

LADY BRACKNELL: I'm sorry if we are a little late, Algernon, but I was obliged to call on dear Lady Harbury. I hadn't been there since her poor husband's death. I never saw a woman so altered; she looks quite twenty years younger. And now I'll have a cup of tea, and one of those nice cucumber sandwiches you promised me.

ALGERNON: Certainly, Aunt Augusta. [*Goes over to tea-table.*]

LADY BRACKNELL: Won't you come and sit here, Gwendolen?

GWENDOLEN: Thanks, mamma, I'm quite comfortable where I am.

ALGERNON: [*Picking up empty plate in horror.*] Good heavens! Lane! Why are there no cucumber sandwiches? I ordered them specially.

LANE: [*Gravely.*] There were no cucumbers in the market this morning, sir. I went down twice.

ALGERNON: No cucumbers!

LANE: No, sir. Not even for ready money.

ALGERNON: That will do, Lane, thank you.

LANE: Thank you, sir.

ALGERNON: I am greatly distressed, Aunt Augusta, about there being no cucumbers, not even for ready money.

LADY BRACKNELL: It really makes no matter, Algernon. I had some crumpets with Lady Harbury, who seems to me to be living entirely for pleasure now.

ALGERNON: I hear her hair has turned quite gold from grief.

LADY BRACKNELL: It certainly has changed its colour. From what cause I, of course, cannot say. [ALGERNON *crosses and hands tea.*] Thank you. I've quite a treat for you to-night, Algernon. I am going to send you down with Mary Farquhar. She is such a nice woman, and so attentive to her husband. It's delightful to watch them.

ALGERNON: I am afraid, Aunt Augusta, I shall have to give up the pleasure of dining with you to-night after all.

LADY BRACKNELL: [*Frowning.*] I hope not, Algernon. It would put my table completely out. Your uncle would have to dine upstairs. Fortunately he is accustomed to that.

ALGERNON: It's a great bore, and, I need hardly say, a terrible disappointment to me, but the fact is I have just had a telegram to say that my poor friend Bunbury is very ill again. [*Exchanges glances with* JACK.] They seem to think I should be with him.

LADY BRACKNELL: It is very strange. This Mr. Bunbury seems to suffer from curiously bad health.

ALGERNON: Yes; poor Bunbury is a dreadful invalid.

LADY BRACKNELL: Well, I must say, Algernon, that I think it is high time that Mr. Bunbury made up his mind whether he was going to live or to die. This shilly-shallying with the question is absurd. Nor do I in any way approve of the modern sympathy with invalids. I consider it morbid. Illness of any kind is hardly a thing to be encouraged in others. Health is the primary duty of life. I am always telling that to your poor uncle, but he never seems to take much notice . . . as far as any improvement in his ailments goes. I should be obliged if you would ask Mr. Bunbury, from me, to be kind enough not to have a relapse on Saturday, for I rely on you to arrange my music for me. It is my last reception, and one wants something that will encourage conversation, particularly at the end of the season when everyone has practically said whatever they had to say, which, in most cases, was probably not much.

ALGERNON: I'll speak to Bunbury, Aunt Augusta, if he is still conscious, and I think I can promise you he'll be all right by Saturday. Of course the music is a great difficulty. You see if one plays good music, people don't listen, and if one plays bad music, people don't talk. But I'll run over the programme I've drawn out, if you will kindly come into the next room for a moment.

LADY BRACKNELL: Thank you, Algernon. It is very thoughtful of you. [*Rising, and following* ALGERNON.] I'm sure the programme will be delightful, after a few expurgations. French songs I cannot possibly allow. People always seem to think that they are improper, and either look shocked, which is vulgar, or laugh, which is worse. But German sounds a thoroughly respectable language, and indeed, I believe is so. Gwendolen, you will accompany me.

GWENDOLEN: Certainly, mamma.

[LADY BRACKNELL *and* ALGERNON *go into the music-room, Gwendolen remains behind.*]

JACK: Charming day it has been, Miss Fairfax.

GWENDOLEN: Pray don't talk to me about the weather, Mr. Worthing. Whenever people talk to me about the weather, I always feel quite certain that they mean something else. And that makes me so nervous.

JACK: I do mean something else.

GWENDOLEN: I thought so. In fact, I am never wrong.

JACK: And I would like to be allowed to take advantage of Lady Bracknell's temporary absence . . .

GWENDOLEN: I would certainly advise you to do so. Mamma has a way of coming back suddenly into a room that I have often had to speak to her about.

JACK: [*Nervously.*] Miss Fairfax, ever since I met you I have admired you more than any girl . . . I have ever met since . . . I met you.

GWENDOLEN: Yes, I am quite aware of the fact. And I often wish that in public, at any rate, you had been more demonstrative. For me you have always had an irresistible fascination. Even before I met you I was far from indifferent to you. [JACK *looks at her in amazement.*] We live, as I hope you know, Mr. Worthing, in an age of ideals. The fact is constantly mentioned in the more expensive monthly magazines, and has reached the provincial pulpits I am told; and my ideal has always been to love some one of the name of Ernest. There is something in that name that inspires absolute confidence. The moment Algernon first mentioned to me that he had a friend called Ernest, I knew I was destined to love you.

JACK: You really love me, Gwendolen?

GWENDOLEN: Passionately!

JACK: Darling! You don't know how happy you've made me.

GWENDOLEN: My own Ernest!

JACK: But you don't really mean to say that you couldn't love me if my name wasn't Ernest?

GWENDOLEN: But your name is Ernest.

JACK: Yes, I know it is. But supposing it was something else? Do you mean to say you couldn't love me then?

GWENDOLEN: [*Glibly*.] Ah! that is clearly a metaphysical speculation, and like most metaphysical speculations has very little reference at all to the actual facts of real life, as we know them.

JACK: Personally, darling, to speak quite candidly, I don't much care about the name of Ernest . . . I don't think the name suits me at all.

GWENDOLEN: It suits you perfectly. It is a divine name. It has a music of its own. It produces vibrations.

JACK: Well, really, Gwendolen, I must say that I think there are lots of other much nicer names. I think Jack, for instance a charming name.

GWENDOLEN: Jack? . . . No, there is very little music in the name Jack, if any at all, indeed. It does not thrill. It produces absolutely no vibrations. . . . I have known several Jacks, and they all, without exception, were more than usually plain. Besides, Jack is a notorious domesticity for John! And I pity any woman who is married to a man called John. She would probably never be allowed to know the entrancing pleasure of a single moment's solitude. The only really safe name is Ernest.

JACK: Gwendolen, I must get christened at once—I mean we must get married at once. There is no time to be lost.

GWENDOLEN: Married, Mr. Worthing?

JACK: [*Astounded*.] Well . . . surely. You know that I love you, and you led me to believe, Miss Fairfax, that you were not absolutely indifferent to me.

GWENDOLEN: I adore you. But you haven't proposed to me yet. Nothing has been said at all about marriage. The subject has not even been touched on.

JACK: Well . . . may I propose to you now?

GWENDOLEN: I think it would be an admirable opportunity. And to spare you any possible disappointment, Mr. Worthing, I think it only fair to tell you quite frankly beforehand that I am fully determined to accept you.

JACK: Gwendolen!

GWENDOLEN: Yes, Mr. Worthing, what have you got to say to me?

JACK: You know what I have got to say to you.

GWENDOLEN: Yes, but you don't say it.

JACK: Gwendolen, will you marry me. [*Goes on his knees*.]

GWENDOLEN: Of course I will, darling. How long you have been about it! I am afraid you have had very little experience in how to propose.

JACK: My own one, I have never loved anyone in the world but you.

GWENDOLEN: Yes, but men often propose for practice. I know my brother Gerald does. All my girl-friends tell me so. What wonderfully blue eyes you have, Ernest! They are quite, quite blue. I hope you will always look at me just like that, especially when there are other people present.

[*Enter* LADY BRACKNELL.]

LADY BRACKNELL: Mr. Worthing! Rise, sir, from this semi-recumbent posture. It is most indecorous.

GWENDOLEN: Mamma! [*He tries to rise; she restrains him.*] I must beg you to retire. This is no place for you. Besides, Mr. Worthing has not quite finished yet.

LADY BRACKNELL: Finished what, may I ask?

GWENDOLEN: I am engaged to Mr. Worthing, mamma. [*They rise together.*]

LADY BRACKNELL: Pardon me, you are not engaged to anyone. When you do become engaged to some one, I, or your father, should his health permit him, will inform you of the fact. An engagement should come on a young girl as a surprise, pleasant or unpleasant, as the case may be. It is hardly a matter that she could be allowed to arrange for herself. . . . And now I have a few questions to put to you, Mr. Worthing. While I am making these inquiries, you, Gwendolen, will wait for me below in the carriage.

GWENDOLEN: [*Reproachfully.*] Mamma!

LADY BRACKNELL: In the carriage, Gwendolen! [GWENDOLEN *goes to the door. She and* JACK *blow kisses to each other behind* LADY BRACKNELL'S *back.* LADY BRACKNELL *looks vaguely about as if she could not understand what the noise was. Finally turns round.*] Gwendolen, the carriage!

GWENDOLEN: Yes, mamma. [*Goes out, looking back at* JACK.]

LADY BRACKNELL: [*Sitting down.*] You can take a seat, Mr. Worthing.

[*Looks in her pocket for note-book and pencil.*]

JACK: Thank you, Lady Bracknell, I prefer standing.

LADY BRACKNELL: [*Pencil and note-book in hand.*] I feel bound to tell you that you are not down on my list of eligible young men, although I have the same list as the dear Duchess of Bolton has. We work together, in fact. However, I am quite ready to enter your name, should your answers be what a really affectionate mother requires. Do you smoke?

JACK: Well, yes, I must admit I smoke.

LADY BRACKNELL: I am glad to hear it. A man should always have an occupation of some kind. There are far soo many idle men in London as it is. How old are you?

JACK: Twenty-nine.

LADY BRACKNELL: A very good age to be married at. I have always been of opinion that a man who desires to get married should know either everything or nothing. Which do you know?

JACK: [*After some hesitation.*] I know nothing, Lady Bracknell.

LADY BRACKNELL: I am pleased to hear it. I do not approve of anything that tampers with natural ignorance. Ignorance is like a delicate exotic fruit; touch it and the bloom is gone. The whole theory of modern education is radically unsound. Fortunately in England, at any rate, education produces no effect whatsoever. If it did, it would prove a serious danger to the upper classes, and probably lead to acts of violence in Grosvenor Square. What is your income?

JACK: Between seven and eight thousand a year.

LADY BRACKNELL: [*Makes a note in her book.*] In land, or in investments?

JACK: In investments, chiefly.

LADY BRACKNELL: That is satisfactory. What between the duties expected of one during one's lifetime, and the duties exacted from one after one's death, land has ceased to be either a profit or a pleasure. It gives one position, and prevents one from keeping it up. That's all that can be said about land.

JACK: I have a country house with some land, of course, attached to it, about fifteen hundred acres, I believe; but I don't depend on that for my real income. In fact, as far as I can make out, the poachers are the only people who make anything out of it.

LADY BRACKNELL: A country house! How many bedrooms? Well, that point can be cleared up afterwards. You have a town house, I hope? A girl with a simple, unspoiled nature, like Gwendolen, could hardly be expected to reside in the country.

JACK: Well, I own a house in Belgrave Square, but it is let by the year to Lady Bloxham. Of course, I can get it back whenever I like, at six months' notice.

LADY BRACKNELL: Lady Bloxham? I don't know her.

JACK: Oh, she goes about very little. She is a lady considerably advanced in years.

LADY BRACKNELL: Ah, now-a-days that is no guarantee of respectability of character. What number in Belgrave Square?

JACK: 149.

LADY BRACKNELL: [*Shaking her head.*] The unfashionable side. I thought there was something. However, that could easily be altered.

JACK: Do you mean the fashion, or the side?

LADY BRACKNELL: [*Sternly.*] Both, if necessary, I presume. What are your politics?

JACK: Well, I am afraid I really have none. I am a Liberal Unionist.

LADY BRACKNELL: Oh, they count as Tories. They dine with us. Or come in the evening, at any rate. Now to minor matters. Are your parents living?

JACK: I have lost both my parents.

LADY BRACKNELL: Both? . . . That seems like carelessness. Who was your father? He was evidently a man of some wealth. Was he born in what the Radical papers call the purple of commerce, or did he rise from the ranks of aristocracy?

JACK: I am afraid I really don't know. The fact is, Lady Bracknell, I said I had lost my parents. It would be nearer the truth to say that my parents seem to have lost me. . . . I don't actually know who I am by birth. I was . . . well, I was found.

LADY BRACKNELL: Found!

JACK: The late Mr. Thomas Cardew, an old gentleman of a very charitable and kindly disposition, found me, and gave me the name of Worthing, because he happened to have a first-class ticket for Worthing in his pocket at the time. Worthing is a place in Sussex. It is a seaside resort.

LADY BRACKNELL: Where did the charitable gentleman who had a first-class ticket for this seaside resort find you?

JACK: [*Gravely.*] In a hand-bag.

LADY BRACKNELL: A hand-bag?

JACK: [*Very seriously.*] Yes, Lady Bracknell. I was in a hand-bag—a somewhat large, black leather hand-bag, with handles to it—an ordinary hand-bag, in fact.

LADY BRACKNELL: In what locality did this Mr. James, or Thomas, Cardew come across this ordinary hand-bag?

JACK: In the cloak-room at Victoria Station. It was given to him in mistake for his own.

LADY BRACKNELL: The cloak-room at Victoria Station?

JACK: Yes. The Brighton line.

LADY BRACKNELL: The line is immaterial. Mr. Worthing, I confess I feel somewhat bewildered by what you have just told me. To be born, or at any rate, bred in a hand-bag, whether it had handles or not, seems to me to display a contempt for the ordinary decencies of family life that remind one of the worst excesses of the French Revolution. And I presume you know what that unfortunate movement led to? As for the particular locality in which the hand-bag was found, a cloak-room at a railway station might serve to conceal a social indiscretion—has probably, indeed, been used for that purpose before now—but it could hardly be regarded as an assured basis for a recognized position in good society.

JACK: May I ask you then what you would advise me to do? I need hardly say I would do anything in the world to ensure Gwendolen's happiness.

LADY BRACKNELL: I would strongly advise you, Mr. Worthing, to try and acquire some relations as soon as possible, and to make a definite effort to produce at any rate one parent, of either sex, before the season is quite over.

JACK: I don't see how I could possibly manage to do that. I can produce the hand-bag at any moment. It is in my dressing-room at home. I really think that should satisfy you, Lady Bracknell.

LADY BRACKNELL: Me, sir! What has it to do with me? You can hardly imagine that I and Lord Bracknell would dream of allowing our only daughter—a girl brought up with the utmost care—to marry into a cloak-room, and form an alliance with a parcel? Good morning, Mr. Worthing!

[LADY BRACKNELL *sweeps out in majestic indignation.*]

JACK: Good morning! [ALGERNON, *from the other room, strikes up the Wedding March.* JACK *looks perfectly furious, and goes to the door.*] For goodness' sake don't play that ghastly tune, Algy! How idiotic you are!

[*The music stops, and* ALGERNON *enters cheerily.*]

ALGERNON: Didn't it go off all right, old boy? You don't mean to say Gwendolen refused you? I know it is a way she has. She is always refusing people. I think it is most ill-natured of her.

JACK: Oh, Gwendolen is as right as a trivet. As far as she is concerned, we are engaged. Her mother is perfectly unbearable. Never met such a Gorgon . . . I don't really know what a Gorgon is like, but I am quite sure that Lady Bracknell is one. In any case, she is a monster, without being a myth, which is rather unfair . . . I beg your pardon, Algy, I suppose I shouldn't talk about your own aunt in that way before you.

ALGERNON: My dear boy, I love hearing my relations abused. It is the only thing that makes me put up with them at all. Relations are simply a tedious pack of people who haven't got the remotest knowledge of how to live, nor the smallest instinct about when to die.

JACK: Oh, that is nonsense!

ALGERNON: It isn't!

JACK: Well, I won't argue about the matter. You always want to argue about things.

ALGERNON: That is exactly what things were originally made for.

JACK: Upon my word, if I thought that, I'd shoot myself . . . [*A pause.*] You don't think there is any chance of Gwendolen becoming like her mother in about a hundred and fifty years, do you, Algy?

ALGERNON: All women become like their mothers. That is their tragedy. No man does. That's his.

JACK: Is that clever?

ALGERNON: It is perfectly phrased! and quite as true as any observation in civilized life should be.

JACK: I am sick to death of cleverness. Everybody is clever now-a-days. You can't go anywhere without meeting clever people. The thing has become an absolute public nuisance. I wish to goodness we had a few fools left.

ALGERNON: We have.

JACK: I should extremely like to meet them. What do they talk about?

ALGERNON: The fools? Oh! about the clever people, of course.

JACK: What fools!

ALGERNON: By the way, did you tell Gwendolen the truth about your being Ernest in town, and Jack in the country?

JACK: [*In a very patronising manner.*] My dear fellow, the truth isn't quite the sort of thing one tells to a nice sweet refined girl. What extraordinary ideas you have about the way to behave to a woman!

ALGERNON: The only way to behave to a woman is to make love to her, if she is pretty, and to someone else if she is plain.

JACK: Oh, that is nonsense.

ALGERNON: What about your brother? What about the profligate Ernest?

JACK: Oh, before the end of the week I shall have got rid of him. I'll say he died in Paris of apoplexy. Lots of people die of apoplexy, quite suddenly, don't they?

ALGERNON: Yes, but it's hereditary, my dear fellow. It's a sort of thing that runs in families. You had much better say a severe chill.

JACK: You are sure a severe chill isn't hereditary, or anything of that kind?

ALGERNON: Of course it isn't!

JACK: Very well, then. My poor brother Ernest is carried off suddenly in Paris, by a severe chill. That gets rid of him.

ALGERNON: But I thought you said that . . . Miss Cardew was a little too much interested in your poor brother, Ernest? Won't she feel his loss a good deal?

JACK: Oh, that is all right. Cecily is not a silly romantic girl, I am glad to say. She has got a capital appetite, goes long walks, and pays no attention at all to her lessons.

ALGERNON: I would rather like to see Cecily.

JACK: I will take very good care you never do. She is excessively pretty, and she is only just eighteen.

ALGERNON: Have you told Gwendolen yet that you have an excessively pretty ward who is only just eighteen?

JACK: Oh! one doesn't blurt these things out to people. Cecily and Gwendolyn are perfectly certain to be extremely great friends. I'll bet you anything you like that half an hour after they have met, they will be calling each other sister.

ALGERNON: Women only do that when they have called each other a lot of other things first. Now, my dear boy, if we want to get a good table at Willis's, we really must go and dress. Do you know it is nearly seven?

JACK: [*Irritably.*] Oh! it always is nearly seven.

ALGERNON: Well, I'm hungry.

JACK: I never knew you when you weren't. . . .

ALGERNON: What shall we do after dinner? Go to the theatre?

JACK: Oh no! I loathe listening.

ALGERNON: Well, let us go to the club?

JACK: Oh, no! I hate talking.

ALGERNON: Well, we might trot round to the Empire at ten?

JACK: Oh no! I can't bear looking at things. It is so silly.

ALGERNON: Well, what shall we do?

JACK: Nothing!

ALGERNON: It is awfully hard work doing nothing. However, I don't mind hard work where there is no definite object of any kind.

[*Enter* LANE.]

LANE: Miss Fairfax.

[*Enter* GWENDOLEN. LANE *goes out.*]

ALGERNON: Gwendolen, upon my word!

GWENDOLEN: Algy, kindly turn your back. I have something very particular to say to Mr. Worthing.

ALGERNON: Really, Gwendolen, I don't think I can allow this at all.

GWENDOLEN: Algy, you always adopt a strictly immoral attitude towards life. You are not quite old enough to do that. [ALGERNON *retires to the fireplace.*]

JACK: My own darling!

GWENDOLEN: Ernest, we may never be married. From the expression on mamma's face I fear we never shall. Few parents now-a-days pay any regard to what their children say to them. The old-fashioned respect for the young is fast dying out. Whatever influence I ever had over mamma, I lost at the age of three. But although she may prevent us from becoming man and wife, and I may marry someone else, and marry often, nothing that she can possibly do can alter my eternal devotion to you.

JACK: Dear Gwendolen!

GWENDOLEN: The story of your romantic origin, as related to me by mamma, with unpleasing comments, has naturally stirred the deeper fibres of my nature. Your Christian name has an irresistible fascination. The simplicity of your character makes you exquisitely incomprehensible to me. Your town address at the Albany I have. What is your address in the country?

JACK: The Manor House, Woolton, Hertfordshire.

[ALGERNON, *who has been carefully listening, smiles to himself, and writes the address on his shirt-cuff. Then picks up the Railway Guide.*]

GWENDOLEN: There is a good postal service, I suppose? It may be necessary to do something desperate. That of course will require serious consideration. I will communicate with you daily.

JACK: My own one!

GWENDOLEN: How long do you remain in town?

JACK: Till Monday.

GWENDOLEN: Good! Algy, you may turn round now.

ALGERNON: Thanks, I've turned round already.

GWENDOLEN: You may also ring the bell.

JACK: You will let me see you to your carriage, my own darling?

GWENDOLEN: Certainly.

JACK: [*To* LANE, *who now enters.*] I will see Miss Fairfax out.

LANE: Yes sir.

[JACK *and* GWENDOLYN *go off.*]

[LANE *presents several letters on a salver to* ALGERNON. *It is to be surmised that they are bills, as* ALGERNON *after looking at the envelopes, tears them up.*]

ALGERNON: A glass of sherry, Lane.

LANE: Yes, sir.

ALGERNON: To-morrow, Lane, I'm going Bunburying.

LANE: Yes, sir.

ALGERNON: I shall probably not be back till Monday. You can put up my dress clothes, my smoking jacket, and all the Bunbury suits. . . .

LANE: Yes, sir. [*Handing sherry*.]

ALGERNON: I hope to-morrow will be a fine day, Lane.

LANE: It never is, sir.

ALGERNON: Lane, you're a perfect pessimist.

LANE: I do my best to give satisfaction, sir.

[*Enter* JACK, LANE *goes off*.]

JACK: There's a sensible, intellectual girl! the only girl I ever cared for in my life. [ALGERNON *is laughing immoderately*.] What on earth are you so amused at?

ALGERNON: Oh, I'm a little anxious about poor Bunbury, that is all.

JACK: If you don't take care, your friend Bunbury will get you into a serious scrape some day.

ALGERNON: I love scrapes. They are the only things that are never serious.

JACK: Oh, that's nonsense, Algy. You never talk anything but nonsense.

ALGERNON: Nobody ever does.

[JACK *looks indignantly at him, and leaves the room*. ALGERNON *lights a cigarette, reads his shirt-cuff, and smiles*.]

ACT-DROP.

SECOND ACT

SCENE—*Garden at the Manor House. A flight of gray stone steps leads up to the house. The garden, an old-fashioned one, full of roses. Time of year, July. Basket chairs, and a table covered with books, are set under a large yew tree.*

[MISS PRISM *discovered seated at the table*. CECILY *is at the back watering flowers*.]

MISS PRISM: [*Calling*.] Cecily, Cecily! Surely such a utilitarian occupation as the watering of flowers is rather Moulton's duty than yours? Especially at a moment when intellectual pleasures await you. Your German grammar is on the table. Pray open it at page fifteen. We will repeat yesterday's lesson.

CECILY: [*Coming over very slowly*.] But I don't like German. It isn't at all a becoming language. I know perfectly well that I look quite plain after my German lesson.

MISS PRISM: Child, you know how anxious your guardian is that you should improve yourself in every way. He laid particular stress on your German, as he was leaving for town yesterday. Indeed, he always lays stress on your German when he is leaving for town.

CECILY: Dear Uncle Jack is so very serious! Sometimes he is so serious that I think he cannot be quite well.

MISS PRISM: [*Drawing herself up*.] Your guardian enjoys the best of health, and his gravity of demeanour is especially to be commended in one so comparatively young as he is. I know no one who has a higher sense of duty and responsibility.

CECILY: I suppose that is why he often looks a little bored when we three are together.

MISS PRISM: Cecily! I am surprised at you. Mr. Worthing has many troubles in his life. Idle merriment and triviality would be out of place in his conversation.

You must remember his constant anxiety about that unfortunate young man his brother.

CECILY: I wish Uncle Jack would allow that unfortunate young man, his brother, to come down here sometimes. We might have a good influence over him, Miss Prism. I am sure you certainly would. You know German, and geology, and things of that kind influence a man very much. [CECILY *begins to write in her diary*.]

MISS PRISM: [*Shaking her head*.] I do not think that even I could produce any effect on a character that according to his own brother's admission is irretrievably weak and vacillating. Indeed I am not sure that I would desire to reclaim him. I am not in favour of this modern mania for turning bad people into good people at a moment's notice. As a man sows so let him reap. You must put away your diary, Cecily. I really don't see why you should keep a diary at all.

CECILY: I keep a diary in order to enter the wonderful secrets of my life. If I didn't write them down I should probably forget all about them.

MISS PRISM: Memory, my dear Cecily, is the diary that we all carry about with us.

CECILY: Yes, but it usually chronicles the things that have never happened, and couldn't possibly have happened. I believe that Memory is responsible for nearly all the three-volume novels that Mudie sends us.

MISS PRISM: Do not speak slightingly of the three-volume novel, Cecily. I wrote one myself in earlier days.

CECILY: Did you really, Miss Prism? How wonderfully clever you are! I hope it did not end happily? I don't like novels that end happily. They depress me so much.

MISS PRISM: The good ended happily, and the bad unhappily. That is what Fiction means.

CECILY: I suppose so. But it seems very unfair. And was your novel ever published?

MISS PRISM: Alas! no. The manuscript unfortunately was abandoned. I use the word in the sense of lost or mislaid. To your work, child, these speculations are profitless.

CECILY: [*Smiling*.] But I see dear Dr. Chasuble coming up through the garden.

MISS PRISM: [*Rising and advancing*.] Dr. Chasuble! This is indeed a pleasure.

[*Enter* CANON CHASUBLE.]

CHASUBLE: And how are we this morning? Miss Prism, you are, I trust, well?

CECILY: Miss Prism has just been complaining of a slight headache. I think it would do her so much good to have a short stroll with you in the Park, Dr. Chasuble.

MISS PRISM: Cecily, I have not mentioned anything about a headache.

CECILY: No, dear Miss Prism, I know that, but I felt instinctively that you had a headache. Indeed I was thinking about that, and not about my German lesson, when the Rector came in.

CHASUBLE: I hope Cecily, you are not inattentive.

CECILY: Oh, I am afraid I am.

CHASUBLE: That is strange. Were I fortunate enough to be Miss Prism's pupil, I would hang upon her lips. [MISS PRISM *glares*.] I spoke metaphorically.—My metaphor was drawn from bees. Ahem! Mr. Worthing I suppose, has not returned from town yet?

MISS PRISM: We do not expect him till Monday afternoon.

CHASUBLE: Ah yes, he usually likes to spend his Sunday in London. He is not one of those whose sole aim is enjoyment, as, by all accounts, that unfortunate young man his brother seems to be. But I must not disturb Egeria and her pupil any longer.

MISS PRISM: Egeria? My name is Laetitia, Doctor.

CHASUBLE: [*Bowing.*] A classical allusion merely, drawn from the Pagan authors. I shall see you both no doubt at Evensong?

MISS PRISM: I think, dear Doctor, I will have a stroll with you. I find I have a headache after all, and a walk might do it good.

CHASUBLE: With pleasure, Miss Prism, with pleasure. We might go as far as the schools and back.

MISS PRISM: That would be delightful. Cecily, you will read your Political Economy in my absence. The chapter on the Fall of the Rupee you may omit. It is somewhat too sensational. Even these metallic problems have their melodramatic side.

[*Goes down the garden with* DR. CHASUBLE.]

CECILY: [*Picks up books and throws them back on table.*] Horrid Political Economy! Horrid Geography! Horrid, horrid German!

[*Enter* MERRIMAN *with a card on a salver.*]

MERR: Mr. Ernest Worthing has just driven over from the station. He has brought his luggage with him.

CECILY: [*Takes the card and reads it.*] "Mr. Ernest Worthing, B. 4 The Albany, W." Uncle Jack's brother! Did you tell him Mr. Worthing was in town?

MERRIMAN: Yes, Miss. He seemed very much disappointed. I mentioned that you and Miss Prism were in the garden. He said he was anxious to speak to you privately for a moment.

CECILY: Ask Mr. Ernest Worthing to come here. I suppose you had better talk to the housekeeper about a room for him.

MERRIMAN: Yes, Miss.

[MERRIMAN *goes off*]

CECILY: I have never met any really wicked person before. I feel rather frightened. I am so afraid he will look just like everyone else.

[*Enter* ALGERNON, *very gay and debonnair.*]

He does!

ALGERNON: [*Raising his hat.*] You are my little cousin Cecily, I'm sure.

CECILY: You are under some strange mistake. I am not little. In fact, I believe I am more than usually tall for my age. [ALGERNON *is rather taken aback.*] But I am your cousin Cecily. You, I see from your card, are Uncle Jack's brother, my cousin Ernest, my wicked cousin Ernest.

ALGERNON: Oh! I am not really wicked at all, cousin Cecily. You mustn't think that I am wicked.

CECILY: If you are not, then you have certainly been deceiving us all in a very inexcusable manner. I hope you have not been leading a double life, pretending to be wicked and being really good all the time. That would be hypocrisy.

ALGERNON: [*Looks at her in amazement.*] Oh! Of course I have been rather reckless.

CECILY: I am glad to hear it.

ALGERNON: In fact, now you mention the subject. I have been very bad in my own small way.

CECILY: I don't think you should be so proud of that, though I am sure it must have been very pleasant.

ALGERNON: It is much pleasanter being here with you.

CECILY: I can't understand how you are here at all. Uncle Jack won't be back till Monday afternoon.

ALGERNON: That is a great disappointment. I am obliged to go up by the first train on Monday morning. I have a business appointment that I am anxious . . . to miss.

CECILY: Couldn't you miss it anywhere but in London?

ALGERNON: No; the appointment is in London.

CECILY: Well, I know, of course, how important it is not to keep a business engagement, if one wants to retain any sense of the beauty of life, but still I think you had better wait till Uncle Jack arrives. I know he wants to speak to you about your emigrating.

ALGERNON: About my what?

CECILY: Your emigrating. He has gone up to buy your outfit.

ALGERNON: I certainly wouldn't let Jack buy my outfit. He has no taste in neckties at all.

CECILY: I don't think you will require neckties. Uncle Jack is sending you to Australia.

ALGERNON: Australia? I'd sooner die.

CECILY: Well, he said at dinner on Wednesday night, that you would have to choose between this world, the next world, and Australia.

ALGERNON: Oh, well! The accounts I have received of Australia and the next world are not particularly encouraging. This world is good enough for me, cousin Cecily.

CECILY: Yes, but are you good enough for it?

ALGERNON: I'm afraid I'm not that. That is why I want you to reform me. You might make that your mission, if you don't mind, cousin Cecily.

CECILY: I'm afraid I've no time, this afternoon.

ALGERNON: Well, would you mind my reforming myself this afternoon?

CECILY: It is rather Quixotic of you. But I think you should try.

ALGERNON: I will. I feel better already.

CECILY: You are looking a little worse.

ALGERNON: That is because I am hungry.

CECILY: How thoughtless of me. I should have remembered that when one is going to lead an entirely new life, one requires regular and wholesome meals. Won't you come in?

ALGERNON: Thank you. Might I have a button-hole first? I never have any appetite unless I have a button-hole first.

CECILY: A Maréchale Niel? [*Picks up scissors.*]

ALGERNON: No, I'd sooner have a pink rose.

CECILY: Why? [*Cuts a flower.*]

ALGERNON: Because you are like a pink rose, cousin Cecily.

CECILY: I don't think it can be right for you to talk to me like that. Miss Prism never says such things to me.

ALGERNON: Then Miss Prism is a short-sighted old lady. [CECILY *puts the rose in his button-hole.*] You are the prettiest girl I ever saw.

CECILY: Miss Prism says that all good looks are a snare.

ALGERNON: They are a snare that every sensible man would like to be caught in.

CECILY: Oh! I don't think I would care to catch a sensible man. I shouldn't know what to talk to him about.

[*They pass into the house.* MISS PRISM *and* DR. CHASUBLE *return.*]

MISS PRISM: You are too much alone, dear Dr. Chasuble. You should get married. A misanthrope I can understand—a womanthrope, never!

CHASUBLE: [*With a scholar's shudder.*] Believe me, I do not deserve so neologistic a phrase. The precept as well as the practice of the Primitive Church was distinctly against matrimony.

MISS PRISM: [*Sententiously.*] That is obviously the reason why the Primitive Church has not lasted up to the present day. And you do not seem to realize, dear Doctor, that by persistently remaining single, a man converts himself into a permanent public temptation. Men should be more careful; this very celibacy leads weaker vessels astray.

CHASUBLE: But is a man not equally attractive when married?

MISS PRISM: No married man is ever attractive except to his wife.

CHASUBLE: And often, I've been told, not even to her.

MISS PRISM: That depends on the intellectual sympathies of the woman. Maturity can always be depended on. Ripeness can be trusted. Young women are green. [DR. CHASUBLE *starts.*] I spoke horticulturally. My metaphor was drawn from fruits. But where is Cecily?

CHASUBLE: Perhaps she followed us to the schools.

[*Enter* JACK *slowly from the back of the garden. He is dressed in the deepest mourning, with crape hatband and black gloves.*]

MISS PRISM: Mr. Worthing!

CHASUBLE: Mr. Worthing?

MISS PRISM: This is indeed a surprise. We did not look for you till Monday afternoon.

JACK: [*Shakes* MISS PRISM'S *hand in a tragic manner.*] I have returned sooner than I expected. Dr. Chasuble, I hope you are well?

CHASUBLE: Dear Mr. Worthing, I trust this garb of woe does not betoken some terrible calamity?

JACK: My brother.

MISS PRISM: More shameful debts and extravagance?

CHASUBLE: Still leading his life of pleasure?

JACK: [*Shaking his head.*] Dead!

CHASUBLE: Your brother Ernest dead?

JACK: Quite dead.

MISS PRISM: What a lesson for him! I trust he will profit by it.

CHASUBLE: Mr. Worthing, I offer you my sincere condolence. You have at least the consolation of knowing that you were always the most generous and forgiving of brothers.

JACK: Poor Ernest! He had many faults, but it is a sad, sad blow.

CHASUBLE: Very sad indeed. Were you with him at the end?

JACK: No. He died abroad; in Paris, in fact. I had a telegram last night from the manager of the Grand Hotel.

CHASUBLE: Was the cause of death mentioned?

JACK: A severe chill, it seems.

MISS PRISM: As a man sows, so shall he reap.

CHASUBLE: [*Raising his hand.*] Charity, dear Miss Prism, charity! None of us are perfect. I myself am peculiarly susceptible to draughts. Will the interment take place here?

JACK: No. He seemed to have expressed a desire to be buried in Paris.

CHASUBLE: In Paris! [*Shakes his head.*] I fear that hardly points to any very serious state of mind at the last. You would no doubt wish me to make some slight allusion to this tragic domestic affliction next Sunday. [JACK *presses his hand convulsively.*] My sermon on the meaning of the manna in the wilderness can be adapted to almost any occasion, joyful, or, as in the present case, distressing. [*All sigh.*] I have preached it at harvest celebrations, christenings, confirmations, on days of humiliation and festal days. The last time I delivered it was in the Cathedral, as a charity sermon on behalf of the Society for the Prevention of Discontent among the Upper Orders. The Bishop, who was present, was much struck by some of the analogies I drew.

JACK: Ah! that reminds me, you mentioned christenings, I think. Dr. Chasuble? I suppose you know how to christen all right? [DR. CHASUBLE *looks astounded.*] I mean, of course, you are continually christening, aren't you?

MISS PRISM: It is, I regret to say, one of the Rector's most constant duties in this parish. I have often spoken to the poorer classes on the subject. But they don't seem to know what thrift is.

CHASUBLE: But is there any particular infant in whom you are interested, Mr. Worthing? Your brother was, I believe, unmarried, was he not?

JACK: Oh yes.

MISS PRISM: [*Bitterly.*] People who live entirely for pleasure usually are.

JACK: But it is not for any child, dear Doctor. I am very fond of children. No! the fact is, I would like to be christened myself, this afternoon, if you have nothing better to do.

CHASUBLE: But surely, Mr. Worthing, you have been christened already?

JACK: I don't remember anything about it.

CHASUBLE: But have you any grave doubts on the subject?

JACK: I certainly intend to have. Of course I don't know if the thing would bother you in any way, or if you think I am a little too old now.

CHASUBLE: Not at all. The sprinkling, and indeed, the immersion of adults is a perfectly canonical practice.

JACK: Immersion!

CHASUBLE: You need have no apprehensions. Sprinkling is all that is necessary, or indeed I think advisable. Our weather is so changeable. At what hour would you wish the ceremony performed?

JACK: Oh, I might trot round about five if that would suit you.

CHASUBLE: Perfectly, perfectly! In fact I have two similar ceremonies to perform at that time. A case of twins that occurred recently in one of the outlying cottages on your own estate. Poor Jenkins the carter, a most hard-working man.

JACK: Oh! I don't see much fun in being christened along with other babies. It would be childish. Would half-past five do?

CHASUBLE: Admirably! Admirably! [*Takes out watch.*] And now, dear Mr. Worthing, I will not intrude any longer into a house of sorrow. I would merely beg you not to be too much bowed down by grief. What seem to us bitter trials are often blessings in disguise.

MISS PRISM: This seems to me a blessing of an extremely obvious kind.

[*Enter* CECILY *from the house.*]

CECILY: Uncle Jack! Oh, I am pleased to see you back. But what horrid clothes you have got on! Do go and change them.

MISS PRISM: Cecily!

CHASUBLE: My child! my child! [*Cecily goes towards Jack; he kisses her brow in a melancholy manner.*]

CECILY: What is the matter, Uncle Jack? Do look happy! You look as if you had toothache, and I have got such a surprise for you. Who do you think is in the dining-room? Your brother!

JACK: Who?

CECILY: Your brother Ernest. He arrived about half an hour ago.

JACK: What nonsense! I haven't got a brother!

CECILY: Oh, don't say that. However badly he may have behaved to you in the past he is still your brother. You couldn't be so heartless as to disown him. I'll tell him to come out. And you will shake hands with him, won't you, Uncle Jack? [*Runs back into the house.*]

CHASUBLE: These are very joyful tidings.

MISS PRISM: After we had all been resigned to his loss, his sudden return seems to me peculiarly distressing.

JACK: My brother is in the dining-room? I don't know what it all means. I think it is perfectly absurd.

[*Enter* ALGERNON *and* CECILY *hand in hand. They come slowly up to* JACK.]

JACK: Good heavens! [*Motions* ALGERNON *away.*]

ALGERNON: Brother John, I have come down from town to tell you that I am very sorry for all the trouble I have given you, and that I intend to lead a better life in the future. [JACK *glares at him and does not take his hand.*]

CECILY: Uncle Jack, you are not going to refuse your own brother's hand?

JACK: Nothing will induce me to take his hand. I think his coming down here disgraceful. He knows perfectly well why.

CECILY: Uncle Jack, do be nice. There is some good in everyone. Ernest has just been telling me about his poor invalid friend Mr. Bunbury whom he goes to visit so often. And surely there must be much good in one who is kind to an invalid, and leaves the pleasures of London to sit by a bed of pain.

JACK: Oh! he has been talking about Bunbury, has he?

CECILY: Yes, he has told me all about poor Mr. Bunbury, and his terrible state of health.

JACK: Bunbury! Well, I won't have him talk to you about Bunbury or about anything else. It is enough to drive one perfectly frantic.

ALGERNON: Of course I admit that the faults were all on my side. But I must say that I think Brother John's coldness to me is peculiarly painful. I expected a more enthusiastic welcome, especially considering it is the first time I have come here.

CECILY: Uncle Jack, if you don't shake hands with Ernest, I will never forgive you.

JACK: Never forgive me?

CECILY: Never, never, never!

JACK: Well, this is the last time I shall ever do it.

[*Shakes hands with* ALGERNON *and glares.*]

CHASUBLE: It is pleasant, is it not, to see so perfect a reconciliation? I think we might leave the two brothers together.

MISS PRISM: Cecily, you will come with us.

CECILY: Certainly, Miss Prism. My little task of reconciliation is over.

CHASUBLE: You have done a beautiful action to-day, dear child.

MISS PRISM: We must not be premature in our judgments.

CECILY: I feel very happy. [*They all go off.*]

JACK: You young scoundrel, Algy, you must get out of this place as soon as possible. I don't allow any Bunburying here.

[*Enter* MERRIMAN.]

MERRIMAN: I have put Mr. Ernest's things in the room next to yours, sir. I suppose that is all right?

JACK: What?

MERRIMAN: Mr. Ernest's luggage, sir, I have unpacked it and put it in the room next to your own.

JACK: His luggage?

MERRIMAN: Yes, sir. Three portmanteaus, a dressing-case, two hat boxes, and a large luncheon-basket.

ALGERNON: I am afraid I can't stay more than a week this time.

JACK: Merriman, order the dog-cart at once. Mr. Ernest has been suddenly called back to town.

MERRIMAN: Yes, sir. [*Goes back into the house.*]

ALGERNON: What a fearful liar you are, Jack. I have not been called back to town at all.

JACK: Yes, you have.

ALGERNON: I haven't heard anyone call me.

JACK: Your duty as a gentleman calls you back.

ALGERNON: My duty as a gentleman has never interfered with my pleasures in the smallest degree.

JACK: I can quite understand that.

ALGERNON: Well, Cecily is a darling.

JACK: You are not to talk of Miss Cardew like that. I don't like it.

ALGERNON: Well, I don't like your clothes. You look perfectly ridiculous in them. Why on earth don't you go up and change? It is perfectly childish to be in deep mourning for a man who is actually staying for a whole week with you in your house as a guest. I call it grotesque.

JACK: You are certainly not staying with me for a whole week as a guest or anything else. You have got to leave . . . by the four-five train.

ALGERNON: I certainly won't leave you so long as you are in mourning. It would be most unfriendly. If I were in mourning you would stay with me, I suppose. I should think it very unkind if you didn't.

JACK: Well, will you go if I change my clothes?

ALGERNON: Yes, if you are not too long. I never saw anybody take so long to dress, and with such little result.

JACK: Well, at any rate, that is better than being always over-dressed as you are.

ALGERNON: If I am occasionally a little over-dressed, I make up for it by being always immensely over-educated.

JACK: Your vanity is ridiculous, your conduct an outrage, and your presence in my garden utterly absurd. However, you have got to catch the four-five, and I hope you will have a pleasant journey back to town. This Bunburying, as you call it, has not been a great success for you.

[*Goes into the house.*]

ALGERNON: I think it has been a great success. I'm in love with Cecily, and that is everything.

[*Enter* CECILY *at the back of the garden. She picks up the can and begins to water the flowers.*]

But I must see her before I go, and make arrangements for another Bunbury. Ah, there she is.

CECILY: Oh, I merely came back to water the roses. I thought you were with Uncle Jack.

ALGERNON: He's gone to order the dog-cart for me.

CECILY: Oh, is he going to take you for a nice drive?

ALGERNON: He's going to send me away.

CECILY: Then have we got to part?

ALGERNON: I am afraid so. It's very painful parting.

CECILY: It is always painful to part from people whom one has known for a very brief space of time. The absence of old friends one can endure with equanimity. But even a momentary separation from anyone to whom one has just been introduced is almost unbearable.

ALGERNON: Thank you.

[*Enter* MERRIMAN.]

MERRIMAN: The dog-cart is at the door, sir. [ALGERNON *looks appealingly at* CECILY.]

CECILY: It can wait, Merriman . . . for . . . five minutes.

MERRIMAN: Yes, Miss. [*Exit* MERRIMAN.]

ALGERNON: I hope, Cecily, I shall not offend you if I state quite frankly and openly that you seem to me to be in every way the visible personification of absolute perfection.

CECILY: I think your frankness does you great credit, Ernest. If you will allow me I will copy your remarks into my diary. [*Goes over to table and begins writing in diary.*]

ALGERNON: Do you really keep a diary? I'd give anything to look at it. May I?

CECILY: Oh no. [*Puts her hand over it.*] You see, it is simply a very young girl's record of her own thoughts and impressions, and consequently meant for publication. When it appears in volume form I hope you will order a copy. But pray, Ernest, don't stop. I delight in taking down from dictation. I have reached "absolute perfection." You can go on. I am quite ready for more.

ALGERNON: [*Somewhat taken aback.*] Ahem! Ahem!

CECILY: Oh, don't cough, Ernest. When one is dictating one should speak fluently and not cough. Besides, I don't know how to spell a cough.

[*Writes as* ALGERNON *speaks.*]

ALGERNON: [*Speaking very rapidly.*] Cecily, ever since I first looked upon your wonderful and incomparable beauty, I have dared to love you wildly, passionately, devotedly, hopelessly.

CECILY: I don't think that you should tell me that you love me wildly, passionately, devotedly, hopelessly. Hopelessly doesn't seem to make much sense, does it?

ALGERNON: Cecily!

[*Enter* MERRIMAN.]

MERRIMAN: The dog-cart is waiting, sir.

ALGERNON: Tell it to come round next week, at the same hour.

MERRIMAN: [*Looks at* CECILY, *who makes no sign.*] Yes, sir.

[MERRIMAN *retires.*]

Cecily: Uncle Jack would be very much annoyed if he knew you were staying on till next week, at the same hour.

Algernon: Oh, I don't care about Jack. I don't care for anybody in the whole world but you. I love you, Cecily. You will marry me, won't you?

Cecily: You silly boy! Of course. Why, we have been engaged for the last three months.

Algernon: For the last three months?

Cecily: Yes, it will be exactly three months on Thursday.

Algernon: But how did we become engaged?

Cecily: Well, ever since dear Uncle Jack first confessed to us that he had a younger brother who was very wicked and bad, you of course have formed the chief topic of conversation between myself and Miss Prism. And of course a man who is much talked about is always very attractive. One feels there must be something in him after all. I daresay it was foolish of me, but I fell in love with you, Ernest.

Algernon: Darling! And when was the engagement actually settled?

Cecily: On the 14th of February last. Worn out by your entire ignorance of my existence, I determined to end the matter one way or the other, and after a long struggle with myself I accepted you under this dear old tree here. The next day I bought this little ring in your name, and this is the little bangle with the true lovers' knot I promised you always to wear.

Algernon: Did I give you this? It's very pretty, isn't it?

Cecily: Yes, you've wonderfully good taste, Ernest. It's the excuse I've always given for your leading such a bad life. And this is the box in which I keep all your dear letters. [*Kneels at table, opens box, and produces letters tied up with blue ribbon.*]

Algernon: My letters! But my own sweet Cecily, I have never written you any letters.

Cecily: You need hardly remind me of that, Ernest. I remember only too well that I was forced to write your letters for you. I always wrote three times a week, and sometimes oftener.

Algernon: Oh, do let me read them, Cecily?

Cecily: Oh, I couldn't possibly. They would make you far too conceited. [*Replaces box.*] The three you wrote me after I had broken off the engagement are so beautiful, and so badly spelled, that even now I can hardly read them without crying a little.

Algernon: But was our engagement ever broken off?

Cecily: Of course it was. On the 22nd of last March. You can see the entry if you like. [*Shows diary.*] "To-day I broke off my engagement with Ernest. I feel it is better to do so. The weather still continues charming."

Algernon: But why on earth did you break it off? What had I done? I had done nothing at all. Cecily, I am very much hurt indeed to hear you broke it off. Particularly when the weather was so charming.

Cecily: It would hardly have been a really serious engagement if it hadn't been broken off at least once. But I forgave you before the week was out.

Algernon: [*Crossing to her, and kneeling.*] What a perfect angel you are, Cecily.

Cecily: You dear romantic boy. [*He kisses her, she puts her fingers through his hair.*] I hope your hair curls naturally, does it?

Algernon: Yes, darling, with a little help from others.

Cecily: I am so glad.

ALGERNON: You'll never break off our engagement again, Cecily?

CECILY: I don't think I could break it off now that I have actually met you. Besides, of course, there is the question of your name.

ALGERNON: Yes, of course. [*Nervously*.]

CECILY: You must not laugh at me, darling, but it had always been a girlish dream of mine to love some one whose name was Ernest. [ALGERNON *rises,* CECILY *also*.] There is something in that name that seems to inspire absolute confidence. I pity any poor married woman whose husband is not called Ernest.

ALGERNON: But, my dear child, do you mean to say you could not love me if I had some other name?

CECILY: But what name?

ALGERNON: Oh, any name you like—Algernon—for instance . . .

CECILY: But I don't like the name of Algernon.

ALGERNON: Well, my own dear, sweet, loving little darling, I really can't see why you should object to the name of Algernon. It is not at all a bad name. In fact, it is rather an aristocratic name. Half of the chaps who get into the Bankruptcy Court are called Algernon. But seriously, Cecily. . . [*Moving to her*.] . . . if my name was Algy, couldn't you love me?

CECILY: [*Rising*.] I might respect you, Ernest, I might admire your character, but I fear that I should not be able to give you my undivided attention.

ALGERNON: Ahem! Cecily! [*Picking up hat*.] Your Rector here is, I suppose, thoroughly experienced in the practice of all the rites and ceremonials of the Church?

CECILY: Oh, yes. Dr. Chasuble is a most learned man. He has never written a single book, so you can imagine how much he knows.

ALGERNON: I must see him at once on a most important christening—I mean on most important business.

CECILY: Oh!

ALGERNON: I shan't be away more than half an hour.

CECILY: Considering that we have been engaged since February the 14th, and that I only met you to-day for the first time, I think it is rather hard that you should leave me for so long a period as half an hour. Couldn't you make it twenty minutes?

ALGERNON: I'll be back in no time.

[*Kisses her and rushes down the garden*.]

CECILY: What an impetuous boy he is! I like his hair so much. I must enter his proposal in my diary.

[*Enter* MERRIMAN.]

MERRIMAN: A Miss Fairfax has just called to see Mr. Worthing. On very important business Miss Fairfax states.

CECILY: Isn't Mr. Worthing in his library?

MERRIMAN: Mr. Worthing went over in the direction of the Rectory some time ago.

CECILY: Pray ask the lady to come out here; Mr. Worthing is sure to be back soon. And you can bring tea.

MERRIMAN: Yes, Miss. [*Goes out*.]

CECILY: Miss Fairfax! I suppose one of the many good elderly women who are associated with Uncle Jack in some of his philanthropic work in London. I don't quite like women who are interested in philanthropic work. I think it is so forward of them.

[*Enter* MERRIMAN.]

MERRIMAN: Miss Fairfax.

[*Enter* GWENDOLEN.] [*Exit* MERRIMAN.]

CECILY: [*Advancing to meet her.*] Pray let me introduce myself to you. My name is Cecily Cardew.

GWENDOLEN: Cecily Cardew? [*Moving to her and shaking hands.*] What a very sweet name! Something tells me that we are going to be great friends. I like you already more than I can say. My first impression of people are never wrong.

CECILY: How nice of you to like me so much after we have known each other such a comparatively short time. Pray sit down.

GWENDOLEN: [*Still standing up.*] I may call you Cecily, may I not?

CECILY: With pleasure!

GWENDOLEN: And you will always call me Gwendolen, won't you?

CECILY: If you wish.

GWENDOLEN: Then that is all quite settled, is it not?

CECILY: I hope so. [*A pause. They both sit down together.*]

GWENDOLEN: Perhaps this might be a favourable opportunity for my mentioning who I am. My father is Lord Bracknell. You have never heard of papa, I suppose?

CECILY: I don't think so.

GWENDOLEN: Outside the family circle, papa, I am glad to say, is entirely unknown. I think that is quite as it should be. The home seems to me to be the proper sphere for the man. And certainly once a man begins to neglect his domestic duties he becomes painfully effeminate, does he not? And I don't like that. It makes men so very attractive. Cecily, mamma, whose views on education are remarkably strict, has brought me up to be extremely short-sighted; it is part of her system; so do you mind my looking at you through my glasses?

CECILY: Oh! not at all, Gwendolen. I am very fond of being looked at.

GWENDOLEN: [*After examining* CECILY *carefully through a lorgnette.*] You are here on a short visit I suppose.

CECILY: Oh no! I live here.

GWENDOLEN: [*Severely.*] Really? Your mother, no doubt, or some female relative of advanced years, resides here also?

CECILY: Oh no! I have no mother, nor, in fact, any relations.

GWENDOLEN: Indeed?

CECILY: My dear guardian, with the assistance of Miss Prism, has the arduous task of looking after me.

GWENDOLEN: Your guardian?

CECILY: Yes, I am Mr. Worthing's ward.

GWENDOLEN: Oh! It is strange he never mentioned to me that he had a ward. How secretive of him! He grows more interesting hourly. I am not sure, however, that the news inspires me with feelings of unmixed delight. [*Rising and going to her.*] I am very fond of you, Cecily; I have liked you ever since I met you! But I am bound to state that now that I know that you are Mr. Worthing's ward, I cannot help expressing a wish you were—well just a little older than you seem to be—and not quite so very alluring in appearance. In fact, if I may speak candidly——

CECILY: Pray do! I think that whenever one has anything unpleasant to say, one should always be quite candid.

GWENDOLEN: Well, to speak with perfect candour, Cecily, I wish that you were fully forty-two, and more than usually plain for your age. Ernest has a strong, upright nature. He is the very soul of truth and honour. Disloyalty would be as impossible to him as deception. But even men of the noblest possible moral character are extremely susceptible to the influence of the physical charms of others. Modern, no less than Ancient History, supplies us with many most painful examples of what I refer to. If it were not so, indeed, History would be quite unreadable.

CECILY: I beg your pardon, Gwendolen, did you say Ernest?

GWENDOLEN: Yes.

CECILY: Oh, but it is not Mr. Ernest Worthing who is my guardian. It is his brother—his elder brother.

GWENDOLEN: [*Sitting down again.*] Ernest never mentioned to me that he had a brother.

CECILY: I am sorry to say they have not been on good terms for a long time.

GWENDOLEN: Ah! that accounts for it. And now that I think of it I have never heard any man mention his brother. The subject seems distasteful to most men. Cecily, you have lifted a load from my mind. I was growing almost anxious. It would have been terrible if any cloud had come across a friendship like ours, would it not? Of course you are quite, quite sure that it is not Mr. Ernest Worthing who is your guardian?

CECILY: Quite sure. [*A pause.*] In fact, I am going to be his.

GWENDOLEN: [*Enquiringly.*] I beg your pardon?

CECILY: [*Rather shy and confidingly.*] Dearest Gwendolen, there is no reason why I should make a secret of it to you. Our little county newspaper is sure to chronicle the fact next week. Mr. Ernest Worthing and I are engaged to be married.

GWENDOLEN: [*Quite politely, rising.*] My darling Cecily, I think there must be some slight error. Mr. Ernest Worthing is engaged to me. The announcement will appear in the "Morning Post" on Saturday at the latest.

CECILY: [*Very politely, rising.*] I am afraid you must be under some misconception. Ernest proposed to me exactly ten minutes ago. [*Shows diary.*]

GWENDOLEN: [*Examines diary through her lorgnette carefully.*] It is certainly very curious, for he asked me to be his wife yesterday afternoon at 5:30. If you would care to verify the incident, pray do so. [*Produces diary of her own.*] I never travel without my diary. One should always have something sensational to read in the train. I am so sorry, dear Cecily, if it is any disappointment to you, but I am afraid *I* have the prior claim.

CECILY: It would distress me more than I can tell you, dear Gwendolen, if it caused you any mental or physical anguish, but I feel bound to point out that since Ernest proposed to you he clearly has changed his mind.

GWENDOLEN: [*Meditatively.*] If the poor fellow has been entrapped into any foolish promise I shall consider it my duty to rescue him at once, and with a firm hand.

CECILY: [*Thoughtfully and sadly.*] Whatever unfortunate entanglement my dear boy may have got into, I will never reproach him with it after we are married.

GWENDOLEN: Do you allude to me, Miss Cardew, as an entanglement? You are presumptuous. On an occasion of this kind it becomes more than a moral duty to speak one's mind. It becomes a pleasure.

CECILY: Do you suggest. Miss Fairfax, that I entrapped Ernest into an engagement? How dare you? This is no time for wearing the shallow mask of manners. When I see a spade I call it a spade.

GWENDOLEN: [*Satirically.*] I am glad to say that I have never seen a spade. It is obvious that our social spheres have been widely different.

[*Enter* MERRIMAN, *followed by the footman. He carries a salver, table cloth, and plate stand.* CECILY *is about to retort. The presence of the servants exercises a restraining influence, under which both girls chafe.*]

MERRIMAN: Shall I lay tea here as usual, Miss?

CECILY: [*Sternly, in a calm voice.*] Yes, as usual. [MERRIMAN *begins to clear table and lay cloth. A long pause.* CECILY *and* GWENDOLEN *glare at each other.*]

GWENDOLEN: Are there many interesting walks in the vicinity, Miss Cardew?

CECILY: Oh! yes! a great many From the top of one of the hills quite close one can see five counties.

GWENDOLEN: Five counties! I don't think I should like that. I hate crowds.

CECILY: [*Sweetly.*] I suppose that is why you live in town? [GWENDOLEN *bites her lip, and beats her foot nervously with her parasol.*]

GWENDOLEN: [*Looking round.*] Quite a well-kept garden this is, Miss Cardew.

CECILY: So glad you like it, Miss Fairfax.

GWENDOLEN: I had no idea there were any flowers in the country.

CECILY: Oh, flowers are as common here. Miss Fairfax, as people are in London.

GWENDOLEN: Personally I cannot understand how anybody manages to exist in the country, if anybody who is anybody does. The country always bores me to death.

CECILY: Ah! This is what the newspapers call agricultural depression, is it not? I believe the aristocracy are suffering very much from it just at present. It is almost an epidemic amongst them, I have been told. May I offer you some tea, Miss Fairfax?

GWENDOLEN: [*With elaborate politeness.*] Thank you. [*Aside.*] Detestable girl! But I require tea!

CECILY: [*Sweetly.*] Sugar?

GWENDOLEN: [*Superciliously.*] No, thank you. Sugar is not fashionable any more.

[CECILY *looks angrily at her, takes up the tongs and puts four lumps of sugar into the cup.*]

CECILY: [*Severely.*] Cake or bread and butter?

GWENDOLEN: [*In a bored manner.*] Bread and butter, please. Cake is rarely seen at the best houses nowadays.

CECILY: [*Cuts a very large slice of cake, and puts it on the tray.*] Hand that to Miss Fairfax.

[MERRIMAN *does so, and goes out with footman.* GWENDOLEN *drinks the tea and makes a grimace. Puts down cup at once, reaches out her hand to the bread and butter, looks at it, and finds it is cake. Rises is in indignation.*]

GWENDOLEN: You have filled my tea with lumps of sugar, and though I asked most distinctly for bread and butter, you have given me cake. I am known for the gentleness of my disposition, and the extraordinary sweetness of my nature, but I warn you Miss Cardew, you may go too far.

CECILY: [*Rising.*] To save my poor, innocent, trusting boy from the machinations of any other girl there are no lengths to which I would no go.

GWENDOLEN: From the moment I saw you I distrusted you. I felt that you were false and deceitful. I am never deceived in such matters. My first impressions of people are invariably right.

CECILY: It seems to me, Miss Fairfax, that I am trespassing on your valuable time. No doubt you have many other calls of a similar character to make in the neighbourhood.

[*Enter* JACK.]

GWENDOLEN: [*Catching sight of him.*] Ernest! My own Ernest!

JACK: Gwendolen! Darling! [*Offers to kiss her.*]

GWENDOLEN: [*Drawing back.*] A moment! May I ask if you are engaged to be married to this young lady? [*Points to* CECILY.]

JACK: [*Laughing.*] To dear little Cecily! Of course not! What could have put such an idea into your pretty little head?

GWENDOLEN: Thank you. You may! [*Offers her cheek.*]

CECILY: [*Very sweetly.*] I knew there must be some misunderstanding, Miss Fairfax. The gentleman whose arm is at present round your waist is my dear guardian, Mr. John Worthing.

GWENDOLEN: I beg your pardon?

CECILY: This is Uncle Jack.

GWENDOLEN: [*Receding.*] Jack! Oh!

[*Enter* ALGERNON.]

CECILY: Here is Ernest.

ALGERNON: [*Goes straight over to* CECILY *without noticing anyone else.*] My own love! [*Offers to kiss her.*]

CECILY: [*Drawing back.*] A moment Ernest! May I ask you—are you engaged to be married to this young lady?

ALGERNON: [*Looking round.*] To what young lady? Good heavens! Gwendolen!

CECILY: Yes! to good heavens, Gwendolen. I mean to Gwendolen.

ALGERNON: [*Laughing.*] Of course not! What could have put such an idea into your pretty little head?

CECILY: Thank you. [*Presenting her cheek to be kissed.*] You may. [ALGERNON *kisses her.*]

GWENDOLEN: I felt there was some slight error, Miss Cardew. The gentleman who is now embracing you is my cousin, Mr. Algernon Moncrieff.

CECILY: [*Breaking away from* ALGERNON.] Algernon Moncrieff! Oh! [*The two girls move towards each other and put their arms round each other's waists as if for protection.*]

CECILY: Are you called Algernon?

ALGERNON: I cannot deny it.

CECILY: Oh!

GWENDOLEN: Is your name really John?

JACK: [*Standing rather proudly.*] I could deny it if I liked. I could deny anything if I liked. But my name certainly is John. It has been John for years.

CECILY: [*To* GWENDOLEN.] A gross deception has been practiced on both of us.

GWENDOLEN: My poor wounded Cecily!

CECILY: My sweet wronged Gwendolen!

GWENDOLEN: [*Slowly and seriously.*] You will call me sister, will you not? [*They embrace.* JACK *and* ALGERNON *groan and walk up and down.*]

CECILY: [*Rather brightly.*] There is just one question I would like to be allowed to ask my guardian.

GWENDOLEN: An admirable idea! Mr. Worthing, there is just one question I would like to be permitted to put to you. Where is your brother Ernest? We are both engaged to be married to your brother Ernest, so it is a matter of some importance to us to know where your brother Ernest is at present.

JACK: [*Slowly and hesitatingly.*] Gwendolen—Cecily—it is very painful for me to be forced to speak the truth. It is the first time in my life that I have ever been reduced to such a painful position, and I am really quite inexperienced in doing anything of the kind. However I will tell you quite frankly that I have no brother Ernest. I have no brother at all. I never had a brother in my life, and I certainly have not the smallest intention of ever having one in the future.

CECILY: [*Surprised.*] No brother at all?

JACK: [*Cheerily.*] None!

GWENDOLEN: [*Severely.*] Had you never a brother of any kind?

JACK: [*Pleasantly.*] Never. Not even of any kind.

GWENDOLEN: I am afraid it is quite clear, Cecily, that neither of us is engaged to be married to anyone.

CECILY: It is not a very pleasant position for a young girl suddenly to find herself in. Is it?

GWENDOLEN: Let us go into the house. They will hardly venture to come after us there.

CECILY: No, men are so cowardly, aren't they?

[*They retire into the house with scornful looks.*]

JACK: This ghastly state of things is what you call Bunburying, I suppose?

ALGERNON: Yes, and a perfectly wonderful Bunbury it is. The most wonderful Bunbury I have ever had in my life.

JACK: Well, you've no right whatsoever to Bunbury here.

ALGERNON: That is absurd. One has a right to Bunbury anywhere one chooses. Every serious Bunburyist knows that.

JACK: Serious Bunburyist! Good heavens!

ALGERNON: Well, one must be serious about something, if one wants to have any amusement in life. I happen to be serious about Bunburying. What on earth you are serious about I haven't got the remotest idea. About everything, I should fancy. You have such an absolutely trivial nature.

JACK: Well, the only small satisfaction I have in the whole of this wretched business is that your friend Bunbury is quite exploded. You won't be able to run down to the country quite so often as you used to do, dear Algy. And a very good thing too.

ALGERNON: Your brother is a little off colour, isn't he, dear Jack? You won't be able to disappear to London quite so frequently as your wicked custom was. And not a bad thing either.

JACK: As for your conduct towards Miss Cardew, I must say that your taking in a sweet, simple, innocent girl like that was quite inexcusable. To say nothing of the fact that she is my ward.

ALGERNON: I can see no possible defence at all for your deceiving a brilliant, clever, thoroughly experienced young lady like Miss Fairfax. To say nothing of the fact that she is my cousin.

JACK: I wanted to be engaged to Gwendolen, that is all. I love her.

ALGERNON: Well, I simply wanted to be engaged to Cecily. I adore her.

JACK: There is certainly no chance of your marrying Miss Cardew.

ALGERNON: I don't think there is much likelihood, Jack, of you and Miss Fairfax being united.

JACK: Well, that is no business of yours.

ALGERNON: If it was my business, I wouldn't talk about it. [*Begins to eat muffins.*] It is very vulgar to talk about one's business. Only people like stockbrokers do that, and then merely at dinner-parties.

JACK: How you can sit there, calmly eating muffins when we are in this horrible trouble, I can't make out. You seem to me to be perfectly heartless.

ALGERNON: Well, I can't eat muffins in an agitated manner. The butter would probably get on my cuffs. One should always eat muffins quite calmly. It is the only way to eat them.

JACK: I say it's perfectly heartless your eating muffins at all, under the circumstances.

ALGERNON: When I am in trouble, eating is the only thing that consoles me. Indeed, when I am in really great trouble, as anyone who knows me intimately will tell you. I refuse everything except food and drink. At the present moment I am eating muffins because I am unhappy. Besides, I am particularly fond of muffins. [*Rising.*]

JACK: [*Rising.*] Well, that is no reason why you should eat them all in that greedy way. [*Takes muffins from* ALGERNON.]

ALGERNON: [*Offering tea-cake.*] I wish you would have tea-cake instead. I don't like tea-cake.

JACK: Good heavens! I suppose a man may eat his own muffins in his own garden.

ALGERNON: But you have just said it was perfectly heartless to eat muffins.

JACK: I said it was perfectly heartless of you, under the circumstances. That is a very different thing.

ALGERNON: That may be. But the muffins are the same. [*He seizes the muffin-dish from* JACK.]

JACK: Algy, I wish to goodness you would go.

ALGERNON: You can't possibly ask me to go without having some dinner. It's absurd. I never go without my dinner. No one ever does, except vegetarians and people like that. Besides I have just made arrangements with Dr. Chasuble to be christened at a quarter to six under the name of Ernest.

JACK: My dear fellow, the sooner you give up that nonsense the better. I made arrangements this morning with Dr. Chasuble to be christened myself at 5.30, and I naturally will take the name of Ernest. Gwendolen would wish it. We can't both be christened Ernest. It's absurd. Besides, I have a perfect right to be christened if I like. There is no evidence at all that I ever have been christened by anybody. I should think it extremely probable I never was, and so does Dr. Chasuble. It is entirely different in your case. You have been christened already.

ALGERNON: Yes, but I have not been christened for years.

JACK: Yes, but you have been christened. That is the important thing.

ALGERNON: Quite so. So I know my constitution can stand it. If you are not quite sure about your ever having been christened, I must say I think it rather dangerous your venturing on it now. It might make you very unwell. You can hardly have forgotten that someone very closely connected with you was very nearly carried off this week in Paris by a severe chill.

JACK: Yes, but you said yourself that a severe chill was not hereditary.

ALGERNON: It usen't to be, I know—but I daresay it is now. Science is always making wonderful improvements in things.

JACK: [*Picking up the muffin-dish.*] Oh, that is nonsense; you are always talking nonsense.

ALGERNON: Jack, you are at the muffins again. I wish you wouldn't. There are only two left. [*Takes them.*] I told you I was particularly fond of muffins.

JACK: But I hate tea-cake.

ALGERNON: Why on earth then do you allow tea-cake to be served up for your guests? What ideas you have of hospitality!

JACK: Algernon! I have already told you to go. I don't want you here. Why don't you go?

ALGERNON: I haven't quite finished my tea yet! and there is still one muffin left.

[JACK *groans, and sinks into a chair.* ALGERNON *still continues eating.*]

ACT-DROP.

THIRD ACT

SCENE—*Morning-room at the Manor House.*

[GWENDOLEN *and* CECILY *are at the window, looking out into the garden.*]

GWENDOLEN: The fact that they did not follow us at once into the house, as anyone else would have done, seems to me to show that they have some sense of shame left.

CECILY: They have been eating muffins. That looks like repentance.

GWENDOLEN: [*After a pause.*] They don't seem to notice us at all. Couldn't you cough?

CECILY: But I haven't got a cough.

GWENDOLEN: They're looking at us. What effrontery!

CECILY: They're approaching. That's very forward of them.

GWENDOLEN: Let us preserve a dignified silence.

CECILY: Certainly. It's the only thing to do now.

[*Enter* JACK *followed by* ALGERNON. *They whistle some dreadful popular air from a British Opera.*]

GWENDOLEN: This dignified silence seems to produce an unpleasant effect.

CECILY: A most distasteful one.

GWENDOLEN: But we will not be the first to speak.

CECILY: Certainly not.

GWENDOLEN: Mr. Worthing, I have something very particular to ask you. Much depends on your reply.

CECILY: Gwendolen, your common sense is invaluable. Mr. Moncrieff, kindly answer me the following question. Why did you pretend to be my guardian's brother?

ALGERNON: In order that I might have an opportunity of meeting you.

CECILY: [*To* GWENDOLEN.] That certainly seems a satisfactory explanation, does it not?

GWENDOLEN: Yes, dear, if you can believe him.

CECILY: I don't. But that does not affect the wonderful beauty of his answer.

GWENDOLEN: True. In matters of grave importance, style, not sincerity is the vital thing. Mr. Worthing, what explanation can you offer to me for pretending to have a brother? Was it in order that you might have an opportunity of coming up to town to see me as often as possible?

JACK: Can you doubt it, Miss Fairfax?

GWENDOLEN: I have the gravest doubts upon the subject. But I intend to crush them. This is not the moment for German scepticism. [*Moving to* CECILY.] Their explanations appear to be quite satisfactory, especially Mr. Worthing's. That seems to me to have the stamp of truth upon it.

CECILY: I am more than content with what Mr. Moncrieff said. His voice alone inspires one with absolute credulity.

GWENDOLEN: Then you think we should forgive them?

CECILY: Yes. I mean no.

GWENDOLEN: True! I had forgotten. There are principles at stake that one cannot surrender. Which of us should tell them? The task is not a pleasant one.

CECILY: Could we not both speak at the same time?

GWENDOLEN: An excellent idea! I nearly always speak at the same time as other people. Will you take the time from me?

CECILY: *Certainly*. [GWENDOLEN *beats time with uplifted finger.*]

GWENDOLEN. AND CECILY: [*Speaking together.*] Your Christian names are still an insuperable barrier. That is all!

JACK AND ALGERNON: [*Speaking together.*] Our Christian names! Is that all? But we are going to be christened this afternoon.

GWENDOLEN: [*To* JACK.] For my sake you are prepared to do this terrible thing?

JACK: I am.

CECILY: [*To* ALGERNON.] To please me you are ready to face this fearful ordeal?

ALGERNON: I am!

GWENDOLEN: How absurd to talk of the equality of the sexes! Where questions of self-sacrifice are concerned, men are infinitely beyond us.

JACK: We are. [*Clasps hands with* ALGERNON.]

CECILY: They have moments of physical courage of which we women know absolutely nothing.

GWENDOLEN: [*To* JACK.] Darling!

ALGERNON: [*To* CECILY.] Darling! [*They fall into each other's arms.*]

[*Enter* MERRIMAN, *When he enters he coughs loudly, seeing the situation.*]

MERRIMAN: Ahem; Ahem! Lady Bracknell!

JACK: Good heavens!

[*Enter* LADY BRACKNELL. *The couples separate in alarm. Exit* MERRIMAN.]

LADY BRACKNELL: Gwendolen! What does this mean?

GWENDOLEN: Merely that I am engaged to be married to Mr. Worthing, mamma.

LADY BRACKNELL: Come here. Sit down. Sit down immediately. Hesitation of any kind is a sign of mental decay in the young, of physical weakness in the old. [*Turns to* JACK.] Apprised, sir, of my daughter's sudden flight by her trusty maid, whose confidence I purchased by means of a small coin, I followed her at once by a luggage train. Her unhappy father is, I am glad to say, under the impression that she is attending a more than usually lengthy lecture by the University Extension Scheme on the Influence of a Permanent Income on Thought. I do not propose to undeceive him. Indeed I have never undeceived him on any question. I would consider it wrong. But of course, you will clearly understand that all communication between yourself and my daughter must cease immediately from this moment. On this point, as indeed on all points, I am firm.

JACK: I am engaged to be married to Gwendolen, Lady Bracknell!

LADY BRACKNELL: You are nothing of the kind, so. And now, as regards Algernon! . . . Algernon!

ALGERNON: Yes, Aunt Augusta.

LADY BRACKNELL: May I ask if it is in this house that your invalid friend Mr. Bunbury resides?

ALGERNON: [*Stammering.*] *Oh! No*! Bunbury doesn't live here. Bunbury is somewhere else at present. In fact, Bunbury is dead.

LADY BRACKNELL: Dead! When did Mr. Bunbury die? His death must have been extremely sudden.

ALGERNON: [*Airily.*] Oh! I killed Bunbury this afternoon. I mean poor Bunbury died this afternoon.

LADY BRACKNELL: What did he die of?

ALGERNON: Bunbury? Oh, he was quite exploded.

LADY BRACKNELL: Exploded! Was he the victim of a revolutionary outrage? I was not aware that Mr. Bunbury was interested in social legislation. If so, he is well punished for his morbidity.

ALGERNON: My dear Aunt Augusta, I mean he was found out! The doctors found out that Bunbury could not live, that is what I mean—so Bunbury died.

LADY BRACKNELL: He seems to have had great confidence in the opinion of his physicians. I am glad, however, that he made up his mind at the last to some definite course of action, and acted under proper medical advice. And now that we have finally got rid of this Mr. Bunbury, may I ask, Mr. Worthing, who is that young person whose hand my nephew Algernon is now holding in what seems to me a peculiarly unnecessary manner?

JACK: That lady is Miss Cecily Cardew, my ward. [LADY BRACKNELL *bows coldly to* CECILY.]

ALGERNON: I am engaged to be married to Cecily, Aunt Augusta.

LADY BRACKNELL: I beg your pardon?

CECILY: Mr. Moncrieff and I are engaged to be married, Lady Bracknell.

LADY BRACKNELL: [*With a shiver, crossing to the sofa and sitting down.*] I do not know whether there is anything peculiarly exciting in the air of this particular part of Hertfordshire, but the number of engagements that go on seems to me considerably above the proper average that statistics have laid down for our guidance. I think some preliminary enquiry on my part would not be out of place. Mr. Worthing, is Miss Cardew at all connected with any of the larger railway stations in London? I merely desire information. Until yesterday I had no idea that there were any families or persons whose origin was a Terminus. [JACK *looks perfectly furious, but restrains himself.*]

JACK: [*In a clear, cold voice.*] Miss Cardew is the granddaughter of the late Mr. Thomas Cardew of 149 Belgrave Square, S.W.; Gervase Park, Dorking, Surrey; and the Sporran, Fifeshire, N.B.

LADY BRACKNELL: That sounds not unsatisfactory. Three addresses always inspire confidence, even in tradesmen. But what proof have I of their authenticity?

JACK: I have carefully preserved the Court Guides of the period. They are open to your inspection, Lady Bracknell.

LADY BRACKNELL: [*Grimly.*] I have known strange errors in that publication.

JACK: Miss Cardew's family solicitors are Messrs. Markby, Markby, and Markby.

LADY BRACKNELL: Markby, Markby, and Markby? A firm of the very highest position in their profession. Indeed I am told that one of the Mr. Markbys is occasionally to be seen at dinner parties. So far I am satisfied.

JACK: [*Very irritably.*] How extremely kind of you, Lady Bracknell! I have also in my possession, you will be pleased to hear, certificates of Miss Cardew's birth, baptism, whooping cough, registration, vaccination, confirmation, and the measles; both the German and the English variety.

LADY BRACKNELL: Ah! A life crowded with incident, I see; though perhaps somewhat too exciting for a young girl. I am not myself in favour of premature experiences. [*Rises, looks at her watch.*] Gwendolen! the time approaches for our departure. We have not a moment to lose. As a matter of form, Mr. Worthing, I had better ask you if Miss Cardew has any little fortune?

JACK: Oh! about a hundred and thirty thousand pounds in the Funds. That is all. Good-bye, Lady Bracknell. So pleased to have seen you.

LADY BRACKNELL: [*Sitting down again.*] A moment, Mr. Worthing. A hundred and thirty thousand pounds! And in the Funds! Miss Cardew seems to me a most attractive young lady, now that I look at her. Few girls of the present day have any really solid qualities, any of the qualities that last, and improve with time. We live, I regret to say, in an age of surfaces. [*To* CECILY.] Come over here, dear. [CECILY *goes across.*] Pretty child! your dress is sadly simple, and your hair seems almost as Nature might have left it. But we can soon alter all that. A thoroughly experienced French maid produces a really marvellous result in a very brief space of time. I remember recommending one to young Lady Lancing, and after three months her own husband did not know her.

JACK: [*Aside.*] And after six months nobody knew her.

LADY BRACKNELL: [*Glares at* JACK *for a few moments. Then bends, with a practised smile, to* CECILY.] Kindly turn round, sweet child. [CECILY *turns completely round.*] No, the side view is what I want. [CECILY *presents her profile.*] Yes, quite as I expected. There are distinct social possibilities in your profile. The two weak points in our age are its want of principle and its want of profile. The chin a little higher, dear. Style largely depends on the way the chin is worn. They are worn very high, just at present. Algernon!

ALGERNON: Yes, Aunt Augusta!

LADY BRACKNELL: There are distinct social possibilities in Miss Cardew's profile.

ALGERNON: Cecily is the sweetest, dearest, prettiest girl in the whole world. And I don't care twopence about social possibilities.

LADY BRACKNELL: Never speak disrespectfully of Society, Algernon. Only people who can't get into it do that. [*To* CECILY.] Dear child, of course you know that Algernon has nothing but his debts to depend upon. But I do not approve of mercenary marriages. When I married Lord Bracknell I had no fortune of any kind. But I never dreamed for a moment of allowing that to stand in my way. Well, I suppose I must give my consent.

ALGERNON: Thank you, Aunt Augusta.

LADY BRACKNELL: Cecily, you may kiss me!

CECILY: [*Kisses her.*] Thank you, Lady Bracknell.

LADY BRACKNELL: You may also address me as Aunt Augusta for the future.

CECILY: Thank you, Aunt Augusta.

LADY BRACKNELL: The marriage, I think, had better take place quite soon.

ALGERNON: Thank you, Aunt Augusta.

CECILY: Thank you, Aunt Augusta.

LADY BRACKNELL: To speak frankly, I am not in favour of long engagements. They give people the opportunity of finding out each other's character before marriage, which I think is never advisable.

JACK: I beg your pardon for interrupting you, Lady Bracknell, but this engagement is quite out of the question. I am Miss Cardew's guardian, and she cannot marry without my consent until she comes of age. That consent I absolutely decline to give.

LADY BRACKNELL: Upon what grounds may I ask? Algernon is an extremely, I may almost say an ostentatiously, eligible young man. He has nothing, but he looks everything. What more can one desire?

JACK: It pains me very much to have to speak frankly to you, Lady Bracknell, about your nephew, but the fact is that I do not approve at all of his moral character. I suspect him of being untruthful. [ALGERNON *and* CECILY *look at him in indignant amazement.*]

LADY BRACKNELL: Untruthful! My nephew Algernon? Impossible! He is an Oxonian.

JACK: I fear there can be no possible doubt about the matter. This afternoon, during my temporary absence in London on an important question of romance, he obtained admission to my house by means of the false pretense of being my brother. Under an assumed name he drank, I've just been informed by my butler, an entire pint bottle of my Perrier Jouet, Brut, '89; a wine I was specially reserving for myself. Continuing his disgraceful deception, he succeeded in the course of the afternoon in alienating the affections of my only ward. He subsequently stayed to tea and devoured every single muffin. And what makes his conduct all the more heartless is, that he was perfectly well aware from the first that I have no brother, that I never had a brother, and that I don't intend to have a brother, not even of any kind. I distinctly told him so myself yesterday afternoon.

LADY BRACKNELL: Ahem! Mr. Worthing, after careful consideration I have decided entirely to overlook my nephew's conduct to you.

JACK: That is very generous of you, Lady Bracknell. My own decision, however, is unalterable. I decline to give my consent.

LADY BRACKNELL: [*To* CECILY.] Come here, sweet child. [CECILY *goes over.*] How old are you, dear?

CECILY: Well, I am really only eighteen, but I always admit to twenty when I go to evening parties.

LADY BRACKNELL: You are perfectly right in making some slight alteration. Indeed, no woman should ever be quite accurate about her age. It looks so calculating. . . . [*In a meditative manner.*] Eighteen, but admitting to twenty at evening parties. Well, it will not be very long before you are of age and free from the restraints of tutelage. So I don't think your guardian's consent is, after all, a matter of any importance.

JACK: Pray excuse me, Lady Bracknell, for interrupting you again, but it is only fair to tell you that according to the terms of her grandfather's will Miss Cardew does not come legally of age till she is thirty-five.

LADY BRACKNELL: That does not seem to one to be a grave objection. Thirty-five is a very attractive age. London society is full of women of the very highest birth who have, of their own free choice, remained thirty-five for years. Lady Dumbleton is an instance in point. To my own knowledge she has been thirty-five ever since she arrived at the age of forty, which was many years ago now. I see no reason why our dear Cecily should not be even still more attractive at the age you mention than she is at present. There will be a large accumulation of property.

CECILY: Algy, could you wait for me till I was thirty-five?

ALGERNON: Of course I could, Cecily. You know I could.

CECILY: Yes. I felt it instinctively, but I couldn't wait all that time. I hate waiting even five minutes for anybody. It always makes me rather cross. I am not punctual myself, I know, but I do like punctuality in others, and waiting, even to be married, is quite out of the question.

ALGERNON: Then what is to be done, Cecily?

CECILY: I don't know, Mr. Moncrieff.

LADY BRACKNELL: My dear Mr. Worthing, as Miss Cardew states positively that she cannot wait till she is thirty-five—a remark which I am bound to say seems to me to show a somewhat impatient nature—I would beg of you to reconsider your decision.

JACK: But, my dear Lady Bracknell, the matter is entirely in your own hands. The moment you consent to my marriage with Gwendolen, I will most gladly allow your nephew to form an alliance with my ward.

LADY BRACKNELL: [*Rising and drawing herself up.*] You must be quite aware that what you propose is out of the question.

JACK: Then a passionate celibacy is all that any of us can look forward to.

LADY BRACKNELL: That is not the destiny I propose for Gwendolen. Algernon, of course, can choose for himself. [*Pulls out her watch.*] Come, dear; [GWENDOLEN *rises.*] we have already missed five, if not six, trains. To miss any more might expose us to comment on the platform.

[*Enter* DR. CHASUBLE.]

CHASUBLE: Everything is quite ready for the christenings.

LADY BRACKNELL: The christenings, sir! Is not that somewhat premature?

CHASUBLE: [*Looking rather puzzled, and pointing to* JACK *and* ALGERNON.] Both these gentlemen have expressed a desire for immediate baptism.

LADY BRACKNELL: At their age? The idea is grotesque and irreligious! Algernon, I forbid you to be baptised. I will not hear of such excesses. Lord Bracknell would be highly displeased if he learned that that was the way in which you wasted your time and money.

CHASUBLE: Am I to understand then that there are to be no christenings at all this afternoon?

JACK: I don't think that, as things are now, it would be of much practical value to either of us, Dr. Chasuble.

CHASUBLE: I am grieved to hear such sentiments from you, Mr. Worthing. They savour of the heretical views of the Anabaptists, views that I have completely refuted in four of my unpublished sermons. However, as your present mood seems to be one peculiarly secular, I will return to the church at once. Indeed, I have just been informed by the pew-opener that for the last hour and a half Miss Prism has been waiting for me in the vestry.

LADY BRACKNELL: [*Starting.*] Miss Prism! Did I hear you mention a Miss Prism?

CHASUBLE: Yes, Lady Bracknell. I am on my way to join her.

LADY BRACKNELL: Pray allow me to detain you for a moment. This matter may prove to be one of vital importance to Lord Bracknell and myself. Is this Miss Prism a female of repellent aspect, remotely connected with education?

CHASUBLE: [*Somewhat indignantly.*] She is the most cultivated of ladies and the very picture of respectability.

LADY BRACKNELL: It is obviously the same person. May I ask what position she holds in your household?

CHASUBLE: [*Severely.*] I am a celibate, madam.

JACK: [*Interposing.*] Miss Prism, Lady Bracknell, has been for the last three years Miss Cardew's esteemed governess and valued companion.

LADY BRACKNELL: In spite of what I hear of her, I must see her at once. Let her be sent for.

CHASUBLE: [*Looking off.*] She approaches; she is nigh.

[*Enter* MISS PRISM *hurriedly.*]

MISS PRISM: I was told you expected me in the vestry, dear Canon. I have been waiting for you there for an hour and three quarters. [*Catches sight of* LADY BRACKNELL *who has fixed her with a stony glare.* MISS PRISM *grows pale and quails. She looks anxiously round as if desirous to escape.*]

LADY BRACKNELL: [*In a severe, judicial voice.*] Prism! [MISS PRISM *bows her head in shame.*] Come here, Prism! [MISS PRISM *approaches in a humble manner.*] Prism! Where is that baby? [*General consternation. The* CANON *starts back in horror.* ALGERNON *and* JACK *pretend to be anxious to shield* CECILY *and* GWENDOLEN *from hearing the details of a terrible public scandal.*] Twenty-eight years ago, Prism, you left Lord Bracknell's house, Number 104, Upper Grosvenor Street, in charge of a perambulator that contained a baby, of the male sex. You never returned. A few weeks later, through the elaborate investigations of the Metropolitan police, the perambulator was discovered at midnight, standing by itself in a remote corner of Bayswater. It contained the manuscript of a three-volume novel of more than usually revolting sentimentality. [MISS PRISM *starts in involuntary indignation.*] But the baby was not there! [*Everyone looks at* MISS PRISM.] Prism! Where is that baby? [*A pause.*]

MISS PRISM: Lady Bracknell, I admit with shame that I do not know. I only wish I did. The plain facts of the case are these. On the morning of the day you mention, a day that is forever branded on my memory, I prepared as usual to take the baby out in its perambulator. I had also with me a somewhat old, but capacious hand-bag, in which I had intended to place the manuscript of a work of fiction that I had written during my few unoccupied hours. In a moment of mental abstraction, for which I can never forgive myself, I deposited the manuscript in the basinette, and placed the baby in the hand-bag.

JACK: [*Who has been listening attentively.*] But where did you deposit the hand-bag?

MISS PRISM: Do not ask me, Mr. Worthing.

JACK: Miss Prism, this is a matter of no small importance to me. I insist on knowing where you deposited the hand-bag that contained that infant.

MISS PRISM: I left it in the cloak room of one of the larger railway stations in London.

JACK: What railway station?

MISS PRISM: [*Quite crushed.*] Victoria. The Brighton line. [*Sinks into a chair.*]

JACK: I must retire to my room for a moment. Gwendolen, wait for me here.

GWENDOLEN: If you are not too long, I will wait here for you all my life.

[*Exit* JACK *in great excitement.*]

CHASUBLE: What do you think this means, Lady Bracknell?

LADY BRACKNELL: I dare not even suspect, Dr. Chasuble. I need hardly tell you that in families of high position strange coincidences are not supposed to occur. They are hardly considered the thing.

[*Noises heard overhead as if someone was throwing trunks about. Everyone looks up.*]

CECILY: Uncle Jack seems strangely agitated.

CHASUBLE: Your guardian has a very emotional nature.

LADY BRACKNELL: This noise is extremely unpleasant. It sounds as if he was having an argument. I dislike arguments of any kind. They are always vulgar, and often convincing.

CHASUBLE: [*Looking up.*] It has stopped now. [*The noise is redoubled.*]

LADY BRACKNELL: I wish he would arrive at some conclusion.

GWENDOLEN: This suspense is terrible. I hope it will last.

[*Enter* JACK *with a hand-bag of black leather in his hand.*]

JACK: [*Rushing over to* MISS PRISM.] Is this the hand-bag, Miss Prism? Examine it carefully before you speak. The happiness of more than one life depends on your answer.

MISS PRISM: [*Calmly.*] It seems to be mine. Yes, here is the injury it received through the upsetting of a Gower Street omnibus in younger and happier days. Here is the stain on the lining caused by the explosion of a temperance beverage, an incident that occurred at Leamington. And here, on the lock, are my initials. I had forgotten that in an extravagant mood I had them placed there. The bag is undoubtedly mine. I am delighted to have it so unexpectedly restored to me. It has been a great inconvenience being without it all these years.

JACK: [*In a pathetic voice.*] Miss Prism, more is restored to you than this hand-bag. I was the baby you placed in it.

MISS PRISM: [*Amazed.*] You?

JACK: [*Embracing her.*] Yes . . . mother!

MISS PRISM: [*Recoiling in indignant astonishment.*] Mr. Worthing! I am unmarried!

JACK: Unmarried! I do not deny that is a serious blow. But after all, who has a right to cast a stone against one who has suffered? Cannot repentance wipe out an act of folly? Why should there be one law for men, and another for women? Mother, I forgive you. [*Tries to embrace her again.*]

MISS PRISM: [*Still more indignant.*] Mr. Worthing, there is some error. [*Pointing to* LADY BRACKNELL.] There is the lady who can tell you who you really are.

JACK: [*After a pause.*] Lady Bracknell, I hate to seem inquisitive, but would you kindly inform me who I am?

LADY BRACKNELL: I am afraid that the news I have to give you will not altogether please you. You are the son of my poor sister, Mrs. Moncrieff, and consequently Algernon's elder brother.

JACK: Algy's elder brother! Then I have a brother after all. I knew I had a brother! I always said I had a brother! Cecily—how could you have ever doubted that I had a brother? [*Seizes hold of* ALGERNON.] Dr. Chasuble, my unfortunate brother. Miss Prism, my unfortunate brother. Gwendolen, my unfortunate brother. Algy, you young scoundrel, you will have to treat me with more respect in the future. You have never behaved to me like a brother in all your life.

ALGERNON: Well, not till today, old boy, I admit. I did my best, however, though I was out of practise. [*Shakes hands.*]

GWENDOLEN: [*To* JACK.] My own! But what own are you? What is your Christian name, now that you have become someone else?

JACK: Good heavens! . . . I had quite forgotten that point. Your decision on the subject of my name is irrevocable, I suppose?

GWENDOLEN: I never change, except in my affections.

CECILY: What a noble nature you have, Gwendolen!

JACK: Then the question had better be cleared up at once. Aunt Augusta, a moment. At the time when Miss Prism left me in the hand-bag, had I been christened already?

LADY BRACKNELL: Every luxury that money could buy, including christening, had been lavished on you by your fond and doting parents.

JACK: Then I was christened! That is settled. Now, what name was I given? Let me know the worst.

LADY BRACKNELL: Being the eldest son you were naturally christened after your father.

JACK: [*Irritably.*] Yes, but what was my father's Christian name?

LADY BRACKNELL: [*Meditatively.*] I cannot at the present moment recall what the General's Christian name was. But I have no doubt he had one. He was eccentric, I admit. But only in later years. And that was the result of the Indian climate, and marriage, and indigestion, and other things of that kind.

JACK: Algy! Can't you recollect what our father's Christian name was?

ALGERNON: My dear boy, we were never even on speaking terms. He died before I was a year old.

JACK: His name would appear in the Army Lists of the period, I suppose. Aunt Augusta?

LADY BRACKNELL: The General was essentially a man of peace, except in his domestic life. But I have no doubt his name would appear in any military directory.

JACK: The Army Lists of the last forty years are here. These delightful records should have been my constant study. [*Rushes to bookcase and tears the books out.*] M. Generals . . . Mallam, Maxbohm, Magley, what ghastly names they have—Markby, Migsby, Mobbs, Moncrieff! Lieutenant 1840, Captain, Lieutenant-Colonel, Colonel, General 1869, Christian names, Ernest John. [*Puts book very quietly down and speaks quite calmly.*] I always told you, Gwendolen, my name was Ernest, didn't I? Well, it is Ernest after all. I mean it naturally is Ernest.

LADY BRACKNELL: Yes, I remember now that the General was called Ernest. I knew I had some particular reason for disliking the name.

GWENDOLEN: Ernest! My own Ernest? I felt from the first that you could have no other name!

JACK: Gwendolen, it is a terrible thing for a man to find out suddenly that all his life he has been speaking nothing but the truth. Can you forgive me?

GWENDOLEN: I can. For I feel that you are sure to change.

JACK: My own one!

CHASUBLE: [*To* MISS PRISM.] Lætitia! [*Embraces her.*]

MISS PRISM: [*Enthusiastically.*] Frederick! At last!

ALGERNON: Cecily! [*Embraces her.*] At last!

JACK: Gwendolen! [*Embraces her.*] At last!

LADY BRACKNELL: My nephew, you seem to be displaying signs of triviality.

JACK: On the contrary, Aunt Augusta. I've now realized for the first time in my life the vital Importance of Being Earnest.

CURTAIN.

HENRIK IBSEN (1828–1906) was born in a small Norwegian timber port south of present-day Oslo. Although his parents were quite wealthy when he was born, by the time Ibsen was a young boy, his father's general store business had collapsed and with it went the family's fortune. Ibsen began to work full-time as a pharmacist's apprentice when he was fifteen, and later tried to enroll at the University of Christiana, but failed to pass the entrance exams. Despite his shortened schooling, Ibsen read and wrote poetry from a young age. Already comfortable in that medium, he composed his first play, *Catiline* (1849), in verse as well. Shortly after writing *Catiline*, Ibsen produced another play *The Burial Mound* (published 1854) and began working as an assistant stage manager at the Norwegian Theater, where, in response to the Norwegians' desire to assert their national identity and independence from Sweden, one of his job requirements was to write an original play each year that celebrated his country's history.

In 1863, after years of hard work managing the theater and writing Norwegian sagas such as *The Feast of Solhaug* (1856), *Lady Inger of Ostraat* (1857), and *The Vikings at Helgeland* (1858), Ibsen convinced the Norwegian government to provide him with a series of grants (which later became an annual stipend) to travel and write so that he could gain a writerly perspective on his homeland and achieve a critical distance from its past. The success of this plan was realized in his pair of plays *Brand* (1866) and *Peer Gynt* (1867). Written soon after he began traveling, these works have been hailed as central texts in Norwegian literature.

The second stage of Ibsen's career as a playwright has been dubbed his **realist** or **naturalist drama** period. In plays such as *Pillars of Society* (1877), *A Dollhouse* (1879), *Ghosts* (1881), and *An Enemy of the People* (1882), Ibsen began to shift his dramatic focus away from historical plot structures, national heroes, and legendary events and toward everyday people in contemporary society and their personal relationships. To give the audience the feeling that they were listening to events that could be happening in their own lives, Ibsen also had to shift from writing verse to writing prose.

A Dollhouse premiered in Copenhagen, Denmark, in December 1879 and in January 1880 at the Christiana Theater in Norway. It was produced in English for the first time in June 1882 as *The Child Wife* in Milwaukee, Wisconsin, but was only performed three times before closing. Like Ibsen himself, *A Dollhouse* is concerned with the place and power of women in the author's society. He supported women's rights as a **feminist** cause; for although Norwegian women had by 1879 gained equal inheritance and the right to an independent living, rising nationalism worked to cast men and women in traditional roles, and unmarried women (or women like Nora and Mrs. Linde) continued to face a bleak situation in a **patriarchal** society. In his revealing Notes for *A Dollhouse*, Ibsen writes that "a woman cannot be herself in the society of the present day, which is an exclusively masculine society, with laws framed by men and with a judicial system that judges feminine conduct from a masculine point of view." Thus, although Nora is proud of having committed forgery to save her husband's life, Torvald, who is guided by a masculine sense of honor and ethics, is horrified at what she has done: "The catastrophe approaches, inexorably, inevitably. Despair, conflict, and destruction."[1]

NOTE

1. Henrik Ibsen, "Notes for the Modern Tragedy," trans. A. G. Chater, in *A Sourcebook on Naturalist Theatre*, ed. Christopher Innes (London and New York: Routledge, 2000), 79.

Related Works: Chopin, "The Story of an Hour"; Mukherjee, "A Wife's Story"; Wideman, "What We Cannot Speak About We Must Pass Over in Silence"; Shakespeare, Sonnet 116; Dickinson, "Hope is the thing with feathers"; Levertov, "The Ache of Marriage"; Shakespeare, *The Taming of the Shrew*.

A Dollhouse (Et Dukkehjem)

Translated by R. Farquharson Sharp

Characters

Torvald Helmer, a lawyer and bank manager
Nora, his wife
Doctor Rank
Mrs. Christine Linde
Nils Krogstad, a lawyer and bank clerk
Ivar, Bob, and Emmy, the Helmers' three young children
Anne, their nurse
Helen, a housemaid
A Porter

The action takes place in Helmer's apartment.

ACT 1

Scene. *A room furnished comfortably and tastefully, but not extravagantly. At the back, a door to the right leads to the entrance hall, another to the left leads to* Helmer's *study. Between the doors stands a piano. In the middle of the left-hand wall is a door, and beyond it a window. Near the window are a round table, armchairs and a small sofa. In the right-hand wall, at the farther end, another door; and on the same side, nearer the footlights, a stove, two easy chairs and a rocking-chair; between the stove and the door, a small table. Engravings on the walls: a cabinet with chair and other small objects: a small book case with well-bound books. The floors are carpeted, and a fire burns in the stove. It is winter.*

A bell rings in the hall; shortly afterwards the door is heard to open. Enter Nora, *humming a tune and in high spirits. She is in outdoor dress and carries a number of parcels; these she lays on the table to the right. She leaves the outer door open after her, and through it is seen a* Porter *who is carrying a Christmas Tree and a basket, which he gives to the* Maid *who has opened the door.*

Nora: Hide the Christmas Tree carefully, Helen. Be sure the children do not see it till this evening, when it is dressed. [*to the* Porter *taking out her purse.*] How much?

Porter: Sixpence.

Nora: There is a shilling. No, keep the change. [*The* Porter *thanks her, and goes out.* Nora *shuts the door. She is laughing to herself, as she takes off her hat and coat. She takes a packet of macaroons from her pocket and eats one or two; then goes cautiously to her husband's door and listens.*] Yes, he is in.

[*Still humming, she goes to the table on the right.*]

Helmer: [*calls out from his room*] Is that my little lark twittering out there?

Nora: [*busy opening some of the parcels*] Yes, it is!

Helmer: Is my little squirrel bustling about?

Nora: Yes!

HELMER: When did my squirrel come home?

NORA: Just now. [*puts the bag of macaroons into her pocket and wipes her mouth.*] Come in here, Torvald, and see what I have bought.

HELMER: Don't disturb me. [*A little later, he opens the door and looks into the room, pen in hand.*] Bought, did you say? All these things? Has my little spendthrift been wasting money again?

NORA: Yes, but, Torvald, this year we really can let ourselves go a little. This is the first Christmas that we have not needed to economise.

HELMER: Still, you know, we can't spend money recklessly.

NORA: Yes, Torvald, we may be a wee bit more reckless now, mayn't we? Just a tiny wee bit! You are going to have a big salary and earn lots and lots of money.

HELMER: Yes, after the New Year; but then it will be a whole quarter before the salary is due.

NORA: Pooh! we can borrow till then.

HELMER: Nora! [*goes up to her and takes her playfully by the ear.*] The same little featherhead! Suppose, now, that I borrowed fifty pounds to-day, and you spent it all in the Christmas week, and then on New Year's Eve a slate fell on my head and killed me, and—

NORA: [*putting her hands over his mouth*] Oh! don't say such horrid things.

HELMER: Still, suppose that happened—what then?

NORA: If that were to happen, I don't suppose I should care whether I owed money or not.

HELMER: Yes, but what about the people who had lent it?

NORA: They? Who would bother about them? I should not know who they were.

HELMER: That is like a woman! But seriously, Nora, you know what I think about that. No debt, no borrowing. There can be no freedom or beauty about a home life that depends on borrowing and debt. We two have kept bravely on the straight road so far, and we will go on the same way for the short time longer that there need be any struggle.

NORA: [*moving towards the stove*] As you please, Torvald.

HELMER: [*following her*] Come, come, my little skylark must not droop her wings. What is this! Is my little squirrel out of temper? [*taking out his purse.*] Nora, what do you think I have got here?

NORA: [*turning around quickly*] Money!

HELMER: There you are. [*gives her some money*] Do you think I don't know what a lot is wanted for housekeeping at Christmas-time?

NORA: [*counting*] Ten shillings—a pound—two pounds! Thank you, thank you. Torvald; that will keep me going for a long time.

HELMER: Indeed it must.

NORA: Yes, yes, it will. But come here and let me show you what I have bought. And all so cheap! Look, here is a new suit for Ivar, and a sword; and a horse and a trumpet for Bob; and a doll and dolly's bedstead for Emmy—they are very plain, but anyway she will soon break them in pieces. And here are dress-lengths and handkerchiefs for the maids; old Anne ought really to have something better.

HELMER: And what is in this parcel?

NORA: [*crying out*] No, no! you mustn't see that till this evening.

HELMER: Very well. But now tell me, you extravagant little person, what would you like for yourself.

NORA: For myself? Oh, I am sure I don't want anything.

HELMER: Yes, but you must. Tell me something reasonable that you would particularly like to have.

NORA: No, I really can't think of anything—unless, Torvald—

HELMER: Well?

NORA: [*playing with his coal buttons, and without raising her eyes to his*] If you really want to give me something, you might—you might—

HELMER: Well, out with it!

NORA: [*speaking quickly*] You might give me money, Torvald. Only just as much as you can afford; and then one of these days I will buy something with it.

HELMER: But, Nora—

NORA: Oh, do! dear Torvald; please, please do! Then I will wrap it up in beautiful gilt paper and hang it on the Christmas Tree. Wouldn't that be fun?

HELMER: What are little people called that are always wasting money?

NORA: Spendthrifts—I know. Let us do as you suggest, Torvald, and then I shall have time to think what I am most in want of. That is a very sensible plan, isn't it?

HELMER: [*smiling*] Indeed it is—that is to say, if you were really to save out of the money I give you, and then really buy something for yourself. But if you spend it all on the housekeeping and any number of unnecessary things, then I merely have to pay up again.

NORA: Oh but, Torvald—

HELMER: You can't deny it, my dear little Nora. [*puts his arm round her waist*] It's a sweet little spendthrift, but she uses up a deal of money. One would hardly believe how expensive such little persons are!

NORA: It's a shame to say that, I do really save all I can.

HELMER: [*laughing*] That's very true—all you can. But you can't save anything!

NORA: [*smiling quietly and happily*] You haven't any idea how many expenses we skylarks and squirrels have, Torvald.

HELMER: You are an odd little soul. Very like your father. You always find some new way of wheedling money out of me, and, as soon as you have got it, it seems to melt in your hands. You never know where it has gone. Still, one must take you as you are. It is in the blood; for indeed it is true that you can inherit these things, Nora.

NORA: Ah, I wish I had inherited many of papa's qualities.

HELMER: And I would not wish you to be anything but just what you are, my sweet little skylark. But, do you know, it strikes me that you are looking rather—what shall I say—rather uneasy to-day?

NORA: Do I?

HELMER: You do, really. Look straight at me.

NORA: [*looks at him*] Well?

HELMER: [*wagging his finger at her*] Hasn't Miss Sweet-Tooth been breaking rules in town to-day?

NORA: No; what makes you think that?

HELMER: Hasn't she paid a visit to the confectioner's?

NORA: No, I assure you, Torvald—

HELMER: Not been nibbling sweets?

NORA: No, certainly not.

HELMER: Not even taken a bite at a macaroon or two?

NORA: No, Torvald, I assure you really—

HELMER: There, there, of course I was only joking

NORA: [*going to the table on the right*] I should not think of going against your wishes.

HELMER: No, I am sure of that! besides, you gave me your word—[*going up to her*] Keep your little Christmas secrets to yourself, my darling. They will all be revealed to-night when the Christmas Tree is lit, no doubt.

NORA: Did you remember to invite Doctor Rank?

HELMER: No. But there is no need; as a matter of course he will come to dinner with us. However, I will ask him when he comes in this morning. I have ordered some good wine. Nora, you can't think how I am looking forward to this evening.

NORA: So am I! And how the children will enjoy themselves, Torvald!

HELMER: It is splendid to feel that one has a perfectly safe appointment, and a big enough income. It's delightful to think of, isn't it?

NORA: It's wonderful!

HELMER: Do you remember last Christmas? For a full three weeks before-hand you shut yourself up every evening till long after midnight, making ornaments for the Christmas Tree and all the other fine things that were to be a surprise to us. It was the dullest three weeks I ever spent!

NORA: I didn't find it dull.

HELMER: [*smiling*] But there was precious little result, Nora.

NORA: Oh, you shouldn't tease me about that again. How could I help the cat's going in and tearing everything to pieces?

HELMER: Of course you couldn't, poor little girl. You had the best of intentions to please us all, and that's the main thing. But it is a good thing that our hard times are over.

NORA: Yes, it is really wonderful.

HELMER: This time I needn't sit here and be dull all alone, and you needn't ruin your dear eyes and your pretty little hands—

NORA: [*clapping her hands*] No, Torvald, I needn't any longer, need I! It's wonderfully lovely to hear you say so! [*taking his arm*] Now I will tell you how I have been thinking we ought to arrange things, Torvald. As soon as Christmas is over—[*A bell rings in the hall.*] There's the bell. [*She tidies the room a little.*] There's someone at the door. What a nuisance!

HELMER: If it is a caller, remember I am not at home.

MAID: [*in the doorway*] A lady to see you, ma'am—a stranger.

NORA: Ask her to come in.

MAID: [*to* HELMER] The doctor came at the same time, sir.

HELMER: Did he go straight into my room?

MAID: Yes sir.

[HELMER *goes into his room. The* MAID *ushers in* MRS. LINDE, *who is in travelling dress, and shuts the door.*]

MRS. LINDE: [*in a dejected and timid voice*] How do you do, Nora?

NORA: [*doubtfully*] How do you do—

MRS. LINDE: You don't recognise me, I suppose.

NORA: No, I don't know—yes, to be sure. I seem to—[*suddenly*] Yes! Christine! Is it really you?

MRS. LINDE: Yes, it is I.

NORA: Christine! To think of my not recognising you! And yet how could I—[*in a gentle voice*] How you have altered, Christine!

MRS. LINDE: Yes, I have indeed. In nine, ten long years—

NORA: Is it so long since we met? I suppose it is. The last eight years have been a happy time for me, I can tell you. And so now you have come into the town, and have taken this long journey in winter—that was plucky of you.

MRS. LINDE: I arrived by steamer this morning.

NORA: To have some fun at Christmas-time, of course. How delightful! We will have such fun together! But take off your things. You are not cold, I hope. [*helps her*] Now we will sit down by the stove, and be cosy. No, take this arm chair; I will sit here in the rocking-chair. [*takes her hands*] Now you look like your old self again; it was only the first moment—You are a little paler, Christine, and perhaps a little thinner.

MRS. LINDE: And much, much older, Nora.

NORA: Perhaps a little older; very, very little; certainly not much. [*stops suddenly and speaks seriously*] What a thoughtless creature I am, chattering away like this. My poor, dear Christine, do forgive me.

MRS. LINDE: What do you mean, Nora?

NORA: [*gently*] Poor Christine, you are a widow.

MRS. LINDE: Yes; it is three years ago now.

NORA: Yes, I knew; I saw it in the papers. I assure you, Christine, I meant ever so often to write to you at the time, but I always put it off and something always prevented me.

MRS. LINDE: I quite understand, dear.

NORA: It was very bad of me, Christine. Poor thing, how you must have suffered. And he left you nothing?

MRS. LINDE: No.

NORA: And no children?

MRS. LINDE: No.

NORA: Nothing at all, then?

MRS. LINDE: Not even any sorrow or grief to live upon.

NORA: [*looking incredulously at her*] But, Christine, is that possible?

MRS. LINDE: [*smiles sadly and strokes her hair*] It sometimes happens, Nora.

NORA: So you are quite alone. How dreadfully sad that must be. I have three lovely children. You can't see them just now, for they are out with their nurse. But now you must tell me all about it.

MRS. LINDE: No, no; I want to hear you.

NORA: No, you must begin. I mustn't be selfish to-day; to-day I must only think of your affairs. But there is one thing I must tell you. Do you know we have just had a great piece of good luck?

MRS. LINDE: No, what is it?

NORA: Just fancy, my husband has been made manager of the Bank!

MRS. LINDE: Your husband? What good luck!

NORA: Yes, tremendous! A barrister's profession is such an uncertain thing, especially if he won't undertake unsavoury cases; and naturally Torvald has never been willing to do that, and I quite agree with him. You may imagine how pleased we are! He is to take up his work in the Bank at the New Year, and then he will have a big salary and lots of commissions. For the future we can live quite differently—we can do just as we like. I feel so relieved and so happy, Christine! It will be splendid to have heaps of money and not need to have any anxiety, won't it?

MRS. LINDE: Yes, anyhow I think it would be delightful to have what one needs.

NORA: No, not only what one needs, but heaps and heaps of money.

MRS. LINDE: [*smiling*] Nora, Nora haven't you learnt sense yet? In our schooldays you were a great spendthrift.

NORA: [*laughing*] Yes, that is what Torvald says now. [*wags her finger at her*] But "Nora, Nora" is not so silly as you think. We have not been in a position for me to waste money. We have both had to work.

MRS. LINDE: You too?

NORA: Yes; odds and ends, needlework, crochet-work, embroidery, and that kind of thing. [*dropping her voice*] And other things as well. You know Torvald left his office when we were married? There was no prospect of promotion there, and he had to try and earn more than before. But during the first year he overworked himself dreadfully. You see, he had to make money every way he could, and he worked early and late; but he couldn't stand it, and fell dreadfully ill, and the doctors said it was necessary for him to go south.

MRS. LINDE: You spent a whole year in Italy didn't you?

NORA: Yes. It was no easy matter to get away, I can tell you. It was just as Ivar was born; but naturally we had to go. It was a wonderfully beautiful journey, and it saved Torvald's life. But it cost a tremendous lot of money, Christine.

MRS. LINDE: So I should think.

NORA: It cost about two hundred and fifty pounds. That's a lot, isn't it?

MRS. LINDE: Yes, and in emergencies like that it is lucky to have the money.

NORA: I ought to tell you that we had it from papa.

MRS. LINDE: Oh, I see. It was just about that time that he died, wasn't it?

NORA: Yes; and, just think of it, I couldn't go and nurse him. I was expecting little Ivar's birth every day and I had my poor sick Torvald to look after. My dear, kind father—I never saw him again, Christine. That was the saddest time I have known since our marriage.

MRS. LINDE: I know how fond you were of him. And then you went off to Italy?

Nora: Yes; you see we had money then, and the doctors insisted on our going, so we started a month later.

Mrs. Linde: And your husband came back quite well?

Nora: As sound as a bell!

Mrs. Linde: But—the doctor?

Nora: What doctor?

Mrs. Linde: I thought your maid said the gentleman who arrived here just as I did was the doctor?

Nora: Yes, that was Doctor Rank, but he doesn't come here professionally. He is our greatest friend, and comes in at least once every day. No, Torvald has not had an hour's illness since then, and our children are strong and healthy and so am I. [*jumps up and claps her hands*] Christine! Christine! it's good to be alive and happy!—But how horrid of me; I am talking of nothing but my own affairs. [*sits on a stool near her, and rests her arms on her knees*] You mustn't be angry with me. Tell me, is it really true that you did not love your husband? Why did you marry him?

Mrs. Linde: My mother was alive then, and was bedridden and helpless, and I had to provide for my two younger brothers; so I did not think I was justified in refusing his offer.

Nora: No, perhaps you were quite right. He was rich at that time, then?

Mrs. Linde: I believe he was quite well off. But his business was a precarious one; and, when he died, it all went to pieces and there was nothing left.

Nora: And then?—

Mrs. Linde: Well, I had to turn my hand to anything I could find—first a small shop, then a small school, and so on. The last three years have seemed like one long working-day, with no rest. Now it is at an end, Nora. My poor mother needs me no more, for she is gone; and the boys do not need me either; they have got situations and can shift for themselves.

Nora: What a relief you must feel it—

Mrs. Linde: No, indeed; I only feel my life unspeakably empty. No one to live for any more. [*gets up restlessly*] That was why I could not stand the life in my little backwater any longer. I hope it may be easier here to find something which will busy me and occupy my thoughts. If only I could have the good luck to get some regular work—office work of some kind—

Nora: But, Christine, that is so frightfully tiring, and you look tired out now. You had far better go away to some watering-place.

Mrs. Linde: [*walking to the window*] I have no father to give me money for a journey, Nora.

Nora: [*rising*] Oh, don't be angry with me.

Mrs. Linde: [*going up to her*] It is you that must not be angry with me, dear. The worst of a position like mine is that it makes one so bitter. No one to work for, and yet obliged to be always on the look-out for chances. One must live, and so one becomes selfish. When you told me of the happy turn your fortunes have taken—you will hardly believe it—I was delighted not so much on your account as on my own.

Nora: How do you mean?—Oh, I understand. You mean that perhaps Torvald could get you something to do.

Mrs. Linde: Yes, that was what I was thinking of.

Nora: He must, Christine. Just leave it to me; I will broach the subject very cleverly—I will think of something that will please him very much. It will make me so happy to be of some use to you.

Mrs. Linde: How kind you are. Nora, to be so anxious to help me! It is doubly kind in you, for you know so little of the burdens and troubles of life.

Nora: I—? I know so little of them?

Mrs. Linde: [*smiling*] My dear! Small household cares and that sort of thing!—You are a child, Nora.

Nora: [*tosses her head and crosses the stage*] You ought not to be so superior.

Mrs. Linde: No?

Nora: You are just like the others. They all think that I am incapable of anything really serious—

Mrs. Linde: Come, come—

Nora: —that I have gone through nothing in this world of cares.

Mrs. Linde: But, my dear Nora, you have just told me all your troubles.

Nora: Pooh!—those were trifles. [*lowrning her voice*] I have not told you the important thing.

Mrs. Linde: The important thing? What do you mean?

Nora: You look down upon me altogether, Christine—but you ought not to. You are proud, aren't you, of having worked so hard and so long for your mother?

Mrs. Linde: Indeed, I don't look down on any one. But it is true that I am both proud and glad to think that I was privileged to make the end of my mother's life almost free from care.

Nora: And you are proud to think of what you have done for your brothers.

Mrs. Linde: I think I have the right to be.

Nora: I think so, too. But now, listen to this; I too have something to be proud of and glad of.

Mrs. Linde: I have no doubt you have. But what do you refer to?

Nora: Speak low. Suppose Torvald were to hear! He mustn't on any account—no one in the world must know, Christine, except you.

Mrs. Linde: But what is it?

Nora: Come here [*pulls her down on the sofa beside her*] Now I will show you that I too have something to be proud and glad of. It was I who saved Torvald's life.

Mrs. Linde: "Saved"? How?

Nora: I told you about our trip to Italy. Torvald would never have recovered if he had not gone there—

Mrs. Linde: Yes, but your father gave you the necessary funds.

Nora: [*smiling*] Yes, that is what Torvald and all the others think, but—

Mrs. Linde: But—

Nora: Papa didn't give us a shilling. It was I who procured the money.

Mrs. Linde: You? All that large sum?

NORA: Two hundred and fifty pounds. What do you think of that?

MRS. LINDE: But, Nora, how could you possibly do it? Did you win a prize in the Lottery?

NORA: [*contemptuously*] In the Lottery? There would have been no credit in that.

MRS. LINDE: But where did you get it from, then?

NORA: [*humming and smiling with an air of mystery*] Hm, hm! Aha!

MRS. LINDE: Because you couldn't have borrowed it.

NORA: Couldn't I? Why not?

MRS. LINDE: No, a wife cannot borrow without her husband's consent.

NORA: [*tossing her head*] Oh, if it is a wife who has any head for business—a wife who has the wit to be a little bit clever—

MRS. LINDE: I don't understand it at all, Nora.

NORA: There is no need you should. I never said I had borrowed the money. I may have got it some other way. [*lies back on the sofa*] Perhaps I got it from some other admirer. When anyone is as attractive as I am—

MRS. LINDE: You are a mad creature.

NORA: Now, you know you're full of curiosity, Christine.

MRS. LINDE: Listen to me, Nora dear. Haven't you been a little bit imprudent?

NORA: [*sits up straight*] Is it imprudent to save your husband's life?

MRS. LINDE: It seems to me imprudent, without his knowledge, to—

NORA: But it was absolutely necessary that he should not know! My goodness, can't you understand that? It was necessary he should have no idea what a dangerous condition he was in. It was to me that the doctors came and said that his life was in danger, and that the only thing to save him was to live in the south. Do you suppose I didn't try, first of all, to get what I wanted as if it were for myself? I told him how much I should love to travel abroad like other young wives; I tried tears and entreaties with him; I told him that he ought to remember the condition I was in, and that he ought to be kind and indulgent to me; I even hinted that he might raise a loan. That nearly made him angry, Christine. He said I was thoughtless, and that it was his duty as my husband not to indulge me in my whims and caprices—as I believe he called them. Very well I thought, you must be saved—and that was how I came to devise a way out of the difficulty—

MRS. LINDE: And did your husband never get to know from your father that the money had not come from him?

NORA: No, never. Papa died just at that time. I had meant to let him into the secret and beg him never to reveal it. But he was so ill then—alas, there never was any need to tell him.

MRS. LINDE: And since then have you never told your secret to your husband?

NORA: Good Heavens, no! How could you think so? A man who has such strong opinions about these things! And besides, how painful and humiliating it would be for Torvald, with his manly independence, to know that he owed me anything! It would upset our mutual relations altogether; our beautiful happy home would no longer be what it is now.

MRS. LINDE: Do you mean never to tell him about it?

NORA: [*meditatively, and with a half smile*] Yes—some day, perhaps, after many years, when I am no longer as nice-looking as I am now. Don't laugh at me! I mean of course, when Torvald is no longer as devoted to me as he is now; when my dancing and dressing-up and reciting have palled on him; then it may be a good thing to have something in reserve—[*breaking off*] What nonsense! That time will never come. Now, what do you think of my great secret, Christine? Do you still think I am of no use? I can tell you, too, that this affair has caused me a lot of worry. It has been by no means easy for me to meet my engagements punctually. I may tell you that there is something that is called, in business, quarterly interest, and another thing called payment in instalments, and it is always so dreadfully difficult to manage them. I have had to save a little here and there, where I could, you understand. I have not been able to put aside much from my housekeeping money, for Torvald must have a good table. I couldn't let my children be shabbily dressed; I have felt obliged to use up all he gave me for them, the sweet little darlings!

MRS. LINDE: So it has all had to come out of your own necessaries of life, poor Nora?

NORA: Of course. Besides, I was the one responsible for it. Whenever Torvald has given me the money for new dresses and such things, I have never spent more than half of it; I have always bought the simplest and cheapest things. Thank Heaven, any clothes look well on me, and so Torvald has never noticed it. But it was often very hard on me, Christine—because it is delightful to be really well dressed, isn't it?

MRS. LINDE: Quite so.

NORA: Well, then I have found other ways of earning money. Last winter I was lucky enough to get a lot of copying to do; so I locked myself up and sat writing every evening until quite late at night. Many a time I was desperately tired; but all the same it was a tremendous pleasure to sit there working and earning money. It was like being a man.

MRS. LINDE: How much have you been able to pay off in that way?

NORA: I can't tell you exactly. You see, it is very difficult to keep an account of a business matter of that kind. I only know that I have paid every penny that I could scrape together. Many a time I was at my wit's end. [*smiles*] Then I used to sit here and imagine that a rich old gentleman had fallen in love with me—

MRS. LINDE: What! Who was it?

NORA: Be quiet!—that he had died; and that when his will was opened it contained, written in big letters, the instruction: "The lovely Mrs. Nora Helmer is to have all I possess paid over to her at once in cash."

MRS. LINDE: But, my dear Nora—who could the man be?

NORA: Good gracious, can't you understand? There was no old gentleman at all; it was only something that I used to sit here and imagine, when I couldn't think of any way of procuring money. But it's all the same now; the tiresome old person can stay where he is, as far as I am concerned; I don't care about him or his will either, for I am free from care now. [*jumps up*] My goodness, it's delightful to think of, Christine! Free from care! To be able to be free from care, quite free from care; to be able to play and romp with the children; to be able to keep the house beautifully and have everything just as Torvald likes it! And, think of it, soon the spring will come and the big blue sky! Perhaps we shall be able to take a little trip—perhaps I shall see the sea again! Oh, it's a wonderful thing to be alive and be happy. [*A bell is heard in the hall.*]

MRS. LINDE: [*rising*] There is the bell; perhaps I had better go.

NORA: No, don't go; no one will come in here; it is sure to be for Torvald.

SERVANT: [*at the hall door*] Excuse me, ma'am—there is a gentleman to see the master, and as the doctor is with him—

NORA: Who is it?

KROGSTAD: [*at the door*] It is I, Mrs. Helmer. [MRS. LINDE *starts, trembles, and turns to the window.*]

NORA: [*takes a step towards him, and speaks in a strained, low voice*] You? What is it? What do you want to see my husband about?

KROGSTAD: Bank business—in a way. I have a small post in the Bank, and I hear your husband is to be our chief now—

NORA: Then it is—

KROGSTAD: Nothing but dry business matters, Mrs. Helmer; absolutely nothing else.

NORA: Be so good as to go into the study, then. [*She bows indifferently to him and shuts the door into the hall; then comes back and makes up the fire in the stove.*]

MRS. LINDE: Nora—who was that man?

NORA: A lawyer, of the name of Krogstad.

MRS. LINDE: Then it really was he.

NORA: Do you know the man?

MRS. LINDE: I used to—many years ago. At one time he was a solicitor's clerk in our town.

NORA: Yes, he was.

MRS. LINDE: He is greatly altered.

NORA: He made a very unhappy marriage.

MRS. LINDE: He is a widower now, isn't he?

NORA: With several children. There now, it is burning up.

[*Shuts the door of the stove and moves the rocking-chair aside.*]

MRS. LINDE: They say he carries on various kinds of business.

NORA: Really! Perhaps he does; I don't know anything about it. But don't let us think of business; it is so tiresome.

DOCTOR RANK: [*comes out of* HELMER'S *study. Before he shuts the door he calls to him.*] No, my dear fellow, I won't disturb you; I would rather go in to your wife for a little while. [*shuts the door and sees* MRS. LINDE] I beg your pardon; I am afraid I am disturbing you too.

NORA: No, not at all. [*introducing him*] Doctor Rank, Mrs. Linde.

RANK: I have often heard Mrs. Linde's name mentioned here. I think I passed you on the stairs when I arrived, Mrs. Linde?

MRS. LINDE: Yes, I go up very slowly; I can't manage stairs well.

RANK: Ah! some slight internal weakness?

MRS. LINDE: No, the fact is I have been overworking myself.

RANK: Nothing more than that? Then I suppose you have come to town to amuse yourself with our entertainments?

MRS. LINDE: I have come to look for work.

RANK: Is that a good cure for overwork?

MRS. LINDE: One must live, Doctor Rank.

RANK: Yes, the general opinion seems to be that it is necessary.

NORA: Look here, Doctor Rank—you know you want to live.

RANK: Certainly. However wretched I may feel, I want to prolong the agony as long as possible. All my patients are like that. And so are those who are morally diseased; one of them, and a bad case too, is at this very moment with Helmer—

MRS. LINDE: [*sadly*] Ah!

NORA: Whom do you mean?

RANK: A lawyer of the name of Krogstad, a fellow you don't know at all. He suffers from a diseased moral character, Mrs. Helmer; but even he began talking of its being highly important that he should live.

NORA: Did he? What did he want to speak to Torvald about?

RANK: I have no idea; I only heard that it was something about the Bank.

NORA: I didn't know this—what's his name—Krogstad had anything to do with the Bank.

RANK: Yes, he has some sort of appointment there. [*to* MRS. LINDE] I don't know whether you find also in your part of the world that there are certain people who go zealously snuffing about to smell out moral corruption, and, as soon as they have found some, put the person concerned into some lucrative position where they can keep their eye on him. Healthy natures are left out in the cold.

MRS. LINDE: Still I think the sick are those who most need taking care of.

RANK: [*shrugging his shoulders*] Yes, there you are. That is the sentiment that is turning Society into a sickhouse.

[NORA, *who has been absorbed in her thoughts, breaks out into smothered laughter and claps her hands.*]

RANK: Why do you laugh at that? Have you any notion what Society really is?

NORA: What do I care about tiresome Society? I am laughing at something quite different, something extremely amusing. Tell me, Doctor Rank, are all the people who are employed in the Bank dependent on Torvald now?

RANK: Is that what you find so extremely amusing?

NORA: [*smiling and humming*] That's my affair! [*walking about the room*] It's perfectly glorious to think that we have—that Torvald has so much power over so many people. [*takes the packet from her pocket*] Doctor Rank, what do you say to a macaroon?

RANK: What, macaroons? I thought they were forbidden here.

NORA: Yes, but these are some Christine gave me.

MRS. LINDE: What! I?—

NORA: Oh, well, don't be alarmed! You couldn't know that Torvald had forbidden them. I must tell you that he is afraid they will spoil my teeth. But, bah!—once in a way—That's so, isn't it, Doctor Rank? By your leave? [*puts a macaroon into his mouth*] You must have one too, Christine. And I shall have one, just a little one—or at most two. [*walking about*] I am tremendously happy. There is just one thing in the world now that I should dearly love to do.

RANK: Well, what is that?

NORA: It's something I should dearly love to say, if Torvald could hear me.

RANK: Well, why can't you say it?

NORA: No, I daren't; it's so shocking.

MRS. LINDE: Shocking?

RANK: Well, I should not advise you to say it. Still, with us you might. What is it you would so much like to say if Torvald could hear you?

NORA: I should just love to say—Well, I'm damned!

RANK: Are you mad?

MRS. LINDE: Nora, dear—!

RANK: Say it, here he is!

NORA: [*hiding the packet*] Hush! Hush! Hush!

[HELMER *comes out of his room, with his coat over his arm and his hat in his hands.*]

NORA: Well, Torvald dear, have you got rid of him?

HELMER: Yes, he has just gone.

NORA: Let me introduce you—this is Christine, who has come to town.

HELMER: Christine—? Excuse me, but I don't know—

NORA: Mrs. Linde, dear; Christine Linde.

HELMER: Of course. A school friend of my wife's, I presume?

MRS. LINDE: Yes, we have known each other since then.

NORA: And just think, she has taken a long journey in order to see you.

HELMER: What do you mean?

MRS. LINDE: No, really, I—

NORA: Christine is tremendously clever at book-keeping, and she is frightfully anxious to work under some clever man, so as to perfect herself—

HELMER: Very sensible, Mrs. Linde.

NORA: And when she heard you had been appointed manager of the Bank—the news was telegraphed, you know—she travelled here as quick as she could. Torvald, I am sure you will be able to do something for Christine, for my sake, won't you?

HELMER: Well, it is not altogether impossible. I presume you are a widow, Mrs. Linde?

MRS. LINDE: Yes.

HELMER: And have had some experience of book-keeping?

MRS. LINDE: Yes, a fair amount.

HELMER: Ah! well, it's very likely I may be able to find something for you—

NORA: [*clapping her hands*] What did I tell you? What did I tell you?

HELMER: You have just come at a fortunate moment, Mrs. Linde.

MRS. LINDE: How am I to thank you?

HELMER: There is no need. [*puts on his coat*] But to-day you must excuse me—

RANK: Wait a minute; I will come with you.

[*Brings his fur coat from the hall and warms it at the fire.*]

NORA: Don't be long away, Torvald dear.

HELMER: About an hour, not more.

NORA: Are you going too, Christine?

MRS. LINDE: [*putting on her cloak*] Yes, I must go and look for a room.

HELMER: Oh, well then, we can walk down the street together.

NORA: [*helping her*] What a pity it is we are so short of space here: I am afraid it is impossible for us—

MRS. LINDE: Please don't think of it! Good-bye, Nora dear, and many thanks.

NORA: Good-bye for the present. Of course you will come back this evening. And you too, Dr. Rank. What do you say? If you are well enough? Oh, you must be! Wrap yourself up well.

[*They go to the door all talking together. Children's voices are heard on the staircase.*]

NORA: There they are. There they are! [*She runs to open the door. The* NURSE *comes in with the children.*] Come in! Come in! [*stoops and kisses them*] Oh, you sweet blessings! Look at them, Christine! Aren't they darlings?

RANK: Don't let us stand here in the draught.

HELMER: Come along, Mrs. Linde; the place will only be bearable for a mother now!

[RANK, HELMER *and* MRS. LINDE *go downstairs. The* NURSE *comes forward with the children;* NORA *shuts the hall door.*]

NORA: How fresh and well you look! Such red cheeks!—like apples and roses. [*The children all talk at once while she speaks to them.*] Have you had great fun? That's splendid! what, you pulled both Emmy and Bob along on the sledge?—both at once?—that was good. You are a clever boy, Ivar. Let me take her for a little, Anne. My sweet little baby doll! [*takes the baby from the* MAID *and dances it up and down*] Yes, yes, mother will dance with Bob too. What! Have you been snow-balling? I wish I had been there too! No, no, I will take their things off, Anne; please let me do it, it is such fun. Go in now, you look half frozen. There is some coffee for you on the stove.

[*The* NURSE *goes into the room on the left.* NORA *takes off the children's things and throws them about, while they all talk to her at once.*]

NORA: Really! Did a big dog run after you? But it didn't bite you? No, dogs don't bite nice little dolly children. You mustn't look at the parcels, Ivar. What are they? Ah, I daresay you would like to know. No, no—it's something nasty! Come, let us have a game! What shall we play at? Hide and Seek? Yes, we'll play Hide and Seek. Bob shall hide first. Must I hide? Very well, I'll hide first.

[*She and the children laugh and shout, and romp in and out of the room; at last* NORA *hides under the table, the children rush in and look for her, but do not see her; they hear her smothered laughter, run to the table, lift up the cloth and find her. Shouts of laughter. She crawls forward and pretends to frighten them. Fresh laughter. Meanwhile there has been a knock at the hall door, but none of them has noticed it. The door is half opened, and* KROGSTAD *appears. He waits a little; the game goes on.*]

KROGSTAD: Excuse me, Mrs. Helmer.

NORA: [*with a stifled cry, turns round and gets up on to her knees*] Ah! what do you want?

KROGSTAD: Excuse me, the outer door was ajar; I suppose someone forgot to shut it.

NORA: [*rising*] My husband is out, Mr. Krogstad.

KROGSTAD: I know that.

NORA: What do you want here, then?

KROGSTAD: A word with you.

NORA: With me?—[*to the children, gently*] Go in to nurse. What? No, the strange man won't do mother any harm. When he has gone we will have another game. [*She takes the children into the room on the left, and shuts the door after them.*] You want to speak to me?

KROGSTAD: Yes, I do.

NORA: To-day? It is not the first of the month yet.

KROGSTAD: No, it is Christmas Eve, and it will depend on yourself what sort of a Christmas you will spend.

NORA: What do you want? To-day it is absolutely impossible for me—

KROGSTAD: We won't talk about that till later on. This is something different. I presume you can give me a moment?

NORA: Yes—yes, I can—although—

KROGSTAD: Good. I was in Olsen's Restaurant and saw your husband going down the street—

NORA: Yes?

KROGSTAD: With a lady.

NORA: What then?

KROGSTAD: May I make so bold as to ask if it was a Mrs. Linde?

NORA: It was.

KROGSTAD: Just arrived in town?

NORA: Yes, to-day.

KROGSTAD: She is a great friend of yours, isn't she?

NORA: She is. But I don't see—

KROGSTAD: I knew her too, once upon a time.

NORA: I am aware of that.

KROGSTAD: Are you? So you know all about it; I thought as much. Then I can ask you, without beating about the bush—is Mrs. Linde to have an appointment in the Bank?

NORA: What right have you to question me. Mr. Krogstad?—You, one of my husband's subordinates! But since you ask, you shall know. Yes, Mrs. Linde *is* to have an appointment. And it was I who pleaded her cause, Mr. Krogstad, let me tell you that.

KROGSTAD: I was right in what I thought, then.

NORA: [*walking up and down the stage*] Sometimes one has a tiny little bit of influence. I should hope. Because one is a woman, it does not necessarily follow that—. When anyone is in a subordinate position, Mr. Krogstad, they should really be careful to avoid offending anyone who—who—

KROGSTAD: Who has influence?

NORA: Exactly.

KROGSTAD: [*changing his tone*] Mrs. Helmer, you will be so good as to use your influence on my behalf.

NORA: What? What do you mean?

KROGSTAD: You will be so kind as to see that I am allowed to keep my subordinate position in the Bank.

NORA: What do you mean by that? Who proposes to take your post away from you?

KROGSTAD: Oh, there is no necessity to keep up the pretence of ignorance. I can quite understand that your friend is not very anxious to expose herself to the chance of rubbing shoulders with me; and I quite understand, too, whom I have to thank for being turned out.

NORA: But I assure you—

KROGSTAD: Very likely; but, to come to the point, the time has come when I should advise you to use your influence to prevent that.

NORA: But, Mr. Krogstad, I *have* no influence.

KROGSTAD: Haven't you? I thought you said yourself just now—

NORA: Naturally I did not mean you to put that construction on it. I! What should make you think I have any influence of that kind with my husband?

KROGSTAD: Oh, I have known your husband from our student days. I don't suppose he is any more unassailable than other husbands.

NORA: If you speak slightingly of my husband, I shall turn you out of the house.

KROGSTAD: You are bold, Mrs. Helmer.

NORA: I am not afraid of you any longer. As soon as the New Year comes, I shall in a very short time be free of the whole thing.

KROGSTAD: [*controlling himself*] Listen to me, Mrs. Helmer. If necessary, I am prepared to fight for my small post in the Bank as if I were fighting for my life.

NORA: So it seems.

KROGSTAD: It is not only for the sake of the money; indeed, that weighs least with me in the matter. There is another reason—well, I may as well tell you. My position is this. I dare-say you know, like everybody else, that once, many years ago, I was guilty of an indiscretion.

NORA: I think I have heard something of the kind.

KROGSTAD: The matter never came into court; but every way seemed to be closed to me after that. So I took to the business that you know of. I had to do something; and, honestly, I don't think I've been one of the worst. But now I must cut myself free from all that. My sons are growing up; for their sake I must try and win back as much respect as I can in the town. This post in the Bank was like the first step up for me—and now your husband is going to kick me downstairs again into the mud.

NORA: But you must believe me, Mr. Krogstad; it is not in my power to help you at all.

KROGSTAD: Then it is because you haven't the will; but I have means to compel you.

NORA: You don't mean that you will tell my husband that I owe you money?

KROGSTAD: Hm!—suppose I were to tell him?

NORA: It would be perfectly infamous of you. [*sobbing*] To think of his learning my secret, which has been my joy and pride, in such an ugly, clumsy way—that he should learn it from you! And it would put me in a horribly disagreeable position—

KROGSTAD: Only disagreeable?

NORA: [*impetuously*] Well, do it, then!—and it will be the worse for you. My husband will see for himself what a blackguard you are, and you certainly won't keep your post then.

KROGSTAD: I asked you if it was only a disagreeable scene at home that you were afraid of?

NORA: If my husband does get to know of it, of course he will at once pay you what is still owing, and we shall have nothing more to do with you.

KROGSTAD: [*coming a step nearer*] Listen to me, Mrs. Helmer. Either you have a very bad memory or you know very little of business. I shall be obliged to remind you of a few details.

NORA: What do you mean?

KROGSTAD: When your husband was ill, you came to me to borrow two hundred and fifty pounds.

NORA: I didn't know any one else to go to.

KROGSTAD: I promised to get you that amount—

NORA: Yes, and you did so.

KROGSTAD: I promised to get you that amount, on certain conditions. Your mind was so taken up with your husband's illness, and you were so anxious to get the money for your journey, that you seem to have paid no attention to the conditions of our bargain. Therefore it will not be amiss if I remind you of them. Now, I promised to get the money on the security of a bond which I drew up.

NORA: Yes, and which I signed.

KROGSTAD: Good. But below your signature there were a few lines constituting your father a surety for the money; those lines your father should have signed.

NORA: Should? He did sign them.

KROGSTAD: I had left the date blank; that is to say your father should himself have inserted the date on which he signed the paper. Do you remember that?

NORA: Yes, I think I remember—

KROGSTAD: Then I gave you the bond to send by post to your father. Is that not so?

NORA: Yes.

KROGSTAD: And you naturally did so at once, because five or six days afterwards you brought me the bond with your father's signature. And then I gave you the money.

NORA: Well, haven't I been paying it off regularly?

KROGSTAD: Fairly so, yes. But—to come back to the matter in hand—that must have been a very trying time for you, Mrs. Helmer?

NORA: It was, indeed.

KROGSTAD: Your father was very ill, wasn't he?

NORA: He was very near his end.

KROGSTAD: And died soon afterwards?

NORA: Yes.

KROGSTAD: Tell me, Mrs. Helmer, can you by any chance remember what day your father died?—on what day of the month, I mean.

NORA: Papa died on the 29th of September.

KROGSTAD: That is correct; I have ascertained it for myself. And, as that is so, there is a discrepancy [*taking a paper from his pocket*] which I cannot account for.

NORA: What discrepancy? I don't know—

KROGSTAD: The discrepancy consists, Mrs. Helmer, in the fact that your father signed this bond three days after his death.

NORA: What do you mean? I don't understand—

KROGSTAD: Your father died on the 29th of September. But, look here; your father has dated his signature the 2nd of October. It is a discrepancy, isn't it? [NORA *is silent.*] Can you explain it to me? [NORA *is still silent.*] It is a remarkable thing, too, that the words "2nd of October," as well as the year, are not written in your father's handwriting but in one that I think I know. Well, of course it can be explained; your father may have forgotten to date his signature, and someone else may have dated it haphazard before they knew of his death. There is no harm in that. It all depends on the signature of the name; and *that* is genuine, I suppose, Mrs. Helmer? It was your father himself who signed his name here?

NORA: [*after a short pause, throws her head up and looks defiantly at him*] No, it was not. It was I that wrote papa's name.

KROGSTAD: Are you aware that is a dangerous confession?

NORA: In what way? You shall have your money soon.

KROGSTAD: Let me ask you a question; why did you not send the paper to your father?

NORA: It was impossible; papa was so ill. If I had asked him for his signature, I should have had to tell him what the money was to be used for; and when he was so ill himself I couldn't tell him that my husband's life was in danger—it was impossible.

KROGSTAD: It would have been better for you if you had given up your trip abroad.

NORA: No, that was impossible. That trip was to save my husband's life; I couldn't give that up.

KROGSTAD: But did it never occur to you that you were committing a fraud on me?

NORA: I couldn't take that into account; I didn't trouble myself about you at all. I couldn't bear you, because you put so many heartless difficulties in my way, although you knew what a dangerous condition my husband was in.

KROGSTAD: Mrs. Helmer, you evidently do not realise clearly what it is that you have been guilty of. But I can assure you that my one false step, which lost me all my reputation, was nothing more or nothing worse than what you have done.

NORA: You? Do you ask me to believe that you were brave enough to run a risk to save your wife's life?

KROGSTAD: The law cares nothing about motives.

NORA: Then it must be a very foolish law.

KROGSTAD: Foolish or not, it is the law by which you will be judged, if I produce this paper in court.

NORA: I don't believe it. Is a daughter not to be allowed to spare her dying father anxiety and care? Is a wife not to be allowed to save her husband's life? I don't know much about law; but I am certain that there must be laws permitting such things as that. Have you no knowledge of such laws—you who are a lawyer? You must be a very poor lawyer, Mr. Krogstad.

KROGSTAD: Maybe. But matters of business—such business as you and I have had together—do you think I don't understand that? Very well. Do as you please. But let me tell you this—if I lose my position a second time, you shall lose yours with me.

[*He bows, and goes out through the hall.*]

NORA: [*appears buried in thought for a short time, then tosses her head*] Nonsense! Trying to frighten me like that!—I am not so silly as he thinks. [*begins to busy herself putting the children's things in order*] And yet—? No, it's impossible! I did it for love's sake.

THE CHILDREN: [*in the doorway on the left*] Mother, the stranger man has gone out through the gate.

NORA: Yes, dears, I know. But, don't tell anyone about the stranger man. Do you hear? Not even papa.

CHILDREN: No, mother; but will you come and play again?

NORA: No, no—not now.

CHILDREN: But, mother, you promised us.

NORA: Yes, but I can't now. Run away in; I have such a lot to do. Run away in, my sweet little darlings. [*She gets them into the room by degrees and shuts the door on them; then sits down on the sofa, takes up a piece of needlework and sews a few stitches, but soon stops.*] No! [*throws down the work, gets up, goes to the hall door and calls out*] Helen! bring the Tree in. [*goes to the table on the left, opens a drawer and stops again*] No, no! it is quite impossible!

MAID: [*coming in with the Tree*] Where shall I put it, ma'am?

NORA: Here, in the middle of the floor.

MAID: Shall I get you anything else?

NORA: No, thank you. I have all I want.

[*Exit* MAID.]

NORA: [*begins dressing the tree*] A candle here—and flowers here—. The horrible man! It's all nonsense—there's nothing wrong. The Tree shall be splendid! I will do everything I can think of to please you, Torvald!—I will sing for you, dance for you— [HELMER *comes in with some papers under his arm*] Oh! are you back already?

HELMER: Yes. Has anyone been here?

NORA: Here? No.

HELMER: That is strange. I saw Krogstad going out of the gate.

NORA: Did you? Oh yes, I forgot, Krogstad was here for a moment.

HELMER: Nora, I can see from your manner that he has been here begging you to say a good word for him.

NORA: Yes.

HELMER: And you were to appear to do it of your own accord; you were to conceal from me the fact of his having been here; didn't he beg that of you too?

NORA: Yes, Torvald, but—

HELMER: Nora, Nora, and you would be a party to that sort of thing? To have any talk with a man like that, and give him any sort of promise? And to tell me a lie into the bargain?

NORA: A lie—?

HELMER: Didn't you tell me no one had been here? [*shakes his finger at her*] My little song-bird must never do that again. A song-bird must have a clean beak to chirp with—no false notes! [*puts his arm round her waist*] That is so, isn't it? Yes, I am sure it is. [*lets her go*] We will say no more about it. [*sits down by the stove*] How warm and snug it is here!

[*Turns over his papers.*]

NORA: [*after a short pause, during which she busies herself with the Christmas Tree*] Torvald!

HELMER: Yes.

NORA: I am looking forward tremendously to the fancy dress ball at the Stenborgs' the day after to-morrow.

HELMER: And I am tremendously curious to see what you are going to surprise me with.

NORA: It was very silly of me to want to do that.

HELMER: What do you mean?

NORA: I can't hit upon anything that will do; everything I think of seems so silly and insignificant.

HELMER: Does my little Nora acknowledge that at last?

NORA: [*standing behind his chair with her arms on the back of it*] Are you very busy, Torvald?

HELMER: Well—

NORA: What are all those papers?

HELMER: Bank business.

NORA: Already?

HELMER: I have got authority from the retiring manager to undertake the necessary changes in the staff and in the rearrangement of the work; and I must make use of the Christmas week for that, so as to have everything in order for the new year.

Nora: Then that was why this poor Krogstad—

Helmer: Hm!

Nora: [*leans against the back of his chair and strokes his hair*] If you hadn't been so busy I should have asked you a tremendously big favour, Torvald.

Helmer: What is that? Tell me.

Nora: There is no one has such good taste as you. And I do so want to look nice at the fancy-dress ball. Torvald, couldn't you take me in hand and decide what I shall go as, and what sort of a dress I shall wear?

Helmer: Aha! so my obstinate little woman is obliged to get someone to come to her rescue?

Nora: Yes, Torvald, I can't get along a bit without your help.

Helmer: Very well, I will think it over, we shall manage to hit upon something.

Nora: That is nice of you. [*Goes to the Christmas Tree. A short pause.*] How pretty the red flowers look—. But, tell me, was it really something very bad that this Krogstad was guilty of?

Helmer: He forged someone's name. Have you any idea what that means?

Nora: Isn't it possible that he was driven to do it by necessity?

Helmer: Yes; or, as in so many cases, by imprudence. I am not so heartless as to condemn a man altogether because of a single false step of that kind.

Nora: No you wouldn't, would you, Torvald?

Helmer: Many a man has been able to retrieve his character, if he has openly confessed his fault and taken his punishment.

Nora: Punishment—?

Helmer: But Krogstad did nothing of that sort; he got himself out of it by a cunning trick, and that is why he has gone under altogether.

Nora: But do you think it would—?

Helmer: Just think how a guilty man like that has to lie and play the hypocrite with everyone, how he has to wear a mask in the presence of those near and dear to him, even before his own wife and children. And about the children—that is the most terrible part of it all, Nora.

Nora: How?

Helmer: Because such an atmosphere of lies infects and poisons the whole life of a home. Each breath the children take in such a house is full of the germs of evil.

Nora: [*coming nearer him*] Are you sure of that?

Helmer: My dear, I have often seen it in the course of my life as a lawyer. Almost everyone who has gone to the bad early in life has had a deceitful mother.

Nora: Why do you only say—mother?

Helmer: It seems most commonly to be the mother's influence, though naturally a bad father's would have the same result. Every lawyer is familiar with the fact. This Krogstad, now, has been persistently poisoning his own children with lies and dissimulation; that is why I say he has lost all moral character. [*holds out his hands to her*] That is why my sweet little Nora must promise me not to plead his cause. Give me your hand on it. Come, come, what is this? Give me your hand. There now, that's settled. I assure you it would be quite impossible for me to work with him; I literally feel physically ill when I am in the company of such people.

NORA: [*takes her hand out of his and goes to the opposite side of the Christmas Tree*] How hot it is in here; and I have such a lot to do.

HELMER: [*getting up and putting his papers in order*] Yes, and I must try and read through some of these before dinner; and I must think about your costume too. And it is just possible I may have something ready in gold paper to hang up on the Tree. [*Puts his hand on her head.*] My precious little singing-bird!

[*He goes into his room and shuts the door after him.*]

NORA: [*after a pause, whispers*] No, no—it isn't true. It's impossible; it must be impossible.

[*The* NURSE *opens the door on the left.*]

NURSE: The little ones are begging so hard to be allowed to come in to mamma.

NORA: No, no, no! Don't let them come in to me! You stay with them, Anne.

NURSE: Very well, ma'am.

[*Shuts the door.*]

NORA: [*pale with terror*] Deprave my little children? Poison my home? [*a short pause. Then she tosses her head.*] It's not true. It can't possibly be true.

ACT 2

THE SAME SCENE. *The Christmas Tree is in the corner by the piano, stripped of its ornaments and with burnt-down candle-ends on its dishevelled branches.* NORA'S *cloak and hat are lying on the sofa. She is alone in the room, walking about uneasily. She stops by the sofa and takes up her cloak.*

NORA: [*drops the cloak*] Someone is coming now! [*goes to the door and listens*] No—it is no one. Of course, no one will come to-day. Christmas Day—nor tomorrow either. But, perhaps—[*opens the door and looks out*] No, nothing in the letter-box; it is quite empty. [*comes forward*] What rubbish! of course he can't be in earnest about it. Such a thing couldn't happen; it is impossible—I have three little children.

[*Enter the* NURSE *from the room on the left, carrying a big cardboard box.*]

NURSE: At last I have found the box with the fancy dress.

NORA: Thanks; put it on the table.

NURSE: [*doing so*] But it is very much in want of mending.

NORA: I should like to tear it into a hundred thousand pieces.

NURSE: What an idea! It can easily be put in order—just a little patience.

NORA: Yes, I will go and get Mrs. Linde to come and help me with it.

NURSE: What, out again? In this horrible weather? You will catch cold, ma'am, and make yourself ill.

NORA: Well, worse than that might happen. How are the children?

NURSE: The poor little souls are playing with their Christmas presents, but—

NORA: Do they ask much for me?

NURSE: You see, they are so accustomed to have their mamma with them.

NORA: Yes, but, nurse, I shall not be able to be so much with them now as I was before.

NURSE: Oh well, young children easily get accustomed to anything.

NORA: Do you think so? Do you think they would forget their mother if she went away altogether?

NURSE: Good heavens!—went away altogether?

NORA: Nurse, I want you to tell me something I have often wondered about—how could you have the heart to put your own child out among strangers?

NURSE: I was obliged to, if I wanted to be little Nora's nurse.

NORA: Yes, but how could you be willing to do it?

NURSE: What, when I was going to get such a good place by it? A poor girl who has got into trouble should be glad to. Besides, that wicked man didn't do a single thing for me.

NORA: But I suppose your daughter has quite forgotten you.

NURSE: No, indeed she hasn't. She wrote to me when she was confirmed, and when she was married.

NORA: [*putting her arms round her neck*] Dear old Anne, you were a good mother to me when I was little.

NURSE: Little Nora, poor dear, had no other mother but me.

NORA: And if my little ones had no other mother, I am sure you would— What nonsense I am talking! [*opens the box*] Go in to them. Now I must—. You will see tomorrow how charming I shall look.

NURSE: I am sure there will be no one at the ball so charming as you, ma'am.

[*Goes into the room on the left.*]

NORA: [*begins to unpack the box, but soon pushes it away from her*] If only I dared go out. If only no one would come. If only I could be sure nothing would happen here in the meantime. Stuff and nonsense! No one will come. Only I mustn't think about it. I will brush my muff. What, lovely gloves! Out of my thoughts, out of my thoughts! One, two, three, four, five, six—[*Screams.*] Ah! there is someone coming—

[*Makes a movement towards the door, but stands irresolute.*]

[*Enter* MRS. LINDE *from the hall, where she has taken off her cloak and hat.*]

NORA: Oh, it's you, Christine. There is no one else out there, is there? How good of you to come?

MRS. LINDE: I heard you were up asking for me.

NORA: Yes, I was passing by. As a matter of fact, it is something you could 30 help me with. Let us sit down here on the sofa. Look here. To-morrow evening there is to be a fancy-dress ball at the Stenborgs', who live above us; and Torvald wants me to go as a Neapolitan fisher-girl, and dance the Tarantella that I learnt at Capri.

MRS. LINDE: I see; you are going to keep up the character.

NORA: Yes, Torvald wants me to. Look, here is the dress; Torvald had it made for me there, but now it is all so torn, and I haven't any idea—

MRS. LINDE: We will easily put that right. It is only some of the trimming come unsewn here and there. Needle and thread? Now then, that's all we want.

NORA: It *is* nice of you.

MRS. LINDE: [*sewing*] So you are going to be dressed up to-morrow, 35 Nora. I will tell you what—I shall come in for a moment and see you in your fine feathers. But I have completely forgotten to thank you for a delightful evening yesterday.

NORA: [*gets up, and crosses the stages*] Well I don't think yesterday was as pleasant as usual. You ought to have come to town a little earlier, Christine. Certainly Torvald does understand how to make a house dainty and attractive.

MRS. LINDE: And so do you, it seems to me; you are not your father's daughter for nothing. But tell me, is Doctor Rank always as depressed as he was yesterday?

NORA: No; yesterday it was very noticeable. I must tell you that he suffers from a very dangerous disease. He has consumption of the spine, poor creature. His father was a horrible man who committed all sorts of excesses; and that is why his son was sickly from childhood, do you understand?

MRS. LINDE: [*dropping her sewing*] But, my dearest Nora, how do you know anything about such things?

NORA: [*walking about*] Pooh! When you have three children, you get visits 40 now and then from—from married women, who know something of medical matters, and they talk about one thing and another.

MRS. LINDE: [*goes on sewing. A short silence*] Does Doctor Rank come here every day?

NORA: Every day regularly. He is Torvald's most intimate friend, and a great friend of mine too. He is just like one of the family.

MRS. LINDE: But tell me this—is he perfectly sincere? I mean, isn't he the kind of man that is very anxious to make himself agreeable?

NORA: Not in the least. What makes you think that?

MRS. LINDE: When you introduced him to me yesterday, he declared he 45 had often heard my name mentioned in this house; but afterwards I noticed that your husband hadn't the slightest idea who I was. So how could Doctor Rank—?

NORA: That is quite right, Christine. Torvald is so absurdly fond of me that he wants me absolutely to himself, as he says. At first he used to seem almost jealous if I mentioned any of the dear folk at home, so naturally I gave up doing so. But I often talk about such things with Doctor Rank, because he likes hearing about them.

MRS. LINDE: Listen to me, Nora. You are still very like a child in many things, and I am older than you in many ways and have a little more experience. Let me tell you this—you ought to make an end of it with Doctor Rank.

NORA: What ought I to make an end of?

MRS. LINDE: Of two things, I think. Yesterday you talked some nonsense about a rich admirer who was to leave you money—

NORA: An admirer who doesn't exist, unfortunately! But what then?

MRS. LINDE: Is Doctor Rank a man of means?

NORA: Yes, he is.

MRS. LINDE: And has no one to provide for?

NORA: No, no one; but—

MRS. LINDE: And comes here every day?

NORA: Yes, I told you so.

MRS. LINDE: But how can this well-bred man be so tactless?

NORA: I don't understand you at all.

MRS. LINDE: Don't prevaricate. Nora. Do you suppose I don't guess who lent you the two hundred and fifty pounds?

NORA: Are you out of your senses? How can you think of such a thing! A friend of ours, who comes here every day! Do you realise what a horribly painful position that would be?

MRS. LINDE: Then it really isn't he?

NORA: No, certainly not. It would never have entered into my head for a moment. Besides, he had no money to lend then; he came into his money afterwards.

MRS. LINDE: Well, I think that was lucky for you, my dear Nora.

NORA: No, it would never have come into my head to ask Doctor Rank. Although I am quite sure that if I had asked him—

MRS. LINDE: But of course you won't.

NORA: Of course not. I have no reason to think it could possibly be necessary. But I am quite sure that if I told Doctor Rank—

MRS. LINDE: Behind your husband's back?

NORA: I *must* make an end of it with the other one, and that will be behind his back too. I *must* make an end of it with him.

MRS. LINDE: Yes, that is what I told you yesterday, but—

NORA: [*walking up and down*] A man can put a thing like that straight much easier than a woman—

MRS. LINDE: One's husband, yes.

NORA: Nonsense! [*standing still*] When you pay off a debt you get your bond back, don't you?

MRS. LINDE: Yes, as a matter of course.

NORA: And can tear it into a hundred thousand pieces, and burn it up—the nasty dirty paper!

MRS. LINDE: [*looks hard at her, lays down her sewing and gets up slowly*] Nora, you are concealing something from me.

NORA: Do I look as if I were?

MRS. LINDE: Something has happened to you since yesterday morning. Nora, what is it?

NORA: [*going nearer to her*] Christine! [*listens*] Hush! there's Torvald come home. Do you mind going in to the children for the present? Torvald can't bear to see dress-making going on. Let Anne help you.

MRS. LINDE: [*gathering some of the things together*] Certainly—but I am not going away from here till we have had it out with one another.

[*She goes into the room on the left, as* HELMER *comes in from the hall.*]

NORA: [*going up to* HELMER] I have wanted you so much, Torvald dear.

HELMER: Was that the dressmaker?

NORA: No, it was Christine; she is helping me to put my dress in order. You will see I shall look quite smart.

HELMER: Wasn't that a happy thought of mine, now?

NORA: Splendid! But don't you think it is nice of me, too, to do as you wish?

HELMER: Nice?—because you do as your husband wishes? Well, well, you little rogue, I am sure you did not mean it in that way. But I am not going to disturb you; you will want to be trying on your dress, I expect.

NORA: I suppose you are going to work.

HELMER: Yes. [*shows her a bundle of papers*] Look at that. I have just been into the bank. [*Turns to go into his room.*]

NORA: Torvald.

HELMER: Yes.

NORA: If your little squirrel were to ask you for something very, very prettily—?

HELMER: What then?

NORA: Would you do it?

HELMER: I should like to hear what it is, first.

NORA: Your squirrel would run about and do all her tricks if you would be nice, and do what she wants.

HELMER: Speak plainly.

NORA: Your skylark would chirp about in every room, with her song rising and falling—

HELMER: Well, my skylark does that anyhow.

NORA: I would play the fairy and dance for you in the moonlight, Torvald.

HELMER: Nora—you surely don't mean that request you made of me this morning?

NORA: [*going near him*] Yes, Torvald, I beg you so earnestly—

HELMER: Have you really the courage to open up that question again?

NORA: Yes, dear, you *must* do as I ask; you *must* let Krogstad keep his post in the Bank.

HELMER: My dear Nora, it is his post that I have arranged Mrs. Linde shall have.

NORA: Yes, you have been awfully kind about that; but you could just as well dismiss some other clerk instead of Krogstad.

HELMER: This is simply incredible obstinacy! Because you chose to give him a thoughtless promise that you would speak for him, I am expected to—

Nora: That isn't the reason, Torvald. It is for your own sake. This fellow writes in the most scurrilous newspapers; you have told me so yourself. He can do you an unspeakable amount of harm. I am frightened to death of him—

Helmer: Ah, I understand; it is recollections of the past that scare you.

Nora: What do you mean?

Helmer: Naturally you are thinking of your father.

Nora: Yes—yes, of course. Just recall to your mind what these malicious creatures wrote in the papers about papa, and how horribly they slandered him. I believe they would have procured his dismissal if the Department had not sent you over to inquire into it, and if you had not been so kindly disposed and helpful to him.

Helmer: My little Nora, there is an important difference between your father and me. Your father's reputation as a public official was not above suspicion. Mine is, and I hope it will continue to be so, as long as I hold my office.

Nora: You never can tell what mischief these men may contrive. We ought to be so well off, so snug and happy here in our peaceful home, and have no cares—you and I and the children, Torvald! That is why I beg you so earnestly—

Helmer: And it is just by interceding for him that you make it impossible for me to keep him. It is already known at the Bank that I mean to dismiss Krogstad. Is it to get about now that the new manager has changed his mind at his wife's bidding—

Nora: And what if it did?

Helmer: Of course!—if only this obstinate little person can get her way! Do you suppose I am going to make myself ridiculous before my whole staff, to let people think that I am a man to be swayed by all sorts of outside influence? I should very soon feel the consequences of it. I can tell you! And besides, there is one thing that makes it quite impossible for me to have Krogstad in the Bank as long as I am manager.

Nora: Whatever is that?

Helmer: His moral failings I might perhaps have overlooked, if necessary—

Nora: Yes, you could—couldn't you?

Helmer: And I hear he is a good worker, too. But I knew him when we were boys. It was one of those rash friendships that so often prove an incubus in after life. I may as well tell you plainly, we were once on very intimate terms with one another. But this tactless fellow lays no restraint on himself when other people are present. On the contrary, he thinks it gives him the right to adopt a familiar tone with me, and every minute it is "I say, Helmer, old fellow!" and that sort of thing. I assure you it is extremely painful for me. He would make my position in the Bank intolerable.

Nora: Torvald, I don't believe you mean that.

Helmer: Don't you? Why not?

Nora: Because it is such a narrow-minded way of looking at things.

Helmer: What are you saying? Narrow-minded? Do you think I am narrow-minded?

Nora: No, just the opposite, dear—and it is exactly for that reason.

HELMER: It's the same thing. You say my point of view is narrow-minded, so I must be so too. Narrow-minded! Very well—I must put an end to this. [*Goes to the hall-door and calls.*] Helen!

NORA: What are you going to do?

HELMER: [*looking among his papers*] Settle it. [*Enter* MAID.] Look here; take this letter and go downstairs with it at once. Find a messenger and tell him to deliver it, and be quick. The address is on it, and here is the money.

MAID: Very well, sir.

[*Exits with the letter.*]

HELMER: [*putting his papers together*] Now then, little Miss Obstinate.

NORA: [*breathlessly*] Torvald—what was that letter?

HELMER: Krogstad's dismissal.

NORA: Call her back, Torvald! There is still time. Oh Torvald, call her back! Do it for my sake—for your own sake—for the children's sake! Do you hear me, Torvald? Call her back!! You don't know what that letter can bring upon us.

HELMER: It's too late.

NORA: Yes, it's too late.

HELMER: My dear Nora, I can forgive the anxiety you are in, although really it is an insult to me. It is, indeed. Isn't it an insult to think that I should be afraid of a starving quill-driver's vengeance? But I forgive you nevertheless, because it is such eloquent witness to your great love for me. [*takes her in his arms*] And that is as it should be, my own darling Nora. Come what will, you may be sure I shall have both courage and strength if they be needed. You will see I am man enough to take everything upon myself.

NORA: [*in a horror-stricken voice*] What do you mean by that?

HELMER: Everything, I say—

NORA: [*recovering herself*] You will never have to do that.

HELMER: That's right. Well, we will share it, Nora, as man and wife should. That is how it shall be. [*caressing her*] Are you content now? There! there!—not these frightened dove's eyes! The whole thing is only the wildest fancy!—Now, you must go and play through the Tarantella and practise with your tambourine. I shall go into the inner office and shut the door, and I shall hear nothing; you can make as much noise as you please. [*turns back at the door*] And when Rank comes, tell him where he will find me.

[*Nods to her, takes his papers and goes into his room, and shuts the door after him*]

NORA: [*bewildered with anxiety, stands as if rooted to the spot, and whispers*] He is capable of doing it. He will do it. He will do it in spite of everything.—No, not that! Never, never! Anything rather than that! Oh, for some help, some way out of it! [*The door-bell rings.*] Doctor Rank! Anything rather than that—anything, whatever it is!

[*She puts her hands over her face, pulls herself together, goes to the door and opens it.* RANK *is standing without, hanging up his coat. During the following dialogue it begins to grow dark.*]

NORA: Good-day, Doctor Rank. I knew your ring. But you mustn't go in to Torvald now; I think he is busy with something.

RANK: And you?

NORA: [*brings him in and shuts the door after him*] Oh, you know very well I always have time for you.

RANK: Thank you. I shall make use of as much of it as I can.

NORA: What do you mean by that? As much of it as you can?

RANK: Well, does that alarm you?

NORA: It was such a strange way of putting it. Is anything likely to happen?

RANK: Nothing but what I have long been prepared for. But I certainly didn't expect it to happen so soon.

NORA: [*gripping him by the arm*] What have you found out? Doctor Rank, you must tell me.

RANK: [*sitting down by the stove*] It is all up with me. And it can't be helped.

NORA: [*with a sigh of relief*] Is it about yourself?

RANK: Who else? It is no use lying to one's self. I am the most wretched of all my patients, Mrs. Helmer. Lately I have been taking stock of my internal economy. Bankrupt! Probably within a month I shall lie rotting in the churchyard.

NORA: What an ugly thing to say!

RANK: The thing itself is cursedly ugly, and the worst of it is that I shall have to face so much more that is ugly before that. I shall only make one more examination of myself; when I have done that, I shall know pretty certainly when it will be that the horrors of dissolution will begin. There is something I want to tell you. Helmer's refined nature gives him an unconquerable disgust at everything that is ugly; I won't have him in my sick-room.

NORA: Oh, but, Doctor Rank—

RANK: I won't have him there. Not on any account. I bar my door to him. As soon as I am quite certain that the worst has come, I shall send you my card with a black cross on it, and then you will know that the loathsome end has begun.

NORA: You are quite absurd to-day. And I wanted you so much to be in a really good humour.

RANK: With death stalking beside me?—To have to pay this penalty for another man's sin! Is there any justice in that? And in every single family, in one way or another, some such inexorable retribution is being exacted—

NORA: [*putting her hands over her ears*] Rubbish! Do talk of something cheerful.

RANK: Oh, it's a mere laughing matter, the whole thing. My poor innocent spine has to suffer for my father's youthful amusements.

NORA: [*sitting at the table on the left*] I suppose you mean that he was too partial to asparagus and pâté de foie gras, don't you.

RANK: Yes, and to truffles.

NORA: Truffles, yes. And oysters too, I suppose?

RANK: Oysters, of course, that goes without saying.

NORA: And heaps of port and champagne. It is sad that all these nice things should take their revenge on our bones.

RANK: Especially that they should revenge themselves on the unlucky bones of those who have not had the satisfaction of enjoying them.

NORA: Yes, that's the saddest part of it all.

RANK: [*with a searching look at her*] Hm!—

NORA: [*after a short pause*] Why did you smile?

RANK: No, it was you that laughed.

NORA: No, it was you that smiled, Doctor Rank!

RANK: [*rising*] You are a greater rascal than I thought.

NORA: I am in a silly mood to-day.

RANK: So it seems.

NORA: [*putting her hands on his shoulders*] Dear, dear Doctor Rank, death mustn't take you away from Torvald and me.

RANK: It is a loss you would easily recover from. Those who are gone are soon forgotten.

NORA: [*looking at him anxiously*] Do you believe that?

RANK: People form new ties, and then—

NORA: Who will form new ties?

RANK: Both you and Helmer, when I am gone. You yourself are already on the high road to it, I think. What did that Mrs. Linde want here last night?

NORA: Oho!—you don't mean to say you are jealous of poor Christine?

RANK: Yes, I am. She will be my successor in this house. When I am done for, this woman will—

NORA: Hush! don't speak so loud. She is in that room.

RANK: To-day again. There, you see.

NORA: She has only come to sew my dress for me. Bless my soul, how unreasonable you are! [*sits down on the sofa*] Be nice now, Doctor Rank, and tomorrow you will see how beautifully I shall dance, and you can imagine I am doing it all for you—and for Torvald too, of course. [*takes various things out of the box*] Doctor Rank, come and sit down here, and I will show you something.

RANK: [*sitting down*] What is it?

NORA: Just look at those!

RANK: Silk stockings.

NORA: Flesh-coloured. Aren't they lovely? It is so dark here now, but to-morrow—. No, no, no! you must only look at the feet. Oh well, you may have leave to look at the legs too.

RANK: Hm!—

NORA: Why are you looking so critical? Don't you think they will fit me?

RANK: I have no means of forming an opinion about that.

NORA: [*looks at him for a moment*] For shame! [*hits him lightly on the ear with the stockings*] That's to punish you. [*folds them up again*]

RANK: And what other nice things am I to be allowed to see?

NORA: Not a single thing more, for being so naughty. [*She looks among the things, humming to herself.*]

RANK: [*after a short silence*] When I am sitting here, talking to you as intimately as this, I cannot imagine for a moment what would have become of me if I had never come into this house.

NORA: [*smiling*] I believe you do feel thoroughly at home with us.

RANK: [*in a lower voice, looking straight in front of him*] And to be obliged to leave it all—

NORA: Nonsense, you are not going to leave it.

RANK: [*as before*] And not be able to leave behind one the slightest token of one's gratitude, scarcely even a fleeting regret—nothing but an empty place which the first comer can fill as well as any other.

NORA: And if I asked you now for a—? No!

RANK: For what?

NORA: For a big proof of your friendship—

RANK: Yes, yes!

NORA: I mean a tremendously big favour—

RANK: Would you really make me so happy for once?

NORA: Ah, but you don't know what it is yet.

RANK: No—but tell me.

NORA: I really can't, Doctor Rank. It is something out of all reason; it means advice, and help, and a favour—

RANK: The bigger a thing it is the better. I can't conceive what it is you mean. Do tell me. Haven't I your confidence?

NORA: More than anyone else. I know you are my truest and best friend, and so I will tell you what it is. Well, Doctor Rank, it is something you must help me to prevent. You know how devotedly, how inexpressibly deeply Torvald loves me; he would never for a moment hesitate to give his life for me.

RANK: [*leaning towards her*] Nora—do you think he is the only one—?

NORA: [*with a slight start*] The only one—?

RANK: The only one who would gladly give his life for your sake.

NORA: [*sadly*] Is that it?

RANK: I was determined you should know it before I went away, and there will never be a better opportunity than this. Now you know it, Nora. And now you know, too, that you can trust me as you would trust no one else.

NORA: [*rises, deliberately and quietly*] Let me pass.

RANK: [*makes room for her to pass him, but sits still*] Nora!

NORA: [*at the hall door*] Helen, bring in the lamp. [*goes over to the stove*] Dear Doctor Rank, that was really horrid of you.

RANK: To have loved you as much as anyone else does? Was that horrid?

NORA: No, but to go and tell me so. There was really no need—

RANK: What do you mean? Did you know—? [MAID *enters with lamp, puts it down on the table, and goes out.*] Nora—Mrs. Helmer—tell me, had you any idea of this?

NORA: Oh, how do I know whether I had or whether I hadn't? I really can't tell you—To think you could be so clumsy, Doctor Rank! We were getting on so nicely.

RANK: Well, at all events you know now that you can command me, body and soul. So won't you speak out?

NORA: [*looking at him*] After what happened?

RANK: I beg you to let me know what it is.

NORA: I can't tell you anything now.

RANK: Yes, yes. You mustn't punish me in that way. Let me have permission to do for you whatever a man may do.

NORA: You can do nothing for me now. Besides, I really don't need any help at all. You will find that the whole thing is merely fancy on my part. It really is so—of course it is! [*Sits down in the rocking-chair, and looks at him with a smile*] You are a nice sort of man, Doctor Rank!—don't you feel ashamed of yourself, now the lamp has come?

RANK: Not a bit. But perhaps I had better go—for ever?

NORA: No, indeed, you shall not. Of course you must come here just as before. You know very well Torvald can't do without you.

RANK: Yes, but you?

NORA: Oh, I am always tremendously pleased when you come.

RANK: It is just that, that put me on the wrong track. You are a riddle to me. I have often thought that you would almost as soon be in my company as in Helmer's.

NORA: Yes—you see there are some people one loves best, and others whom one would almost always rather have as companions.

RANK: Yes, there is something in that.

NORA: When I was at home, of course I loved papa best. But I always thought it tremendous fun if I could steal down into the maid's room, because they never moralised at all, and talked to each other about such entertaining things.

RANK: I see—it is *their* place I have taken.

NORA: [*jumping up and going to him*] Oh, dear, nice Doctor Rank. I never meant that at all. But surely you can understand that being with Torvald is a little like being with papa—

[*Enter* MAID *from the hall*]

MAID: If you please, ma'am. [*whispers and hands her a card*]

NORA: [*glancing at the card*] Oh! [*puts it in her pocket*]

RANK: Is there anything wrong?

NORA: No, no, not in the least. It is only something—it is my new dress—

RANK: What? Your dress is lying there.

NORA: Oh, yes, that one; but this is another. I ordered it. Torvald mustn't know about it—

RANK: Oho! Then that was the great secret.

NORA: Of course. Just go in to him; he is sitting in the inner room. Keep him as long as—

RANK: Make your mind easy; I won't let him escape. [*goes into* HELMER'S *room*]

NORA: [*to the* MAID] And he is standing waiting in the kitchen?

MAID: Yes; he came up the back stairs.

NORA: But didn't you tell him no one was in?

MAID: Yes, but it was no good.

NORA: He won't go away?

MAID: No; he says he won't until he has seen you, ma'am.

NORA: Well, let him come in—but quietly. Helen, you mustn't say anything about it to anyone. It is a surprise for my husband.

MAID: Yes, ma'am. I quite understand. [*Exit.*]

NORA: This dreadful thing is going to happen! It will happen in spite of me! No, no, no, it can't happen—it shan't happen!

[*She bolts the door of* HELMER'S *room. The* MAID *opens the hall door for* KROGSTAD *and shuts it after him. He is wearing a fur coat, high boots and a fur cap.*]

NORA: [*advancing towards him*] Speak low—my husband is at home.
KROGSTAD: No matter about that.
NORA: What do you want of me?
KROGSTAD: An explanation of something.
NORA: Make haste then. What is it?
KROGSTAD: You know, I suppose, that I have got my dismissal.
NORA: I couldn't prevent it, Mr. Krogstad. I fought as hard as I could on your side, but it was no good.
KROGSTAD: Does your husband love you so little, then? He knows that what I can expose you to, and yet he ventures—
NORA: How can you suppose that he has any knowledge of the sort?
KROGSTAD: I didn't suppose so at all. It would not be the least like our dear Torvald Helmer to show so much courage—
NORA: Mr. Krogstad, a little respect for my husband, please.
KROGSTAD: Certainly—all the respect he deserves. But since you have kept the matter so carefully to yourself, I make bold to suppose that you have a little clearer idea, than you had yesterday, of what it actually is that you have done?
NORA: More than you could ever teach me.
KROGSTAD: Yes, such a bad lawyer as I am.
NORA: What is it you want of me?
KROGSTAD: Only to see how you were, Mrs. Helmer. I have been thinking about you all day long. A mere cashier, a quill-driver, a—well, a man like me—even he has a little of what is called feeling, you know.
NORA: Show it, then; think of my little children.
KROGSTAD: Have you and your husband thought of mine? But never mind about that. I only wanted to tell you that you need not take this matter too seriously. In the first place there will be no accusation made on my part.
NORA: No, of course not; I was sure of that.
KROGSTAD: The whole thing can be arranged amicably; there is no reason why anyone should know anything about it. It will remain a secret between us three.
NORA: My husband must never get to know anything about it.
KROGSTAD: How will you be able to prevent it? Am I to understand that you can pay the balance that is owing?
NORA: No, not just at present.
KROGSTAD: Or perhaps that you have some expedient for raising the money soon?
NORA: No expedient that I mean to make use of
KROGSTAD: Well, in any case, it would have been of no use to you now. If you stood there with ever so much money in your hand, I would never part with your bond.
NORA: Tell me what purpose you mean to put it to.

KROGSTAD: I shall only preserve it—keep it in my possession. No one who is not concerned in the matter shall have the slightest hint of it. So that if the thought of it has driven you to any desperate resolution—

NORA: It has.

KROGSTAD: If you had it in your mind to run away from your home—

NORA: I had.

KROGSTAD: Or even something worse—

NORA: How could you know that?

KROGSTAD: Give up the idea.

NORA: How did you know I had thought of *that*?

KROGSTAD: Most of us think of that at first. I did, too—but I hadn't the courage.

NORA: [*faintly*] No more had I.

KROGSTAD: [*in a tone of relief*] No, that's it, isn't it—you hadn't the courage either?

NORA: No, I haven't—I haven't.

KROGSTAD: Besides, it would have been a great piece of folly. Once the first storm at home is over—. I have a letter for your husband in my pocket.

NORA: Telling him everything?

KROGSTAD: In as lenient a manner as I possibly could.

NORA: [*quickly*] He mustn't get the letter. Tear it up. I will find some means of getting money.

KROGSTAD: Excuse me, Mrs. Helmer, but I think I told you just now—

NORA: I am not speaking of what I owe you. Tell me what sum you are asking my husband for and I will get the money.

KROGSTAD: I am not asking your husband for a penny.

NORA: What do you want, then?

KROGSTAD: I will tell you. I want to rehabilitate myself, Mrs. Helmer; I want to get on; and in that your husband must help me. For the last year and a half I have not had a hand in anything dishonourable, and all that time I have been struggling in most restricted circumstances. I was content to work my way up step by step. Now I am turned out, and I am not going to be satisfied with merely being taken into favour again. I want to get on, I tell you. I want to get into the Bank again, in a higher position. Your husband must make a place for me—

NORA: That he will never do!

KROGSTAD: He will; I know him; he dare not protest. And as soon as I am in there again with him, then you will see! Within a year I shall be the manager's right hand. It will be Nils Krogstad and not Torvald Helmer who manages the Bank.

NORA: That's a thing you will never see!

KROGSTAD: Do you mean that you will—

NORA: I have courage enough for it now.

KROGSTAD: Oh, you can't frighten me. A fine, spoilt lady like you—

NORA: You will see, you will see.

KROGSTAD: Under the ice, perhaps? Down into the cold, coal-black water? And then, in the spring, to float up to the surface, all horrible and unrecognisable, with your hair fallen out—

NORA: You can't frighten me.

KROGSTAD: Nor you me. People don't do such things, Mrs. Helmer. Besides, what use would it be? I should have him completely in my power all the same.

NORA: Afterwards? When I am no longer—

KROGSTAD: Have you forgotten that it is I who have the keeping of your reputation? [NORA *stands speechlessly looking at him.*] Well, now, I have warned you. Do not do anything foolish. When Helmer has had my letter, I shall expect a message from him. And be sure you remember that it is your husband himself who has forced me into such ways as this again. I will never forgive him for that. Good-bye, Mrs. Helmer.

[*Exit through the hall.*]

NORA: [*goes to the hall door, opens it slightly and listens*] He is going. He is not putting the letter in the box. Oh no, no! that's impossible! [*opens the door by degrees*] What is that? He is standing outside. He is not going downstairs. Is he hesitating? Can he—

[*A letter drops into the box; then* KROGSTAD'S *footsteps are heard, till they die away as he goes down-stairs.* NORA *utters a stifled cry and runs across the room to the table by the sofa. A short pause.*]

NORA: In the letter-box. [*steals across to the hall door*] There it lies—Torvald, Torvald, there is no hope for us now!

[MRS. LINDE *comes in from the room on the left, carrying the dress.*]

MRS. LINDE: There, I can't see anything more to mend now. Would you like to try it on—?

NORA: [*in a hoarse whisper*] Christine, come here.

MRS. LINDE: [*throwing the dress down on the sofa*] What is the matter with you? You look so agitated!

NORA: Come here. Do you see that letter? There, look—you can see it through the glass in the letter-box.

MRS. LINDE: Yes, I see it.

NORA: That letter is from Krogstad.

MRS. LINDE: Nora—it was Krogstad who lent you the money!

NORA: Yes, and now Torvald will know all about it.

MRS. LINDE: Believe me, Nora, that's the best thing for both of you.

NORA: You don't know all. I forged a name.

MRS. LINDE: Good heavens—!

NORA: I only want to say this to you, Christine—you must be my witness.

MRS. LINDE: Your witness? What do you mean? What am I to—?

NORA: If I should go out of my mind—and it might easily happen—

MRS. LINDE: Nora!

NORA: Or if anything else should happen to me—anything, for instance, that might prevent my being here—

MRS. LINDE: Nora! Nora! you are quite out of your mind.

NORA: And if it should happen that there were someone who wanted to take all the responsibility, all the blame, you understand—

MRS. LINDE: Yes, yes—but how can you suppose—?

NORA: Then you must be my witness, that it is not true. Christine. I am not out of my mind at all; I am in my right senses now, and I tell you no one else has known anything about it; I, and I alone, did the whole thing. Remember that.

MRS. LINDE: I will, indeed. But I don't understand all this.

NORA: How should you understand it? A wonderful thing is going to happen.

MRS. LINDE: A wonderful thing?

NORA: Yes, a wonderful thing!—But it is so terrible. Christine; it *mustn't* happen, not for all the world.

MRS. LINDE: I will go at once and see Krogstad.

NORA: Don't go to him: he will do you some harm.

MRS. LINDE: There was a time when he would gladly do anything for my sake.

NORA: He?

MRS. LINDE: Where does he live?

NORA: How should I know—? Yes [*feeling in her pocket*] here is his card. But the letter, the letter—!

HELMER: [*calls from his room, knocking at the door*] Nora!

NORA: [*cries out anxiously*] Oh, what's that? What do you want?

HELMER: Don't be so frightened. We are not coming in; you have locked the door. Are you trying on your dress?

NORA: Yes, that's it. I look so nice, Torvald.

MRS. LINDE: [*who has read the card*] I see he lives at the corner here.

NORA: Yes, but it's no use. It is hopeless. The letter is lying there in the box.

MRS. LINDE: And your husband keeps the key?

NORA: Yes, always.

MRS. LINDE: Krogstad must ask for his letter back unread, he must find some pretence—

NORA: But it is just at this time that Torvald generally—

MRS. LINDE: You must delay him. Go in to him in the meantime. I will come back as soon as I can.

[*She goes out hurriedly through the hall door.*]

NORA: [*goes to* HELMER'S *door, opens it and peeps in*] Torvald!

HELMER: [*from the inner room*] Well? May I venture at last to come into my own room again? Come along, Rank, now you will see—[*halting in the doorway*] But what is this?

NORA: What is what, dear?

HELMER: Rank led me to expect a splendid transformation.

RANK: [*in the doorway*] I understood so, but evidently I was mistaken.

NORA: Yes, nobody is to have the chance of admiring me in my dress until tomorrow.

HELMER: But, my dear Nora, you look so worn out. Have you been practising too much?

NORA: No, I have not practised at all.

HELMER: But you will need to—

NORA: Yes, indeed I shall, Torvald. But I can't get on a bit without you to help me; I have absolutely forgotten the whole thing.

Helmer: Oh, we will soon work it up again.

Nora: Yes, help me, Torvald. Promise that you will! I am so nervous about it—all the people—. You must give yourself up to me entirely this evening. Not the tiniest bit of business—you mustn't even take a pen in your hand. Will you promise, Torvald dear?

Helmer: I promise. This evening I will be wholly and absolutely at your service, you helpless little mortal. Ah, by the way, first of all I will just—

[*Goes towards the hall door*]

Nora: What are you going to do there?

Helmer: Only see if any letters have come.

Nora: No, no! don't do that, Torvald!

Helmer: Why not?

Nora: Torvald, please don't. There is nothing there.

Helmer: Well, let me look [*Turns to go to the letter-box.* Nora, *at the piano, plays the first bars of the Tarantella.* Helmer *stops in the doorway.*] Aha!

Nora: I can't dance to-morrow if I don't practise, with you.

Helmer: [*going up to her*] Are you really so afraid of it, dear.

Nora: Yes, so dreadfully afraid of it. Let me practise at once; there is time now, before we go to dinner. Sit down and play for me, Torvald dear; criticise me, and correct me as you play.

Helmer: With great pleasure, if you wish me to.

[*Sits down at the piano.*]

Nora: [*takes out of the box a tambourine and a long variegated shawl. She hastily drapes the shawl round her. Then she springs to the front of the stage and calls out.*] Now play for me! I am going to dance!

[Helmer *plays and* Nora *dances.* Rank *stands by the piano behind* Helmer *and looks on.*]

Helmer: [*as he plays*] Slower, slower!

Nora: I can't do it any other way.

Helmer: Not so violently, Nora!

Nora: This is the way.

Helmer: [*stops playing*] No, no—that is not a bit right.

Nora: [*laughing and swinging the tambourine*] Didn't I tell you so?

Rank: Let me play for her.

Helmer: [*getting up*] Yes, do. I can correct her better then.

[Rank *sits down at the piano and plays.* Nora *dances more and more wildly.* Helmer *has taken up a position beside the stove, and during her dance gives her frequent instructions. She does not seem to hear him; her hair comes down and falls over her shoulders; she pays no attention to it, but goes on dancing. Enter* Mrs. Linde.]

Mrs. Linde: [*standing as if spell-bound in the doorway*] Oh!—

Nora: [*as she dances*] Such fun, Christine!

Helmer: My dear darling Nora, you are dancing as if your life depended on it.

NORA: So it does.

HELMER: Stop, Rank; this is sheer madness. Stop, I tell you! [RANK *stops playing and* NORA *suddenly stands still.* HELMER *goes up to her.*] I could never have believed it. You have forgotten everything I taught you.

NORA: [*throwing away the tambourine*] There, you see.

HELMER: You will want a lot of coaching.

NORA: Yes, you see how much I need it. You must coach me up to the last minute. Promise me that, Torvald!

HELMER: You can depend on me.

NORA: You must not think of anything but me, either to-day or to-morrow; you mustn't open a single letter—not even open the letter-box—

HELMER: Ah, you are still afraid of that fellow—

NORA: Yes, indeed I am.

HELMER: Nora, I can tell from your looks that there is a letter from him lying there.

NORA: I don't know: I think there is; but you must not read anything of that kind now. Nothing horrid must come between us till this is all over.

RANK: [*whispers to* HELMER] You mustn't contradict her.

HELMER: [*taking her in his arms*] The child shall have her way. But to-morrow night, after you have danced—

NORA: Then you will be free.

[MAID *appears in the doorway to the right.*]

MAID: Dinner is served, ma'am.

NORA: We will have champagne, Helen.

MAID: Very good, ma'am.

[*Exit.*]

HELMER: Hullo!—are we going to have a banquet?

NORA: Yes, a champagne banquet till the small hours. [*calls out*] And a few macaroons, Helen—lots, just for once!

HELMER: Come, come, don't be so wild and nervous. Be my own little skylark, as you used.

NORA: Yes, dear, I will. But go in now and you too, Doctor Rank. Christine, you must help me to do up my hair.

RANK: [*whispers to* HELMER *as they go out*] I suppose there is nothing—she is not expecting anything?

HELMER: Far from it, my dear fellow, it is simply nothing more than this childish nervousness I was telling you of.

[*They go into the right-hand room.*]

NORA: Well!

MRS. LINDE: Gone out of town.

NORA: I could tell from your face.

MRS. LINDE: He is coming home to-morrow evening. I wrote a note for him.

NORA: You should have let it alone, you must prevent nothing. After all, it is splendid to be waiting for a wonderful thing to happen.

MRS. LINDE: What is it that you are waiting for?

NORA: Oh, you wouldn't understand. Go in to them. I will come in a moment. [MRS. LINDE *goes into the dining-room.* NORA *stands still for a little while, as if to compose herself. Then she looks at her watch.*] Five o'clock. Seven hours till midnight; and then four-and-twenty hours till the next midnight. Then the Tarantella will be over. Twenty-four and seven? Thirty-one hours to live.

HELMER: [*from the doorway on the right*] Where's my little skylark?

NORA: [*going to him with her arms outstretched*] Here she is!

ACT 3

THE SAME SCENE: *The table has been placed in the middle of the stage, with chairs round it. A lamp is burning on the table. The door into the hall stands open. Dance music is heard in the room above.* MRS. LINDE *is sitting at the table idly turning over the leaves of a book; she tries to read, but does not seem able to collect her thoughts. Every now and then she listens intently for a sound at the outer door.*

MRS. LINDE: [*looking at her watch*] Not yet—and the time is nearly up. If only he does not—. [*listens again*] Ah, there he is. [*Goes into the hall and opens the outer door carefully. Light footsteps are heard on the stairs. She whispers.*] Come in. There is no one here.

KROGSTAD: [*in the doorway*] I found a note from you at home. What does this mean?

MRS. LINDE: It is absolutely necessary that I should have a talk with you.

KROGSTAD: Really? And is it absolutely necessary that it should be here?

MRS. LINDE: It is impossible where I live; there is no private entrance to my rooms. Come in; we are quite alone. The maid is asleep, and the Helmers are at the dance upstairs.

KROGSTAD: [*coming into the room*] Are the Helmers really at a dance to-night?

MRS. LINDE: Yes, why not?

KROGSTAD: Certainly—why not?

MRS. LINDE: Now, Nils, let us have a talk.

KROGSTAD: Can we two have anything to talk about?

MRS. LINDE: We have a great deal to talk about.

KROGSTAD: I shouldn't have thought so.

MRS. LINDE: No, you have never properly understood me.

KROGSTAD: Was there anything else to understand except what was obvious to all the world—a heartless woman jilts a man when a more lucrative chance turns up?

MRS. LINDE: Do you believe I am as absolutely heartless as all that? And do you believe that I did it with a light heart?

KROGSTAD: Didn't you?

MRS. LINDE: Nils, did you really think that?

KROGSTAD: If it were as you say, why did you write to me as you did at the time?

MRS. LINDE: I could do nothing else. As I had to break with you, it was my duty also to put an end to all that you felt for me.

KROGSTAD: [*wringing his hands*] So that was it, and all this—only for the sake of money!

MRS. LINDE: You must not forget that I had a helpless mother and two little brothers. We couldn't wait for you, Nils; your prospects seemed hopeless then.

KROGSTAD: That may be so, but you had no right to throw me over for any one else's sake.

MRS. LINDE: Indeed I don't know. Many a time did I ask myself if I had the right to do it.

KROGSTAD: [*more gently*] When I lost you, it was as if all the solid ground went from under my feet. Look at me now—I am a shipwrecked man clinging to a bit of wreckage.

MRS. LINDE: But help may be near.

KROGSTAD: It *was* near; but then you came and stood in my way.

MRS. LINDE: Unintentionally, Nils. It was only to-day that I learnt it was your place I was going to take in the Bank.

KROGSTAD: I believe you, if you say so. But now that you know it, are you not going to give it up to me?

MRS. LINDE: No, because that would not benefit you in the least.

KROGSTAD: Oh, benefit, benefit—I would have done it whether or no.

MRS. LINDE: I have learnt to act prudently. Life, and hard, bitter necessity have taught me that.

KROGSTAD: And life has taught me not to believe in fine speeches.

MRS. LINDE: Then life has taught you something very reasonable. But deeds you must believe in?

KROGSTAD: What do you mean by that?

MRS. LINDE: You said you were like a shipwrecked man clinging to some wreckage.

KROGSTAD: I had good reason to say so.

MRS. LINDE: Well, I am like a shipwrecked woman clinging to some wreckage—no one to mourn for, no one to care for.

KROGSTAD: It was your own choice.

MRS. LINDE: There was no other choice—then.

KROGSTAD: Well, what now?

MRS. LINDE: Nils, how would it be if we two shipwrecked people could join forces?

KROGSTAD: What are you saying?

MRS. LINDE: Two on the same piece of wreckage would stand a better chance than each on their own.

KROGSTAD: Christine!

MRS. LINDE: What do you suppose brought me to town?

KROGSTAD: Do you mean that you gave me a thought?

MRS. LINDE: I could not endure life without work. All my life, as long as I can remember, I have worked, and it has been my greatest and only pleasure. But now I am quite alone in the world—my life is so dreadfully empty and I feel so forsaken. There is not the least pleasure in working for one's self. Nils, give me someone and something to work for.

KROGSTAD: I don't trust that. It is nothing but a woman's overstrained sense of generosity that prompts you to make such an offer of yourself.

MRS. LINDE: Have you ever noticed anything of the sort in me?

KROGSTAD: Could you really do it? Tell me—do you know all about my past life?

MRS. LINDE: Yes.

KROGSTAD: And do you know what they think of me here?

MRS. LINDE: You seemed to me to imply that with me you might have been quite another man.

KROGSTAD: I am certain of it.

MRS. LINDE: Is it too late now?

KROGSTAD: Christine, are you saying this deliberately? Yes, I am sure you are. I see it in your face. Have you really the courage, then—?

MRS. LINDE: I want to be a mother to someone, and your children need a mother. We two need each other. Nils, I have faith in your real character—I can dare anything together with you.

KROGSTAD: [*grasps her hands*] Thanks, thanks, Christine! Now I shall find a way to clear myself in the eyes of the world. Ah, but I forgot—

MRS. LINDE: [*listening*] Hush! The Tarantella! Go, go!

KROGSTAD: Why? What is it?

MRS. LINDE: Do you hear them up there? When that is over, we may expect them back.

KROGSTAD: Yes, yes—I will go. But it is all no use. Of course you are not aware what steps I have taken in the matter of the Helmers.

MRS. LINDE: Yes, I know all about that.

KROGSTAD: And in spite of that have you the courage to—?

MRS. LINDE: I understand very well to what lengths a man like you might be driven by despair.

KROGSTAD: If I could only undo what I have done?

MRS. LINDE: You can. Your letter is lying in the letter-box now.

KROGSTAD: Are you sure of that?

MRS. LINDE: Quite sure, but—

KROGSTAD: [*with a searching look at her*] Is that what it all means?—that you want to save your friend at any cost? Tell me frankly. Is that it?

MRS. LINDE: Nils, a woman who has once sold herself for another's sake, doesn't do it a second time.

KROGSTAD: I will ask for my letter back.

MRS. LINDE: No, no.

KROGSTAD: Yes, of course I will. I will wait here till Helmer comes; I will tell him he must give me my letter back—that it only concerns my dismissal—that he is not to read it—

MRS. LINDE: No, Nils, you must not recall your letter.

KROGSTAD: But, tell me, wasn't it for that very purpose that you asked me to meet you here?

MRS. LINDE: In my first moment of fright, it was. But twenty-four hours have elapsed since then, and in that time I have witnessed incredible things in this house. Helmer must know all about it. This unhappy secret must be disclosed; they must have a complete understanding between them, which is impossible with all this concealment and falsehood going on.

KROGSTAD: Very well, if you will take the responsibility. But there is one thing I can do in any case, and I shall do it at once.

MRS. LINDE: [*listening*] You must be quick and go! The dance is over; we are not safe a moment longer.

KROGSTAD: I will wait for you below.

MRS. LINDE: Yes, do. You must see me back to my door.

KROGSTAD: I have never had such an amazing piece of good fortune in my life.

[*Goes out through the outer door. The door between the room and the hall remains open.*]

MRS. LINDE: [*tidying up the room and laying her hat and clock ready*] What a difference! what a difference! Someone to work for and live for—a home to bring comfort into. That I will do, indeed. I wish they would be quick and come—[*listens*] Ah, there they are now. I must put on my things.

[*Takes up her hat and cloak.* HELMER'S *and* NORA'S *voices are heard outside; a key is turned, and* HELMER *brings* NORA *almost by force into the hall. She is in an Italian costume with a large black shawl round her; he is in evening dress and a black domino which is flying open.*]

NORA: [*hanging back in the doorway, and struggling with him*] No, no, no!—don't take me in. I want to go upstairs again; I don't want to leave so early.

HELMER: But, my dearest Nora—

NORA: Please, Torvald dear—please, *please*—only an hour more.

HELMER: Not a single minute, my sweet Nora. You know that was our agreement. Come along into the room; you are catching cold standing there.

[*He brings her gently into the room, in spite of her resistance.*]

MRS. LINDE: Good evening.

NORA: Christine!

HELMER: You here, so late, Mrs. Linde?

MRS. LINDE: Yes, you must excuse me; I was so anxious to see Nora in her dress.

NORA: Have you been sitting here waiting for me?

MRS. LINDE: Yes, unfortunately I came too late, you had already gone upstairs; and I thought I couldn't go away without having seen you.

HELMER: [*taking off* NORA'S *shawl*] Yes, take a good look at her. I think she is worth looking at. Isn't she charming, Mrs. Linde?

MRS. LINDE: Yes, indeed she is.

HELMER: Doesn't she look remarkably pretty? Everyone thought so at the dance. But she is terribly self-willed, this sweet little person. What are we to do with her? You will hardly believe that I had almost to bring her away by force.

NORA: Torvald, you will repent not having let me stay, even if it were only for half an hour.

HELMER: Listen to her, Mrs. Linde! She had danced her Tarantella, and it had been a tremendous success, as it deserved—although possibly the performance was a trifle too realistic—a little more so, I mean, than was strictly compatible with the limitations of art. But never mind about that! The chief thing is, she had made a success—she had made a tremendous success. Do you think I was going to let her remain there after that, and spoil the effect? No indeed! I took my charming little Capri maiden—my capricious little Capri maiden, I should say—on my arm; took one quick turn round the room; a curtsey on either side, and, as they say in novels, the beautiful apparition disappeared. An exit ought always to be effective, Mrs. Linde; but that is what I cannot make Nora understand. Pooh! this room is hot. [*throws his domino on a chair and opens the door of his room*] Hullo! it's all dark in here. Oh, of course—excuse me—.

[*He goes in and lights some candles.*]

NORA: [*in a hurried and breathless whisper*] Well?
MRS. LINDE: [*in a low voice*] I have had a talk with him.
NORA: Yes, and—
MRS. LINDE: Nora, you must tell your husband all about it.
NORA: [*in an expressionless voice*] I knew it.
MRS. LINDE: You have nothing to be afraid of as far as Krogstad is concerned; but you must tell him.
NORA: I won't tell him.
MRS. LINDE: Then the letter will.
NORA: Thank you, Christine. Now I know what I must do. Hush—!
HELMER: [*coming in again*] Well. Mrs. Linde, have you admired her?
MRS. LINDE: Yes, and now I will say good-night.
HELMER: What already? Is this yours, this knitting?
MRS. LINDE: [*taking it*] Yes, thank you, I had very nearly forgotten it.
HELMER: So you knit?
MRS. LINDE: Of course.
HELMER: Do you know, you ought to embroider.
MRS. LINDE: Really? Why?
HELMER: Yes, it's far more becoming. Let me show you. You hold the embroidery thus in your left hand, and use the needle with the right—like this—with a long, easy sweep. Do you see?
MRS. LINDE: Yes, perhaps—
HELMER: But in the case of knitting—that can never be anything but ungraceful; look here—the arms close together, the knitting-needles going up and down—it has a sort of Chinese effect—. That was really excellent champagne they gave us.
MRS. LINDE: Well,—good-night, Nora, and don't be self-willed any more.
HELMER: That's right, Mrs. Linde.
MRS. LINDE: Good-night, Mr. Helmer.
HELMER: [*accompanying her to the door*] Good-night, good-night. I hope you will get home all right. I should be very happy to—but you haven't any great distance to go. Good-night, good-night. [*She goes out; he shuts the door after her, and comes in again.*] Ah!—at last we have got rid of her. She is a frightful bore, that woman.

NORA: Aren't you very tired, Torvald?

HELMER: No, not in the least.

NORA: Nor sleepy?

HELMER: Not a bit. On the contrary, I feel extraordinarily lively. And you?—you really look both tired and sleepy.

NORA: Yes, I am very tired. I want to go to sleep at once.

HELMER: There, you see it was quite right of me not to let you stay there any longer.

NORA: Everything you do is quite right, Torvald.

HELMER: [*kissing her on the forehead*] Now my little skylark is speaking reasonably. Did you notice what good spirits Rank was in this evening?

NORA: Really? Was he? I didn't speak to him at all.

HELMER: And I very little, but I have not for a long time seen him in such good form. [*looks for a while at her and then goes nearer to her*] It is delightful to be at home by ourselves again, to be all alone with you—you fascinating, charming little darling!

NORA: Don't look at me like that, Torvald.

HELMER: Why shouldn't I look at my dearest treasure?—at all the beauty that is mine, all my very own?

NORA: [*going to the other side of the table*] You mustn't say things like that to me to-night.

HELMER: [*following her*] You have still got the Tarantella in your blood, I see. And it makes you more captivating than ever. Listen—the guests are beginning to go now. [*in a lower voice*] Nora—soon the whole house will be quiet.

NORA: Yes. I hope so.

HELMER: Yes, my own darling Nora. Do you know, when I am out at a party with you like this, why I speak so little to you, keep away from you, and only send a stolen glance in your direction now and then?—do you know why I do that? It is because I make believe to myself that we are secretly in love, and you are my secretly promised bride, and that no one suspects there is anything between us.

NORA: Yes, yes—I know very well your thoughts are with me all the time.

HELMER: And when we are leaving, and I am putting the shawl over your beautiful young shoulders—on your lovely neck—then I imagine that you are my young bride and that we have just come from the wedding, and I am bringing you for the first time into our home—to be alone with you for the first time—quite alone with my shy little darling! All this evening I have longed for nothing but you. When I watched the seductive figures of the Tarantella, my blood was on fire; I could endure it no longer, and that was why I brought you down so early—

NORA: Go away, Torvald! You must let me go. I won't—

HELMER: What's that? You're joking, my little Nora! You won't—you won't? Am I not your husband—?

[*A knock is heard at the outer door.*]

NORA: [*starting*] Did you hear—?

HELMER: [*going into the hall*] Who is it?

Rank: [*outside*] It is I. May I come in for a moment?

Helmer: [*in a fretful whisper*] Oh, what does he want now? [*aloud*] Wait a minute! [*unlocks the door*] Come, that's kind of you not to pass by our door.

Rank: I thought I heard your voice, and felt as if I should like to look in. [*with a swift glance round*] Ah, yes!—these dear familiar rooms. You are very happy and cosy in here, you two.

Helmer: It seems to me that you looked after yourself pretty well upstairs too.

Rank: Excellently. Why shouldn't I? Why shouldn't one enjoy everything in this world?—at any rate as much as one can, and as long as one can. The wine was capital—

Helmer: Especially the champagne.

Rank: So you noticed that too? It is almost incredible how much I managed to put away!

Nora: Torvald drank a great deal of champagne tonight, too.

Rank: Did he?

Nora: Yes, and he is always in such good spirits afterwards.

Rank: Well, why should one not enjoy a merry evening after a well-spent day?

Helmer: Well spent? I am afraid I can't take credit for that.

Rank: [*clapping him on the back*] But I can, you know!

Nora: Doctor Rank, you must have been occupied with some scientific investigation to-day.

Rank: Exactly.

Helmer: Just listen!—little Nora talking about scientific investigations!

Nora: And may I congratulate you on the result?

Rank: Indeed you may.

Nora: Was it favourable, then?

Rank: The best possible, for both doctor and patient—certainty.

Nora: [*quickly and searchingly*] Certainty?

Rank: Absolute certainty. So wasn't I entitled to make a merry evening of it after that?

Nora: Yes, you certainly were, Doctor Rank.

Helmer: I think so too, so long as you don't have to pay for it in the morning.

Rank: Oh well, one can't have anything in this life without paying for it.

Nora: Doctor Rank—are you fond of fancy-dress balls?

Rank: Yes, if there is a fine lot of pretty costumes.

Nora: Tell me—what shall we two wear at the next?

Helmer: Little featherbrain!—are you thinking of the next already?

Rank: We two? Yes, I can tell you. You shall go as a good fairy—

Helmer: Yes, but what do you suggest as an appropriate costume for that?

Rank: Let your wife go dressed just as she is in everyday life.

Helmer: That was really very prettily turned. But can't you tell us what you will be?

Rank: Yes, my dear friend, I have quite made up my mind about that.

Helmer: Well?

Rank: At the next fancy dress ball I shall be invisible.

HELMER: That's a good joke!

RANK: There is a big black hat—have you never heard of hats that make you invisible? If you put one on, no one can see you.

HELMER: [*suppressing a smile*] Yes, you are quite right.

RANK: But I am clean forgetting what I came for. Helmer, give me a cigar—one of the dark Havanas.

HELMER: With the greatest pleasure. [*offers him his case*]

RANK: [*takes a cigar and cuts off the end*] Thanks.

NORA: [*striking a match*] Let me give you a light.

RANK: Thank you. [*She holds the match for him to light his cigar.*] And now good-bye!

HELMER: Good-bye, good-bye, dear old man!

NORA: Sleep well, Doctor Rank.

RANK: Thank you for that wish.

NORA: Wish me the same.

RANK: You? Well, if you want me to: sleep well! And thanks for the light.

[*He nods to them both and goes out.*]

HELMER: [*in a subdued voice*] He has drunk more than he ought.

NORA: [*absently*] Maybe. [HELMER *takes a bunch of keys out of his pocket and goes into the hall.*] Torvald! what are you going to do there?

HELMER: Empty the letter box; it is quite full; there will be no room to put the newspaper in to-morrow morning.

NORA: Are you going to work to-night?

HELMER: You know quite well I'm not. What is this? Some one has been at the lock.

NORA: At the lock—?

HELMER: Yes, someone has. What can it mean? I should never have thought the maid—. Here is a broken hairpin. Nora, it is one of yours.

NORA: [*quickly*] Then it must have been the children—

HELMER: Then you must get them out of those ways. There, at last I have got it open. [*Takes out the contents of the letter-box, and calls to the kitchen.*] Helen!—Helen, put out the light over the front door. [*Goes back into the room and shuts the door into the hall. He holds out his hand full of letters.*] Look at that—look what a heap of them there are. [*turning them over*] What on earth is that?

NORA: [*at the window*] The letter—No! Torvald, no!

HELMER: Two cards—of Rank's.

NORA: Of Doctor Rank's?

HELMER: [*looking at them*] Doctor Rank. They were on the top. He must have put them in when he went out.

NORA: Is there anything written on them?

HELMER: There is a black cross over the name. Look there—what an uncomfortable idea! It looks as if he were announcing his own death.

NORA: It is just what he is doing.

HELMER: What? Do you know anything about it? Has he said anything to you?

NORA: Yes. He told me that when the cards came it would be his leave-taking from us. He means to shut himself up and die.

Helmer: My poor old friend. Certainly I knew we should not have him very long with us. But so soon? And so he hides himself away like a wounded animal.

Nora: If it has to happen, it is best it should be without a word—don't you think so, Torvald?

Helmer: [*walking up and down*] He had so grown into our lives. I can't think of him as having gone out of them. He, with his sufferings and his loneliness, was like a cloudy background to our sunlit happiness. Well, perhaps it is best so. For him, anyway. [*standing still*] And perhaps for us too, Nora. We two are thrown quite upon each other now. [*puts his arms round her*] My darling wife, I don't feel as if I could hold you tight enough. Do you know, Nora, I have often wished that you might be threatened by some great danger, so that I might risk my life's blood, and everything, for your sake.

Nora: [*disengages herself, and says firmly and decidedly*] Now you must read your letters, Torvald.

Helmer: No, no; not to-night. I want to be with you, my darling wife.

Nora: With the thought of your friend's death—

Helmer: You are right, it has affected us both. Something ugly has come between us—the thought of the horrors of death. We must try and rid our minds of that. Until then—we will each go to our own room.

Nora: [*hanging on his neck*] Good-night, Torvald—Good-night!

Helmer: [*kissing her on the forehead.*] Good-night, my little singing-bird. Sleep sound, Nora. Now I will read my letters through.

[*He takes his letters and goes into his room, shutting the door after him.*]

Nora: [*gropes distractedly about, seizes* Helmer's *domino, throws it round her, while she says in quick, hoarse, spasmodic whispers*] Never to see him again. Never! Never! [*puts her shawl over her head*] Never to see my children again either—never again. Never! Never!—Ah! the icy, black water—the unfathomable depths—If only it were over! He has got it now—now he is reading it. Good-bye, Torvald and my children!

[*She is about to rush out through the hall, when* Helmer *opens his door hurriedly and stands with an open letter in his hand.*]

Helmer: Nora!

Nora: Ah!—

Helmer: What is this? Do you know what is in this letter?

Nora: Yes, I know. Let me go! Let me get out!

Helmer: [*holding her back*] Where are you going?

Nora: [*trying to get free*] You shan't save me, Torvald!

Helmer: [*reeling*] True? Is this true, that I read here? Horrible! No, no—it is impossible that it can be true.

Nora: It is true. I have loved you above everything else in the world.

Helmer: Oh, don't let us have any silly excuses.

Nora: [*taking a step towards him*] Torvald—!

Helmer: Miserable creature—what have you done?

Nora: Let me go. You shall not suffer for my sake. You shall not take it upon yourself.

HELMER: No tragedy airs, please. [*locks the hall door*] Here you shall stay and give me an explanation. Do you understand what you have done? Answer me? Do you understand what you have done?

NORA: [*looks steadily at him and says with a growing look of coldness in her face*] Yes, now I am beginning to understand thoroughly.

HELMER: [*walking about the room*] What a horrible awakening! All these eight years—she who was my joy and pride—a hypocrite, a liar—worse, worse—a criminal! The unutterable ugliness of it all! For shame! For shame! [NORA *is silent and looks steadily at him. He stops in front of her.*] I ought to have suspected that something of the sort would happen. I ought to have foreseen it. All your father's want of principle—be silent!—all your father's want of principle has come out in you. No religion, no morality, no sense of duty—. How I am punished for having winked at what he did! I did it for your sake, and this is how you repay me.

NORA: Yes, that's just it.

HELMER: Now you have destroyed all my happiness. You have ruined all my future. It is horrible to think of! I am in the power of an unscrupulous man; he can do what he likes with me, ask anything he likes of me, give me any orders he pleases—I dare not refuse. And I must sink to such miserable depths because of a thoughtless woman!

NORA: When I am out of the way, you will be free.

HELMER: No fine speeches, please. Your father had always plenty of those ready, too. What good would it be to me if you were out of the way, as you say? Not the slightest. He can make the affair known everywhere; and if he does, I may be falsely suspected of having been a party to your criminal action. Very likely people will think I was behind it all—that it was I who prompted you! And I have to thank you for all this—you whom I have cherished during the whole of our married life. Do you understand now what it is you have done for me?

NORA: [*coldly and quietly*] Yes.

HELMER: It is so incredible that I can't take it in. But we must come to some understanding. Take off that shawl. Take it off, I tell you. I must try and appease him some way or another. The matter must be hushed up at any cost. And as for you and me, it must appear as if everything between us were just as before—but naturally only in the eyes of the world. You will still remain in my house, that is a matter of course. But I shall not allow you to bring up the children; I dare not trust them to you. To think that I should be obliged to say so to one whom I have loved so dearly, and whom I still—. No, that is all over. From this moment happiness is not the question; all that concerns us is to save the remains, the fragments, the appearance—

[*A ring is heard at the front-door bell.*]

HELMER: [*with a start*] What is that? So late! Can the worst—? Can he—? Hide yourself, Nora. Say you are ill.

[NORA *stands motionless.* HELMER *goes and unlocks the hall door.*]

MAID: [*half-dressed, comes to the door*] A letter for the mistress.

HELMER: Give it to me. [*takes the letter, and shuts the door*] Yes, it is from him. You shall not have it; I will read it myself.

NORA: Yes, read it.

HELMER: [*standing by the lamp*] I scarcely have the courage to do it. It may mean ruin for both of us. No, I must know. [*tears open the letter, runs his eye over a few lines, looks at a paper enclosed and gives a shout of joy*] Nora! [*She looks at him questioningly.*] Nora!—No, I must read it once again—. Yes, it is true! I am saved! Nora, I am saved!

NORA: And I?

HELMER: You too, of course; we are both saved, both you and I. Look, he sends you your bond back. He says he regrets and repents—that a happy change in his life—never mind what he says! We are saved, Nora! No one can do anything to you. Oh, Nora, Nora!—no, first I must destroy these hateful things. Let me see—[*takes a look at the bond*] No, no, I won't look at it. The whole thing shall be nothing but a bad dream to me. [*tears up the bond and both letters, throws them all into the stove, and watches them burn*] There—now it doesn't exist any longer. He says that since Christmas Eve you—. These must have been three dreadful days for you, Nora.

NORA: I have fought a hard fight these three days.

HELMER: And suffered agonies, and seen no way out but—. No, we won't call any of the horrors to mind. We will only shout with joy, and keep saying "It's all over! It's all over!" Listen to me, Nora. You don't seem to realise that it is all over. What is this?—such a cold, set face! My poor little Nora, I quite understand; you don't feel as if you could believe that I have forgiven you. But it is true. Nora, I swear it; I have forgiven you everything. I know that what you did, you did out of love for me.

NORA: That is true.

HELMER: You have loved me as a wife ought to love her husband. Only you had not sufficient knowledge to judge of the means you used. But do you suppose you are any the less dear to me, because you don't understand how to act on your own responsibility? No, no; only lean on me; I will advise you and direct you. I should not be a man if this womanly helplessness did not just give you a double attractiveness in my eyes. You must not think any more about the hard things I said in my first moment of consternation, when I thought everything was going to overwhelm me. I have forgiven you, Nora; I swear to you I have forgiven you.

NORA: Thank you for your forgiveness.

[*She goes out through the door to the right.*]

HELMER: No, don't go—. [*looks in*] What are you doing in there?

NORA: [*from within*] Taking off my fancy dress.

HELMER: [*standing at the open door*] Yes, do. Try and calm yourself, and make your mind easy again, my frightened little singing-bird. Be at rest, and feel secure; I have broad wings to shelter you under. [*walks up and down by the door*] How warm and cosy our home is, Nora. Here is shelter for you; here I will protect you like a hunted dove that I have saved from a hawk's claws. I will bring peace to your poor beating heart. It will come, little by little, Nora, believe me.

Tomorrow morning you will look upon it all quite differently; soon everything will be just as it was before. Very soon you won't need me to assure you that I have forgiven you; you will yourself feel the certainty that I have done so. Can you suppose I should ever think of such a thing as repudiating you, or even reproaching you? You have no idea what a true man's heart is like, Nora. There is something so indescribably sweet and satisfying, to a man, in the knowledge that he has forgiven his wife—forgiven her freely, and with all his heart. It seems as if that had made her, as it were, doubly his own; he has given her a new life, so to speak; and she has in a way become both wife and child to him. So you shall be for me after this, my little scared, helpless darling. Have no anxiety about anything, Nora; only be frank and open with me, and I will serve as will and conscience both to you—. What is this? Not gone to bed? Have you changed your things?

NORA: [*in everyday dress*] Yes, Torvald, I have changed my things now.

HELMER: But what for?—so late as this.

NORA: I shall not sleep to-night.

HELMER: But, my dear Nora—

NORA: [*looking at her watch*] It is not so very late. Sit down here, Torvald. You and I have much to say to one another.

[*She sits down at one side of the table.*]

HELMER: Nora—what is this?—this cold, set face?

NORA: Sit down; it will take some time; I have a lot to talk over with you.

HELMER: [*sits down at the opposite side of the table*] You alarm me, Nora!—and I don't understand you.

NORA: No, that is just it. You don't understand me, and I have never understood you either—before to-night. No, you mustn't interrupt me. You must simply listen to what I say. Torvald, this is a settling of accounts.

HELMER: What do you mean by that?

NORA: [*after a short silence*] Isn't there one thing that strikes you as strange in our sitting here like this?

HELMER: What is that?

NORA: We have been married now eight years. Does it not occur to you that this is the first time we two, you and I, husband and wife, have had a serious conversation?

HELMER: What do you mean by serious?

NORA: In all these eight years—longer than that—from the very beginning of our acquaintance, we have never exchanged a word on any serious subject.

HELMER: Was it likely that I would be continually and for ever telling you about worries that you could not help me to bear?

NORA: I am not speaking about business matters. I say that we have never sat down in earnest together to try and get at the bottom of anything.

HELMER: But, dearest Nora, would it have been any good to you?

NORA: That is just it; you have never understood me. I have been greatly wronged, Torvald—first by papa and then by you.

HELMER: What! By us two—by us two, who have loved you better than anyone else in the world?

NORA: [*shaking her head*] You have never loved me. You have only thought it pleasant to be in love with me.

HELMER: Nora, what do I hear you saying?

NORA: It is perfectly true, Torvald. When I was at home with papa, he told me his opinion about everything, and so I had the same opinions; and if I differed from him I concealed the fact, because he would not have liked it. He called me his doll-child, and he played with me just as I used to play with my dolls. And when I came to live with you—

HELMER: What sort of an expression is that to use about our marriage?

NORA: [*undisturbed*] I mean that I was simply transferred from papa's hands into yours. You arranged everything according to your own taste, and so I got the same tastes as you—or else I pretended to, I am really not quite sure which—I think sometimes the one and sometimes the other. When I look back on it, it seems to me as if I had been living here like a poor woman—just from hand to mouth. I have existed merely to perform tricks for you, Torvald. But you would have it so. You and papa have committed a great sin against me. It is your fault that I have made nothing of my life.

HELMER: How unreasonable and how ungrateful you are, Nora! Have you not been happy here?

NORA: No, I have never been happy. I thought I was, but it has never really been so.

HELMER: Not—not happy!

NORA: No, only merry. And you have always been so kind to me. But our home has been nothing but a playroom. I have been your doll-wife, just as at home I was papa's doll-child; and here the children have been my dolls. I thought it great fun when you played with me, just as they thought it great fun when I played with them. That is what our marriage has been, Torvald.

HELMER: There is some truth in what you say—exaggerated and strained as your view of it is. But for the future it shall be different. Playtime shall be over, and lesson-time shall begin.

NORA: Whose lessons? Mine, or the children's?

HELMER: Both yours and the children's, my darling Nora.

NORA: Alas, Torvald, you are not the man to educate me into being a proper wife for you.

HELMER: And you can say that!

NORA: And I—how am I fitted to bring up the children?

HELMER: Nora!

NORA: Didn't you say so yourself a little while ago—that you dare not trust me to bring them up?

HELMER: In a moment of anger! Why do you pay any heed to that?

NORA: Indeed, you were perfectly right. I am not fit for the task. There is another task I must undertake first. I must try and educate myself—you are not the man to help me in that. I must do that for myself. And that is why I am going to leave you now.

Helmer: [*springing up*] What do you say?

Nora: I must stand quite alone, if I am to understand myself and everything about me. It is for that reason that I cannot remain with you any longer.

Helmer: Nora! Nora!

Nora: I am going away from here now, at once. I am sure Christine will take me in for the night—

Helmer: You are out of your mind! I won't allow it! I forbid you!

Nora: It is no use forbidding me anything any longer. I will take with me what belongs to myself. I will take nothing from you, either now or later.

Helmer: What sort of madness is this!

Nora: To-morrow I shall go home—I mean, to my old home. It will be easiest for me to find something to do there.

Helmer: You blind, foolish woman!

Nora: I must try and get some sense, Torvald.

Helmer: To desert your home, your husband and your children! And you don't consider what people will say!

Nora: I cannot consider that at all. I only know that it is necessary for me.

Helmer: It's shocking. This is how you would neglect your most sacred duties.

Nora: What do you consider my most sacred duties?

Helmer: Do I need to tell you that? Are they not your duties to your husband and your children?

Nora: I have other duties just as sacred.

Helmer: That you have not. What duties could those be?

Nora: Duties to myself.

Helmer: Before all else, you are a wife and a mother.

Nora: I don't believe that any longer. I believe that before all else I am a reasonable human being, just as you are—or, at all events, that I must try and become one. I know quite well, Torvald, that most people would think you right, and that views of that kind are to be found in books; but I can no longer content myself with what most people say, or with what is found in books. I must think over things for myself and get to understand them.

Helmer: Can you not understand your place in your own home? Have you not a reliable guide in such matters as that?—have you no religion?

Nora: I am afraid, Torvald, I do not exactly know what religion is.

Helmer: What are you saying?

Nora: I know nothing but what the clergyman said when I went to be confirmed. He told us that religion was this, and that, and the other. When I am away from all this, and am alone, I will look into that matter too. I will see if what the clergyman said is true, or at all events if it is true for me.

Helmer: This is unheard of in a girl of your age! But if religion cannot lead you aright, let me try and awaken your conscience. I suppose you have some moral sense? Or—answer me—am I to think you have none?

NORA: I assure you, Torvald, that is not an easy question to answer. I really don't know. The thing perplexes me altogether. I only know that you and I look at it in quite a different light. I am learning, too, that the law is quite another thing from what I supposed; but I find it impossible to convince myself that the law is right. According to it a woman has no right to spare her old dying father, or to save her husband's life. I can't believe that.

HELMER: You talk like a child. You don't understand the conditions of the world in which you live.

NORA: No, I don't. But now I am going to try. I am going to see if I can make out who is right, the world or I.

HELMER: You are ill, Nora; you are delirious; I almost think you are out of your mind.

NORA: I have never felt my mind so clear and certain as to-night.

HELMER: And is it with a clear and certain mind that you forsake your husband and your children?

NORA: Yes, it is.

HELMER: Then there is only one possible explanation.

NORA: What is that?

HELMER: You do not love me any more.

NORA: No, that is just it.

HELMER: Nora!—and you can say that?

NORA: It gives me great pain, Torvald, for you have always been so kind to me, but I cannot help it. I do not love you any more.

HELMER: [*regaining his composure*] Is that a clear and certain conviction too?

NORA: Yes, absolutely clear and certain. That is the reason why I will not stay here any longer.

HELMER: And can you tell me what I have done to forfeit your love?

NORA: Yes, indeed I can. It was to-night, when the wonderful thing did not happen; then I saw you were not the man I had thought you.

HELMER: Explain yourself better—I don't understand you.

NORA: I have waited so patiently for eight years; for goodness knows, I knew very well that wonderful things don't happen every day. Then this horrible misfortune came upon me; and then I felt quite certain that the wonderful thing was going to happen at last. When Krogstad's letter was lying out there, never for a moment did I imagine that you would consent to accept this man's conditions. I was so absolutely certain that you would say to him: Publish the thing to the whole world. And when that was done—

HELMER: Yes, what then?—when I had exposed my wife to shame and disgrace?

NORA: When that was done, I was so absolutely certain, you would come forward and take everything upon yourself, and say: I am the guilty one.

HELMER: Nora—!

NORA: You mean that I would never have accepted such a sacrifice on your part? No, of course not. But what would my assurances have been worth against yours? That was the wonderful thing which I hoped for and feared; and it was to prevent that, that I wanted to kill myself.

HELMER: I would gladly work night and day for you, Nora—bear sorrow and want for your sake. But no man would sacrifice his honour for the one he loves.

NORA: It is a thing hundreds of thousands of women have done.

HELMER: Oh, you think and talk like a heedless child.

NORA: Maybe. But you neither think nor talk like the man I could bind myself to. As soon as your fear was over—and it was not fear for what threatened me, but for what might happen to you—when the whole thing was past, as far as you were concerned it was exactly as if nothing at all had happened. Exactly as before, I was your little skylark, your doll, which you would in future treat with doubly gentle care, because it was so brittle and fragile. [*getting up*] Torvald—it was then it dawned upon me that for eight years I had been living here with a strange man, and had borne him three children—. Oh, I can't bear to think of it! I could tear myself into little bits!

HELMER: [*sadly*] I see, I see. An Abyss has opened between us—there is no denying it. But, Nora, would it not be possible to fill it up?

NORA: As I am now, I am no wife for you.

HELMER: I have it in me to become a different man.

NORA: Perhaps—if your doll is taken away from you.

HELMER: But to part!—to part from you! No, no, Nora, I can't understand that idea.

NORA: [*going out to the right*] That makes it all the more certain that it must be done.

[*She comes back with her cloak and hat and a small bag which she puts on a chair by the table.*]

HELMER: Nora, Nora, not now! Wait till to-morrow.

NORA: [*putting on her cloak*] I cannot spend the night in a strange man's room.

HELMER: But can't we live here like brother and sister—?

NORA: [*putting on her hat*] You know very well that would not last long. [*puts the shawl round her*] Good-bye, Torvald. I won't see the little ones. I know they are in better hands than mine. As I am now, I can be of no use to them.

HELMER: But some day, Nora—some day?

NORA: How can I tell? I have no idea what is going to become of me.

HELMER: But you are my wife, whatever becomes of you.

NORA: Listen, Torvald. I have heard that when a wife deserts her husband's house, as I am doing now, he is legally freed from all obligations towards her. In any case I set you free from all your obligations. You are not to feel yourself bound in the slightest way, any more than I shall. There must be perfect freedom on both sides. See here is your ring back. Give me mine.

HELMER: That too?

NORA: That too.

HELMER: Here it is.

Nora: That's right. Now it is all over. I have put the keys here. The maids know all about everything in the house—better than I do. To-morrow, after I have left her, Christine will come here and pack up my own things that I brought with me from home. I will have them sent after me.

Helmer: All over! All over!—Nora, shall you never think of me again?

Nora: I know I shall often think of you and the children and this house.

Helmer: May I write to you, Nora?

Nora: No—never. You must not do that.

Helmer: But at least let me send you—

Nora: Nothing—nothing—

Helmer: Let me help you if you are in want.

Nora: No. I can receive nothing from a stranger.

Helmer: Nora—can I never be anything more than a stranger to you?

Nora: [*taking her bag*] Ah, Torvald, the most wonderful thing of all would have to happen.

Helmer: Tell me what that would be!

Nora: Both you and I would have to be so changed that—. Oh, Torvald, I don't believe any longer in wonderful things happening.

Helmer: But I will believe in it. Tell me? So changed that—?

Nora: That our life together would be a real wedlock. Good-bye.

[*She goes out through the hall.*]

Helmer: [*sinks down on a chair at the door and buries his face in his hands*] Nora! Nora! [*looks round, and rises*] Empty. She is gone. [*A hope flashes across his mind.*] The most wonderful thing of all—?

[*The sound of a door slamming is heard from below.*]

Arthur Miller (1915–2005) was born in Manhattan into an upper-middle-class family of Jewish and Polish ethnicity, whose wealth came from a family-owned clothing factory. After the business failed in 1928, the family moved to Brooklyn. The Depression, the social environment of Brooklyn, and American anti-Semitism—which Miller experienced at this point in his life—all play a central role in his work. Because of family finances, Miller did not attend college and worked a series of jobs until 1934, when he entered the University of Michigan; there Miller worked his way through college by washing dishes and feeding laboratory mice. At Michigan he also began his career as a playwright. After graduation, Miller became part of the Federal Theater Project, where he wrote about Adolf Hitler. In 1940, he married Mary Grace Slattery. In the mid 1950s, Miller experienced trouble with the U.S. government over his purported ties to communism. He gave testimony before the House Committee on Un-American Activities, where he admitted to having attended a meeting of communist writers, but refused to give other names and defended his right of free speech. In 1956 Miller married the actress Marilyn Monroe (divorced 1961) and later married Ingeborg Morath, a photojournalist. He continued to write prolifically in different genres; in 2004, Miller's play *Finishing the Picture* was produced, and he received the Peggy V. Helmerich Distinguished Author Award for his collected works.

Death of a Salesman premiered on February 10, 1949, and ran for 742 performances on Broadway. The director was Elia Kazan, the designer Jo Mielziner, and the composer Alex North. The Broadway cast included Lee J. Cobb as Willy, Mildred Dunnock as Linda, Arthur Kennedy as Biff, and Cameron Mitchell as Hap. *Salesman* won the Pulitzer Prize and the New York Drama Critics Circle Award for best play of that year. Since then, it has been performed in many countries, including Australia, England, France, Germany, Russia, and China, where Miller himself directed the production. In 1999, the play's fiftieth anniversary, *Salesman* was revived on Broadway and won a Tony for Best Revival of a Play. There have been several film and television versions, including an excellent 1985 television version with Dustin Hoffman, Kate Reid, and John Malkovich.

Technically, *Death of a Salesman* is notable for two dramatic innovations. The first is Miller's development of **subjective realism** as a structural technique. The other is the stage set, which used **abstract realism**.

In some cases, as in Arthur Miller's *Death of a Salesman*, the stage itself attracts so much of the audience's attention that it becomes almost another character in the play. *Death of a Salesman* ranges widely in time and place, but uses staging to keep the action unified. Stage designer Jo Mielziner observed that although the play explores both past and present through dramatized **flashbacks**, the drama's unity could be enhanced by avoiding scene changes. Recognizing that the play's most important visual symbol was Willy Loman's house, Mielziner made the temporal shifts easily comprehensible by placing other scenes—the graveyard, the hotel room in Boston, etc.—on a forestage contiguous with the house. Lighting changes made the move from one place to another, and from past to present, seamless but significant.

Death of a Salesman was instantly recognized as a classic drama because it touched on timely and enduring themes, mostly centered around the disparity between reality and the ideal: some examples include the tragedy of the common man, the American Dream and the Protestant Work Ethic, the family under democracy, and the city versus the Western frontier.

Related Works: Auden, "The Unknown Citizen"; cummings, "Buffalo Bill's" and "Next of course god america I"; Eliot, "The Love Song of J. Alfred Prufrock"; *Everyman*; Ginsberg, "Howl"; Hughes, "Harlem"; McKay, "America"; Sophocles, *Antigone*; Wilson, *The Piano Lesson*.

Death of a Salesman

ACT ONE

A melody is heard, played upon a flute. It is small and fine, telling of grass and trees and the horizon. The curtain rises.

Before us is the SALESMAN'S *house. We are aware of towering, angular shapes behind it, surrounding it on all sides. Only the blue light of the sky falls upon the house and forestage; the surrounding area shows an angry glow of orange. As more light appears, we see a solid vault of apartment houses around the small, fragile-seeming home. An air of the dream clings to the place, a dream rising out of reality. The kitchen at center seems actual*

Stage set from *Death of a Salesman*

enough, for there is a kitchen table with three chairs, and a refrigerator. But no other fixtures are seen. At the back of the kitchen there is a draped entrance, which leads to the living-room. To the right of the kitchen, on a level raised two feet, is a bedroom furnished only with a brass bedstead and a straight chair. On a shelf over the bed a silver athletic trophy stands. A window opens on to the apartment house at the side.

Behind the kitchen, on a level raised six and a half feet, is the boys' bedroom, at present barely visible. Two beds are dimly seen, and at the back of the room a dormer window. (This bedroom is above the unseen living-room.) At the left a stairway curves up to it from the kitchen.

The entire setting is wholly or, in some places, partially transparent. The roof-line of the house is one-dimensional; under and over it we see the apartment buildings. Before the house lies an apron, curving beyond the forestage into the orchestra. This forward area serves as the back yard as well as the locale of all Willy's imaginings and of his city scenes. Whenever the action is in the present the actors observe the imaginary wall-lines, entering the house only through its door at the left. But in the scenes of the past these boundaries are broken, and characters enter or leave a room by stepping "through" a wall on to the forestage.

The action takes place in Willy Loman's house and yard and in various places he visits in the New York and Boston of today.

Throughout the play, in the stage directions, left and right mean stage left and stage right.

[*From the right,* WILLY LOMAN, *the Salesman, enters, carrying two large sample cases. The flute plays on. He hears but is not aware of it. He is past sixty years of age, dressed quietly. Even as he crosses the stage to the doorway of the house, his exhaustion is apparent. He unlocks the door, comes into the kitchen, and thankfully lets his burden down, feeling the soreness of his palms. A word-sigh escapes his lips—it might be* "Oh, boy, oh, boy." *He closes the door, then carries his cases out into the living-room, through the draped kitchen doorway.* LINDA, *his wife, has stirred in her bed at the right. She gets out and puts on a robe, listening. Most often jovial, she has developed an iron repression of her exceptions to* WILLY'S *behavior—she more than loves him, she admires him, as though his mercurial nature, his temper, his massive dreams and little cruelties, served her only as sharp reminders of the turbulent longings within him, longings which she shares but lacks the temperament to utter and follow to their end.*]

LINDA [*hearing* WILLY *outside the bedroom, calls with some trepidation*]: Willy!

WILLY: It's all right. I came back.

LINDA: Why? What happened? [*Slight pause.*] Did something happen, Willy?

WILLY: No, nothing happened.

LINDA: You didn't smash the car, did you?

WILLY: [*with casual irritation*]: I said nothing happened. Didn't you hear me?

LINDA: Don't you feel well?

WILLY: I'm tired to the death. [*The flute has faded away. He sits on the bed beside her, a little numb.*] I couldn't make it. I just couldn't make it, Linda.

LINDA [*very carefully, delicately*]: Where were you all day? You look terrible.

WILLY: I got as far as a little above Yonkers. I stopped for a cup of coffee. Maybe it was the coffee.

LINDA: What?

WILLY [*after a pause*]: I suddenly couldn't drive any more. The car kept going off on to the shoulder, y'know?

LINDA [*helpfully*]: Oh. Maybe it was the steering again. I don't think Angelo knows the Studebaker.

WILLY: No, it's me, it's me. Suddenly I realize I'm goin' sixty miles an hour and I don't remember the last five minutes. I'm—I can't seem to—keep my mind to it.

LINDA: Maybe it's your glasses. You never went for your new glasses.

WILLY: No, I see everything. I came back ten miles an hour. It took me nearly four hours from Yonkers.

LINDA [*resigned*]: Well, you'll just have to take a rest, Willy, you can't continue this way.

WILLY: I just got back from Florida.

LINDA: But you didn't rest your mind. Your mind is overactive, and the mind is what counts, dear.

WILLY: I'll start out in the morning. Maybe I'll feel better in the morning. [*She is taking off his shoes.*] These goddam arch supports are killing me.

LINDA: Take an aspirin. Should I get you an aspirin? It'll soothe you.

WILLY [*with wonder*]: I was driving along, you understand? And I was fine. I was even observing the scenery. You can imagine, me looking at scenery, on the road every week of my life. But it's so beautiful up there, Linda, the trees are so thick, and the sun is warm. I opened the windshield and just let the warm air bathe over me. And then all of a sudden I'm goin' off the road! I'm tellin' ya. I absolutely forgot I was driving. If I'd've gone the other way over the white line I might've killed somebody. So I went on again—and five minutes later I'm dreamin' again, and I nearly—[*He presses two fingers against his eyes.*] I have such thoughts, I have such strange thoughts.

LINDA: Willy, dear. Talk to them again. There's no reason why you can't work in New York.

WILLY: They don't need me in New York. I'm the New England man. I'm vital in New England.

LINDA: But you're sixty years old. They can't expect you to keep traveling every week.

WILLY: I'll have to send a wire to Portland. I'm supposed to see Brown and Morrison tomorrow morning at ten o'clock to show the line. Goddammit. I could sell them! [*He starts putting on his jacket.*]

LINDA [*taking the jacket from him*]: Why don't you go down to the place tomorrow and tell Howard you've simply got to work in New York? You're too accommodating, dear.

WILLY: If old man Wagner was alive I'd a been in charge of New York now! That man was a prince, he was a masterful man. But that boy of his, that Howard, he don't appreciate. When I went north the first time, the Wagner Company didn't know where New England was!

LINDA: Why don't you tell those things to Howard, dear?

WILLY [*encouraged*]: I will, I definitely will. Is there any cheese?

LINDA: I'll make you a sandwich.

WILLY: No, go to sleep. I'll take some milk. I'll be up right away. The boys in?

LINDA: They're sleeping. Happy took Biff on a date to-night.

WILLY [*interested*]: That so?

LINDA: It was so nice to see them shaving together, one behind the other, in the bathroom. And going out together. You notice? The whole house smells of shaving lotion.

WILLY: Figure it out. Work a lifetime to pay off a house. You finally own it, and there's nobody to live in it.

LINDA: Well, dear, life is a casting off. It's always that way.

WILLY: No, no, some people—some people accomplish something. Did Biff say anything after I went this morning?

LINDA: You shouldn't have criticized him, Willy, especially after he just got off the train. You mustn't lose your temper with him.

WILLY: When the hell did I lose my temper? I simply asked him if he was making any money. Is that a criticism?

LINDA: But, dear, how could he make any money?

WILLY [*worried and angered*]: There's such an undercurrent in him. He became a moody man. Did he apologize when I left this morning?

LINDA: He was crestfallen, Willy. You know how he admires you. I think if he finds himself, then you'll both be happier and not fight any more.

WILLY: How can he find himself on a farm? Is that a life? A farmhand? In the beginning, when he was young, I thought, well, a young man, it's good for him to tramp around, take a lot of different jobs. But it's more than ten years now and he has yet to make thirty-five dollars a week!

LINDA: He's finding himself, Willy.

WILLY: Not finding yourself at the age of thirty-four is a disgrace!

LINDA: Shh!

WILLY: The trouble is he's lazy, goddammit!

LINDA: Willy, please!

WILLY: Biff is a lazy bum!

LINDA: They're sleeping. Get something to eat. Go on down.

WILLY: Why did he come home? I would like to know what brought him home.

LINDA: I don't know. I think he's still lost. Willy, I think he's very lost.

WILLY: Biff Loman is lost. In the greatest country in the world a young man with such—personal attractiveness, gets lost. And such a hard worker. There's one thing about Biff—he's not lazy.

LINDA: Never.

WILLY [*with pity and resolve*]: I'll see him in the morning; I'll have a nice talk with him. I'll get him a job selling. He could be big in no time. My God! Remember how they used to follow him around in high school? When he smiled at one of them their faces lit up. When he walked down the street . . . [*He loses himself in reminiscences.*]

LINDA [*trying to bring him out of it*]: Willy, dear. I got a new kind of American-type cheese today. It's whipped.

WILLY: Why do you get American when I like Swiss?

LINDA: I just thought you'd like a change—

WILLY: I don't want a change! I want Swiss cheese. Why am I always being contradicted?

LINDA [*with a covering laugh*]: I thought it would be a surprise.

WILLY: Why don't you open a window in here, for God's sake?

LINDA [*with infinite patience*]: They're all open, dear.

WILLY: The way they boxed us in here. Bricks and windows, windows and bricks.

LINDA: We should've bought the land next door.

WILLY: The street is lined with cars. There's not a breath of fresh air in the neighborhood. The grass don't grow any more, you can't raise a carrot in the back yard. They should've had a law against apartment houses. Remember those two beautiful elm trees out there? When I and Biff hung the swing between them?

LINDA: Yeah, like being a million miles from the city.

WILLY: They should've arrested the builder for cutting those down. They massacred the neighborhood. [*Lost*] More and more I think of those days, Linda. This time of year it was lilac and wisteria. And then the peonies would come out, and the daffodils. What fragrance in this room!

LINDA: Well, after all, people had to move somewhere.

WILLY: No, there's more people now.

LINDA: I don't think there's more people. I think—

WILLY: There's more people! That's what's ruining this country! Population is getting out of control. The competition is maddening! Smell the stink from that apartment house! And another one on the other side . . . How can they whip cheese?

[*On* WILLY'S *last line*, BIFF *and* HAPPY *raise themselves up in their beds, listening.*]

LINDA: Go down, try it. And be quiet.

WILLY [*turning to* LINDA, *guiltily*]: You're not worried about me, are you, sweetheart?

BIFF: What's the matter?

HAPPY: Listen!

LINDA: You've got too much on the ball to worry about.

WILLY: You're my foundation and my support, Linda.

LINDA: Just try to relax, dear. You make mountains out of molehills.

WILLY: I won't fight with him any more. If he wants to go back to Texas, let him go.

LINDA: He'll find his way.

WILLY: Sure. Certain men just don't get started till later in life. Like Thomas Edison, I think. Or B. F. Goodrich. One of them was deaf. [*He starts for the bedroom doorway.*] I'll put my money on Biff.

LINDA: And Willy—if it's warm Sunday we'll drive in the country. And we'll open the windshield, and take lunch.

WILLY: No, the windshields don't open on the new cars.

LINDA: But you opened it today.

WILLY: Me? I didn't [*He stops.*] Now isn't that peculiar! Isn't that a remarkable— [*He breaks off in amazement and fright as the flute is heard distantly.*]

LINDA: What, darling?

WILLY: That is the most remarkable thing.

LINDA: What, dear?

WILLY: I was thinking of the Chevvy. [*Slight pause.*] Nineteen twenty-eight . . . when I had that red Chevvy—[*Breaks off.*] That funny? I coulda sworn I was driving that Chevvy today.

LINDA: Well, that's nothing. Something must've reminded you.

WILLY: Remarkable. Ts. Remember those days? The way Biff used to simonize that car? The dealer refused to believe there was eighty thousand miles on it. [*He shakes his head.*] Heh! [*To* LINDA] Close your eyes. I'll be right up. [*He walks out of the bedroom.*]

HAPPY [*to* BIFF]: Jesus, maybe he smashed up the car again!

LINDA [*calling after* WILLY]: Be careful on the stairs, dear! The cheese is on the middle shelf! [*She turns, goes over to the bed, takes his jacket, and goes out of the bedroom.*]

[*Light has risen on the boys' room. Unseen,* WILLY *is heard talking to himself,* "Eighty thousand miles," *and a little laugh.* BIFF *gets out of bed, comes downstage a bit, and stands attentively.* BIFF *is two years older than his brother,* HAPPY, *well built, but in these days bears a worn air and seems less self-assured. He has succeeded less, and his dreams are stronger and less acceptable than* HAPPY'S. HAPPY *is tall, powerfully made. Sexuality is like a visible color on him, or a scent that many women have discovered. He, like his brother, is lost, but in a different way, for he has never allowed himself to turn his face toward defeat and is thus more confused and hard-skinned, although seemingly more content.*]

HAPPY [*getting out of bed*]: He's going to get his licence taken away if he keeps that up. I'm getting nervous about him, y'know, Biff?

BIFF: His eyes are going.

HAPPY: No, I've driven with him. He sees all right. He just doesn't keep his mind on it. I drove into the city with him last week. He stops at a green light and then it turns red and he goes. [*He laughs.*]

BIFF: Maybe he's color-blind.

HAPPY: Pop? Why, he's got the finest eye for color in the business. You know that.

BIFF [*sitting down on his bed*]: I'm going to sleep.

HAPPY: You're not still sour on Dad, are you, Biff?

BIFF: He's all right, I guess.

WILLY [*underneath them, in the living-room*]: Yes, sir, eighty thousand miles—eighty-two thousand!

BIFF: You smoking?

HAPPY [*holding out a pack of cigarettes*]: Want one?

BIFF [*taking a cigarette*]: I can never sleep when I smell it.

WILLY: What a simonizing job, heh!

HAPPY [*with deep sentiment*]: Funny, Biff, y'know? Us sleeping in here again? The old beds. [*He pats his bed affectionately.*] All the talk that went across those two beds, huh? Our whole lives.

BIFF: Yeah. Lotta dreams and plans.

HAPPY [*with a deep and masculine laugh*]: About five hundred women would like to know what was said in this room.

[*They share a soft laugh.*]

BIFF: Remember that big Betsy something—what the hell was her name—over on Bushwick Avenue?

HAPPY [*combing his hair*]: With the collie dog!

BIFF: That's the one. I got you in there, remember?

HAPPY: Yeah, that was my first time—I think. Boy, there was a pig! [*They laugh, almost crudely.*] You taught me everything I know about women. Don't forget that.

BIFF: I bet you forgot how bashful you used to be. Especially with girls.

HAPPY: Oh, I still am, Biff.

BIFF: Oh, go on.

HAPPY: I just control it, that's all. I think I got less bashful and you got more so. What happened, Biff? Where's the old humor, the old confidence? [*He shakes* BIFF'S *knee.* BIFF *gets up and moves restlessly about the room.*] What's the matter?

BIFF: Why does Dad mock me all the time?

HAPPY: He's not mocking you, he—

BIFF: Everything I say there's a twist of mockery on his face. I can't get near him.

HAPPY: He just wants you to make good, that's all. I wanted to talk to you about Dad for a long time, Biff. Something's—happening to him. He—talks to himself.

BIFF: I noticed that this morning. But he always mumbled.

HAPPY: But not so noticeable. It got so embarrassing I sent him to Florida. And you know something? Most of the time he's talking to you.

BIFF: What's he say about me?

HAPPY: I can't make it out.

BIFF: What's he say about me?

HAPPY: I think the fact that you're not settled, that you're still kind of up in the air . . .

BIFF: There's one or two other things depressing him, Happy.

HAPPY: What do you mean?

BIFF: Never mind. Just don't lay it all to me.

HAPPY: But I think if you got started—I mean—is there any future for you out there?

BIFF: I tell ya, Hap, I don't know what the future is. I don't know—what I'm supposed to want.

HAPPY: What do you mean?

BIFF: Well, I spent six or seven years after high school trying to work myself up. Shipping clerk, salesman, business of one kind or another. And it's a measly manner of existence. To get on that subway on the hot mornings in summer. To devote your whole life to keeping stock, or making phone calls, or selling or buying. To suffer fifty weeks of the year for the sake of a two-week vacation, when all you really desire is to be outdoors, with your shirt off. And always to have to get ahead of the next fella. And still—that's how you build a future.

HAPPY: Well, you really enjoy it on a farm? Are you content out there?

BIFF [*with rising agitation*]: Hap, I've had twenty or thirty different kinds of job since I left home before the war, and it always turns out the same. I just realized it lately. In Nebraska when I herded cattle, and the Dakotas, and Arizona, and now in Texas. It's why I came home now, I guess, because I realized it. This farm I work on, it's spring there now, see? And they've got about fifteen new colts. There's nothing more inspiring or—beautiful than the sight of a mare and a new colt. And it's cool there now, see? Texas is cool now, and it's spring. And whenever spring comes to where I am, I suddenly get the feeling, my God, I'm not gettin' anywhere! What the hell am I doing, playing around with horses, twenty-eight dollars a week! I'm thirty-four years old, I oughta be makin' my future. That's when I come running home. And now, I get here, and I don't know what to do with myself. [*After a pause*] I've always made a point of not wasting my life, and everytime I come back here I know that all I've done is to waste my life.

HAPPY: You're a poet, you know that, Biff? You're a— you're an idealist!

BIFF: No, I'm mixed up very bad. Maybe I oughta get married. Maybe I oughta get stuck into something. Maybe that's my trouble. I'm like a boy. I'm not married, I'm not in business. I just—I'm like a boy. Are you content, Hap? You're a success, aren't you? Are you content?

HAPPY: Hell, no!

BIFF: Why? You're making money, aren't you?

HAPPY [*moving about with energy, expressiveness*]: All I can do now is wait for the merchandise manager to die. And suppose I get to be merchandise manager? He's a good friend of mine, and he just built a terrific estate on Long Island. And he lived there about two months and sold it, and now he's building another one. He can't enjoy it once it's finished. And I know that's just what I would do. I don't know what the hell I'm workin' for. Sometimes I sit in my apartment—all alone. And I think of the rent I'm paying. And it's crazy. But then, it's what I always wanted. My own apartment, a car, and plenty of women. And still, goddammit, I'm lonely.

BIFF [*with enthusiasm*]: Listen, why don't you come out West with me?

HAPPY: You and I, heh?

BIFF: Sure, maybe we could buy a ranch. Raise cattle, use our muscles. Men built like we are should be working out in the open.

HAPPY [*avidly*]: The Loman Brothers, heh?

BIFF [*with vast affection*]: Sure, we'd be known all over the counties!

HAPPY [*enthralled*]: That's what I dream about, Biff. Sometimes I want to just rip my clothes off in the middle of the store and outbox that goddam merchandise manager. I mean I can outbox, outrun, and outlift anybody in that store, and I have to take orders from those common, petty sons-of-bitches till I can't stand it any more.

BIFF: I'm tellin' you, kid, if you were with me I'd be happy out there.

HAPPY [*enthused*]: See, Biff, everybody around me is so false that I'm constantly lowering my ideals . . .

BIFF: Baby, together we'd stand up for one another, we'd have someone to trust.

HAPPY: If I were around you—

BIFF: Hap, the trouble is we weren't brought up to grub for money. I don't know how to do it.

HAPPY: Neither can I!

BIFF: Then let's go!

HAPPY: The only thing is—what can you make out there?

BIFF: But look at your friend. Builds an estate and then hasn't the peace of mind to live in it.

HAPPY: Yeah, but when he walks into the store the waves part in front of him. That's fifty-two thousand dollars a year coming through the revolving door, and I got more in my pinky finger than he's got in his head.

BIFF: Yeah, but you just said—

HAPPY: I gotta show some of those pompous, self-important executives over there that Hap Loman can make the grade. I want to walk into the store the way he walks in. Then I'll go with you, Biff. We'll be together yet, I swear. But take those two we had tonight. Now weren't they gorgeous creatures?

BIFF: Yeah, yeah, most gorgeous I've had in years.

HAPPY: I get that any time I want, Biff. Whenever I feel disgusted. The only trouble is, it gets like bowling or something. I just keep knockin' them over and it doesn't mean anything. You still run around a lot?

BIFF: Naa. I'd like to find a girl—steady, somebody with substance.

HAPPY: That's what I long for.

BIFF: Go on! You'd never come home.

HAPPY: I would! Somebody with character, with resistance! Like Mom, y'know? You're gonna call me a bastard when I tell you this. That girl Charlotte I was with tonight is engaged to be married in five weeks. [*He tries on his new hat.*]

BIFF: No kiddin'!

HAPPY: Sure, the guy's in line for the vice-presidency of the store. I don't know what gets into me, maybe I just have an overdeveloped sense of competition or something, but I went and ruined her, and furthermore I can't get rid of her. And he's the third executive I've done that to. Isn't that a crummy characteristic? And to top it all, I go to their weddings! [*Indignantly, but laughing*] Like I'm not supposed to take bribes. Manufacturers offer me a hundred-dollar bill now and then to throw an order their way. You know how honest I am, but it's like this girl, see. I hate myself for it. Because I don't want the girl, and still, I take it and—I love it!

BIFF: Let's go to sleep.

HAPPY: I guess we didn't settle anything, heh?

BIFF: I just got one idea that I think I'm going to try.

HAPPY: What's that?

BIFF: Remember Bill Oliver?

HAPPY: Sure, Oliver is very big now. You want to work for him again?

BIFF: No, but when I quit he said something to me. He put his arm on my shoulder, and he said, "Biff, if you ever need anything, come to me."

HAPPY: I remember that. That sounds good.

BIFF: I think I'll go to see him. If I could get ten thousand or ever seven or eight thousand dollars I could buy a beautiful ranch.

HAPPY: I bet he'd back you. 'Cause he thought highly of you, Biff. I mean, they all do. You're well liked, Biff. That's why I say to come back here, and we both have the apartment. And I'm tellin' you, Biff, any babe you want . . .

BIFF: No, with a ranch I could do the work I like and still be something. I just wonder though. I wonder if Oliver still thinks I stole that carton of basketballs.

HAPPY: Oh, he probably forgot that long ago. It's almost ten years. You're too sensitive. Anyway, he didn't really fire you.

BIFF: Well, I think he was going to. I think that's why I quit. I was never sure whether he knew or not. I know he thought the world of me, though. I was the only one he'd let lock up the place.

WILLY [*below*]: You gonna wash the engine, Biff?

HAPPY: Shh!

[BIFF *looks at* HAPPY, *who is gazing down, listening.* WILLY *is mumbling in the parlor.*]

HAPPY: You hear that?

[*They listen.* WILLY *laughs warmly.*]

BIFF [*growing angry*]: Doesn't he know Mom can hear that?

WILLY: Don't get your sweater dirty, Biff!

[*A look of pain crosses* BIFF'S *face.*]

HAPPY: Isn't that terrible? Don't leave again, will you? You'll find a job here. You gotta stick around. I don't know what to do about him, it's getting embarrassing.

WILLY: What a simonizing job!

BIFF: Mom's hearing that!

WILLY: No kiddin', Biff, you got a date? Wonderful!

HAPPY: Go on to sleep. But talk to him in the morning, will you?

BIFF [*reluctantly getting into bed*]: With her in the house. Brother!

HAPPY [*getting into bed*]: I wish you'd have a good talk with him.

[*The light on their room begins to fade.*]

BIFF [*to himself in bed*]: That selfish, stupid . . .

HAPPY: Sh . . . Sleep, Biff.

[*Their light is out. Well before they have finished speaking,* WILLY'S *form is dimly seen below in the darkened kitchen. He opens the refrigerator, searches in there, and takes out a bottle of milk. The apartment houses are fading out, and the entire house and surroundings become covered with leaves. Music insinuates itself as the leaves appear.*]

WILLY: Just wanna be careful with those girls, Biff, that's all. Don't make any promises. No promises of any kind. Because a girl, y'know, they always believe what you tell 'em, and you're very young. Biff, you're too young to be talking seriously to girls.

[*Light rises on the kitchen.* WILLY, *talking, shuts the refrigerator door and comes downstage to the kitchen table. He pours milk into a glass. He is totally immersed in himself, smiling faintly.*]

WILLY: Too young entirely, Biff. You want to watch your schooling first. Then when you're all set, there'll be plenty of girls for a boy like you. [*He smiles broadly at a kitchen chair.*] That so? The girls pay for you? [*He laughs.*] Boy, you must really be makin' a hit.

[WILLY *is gradually addressing—physically—a point offstage, speaking through the wall of the kitchen, and his voice has been rising in volume to that of a normal conversation.*]

WILLY: I been wondering why you polish the car so careful. Ha! Don't leave the hubcaps, boys. Get the chamois to the hubcaps. Happy, use newspaper on the windows, it's the easiest thing. Show him how to do it, Biff! You see, Happy?

Pad it up, use it like a pad. That's it, that's it, good work. You're doin' all right, Hap. [*He pauses, then nods in approbation for a few seconds, then looks upward.*] Biff, first thing we gotta do when we get time is clip that big branch over the house. Afraid it's gonna fall in a storm and hit the roof. Tell you what. We get a rope and sling her around, and then we climb up there with a couple of saws and take her down. Soon as you finish the car, boys. I wanna see ya. I got a surprise for you, boys.

BIFF [*offstage*]: Whatta ya got, Dad?

WILLY: No, you finish first. Never leave a job till you're finished—remember that. [*Looking toward the "big trees"*] Biff, up in Albany I saw a beautiful hammock. I think I'll buy it next trip, and we'll hang it right between those two elms. Wouldn't that be something? Just swingin' there under those branches. Boy, that would be . . .

[YOUNG BIFF *and* YOUNG HAPPY *appear from the direction* WILLY *was addressing.* HAPPY *carries rags and a pail of water.* BIFF, *wearing a sweater with a block "S," carries a football.*]

BIFF [*pointing in the direction of the car offstage*]: How's that, Pop, professional?

WILLY: Terrific. Terrific job, boys. Good work, Biff.

HAPPY: Where's the surprise, Pop?

WILLY: In the back seat of the car.

HAPPY: Boy! [*He runs off.*]

BIFF: What is it, Dad? Tell me, what'd you buy?

WILLY [*laughing, cuffs him*]: Never mind, something I want you to have.

BIFF [*turns and starts off*]: What is it, Hap?

HAPPY [*offstage*]: It's a punching bag!

BIFF: Oh, Pop!

WILLY: It's got Gene Tunney's signature on it!

[HAPPY *runs onstage with a punching bag.*]

BIFF: Gee, how'd you know we wanted a punching bag?

WILLY: Well, it's the finest thing for the timing.

HAPPY [*lies down on his back and pedals with his feet*]: I'm losing weight, you notice, Pop?

WILLY [*to* HAPPY]: Jumping rope is good, too.

BIFF: Did you see the new football I got?

WILLY [*examining the ball*]: Where'd you get a new ball?

BIFF: The coach told me to practice my passing.

WILLY: That so? And he gave you the ball, heh?

BIFF: Well, I borrowed it from the locker room. [*He laughs confidentially.*]

WILLY [*laughing with him at the theft*]: I want you to return that.

HAPPY: I told you he wouldn't like it!

BIFF [*angrily*]: Well, I'm bringing it back!

WILLY [*stopping the incipient argument, to* HAPPY]: Sure, he's gotta practice with a regulation ball, doesn't he? [*To* BIFF] Coach'll probably congratulate you on your initiative!

BIFF: Oh, he keeps congratulating my initiative all the time, Pop.

WILLY: That's because he likes you. If somebody else took that ball there'd be an uproar. So what's the report, boys, what's the report?

BIFF: Where'd you go this time, Dad? Gee, we were lonesome for you.

WILLY [*pleased, puts an arm around each boy and they come down to the apron*]: Lonesome, heh?

BIFF: Missed you every minute.

WILLY: Don't say? Tell you a secret, boys. Don't breathe it to a soul. Someday I'll have my own business, and I'll never have to leave home any more.

HAPPY: Like Uncle Charley, heh?

WILLY: Bigger than Uncle Charley! Because Charley is not—liked. He's liked, but he's not—well liked.

BIFF: Where'd you go this time, Dad?

WILLY: Well, I got on the road, and I went north to Providence. Met the Mayor.

BIFF: The Mayor of Providence!

WILLY: He was sitting in the hotel lobby.

BIFF: What'd he say?

WILLY: He said, "Morning!" And I said, "You got a fine city here, Mayor." And then he had coffee with me. And then I went to Waterbury. Waterbury is a fine city. Big clock city, the famous Waterbury clock. Sold a nice bill there. And then Boston—Boston is the cradle of the Revolution. A fine city. And a couple of other towns in Mass., and on to Portland and Bangor and straight home!

BIFF: Gee, I'd love to go with you sometime, Dad.

WILLY: Soon as summer comes.

HAPPY: Promise?

WILLY: You and Hap and I, and I'll show you all the towns. America is full of beautiful towns and fine, upstanding people. And they know me, boys, they know me up and down New England. The finest people. And when I bring you fellas up, there'll be open sesame for all of us, 'cause one thing, boys: I have friends. I can park my car in any street in New England, and the cops protect it like their own. This summer, heh?

BIFF AND HAPPY [*together*]: Yeah! You bet!

WILLY: We'll take our bathing suits.

HAPPY: We'll carry your bags, Pop!

WILLY: Oh, won't that be something! Me comin' into the Boston stores with you boys carryin' my bags. What a sensation!

[BIFF *is prancing around, practicing passing the ball.*]

WILLY: You nervous, Biff, about the game?

BIFF: Not if you're gonna be there.

WILLY: What do they say about you in school, now that they made you captain?

HAPPY: There's a crowd of girls behind him every time the classes change.

BIFF [*taking* WILLY'S *hand*]: This Saturday, Pop, this Saturday—just for you, I'm going to break through for a touchdown.

HAPPY: You're supposed to pass.

BIFF: I'm takin' one play for Pop. You watch me, Pop, and when I take off my helmet, that means I'm breakin' out. Then you watch me crash through that line!

WILLY [*kisses* BIFF]: Oh, wait'll I tell this in Boston!

[BERNARD *enters in knickers. He is younger than* BIFF, *earnest and loyal, a worried boy.*]

BERNARD: Biff, where are you? You're supposed to study with me today.

WILLY: Hey, looka Bernard. What're you lookin' so anemic about, Bernard?

BERNARD: He's gotta study, Uncle Willy. He's got Regents next week.

HAPPY [*tauntingly, spinning* BERNARD *around*]: Let's box, Bernard!

BERNARD: Biff! [*He gets away from* HAPPY.] Listen, Biff, I heard Mr. Birnbaum say that if you don't start studyin' math he's gonna flunk you, and you won't graduate. I heard him!

WILLY: You better study with him, Biff. Go ahead now.
BERNARD: I heard him!
BIFF: Oh, Pop, you didn't see my sneakers! [*He holds up a foot for* WILLY *to look at.*]
WILLY: Hey, that's a beautiful job of printing!
BERNARD [*wiping his glasses*]: Just because he printed University of Virginia on his sneakers doesn't mean they've got to graduate him, Uncle Willy!
WILLY [*angrily*]: What're you talking about? With scholarships to three universities they're gonna flunk him?
BERNARD: But I heard Mr. Birnbaum say—
WILLY: Don't be a pest, Bernard! [*To his boys*] What an anemic!
BERNARD: Okay, I'm waiting for you in my house, Biff.

[BERNARD *goes off. The* LOMANS *laugh.*]

WILLY: Bernard is not well liked, is he?
BIFF: He's liked, but he's not well liked.
HAPPY: That's right, Pop.
WILLY: That's just what I mean, Bernard can get the best marks in school, y'understand, but when he gets out in the business world, y'understand, you are going to be five times ahead of him. That's why I thank Almighty God you're both built like Adonises. Because the man who makes an appearance in the business world, the man who creates personal interest, is the man who gets ahead. Be liked and you will never want. You take me, for instance. I never have to wait in line to see a buyer. "Willy Loman is here!" That's all they have to know, and I go right through.
BIFF: Did you knock them dead, Pop?
WILLY: Knocked 'em cold in Providence, slaughtered 'em in Boston.
HAPPY [*on his back, pedaling again*]: I'm losing weight, you notice, Pop?

[LINDA *enters, as of old, a ribbon in her hair, carrying a basket of washing.*]

LINDA [*with youthful energy*]: Hello, dear!
WILLY: Sweetheart!
LINDA: How'd the Chevvy run?
WILLY: Chevrolet, Linda, is the greatest car ever built. [*To the boys*] Since when do you let your mother carry wash up the stairs?
BIFF: Grab hold there, boy!
HAPPY: Where to, Mom?
LINDA: Hang them up on the line. And you better go down to your friends, Biff. The cellar is full of boys. They don't know what to do with themselves.
BIFF: Ah, when Pop comes home they can wait!
WILLY [*laughs appreciatively*]: You better go down and tell them what to do, Biff.
BIFF: I think I'll have them sweep out the furnace room.
WILLY: Good work, Biff.
BIFF [*goes through wall-line of kitchen to doorway at back and calls down*]: Fellas! Everybody sweep out the furnace room! I'll be right down!
VOICES: All right! Okay, Biff.
BIFF: George and Sam and Frank, come out back! We're hangin' up the wash! Come on, Hap, on the double! [*He and* HAPPY *carry out the basket.*]
LINDA: The way they obey him!
WILLY: Well, that's training, the training. I'm tellin' you, I was sellin' thousands and thousands, but I had to come home.
LINDA: Oh, the whole block'll be at that game. Did you sell anything?

WILLY: I did five hundred gross in Providence and seven hundred gross in Boston.

LINDA: No! Wait a minute, I've got a pencil. [*She pulls pencil and paper out of her apron pocket.*] That makes your commission . . . Two hundred—my God! Two hundred and twelve dollars!

WILLY: Well, I didn't figure it yet, but . . .

LINDA: How much did you do?

WILLY: Well, I—I did—about a hundred and eighty gross in Providence. Well, no—it came to—roughly two hundred gross on the whole trip.

LINDA [*without hesitation*]: Two hundred gross. That's . . . [*She figures.*]

WILLY: The trouble was that three of the stores were half closed for inventory in Boston. Otherwise I woulda broke records.

LINDA: Well, it makes seventy dollars and some pennies. That's very good.

WILLY: What do we owe?

LINDA: Well, on the first there's sixteen dollars on the refrigerator—

WILLY: Why sixteen?

LINDA: Well, the fan belt broke, so it was a dollar eighty.

WILLY: But it's brand new.

LINDA: Well, the man said that's the way it is. Till they work themselves in, y'know. [*They move through the wall-line into the kitchen.*]

WILLY: I hope we didn't get stuck on that machine.

LINDA: They got the biggest ads of any of them!

WILLY: I know, it's a fine machine. What else?

LINDA: Well, there's nine-sixty for the washing machine. And for the vacuum cleaner there's three and a half due on the fifteenth. Then the roof, you got twenty-one dollars remaining.

WILLY: It don't leak, does it?

LINDA: No, they did a wonderful job. Then you owe Frank for the carburetor.

WILLY: I'm not going to pay that man! That goddam Chevrolet, they ought to prohibit the manufacture of that car!

LINDA: Well, you owe him three and a half. And odds and ends, comes to around a hundred and twenty dollars by the fifteenth.

WILLY: A hundred and twenty dollars! My God, if business don't pick up I don't know what I'm gonna do!

LINDA: Well, next week you'll do better.

WILLY: Oh, I'll knock 'em dead next week. I'll go to Hartford. I'm very well liked in Hartford. You know, the trouble is, Linda, people don't seem to take to me. [*They move onto the forestage.*]

LINDA: Oh, don't be foolish.

WILLY: I know it when I walk in. They seem to laugh at me.

LINDA: Why? Why would they laugh at you? Don't talk that way, Willy. [WILLY *moves to the edge of the stage.* LINDA *goes into the kitchen and starts to darn stockings.*]

WILLY: I don't know the reason for it, but they just pass me by. I'm not noticed.

LINDA: But you're doing wonderful, dear. You're making seventy to a hundred dollars a week.

WILLY: But I gotta be at it ten, twelve hours a day. Other men—I don't know—they do it easier. I don't know why—I can't stop myself—I talk too much. A man oughta come in with a few words. One thing about Charley. He's a man of few words, and they respect him.

LINDA: You don't talk too much, you're just lively.

WILLY [*smiling*]: Well, I figure, what the hell, life is short, a couple of jokes. [*To himself*] I joke too much! [*The smile goes.*]

LINDA: Why? You're—

WILLY: I'm fat. I'm very—foolish to look at, Linda. I didn't tell you, but Christmas time I happened to be calling on F. H. Stewarts, and a salesman I know, as I was going in to see the buyer I heard him say something about—walrus. And I—I cracked him right across the face. I won't take that. I simply will not take that. But they do laugh at me. I know that.

LINDA: Darling . . .

WILLY: I gotta overcome it. I know I gotta overcome it. I'm not dressing to advantage, maybe.

LINDA: Willy, darling, you're the handsomest man in the world—

WILLY: Oh, no, Linda.

LINDA: To me you are. [*Slight pause.*] The handsomest.

[*From the darkness is heard the laughter of a woman.* WILLY *doesn't turn to it, but it continues through* LINDA'S *lines.*]

LINDA: And the boys, Willy. Few men are idolized by their children the way you are.

[*Music is heard as behind a scrim, to the left of the house,* THE WOMAN, *dimly seen, is dressing.*]

WILLY [*with great feeling*]: You're the best there is, Linda, you're a pal, you know that? On the road—on the road I want to grab you sometimes and just kiss the life outa you.

[*The laughter is loud now, and he moves into a brightening area at the left, where* THE WOMAN *has come from behind the scrim and is standing, putting on her hat, looking into a "mirror," and laughing.*]

WILLY: 'Cause I get so lonely—especially when business is bad and there's nobody to talk to. I get the feeling that I'll never sell anything again, that I won't make a living for you, or a business, a business for the boys. [*He talks through* THE WOMAN'S *subsiding laughter*: THE WOMAN *primps at the "mirror."*] There's so much I want to make for—

THE WOMAN: Me? You didn't make me, Willy. I picked you.

WILLY [*pleased*]: You picked me?

THE WOMAN [*who is quite proper-looking, Willy's age*]: I did. I've been sitting at that desk watching all the salesmen go by, day in, day out. But you've got such a sense of humor, and we do have such a good time together, don't we?

WILLY: Sure, sure. [*He takes her in his arms.*] Why do you have to go now?

THE WOMAN: It's two o'clock . . .

WILLY: No, come on in! [*He pulls her.*]

THE WOMAN: . . . my sisters'll be scandalized. When'll you be back?

WILLY: Oh, two weeks about. Will you come up again?

THE WOMAN: Sure thing. You do make me laugh. It's good for me. [*She squeezes his arm, kisses him.*] And I think you're a wonderful man.

WILLY: You picked me, heh?

THE WOMAN: Sure. Because you're so sweet. And such a kidder.

WILLY: Well, I'll see you next time I'm in Boston.

THE WOMAN: I'll put you right through to the buyers.

WILLY [*slapping her bottom*]: Right. Well, bottoms up!

THE WOMAN [*slaps him gently and laughs*]: You just kill me, Willy. [*He suddenly grabs her and kisses her roughly.*] You kill me. And thanks for the stockings. I love a lot of stockings. Well, good night.

WILLY: Good night. And keep your pores open!

THE WOMAN: Oh, Willy!

[THE WOMAN *bursts out laughing, and* LINDA'S *laughter blends in.* THE WOMAN *disappears into the dark. Now the area at the kitchen table brightens.* LINDA *is sitting where she was at the kitchen table, but now is mending a pair of her silk stockings.*]

LINDA: You are, Willy. The handsomest man. You've got no reason to feel that—

WILLY [*coming out of* THE WOMAN'S *dimming area and going over to* LINDA]: I'll make it all up to you, Linda, I'll—

LINDA: There's nothing to make up, dear. You're doing fine, better than—

WILLY [*noticing her mending*]: What's that?

LINDA: Just mending my stockings. They're so expensive—

WILLY [*angrily, taking them from her*]: I won't have you mending stockings in this house! Now throw them out!

[LINDA *puts the stockings in her pocket.*]

BERNARD [*entering on the run*]: Where is he? If he doesn't study!

WILLY [*moving to the forestage, with great agitation*]: You'll give him the answers!

BERNARD: I do, but I can't on a Regents! That's a state exam! They're liable to arrest me!

WILLY: Where is he? I'll whip him, I'll whip him!

LINDA: And he'd better give back that football, Willy, it's not nice.

WILLY: Biff! Where is he? Why is he taking everything?

LINDA: He's too rough with the girls, Willy. All the mothers are afraid of him!

WILLY: I'll whip him!

BERNARD: He's driving the car without a license!

[THE WOMAN'S *laugh is heard.*]

WILLY: Shut up!

LINDA: All the mothers—

WILLY: Shut up!

BERNARD [*backing quietly away and out*]: Mr. Birnbaum says he's stuck up.

WILLY: Get outa here!

BERNARD: If he doesn't buckle down he'll flunk math! [*He goes off.*]

LINDA: He's right. Willy, you've gotta—

WILLY [*exploding at her*]: There's nothing the matter with him! You want him to be a worm like Bernard? He's got spirit, personality . . .

[*As he speaks,* LINDA, *almost in tears, exits into the living-room.* WILLY *is alone in the kitchen, wilting and staring. The leaves are gone. It is night again, and the apartment houses look down from behind.*]

WILLY: Loaded with it. Loaded! What is he stealing? He's giving it back, isn't he? Why is he stealing? What did I tell him? I never in my life told him anything but decent things.

[HAPPY *in pajamas has come down the stairs;* WILLY *suddenly becomes aware of* HAPPY'S *presence.*]

HAPPY: Let's go now, come on.

WILLY [*sitting down at the kitchen table*]: Huh! Why did she have to wax the floors herself? Everytime she waxes the floors she keels over. She knows that!

HAPPY: Shh! Take it easy. What brought you back tonight?

WILLY: I got an awful scare. Nearly hit a kid in Yonkers. God! Why didn't I go to Alaska with my brother Ben that time! Ben! That man was a genius, that man was success incarnate! What a mistake! He begged me to go.

HAPPY: Well, there's no use in—

WILLY: You guys! There was a man started with the clothes on his back and ended up with diamond mines?

HAPPY: Boy, someday I'd like to know how he did it.

WILLY: What's the mystery? The man knew what he wanted and went out and got it! Walked into a jungle, and comes out, the age of twenty-one, and he's rich! The world is an oyster, but you don't crack it open on a mattress!

HAPPY: Pop, I told you I'm gonna retire you for life.

WILLY: You'll retire me for life on seventy goddam dollars a week? And your women and your car and your apartment, and you'll retire me for life! Christ's sake. I couldn't get past Yonkers today! Where are you guys, where are you? The woods are burning! I can't drive a car!

[CHARLEY *has appeared in the doorway. He is a large man, slow of speech, laconic, immovable. In all he says, despite what he says, there is pity, and, now, trepidation. He has a robe over pajamas, slippers on his feet. He enters the kitchen.*]

CHARLEY: Everything all right?

HAPPY: Yeah, Charley, everything's . . .

WILLY: What's the matter?

CHARLEY: I heard some noise. I thought something happened. Can't we do something about the walls? You sneeze in here, and in my house hats blow off.

HAPPY: Let's go to bed, Dad. Come on.

[CHARLEY *signals to* HAPPY *to go.*]

WILLY: You go ahead, I'm not tired at the moment.

HAPPY: [*to* WILLY]: Take it easy, huh?

[*He exits.*]

WILLY: What're you doin' up?

CHARLEY [*sitting down at the kitchen table opposite* WILLY]: Couldn't sleep good. I had a heartburn.

WILLY: Well, you don't know how to eat.

CHARLEY: I eat with my mouth.

WILLY: No, you're ignorant. You gotta know about vitamins and things like that.

CHARLEY: Come on, let's shoot. Tire you out a little.

WILLY [*hesitantly*]: All right. You got cards?

CHARLEY [*taking a deck from his pocket*]: Yeah, I got them. Someplace. What is it with those vitamins?

WILLY [*dealing*]: They build up your bones. Chemistry.

CHARLEY: Yeah, but there's no bones in a heartburn.

WILLY: What are you talkin' about? Do you know the first thing about it?

CHARLEY: Don't get insulted.

WILLY: Don't talk about something you don't know anything about.

[*They are playing. Pause.*]

CHARLEY: What're you doin' home?

WILLY: A little trouble with the car.

CHARLEY: Oh. [*Pause.*] I'd like to take a trip to California.

WILLY: Don't say.

CHARLEY: You want a job?

WILLY: I got a job, I told you that. [*After a slight pause*] What the hell are you offering me a job for?

CHARLEY: Don't get insulted.

WILLY: Don't insult me.

CHARLEY: I don't see no sense in it. You don't have to go on this way.

WILLY: I got a good job. [*Slight pause.*] What do you keep comin' in here for?

CHARLEY: You want me to go?

WILLY: [*after a pause, withering*]: I can't understand it. He's going back to Texas again. What the hell is that?

CHARLEY: Let him go.

WILLY: I got nothin' to give him. Charley, I'm clean, I'm clean.

CHARLEY: He won't starve. None a them starve. Forget about him.

WILLY: Then what have I got to remember?

CHARLEY: You take it too hard. To hell with it. When a deposit bottle is broken you don't get your nickel back.

WILLY: That's easy enough for you to say.

CHARLEY: That ain't easy for me to say.

WILLY: Did you see the ceiling I put up in the living-room?

CHARLEY: Yeah, that's a piece of work. To put up a ceiling is a mystery to me. How do you do it?

WILLY: What's the difference?

CHARLEY: Well, talk about it.

WILLY: You gonna put up a ceiling?

CHARLEY: How could I put up a ceiling?

WILLY: Then what the hell are you bothering me for?

CHARLEY: You're insulted again.

WILLY: A man who can't handle tools is not a man. You're disgusting.

CHARLEY: Don't call me disgusting, Willy.

[UNCLE BEN, *carrying a valise and an umbrella, enters the forestage from around the right corner of the house. He is a stolid man, in his sixties, with a mustache and an authoritative air. He is utterly certain of his destiny, and there is an aura of far places about him. He enters exactly as* WILLY *speaks.*]

WILLY: I'm getting awfully tired, Ben.

[BEN'S *music is heard.* BEN *looks around at everything.*]

CHARLEY: Good, keep playing; you'll sleep better. Did you call me Ben?

[BEN *looks at his watch.*]

WILLY: That's funny. For a second there you reminded me of my brother Ben.

BEN: I only have a few minutes. [*He strolls, inspecting the place.* WILLY *and* CHARLEY *continue playing.*]

CHARLEY: You never heard from him again, heh? Since that time?

WILLY: Didn't Linda tell you? Couple of weeks ago we got a letter from his wife in Africa. He died.

CHARLEY: That so.

BEN [*chuckling*]: So this is Brooklyn, eh?

CHARLEY: Maybe you're in for some of his money.

WILLY: Naa, he had seven sons. There's just one opportunity I had with that man . . .

BEN: I must make a train, William. There are several properties I'm looking at in Alaska.

WILLY: Sure, sure! If I'd gone with him to Alaska that time, everything would've been totally different.
CHARLEY: Go on, you'd froze to death up there.
WILLY: What're you talking about?
BEN: Opportunity is tremendous in Alaska, William. Surprised you're not up there.
WILLY: Sure, tremendous.
CHARLEY: Heh?
WILLY: There was the only man I ever met who knew the answers.
CHARLEY: Who?
BEN: How are you all?
WILLY [*taking a pot, smiling*]: Fine, fine.
CHARLEY: Pretty sharp tonight.
BEN: Is Mother living with you?
WILLY: No, she died a long time ago.
CHARLEY: Who?
BEN: That's too bad. Fine specimen of a lady, Mother.
WILLY [*to* CHARLEY]: Heh?
BEN: I'd hoped to see the old girl.
CHARLEY: Who died?
BEN: Heard anything from Father, have you?
WILLY [*unnerved*]: What do you mean, who died?
CHARLEY [*taking a pot*]: What're you talkin' about?
BEN [*looking at his watch*]: William, it's half past eight!
WILLY [*as though to dispel his confusion he angrily stops* CHARLEY'S *hand*]: That's my build!
CHARLEY: I put the ace—
WILLY: If you don't know how to play the game I'm not gonna throw my money away on you!
CHARLEY [*rising*]: It was my ace, for God's sake!
WILLY: I'm through, I'm through!
BEN: When did Mother die?
WILLY: Long ago. Since the beginning you never knew how to play cards.
CHARLEY [*picks up the cards and goes to the door*]: All right! Next time I'll bring a deck with five aces.
WILLY: I don't play that kind of game!
CHARLEY [*turning to him*]: You ought to be ashamed of yourself!
WILLY: Yeah?
CHARLEY: Yeah! [*He goes out.*]
WILLY [*slamming the door after him*]: Ignoramus!
BEN [*as* WILLY *comes toward him through the wall-line of the kitchen*]: So you're William.
WILLY [*shaking* BEN'S *hand*]: Ben! I've been waiting for you so long! What's the answer? How did you do it?
BEN: Oh, there's a story in that.

[LINDA *enters the forestage, as of old, carrying the wash basket.*]

LINDA: Is this Ben?
BEN [*gallantly*]: How do you do, my dear.
LINDA: Where've you been all these years? Willy's always wondered why you—

WILLY [*pulling* BEN *away from her impatiently*]: Where is Dad? Didn't you follow him? How did you get started?

BEN: Well, I don't know how much you remember.

WILLY: Well, I was just a baby, of course, only three or four years old—

BEN: Three years and eleven months.

WILLY: What a memory, Ben!

BEN: I have many enterprises, William, and I have never kept books.

WILLY: I remember I was sitting under the wagon in—was it Nebraska?

BEN: It was South Dakota, and I gave you a bunch of wildflowers.

WILLY: I remember you walking away down some open road.

BEN [*laughing*]: I was going to find Father in Alaska.

WILLY: Where is he?

BEN: At that age I had a very faulty view of geography, William. I discovered after a few days that I was heading due south, so instead of Alaska, I ended up in Africa.

LINDA: Africa!

WILLY: The Gold Coast!

BEN: Principally diamond mines.

LINDA: Diamond mines!

BEN: Yes, my dear. But I've only a few minutes—

WILLY: No! Boys! Boys! [YOUNG BIFF *and* HAPPY *appear.*] Listen to this. This is your Uncle Ben, a great man! Tell my boys, Ben!

BEN: Why boys, when I was seventeen I walked into the jungle, and when I was twenty-one I walked out. [*He laughs.*] And by God I was rich.

WILLY [*to the boys*]: You see what I been talking about? The greatest things can happen!

BEN [*glancing at his watch*]: I have an appointment in Ketchikan Tuesday week.

WILLY: No, Ben! Please tell about Dad. I want my boys to hear. I want them to know the kind of stock they spring from. All I remember is a man with a big beard, and I was in Mamma's lap, sitting around a fire, and some kind of high music.

BEN: His flute. He played the flute.

WILLY: Sure, the flute, that's right!

[*New music is heard, a high, rollicking tune.*]

BEN: Father was a very great and a very wild-hearted man. We would start in Boston, and he'd toss the whole family into the wagon, and then he'd drive the team right across the country; through Ohio, and Indiana, Michigan, Illinois, and all the Western states. And we'd stop in the towns and sell the flutes that he'd made on the way. Great inventor, Father. With one gadget he made more in a week than a man like you could make in a lifetime.

WILLY: That's just the way I'm bringing them up, Ben—rugged, well liked, all-around.

BEN: Yeah? [*To* BIFF] Hit that, boy—hard as you can. [*He pounds his stomach.*]

BIFF: Oh, no, sir!

BEN [*taking boxing stance*]: Come on, get to me! [*He laughs.*]

WILLY: Go to it. Biff! Go ahead, show him!

BIFF: Okay! [*He cocks his fists and starts in.*]

LINDA [*to* WILLY]: Why must he fight, dear?

BEN [*sparring with* BIFF]: Good boy! Good boy!

WILLY: How's that, Ben, heh?

HAPPY: Give him the left, Biff!

LINDA: Why are you fighting?

BEN: Good boy! [*Suddenly comes in, trips* BIFF, *and stands over him, the point of his umbrella poised over* BIFF'S *eye.*]

LINDA: Look out, Biff!

BIFF: Gee!

BEN [*patting* BIFF'S *knee*]: Never fight fair with a stranger, boy. You'll never get out of the jungle that way. [*Taking* LINDA'S *hand and bowing*] It was an honor and a pleasure to meet you, Linda.

LINDA [*withdrawing her hand coldly, frightened*]: Have a nice—trip.

BEN [*to* WILLY]: And good luck with your—what do you do?

WILLY: Selling.

BEN: Yes. Well . . . [*He raises his hand in farewell to all.*]

WILLY: No, Ben, I don't want you to think . . . [*He takes* BEN'S *arm to show him.*] It's Brooklyn, I know, but we hunt too.

BEN: Really, now.

WILLY: Oh, sure, there's snakes and rabbits and—that's why I moved out here. Why, Biff can fell any one of these trees in no time! Boys! Go right over to where they're building the apartment house and get some sand. We're gonna rebuild the entire front stoop right now! Watch this, Ben!

BIFF: Yes, sir! On the double, Hap!

HAPPY [*as he and* BIFF *run off*]: I lost weight, Pop, you notice?

[CHARLEY *enters in knickers, even before the boys are gone.*]

CHARLEY: Listen, if they steal any more from that building the watchman'll put the cops on them!

LINDA [*to* WILLY]: Don't let Biff . . .

[BEN *laughs lustily.*]

WILLY: You shoulda seen the lumber they brought home last week. At least a dozen six-by-tens worth all kinds a money.

CHARLEY: Listen, if that watchman—

WILLY: I gave them hell, understand. But I got a couple of fearless characters there.

CHARLEY: Willy, the jails are full of fearless characters.

BEN [*clapping* WILLY *on the back, with a laugh at* CHARLEY]: And the stock exchange, friend!

WILLY [*joining in* BEN'S *laughter*]: Where are the rest of your pants?

CHARLEY: My wife bought them.

WILLY: Now all you need is a golf club and you can go upstairs and go to sleep. [*To* BEN] Great athlete! Between him and his son Bernard they can't hammer a nail!

BERNARD [*rushing in*]: The watchman's chasing Biff!

WILLY [*angrily*]: Shut up! He's not stealing anything!

LINDA [*alarmed, hurrying off left*]: Where is he? Biff, dear! [*She exits.*]

WILLY [*moving toward the left, away from* BEN]: There's nothing wrong. What's the matter with you?

BEN: Nervy boy. Good!

WILLY [*laughing*]: Oh, nerves of iron, that Biff!

CHARLEY: Don't know what it is. My New England man comes back and he's bleedin', they murdered him up there.

WILLY: It's contacts, Charley. I got important contacts!

CHARLEY [*sarcastically*]: Glad to hear it, Willy. Come in later, we'll shoot a little casino. I'll take some of your Portland money. [*He laughs at* WILLY *and exits.*]

WILLY [*turning to* BEN]: Business is bad, it's murderous. But not for me, of course.

BEN: I'll stop by on my way back to Africa.

WILLY [*longingly*]: Can't you stay a few days? You're just what I need, Ben, because I—I have a fine position here, but I—well, Dad left when I was such a baby and I never had a chance to talk to him and I still feel—kind of temporary about myself.

BEN: I'll be late for my train.

[*They are at opposite ends of the stage.*]

WILLY: Ben, my boys—can't we talk? They'd go into the jaws of hell for me, see, but I—

BEN: William, you're being first-rate with your boys. Outstanding, manly chaps!

WILLY [*hanging on to his words*]: Oh, Ben, that's good to hear! Because sometimes I'm afraid that I'm not teaching them the right kind of—Ben, how should I teach them?

BEN [*giving great weight to each word, and with a certain vicious audacity*]: William, when I walked into the jungle, I was seventeen. When I walked out I was twenty-one. And, by God, I was rich! [*He goes off into darkness around the right corner of the house.*]

WILLY: . . . was rich! That's just the spirit I want to imbue them with! To walk into a jungle! I was right! I was right! I was right!

[BEN *is gone, but* WILLY *is still speaking to him as* LINDA, *in nightgown and robe, enters the kitchen, glances around for* WILLY, *then goes to the door of the house, looks out and sees him. Comes down to his left. He looks at her.*]

LINDA: Willy, dear? Willy?

WILLY: I was right!

LINDA: Did you have some cheese? [*He can't answer.*] It's very late, darling. Come to bed, heh?

WILLY [*looking straight up*]: Gotta break your neck to see a star in this yard.

LINDA: You coming in?

WILLY: Whatever happened to that diamond watch fob? Remember? When Ben came from Africa that time? Didn't he give me a watch fob with a diamond in it?

LINDA: You pawned it, dear. Twelve, thirteen years ago. For Biff's radio correspondence course.

WILLY: Gee, that was a beautiful thing. I'll take a walk.

LINDA: But you're in your slippers.

WILLY [*starting to go around the house at the left*]: I was right! I was! [*Half to* LINDA, *as he goes, shaking his head*] What a man! There was a man worth talking to. I was right!

LINDA [*calling after* WILLY]: But in your slippers, Willy!

[WILLY *is almost gone when* BIFF, *in his pajamas, comes down the stairs and enters the kitchen.*]

BIFF: What is he doing out there?

LINDA: Sh!

BIFF: God Almighty, Mom, how long has he been doing this?

LINDA: Don't, he'll hear you.

BIFF: What the hell is the matter with him?

LINDA: It'll pass by morning.

BIFF: Shouldn't we do anything?

LINDA: Oh, my dear, you should do a lot of things, but there's nothing to do, so go to sleep.

[HAPPY *comes down the stairs and sits on the steps.*]

HAPPY: I never heard him so loud, Mom.

LINDA: Well, come around more often; you'll hear him.

[*She sits down at the table and mends the lining of* WILLY'S *jacket.*]

BIFF: Why didn't you ever write me about this, Mom?

LINDA: How would I write to you? For over three months you had no address.

BIFF: I was on the move. But you know I thought of you all the time. You know that, don't you, pal?

LINDA: I know, dear, I know. But he likes to have a letter. Just to know that there's still a possibility for better things.

BIFF: He's not like this all the time, is he?

LINDA: It's when you come home he's always the worst.

BIFF: When I come home?

LINDA: When you write you're coming, he's all smiles, and talks about the future, and—he's just wonderful. And then the closer you seem to come, the more shaky he gets, and then, by the time you get here, he's arguing, and he seems angry at you. I think it's just that maybe he can't bring himself to—to open up to you. Why are you so hateful to each other? Why is that?

BIFF [*evasively*]: I'm not hateful, Mom.

LINDA: But you no sooner come in the door than you're fighting!

BIFF: I don't know why. I mean to change. I'm tryin', Mom, you understand?

LINDA: Are you home to stay now?

BIFF: I don't know. I want to look around, see what's doin'.

LINDA: Biff, you can't look around all your life, can you?

BIFF: I just can't take hold, Mom. I can't take hold of some kind of a life.

LINDA: Biff, a man is not a bird, to come and go with the springtime.

BIFF: Your hair . . . [*He touches her hair.*] Your hair got so gray.

LINDA: Oh, it's been gray since you were in high school. I just stopped dyeing it, that's all.

BIFF: Dye it again, will ya? I don't want my pal looking old. [*He smiles.*]

LINDA: You're such a boy! You think you can go away for a year and . . . You've got to get it into your head now that one day you'll knock on this door and there'll be strange people here—

BIFF: What are you talking about? You're not even sixty, Mom.

LINDA: But what about your father?

BIFF [*lamely*]: Well, I meant him too.

HAPPY: He admires Pop.

LINDA: Biff, dear, if you don't have any feeling for him, then you can't have any feeling for me.

BIFF: Sure I can, Mom.

LINDA: No. You can't just come to see me, because I love him. [*With a threat, but only a threat, of tears*] He's the dearest man in the world to me, and I won't have anyone making him feel unwanted and low and blue. You've got to make up your mind now, darling, there's no leeway any more. Either he's your father and you pay him that respect, or else you're not to come here. I know he's not easy to get along with—nobody knows that better than me—but . . .

WILLY [*from the left, with a laugh*]: Hey, hey, Biffo!

BIFF [*starting to go out after* WILLY]: What the hell is the matter with him? [HAPPY *stops him.*]

LINDA: Don't—don't go near him!

BIFF: Stop making excuses for him! He always, always wiped the floor with you. Never had an ounce of respect for you.

HAPPY: He's always had respect for—

BIFF: What the hell do you know about it?

HAPPY [*surlily*]: Just don't call him crazy!

BIFF: He's got no character—Charley wouldn't do this. Not in his own house—spewing out that vomit from his mind.

HAPPY: Charley never had to cope with what he's got to.

BIFF: People are worse off than Willy Loman. Believe me, I've seen them!

LINDA: Then make Charley your father, Biff. You can't do that, can you? I don't say he's a great man. Willy Loman never made a lot of money. His name was never in the paper. He's not the finest character that ever lived. But he's a human being, and a terrible thing is happening to him. So attention must be paid. He's not to be allowed to fall into his grave like an old dog. Attention, attention must be finally paid to such a person. You called him crazy—

BIFF: I didn't mean—

LINDA: No, a lot of people think he's lost his—balance. But you don't have to be very smart to know what his trouble is. The man is exhausted.

HAPPY: Sure!

LINDA: A small man can be just as exhausted as a great man. He works for a company thirty-six years this March, opens up unheard-of territories to their trademark, and now in his old age they take his salary away.

HAPPY [*indignantly*]: I didn't know that, Mom.

LINDA: You never asked, my dear! Now that you get your spending money someplace else you don't trouble your mind with him.

HAPPY: But I gave you money last—

LINDA: Christmas time, fifty dollars! To fix the hot water it cost ninety seven fifty! For five weeks he's been on straight commission, like a beginner, an unknown!

BIFF: Those ungrateful bastards!

LINDA: Are they any worse than his sons? When he brought them business, when he was young, they were glad to see him. But now his old friends, the old buyers that loved him so and always found some order to hand him in a pinch—they're all dead, retired. He used to be able to make six, seven calls a day in Boston. Now he takes his valises out of the car and puts them back and takes them out again and he's exhausted. Instead of walking he talks now. He drives seven hundred miles, and when he gets there no one knows him any more, no one welcomes him. And what goes through a man's mind, driving seven hundred miles home without having earned a cent? Why shouldn't he talk to himself? Why? When he has to go to Charley and borrow fifty dollars a week and pretend to me that it's his pay? How long can that go on? How long? You see what I'm sitting here and waiting for? And you tell me he has no character? The man who never worked a day but for your benefit? When does he get the medal for that? Is this his reward—to turn around at the age of sixty-three and find his sons, who he loved better than his life, one a philandering bum—

HAPPY: Mom!

LINDA: That's all you are, my baby! [*To* BIFF] And you! What happened to the love you had for him? You were such pals! How you used to talk to him on the phone every night! How lonely he was till he could come home to you!

BIFF: All right, Mom. I'll live here in my room, and I'll get a job. I'll keep away from him, that's all.

LINDA: No, Biff. You can't stay here and fight all the time.

BIFF: He threw me out of this house, remember that.

LINDA: Why did he do that? I never knew why.

BIFF: Because I know he's a fake and he doesn't like anybody around who knows!

LINDA: Why a fake? In what way? What do you mean?

BIFF: Just don't lay it all at my feet. It's between me and him—that's all I have to say. I'll chip in from now on. He'll settle for half my pay check. He'll be all right. I'm going to bed. [*He starts for the stairs.*]

LINDA: He won't be all right.

BIFF [*turning on the stairs, furiously*]: I hate this city and I'll stay here. Now what do you want?

LINDA: He's dying, Biff.

[HAPPY *turns quickly to her, shocked.*]

BIFF [*after a pause*]: Why is he dying?

LINDA: He's been trying to kill himself.

BIFF [*with great horror*]: How?

LINDA: I live from day to day.

BIFF: What're you talking about?

LINDA: Remember I wrote you that he smashed up the car again? In February?

BIFF: Well?

LINDA: The insurance inspector came. He said that they have evidence. That all these accidents in the last year—weren't—weren't—accidents.

HAPPY: How can they tell that? That's a lie.

LINDA: It seems there's a woman . . . [*She takes a breath as*]

BIFF [*sharply but contained*]: } What woman? . . .
LINDA [*simultaneously*]: } . . . and this woman . . .

LINDA: What?

BIFF: Nothing. Go ahead.

LINDA: What did you say?

BIFF: Nothing. I just said what woman?

HAPPY: What about her?

LINDA: Well, it seems she was walking down the road and saw his car. She says that he wasn't driving fast at all, and that he didn't skid. She says he came to that little bridge, and then deliberately smashed into the railing, and it was only the shallowness of the water that saved him.

BIFF: Oh, no, he probably just fell asleep again.

LINDA: I don't think he fell asleep.

BIFF: Why not?

LINDA: Last month . . . [*With great difficulty*] Oh, boys, it's so hard to say a thing like this! He's just a big stupid man to you, but I tell you there's more good in him than in many other people. [*She chokes, wipes her eyes.*] I was looking for a fuse. The lights blew out, and I went down the cellar. And behind the fuse box—it happened to fall out—was a length of rubber pipe—just short.

HAPPY: No kidding?

LINDA: There's a little attachment on the end of it. I knew right away. And sure enough, on the bottom of the water heater there's a new little nipple on the gas pipe.

HAPPY [*angrily*]: That—jerk.

BIFF: Did you have it taken off?

LINDA: I'm—I'm ashamed to. How can I mention it to him? Every day I go down and take away that little rubber pipe. But, when he comes home, I put it back where it was. How can I insult him that way? I don't know what to do. I live from day to day, boys. I tell you, I know every thought in his mind. It sounds so old-fashioned and silly, but I tell you he put his whole life into you and you've turned your backs on him. [*She is bent over in the chair, weeping, her face in her hands.*] Biff, I swear to God! Biff, his life is in your hands!

HAPPY [*to* BIFF]: How do you like that damned fool!

BIFF [*kissing her*]: All right, pal, all right. It's all settled now. I've been remiss. I know that, Mom. But now I'll stay, and I swear to you, I'll apply myself. [*Kneeling in front of her, in a fever of self-reproach*] It's just—you see, Mom, I don't fit in business. Not that I won't try. I'll try, and I'll make good.

HAPPY: Sure you will. The trouble with you in business was you never tried to please people.

BIFF: I know, I—

HAPPY: Like when you worked for Harrison's. Bob Harrison said you were tops, and then you go and do some damn fool thing like whistling whole songs in the elevator like a comedian.

BIFF [*against* HAPPY]: So what? I like to whistle sometimes.

HAPPY: You don't raise a guy to a responsible job who whistles in the elevator!

LINDA: Well, don't argue about it now.

HAPPY: Like when you'd go off and swim in the middle of the day instead of taking the line around.

BIFF [*his resentment rising*]: Well, don't you run off? You take off sometimes, don't you? On a nice summer day?

HAPPY: Yeah, but I cover myself!

LINDA: Boys!

HAPPY: If I'm going to take a fade the boss can call any number where I'm supposed to be and they'll swear to him that I just left. I'll tell you something that I hate to say, Biff, but in the business world some of them think you're crazy.

BIFF [*angered*]: Screw the business world!

HAPPY: All right, screw it! Great, but cover yourself!

LINDA: Hap, Hap!

BIFF: I don't care what they think! They've laughed at Dad for years, and you know why? Because we don't belong in this nuthouse of a city! We should be mixing cement on some open plain, or—or carpenters. A carpenter is allowed to whistle!

[WILLY *walks in from the entrance of the house, at left.*]

WILLY: Even your grandfather was better than a carpenter. [*Pause. They watch him.*] You never grew up. Bernard does not whistle in the elevator, I assure you.

BIFF [*as though to laugh* WILLY *out of it*]: Yeah, but you do, Pop.

WILLY: I never in my life whistled in an elevator! And who in the business world thinks I'm crazy?

BIFF: I didn't mean it like that. Pop. Now don't make a whole thing out of it, will ya?

WILLY: Go back to the West! Be a carpenter, a cowboy, enjoy yourself!

LINDA: Willy, he was just saying—

WILLY: I heard what he said!

HAPPY [*trying to quiet* WILLY]: Hey, Pop, come on now . . .

WILLY [*continuing over* HAPPY'S *line*]: They laugh at me, heh? Go to Filene's, go to the Hub, go to Slattery's, Boston. Call out the name Willy Loman and see what happens! Big shot!

BIFF: All right, Pop.

WILLY: Big!

BIFF: All right!

WILLY: Why do you always insult me?

BIFF: I didn't say a word. [*To* LINDA] Did I say a word?

LINDA: He didn't say anything, Willy.

WILLY [*going to the doorway of the living-room*]: All right, good night, good night.

LINDA: Willy, dear, he just decided . . .

WILLY [*to* BIFF]: If you get tired hanging around tomorrow, paint the ceiling I put up in the living-room.

BIFF: I'm leaving early tomorrow.

HAPPY: He's going to see Bill Oliver, Pop.

WILLY [*interestedly*]: Oliver? For what?

BIFF [*with reserve, but trying, trying*]: He always said he'd stake me. I'd like to go into business, so maybe I can take him up on it.

LINDA: Isn't that wonderful?

WILLY: Don't interrupt. What's wonderful about it? There's fifty men in the City of New York who'd stake him. [*To* BIFF] Sporting goods?

BIFF: I guess so. I know something about it and—

WILLY: He knows something about it! You know sporting goods better than Spalding, for God's sake! How much is he giving you?

BIFF: I don't know, I didn't even see him yet, but—

WILLY: Then what're you talkin' about?

BIFF [*getting angry*]: Well, all I said was I'm gonna see him, that's all!

WILLY [*turning away*]: Ah, you're counting your chickens again.

BIFF [*starting left for the stairs*]: Oh, Jesus, I'm going to sleep!

WILLY [*calling after him*]: Don't curse in this house!

BIFF [*turning*]: Since when did you get so clean?

HAPPY [*trying to stop them*]: Wait a . . .

WILLY: Don't use that language to me! I won't have it!

HAPPY [*grabbing* BIFF, *shouts*]: Wait a minute! I got an idea. I got a feasible idea. Come here, Biff, let's talk this over now, let's talk some sense here. When I was down in Florida last time, I thought of a great idea to sell sporting goods. It just came back to me. You and I, Biff—we have a line, the Loman Line. We train a couple of weeks, and put on a couple of exhibitions, see?

WILLY: That's an idea!

HAPPY: Wait! We form two basketball teams, see? Two water-polo teams. We play each other. It's a million dollars' worth of publicity. Two brothers, see? The Loman Brothers. Displays in the Royal Palms—all the hotels. And banners over the ring and the basketball court: "Loman Brothers." Baby, we could sell sporting goods!

WILLY: That is a one-million-dollar idea!

LINDA: Marvelous!

BIFF: I'm in great shape as far as that's concerned.

HAPPY: And the beauty of it is, Biff, it wouldn't be like a business. We'd be out playin' ball again . . .

BIFF [*enthused*]: Yeah, that's . . .

WILLY: Million-dollar . . .

HAPPY: And you wouldn't get fed up with it, Biff. It'd be the family again. There'd be the old honor, and comradeship, and if you wanted to go off for a swim or somethin'—well you'd do it! Without some smart cooky gettin' up ahead of you!

WILLY: Lick the world! You guys together could absolutely lick the civilized world.

BIFF: I'll see Oliver tomorrow. Hap, if we could work that out . . .

LINDA: Maybe things are beginning to—

WILLY [*wildly enthused, to* LINDA]: Stop interrupting! [*To* BIFF] But don't wear sport jacket and slacks when you see Oliver.

BIFF: No, I'll—

WILLY: A business suit, and talk as little as possible, and don't crack any jokes.

BIFF: He did like me. Always liked me.

LINDA: He loved you!

WILLY [*to* LINDA]: Will you stop! [*To* BIFF] Walk in very serious. You are not applying for a boy's job. Money is to pass. Be quiet, fine, and serious. Everybody likes a kidder, but nobody lends him money.

HAPPY: I'll try to get some myself, Biff. I'm sure I can.

WILLY: I see great things for you kids. I think your troubles are over. But remember, start big and you'll end big. Ask for fifteen. How much you gonna ask for?

BIFF: Gee, I don't know—

WILLY: And don't say "Gee." "Gee" is a boy's word. A man walking in for fifteen thousand dollars does not say "Gee"!

BIFF: Ten, I think, would be top though.

WILLY: Don't be so modest. You always started too low. Walk in with a big laugh. Don't look worried. Start off with a couple of your good stories to lighten things up. It's not what you say, it's how you say it—because personality always wins the day.

LINDA: Oliver always thought the highest of him—

WILLY: Will you let me talk?

BIFF: Don't yell at her, Pop, will ya?

WILLY [*angrily*]: I was talking, wasn't I?

BIFF: I don't like you yelling at her all the time, and I'm tellin' you, that's all.

WILLY: What're you, takin' over this house?

LINDA: Willy—

WILLY [*turning on her*]: Don't take his side all the time, goddammit!

BIFF [*furiously*]: Stop yelling at her!

WILLY [*suddenly pulling on his cheek, beaten down, guilt ridden*]: Give my best to Bill Oliver—he may remember me. [*He exits through the living-room doorway.*]

LINDA [*her voice subdued*]: What'd you have to start that for? [BIFF *turns away.*] You see how sweet he was as soon as you talked hopefully? [*She goes over to* BIFF.] Come up and say good night to him. Don't let him go to bed that way.

HAPPY: Come on, Biff, let's buck him up.

LINDA: Please, dear. Just say good night. It takes so little to make him happy. Come. [*She goes through the living-room doorway, calling upstairs from within the living-room.*] Your pajamas are hanging in the bathroom, Willy!

HAPPY [*looking toward where* LINDA *went out*]: What a woman! They broke the mold when they made her. You know that, Biff?

BIFF: He's off salary. My God, working on commission!

HAPPY: Well, let's face it; he's no hot-shot selling man. Except that sometimes, you have to admit, he's a sweet personality.

BIFF [*deciding*]: Lend me ten bucks, will ya? I want to buy some new ties.

HAPPY: I'll take you to a place I know. Beautiful stuff. Wear one of my striped shirts tomorrow.

BIFF: She got gray. Mom got awful old. Gee, I'm gonna go in to Oliver tomorrow and knock him for a—

HAPPY: Come on up. Tell that to Dad. Let's give him a whirl. Come on.

BIFF [*steamed up*]: You know, with ten thousand bucks, boy!

HAPPY [*as they go into the living-room*]: That's the talk, Biff, that's the first time I've heard the old confidence out of you! [*From within the living-room, fading off*] You're gonna live with me, kid, and any babe you want just say the word . . . [*The last lines are hardly heard. They are mounting the stairs to their parents' bedroom.*]

LINDA [*entering her bedroom and addressing* WILLY, *who is in the bathroom. She is straightening the bed for him.*] Can you do anything about the shower? It drips.

WILLY [*from the bathroom*]: All of a sudden everything falls to pieces! Goddam plumbing, oughta be sued, those people. I hardly finished putting it in and the thing . . . [*His words rumble off.*]

LINDA: I'm just wondering if Oliver will remember him. You think he might?

WILLY [*coming out of the bathroom in his pajamas*]: Remember him? What's the matter with you, you crazy? If he'd've stayed with Oliver he'd be on top by now! Wait'll Oliver gets a look at him. You don't know the average caliber any more. The average young man today—[*he is getting into bed*]—is got a caliber of zero. Greatest thing in the world for him was to bum around.

[BIFF *and* HAPPY *enter the bedroom. Slight pause.*]

WILLY [*stops short, looking at* BIFF]: Glad to hear it, boy.

HAPPY: He wanted to say good night to you, sport.

WILLY [*to* BIFF]: Yeah. Knock him dead, boy. What'd you want to tell me?

BIFF: Just take it easy, Pop. Good night. [*He turns to go.*]

WILLY [*unable to resist*]: And if anything falls off the desk while you're talking to him—like a package or something—don't you pick it up. They have office boys for that.

LINDA: I'll make a big breakfast—

WILLY: Will you let me finish? [*To* BIFF] Tell him you were in the business in the West. Not farm work.

BIFF: All right, Dad.

LINDA: I think everything—

WILLY [*going right through her speech*]: And don't undersell yourself. No less than fifteen thousand dollars.

BIFF [*unable to bear him*]: Okay. Good night. Mom. [*He starts moving.*]

WILLY: Because you got a greatness in you, Biff, remember that. You got all kinds a greatness . . . [*He lies back, exhausted.* BIFF *walks out.*]

LINDA [*calling after* BIFF]: Sleep well, darling!

HAPPY: I'm gonna get married, Mom. I wanted to tell you.
LINDA: Go to sleep, dear.
HAPPY [*going*]: I just wanted to tell you.
WILLY: Keep up the good work. [HAPPY *exits.*] God . . . remember that Ebbets Field game? The championship of the city?
LINDA: Just rest. Should I sing to you?
WILLY: Yeah. Sing to me. [LINDA *hums a soft lullaby.*] When that team came out—he was the tallest, remember?
LINDA: Oh, yes. And in gold.

[BIFF *enters the darkened kitchen, takes a cigarette, and leaves the house. He comes downstage into a golden pool of light. He smokes, staring at the night.*]

WILLY: Like a young god. Hercules—something like that. And the sun, the sun all around him. Remember how he waved to me? Right up from the field, with the representatives of three colleges standing by? And the buyers I brought, and the cheers when he came out—Loman, Loman, Loman! God Almighty, he'll be great yet. A star like that, magnificent, can never really fade away!

[*The light on* WILLY *is fading. The gas heater begins to glow through the kitchen wall, near the stairs, a blue flame beneath red coils.*]

LINDA [*timidly*]: Willy dear, what has he got against you?
WILLY: I'm so tired. Don't talk any more.

[BIFF *slowly returns to the kitchen. He stops, stares toward the heater.*]

LINDA: Will you ask Howard to let you work in New York?
WILLY: First thing in the morning. Everything'll be all right.

[BIFF *reaches behind the heater and draws out a length of rubber tubing. He is horrified and turns his head toward* WILLY'S *room, still dimly lit, from which the strains of* LINDA'S *desperate but monotonous humming rise.*]

WILLY [*staring through the window into the moonlight*]: Gee, look at the moon moving between the buildings!

[BIFF *wraps the tubing around his hand and quickly goes up the stairs.*]

CURTAIN

ACT TWO

Music is heard, gay and bright. The curtain rises as the music fades away.

[WILLY, *in shirt sleeves, is sitting at the kitchen table, sipping coffee, his hat in his lap.* LINDA *is filling his cup when she can.*]

WILLY: Wonderful coffee. Meal in itself.
LINDA: Can I make you some eggs?
WILLY: No. Take a breath.
LINDA: You look so rested, dear.
WILLY: I slept like a dead one. First time in months. Imagine, sleeping till ten on a Tuesday morning. Boys left nice and early, heh?
LINDA: They were out of here by eight o'clock.
WILLY: Good work!
LINDA: It was so thrilling to see them leaving together. I can't get over the shaving lotion in this house!
WILLY [*smiling*]: Mmm—

LINDA: Biff was very changed this morning. His whole attitude seemed to be hopeful. He couldn't wait to get downtown to see Oliver.

WILLY: He's heading for a change. There's no question, there simply are certain men that take longer to get—solidified. How did he dress?

LINDA: His blue suit. He's so handsome in that suit. He could be a—anything in that suit!

[WILLY *gets up from the table.* LINDA *holds his jacket for him.*]

WILLY: There's no question, no question at all. Gee, on the way home tonight I'd like to buy some seeds.

LINDA [*laughing*]: That'd be wonderful. But not enough sun gets back there. Nothing'll grow any more.

WILLY: You wait, kid, before it's all over we're gonna get a little place out in the country, and I'll raise some vegetables, a couple of chickens . . .

LINDA: You'll do it yet, dear.

[WILLY *walks out of his jacket.* LINDA *follows him.*]

WILLY: And they'll get married, and come for a weekend. I'd build a little guest house. 'Cause I got so many fine tools, all I'd need would be a little lumber and some peace of mind.

LINDA [*joyfully*]: I sewed the lining . . .

WILLY: I could build two guest, houses, so they'd both come. Did he decide how much he's going to ask Oliver for?

LINDA [*getting him into the jacket*]: He didn't mention it, but I imagine ten or fifteen thousand. You going to talk to Howard today?

WILLY: Yeah. I'll put it to him straight and simple. He'll just have to take me off the road.

LINDA: And Willy, don't forget to ask for a little advance, because we've got the insurance premium. It's the grace period now.

WILLY: That's a hundred . . . ?

LINDA: A hundred and eight, sixty-eight. Because we're a little short again.

WILLY: Why are we short?

LINDA: Well, you had the motor job on the car . . .

WILLY: That goddam Studebaker!

LINDA: And you got one more payment on the refrigerator . . .

WILLY: But it just broke again!

LINDA: Well, it's old, dear.

WILLY: I told you we should've bought a well-advertised machine. Charley bought a General Electric and it's twenty years old and it's still good, that son-of-a-bitch.

LINDA: But, Willy—

WILLY: Whoever heard of a Hastings refrigerator? Once in my life I would like to own something outright before it's broken! I'm always in a race with the junkyard! I just finished paying for the car and it's on its last legs. The refrigerator consumes belts like a goddam maniac. They time those things. They time them so when you finally paid for them, they're used up.

LINDA [*buttoning up his jacket as he unbuttons it*]: All told, about two hundred dollars would carry us, dear. But that includes the last payment on the mortgage. After this payment, Willy, the house belongs to us.

WILLY: It's twenty-five years!

LINDA: Biff was nine years old when we bought it.

WILLY: Well, that's a great thing. To weather a twenty-five-year mortgage is—

LINDA: It's an accomplishment.

WILLY: All the cement, the lumber, the reconstruction I put in this house! There ain't a crack to be found in it any more.

LINDA: Well, it served its purpose.

WILLY: What purpose? Some stranger'll come along, move in, and that's that. If only Biff would take this house, and raise a family . . . [*He starts to go.*] Good-bye, I'm late.

LINDA [*suddenly remembering*]: Oh, I forgot! You're supposed to meet them for dinner.

WILLY: Me?

LINDA: At Frank's Chop House on Forty-eighth near Sixth Avenue.

WILLY: Is that so! How about you?

LINDA: No, just the three of you. They're gonna blow you to a big meal!

WILLY: Don't say! Who thought of that?

LINDA: Biff came to me this morning, Willy, and he said, "Tell Dad, we want to blow him to a big meal." Be there six o'clock. You and your two boys are going to have dinner.

WILLY: Gee whiz! That's really somethin'. I'm gonna knock Howard for a loop, kid. I'll get an advance, and I'll come home with a New York job. Goddammit, now I'm gonna do it!

LINDA: Oh, that's the spirit, Willy!

WILLY: I will never get behind a wheel the rest of my life!

LINDA: It's changing, Willy. I can feel it changing!

WILLY: Beyond a question. G'bye, I'm late. [*He starts to go again.*]

LINDA [*calling after him as she runs to the kitchen table for a handkerchief*]: You got your glasses?

WILLY [*feels for them, then comes back in*]: Yeah, yeah, got my glasses.

LINDA [*giving him the handkerchief*]: And a handkerchief.

WILLY: Yeah, handkerchief.

LINDA: And your saccharine?

WILLY: Yeah, my saccharine.

LINDA: Be careful on the subway stairs.

[*She kisses him, and a silk stocking is seen hanging from her hand.* WILLY *notices it.*]

WILLY: Will you stop mending stockings? At least while I'm in the house. It gets me nervous. I can't tell you. Please.

[LINDA *hides the stocking in her hand as she follows* WILLY *across the forestage in front of the house.*]

LINDA: Remember, Frank's Chop House.

WILLY [*passing the apron*]: Maybe beets would grow out there.

LINDA [*laughing*]: But you tried so many times.

WILLY: Yeah. Well, don't work hard today. [*He disappears around the right corner of the house.*]

LINDA: Be careful!

[*As* WILLY *vanishes,* LINDA *waves to him. Suddenly the phone rings. She runs across the stage and into the kitchen and lifts it.*]

LINDA: Hello? Oh, Biff! I'm so glad you called, I just . . . Yes, sure, I just told him. Yes, he'll be there for dinner at six o'clock, I didn't forget. Listen, I was just dying to tell you. You know that little rubber pipe I told you about? That he connected to the gas heater? I finally decided to go down the cellar this morning and take it away and destroy it. But it's gone! Imagine? He took it away himself, it isn't there! [*She listens.*] When? Oh, then you took it. Oh—nothing, it's just that I'd hoped he'd taken it away himself. Oh, I'm not worried, darling, because this morning he left in such high spirits, it was like the old days! I'm not afraid any more. Did Mr. Oliver see you? . . . Well, you wait there then. And make a nice impression on him, darling. Just don't perspire too much before you see him. And have a nice time with Dad. He may have big news too! . . . That's right, a New York job. And be sweet to him tonight, dear. Be loving to him. Because he's only a little boat looking for a harbor. [*She is trembling with sorrow and joy.*] Oh, that's wonderful, Biff, you'll save his life. Thanks, darling. Just put your arm around him when he comes into the restaurant. Give him a smile. That's the boy . . . Good-bye, dear . . . You got your comb? . . . That's fine. Good-bye, Biff dear.

[*In the middle of her speech,* HOWARD WAGNER, *thirty-six, wheels in a small typewriter table on which is a wire-recording machine and proceeds to plug it in. This is on the left forestage. Light slowly fades on* LINDA *as it rises on* HOWARD. HOWARD *is intent on threading the machine and only glances over his shoulder as* WILLY *appears.*]

WILLY: Pst! Pst!

HOWARD: Hello, Willy, come in.

WILLY: Like to have a little talk with you, Howard.

HOWARD: Sorry to keep you waiting. I'll be with you in a minute.

WILLY: What's that, Howard?

HOWARD: Didn't you ever see one of these? Wire recorder.

WILLY: Oh. Can we talk a minute?

HOWARD: Records things. Just got delivery yesterday. Been driving me crazy, the most terrific machine I ever saw in my life. I was up all night with it.

WILLY: What do you do with it?

HOWARD: I bought it for dictation, but you can do anything with it. Listen to this. I had it home last night. Listen to what I picked up. The first one is my daughter. Get this. [*He flicks the switch and "Roll out the Barrel" is heard being whistled.*] Listen to that kid whistle.

WILLY: That is lifelike, isn't it?

HOWARD: Seven years old. Get that tone.

WILLY: Ts, ts. Like to ask a little favor if you . . .

[*The whistling breaks off, and the voice of* HOWARD'S *daughter is heard.*]

HIS DAUGHTER: "Now you, Daddy."

HOWARD: She's crazy for me! [*Again the same song is whistled.*] That's me! Ha! [*He winks.*]

WILLY: You're very good!

[*The whistling breaks off again. The machine runs silent for a moment.*]

HOWARD: Sh! Get this now, this my son.

HIS SON: "The capital of Alabama is Montgomery; the capital of Arizona is Phoenix; the capital of Arkansas is Little Rock; the capital of California is Sacramento . . ." [*and on, and on.*]

HOWARD [*holding up five fingers*]: Five years old, Willy!

WILLY: He'll make an announcer some day!

HIS SON [*continuing*]: "The capital . . ."

HOWARD: Get that—alphabetical order! [*The machine breaks off suddenly.*] Wait a minute. The maid kicked the plug out.

WILLY: It certainly is a—

HOWARD: Sh, for God's sake!

HIS SON: "It's nine o'clock, Bulova watch time. So I have to go to sleep."

WILLY: That really is—

HOWARD: Wait a minute! The next is my wife.

[*They wait.*]

HOWARD'S VOICE: "Go on, say something." [*Pause.*] "Well, you gonna talk?"

HIS WIFE: "I can't think of anything."

HOWARD'S VOICE: "Well, talk—it's turning."

HIS WIFE [*shyly, beaten*]: "Hello." [*Silence.*] "Oh, Howard, I can't talk into this . . ."

HOWARD [*snapping the machine off*]: That was my wife.

WILLY: That is a wonderful machine. Can we—

HOWARD: I tell you, Willy, I'm gonna take my camera, and my bandsaw, and all my hobbies, and out they go. This is the most fascinating relaxation I ever found.

WILLY: I think I'll get one myself.

HOWARD: Sure, they're only a hundred and a half. You can't do without it. Supposing you wanna hear Jack Benny, see? But you can't be at home at that hour. So you tell the maid to turn the radio on when Jack Benny comes on, and this automatically goes on with the radio . . .

WILLY: And when you come home you . . .

HOWARD: You can come home twelve o'clock, one o'clock, any time you like, and you get yourself a Coke and sit yourself down, throw the switch, and there's Jack Benny's program in the middle of the night!

WILLY: I'm definitely going to get one. Because lots of time I'm on the road, and I think to myself, what I must be missing on the radio!

HOWARD: Don't you have a radio in the car?

WILLY: Well, yeah, but who ever thinks of turning it on?

HOWARD: Say, aren't you supposed to be in Boston?

WILLY: That's what I want to talk to you about, Howard. You got a minute? [*He draws a chair in from the wing.*]

HOWARD: What happened? What're you doing here?

WILLY: Well . . .

HOWARD: You didn't crack up again, did you?

WILLY: Oh, no. No . . .

HOWARD: Geez, you had me worried there for a minute. What's the trouble?

WILLY: Well, tell you the truth, Howard. I've come to the decision that I'd rather not travel any more.

HOWARD: Not travel! Well, what'll you do?

WILLY: Remember, Christmas time, when you had the party here? You said you'd try to think of some spot for me here in town.

HOWARD: With us?

WILLY: Well, sure.

HOWARD: Oh, yeah, yeah. I remember. Well, I couldn't think of anything for you, Willy.

WILLY: I tell ya, Howard. The kids are all grown up, y'know. I don't need much any more. If I could take home—well, sixty-five dollars a week. I could swing it.

HOWARD: Yeah, but Willy, see I—

WILLY: I tell ya why, Howard. Speaking frankly and between the two of us, y'know—I'm just a little tired.

HOWARD: Oh, I could understand that, Willy. But you're a road man, Willy, and we do a road business. We've only got a half-dozen salesmen on the floor here.

WILLY: God knows, Howard, I never asked a favor of any man. But I was with the firm when your father used to carry you in here in his arms.

HOWARD: I know that, Willy, but—

WILLY: Your father came to me the day you were born and asked me what I thought of the name of Howard, may he rest in peace.

HOWARD: I appreciate that, Willy, but there just is no spot here for you. If I had a spot I'd slam you right in, but I just don't have a single solitary spot.

[*He looks for his lighter.* WILLY *has picked it up and gives it to him. Pause.*]

WILLY [*with increasing anger*]: Howard, all I need to set my table is fifty dollars a week.

HOWARD: But where am I going to put you, kid?

WILLY: Look, it isn't a question of whether I can sell merchandise, is it?

HOWARD: No, but it's a business, kid, and everybody's gotta pull his own weight.

WILLY [*desperately*]: Just let me tell you a story, Howard—

HOWARD: 'Cause you gotta admit, business is business.

WILLY [*angrily*]: Business is definitely business, but just listen for a minute. You don't understand this. When I was a boy—eighteen, nineteen—I was already on the road. And there was a question in my mind as to whether selling had a future for me. Because in those days I had a yearning to go to Alaska. See, there were three gold strikes in one month in Alaska, and I felt like going out. Just for the ride, you might say.

HOWARD [*barely interested*]: Don't say.

WILLY: Oh, yeah, my father lived many years in Alaska. He was an adventurous man. We've got quite a little streak of self-reliance in our family. I thought I'd go out with my older brother and try to locate him, and maybe settle in the North with the old man. And I was almost decided to go, when I met a salesman in the Parker House. His name was Dave Singleman. And he was eighty-four years old, and he'd drummed merchandise in thirty-one states. And old Dave, he'd go up to his room, y'understand, put on his green velvet slippers—I'll never forget—and pick up his phone and call the buyers, and without ever leaving his room, at the age of eighty-four, he made his living. And when I saw that, I realized that selling was the greatest career a man could want. 'Cause what could be more satisfying than to be able to go, at the age of eighty-four, into twenty or thirty different cities, and pick up a phone, and be remembered and loved and helped by so many different people? Do you know? when he died—and by the way he died the death of a salesman, in his green velvet slippers in the smoker of the New York, New Haven, and Hartford, going into Boston—when he died, hundreds of salesmen and buyers were at his funeral. Things were sad on a lotta trains for months after that. [*He stands up.* HOWARD *has not looked at him.*] In those days there was personality in it, Howard. There was respect, and comradeship, and gratitude in it. Today, it's all cut and dried, and there's no chance for bringing friendship to bear—or personality. You see what I mean? They don't know me any more.

HOWARD [*moving away, to the right*]: That's just the thing, Willy.

WILLY: If I had forty dollars a week—that's all I'd need. Forty dollars, Howard.

HOWARD: Kid, I can't take blood from a stone, I—

WILLY [*desperation is on him now*]: Howard, the year Al Smith was nominated, your father came to me and—

HOWARD [*starting to go off*]: I've got to see some people, kid.

WILLY [*stopping him*]: I'm talking about your father! There were promises made across this desk! You mustn't tell me you've got people to see—I put thirty-four years into this firm, Howard, and now I can't pay my insurance! You can't eat the orange and throw the peel away—a man is not a piece of fruit! [*After a pause*] Now pay attention. Your father—in 1928 I had a big year. I averaged a hundred and seventy dollars a week in commissions.

HOWARD [*impatiently*]: Now. Willy, you never averaged—

WILLY [*banging his hand on the desk*]: I averaged a hundred and seventy dollars a week in the year of 1928! And your father came to me—or rather, I was in the office here—it was right over this desk—and he put his hand on my shoulder—

HOWARD [*getting up*]: You'll have to excuse me, Willy, I gotta see some people. Pull yourself together. [*Going out*] I'll be back in a little while.

[*On* HOWARD'S *exit, the light on his chair grows very bright and strange.*]

WILLY: Pull myself together! What the hell did I say to him? My God, I was yelling at him! How could I! [WILLY *breaks off, staring at the light, which occupies the chair, animating it. He approaches this chair, standing across the desk from it.*] Frank. Frank, don't you remember what you told me that time? How you put your hand on my shoulder, and Frank . . . [*He leans on the desk and as he speaks the dead man's name he accidentally switches on the recorder, and instantly*—]

HOWARD'S SON: ". . . of New York is Albany. The capital of Ohio is Cincinnati, the capital of Rhode Island is . . ." [*The recitation continues.*]

WILLY [*leaping away with fright, shouting*]: Ha! Howard! Howard! Howard!

HOWARD [*rushing in*]: What happened?

WILLY [*pointing at the machine, which continues nasally, childishly, with the capital cities*]: Shut it off! Shut it off!

HOWARD [*pulling the plug out*]: Look, Willy . . .

WILLY [*pressing his hands to his eyes*]: I gotta get myself some coffee. I'll get some coffee . . .

[WILLY *starts to walk out.* HOWARD *stops him.*]

HOWARD [*rolling up the cord*]: Willy, look . . .

WILLY: I'll go to Boston.

HOWARD: Willy, you can't go to Boston for us.

WILLY: Why can't I go?

HOWARD: I don't want you to represent us. I've been meaning to tell you for a long time now.

WILLY: Howard, are you firing me?

HOWARD: I think you need a good long rest, Willy.

WILLY: Howard—

HOWARD: And when you feel better, come back, and we'll see if we can work something out.

WILLY: But I gotta earn money, Howard. I'm in no position to—

HOWARD: Where are your sons? Why don't your sons give you a hand?

WILLY: They're working on a very big deal.

HOWARD: This is no time for false pride, Willy. You go to your sons and you tell them that you're tired. You've got two great boys, haven't you?

WILLY: Oh, no question, no question, but in the meantime . . .

HOWARD: Then that's that, heh?

WILLY: All right. I'll go to Boston tomorrow.

HOWARD: No, no.

WILLY: I can't throw myself on my sons. I'm not a cripple!

HOWARD: Look, kid. I'm busy this morning.

WILLY [*grasping* HOWARD'S *arm*]: Howard, you've got to let me go to Boston!

HOWARD [*hard, keeping himself under control*]: I've got a line of people to see this morning. Sit down, take five minutes, and pull yourself together, and then go home, will ya? I need the office, Willy. [*He starts to go, turns, remembering the recorder, starts to push off the table holding the recorder.*] Oh, yeah. Whenever you can this week, stop by and drop off the samples. You'll feel better, Willy, and then come back and we'll talk. Pull yourself together, kid, there's people outside.

[HOWARD *exits, pushing the table off left.* WILLY *stares into space, exhausted. Now the music is heard*—BEN'S *music*—*first distantly, then closer, closer. As* WILLY *speaks*, BEN *enters from the right. He carries valise and umbrella.*]

WILLY: Oh, Ben, how did you do it? What is the answer? Did you wind up the Alaska deal already?

BEN: Doesn't take much time if you know what you're doing. Just a short business trip. Boarding ship in an hour. Wanted to say good-bye.

WILLY: Ben, I've got to talk to you.

BEN [*glancing at his watch*]: Haven't the time, William.

WILLY [*crossing the apron to* BEN]: Ben, nothing's working out. I don't know what to do.

BEN: Now, look here, William. I've bought timberland in Alaska and I need a man to look after things for me.

WILLY: God, timberland! Me and my boys in those grand outdoors!

BEN: You've a new continent at your doorstep, William. Get out of these cities, they're full of talk and time payments and courts of law. Screw on your fists and you can fight for a fortune up there.

WILLY: Yes, yes! Linda, Linda!

[LINDA *enters as of old, with the wash.*]

LINDA: Oh, you're back?

BEN: I haven't much time.

WILLY: No, wait! Linda, he's got a proposition for me in Alaska.

LINDA: But you've got—[*To* BEN] He's got a beautiful job here.

WILLY: But in Alaska, kid, I could—

LINDA: You're doing well enough, Willy!

BEN [*to* LINDA]: Enough for what, my dear?

LINDA [*frightened of* BEN *and angry at him*]: Don't say those things to him! Enough to be happy right here, right now. [*To* WILLY, *while* BEN *laughs*] Why must everybody conquer the world? You're well liked, and the boys love you, and someday—[*to* BEN]—why, old man Wagner told him just the other day that if he keeps it up he'll be a member of the firm, didn't he, Willy?

WILLY: Sure, sure. I am building something with this firm, Ben, and if a man is building something he must be on the right track, mustn't he?

BEN: What are you building? Lay your hand on it. Where is it?

WILLY [*hesitantly*]: That's true, Linda, there's nothing.
LINDA: Why? [*To* BEN] There's a man eighty-four years old—
WILLY: That's right, Ben, that's right. When I look at that man I say, what is there to worry about?
BEN: Bah!
WILLY: It's true, Ben. All he has to do is go into any city, pick up the phone, and he's making his living and you know why?
BEN [*picking up his valise*]: I've got to go.
WILLY [*holding* BEN *back*]: Look at this boy!

[BIFF, *in his high school sweater, enters carrying suitcase.* HAPPY *carries* BIFF'S *shoulder guards, gold helmet, and football pants.*]

WILLY: Without a penny to his name, three great universities are begging for him, and from there the sky's the limit, because it's not what you do, Ben. It's who you know and the smile on your face! It's contacts, Ben, contacts! The whole wealth of Alaska passes over the lunch table at the Commodore Hotel, and that's the wonder, the wonder of this country, that a man can end with diamonds here on the basis of being liked! [*He turns to* BIFF.] And that's why when you get out on that field today it's important. Because thousands of people will be rooting for you and loving you. [*To* BEN, *who has again begun to leave*] And Ben! when he walks into a business office his name will sound out like a bell and all the doors will open to him! I've seen it, Ben, I've seen it a thousand times! You can't feel it with your hand like timber, but it's there!
BEN: Good-bye, William.
WILLY: Ben, am I right? Don't you think I'm right? I value your advice.
BEN: There's a new continent at your doorstep, William. You could walk out rich. Rich! [*He is gone.*]
WILLY: We'll do it here, Ben! You hear me? We're gonna do it here!

[*Young* BERNARD *rushes in. The gay music of the boys is heard.*]

BERNARD: Oh, gee. I was afraid you left already!
WILLY: Why? What time is it?
BERNARD: It's half-past one!
WILLY: Well, come on, everybody! Ebbets Field next stop! Where's the pennants?

[*He rushes through the wall-line of the kitchen and out into the living-room.*]

LINDA [*to* BIFF]: Did you pack fresh underwear?
BIFF [*who has been limbering up*]: I want to go!
BERNARD: Biff, I'm carrying your helmet, ain't I?
HAPPY: No, I'm carrying the helmet.
BERNARD: Oh, Biff, you promised me.
HAPPY: I'm carrying the helmet.
BERNARD: How am I going to get in the locker room?
LINDA: Let him carry the shoulder guards. [*She puts her coat and hat on in the kitchen.*]
BERNARD: Can I, Biff? 'Cause I told everybody I'm going to be in the locker room.
HAPPY: In Ebbets Field it's the clubhouse.
BERNARD: I meant the clubhouse, Biff!
HAPPY: Biff!
BIFF [*grandly, after a slight pause*]: Let him carry the shoulder guards.
HAPPY [*as he gives* BERNARD *the shoulder guards*]: Stay close to us now.

[WILLY *rushes in with the pennants.*]

WILLY [*handing them out*]: Everybody wave when Biff comes out on the field. [HAPPY *and* BERNARD *run off.*] You set now, boy?

[*The music has died away.*]

BIFF: Ready to go, Pop. Every muscle is ready.

WILLY [*at the edge of the apron*]: You realize what this means?

BIFF: That's right, Pop.

WILLY [*feeling* BIFF'S *muscles*]: You're comin' home this afternoon captain of the All-Scholastic Championship Team of the City of New York.

BIFF: I got it, Pop. And remember, pal, when I take off my helmet, that touchdown is for you.

WILLY: Let's go! [*He is starting out, with his arm around* BIFF, *when* CHARLEY *enters, as of old, in knickers.*] I got no room for you, Charley.

CHARLEY: Room? For what?

WILLY: In the car.

CHARLEY: You goin' for a ride? I wanted to shoot some casino.

WILLY [*furiously*]: Casino! [*Incredulously*] Don't you realize what today is?

LINDA: Oh, he knows, Willy. He's just kidding you.

WILLY: That's nothing to kid about!

CHARLEY: No. Linda, what's goin' on?

LINDA: He's playing in Ebbets Field.

CHARLEY: Baseball in this weather?

WILLY: Don't talk to him. Come on, come on! [*He is pushing them out.*]

CHARLEY: Wait a minute, didn't you hear the news?

WILLY: What?

CHARLEY: Don't you listen to the radio? Ebbets Field just blew up.

WILLY: You go to hell! [CHARLEY *laughs. Pushing them out*] Come on, come on! We're late.

CHARLEY [*as they go*]: Knock a homer, Biff, knock a homer!

WILLY [*the last to leave, turning to* CHARLEY]: I don't think that was funny, Charley. This is the greatest day of his life.

CHARLEY: Willy, when are you going to grow up?

WILLY: Yeah, heh? When this game is over, Charley, you'll be laughing out of the other side of your face. They'll be calling him another Red Grange. Twenty-five thousand a year.

CHARLEY [*kidding*]: Is that so?

WILLY: Yeah, that's so.

CHARLEY: Well, then, I'm sorry, Willy. But tell me something.

WILLY: What?

CHARLEY: Who is Red Grange?

WILLY: Put up your hands. Goddam you, put up your hands!

[CHARLEY, *chuckling, shakes his head and walks away, around the left corner of the stage.* WILLY *follows him. The music rises to a mocking frenzy.*]

WILLY: Who the hell do you think you are, better than everybody else? You don't know everything, you big, ignorant, stupid . . . Put up your hands!

[*Light rises, on the right side of the forestage, on a small table in the reception room of* CHARLEY'S *office. Traffic sounds are heard.* BERNARD, *now mature, sits whistling to himself. A pair of tennis rackets and an overnight bag are on the floor beside him.*]

WILLY [*offstage*]: What are you walking away for? Don't walk away! If you're going to say something say it to my face! I know you laugh at me behind my back.

You'll laugh out of the other side of your goddam face after this game. Touchdown! Touchdown! Eighty thousand people! Touchdown! Right between the goal posts.

[BERNARD *is a quiet, earnest, but self-assured young man.* WILLY'S *voice is coming from right upstage now,* BERNARD *lowers his feet off the table and listens.* JENNY, *his father's secretary, enters.*]

JENNY [*distressed*]: Say, Bernard, will you go out in the hall?

BERNARD: What is that noise? Who is it?

JENNY: Mr. Loman. He just got off the elevator.

BERNARD [*getting up*]: Who's he arguing with?

JENNY: Nobody. There's nobody with him. I can't deal with him any more, and your father gets all upset everytime he comes. I've got a lot of typing to do, and your father's waiting to sign it. Will you see him?

WILLY [*entering*]: Touchdown! Touch—[*He sees* JENNY.] Jenny, Jenny, good to see you. How're ya? Workin'? Or still honest?

JENNY: Fine. How've you been feeling?

WILLY: Not much any more, Jenny. Ha, ha! [*He is surprised to see the rackets.*]

BERNARD: Hello, Uncle Willy.

WILLY [*almost shocked*]: Bernard! Well, look who's here! [*He comes quickly, guiltily, to* BERNARD *and warmly shakes his hand.*]

BERNARD: How are you? Good to see you.

WILLY: What are you doing here?

BERNARD: Oh, just stopped by to see Pop. Get off my feet till my train leaves. I'm going to Washington in a few minutes.

WILLY: Is he in?

BERNARD: Yes, he's in his office with the accountant. Sit down.

WILLY [*sitting down*]: What're you going to do in Washington?

BERNARD: Oh, just a case I've got there, Willy.

WILLY: That so? [*indicating the rackets*] You going to play tennis there?

BERNARD: I'm staying with a friend who's got a court.

WILLY: Don't say. His own tennis court. Must be fine people, I bet.

BERNARD: They are, very nice. Dad tells me Biff's in town.

WILLY [*with a big smile*]: Yeah, Biff's in. Working on a very big deal, Bernard.

BERNARD: What's Biff doing?

WILLY: Well, he's been doing very big things in the West. But he decided to establish himself here. Very big. We're having dinner. Did I hear your wife had a boy?

BERNARD: That's right. Our second.

WILLY: Two boys! What do you know!

BERNARD: What kind of a deal has Biff got?

WILLY: Well, Bill Oliver—very big sporting-goods man—he wants Biff very badly. Called him in from the West. Long distance, carte blanche, special deliveries. Your friends have their own private tennis court?

BERNARD: You still with the old firm, Willy?

WILLY [*after a pause*]: I'm—I'm overjoyed to see how you made the grade, Bernard, overjoyed. It's an encouraging thing to see a young man really—really—Looks very good for Biff—very—[*He breaks off, then*] Bernard—[*He is so full of emotion, he breaks off again.*]

BERNARD: What is it, Willy?

WILLY [*small and alone*]: What—what's the secret?

BERNARD: What secret?

WILLY: How—how did you? Why didn't he ever catch on?

BERNARD: I wouldn't know that, Willy.

WILLY [*confidentially, desperately*]: You were his friend, his boyhood friend. There's something I don't understand about it. His life ended after that Ebbets Field game. From the age of seventeen nothing good ever happened to him.

BERNARD: He never trained himself for anything.

WILLY: But he did, he did. After high school he took so many correspondence courses. Radio mechanics; television; God knows what, and never made the slightest mark.

BERNARD [*taking off his glasses*]: Willy, do you want to talk candidly?

WILLY [*rising, faces* BERNARD]: I regard you as a very brilliant man, Bernard. I value your advice.

BERNARD: Oh, the hell with the advice, Willy. I couldn't advise you. There's just one thing I've always wanted to ask you. When he was supposed to graduate, and the math teacher flunked him—

WILLY: Oh, that son-of-a-bitch ruined his life.

BERNARD: Yeah, but, Willy, all he had to do was to go to summer school and make up that subject.

WILLY: That's right, that's right.

BERNARD: Did you tell him not to go to summer school?

WILLY: Me? I begged him to go. I ordered him to go!

BERNARD: Then why wouldn't he go?

WILLY: Why? Why! Bernard, that question has been trailing me like a ghost for the last fifteen years. He flunked the subject, and laid down and died like a hammer hit him!

BERNARD: Take it easy, kid.

WILLY: Let me talk to you—I got nobody to talk to. Bernard, Bernard, was it my fault? Y'see? It keeps going around in my mind, maybe I did something to him. I got nothing to give him.

BERNARD: Don't take it so hard.

WILLY: Why did he lay down? What is the story there? You were his friend!

BERNARD: Willy, I remember, it was June, and our grades came out. And he'd flunked math.

WILLY: That son-of-a-bitch!

BERNARD: No, it wasn't right then. Biff just got very angry, I remember, and he was ready to enroll in summer school.

WILLY [*surprised*]: He was?

BERNARD: He wasn't beaten by it at all. But then, Willy, he disappeared from the block for almost a month. And I got the idea that he'd gone up to New England to see you. Did he have a talk with you then?

[WILLY *stares in silence.*]

BERNARD: Willy?

WILLY [*with a strong edge of resentment in his voice*]: Yeah, he came to Boston. What about it?

BERNARD: Well, just that when he came back—I'll never forget this, it always mystifies me. Because I'd thought so well of Biff, even though he'd always taken advantage of me. I loved him, Willy, y'know? And he came back after that month and took his sneakers—remember those sneakers with "University of Virginia" printed on them? He was so proud of those, wore them every day. And he took them down in the cellar, and burned them up in the furnace. We had a fist fight. It lasted at least half an hour. Just the two of us, punching each other down the cellar, and crying right through it. I've often thought of how strange it was that I knew he'd given up his life. What happened in Boston, Willy?

[WILLY *looks at him as at an intruder.*]

BERNARD: I just bring it up because you asked me.

WILLY [*angrily*]: Nothing. What do you mean, "What happened?" What's that got to do with anything?

BERNARD: Well, don't get sore.

WILLY: What are you trying to do, blame it on me? If a boy lays down is that my fault?

BERNARD: Now, Willy, don't get—

WILLY: Well, don't—don't talk to me that way! What does that mean, "What happened?"

[CHARLEY *enters. He is in his vest, and he carries a bottle of bourbon.*]

CHARLEY: Hey, you're going to miss that train. [*He waves the bottle.*]

BERNARD: Yeah, I'm going. [*He takes the bottle.*] Thanks, Pop. [*He picks up his rackets and bag.*] Good-bye, Willy, and don't worry about it. You know, "If at first you don't succeed . . ."

WILLY: Yes, I believe in that.

BERNARD: But sometimes, Willy, it's better for a man just to walk away.

WILLY: Walk away?

BERNARD: That's right.

WILLY: But if you can't walk away?

BERNARD [*after a slight pause*]: I guess that's when it's tough.

[*Extending his hand*] Good-bye, Willy.

WILLY [*shaking* BERNARD'S *hand*]: Good-bye, boy.

CHARLEY [*an arm on* BERNARD'S *shoulder*]: How do you like this kid? Gonna argue a case in front of the Supreme Court.

BERNARD [*protesting*]: Pop!

WILLY [*genuinely shocked, pained, and happy*]: No! The Supreme Court!

BERNARD: I gotta run. 'Bye, Dad!

CHARLEY: Knock 'em dead, Bernard!

[BERNARD *goes off.*]

WILLY [*as* CHARLEY *takes out his wallet*]: The Supreme Court! And he didn't even mention it!

CHARLEY [*counting out money on the desk*]: He don't have to—he's gonna do it.

WILLY: And you never told him what to do, did you? You never took any interest in him.

CHARLEY: My salvation is that I never took any interest in anything. There's some money—fifty dollars. I got an accountant inside.

WILLY: Charley, look . . . [*With difficulty*] I got my insurance to pay. If you can manage it—I need a hundred and ten dollars.

[CHARLEY *doesn't reply for a moment; merely stops moving.*]

WILLY: I'd draw it from my bank but Linda would know, and I . . .

CHARLEY: Sit down, Willy.

WILLY [*moving toward the chair*]: I'm keeping an account of everything, remember. I'll pay every penny back. [*He sits.*]

CHARLEY: Now listen to me, Willy.

WILLY: I want you to know I appreciate . . .

CHARLEY [*sitting down on the table*]: Willy, what're you doin'? What the hell is goin' on in your head?

WILLY: Why? I'm simply . . .

CHARLEY: I offered you a job. You can make fifty dollars a week. And I won't send you on the road.

WILLY: I've got a job.

CHARLEY: Without pay? What kind of a job is a job without pay? [*He rises.*] Now, look, kid, enough is enough. I'm no genius but I know when I'm being insulted.

WILLY: Insulted!

CHARLEY: Why don't you want to work for me?

WILLY: What's the matter with you? I've got a job.

CHARLEY: Then what're you walkin' in here every week for?

WILLY [*getting up*]: Well, if you don't want me to walk in here—

CHARLEY: I am offering you a job.

WILLY: I don't want your goddam job!

CHARLEY: When the hell are you going to grow up?

WILLY [*furiously*]: You big ignoramus, if you say that to me again I'll rap you one! I don't care how big you are! [*He's ready to fight.*]

[*Pause.*]

CHARLEY [*kindly, going to him*]: How much do you need, Willy?

WILLY: Charley, I'm strapped, I'm strapped. I don't know what to do. I was just fired.

CHARLEY: Howard fired you?

WILLY: That snotnose. Imagine that? I named him. I named him Howard.

CHARLEY: Willy, when're you gonna realize that them things don't mean anything? You named him Howard, but you can't sell that. The only thing you got in this world is what you can sell. And the funny thing is that you're a salesman, and you don't know that.

WILLY: I've always tried to think otherwise, I guess, I always felt that if a man was impressive, and well liked, that nothing—

CHARLEY: Why must everybody like you? Who liked J. P. Morgan? Was he impressive? In a Turkish bath he'd look like a butcher. But with his pockets on he was very well liked. Now listen, Willy, I know you don't like me, and nobody can say I'm in love with you, but I'll give you a job because—just for the hell of it, put it that way. Now what do you say?

WILLY: I—I just can't work for you, Charley.

CHARLEY: What're you, jealous of me?

WILLY: I can't work for you, that's all, don't ask me why.

CHARLEY [*angered, takes out more bills*]: You been jealous of me all your life, you damned fool! Here, pay your insurance. [*He puts the money in* WILLY'S *hand.*]

WILLY: I'm keeping strict accounts.

CHARLEY: I've got some work to do. Take care of yourself. And pay your insurance.

WILLY [*moving to the right*]: Funny, y'know? After all the highways, and the trains, and the appointments, and the years, you end up worth more dead than alive.

CHARLEY: Willy, nobody's worth nothin' dead. [*After a slight pause*] Did you hear what I said?

[WILLY *stands still, dreaming.*]

CHARLEY: Willy!

WILLY: Apologize to Bernard for me when you see him. I didn't mean to argue with him. He's a fine boy. They're all fine boys, and they'll end up big—all of them. Someday they'll all play tennis together. Wish me luck, Charley. He saw Bill Oliver today.

CHARLEY: Good luck.

WILLY [*on the verge of tears*]: Charley, you're the only friend I got. Isn't that a remarkable thing? [*He goes out.*]

CHARLEY: Jesus!

[CHARLEY *stares after him a moment and follows. All light blacks out. Suddenly raucous music is heard, and a red glow rises behind the screen at right.* STANLEY, *a young waiter, appears, carrying a table, followed by* HAPPY, *who is carrying two chairs.*]

STANLEY [*putting the table down*]: That's all right, Mr. Loman, I can handle it myself. [*He turns and takes the chairs from* HAPPY *and places them at the table.*]

HAPPY [*glancing around*]: Oh, this is better.

STANLEY: Sure, in the front there you're in the middle of all kinds a noise. Whenever you got a party, Mr. Loman, you just tell me and I'll put you back here. Y'know, there's a lotta people they don't like it private, because when they go out they like to see a lotta action around them because they're sick and tired to stay in the house by theirself. But I know you, you ain't from Hackensack. You know what I mean?

HAPPY [*sitting down*]: So how's it coming, Stanley?

STANLEY: Ah, it's a dog's life. I only wish during the war they'd a took me in the Army. I coulda been dead by now.

HAPPY: My brother's back, Stanley.

STANLEY: Oh, he come back, heh? From the Far West.

HAPPY: Yeah, big cattle man, my brother, so treat him right. And my father's coming too.

STANLEY: Oh, your father too!

HAPPY: You got a couple of nice lobsters?

STANLEY: Hundred percent, big.

HAPPY: I want them with the claws.

STANLEY: Don't worry. I don't give you no mice. [HAPPY *laughs.*] How about some wine? It'll put a head on the meal.

HAPPY: No. You remember, Stanley, that recipe I brought you from overseas? With the champagne in it?

STANLEY: Oh, yeah, sure. I still got it tacked up yet in the kitchen. But that'll have to cost a buck apiece anyways.

HAPPY: That's all right.

STANLEY: What'd you, hit a number or somethin'?

HAPPY: No, it's a little celebration. My brother is—I think he pulled off a big deal today. I think we're going into business together.

STANLEY: Great! That's the best for you. Because a family business, you know what I mean?—that's the best.

HAPPY: That's what I think.

STANLEY: 'Cause what's the difference? Somebody steals? It's in the family. Know what I mean? [*Sotto voce*] Like this bartender here. The boss is goin' crazy what kinda leak he's got in the cash register. You put it in but it don't come out.

HAPPY [*raising his head*]: Sh!

STANLEY: What?

HAPPY: You notice I wasn't lookin' right or left, was I?

STANLEY: No.

HAPPY: And my eyes are closed.

STANLEY: So what's the—?

HAPPY: Strudel's comin'.

STANLEY [*catching on, looks around*]: Ah, no, there's no— [*He breaks off as a furred, lavishly dressed girl enters and sits at the next table. Both follow her with their eyes.*]

STANLEY: Geez, how'd ya know?

HAPPY: I got radar or something. [*Staring directly at her profile*] Oooooooo . . . Stanley.

STANLEY: I think that's for you, Mr. Loman.

HAPPY: Look at that mouth. Oh, God. And the binoculars.

STANLEY: Geez, you got a life, Mr. Loman.

HAPPY: Wait on her.

STANLEY [*going to the girl's table*]: Would you like a menu, ma'am?

GIRL: I'm expecting someone, but I'd like a—

HAPPY: Why don't you bring her—excuse me, miss, do you mind? I sell champagne, and I'd like you to try my brand. Bring her a champagne, Stanley.

GIRL: That's awfully nice of you.

HAPPY: Don't mention it. It's all company money. [*He laughs.*]

GIRL: That's a charming product to be selling, isn't it?

HAPPY: Oh, gets to be like everything else. Selling is selling, y'know.

GIRL: I suppose.

HAPPY: You don't happen to sell, do you?

GIRL: No, I don't sell.

HAPPY: Would you object to a compliment from a stranger? You ought to be on a magazine cover.

GIRL [*looking at him a little archly*]: I have been.

[STANLEY *comes in with a glass of champagne.*]

HAPPY: What'd I say before, Stanley? You see? She's a cover girl.

STANLEY: Oh, I could see, I could see.

HAPPY [*to the* GIRL]: What magazine?

GIRL: Oh, a lot of them. [*She takes the drink.*] Thank you.

HAPPY: You know what they say in France, don't you? "Champagne is the drink of the complexion"—Hya, Biff!

[BIFF *has entered and sits with* HAPPY.]

BIFF: Hello, kid. Sorry I'm late.

HAPPY: I just got here. Uh, Miss—?

GIRL: Forsythe.

HAPPY: Miss Forsythe, this is my brother.

BIFF: Is Dad here?

HAPPY: His name is Biff. You might've heard of him. Great football player.

GIRL: Really? What team?

HAPPY: Are you familiar with football?

GIRL: No, I'm afraid I'm not.

HAPPY: Biff is quarterback with the New York Giants.

GIRL: Well, that is nice, isn't it? [*She drinks.*]

HAPPY: Good health.

GIRL: I'm happy to meet you.

HAPPY: That's my name. Hap. It's really Harold, but at West Point they called me Happy.

GIRL [*now really impressed*]: Oh, I see. How do you do? [*She turns her profile.*]

BIFF: Isn't Dad coming?

HAPPY: You want her?

BIFF: Oh, I could never make that.

HAPPY: I remember the time that idea would never come into your head. Where's the old confidence, Biff?

BIFF: I just saw Oliver—

HAPPY: Wait a minute. I've got to see that old confidence again. Do you want her? She's on call.

BIFF: Oh, no. [*He turns to look at the* GIRL.]

HAPPY: I'm telling you. Watch this. [*Turning to the* GIRL.] Honey? [*She turns to him.*] Are you busy?

GIRL: Well, I am . . . but I could make a phone call.

HAPPY: Do that, will you, honey? And see if you can get a friend. We'll be here for a while. Biff is one of the greatest football players in the country.

GIRL [*standing up*]: Well, I'm certainly happy to meet you.

HAPPY: Come back soon.

GIRL: I'll try.

HAPPY: Don't try, honey, try hard.

[*The* GIRL *exits.* STANLEY *follows, shaking his head in bewildered admiration.*]

HAPPY: Isn't that a shame now? A beautiful girl like that? That's why I can't get married. There's not a good woman in a thousand. New York is loaded with them, kid!

BIFF: Hap, look—

HAPPY: I told you she was on call!

BIFF [*strangely unnerved*]: Cut it out, will ya? I want to say something to you.

HAPPY: Did you see Oliver?

BIFF: I saw him all right. Now look, I want to tell Dad a couple of things and I want you to help me.

HAPPY: What? Is he going to back you?

BIFF: Are you crazy? You're out of your goddam head, you know that?

HAPPY: Why? What happened?

BIFF [*breathlessly*]: I did a terrible thing today, Hap. It's been the strangest day I ever went through. I'm all numb, I swear.

HAPPY: You mean he wouldn't see you?

BIFF: Well, I waited six hours for him, see? All day. Kept sending my name in. Even tried to date his secretary so she'd get me to him, but no soap.

HAPPY: Because you're not showin' the old confidence, Biff. He remembered you, didn't he?

BIFF [*stopping* HAPPY *with a gesture*]: Finally, about five o'clock, he comes out. Didn't remember who I was or anything. I felt like such an idiot, Hap.

HAPPY: Did you tell him my Florida idea?

BIFF: He walked away. I saw him for one minute. I got so mad I could've torn the walls down! How the hell did I ever get the idea I was a salesman there? I even believed myself that I'd been a salesman for him! And then he gave me one look and—I realized what a ridiculous lie my whole life has been. We've been talking in a dream for fifteen years. I was a shipping clerk.
HAPPY: What'd you do?
BIFF [*with great tension and wonder*]: Well, he left, see. And the secretary went out. I was all alone in the waiting-room. I don't know what came over me, Hap. The next thing I know I'm in his office—paneled walls, everything. I can't explain it. I—Hap, I took his fountain pen.
HAPPY: Geez, did he catch you?
BIFF: I ran out. I ran down all eleven flights. I ran and ran and ran.
HAPPY: That was an awful dumb—what'd you do that for?
BIFF [*agonized*]: I don't know. I just—wanted to take something, I don't know. You gotta help me, Hap. I'm gonna tell Pop.
HAPPY: You crazy? What for?
BIFF: Hap, he's got to understand that I'm not the man somebody lends that kind of money to. He thinks I've been spiting him all these years and it's eating him up.
HAPPY: That's just it. You tell him something nice.
BIFF: I can't.
HAPPY: Say you got a lunch date with Oliver tomorrow.
BIFF: So what do I do tomorrow?
HAPPY: You leave the house tomorrow and come back at night and say Oliver is thinking it over. And he thinks it over for a couple of weeks, and gradually it fades away and nobody's the worse.
BIFF: But it'll go on for ever!
HAPPY: Dad is never so happy as when he's looking forward to something!
[WILLY *enters.*]
HAPPY: Hello, scout!
WILLY: Gee, I haven't been here in years!
[STANLEY *has followed* WILLY *in and sets a chair for him.* STANLEY *starts off but* HAPPY *stops him.*]
HAPPY: Stanley!
[STANLEY *stands by, waiting for an order.*]
BIFF [*going to* WILLY *with guilt, as to an invalid*]: Sit down, Pop. You want a drink?
WILLY: Sure, I don't mind.
BIFF: Let's get a load on.
WILLY: You look worried.
BIFF: N-no. [*To* STANLEY] Scotch all around. Make it doubles.
STANLEY: Doubles, right. [*He goes.*]
WILLY: You had a couple already, didn't you?
BIFF: Just a couple, yeah.
WILLY: Well, what happened, boy? [*Nodding affirmatively, with a smile*] Everything go all right?
BIFF [*takes a breath, then reaches out and grasps* WILLY'S *hand*]: Pal . . . [*He is smiling bravely, and* WILLY *is smiling too.*] I had an experience today.
HAPPY: Terrific, Pop.
WILLY: That so? What happened?

BIFF: [*high, slightly alcoholic, above the earth*]: I'm going to tell you everything from first to last. It's been a strange day. [*Silence. He looks around, composes himself as best he can, but his breath keeps breaking the rhythm of his voice.*] I had to wait quite a while for him, and—

WILLY: Oliver?

BIFF: Yeah, Oliver. All day, as a matter of cold fact. And a lot of—instances—facts. Pop, facts about my life came back to me. Who was it, Pop? Who ever said I was a salesman with Oliver?

WILLY: Well, you were.

BIFF: No, Dad, I was a shipping clerk.

WILLY: But you were practically—

BIFF [*with determination*]: Dad, I don't know who said it first, but I was never a salesman for Bill Oliver.

WILLY: What're you talking about?

BIFF: Let's hold on to the facts tonight, Pop. We're not going to get anywhere bullin' around. I was a shipping clerk.

WILLY [*angrily*]: All right, now listen to me—

BIFF: Why don't you let me finish?

WILLY: I'm not interested in stories about the past or any crap of that kind because the woods are burning, boys, you understand? There's a big blaze going on all around. I was fired today.

BIFF [*shocked*]: How could you be?

WILLY: I was fired, and I'm looking for a little good news to tell your mother, because the woman has waited and the woman has suffered. The gist of it is that I haven't got a story left in my head, Biff. So don't give me a lecture about facts and aspects. I am not interested. Now what've you got to say to me?

[STANLEY *enters with three drinks. They wait until he leaves.*]

WILLY: Did you see Oliver?

BIFF: Jesus, Dad!

WILLY: You mean you didn't go up there?

HAPPY: Sure he went up there.

BIFF: I did. I—saw him. How could they fire you?

WILLY [*on the edge of his chair*]: What kind of a welcome did he give you?

BIFF: He won't even let you work on commission?

WILLY: I'm out! [*Driving*] So tell me, he gave you a warm welcome?

HAPPY: Sure, Pop, sure!

BIFF [*driven*]: Well, it was kind of—

WILLY: I was wondering if he'd remember you. [*To* HAPPY] Imagine, man doesn't see him for ten, twelve years and gives him that kind of a welcome!

HAPPY: Damn right!

BIFF [*trying to return to the offensive*]: Pop, look—

WILLY: You know why he remembered you, don't you? Because you impressed him in those days.

BIFF: Let's talk quietly and get this down to the facts, huh?

WILLY [*as though* BIFF *had been interrupting*]: Well, what happened? It's great news, Biff. Did he take you into his office or'd you talk in the waiting-room?

BIFF: Well, he came in, see, and—

WILLY [*with a big smile*]: What'd he say? Betcha he threw his arm around you.

BIFF: Well, he kinda—

WILLY: He's a fine man. [*To* HAPPY] Very hard man to see, y'know.

HAPPY [*agreeing*]: Oh, I know.

WILLY [*to* BIFF]: Is that where you had the drinks?

BIFF: Yeah, he gave me a couple of—no, no!

HAPPY [*cutting in*]: He told him my Florida idea.

WILLY: Don't interrupt. [*To* BIFF] How'd he react to the Florida idea?

BIFF: Dad, will you give me a minute to explain?

WILLY: I've been waiting for you to explain since I sat down here! What happened? He took you into his office and what?

BIFF: Well—I talked. And—and he listened, see.

WILLY: Famous for the way he listens, y'know. What was his answer?

BIFF: His answer was—[*He breaks off, suddenly angry.*] Dad, you're not letting me tell you what I want to tell you!

WILLY [*accusing, angered*]: You didn't see him, did you?

BIFF: I did see him!

WILLY: What'd you insult him or something? You insulted him, didn't you?

BIFF: Listen, will you let me out of it, will you just let me out of it!

HAPPY: What the hell!

WILLY: Tell me what happened!

BIFF [*to* HAPPY]: I can't talk to him!

[*A single trumpet note jars the ear. The light of green leaves stains the house, which holds the air of night and a dream.* YOUNG BERNARD *enters and knocks on the door of the house.*]

YOUNG BERNARD [*frantically*]: Mrs. Loman, Mrs. Loman!

HAPPY: Tell him what happened!

BIFF [*to* HAPPY]: Shut up and leave me alone!

WILLY: No, no! You had to go and flunk math!

BIFF: What math? What're you talking about?

YOUNG BERNARD: Mrs. Loman, Mrs. Loman!

[LINDA *appears in the house, as of old.*]

WILLY [*wildly*]: Math, math, math!

BIFF: Take it easy, Pop!

YOUNG BERNARD: Mrs. Loman!

WILLY [*furiously*]: If you hadn't flunked you'd've been set by now!

BIFF: Now, look. I'm gonna tell you what happened, and you're going to listen to me.

YOUNG BERNARD: Mrs. Loman!

BIFF: I waited six hours—

HAPPY: What the hell are you saying?

BIFF: I kept sending in my name but he wouldn't see me. So finally he . . . [*He continues unheard as light fades low on the restaurant.*]

YOUNG BERNARD: Biff flunked math!

LINDA: No!

YOUNG BERNARD: Birnbaum flunked him! They won't graduate him!

LINDA: But they have to. He's gotta go to the university. Where is he? Biff! Biff!

YOUNG BERNARD: No, he left. He went to Grand Central.

LINDA: Grand—You mean he went to Boston!

YOUNG BERNARD: Is Uncle Willy in Boston?

LINDA: Oh, maybe Willy can talk to the teacher. Oh, the poor, poor boy!

[*Light on house area snaps out.*]

BIFF [*at the table, now audible, holding up a gold fountain pen*]: . . . so I'm washed up with Oliver, you understand? Are you listening to me?

WILLY [*at a loss*]: Yeah, sure. If you hadn't flunked—

BIFF: Flunked what? What're you talking about?

WILLY: Don't blame everything on me! I didn't flunk math—you did! What pen?

HAPPY: That was awful dumb, Biff, a pen like that is worth—

WILLY [*seeing the pen for the first time*]: You took Oliver's pen?

BIFF [*weakening*]: Dad, I just explained it to you.

WILLY: You stole Bill Oliver's fountain pen!

BIFF: I didn't exactly steal it! That's just what I've been explaining to you!

HAPPY: He had it in his hand and just then Oliver walked in, so he got nervous and stuck it in his pocket!

WILLY: My God, Biff!

BIFF: I never intended to do it, Dad!

OPERATOR'S VOICE: Standish Arms, good evening!

WILLY [*shouting*]: I'm not in my room!

BIFF [*frightened*]: Dad, what's the matter? [*He and* HAPPY *stand up.*]

OPERATOR: Ringing Mr. Loman for you!

WILLY: I'm not there, stop it!

BIFF [*horrified, gets down on one knee before* WILLY]: Dad, I'll make good, I'll make good. [WILLY *tries to get to his feet.* BIFF *holds him down.*] Sit down now.

WILLY: No, you're no good, you're no good for anything.

BIFF: I am, Dad, I'll find something else, you understand? Now don't worry about anything. [*He holds up* WILLY'S *face.*] Talk to me, Dad.

OPERATOR: Mr. Loman does not answer. Shall I page him?

WILLY [*attempting to stand, as though to rush and silence the* OPERATOR]: No, no, no!

HAPPY: He'll strike something, Pop.

WILLY: No, no . . .

BIFF [*desperately, standing over* WILLY]: Pop, listen! Listen to me! I'm telling you something good. Oliver talked to his partner about the Florida idea. You listening? He—he talked to his partner, and he came to me . . . I'm going to be all right, you hear? Dad, listen to me, he said it was just a question of the amount!

WILLY: Then you . . . got it?

HAPPY: He's gonna be terrific, Pop!

WILLY [*trying to stand*]: Then you got it, haven't you? You got it! You got it!

BIFF [*agonized, holds* WILLY *down*]: No, no. Look, Pop. I'm supposed to have lunch with them tomorrow. I'm just telling you this so you'll know that I can still make an impression, Pop. And I'll make good somewhere, but I can't go tomorrow, see?

WILLY: Why not? You simply—

BIFF: But the pen, Pop!

WILLY: You give it to him and tell him it was an oversight!

HAPPY: Sure, have lunch tomorrow!

BIFF: I can't say that—

WILLY: You were doing a crossword puzzle and accidentally used his pen!

BIFF: Listen, kid, I took those balls years ago, now I walk in with his fountain pen? That clinches it, don't you see? I can't face him like that! I'll try elsewhere.

PAGE'S VOICE: Paging Mr. Loman!
WILLY: Don't you want to be anything?
BIFF: Pop, how can I go back?
WILLY: You don't want to be anything, is that what's behind it?
BIFF [*now angry at* WILLY *for not crediting his sympathy*]: Don't take it that way! You think it was easy walking into that office after what I'd done to him? A team of horses couldn't have dragged me back to Bill Oliver!
WILLY: Then why'd you go?
BIFF: Why did I go? Why did I go! Look at you! Look at what's become of you!
[*Off left,* THE WOMAN *laughs.*]
WILLY: Biff, you're going to go to that lunch tomorrow, or—
BIFF: I can't go. I've got no appointment!
HAPPY: Biff, for . . . !
WILLY: Are you spiting me?
BIFF: Don't take it that way! Goddammit!
WILLY [*strikes* BIFF *and falters away from the table*]: You rotten little louse! Are you spiting me?
THE WOMAN: Someone's at the door, Willy!
BIFF: I'm no good, can't you see what I am?
HAPPY [*separating them*]: Hey, you're in a restaurant! Now cut it out, both of you! [*The girls enter.*] Hello, girls, sit down.
[THE WOMAN *laughs, off left.*]
MISS FORSYTHE: I guess we might as well. This is Letta.
THE WOMAN: Willy, are you going to wake up?
BIFF [*ignoring* WILLY]: How're ya, miss, sit down. What do you drink?
MISS FORSYTHE: Letta might not be able to stay long.
LETTA: I gotta get up very early tomorrow. I got jury duty. I'm so excited! Were you fellows ever on a jury?
BIFF: No, but I been in front of them! [*The girls laugh.*] This is my father.
LETTA: Isn't he cute? Sit down with us, Pop.
HAPPY: Sit him down, Biff!
BIFF [*going to him*]: Come on, slugger, drink us under the table. To hell with it! Come on, sit down, pal.
[*On* BIFF'S *last insistence,* WILLY *is about to sit.*]
THE WOMAN [*now urgently*]: Willy, are you going to answer the door!
[THE WOMAN'S *call pulls* WILLY *back. He starts right, befuddled.*]
BIFF: Hey, where are you going?
WILLY: Open the door.
BIFF: The door?
WILLY: The washroom . . . the door . . . where's the door?
BIFF [*leading* WILLY *to the left*]: Just go straight down.
[WILLY *moves left.*]
THE WOMAN: Willy, Willy, are you going to get up, get up, get up, get up?
[WILLY *exits left.*]
LETTA: I think it's sweet you bring your daddy along.
MISS FORSYTHE: Oh, he isn't really your father!
BIFF [*at left, turning to her resentfully*]: Miss Forsythe, you've just seen a prince walk by. A fine, troubled prince. A hard-working, unappreciated prince. A pal, you understand? A good companion. Always for his boys.

LETTA: That's so sweet.

HAPPY: Well, girls, what's the program? We're wasting time. Come on, Biff. Gather round. Where would you like to go?

BIFF: Why don't you do something for him?

HAPPY: Me!

BIFF: Don't you give a damn for him, Hap?

HAPPY: What're you talking about? I'm the one who—

BIFF: I sense it, you don't give a good goddam about him. [*He takes the rolled-up hose from his pocket and puts it on the table in front of* HAPPY.] Look what I found in the cellar, for Christ's sake. How can you bear to let it go on?

HAPPY: Me? Who goes away? Who runs off and—

BIFF: Yeah, but he doesn't mean anything to you. You could help him—I can't. Don't you understand what I'm talking about? He's going to kill himself, don't you know that?

HAPPY: Don't I know it! Me!

BIFF: Hap, help him! Jesus . . . help him . . . Help me, help me, I can't bear to look at his face! [*Ready to weep, he hurries out, up right.*]

HAPPY [*starting after him*]: Where are you going?

MISS FORSYTHE: What's he so mad about?

HAPPY: Come on, girls, we'll catch up with him.

MISS FORSYTHE [*as* HAPPY *pushes her out*]: Say, I don't like that temper of his!

HAPPY: He's just a little overstrung, he'll be all right!

WILLY [*off left, as* THE WOMAN *laughs*]: Don't answer! Don't answer!

LETTA: Don't you want to tell your father—

HAPPY: No, that's not my father. He's just a guy. Come on, we'll catch Biff, and, honey, we're going to paint this town! Stanley, where's the check! Hey, Stanley!

[*They exit.* STANLEY *looks toward left.*]

STANLEY [*calling to* HAPPY *indignantly*]: Mr. Loman! Mr. Loman!

[STANLEY *picks up a chair and follows them off. Knocking is heard off left.* THE WOMAN *enters, laughing.* WILLY *follows her. She is in a black slip; he is buttoning his shirt. Raw, sensuous music accompanies their speech.*]

WILLY: Will you stop laughing? Will you stop?

THE WOMAN: Aren't you going to answer the door? He'll wake the whole hotel.

WILLY: I'm not expecting anybody.

THE WOMAN: Whyn't you have another drink, honey, and stop being so damn self-centered?

WILLY: I'm so lonely.

THE WOMAN: You know you ruined me, Willy? From now on, whenever you come to the office, I'll see that you go right through to the buyers. No waiting at my desk any more, Willy. You ruined me.

WILLY: That's nice of you to say that.

THE WOMAN: Gee, you are self-centered! Why so sad? You are the saddest, self-centeredest soul I ever did see-saw. [*She laughs. He kisses her.*] Come on inside, drummer boy. It's silly to be dressing in the middle of the night. [*As knocking is heard*] Aren't you going to answer the door?

WILLY: They're knocking on the wrong door.

THE WOMAN: But I felt the knocking. And he heard us talking in here. Maybe the hotel's on fire!

WILLY [*his terror rising*]: It's a mistake.

THE WOMAN: Then tell him to go away!

WILLY: There's nobody there.

THE WOMAN: It's getting on my nerves, Willy. There's somebody standing out there and it's getting on my nerves!

WILLY [*pushing her away from him*]: All right, stay in the bathroom here, and don't come out. I think there's a law in Massachusetts about it, so don't come out. It may be that new room clerk. He looked very mean. So don't come out. It's a mistake, there's no fire.

[*The knocking is heard again. He takes a few steps away from her, and she vanishes into the wing. The light follows him, and now he is facing* YOUNG BIFF, *who carries a suitcase.* BIFF *steps toward him. The music is gone.*]

BIFF: Why didn't you answer?

WILLY: Biff! What are you doing in Boston?

BIFF: Why didn't you answer? I've been knocking for five minutes. I called you on the phone—

WILLY: I just heard you. I was in the bathroom and had the door shut. Did anything happen home?

BIFF: Dad—I let you down.

WILLY: What do you mean?

BIFF: Dad . . .

WILLY: Biffo, what's this about? [*Putting his arm around* BIFF] Come on, let's go downstairs and get you a malted.

BIFF: Dad, I flunked math.

WILLY: Not for the term?

BIFF: The term. I haven't got enough credits to graduate.

WILLY: You mean to say Bernard wouldn't give you the answers?

BIFF: He did, he tried, but I only got a sixty-one.

WILLY: And they wouldn't give you four points?

BIFF: Birnbaum refused absolutely. I begged him, Pop, but he won't give me those points. You gotta talk to him before they close the school. Because if he saw the kind of man you are, and you just talked to him in your way, I'm sure he'd come through for me. The class came right before practice, see, and I didn't go enough. Would you talk to him? He'd like you, Pop. You know the way you could talk.

WILLY: You're on. We'll drive right back.

BIFF: Oh, Dad, good work! I'm sure he'll change it for you!

WILLY: Go downstairs and tell the clerk I'm checkin' out. Go right down.

BIFF: Yes, sir! See, the reason he hates me, Pop—one day he was late for class so I got up at the blackboard and imitated him. I crossed my eyes and talked with a lithp.

WILLY [*laughing*]: You did? The kids like it?

BIFF: They nearly died laughing!

WILLY: Yeah? What'd you do?

BIFF: The thquare root of thixthy twee is . . . [WILLY *bursts out laughing;* BIFF *joins him.*] And in the middle of it he walked in!

[WILLY *laughs and* THE WOMAN *joins in offstage.*]

WILLY [*without hesitation*]: Hurry downstairs and—

BIFF: Somebody in there?

WILLY: No, that was next door.

[THE WOMAN *laughs offstage.*]

BIFF: Somebody got in your bathroom!

WILLY: No, it's the next room, there's a party—

THE WOMAN [*enters, laughing. She lisps this*]: Can I come in? There's something in the bathtub, Willy, and it's moving!

[WILLY *looks at* BIFF, *who is staring open-mouthed and horrified at* THE WOMAN.]

WILLY: Ah—you better go back to your room. They must be finished painting by now. They're painting her room so I let her take a shower here. Go back, go back . . . [*He pushes her.*]

THE WOMAN [*resisting*]: But I've got to get dressed, Willy, I can't—

WILLY: Get out of here! Go back, go back . . . *Suddenly striving for the ordinary*] This is Miss Francis, Biff, she's a buyer. They're painting her room. Go back, Miss Francis, go back . . .

THE WOMAN: But my clothes, I can't go out naked in the hall!

WILLY [*pushing her offstage*]: Get outa here! Go back, go back!

[BIFF *slowly sits down on his suitcase as the argument continues offstage.*]

THE WOMAN: Where's my stockings? You promised me stockings, Willy!

WILLY: I have no stockings here!

THE WOMAN: You had two boxes of size nine sheers for me, and I want them!

WILLY: Here, for God's sake, will you get outa here!

THE WOMAN [*enters holding a box of stockings*]: I just hope there's nobody in the hall. That's all I hope. [*To* BIFF] Are you football or baseball?

BIFF: Football.

THE WOMAN [*angry, humiliated*]: That's me too. G'night. [*She snatches her clothes from* WILLY, *and walks out.*]

WILLY [*after a pause*]: Well, better get going. I want to get to the school first thing in the morning. Get my suits out of the closet. I'll get my valise. [BIFF *doesn't move.*] What's the matter? [BIFF *remains motionless, tears falling.*] She's a buyer. Buys for J. H. Simmons. She lives down the hall—they're painting. You don't imagine—[*He breaks off. After a pause*] Now listen, pal, she's just a buyer. She sees merchandise in her room and they have to keep it looking just so . . . [*Pause. Assuming command*] All right, get my suits. [BIFF *doesn't move.*] Now stop crying and do as I say. I gave you an order. Biff, I gave you an order! Is that what you do when I give you an order? How dare you cry? [*Putting his arm around* BIFF] Now look, Biff, when you grow up you'll understand about these things. You mustn't—you mustn't overemphasize a thing like this. I'll see Birnbaum first thing in the morning.

BIFF: Never mind.

WILLY [*getting down beside* BIFF]: Never mind! He's going to give you those points. I'll see to it.

BIFF: He wouldn't listen to you.

WILLY: He certainly will listen to me. You need those points for the U. of Virginia.

BIFF: I'm not going there.

WILLY: Heh? If I can't get him to change that mark you'll make it up in summer school. You've got all summer to—

BIFF [*his weeping breaking from him*]: Dad . . .

WILLY [*infected by it*]: Oh, my boy . . .

BIFF: Dad . . .

WILLY: She's nothing to me, Biff. I was lonely, I was terribly lonely.

BIFF: You—you gave her Mama's stockings! [*His tears break through and he rises to go.*]

WILLY [*grabbing for* BIFF]: I gave you an order!

BIFF: Don't touch me, you—liar!

WILLY: Apologize for that!

BIFF: You fake! You phony little fake! You fake! [*Overcome, he turns quickly and weeping fully goes out with his suitcase.* WILLY *is left on the floor on his knees.*]

WILLY: I gave you an order! Biff, come back here or I'll beat you! Come back here! I'll whip you!

[STANLEY *comes quickly in from the right and stands in front of* WILLY.]

WILLY [*shouts at* STANLEY]: I gave you an order. . .

STANLEY: Hey, let's pick it up, pick it up, Mr. Loman. [*He helps* WILLY *to his feet.*] Your boys left with the chippies. They said they'll see you home.

[*A second waiter watches some distance away.*]

WILLY: But we were supposed to have dinner together.

[*Music is heard,* WILLY'S *theme.*]

STANLEY: Can you make it?

WILLY: I'll—sure, I can make it. [*Suddenly concerned about his clothes.*] Do I—I look all right?

STANLEY: Sure, you look all right. [*He flicks a speck off* WILLY'S *lapel.*]

WILLY: Here—here's a dollar.

STANLEY: Oh, your son paid me. It's all right.

WILLY [*putting it in* STANLEY'S *hand*]: No, take it. You're a good boy.

STANLEY: Oh, no, you don't have to . . .

WILLY: Here—here's some more. I don't need it any more. [*After a slight pause*] Tell me—is there a seed store in the neighborhood?

STANLEY: Seeds? You mean like to plant?

[*As* WILLY *turns,* STANLEY *slips the money back into his jacket pocket.*]

WILLY: Yes. Carrots, peas . . .

STANLEY: Well, there's hardware stores on Sixth Avenue, but it may be too late now.

WILLY [*anxiously*]: Oh, I'd better hurry. I've got to get some seeds. [*He starts off to the right.*] I've got to get some seeds, right away. Nothing's planted. I don't have a thing in the ground.

[WILLY *hurries out as the light goes down.* STANLEY *moves over to the right after him, watches him off. The other waiter has been staring at* WILLY.]

STANLEY [*to the waiter*]: Well, whatta you looking at?

[*The waiter picks up the chairs and moves off right.* STANLEY *takes the table and follows him. The light fades on this area. There is a long pause, the sound of the flute coming over. The light gradually rises on the kitchen, which is empty.* HAPPY *appears at the door of the house, followed by* BIFF. HAPPY *is carrying a large bunch of long-stemmed roses. He enters the kitchen, looks around for* LINDA. *Not seeing her, he turns to* BIFF, *who is just outside the house door, and makes a gesture with his hands, indicating "Not here, I guess." He looks into the living-room and freezes. Inside,* LINDA, *unseen, is seated,* WILLY'S *coat on her lap. She rises ominously and quietly and moves toward* HAPPY, *who backs up into the kitchen, afraid.*]

HAPPY: Hey, what're you doing up? [LINDA *says nothing but moves toward him implacably.*] Where's Pop? [*He keeps backing to the right, and now* LINDA *is in full view in the doorway to the living-room.*] Is he sleeping?

LINDA: Where were you?

HAPPY [*trying to laugh it off*]: We met two girls, Mom, very fine types. Here, we brought you some flowers. [*Offering them to her*] Put them in your room, Ma.

[*She knocks them to the floor at* BIFF'S *feet. He has now come inside and closed the door behind him. She stares at* BIFF, *silent.*]

HAPPY: Now what'd you do that for? Mom, I want you to have some flowers—

LINDA [*cutting* HAPPY *off, violently to* BIFF]: Don't you care whether he lives or dies?

HAPPY [*going to the stairs*]: Come upstairs, Biff.

BIFF [*with a flare of disgust, to* HAPPY]: Go away from me! [*To* LINDA] What do you mean, lives or dies? Nobody's dying around here, pal.

LINDA: Get out of my sight! Get out of here!

BIFF: I wanna see the boss.

LINDA: You're not going near him!

BIFF: Where is he? [*He moves into the living-room and* LINDA *follows.*]

LINDA [*shouting after* BIFF]: You invite him to dinner. He looks forward to it all day—[BIFF *appears in his parents' bedroom, looks around, and exists*]—and then you desert him there. There's no stranger you'd do that to!

HAPPY: Why? He had a swell time with us. Listen, when I—[LINDA *comes back into the kitchen*]—desert him I hope I don't outlive the day!

LINDA: Get out of here!

HAPPY: Now look, Mom . . .

LINDA: Did you have to go to women tonight? You and your lousy rotten whores!

[BIFF *reenters the kitchen.*]

HAPPY: Mom, all we did was follow Biff around trying to cheer him up! [*To* BIFF] Boy, what a night you gave me!

LINDA: Get out of here, both of you, and don't come back! I don't want you tormenting him any more. Go on now, get your things together! [*To* BIFF] You can sleep in his apartment. [*She starts to pick up the flowers and stops herself.*] Pick up this stuff, I'm not your maid any more. Pick it up, you bum, you!

[HAPPY *turns his back to her in refusal.* BIFF *slowly moves over and gets down on his knees, picking up the flowers.*]

LINDA: You're a pair of animals! Not one, not another living soul would have had the cruelty to walk out on that man in a restaurant!

BIFF [*not looking at her*]: Is that what he said?

LINDA: He didn't have to say anything. He was so humiliated he nearly limped when he came in.

HAPPY: But, Mom, he had a great time with us—

BIFF [*cutting him off violently*]: Shut up!

[*Without another word,* HAPPY *goes upstairs.*]

LINDA: You! You didn't even go in to see if he was all right!

BIFF [*still on the floor in front of* LINDA, *the flowers in his hand; with self-loathing*]: No. Didn't. Didn't do a damned thing. How do you like that, heh? Left him babbling in a toilet.

LINDA: You louse. You . . .

BIFF: Now you hit it on the nose! [*He gets up, throws the flowers in the wastebasket.*] The scum of the earth, and you're looking at him!

LINDA: Get out of here!

BIFF: I gotta talk to the boss, Mom. Where is he?

LINDA: You're not going near him. Get out of this house!

BIFF [*with absolute assurance, determination*]: No. We're gonna have an abrupt conversation, him and me.

LINDA: You're not talking to him!

[*Hammering is heard from outside the house, off right.* BIFF *turns toward the noise.*]

LINDA [*suddenly pleading*]: Will you please leave him alone?

BIFF: What's he doing out there?

LINDA: He's planting the garden!

BIFF [*quietly*]: Now? Oh, my God!

[BIFF *moves outside,* LINDA *following. The light dies down on them and comes up on the center of the apron as* WILLY *walks into it. He is carrying a flashlight, a hoe, and a handful of seed packets. He raps the top of the hoe sharply to fix it firmly, and then moves to the left, measuring off the distance with his foot. He holds the flashlight to look at the seed packets, reading off the instructions. He is in the blue of night.*]

WILLY: Carrots . . . quarter-inch apart. Rows . . . one-foot rows. [*He measures it off.*] One foot. [*He puts down a package and measures off.*] Beets. [*He puts down another package and measures again.*] Lettuce. [*He reads the package, puts it down.*] One foot—[*He breaks off as* BEN *appears at the right and moves slowly down to him.*] What a proposition, ts, ts. Terrific, terrific. 'Cause she's suffered, Ben, the woman has suffered. You understand me? A man can't go out the way he came in, Ben, a man has got to add up to something. You can't, you can't—[BEN *moves toward him as though to interrupt.*] You gotta consider, now. Don't answer so quick. Remember, it's a guaranteed twenty-thousand-dollar proposition. Now look, Ben, I want you to go through the ins and outs of this thing with me. I've got nobody to talk to, Ben, and the woman has suffered, you hear me?

BEN [*standing still, considering*]: What's the proposition?

WILLY: It's twenty thousand dollars on the barrelhead. Guaranteed, gilt-edged, you understand?

BEN: You don't want to make a fool of yourself. They might not honor the policy.

WILLY: How can they dare refuse? Didn't I work like a coolie to meet every premium on the nose? And now they don't pay off? Impossible!

BEN: It's called a cowardly thing, William.

WILLY: Why? Does it take more guts to stand here the rest of my life ringing up a zero?

BEN [*yielding*]: That's a point, William. [*He moves, thinking, turns.*] And twenty thousand—that *is* something one can feel with the hand, it is there.

WILLY [*now assured, with rising power*]: Oh, Ben, that's the whole beauty of it! I see it like a diamond, shining in the dark, hard and rough, that I can pick up and touch in my hand. Not like—like an appointment! This would not be another damned-fool appointment, Ben, and it changes all the aspects. Because he thinks I'm nothing, see, and so he spites me. But the funeral—[*Straightening up*] Ben, that funeral will be massive! They'll come from Maine, Massachusetts, Vermont. New Hampshire! All the old-timers with the strange license plates—that boy will be thunderstruck, Ben, because he never realized—I am known! Rhode Island, New York, New Jersey—I am known, Ben, and he'll see it with his eyes once and for all. He'll see what I am, Ben! He's in for a shock, that boy!

BEN [*coming down to the edge of the garden*]: He'll call you a coward.

WILLY [*suddenly fearful*]: No, that would be terrible.

BEN: Yes. And a damned fool.

WILLY: No, no, he mustn't. I won't have that! [*He is broken and desperate.*]

BEN: He'll hate you, William.

[*The gay music of the boys is heard.*]

WILLY: Oh, Ben, how do we get back to all the great times? Used to be so full of light, and comradeship, the sleigh-riding in winter, and the ruddiness on his cheeks. And always some kind of good news coming up, always something nice coming up ahead. And never even let me carry the valises in the house, and simonizing, simonizing that little red car! Why, why can't I give him something and not have him hate me?

BEN: Let me think about it. [*He glances at his watch.*] I still have a little time. Remarkable proposition, but you've got to be sure you're not making a fool of yourself.

[BEN *drifts off upstage and goes out of sight.* BIFF *comes down from the left.*]

WILLY [*suddenly conscious of* BIFF, *turns and looks up at him, then begins picking up the packages of seeds in confusion*]: Where the hell is that seed? [*Indignantly*] You can't see nothing out here! They boxed in the whole goddam neighborhood!

BIFF: There are people all around here. Don't you realize that?

WILLY: I'm busy. Don't bother me.

BIFF [*taking the hoe from* WILLY]: I'm saying good-bye to you, Pop. [WILLY *looks at him, silent, unable to move.*] I'm not coming back any more.

WILLY: You're not going to see Oliver tomorrow?

BIFF: I've got no appointment, Dad.

WILLY: He put his arm around you, and you've got no appointment?

BIFF: Pop, get this now, will you? Everytime I've left it's been a fight that sent me out of here. Today I realized something about myself and I tried to explain it to you and I—I think I'm just not smart enough to make any sense out of it for you. To hell with whose fault it is or anything like that. [*He takes* WILLY'S *arm.*] Let's just wrap it up, heh? Come on in, we'll tell Mom. [*He gently tries to pull* WILLY *to left.*]

WILLY [*frozen, immobile, with guilt in his voice*]: No, I don't want to see her.

BIFF: Come on! [*He pulls again, and* WILLY *tries to pull away.*]

WILLY [*highly nervous*]: No, no. I don't want to see her.

BIFF [*tries to look into* WILLY'S *face, as if to find the answer there*]: Why don't you want to see her?

WILLY [*more harshly now*]: Don't bother me, will you?

BIFF: What do you mean, you don't want to see her? You don't want them calling you yellow, do you? This isn't your fault: it's me, I'm a bum. Now come inside! [WILLY *strains to get away.*] Did you hear what I said to you?

[WILLY *pulls away and quickly goes by himself into the house,* BIFF *follows.*]

LINDA [*to* WILLY]: Did you plant, dear?

BIFF [*at the door, to* LINDA]: All right, we had it out. I'm going and I'm not writing any more.

LINDA [*going to* WILLY *in the kitchen*]: I think that's the best way, dear. 'Cause there's no use drawing it out, you'll just never get along.

[WILLY *doesn't respond.*]

BIFF: People ask where I am and what I'm doing, you don't know, and you don't care. That way it'll be off your mind and you can start brightening up again. All right? That clears it, doesn't it? [WILLY *is silent, and* BIFF *goes to him.*] You gonna wish me luck, scout? [*He extends his hand*] What do you say?

LINDA: Shake his hand, Willy.

WILLY [*turning to her, seething with hurt*]: There's no necessity to mention the pen at all, y'know.

BIFF [*gently*]: I've got no appointment, Dad.

WILLY [*erupting fiercely*]: He put his arm around . . . ?

BIFF: Dad, you're never going to see what I am, so what's the use of arguing? If I strike oil I'll send you a check. Meantime forget I'm alive.

WILLY [*to* LINDA]: Spite, see?

BIFF: Shake hands, Dad.

WILLY: Not my hand.

BIFF: I was hoping not to go this way.

WILLY: Well, this is the way you're going. Good-bye.

[BIFF *looks at him a moment, then turns sharply and goes to the stairs.*]

WILLY [*stops him with*]: May you rot in hell if you leave this house!

BIFF [*turning*]: Exactly what is it that you want from me?

WILLY: I want you to know, on the train, in the mountains, in the valleys, wherever you go, that you cut down your life for spite!

BIFF: No, no.

WILLY: Spite, spite, is the word of your undoing! And when you're down and out, remember what did it. When you're rotting somewhere beside the railroad tracks, remember, and don't you dare blame it on me!

BIFF: I'm not blaming it on you!

WILLY: I won't take the rap for this, you hear?

[HAPPY *comes down the stairs and stands on the bottom step, watching.*]

BIFF: That's just what I'm telling you!

WILLY [*sinking into a chair at the table, with full accusation*]: You're trying to put a knife in me—don't think I don't know what you're doing!

BIFF: All right, phony! Then let's lay it on the line. [*He whips the rubber tube out of his pocket and puts it on the table.*]

HAPPY: You crazy—

LINDA: Biff! [*She moves to grab the hose, but* BIFF *holds it down with his hand.*]

BIFF: Leave it there! Don't move it!

WILLY [*not looking at it*]: What is that?

BIFF: You know goddam well what that is.

WILLY [*caged, wanting to escape*]: I never saw that.

BIFF: You saw it. The mice didn't bring it into the cellar! What is this supposed to do, make a hero out of you? This supposed to make me sorry for you?

WILLY: Never heard of it.

BIFF: There'll be no pity for you, you hear it? No pity!

WILLY [*to* LINDA]: You hear the spite!

BIFF: No, you're going to hear the truth—what you are and what I am!

LINDA: Stop it!

WILLY: Spite!

HAPPY [*coming down toward* BIFF]: You cut it now!

BIFF [*to* HAPPY]: The man don't know who we are! The man is gonna know! [*To* WILLY] We never told the truth for ten minutes in this house!

HAPPY: We always told the truth!

BIFF [*turning on him*]: You big blow, are you the assistant buyer? You're one of the two assistants to the assistant, aren't you?

HAPPY: Well, I'm practically—

BIFF: You're practically full of it! We all are! And I'm through with it. [*To* WILLY] Now hear this, Willy, this is me.

WILLY: I know you!

BIFF: You know why I had no address for three months? I stole a suit in Kansas City and I was in jail. [*To* LINDA, *who is sobbing*] Stop crying. I'm through with it.

[LINDA *turns away from them, her hands covering her face.*]

WILLY: I suppose that's my fault!

BIFF: I stole myself out of every good job since high school!

WILLY: And whose fault is that?

BIFF: And I never got anywhere because you blew me so full of hot air I could never stand taking orders from anybody! That's whose fault it is!

WILLY: I hear that!

LINDA: Don't, Biff!

BIFF: It's goddam time you heard that! I had to be boss big shot in two weeks, and I'm through with it!

WILLY: Then hang yourself! For spite, hang yourself!

BIFF: No! Nobody's hanging himself, Willy! I ran down eleven flights with a pen in my hand today. And suddenly I stopped, you hear me? And in the middle of that office building, do you hear this? I stopped in the middle of that building and I saw—the sky. I saw the things that I love in this world. The work and the food and time to sit and smoke. And I looked at the pen and said to myself, what the hell am I grabbing this for? Why am I trying to become what I don't want to be? What am I doing in an office, making a contemptuous, begging fool of myself, when all I want is out there, waiting for me the minute I say I know who I am! Why can't I say that, Willy? [*He tries to make* WILLY *face him, but* WILLY *pulls away and moves to the left.*]

WILLY [*with hatred, threateningly*]: The door of your life is wide open!

BIFF: Pop! I'm a dime a dozen, and so are you!

WILLY [*turning on him now in an uncontrolled outburst*]: I am not a dime a dozen! I am Willy Loman, and you are Biff Loman!

[BIFF *starts for* WILLY, *but is blocked by* HAPPY. *In his fury,* BIFF *seems on the verge of attacking his father.*]

BIFF: I am not a leader of men, Willy, and neither are you. You were never anything but a hard-working drummer who landed in the ash can like all the rest of them! I'm one dollar an hour, Willy! I tried seven states and couldn't raise it. A buck an hour! Do you gather my meaning? I'm not bringing home any prizes any more, and you're going to stop waiting for me to bring them home!

WILLY [*directly to* BIFF]: You vengeful, spiteful mut!

[BIFF *breaks from* HAPPY. WILLY, *in fright, starts up the stairs.* BIFF *grabs him.*]

BIFF [*at the peak of his fury*]: Pop, I'm nothing! I'm nothing, Pop. Can't you understand that? There's no spite in it any more. I'm just what I am, that's all.

[BIFF'S *fury has spent itself, and he breaks down, sobbing, holding on to* WILLY, *who dumbly fumbles for* BIFF'S *face.*]

WILLY [*astonished*]: What're you doing? What're you doing? [*To* LINDA] Why is he crying?

BIFF [*crying, broken*]: Will you let me go, for Christ's sake? Will you take that phony dream and burn it before something happens? [*Struggling to contain himself, he pulls away and moves to the stairs.*] I'll go in the morning. Put him—put him to bed. [*Exhausted,* BIFF *moves up the stairs to his room.*]

WILLY [*after a long pause astonished, elevated*]: Isn't that—isn't that remarkable? Biff—he likes me!

LINDA: He loves you, Willy!

HAPPY [*deeply moved*]: Always did, Pop.

WILLY: Oh, Biff! [*Staring wildly*] He cried! Cried to me. [*He is choking with his love, and now cries out his promise.*] That boy—that boy is going to be magnificent!

[BEN *appears in the light just outside the kitchen.*]

BEN: Yes, outstanding, with twenty thousand behind him.

LINDA [*sensing the racing of his mind, fearfully, carefully*]: Now come to bed, Willy. It's all settled now.

WILLY [*finding it difficult not to rush out of the house*]: Yes, we'll sleep. Come on. Go to sleep, Hap.

BEN: And it does take a great kind of a man to crack the jungle.

[*In accents of dread,* BEN'S *idyllic music starts up.*]

HAPPY [*his arm around* LINDA]: I'm getting married, Pop, don't forget it. I'm changing everything. I'm gonna run that department before the year is up. You'll see, Mom. [*He kisses her.*]

BEN: The jungle is dark but full of diamonds, Willy.

[WILLY *turns, moves, listening to* BEN.]

LINDA: Be good. You're both good boys, just act that way, that's all.

HAPPY: 'Night, Pop. [*He goes upstairs.*]

LINDA [*to* WILLY]: Come, dear.

BEN [*with greater force*]: One must go in to fetch a diamond out.

WILLY [*to* LINDA, *as he moves slowly along the edge of the kitchen, toward the door*]: I just want to get settled down, Linda. Let me sit alone for a little.

LINDA [*almost uttering her fear*]: I want you upstairs.

WILLY [*taking her in his arms*]: In a few minutes, Linda. I couldn't sleep right now. Go on, you look awful tired. [*He kisses her.*]

BEN: Not like an appointment at all. A diamond is rough and hard to the touch.

WILLY: Go on now. I'll be right up.

LINDA: I think this is the only way, Willy.

WILLY: Sure, it's the best thing.

BEN: Best thing!

WILLY: The only way. Everything is gonna be—go on, kid, get to bed. You look so tired.

LINDA: Come right up.

WILLY: Two minutes.

[LINDA *goes into the living-room, then reappears in her bedroom.* WILLY *moves just outside the kitchen door.*]

WILLY: Loves me. [*Wonderingly*] Always loved me. Isn't that a remarkable thing? Ben, he'll worship me for it!

BEN [*with promise*]: It's dark there, but full of diamonds.

WILLY: Can you imagine that magnificence with twenty thousand dollars in his pocket?

LINDA [*calling from her room*]: Willy! Come up!

WILLY [*calling into the kitchen*]: Yes! Yes. Coming! It's very smart, you realize that, don't you, sweetheart? Even Ben sees it. I gotta go, baby. 'Bye! Bye! [*Going over to* BEN, *almost dancing*] Imagine? When the mail comes he'll be ahead of Bernard again!

BEN: A perfect proposition all around.

WILLY: Did you see how he cried to me? Oh, if I could kiss him, Ben!

BEN: Time, William, time!

WILLY: Oh, Ben, I always knew one way or another we were gonna make it, Biff and I!

BEN [*looking at his watch*]: The boat. We'll be late. [*He moves slowly off into the darkness.*]

WILLY [*elegiacally, turning to the house*]: Now when you kick off, boy, I want a seventy-yard boot, and get right down the field under the ball, and when you hit, hit low and hit hard, because it's important, boy. [*He swings around and faces the audience.*] There's all kinds of important people in the stands, and the first thing you know . . . [*Suddenly realizing he is alone*] Ben! Ben, where do I . . . ? [*He makes a sudden movement of search.*] Ben, how do I . . . ?

LINDA [*calling*]: Willy, you coming up?

WILLY [*uttering a gasp of fear, whirling about as if to quiet her*]: Sh! [*He turns around as if to find his way; sounds, faces, voices seem to be swarming in upon him and he flicks at them, crying,* "Sh! Sh!" *Suddenly music, faint and high, stops him. It rises in intensity, almost to an unbearable scream. He goes up and down on his toes, and rushes off around the house.*] Shhh!

LINDA: Willy?

[*There is no answer.* LINDA *waits.* BIFF *gets up off his bed. He is still in his clothes.* HAPPY *sits up.* BIFF *stands listening.*]

LINDA [*with real fear*]: Willy, answer me! Willy!

[*There is the sound of a car starting and moving away at full speed.*]

LINDA: No!

BIFF [*rushing down the stairs*]: Pop!

[*As the car speeds off, the music crashes down in a frenzy of sound, which becomes the soft pulsation of a single cello string.* BIFF *slowly returns to his bedroom. He and* HAPPY *gravely don their jackets.* LINDA *slowly walks out of her room. The music has developed into a dead march. The leaves of day are appearing over everything.* CHARLEY *and* BERNARD, *somberly dressed, appear and knock on the kitchen door.* BIFF *and* HAPPY *slowly descend the stairs to the kitchen as* CHARLEY *and* BERNARD *enter. All stop a moment when* LINDA, *in clothes of mourning, bearing a little bunch of roses, comes through the draped doorway into the kitchen. She goes to* CHARLEY *and takes his arm. Now all move toward the audience, through the wall-line of the kitchen. At the limit of the apron,* LINDA *lays down the flowers, kneels, and sits back on her heels. All stare down at the grave.*]

REQUIEM

CHARLEY: It's getting dark, Linda.

[LINDA *doesn't react. She stares at the grave.*]

BIFF: How about it, Mom? Better get some rest, heh? They'll be closing the gate soon.

[LINDA *makes no move. Pause.*]

HAPPY [*deeply angered*]: He had no right to do that. There was no necessity for it. We would've helped him.

CHARLEY [*grunting*]: Hmmm.

BIFF: Come along, Mom.

LINDA: Why didn't anybody come?

CHARLEY: It was a very nice funeral.

LINDA: But where are all the people he knew? Maybe they blame him.

CHARLEY: Naa. It's a rough world, Linda. They wouldn't blame him.

LINDA: I can't understand it. At this time especially. First time in thirty-five years we were just about free and clear. He only needed a little salary. He was even finished with the dentist.

CHARLEY: No man only needs a little salary.

LINDA: I can't understand it.

BIFF: There were a lot of nice days. When he'd come home from a trip; or on Sundays, making the stoop; finishing the cellar; putting on the new porch; when he built the extra bathroom; and put up the garage. You know something, Charley, there's more of him in that front stoop than in all the sales he ever made.

CHARLEY: Yeah. He was a happy man with a batch of cement.

LINDA: He was so wonderful with his hands.

BIFF: He had the wrong dreams. All, all, wrong.

HAPPY [*almost ready to fight* BIFF]: Don't say that!

BIFF: He never knew who he was.

CHARLEY [*stopping* HAPPY'S *movement and reply. To* BIFF]: Nobody dast blame this man. You don't understand: Willy was a salesman. And for a salesman, there is no rock bottom to the life. He don't put a bolt to a nut, he don't tell you the law or give you medicine. He's a man way out there in the blue, riding on a smile and a shoeshine. And when they start not smiling back—that's an earthquake. And then you get yourself a couple of spots on your hat, and you're finished. Nobody dast blame this man. A salesman is got to dream, boy. It comes with the territory.

BIFF: Charley, the man didn't know who he was.

HAPPY [*infuriated*]: Don't say that!

BIFF: Why don't you come with me, Happy?

HAPPY: I'm not licked that easily. I'm staying right in this city, and I'm gonna beat this racket! [*He looks at* BIFF, *his chin set.*] The Loman Brothers!

BIFF: I know who I am, kid

HAPPY: All right, boy. I'm gonna show you and everybody else that Willy Loman did not die in vain. He had a good dream. It's the only dream you can have—to come out number-one man. He fought it out here, and this is where I'm gonna win it for him.

BIFF [*with a hopeless glance at* HAPPY, *bends toward his mother*]: Let's go, Mom.

LINDA: I'll be with you in a minute. Go on, Charley. [*He hesitates.*] I want to, just for a minute. I never had a chance to say good-bye.

[CHARLEY *moves away, followed by* HAPPY. BIFF *remains a slight distance up and left of* LINDA. *She sits there, summoning herself. The flute begins, not far away, playing behind her speech.*]

LINDA: Forgive me, dear. I can't cry. I don't know what it is, but I can't cry. I don't understand it. Why did you ever do that? Help me, Willy, I can't cry. It seems to me that you're just on another trip. I keep expecting you. Willy, dear, I can't cry. Why did you do it? I search and search and I search, and I can't understand it,

Willy. I made the last payment on the house today. Today, dear. And there'll be nobody home. [*A sob rises in her throat.*] We're free and clear. [*Sobbing more fully, released*] We're free. [BIFF *comes slowly toward her.*] We're free . . . We're free . . .

[BIFF *lifts her to her feet and moves out up right with her in his arms.* LINDA *sobs quietly.* BERNARD *and* CHARLEY *come together and follow them, followed by* HAPPY. *Only the music of the flute is left on the darkening stage as over the house the hard towers of the apartment buildings rise into sharp focus.*]

CURTAIN

TENNESSEE WILLIAMS (1911–1983) was born as Thomas Lanier Williams in Columbus, Mississippi, to Cornelius Coffin (a traveling salesman) and Edwina Williams. As his father traveled frequently, Williams was raised by his mother and her parents at the grandfather's Episcopal rectory. When he was twelve, the family

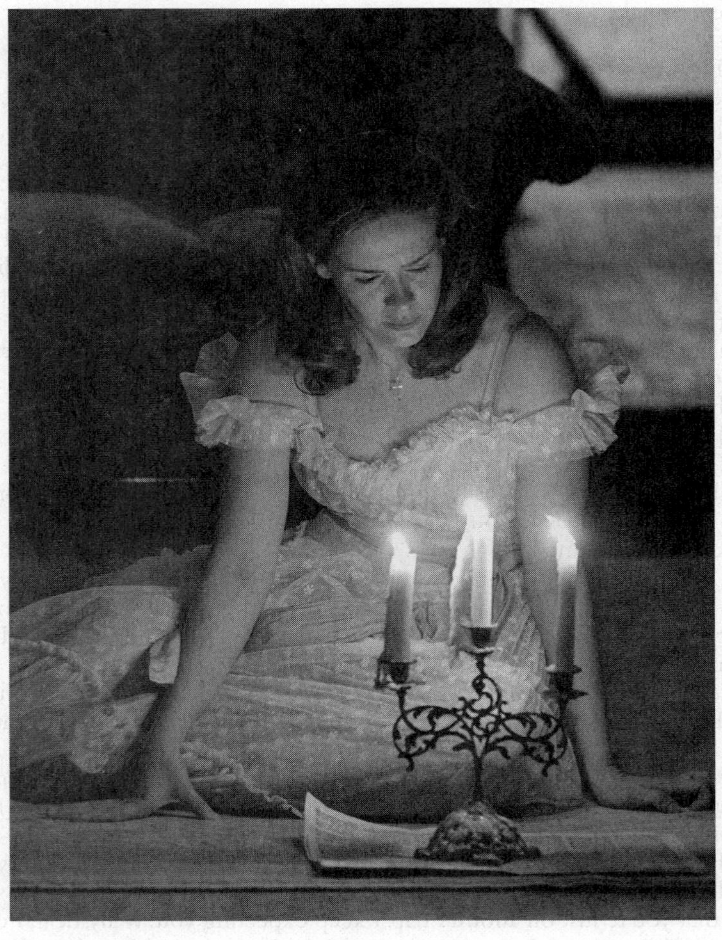

The Glass Menagerie

moved to St. Louis; he made a poor adjustment to urban life, and in response to his alienation the young Williams began to write poems and short stories. Tennessee Williams attended the University of Missouri and Washington University in St. Louis, then received his B.A. degree from the University of Iowa in 1938. He was, however, also familiar with lower-class jobs like the one held by Tom in *The Glass Menagerie*. He worked in a St. Louis shoe store, then as a manual laborer, clerical worker, waiter, elevator operator, and theater usher before becoming a screenwriter for Metro-Goldwyn-Mayer. It was during his unsuccessful stint as a screenwriter that Williams produced *The Glass Menagerie*, which won the New York Drama Critics Circle Award in 1945. Williams had a prolific and successful career writing plays, short stories, and poetry. He also won many awards, including two Pulitzer Prizes for his plays. Tennessee Williams died in New York, from choking, in 1983.

The Glass Menagerie was produced in Chicago in 1944 and then played on Broadway in 1945. The play has enjoyed numerous revivals and has been produced for both film and television; with Oscar Saul, Williams himself wrote the screenplay for the Warner Brothers film of *The Glass Menagerie* (1950). The language of *The Glass Menagerie* is poetic, drawing on imagery and **symbolism**. Laura's glass menagerie, although part of the plot and a simple stage **prop**, also stands for her fragile, innocent character. Tom's statement that "America is matriculating in a school for the blind" is a poetic **metaphor** that assigns a negative moral value to the realistic urban setting of Williams's play. *The Glass Menagerie* has also been called a memory play because the **dramatic frame**, in which Tom reflects back on the principal action, characterizes that action as the product of Tom's memories rather than a separate reality.

Staging is particularly important to the emotional effect of Williams's *The Glass Menagerie*. The distancing effect produced by the dramatic frame in which Tom acts as a chorus, narrator, or even historical guide is reinforced by what Williams himself called "plastic theater," the symbolic use of staging, props, even lighting and sound that is characteristic of **expressionist drama**. The most unusual feature, abandoned in the original production but used successfully in revivals of *The Glass Menagerie*, is the use of images and titles projected on a screen that comment on the characters' statements and actions.

Related Works: Hemingway, "A Clean, Well-Lighted Place"; Steinbeck, "The Chrysanthemums"; Donne, "A Valediction: Forbidding Mourning"; Auden, "The Unknown Citizen"; Bishop, "One Art" and "Sestina"; Miller, *Death of a Salesman.*

The Glass Menagerie

Characters

AMANDA WINGFIELD, the mother. A little woman of great but confused vitality clinging frantically to another time and place. Her characterization must be carefully created, not copied from type. She is not paranoiac, but her life is paranoia. There is much to admire in AMANDA, and as much to love and pity as there is to laugh at. Certainly she has endurance and a kind of heroism, and though her foolishness makes her unwittingly cruel at times, there is tenderness in her slight person.

LAURA WINGFIELD, her daughter. AMANDA, having failed to establish contact with reality, continues to live vitally in her illusions, but LAURA'S situation is even graver. A childhood illness has left her crippled, one leg slightly shorter than the other, and held in a brace. This defect need not be more than suggested on the stage. Stemming from this, LAURA'S separation increases till she is like a piece of her own glass collection, too exquisitely fragile to move from the shelf.

TOM WINGFIELD, her son, and the narrator of the play. A poet with a job in a warehouse. His nature is not remorseless, but to escape from a trap he has to act without pity.

JIM O'CONNOR, the gentleman caller. A nice, ordinary, young man.

SCENE: *An alley in St. Louis.*
PART I: *Preparation for a gentleman caller.*
PART II: *The gentleman calls.*
TIME: *Now and the past.*

Author's Production Notes

Being a "memory play," *The Glass Menagerie* can be presented with unusual freedom of convention. Because of its considerably delicate or tenuous material, atmospheric touches and subtleties of direction play a particularly important part. Expressionism and all other unconventional techniques in drama have only one valid aim, and that is a closer approach to truth. When a play employs unconventional techniques, it is not, or certainly shouldn't be, trying to escape its responsibility of dealing with reality, or interpreting experience, but is actually or should be attempting to find a closer approach, a more penetrating and vivid expression of things as they are. The straight realistic play with its genuine frigidaire and authentic ice-cubes, its characters that speak exactly as its audience speaks, corresponds to the academic landscape and has the same virtue of a photographic likeness. Everyone should know nowadays the unimportance of the photographic in art: that truth, life, or reality is an organic thing which the poetic imagination can represent or suggest, in essence, only through transformation, through changing into other forms than those which were merely present in appearance.

These remarks are not meant as a preface only to this particular play. They have to do with a conception of a new, plastic theatre which must take the place of the exhausted theatre of realistic conventions if the theatre is to resume vitality as a part of our culture.

The Screen Device. There is *only one important difference between the original and acting version of the play* and that is the *omission* in the latter of the device which I tentatively included in my *original* script. This device was the use of a screen on which were projected magic-lantern slides bearing images or titles. I do not regret the omission of this device from the present Broadway production. The extraordinary power of Miss Taylor's performance made it suitable to have the utmost simplicity in the physical production. But I think it may be interesting to some readers to see how this device was conceived. So I am putting it into the published manuscript. These images and legends, projected from behind, were cast on a section of wall between the front-room and dining-room areas, which should be indistinguishable from the rest when not in use.

The purpose of this will probably be apparent. It is to give accent to certain values in each scene. Each scene contains a particular point (or several) which is structurally the most important. In an episodic play, such as this, the basic structure or narrative line may be obscured from the audience; the effect may seem fragmentary rather than architectural. This may not be the fault of the play so much as a lack of attention in the audience. The legend or image upon the screen will strengthen the effect of what is merely allusion in the writing and allow the primary point to be made more simply and lightly than if the entire responsibility were on the spoken lines. Aside from this structural value, I think the screen will have a definite emotional appeal, less definable but just as important. An imaginative producer or director may invent many other uses for this device than those indicated in the present script. In fact the possibilities of the device seem much larger to me than the instance of this play can possibly utilize.

The Music: Another extra-literary accent in this play is provided by the use of music. A single recurring tune, "The Glass Menagerie," is used to give emotional emphasis to suitable passages. This tune is like circus music, not when you are on the grounds or in the immediate vicinity of the parade, but when you are at some distance and very likely thinking of something else. It seems under those circumstances to continue almost interminably and it weaves in and out of your preoccupied consciousness; then it is the lightest, most delicate music in the world and perhaps the saddest. It expresses the surface vivacity of life with the underlying strain of immutable and inexpressible sorrow. When you look at a piece of delicately spun glass you think of two things: how beautiful it is and how easily it can be broken. Both of those ideas should be woven into the recurring tune, which dips in and out of the play as if it were carried on a wind that changes. It serves as a thread of connection and allusion between the narrator with his separate point in time and space and the subject of his story. Between each episode it returns as reference to the emotion, nostalgia, which is the first condition of the play. It is primarily LAURA'S music and therefore comes out most clearly when the play focuses upon her and the lovely fragility of glass which is her image.

The Lighting. The lighting in the play is not realistic. In keeping with the atmosphere of memory, the stage is dim. Shafts of light are focused on selected areas or actors, sometimes in contradistinction to what is the apparent center. For instance, in the quarrel scene between TOM and AMANDA, in which LAURA has no active part, the clearest pool of light is on her figure. This is also true of the supper scene, when her silent figure on the sofa should remain the visual center. The light upon LAURA should be distinct from the others, having a peculiar pristine clarity such as light used in early religious portraits of female saints or madonnas. A certain correspondence to light in religious paintings, such as El Greco's, where the figures are radiant in atmosphere that is relatively dusky, could be effectively used throughout the play. (It will also permit a more effective use of the screen.) A free, imaginative use of light can be of enormous value in giving a mobile, plastic quality to plays of a more or less static nature.

T. W.

SCENE 1

The Wingfield apartment is in the rear of the building, one of those vast hive-like conglomerations of cellular living-units that flower as warty growths in overcrowded urban centers of lower middle-class population and are symptomatic of the impulse of this largest and fundamentally enslaved section of American society to avoid fluidity and differentiation and to exist and function as one interfused mass of automatism.

The apartment faces an alley and is entered by a fire-escape, a structure whose name is a touch of accidental poetic truth, for all of these huge buildings are always burning with the slow and implacable fires of human desperation. The fire-escape is included in the set—that is, the landing of it and steps descending from it.

The scene is memory and is therefore nonrealistic. Memory takes a lot of poetic license. It omits some details; others are exaggerated, according to the emotional value of the articles it touches, for memory is seated and predominantly in the heart. The interior is therefore rather dim and poetic.

At the rise of the curtain, the audience is faced with the dark, grim rear wall of the Wingfield tenement. This building, which runs parallel to the footlights, is flanked on both sides by dark, narrow alleys which run into murky canyons of tangled clotheslines, garbage cans and the sinister lattice work of neighboring fire-escapes. It is up and down these side alleys that exterior entrances and exits are made, during the play. At the end of TOM'S *opening commentary, the dark tenement wall slowly reveals (by means of a transparency) the interior of the ground floor Wingfield apartment.*

Downstage is the living room, which also serves as a sleeping room for LAURA, *the sofa unfolding to make her bed. Upstage, center, and divided by a wide arch or second proscenium with transparent faded portieres (or second curtain), is the dining room. In an old-fashioned what-not in the living room are seen scores of transparent glass animals. A blown-up photograph of the father hangs on the wall of the living room, facing the audience, to the left of the archway. It is the face of a very handsome young man in a doughboy's First World War cap. He is gallantly smiling, ineluctably smiling, as if to say, "I will be smiling forever."*

The audience hears and sees the opening scene in the dining room through both the transparent fourth wall of the building and the transparent gauze portieres of the dining-room arch. It is during this revealing scene that the fourth wall slowly ascends, out of sight. This transparent exterior wall is not brought down again until the very end of the play, during TOM'S *final speech.*

The narrator is an undisguised convention of the play. He takes whatever license with dramatic convention as is convenient to his purposes.

TOM *enters dressed as a merchant sailor from alley, stage left, and strolls across the front of the stage to the fire-escape. There he stops and lights a cigarette. He addresses the audience.*

TOM: Yes, I have tricks in my pocket, I have things up my sleeve. But I am the opposite of a stage magician. He gives you illusion that has the appearance of truth. I give you truth in the pleasant disguise of illusion. To begin with, I turn back time. I reverse it to that quaint period, the thirties, when the huge middle class of America was matriculating in a school for the blind. Their eyes had failed them, or they had failed their eyes, and so they were having their fingers pressed forcibly down on the fiery Braille alphabet of a dissolving economy. In Spain there was revolution. Here there was only shouting and confusion. In Spain there was Guernica. Here there were disturbances of labor, sometimes pretty violent, in otherwise peaceful cities such as Chicago, Cleveland, Saint Louis . . . This is the social background of the play.

(*Music*)

The play is memory. Being a memory play, it is dimly lighted, it is sentimental, it is not realistic. In memory everything seems to happen to music. That explains the fiddle in the wings. I am the narrator of the play, and also a character in it. The other characters are my mother, Amanda, my sister, Laura, and a gentleman caller who appears in the final scenes. He is the most realistic character in the play, being an emissary from a world of reality that we were somehow set apart from. But since I have a poet's weakness for symbols, I am using this character also as a symbol; he is the long delayed but always expected something that we live for. There is a fifth character in the play who doesn't appear except in this larger-than-life-size photograph over the mantel. This is our father who left us a long time ago. He was a telephone man who fell in love with long distances; he gave up his job with the telephone company and skipped the light fantastic out of town . . . The last we heard of him was a picture post-card from Mazatlan, on the Pacific coast of Mexico, containing a message of two words—"Hello—Good-bye!" and no address. I think the rest of the play will explain itself . . .

AMANDA'S *voice becomes audible through the portieres.*

(*Legend on screen: "Où sont les neiges."*)

He divides the portieres and enters the upstage area.

AMANDA *and* LAURA *are seated at a drop-leaf table. Eating is indicated by gestures without food or utensils.* AMANDA *faces the audience.* TOM *and* LAURA *are seated in profile.*

The interior has lit up softly and through the scrim we see AMANDA *and* LAURA *seated at the table in the upstage area.*

AMANDA (*calling*): Tom?

TOM: Yes, Mother.

AMANDA: We can't say grace until you come to the table!

TOM: Coming, Mother. (*He bows slightly and withdraws, reappearing a few moments later in his place at the table.*)

AMANDA (*to her son*): Honey, don't *push* with your *fingers*. If you have to push with something, the thing to push with is a crust of bread. And chew—chew! Animals have sections in their stomachs which enable them to digest food without mastication, but human beings are supposed to chew their food before they swallow it down. Eat food leisurely, son, and really enjoy it. A well-cooked meal has lots of delicate flavors that have to be held in the mouth for appreciation. So chew your food and give your salivary glands a chance to function!

TOM *deliberately lays his imaginary fork down and pushes his chair back from the table.*

TOM: I haven't enjoyed one bite of this dinner because of your constant directions on how to eat it. It's you that make me rush through meals with your hawk-like attention to every bite I take: Sickening—spoils my appetite—all this discussion of—animals' secretion—salivary glands—mastication!

AMANDA (*lightly*): Temperament like a Metropolitan star! (*He rises and crosses downstage.*) You're not excused from the table.

TOM: I'm getting a cigarette.

AMANDA: You smoke too much.

LAURA *rises.*

LAURA: I'll bring in the blanc mange.

He remains standing with his cigarette by the portieres during the following.

AMANDA (*rising*): No, sister, no, sister—you be the lady this time and I'll be the darky.

LAURA: I'm already up.

AMANDA: Resume your seat, little sister—I want you to stay fresh and pretty—for gentlemen callers!

LAURA: I'm not expecting any gentlemen callers.

AMANDA (*Crossing out to kitchenette. Airily.*): Sometimes they come when they are least expected! Why, I remember one Sunday afternoon in Blue Mountain—(*enters kitchenette*)

TOM: I know what's coming!

LAURA: Yes, But let her tell it.

TOM: Again?

LAURA: She loves to tell it.

AMANDA *returns with bowl of dessert.*

AMANDA: One Sunday afternoon in Blue Mountain—your mother received—*seventeen*!—gentlemen callers! Why, sometimes there weren't chairs enough to accommodate them all. We had to send the nigger over to bring in folding chairs from the parish house.

TOM (*remaining at portieres*): How did you entertain those gentlemen callers?

AMANDA: I understood the art of conversation!

TOM: I bet you could talk.

AMANDA: Girls in those days *knew* how to talk, I can tell you.

TOM: Yes?

(*Image*: AMANDA *as a girl on a porch, greeting callers.*)

AMANDA: They knew how to entertain their gentlemen callers. It wasn't enough for a girl to be possessed of a pretty face and a graceful figure—although I wasn't slighted in either respect. She also needed to have a nimble wit and a tongue to meet all occasions.

TOM: What did you talk about?

AMANDA: Things of importance going on in the world! Never anything coarse or common or vulgar. (*She addresses* TOM *as though he were seated in the vacant chair at the table though he remains by portieres. He plays this scene as though he held the book.*) My callers were gentlemen—all! Among my callers were some of the most prominent young planters of the Mississippi Delta—planters and sons of planters!

TOM *motions for music and a spot of light on* AMANDA.

Her eyes lift, her face glows, her voice becomes rich and elegiac.

(*Screen legend: "Où sont les neiges."*)

There was young Champ Laughlin who later became vice-president of the Delta Planters Bank. Hadley Stevenson who was drowned in Moon Lake and left his widow one hundred and fifty thousand in Government bonds. There were the Cutrere brothers, Wesley and Bates. Bates was one of my bright particular beaux! He got in a quarrel with that wild Wainwright boy. They shot it out on the floor of Moon Lake Casino. Bates was shot through the stomach. Died in the ambulance on his way to Memphis. His widow was also well-provided for, came into eight or ten thousand acres, that's all. She married him on the rebound—never loved her—carried my picture on him the night he died! And there was that boy that every girl in the Delta had set her cap for! That beautiful, brilliant young Fitzhugh boy from Greene County!

TOM: What did he leave his widow?

AMANDA: He never married! Gracious, you talk as though all of my old admirers had turned up their toes to the daisies!

TOM: Isn't this the first you've mentioned that still survives?

AMANDA: That Fitzhugh boy went North and made a fortune—came to be known as the Wolf of Wall Street! He had the Midas touch, whatever he touched turned to gold!

And I could have been Mrs. Duncan J. Fitzhugh, mind you! But—I picked your *father!*

LAURA (*rising*): Mother, let me clear the table.

AMANDA: No, dear, you go in front and study your typewriter chart. Or practice your shorthand a little. Stay fresh and pretty!—It's almost time for our gentlemen callers to start arriving. (*She flounces girlishly toward the kitchenette.*) How many do you suppose we're going to entertain this afternoon?

TOM *throws down the paper and jumps up with a groan.*

LAURA (*alone in the dining room*): I don't believe we're going to receive any, Mother.

AMANDA (*reappearing, airily*): What? No one—not one? You must be joking! (LAURA *nervously echoes her laugh. She slips in a fugitive manner through the half-open portieres and draws them gently behind her. A shaft of very clear light is thrown on her face against the faded tapestry of the curtains.*) (*Music: "The Glass Menagerie" under faintly.*) (*lightly*) Not one gentleman caller? It can't be true! There must be a flood, there must have been a tornado!

LAURA: It isn't a flood, it's not a tornado, Mother. I'm just not popular like you were in Blue Mountain. . . . (TOM *utters another a groan.* LAURA *glances at him with a faint, apologetic smile. Her voice catching a little.*) Mother's afraid I'm going to be an old maid.

(*The scene dims out with "Glass Menagerie" music.*)

SCENE 2

"LAURA, HAVEN'T YOU EVER LIKED SOME BOY?"

On the dark stage the screen is lighted with the image of blue roses.

Gradually LAURA'S *figure becomes apparent and the screen goes out.*

The music subsides.

LAURA *is seated in the delicate ivory chair at the small claw-foot table.*

She wears a dress of soft violet material for a kimono—her hair tied back from her forehead with a ribbon.

She is washing and polishing her collection of glass.

AMANDA *appears on the fire-escape steps. At the sound of her ascent,* LAURA *catches her breath, thrusts the bowl of ornaments away and seats herself stiffly before the diagram of the typewriter keyboard as though it held her spellbound.*

Something has happened to AMANDA. *It is written in her face as she climbs to the landing a look that is grim and hopeless and a little absurd.*

She has on one of those cheap or imitation velvety-looking cloth coats with imitation fur collar. Her hat is five or six years old, one of those dreadful cloche hats that were worn in the late twenties and she is clasping an enormous black patent-leather pocketbook with nickel clasps and initials. This is her full-dress outfit, the one she usually wears to the D.A.R.

Before entering she looks through the door.

She purses her lips, opens her eyes very wide, rolls them upward and shakes her head.

Then she slowly lets herself in the door. Seeing her mother's expression LAURA *touches her lips with a nervous gesture.*

LAURA: Hello, Mother, I was—(*She makes a nervous gesture toward the chart on the wall.* AMANDA *leans against the shut door and stares at* LAURA *with a martyred look.*)

AMANDA: Deception? Deception? (*She slowly removes her hat and gloves, continuing the sweet suffering stare. She lets the hat and gloves fall on the floor—a bit of acting.*)

LAURA (*shakily*): How was the D.A.R. meeting? (AMANDA *slowly opens her purse and removes a dainty white handkerchief which she shakes out delicately and delicately touches to her lips and nostrils.*) Didn't you go to the D.A.R. meeting, Mother?

AMANDA (*faintly, almost inaudibly*): —No.—No. (*then more forcibly*) I did not have the strength—to go to the D.A.R. In fact, I did not have the courage! I wanted to find a hole in the ground and hide myself in it forever! (*She crosses slowly to the wall and removes the diagram of the typewriter keyboard. She holds it in front of her for a second, staring at it sweetly and sorrowfully—then bites her lips and tears it in two pieces.*)

LAURA (*faintly*): Why did you do that, Mother? (AMANDA *repeats the same procedure with the chart of the Gregg Alphabet.*) Why are you—

AMANDA: Why? Why? How old are you, Laura?

LAURA: Mother, you know my age.

AMANDA: I thought that you were an adult; it seems that I was mistaken. (*She crosses slowly to the sofa and sinks down and stares at* LAURA.)

LAURA: Please don't stare at me, Mother.

AMANDA *closes her eyes and lowers her head. Count ten.*

AMANDA: What are we going to do, what is going to become of us, what is the future?

Count ten.

LAURA: Has something happened, Mother? (AMANDA *draws a long breath and takes out the handkerchief again. Dabbing process.*) Mother, has—something happened?

AMANDA: I'll be all right in a minute, I'm just bewildered—(*count five*)—by life. . . .

LAURA: Mother, I wish that you would tell me what's happened!

AMANDA: As you know, I was supposed to be inducted into my office at the D.A.R. this afternoon. (*Image: A swarm of typewriters.*) But I stopped off at Rubicam's business college to speak to your teachers about your having a cold and ask them what progress they thought you were making down there.

LAURA: Oh. . . .

AMANDA: I went to the typing instructor and introduced myself as your mother. She didn't know who you were. Wingfield, she said. We don't have any such student enrolled at the school! I assured her she did, that you had been going to classes since early in January. "I wonder," she said, "if you could be talking about that terribly shy little girl who dropped out of school after only a few days attendance?" "No." I said, "Laura, my daughter, has been going to school every day for the past six weeks!" "Excuse me," she said. She took the attendance book out and there was your name, unmistakably printed, and all the dates you were absent until they decided that you had dropped out of school. I still said, "No, there must have been some mistake! There must have been some mix-up in the records!" And she said, "No—I remember her perfectly now. Her hands shook so that she couldn't hit the right keys! The first time we gave a speed-test, she broke down completely—was sick at the stomach and almost had to be carried into the wash-room! After that morning she never showed up any more. We phoned the house but never got any answer—while I was working at Famous and Barr, I suppose, demonstrating those—Oh!" I felt so weak I could barely keep on my feet! I had to sit down while they got me a glass of water! Fifty dollars' tuition, all of our plans—my hopes and ambitions for you—just gone up the spout, just gone up the spout like that. (LAURA *draws a long breath and gets awkwardly to her feet. She crosses to the victrola and winds it up.*) What are you doing?

LAURA: Oh! (*She releases the handle and returns to her seat.*)

AMANDA: Laura, where have you been going when you've gone out pretending that you were going to business college?

LAURA: I've just been going out walking.

AMANDA: That's not true.

LAURA: It is. I just went walking.

AMANDA: Walking? Walking? In winter? Deliberately courting pneumonia in that light coat? Where did you walk to, Laura?

LAURA: All sorts of places—mostly in the park.

AMANDA: Even after you'd started catching that cold?

LAURA: It was the lesser of two evils, Mother. (*Image: Winter scene in the park.*) I couldn't go back up. I—threw up—on the floor!

AMANDA: From half past seven till after five every day you mean to tell me you walked around in the park, because you wanted to make me think that you were still going to Rubicam's Business College?

LAURA: It wasn't as bad as it sounds. I went inside places to get warmed up.

AMANDA: Inside where?

LAURA: I went in the art museum and the bird-houses at the Zoo. I visited the penguins every day! Sometimes I did without lunch and went to the movies. Lately I've been spending most of my afternoons in the Jewelbox, that big glass house where they raise the tropical flowers.

AMANDA: You did all this to deceive me, just for deception? (LAURA *looks down.*) Why?

LAURA: Mother, when you're disappointed, you get that awful suffering look on your face, like the picture of Jesus' mother in the museum!

AMANDA: Hush!

LAURA: I couldn't face it.

Pause. A whisper of strings.

(*Legend: "The Crust of Humility."*)

AMANDA (*hopelessly fingering the huge pocketbook*): So what are we going to do the rest of our lives? Stay home and watch the parades go by? Amuse ourselves with the glass menagerie, darling? Eternally play those wornout phonograph records your father left as a painful reminder of him? We won't have a business career—we've given that up because it gave us nervous indigestion! (*laughs wearily*) What is there left but dependency all our lives? I know so well what becomes of unmarried women who aren't prepared to occupy a position. I've seen such pitiful cases in the South—barely tolerated spinsters living upon the grudging patronage of sister's husband or brother's wife!—stuck away in some little mouse-trap of a room—encouraged by one in-law to visit another—little birdlike women without any nest—eating the crust of humility all their life! Is that the future that we've mapped out for ourselves? I swear it's the only alternative I can think of! It isn't a very pleasant alternative, is it? Of course—some girls *do marry*. (LAURA *twists her hands nervously*.) Haven't you ever liked some boy?

LAURA: Yes. I liked one once. (*rises*) I came across his picture a while ago.

AMANDA (*with some interest*): He gave you his picture?

LAURA: No, it's in the year-book.

AMANDA (*disappointed*): Oh—a high-school boy.

(*Screen image*: JIM *as high-school hero bearing a silver cup*.)

LAURA: Yes. His name was Jim. (LAURA *lifts the heavy annual from the claw-foot table*.) Here he is in *The Pirates of Penzance*.

AMANDA (*absently*): The what?

LAURA The operetta the senior class put on. He had a wonderful voice and we sat across the aisle from each other Mondays, Wednesdays and Fridays in the Aud. Here he is with the silver cup for debating! See his grin?

AMANDA (*absently*): He must have had a jolly disposition.

LAURA: He used to call me—Blue Roses.

(*Image: Blue roses*.)

AMANDA: Why did he call you such a name as that?

LAURA: When I had that attack of pleurosis—he asked me what was the matter when I came back. I said pleurosis—he thought that I said Blue Roses! So that's what he always called me after that. Whenever he saw me, he'd holler, "Hello, Blue Roses!" I didn't care for the girl that he went out with. Emily Meisenbach. Emily was the best-dressed girl at Soldan. She never struck me, though, as being sincere . . . It says in the Personal Section—they're engaged. That's—six years ago! They must be married by now.

AMANDA: Girls that aren't cut out for business careers usually wind up married to some nice man. (*gets up with a spark of revival*) Sister, that's what you'll do!

LAURA *utters a startled, doubtful laugh. She reaches quickly for a piece of glass*.

LAURA: But, Mother—

AMANDA: Yes? (*crossing to photograph*)

LAURA (*in a tone of frightened apology*): I'm—crippled!

(*Image: Screen*.)

AMANDA: Nonsense! Laura, I've told you never, never to use that word. Why, you're not crippled, you just have a little defect—hardly noticeable, even! When people have some slight disadvantage like that, they cultivate other things to make up for it—develop charm—and vivacity—and—*charm*! That's all you have to do! (*She turns again to the photograph*.) One thing your father had *plenty of—was charm*!

TOM *motions to the fiddle in the winds*.

(*The scene fades out with music*.)

SCENE 3

(*Legend on screen: "After the Fiasco—"*)

TOM *speaks from the fire-escape landing.*

TOM: After the fiasco at Rubicam's Business College, the idea of getting a gentleman caller for Laura began to play a more and more important part in Mother's calculations. It became an obsession. Like some archetype of the universal unconscious, the image of the gentleman caller haunted our small apartment. . . . (*Image: Young man at door with flowers.*) An evening at home rarely passed without some allusion to this image, this spectre, this hope. . . . Even when he wasn't mentioned, his presence hung in Mother's preoccupied look and in my sister's frightened, apologetic manner—hung like a sentence passed upon the Wingfields! Mother was a woman of action as well as words. She began to take logical steps in the planned direction. Late that winter and in the early spring—realizing that extra money would be needed to properly feather the nest and plume the bird—she conducted a vigorous campaign on the telephone, roping in subscribers to one of those magazines for matrons called *The Home-maker's Companion*, the type of journal that features the serialized sublimations of ladies of letters who think in terms of delicate cup-like breasts, slim, tapering waists, rich, creamy thighs, eyes like wood-smoke in autumn, fingers that soothe and caress like strains of music, bodies as powerful as Etruscan sculpture.

(*Screen image*: Glamor *magazine cover.*)

AMANDA *enters with phone on long extension cord. She is spotted in the dim stage.*

AMANDA: Ida Scott? This is Amanda Wingfield! We *missed* you at the D.A.R. last Monday! I said to myself: She's probably suffering with that sinus condition! How is that sinus condition? Horrors! Heaven have mercy!—You're a Christian martyr, yes, that's what you are, a Christian martyr! Well, I just now happened to notice that your subscription to the *Companion's* about to expire! Yes, it expires with the next issue, honey!—just when that wonderful new serial by Bessie Mae Hopper is getting off to such an exciting start. Oh, honey, it's something that you can't miss! You remember how *Gone With the Wind* took everybody by storm? You simply couldn't go out if you hadn't read it. All everybody *talked* was Scarlett O'Hara. Well, this is a book that critics already compare to *Gone With the Wind*. It's the *Gone With the Wind* of the post-World War generation!—What?—Burning?—Oh, honey, don't let them burn, go take a look in the oven and I'll hold the wire! Heavens—I think she's hung up!

(*Dim out.*)

(*Legend on screen: "You think I'm in love with continental shoemakers?"*)

Before the stage is lighted, the violent voices of TOM *and* AMANDA *are heard. They are quarreling behind the portieres. In front of them stands* LAURA *with clenched hands and panicky expression.*

A clear pool of light on her figure throughout this scene.

TOM: What in Christ's name am I—

AMANDA (*shrilly*): Don't you use that—

TOM: Supposed to do!

AMANDA: Expression! Not in my—

TOM: Ohhh!

AMANDA: Presence! Have you gone out of your senses?

TOM: I have, that's true, *driven* out!

AMANDA: What is the matter with you, you—big—big—IDIOT!

TOM: Look—I've got *no thing,* no single thing—

AMANDA: Lower your voice!

TOM: In my life here that I can call my own! Everything is—

AMANDA: Stop that shouting!

TOM: Yesterday you confiscated my books! You had the nerve to—

AMANDA: I took that horrible novel back to the library—yes! That hideous book by that insane Mr. Lawrence. (TOM *laughs wildly.*) I cannot control the output of diseased minds or people who cater to them—(TOM *laughs still more wildly.*) BUT I WON'T ALLOW SUCH FILTH BROUGHT INTO MY HOUSE! No, no, no, no, no!

TOM: House, house! Who pays rent on it, who makes a slave of himself to—

AMANDA (*fairly screeching*): Don't you DARE to—

TOM: No, no, *I* mustn't say things! *I've* got to just—

AMANDA: Let me tell you—

TOM: I don't want to hear any more! (*He tears the portieres open. The upstage area is lit with a turgid smoky red glow.*)

AMANDA'S *hair is in metal curlers and she wears a very old bathrobe, much too large for her slight figure, a relic of the faithless Mr. Wingfield.*

An upright typewriter and a wild disarray of manuscripts is on the drop-leaf table. The quarrel was probably precipitated by AMANDA'S *interruption of his creative labor. A chair lying overthrown on the floor.*

Their gesticulating shadows are cast on the ceiling by the fiery glow.

AMANDA: You *will* hear more. you—

TOM: No, I won't hear more. I'm going out!

AMANDA: You come right back in—

TOM: Out, out, out! Because I'm—

AMANDA: Come back here, Tom Wingfield! I'm not through talking to you!

TOM: Oh, go—

LAURA (*desperately*): —*Tom*!

AMANDA: You're going to listen and no more insolence from you! I'm at the end of my patience! (*He comes back toward her.*)

TOM: What do you think I'm at? Aren't I supposed to have any patience to reach the end of, Mother? I know, I know. It seems unimportant to you, what I'm *doing*—what I *want* to do—having a little *difference* between them! You don't think that—

AMANDA: I think you've been doing things that you're ashamed of. That's why you act like this. I don't believe that you go every night to the movies. Nobody goes to the movies night after night. Nobody in their right minds goes to the movies as often as you pretend to. People don't go to the movies at nearly midnight, and movies don't let out at two A.M. Come in stumbling. Muttering to yourself like a maniac! You get three hours' sleep and then go to work. Oh, I can picture the way you're doing down there. Moping, doping, because you're in no condition.

TOM (*wildly*): No, I'm in no condition!

AMANDA: What right have you got to jeopardize your job? Jeopardize the security of us all? How do you think we'd manage if you were—

TOM: Listen! You think I'm crazy *about the warehouse?* (*He bends fiercely toward her slight figure.*) You think I'm in love with the Continental Shoemakers? You think I want to spend fifty-five *years* down there in that—*celotex interior*! with—*fluorescent*—*tubes*! Look! I'd rather somebody picked up a crowbar and battered out my brains—than go back mornings! I *go*! Every time you come in yelling that God damn *"Rise and Shine!" "Rise and Shine!"* I say to myself, "How *lucky dead* people are!" But I get up. I *go*! For sixty-five dollars a month I give up all that I dream of doing and being *ever*! And you say self—*self's* all I ever think of. Why, listen, if self is what I thought of, Mother, I'd be where he is—GONE! (*pointing to father's picture*) As far as the system of transportation reaches! (*He starts past her. She grabs his arm.*) Don't grab at me, Mother!

AMANDA: Where are you going?

TOM: I'm going to the *movies*!

AMANDA: I don't believe that lie!

TOM (*Crouching toward her, overtowering her tiny figure. She backs away, gasping.*): I'm going to opium dens! Yes, opium dens, dens of vice and criminals' hang-outs, Mother. I've joined the Hogan gang, I'm a hired assassin, I carry a tommy-gun in a violin case! I run a string of cat-houses in the Valley! They call me Killer, Killer Wingfield, I'm leading a double-life, a simple, honest warehouse worker by day, by night a dynamic *czar* of the *underworld, Mother* I go to gambling casinos, I spin away fortunes on the roulette table! I wear a patch over one eye and a false mustache, sometimes I put on green whiskers. On those occasions they call me—*El Diablo!* Oh, I could tell you things to make you sleepless! My enemies plan to dynamite this place. They're going to blow us all sky-high some night! I'll be glad, very happy, and so will you! You'll go up, up on a broomstick, over Blue Mountain with seventeen gentlemen callers! You ugly—babbling old—*witch*. . . . (*He goes through a series of violent, clumsy movements, seizing his overcoat, lunging to the door, pulling it fiercely open. The women watch him, aghast. His arm catches in the sleeve of the coat as he struggles to pull it on. For a moment he is pinioned by the bulky garment. With an outraged groan he tears the coat off again, splitting the shoulder of it, and hurls it across the room. It strikes against the shelf of* LAURA'S *glass collection, there is a tinkle of shattering glass.* LAURA *cries out as if wounded.*)

(*Music Legend: "The Glass Menagerie."*)

LAURA (*shrilly*): *My glass!*—menagerie. . . . (*She covers her face and turns away.*)

But AMANDA *is still stunned and stupefied by the "ugly witch" so that she barely notices this occurrence. Now she recovers her speech.*

AMANDA (*in an awful voice*): I won't speak to you—until you apologize! (*She crosses through portieres and draws them together behind her.* TOM *is left with* LAURA. LAURA *clings weakly to the mantel with her face averted.* TOM *stares at her stupidly for a moment. Then he crosses to shelf. Drops awkwardly on his knees to collect the fallen glass, glancing at* LAURA *as if he would speak but couldn't.*)

"The Glass Menagerie" steals in as

(*The scene dims out.*)

SCENE 4

The interior is dark. Faint light in the alley.

A deep-voiced bell in a church is tolling the hour of five as the scene commences.

TOM *appears at the top of the alley. After each solemn boom of the bell in the tower, he shakes a little noise-maker or rattle as if to express the tiny spasm of man in contrast to the sustained power and dignity of the Almighty. This and the unsteadiness of his advance make it evident that he has been drinking.*

As he climbs the few steps to the fire-escape landing light steals up inside. LAURA *appears in night-dress, observing* TOM'S *empty bed in the front room.*

TOM *fishes in his pockets for door-key, removing a motley assortment of articles in the search, including a perfect shower of movie-ticket stubs and an empty bottle. At last he finds the key, but just as he is about to insert it, it slips from his fingers. He strikes a match and crouches below the door.*

TOM (*bitterly*): One crack—and it falls through!

LAURA *opens the door.*

LAURA: Tom! Tom, what are you doing?

TOM: Looking for a door-key.

LAURA: Where have you been all this time?

TOM: I have been to the movies.

LAURA: All this time at the movies?

TOM: There was a very long program. There was a Garbo picture and a Mickey Mouse and a travelogue and a newsreel and a preview of coming attractions. And there was an organ solo and a collection for the milk-fund—simultaneously—which ended up in a terrible fight between a fat lady and an usher!

LAURA (*innocently*): Did you have to stay through everything?

TOM: Of course! And, oh, I forgot! There was a big stage show! The headliner on this stage show was Malvolio the Magician. He performed wonderful tricks, many of them, such as pouring water back and forth between pitchers. First it turned to wine and then it turned to beer and then it turned to whiskey. I know it was whiskey it finally turned into because he needed somebody to come up out of the audience to help him, and I came up—both shows! It was Kentucky Straight Bourbon. A very generous fellow, he gave souvenirs. (*He pulls from his back pocket a shimmering rainbow-colored scarf.*) He gave me this. This is his magic scarf. You can have it, Laura. You wave it over a canary cage and you get a bowl of gold-fish. You wave it over the gold-fish bowl and they fly away canaries . . . But the wonderfullest trick of all was the coffin trick. We nailed him into a coffin and he got out of the coffin without removing one nail. (*He has come inside.*) There is a trick that would come in handy for me—get me out of this 2 by 4 situation! (*flops onto bed and starts removing shoes*)

LAURA: Tom—Shhh!

TOM: What're you shushing me for?

LAURA: You'll wake up Mother.

TOM: Goody, goody! Pay'er back for all those "Rise an' Shines." (*lies down, groaning*) You know it don't take much intelligence to get yourself into a nailed-up coffin, Laura. But who in hell ever got himself out of one without removing one nail?

As if in answer, the father's grinning photograph lights up.

(*Scene dims out.*)

Immediately following: The church bell is heard striking six. At the sixth stroke the alarm clock goes off in AMANDA'S *room, and after a few moments we hear her calling: "Rise and Shine! Rise and Shine! Laura, go tell your brother to rise and shine!"*

TOM (*sitting up slowly*): I'll rise—but I won't shine.

The light increases.

AMANDA: Laura, tell your brother his coffee is ready.

LAURA *slips into front room.*

LAURA: Tom—It's nearly seven. Don't make Mother nervous. (*He stares at her stupidly. Beseechingly.*) Tom, speak to Mother this morning. Make up with her, apologize, speak to her!

TOM: She won't to me. It's her that started not speaking.

LAURA: If you just say you're sorry she'll start speaking.

TOM: Her not speaking—is that such a tragedy?

LAURA: Please—please!

AMANDA (*calling from kitchenette*): Laura, are you going to do what I asked you to do, or do I have to get dressed and go out myself?

LAURA: Going, going—soon as I get on my coat! (*She pulls on a shapeless felt hat with nervous, jerky movement, pleadingly glancing at* TOM. *Rushes awkwardly for coat. The coat is one of* AMANDA'S, *inaccurately made-over, the sleeves too short for* LAURA.) Butter and what else?

AMANDA (*entering upstage*): Just butter. Tell them to charge it.

LAURA: Mother, they make such faces when I do that.

AMANDA: Sticks and stones can break our bones, but the expression on Mr. Garfinkel's face won't harm us! Tell your brother his coffee is getting cold.

LAURA (*at door*): Do what I asked you, will you, will you, Tom?

He looks sullenly away.

AMANDA: Laura, go now or just don't go at all!

LAURA (*rushing out*): Going—going! (*A second later she cries out.* TOM *springs up and crosses to door.* AMANDA *rushes anxiously in.* TOM *opens the door.*)

TOM: Laura?

LAURA: I'm all right. I slipped, but I'm all right.

AMANDA (*peering anxiously after her*): If anyone breaks a leg on those fire-escape steps, the landlord ought to be sued for every cent he possesses! (*She shuts door. Remembers she isn't speaking and returns to other room.*)

As TOM *enters listlessly for his coffee, she turns her back to him and stands rigidly facing the window on the gloomy gray vault of the areaway. Its light on her face with its aged but childish features is cruelly sharp, satirical as a Daumier print.*

(*Music under: "Ave Maria."*)

TOM *glances sheepishly but sullenly at her averted figure and slumps at the table. The coffee is scalding hot; he sips it and gasps and spits it back in the cup. At his gasp,* AMANDA *catches her breath and half turns. Then catches herself and turns back to window.*

Tom *blows on his coffee, glancing sidewise at his mother. She clears her throat.* Tom *clears his. He starts to rise. Sinks back down again, scratches his head, clears his throat again.* Amanda *coughs.* Tom *raises his cup in both hands to blow on it, his eyes staring over the rim of it at his mother for several moments. Then he slowly sets the cup down and awkwardly and hesitantly rises from the chair.*

Tom (*hoarsely*): Mother. I—I apologize, Mother. (Amanda *draws a quick, shuddering breath. Her face works grotesquely. She breaks into childlike tears.*) I'm sorry for what I said, for everything that I said, I didn't mean it.

Amanda (*sobbingly*): My devotion has made me a witch and so I make myself hateful to my children!

Tom: *No*, you *don't.*

Amanda: I worry so much, don't sleep, it makes me nervous!

Tom (*gently*): I understand that.

Amanda: I've had to put up a solitary battle all these years. But you're my right-hand bower! Don't fall down, don't fail!

Tom (*gently*): I try, Mother.

Amanda (*with great enthusiasm*): Try and you will SUCCEED! (*The notion makes her breathless.*) Why, you—you're just *full* of natural endowments! Both of my children—they're *unusual* children! Don't you think I know it? I'm so—*proud!* Happy and—feel I've—so much to be thankful for but—Promise me one thing, Son!

Tom: What, Mother?

Amanda: Promise, son, you'll—never be a drunkard!

Tom (*turns to her grinning*): I will never be a drunkard, Mother.

Amanda: That's what frightened me so, that you'd be drinking! Eat a bowl of Purina!

Tom: Just coffee, Mother.

Amanda: Shredded wheat biscuit?

Tom: No. No, Mother, just coffee.

Amanda: You can't put in a day's work on an empty stomach. You've got ten minutes—don't gulp! Drinking too-hot liquids makes cancer of the stomach. . . . Put cream in.

Tom: No, thank you.

Amanda: To cool it.

Tom: No! No, thank you, I want it black.

Amanda: I know, but it's not good for you. We have to do all that we can to build ourselves up. In these trying times we live in, all that we have to cling to is—each other. . . . That's why it's so important to—Tom, I—I sent out your sister so I could discuss something with you. If you hadn't spoken I would have spoken to you. (*sits down*)

Tom (*gently*): What is it, Mother, that you want to discuss?

Amanda: *Laura!*

Tom *puts his cup down slowly.*

(*Legend on screen: "Laura."*)

(*Music: "The Glass Menagerie."*)

Tom: —Oh.—Laura . . .

AMANDA (*touching his sleeve*): You know how Laura is. So quiet but—still water runs deep! She notices things and I think she—broods about them. (TOM *looks up.*) A few days ago I came in and she was crying.

TOM: What about?

AMANDA: You.

TOM: Me?

AMANDA: She has an idea that you're not happy here.

TOM: What gave her that idea?

AMANDA: What gives her any idea? However, you do act strangely. I—I'm not criticizing, understand *that*! I know your ambitions do not lie in the warehouse, that like everybody in the whole wide world—you've had to—make sacrifices, but—Tom—Tom—life's not easy, it calls for—Spartan endurance! There's so many things in my heart that I cannot describe to you! I've never told you but I—*loved* your father. . . .

TOM (*gently*): I know that, Mother.

AMANDA: And you—when I see you taking after his ways! Staying out late—and—well, you *had* been drinking the night you were in that—terrifying condition! Laura says that you hate the apartment and that you go out nights to get away from it! Is that true, Tom?

TOM: No. You say there's so much in your heart that you can't describe to me. That's true of me, too. There's so much in my heart that I can't describe to *you*! So let's respect each other's—

AMANDA: But, why—*why*, Tom—are you always so *restless?* Where do you go to, nights?

TOM: I—go to the movies.

AMANDA: Why do you go to the movies so much, Tom?

TOM: I go to the movies because—I like adventure. Adventure is something I don't have much of at work, so I go to the movies.

AMANDA: But, Tom, you go to the movies *entirely* too much!

TOM: I like a lot of adventure.

AMANDA *looks baffled, then hurt. As the familiar inquisition resumes he becomes hard and impatient again.* AMANDA *slips back into her querulous attitude toward him.*
(*Image on screen: Sailing vessel with Jolly Roger.*)

AMANDA: Most young men find adventure in their careers.

TOM: Then most young men are not employed in a warehouse.

AMANDA: The world is full of young men employed in warehouses and offices and factories.

TOM: Do all of them find adventure in their careers?

AMANDA: They do or they do without it! Not everybody has a craze for adventure.

TOM: Man is by instinct a lover, a hunter, a fighter, and none of those instincts are given much play at the warehouse!

AMANDA: Man is by instinct! Don't quote instinct to me! Instinct is something that people have got away from! It belongs to animals! Christian adults don't want it!

TOM: What do Christian adults want, then, Mother?

AMANDA: Superior things! Things of the mind and the spirit! Only animals have to satisfy instincts! Surely your aims are somewhat higher than theirs! Than monkeys—pigs—

TOM: I reckon they're not.

AMANDA: You're joking. However, that isn't what I wanted to discuss.

TOM (*rising*): I haven't much time.

AMANDA (*pushing his shoulders*): Sit down.

TOM: You want me to punch in red at the warehouse, Mother?

AMANDA: You have five minutes. I want to talk about Laura.

(*Legend: "Plans and Provisions."*)

TOM: All right! What about Laura?

AMANDA: We have to be making some plans and provisions for her. She's older than you, two years, and nothing has happened. She just drifts along doing nothing. It frightens me terribly how she just drifts along.

TOM: I guess she's the type that people call home girls.

AMANDA: There's no such type, and if there is, it's a pity! That is unless the home is hers, with a husband!

TOM: What?

AMANDA: Oh, I can see the handwriting on the wall as plain as I see the nose in front of my face! It's terrifying! More and more you remind me of your father! He was out all hours without explanation!—Then *left! Good-bye!* And me with the bag to hold. I saw that letter you got from the Merchant Marine. I know what you're dreaming of. I'm not standing here blindfolded. Very well, then. Then *do* it! But not till there's somebody to take your place.

TOM: What do you mean?

AMANDA: I mean that as soon as Laura has got somebody to take care of her, married, a home of her own, independent—why, then you'll be free to go wherever you please, on land, on sea, whichever way the wind blows you! But until that time you've got to look out for your sister. I don't say me because I'm old and don't matter! I say for your sister because she's young and dependent. I put her in business college—a dismal failure! Frightened her so it made her sick at the stomach. I took her over to the Young People's League at the church. Another fiasco. She spoke to nobody, nobody spoke to her. Now all she does is fool with those pieces of glass and play those worn-out records. What kind of a life is that for a girl to lead?

TOM: What can I do about it?

AMANDA: Overcome selfishness! Self, self, self is all that you ever think of! (TOM *springs up and crosses to get his coat. It is ugly and bulky. He pulls on a cap with earmuffs.*) Where is your muffler? Put your wool muffler on! (*He snatches it angrily from the closet and tosses it around his neck and pulls both ends tight.*) Tom! I haven't said what I had in mind to ask you.

TOM: I'm too late to—

AMANDA (*Catching his arm—very importunately. Then shyly.*): Down at the warehouse, aren't there some—nice young men?

TOM: No!

AMANDA: There *must* be—*some* . . .

TOM: Mother—

Gesture.

AMANDA: Find out one that's clean-living—doesn't drink and—ask him out for sister!

TOM: What?

AMANDA: For *sister!* To *meet!* Get *acquainted!*

TOM (*stamping to door*): Oh, my *go-osh!*

AMANDA: Will you? (*He opens door. Imploringly.*) *Will you?* (*He starts down.*) Will you? *Will* you, dear?

TOM (*calling back*): YES!

AMANDA *closes the door hesitantly and with a troubled but faintly hopeful expression.*

(*Screen image*: Glamor *magazine cover.*)

Spot AMANDA *at phone.*

AMANDA: Ella Cartwright? This is Amanda Wingfield! How are you, honey? How is that kidney condition? (*count five*) *Horrors!* (*count five*) You're a Christian martyr, yes, honey, that's what you are, a Christian martyr! Well, I just now happened to notice in my little red book that your subscription to the *Companion* has just run out! I knew that you wouldn't want to miss out on the wonderful serial starting in this new issue. It's by Bessie Mae Hopper, the first thing she's written since *Honeymoon for Three.* Wasn't that a strange and interesting story? Well, this one is even lovelier, I believe. It has a sophisticated, society background. It's all about the horsey set on Long Island!

(*Fade out.*)

SCENE 5

(*Legend on screen: "Annunciation."*) *Fade with music.*

It is early dusk of a spring evening. Supper has just been finished in the Wingfield apartment. AMANDA *and* LAURA *in light-colored dresses are removing dishes from the table, in the upstage area, which is shadowy, their movements formalized almost as a dance or ritual, their moving forms as pale and silent as moths.*

TOM, *in white shirt and trousers, rises from the table and crosses toward the fire-escape.*

AMANDA (*as he passes her*): Son, will you do me a favor?

TOM: What?

AMANDA: Comb your hair! You look so pretty when your hair is combed! (TOM *slouches on sofa with evening paper. Enormous caption "Franco Triumphs."*) There is only one respect in which I would like you to emulate your father.

TOM: What respect is that?

AMANDA: The care he always took of his appearance. He never allowed himself to look untidy. (*He throws down the paper and crosses to fire-escape.*) Where are you going?

TOM: I'm going out to smoke.

AMANDA: You smoke too much. A pack a day at fifteen cents a pack. How much would that amount to in a month? Thirty times fifteen is how much, Tom? Figure it out and you will be astounded at what you could save. Enough to give you a night-school course in accounting at Washington U! Just think what a wonderful thing that would be for you, Son!

TOM *is unmoved by the thought.*

TOM: I'd rather smoke. (*He steps out on landing, letting the screen door slam.*)

AMANDA (*sharply*): I know! That's the tragedy of it. . . . (*Alone, she turns to look at her husband's picture.*)

(*Dance music: "All the world is waiting for the sunrise!"*)

TOM (*to the audience*): Across the alley from us was the Paradise Dance Hall. On evenings in spring the windows and doors were open and the music came outdoors. Sometimes the lights were turned out except for a large glass sphere that hung from the ceiling. It would turn slowly about and filter the dusk with delicate rainbow colors. Then the orchestra played a waltz or a tango, something that had a slow and sensuous rhythm. Couples would come outside, to the relative privacy of the alley. You could see them kissing behind ash-pits and telephone poles. This was the compensation for lives that passed like mine, without any change or adventure. Adventure and change were imminent in this year. They were waiting around the corner for all these kids. Suspended in the mist over Berchtesgaden, caught in the folds of Chamberlain's umbrella—In Spain there was Guernica! But here there was only hot swing music and liquor, dance halls, bars, and movies, and sex that hung in the gloom like a chandelier and flooded the world with brief, deceptive rainbows. . . . All the world was waiting for bombardments!

AMANDA *turns from the picture and comes outside.*

AMANDA (*sighing*): A fire-escape landing's a poor excuse for a porch. (*She spreads a newspaper on a step and sits down, gracefully and demurely as if she were settling into a swing on a Mississippi veranda.*) What are you looking at?

TOM: The moon.

AMANDA: Is there a moon this evening?

TOM: It's rising over Garfinkel's Delicatessen.

AMANDA: So it is! A little silver slipper of a moon. Have you made a wish on it yet?

TOM: Um-hum.

AMANDA: What did you wish for?

TOM: That's a secret.

AMANDA: A secret, huh? Well, I won't tell mine either. I will be just as mysterious as you.

TOM: I bet I can guess what yours is.

AMANDA: Is my head so transparent?

TOM: You're not a sphinx.

AMANDA: No, I don't have secrets. I'll tell you what I wished for on the moon. Success and happiness for my precious children! I wish for that whenever there's a moon, and when there isn't a moon, I wish for it, too.

TOM: I thought perhaps you wished for a gentleman caller.

AMANDA: Why do you say that?

TOM: Don't you remember asking me to fetch one?

AMANDA: I remember suggesting that it would be nice for your sister if you brought home some nice young man from the warehouse. I think that I've made that suggestion more than once.

TOM: Yes, you have made it repeatedly.

AMANDA: Well?

TOM: We are going to have one.

AMANDA: *What?*

TOM: A gentleman caller!

(*The annunciation is celebrated with music.*)

AMANDA *rises.*

(*Image on screen. Caller with bouquet.*)

AMANDA: You mean you have asked some nice young man to come over?

TOM: Yep. I've asked him to dinner.

AMANDA: You really did?

TOM: I did!

AMANDA: You did, and did he—*accept?*

TOM: He did!

AMANDA: Well, well—well, well! That's—lovely!

TOM: I thought that you would be pleased.

AMANDA: It's definite, then?

TOM: Very definite.

AMANDA: Soon?

TOM: Very soon.

AMANDA: For heaven's sake, stop putting on and tell me some things, will you?

TOM: What things do you want me to tell you?

AMANDA: *Naturally* I would like to know when he's *coming!*

TOM: He's coming tomorrow.

AMANDA: *Tomorrow?*

TOM: Yep. Tomorrow.

AMANDA: But, Tom!

TOM: Yes, Mother?

AMANDA: Tomorrow gives me no time!

TOM: Time for what?

AMANDA: Preparations! Why didn't you phone me at once, as soon as you asked him, the minute that he accepted? Then, don't you see, I could have been getting ready!

TOM: You don't have to make any fuss.

AMANDA: Oh, Tom, Tom, Tom, of course I have to make a fuss! I want things nice, not sloppy! Not thrown together. I'll certainly have to do some fast thinking, won't I?

TOM: I don't see why you have to think at all.

AMANDA: You just don't know. We can't have a gentleman caller in a pig-sty! All my wedding silver has to be polished, the monogrammed table linen ought to be laundered! The windows have to be washed and fresh curtains put up. And how about clothes? We have to *wear* something, don't we?

TOM: Mother, this boy is no one to make a fuss over!

AMANDA: Do you realize he's the first young man we've introduced to your sister? It's terrible, dreadful, disgraceful the poor little sister has never received a single gentleman caller! Tom, come inside! (*She opens the screen door.*)

TOM: What for?

AMANDA: I want to ask you some things.

TOM: If you're going to make such a fuss, I'll call it off, I'll tell him not to come!

AMANDA: You certainly won't do anything of the kind. Nothing offends people worse than broken engagements. It simply means I'll have to work like a Turk! We won't be brilliant, but we will pass inspection. Come on inside. (TOM *follows, groaning.*) Sit down.

TOM: Any particular place you would like me to sit?

AMANDA: Thank heavens I've got that new sofa! I'm also making payments on a floor lamp I'll have sent out! And put the chintz covers on, they'll brighten things up! Of course I'd hoped to have these walls re-papered. . . . What is the young man's name?

TOM: His name is O'Connor.

AMANDA: That, of course, means fish—tomorrow is Friday! I'll have that salmon loaf—with Durkee's dressing! What does he do? He works at the warehouse?

TOM: Of course! How else would I—

AMANDA: Tom, he—doesn't drink?

TOM: Why do you ask me that?

AMANDA: Your father *did!*

TOM: Don't get started on that!

AMANDA: He *does* drink, then?

TOM: Not that I know of!

AMANDA: Make sure, be certain! The last thing I want for my daughter's a boy who drinks!

TOM: Aren't you being a little bit premature? Mr. O'Connor has not yet appeared on the scene!

AMANDA: But will tomorrow. To meet your sister, and what do I know about his character? Nothing! Old maids are better off than wives of drunkards!

TOM: Oh, my God!

AMANDA: Be still!

TOM (*leaning forward to whisper*): Lots of fellows meet girls whom they don't marry!

AMANDA: Oh, talk sensibly, Tom—and don't be sarcastic! (*She has gotten a hairbrush.*)

TOM: What are you doing?

AMANDA: I'm brushing that cow-lick down! What is this young man's position at the warehouse?

TOM (*submitting grimly to the brush and the interrogation*): This young man's position is that of a shipping clerk, Mother.

AMANDA: Sounds to me like a fairly responsible job, the sort of a job *you* would be in if you just had more *get-up*. What is his salary? Have you any idea?

TOM: I would judge it to be approximately eighty-five dollars a month.

AMANDA: Well—not princely, but—

TOM: Twenty more than I make.

AMANDA: Yes, how well I know! But for a family man, eighty-five dollars a month is not much more than you can just get by on. . . .

TOM: Yes, but Mr. O'Connor is not a family man.

AMANDA: He might be, mightn't he? Some time in the future?

TOM: I see. Plans and provisions.

AMANDA: You are the only young man that I know of who ignores the fact that the future becomes the present, the present the past, and the past turns into everlasting regret if you don't plan for it!

TOM: I will think that over and see what I can make of it.

AMANDA: Don't be supercilious with your mother! Tell me some more about this—what do you call him?

TOM: James D. O'Connor. The D. is for Delaney.

AMANDA: Irish on *both* sides! *Gracious!* And doesn't drink?

TOM: Shall I call him up and ask him right this minute?

AMANDA: The only way to find out about those things is to make discreet inquiries at the proper moment. When I was a girl in Blue Mountain and it was suspected that a young man drank, the girl whose attentions he had been receiving, if any girl *was*, would sometimes speak to the minister of his church, or rather her father would if her father was living, and sort of feel him out on the young man's character. That is the way such things are discreetly handled to keep a young woman from making a tragic mistake!

TOM: Then how did you happen to make a tragic mistake?

AMANDA: That innocent look of your father's had everyone fooled! He *smiled*—the world was *enchanted!* No girl can do worse than put herself at the mercy of a handsome appearance! I hope that Mr. O'Connor is not too good-looking.

TOM: No, he's not too good-looking. He's covered with freckles and hasn't too much of a nose.

AMANDA: He's not right-down homely, though?

TOM: Not right-down homely. Just medium homely, I'd say.

AMANDA: Character's what to look for in a man.

TOM: That's what I've always said, Mother.

AMANDA: You've never said anything of the kind and I suspect you would never give it a thought.

TOM: Don't be so suspicious of me.

AMANDA: At least I hope he's the type that's up and coming.

TOM: I think he really goes in for self-improvement.

AMANDA: What reason have you to think so?

TOM: He goes to night school.

AMANDA (*beaming*): Splendid! What does he do, I mean study?

TOM: Radio engineering and public speaking!

AMANDA: Then he has visions of being advanced in the world! Any young man who studies public speaking is aiming to have an executive job some day! And radio engineering? A thing for the future! Both of these facts are very illuminating. Those are the sort of things that a mother should know concerning any young man who comes to call on her daughter. Seriously or—not.

TOM: One little warning. He doesn't know about Laura. I didn't let on that we had dark ulterior motives. I just said, why don't you come and have dinner with us? He said okay and that was the whole conversation.

AMANDA: I bet it was! You're eloquent as an oyster. However, he'll know about Laura when he gets here. When he sees how lovely and sweet and pretty she is, he'll thank his lucky stars he was asked to dinner.

TOM: Mother, you mustn't expect too much of Laura.

AMANDA: What do you mean?

TOM: Laura seems all those things to you and me because she's ours and we love her. We don't even notice she's crippled any more.

AMANDA: Don't say crippled! You know that I never allow that word to be used!

TOM: But face facts, Mother. She is and—that's not all—

AMANDA: What do you mean "not all"?

TOM: Laura is very different from other girls.

AMANDA: I think the difference is all to her advantage.

TOM: Not quite all—in the eyes of others—strangers—she's terribly shy and lives in a world of her own and those things make her seem a little peculiar to people outside the house.

AMANDA: Don't say peculiar.

TOM: Face the facts. She is.

(*The dance-hall music changes to a tango that has a minor and somewhat ominous tone.*)

AMANDA: In what way is she peculiar—may I ask?

TOM (*gently*): She lives in a world of her own—a world of—little glass ornaments, Mother. . . . (*Gets up.* AMANDA *remains holding brush, looking at him, troubled.*) She plays old phonograph records and—that's about all—(*He glances at himself in the mirror and crosses to door.*)

AMANDA (*sharply*): Where are you going?

TOM: I'm going to the movies. (*out screen door*)

AMANDA: Not to the movies, every night to the movies! (*follows quickly to screen door*) I don't believe you always go to the movies! (*He is gone.* AMANDA *looks worriedly after him for a moment. Then vitality and optimism return and she turns from the door. Crossing to portieres.*) Laura! Laura! (LAURA *answers from kitchenette.*)

LAURA: Yes, Mother.

AMANDA: Let those dishes go and come in front! (LAURA *appears with dish towel Gaily.*) Laura, come here and make a wish on the moon!

(*Screen image: Moon.*)

LAURA (*entering*): Moon—moon?

AMANDA: A little silver slipper of a moon. Look over your left shoulder, Laura, and make a wish! (LAURA *looks faintly puzzled as if called out of sleep.* AMANDA *seizes her shoulders and turns her at an angle by the door.*) Now! Now, darling, *wish!*

LAURA: What shall I wish for, Mother?

AMANDA (*her voice trembling and her eyes suddenly filling with tears*): Happiness! Good fortune!

(*The violin rises and the stage dims out.*)

SCENE 6

(*Image: High school hero.*)

TOM: And so the following evening I brought Jim home to dinner. I had known Jim slightly in high school. In high school Jim was a hero. He had tremendous Irish good nature and vitality with the scrubbed and polished look of white chinaware. He seemed to move in a continual spot-light. He was a star in basketball, captain of the debating club, president of the senior class and the glee club and he sang the male lead in the annual light operas. He was always running or bounding, never just walking. He seemed always at the point of defeating the law of gravity. He was shooting with such velocity through his adolescence that you would logically expect him to arrive at nothing short of the White House by the time he was thirty. But Jim apparently ran into more interference after his graduation from Soldan. His speed had definitely slowed. Six years after he left high school he was holding a job that wasn't much better than mine.

(*Image: Clerk.*)

He was the only one at the warehouse with whom I was on friendly terms. I was valuable to him as someone who could remember his former glory, who had seen him win basketball games and the silver cup in debating. He knew of my secret practice of retiring to a cabinet of the wash-room to work on poems when business was slack in the warehouse. He called me Shakespeare. And while the other boys in the warehouse regarded me with suspicious hostility, Jim took a humorous attitude toward me. Gradually his attitude affected the others, their hostility wore off and they also began to smile at me as people smile at an oddly fashioned dog who trots across their path at some distance.

I knew that Jim and Laura had known each other at Soldan, and I had heard Laura speak admiringly of his voice. I didn't know if Jim remembered her or not. In high school Laura had been as unobtrusive as Jim had been astonishing. If he did remember Laura, it was not as my sister, for when I asked him to dinner, he grinned and said, "You know, Shakespeare, I never thought of you as having folks!" He was about to discover that I did. . . .

(*Light up stage.*)

(*Legend on screen: "The Accent of a Coming Foot."*)

Friday evening. It is about five o'clock of a late spring evening which comes "scattering poems in the sky."

A delicate lemony light is in the Wingfield apartment.

AMANDA *has worked like a Turk in preparation for the gentleman caller. The results are astonishing. The new floor lamp with its rose-silk shade is in place, a colored paper lantern conceals the broken light fixture in the ceiling, new billowing white curtains are at the windows, chintz covers are on chairs and sofa, a pair of new sofa pillows make their initial appearance.*

Open boxes and tissue paper are scattered on the floor.

LAURA *stands in the middle with lifted arms while* AMANDA *crouches before her, adjusting the hem of the new dress, devout and ritualistic. The dress is colored and designed by memory. The arrangement of* LAURA'S *hair is changed; it is softer and more becoming. A fragile, unearthly prettiness has come out in* LAURA: *she is like a piece of translucent glass touched by light, given a momentary radiance, not actual, not lasting.*

AMANDA (*impatiently*): Why are you trembling?

LAURA: Mother, you've made me so nervous!

AMANDA: How have I made you nervous?

LAURA: By all this fuss! You make it seem so important!

AMANDA: I don't understand you, Laura. You couldn't be satisfied with just sitting home, and yet whenever I try to arrange something for you, you seem to resist it.

She gets up.

Now take a look at yourself. No, wait! Wait just a moment—I have an idea!

LAURA: What is it now?

AMANDA *produces two powder puffs which she wraps in handkerchiefs and stuffs in* LAURA'S *bosom.*

LAURA: Mother, what are you doing?

AMANDA: They call them "Gay Deceivers"!

LAURA: I won't wear them!

AMANDA: You will!

LAURA: Why should I?

AMANDA: Because, to be painfully honest, your chest is flat.

LAURA: You make it seem like we were setting a trap.

AMANDA: All pretty girls are a trap, a pretty trap, and men expect them to be. (*Legend: "A Pretty Trap."*) Now look at yourself, young lady. This is the prettiest you will ever be! I've got to fix myself now! You're going to be surprised by your mother's appearance! (*She crosses through portieres, humming gaily.*)

LAURA *moves slowly to the long mirror and stares solemnly at herself.*

A wind blows the white curtains inward in a slow, graceful motion and with a faint, sorrowful sighing.

AMANDA (*off stage*): It isn't dark enough yet. (*She turns slowly before the mirror with a troubled look.*)

(*Legend on screen: "This Is My Sister: Celebrate Her with Strings!" Music.*)

AMANDA (*laughing, off*): I'm going to show you something. I'm going to make a spectacular appearance!

LAURA: What is it, Mother?

AMANDA: Possess your soul in patience—you will see! Something I've resurrected from that old trunk! Styles haven't changed so terribly much after all. . . . (*She parts the portieres.*) Now just look at your mother! (*She wears a girlish frock of yellowed voile with a blue silk sash. She carries a bunch of jonquils—the legend of her youth is nearly revived. Feverishly.*) This is the dress in which I led the cotillion. Won the cakewalk twice at Sunset Hill, wore one spring to the Governor's ball in Jackson! See how I sashayed around the ballroom, Laura? (*She raises her skirt and does a mincing step around the room.*) I wore it on Sundays for my gentlemen callers! I had it on the day I met your father—I had malaria fever all that spring. The change of climate from East Tennessee to the Delta—weakened resistance—I had a little temperature all the time—not enough to be serious—just enough to make me restless and giddy!—Invitations poured in—parties all over the Delta!—"Stay in bed," said Mother, "you have fever!"—but I just wouldn't.—I took quinine but kept on going, going!—Evenings, dances!—Afternoons, long, long rides! Picnics—lovely!—So lovely, that country in May.—All lacy with dogwood, literally flooded with jonquils!—That was the spring I had the craze for jonquils. Jonquils became an absolute obsession. Mother said, "Honey, there's no more room for jonquils." And still I kept on bringing in more jonquils. Whenever, wherever I saw them, I'd say, "Stop! Stop! I see jonquils!" I made the young men help me gather the jonquils! It was a joke, Amanda and her jonquils! Finally there were no more vases to hold them, every available space was filled with jonquils. No vases to hold them? All right, I'll hold them myself! And then I—(*She stops in front of the picture. Music.*) met your father! Malaria fever and jonquils and then—this—boy. . . . (*She switches on the rose-colored lamp.*) I hope they get here before it starts to rain. (*She crosses upstage and places the jonquils in bowl on table.*) I gave your brother a little extra change so he and Mr. O'Connor could take the service car home.

LAURA (*with altered look*): What did you say his name was?

AMANDA: O'Connor.

LAURA: What is his first name?

AMANDA: I don't remember, Oh, yes, I do. It was—Jim!

LAURA *sways slightly and catches hold of a chair.*

(*Legend on screen. "Not Jim!"*)

LAURA (*faintly*): Not—Jim!

AMANDA: Yes, that was it, it was Jim! I've never known a Jim that wasn't nice!

(*Music: Ominous.*)

LAURA: Are you sure his name is Jim O'Connor?

AMANDA: Yes. Why?

LAURA: Is he the one that Tom used to know in high school?

AMANDA: He didn't say so. I think he just got to know him at the warehouse.

LAURA: There was a Jim O'Connor we both knew in high school—(*then, with effort*) If that is the one that Tom is bringing to dinner—you'll have to excuse me, I won't come to the table.

AMANDA: What sort of nonsense is this?

LAURA: You asked me once if I'd ever liked a boy. Don't you remember I showed you this boy's picture?

AMANDA: You mean the boy you showed me in the year book?

LAURA: Yes, that boy.

AMANDA: Laura, Laura, were you in love with that boy?

LAURA: I don't know, Mother. All I know is I couldn't sit at the table if it was him!

AMANDA: It won't be him! It isn't the least bit likely. But whether it is or not, you will come to the table. You will not be excused.

LAURA: I'll have to be, Mother.

AMANDA: I don't intend to humor your silliness, Laura. I've had too much from you and your brother, both! So just sit down and compose yourself till they come. Tom has forgotten his key so you'll have to let them in, when they arrive.

LAURA (*panicky*): Oh, Mother—*you* answer the door!

AMANDA (*lightly*): I'll be in the kitchen—busy!

LAURA: Oh, Mother, please answer the door, don't make me do it!

AMANDA (*crossing into kitchenette*): I've got to fix the dressing for the salmon. Fuss, fuss—silliness!—over a gentleman caller!

Door swings shut. LAURA *is left alone.*

(*Legend: "Terror!"*)

She utters a low moan and turns off the lamp—sits stiffly on the edge of the sofa, knotting her fingers together.

(*Legend on screen: "The Opening of a Door!"*)

TOM *and* JIM *appear on the fire-escape steps and climb to landing. Hearing their approach,* LAURA *rises with a panicky gesture. She retreats to the portieres.*

The doorbell. LAURA *catches her breath and touches her throat. Low drums.*

AMANDA (*calling*): Laura. sweetheart! The door!

LAURA *stares at it without moving.*

JIM: I think we just beat the rain.

TOM: Uh-huh. (*He rings again, nervously.* JIM *whistles and fishes for a cigarette.*)

AMANDA (*very, very gaily*): Laura, that is your brother and Mr. O'Connor! Will you let them in, darling?

LAURA *crosses toward kitchenette door.*

LAURA (*breathlessly*): Mother—you go to the door!

AMANDA *steps out of kitchenette and stares furiously at* LAURA. *She points imperiously at the door.*

LAURA: Please, please!

AMANDA (*in a fierce whisper*): What is the matter with you, you silly thing?

LAURA (*desperately*): Please, you answer it, *please!*

AMANDA: I told you I wasn't going to humor you, Laura. Why have you chosen this moment to lose your mind?

LAURA: Please, please, please, you go!

AMANDA: You'll have to go to the door because I can't!

LAURA (*despairingly*): I can't either!

AMANDA: *Why?*

LAURA: I'm *sick!*

AMANDA: I'm sick, too—of your nonsense! Why can't you and your brother be normal people? Fantastic whims and behavior! (TOM *gives a long ring.*) Preposterous goings on! Can you give me one reason—(*calls out lyrically*) COMING! JUST ONE SECOND!—why you should be afraid to open a door? Now you answer it, Laura!

LAURA: Oh, oh, oh . . . (*She returns through the portieres. Darts to the victrola and winds it frantically and turns it on.*)

AMANDA: Laura Wingfield, you march right to that door!

LAURA: Yes—yes. Mother!

A faraway, scratchy rendition of "Dardanella" softens the air and gives her strength to move through it. She slips to the door and draws it cautiously open.

TOM *enters with the caller,* JIM O'CONNOR.

TOM: Laura, this is Jim. Jim, this is my sister, Laura.

JIM (*stepping inside*): I didn't know that Shakespeare had a sister!

LAURA (*retreating stiff and trembling from the door*): How—how do you do?

JIM (*heartily extending his hand*): Okay!

LAURA *touches it hesitantly with hers.*

JIM: Your hand's *cold,* Laura!

LAURA: Yes, well—I've been playing the victrola. . . .

JIM: Must have been playing classical music on it! You ought to play a little hot swing music to warm you up!

LAURA: Excuse me—I haven't finished playing the victrola. . . . (*She turns awkwardly and hurries into the front room. She pauses a second by the victrola. Then catches her breath and darts through the portieres like a frightened deer.*)

JIM (*grinning*): What was the matter?

TOM: Oh—with Laura? Laura is—terribly shy.

JIM: Shy, huh? It's unusual to meet a shy girl nowadays. I don't believe you ever mentioned you had a sister.

TOM: Well, now you know. I have one. Here is the *Post Dispatch.* You want a piece of it?

JIM: Uh-huh.

TOM: What piece? The comics?

JIM: Sports! (*glances at it*) Ole Dizzy Dean is on his bad behavior.

TOM (*disinterest*): Yeah? (*lights cigarette and crosses back to fire-escape door*)

JIM: Where are *you* going?

TOM: I'm going out on the terrace.

JIM (*goes after him*): You know, Shakespeare—I'm going to sell you a bill of goods!

TOM: What goods?

JIM: A course I'm taking.

TOM: Huh?

JIM: In public speaking! You and me, we're not the warehouse type.

TOM: Thanks—that's good news. But what has public speaking got to do with it?

JIM: It fits you for—executive positions!

TOM: Awww.

JIM: I tell you it's done a helluva lot for me.

(*Image: Executive at desk.*)

TOM: In what respect?

JIM: In every! Ask yourself what is the difference between you an' me and men in the office down front? Brains?—No!—Ability?—No! Then what? Just one little thing—

TOM: What is that one little thing?

JIM: Primarily it amounts to—social poise! Being able to square up to people and hold your own on any social level!

AMANDA (*off stage*): Tom?

TOM: Yes, Mother?

AMANDA: Is that you and Mr. O'Connor?

TOM: Yes, Mother.

AMANDA: Well, you just make yourselves comfortable in there.

TOM: Yes, Mother.

AMANDA: Ask Mr. O'Connor if he would like to wash his hands.

JIM: Aw, no—no—thank you—I took care of that at the warehouse. Tom—

TOM: Yes?

JIM: Mr. Mendoza was speaking to me about you.

TOM: Favorably?

JIM: What do you think?

TOM: Well—

JIM: You're going to be out of a job if you don't wake up.

TOM: I am waking up—

JIM: You show no signs.

TOM: The signs are interior.

(*Image on screen: The sailing vessel with Jolly Roger again.*)

TOM: I'm planning to change. (*He leans over the rail speaking with quiet exhilaration. The incandescent marquees and signs of the first-run movie houses light his face from across the alley. He looks like a voyager.*) I'm right at the point of committing myself to a future that doesn't include the warehouse and Mr. Mendoza or even a night-school course in public speaking.

JIM: What are you gassing about?

TOM: I'm tired of the movies.

JIM: Movies!

TOM: Yes, movies! Look at them—(*a wave toward the marvels of Grand Avenue*) All of those glamorous people—having adventures—hogging it all, gobbling the whole thing up! You know what happens? People go to the *movies* instead of *moving!* Hollywood characters are supposed to have all the adventures for everybody in America, while everybody in America sits in a dark room and watches them have them! Yes, until there's a war. That's when adventure becomes available to the masses! *Everyone's* dish, not only Gable's! Then the people in the dark room come out of the dark room to have some adventures themselves—Goody, goody!—It's our turn now, to go to the South Sea Island—to make a safari—to be exotic, far-off!—But I'm not patient. I don't want to wait till then. I'm tired of the *movies* and I am *about* to *move!*

JIM (*incredulously*): Move?

TOM: Yes.

JIM: When?

TOM: Soon!

JIM: Where? Where?

(*Theme three music seems to answer to question, while* TOM *thinks it over. He searches among his pockets.*)

TOM: I'm starting to boil inside. I know I seem dreamy, but inside—well, I'm boiling!—Whenever I pick up a shoe, I shudder a little thinking how short life is and what I am doing!—Whatever that means, I know it doesn't mean shoes—except as something to wear on a traveler's feet! (*finds paper*) Look—

JIM: What?

TOM: I'm a member.

JIM (*reading*): The Union of Merchant Seamen.

TOM: I paid my dues this month, instead of the light bill.

JIM: You will regret it when they turn the lights off.

TOM: I won't be here.

JIM: How about your mother?

TOM: I'm like my father. The bastard son of a bastard! See how he grins? And he's been absent going on sixteen years!

JIM: You're just talking, you drip. How does your mother feel about it?

TOM: Shhh!—Here comes Mother! Mother is not acquainted with my plans!

AMANDA (*enters portieres*): Where are you all?

TOM: On the terrace, Mother.

They start inside. She advances to them. TOM *is distinctly shocked at her appearance. Even* JIM *blinks a little. He is making his first contact with girlish Southern vivacity and in spite of the night-school course in public speaking is somewhat thrown off the beam by the unexpected outlay of social charm.*

Certain responses are attempted by JIM *but are swept aside by* AMANDA'S *gay laughter and chatter.* TOM *is embarrassed but after the first shock* JIM *reacts very warmly. Grins and chuckles, is altogether won over.*

(*Image:* AMANDA *as a girl.*)

AMANDA (*coyly smiling, shaking her girlish ringlets*): Well, well, well, so this is Mr. O'Connor. Introductions entirely unnecessary. I've heard so much about you from my boy. I finally said to him, Tom—good gracious!—why don't you bring this paragon to supper? I'd like to meet this nice young man at the warehouse!—Instead of just hearing him sing your praises so much! I don't know why my son is so stand-offish—that's not Southern behavior! Let's sit down and—I think we could stand a little more air in here! Tom, leave the door open. I felt a nice fresh breeze a moment ago. Where has it gone to? Mmm, so warm already! And not quite summer, even. We're going to burn up when summer really gets started. However, we're having—we're having a very light supper. I think light things are better fo' this time of year. The same as light clothes are. Light clothes an' light food are what warm weather calls fo'. You know our blood gets so thick during th' winter—it takes a while fo' us to *adjust* ou'selves!—when the season changes. . . . It's come so quick this year. I wasn't prepared. All of a sudden—heavens! Already summer!—I ran to the trunk an' pulled out this light dress—Terribly old! Historical almost! But feels so good—so good an' co-ol, y' know. . . .

TOM: Mother—

AMANDA: Yes, honey?

TOM: How about—supper?

AMANDA: Honey, you go ask Sister if supper is ready! You know that Sister is in full charge of supper! Tell her you hungry boys are waiting for it. (*to* JIM) Have you met Laura?

JIM: She—

AMANDA: Let you in? Oh, good, you've met already! It's rare for a girl as sweet an' pretty as Laura to be domestic! But Laura is, thank heavens, not only pretty but also very domestic. I'm not at all. I never was a bit. I never could make a thing but angel-food cake. Well, in the South we had so many servants. Gone, gone, gone. All vestige of gracious living! Gone completely! I wasn't prepared for what the future brought me. All of my gentlemen callers were sons of planters and so of course I assumed that I would be married to one and raise my family on a large piece of land with plenty of servants. But man proposes—and woman accepts the proposal!—To vary that old, old saying a little bit—I married no planter! I married a man who worked for the telephone company!—That gallantly smiling gentleman over there! (*points to the picture*) A telephone man who—fell in love with long-distance!—Now he travels and I don't even know where!—But what am I going on for about my—tribulations? Tell me yours—I hope you don't have any! Tom?

TOM (*returning*): Yes, Mother?

AMANDA: Is supper nearly ready?

TOM: It looks to me like supper is on the table.

AMANDA: Let me look—(*She rises prettily and looks through portieres.*) Oh, lovely!—But where is Sister?

TOM: Laura is not feeling well and she says that she thinks she'd better not come to the table.

AMANDA: What?—Nonsense—Laura? Oh, Laura!

LAURA (*off stage, faintly*): Yes, Mother.

AMANDA: You really must come to the table. We won't be seated until you come to the table! Come in, Mr. O'Connor. You sit over there, and I'll—Laura?

Laura Wingfield! You're keeping us waiting, honey! We can't say grace until you come to the table!

The back door is pushed weakly open and LAURA *comes in. She is obviously quite faint, her lips trembling, her eyes wide and staring. She moves unsteadily toward the table.*

(*Legend: "Terror!"*)

Outside a summer storm is coming abruptly. The white curtains billou inward at the windows and there is a sorrowful murmur and deep blue dusk.

LAURA *suddenly stumbles—she catches at a chair with a faint moan.*

TOM: Laura!

AMANDA: Laura! (*There is a clap of thunder.*) (*Legend: "Ah!"*) (*despairingly*) Why, Laura, you *are* sick, darling! Tom, help your sister into the living room, dear! Sit in the living room, Laura—rest on the sofa. Well! (*to the gentleman caller*) Standing over the hot stove made her ill!—I told her that it was just too warm this evening, but—(TOM *comes back in.* LAURA *is on the sofa.*) Is Laura all right now?

TOM: Yes.

AMANDA: What *is* that? Rain? A nice cool rain has come up! (*She gives the gentleman caller a frightened look.*) I think we may—have grace—now . . . (TOM *looks at her stupidly.*) Tom, honey—you say grace!

TOM: Oh . . . "For these and all thy mercies—" (*They bow their heads,* AMANDA *stealing a nervous glance at* JIM. *In the living room* LAURA, *stretched on the sofa, clenches her hand to her lips, to hold back a shuddering sob.*) God's Holy Name be praised—

(*The scene dims out.*)

SCENE 7

A SOUVENIR

Half an hour later. Dinner is just being finished in the upstage area which is concealed by the drawn portieres.

As the curtain rises LAURA *is still huddled upon the sofa, her feet drawn under her, her head resting on a pale blue pillow, her eyes wide and mysteriously watchful. The new floor lamp with its shade of rose-colored silk gives a soft, becoming light to her face, bringing out the fragile, unearthly prettiness which usually escapes attention. There is a steady murmur of rain, but it is slackening and stops soon after the scene begins; the air outside becomes pale and luminous as the moon breaks out.*

A moment after the curtain rises, the lights in both rooms flicker and go out.

JIM: Hey, there, Mr. Light Bulb!

AMANDA *laughs nervously.*

(*Legend: "Suspension of a Public Service."*)

AMANDA: Where was Moses when the lights went out? Ha-ha. Do you know the answer to that one, Mr. O'Connor?

JIM: No, Ma'am, what's the answer?

AMANDA: In the dark! (JIM *laughs appreciatively.*) Everybody sit still. I'll light the candles. Isn't it lucky we have them on the table? Where's a match? Which of you gentleman can provide a match?

JIM: Here.

AMANDA: Thank you, sir.

JIM: Not at all, Ma'am!

AMANDA: I guess the fuse has burnt out. Mr. O'Connor, can you tell a burntout fuse? I know I can't and Tom is a total loss when it comes to mechanics. (*Sound: Getting up: Voices recede a little to kitchenette.*) Oh, be careful you don't bump into something. We don't want our gentleman caller to break his neck. Now wouldn't that be a fine howdy-do?

JIM: Ha-ha! Where is the fuse-box?

AMANDA: Right here next to the stove. Can you see anything?

JIM: Just a minute.

AMANDA: Isn't electricity a mysterious thing? Wasn't it Benjamin Franklin who tied a key to a kite? We live in such a mysterious universe, don't we? Some people say that science clears up all the mysteries for us. In my opinion it only creates more! Have you found it yet?

JIM: No, Ma'am. All these fuses look okay to me.

AMANDA: Tom!

TOM: Yes, Mother?

AMANDA: That light bill I gave you several days ago. The one I told you we got the notices about?

(*Legend: "Ha!"*)

TOM: Oh.—Yeah.

AMANDA: You didn't neglect to pay it by any chance?

TOM: Why, I—

AMANDA: Didn't! I might have known it!

JIM: Shakespeare probably wrote a poem on that light bill, Mrs. Wingfield.

AMANDA: I might have known better than to trust him with it! There's such a high price for negligence in this world!

JIM: Maybe the poem will win a ten-dollar prize.

AMANDA: We'll just have to spend the remainder of the evening in the nineteenth century, before Mr. Edison made the Mazda lamp!

JIM: Candlelight is my favorite kind of light.

AMANDA: That shows you're romantic! But that's no excuse for Tom. Well, we got through dinner. Very considerate of them to let us get through dinner before they plunged us into everlasting darkness, wasn't it, Mr. O'Connor?

JIM: Ha-ha!

AMANDA: Tom, as a penalty for your carelessness you can help me with the dishes.

JIM: Let me give you a hand.

AMANDA: Indeed you will not!

JIM: I ought to be good for something.

AMANDA: Good for something? (*Her tone is rhapsodic.*) *You?* Why, Mr. O'Connor, nobody, *nobody's* given me this much entertainment in years—as you have!

JIM: Aw, now, Mrs. Wingfield!

AMANDA: I'm not exaggerating, not one bit! But Sister is all by her lonesome. You go keep her company in the parlor! I'll give you this lovely old candelabrum that used to be on the altar at the church of the Heavenly Rest. It was melted a little out of shape when the church burnt down. Lightning struck it one spring. Gypsy Jones was holding a revival at the time and he intimated that the church was destroyed because the Episcopalians gave card parties.

JIM: Ha-ha.

AMANDA: And how about you coaxing Sister to drink a little wine? I think it would be good for her! Can you carry both at once?

JIM: Sure. I'm Superman!

AMANDA: Now, Thomas, get into this apron!

The door of kitchenette swings closed on AMANDA'S *gay laughter, the flickering light approaches the portieres.*

LAURA *sits up nervously as he enters. Her speech at first is low and breathless from the almost intolerable strain of being alone with a stranger.*

(*The legend: "I Don't Suppose You Remember Me at All!"*)

In her first speeches in this scene, before JIM'S *warmth overcomes her paralyzing shyness,* LAURA'S *voice is thin and breathless as though she has just run up a steep flight of stairs.*

JIM'S *attitude is gently humorous. In playing this scene it should be stressed that while the incident is apparently unimportant, it is to* LAURA *the climax of her secret life.*

JIM: Hello, there, Laura.

LAURA (*faintly*): Hello. (*She clears her throat.*)

JIM: How are you feeling now? Better?

LAURA: Yes. Yes, thank you.

JIM: This is for you. A little dandelion wine. (*He extends it toward her with extravagant gallantry.*)

LAURA: Thank you.

JIM: Drink it—but don't get drunk! (*He laughs heartily.* LAURA *takes the glass uncertainly; laughs shyly.*) Where shall I set the candles?

LAURA: Oh—oh, anywhere . . .

JIM: How about here on the floor? Any objections?

LAURA: No.

JIM: I'll spread a newspaper under to catch the drippings. I like to sit on the floor. Mind if I do?

LAURA: Oh, no.

JIM: Give me a pillow?

LAURA: What?

JIM: A pillow!

LAURA: Oh . . . (*hands him one quickly*)

JIM: How about you? Don't you like to sit on the floor?

LAURA: Oh—yes.

JIM: Why don't you, then?

LAURA: I—will.

JIM: Take a pillow! (LAURA *does. Sits on the other side of the candelabrum.* JIM *crosses his legs and smiles engagingly at her.*) I can't hardly see you sitting way over there.

LAURA: I can—see you.

JIM: I know, but that's not fair, I'm in the limelight. (LAURA *moves her pillow closer.*) Good! Now I can see you! Comfortable?

LAURA: Yes.

JIM: So am I. Comfortable as a cow! Will you have some gum?

LAURA: No, thank you.

JIM: I think that I will indulge, with your permission. (*musingly unwraps it and holds it up*) Think of the fortune made by the guy that invented the first piece of chewing gum. Amazing, huh? The Wrigley Building is one of the sights of Chicago—I saw it summer before last when I went up to the Century of Progress. Did you take in the Century of Progress?

LAURA: No, I didn't.

JIM: Well, it was quite a wonderful exposition. What impressed me most was the Hall of Science. Gives you an idea of what the future will be in America, even more wonderful than the present time is! (*Pause. Smiling at her.*) Your brother tells me you're shy. Is that right, Laura?

LAURA: I—don't know.

JIM: I judge you to be an old-fashioned type of girl. Well, I think that's a pretty good type to be. Hope you don't think I'm being too personal—do you?

LAURA (*hastily, out of embarrassment*): I believe I *will* take a piece of gum, if you—don't mind. (*clearing her throat*) Mr. O'Connor, have you—kept up with your singing?

JIM: Singing? Me?

LAURA: Yes. I remember what a beautiful voice you had.

JIM: When did you hear me sing?

(*Voice off stage in the pause.*)

VOICE (*off stage*): O blow, ye winds, heigh-ho,
A-roving I will go!
I'm off to my love
With a boxing glove—
Ten thousand miles away!

JIM: You say you've heard me sing?

LAURA: Oh, yes! Yes, very often . . . I—don't suppose—you remember me—at all?

JIM (*smiling doubtfully*): You know I have an idea I've seen you before. I had that idea soon as you opened the door. It seemed almost like I was about to remember your name. But the name that I started to call you—wasn't a name! And so I stopped myself before I said it.

LAURA: Wasn't it—Blue Roses?

JIM (*springs up, grinning*): Blue Roses!—My gosh, yes—Blue Roses! That's what I had on my tongue when you opened the door! Isn't it funny what tricks your memory plays? I didn't connect you with high school somehow or other. But that's where it was; it was high school. I didn't even know you were Shakespeare's sister! Gosh, I'm sorry.

LAURA: I didn't expect you to. You—barely knew me!

JIM: But we did have a speaking acquaintance, huh?

LAURA: Yes, we—spoke to each other.

JIM: When did you recognize me?

LAURA: Oh, right away!

JIM: Soon as I came in the door?

LAURA: When I heard your name I thought it was probably you. I knew that Tom used to know you a little in high school. So when you came in the door—Well, then I was—sure.

JIM: Why didn't you *say* something, then?

Laura (*breathlessly*): I didn't know what to say, I was—too surprised!
Jim: For goodness' sakes! You know, this sure is funny!
Laura: Yes! Yes, isn't it, though . . .
Jim: Didn't we have a class in something together?
Laura: Yes, we did.
Jim: What class was that?
Laura: It was—singing—Chorus!
Jim: Aw.
Laura: I sat across the aisle from you in the Aud.
Jim: Aw!
Laura: Mondays, Wednesdays and Fridays.
Jim: Now I remember—you always came in late.
Laura: Yes, it was so hard for me, getting upstairs. I had that brace on my leg—it clumped so loud!
Jim: I never heard any clumping!
Laura (*wincing at the recollection*): To me it sounded like—thunder!
Jim: Well, well, well, I never even noticed.
Laura: And everybody was seated before I came in. I had to walk in front of all those people. My seat was in the back row. I had to go clumping all the way up the aisle with everyone watching!
Jim: You shouldn't have been self-conscious.
Laura: I know, but I was. It was always such a relief when the singing started.
Jim: Aw, yes, I've placed you now! I used to call you Blue Roses. How was it that I got started calling you that?
Laura: I was out of school a little while with pleurosis. When I came back you asked me what was the matter. I said I had pleurosis—you thought I said Blue Roses. That's what you always called me after that!
Jim: I hope you didn't mind.
Laura: Oh, no—I liked it. You see, I wasn't acquainted with many—people. . . .
Jim: As I remember you sort of stuck by yourself.
Laura: I—I—never have had much luck at—making friends.
Jim: I don't see why you wouldn't.
Laura: Well, I—started out badly.
Jim: You mean being—
Laura: Yes, it sort of—stood between me—
Jim: You shouldn't have let it!
Laura: I know, but it did, and—
Jim: You were shy with people!
Laura: I tried not to be but never could—
Jim: Overcome it?
Laura: No, I—I never could!
Jim: I guess being shy is something you have to work out of kind of gradually.
Laura (*sorrowfully*): Yes—I guess it—
Jim: Takes time!
Laura: Yes—
Jim: People are not so dreadful when you know them. That's what you have to remember! And everybody has problems, not just you, but practically everybody has got some problems. You think of yourself as having the only problems, as being the only one who is disappointed. But just look around you and you will

see lots of people as disappointed as you are. For instance, I hoped when I was going to high school that I would be further along at this time, six years later, than I am now—You remember that wonderful write-up I had in *The Torch?*

LAURA: Yes! (*She rises and crosses to table.*)

JIM: It said I was bound to succeed in anything I went into! (LAURA *returns with the annual.*) Holy Jeez! *The Torch!* (*He accepts it reverently. They smile across it with mutual wonder.* LAURA *crouches beside him and they begin to turn through it.* LAURA'S *shyness is dissolving in his warmth.*)

LAURA: Here you are in *The Pirates of Penzance!*

JIM (*wistfully*): I sang the baritone lead in that operetta.

LAURA (*raptly*): So—*beautifully!*

JIM (*protesting*): Aw—

LAURA: Yes, yes—beautifully—beautifully!

JIM: You heard me?

LAURA: All three times!

JIM: No!

LAURA: Yes!

JIM: All three performances?

LAURA (*looking down*): Yes.

JIM: Why?

LAURA: I—wanted to ask you to—autograph my program.

JIM: Why didn't you ask me to?

LAURA: You were always surrounded by your own friends so much that I never had a chance to.

JIM: You should have just—

LAURA: Well, I—thought you might think I was—

JIM: Thought I might think you was—what?

LAURA: Oh—

JIM (*with reflective relish*): I was beleaguered by females in those days.

LAURA: You were terribly popular!

JIM: Yeah—

LAURA: You had such a—friendly way—

JIM: I was spoiled in high school.

LAURA: Everybody—liked you!

JIM: Including you?

LAURA: I—yes, I—I did, too—(*She gently closes the book in her lap.*)

JIM: Well, well, well!—Give me that program, Laura. (*She hands it to him. He signs it with a flourish.*) There you are—better late than never!

LAURA: Oh, I—what a—surprise!

JIM: My signature isn't worth very much right now. But some day—maybe—it will increase in value! Being disappointed is one thing and being discouraged is something else. I am disappointed but I am not discouraged. I'm twenty-three years old. How old are you?

LAURA: I'll be twenty-four in June.

JIM: That's not old age!

LAURA: No, but—

JIM: You finished high school?

LAURA (*with difficulty*): I didn't go back.

JIM: You mean you dropped out?

LAURA: I made bad grades in my final examinations. (*She rises and replaces the book and the program. Her voice strained.*) How is—Emily Meisenbach getting along?

JIM: Oh, that kraut-head!

LAURA: Why do you call her that?

JIM: That's what she was.

LAURA: You're not still—going with her?

JIM: I never see her.

LAURA: It said in the Personal Section that you were—engaged!

JIM: I know, but I wasn't impressed by that—propaganda!

LAURA: It wasn't—the truth?

JIM: Only in Emily's optimistic opinion!

LAURA: Oh—

(*Legend: "What Have You Done Since High School?"*)

JIM *lights a cigarette and leans indolently back on his elbows smiling at* LAURA *with a warmth and charm which lights her inwardly with altar candles. She remains by the table and turns in her hands a piece of glass to cover her tumult.*

JIM (*after several reflective puffs on a cigarette*): What have you done since high school? (*She seems not to hear him.*) Huh? (LAURA *looks up.*) I said what have you done since high school, Laura?

LAURA: Nothing much.

JIM: You must have been doing something these six long years.

LAURA: Yes.

JIM: Well, then, such as what?

LAURA: I took a business course at business college—

JIM: How did that work out?

LAURA: Well, not very—well—I had to drop out, it gave me—indigestion—

JIM *laughs gently.*

JIM: What are you doing now?

LAURA: I don't do anything—much. Oh, please don't think I sit around doing nothing! My glass collection takes up a good deal of time. Glass is something you have to take good care of.

JIM: What did you say—about glass?

LAURA: Collection I said—I have one—(*She clears her throat and turns away again, acutely shy.*)

JIM (*abruptly*): You know what I judge to be the trouble with you? Inferiority complex! Know what that is? That's what they call it when someone low-rates himself! I understand it because I had it, too. Although my case was not so aggravated as yours seems to be. I had it until I took up public speaking, developed my voice, and learned that I had an aptitude for science. Before that time I never thought of myself as being outstanding in any way whatsoever! Now I've never made a regular study of it, but I have a friend who says I can analyze people better than doctors that make a profession of it. I don't claim that to be necessarily true, but I can sure guess a person's psychology, Laura! (*takes out his gum*) Excuse me, Laura. I always take it out when the flavor is gone. I'll use this scrap of paper to wrap it in. I know how it is to get it stuck on a shoe. Yep—that's what I judge to be your principal trouble. A lack of confidence in yourself as a person. You don't have the proper amount of faith in yourself. I'm basing that fact on a number of your remarks and also on certain observations I've made. For instance that clumping you thought was so awful in high school. You say that you even dreaded to walk into class. You see what you did? You dropped out of school, you gave up an education because of a clump, which as far as I know was practically nonexistent! A little physical defect is what you have. Hardly noticeable even! Magnified thousands of times by imagination! You know what my strong advice to you is? Think of yourself as *superior* in some way!

LAURA: In what way would I think?

JIM: Why, man alive, Laura! Just look about you a little. What do you see? A world full of common people! All of 'em born and all of 'em going to die! Which of them has one-tenth of your good points! Or mine! Or anyone else's, as far as that goes—Gosh! Everybody excels in some one thing. Some in many! (*unconsciously glances at himself in the mirror*) All you've got to do is discover in *what*! Take me, for instance. (*He adjusts his tie at the mirror.*) My interest happens to lie in electrodynamics. I'm taking a course in radio engineering at night school, Laura, on top of a fairly responsible job at the warehouse. I'm taking that course and studying public speaking.

LAURA: Ohhhh.

JIM: Because I believe in the future of television! (*turning back to her*) I wish to be ready to go up right along with it. Therefore I'm planning to get in on the ground floor. In fact I've already made the right connections and all that remains is for the industry itself to get under way! Full steam—(*His eyes are starry.*) *Knowledge*—ZZZZZP! *Money*—ZZZZZZP!—*Power!* That's the cycle democracy is built on! (*His attitude is convincingly dynamic.* LAURA *stares at him, even her shyness eclipsed in her absolute wonder. He suddenly grins.*) I guess you think I think a lot of myself!

LAURA: No—o-o-o, I—

JIM: Now how about you? Isn't there something you take more interest in than anything else?

LAURA: Well, I do—as I said—have my—glass collection—

A peal of girlish laughter from the kitchen.

JIM: I'm not right sure I know what you're talking about. What kind of glass is it?

LAURA: Little articles of it, they're ornaments mostly! Most of them are little animals made out of glass, the tiniest little animals in the world. Mother calls them a glass menagerie! Here's an example of one, if you'd like to see it! This one is one of the oldest. It's nearly thirteen. (*Music: "The Glass Menagerie."*) (*He stretches out his hand.*) Oh, be careful—if you breathe, it breaks!

JIM: I'd better not take it. I'm pretty clumsy with things.

LAURA: Go on. I trust you with him! (*places it in his palm*) There now—you're holding him gently! Hold him over the light, he loves the light! You see how the light shines through him?

JIM: It sure does shine!

LAURA: I shouldn't be partial, but he is my favorite one.

JIM: What kind of a thing is this one supposed to be?

LAURA: Haven't you noticed the single horn on his forehead?

JIM: A unicorn. huh?

LAURA: Mmm-hmmm!

JIM: Unicorns, aren't they extinct in the modern world?

LAURA: I know!

JIM: Poor little fellow, he must feel sort of lonesome.

LAURA (*smiling*): Well, if he does he doesn't complain about it. He stays on a shelf with some horses that don't have horns and all of them seem to get along nicely together.

JIM: How do you know?

LAURA (*lightly*): I haven't heard any arguments among them!

JIM (*grinning*): No arguments, huh? Well, that's a pretty good sign! Where shall I set him?

LAURA: Put him on the table. They all like a change of scenery once in a while!

JIM (*stretching*): Well, well, well, well—Look how big my shadow is when I stretch!

LAURA: Oh, oh, yes—it stretches across the ceiling!

JIM (*crossing to door*): I think it's stopped raining. (*opens fire-escape door*) Where does the music come from?

LAURA: From the Paradise Dance Hall across the alley.

JIM: How about cutting the rug a little, Miss Wingfield?

LAURA: Oh, I—

JIM: Or is your program filled up? Let me have a look at it. (*grasps imaginary card*) Why, every dance is taken! I'll just have to scratch some out. (*Waltz music: "La Colondrina."*) Ahhh, a waltz! (*He executes some sweeping turns by himself then holds his arms toward* LAURA.)

LAURA (*breathlessly*): I—can't dance!

JIM: There you go, that inferiority stuff!

LAURA: I've never danced in my life!

JIM: Come on, try!

LAURA: Oh, but I'd step on you!

JIM: I'm not made out of glass.

LAURA: How—how—how do we start?

JIM: Just leave it to me. You hold your arms out a little.

LAURA: Like this?

JIM: A little bit higher. Right. Now don't tighten up, that's the main thing about it—relax.

LAURA (*laughing breathlessly*): It's hard not to.

JIM: Okay.

LAURA: I'm afraid you can't budge me.

JIM: What do you bet I can't? (*He swings her into motion*).

LAURA: Goodness, yes, you can!

JIM: Let yourself go, now, Laura, just let yourself go.

LAURA: I'm—

JIM: Come on!

LAURA: Trying!

JIM: Not so stiff—Easy does it!

LAURA: I know but I'm—

JIM: Loosen th' backbone! There now, that's a lot better.

LAURA: Am I?

JIM: Lots, lots better! (*He moves her about the room in a clumsy waltz.*)

LAURA: Oh, my!

JIM: Ha-ha!

JIM: I hope that it wasn't the little glass horse with the horn!
LAURA: Yes.
JIM: Aw, aw, aw. Is it broken?
LAURA: Now it is just like all the other horses.
JIM: It's lost its—
LAURA: Horn! It doesn't matter. Maybe it's a blessing in disguise.
JIM: You'll never forgive me. I bet that was your favorite piece of glass.
LAURA: I don't have favorites much. It's no tragedy, Freckles. Glass breaks so easily. No matter how careful you are. The traffic jars the shelves and things fall off them.
JIM: Still I'm awfully sorry that I was the cause.
LAURA (*smiling*): I'll just imagine he had an operation. The horn was removed to make him feel less—freakish! (*They both laugh.*) Now he will feel more at home with the other horses, the ones that don't have horns. . . .
JIM: Ha-ha, that's very funny! (*suddenly serious*) I'm glad to see that you have a sense of humor. You know—you're—well—very different! Surprisingly different from anyone else I know! (*His voice becomes soft and hesitant with a genuine feeling.*) Do you mind me telling you that? (LAURA *is abashed beyond speech.*) I mean it in a nice way . . . (LAURA *nods shyly, looking away.*) You make me feel sort of—I don't know how to put it! I'm usually pretty good at expressing things, but—This is something that I don't know how to say! (LAURA *touches her throat and clears it—turns the broken unicorn in her hands.*) (*even softer*) Has anyone ever told you that you were pretty? (*Pause: Music.*) (LAURA *looks up slowly, with wonder, and shakes her head.*) Well, you are! In a very different way from anyone else. And all the nicer because of the difference, too. (*His voice becomes low and husky.* LAURA *turns away, nearly faint with the novelty of her emotions.*) I wish that you were my sister. I'd teach you to have some confidence in yourself. The different people are not like other people, but being different is nothing to be ashamed of. Because other people are not such wonderful people. They're one hundred times one thousand. You're one times one! They walk all over the earth. You just stay here. They're common as—weeds, but—you—well, you're—*Blue Roses*!

(*Image on screen: Blue roses.*)

(*Music changes.*)

LAURA: But blue is wrong for—roses . . .
JIM: It's right for you!—You're—pretty!
LAURA: In what respect am I pretty?
JIM: In all respects—believe me! Your eyes—your hair—are pretty! Your hands are pretty! (*He catches hold of her hand.*) You think I'm making this up because I'm invited to dinner and have to be nice. Oh, I could do that I could put on an act for you, Laura, and say lots of things without being very sincere. But this time I am. I'm talking to you sincerely. I happened to notice you had this inferiority complex that keeps you from feeling comfortable with people. Somebody needs to build your confidence up and make you proud instead of shy and turning away and—blushing—Somebody—Ought to—Ought to—*kiss* you, Laura! (*His hand slips slowly up her arm to her shoulder.*) (*Music swells tumultuously.*) (*He suddenly turns her about and kisses her on the lips. When he releases her,* LAURA *sinks on the sofa with a bright, dazed look.* JIM *backs away and fishes in his pocket for a cigarette.*) (*Legend on screen: Souvenir.*) Stumble-john!

(*He lights the cigarette, avoiding her look. There is a peal of girlish laughter from* AMANDA *in the kitchen.* LAURA *slowly raises and opens her hand. It still contains the little broken glass animal. She looks at it with a tender, bewildered expression.*) Stumble-john! I shouldn't have done that—That was way off the beam. You don't smoke, do you? (*She looks up, smiling, not hearing the question. He sits beside her a little gingerly. She looks at him speechlessly—waiting. He coughs decorously and moves a little farther aside as he considers the situation and senses her feelings, dimly, with perturbation.*) (*gently*) *Would you—care for a—mint?* (*She doesn't seem to hear him but her look grows brighter even.*) Peppermint—LifeSaver? My pocket's a regular drug store—wherever I go . . . (*He pops a mint in his mouth. Then gulps and decides to make a clean breast of it. He speaks slowly and gingerly.*) Laura, you know, if I had a sister like you, I'd do the same thing as Tom. I'd bring out fellows and—introduce her to them. The right type of boys of a type to—appreciate her. Only—well—he made a mistake about me. Maybe I've got no call to be saying this. That may not have been the idea in having me over. But what if it was? There's nothing wrong about that. The only trouble is that is my case—I'm not in a situation to—do the right thing. I can't take down your number and say I'll phone. I can't call up next week and—ask for a date. I thought I had better explain the situation in case you—misunderstood it and—hurt your feelings. . . . (*pause*) (*Slowly, very slowly,* LAURA'S *look changes, her eyes returning slowly from his to the ornament in her palm.*) (AMANDA *utters another gay laugh in the kitchen.*)

LAURA (*faintly*): You—won't—call again?

JIM: No, Laura, I can't. (*He rises from the sofa.*) As I was just explaining, I've—got strings on me. Laura, I've—been going steady! I go out all of the time with a girl named Betty. She's a home-girl like you, and Catholic, and Irish, and in a great many ways we—get along fine. I met her last summer on a moonlight boat trip up the river to Alton, on the *Majestic.* Well—right away from the start it was—love! (*Legend: Love!*) (LAURA *sways slightly forward and grips the arm of the sofa. He fails to notice, now enrapt in his own comfortable being.*) Being in love has made a new man of me! (*Leaning stiffly forward, clutching the arm of the sofa,* LAURA *struggles visibly with her storm. But* JIM *is oblivious, she is a long way off.*) The power of love is really pretty tremendous! Love is something that—changes the whole world, Laura! (*The storm abates a little and* LAURA *leans back. He notices her again.*) It happened that Betty's aunt took sick, she got a wire and had to go to Centralia. So Tom—when he asked me to dinner—I naturally just accepted the invitation, not knowing that you—that he—that I—(*He stops awkwardly.*) Huh—I'm a stumble-john! (*He flops back on the sofa.*) (*The holy candles in the altar of* LAURA'S *face have been snuffed out. There is a look of almost infinite desolation.*) (JIM *glances at her uneasily.*) I wish that you would—say something. (*She bites her lip which was trembling and then bravely smiles. She opens her hand again on the broken glass ornament. Then she gently takes his hand and raises it level with her own. She carefully places the unicorn in the palm of his hand, then pushes his fingers closed upon it.*) What are you—doing that for? You want me to have him?—Laura? (*She nods.*) What for?

LAURA: A—souvenir . . .

She rises unsteadily and crouches beside the victrola to wind it up.

(*Legend on screen: "Things Have a Way of Turning Out So Badly!"*)

(Or image: "Gentleman Caller Waving Good-bye!—Gaily.")

At this moment AMANDA *rushes brightly back in the front room. She bears a pitcher of fruit punch in an old-fashioned cut-glass pitcher and a plate of macaroons. The plate has a gold border and poppies painted on it.*

AMANDA: Well, well, well! Isn't the air delightful after the shower? I've made you children a little liquid refreshment. (*turns gaily to the gentleman caller*) Jim, do you know that song about lemonade?

"Lemonade, lemonade
Made in the shade and stirred with a spade—
Good enough for any old maid!"

JIM (*uneasily*): Ha-ha! No—I never heard it.

AMANDA: Why, Laura! You look so serious!

JIM: We were having a serious conversation.

AMANDA: Good! Now you're better acquainted!

JIM (*uncertainly*): Ha-ha! Yes.

AMANDA: You modern young people are much more serious-minded than my generation. I was so gay as a girl!

JIM: You haven't changed, Mrs. Wingfield.

AMANDA: Tonight I'm rejuvenated! The gaiety of the occasion, Mr. O'Connor! (*She tosses her head with a peal of laughter. Spills lemonade.*) Oooo! I'm baptizing myself!

JIM: Here—let me—

AMANDA (*setting the pitcher down*): There now, I discovered we had some maraschino cherries. I dumped them in, juice and all!

JIM: You shouldn't have gone to that trouble, Mrs. Wingfield.

AMANDA: Trouble, trouble? Why, it was loads of fun! Didn't you hear me cutting up in the kitchen? I bet your ears were burning! I told Tom how outdone with him I was for keeping you to himself so long a time! He should have brought you over much, much sooner! Well, now that you've found your way, I want you to be a very frequent caller! Not just occasional but all the time. Oh, we're going to have a lot of gay times together! I see them coming! Mmm, just breathe that air! So fresh, and the moon's so pretty! I'll skip back out—I know where my place is when young folks are having a—serious conversation!

JIM: Oh, don't go out, Mrs. Wingfield. The fact of the matter is I've got to be going.

AMANDA: Going, now? You're joking! Why, it's only the shank of the evening, Mr. O'Connor!

JIM: Well, you know how it is.

AMANDA: You mean you're a young workingman and have to keep workingmen's hours. We'll let you off early tonight. But only on the condition that next time you stay later. What's the best night for you? Isn't Saturday night the best night for you workingmen?

JIM: I have a couple of time-clocks to punch, Mrs. Wingfield. One at morning, another one at night!

AMANDA: My, but you *are* ambitious! You work at night, too?

JIM: No, Ma'am, not work but—Betty! (*He crosses deliberately to pick up his hat. The band at the Paradise Dance Hall goes into a tender waltz.*)

AMANDA: Betty? Betty? Who's—Betty! (*There is an ominous cracking sound in the sky.*)

JIM: Oh, just a girl. The girl I go steady with! (*He smiles charmingly. The sky falls.*) (*Legend: "The Sky Falls."*)

AMANDA (*a long-drawn exhalation*): Ohhhh . . . Is it a serious romance, Mr. O'Connor?

JIM: We're going to be married the second Sunday in June.

AMANDA: Ohhhh—how nice! Tom didn't mention that you were engaged to be married.

JIM: The cat's not out of the bag at the warehouse yet. You know how they are. They call you Romeo and stuff like that. (*He stops at the oval mirror to put on his hat. He carefully shapes the brim and the crown to give a discreetly dashing effect.*) It's been a wonderful evening, Mrs. Wingfield. I guess this is what they mean by Southern hospitality.

AMANDA: It really wasn't anything at all.

JIM: I hope it don't seem like I'm rushing off. But I promised Betty I'd pick her up at the Wabash depot, an' by the time I get my jalopy down there her train'll be in. Some women are pretty upset if you keep 'em waiting.

AMANDA: Yes, I know—The tyranny of women! (*extends her hand*) Good-bye, Mr. O'Connor. I wish you luck—and happiness—and success! All three of them, and so does Laura!—Don't you, Laura?

LAURA: Yes!

JIM (*taking her hand*): Good-bye, Laura. I'm certainly going to treasure that souvenir. And don't you forget the good advice I gave you. (*raises his voice to a cheery shout*) So long, Shakespeare! Thanks again, ladies—Good night!

He grins and ducks jauntily out.

Still bravely grimacing, AMANDA *closes the door on the gentleman caller. Then she turns back to the room with a puzzled expression. She and* LAURA *don't dare to face each other.* LAURA *crouches beside the victrola to wind it.*

AMANDA (*faintly*): Things have a way of turning out so badly. I don't believe that I would play the victrola. Well, well—well—Our gentleman caller was engaged to be married! Tom!

TOM (*from back*): Yes, Mother?

AMANDA: Come in here a minute. I want to tell you something awfully funny.

TOM (*enters with macaroon and a glass of the lemonade*): Has the gentleman caller gotten away already?

AMANDA: The gentleman caller has made an early departure. What a wonderful joke you played on us!

TOM: How do you mean?

AMANDA: You didn't mention that he was engaged to be married.

TOM: Jim? Engaged?

AMANDA: That's what he just informed us.

TOM: I'll be jiggered! I didn't know about that.

AMANDA: That seems very peculiar.

TOM: What's peculiar about it?

AMANDA: Didn't you call him your best friend down at the warehouse?

TOM: He is, but how did I know?

AMANDA: It seems extremely peculiar that you wouldn't know your best friend was going to be married!

TOM: The warehouse is where I work, not where I know things about people!

AMANDA: You don't know things anywhere! You live in a dream; you manufacture illusions! (*He crosses to door.*) Where are you going?

TOM: I'm going to the movies.

AMANDA: That's right, now that you've had us make such fools of ourselves. The effort, the preparations, all the expense! The new floor lamp, the rug, the clothes for Laura! All for what? To entertain some other girl's fiancé! Go to the movies, go! Don't think about us, a mother deserted, an unmarried sister who's crippled and has no job! Don't let anything interfere with your selfish pleasure! Just go, go, go—to the movies!

TOM: All right. I will! The more you shout about my selfishness to me the quicker I'll go and I won't go to the movies!

AMANDA: Go, then! Then go to the moon—you selfish dreamer!

TOM *smashes his glass on the floor. He plunges out on the fire-escape, slamming the door.* LAURA *screams—cut by door.*

Dance-hall music up. TOM *goes to the rail and grips it desperately, lifting his face in the chill white moonlight penetrating the narrow abyss of the alley.*

(*Legend on screen: "And So Good-bye . . ."*)

(TOM'S *closing speech is timed with the interior pantomime. The interior scene is played as though viewed through soundproof glass.* AMANDA *appears to be making a comforting speech to* LAURA *who is huddled upon the sofa. Now that we cannot hear the mother's speech, her silliness is gone and she has dignity and tragic beauty.* LAURA'S *dark hair hides her face until at the end of the speech she lifts it to smile at her mother.* AMANDA'S *gestures are slow and graceful, almost dancelike, as she comforts the daughter. At the end of her speech she glances a moment at the father's picture—then withdraws through the portieres. At close of* TOM'S *speech,* LAURA *blows out the candles, ending the play.*)

TOM: I didn't go to the moon, I went much further—for time is the longest distance between two places—Not long after that I was fired for writing a poem on the lid of a shoe-box. I left Saint Louis. I descended the steps of this fire-escape for a last time and followed, from then on, in my father's footsteps attempting to find in motion what was lost in space—I traveled around a great deal. The cities swept about me like dead leaves, leaves that were brightly colored but torn away from the branches. I would have stopped, but I was pursued by something. It always came upon me unawares, taking me altogether by surprise. Perhaps it was a familiar bit of music. Perhaps it was only a piece of transparent glass—Perhaps I am walking along a street at night, in some strange city, before I have found companions. I pass the lighted window of a shop where perfume is sold. The window is filled with pieces of colored glass, tiny transparent bottles in delicate colors, like bits of a shattered rainbow. Then all at once my sister touches my shoulder. I turn around and look into her eyes . . . Oh, Laura, Laura, I tried to leave you behind me, but I am more faithful than I intended to be! I reach for a cigarette, I cross the street, I run into the movies or a bar, I buy a drink, I speak to the nearest stranger—anything that can blow your candles out! (LAURA *bends over the candles.*)—for nowadays the world is lit by lightning! Blow out your candles, Laura—and so goodbye . . . (*She blows the candles out.*)

(*The scene dissolves.*)

Brenda Blethyn as Thelma Cates and Edie Falco as her daughter, Jessie, in *'Night, Mother*

MARSHA NORMAN (b. 1947) was born and grew up in Louisville, Kentucky. Her father, Billie Williams, sold insurance and real estate, and her mother, Bertha, stayed home with the four children. After a sheltered childhood in her fundamentalist family, Norman attended Agnes Scott College in Atlanta, Georgia, where she earned a B.A. in philosophy. In 1969 Marsha Williams married Michael Norman (from whom she was divorced in 1974) and returned to Louisville, where she earned a master's degree in education; she taught disturbed children for Kentucky Central State Hospital, worked with gifted children at the Brown School, and made movies with children for the Kentucky Arts Commission. Norman also wrote book reviews for the *Louisville Times*.

With encouragement from Jon Jory of the ATL (Actors Theater of Louisville), Norman began writing plays. *Getting Out* (1977) features a former prisoner with a history of violence who must adjust to freedom and come to terms with her past. *'Night Mother* (1982), which premiered at the American Repertory Theatre in Cambridge, Massachusetts, was directed by Tom Moore and starred Anne Pitoniak as Thelma and Kathy Bates as Jessie Cates. In 1983, *'Night Mother* won the Pulitzer Prize for drama.

'Night Mother is a study of suicide that may or may not have some inspiration in life; in either case, many viewers who have lost loved ones to suicide confirm the realism of Jessie's action and motives. Some critics fault Norman for making her main character capitulate passively to social norms that deem her a failure, but in public statements, Norman herself has agreed with Jessie that the suicide is a triumph, a positive act of freedom. Jessie chooses to say "no" to life, and she also reaches an understanding with Mama. A tightly **plotted** drama of one act that

observes the **dramatic unities,** *'Night Mother* relies on **dialogue, flashbacks**, and a **setting** that is at once realistic and symbolic to articulate a complex relationship between mother and daughter.

Related Works: Bishop, "Sestina"; Dickinson, "Because I could not stop for Death"; *Everyman*; Kafka, "Metamorphosis"; Miller, *Death of a Salesman*; Porter, "The Jilting of Granny Weatherall"; Thomas, "Do Not Go Gentle into That Good Night"; Tichborne, "Elegy."

'Night, Mother

The play takes place in a relatively new house built way out on a country road, with a living room and connecting kitchen, and a center hall that leads off to the bedrooms. A pull cord in the hall ceiling releases a ladder which leads to the attic. One of these bedrooms opens directly onto the hall, and its entry should be visible to everyone in the audience. It should be, in fact, the focal point of the entire set, and the lighting should make it disappear completely at times and draw the entire set into it at others. It is a point of both threat and promise. It is an ordinary door that opens onto absolute nothingness. That door is the point of all the action, and the utmost care should be given to its design and construction.

The living room is cluttered with magazines and needlework catalogues, ashtrays and candy dishes. Examples of Mama's needlework are everywhere—pillows, afghans, and quilts, doilies and rugs, and they are quite nice examples. The house is more comfortable than messy, but there is quite a lot to keep in place here. It is more personal than charming. It is not quaint. Under no circumstances should the set and its dressing make a judgment about the intelligence or taste of Jessie and Mama. It should simply indicate that they are very specific real people who happen to live in a particular part of the country. Heavy accents, which would further distance the audience from Jessie and Mama, are also wrong.

The time is the present, with the action beginning about 8:15. Clocks onstage in the kitchen and on a table in the living room should run throughout the performance and be visible to the audience.

There will be no intermission.

Characters

JESSIE CATES, in her late thirties or early forties, is pale and vaguely unsteady physically. It is only in the last year that Jessie has gained control of her mind and body, and tonight she is determined to hold on to that control. She wears pants and a long black sweater with deep pockets, which contain scraps of paper, and there may be a pencil behind her ear or a pen clipped to one of the pockets of the sweater.

As a rule, Jessie doesn't feel much like talking. Other people have rarely found her quirky sense of humor amusing. She has a peaceful energy on this night, a sense of purpose, but is clearly aware of the time passing moment by moment. Oddly enough, Jessie has never been as communicative or as enjoyable as she is on this evening, but we must know she has not always been this way. There is a familiarity between these two women that comes from having lived together for a long time. There is a shorthand to the talk and a sense of routine comfort in the way they relate to each other physically. Naturally, there are also routine aggravations.

THELMA CATES, "MAMA," is Jessie's mother, in her late fifties or early sixties. She has begun to feel her age and so takes it easy when she can, or when it serves her purpose to let someone help her. But she speaks quickly and enjoys talking. She believes that things *are* what she says they are. Her sturdiness is more a mental quality than a physical one, finally. She is chatty and nosy, and this is *her* house.

MAMA *stretches to reach the cupcakes in a cabinet in the kitchen. She can't see them, but she can feel around for them, and she's eager to have one, so she's working pretty hard at it. This may be the most serious exercise* MAMA *ever gets. She finds a cupcake, the coconut-covered, raspberry-and-marshmallow-filled kind known as a snowball, but sees that there's one missing from the package. She calls to* JESSIE, *who is apparently somewhere else in the house.*

MAMA (*Unwrapping the cupcake*): Jessie, it's the last snowball, sugar. Put it on the list, O.K.? And we're out of Hershey bars, and where's that peanut brittle? I think maybe Dawson's been in it again. I ought to put a big mirror on the refrigerator door. That'll keep him out of my treats, won't it? You hear me, honey? (*Then more to herself*) I hate it when the coconut falls off. Why does the coconut fall off?

(JESSIE *enters from her bedroom, carrying a stack of newspapers*)

JESSIE: We got any old towels?

MAMA: There you are!

JESSIE: (*Holding a towel that was on the stack of newspapers*): Towels you don't want anymore. (*Picking up* MAMA'S *snowball wrapper*) How about this swimming towel Loretta gave us? Beach towel, that's the name of it. You want it? (MAMA *shakes her head no*)

MAMA: What have you been doing in there?

JESSIE: And a big piece of plastic like a rubber sheet or something. Garbage bags would do if there's enough.

MAMA: Don't go making a big mess, Jessie. It's eight o'clock already.

JESSIE: Maybe an old blanket or towels we got in a soap box sometime?

MAMA: I said don't make a mess. Your hair is black enough, hon.

JESSIE (*Continuing to search the kitchen cabinets, finding two or three more towels to add to her stack*): It's not for my hair, Mama. What about some old pillows anywhere, or a foam cushion out of a yard chair would be real good.

MAMA: You haven't forgot what night it is, have you? (*Holding up her fingernails*) They're all chipped, see? I've been waiting all week, Jess. It's Saturday night, sugar.

JESSIE: I know. I got it on the schedule.

MAMA (*Crossing to the living room*): You want me to wash 'em now or are you making your mess first? (*Looking at the snowball*) We're out of these. Did I say that already?

JESSIE: There's more coming tomorrow. I ordered you a whole case.

MAMA (*Checking the* TV Guide): A whole case will go stale, Jessie.

JESSIE: They can go in the freezer till you're ready for them. Where's Daddy's gun?

MAMA: In the attic.

JESSIE: Where in the attic? I looked your whole nap and couldn't find it anywhere.

MAMA: One of his shoeboxes, I think.

JESSIE: Full of his shoes. I looked already.

MAMA: Well, you didn't look good enough, then. There's that box from the ones he wore to the hospital. When he died, they told me I could have them back, but I never did like those shoes.

JESSIE (*Pulling them out of her pocket*): I found the bullets. They were in an old milk can.

MAMA (*As* JESSIE *starts for the hall*): Dawson took the shotgun, didn't he? Hand me that basket, hon.

JESSIE (*Getting the basket for her*): Dawson better not've taken that pistol.

MAMA (*Stopping her again*): Now my glasses, please. (JESSIE *returns to get the glasses*) I told him to take those rubber boots, too, but he said they were for fishing. I told him to take up fishing.

(JESSIE *reaches for the cleaning spray, and cleans* MAMA'S *glasses for her*)

JESSIE: He's just too lazy to climb up there, Mama. Or maybe he's just being smart. That floor's not very steady.

MAMA (*Getting out a piece of knitting*): It's not a floor at all, hon, it's a board now and then. Measure this for me. I need six inches.

JESSIE (*As she measures*): Dawson could probably use some of those clothes up there. Somebody should have them. You ought to call the Salvation Army before the whole thing falls in on you. Six inches exactly.

MAMA: It's plenty safe! As long as you don't go up there.

JESSIE (*Turning to go again*): I'm careful.

MAMA: What do you want the gun for, Jess?

JESSIE (*Not returning this time. Opening the ladder in the hall*): Protection. (*She steadies the ladder as* MAMA *talks*)

MAMA: You take the TV way too serious, hon. I've never seen a criminal in my life. This is way too far to come for what's out here to steal. Never seen a one.

JESSIE (*Taking her first step up*): Except for Ricky.

MAMA: Ricky is mixed up. That's not a crime.

JESSIE: Get your hands washed. I'll be right back. And get 'em real dry. You dry your hands till I get back or it's no go, all right?

MAMA: I thought Dawson told you not to go up those stairs.

JESSIE (*Going up*): He did.

MAMA: I don't like the idea of a gun, Jess.

JESSIE (*Calling down from the attic*): Which shoebox, do you remember?

MAMA: Black.

JESSIE: The box was black?

MAMA: The shoes were black.

JESSIE: That doesn't help much, Mother.

MAMA: I'm not trying to help, sugar. (*No answer*) We don't have anything anybody'd want, Jessie. I mean, I don't even want what we got, Jessie.

JESSIE: Neither do I. Wash your hands. (MAMA *gets up and crosses to stand under the ladder*)

MAMA: You come down from there before you have a fit. I can't come up and get you, you know.

JESSIE: I know.

MAMA: We'll just hand it over to them when they come, how's that? Whatever they want, the criminals.

JESSIE: That's a good idea, Mama.

MAMA: Ricky will grow out of this and be a real fine boy, Jess. But I have to tell you, I wouldn't want Ricky to know we had a gun in the house.

JESSIE: Here it is. I found it.

MAMA: It's just something Ricky's going through. Maybe he's in with some bad people. He just needs some time, sugar. He'll get back in school or get a job or one day you'll get a call and he'll say he's sorry for all the trouble he's caused and invite you out for supper someplace dress-up.

JESSIE (*Coming back down the steps*): Don't worry. It's not for him, it's for me.

MAMA: I didn't think you would shoot your own boy, Jessie. I know you've felt like it, well, we've all felt like shooting somebody, but we don't do it. I just don't think we need . . .

JESSIE (*Interrupting*): Your hands aren't washed. Do you want a manicure or not?

MAMA: Yes, I do, but . . .

JESSIE (*Crossing to the chair*): Then wash your hands and don't talk to me any more about Ricky. Those two rings he took were the last valuable things *I* had, so now he's started in on other people, door to door. I hope they put him away sometime. I'd turn him in myself if I knew where he was.

MAMA: You don't mean that.

JESSIE: Every word. Wash your hands and that's the last time I'm telling you.

(JESSIE *sits down with the gun and starts cleaning it, pushing the cylinder out, checking to see that the chambers and barrel are empty, then putting some oil on a small patch of cloth and pushing it through the barrel with the push rod that was in the box.* MAMA *goes to the kitchen and washes her hands, as instructed, trying not to show her concern about the gun*)

MAMA: I shoulda got you to bring down that milk can. Agnes Fletcher sold hers to somebody with a flea market for forty dollars apiece.

JESSIE: I'll go back and get it in a minute. There's a wagon wheel up there, too. There's even a churn. I'll get it all if you want.

MAMA (*Coming over, now, taking over now*): What are you doing?

JESSIE: The barrel has to be clean, Mama. Old powder, dust gets in it . . .

MAMA: What for?

JESSIE: I told you.

MAMA (*Reaching for the gun*): And I told you, we don't get criminals out here.

JESSIE (*Quickly pulling it to her*): And I told you . . . (*Then trying to be calm*) The gun is for me.

MAMA: Well, you can have it if you want. When I die, you'll get it all, anyway.

JESSIE: I'm going to kill myself, Mama.

MAMA (*Returning to the sofa*): Very funny. Very funny.

JESSIE: I am.

MAMA: You are not! Don't even say such a thing, Jessie.

JESSIE: How would you know if I didn't say it? You want it to be a surprise? You're lying there in your bed or maybe you're just brushing your teeth and you hear this . . . noise down the hall?

MAMA: Kill yourself.

JESSIE: Shoot myself. In a couple of hours.

MAMA: It must be time for your medicine.

JESSIE: Took it already.

MAMA: What's the matter with you?

JESSIE: Not a thing. Feel fine.

MAMA: You feel fine. You're just going to kill yourself.

JESSIE: Waited until I felt good enough, in fact.

MAMA: Don't make jokes, Jessie. I'm too old for jokes.

JESSIE: It's not a joke, Mama.

(MAMA *watches for a moment in silence*)

MAMA: That gun's no good, you know. He broke it right before he died. He dropped it in the mud one day.

JESSIE: Seems O.K. (*She spins the chamber, cocks the pistol, and pulls the trigger. The gun is not yet loaded, so all we hear is the click, but it will definitely work. It's also obvious that* JESSIE *knows her way around a gun.* MAMA *cannot speak*) I had Cecil's all ready in there, just in case I couldn't find this one, but I'd rather use Daddy's.

MAMA: Those bullets are at least fifteen years old.

JESSIE (*Pulling out another box*): These are from last week.

MAMA: Where did you get those?

JESSIE: Feed store Dawson told me about.

MAMA: Dawson!

JESSIE: I told him I was worried about prowlers. He said he thought it was a good idea. He told me what kind to ask for.

MAMA: If he had any idea . . . .

JESSIE: He took it as a compliment. He thought I might be taking an interest in things. He got through telling me all about the bullets and then he said we ought to talk like this more often.

MAMA: And where was I while this was going on?

JESSIE: On the phone with Agnes. About the milk can, I guess. Anyway, I asked Dawson if he thought they'd send me some bullets and he said he'd just call for me, because he knew they'd send them if he told them to. And he was absolutely right. Here they are.

MAMA: How could he do that?

JESSIE: Just trying to help, Mama.

MAMA: And then I told you where the gun was.

JESSIE (*Smiling, enjoying this joke*): See? Everybody's doing what they can.

MAMA: You told me it was for protection!

JESSIE: It *is*! I'm still doing your nails, though. Want to try that new Chinaberry color?

MAMA: Well, I'm calling Dawson right now. We'll just see what he has to say about this little stunt.

JESSIE: Dawson doesn't have any more to do with this.

MAMA: He's your brother.

JESSIE: And that's all.

MAMA (*Stands up, moves toward the phone*): Dawson will put a stop to this. Yes he will. He'll take the gun away.

JESSIE: If you call him, I'll just have to do it before he gets here. Soon as you hang up the phone, I'll just walk in the bedroom and lock the door. Dawson will get here just in time to help you clean up. Go ahead, call him. Then call the police. Then call the funeral home. Then call Loretta and see if *she'll* do your nails.

MAMA: You will not! This is crazy talk, Jessie!

(MAMA *goes directly to the telephone and starts to dial, but* JESSIE *is fast, coming up behind her and taking the receiver out of her hand, putting it back down*)

JESSIE (*Firm and quiet*): I said no. This is private. Dawson is not invited.

MAMA: Just me.

JESSIE: I don't want anybody else over here. Just you and me. If Dawson comes over, it'll make me feel stupid for not doing it ten years ago.

MAMA: I think we better call the doctor. Or how about the ambulance. You like that one driver, I know. What's his name, Timmy? Get you somebody to talk to.

JESSIE (*Going back to her chair*): I'm through talking, Mama. You're it. No more.

MAMA: We're just going to sit around like every other night in the world and then you're going to kill yourself? (JESSIE *doesn't answer*) You'll miss. (*Again there is no response*) You'll just wind up a vegetable. How would you like that? Shoot your ear off? You know what the doctor said about getting excited. You'll cock the pistol and have a fit.

JESSIE: I think I can kill myself, Mama.

MAMA: You're not going to kill yourself, Jessie. You're not even upset! (JESSIE *smiles, or laughs quietly, and* MAMA *tries a different approach*) People don't really kill themselves, Jessie. No, mam, doesn't make sense, unless you're retarded or deranged, and you're as normal as they come, Jessie, for the most part. We're all *afraid* to die.

JESSIE: I'm not, Mama. I'm cold all the time, anyway.

MAMA: That's ridiculous.

JESSIE: It's exactly what I want. It's dark and quiet.

MAMA: So is the back yard, Jessie! Close your eyes. Stuff cotton in your ears. Take a nap! It's quiet in your room. I'll leave the TV off all night.

JESSIE: So quiet I don't know it's quiet. So nobody can get me.

MAMA: You don't know what dead is like. It might not be quiet at all. What if it's like an alarm clock and you can't wake up so you can't shut it off. Ever.

JESSIE: Dead is everybody and everything I ever knew, gone. Dead is dead quiet.

MAMA: It's a sin. You'll go to hell.

JESSIE: Uh-huh.

MAMA: You will!

JESSIE: Jesus was a suicide, if you ask me.

MAMA: You'll go to hell just for saying that. Jessie!

JESSIE (*With genuine surprise*): I didn't know I thought that.

MAMA: Jessie!

(JESSIE *doesn't answer. She puts the now-loaded gun back in the box and crosses to the kitchen. But* MAMA *is afraid she's headed for the bedroom*)

MAMA (*In a panic*): You can't use my towels! They're my towels. I've had them for a long time. I like my towels.

JESSIE: I asked you if you wanted that swimming towel and you said you didn't.

MAMA: And you can't use your father's gun, either. It's mine now, too. And you can't do it in my house.

JESSIE: Oh, come on.

MAMA: No. You can't do it. I won't let you. The house is in my name.

JESSIE: I have to go in the bedroom and lock the door behind me so they won't arrest you for killing me. They'll probably test your hands for gunpowder, anyway, but you'll pass.

MAMA: Not in my house!

JESSIE: If I'd known you were going to act like this, I wouldn't have told you.

MAMA: How am I supposed to act? Tell you to go ahead? O.K. by me, sugar? Might try it myself. What took you so long?

JESSIE: There's just no point in fighting me over it, that's all. Want some coffee?

MAMA: Your birthday's coming up, Jessie. Don't you want to know what we got you?

JESSIE: You got me dusting powder, Loretta got me a new housecoat, pink probably, and Dawson got me new slippers, too small, but they go with the robe, he'll say. (MAMA *cannot speak*) Right? (*Apparently* JESSIE *is right*) Be back in a minute.

(JESSIE *takes the gun box, puts it on top of the stack of towels and garbage bags, and takes them into her bedroom.* MAMA, *alone for a moment, goes to the phone, picks up the receiver, looks toward the bedroom, starts to dial, and then replaces the receiver in its cradle as* JESSIE *walks back into the room.* JESSIE *wonders, silently. They have lived together for so long there is very rarely any reason for one to ask what the other was about to do*)

MAMA: I started to, but I didn't. I didn't call him.

JESSIE: Good. Thank you.

MAMA (*Starting over, a new approach*): What's this all about, Jessie?

JESSIE: About?

(JESSIE *now begins the next task she had "on the schedule," which is refilling all the candy jars, taking the empty papers out of the boxes of chocolates, etc.* MAMA *generally snitches when* JESSIE *does this. Not tonight, though. Nevertheless,* JESSIE *offers*)

MAMA: What did I do?

JESSIE: Nothing. Want a caramel?

MAMA (*Ignoring the candy*): You're mad at me.

JESSIE: Not a bit. I am worried about you, but I'm going to do what I can before I go. We're not just going to sit around tonight. I made a list of things.

MAMA: What things?

JESSIE: How the washer works. Things like that.

MAMA: I know how the washer works. You put the clothes in. You put the soap in. You turn it on. You wait.

JESSIE: You do something else. You don't just wait.

MAMA: Whatever else you find to do, you're still mainly waiting. The waiting's the worst part of it. The waiting's what you pay somebody else to do, if you can.

JESSIE (*Nodding*): O.K. Where do we keep the soap?

MAMA: I could find it.

JESSIE: See?

MAMA: If you're mad about doing the wash, we can get Loretta to do it.

JESSIE: Oh now, that might be worth staying to see.

MAMA: She'd never in her life, would she?

JESSIE: Nope.

MAMA: What's the matter with her?

JESSIE: She thinks she's better than we are. She's not.

MAMA: Maybe if she didn't wear that yellow all the time.

JESSIE: The washer repair number is on a little card taped to the side of the machine.

MAMA: Loretta doesn't ever have to come over here again. Dawson can just leave her at home when he comes. And we don't ever have to see Dawson either if he bothers you. Does he bother you?

JESSIE: Sure he does. Be sure you clean out the lint tray every time you use the dryer. But don't ever put your house shoes in, it'll melt the soles.

MAMA: What does Dawson do, that bothers you?

JESSIE: He just calls me Jess like he knows who he's talking to. He's always wondering what I do all day. I mean, I wonder that myself, but it's my day, so it's mine to wonder about, not his.

MAMA: Family is just accident, Jessie. It's nothing personal, hon. They don't mean to get on your nerves. They don't even mean to be your family, they just are.

JESSIE: They know too much.

MAMA: About what?

JESSIE: They know things about you, and they learned it before you had a chance to say whether you wanted them to know it or not. They were there when it happened and it don't belong to them, it belongs to you, only they got it. Like my mail-order bra got delivered to their house.

MAMA: By accident!

JESSIE: All the same . . . they opened it. They saw the little rosebuds on it. (*Offering her another candy*) Chewy mint?

MAMA (*Shaking her head no*): What do they know about you? I'll tell them never to talk about it again. Is it Ricky or Cecil or your fits or your hair is falling out or you drink too much coffee or you never go out of the house or what?

JESSIE: I just don't like their talk. The account at the grocery is in Dawson's name when you call. The number's on a whole list of numbers on the back cover of the phone book.

MAMA: Well! Now we're getting somewhere. They're none of them ever setting foot in this house again.

JESSIE: It's not them, Mother. I wouldn't kill myself just to get away from them.

MAMA: You leave the room when they come over, anyway.

JESSIE: I stay as long as I can. Besides, it's you they come to see.

MAMA: That's because I stay in the room when they come.

JESSIE: It's not them.

MAMA: Then what is it?

JESSIE (*Checking the list on her note pad*): The grocery won't deliver on Saturday anymore. And if you want your order the same day, you have to call before ten. And they won't deliver less than fifteen dollars' worth. What I do is tell them what we need and tell them to add on cigarettes until it gets to fifteen dollars.

MAMA: It's Ricky. You're trying to get through to him.

JESSIE: If I thought I could do that, I would stay.

MAMA: Make him sorry he hurt you, then. That's it, isn't it?

JESSIE: He's hurt me, I've hurt him. We're about even.

MAMA: You'll be telling him killing is O.K. with you, you know. Want him to start killing next? Nothing wrong with it. Mom did it.

JESSIE: Only a matter of time, anyway, Mama. When the call comes, you let Dawson handle it.

MAMA: Honey, nothing says those calls are always going to be some new trouble he's into. You could get one that he's got a job, that he's getting married, or how about he's joined the army, wouldn't that be nice?

JESSIE: If you call the Sweet Tooth before you call the grocery, that Susie will take your fudge next door to the grocery and it'll all come out together. Be sure you talk to Susie, though. She won't let them put it in the bottom of a sack like that one time, remember?

MAMA: Ricky could come over, you know. What if he calls us?

JESSIE: It's not Ricky, Mama.

MAMA: Or anybody could call us, Jessie.

JESSIE: Not on Saturday night, Mama.

MAMA: Then what is it? Are you sick? If your gums are swelling again, we can get you to the dentist in the morning.

JESSIE: No. Can you order your medicine or do you want Dawson to? I've got a note to him. I'll add that to it if you want.

MAMA: Your eyes don't look right. I thought so yesterday.

JESSIE: That was just the ragweed. I'm not sick.

MAMA: Epilepsy is sick, Jessie.

JESSIE: It won't kill me. (*A pause*) If it would, I wouldn't have to.

MAMA: You don't *have* to.

JESSIE: No, I don't. That's what I like about it.

MAMA: Well, I won't let you!

JESSIE: It's not up to you.

MAMA: Jessie!

JESSIE: I want to hang a big sign around my neck, like Daddy's on the barn. GONE FISHING.

MAMA: You don't like it here.

JESSIE (*Smiling*): Exactly.

MAMA: I meant here in my house.

JESSIE: I know you did.

MAMA: You never should have moved back in here with me. If you'd kept your little house or found another place when Cecil left you, you'd have made some new friends at least. Had a life to lead. Had your own things around you. Give Ricky a place to come see you. You never should've come here.

JESSIE: Maybe.

MAMA: But I didn't force you, did I?

JESSIE: If it was a mistake, we made it together. You took me in. I appreciate that.

MAMA: You didn't have any business being by yourself right then, but I can see how you might want a place of your own. A grown woman should . . .

JESSIE: Mama . . . I'm just not having a very good time and I don't have any reason to think it'll get anything but worse. I'm tired. I'm hurt. I'm sad. I feel used.

MAMA: Tired of what?

JESSIE: It all.

MAMA: What does that mean?

JESSIE: I can't say it any better.

MAMA: Well, you'll have to say it better because I'm not letting you alone till you do. What were those other things? Hurt . . . (*Before* JESSIE *can answer*) You had this all ready to say to me, didn't you? Did you write this down? How long have you been thinking about this?

JESSIE: Off and on, ten years. On all the time, since Christmas.

MAMA: What happened at Christmas?

JESSIE: Nothing.

MAMA: So why Christmas?

JESSIE: That's it. On the nose.

(*A pause.* MAMA *knows exactly what* JESSIE *means. She was there, too, after all*)

JESSIE (*Putting the candy sacks away*): See where all this is? Red hots up front, sour balls and horehound mixed together in this one sack. New packages of toffee and licorice right in back there.

MAMA: Go back to your list. You're hurt by what?

JESSIE (MAMA *knows perfectly well*): Mama . . .

MAMA: O.K. Sad about what? There's nothing real sad going on right now. If it was after your divorce or something, that would make sense.

JESSIE (*Looking at her list, then opening the drawer*): Now, this drawer has everything in it that there's no better place for. Extension cords, batteries for the radio, extra lighters, sandpaper, masking tape, Elmer's glue, thumbtacks, that kind of stuff. The mousetraps are under the sink, but you call Dawson if you've got one and let him do it.

MAMA: Sad about what?

JESSIE: The way things are.

MAMA: Not good enough. What things?

JESSIE: Oh, everything from you and me to Red China.

MAMA: I think we can leave the Chinese out of this.

JESSIE (*Crosses back into the living room*): There's extra light bulbs in a box in the hall closet. And we've got a couple of packages of fuses in the fuse box. There's candles and matches in the top of the broom closet, but if the lights go out, just call Dawson and sit tight. But don't open the refrigerator door. Things will stay cool in there as long as you keep the door shut.

MAMA: I asked you a question.

JESSIE: I read the paper. I don't like how things are. And they're not any better out there than they are in here.

MAMA: If you're doing this because of the newspapers, I can sure fix that!

JESSIE: There's just more of it on TV.

MAMA (*Kicking the television set*): Take it out, then!

JESSIE: You wouldn't do that.

MAMA: Watch me.

JESSIE: What would you do all day?

MAMA (*Desperately*): Sing. (JESSIE *laughs*) I would, too. You want to watch? I'll sing till morning to keep you alive, Jessie, please!

JESSIE: No. (*Then affectionately*) It's a funny idea, though. What do you sing?

MAMA (*Has no idea how to answer this*): We've got a good life here!

JESSIE (*Going back into the kitchen*): I called this morning and canceled the papers, except for Sunday, for your puzzles; you'll still get that one.

MAMA: Let's get another dog, Jessie! You liked a big dog, now, didn't you? That King dog, didn't you?

JESSIE (*Washing her hands*): I did like that King dog, yes.

MAMA: I'm so dumb. He's the one run under the tractor.

JESSIE: That makes him dumb, not you.

MAMA: For bringing it up.

JESSIE: It's O.K. Handi-Wipes and sponges under the sink.

MAMA: We could get a new dog and keep him in the house. Dogs are cheap!

JESSIE (*Getting big pill jars out of the cabinet*): No.

MAMA: Something for you to take care of.

JESSIE: I've had you, Mama.

MAMA (*Frantically starting to fill pill bottles*): You do too much for me. I can fill pill bottles all day, Jessie, and change the shelf paper and wash the floor when I get through. You just watch me. You don't have to do another thing in this house if you don't want to. You don't have to take care of me, Jessie.

JESSIE: I know that. You've just been letting me do it so I'll have something to do, haven't you?

MAMA (*Realizing this was a mistake*): I don't do it as well as you. I just meant if it tires you out or makes you feel used . . .

JESSIE: Mama, I know you used to ride the bus. Riding the bus and it's hot and bumpy and crowded and too noisy and more than anything in the world you want to get off and the only reason in the world you don't get off is it's still fifty blocks from where you're going? Well, I can get off right now if I want to, because even if I ride fifty more years and get off then, it's the same place when I step down to it. Whenever I feel like it, I can get off. As soon as I've had enough, it's my stop. I've had enough.

MAMA: You're feeling sorry for yourself!

JESSIE: The plumber's helper is under the sink, too.

MAMA: You're not having a good time! Whoever promised you a good time? Do you think I've had a good time?

JESSIE: I think you're pretty happy, yeah. You have things you like to do.

MAMA: Like what?

JESSIE: Like crochet.

MAMA: I'll teach you to crochet.

JESSIE: I can't do any of that nice work, Mama.

MAMA: Good time don't come looking for you, Jessie. You could work some puzzles or put in a garden or go to the store. Let's call a taxi and go to the A&P!

JESSIE: I shopped you up for about two weeks already. You're not going to need toilet paper till Thanksgiving.

MAMA (*Interrupting*): You're acting like some little brat, Jessie. You're mad and everybody's boring and you don't have anything to do and you don't like me and you don't like going out and you don't like staying in and you never talk on the phone and you don't watch TV and you're miserable and it's your own sweet fault.

JESSIE: And it's time I did something about it.

MAMA: Not something like killing yourself. Something like . . . buying us all new dishes! I'd like that. Or maybe the doctor would let you get a driver's license now, or I know what let's do right this minute, let's rearrange the furniture.

JESSIE: I'll do that. If you want. I always thought if the TV was somewhere else, you wouldn't get such a glare on it during the day. I'll do whatever you want before I go.

MAMA (*Badly frightened by those words*): You could get a job!

JESSIE: I took that telephone sales job and I didn't even make enough money to pay the phone bill, and I tried to work at the gift shop at the hospital and they said I made people real uncomfortable smiling at them the way I did.

MAMA: You could keep books. You kept your dad's books.

JESSIE: But nobody ever checked them.

MAMA: When he died, they checked them.

JESSIE: And that's when they took the books away from me.

MAMA: That's because without him there wasn't any business, Jessie!

JESSIE (*Putting the pill bottles away*): You know I couldn't work. I can't do anything. I've never been around people my whole life except when I went to the hospital. I could have a seizure any time. What good would a job do? The kind of job I could get would make me feel worse.

MAMA: Jessie!

JESSIE: It's true!

MAMA: It's what you think is true!

JESSIE (*Struck by the clarity of that*): That's right. It's what I think is true.

MAMA (*Hysterically*): But I can't do anything about that!

JESSIE (*Quietly*): No. You can't. (MAMA *slumps, if not physically, at least emotionally*) And I can't do anything either, about my life, to change it, make it better, make me feel better about it. Like it better, make it work. But I can stop it. Shut it down, turn it off like the radio when there's nothing on I want to listen to. It's all I really have that belongs to me and I'm going to say what happens to it. And it's going to stop. And I'm going to stop it. So. Let's just have a good time.

MAMA: Have a good time.

JESSIE: We can't go on fussing all night. I mean, I could ask you things I always wanted to know and you could make me some hot chocolate. The old way.

MAMA (*In despair*): It takes cocoa, Jessie.

JESSIE (*Gets it out of the cabinet*): I bought cocoa, Mama. And I'd like to have a caramel apple and do your nails.

MAMA: You didn't eat a bite of supper.

JESSIE: Does that mean I can't have a caramel apple?

MAMA: Of course not. I mean . . . (*Smiling a little*) Of course you can have a caramel apple.

JESSIE: I thought I could.

MAMA: I make the best caramel apples in the world.

JESSIE: I know you do.

MAMA: Or used to. And you don't get cocoa like mine anywhere anymore.

JESSIE: It takes time, I know, but . . .

MAMA: The salt is the trick.

JESSIE: Trouble and everything.

MAMA (*Backing away toward the stove*): It's no trouble. What trouble? You put it in the pan and stir it up. All right. Fine. Caramel apples. Cocoa. O.K.

(JESSIE *walks to the counter to retrieve her cigarettes as* MAMA *looks for the right pan. There are brief near-smiles, and maybe* MAMA *clears her throat. We have a truce, for the moment. A genuine but nevertheless uneasy one.* JESSIE, *who has been in constant motion since the beginning, now seems content to sit.*

MAMA *starts looking for a pan to make the cocoa, getting out all the pans in the cabinets in the process. It looks like she's making a mess on purpose so* JESSIE *will have to put them all away again.* MAMA *is buying time, or trying to, and entertaining)*

JESSIE: You talk to Agnes today?

MAMA: She's calling me from a pay phone this week. God only knows why. She has a perfectly good Trimline at home.

JESSIE (*Laughing*): Well, how is she?

MAMA: How is she every day, Jessie? Nuts.

JESSIE: Is she really crazy or just silly?

MAMA: No, she's really crazy. She was probably using the pay phone because she had another little fire problem at home.

JESSIE: Mother . . .

MAMA: I'm serious! Agnes Fletcher's burned down every house she ever lived in. Eight fires, and she's due for a new one any day now.

JESSIE (*Laughing*): No!

MAMA: Wouldn't surprise me a bit.

JESSIE (*Laughing*): Why didn't you tell me this before? Why isn't she locked up somewhere?

MAMA: 'Cause nobody ever got hurt, I guess. Agnes woke everybody up to watch the fires as soon as she set 'em. One time she set out porch chairs and served lemonade.

JESSIE (*Shaking her head*): Real lemonade?

MAMA: The houses they lived in, you knew they were going to fall down anyway, so why wait for it, is all I could ever make out about it. Agnes likes a feeling of accomplishment.

JESSIE: Good for her.

MAMA (*Finding the pan she wants*): Why are you asking about Agnes? One cup or two?

JESSIE: One. She's your friend. No marshmallows.

MAMA (*Getting the milk, etc.*): You have to have marshmallows. That's the old way, Jess. Two or three? Three is better.

JESSIE: Three, then. Her whole house burns up? Her clothes and pillows and everything? I'm not sure I believe this.

MAMA: When she was a girl, Jess, not now. Long time ago. But she's still got it in her, I'm sure of it.

JESSIE: She wouldn't burn her house down now. Where would she go? She can't get Buster to build her a new one, he's dead. How could she burn it up?

MAMA: Be exciting, though, if she did. You never know.

JESSIE: You do too know, Mama. She wouldn't do it.

MAMA (*Forced to admit, but reluctant*): I guess not.

JESSIE: What else? Why does she wear all those whistles around her neck?

MAMA: Why does she have a house full of birds?

JESSIE: I didn't know she had a house full of birds!

MAMA: Well, she does. And she says they just follow her home. Well, I know for a fact she's still paying on the last parrot she bought. You gotta keep your life filled up, she says. She says a lot of stupid things. (JESSIE *laughs*, MAMA *continues, convinced she's getting somewhere*) It's all that okra she eats. You can't just willy-nilly eat okra two meals a day and expect to get away with it. Made her crazy.

JESSIE: She really eats okra twice a day? Where does she get it in the winter?

MAMA: Well, she eats it a lot. Maybe not two meals, but . . .

JESSIE: More than the average person.

MAMA (*Beginning to get irritated*): I don't know how much okra the average person eats.

JESSIE: Do you know how much okra Agnes eats?

MAMA: No.

JESSIE: How many birds does she have?

MAMA: Two.

JESSIE: Then what are the whistles for?

MAMA: They're not real whistles. Just little plastic ones on a necklace she won playing Bingo, and I only told you about it because I thought I might get a laugh out of you for once even if it wasn't the truth, Jessie. Things don't have to be true to talk about 'em, you know.

JESSIE: Why won't she come over here?

(MAMA *is suddenly quiet, but the cocoa and milk are in the pan now, so she lights the stove and starts stirring*)

MAMA: Well now, what a good idea. We should've had more cocoa. Cocoa is perfect.

JESSIE: Except you don't like milk.

MAMA (*Another attempt, but not as energetic*): I hate milk. Coats your throat as bad as okra. Something just downright disgusting about it.

JESSIE: It's because of me, isn't it?

MAMA: No, Jess.

JESSIE: Yes, Mama.

MAMA: O.K. Yes, then, but she's crazy. She's as crazy as they come. She's a lunatic.

JESSIE: What is it exactly? Did I say something, sometime? Or did she see me have a fit and's afraid I might have another one if she came over, or what?

MAMA: I guess.

JESSIE: You guess what? What's she ever said? She must've given you some reason.

MAMA: Your hands are cold.

JESSIE: What difference does that make?

MAMA: "Like a corpse," she says, "and I'm gonna be one soon enough as it is."

JESSIE: That's crazy.

MAMA: That's Agnes. "Jessie's shook the hand of death and I can't take the chance it's catching, Thelma, so I ain't comin' over, and you can understand or not, but I ain't comin'. I'll come up the driveway, but that's as far as I go."

JESSIE (*Laughing, relieved*): I thought she didn't like me! She's scared of me! How about that! Scared of me.

MAMA: I could make her come over here, Jessie. I could call her up right now and she could bring the birds and come visit. I didn't know you ever thought about her at all. I'll tell her she just has to come and she'll come, all right. She owes me one.

JESSIE: No, that's all right. I just wondered about it. When I'm in the hospital, does she come over here?

MAMA: Her kitchen is just a tiny thing. When she comes over here, she feels like . . . (*Toning it down a little*) Well, we all like a change of scene, don't we?

JESSIE (*Playing along*): Sure we do. Plus there's no birds diving around.

MAMA: I hate those birds. She says I don't understand them. What's there to understand about birds?

JESSIE: Why Agnes likes them, for one thing. Why they stay with her when they could be outside with the other birds. What their singing means. How they fly. What they think Agnes is.

MAMA: Why do you have to know so much about things, Jessie? There's just not that much *to* things that I could ever see.

JESSIE: That you could ever *tell*, you mean. You didn't have to lie to me about Agnes.

MAMA: I didn't lie. You never asked before!

JESSIE: You lied about setting fire to all those houses and about how many birds she has and how much okra she eats and why she won't come over here. If I have to keep dragging the truth out of you, this is going to take all night.

MAMA: That's fine with me. I'm not a bit sleepy.

JESSIE: Mama . . .

MAMA: All right. Ask me whatever you want. Here.

(*They come to an awkward stop, as the cocoa is ready and* MAMA *pours it into the cups* JESSIE *has set on the table*)

JESSIE (*As* MAMA *takes her first sip*): Did you love Daddy?

MAMA: No.

JESSIE (*Pleased that* MAMA *understands the rules better now*): I didn't think so. Were you really fifteen when you married him?

MAMA: The way he told it? I'm sitting in the mud, he comes along, drags me in the kitchen, "She's been there ever since"?

JESSIE: Yes.

MAMA: No. It was a big fat lie, the whole thing. He just thought it was funnier that way. God, this milk in here.

JESSIE: The cocoa helps.

MAMA (*Pleased that they agree on this, at least*): Not enough, though, does it? You can still taste it, can't you?

JESSIE: Yeah, it's pretty bad. I thought it was my memory that was bad, but it's not. It's the milk, all right.

MAMA: It's a real waste of chocolate. You don't have to finish it.

JESSIE (*Putting her cup down*): Thanks, though.

MAMA: I should've known not to make it. I knew you wouldn't like it. You never did like it.

JESSIE: You didn't ever love him, or he did something and you stopped loving him, or what?

MAMA: He felt sorry for me. He wanted a plain country woman and that's what he married, and then he held it against me the rest of my life like I was supposed to change and surprise him somehow. Like I remember this one day he was standing on the porch and I told him to get a shirt on and he went in and got one and then he said, real peaceful, but to the point, "You're right, Thelma. If God had meant for people to go around without any clothes on, they'd have been born that way."

JESSIE (*Sees* MAMA'S *hurt*): He didn't mean anything by that, Mama.

MAMA: He never said a word he didn't have to, Jessie. That was probably all he'd said to me all day, Jessie. So if he said it, there was something to it, but I never did figure that one out. What did that mean?

JESSIE: I don't know. I liked him better than you did, but I didn't know him any better.

MAMA: How could I love him, Jessie. I didn't have a thing he wanted. (JESSIE *doesn't answer*) He got his share, though. You loved him enough for both of us. You followed him around like some . . . Jessie, all the man ever did was farm and sit . . . and try to think of somebody to sell the farm to.

JESSIE: Or make me a boyfriend out of pipe cleaners and sit back and smile like the stick man was about to dance and wasn't I going to get a kick out of that. Or sit up with a sick cow all night and leave me a chain of sleepy stick elephants on my bed in the morning.

MAMA: Or just sit.

JESSIE: I liked him sitting. Big old faded blue man in the chair. Quiet.

MAMA: Agnes gets more talk out of her birds than I got from the two of you. He could've had that GONE FISHING sign around his neck in that chair. I saw him stare off at the water. I saw him look at the weather rolling in. I got where I could practically see the boat myself. But you, you knew what he was thinking about and you're going to tell me.

JESSIE: I don't know, Mama! His life, I guess. His corn. His boots. Us. Things. You know.

MAMA: No, I don't know, Jessie! You had those quiet little conversations after supper every night. What were you whispering about?

JESSIE: We weren't whispering, you were just across the room.

MAMA: What did you talk about?

JESSIE: We talked about why black socks are warmer than blue socks. Is that something to go tell Mother? You were just jealous because I'd rather talk to him than wash the dishes with you.

MAMA: I was jealous because you'd rather talk to him than anything! (JESSIE *reaches across the table for the small clock and starts to wind it*) If I had died instead of him, he wouldn't have taken you in like I did.

JESSIE: I wouldn't have expected him to.

MAMA: Then what would you have done?

JESSIE: Come visit.

MAMA: Oh, I see. He died and left you stuck with me and you're mad about it.

JESSIE (*Getting up from the table*): Not anymore. He didn't mean to. I didn't have to come here. We've been through this.

MAMA: He felt sorry for you, too, Jessie, don't kid yourself about that. He said you were a runt and he said it from the day you were born and he said you didn't have a chance.

JESSIE (*Getting the canister of sugar and starting to refill the sugar bowl*): I know he loved me.

MAMA: What if he did? It didn't change anything.

JESSIE: It didn't have to. I miss him.

MAMA: He never really went fishing, you know. Never once. His tackle box was full of chewing tobacco and all he ever did was drive out to the lake and sit in his car. Dawson told me. And Bennie at the bait shop, he told Dawson. They all laughed about it. And he'd come back from fishing and all he'd have to show for it was . . . a whole pipe-cleaner *family*—chickens, pigs, a dog with a bad leg—it was creepy strange. It made me sick to look at them and I hid his pipe cleaners a couple of times but he always had more somewhere.

JESSIE: I thought it might be better for you after he died. You'd get interested in things. Breathe better. Change somehow.

MAMA: Into what? The Queen? A clerk in a shoe store? Why should I? Because he said to? Because you said to? (JESSIE *shakes her head*) Well I wasn't here for his entertainment and I'm not here for yours either, Jessie. I don't know what I'm here for, but then I don't think about it. (*Realizing what all this means*) But I bet you wouldn't be killing yourself if he were still alive. That's a fine thing to figure out, isn't it?

JESSIE (*Filling the honey jar now*): That's not true.

MAMA: Oh no? Then what were you asking about him for? Why did you want to know if I loved him?

JESSIE: I didn't think you did, that's all.

MAMA: Fine then. You were right. Do you feel better now?

JESSIE (*Cleaning the honey jar carefully*): It feels good to be right about it.

MAMA: It didn't matter whether I loved him. It didn't matter to me and it didn't matter to him. And it didn't mean we didn't get along. It wasn't important. We didn't talk about it. (*Sweeping the pots off the cabinet*) Take all these pots out to the porch!

JESSIE: What for?

MAMA: Just leave me this one pan. (*She jerks the silverware drawer open*) Get me one knife, one fork, one big spoon, and the can opener, and put them out where I can get them. (*Starts throwing knives and forks in one of the pans*)

JESSIE: Don't do that! I just straightened that drawer!

MAMA (*Throwing the pan in the sink*): And throw out all the plates and cups. I'll use paper. Loretta can have what she wants and Dawson can sell the rest.

JESSIE (*Calmly*): What are you doing?

MAMA: I'm not going to cook. I never liked it, anyway. I like candy. Wrapped in plastic or coming in sacks. And tuna. I like tuna. I'll eat tuna, thank you.

JESSIE (*Taking the pan out of the sink*): What if you want to make apple butter? You can't make apple butter in that little pan. What if you leave carrots on cooking and burn up that pan?

MAMA: I don't like carrots.

JESSIE: What if the strawberries are good this year and you want to go picking with Agnes.

MAMA: I'll tell her to bring a pan. You said you would do whatever I wanted! I don't want a bunch of pans cluttering up my cabinets I can't get down to, anyway. Throw them out. Every last one.

JESSIE (*Gathering up the pots*): I'm putting them all back in. I'm not taking them to the porch. If you want them, they'll be here. You'll bend down and get them, like you got the one for the cocoa. And if somebody else comes over here to cook, they'll have something to cook in, and that's the end of it!

MAMA: Who's going to come cook here?

JESSIE: Agnes.

MAMA: In my pots. Not on your life.

JESSIE: There's no reason why the two of you couldn't just live here togther. Be cheaper for both of you and somebody to talk to. And if the birds bothered you, well, one day when Agnes is out getting her hair done, you could take them all for a walk!

MAMA (*As* JESSIE *straightens the silverware*): So that's why you're pestering me about Agnes. You think you can rest easy if you get me a new babysitter? Well,

I don't want to live with Agnes. I barely want to talk with Agnes. She's just around. We go back, that's all. I'm not letting Agnes near this place. You don't get off as easy as that, child.

JESSIE: O.K., then. It's just something to think about.

MAMA: I don't like things to think about. I like things to go on.

JESSIE (*Closing the silverware drawer*): I want to know what Daddy said to you the night he died. You came storming out of his room and said I could wait it out with him if I wanted to, but you were going to watch *Gunsmoke*. What did he say to you?

MAMA: He didn't have *anything* to say to me, Jessie. That's why I left. He didn't say a thing. It was his last chance not to talk to me and he took full advantage of it.

JESSIE (*After a moment*): I'm sorry you didn't love him. Sorry for you, I mean. He seemed like a nice man.

MAMA (*As* JESSIE *walks to the refrigerator*): Ready for your apple now?

JESSIE: Soon as I'm through here, Mama.

MAMA: You won't like the apple, either. It'll be just like the cocoa. You never liked eating at all, did you? Any of it! What have you been living on all these years, toothpaste?

JESSIE (*As she starts to clean out the refrigerator*): Now, you know the milkman comes on Wednesdays and Saturdays, and he leaves the order blank in an egg box, and you give the bills to Dawson once a month.

MAMA: Do they still make that orangeade?

JESSIE: It's not orangeade, it's just orange.

MAMA: I'm going to get some. I thought they stopped making it. You just stopped ordering it.

JESSIE: You should drink milk.

MAMA: Not anymore, I'm not. That hot chocolate was the last. Hooray.

JESSIE (*Getting the garbage can from under the sink*): I told them to keep delivering a quart a week no matter what you said. I told them you'd run out of Cokes and you'd have to drink it. I told them I knew you wouldn't pour it on the ground . . .

MAMA (*Finishing her sentence*): And you told them you weren't going to be ordering anymore?

JESSIE: I told them I was taking a little holiday and to look after you.

MAMA: And they didn't think something was funny about that? You who doesn't go to the front steps? You, who only sees the driveway looking down from a stretcher passed out cold?

JESSIE (*Enjoying this, but not laughing*): They said it was about time, but why didn't I take you with me? And I said I didn't think you'd want to go, and they said, "Yeah, everybody's got their own idea of vacation."

MAMA: I guess you think that's funny.

JESSIE (*Pulling jars out of the refrigerator*): You know there never was any reason to call the ambulance for me. All they ever did for me in the emergency room was let me wake up. I could've done that here. Now, I'll just call them out and you say yes or no. I know you like pickles. Ketchup?

MAMA: Keep it.

JESSIE: We've had this since last Fourth of July.

MAMA: Keep the ketchup. Keep it all.

JESSIE: Are you going to drink ketchup from the bottle or what? How can you want your food and not want your pots to cook it in? This stuff will all spoil in here, Mother.

MAMA: Nothing I ever did was good enough for you and I want to know why.

JESSIE: That's not true.

MAMA: And I want to know why you've lived here this long feeling the way you do.

JESSIE: You have no earthly idea how I feel.

MAMA: Well, how could I? You're real far back there, Jessie.

JESSIE: Back where?

MAMA: What's it like over there, where you are? Do people always say the right thing or get whatever they want, or what?

JESSIE: What are you talking about?

MAMA: Why do you read the newspaper? Why don't you wear that sweater I made for you? Do you remember how I used to look, or am I just any old woman now? When you have a fit, do you see stars or what? How did you fall off the horse, really? Why did Cecil leave you? Where did you put my old glasses?

JESSIE (*Stunned by* MAMA'S *intensity*): They're in the bottom drawer of your dresser in an old Milk of Magnesia box. Cecil left me because he made me choose between him and smoking.

MAMA: Jessie, I know he wasn't that dumb.

JESSIE: I never understood why he hated it so much when it's so good. Smoking is the only thing I know that's always just what you think it's going to be. Just like it was the last time, right there when you want it and real quiet.

MAMA: Your fits made him sick and you know it.

JESSIE: Say seizures, not fits. Seizures.

MAMA: It's the same thing. A seizure in the hospital is a fit at home.

JESSIE: They didn't bother him at all. Except he did feel responsible for it. It *was* his idea to go horseback riding that day. It was his idea I could do *anything* if I just made up my mind to. I fell off the horse because I didn't know how to hold on. Cecil left for pretty much the same reason.

MAMA: He had a girl, Jessie. I walked right in on them in the toolshed.

JESSIE (*After a moment*): O.K. That's fair. (*Lighting another cigarette*) Was she very pretty?

MAMA: She was Agnes's girl, Carlene. Judge for yourself.

JESSIE (*As she walks to the living room*): I guess you and Agnes had a good talk about that, huh?

MAMA: I never thought he was good enough for you. They moved here from Tennessee, you know.

JESSIE: What are you talking about? You liked him better than I did. You flirted him out here to build your porch or I'd never even met him at all. You thought maybe he'd help you out around the place, come in and get some coffee and talk to you. God knows what you thought. All that curly hair.

MAMA: He's the best carpenter I ever saw. That little house of yours will still be standing at the end of the world, Jessie.

JESSIE: You didn't need a porch, Mama.

MAMA: All right! I wanted you to have a husband.

JESSIE: And I couldn't get one on my own, of course.

MAMA: How were you going to get a husband never opening your mouth to a living soul?

JESSIE: So I was quiet about it, so what?

MAMA: So I should have let you just sit here? Sit like your daddy? Sit here?

JESSIE: Maybe.

MAMA: Well, I didn't think so.

JESSIE: Well, what did you know?

MAMA: I never said I knew much. How was I supposed to learn anything living out here? I didn't know enough to do half the things I did in my life. Things happen. You do what you can about them and you see what happens next. I married you off to the wrong man, I admit that. So I took you in when he left. I'm sorry.

JESSIE: He wasn't the wrong man.

MAMA: He didn't love you, Jessie, or he wouldn't have left.

JESSIE: He wasn't the wrong man, Mama. I loved Cecil so much. And I tried to get more exercise and I tried to stay awake. I tried to learn to ride a horse. And I tried to stay outside with him, but he always knew I was trying, so it didn't work.

MAMA: He was a selfish man. He told me once he hated to see people move into his houses after he built them. He knew they'd mess them up.

JESSIE: I loved that bridge he built over the creek in back of the house. It didn't have to be anything special, a couple of boards would have been just fine, but he used that yellow pine and rubbed it so smooth . . .

MAMA: He had responsibilities here. He had a wife and son here and he failed you.

JESSIE: Or that baby bed he built for Ricky. I told him he didn't have to spend so much time on it, but he said it had to last, and the thing ended up weighing two hundred pounds and I couldn't move it. I said, "How long does a baby bed have to last, anyway?" But maybe he thought if it was strong enough, it might keep Ricky a baby.

MAMA: Ricky is too much like Cecil.

JESSIE: He is not. Ricky is as much like me as it's possible for any human to be. We even wear the same size pants. These are his, I think.

MAMA: That's just the same size. That's not you're the same person.

JESSIE: I see it on his face. I hear it when he talks. We look out at the world and we see the same thing: Not Fair. And the only difference between us is Ricky's out there trying to get even. And he knows not to trust anybody and he got it straight from me. And he knows not to try to get work, and guess where he got that. He walks around like there's loose boards in the floor, and you know who laid that floor, I did.

MAMA: Ricky isn't through yet. You don't know how he'll turn out!

JESSIE (*Going back to the kitchen*): Yes I do and so did Cecil. Ricky is the two of us together for all time in too small a space. And we're tearing each other apart, like always, inside that boy, and if you don't see it, then you're just blind.

MAMA: Give him time, Jess.

JESSIE: Oh, he'll have plenty of that. Five years for forgery, ten years for armed assault . . .

MAMA (*Furious*): Stop that! (*Then pleading*) Jessie, Cecil might be ready to try it again, honey, that happens sometimes. Go downtown. Find him. Talk to him.

He didn't know what he had in you. Maybe he sees things different now, but you're not going to know that till you go see him. Or call him up! Right now! He might be home.

JESSIE: And say what? Nothing's changed, Cecil, I'd just like to look at you, if you don't mind? No. He loved me, Mama. He just didn't know how things fall down around me like they do. I think he did the right thing. He gave himself another chance, that's all. But I did beg him to take me with him. I did tell him I would leave Ricky and you and everything I loved out here if only he would take me with him, but he couldn't and I understood that. (*Pause*) I wrote that note I showed you, I wrote it. Not Cecil. I said "I'm sorry, Jessie, I can't fix it all for you." I said I'd always love me, not Cecil. But that's how he felt.

MAMA: Then he should've taken you with him!

JESSIE (*Picking up the garbage bag she has filled*): Mama, you don't pack your garbage when you move.

MAMA: You will not call yourself garbage, Jessie.

JESSIE (*Taking the bag to the big garbage can near the back door*): Just a way of saying it, Mama. Thinking about my list, that's all. (*Opening the can, putting the garbage in, then securing the lid*) Well, a little more than that. I was trying to say it's all right that Cecil left. It was . . . a relief in a way. I never was what he wanted to see, so it was better when he wasn't looking at me all the time.

MAMA: I'll make your apple now.

JESSIE: No thanks. You get the manicure stuff and I'll be right there.

(JESSIE *ties up the big garbage bag in the can and replaces the small garbage bag under the sink, all the time trying desperately to regain her calm.* MAMA *watches, from a distance, her hand reaching unconsciously for the phone. Then she has a better idea. Or rather she thinks of the only other thing left and is willing to try it. Maybe she is even convinced it will work*)

MAMA: Jessie, I think your daddy had little . . .

JESSIE (*Interrupting her*): Garbage night is Tuesday. Put it out as late as you can. The Davis's dogs get in it if you don't. (*Replacing the garbage bag in the can under the sink*) And keep ordering the heavy black bags. It doesn't pay to buy the cheap ones. And I've got all the ties here with the hammers and all. Take them out of the box as soon as you open a new one and put them in this drawer. They'll get lost if you don't, and rubber bands or something else won't work.

MAMA: I think your daddy had fits, too. I think he sat in his chair and had little fits. I read this a long time ago in a magazine, how little fits go, just little blackouts where maybe their eyes don't even close and people just call them "thinking spells."

JESSIE (*Getting the slipcover out of the laundry basket*): I don't think you want this manicure we've been looking forward to. I washed this cover for the sofa, but it'll take both of us to get it back on.

MAMA: I watched his eyes. I know that's what it was. The magazine said some people don't even know they've had one.

JESSIE: Daddy would've known if he'd had fits, Mama.

MAMA: The lady in this story had kept track of hers and she'd had eighty thousand of them in the last eleven years.

JESSIE: Next time you wash this cover, it'll dry better if you put it on wet.

MAMA: Jessie, listen to what I'm telling you. This lady had anywhere between five and five hundred fits a day and they lasted maybe fifteen seconds apiece, so that out of her life, she'd only lost about two weeks altogether, and she had a full-time secretary job and an IQ of 120.

JESSIE (*Amused by* MAMA'S *approach*): You want to talk about fits, is that it?

MAMA: Yes. I do. I want to say . . .

JESSIE (*Interrupting*): Most of the time I wouldn't even know I'd had one, except I wake up with different clothes on, feeling like I've been run over. Sometimes I feel my head start to turn around or hear myself scream. And sometimes there *is* this dizzy stupid feeling a little before it, but if the TV's on, well, it's easy to miss. (*As* JESSIE *and* MAMA *replace the slipcover on the sofa and the afghan on the chair, the physical struggle somehow mirrors the emotional one in the conversation*)

MAMA: I can tell when you're about to have one. Your eyes get this big! But, Jessie, you haven't . . .

JESSIE (*Taking charge of this*): What do they look like? The seizures.

MAMA (*Reluctant*): Different each time, Jess.

JESSIE: O.K. Pick one, then. A good one. I think I want to know now.

MAMA: There's not much to tell. You just . . . crumple, in a heap, like a puppet and somebody cut the strings all at once, or like the firing squad in some Mexican movie, you just slide down the wall, you know. You don't know what happens? How can you not know what happens?

JESSIE: I'm busy.

MAMA: That's not funny.

JESSIE: I'm not laughing. My head turns around and I fall down and then what?

MAMA: Well, your chest squeezes in and out, and you sound like you're gagging, sucking air in and out like you can't breathe.

JESSIE: Do it for me. Make the sound for me.

MAMA: I will not. It's awful-sounding.

JESSIE: Yeah. It felt like it might be. What's next?

MAMA: Your mouth bites down and I have to get your tongue out of the way fast, so you don't bite yourself.

JESSIE: Or you, I bite you, too, don't I?

MAMA: You got me once real good. I had to get a tetanus! But I know what to watch for now. And then you turn blue and the jerks start up. Like I'm standing there poking you with a cattle prod or you're sticking your finger in a light socket as fast as you can . . .

JESSIE: Foaming like a mad dog the whole time.

MAMA: It's bubbling, Jess, not foam like the washer overflowed, for God's sake; it's bubbling like a baby spitting up. I go get a wet washcloth, that's all. And then the jerks slow down and you wet yourself and it's over. Two minutes tops.

JESSIE: How do I get to the bed?

MAMA: How do you think?

JESSIE: I'm too heavy for you now. How do you do it?

MAMA: I call Dawson. But I get you cleaned up before he gets here and I make him leave before you wake up.

JESSIE: You could just leave me on the floor.

MAMA: I want you to wake up someplace nice, O.K.? (*Then making a real effort*) But, Jessie, and this is the reason I even brought this up! You haven't had a seizure for a solid year. A whole year, do you realize that?

JESSIE: Yeah, the phenobarb's about right now, I guess.

MAMA: You bet it is. You might never have another one, ever! You might be through with it for all time!

JESSIE: Could be.

MAMA: You are. I know you are!

JESSIE: I sure am feeling good. I really am. The double vision's gone and my gums aren't swelling. No rashes or anything. I'm feeling as good as I ever felt in my life. I'm even feeling like worrying or getting mad and I'm not afraid it will start a fit if I do, I just go ahead.

MAMA: Of course you do! You can even scream at me, if you want to. I can take it. You don't have to act like you're just visiting here, Jessie. This is your house, too.

JESSIE: The best part is, my memory's back.

MAMA: Your memory's always been good. When couldn't you remember things? You're always reminding me what . . .

JESSIE: Because I've made lists for everything. But now I remember what things mean on my lists. I see "dish towels," and I used to wonder whether I was supposed to wash them, buy them, or look for them because I wouldn't remember where I put them after I washed them, but now I know it means wrap them up, they're a present for Loretta's birthday.

MAMA (*Finished with the sofa now*): You used to go looking for your lists, too, I've noticed that. You always know where they are now! (*Then suddenly worried*) Loretta's birthday isn't coming up, is it?

JESSIE: I made a list of all the birthdays for you. I even put yours on it. (*A small smile*) So you can call Loretta and remind her.

MAMA: Let's take Loretta to Howard Johnson's and have those fried clams. I *know* you love that clam roll.

JESSIE (*Slight pause*): I won't be here, Mama.

MAMA: What have we just been talking about? You'll be here. You're well, Jessie. You're starting all over. You said it yourself. You're remembering things and . . .

JESSIE: I won't be here. If I'd ever had a year like this, to think straight and all, before now, I'd be gone already.

MAMA (*Not pleading, commanding*): No, Jessie.

JESSIE (*Folding the rest of the laundry*): Yes, Mama. Once I started remembering, I could see what it all added up to.

MAMA: The fits are over!

JESSIE: It's not the fits, Mama.

MAMA: Then it's me for giving them to you, but I didn't do it!

JESSIE: It's not the fits! You said it yourself, the medicine takes care of the fits.

MAMA (*Interrupting*): Your daddy gave you those fits, Jessie. He passed it down to you like your green eyes and your straight hair. It's not my fault!

JESSIE: So what if he had little fits? It's not inherited. I fell off the horse. It was an accident.

MAMA: The horse wasn't the first time, Jessie. You had a fit when you were five years old.

JESSIE: I did not.

MAMA: You did! You were eating a popsicle and down you went. He gave it to you. It's *his* fault, not mine.

JESSIE: Well, you took your time telling me.

MAMA: How do you tell that to a five-year-old?

JESSIE: What did the doctor say?

MAMA: He said kids have them all the time. He said there wasn't anything to do but wait for another one.

JESSIE: But I didn't have another one.

(*Now there is a real silence*)

JESSIE: You mean to tell me I had fits all the time as a kid and you just told me. I fell down or something and it wasn't till I had the fit when Cecil was looking that anybody bothered to find out what was the matter with me?

MAMA: It wasn't *all the time*, Jessie. And they changed when you started to school. More like your daddy's. Oh, that was some swell time, sitting here with the two of you turning off and on like light bulbs some nights.

JESSIE: How many fits did I have?

MAMA: You never hurt yourself. I never let you out of my sight. I caught you every time.

JESSIE: But you didn't tell anybody.

MAMA: It was none of their business.

JESSIE: You were ashamed.

MAMA: I didn't want anybody to know. Least of all you.

JESSIE: Least of all me. Oh, right. That was mine to know, Mama, not yours. Did Daddy know?

MAMA: He thought you were . . . you fell down a lot. That's what he thought. You were careless. Or maybe he thought I beat you. I don't know what he thought. He didn't think about it.

JESSIE: Because you didn't tell him!

MAMA: If I told him about you, I'd have to tell him about him!

JESSIE: I don't like this. I don't like this one bit.

MAMA: I didn't think you'd like it. That's why I didn't tell you.

JESSIE: If I'd known I was an epileptic, Mama, I wouldn't have ridden any horses.

MAMA: Make you feel like a freak, is that what I should have done?

JESSIE: Just get the manicure tray and sit down!

MAMA (*Throwing it to the floor*): I don't want a manicure!

JESSIE: Doesn't look like you do, no.

MAMA: Maybe I did drop you, you don't know.

JESSIE: If you say you didn't, you didn't.

MAMA (*Beginning to break down*): Maybe I fed you the wrong thing. Maybe you had a fever sometime and I didn't know it soon enough. Maybe it's a punishment.

JESSIE: For what?

MAMA: I don't know. Because of how I felt about your father. Because I didn't want any more children. Because I smoked too much or didn't eat right when I was carrying you. It has to be something I did.

JESSIE: It does not. It's just a sickness, not a curse. Epilepsy doesn't mean anything. It just is.

MAMA: I'm not talking about the fits here, Jessie! I'm talking about this killing yourself. It has to be me that's the matter here. You wouldn't be doing this if it wasn't. I didn't tell you things or I married you off to the wrong man or I took you in and let your life get away from you or all of it put together. I don't know what I did, but I did it, I know. This is all my fault, Jessie, but I don't know what to do about it now!

JESSIE (*Exasperated at having to say this again*): It doesn't have anything to do with you!

MAMA: Everything you do has to do with me, Jessie. You can't do *anything*, wash your face or cut your finger, without doing it to me. That's right! You might as well kill me as you, Jessie, it's the same thing. This has to do with me, Jessie.

JESSIE: Then what if it does! What if it has everything to do with you! What if you are all I have and you're not enough? What if I could take all the rest of it if only I didn't have you here? What if the only way I can get away from you for good is to kill myself? What if it is? I can *still* do it!

MAMA (*In desperate tears*): Don't leave me, Jessie! (JESSIE *stands for a moment, then turns for the bedroom*) No! (*She grabs* JESSIE'S *arm*)

JESSIE (*Carefully taking her arm away*): I have a box of things I want people to have. I'm just going to go get it for you. You . . . just rest a minute.

(JESSIE *is gone.* MAMA *heads for the telephone, but she can't even pick up the receiver this time and, instead, stoops to clean up the bottles that have spilled out of the manicure tray*

JESSIE *returns, carrying a box that groceries were delivered in. It probably says Hershey Kisses or Starkist Tuna.* MAMA *is still down on the floor cleaning up, hoping that maybe if she just makes it look nice enough,* JESSIE *will stay*)

MAMA: Jessie, how can I live here without you? I need you! You're supposed to tell me to stand up straight and say how nice I look in my pink dress, and drink my milk. You're supposed to go around and lock up so I know we're safe for the night, and when I wake up, you're supposed to be out there making the coffee and watching me get older every day, and you're supposed to help me die when the time comes. I can't do that by myself, Jessie. I'm not like you, Jessie. I hate the quiet and I don't want to die and I don't want you to go, Jessie. How can I . . . (*Has to stop a moment*) How can I get up every day knowing you had to kill yourself to make it stop hurting and I was here all the time and I never even saw it. And then you gave me this chance to make it better, convince you to stay alive, and I couldn't do it. How can I live with myself after this, Jessie?

JESSIE: I only told you so I could explain it, so you wouldn't blame yourself, so you wouldn't feel bad. There wasn't anything you could say to change my mind. I didn't want you to save me. I just wanted you to know.

MAMA: Stay with me just a little longer. Just a few more years. I don't have that many more to go, Jessie. And as soon as I'm dead, you can do whatever you want. Maybe with me gone, you'll have all the quiet you want, right here in the house. And maybe one day you'll put in some begonias up the walk and get just the right rain for them all summer. And Ricky will be married by then and he'll bring your grandbabies over and you can sneak them a piece of candy when their daddy's not looking and then be real glad when they've gone home and left you to your quiet again.

JESSIE: Don't you see, Mama, everything I do winds up like this. How could I think you would understand? How could I think you would want a manicure? We could hold hands for an hour and then I could go shoot myself? I'm sorry about tonight, Mama, but it's exactly why I'm doing it.

MAMA: If you've got the guts to kill yourself, Jessie, you've got the guts to stay alive.

JESSIE: I know that. So it's really just a matter of where I'd rather be.

MAMA: Look, maybe I can't think of what you should do, but that doesn't mean there isn't something that would help. *You* find it. *You* think of it. You can keep trying. You can get brave and try some more. You don't have to give up!

JESSIE: I'm *not* giving up! This *is* the other thing I'm trying. And I'm sure there are some other things that might work, but *might* work isn't good enough anymore. I need something that *will* work. *This* will work. That's why I picked it.

MAMA: But something might happen. Something that could change everything. Who knows what it might be, but it might be worth waiting for! (JESSIE *doesn't respond*) Try it for two more weeks. We could have more talks like tonight.

JESSIE: No, Mama.

MAMA: I'll pay more attention to you. Tell the truth when you ask me. Let you have your say.

JESSIE: No, Mama! We wouldn't have more talks like tonight, because it's this next part that's made this last part so good, Mama. No, Mama. *This* is how I have my say. This is how I say what I thought about it *all* and I say no. To Dawson and Loretta and the Red Chinese and epilepsy and Ricky and Cecil and you. And me. And hope. I say no! (*Then going to Mama on the sofa*) Just let me go easy, Mama.

MAMA: How can I let you go?

JESSIE: You can because you have to. It's what you've always done.

MAMA: You are my child!

JESSIE: I am what became of your child. (MAMA *cannot answer*) I found an old baby picture of me. And it was somebody else, not me. It was somebody pink and fat who never heard of sick or lonely, somebody who cried and got fed, and reached up and got held and kicked but didn't hurt anybody, and slept whenever she wanted to, just by closing her eyes. Somebody who mainly just laid there and laughed at the colors waving around over her head and chewed on a polka-dot whale and woke up knowing some new trick nearly every day, and rolled over and drooled on the sheet and felt your hand pulling my quilt back up over me. That's who I started out and this is who is left. (*There is no self-pity here*) That's what this is about. It's somebody I lost, all right, it's my own self. Who I never was. Or who I tried to be and never got there. Somebody I waited for who never came. And never will. So, see, it doesn't much matter what else happens in the world or in this house, even. I'm what was worth waiting for and I didn't make it. Me . . . who might have made a difference to me . . . I'm not going to show up, so there's no reason to stay, except to keep you company, and that's . . . not reason enough because I'm not . . . very good company. (*Pause*) Am I.

MAMA (*Knowing she must tell the truth*): No. And neither am I.

JESSIE: I had this strange little thought, well, maybe it's not so strange. Anyway, after Christmas, after I decided to do this, I would wonder, sometimes, what might keep me here, what might be worth staying for, and you know what it was? It was maybe if there was something I really liked, like maybe if I really liked rice pudding or cornflakes for breakfast or something, that might be enough.

MAMA: Rice pudding is good.

JESSIE: Not to me.

MAMA: And you're not afraid?

JESSIE: Afraid of what?

MAMA: I'm afraid of it, for me, I mean. When my time comes. I know it's coming, but . . .

JESSIE: You don't know when. Like in a scary movie.

MAMA: Yeah, sneaking up on me like some killer on the loose, hiding out in the back yard just waiting for me to have my hands full someday and how am I supposed to protect myself anyhow when I don't know what he looks like and I don't know how he sounds coming up behind me like that or if it will hurt or take very long or what I don't get done before it happens.

JESSIE: You've got plenty of time left.

MAMA: I forget what for, right now.

JESSIE: For whatever happens, I don't know. For the rest of your life. For Agnes burning down one more house or Dawson losing his hair or . . .

MAMA (*Quickly*): Jessie. I can't just sit here and say O.K., kill yourself if you want to.

JESSIE: Sure you can. You just did. Say it again.

MAMA (*Really startled*): Jessie! (*Quiet horror*) How dare you! (*Furious*) How dare you! You think you can just leave whenever you want, like you're watching television here? No, you can't, Jessie. You make me feel like a fool for being alive, child, and you are so wrong! I like it here, and I will stay here until they make me go, until they drag me screaming and I mean screeching into my grave, and you're real smart to get away before then because, I mean, honey, you've never heard noise like that in your life. (JESSIE *turns away*) Who am I talking to? You're gone already, aren't you? I'm looking right through you! I can't stop you because you're already gone! I guess you think they'll all have to talk about you now! I guess you think this will really confuse them. Oh yes, ever since Christmas you've been laughing to yourself and thinking, "Boy, are they all in for a surprise." Well, nobody's going to be a bit surprised, sweetheart. This is just like you. Do it the hard way, that's my girl, all right. (JESSIE *gets up and goes into the kitchen, but* MAMA *follows her*) You know who they're going to feel sorry for? Me! How about that! Not you, me! They're going to be *ashamed* of you. Yes. *Ashamed!* If somebody asks Dawson about it, he'll change the subject as fast as he can. He'll talk about how much he has to pay to park his car these days.

JESSIE: Leave me alone.

MAMA: It's the truth!

JESSIE: I should've just left you a note!

MAMA (*Screaming*): Yes! (*Then suddenly understanding what she has said, nearly paralyzed by the thought of it, she turns slowly to face* JESSIE *nearly whispering*) No. No. I . . . might not have thought of all the things you've said.

JESSIE: It's O.K., Mama.

(MAMA *is nearly unconscious from the emotional devastation of these last few moments. She sits down at the kitchen table, hurt and angry and desperately afraid. But she looks almost numb. She is so far beyond what is known as pain that she is virtually unreachable and* JESSIE *knows this, and talks quietly, watching for signs of recovery*)

JESSIE (*Washes her hands in the sink*): I remember you liked that preacher who did Daddy's, so if you want to ask him to do the service, that's O.K. with me.

MAMA (*Not an answer, just a word*): What.

JESSIE (*Putting on hand lotion as she talks*): And pick some songs you like or let Agnes pick, she'll know exactly which ones. Oh, and I had your dress cleaned that you wore to Daddy's. You looked real good in that.

MAMA: I don't remember, hon.

JESSIE: And it won't be so bad once your friends start coming to the funeral home. You'll probably see people you haven't seen for years, but I thought about what you should say to get you over that nervous part when they first come in.

MAMA (*Simply repeating*): Come in.

JESSIE: Take them up to see their flowers, they'd like that. And when they say, "I'm so sorry, Thelma," you just say, "I appreciate your coming, Connie." And then ask how their garden was this summer or what they're doing for Thanksgiving or how their children . . .

MAMA: I don't think I should ask about their children. I'll talk about what they have on, that's always good. And I'll have some crochet work with me.

JESSIE: And Agnes will be there, so you might not have to talk at all.

MAMA: Maybe if Connie Richards does come, I can get her to tell me where she gets that Irish yarn, she calls it. I know it doesn't come from Ireland. I think it just comes with a green wrapper.

JESSIE: And be sure to invite enough people home afterward so you get enough food to feed them all and have some left for you. But don't let anybody take anything home, especially Loretta.

MAMA: Loretta will get all the food set up, honey. It's only fair to let her have some macaroni or something.

JESSIE: No, Mama. You have to be more selfish from now on. (*Sitting at the table with* MAMA) Now, somebody's bound to ask you why I did it and you just say you don't know. That you loved me and you know I loved you and we just sat around tonight like every other night of our lives, and then I came over and kissed you and said, "'Night, Mother," and you heard me close my bedroom door and the next thing you heard was the shot. And whatever reasons I had, well, you guess I just took them with me.

MAMA (*Quietly*): It was something personal.

JESSIE: Good. That's good, Mama.

MAMA: That's what I'll say, then.

JESSIE: Personal. Yeah.

MAMA: Is that what I tell Dawson and Loretta, too? We sat around, you kissed me, "'Night, Mother"? They'll want to know more, Jessie. They won't believe it.

JESSIE: Well, then, tell them what we did. I filled up the candy jars. I cleaned out the refrigerator. We made some hot chocolate and put the cover back on the sofa. You had no idea. All right? I really think it's better that way. If they know we talked about it, they really won't understand how you let me go.

MAMA: I guess not.

JESSIE: It's private. Tonight is private, yours and mine, and I don't want anybody else to have any of it.

MAMA: O.K., then.

JESSIE (*Standing behind* MAMA *now, holding her shoulders*): Now, when you hear the shot, I don't want you to come in. First of all, you won't be able to get in by yourself, but I don't want you trying. Call Dawson, then call the police, and then call Agnes. And then you'll need something to do till somebody gets here, so wash the hot-chocolate pan. You wash that pan till you hear the doorbell ring and I don't care if it's an hour, you keep washing that pan.

MAMA: I'll make my calls and then I'll just sit. I won't need something to do. What will the police say?

JESSIE: They'll do that gunpowder test, I guess, and ask you what happened, and by that time, the ambulance will be here and they'll come in and get me and you know how that goes. You stay out here with Dawson and Loretta. You keep Dawson out here. I want the police in the room first, not Dawson, O.K.?

MAMA: What if Dawson and Loretta want me to go home with them?

JESSIE (*Returning to the living room*): That's up to you.

MAMA: I think I'll stay here. All they've got is Sanka.

JESSIE: Maybe Agnes could come stay with you for a few days.

MAMA (*Standing up, looking into the living room*): I'd rather be by myself, I think. (*Walking toward the box* JESSIE *brought in earlier*) You want me to give people those things?

JESSIE (*They sit down on the sofa,* JESSIE *holding the box on her lap*): I want Loretta to have my little calculator. Dawson bought it for himself, you know, but then he saw one he liked better and he couldn't bring both of them home with Loretta counting every penny the way she does, so he gave the first one to me. Be funny for her to have it now, don't you think? And all my house slippers are in a sack for her in my closet. Tell her I know they'll fit and I've never worn any of them, and make sure Dawson hears you tell her that. I'm glad he loves Loretta so much, but I wish he knew not everybody has her size feet.

MAMA (*Taking the calculator*): O.K.

JESSIE (*Reaching into the box again*): This letter is for Dawson, but it's mostly about you, so read it if you want. There's a list of presents for you for at least twenty more Christmases and birthdays, so if you want anything special you better add it to this list before you give it to him. Or if you want to be surprised, just don't read that page. This Christmas, you're getting mostly stuff for the house, like a new rug in your bathroom and needlework, but next Christmas, you're really going to cost him next Christmas. I think you'll like it a lot and you'd never think of it.

MAMA: And you think he'll go for it?

JESSIE: I think he'll feel like a real jerk if he doesn't. Me telling him to, like this and all. Now, this number's where you call Cecil. I called it last week and he answered, so I know he still lives there.

MAMA: What do you want me to tell him?

JESSIE: Tell him we talked about him and I only had good things to say about him, but mainly tell him to find Ricky and tell him what I did, and tell Ricky you have something for him, out here, from me, and to come get it. (*Pulls a sack out of the box*)

MAMA (*The sack feels empty*): What is it?

JESSIE (*Taking it off*): My watch. (*Putting it in the sack and taking a ribbon out of the sack to tie around the top of it*)

MAMA: He'll sell it!

JESSIE: That's the idea. I appreciate him not stealing it already. I'd like to buy him a good meal.

MAMA: He'll buy dope with it!

JESSIE: Well, then, I hope he gets some good dope with it, Mama. And the rest of this is for you. (*Handing* MAMA *the box now.* MAMA *picks up the things and looks at them*)

MAMA (*Surprised and pleased*): When did you do all this? During my naps, I guess.

JESSIE: I guess. I tried to be quiet about it. (*As* MAMA *is puzzled by the presents*) Those are just little presents. For whenever you need one. They're not bought presents, just things I thought you might like to look at, pictures or things you think you've lost. Things you didn't know you had, even. You'll see.

MAMA: I'm not sure I want them. They'll make me think of you.

JESSIE: No they won't. They're just things, like a free tube of toothpaste I found hanging on the door one day.

MAMA: Oh. All right, then.

JESSIE: Well, maybe there's one nice present in there somewhere. It's Granny's ring she gave me and I thought you might like to have it, but I didn't think you'd wear it if I gave it to you right now.

MAMA (*Taking the box to a table nearby*): No. Probably not. (*Turning back to face her*) I'm ready for my manicure, I guess. Want me to wash my hands again?

JESSIE (*Standing up*): It's time for me to go, Mama.

MAMA (*Starting for her*): No, Jessie, you've got all night!

JESSIE (*As* MAMA *grabs her*): No, Mama.

MAMA: It's not even ten o'clock.

JESSIE (*Very calm*): Let me go, Mama.

MAMA: I can't. You can't go. You can't do this. You didn't say it would be so soon, Jessie. I'm scared. I love you.

JESSIE (*Takes her hands away*): Let go of me, Mama. I've said everything I had to say.

MAMA (*Standing still a minute*): You said you wanted to do my nails.

JESSIE (*Taking a small step backward*): I can't. It's too late.

MAMA: It's not too late!

JESSIE: I don't want you to wake Dawson and Loretta when you call. I want them to still be up and dressed so they can get right over.

MAMA (*As* JESSIE *backs up,* MAMA *moves in on her, but carefully*): They wake up fast, Jessie, if they have to. They don't matter here, Jessie. You do. I do. We're not through yet. We've got a lot of things to take care of here. I don't know where my prescriptions are and you didn't tell me what to tell Dr. Davis when he calls or how much you want me to tell Ricky or who I call to rake the leaves or . . .

JESSIE: Don't try and stop me, Mama, you can't do it.

MAMA (*Grabbing her again, this time hard*): I can too! I'll stand in front of this hall and you can't get past me. (*They struggle*) You'll have to knock me down to get away from me, Jessie. I'm not about to let you . . .

(MAMA *struggles with* JESSIE *at the door and in the struggle* JESSIE *gets away from her and—*

JESSIE (*Almost a whisper*): 'Night, Mother. (*She vanishes into her bedroom and we hear the door lock just as* MAMA *gets to it*)

MAMA (*Screams*): Jessie! (*Pounding on the door*) Jessie, you let me in there. Don't you do this, Jessie. I'm not going to stop screaming until you open this door, Jessie. Jessie! Jessie! What if I don't do any of the things you told me to do! I'll tell Cecil what a miserable man he was to make you feel the way he did and I'll give Ricky's watch to Dawson if I feel like it and the only way you can make sure I do what you want is you come out here and make me, Jessie! (*Pounding again*) Jessie! Stop this! I didn't know! I was here with you all the time. How could I know you were so alone?

(*And* MAMA *stops for a moment, breathless and frantic, putting her ear to the door, and when she doesn't hear anything, she stands up straight again and screams once more*)

Jessie! Please!

(*And we hear the shot, and it sounds like an answer, it sounds like No.*

MAMA *collapses against the door, tears streaming down her face, but not screaming anymore. In shock now*)

Jessie, Jessie, child . . . Forgive me. (*Pause*) I thought you were mine.

(*And she leaves the door and makes her way through the living room, around the furniture, as though she didn't know where it was, not knowing what to do. Finally, she goes to the stove in the kitchen and picks up the hot-chocolate pan and carries it with her to the telephone, and holds on to it while she dials the number. She looks down at the pan, holding it tight like her life depended on it. She hears Loretta answer*)

MAMA: Loretta, let me talk to Dawson, honey.

AUGUST WILSON (1945–2005) was born as Frederick August Kittel in Pittsburgh to an African American mother and a white German father, who soon abandoned the family. He grew up in poverty, but could read at the age of four. When his mother was remarried, Wilson's family moved to a predominantly white suburb, where he spent his high school career experiencing racism on a daily basis. He

Romare Bearden, *The Piano Lesson* (1983)

dropped out of school at fifteen, after having been accused of plagiarism, and began to educate himself. At twenty, Wilson moved out of his mother's house, bought a typewriter and a used Victrola; he became involved with a group of African American intellectuals and writers and developed his interest in the blues as an African American musical form. Wilson was also influenced by Malcolm X and the **Black Power movement**. With Rob Penny, Wilson founded the Black Horizon on the Hill Theater, which produced his plays between 1968 and 1978. When his mother died in 1983, he took her maiden name. Wilson's first success was *Ma Rainey's Black Bottom* (1984), which won the New York Drama Critics Circle Award. Other plays include *Fences* (1987), which won the Pulitzer Prize, and *Joe Turner's Come and Gone* (1988). *The Piano Lesson* (1990) also won the Pulitzer Prize. The title of *The Piano Lesson* was inspired by Romare Bearden's 1983 collage of the same name, whose central subject may be another Pittsburgh native, jazz pianist Mary Lou Williams.

The Piano Lesson, as part of Wilson's cycle of historical plays, takes place in the Pittsburgh neighborhood where Wilson grew up. Its prominent themes are racial injustice, the search for identity, overcoming the damaging legacy of slavery, and the power of language and the blues in African American culture. Despite the inclusion of supernatural elements, *The Piano Lesson* focuses largely on the daily rituals of the characters' lives and on **African American folkways**. Wilson is a master of dramatic **dialogue** modeled on African American call and response; he communicates the heroism of his characters strictly through their everyday encounters within domestic interiors. Like *The Glass Menagerie, The Piano Lesson* centers around the richly symbolic **prop** of the family piano, which embodies the family's tragic history and perilously fragile identity. Music, and in particular the blues, also plays a central role in resolving the characters' sense of person and place.

Related Works: Clifton, "my mama moved among the days"; Cofer, "Tales Told Under the Mango Tree"; Dunbar, "We wear the mask"; Ellison, "Battle Royal"; Shakespeare, *Hamlet*; Williams, *The Glass Menagerie*.

The Piano Lesson

The Setting

The action of the play takes place in the kitchen and parlor of the house where DOAKER CHARLES lives with his niece, BERNIECE and her eleven-year-old daughter, MARETHA. The house is sparsely furnished, and although there is evidence of a woman's touch, there is a lack of warmth and vigor. BERNIECE and MARETHA occupy the upstairs rooms. DOAKER's room is prominent and opens onto the kitchen. Dominating the parlor is an old upright piano. On the legs of the piano, carved in the manner of African sculpture, are mask-like figures resembling totems. The carvings are rendered with a grace and power of invention that lifts them out of the realm of craftsmanship and into the realm of art. At left is a staircase leading to the upstairs.

ACT ONE

SCENE 1

(*The lights come up on the Charles household. It is five o'clock in the morning. The dawn is beginning to announce itself, but there is something in the air that belongs to the night. A stillness that is a portent, a gathering, a coming together of something akin to a storm. There is a loud knock at the door.*)

BOY WILLIE: (*Off stage, calling.*) Hey, Doaker . . . Doaker!

(*He knocks again and calls.*)

Hey, Doaker! Hey, Berniece! Berniece!

(DOAKER *enters from his room. He is a tall, thin man of forty-seven, with severe features, who has for all intents and purposes retired from the world though he works full-time as a railroad cook.*)

DOAKER: Who is it?

BOY WILLIE: Open the door, nigger! It's me . . . Boy Willie!

DOAKER: Who?

BOY WILLIE: Boy Willie! Open the door!

(DOAKER *opens the door and* BOY WILLIE *and* LYMON *enter.* BOY WILLIE *is thirty years old. He has an infectious grin and a boyishness that is apt for his name. He is brash and impulsive, talkative and somewhat crude in speech and manner.* LYMON *is twenty-nine.* BOY WILLIE*'s partner, he talks little, and then with a straightforwardness that is often disarming.*)

DOAKER: What you doing up here?

BOY WILLIE: I told you, Lymon. Lymon talking about you might be sleep. This is Lymon. You remember Lymon Jackson from down home? This my Uncle Doaker.

DOAKER: What you doing up here? I couldn't figure out who that was. I thought you was still down in Mississippi.

BOY WILLIE: Me and Lymon selling watermelons. We got a truck out there. Got a whole truckload of watermelons. We brought them up here to sell. Where's Berniece?

(*Calls.*)

Hey, Berniece!

DOAKER: Berniece up there sleep.

BOY WILLIE: Well, let her get up.

(*Calls.*)

Hey, Berniece!

DOAKER: She got to go to work in the morning.

BOY WILLIE: Well she can get up and say hi. It's been three years since I seen her.

(*Calls.*)

Hey, Berniece! It's me . . . Boy Willie.

DOAKER: Berniece don't like all that hollering now. She got to work in the morning.

BOY WILLIE: She can go on back to bed. Me and Lymon been riding two days in that truck . . . the least she can do is get up and say hi.

DOAKER: (*Looking out the window.*) Where you all get that truck from?

BOY WILLIE: It's Lymon's. I told him let's get a load of watermelons and bring them up here.

LYMON: Boy Willie say he going back, but I'm gonna stay. See what it's like up here.

BOY WILLIE: You gonna carry me down there first.

LYMON: I told you I ain't going back down there and take a chance on that truck breaking down again. You can take the train. Hey, tell him Doaker, he can take the train back. After we sell them watermelons he have enough money he can buy him a whole railroad car.

DOAKER: You got all them watermelons stacked up there no wonder the truck broke down. I'm surprised you made it this far with a load like that. Where you break down at?

BOY WILLIE: We broke down three times! It took us two and a half days to get here. It's a good thing we picked them watermelons fresh.

LYMON: We broke down twice in West Virginia. The first time was just as soon as we got out of Sunflower. About forty miles out she broke down. We got it going and got all the way to West Virginia before she broke down again.

BOY WILLIE: We had to walk about five miles for some water.

LYMON: It got a hole in the radiator but it runs pretty good. You have to pump the brakes sometime before they catch. Boy Willie have his door open and be ready to jump when that happens.

BOY WILLIE: Lymon think that's funny. I told the nigger I give him ten dollars to get the brakes fixed. But he thinks that funny.

LYMON: They don't need fixing. All you got to do is pump them till they catch.

(BERNIECE *enters on the stairs. Thirty-five years old, with an eleven-year-old daughter, she is still in mourning for her husband after three years.*)

BERNIECE: What you doing all that hollering for?

BOY WILLIE: Hey, Berniece. Doaker said you was sleep. I said at least you could get up and say hi.

BERNIECE: It's five o'clock in the morning and you come in here with all this noise. You can't come like normal folks. You got to bring all that noise with you.

BOY WILLIE: Hell, I ain't done nothing but come in and say hi. I ain't got in the house good.

BERNIECE: That's what I'm talking about. You start all that hollering and carry on as soon as you hit the door.

BOY WILLIE: Aw hell, woman, I was glad to see Doaker. You ain't had to come down if you didn't want to. I come eighteen hundred miles to see my sister I figure she might want to get up and say hi. Other than that you can go back upstairs. What you got, Doaker? Where your bottle? Me and Lymon want a drink.

(*To* BERNIECE.)

This is Lymon. You remember Lymon Jackson from down home.

LYMON: How you doing, Berniece. You look just like I thought you looked.

BERNIECE: Why you all got to come in hollering and carrying on? Waking the neighbors with all that noise.

BOY WILLIE: They can come over and join the party. We fixing to have a party. Doaker, where your bottle? Me and Lymon celebrating. The Ghosts of the Yellow Dog got Sutter.

BERNIECE: Say what?

BOY WILLIE: Ask Lymon, they found him the next morning. Say he drowned in his well.

DOAKER: When this happen, Boy Willie?

BOY WILLIE: About three weeks ago. Me and Lymon was over in Stoner County when we heard about it. We laughed. We thought it was funny. A great big old three-hundred-and-forty-pound man gonna fall down his well.

LYMON: It remind me of Humpty Dumpty.

BOY WILLIE: Everybody say the Ghosts of the Yellow Dog pushed him.

BERNIECE: I don't want to hear that nonsense. Somebody down there pushing them people in their wells.

DOAKER: What was you and Lymon doing over in Stoner County?

BOY WILLIE: We was down there working. Lymon got some people down there.

LYMON: My cousin got some land down there. We was helping him.

BOY WILLIE: Got near about a hundred acres. He got it set up real nice. Me and Lymon was down there chopping down trees. We was using Lymon's truck to haul the wood. Me and Lymon used to haul wood all around them parts.
(*To* BERNIECE.)
Me and Lymon got a truckload of watermelons out there.
(BERNIECE *crosses to the window to the parlor.*)
Doaker, where your bottle? I know you got a bottle stuck up in your room. Come on, me and Lymon want a drink.

(DOAKER *exits into his room.*)

BERNIECE: Where you all get that truck from?

BOY WILLIE: I told you it's Lymon's.

BERNIECE: Where you get the truck from, Lymon?

LYMON: I bought it.

BERNIECE: Where he get that truck from, Boy Willie?

BOY WILLIE: He told you he bought it. Bought it for a hundred and twenty dollars. I can't say where he got that hundred and twenty dollars from . . . but he bought that old piece of truck from Henry Porter. (*To* LYMON.) Where you get that hundred and twenty dollars from, nigger?

LYMON: I got it like you get yours. I know how to take care of money.
(DOAKER *brings a bottle and sets it on the table.*)

BOY WILLIE: Aw hell, Doaker got some of that good whiskey. Don't give Lymon none of that. He ain't used to good whiskey. He liable to get sick.

LYMON: I done had good whiskey before.

BOY WILLIE: Lymon bought that truck so he have him a place to sleep. He down there wasn't doing no work or nothing. Sheriff looking for him. He bought that truck to keep away from the sheriff. Got Stovall looking for him too. He down there sleeping in that truck ducking and dodging both of them. I told him come on let's go up and see my sister.

BERNIECE: What the sheriff looking for you for, Lymon?

BOY WILLIE: The man don't want you to know all his business. He's my company. He ain't asking you no questions.

LYMON: It wasn't nothing. It was just a misunderstanding.

BERNIECE: He in my house. You say the sheriff looking for him, I wanna know what he looking for him for. Otherwise you all can go back out there and be where nobody don't have to ask you nothing.

LYMON: It was just a misunderstanding. Sometimes me and the sheriff we don't think alike. So we just got crossed on each other.

BERNIECE: Might be looking for him about that truck. He might have stole that truck.

BOY WILLIE: We ain't stole no truck, woman. I told you Lymon bought it.

DOAKER: Boy Willie and Lymon got more sense than to ride all the way up here in a stolen truck with a load of watermelons. Now they might have stole them watermelons, but I don't believe they stole that truck.

BOY WILLIE: You don't even know the man good and you calling him a thief. And we ain't stole them watermelons either. Them old man Pitterford's watermelons. He give me and Lymon all we could load for ten dollars.

DOAKER: No wonder you got them stacked up out there. You must have five hundred watermelons stacked up out there.

BERNIECE: Boy Willie, when you and Lymon planning on going back?

BOY WILLIE: Lymon say he staying. As soon as we sell them watermelons I'm going on back.

BERNIECE: (*Starts to exit up the stairs.*) That's what you need to do. And you need to do it quick. Come in here disrupting the house. I don't want all that loud carrying on around here. I'm surprised you ain't woke Maretha up.

BOY WILLIE: I was fixing to get her now.

(*Calls.*)

Hey, Maretha!

DOAKER: Berniece don't like all that hollering now.

BERNIECE: Don't you wake that child up!

BOY WILLIE: You going up there . . . wake her up and tell her her uncle's here. I ain't seen her in three years. Wake her up and send her down here. She can go back to bed.

BERNIECE: I ain't waking that child up . . . and don't you be making all that noise. You and Lymon need to sell them watermelons and go on back.

(BERNIECE *exits up the stairs.*)

BOY WILLIE: I see Berniece still try to be stuck up.

DOAKER: Berniece alright. She don't want you making all that noise. Maretha up there sleep. Let her sleep until she get up. She can see you then.

BOY WILLIE: I ain't thinking about Berniece. You hear from Wining Boy? You know Cleotha died?

DOAKER: Yeah, I heard that. He come by here about a year ago. Had a whole sack of money. He stayed here about two weeks. Ain't offered nothing. Berniece asked him for three dollars to buy some food and he got mad and left.

LYMON: Who's Wining Boy?

BOY WILLIE: That's my uncle. That's Doaker's brother. You heard me talk about Wining Boy. He play piano. He done made some records and everything. He still doing that, Doaker?

DOAKER: He made one or two records a long time ago. That's the only ones I ever known him to make. If you let him tell it he a big recording star.

BOY WILLIE: He stopped down home about two years ago. That's what I hear. I don't know. Me and Lymon was up on Parchman Farm doing them three years.

DOAKER: He don't never stay in one place. Now, he been here about eight months ago. Back in the winter. Now, you subject not to see him for another two years. It's liable to be that long before he stop by.

BOY WILLIE: If he had a whole sack of money you liable never to see him. You ain't gonna see him until he get broke. Just as soon as that sack of money is gone you look up and he be on your doorstep.

LYMON: (*Noticing the piano.*) Is that the piano?

BOY WILLIE: Yeah . . . look here, Lymon. See how it got all those carvings on it. See, that's what I was talking about. See how it's carved up real nice and polished and everything? You never find you another piano like that.

LYMON: Yeah, that look real nice.

BOY WILLIE: I told you. See how it's polished? My mama used to polish it every day. See all them pictures carved on it? That's what I was talking about. You can get a nice price for that piano.

LYMON: That's all Boy Willie talked about the whole trip up here. I got tired of hearing him talk about the piano.

BOY WILLIE: All you want to talk about is women. You ought to hear this nigger, Doaker. Talking about all the women he gonna get when he get up here. He ain't had none down there but he gonna get a hundred when he get up here.

DOAKER: How your people doing down there, Lymon?

LYMON: They alright. They still there. I come up here to see what it's like up here. Boy Willie trying to get me to go back and farm with him.

BOY WILLIE: Sutter's brother selling the land. He say he gonna sell it to me. That's why I come up here. I got one part of it. Sell them watermelons and get me another part. Get Berniece to sell that piano and I'll have the third part.

DOAKER: Berniece ain't gonna sell that piano.

BOY WILLIE: I'm gonna talk to her. When she see I got a chance to get Sutter's land she'll come around.

DOAKER: You can put that thought out your mind. Berniece ain't gonna sell that piano.

BOY WILLIE: I'm gonna talk to her. She been playing on it?

DOAKER: You know she won't touch that piano. I ain't never known her to touch it since Mama Ola died. That's over seven years now. She say it got blood on it. She got Maretha playing on it though. Say Maretha can go on and do everything she can't do. Got her in an extra school down at the Irene Kaufman Settlement House. She want Maretha to grow up and be a schoolteacher. Say she good enough she can teach on the piano.

BOY WILLIE: Maretha don't need to be playing on no piano. She can play on the guitar.

DOAKER: How much land Sutter got left?

BOY WILLIE: Got a hundred acres. Good land. He done sold it piece by piece, he kept the good part for himself. Now he got to give that up. His brother come down from Chicago for the funeral . . . he up there in Chicago got some kind of business with soda fountain equipment. He anxious to sell the land, Doaker. He don't want to be bothered with it. He called me to him and said cause of how long our families done known each other and how we been good friends and all, say he wanted to sell the land to me. Say he'd rather see me with it than Jim Stovall. Told me he'd let me have it for two thousand dollars cash money. He don't know I found out the most Stovall would give him for it was fifteen hundred dollars. He trying to get that extra five hundred out of me telling me he doing me a favor. I thanked him just as nice. Told him what a good man Sutter was and how he had my sympathy and all.

Told him to give me two weeks. He said he'd wait on me. That's why I come up here. Sell them watermelons. Get Berniece to sell that piano. Put them two parts with the part I done saved. Walk in there. Tip my hat. Lay my money down on the table. Get my deed and walk on out. This time I get to keep all the cotton. Hire me some men to work it for me. Gin my cotton. Get my seed. And I'll see you again next year. Might even plant some tobacco or some oats.

DOAKER: You gonna have a hard time trying to get Berniece to sell that piano. You know Avery Brown from down there don't you? He up here now. He followed Berniece up here trying to get her to marry him after Crawley got killed. He been up here about two years. He call himself a preacher now.

BOY WILLIE: I know Avery. I know him from when he used to work on the Willshaw place. Lymon know him too.

DOAKER: He after Berniece to marry him. She keep telling him no but he won't give up. He keep pressing her on it.

BOY WILLIE: Avery think all white men is bigshots. He don't know there some white men ain't got as much as he got.

DOAKER: He supposed to come past here this morning. Berniece going down to the bank with him to see if he can get a loan to start his church. That's why I know Berniece ain't gonna sell that piano. He tried to get her to sell it to help him start his church. Sent the man around and everything.

BOY WILLIE: What man?

DOAKER: Some white fellow was going around to all the colored people's houses looking to buy up musical instruments. He'd buy anything. Drums. Guitars. Harmonicas. Pianos. Avery sent him past here. He looked at the piano and got excited. Offered her a nice price. She turned him down and got on Avery for sending him past. The man kept on her about two weeks. He seen where she wasn't gonna sell it, he gave her his number and told her if she ever wanted to sell it to call him first. Say he'd go one better than what anybody else would give her for it.

BOY WILLIE: How much he offer her for it?

DOAKER: Now you know me. She didn't say and I didn't ask. I just know it was a nice price.

LYMON: All you got to do is find out who he is and tell him somebody else wanna buy it from you. Tell him you can't make up your mind who to sell it to, and if he like Doaker say, he'll give you anything you want for it.

BOY WILLIE: That's what I'm gonna do. I'm gonna find out who he is from Avery.

DOAKER: It ain't gonna do you no good. Berniece ain't gonna sell that piano.

BOY WILLIE: She ain't got to sell it. I'm gonna sell it. I own just as much of it as she does.

BERNIECE: (*Offstage, hollers.*) Doaker! Go on get away. Doaker!

DOAKER: (*Calling.*) Berniece?

(DOAKER *and* BOY WILLIE *rush to the stairs,* BOY WILLIE *runs up the stairs, passing* BERNIECE *as she enters, running.*)

DOAKER: Berniece, what's the matter? You alright? What's the matter?

(BERNIECE *tries to catch her breath. She is unable to speak.*)

DOAKER: That's alright. Take your time. You alright. What's the matter?

(*He calls.*)

Hey, Boy Willie?

BOY WILLIE: (*Offstage.*) Ain't nobody up here.

BERNIECE: Sutter . . . Sutter's standing at the top of the steps.

DOAKER: (*Calls.*) Boy Willie!

(LYMON *crosses to the stairs and looks up.* BOY WILLIE *enters from the stairs.*)

BOY WILLIE: Hey Doaker, what's wrong with her? Berniece, what's wrong? Who was you talking to?

DOAKER: She say she seen Sutter's ghost standing at the top of the stairs.

BOY WILLIE: Seen what? Sutter? She ain't seen no Sutter.

BERNIECE: He was standing right up there.

BOY WILLIE: (*Entering on the stairs.*) That's all in Berniece's head. Ain't nobody up there. Go on up there, Doaker.

DOAKER: I'll take your word for it. Berniece talking about what she seen. She say Sutter's ghost standing at the top of the steps. She ain't just make all that up.

BOY WILLIE: She up there dreaming. She ain't seen no ghost.

LYMON: You want a glass of water, Berniece? Get her a glass of water, Boy Willie.

BOY WILLIE: She don't need no water. She ain't seen nothing. Go on up there and look. Ain't nobody up there but Maretha.

DOAKER: Let Berniece tell it.

BOY WILLIE: I ain't stopping her from telling it.

DOAKER: What happened, Berniece?

BERNIECE: I come out my room to come back down here and Sutter was standing there in the hall.

BOY WILLIE: What he look like?

BERNIECE: He look like Sutter. He look like he always look.

BOY WILLIE: Sutter couldn't find his way from Big Sandy to Little Sandy. How he gonna find his way all the way up here to Pittsburgh? Sutter ain't never even heard of Pittsburgh.

DOAKER: Go on, Berniece.

BERNIECE: Just standing there with the blue suit on.

BOY WILLIE: The man ain't never left Marlin County when he was living . . . and he's gonna come all the way up here now that he's dead?

DOAKER: Let her finish. I want to hear what she got to say.

BOY WILLIE: I'll tell you this. If Berniece had seen him like she think she seen him she'd still be running.

DOAKER: Go on, Berniece. Don't pay Boy Willie no mind.

BERNIECE: He was standing there . . . had his hand on top of his head. Look like he might have thought if he took his hand down his head might have fallen off.

LYMON: Did he have on a hat?

BERNIECE: Just had on that blue suit . . . I told him to go away and he just stood there looking at me . . . calling Boy Willie's name.

BOY WILLIE: What he calling my name for?

BERNIECE: I believe you pushed him in the well.

BOY WILLIE: Now what kind of sense that make? You telling me I'm gonna go out there and hide in the weeds with all them dogs and things he got around there . . . I'm gonna hide and wait till I catch him looking down his well just right . . . then I'm gonna run over and push him in. A great big old three-hundred-and-forty-pound man.

BERNIECE: Well, what he calling your name for?

BOY WILLIE: He bending over looking down his well, woman . . . how he know who pushed him? It could have been anybody. Where was you when Sutter fell in his well? Where was Doaker? Me and Lymon was over in Stoner County. Tell her, Lymon. The Ghosts of the Yellow Dog got Sutter. That's what happened to him.

BERNIECE: You can talk all that Ghosts of the Yellow Dog stuff if you want. I know better.

LYMON: The Ghosts of the Yellow Dog pushed him. That's what the people say. They found him in his well and all the people say it must be the Ghosts of the Yellow Dog. Just like all them other men.

BOY WILLIE: Come talking about he looking for me. What he come all the way up here for? If he looking for me all he got to do is wait. He could have saved himself a trip if he looking for me. That ain't nothing but in Berniece's head. Ain't no telling what she liable to come up with next.

BERNIECE: Boy Willie, I want you and Lymon to go ahead and leave my house. Just go on somewhere. You don't do nothing but bring trouble with you everywhere you go. If it wasn't for you Crawley would still be alive.

BOY WILLIE: Crawley what? I ain't had nothing to do with Crawley getting killed. Crawley three time seven. He had his own mind.

BERNIECE: Just go on and leave. Let Sutter go somewhere else looking for you.

BOY WILLIE: I'm leaving. Soon as we sell them watermelons. Other than that I ain't going nowhere. Hell, I just got here. Talking about Sutter looking for me. Sutter was looking for that piano. That's what he was looking for. He had to die to find out where that piano was at . . . If I was you I'd get rid of it. That's the way to get rid of Sutter's ghost. Get rid of that piano.

BERNIECE: I want you and Lymon to go on and take all this confusion out of my house!

BOY WILLIE: Hey, tell her, Doaker. What kind of sense that make? I told you, Lymon, as soon as Berniece see me she was gonna start something. Didn't I tell you that? Now she done made up that story about Sutter just so she could tell me to leave her house. Well, hell, I ain't going nowhere till I sell them watermelons.

BERNIECE: Well why don't you go out there and sell them! Sell them and go on back!

BOY WILLIE: We waiting till the people get up.

LYMON: Boy Willie say if you get out there too early and wake the people up they get mad at you and won't buy nothing from you.

DOAKER: You won't be waiting long. You done let the sun catch up with you. This the time everybody be getting up around here.

BERNIECE: Come on, Doaker, walk up here with me. Let me get Maretha up and get her started. I got to get ready myself. Boy Willie, just go on out there and sell them watermelons and you and Lymon leave my house.

(BERNIECE *and* DOAKER *exit up the stairs.*)

BOY WILLIE: (*Calling after them.*) If you see Sutter up there . . . tell him I'm down here waiting on him.

LYMON: What if she see him again?

BOY WILLIE: That's all in her head. There ain't no ghost up there.

(*Calls.*)

Hey, Doaker . . . I told you ain't nothing up there.

LYMON: I'm glad he didn't say he was looking for me.

BOY WILLIE: I wish I would see Sutter's ghost. Give me a chance to put a whupping on him.

LYMON: You ought to stay up here with me. You be down there working his land . . . he might come looking for you all the time.

BOY WILLIE: I ain't thinking about Sutter. And I ain't thinking about staying up here. You stay up here. I'm going back and get Sutter's land. You think you ain't got to work up here. You think this the land of milk and honey. But I ain't scared of work. I'm going back and farm every acre of that land.

(DOAKER *enters from the stairs.*)

I told you there ain't nothing up there, Doaker. Berniece dreaming all that.

DOAKER: I believe Berniece seen something. Berniece level- headed. She ain't just made all that up. She say Sutter had on a suit. I don't believe she ever seen Sutter in a suit. I believe that's what he was buried in, and that's what Berniece saw.

BOY WILLIE: Well, let her keep on seeing him then. As long as he don't mess with me.

(DOAKER *starts to cook his breakfast.*)

I heard about you, Doaker. They say you got all the women looking out for you down home. They be looking to see you coming. Say you got a different one every two weeks. Say they be fighting one another for you to stay with them.

(*To* LYMON.)

Look at him, Lymon. He know it's true.

DOAKER: I ain't thinking about no women. They never get me tied up with them. After Coreen I ain't got no use for them. I stay up on Jack Slattery's place when I be down there. All them women want is somebody with a steady payday.

BOY WILLIE: That ain't what I hear. I hear every two weeks the women all put on their dresses and line up at the railroad station.

DOAKER: I don't get down there but once a month. I used to go down there every two weeks but they keep switching me around. They keep switching all the fellows around.

BOY WILLIE: Doaker can't turn that railroad loose. He was working the railroad when I was walking around crying for sugartit. My mama used to brag on him.

DOAKER: I'm cooking now, but I used to line track. I pieced together the Yellow Dog stitch by stitch. Rail by rail. Line track all up around there. I lined track all up around Sunflower and Clarksdale. Wining Boy worked with me. He helped put in some of that track. He'd work it for six months and quit. Go back to playing piano and gambling.

BOY WILLIE: How long you been with the railroad now?

DOAKER: Twenty-seven years. Now, I'll tell you something about the railroad. What I done learned after twenty-seven years. See, you got North. You got West. You look over here you got South. Over there you got East. Now, you can start from anywhere. Don't care where you at. You got to go one of them four ways. And whichever way you decide to go they got a railroad that will take you there. Now, that's something simple. You think anybody would be able to understand that. But you'd be surprised how many people trying to go North get on a train going West. They think the train's supposed to go where they going rather than where it's going.

Now, why people going? Their sister's sick. They leaving before they kill somebody . . . and they sitting across from somebody who's leaving to keep from getting killed. They leaving cause they can't get satisfied. They going to meet someone. I wish I had a dollar for every time that someone wasn't at the station to meet them. I done seen that a lot. In between the time they sent the telegram and the time the person get there . . . they done forgot all about them.

They got so many trains out there they have a hard time keeping them from running into each other. Got trains going every whichaway. Got people on all of them. Somebody going where somebody just left. If everybody stay in one place I believe this would be a better world. Now what I done learned after twenty-seven years of railroading is this . . . if the train stays on the track . . . it's going to get where it's going. It might not be where you going. If it ain't, then all you got to do is sit and wait cause the train's coming back to get you. The train don't never stop. It'll come back every time. Now I'll tell you another thing . . .

BOY WILLIE: What you cooking over there, Doaker? Me and Lymon's hungry.

DOAKER: Go on down there to Wylie and Kirkpatrick to Eddie's restaurant. Coffee cost a nickel and you can get two eggs, sausage, and grits for fifteen cents. He even give you a biscuit with it.

BOY WILLIE: That look good what you got. Give me a little piece of that grilled bread.

DOAKER: Here . . . go on take the whole piece.

BOY WILLIE: Here you go, Lymon . . . you want a piece?

(*He gives* LYMON *a piece of toast.* MARETHA *enters from the stairs.*)

BOY WILLIE: Hey, sugar. Come here and give me a hug. Come on give Uncle Boy Willie a hug. Don't be shy. Look at her, Doaker. She done got bigger. Ain't she got big?

DOAKER: Yeah, she getting up there.

BOY WILLIE: How you doing, sugar?

MARETHA: Fine.

BOY WILLIE: You was just a little old thing last time I seen you. You remember me, don't you? This your Uncle Boy Willie from down South. That there's Lymon. He my friend. We come up here to sell watermelons. You like watermelons?

(MARETHA *nods.*)

We got a whole truckload out front. You can have as many as you want. What you been doing?

MARETHA: Nothing.

BOY WILLIE: Don't be shy now. Look at you getting all big. How old is you?

MARETHA: Eleven. I'm gonna be twelve soon.

BOY WILLIE: You like it up here? You like the North?

MARETHA: It's alright.

BOY WILLIE: That there's Lymon. Did you say hi to Lymon?

MARETHA: Hi.

LYMON: How you doing? You look just like your mama. I remember you when you was wearing diapers.

BOY WILLIE: You gonna come down South and see me? Uncle Boy Willie gonna get him a farm. Gonna get a great big old farm. Come down there and I'll teach you how to ride a mule. Teach you how to kill a chicken, too.

MARETHA: I seen my mama do that.

BOY WILLIE: Ain't nothing to it. You just grab him by his neck and twist it. Get you a real good grip and then you just wring his neck and throw him in the pot. Cook him up. Then you got some good eating. What you like to eat? What kind of food you like?

MARETHA: I like everything . . . except I don't like no black-eyed peas.

BOY WILLIE: Uncle Doaker tell me your mama got you playing that piano. Come on play something for me.

(BOY WILLIE *crosses over to the piano followed by* MARETHA.)

Show me what you can do. Come on now. Here . . . Uncle Boy Willie give you a dime . . . show me what you can do. Don't be bashful now. That dime say you can't be bashful.

(MARETHA *plays. It is something any beginner first learns.*)

Here, let me show you something.

(BOY WILLIE *sits and plays a simple boogie-woogie.*)

See that? See what I'm doing? That's what you call the boogie-woogie. See now . . . you can get up and dance to that. That's how good it sound. It sound like you wanna dance. You can dance to that. It'll hold you up. Whatever kind of dance you wanna do you can dance to that right there. See that? See how it go? Ain't nothing to it. Go on you do it.

MARETHA: I got to read it on the paper.

BOY WILLIE: You don't need no paper. Go on. Do just like that there.

BERNIECE: Maretha! You get up here and get ready to go so you be on time. Ain't no need you trying to take advantage of company.

MARETHA: I got to go.

BOY WILLIE: Uncle Boy Willie gonna get you a guitar. Let Uncle Doaker teach you how to play that. You don't need to read no paper to play the guitar. Your mama told you about that piano? You know how them pictures got on there?

MARETHA: She say it just always been like that since she got it.

BOY WILLIE: You hear that, Doaker? And you sitting up here in the house with Berniece.

DOAKER: I ain't got nothing to do with that. I don't get in the way of Berniece's raising her.

BOY WILLIE: You tell your mama to tell you about that piano. You ask her how them pictures got on there. If she don't tell you I'll tell you.

BERNIECE: Maretha!

MARETHA: I got to get ready to go.

BOY WILLIE: She getting big, Doaker. You remember her, Lymon?

LYMON: She used to be real little.

(*There is a knock on the door.* DOAKER *goes to answer it.* AVERY *enters. Thirty-eight years old, honest and ambitious, he has taken to the city like a fish to water, finding in it opportunities for growth and advancement that did not exist for him in the rural South. He is dressed in a suit and tie with a gold cross around his neck. He carries a small Bible.)*

DOAKER: Hey, Avery, come on in. Berniece upstairs.

BOY WILLIE: Look at him . . . look at him . . . he don't know what to say. He wasn't expecting to see me.

AVERY: Hey, Boy Willie. What you doing up here?

BOY WILLIE: Look at him, Lymon.

AVERY: Is that Lymon? Lymon Jackson?

BOY WILLIE: Yeah, you know Lymon.

DOAKER: Berniece be ready in a minute, Avery.

BOY WILLIE: Doaker say you a preacher now. What . . . we supposed to call you Reverend? You used to be plain old Avery. When you get to be a preacher, nigger?

LYMON: Avery say he gonna be a preacher so he don't have to work.

BOY WILLIE: I remember when you was down there on the Willshaw place planting cotton. You wasn't thinking about no Reverend then.

AVERY: That must be your truck out there. I saw that truck with them watermelons, I was trying to figure out what it was doing in front of the house.

BOY WILLIE: Yeah, me and Lymon selling watermelons. That's Lymon's truck.

DOAKER: Berniece say you all going down to the bank.

AVERY: Yeah, they give me a half day off work. I got an appointment to talk to the bank about getting a loan to start my church.

BOY WILLIE: Lymon say preachers don't have to work. Where you working at, nigger?

DOAKER: Avery got him one of them good jobs. He working at one of them skyscrapers downtown.

AVERY: I'm working down there at the Gulf Building running an elevator. Got a pension and everything. They even give you a turkey on Thanksgiving.

LYMON: How you know the rope ain't gonna break? Ain't you scared the rope's gonna break?

AVERY: That's steel. They got steel cables hold it up. It take a whole lot of breaking to break that steel. Naw, I ain't worried about nothing like that. It ain't nothing but a little old elevator. Now, I wouldn't get in none of them airplanes. You couldn't pay me to do nothing like that.

LYMON: That be fun. I'd rather do that than ride in one of them elevators.

BOY WILLIE: How many of them watermelons you wanna buy?

AVERY: I thought you was gonna give me one seeing as how you got a whole truck full.

BOY WILLIE: You can get one, get two. I'll give you two for a dollar.

AVERY: I can't eat but one. How much are they?

BOY WILLIE: Aw, nigger, you know I'll give you a watermelon. Go on, take as many as you want. Just leave some for me and Lymon to sell.

AVERY: I don't want but one.

BOY WILLIE: How you get to be a preacher, Avery? I might want to be a preacher one day. Have everybody call me Reverend Boy Willie.

AVERY: It come to me in a dream. God called me and told me he wanted me to be a shepherd for his flock. That's what I'm gonna call my church . . . The Good Shepherd Church of God in Christ.

DOAKER: Tell him what you told me. Tell him about the three hobos.

AVERY: Boy Willie don't want to hear all that.

LYMON: I do. Lots a people say your dreams can come true.

AVERY: Naw. You don't want to hear all that.

DOAKER: Go on. I told him you was a preacher. He didn't want to believe me. Tell him about the three hobos.

AVERY: Well, it come to me in a dream. See . . . I was sitting out in this railroad yard watching the trains go by. The train stopped and these three hobos got off. They told me they had come from Nazareth and was on their way to Jerusalem. They had three candles. They gave me one and told me to light it . . . but to be careful that it didn't go out. Next thing I knew I was standing in front of this house. Something told me to go knock on the door. This old woman opened the door and said they had been waiting on me. Then she led me into this room. It was a big room and it was full of all kinds of different people. They looked like anybody else except they all had sheep heads and was making noise like sheep make. I heard somebody call my name. I looked around and there was these same three hobos. They told me to take off my clothes and they give me a blue robe with gold thread. They washed my feet and combed my hair. Then they showed me these three doors and told me to pick one.

I went through one of them doors and that flame leapt off that candle and it seemed like my whole head caught fire. I looked around and there was four or five other men standing there with these same blue robes on. Then we heard a voice tell us to look out across this valley. We looked out and saw the valley was full of wolves. The voice told us that these sheep people that I had seen in the other room had to go over to the other side of this valley and somebody had to take them. Then I heard another voice say, "Who shall I send?" Next thing I knew I said, "Here I am. Send me." That's when I met Jesus. He say, "If you go, I'll go with you." Something told me to say, "Come on. Let's go." That's when I woke up. My head still felt like it was on fire . . . but I had a peace about myself that was hard to explain. I knew right then that I had been filled with the Holy Ghost and called to be a servant of the Lord. It took me a while before I could accept that. But then a lot of little ways God showed me that it was true. So I became a preacher.

LYMON: I see why you gonna call it the Good Shepherd Church. You dreaming about them sheep people. I can see that easy.

BOY WILLIE: Doaker say you sent some white man past the house to look at that piano. Say he was going around to all the colored people's houses looking to buy up musical instruments.

AVERY: Yeah, but Berniece didn't want to sell that piano. After she told me about it . . . I could see why she didn't want to sell it.

BOY WILLIE: What's this man's name?

AVERY: Oh, that's a while back now. I done forgot his name. He give Berniece a card with his name and telephone number on it, but I believe she throwed it away.

(BERNIECE *and* MARETHA *enter from the stairs.*)

BERNIECE: Maretha, run back upstairs and get my pocketbook. And wipe that hair grease off your forehead. Go ahead, hurry up.

(MARETHA *exits up the stairs.*)

How you doing, Avery? You done got all dressed up. You look nice. Boy Willie, I thought you and Lymon was going to sell them watermelons.

BOY WILLIE: Lymon done got sleepy. We liable to get some sleep first.

LYMON: I ain't sleepy.

DOAKER: As many watermelons as you got stacked up on that truck out there, you ought to have been gone.

BOY WILLIE: We gonna go in a minute. We going.

BERNIECE: Doaker. I'm gonna stop down there on Logan Street. You want anything?

DOAKER: You can pick up some ham hocks if you going down there. See if you can get the smoked ones. If they ain't got that get the fresh ones. Don't get the ones that got all that fat under the skin. Look for the long ones. They nice and lean.

(*He gives her a dollar.*)

Don't get the short ones lessen they smoked. If you got to get the fresh ones make sure that they the long ones. If they ain't got them smoked then go ahead and get the short ones.

(*Pause.*)

You may as well get some turnip greens while you down there. I got some buttermilk . . . if you pick up some cornmeal I'll make me some cornbread and cook up them turnip greens.

(MARETHA *enters from the stairs.*)

MARETHA: We gonna take the streetcar?

BERNIECE: Me and Avery gonna drop you off at the settlement house. You mind them people down there. Don't be going down there showing your color. Boy Willie, I done told you what to do. I'll see you later, Doaker.

AVERY: I'll be seeing you again, Boy Willie.

BOY WILLIE: Hey, Berniece . . . what's the name of that man Avery sent past say he want to buy the piano?

BERNIECE: I knew it. I knew it when I first seen you. I knew you was up to something.

BOY WILLIE: Sutter's brother say he selling the land to me. He waiting on me now. Told me he'd give me two weeks. I got one part. Sell them watermelons get me another part. Then we can sell that piano and I'll have the third part.

BERNIECE: I ain't selling that piano, Boy Willie. If that's why you come up here you can just forget about it.

(*To* DOAKER.)

Doaker, I'll see you later. Boy Willie ain't nothing but a whole lot of mouth. I ain't paying him no mind. If he come up here thinking he gonna sell that piano then he done come up here for nothing.

(BERNIECE, AVERY, *and* MARETHA *exit the front door.*)

BOY WILLIE: Hey, Lymon! You ready to go sell these watermelons.

(BOY WILLIE *and* LYMON *start to exit. At the door* BOY WILLIE *turns to* DOAKER.)

Hey, Doaker . . . if Berniece don't want to sell that piano . . . I'm gonna cut it in half and go on and sell my half.

(BOY WILLIE *and* LYMON *exit.*)

(*The lights go down on the scene.*)

Scene 2

(*The lights come up on the kitchen. It is three days later.* Wining Boy *sits at the kitchen table. There is a half-empty pint bottle on the table.* Doaker *busies himself washing pots.* Wining Boy *is fifty-six years old.* Doaker's *older brother, he tries to present the image of a successful musician and gambler, but his music, his clothes, and even his manner of presentation are old. He is a man who looking back over his life continues to live it with an odd mixture of zest and sorrow.*)

Wining Boy: So the Ghosts of the Yellow Dog got Sutter. That just go to show you I believe I always lived right. They say every dog gonna have his day and time it go around it sure come back to you. I done seen that a thousand times. I know the truth of that. But I'll tell you outright . . . if I see Sutter's ghost I'll be on the first thing I find that got wheels on it.

(Doaker *enters from his room.*)

Doaker: Wining Boy!

Wining Boy: And I'll tell you another thing . . . Berniece ain't gonna sell that piano.

Doaker: That's what she told him. He say he gonna cut it in half and go on and sell his half. They been around here three days trying to sell them watermelons. They trying to get out to where the white folks live but the truck keep breaking down. They go a block or two and it break down again. They trying to get out to Squirrel Hill and can't get around the corner. He say soon as he can get that truck empty to where he can set the piano up in there he gonna take it out of here and go sell it.

Wining Boy: What about them boys Sutter got? How come they ain't farming that land?

Doaker: One of them going to school. He left down there and come North to school. The other one ain't got as much sense as that frying pan over yonder. That is the dumbest white man I ever seen. He'd stand in the river and watch it rise till it drown him.

Wining Boy: Other than seeing Sutter's ghost how's Berniece doing?

Doaker: She doing alright. She still got Crawley on her mind. He been dead three years but she still holding on to him. She need to go out here and let one of these fellows grab a whole handful of whatever she got. She act like it done got precious.

Wining Boy: They always told me any fish will bite if you got good bait.

Doaker: She stuck up on it. She think it's better than she is. I believe she messing around with Avery. They got something going. He a preacher now. If you let him tell it the Holy Ghost sat on his head and heaven opened up with thunder and lightning and God was calling his name. Told him to go out and preach and tend to his flock. That's what he gonna call his church. The Good Shepherd Church.

Wining Boy: They had that joker down in Spear walking around talking about he Jesus Christ. He gonna live the life of Christ. Went through the Last Supper and everything. Rented him a mule on Palm Sunday and rode through the town. Did everything . . . talking about he Christ. He did everything until they got up to that crucifixion part. Got up to that part and told everybody to go home and quit pretending. He got up to the crucifixion part and changed his mind. Had a whole bunch of folks come down there to see him get nailed to the cross. I don't know who's the worse fool. Him or them. Had all them folks come down there . . . even carried the cross up this little hill. People standing around waiting to see him get nailed to the cross and he stop everything and preach a little sermon and told everybody to go home. Had enough nerve to tell them to come to church on Easter Sunday to celebrate his resurrection.

DOAKER: I'm surprised Avery ain't thought about that. He trying every little thing to get him a congregation together. They meeting over at his house till he get him a church.

WINING BOY: Ain't nothing wrong with being a preacher. You got the preacher on one hand and the gambler on the other. Sometimes there ain't too much difference in them.

DOAKER: How long you been in Kansas City?

WINING BOY: Since I left here. I got tied up with some old gal down there.

(*Pause.*)

You know Cleotha died.

DOAKER: Yeah, I heard that last time I was down there. I was sorry to hear that.

WINING BOY: One of her friends wrote and told me. I got the letter right here.

(*He takes the letter out of his pocket.*)

I was down in Kansas City and she wrote and told me Cleotha had died. Name of Willa Bryant. She say she know cousin Rupert.

(*He opens the letter and reads.*)

Dear Wining Boy: I am writing this letter to let you know Miss Cleotha Holman passed on Saturday the first of May she departed this world in the loving arms of her sister Miss Alberta Samuels. I know you would want to know this and am writing as a friend of Cleotha. There have been many hardships since last you seen her but she survived them all and to the end was a good woman whom I hope have God's grace and is in His Paradise. Your cousin Rupert Bates is my friend also and he give me your address and I pray this reaches you about Cleotha. Miss Willa Bryant. A friend.

(*He folds the letter and returns it to his pocket.*)

They was nailing her coffin shut by the time I heard about it. I never knew she was sick. I believe it was that yellow jaundice. That's what killed her mama.

DOAKER: Cleotha wasn't but forty-some.

WINING BOY: She was forty-six. I got ten years on her. I met her when she was sixteen. You remember I used to run around there. Couldn't nothing keep me still. Much as I loved Cleotha I loved to ramble. Couldn't nothing keep me still. We got married and we used to fight about it all the time. Then one day she asked me to leave. Told me she loved me before I left. Told me, Wining Boy, you got a home as long as I got mine. And I believe in my heart I always felt that and that kept me safe.

DOAKER: Cleotha always did have a nice way about her.

WINING BOY: Man that woman was something. I used to thank the Lord. Many a night I sat up and looked out over my life. Said, well, I had Cleotha. When it didn't look like there was nothing else for me, I said, thank God, at least I had that. If ever I go anywhere in this life I done known a good woman. And that used to hold me till the next morning.

(*Pause.*)

What you got? Give me a little nip. I know you got something stuck up in your room.

DOAKER: I ain't seen you walk in here and put nothing on the table. You done sat there and drank up your whiskey. Now you talking about what you got.

WINING BOY: I got plenty money. Give me a little nip.

(DOAKER *carries a glass into his room and returns with it half-filled. He sets it on the table in front of* WINING BOY.)

WINING BOY: You hear from Coreen?

DOAKER: She up in New York. I let her go from my mind.

WINING BOY: She was something back then. She wasn't too pretty but she had a way of looking at you made you know there was a whole lot of woman there. You got married and snatched her out from under us and we all got mad at you.

DOAKER: She up in New York City. That's what I hear.

(*The door opens and* BOY WILLIE *and* LYMON *enter.*)

BOY WILLIE: Aw hell . . . look here! We was just talking about you. Doaker say you left out of here with a whole sack of money. I told him we wasn't going see you till you got broke.

WINING BOY: What you mean broke? I got a whole pocketful of money.

DOAKER: Did you all get that truck fixed?

BOY WILLIE: We got it running and got halfway out there on Centre and it broke down again. Lymon went out there and messed it up some more. Fellow told us we got to wait till tomorrow to get it fixed. Say he have it running like new. Lymon going back down there and sleep in the truck so the people don't take the watermelons.

LYMON: Lymon nothing. You go down there and sleep in it.

BOY WILLIE: You was sleeping in it down home, nigger! I don't know nothing about sleeping in no truck.

LYMON: I ain't sleeping in no truck.

BOY WILLIE: They can take all the watermelons. I don't care. Wining Boy, where you coming from? Where you been?

WINING BOY: I been down in Kansas City.

BOY WILLIE: You remember Lymon? Lymon Jackson.

WINING BOY: Yeah, I used to know his daddy.

BOY WILLIE: Doaker say you don't never leave no address with nobody. Say he got to depend on your whim. See when it strike you to pay a visit.

WINING BOY: I got four or five addresses.

BOY WILLIE: Doaker say Berniece asked you for three dollars and you got mad and left.

WINING BOY: Berniece try and rule over you too much for me. That's why I left. It wasn't about no three dollars.

BOY WILLIE: Where you getting all these sacks of money from? I need to be with you. Doaker say you had a whole sack of money . . . turn some of it loose.

WINING BOY: I was just fixing to ask you for five dollars.

BOY WILLIE: I ain't got no money. I'm trying to get some. Doaker tell you about Sutter? The Ghosts of the Yellow Dog got him about three weeks ago. Berniece done seen his ghost and everything. He right upstairs.

(*Calls.*)

Hey Sutter! Wining Boy's here. Come on, get a drink!

WINING BOY: How many that make the Ghosts of the Yellow Dog done got?

BOY WILLIE: Must be about nine or ten, eleven or twelve. I don't know.

DOAKER: You got Ed Saunders. Howard Peterson. Charlie Webb.

WINING BOY: Robert Smith. That fellow that shot Becky's boy . . . say he was stealing peaches . . .

DOAKER: You talking about Bob Mallory.

BOY WILLIE: Berniece say she don't believe all that about the Ghosts of the Yellow Dog.

WINING BOY: She ain't got to believe. You go ask them white folks in Sunflower County if they believe. You go ask Sutter if he believe. I don't care if Berniece believe or not. I done been to where the Southern cross the Yellow Dog and called out their names. They talk back to you, too.

LYMON: What they sound like? The wind or something?

BOY WILLIE: You done been there for real, Wining Boy?

WINING BOY: Nineteen thirty. July of nineteen thirty I stood right there on that spot. It didn't look like nothing was going right in my life. I said everything can't go wrong all the time . . . let me go down there and call on the Ghosts of the Yellow Dog, see if they can help me. I went down there and right there where them two railroads cross each other . . . I stood right there on that spot and called out their names. They talk back to you, too.

LYMON: People say you can ask them questions. They talk to you like that?

WINING BOY: A lot of things you got to find out on your own. I can't say how they talked to nobody else. But to me it just filled me up in a strange sort of way to be standing there on that spot. I didn't want to leave. It felt like the longer I stood there the bigger I got. I seen the train coming and it seem like I was bigger than the train. I started not to move. But something told me to go ahead and get on out the way. The train passed and I started to go back up there and stand some more. But something told me not to do it. I walked away from there feeling like a king. Went on and had a stroke of luck that run on for three years. So I don't care if Berniece believe or not. Berniece ain't got to believe. I know cause I been there. Now Doaker'll tell you about the Ghosts of the Yellow Dog.

DOAKER: I don't try and talk that stuff with Berniece. Avery got her all tied up in that church. She just think it's a whole lot of nonsense.

BOY WILLIE: Berniece don't believe in nothing. She just think she believe. She believe in anything if it's convenient for her to believe. But when that convenience run out then she ain't got nothing to stand on.

WINING BOY: Let's not get on Berniece now. Doaker tell me you talking about selling that piano.

BOY WILLIE: Yeah . . . hey, Doaker, I got the name of that man Avery was talking about. The man what's fixing the truck gave me his name. Everybody know him. Say he buy up anything you can make music with. I got his name and his telephone number. Hey, Wining Boy, Sutter's brother say he selling the land to me. I got one part. Sell them watermelons get me the second part. Then . . . soon as I get them watermelons out that truck I'm gonna take and sell that piano and get the third part.

DOAKER: That land ain't worth nothing no more. The smart white man's up here in these cities. He cut the land loose and step back and watch you and the dumb white man argue over it.

WINING BOY: How you know Sutter's brother ain't sold it already? You talking about selling the piano and the man's liable to sold the land two or three times.

BOY WILLIE: He say he waiting on me. He say he give me two weeks. That's two weeks from Friday. Say if I ain't back by then he might gonna sell it to somebody else. He say he wanna see me with it.

WINING BOY: You know as well as I know the man gonna sell the land to the first one walk up and hand him the money.

BOY WILLIE: That's just who I'm gonna be. Look, you ain't gotta know he waiting on me. I know. Okay. I know what the man told me. Stoval already done tried to buy the land from him and he told him no. The man say he waiting on me . . . he waiting on me. Hey, Doaker . . . give me a drink. I see Wining Boy got his glass.

(DOAKER *exits into his room.*)

Wining Boy, what you doing in Kansas City? What they got down there?

LYMON: I hear they got some nice-looking women in Kansas City. I sure like to go down there and find out.

WINING BOY: Man, the women down there is something else.

(DOAKER *enters with a bottle of whiskey. He sets it on the table with some glasses.*)

DOAKER: You wanna sit up here and drink up my whiskey, leave a dollar on the table when you get up.

BOY WILLIE: You ain't doing nothing but showing your hospitality. I know we ain't got to pay for your hospitality.

WINING BOY: Doaker say they had you and Lymon down on the Parchman Farm. Had you on my old stomping grounds.

BOY WILLIE: Me and Lymon was down there hauling wood for Jim Miller and keeping us a little bit to sell. Some white fellows tried to run us off of it. That's when Crawley got killed. They put me and Lymon in the penitentiary.

LYMON: They ambushed us right there where that road dip down and around that bend in the creek. Crawley tried to fight them. Me and Boy Willie got away but the sheriff got us. Say we was stealing wood. They shot me in my stomach.

BOY WILLIE: They looking for Lymon down there now. They rounded him up and put him in jail for not working.

LYMON: Fined me a hundred dollars. Mr. Stovall come and paid my hundred dollars and the judge say I got to work for him to pay him back his hundred dollars. I told them I'd rather take my thirty days but they wouldn't let me do that.

BOY WILLIE: As soon as Stovall turned his back, Lymon was gone. He down there living in that truck dodging the sheriff and Stovall. He got both of them looking for him. So I brought him up here.

LYMON: I told Boy Willie I'm gonna stay up here. I ain't going back with him.

BOY WILLIE: Ain't nobody twisting your arm to make you go back. You can do what you want to do.

WINING BOY: I'll go back with you. I'm on my way down there. You gonna take the train? I'm gonna take the train.

LYMON: They treat you better up here.

BOY WILLIE: I ain't worried about nobody mistreating me. They treat you like you let them treat you. They mistreat me I mistreat them right back. Ain't no difference in me and the white man.

WINING BOY: Ain't no difference as far as how somebody supposed to treat you. I agree with that. But I'll tell you the difference between the colored man and the white man. Alright. Now you take and eat some berries. They taste real good to you. So you say I'm gonna go out and get me a whole pot of these berries and cook them up to make a pie or whatever. But you ain't looked to see them berries is sitting in the white fellow's yard. Ain't got no fence around them. You figure anybody want something they'd fence it in. Alright. Now the white man come along and say that's my land. Therefore everything that grow on it belong to me. He tell the sheriff, "I want you to put this nigger in jail as a warning to all the other niggers. Otherwise first thing you know these niggers have everything that belong to us."

BOY WILLIE: I'd come back at night and haul off his whole patch while he was sleep.

WINING BOY: Alright. Now Mr. So and So, he sell the land to you. And he come to you and say, "John, you own the land. It's all yours now. But them is my berries. And come time to pick them I'm gonna send my boys over. You got the land . . . but them berries, I'm gonna keep them. They mine." And he go and fix it with the law that them is his berries. Now that's the difference between the colored man and the white man. The colored man can't fix nothing with the law.

BOY WILLIE: I don't go by what the law say. The law's liable to say anything. I go by if it's right or not. It don't matter to me what the law say. I take and look at it for myself.

LYMON: That's why you gonna end up back down there on the Parchman Farm.

BOY WILLIE: I ain't thinking about no Parchman Farm. You liable to go back before me.

LYMON: They work you too hard down there. All that weeding and hoeing and chopping down trees. I didn't like all that.

WINING BOY: You ain't got to like your job on Parchman. Hey, tell him, Doaker, the only one got to like his job is the waterboy.

DOAKER: If he don't like his job he need to set that bucket down.

BOY WILLIE: That's what they told Lymon. They had Lymon on water and everybody got mad at him cause he was lazy.

LYMON: That water was heavy.

BOY WILLIE: They had Lymon down there singing:

(*Sings.*)

O Lord Berta Berta O Lord gal oh-ah
O Lord Berta Berta O Lord gal well

(LYMON *and* WINING BOY *join in.*)

Go 'head marry don't you wait on me oh-ah
Go 'head marry don't you wait on me well
Might not want you when I go free oh-ah
Might not want you when I go free well

BOY WILLIE: Come on, Doaker. Doaker know this one.

(*As* DOAKER *joins in the men stamp and clap to keep time. They sing in harmony with great fervor and style.*)

O Lord Berta Berta O Lord gal oh-ah
O Lord Berta Berta O Lord gal well

Raise them up higher, let them drop on down oh-ah
Raise them up higher, let them drop on down well
Don't know the difference when the sun go down oh-ah
Don't know the difference when the sun go down well

Berta in Meridan and she living at ease oh-ah
Berta in Meridan and she living at ease well
I'm on old Parchman, got to work or leave oh-ah
I'm on old Parchman, got to work or leave well

O Alberta, Berta, O Lord gal oh-ah
O Alberta, Berta, O Lord gal well

When you marry, don't marry no farming man oh-ah
When you marry, don't marry no farming man well
Everyday Monday, hoe handle in your hand oh-ah
Everyday Monday, hoe handle in your hand well

When you marry, marry a railroad man, oh-ah
When you marry, marry a railroad man, well
Everyday Sunday, dollar in your hand oh-ah
Everyday Sunday, dollar in your hand well

O Alberta, Berta, O Lord gal oh-ah
O Alberta, Berta, O Lord gal well

BOY WILLIE: Doaker like that part. He like that railroad part.

LYMON: Doaker sound like Tangleye. He can't sing a lick.

BOY WILLIE: Hey, Doaker, they still talk about you down on Parchman. They ask me, "You Doaker Boy's nephew?" I say, "Yeah, me and him is family." They treated me alright soon as I told them that. Say, "Yeah, he my uncle."

DOAKER: I don't never want to see none of them niggers no more.

BOY WILLIE: I don't want to see them either. Hey, Wining Boy, come on play some piano. You a piano player, play some piano. Lymon wanna hear you.

WINING BOY: I give that piano up. That was the best thing that ever happened to me, getting rid of that piano. That piano got so big and I'm carrying it around on my back. I don't wish that on nobody. See, you think it's all fun being a recording star. Got to carrying that piano around and man did I get slow. Got just like molasses. The world just slipping by me and I'm walking around with that piano. Alright. Now, there ain't but so many places you can go. Only so many road wide enough for you and that piano. And that piano get heavier and heavier. Go to a place and they find out you play piano, the first thing they want to do is give you a drink, find you a piano, and sit you right down. And that's where you gonna be for the next eight hours. They ain't gonna let you get up! Now, the first three or four years of that is fun. You can't get enough whiskey and you can't get enough women and you don't never get tired of playing that piano. But that only last so long. You look up one day and you hate the whiskey, and you hate the women, and you hate the piano. But that's all you got. You can't do nothing else. All you know how to do is play that piano. Now, who am I? Am I me? Or am I the piano player? Sometime it seem like the only thing to do is shoot the piano player cause he the cause of all the trouble I'm having.

DOAKER: What you gonna do when your troubles get like mine?

LYMON: If I knew how to play it, I'd play it. That's a nice piano.

BOY WILLIE: Whoever playing better play quick. Sutter's brother say he waiting on me. I sell them watermelons. Get Berniece to sell that piano. Put them two parts with the part I done saved . . .

WINING BOY: Berniece ain't gonna sell that piano. I don't see why you don't know that.

BOY WILLIE: What she gonna do with it? She ain't doing nothing but letting it sit up there and rot. That piano ain't doing nobody no good.

LYMON: That's a nice piano. If I had it I'd sell it. Unless I knew how to play like Wining Boy. You can get a nice price for that piano.

DOAKER: Now I'm gonna tell you something, Lymon don't know this . . . but I'm gonna tell you why me and Wining Boy say Berniece ain't gonna sell that piano.

BOY WILLIE: She ain't got to sell it! I'm gonna sell it! Berniece ain't got no more rights to that piano than I do.

DOAKER: I'm talking to the man . . . let me talk to the man. See, now . . . to understand why we say that . . . to understand about that piano . . . you got to go back to slavery time. See, our family was owned by a fellow named Robert Sutter. That was Sutter's grandfather. Alright. The piano was owned by a fellow named Joel Nolander. He was one of the Nolander brothers from down in Georgia. It was coming up on Sutter's wedding anniversary and he was looking to buy his wife . . . Miss Ophelia was her name . . . he was looking to buy her an anniversary present. Only thing with him . . . he ain't had no money. But he had some niggers. So he asked Mr. Nolander to see if maybe he could trade off some of his niggers for that piano. Told him he would give him one and a half niggers for it. That's the way he told him. Say he could have one full grown and one half grown. Mr. Nolander agreed only he say he had to pick them. He didn't want Sutter to give him just any old nigger. He say he wanted to have the pick of the litter. So Sutter lined up his niggers and Mr. Nolander looked them over and out of the whole bunch he picked my grandmother . . . her name was Berniece . . . same like Berniece . . . and he picked my daddy when he wasn't nothing but a little boy nine years old. They made the trade off and Miss Ophelia was so happy with that piano that it got to be just about all she would do was play on that piano.

WINING BOY: Just get up in the morning, get all dressed up and sit down and play on that piano.

DOAKER: Alright. Time go along. Time go along. Miss Ophelia got to missing my grandmother . . . the way she would cook and clean the house and talk to her and what not. And she missed having my daddy around the house to fetch things for her. So she asked to see if maybe she could trade back that piano and get her niggers back. Mr. Nolander said no. Said a deal was a deal. Him and Sutter had a big falling out about it and Miss Ophelia took sick to the bed. Wouldn't get out of the bed in the morning. She just lay there. The doctor said she was wasting away.

WINING BOY: That's when Sutter called our granddaddy up to the house.

DOAKER: Now, our granddaddy's name was Boy Willie. That's who Boy Willie's named after . . . only they called him Willie Boy. Now, he was a worker of wood. He could make you anything you wanted out of wood. He'd make you a desk. A table. A lamp. Anything you wanted. Them white fellows around there used to come up to Mr. Sutter and get him to make all kinds of things for them. Then they'd pay Mr. Sutter a nice price. See, everything my granddaddy made Mr. Sutter owned cause he owned him. That's why when Mr. Nolander offered to buy him to keep the family together Mr. Sutter wouldn't sell him. Told Mr. Nolander he didn't have enough money to buy him. Now . . . am I telling it right, Wining Boy?

WINING BOY: You telling it.

DOAKER: Sutter called him up to the house and told him to carve my grandmother and my daddy's picture on the piano for Miss Ophelia. And he took and carved this . . . (DOAKER *crosses over to the piano.*) See that right there? That's my grandmother, Berniece. She looked just like that. And he put a picture of my daddy when he wasn't nothing but a little boy the way he remembered him. He made them up out of his memory. Only thing . . . he didn't stop there. He carved all this. He got a picture of his mama . . . Mama Esther . . . and his daddy, Boy Charles.

WINING BOY: That was the first Boy Charles.

DOAKER: Then he put on the side here all kinds of things. See that? That's when him and Mama Berniece got married. They called it jumping the broom. That's how you got married in them days. Then he got here when my daddy was born . . . and here he got Mama Esther's funeral . . . and down here he got Mr. Nolander taking Mama Berniece and my daddy away down to his place in Georgia. He got all kinds of things what happened with our family. When Mr. Sutter seen the piano with all them carvings on it he got mad. He didn't ask for all that. But see . . . there wasn't nothing he could do about it. When Miss Ophelia seen it . . . she got excited. Now she had her piano and her niggers too. She took back to playing it and played on it right up till the day she died. Alright . . . now see, our brother Boy Charles . . . that's Berniece and Boy Willie's daddy . . . he was the oldest of us three boys. He's dead now. But he would have been fifty-seven if he had lived. He died in 1911 when he was thirty-one years old. Boy Charles used to talk about that piano all the time. He never could get it off his mind. Two or three months go by and he be talking about it again. He be talking about taking it out of Sutter's house. Say it was the story of our whole family and as long as Sutter had it . . . he had us. Say we was still in slavery. Me and Wining Boy tried to talk him out of it but it wouldn't do any good. Soon as he quiet down about it he'd start up again. We seen where he wasn't gonna get it off his mind . . . so, on the

Fourth of July, 1911 . . . when Sutter was at the picnic what the county give every year . . . me and Wining Boy went on down there with him and took that piano out of Sutter's house. We put it on a wagon and me and Wining Boy carried it over into the next county with Mama Ola's people. Boy Charles decided to stay around there and wait until Sutter got home to make it look like business as usual.

Now, I don't know what happened when Sutter came home and found that piano gone. But somebody went up to Boy Charles's house and set it on fire. But he wasn't in there. He must have seen them coming cause he went down and caught the 3:57 Yellow Dog. He didn't know they was gonna come down and stop the train. Stopped the train and found Boy Charles in the boxcar with four of them hobos. Must have got mad when they couldn't find the piano cause they set the boxcar afire and killed everybody. Now, nobody know who done that. Some people say it was Sutter cause it was his piano. Some people say it was Sheriff Carter. Some people say it was Robert Smith and Ed Saunders. But don't nobody know for sure. It was about two months after that that Ed Saunders fell down his well. Just upped and fell down his well for no reason. People say it was the ghost of them men who burned up in the boxcar that pushed him in his well. They started calling them the Ghosts of the Yellow Dog. Now, that's how all that got started and that why we say Berniece ain't gonna sell that piano. Cause her daddy died over it.

BOY WILLIE: All that's in the past. If my daddy had seen where he could have traded that piano in for some land of his own, it wouldn't be sitting up here now. He spent his whole life farming on somebody else's land. I ain't gonna do that. See, he couldn't do no better. When he come along he ain't had nothing he could build on. His daddy ain't had nothing to give him. The only thing my daddy had to give me was that piano. And he died over giving me that. I ain't gonna let it sit up there and rot without trying to do something with it. If Berniece can't see that, then I'm gonna go ahead and sell my half. And you and Wining Boy know I'm right.

DOAKER: Ain't nobody said nothing about who's right and who's wrong. I was just telling the man about the piano. I was telling him why we say Berniece ain't gonna sell it.

LYMON: Yeah, I can see why you say that now. I told Boy Willie he ought to stay up here with me.

BOY WILLIE: You stay! I'm going back! That's what I'm gonna do with my life! Why I got to come up here and learn to do something I don't know how to do when I already know how to farm? You stay up here and make your own way if that's what you want to do. I'm going back and live my life the way I want to live it.

(WINING BOY *gets up and crosses to the piano.*)

WINING BOY: Let's see what we got here. I ain't played on this thing for a while.

DOAKER: You can stop telling that. You was playing on it the last time you was through here. We couldn't get you off of it. Go on and play something.

(WINING BOY *sits down at the piano and plays and sings. The song is one which has put many dimes and quarters in his pocket, long ago, in dimly remembered towns and way stations. He plays badly, without hesitation, and sings in a forceful voice.*)

WINING BOY: (*Singing.*)

I am a rambling gambling man
I gambled in many towns
I rambled this wide world over
I rambled this world around
I had my ups and downs in life
And bitter times I saw
But I never knew what misery was
Till I lit on old Arkansas.

I started out one morning
to meet that early train
He said, "You better work for me
I have some land to drain.
I'll give you fifty cents a day,
Your washing, board and all
And you shall be a different man
In the state of Arkansas."

I worked six months for the rascal
Joe Herrin was his name
He fed me old corn dodgers
They was hard as any rock
My tooth is all got loosened
And my knees begin to knock
That was the kind of hash I got
In the state of Arkansas.

Traveling man
I've traveled all around this world
Traveling man
I've traveled from land to land
Traveling man
I've traveled all around this world
Well it ain't no use
writing no news
I'm a traveling man.

(*The door opens and* BERNIECE *enters with* MARETHA.)

BERNIECE: Is that . . . Lord, I know that ain't Wining Boy sitting there.

WINING BOY: Hey, Berniece.

BERNIECE: You all had this planned. You and Boy Willie had this planned.

WINING BOY: I didn't know he was gonna be here. I'm on my way down home. I stopped by to see you and Doaker first.

DOAKER: I told the nigger he left out of here with that sack of money, we thought we might never see him again. Boy Willie say he wasn't gonna see him till he got broke. I looked up and seen him sitting on the doorstep asking for two dollars. Look at him laughing. He know it's the truth.

BERNIECE: Boy Willie, I didn't see that truck out there. I thought you was out selling watermelons.

BOY WILLIE: We done sold them all. Sold the truck too.

BERNIECE: I don't want to go through none of your stuff. I done told you to go back where you belong.

BOY WILLIE: I was just teasing you, woman. You can't take no teasing?

BERNIECE: Wining Boy, when you get here?

WINING BOY: A little while ago. I took the train from Kansas City.

BERNIECE: Let me go upstairs and change and then I'll cook you something to eat.

BOY WILLIE: You ain't cooked me nothing when I come.

BERNIECE: Boy Willie, go on and leave me alone. Come on, Maretha, get up here and change your clothes before you get them dirty.

(BERNIECE *exits up the stairs, followed by* MARETHA.)

WINING BOY: Maretha sure getting big, ain't she, Doaker. And just as pretty as she want to be. I didn't know Crawley had it in him.

(BOY WILLIE *crosses to the piano.*)

BOY WILLIE: Hey, Lymon . . . get up on the other side of this piano and let me see something.

WINING BOY: Boy Willie, what is you doing?

BOY WILLIE: I'm seeing how heavy this piano is. Get up over there, Lymon.

WINING BOY: Go on and leave that piano alone. You ain't taking that piano out of here and selling it.

BOY WILLIE: Just as soon as I get them watermelons out that truck.

WINING BOY: Well, I got something to say about that.

BOY WILLIE: This my daddy's piano.

WINING BOY: He ain't took it by himself. Me and Doaker helped him.

BOY WILLIE: He died by himself. Where was you and Doaker at then? Don't come telling me nothing about this piano. This is me and Berniece's piano. Am I right, Doaker?

DOAKER: Yeah, you right.

BOY WILLIE: Let's see if we can lift it up, Lymon. Get a good grip on it and pick it up on your end. Ready? Lift!

(*As they start to move the piano, the sound of* SUTTER'S GHOST *is heard.* DOAKER *is the only one to hear it. With difficulty they move the piano a little bit so it is out of place.*)

BOY WILLIE: What you think?

LYMON: It's heavy . . . but you can move it. Only it ain't gonna be easy.

BOY WILLIE: It wasn't that heavy to me. Okay, let's put it back.

(*The sound of* SUTTER'S GHOST *is heard again. They all hear it as* BERNIECE *enters on the stairs.*)

BERNIECE: Boy Willie . . . you gonna play around with me one too many times. And then God's gonna bless you and West is gonna dress you. Now set that piano back over there. I done told you a hundred times I ain't selling that piano.

BOY WILLIE: I'm trying to get me some land, woman. I need that piano to get me some money so I can buy Sutter's land.

BERNIECE: Money can't buy what that piano cost. You can't sell your soul for money. It won't go with the buyer. It'll shrivel and shrink to know that you ain't taken on to it. But it won't go with the buyer.

BOY WILLIE: I ain't talking about all that, woman. I ain't talking about selling my soul. I'm talking about trading that piece of wood for some land. Get something under your feet. Land the only thing God ain't making no more of. You can always get you another piano. I'm talking about some land. What you get something out the ground from. That's what I'm talking about. You can't do nothing with that piano but sit up there and look at it.

BERNIECE: That's just what I'm gonna do. Wining Boy, you want me to fry you some pork chops?

BOY WILLIE: Now, I'm gonna tell you the way I see it. The only thing that make that piano worth something is them carvings Papa Willie Boy put on there. That's what make it worth something. That was my great-grandaddy. Papa Boy Charles brought that piano into the house. Now, I'm supposed to build on what they left me. You can't do nothing with that piano sitting up here in the house. That's just like if I let them watermelons sit out there and rot. I'd be a fool. Alright now, if you say to me, Boy Willie, I'm using that piano. I give out lessons on it and that help me make my rent or whatever. Then that be something else, I'd have to go on and say, well, Berniece using that piano. She building on it. Let her go on and use it. I got to find another way to get Sutter's land. But Doaker say you ain't touched that piano the whole time it's been up here. So why you wanna stand in my way? See, you just looking at the sentimental value. See, that's good. That's alright. I take my hat off whenever somebody say my daddy's name. But I ain't gonna be no fool about no sentimental value. You can sit up here and look at the piano for the next hundred years and it's just gonna be a piano. You can't make more than that. Now I want to get Sutter's land with that piano. I get Sutter's land and I can go down and cash in the crop and get my seed. As long as I got the land and the seed then I'm alright. I can always get me a little something else. Cause that land give back to you. I can make me another crop and cash that in. I still got the land and the seed. But that piano don't put out nothing else. You ain't got nothing working for you. Now, the kind of man my daddy was he would have understood that. I'm sorry you can't see it that way. But that's why I'm gonna take that piano out of here and sell it.

BERNIECE: You ain't taking that piano out of my house.

(*She crosses to the piano.*)

Look at this piano. Look at it. Mama Ola polished this piano with her tears for seventeen years. For seventeen years she rubbed on it till her hands bled. Then she rubbed the blood in . . . mixed it up with the rest of the blood on it. Every day that God breathed life into her body she rubbed and cleaned and polished and prayed over it. Play something for me, Berniece. Play something for me, Berniece." Every day. "I cleaned it up for you, play something for me, Berniece." You always talking about your daddy but you ain't never stopped to look at what his foolishness cost your mama. Seventeen years' worth of cold nights and an empty bed. For what? For a piano? For a piece of wood? To get even with somebody? I look at you and you're all the same. You, Papa Boy Charles, Wining Boy, Doaker, Crawley . . . you're all alike. All this thieving and killing and thieving and killing. And what it ever lead to? More killing and more thieving. I ain't never seen it come to nothing. People getting burned up. People getting shot. People falling down their wells. It don't never stop.

DOAKER: Come on now, Berniece, ain't no need in getting upset.

BOY WILLIE: I done a little bit of stealing here and there, but I ain't never killed nobody. I can't be speaking for nobody else. You all got to speak for yourself, but I ain't never killed nobody.

BERNIECE: You killed Crawley just as sure as if you pulled the trigger.

BOY WILLIE: See, that's ignorant. That's downright foolish for you to say something like that. You ain't doing nothing but showing your ignorance. If the nigger was here I'd whup his ass for getting me and Lymon shot at.

BERNIECE: Crawley ain't knew about the wood.

BOY WILLIE: We told the man about the wood. Ask Lymon. He knew all about the wood. He seen we was sneaking it. Why else we gonna be out there at night? Don't come telling me Crawley ain't knew about the wood. Them fellows come up on us and Crawley tried to bully them. Me and Lymon seen the sheriff with them and give in. Wasn't no sense in getting killed over fifty dollars' worth of wood.

BERNIECE: Crawley ain't knew you stole that wood.

BOY WILLIE: We ain't stole no wood. Me and Lymon was hauling wood for Jim Miller and keeping us a little bit on the side. We dumped our little bit down there by the creek till we had enough to make a load. Some fellows seen us and we figured we better get it before they did. We come up there and got Crawley to help us load it. Figured we'd cut him in. Crawley trying to keep the wolf from his door . . . we was trying to help him.

LYMON: Me and Boy Willie told him about the wood. We told him some fellows might be trying to beat us to it. He say let me go back and get my thirty-eight. That's what caused all the trouble.

BOY WILLIE: If Crawley ain't had the gun he'd be alive today.

LYMON: We had it about half loaded when they come up on us. We seen the sheriff with them and we tried to get away. We ducked around near the bend in the creek . . . but they was down there too. Boy Willie say let's give in. But Crawley pulled out his gun and started shooting. That's when they started shooting back.

BERNIECE: All I know is Crawley would be alive if you hadn't come up there and got him.

BOY WILLIE: I ain't had nothing to do with Crawley getting killed. That was his own fault.

BERNIECE: Crawley's dead and in the ground and you still walking around here eating. That's all I know. He went off to load some wood with you and ain't never come back.

BOY WILLIE: I told you, woman . . . I ain't had nothing to do with . . .

BERNIECE: He ain't here, is he? He ain't here!

(BERNIECE *hits* BOY WILLIE.)

I said he ain't here. Is he?

(BERNIECE *continues to hit* BOY WILLIE, *who doesn't move to defend himself, other than back up and turning his head so that most of the blows fall on his chest and arms.*)

DOAKER: (*Grabbing* BERNIECE.) Come on, Berniece . . . let it go, it ain't his fault.

BERNIECE: He ain't here, is he? Is he?

BOY WILLIE: I told you I ain't responsible for Crawley.

BERNIECE: He ain't here.

BOY WILLIE: Come on now, Berniece . . . don't do this now. Doaker get her. I ain't had nothing to do with Crawley . . .

BERNIECE: You come up there and got him!

BOY WILLIE: I done told you now. Doaker, get her. I ain't playing.

DOAKER: Come on. Berniece.

(MARETHA *is heard screaming upstairs. It is a scream of stark terror.*)

MARETHA: Mama! . . . Mama!

(*The lights go down to black. End of Act One.*)

ACT TWO

SCENE ONE

(*The lights come up on the kitchen. It is the following morning.* DOAKER *is ironing the pants to his uniform. He has a pot cooking on the stove at the same time. He is singing a song. The song provides him with the rhythm for his work and he moves about the kitchen with the ease born of many years as a railroad cook*)

DOAKER:

Gonna leave Jackson Mississippi
and go to Memphis
and double back to Jackson
Come on down to Hattiesburg
Change cars on the Y.D.
coming through the territory to
Meridian
and Meridian to Greenville
and Greenville to Memphis
I'm on my way and I know where

Change cars on the Katy
Leaving Jackson
and going through Clarksdale
Hello Winona!
Courtland!
Bateville!
Como!
Senitobia!
Lewisberg!
Sunflower!
Glendora!
Sharkey!
And double back to Jackson
Hello Greenwood
I'm on my way Memphis
Clarksdale
Moorhead

Indianola
Can a highball pass through?
Highball on through sir
Grand Carson!
Thirty First Street Depot
Fourth Street Depot
Memphis!

(WINING BOY *enters carrying a suit of clothes.*)

DOAKER: I thought you took that suit to the pawnshop?

WINING BOY: I went down there and the man tell me the suit is too old. Look at this suit. This is one hundred percent silk! How a silk suit gonna get too old? I know what it was he just didn't want to give me five dollars for it. Best he wanna give me is three dollars. I figure a silk suit is worth five dollars all over the world. I wasn't gonna part with it for no three dollars so I brought it back.

DOAKER: They got another pawnshop up on Wylie.

WINING BOY: I carried it up there. He say he don't take no clothes. Only thing he take is guns and radios. Maybe a guitar or two. Where's Berniece?

DOAKER: Berniece still at work. Boy Willie went down there to meet Lymon this morning. I guess they got that truck fixed, they been out there all day and ain't come back yet. Maretha scared to sleep up there now. Berniece don't know, but I seen Sutter before she did.

WINING BOY: Say what?

DOAKER: About three weeks ago. I had just come back from down there. Sutter couldn't have been dead more than three days. He was sitting over there at the piano. I come out to go to work . . . and he was sitting right there. Had his hand on top of his head just like Berniece said. I believe he broke his neck when he fell in the well. I kept quiet about it. I didn't see no reason to upset Berniece.

WINING BOY: Did he say anything? Did he say he was looking for Boy Willie?

DOAKER: He was just sitting there. He ain't said nothing. I went on out the door and left him sitting there. I figure as long as he was on the other side of the room everything be alright. I don't know what I would have done if he had started walking toward me.

WINING BOY: Berniece say he was calling Boy Willie's name.

DOAKER: I ain't heard him say nothing. He was just sitting there when I seen him. But I don't believe Boy Willie pushed him in the well. Sutter here cause of that piano. I heard him playing on it one time. I thought it was Berniece but then she don't play that kind of music. I come out here and ain't seen nobody, but them piano keys was moving a mile a minute. Berniece need to go on and get rid of it. It ain't done nothing but cause trouble.

WINING BOY: I agree with Berniece. Boy Charles ain't took it to give it back. He took it cause he figure he had more right to it than Sutter did. If Sutter can't understand that . . . then that's just the way that go. Sutter dead and in the ground . . . don't care where his ghost is. He can hover around and play on the piano all he want. I want to see him carry it out the house. That's what I want to see. What time Berniece get home? I don't see how I let her get away from me this morning.

DOAKER: You up there sleep. Berniece leave out of here early in the morning. She out there in Squirrel Hill cleaning house for some bigshot down there at the steel mill. They don't like you to come late. You come late they won't give you your carfare. What kind of business you got with Berniece?

WINING BOY: My business. I ain't asked you what kind of business you got.

DOAKER: Berniece ain't got no money. If that's why you was trying to catch her. She having a hard enough time trying to get by as it is. If she go ahead and marry Avery . . . he working every day . . . she go ahead and marry him they could do alright for themselves. But as it stands she ain't got no money.

WINING BOY: Well, let me have five dollars.

DOAKER: I just give you a dollar before you left out of here. You ain't gonna take my five dollars out there and gamble and drink it up.

WINING BOY: Aw, nigger, give me five dollars. I'll give it back to you.

DOAKER: You wasn't looking to give me five dollars when you had that sack of money. You wasn't looking to throw nothing my way. Now you wanna come in here and borrow five dollars. If you going back with Boy Willie you need to be trying to figure out how you gonna get train fare.

WINING BOY: That's why I need the five dollars. If I had five dollars I could get me some money.

(DOAKER *goes into his pocket.*)

Make it seven.

DOAKER: You take this five dollars . . . and you bring my money back here too.

(BOY WILLIE *and* LYMON *enter. They are happy and excited. They have money in all of their pockets and are anxious to count it.*)

DOAKER: How'd you do out there?

BOY WILLIE: They was lining up for them.

LYMON: Me and Boy Willie couldn't sell them fast enough. Time we got one sold we'd sell another.

BOY WILLIE: I seen what was happening and told Lymon to up the price on them.

LYMON: Boy Willie say charge them a quarter more. They didn't care. A couple of people give me a dollar and told me to keep the change.

BOY WILLIE: One fellow bought five. I say now what he gonna do with five watermelons? He can't eat them all. I sold him the five and asked him did he want to buy five more.

LYMON: I ain't never seen nobody snatch a dollar fast as Boy Willie.

BOY WILLIE: One lady asked me say, "Is they sweet?" I told her say, "Lady, where we grow these watermelons we put sugar in the ground." You know, she believed me. Talking about she had never heard of that before. Lymon was laughing his head off. I told her, "Oh, yeah, we put the sugar right in the ground with the seed." She say, "Well, give me another one." Them white folks is something else . . . ain't they, Lymon?

LYMON: Soon as you holler watermelons they come right out their door. Then they go and get their neighbors. Look like they having a contest to see who can buy the most.

WINING BOY: I got something for Lymon.

(WINING BOY *goes to get his suit.* BOY WILLIE *and* LYMON *continue to count their money.*)

BOY WILLIE: I know you got more than that. You ain't sold all them watermelons for that little bit of money.

LYMON: I'm still looking. That ain't all you got either. Where's all them quarters?

BOY WILLIE: You let me worry about the quarters. Just put the money on the table.

WINING BOY: (*Entering with his suit.*) Look here, Lymon . . . see this? Look at his eyes getting big. He ain't never seen a suit like this. This is one hundred percent silk. Go ahead . . . put it on. See if it fit you.

(LYMON *tries the suit coat on.*)

Look at that. Feel it. That's one hundred percent genuine silk. I got that in Chicago. You can't get clothes like that nowhere but New York and Chicago. You can't get clothes like that in Pittsburgh. These folks in Pittsburgh ain't never seen clothes like that.

LYMON: This is nice, feel real nice and smooth.

WINING BOY: That's a fifty-five-dollar suit. That's the kind of suit the bigshots wear. You need a pistol and a pocketful of money to wear that suit. I'll let you have it for three dollars. The women will fall out their windows they see you in a suit like that. Give me three dollars and go on and wear it down the street and get you a woman.

BOY WILLIE: That looks nice, Lymon. Put the pants on. Let me see it with the pants.

(LYMON *begins to try on the pants.*)

WINING BOY: Look at that . . . see how it fits you? Give me three dollars and go on and take it. Look at that, Doaker . . . don't he look nice?

DOAKER: Yeah . . . that's a nice suit.

WINING BOY: Got a shirt to go with it. Cost you an extra dollar. Four dollars you got the whole deal.

LYMON: How this look, Boy Willie?

BOY WILLIE: That look nice . . . if you like that kind of thing. I don't like them dress-up kind of clothes. If you like it, look real nice.

WINING BOY: That's the kind of suit you need for up here in the North.

LYMON: Four dollars for everything? The suit and the shirt?

WINING BOY: That's cheap. I should be charging you twenty dollars. I give you a break cause you a homeboy. That's the only way I let you have it for four dollars.

LYMON: (*Going into his pocket.*) Okay . . . here go the four dollars.

WINING BOY: You got some shoes? What size you wear?

LYMON: Size nine.

WINING BOY: That's what size I got! Size nine. I let you have them for three dollars.

LYMON: Where they at? Let me see them.

WINING BOY: They real nice shoes, too. Got a nice tip to them. Got pointy toe just like you want.

(WINING BOY *goes to get his shoes.*)

LYMON: Come on, Boy Willie, let's go out tonight. I wanna see what it looks like up here. Maybe we go to a picture show. Hey, Doaker, they got picture shows up here?

DOAKER: The Rhumba Theater. Right down there on Fullerton Street. Can't miss it. Got the speakers outside on the sidewalk. You can hear it a block away. Boy Willie know where it's at.

(DOAKER *exits into his room.*)

LYMON: Let's go to the picture show, Boy Willie. Let's go find some women.

BOY WILLIE: Hey, Lymon, how many of them watermelons would you say we got left? We got just under a half a load . . . right?

LYMON: About that much. Maybe a little more.

BOY WILLIE: You think that piano will fit up in there?

LYMON: If we stack them watermelons you can sit it up in the front there.

BOY WILLIE: I'm gonna call that man tomorrow.

WINING BOY: (*Returns with his shoes.*) Here you go . . . size nine. Put them on. Cost you three dollars. That's a Florsheim shoe. That's the kind Staggerlee wore.

LYMON: (*Trying on the shoes.*) You sure these size nine?

WINING BOY: You can look at my feet and see we wear the same size. Man, you put on that suit and them shoes and you got something there. You ready for whatever's out there. But is they ready for you? With them shoes on you be the King of the Walk. Have everybody stop to look at your shoes. Wishing they had a pair. I'll give you a break. Go on and take them for two dollars.

(LYMON *pays* WINING BOY *two dollars.*)

LYMON: Come on, Boy Willie . . . let's go find some women. I'm gonna go upstairs and get ready. I'll be ready to go in a minute. Ain't you gonna get dressed?

BOY WILLIE: I'm gonna wear what I got on. I ain't dressing up for these city niggers.

(LYMON *exits up the stairs.*)

That's all Lymon think about is women.

WINING BOY: His daddy was the same way. I used to run around with him. I know his mama too. Two strokes back and I would have been his daddy! His daddy's dead now . . . but I got the nigger out of jail one time. They was fixing to name him Daniel and walk him through the Lion's Den. He got in a tussle with one of them white fellows and the sheriff lit on him like white on rice. That's how the whole thing come about between me and Lymon's mama. She knew me and his daddy used to run together and he got in jail and she went down there and took the sheriff a hundred dollars. Don't get me to lying about where she got it from. I don't know. The sheriff *looked at that hundred dollars and turned his nose up* Told her, say, "That ain't gonna do him no good. You got to put another hundred on top of that." She come up *there and got me where I was playing at this saloon* . . . said she had all but fifty dollars and asked me if I could help. Now the way I figured it . . . without that fifty dollars the sheriff was gonna turn him over to Parchman. The sheriff turn him over to Parchman it be three years before anybody see him again. Now I'm gonna say it right . . . I will give anybody fifty dollars to keep them out of jail for three years. I give her the fifty dollars and she told me to come over to the house. I ain't asked her. I figure if she was nice enough to invite me I ought to go. I ain't had to say a word. She invited me over just as nice. Say, "Why don't you come over to the house?" She ain't had to say nothing else. Them words rolled off her tongue just as nice. I went on down there and sat about three hours. Started to leave and changed my mind. She grabbed hold to me and say, "Baby, it's all night long." That was one of the shortest nights I have ever spent on this earth! I could have used another eight hours. Lymon's daddy didn't even say nothing to me when he got out. He just looked at me funny. He had a good notion something had happened between me an' her. L. D. Jackson. That was one bad-luck nigger. Got killed at some dance. Fellow walked in and shot him thinking he was somebody else.

(DOAKER *enters from his room.*)

Hey, Doaker, you remember L. D. Jackson?

DOAKER: That's Lymon's daddy. That was one bad-luck nigger.

BOY WILLIE: Look like you ready to railroad some.

DOAKER: Yeah, I got to make that run.

(LYMON *enters from the stairs. He is dressed in his new suit and shoes, to which he has added a cheap straw hat.*)

LYMON: How I look?

WINING BOY: You look like a million dollars. Don't he look good, Doaker? Come on, let's play some cards. You wanna play some cards?

BOY WILLIE: We ain't gonna play no cards with you. Me and Lymon gonna find some women. Hey, Lymon, don't play no cards with Wining Boy. He'll take all your money.

WINING BOY: (*To* LYMON.) You got a magic suit there. You can get you a woman easy with that suit . . . but you got to know the magic words. You know the magic words to get you a woman?

LYMON: I just talk to them to see if I like them and they like me.

WINING BOY: You just walk right up to them and say, "If you got the harbor I got the ship." If that don't work ask them if you can put them in your pocket. The first thing they gonna say is, "It's too small." That's when you look them dead in the eye and say, "Baby, ain't nothing small about me." If that don't work then you move on to another one. Am I telling him right, Doaker?

DOAKER: That man don't need you to tell him nothing about no women. These women these days ain't gonna fall for that kind of stuff. You got to buy them a present. That's what they looking for these days.

BOY WILLIE: Come on, I'm ready. You ready, Lymon? Come on, let's go find some women.

WINING BOY: Here, let me walk out with you. I wanna see the women fall out their window when they see Lymon.

(*They all exit and the lights go down on the scene.*)

SCENE 2

(*The lights come up on the kitchen. It is late evening of the same day.* BERNIECE *has set a tub for her bath in the kitchen. She is heating up water on the stove. There is a knock at the door.*)

BERNIECE: Who is it?

AVERY: It's me, Avery.

(BERNIECE *opens the door and lets him in.*)

BERNIECE: Avery, come on in. I was just fixing to take my bath.

AVERY: Where Boy Willie? I see that truck out there almost empty. They done sold almost all them watermelons.

BERNIECE: They was gone when I come home. I don't know where they went off to. Boy Willie around here about to drive me crazy.

AVERY: They sell them watermelons . . . he'll be gone soon.

BERNIECE: What Mr. Cohen say about letting you have the place?

AVERY: He say he'll let me have it for thirty dollars a month. I talked him out of thirty-five and he say he'll let me have it for thirty.

BERNIECE: That's a nice spot next to Benny Diamond's store.

AVERY: Berniece . . . I be at home and I get to thinking you up here an' I'm down there. I get to thinking how that look to have a preacher that ain't married. It makes for a better congregation if the preacher was settled down and married.

BERNIECE: Avery . . . not now. I was fixing to take my bath.

AVERY: You know how I feel about you, Berniece. Now . . . I done got the place from Mr. Cohen. I get the money from the bank and I can fix it up real nice. They give me a ten cents a hour raise down there on the job . . . now Berniece, I ain't got much in the way of comforts. I got a hole in my pockets near about as far as money is concerned. I ain't never found no way through life to a woman I care about like I care about you. I need that. I need somebody on my bond side. I need a woman that fits in my hand.

BERNIECE: Avery, I ain't ready to get married now.

AVERY: You too young a woman to close up, Berniece.

BERNIECE: I ain't said nothing about closing up. I got a lot of woman left in me.

AVERY: Where's it at? When's the last time you looked at it?

BERNIECE: (*Stunned by his remark.*) That's a nasty thing to say. And you call yourself a preacher.

AVERY: Anytime I get anywhere near you . . . you push me away.

BERNIECE: I got enough on my hands with Maretha. I got enough people to love and take care of.

AVERY: Who you got to love you? Can't nobody get close enough to you. Doaker can't half say nothing to you. You jump all over Boy Willie. Who you got to love you, Berniece?

BERNIECE: You trying to tell me a woman can't be nothing without a man. But you alright, huh? You can just walk out of here without me—without a woman—and still be a man. That's alright. Ain't nobody gonna ask you, "Avery, who you got to love you?" That's alright for you. But everybody gonna be worried about Berniece. "How Berniece gonna take care of herself? How she gonna raise that child without a man? Wonder what she do with herself. How she gonna live like that?" Everybody got all kinds of questions for Berniece. Everybody telling me I can't be a woman unless I got a man. Well, you tell me, Avery—you know—how much woman am I?

AVERY: It wasn't me, Berniece. You can't blame me for nobody else. I'll own up to my own shortcomings. But you can't blame me for Crawley or nobody else.

BERNIECE: I ain't blaming nobody for nothing. I'm just stating the facts.

AVERY: How long you gonna carry Crawley with you, Berniece? It's been over three years. At some point you got to let go and go on. Life's got all kinds of twists and turns. That don't mean you stop living. That don't mean you cut yourself off from life. You can't go through life carrying Crawley's ghost with you. Crawley's been dead three years. Three years, Berniece.

BERNIECE: I know how long Crawley's been dead. You ain't got to tell me that. I just ain't ready to get married right now.

AVERY: What is you ready for, Berniece? You just gonna drift along from day to day. Life is more than making it from one day to another. You gonna look up one day and it's all gonna be past you. Life's gonna be gone out of your hands—there won't be enough to make nothing with. I'm standing here now, Berniece—but I don't know how much longer I'm gonna be standing here waiting on you.

BERNIECE: Avery, I told you . . . when you get your church we'll sit down and talk about this. I got too many other things to deal with right now. Boy Willie and the piano . . . and Sutter's ghost. I thought I might have been seeing things, but Maretha done seen Sutter's ghost, too.

AVERY: When this happen, Berniece?

BERNIECE: Right after I came home yesterday. Me and Boy Willie was arguing about the piano and Sutter's ghost was standing at the top of the stairs. Maretha scared to sleep up there now. Maybe if you bless the house he'll go away.

AVERY: I don't know, Berniece. I don't know if I should fool around with something like that.

BERNIECE: I can't have Maretha scared to go to sleep up there. Seem like if you bless the house he would go away.

AVERY: You might have to be a special kind of preacher to do something like that.

BERNIECE: I keep telling myself when Boy Willie leave he'll go on and leave with him. I believe Boy Willie pushed him in the well.

AVERY: That's been going on down there a long time. The Ghosts of the Yellow Dog been pushing people in their wells long before Boy Willie got grown.

BERNIECE: Somebody down there pushing them people in their wells. They ain't just upped and fell. Ain't no wind pushed nobody in their well.

AVERY: Oh, I don't know. God works in mysterious ways.

BERNIECE: He ain't pushed nobody in their wells.

AVERY: He caused it to happen. God is the Great Causer. He can do anything. He parted the Red Sea. He say I will smite my enemies. Reverend Thompson used to preach on the Ghosts of the Yellow Dog as the hand of God.

BERNIECE: I don't care who preached what. Somebody down there pushing them people in their wells. Somebody like Boy Willie. I can see him doing something like that. You ain't gonna tell me that Sutter just upped and fell in his well. I believe Boy Willie pushed him so he could get his land.

AVERY: What Doaker say about Boy Willie selling the piano?

BERNIECE: Doaker don't want no part of that piano. He ain't never wanted no part of it. He blames himself for not staying behind with Papa Boy Charles. He washed his hands of that piano a long time ago. He didn't want me to bring it up here—but I wasn't gonna leave it down there.

AVERY: Well, it seems to me somebody ought to be able to talk to Boy Willie.

BERNIECE: You can't talk to Boy Willie. He been that way all his life. Mama Ola had her hands full trying to talk to him. He don't listen to nobody. He just like my daddy. He get his mind fixed on something and can't nobody turn him from it.

AVERY: You ought to start a choir at the church. Maybe if he seen you was doing something with it—if you told him you was gonna put it in my church—maybe he'd see it different. You ought to put it down in the church and start a choir. The Bible say "Make a joyful noise unto the Lord." Maybe if Boy Willie see you was doing something with it he'd see it different.

BERNIECE: I done told you I don't play on that piano. Ain't no need in you to keep talking this choir stuff. When my mama died I shut the top on that piano and I ain't never opened it since. I was only playing it for her. When my daddy died seem like all her life went into that piano. She used to have me playing on it . . . had Miss Eula come in and teach me . . . say when I played it she could hear my daddy talking to her. I used to think them pictures came alive and walked through the house. Sometime late at night I could hear my mama talking to them. I said that wasn't gonna happen to me. I don't play that piano 'cause I don't want to wake them spirits. They never be walking around in this house.

AVERY: You got to put all that behind you, Berniece.

BERNIECE: I got Maretha playing on it. She don't know nothing about it. Let her go on and be a schoolteacher or something. She don't have to carry all of that with her. She got a chance I didn't have. I ain't gonna burden her with that piano.

AVERY: You got to put all of that behind you, Berniece. That's the same thing like Crawley. Everybody got stones in their passway. You got to step over them or walk around them. You picking them up and carrying them with you. All you got to do is set them down by the side of the road. You ain't got to carry them with you. You can walk over there right now and play that piano. You can walk over there right now and God will walk over there with you. Right now you can set that sack of stones down by the side of the road and walk away from it. You don't have to carry it with you. You can do it right now.

(AVERY *crosses over to the piano and raises the lid.*)

Come on, Berniece . . . set it down and walk away from it. Come on, play "Old Ship of Zion." Walk over here and claim it as an instrument of the Lord. You can walk over here right now and make it into a celebration.

(BERNIECE *moves toward the piano.*)

BERNIECE: Avery . . . I done told you I don't want to play that piano. Now or no other time.

AVERY: The Bible say, "The Lord is my refuge . . . and my strength!" With the strength of God you can put the past behind you, Berniece. With the strength of God you can do anything! God got a bright tomorrow. God don't ask what you done . . . God ask what you gonna do. The strength of God can move mountains! God's got a bright tomorrow for you . . . all you got to do is walk over here and claim it.

BERNIECE: Avery, just go on and let me finish my bath. I'll see you tomorrow.

AVERY: Okay, Berniece. I'm gonna go home. I'm gonna go home and read up on my Bible. And tomorrow . . . if the good Lord give me strength tomorrow . . . I'm gonna come by and bless the house . . . and show you the power of the Lord.

(AVERY *crosses to the door.*)

It's gonna be alright, Berniece. God say he will soothe the troubled waters. I'll come by tomorrow and bless the house.

(*The lights go down to black.*)

SCENE 3

(*Several hours later. The house is dark.* BERNIECE *has retired for the night.* BOY WILLIE *enters the darkened house with* GRACE.)

BOY WILLIE: Come on in. This my sister's house. My sister live here. Come on, I ain't gonna bite you.

GRACE: Put some light on. I can't see.

BOY WILLIE: You don't need to see nothing, baby. This here is all you need to see. All you need to do is see me. If you can't see me you can feel me in the dark. How's that, sugar?

(*He attempts to kiss her.*)

GRACE: Go on now . . . wait!

BOY WILLIE: Just give me one little old kiss.

GRACE: (*Pushing him away.*) Come on, now. Where I'm gonna sleep at?

BOY WILLIE: We got to sleep out here on the couch. Come on, my sister don't mind. Lymon come back he just got to sleep on the floor. He run off with Dolly somewhere he better stay there. Come on, sugar.

GRACE: Wait now . . . you ain't told me nothing about no couch. I thought you had a bed. Both of us can't sleep on that little old couch.

BOY WILLIE: It don't make no difference. We can sleep on the floor. Let Lymon sleep on the couch.

GRACE: You ain't told me nothing about no couch.

BOY WILLIE: What difference it make? You just wanna be with me.

GRACE: I don't want to be with you on no couch. Ain't you got no bed?

BOY WILLIE: You don't need no bed, woman. My granddaddy used to take women on the backs of horses. What you need a bed for? You just want to be with me.

GRACE: You sure is country. I didn't know you was this country.

BOY WILLIE: There's a lot of things you don't know about me. Come on, let me show you what this country boy can do.

GRACE: Let's go to my place. I got a room with a bed if Leroy don't come back there.

BOY WILLIE: Who's Leroy? You ain't said nothing about no Leroy.

GRACE: He used to be my man. He ain't coming back. He gone off with some other gal.

BOY WILLIE: You let him have your key?

GRACE: He ain't coming back.

BOY WILLIE: Did you let him have your key?

GRACE: He got a key but he ain't coming back. He took off with some other gal.

BOY WILLIE: I don't wanna go nowhere he might come. Let's stay here. Come on, sugar.

(*He pulls her over to the couch.*)

Let me heist your hood and check your oil. See if your battery needs charged.

(*He pulls her to him: They kiss and tug at each other's clothing. In their anxiety they knock over a lamp.*)

BERNIECE: Who's that . . . Wining Boy?

BOY WILLIE: It's me . . . Boy Willie. Go on back to sleep. Everything's alright.

(*To* GRACE.)

That's my sister. Everything's alright, Berniece. Go on back to sleep.

BERNIECE: What you doing down there? What you done knocked over?

BOY WILLIE: It wasn't nothing. Everything's alright. Go on back to sleep.

(*To* GRACE.)

That's my sister. We alright. She gone back to sleep.

(*They begin to kiss.* BERNIECE *enters from the stairs dressed in a nightgown. She cuts on the light.*)

BERNIECE: Boy Willie, what you doing down here?

BOY WILLIE: It was just that there lamp. It ain't broke. It's okay. Everything's alright. Go on back to bed.

BERNIECE: Boy Willie, I don't allow that in my house. You gonna have to take your company someplace else.

BOY WILLIE: It's alright. We ain't doing nothing. We just sitting here talking. This here is Grace. That's my sister Berniece.

BERNIECE: You know I don't allow that kind of stuff in my house.

BOY WILLIE: Allow what? We just sitting here talking.

BERNIECE: Well, your company gonna have to leave. Come back and talk in the morning.

BOY WILLIE: Go on back upstairs now.

BERNIECE: I got an eleven-year-old girl upstairs. I can't allow that around here.

BOY WILLIE: Ain't nobody said nothing about that. I told you we just talking.

GRACE: Come on . . . let's go to my place. Ain't nobody got to tell me to leave but once.

BOY WILLIE: You ain't got to be like that, Berniece.

BERNIECE: I'm sorry, Miss. But he know I don't allow that in here.

GRACE: You ain't got to tell me but once. I don't stay nowhere I ain't wanted.

BOY WILLIE: I don't know why you want to embarrass me in front of my company.

GRACE: Come on, take me home.

BERNIECE: Go on, Boy Willie. Just go on with your company.

(BOY WILLIE *and* GRACE *exit.* BERNIECE *puts the light on in the kitchen and puts on the teakettle. Presently there is a knock at the door.* BERNIECE *goes to answer it.* BERNIECE *opens the door.* LYMON *enters.*)

LYMON: How you doing, Berniece? I thought you'd be asleep. Boy Willie been back here?

BERNIECE: He just left out of here a minute ago.

LYMON: I went out to see a picture show and never got there. We always end up doing something else. I was with this woman she just wanted to drink up all my money. So I left her there and came back looking for Boy Willie.

BERNIECE: You just missed him. He just left out of here.

LYMON: They got some nice-looking women in this city. I'm gonna like it up here real good. I like seeing them with their dresses on. Got them high heels. I like that. Make them look like they real precious. Boy Willie met a real nice one today. I wish I had met her before he did.

BERNIECE: He come by here with some woman a little while ago. I told him to go on and take all that out of my house.

LYMON: What she look like, the woman he was with? Was she a brown-skinned woman about this high? Nice and healthy? Got nice hips on her?

BERNIECE: She had on a red dress.

LYMON: That's her! That's Grace. She real nice. Laugh a lot. Lot of fun to be with. She don't be trying to put on. Some of these woman act like they the Queen of Sheba. I don't like them kind. Grace ain't like that. She real nice with herself.

BERNIECE: I don't know what she was like. He come in here all drunk knocking over the lamp, and making all kind of noise. I told them to take that somewhere else. I can't really say what she was like.

LYMON: She real nice. I seen her before he did. I was trying not to act like I seen her. I wanted to look at her a while before I said something. She seen me when I come into the saloon. I tried to act like I didn't see her. Time I looked around Boy Willie was talking to her. She was talking to him kept looking at me. That's when her friend Dolly came. I asked her if she wanted to go to the picture show. She told me to buy her a drink while she thought about it. Next thing I knew she done had three drinks talking about she too tired to go. I bought her another drink, then I left. Boy Willie was gone and I thought he might have come back here. Doaker gone, huh? He say he had to make a trip.

BERNIECE: Yeah, he gone on his trip. This is when I can usually get me some peace and quiet, Maretha asleep.

LYMON: She look just like you. Got them big eyes. I remember her when she was in diapers.

BERNIECE: Time just keep on. It go on with or without you. She going on twelve.

LYMON: She sure is pretty. I like kids.

BERNIECE: Boy Willie say you staying . . . what you gonna do up here in this big city? You thought about that?

LYMON: They never get me back down there. The sheriff looking for me. All because they gonna try and make me work for somebody when I don't want to. They gonna try and make me work for Stovall when he don't pay nothing. It ain't like that up here. Up here you more or less do what you want to. I figure I find me a job and try to get set up and then see what the year brings. I tried to do that two or three times down there . . . but it never would work out. I was always in the wrong place.

BERNIECE: This ain't a bad city once you get to know your way around.

LYMON: Up here is different. I'm gonna get me a job unloading boxcars or something. One fellow told me say he know a place. I'm gonna go over there with him next week. Me and Boy Willie finish selling them watermelons I'll have enough money to hold me for a while. But I'm gonna go over there and see what kind of jobs they have.

BERNIECE: You shouldn't have too much trouble finding a job. It's all in how you present yourself. See now, Boy Willie couldn't get no job up here. Somebody hire him they got a pack of trouble on their hands. Soon as they find that out they fire him. He don't want to do nothing unless he do it his way.

LYMON: I know. I told him let's go to the picture show first and see if there was any women down there. They might get tired of sitting at home and walk down to the picture show. He say he wanna look around first. We never did get down there. We tried a couple of places and then we went to this saloon where he met Grace. I tried to meet her before he did but he beat me to her. We left Wining Boy sitting down there running his mouth. He told me if I wear this suit I'd find me a woman. He was almost right.

BERNIECE: You don't need to be out there in them saloons. Ain't no telling what you liable to run into out there. This one liable to cut you as quick as that one shoot you. You don't need to be out there. You start out that fast life you can't keep it up. It makes you old quick. I don't know what them women out there be thinking about.

LYMON: Mostly they be lonely and looking for somebody to spend the night with them. Sometimes it matters who it is and sometimes it don't. I used to be the same way. Now it got to matter. That's why I'm here now. Dolly liable not to even recognize me if she sees me again. I don't like women like that. I like my women to be with me in a nice and easy way. That way we can both enjoy ourselves. The way I see it we the only two people like us in the world. We got to see how we fit together. A woman that don't want to take the time to do that I don't bother with. Used to. Used to bother with all of them. Then I woke up one time with this woman and I didn't know who she was. She was the prettiest woman I had ever seen in my life. I spent the whole night with her and didn't even know it. I had never taken the time to look at her. I guess she kinda knew I ain't never really looked at her. She must have known that cause she ain't wanted to see me no more. If she had wanted to see me I believe we might have got married. How come you ain't married? It seem like to me you would be married. I remember Avery from down home. I used to call him plain old Avery. Now he Reverend Avery. That's kinda funny about him becoming a preacher. I like when he told about how that come to him in a dream about them sheep people and them hobos. Nothing ever come to me in a dream like that. I just dream about women. Can't never seem to find the right one.

BERNIECE: She out there somewhere. You just got to get yourself ready to meet her. That's what I'm trying to do. Avery's alright. I ain't really got nobody in mind.

LYMON: I get me a job and a little place and get set up to where I can make a woman comfortable I might get married. Avery's nice. You ought to go ahead and get married. You be a preacher's wife you won't have to work. I hate living by myself. I didn't want to be no strain on my mama so I left home when I was about sixteen. Everything I tried seem like it just didn't work out. Now I'm trying this.

BERNIECE: You keep trying it'll work out for you.

LYMON: You ever go down there to the picture show?

BERNIECE: I don't go in for all that.

LYMON: Ain't nothing wrong with it. It ain't like gambling and sinning. I went to one down in Jackson once. It was fun.

BERNIECE: I just stay home most of the time. Take care of Maretha.

LYMON: It's getting kind of late. I don't know where Boy Willie went off to. He's liable not to come back. I'm gonna take off these shoes. My feet hurt. Was you in bed? I don't mean to be keeping you up.

BERNIECE: You ain't keeping me up. I couldn't sleep after that Boy Willie woke me up.

LYMON: You got on that nightgown. I likes women when they wear them fancy nightclothes and all. It makes their skin look real pretty.

BERNIECE: I got this at the five-and-ten-cents store. It ain't so fancy.

LYMON: I don't too often get to see a woman dressed like that.

(*There is a long pause.* LYMON *takes off his suit coat.*)

Well, I'm gonna sleep here on the couch. I'm supposed to sleep on the floor but I don't reckon Boy Willie's coming back tonight. Wining Boy sold me this suit. Told me it was a magic suit. I'm gonna put it on again tomorrow. Maybe it bring me a woman like he say.

(*He goes into his coat pocket and takes out a small bottle of perfume.*)

I almost forgot I had this. Some man sold me this for a dollar. Say it come from Paris. This is the same kind of perfume the Queen of France wear. That's what he told me. I don't know if it's true or not. I smelled it. It smelled good to me. Here . . . smell it see if you like it. I was gonna give it to Dolly. But I didn't like her too much.

BERNIECE: (*Takes the bottle.*) It smells nice.

LYMON: I was gonna give it to Dolly if she had went to the picture with me. Go on, you take it.

BERNIECE: I can't take it. Here . . . go on you keep it. You'll find somebody to give it to.

LYMON: I wanna give it to you. Make you smell nice.

(*He takes the bottle and puts perfume behind* BERNIECE'S *ear.*)

They tell me you supposed to put it right here behind your ear. Say if you put it there you smell nice all day.

(BERNIECE *stiffens at his touch.* LYMON *bends down to smell her.*)

There . . . you smell real good now.

(*He kisses her neck.*)

You smell real good for Lymon.

(*He kisses her again.* BERNIECE *returns the kiss, then breaks the embrace and crosses to the stairs. She turns and they look silently at each other.* LYMON *hands her the bottle of perfume.* BERNIECE *exits up the stairs.* LYMON *picks up his suit coat and strokes it lovingly with the full knowledge that it is indeed a magic suit. The lights go down on the scene.*)

SCENE 4

(*It is late the next morning. The lights come up on the parlor.* LYMON *is asleep on the sofa.* BOY WILLIE *enters the front door.*)

BOY WILLIE: Hey, Lymon! Lymon, come on get up.

LYMON: Leave me alone.

BOY WILLIE: Come on, get up, nigger! Wake up, Lymon.

LYMON: What you want?

BOY WILLIE: Come on, let's go. I done called the man about the piano.

LYMON: What piano?

BOY WILLIE (*Dumps* LYMON *on the floor.*) Come on, get up!

LYMON: Why you leave, I looked around and you was gone.

BOY WILLIE: I come back here with Grace, then I went looking for you. I figured you'd be with Dolly.

LYMON: She just want to drink and spend up your money. I come on back here looking for you to see if you wanted to go to the picture show.

BOY WILLIE: I been up at Grace's house. Some nigger named Leroy come by but I had a chair up against the door. He got mad when he couldn't get in. He went off somewhere and I got out of there before he could come back. Berniece got mad when we came here.

LYMON: She say you was knocking over the lamp busting up the place.

BOY WILLIE: That was Grace doing all that.

LYMON: Wining Boy seen Sutter's ghost last night.

BOY WILLIE: Wining Boy's liable to see anything. I'm surprised he found the right house. Come on, I done called the man about the piano.

LYMON: What he say?

BOY WILLIE: He say to bring it on out. I told him I was calling for my sister, Miss Berniece Charles. I told him some man wanted to buy it for eleven hundred dollars and asked him if he would go any better. He said yeah, he would give me eleven hundred and fifty dollars for it if it was the same piano. I described it to him again and he told me to bring it out.

LYMON: Why didn't you tell him to come and pick it up?

BOY WILLIE: I didn't want to have no problem with Berniece. This way we just take it on out there and it be out the way. He want to charge twenty-five dollars to pick it up.

LYMON: You should have told him the man was gonna give you twelve hundred for it.

BOY WILLIE: I figure I was taking a chance with that eleven hundred. If I had told him twelve hundred he might have run off. Now I wish I had told him twelve-fifty. It's hard to figure out white folks sometimes.

LYMON: You might have been able to tell him anything. White folks got a lot of money.

BOY WILLIE: Come on, let's get it loaded before Berniece come back. Get that end over there. All you got to do is pick it up on that side. Don't worry about this side. You wanna stretch you' back for a minute?

LYMON: I'm ready.

BOY WILLIE: Get a real good grip on it now.

(*The sound of* SUTTER'S GHOST *is heard. They do not hear it.*)

LYMON: I got this end. You get that end.

BOY WILLIE: Wait till I say ready now. Alright. You got it good? You got a grip on it?

LYMON: Yeah, I got it. You lift up on that end.

BOY WILLIE: Ready? Lift!

(*The piano will not budge.*)

LYMON: Man, this piano is heavy! It's gonna take more than me and you to move this piano.

BOY WILLIE: We can do it. Come on—we did it before.

LYMON: Nigger—you crazy! That piano weighs five hundred pounds!

BOY WILLIE: I got three hundred pounds of it! I know you can carry two hundred pounds! You be lifting them cotton sacks! Come on lift this piano!

(*They try to move the piano again without success.*)

LYMON: It's stuck. Something holding it.

BOY WILLIE: How the piano gonna be stuck? We just moved it. Slide you' end out.

LYMON: Naw—we gonna need two or three more people. How this big old piano get in the house?

BOY WILLIE: I don't know how it got in the house. I know how it's going out though! You get on this end. I'll carry three hundred and fifty pounds of it. All you got to do is slide your end out. Ready?

(*They switch sides and try again without success.* DOAKER *enters from his room as they try to push and shove it.*)

LYMON: Hey, Doaker . . . how this piano get in the house?

DOAKER: Boy Willie, what you doing?

BOY WILLIE: I'm carrying this piano out the house. What it look like I'm doing? Come on, Lymon, let's try again.

DOAKER: Go on let the piano sit there till Berniece come home.

BOY WILLIE: You ain't got nothing to do with this, Doaker. This my business.

DOAKER: This is my house, nigger! I ain't gonna let you or nobody else carry nothing out of it. You ain't gonna carry nothing out of here without my permission!

BOY WILLIE: This is my piano. I don't need your permission to carry my belongings out of your house. This is mine. This ain't got nothing to do with you.

DOAKER: I say leave it over there till Berniece come home. She got part of it too. Leave it set there till you see what she say.

BOY WILLIE: I don't care what Berniece say. Come on, Lymon. I got this side.

DOAKER: Go on and cut it half in two if you want to. Just leave Berniece's half sitting over there. I can't tell you what to do with your piano. But I can't let you take her half out of here.

BOY WILLIE: Go on, Doaker. You ain't got nothing to do with this. I don't want you starting nothing now. Just go on and leave me alone. Come on, Lymon. I got this end.

(DOAKER *goes into his room.* BOY WILLIE *and* LYMON *prepare to move the piano.*)

LYMON: How we gonna get it in the truck?

BOY WILLIE: Don't worry about how we gonna get it on the truck. You got to get it out the house first.

LYMON: It's gonna take more than me and you to move this piano.

BOY WILLIE: Just lift up on that end, nigger!

(DOAKER *comes to the doorway of his room and stands.*)

DOAKER: (*Quietly with authority.*) Leave that piano set over there till Berniece come back. I don't care what you do with it then. But you gonna leave it sit over there right now.

BOY WILLIE: Alright . . . I'm gonna tell you this, Doaker. I'm going out of here . . . I'm gonna get me some rope . . . find me a plank and some wheels . . . and I'm coming back. Then I'm gonna carry that piano out of here . . . sell it and give Berniece half the money. See . . . now that's what I'm gonna do. And you . . . or nobody else is gonna stop me. Come on, Lymon . . . let's go get some rope and stuff. I'll be back, Doaker.

(BOY WILLIE *and* LYMON *exit. The lights go down on the scene.*)

SCENE 5

(*The lights come up.* BOY WILLIE *sits on the sofa, screwing casters on a wooden plank.* MARETHA *is sitting on the piano stool.* DOAKER *sits at the table playing solitaire.*)

BOY WILLIE: (*To* MARETHA.) Then after that them white folks down around there started falling down their wells. You ever seen a well? A well got a wall around it. It's hard to fall down a well. You got to be leaning way over. Couldn't nobody figure out too much what was making these fellows fall down their well . . . so everybody says the Ghosts of the Yellow Dog must have pushed them. That's what everybody called them four men what got burned up in the boxcar.

MARETHA: Why they call them that?

BOY WILLIE: Cause the Yazoo Delta railroad got yellow boxcars. Sometime the way the whistle blow sound like an old dog howling so the people call it the Yellow Dog.

MARETHA: Anybody ever see the Ghosts?

BOY WILLIE: I told you they like the wind. Can you see the wind?

MARETHA: No.

BOY WILLIE: They like the wind you can't see them. But sometimes you be in trouble they might be around to help you. They say if you go where the Southern cross the Yellow Dog . . . you go to where them two railroads cross each other . . . and call out their names . . . they say they talk back to you. I don't know, I ain't never done that. But Uncle Wining Boy he say he been down there and talked to them. You have to ask him about that part.

(BERNIECE *has entered from the front door.*)

BERNIECE: Maretha, you go on and get ready for me to do your hair.

(MARETHA *crosses to the steps.*)

Boy Willie, I done told you to leave my house.

(*To* MARETHA.)

Go on, Maretha.

(MARETHA *is hesitant about going up the stairs.*)

BOY WILLIE: Don't be scared. Here, I'll go up there with you. If we see Sutter's ghost I'll put a whupping on him. Come on, Uncle Boy Willie going with you.

(BOY WILLIE *and* MARETHA *exit up the stairs.*)

BERNIECE: Doaker—what is going on here?

DOAKER: I come home and him and Lymon was moving the piano. I told them to leave it over there till you got home. He went out and got that board and them wheels. He say he gonna take that piano out of here and ain't nobody gonna stop him.

BERNIECE: I ain't playing with Boy Willie. I got Crawley's gun upstairs. He don't know but I'm through with it. Where Lymon go?

DOAKER: Boy Willie sent him for some rope just before you come in.

BERNIECE: I ain't studying Boy Willie or Lymon—or the rope. Boy Willie ain't taking that piano out this house. That's all there is to it.

(BOY WILLIE *and* MARETHA *enter on the stairs.* MARETHA *carries a hot comb and a can of hair grease.* BOY WILLIE *crosses over and continues to screw the wheels on the board.*)

MARETHA: Mama, all the hair grease is gone. There ain't but this little bit left.

BERNIECE: (*Gives her a dollar.*) Here . . . run across the street and get another can. You come straight back, too. Don't you be playing around out there. And watch the cars. Be careful when you cross the street.

(MARETHA *exits out the front door.*)

Boy Willie, I done told you to leave my house.

BOY WILLIE: I ain't in you' house. I'm in Doaker's house. If he ask me to leave then I'll go on and leave. But consider me done left your part.

BERNIECE: Doaker, tell him to leave. Tell him to go on.

DOAKER: Boy Willie ain't done nothing for me to put him out of the house. I told you if you can't get along just go on and don't have nothing to do with each other.

BOY WILLIE: I ain't thinking about Berniece.

(*He gets up and draws a line across the floor with his foot.*)

There! Now I'm out of your part of the house. Consider me done left your part. Soon as Lymon come back with that rope. I'm gonna take that piano out of here and sell it.

BERNIECE: You ain't gonna touch that piano.

BOY WILLIE: Carry it out of here just as big and bold. Do like my daddy would have done come time to get Sutter's land.

BERNIECE: I got something to make you leave it over there.

BOY WILLIE: It's got to come better than this thirty-two-twenty.

DOAKER: Why don't you stop all that! Boy Willie, go on and leave her alone. You know how Berniece get. Why you wanna sit there and pick with her?

BOY WILLIE: I ain't picking with her. I told her the truth. She the one talking about what she got. I just told her what she better have.

BERNIECE: That's alright, Doaker. Leave him alone.

BOY WILLIE: She trying to scare me. Hell, I ain't scared of dying. I look around and see people dying every day. You got to die to make room for somebody else. I had a dog that died. Wasn't nothing but a puppy. I picked it up and put it in a bag and carried it up there to Reverend C. L. Thompson's church. I carried it up there and prayed and asked Jesus to make it live like he did the man in the Bible. I prayed real hard. Knelt down and everything. Say ask in Jesus' name. Well, I must have called Jesus' name two hundred times. I called his name till my mouth got sore. I got up and looked in the bag and the dog still dead. It ain't moved a muscle! I say, "Well, ain't nothing precious." And then I went out and killed me a cat. That's when I discovered the power of death. See, a nigger that ain't afraid to die is the worse kind of nigger for the white man. He can't hold that power over you. That's what I learned when I killed that cat. I got the power of death too. I can command him. I can call him up. The white man don't like to see that. He don't like for you to stand up and look him square in the eye and say, "I got it too." Then he got to deal with you square up.

BERNIECE: That's why I don't talk to him, Doaker. You try and talk to him and that's the only kind of stuff that comes out his mouth.

DOAKER: You say Avery went home to get his Bible?

BOY WILLIE: What Avery gonna do? Avery can't do nothing with me. I wish Avery would say something to me about this piano.

DOAKER: Berniece ain't said about that. Avery went home to get his Bible. He coming by to bless the house see if he can get rid of Sutter's ghost.

BOY WILLIE: Ain't nothing but a house full of ghosts down there at the church. What Avery look like chasing away somebody's ghost?

(MARETHA *enters the front door.*)

BERNIECE: Light that stove and set that comb over there to get hot. Get something to put around your shoulders.

BOY WILLIE: The Bible say an eye for an eye, a tooth for a tooth, and a life for a life. Tit for tat. But you and Avery don't want to believe that. You gonna pass up that part and pretend it ain't in there. Everything else you gonna agree with.

But if you gonna agree with part of it you got to agree with all of it. You can't do nothing halfway. You gonna go at the Bible halfway. You gonna act like that part ain't in there. But you pull out the Bible and open it and see what it say. Ask Avery. He a preacher. He'll tell you it's in there. He the Good Shepherd. Unless he gonna shepherd you to heaven with half the Bible.

BERNIECE: Maretha, bring me that comb. Make sure it's hot.

(MARETHA *brings the comb.* BERNIECE *begins to do her hair.*)

BOY WILLIE: I will say this for Avery. He done figured out a path to go through life. I don't agree with it. But he done fixed it so he can go right through it real smooth. Hell, he liable to end up with a million dollars that he done got from selling bread and wine.

MARETHA: OWWWWWW!

BERNIECE: Be still, Maretha. If you was a boy I wouldn't be going through this.

BOY WILLIE: Don't you tell that girl that. Why you wanna tell her that?

BERNIECE: You ain't got nothing to do with this child.

BOY WILLIE: Telling her you wished she was a boy. How's that gonna make her feel?

BERNIECE: Boy Willie, go on and leave me alone.

DOAKER: Why don't you leave her alone? What you got to pick with her for? Why don't you go on out and see what's out there in the streets? Have something to tell the fellows down home.

BOY WILLIE: I'm waiting on Lymon to get back with that truck. Why don't you go on out and see what's out there in the streets? You ain't got to work tomorrow. Talking about me . . . why don't you go out there? It's Friday night.

DOAKER: I got to stay around here and keep you all from killing one another.

BOY WILLIE: You ain't got to worry about me. I'm gonna be here just as long as it takes Lymon to get back here with that truck. You ought to be talking to Berniece. Sitting up there telling Maretha she wished she was a boy. What kind of thing is that to tell a child? If you want to tell her something tell her about that piano. You ain't even told her about that piano. Like that's something to be ashamed of. Like she supposed to go off and hide somewhere about that piano. You ought to mark down on the calendar the day that Papa Boy Charles brought that piano into the house. You ought to mark that day down and draw a circle around it . . . and every year when it come up throw a party. Have a celebration. If you did that she wouldn't have no problem in life. She could walk around here with her head held high. I'm talking about a big party!

Invite everybody! Mark that day down with a special meaning. That way she know where she at in the world. You got her going out here thinking she wrong in the world. Like there ain't no part of it belong to her.

BERNIECE: Let me take care of my child. When you get one of your own then you can teach it what you want to teach it.

(DOAKER *exits into his room.*)

BOY WILLIE: What I want to bring a child into this world for? Why I wanna bring somebody else into all this for? I'll tell you this . . . If I was Rockefeller I'd have forty or fifty. I'd make one every day. Cause they gonna start out in life with all the advantages. I ain't got no advantages to offer nobody. Many is the time I looked at my daddy and seen him staring off at his hands. I got a little older I know what he was thinking. He sitting there saying, "I got these big old hands but what I'm gonna do with them? Best I can do is make a fifty-acre crop for Mr. Stovall. Got these big old hands capable of doing anything. I can take and build something with these hands. But where's the tools? All I got is these hands. Unless I go out here and kill me somebody and take what they got . . . it's a long row to hoe for me to get something of my own. So what I'm gonna do with these big old hands? What would you do?"

See now . . . if he had his own land he wouldn't have felt that way. If he had something under his feet that belonged to him he could stand up taller. That's what I'm talking about. Hell, the land is there for everybody. All you got to do is figure out how to get you a piece. Ain't no mystery to life. You just got to go out and meet it square on. If you got a piece of land you'll find everything else fall right into place. You can stand right up next to the white man and talk about the price of cotton . . . the weather, and anything else you want to talk about. If you teach that girl that she living at the bottom of life, she's gonna grow up and hate you.

BERNIECE: I'm gonna teach her the truth. That's just where she living. Only she ain't got to stay there.

(*To* MARETHA.)

Turn you' head over to the other side.

BOY WILLIE: This might be your bottom but it ain't mine. I'm living at the top of life. I ain't gonna just take my life and throw it away at the bottom. I'm in the world like everybody else. The way I see it everybody else got to come up a little taste to be where I am.

BERNIECE: You right at the bottom with the rest of us.

BOY WILLIE: I'll tell you this . . . and ain't a living soul can put a come back on it. If you believe that's where you at then you gonna act that way. If you act that way then that's where you gonna be. It's as simple as that. Ain't no mystery to life. I don't know how you come to believe that stuff. Crawley didn't think like that. He wasn't living at the bottom of life. Papa Boy Charles and Mama Ola wasn't living at the bottom of life. You ain't never heard them say nothing like that. They would have taken a strap to you if they heard you say something like that.

(DOAKER *enters from his room.*)

Hey, Doaker . . . Berniece say the colored folks is living at the bottom of life. I tried to tell her if she think that . . . that's where she gonna be. You think you living at the bottom of life? Is that how you see yourself?

DOAKER: I'm just living the best way I know how. I ain't thinking about no top or no bottom.

BOY WILLIE: That's what I tried to tell Berniece. I don't know where she got that from. That sound like something Avery would say. Avery think cause the white man give him a turkey for Thanksgiving that makes him better than everybody else. That's gonna raise him out of the bottom of life. I don't need nobody to give me a turkey. I can get my own turkey. All you have to do is get out my way. I'll get me two or three turkeys.

BERNIECE: You can't even get a chicken let alone two or three turkeys. Talking about get out your way. Ain't nobody in your way.

(*To* MARETHA.)

Straighten your head, Maretha! Don't be bending down like that. Hold your head up!

(*To* BOY WILLIE.)

All you got going for you is talk. You' whole life that's all you ever had going for you.

BOY WILLIE: See now . . . I'll tell you something about me. I done strung along and strung along. Going this way and that. Whatever way would lead me to a moment of peace. That's all I want. To be as easy with everything. But I wasn't born to that. I was born to a time of fire.

The world ain't wanted no part of me. I could see that since I was about seven. The world say it's better off without me. See, Berniece accept that. She trying to come up to where she can prove something to the world. Hell, the world a better place cause of me. I don't see it like Berniece. I got a heart that beats here and it beats just as loud as the next fellow's. Don't care if he black or white. Sometime it beats louder. When it beats louder, then everybody can hear it. Some people get scared of that. Like Berniece. Some people get scared to hear a nigger's heart beating. They think you ought to lay low with that heart. Make it beat quiet and go along with everything the way it is. But my mama ain't birthed me for nothing. So what I got to do? I got to mark my passing on the road. Just like you write on a tree, "Boy Willie was here."

That's all I'm trying to do with that piano. Trying to put my mark on the road. Like my daddy done. My heart say for me to sell that piano and get me some land so I can make a life for myself to live in my own way. Other than that I ain't thinking about nothing Berniece got to say.

(*There is a knock at the door.* BOY WILLIE *crosses to it and yanks it open thinking it is* LYMON. AVERY *enters. He carries a Bible.*)

BOY WILLIE: Where you been, nigger? Aw . . . I thought you was Lymon. Hey, Berniece, look who's here.

BERNIECE: Come on in, Avery. Don't you pay Boy Willie no mind.

BOY WILLIE: Hey . . . Hey, Avery . . . tell me this . . . can you get to heaven with half the Bible?

BERNIECE: Boy Willie . . . I done told you to leave me alone.

BOY WILLIE: I just ask the man a question. He can answer. He don't need you to speak for him. Avery . . . if you only believe on half the Bible and don't want to accept the other half . . . you think God let you in heaven? Or do you got to have the whole Bible? Tell Berniece . . . if you only believe in part of it . . . when you see God he gonna ask you why you ain't believed in the other part . . . then he gonna send you straight to Hell.

AVERY: You got to be born again. Jesus say unless a man be born again he cannot come unto the Father and who so ever heareth my words and believeth them not shall be cast into a fiery pit.

BOY WILLIE: That's what I was trying to tell Berniece. You got to believe in it all. You can't go at nothing halfway. She think she going to heaven with half the Bible.

(*To* BERNIECE.)

You hear that . . . Jesus say you got to believe in it all.

BERNIECE: You keep messing with me.

BOY WILLIE: I ain't thinking about you.

DOAKER: Come on in, Avery, and have a seat. Don't pay neither one of them no mind. They been arguing all day.

BERNIECE: Come on in, Avery.

AVERY: How's everybody in here?

BERNIECE: Here, set this comb back over there on that stove.

(*To* AVERY.)

Don't pay Boy Willie no mind. He been around here bothering me since I come home from work.

BOY WILLIE: Boy Willie ain't bothering you. Boy Willie ain't bothering nobody. I'm just waiting on Lymon to get back. I ain't thinking about you. You heard the man say I was right and you still don't want to believe it. You just wanna go and make up anythin'. Well there's Avery . . . there's the preacher . . . go on and ask him.

AVERY: Berniece believe in the Bible. She been baptized.

BOY WILLIE: What about that part that say an eye for an eye a tooth for a tooth and a life for a life? Ain't that in there?

DOAKER: What they say down there at the bank, Avery?

AVERY: Oh, they talked to me real nice. I told Berniece . . . they say maybe they let me borrow the money. They done talked to my boss down at work and everything.

DOAKER: That's what I told Berniece. You working every day you ought to be able to borrow some money.

AVERY: I'm getting more people in my congregation every day. Berniece says she gonna be the Deaconess. I get me my church I can get married and settled down. That's what I told Berniece.

DOAKER: That be nice. You all ought to go ahead and get married. Berniece don't need to be by herself. I tell her that all the time.

BERNIECE: I ain't said nothing about getting married. I said I was thinking about it.

DOAKER: Avery get him his church you all can make it nice.

(*To* AVERY.)

Berniece said you was coming by to bless the house.

AVERY: Yeah, I done read up on my Bible. She asked me to come by and see if I can get rid of Sutter's ghost.

BOY WILLIE: Ain't no ghost in this house. That's all in Berniece's head. Go on up there and see if you see him. I'll give you a hundred dollars if you see him. That's all in her imagination.

DOAKER: Well, let her find that out then. If Avery blessing the house is gonna make her feel better . . . what you got to do with it?

AVERY: Berniece say Maretha seen him too. I don't know, but I found a part in the Bible to bless the house. If he is here then that ought to make him go.

BOY WILLIE: You worse than Berniece believing all that stuff. Talking about . . . if he here. Go on up there and find out. I been up there I ain't seen him. If you reading from that Bible gonna make him leave out of Berniece imagination, well, you might be right. But if you talking about . . .

DOAKER: Boy Willie, why don't you just be quiet? Getting all up in the man's business. This ain't got nothing to do with you. Let him go ahead and do what he gonna do.

BOY WILLIE: I ain't stopping him. Avery ain't got no power to do nothing.

AVERY: Oh, I ain't got no power. God got the power! God got power over everything in His creation. God can do anything. God say, "As I commandeth so it shall be." God said, "Let there be light," and there was light. He made the world in six days and rested on the seventh. God's got a wonderful power. He got power over life and death. Jesus raised Lazareth from the dead. They was getting ready to bury him and Jesus told him say, "Rise up and walk." He got up and walked and the people made great rejoicing at the power of God. I ain't worried about him chasing away a little old ghost!

(*There is a knock at the door.* BOY WILLIE *goes to answer it.* LYMON *enters carrying a coil of rope.*)

BOY WILLIE: Where you been? I been waiting on you and you run off somewhere.

LYMON: I ran into Grace. I stopped and bought her drink. She say she gonna go to the picture show with me.

BOY WILLIE: I ain't thinking about no Grace nothing.

LYMON: Hi, Berniece.

BOY WILLIE: Give me that rope and get up on this side of the piano.

DOAKER: Boy Willie, don't start nothing now. Leave the piano alone.

BOY WILLIE: Get that board there, Lymon. Stay out of this, Doaker.

(BERNIECE *exits up the stairs.*)

DOAKER: You just can't take the piano. How you gonna take the piano? Berniece ain't said nothing about selling that piano.

BOY WILLIE: She ain't got to say nothing. Come on, Lymon. We got to lift one end at a time up on the board. You got to watch so that the board don't slide up under there.

LYMON: What we gonna do with the rope?

BOY WILLIE: Let me worry about the rope. You just get up on this side over here with me.

(BERNIECE *enters from the stairs. She has her hand in her pocket where she has Crawley's gun.*)

AVERY: Boy Willie . . . Berniece . . . why don't you all sit down and talk this out now?

BERNIECE: Ain't nothing to talk out.

BOY WILLIE: I'm through talking to Berniece. You can talk to Berniece till you get blue in the face, and it don't make no difference. Get up on that side, Lymon. Throw that rope around there and tie it to the leg.

LYMON: Wait a minute . . . wait a minute, Boy Willie. Berniece got to say. Hey, Berniece . . . did you tell Boy Willie he could take this piano?

BERNIECE: Boy Willie ain't taking nothing out of my house but himself. Now you let him go ahead and try.

BOY WILLIE: Come on, Lymon, get up on this side with me.

(LYMON *stands undecided.*)

Come on, nigger! What you standing there for?

LYMON: Maybe Berniece is right, Boy Willie. Maybe you shouldn't sell it.

AVERY: You all ought to sit down and talk it out. See if you can come to an agreement.

DOAKER: That's what I been trying to tell them. Seem like one of them ought to respect the other one's wishes.

BERNIECE: I wish Boy Willie would go on and leave my house. That's what I wish. Now, he can respect that. Cause he's leaving here one way or another.

BOY WILLIE: What you mean one way or another? What's that supposed to mean? I ain't scared of no gun.

DOAKER: Come on, Berniece, leave him alone with that.

BOY WILLIE: I don't care what Berniece say. I'm selling my half. I can't help it if her half got to go along with it. It ain't like I'm trying to cheat her out of her half. Come on, Lymon.

LYMON: Berniece . . . I got to do this . . . Boy Willie say he gonna give you half of the money . . . say he want to get Sutter's land.

BERNIECE: Go on, Lymon. Just go on . . . I done told Boy Willie what to do.

BOY WILLIE: Here, Lymon . . . put that rope up over there.

LYMON: Boy Willie, you sure you want to do this? The way I figure it . . . I might be wrong . . . but I figure she gonna shoot you first.

BOY WILLIE: She just gonna have to shoot me.

BERNIECE: Maretha, get on out the way. Get her out the way, Doaker.

DOAKER: Go on, do what your mama told you.

BERNIECE: Put her in your room.

(MARETHA *exits to Doaker's room.* BOY WILLIE *and* LYMON *try to lift the piano. The door opens and* WINING BOY *enters. He has been drinking.*)

WINING BOY: Man, these niggers around here! I stopped down there at Seefus. . . . These folks standing around talking about Patchneck Red's coming. They jumping back and getting off the sidewalk talking about Patchneck Red this and Patchneck Red that. Come to find out . . . you know who they was talking about? Old John D. from up around Tyler! Used to run around with Otis Smith. He got everybody scared of him. Calling him Patchneck Red. They don't know I whupped the nigger's head in one time.

BOY WILLIE: Just make sure that board don't slide, Lymon.

LYMON: I got this side. You watch that side.

WINING BOY: Hey, Boy Willie, what you got? I know you got a pint stuck up in your coat.

BOY WILLIE: Wining Boy, get out the way!

WINING BOY: Hey, Doaker. What you got? Gimme a drink. I want a drink.

DOAKER: It look like you had enough of whatever it was. Come talking about "What you got?" You ought to be trying to find somewhere to lay down.

WINING BOY: I ain't worried about no place to lay down. I can always find me a place to lay down in Berniece's house. Ain't that right, Berniece?

BERNIECE: Wining Boy, sit down somewhere. You been out there drinking all day. Come in here smelling like an old polecat. Sit on down there, you don't need nothing to drink.

DOAKER: You know Berniece don't like all that drinking.

WINING BOY: I ain't disrespecting Berniece. Berniece, am I disrespecting you? I'm just trying to be nice. I been with strangers all day and they treated me like family. I come in here to family and you treat me like a stranger. I don't need your whiskey. I can buy my own. I wanted your company, not your whiskey.

DOAKER: Nigger, why don't you go upstairs and lay down? You don't need nothing to drink.

WINING BOY: I ain't thinking about no laying down. Me and Boy Willie fixing to party. Ain't that right, Boy Willie? Tell him. I'm fixing to play me some piano. Watch this.

(WINING BOY *sits down at the piano.*)

BOY WILLIE: Come on, Wining Boy! Me and Lymon fixing to move the piano.

WINING BOY: Wait a minute . . . wait a minute. This a song I wrote for Cleotha. I wrote this song in memory of Cleotha.

(*He begins to play and sing.*)

Hey little woman what's the matter with you now
Had a storm last night and blowed the line all down

Tell me how long
Is I got to wait
Can I get it now
Or must I hesitate

It takes a hesitating stocking in her hesitating shoe
It takes a hesitating woman wanna sing the blues

Tell me how long
Is I got to wait
Can I kiss you now
Or must I hesitate.

BOY WILLIE: Come on, Wining Boy, get up! Get up, Wining Boy! Me and Lymon's fixing to move the piano.

WINING BOY: Naw . . . Naw . . . you ain't gonna move this piano!

BOY WILLIE: Get out the way, Wining Boy.

(WINING BOY, *his back to the piano, spreads his arms out over the piano.*)

WINING BOY: You ain't taking this piano out the house. You got to take me with it!

BOY WILLIE: Get on out the way, Wining Boy! Doaker get him!

(*There is a knock on the door.*)

BERNIECE: I got him, Doaker. Come on, Wining Boy. I done told Boy Willie he ain't taking the piano.

(BERNIECE *tries to take* WINING BOY *away from the piano.*)

WINING BOY: He got to take me with it!

(DOAKER *goes to answer the door.* GRACE *enters.*)

GRACE: Is Lymon here?

DOAKER: Lymon.

WINING BOY: He ain't taking that piano.

BERNIECE: I ain't gonna let him take it.

GRACE: I thought you was coming back. I ain't gonna sit in that truck all day.

LYMON: I told you I was coming back.

GRACE: (*Sees* BOY WILLIE.) Oh, hi, Boy Willie. Lymon told me you was gone back down South.

LYMON: I said he was going back. I didn't say he had left already.

GRACE: That's what you told me.

BERNIECE: Lymon, you got to take your company someplace else.

LYMON: Berniece, this is Grace. That there is Berniece. That's Boy Willie's sister.

GRACE: Nice to meet you.

(*To* LYMON.)

I ain't gonna sit out in that truck all day. You told me you was gonna take me to the movie.

LYMON: I told you I had something to do first. You supposed to wait on me.

BERNIECE: Lymon, just go on and leave. Take Grace or whoever with you. Just go on get out my house.

BOY WILLIE: You gonna help me move this piano first, nigger!

LYMON: (*To* GRACE.) I got to help Boy Willie move the piano first.

(*Everybody but* GRACE *suddenly senses* SUTTER'S *presence.*)

GRACE: I ain't waiting on you. Told me you was coming right back. Now you got to move a piano. You just like all the other men.

(GRACE *now senses something.*)

Something ain't right here. I knew I shouldn't have come back up in this house.

(GRACE *exits.*)

LYMON: Hey, Grace! I'll be right back, Boy Willie.

BOY WILLIE: Where you going, nigger?

LYMON: I'll be back. I got to take Grace home.

BOY WILLIE: Come on, let's move the piano first!

LYMON: I got to take Grace home. I told you I'll be back.

(LYMON *exits.* BOY WILLIE *exits and calls after him.*)

BOY WILLIE: Come on, Lymon! Hey . . . Lymon! Lymon . . . come on!

(*Again, the presence of* SUTTER *is felt.*)

WINING BOY: Hey, Doaker, did you feel that? Hey, Berniece . . . did you get cold? Hey, Doaker . . .

DOAKER: What you calling me for?

WINING BOY: I believe that's Sutter.

DOAKER: Well, let him stay up there. As long as he don't mess with me.

BERNIECE: Avery, go on and bless the house.

DOAKER: You need to bless that piano. That's what you need to bless. It ain't done nothing but cause trouble. If you gonna bless anything go on and bless that.

WINING BOY: Hey, Doaker, if he gonna bless something let him bless everything. The kitchen . . . the upstairs. Go on and bless it all.

BOY WILLIE: Ain't no ghost in this house. He need to bless Berniece's head. That's what he need to bless.

AVERY: Seem like that piano's causing all the trouble. I can bless that. Berniece, put me some water in that bottle.

(AVERY *takes a small bottle from his pocket and hands it to* BERNIECE, *who goes into the kitchen to get water.* AVERY *takes a candle from his pocket and lights it. He gives it to* BERNIECE *as she gives him the water.*)

Hold this candle. Whatever you do make sure it don't go out.

O Holy Father we gather here this evening in the Holy Name to cast out the spirit of one James Sutter. May this vial of water be empowered with thy spirit. May each drop of it be a weapon and a shield against the presence of all evil and may it be a cleansing and blessing of this humble abode.

Just as Our Father taught us how to pray so He say, "I will prepare a table for you in the midst of mine enemies," and in His hands we place ourselves to come unto his presence. Where there is Good so shall it cause Evil to scatter to the Four Winds.

(*He throws water at the piano at each commandment.*)

AVERY: Get thee behind me, Satan! Get thee behind the face of Righteousness as we Glorify His Holy Name! Get thee behind the Hammer of Truth that breaketh down the Wall of Falsehood! Father. Father. Praise. Praise.

We ask in Jesus' name and call forth the power of the Holy Spirit as it is written . . .

(*He opens the Bible and reads from it.*)

I will sprinkle clean water upon thee and ye shall be clean.

BOY WILLIE: All this old preaching stuff. Hell, just tell him to leave.

(AVERY *continues reading throughout* BOY WILLIE'S *outburst.*)

AVERY: I will sprinkle clean water upon you and you shall be clean: from all your uncleanliness, and from all your idols, will I cleanse you. A new heart also will I give you, and a new spirit will I put within you: and I will take out of your flesh the heart of stone, and I will give you a heart of flesh. And I will put my spirit within you, and cause you to walk in my statutes, and ye shall keep my judgments, and do them.

(BOY WILLIE *grabs a pot of water from the stove and begins to fling it around the room.*)

BOY WILLIE: Hey Sutter! Sutter! Get your ass out this house! Sutter! Come on and get some of this water! You done drowned in the well, come on and get some more of this water!

(BOY WILLIE *is working himself into a frenzy as he* runs around the room throwing water and calling SUTTER'S *name.* AVERY *continues reading.*)

BOY WILLIE: Come on, Sutter!

(*He starts up the stairs.*)

Come on, get some water! Come on, Sutter!

(*The sound of* SUTTER'S GHOST *is heard. As* BOY WILLIE *approaches the steps he is suddenly thrown back by the unseen force, which is choking him. As he struggles he frees himself, then dashes up the stairs.*)

BOY WILLIE: Come on, Sutter!

AVERY: (*Continuing.*) A new heart also will I give you and a new spirit will I put within you: and I will take out of your flesh the heart of stone, and I will give you a heart of flesh. And I will put my spirit within you, and cause you to walk in my statutes, and ye shall keep my judgments, and do them.

(*There are loud sounds heard from upstairs as* BOY WILLIE *begins to wrestle with* SUTTER'S GHOST. *It is a life-and-death struggle fraught with perils and faultless terror.* BOY WILLIE *is thrown down the stairs.* AVERY *is stunned into silence.* BOY WILLIE *picks himself up and dashes back upstairs.*)

AVERY: Berniece, I can't do it.

(*There are more sounds heard from upstairs.* DOAKER *and* WINING BOY *stare at one another in stunned disbelief. It is in this moment, from somewhere old, that* BERNIECE *realizes what she must do. She crosses to the piano. She begins to play. The song is found piece by piece. It is an old urge to song that is both a commandment and a plea. With each repetition it gains in strength. It is intended as an exorcism and a dressing for battle. A rustle of wind blowing across two continents.*)

BERNIECE: (*Singing.*)

I want you to help me
I want you to help me
I want you to help me
I want you to help me
I want you to help me
I want you to help me

Mama Berniece
I want you to help me
Mama Esther
I want you to help me
Papa Boy Charles
I want you to help me
Mama Ola
I want you to help me

I want you to help me
I want you to help me
I want you to help me
I want you to help me
I want you to help me
I want you to help me
I want you to help me
I want you to help me

(*The sound of a train approaching is heard. The noise upstairs subsides.*)

BOY WILLIE: Come on, Sutter! Come back, Sutter!

(BERNIECE *begins to chant:*)

BERNIECE:

Thank you.
Thank you.
Thank you.

(*A calm comes over the house.* MARETHA *enters from* DOAKER'S *room.* BOY WILLIE *enters on the stairs. He pauses a moment to watch* BERNIECE *at the piano.*)

BERNIECE:

Thank you.
Thank you.

BOY WILLIE: Wining Boy, you ready to go back down home? Hey, Doaker, what time the train leave?

DOAKER: You still got time to make it.

(MARETHA *crosses and embraces* BOY WILLIE.)

BOY WILLIE: Hey Berniece . . . if you and Maretha don't keep playing on that piano . . . ain't no telling . . . me and Sutter both liable to be back.

(*He exits.*)

BERNIECE: Thank you.

(*The lights go down to black.*)

CHAPTER 10

Literary Research and Documentation

INTRODUCTION

At the beginning of this course, your instructor may want to foster your abilities as a critical reader by restricting the sources of evidence for your essays to the literary text(s) themselves. However, later on, after close and careful reading, class discussion, peer consultation, and teacher conferences, you will have developed sophistication and confidence as a critical reader and writer, and your teacher may ask you to broaden the scope of your textual studies by doing further research.

Conducting research on the literary works that you are reading and writing about enhances both experiences. Like reading and writing, research takes time and effort, but, like the time and effort spent on reading and writing, the rewards are plentiful. The research process not only helps you to increase your understanding of and engagement with the literature, but also can serve as a stimulus for your own ideas or help you to articulate those ideas better.

Like the writing process, the research process begins with your reading of the literary text(s) and your initial prewriting phases. Before you head to the library or log on to the Web, you ought to have an initial focus. Simply typing the name of the text or author into a library catalog or online search engine will usually generate an unwieldy amount of material. Rather than using this highly imprecise approach, begin by concentrating your research efforts on the questions you posed in your prewriting, the aspect of the text that most intrigued you, or the topic of the writing assignment provided by your instructor. For example, you may want to focus on researching the author's biographical details, the historical period during which the author was writing, or the period during which the events of the text take place. You may want to study the social or political circumstances of the text, or review critical works about one or more of the formal elements of the text. Although these research categories are still broad, choosing one will help make your research process more manageable. Taking some time to talk over your ideas with your instructor before you begin will also provide you with a more focused research objective.

Once you have settled on an initial topic and a focus for your research, we suggest that you go to the research section of your library and consult with a research librarian. These experts will point you in the right direction for both print and electronic sources and can offer useful tips and guidelines for searching your library's online catalog and electronic databases. You might also peruse Nancy L. Baker's and Nancy Huling's reference text *A Research Guide for Undergraduate Students: English and American Literature* to find some helpful research suggestions.

Making careful notes is a key to useful research; be sure to take along a stack of note cards, a tablet of paper, or your laptop, so that you can keep a running record of your research efforts. Your notes will most likely consist of **paraphrases, summaries**, and **quotations** from the sources, as well as any bibliographic information necessary for proper documentation (see below). It is important to write down *complete* bibliographical citations to useful information as you find it—including inclusive page numbers and the exact page(s) from which your information or quotation comes—as later you may not remember where you found what. Just as in the early drafting stages of an essay, you may find that, at first, you will collect more information than you need, and, as you incorporate other information, you may find that you need to go back and do more research.

LOCATING AND EVALUATING PRINT SOURCES

The research section of your library is not only a useful place to begin because of its human resources, but also a helpful place to begin locating quick reference guides to literary texts and criticism, such as *A Handbook to Literature*, the *Twayne Companion to Contemporary World Literature*, the *Oxford Companion to American Literature*, the *Oxford Companion to English Literature*, *Contemporary Authors*, and *Contemporary Literary Criticism*.

If you are conducting research on the author's life and works, try the *Dictionary of Literary Biography* (also available online at subscribing libraries) or the *Biographical Companion to Literature in English*.

If you are researching a formal element of the text, try the Gale Research Group's series on literary criticism, including *Contemporary Literary Criticism, Poetry Criticism*, and *Short Story Criticism*.

After spending some time with these general research materials, you may find it helpful to search the library catalog for specific books on your topic. You might, for example, search for book-length biographies on Nathaniel Hawthorne by selecting "Nathaniel Hawthorne" and "biography" as search terms. Or, if you're interested in the theme of death in Emily Dickinson's poems, you might use "Emily Dickinson," "death," and "poetry" as your key words. Another benefit of doing library research is that the books on the shelves are organized by similar categories, so as you scan the shelf for a book on your list, you might just happen upon another valuable source that did not appear in your initial catalog search.

In addition to finding useful books, you might also want to search for relevant journal articles. Several writers have periodicals dedicated solely to their works, such as the *Nathaniel Hawthorne Journal* and *Dickinson Studies*. But, since you cannot possibly search through years of these publications by hand, you will want to use a guide such as the *MLA International Bibliography of Books and Articles on the Modern Languages and Literatures* (also available as an online database in some libraries) to narrow your search. Undoubtedly, these searches will retrieve more than one potentially helpful source, so your task then becomes selecting those sources you think will be most relevant and credible.

The good news about print sources in the library is that you can be reasonably confident that the books and journals the library has purchased are sufficiently authoritative and scholarly. The books and journals available in your library had to go through a fairly rigorous screening process for publication (such as peer review by other experts in the field), and the librarians who purchase these texts not only are familiar with the credible publishing houses, but also often rely on suggestions from local scholars and subject-matter experts when selecting texts and periodicals for the library's permanent collection.

Since you can be reasonably confident in the trustworthiness of sources that you find in the library, how do you decide which books and articles are the best ones to use for your current research project? To make this decision, you will want to return to the notes you've taken and the questions you're trying to answer. Then, you can try to narrow your selection by glancing over the introductions to the books—paying particular attention to the paragraphs that summarize each chapter (as is common in many scholarly texts)—and by reading journal article abstracts (if they are provided). If these helpful "snapshots" are not available, you may have to spend a bit longer skimming through the journal articles or the indexes and applicable chapters of the books to determine which ones will be worth spending more time on.

LOCATING AND EVALUATING ELECTRONIC SOURCES

Libraries aren't just great repositories for printed books and journals; they also subscribe to Web-based databases. Unlike other Internet sites, which can be created by anyone for any purpose, the databases accessible through your library are licensed, commercial databases from reputable publishers and information sources; therefore, the publications that can be accessed through the library databases have undergone some kind of credible editorial review to ensure their accuracy and legitimacy. Consequently, you can usually rely on the scholarly merit of the information you access through these subscription databases.

In addition to the *MLA International Bibliography*, mentioned earlier, your library may subscribe to other databases that are particularly useful for literary research, such as *Academic Search Premier*, the *Johns Hopkins Guide to Literary Criticism*, the *Literature Resource Center*, and *JSTOR*. Many of these databases allow you to access and read full-text articles from journals and reference books. Most libraries offer their patrons password-protected, off-site access to these databases from any computer with Internet access, which means you can even save yourself a trip to the actual library building! (Note: Although it may be tempting to cut and paste information from these sites, be sure you accurately and fully document your use of these sources, as is explained later in this chapter.)

In addition to accessing the library's electronic databases, you may choose to conduct some of your Internet research directly on the World Wide Web. This option, however, has several drawbacks. First, doing a keyword search on an Internet search engine such as *Google*, *Yahoo*, *MSN*, or *Dogpile* generally produces an unmanageable number of options or "hits." Second, these sites, although potentially useful, are not organized according to any principle of scholarly value; they have not been professionally filtered and reviewed for accuracy and validity. One exception is *Google Scholar*, which allows you "to broadly search for scholarly literature across many disciplines and sources: peer-reviewed papers, theses, books, abstracts and articles, from academic publishers, professional societies, preprint repositories, universities and other scholarly organizations" (http://scholar.google.com/scholar/about.html). In general, however, *you* will need to determine the merit of the information provided by the sites you find through a keyword Internet engine search.

One way to begin your evaluation is to examine the final extension on the Web address, or URL (Uniform Resource Locator), to see what kind of institution or individual is hosting the site. Sites with an ".edu" extension are hosted by educational institutions and are often considered to be fairly reliable. Be aware, however, that many institutions allow students to store their coursework, personal pages, and so forth on the institutional server, so you need to be cautious. Try to ascertain as much specific information as possible about the *author of the site*, the *intended audience* for the site, the *currency of the information* on the site, and the *documentation* on the site. If you have trouble determining any of the preceding information, or you can't ascertain the sources of the site's "facts" or claims, you may want to choose another site.

Other common Web site extensions include ".org" (organizations), ".gov" (government), ".com" (commercial), and ".net" (commercial networks). Each of these sources has a potential for institutional bias, corporate influence, or political appropriation; therefore, you should evaluate each site carefully. One way to establish a sense of legitimacy for your Web resources is to compare the information contained on the sites with information you have gathered from trustworthy print resources. Compare the level of diction and the depth of analysis, the documentation, and references to other scholarly works or other works by the author to see whether the Web site information matches the quality of the print sources.

Some well-established Internet sites that contain reliable links for scholarly research include: *The Voice of the Shuttle: Web Pages for Humanities Research* (http://vos.ucsb.edu), Jack Lynch's *Literary Resources on the Net* (http://andromeda.rutgers.edu/~jlynch/Lit/), and the Buley Library's *American and English Language Internet Resources* (http://library.scsu.ctstateu.edu/litbib.html).

We suggest that you resist the temptation to use the simplistic summaries and analyses of literary texts available through online study guides such as *Sparks Notes*, *CliffsNotes*, or *eNotes Literature*. These sites are not suitable substitutes for close readings of the literary works, and your instructor is certainly familiar with their clichéd interpretations. Be cautious, too, when using online encyclopedia entries such as those found on *Encarta*, *Encyclopedia Britannica*, and *Wikipedia*. Of course, if you do borrow any ideas from these sites, you must be sure to document them.

DOCUMENTING SOURCES

Whenever you borrow ideas—**quote** directly from a source, **paraphrase** or **summarize** a source, or include any information or facts that cannot be considered "common knowledge"[1]—you must indicate that the material is not your own. You must also provide your readers with enough information about each of your sources so that they can find and consult them on their own. *Failure to distinguish borrowed material from your own work, even if done unintentionally, constitutes* ***plagiarism****, a serious academic violation.* To avoid any risky oversights, take careful notes as you are conducting your research, be sure to place quotation marks around direct quotes, and ensure that you have all of the necessary information to identify the original source. You should also document your in-text citations immediately so that you can distinguish your own ideas and analysis from those that you have borrowed; you might even use your word processor to format the source material—especially that material that is not offset by quotation marks—in a different color so that as you revise and reorganize your drafts, you don't inadvertently present the source material as your own. Finally, do not let the research material take over the paper; try to ensure that *your own* thoughts and conclusions about the literary text(s) remain at the forefront of your essay and that you are not just rehashing or restating existing scholarly opinions. Always make it clear that you are using the sources to support and augment *your way* of reading and interpreting the texts.

The most common convention or "style" for literary research documentation is the Modern Language Association (MLA) style, which includes standards for in-text parenthetical citations and a bibliographic reference list, or "Works Cited" page.

IN-TEXT PARENTHETICAL CITATIONS

The purpose of the in-text parenthetical citations is to provide your readers with a brief identification of your source and to direct him or her to the complete citation on your Works Cited page. The source material should be placed within the context of the sentence or paragraph in which it is incorporated, and the parenthetical citation should be placed as close to the source material as possible without being disruptive to the reader. If you are **paraphrasing** or **summarizing** instead of **quoting** directly, the parenthetical citation should appear as close to the conclusion of the paraphrase or summary as possible. Indicate any modifications to direct quotations with square brackets [ ]. Here are some examples of common in-text parenthetical citations:

1. When an author's name is mentioned in the sentence, cite only the page number(s) on which the source material appears: `Ellison describes the fight in "Battle Royal" as "a vital part of behavior pattern in the South... a ritual in preservation of caste lines" (175).` Note that the close quotation marks come before the parentheses and the period comes after.

2. When an author's name is not mentioned, cite the author's name and the page number(s) on which the source material appears: `The fictional fight scene in "Battle Royal" mimics other such fights that were "a vital part of behavior pattern in the South... a ritual in preservation of caste lines" (Ellison 175).` Note that no punctuation separates the author's name from the page number(s).

3. If you have more than one source by the same author in your Works Cited list (e.g., Ellison's short story and his interview), state the title of the work in the parenthetical citation too: `The fictional fight scene in "Battle Royal" mimics other such fights that were "a vital part of behavior pattern in the South... a ritual in preservation of caste lines" (Ellison,` *`Shadow and Act`* `175).` Note that when you are quoting from a work reprinted in an anthology, you use the name of the author of the work, not the editor(s) of the anthology.

4. If you don't know the author's name, use the title of the work or enough information for the readers to find the source on the Works Cited page: `Ellison`

strove to produce "literature that explores and affirms the complex, often contradictory frontier of an identity at once black and American and universally human" (*Contemporary Authors*).

5. If you are quoting a direct quote contained within a source, use the abbreviation *qtd. in*: John F. Callahan commented that Ellison was a "moral historian" (qtd. in *Contemporary Authors*).

6. According to MLA style, prose quotations longer than four lines must be formatted as block quotations. Block quotations begin on a new line and each line of the quotation is indented one inch from the left margin. Such long quotations are usually introduced by a signal phrase followed by a colon: When responding to angry contentions that the work of his fellow black authors had been rejected because of racial discrimination, Ellison claimed that:

> protest is not the source of the inadequacy characteristic of most novels by Negroes, but the simple failure of craft, bad writing; the desire to have protest perform the difficult tasks of art; the belief that racial suffering, social injustice, or ideologies of whatever mammy-made variety, is enough. (*Shadow and Act* 142)

Note that a block quotation has no quotation marks and that the period comes *before* the parentheses, at the end of the sentence and before the beginning of the citation.

7. When citing poetry, for quotations of four lines or fewer separate the lines with slashes and cite the line number(s) after the word *line(s)* in the parenthetical citation: The narrator of Marvell's poem tries to pacify his lover by explaining, "Had we but world enough, and time / This coyness, lady, were no crime" (lines 1-2). If the poem is separated into parts, cite the part first and then the line number(s). Place a period between the part and the line(s): The moral of the poem is "'Beauty is truth, truth beauty,'—that is all/ Ye know on earth, and all ye need to know" (Keats 5.49-50). Note that the quotation must be incorporated into and make grammatical sense within the context of your whole sentence. Read the sentence aloud, as if the quotation marks were not there. Does it sound right? Does it make sense as a sentence?

8. When citing a play in verse, for quotations of four lines or fewer separate the act, scene, and line numbers with periods: When queried about the appearance of the ghost, Horatio describes for Marcellus how the apparition is dressed: "Such was the very armor he had on / When he the ambitious Norway combated. / So frowned he once, when, in an angry parle, / He smote the sledded Polacks on the ice" (*Hamlet* 1.1.59-63).

9. In the case of both poems and poetic drama, quotations of more than four lines should be indented twice from the margin and the line divisions should be observed: When queried about the appearance of the ghost, Horatio explains to Marcellus that it is as much like the king

> As thou art to thyself:
> Such was the very armor he had on
> When he the ambitious Norway combated.
> So frown'd he once, when, in an angry parle,

```
He smote the sledded Polacks on the ice.
'Tis strange. (Hamlet 1.1.59-64)
```

There are no quotation marks surrounding indented quotations of poetry; note as well that the period comes at the end of the last sentence, before the parenthesis. Indented longer quotations of poetry are formatted in exactly the same manner.

We discourage you from using long block quotations very often because shorter quotations incorporated into your own sentences focus your reader's attention on the words and phrases that you want to emphasize and because within any given paragraph, there is more explanation in proportion to quotation, which means that you are analyzing rather than simply quoting the literary text.

10. Prose quotations from plays, when incorporated into your own sentence, are formatted just like in-line quotations, omitting the slash marks that, in the play text, mark line divisions: Deflecting his friends'probing questions, Hamlet offers a philosophical evaluation of humanity, beginning with the exclamation "What a piece of work is a man, How noble in reason, how infinite in faculty, in form and moving how express and admirable" (*Hamlet* 2.2.273-75). The prose is "run together" so that it fits the formatting of your paragraph.

Prose quotations from plays that are longer than four lines long are indented as block quotations: Deflecting his friends'probing questions, Hamlet offers a philosophical evaluation of humanity:

> What piece of work is a man, how noble in reason, how infinite in faculties, in form and moving how express and admirable, in action how like an angel, in apprehension how like a god: the beauty of the world, the paragon of animals! And yet to me what is this quintessence of dust? Man delights not me—no, nor woman neither, though by your smiling you seem to say so. (*Hamlet* 2.2.273-80)

Again, there are no quotation marks, and the final period comes at the end of the quotation rather than at the end of the citation. The prose lines are run together; there are no slash marks to signify line divisions.

WORKS CITED PAGE

The Works Cited page is an alphabetical listing of the complete bibliographic information for the sources cited in your essay. The list of works cited should begin on a new page after the completion of the text of your essay. The first line of each entry should be flush with the left margin, and each additional line should be indented five spaces. Here are some sample Works Cited entries:

1. The entry for a book begins with the author's last name, followed by a comma and then his or her first name and a period, then the title of the book (underlined or italicized) followed by a period, and finally the publication information (city of publication followed by a colon, publisher's name followed by a comma, and year of publication followed by a period):

Ellison, Ralph. *Shadow and Act*. New York: Signet, 1964.

2. An essay or work of literature that appears in an anthology or a chapter in a book with an editor or editors begins with the name of the author of the work, followed by the title of the selection in quotation marks, then the title of the anthology or book (underlined or italicized), the notation *Ed.*, and the names of the editor(s), then the publication information, and the inclusive page numbers of the selection:

Miller, J. Hillis. "Narrative." *Critical Terms for Literary Study.* 2nd ed. Ed. Frank Lentricchia and Thomas McLaughlin. Chicago: U of Chicago P, 1995. 66-79.

Note that this is the second edition of this book, as indicated by the notation *2nd ed.*

3. For periodicals (such as journals), list the author's last name followed by a comma and then his or her first name followed by a period, the title of the article enclosed in double quotation marks, then the title of the periodical (underlined or italicized), the volume or issue number plus publication date (if applicable), and the inclusive page numbers:

Blake, Susan L. "Ritual and Rationalization: Black Folklore in the Works of Ralph Ellison." *PMLA* 94.1 (1979): 121-36.

4. To cite an entry in a reference work, list the author of the selection, if identified, followed by the title of the entry, the title of the publication, the edition number, and the date of publication:

"Ralph Ellison." *Dictionary of Literary Biography, Volume 227: American Novelists Since World War II, Sixth Series.* 2000.

5. For a Web site, include the name of the person who made or maintains the site, if identifiable; the title of the page, if applicable; the title of the site; the date of the latest update, if listed; the name of any institution or organization affiliated with the site, if identifiable; the date you accessed the site; and the Web address, or URL, in angle brackets:

Potts, Claude Henry. "Introduction." Ralph Ellison Webliography. Graduate School of Education and Information Studies, University of California, Los Angeles. 9 Jan. 2005 <http://www.centerx.gseis.ucla.edu/weblio/ellison.html>.

CONCLUSION

By taking careful notes during the process of research, you will ensure that you can document your sources fully and accurately, and you will demonstrate your credibility as a literary critic by having joined in the critical conversation, thereby enriching not only your own encounter with the text, but others' encounters as well.

NOTE

1. An author's birthplace, for example, would fall into the category of common knowledge, but specific theories about how his or her place of birth affected his or her writing would not.

CHAPTER 11

Reading and Writing Intertextually and across Genres

THE WHOLE CITY IS TALKING ABOUT THE BUMSTEADS' ANNIVERSARY PARTY
I HEAR IT WILL BE QUITE AN EVENT
www.Blondie.com
8-22

©2005 by King Features Syndicate, Inc. World Rights reserved
I WONDER WHICH HOUSE IS THEIRS?

Intertextuality: The Comics Come to Blondie's Seventy-Fifth Anniversary Party

?
SLURP
SLURP

©2005 by King Features Syndicate, Inc. World Rights reserved
I'M JUST HAVING A NIGHTCAP

BOY, I SURE WILL BE GLAD WHEN THIS ANNIVERSARY PARTY IS OVER!
SLURP
SLURP
www.Blondie.com
8-25

Intertextuality: A "Dialogue" Between Dagwood and Grimm

INTRODUCTION

Although *Literature Portfolio: An Anthology of Readings* is arranged by genre, neither writers nor readers need be bound by this restriction. Many writers, indeed, work in several genres. If you look through the Table of Contents, you will find a number of authors who are included in two different sections of the anthology, and we invite you to cross generic boundaries and read their work as a unified whole. In this chapter, we offer as well casebooks for three writers from different historical periods—William Shakespeare, Edgar Allan Poe, and Judith Ortiz Cofer—who are represented by pieces in two genres.

Although comparing works of different types by the same author seems natural, works and authors also invite comparison with one another in other ways. The idea that works of literature refer to one another, either overtly or unobtrusively, is called **intertextuality**. The venerable comic strip Blondie recently had its seventy-fifth anniversary. As part of the celebration, characters in other comic strips referred to Blondie's upcoming anniversary party and also made guest appearances in *Blondie*. We can see intertextuality at work when Hagar the Horrible, Dilbert, Garfield, and other recognizable figures descend together on the Bumstead home in anticipation of the upcoming revels, as in the first comic strip above. In the second strip, however, the dog from *Mother Goose and Grimm* is interrupted by Dagwood in the act of taking a drink from the Bumstead toilet. This more subtle, complicated intertextual reference requires us not only to know about canine behavior and Grimm's behavior at home with Mother Goose, but also to recognize the strip's reference to a standard Blondie gag, in which either Dagwood or Blondie is regularly interrupted by other characters while trying to take a relaxing bath. We get the joke by understanding the two plot lines in relation to one another. In literature, intertextual references work in a similar way and can occur on many levels, ranging from a single word or phrase to broad structural and thematic principles.

INTERTEXTUAL REFERENCES

In its consideration of intertextual relations between texts and cross-genre explorations, this chapter moves from a consideration of small, focused connections between texts—at the level of the word or phrase—to broader principles for reading texts together.

Citations, References, and Quotations

The most specific and focused kinds of intertextual reference are citation, **quotation**, and **allusion**. The distinction between citation and quotation is a fine one. A citation, like an in-text citation of a source within the body of your own essay, is a shorthand reference that *points toward* another work. A quotation, by contrast, *repeats at greater length the exact words* of another work and usually *calls attention to* the exactness of its repetition; it puts the material within imaginary quotation marks. The title of Lorraine Hansberry's well-known play *A Raisin in the Sun* is a citation to a phrase in Langston Hughes's poem "Harlem" (included in this anthology), which serves as an **epigraph** to the printed play; with this gesture, Hansberry claims an intellectual kinship with the poet and his political concerns. We would call the reference a citation rather than a quotation because although the title "points" us toward the Hughes poem, the reference is brief and not developed at length. We understand the reference completely only when we compare the title and epigraph. In a similar way, Kevin Young's poem "Langston Hughes" cites the title of a famous Hughes poem when Young's speaker addresses the poet as "Mr. Theme for English B."

In "Gertrude Talks Back," by contrast, the Queen's monologue quotes directly and liberally from Hamlet's famous criticisms against his mother in the closet scene. Atwood's Gertrude throws back in Hamlet's face his own words, so to speak. The joke, in this intertextual quotation, rests in part on our understanding that while Gertrude is quoting her son Hamlet, Atwood is also quoting Shakespeare.

A good example of an allusion might be Prufrock's self-deprecating statement that "I am not Prince Hamlet, nor was meant to be" in "The Love Song of J. Alfred Prufrock." Eliot's line does not cite author or title, nor does it quote directly from the play text of *Hamlet*; rather, Prufrock's statement gestures broadly in the direction of Shakespeare's play and asks readers to draw on their critical understanding of the character Hamlet, his status, and his problems in order to comprehend Prufrock's self-evaluation. An allusion is both less precise and more wide-ranging than a citation or quotation.

Citations, quotations, and allusions entice us to think about *why* an author or character is pointing us toward another literary text. In Judith Ortiz Cofer's short story, "Arturo's Flight," the young hero has been studying Shakespeare and John Donne; the crisis that makes him flee El Building and the neighborhood involves Donne's humorously erotic poem, "The Flea" (also reproduced in this anthology). The fact that Cofer's character reads, quotes from, and reacts to Donne and to this particular poem could be sheer accident. But a curious reader could easily find reasons why the choice is appropriate to both the character and the story's main themes. Citations, allusions, and quotations, however, need not be necessarily reverential or appreciative. "The Book of Yolek"—Anthony Hecht's poem about the Holocaust—has as its **epigraph** a German-language citation from the New Testament or Christian Bible. The line, from John 19.7, exists in a bitterly ironic relation to the events described in the body of this poem. And sometimes references can be subtle or "unmarked." The title of Robert Frost's poem "Out, Out—," for instance, probably refers to a famous line spoken by Shakespeare's Macbeth: "Out, out, brief candle," which comments on the brevity of man's life.

Finally, allusions can be tentative, debatable, or multi-layered. The title of Countee Cullen's poem "To the Dark Tower" probably refers primarily to the newspaper column of the same name that Cullen wrote for *Opportunity*. Some readers think the "dark tower" also represents an ironic reference to the "ivory tower" of academia. (The poem was dedicated to Charles S. Johnson of Fisk University.) But the poem's title could also evoke the dominant symbol of Robert Browning's "Childe Roland," another elegy to unsung heroes, or even Browning's own source, the song of Edgar in his disguise as the beggar Poor Tom in Shakespeare's *King Lear*: "Child Rowland to the dark tower came, / His word was still,—Fie, foh, and fum, / I smell the blood of a British man." Your job, as literary detective, would be to decide what connection, if any, informs these literary echoes and to explain that connection, largely by means of comparison-and-contrast between the different works.

Connections Established by External Evidence

Sometimes a writer herself or a critic of her work will make a direct comparison between authors or works. Arthur Miller, in his op-ed piece "Tragedy and the Common Man," encourages a direct comparison between *Death of a Salesman* and ancient Greek drama by defending Willy Loman's status as a modern "tragic hero," who differs greatly from the hero described by Aristotle, but nevertheless exhibits his own kind of "greatness" by claiming a place for himself in society: "As a general rule, to which there may be exceptions unknown to me, I think the tragic feeling is evoked in us when we are in the presence of a character who is ready to lay down his life, if need be, to secure one thing—his sense of personal dignity. From Orestes to Hamlet, Medea to Macbeth, the underlying struggle is that of the individual attempting to gain his 'rightful' position in his society." Comments such as these invite readers to perform a sustained comparison and contrast between works from different traditions or time periods.

External evidence can also suggest links between one author or work and another based on admiration or influence. Miller, for instance, has indicated his appreciation of Ibsen and his work. In the Introduction to his *Collected Plays*, he writes that he appreciates Ibsen's "ability to forge a play upon a factual bedrock" (Miller 131). Miller likes especially Ibsen's ability to convey a "contrast between past and present" and an understanding "of the process by which the present has become what it is" (133). A comparable emphasis can easily be seen in *Death of a Salesman*, inviting a direct comparison between the two works on this point.

Dialogues between Texts

Critics who talk about intertextuality often use metaphors of **dialogue** or conversation to explain the way in which texts respond to previous texts and, in turn, invite the responses of later writers. The later work may echo the earlier one, but in most cases the author also wants to "talk back" in some way to her or his predecessor: to update the source's perspective, to correct a misconception, or even to offer a radically different view of life. Two poems in this anthology, Christopher Marlowe's "The Passionate Shepherd" and Walter Ralegh's "The Nymph's Reply," dramatize the dynamics of such a dialogue. Pastoral shepherds are by nature clever poets, whereas pastoral nymphs are more notable for being chased by gods and seduced by shepherds. The fictional nymph of Ralegh's poem, surprisingly, is at once eloquent and admirably clear-sighted about the nature of the love offered to her by Marlowe's fictional shepherd. In Matthew Arnold's "Dover Beach" and Anthony Hecht's "The Dover Bitch," we see an even tenser, but at the same time humorous, relationship between the two texts, which are linked explicitly by their titles. **Parody**, as a genre, depends for its punch on intertextual connections.

Intertextuality can occur between two works in the same genre, works in different genres, or even works in different media. W. H. Auden's "Musée des Beaux Arts," for instance, not only alludes to "The Fall of Icarus," a painting by sixteenth-century Flemish artist Peter Brueghel, but also expects the reader of his poem to possess a rather complete visual recall of the painting—or at least access to a reproduction—and a general ability to analyze paintings. Cathy Song's poem, "Girl Powdering Her Neck," asks for a comparable knowledge of Japanese art and of a specific work by Kitagawa Utamaro.

In some cases, formal qualities themselves can invite intertextual examinations of different literary works. Elizabeth Bishop was famous for her command of complex poetic forms, such as the **sestina** and **villanelle**. *Prentice Hall Literature Portfolio* contains Bishop's villanelle, "One Art." The anthology contains as well two other poems that are identified, by their titles, as villanelles: John Yau's "Chinese Villanelle" and Marilyn Hacker's "Villanelle for D. G. B." To write in a specific form is to place oneself within a poetic tradition, and critical readers should be aware of possible connections established by the rules of literary form.

Finally, source study invites direct comparison and contrast between literary texts and other texts, sometimes but not necessarily literary in nature. Tennessee Williams's *The Glass Menagerie*, for instance, was preceded by a short story entitled "Portrait of a Girl in Glass." Susan Glaspell wrote a newspaper article about the real-life event that inspired her play *Trifles*. *Hamlet* is based, at least in part, on bits of Saxo Grammaticus's *Historiae Danicae*. Source study is especially interesting because it allows critics to do a focused and detailed comparison and contrast between two or more texts.

Thematic Connections

The broadest form of intertextual relation between two literary texts takes place at the level of theme. Some thematic connections are the result of direct influence. A number of writers, such as Kevin Young in this volume, are indebted to the work and poetry of Langston Hughes. In these cases, the writers implicitly or explicitly acknowledge Hughes as a predecessor or influence on their own art. Sometimes thematic connections are caused by broader movements in literary history. Many of the Renaissance poems represented in this anthology, for instance, draw on or resist the rules of Petrarchan love, a genre in which the poet worships a cold, distant, and ideal beloved, whom he places on a metaphorical pedestal. The lover, by contrast, suffers cold shakes and hot fevers and is perfectly miserable, although at the same time faithful to his ideal lady. Almost anyone writing in the sonnet tradition—Shakespeare, for instance—would know the themes and situations of Petrarchan poetry. Sonnet 18 responds to the tradition by recasting the beloved as a young man who is both fairer and more constant than any woman, whereas Sonnet 130 defends the worth of a woman who does not fit at all the physical type of the female beloved in the Petrarchan tradition. When John Donne writes his Holy Sonnet 14, "Batter my heart," he self-consciously adapts the love poem to the subject of divine love. Finally, Countee Cullen adapts the Petrarchan sonnet form and imagery (e.g., night and stars) to a very different kind of subject: racial injustice.

WRITING ABOUT INTERTEXTUALITY AND ACROSS GENERIC BOUNDARIES

Readers and writers of literature often have a favorite genre. Some people read short stories, some poetry. Some like the excitement of theater, whereas some prefer reading books under their favorite tree. As students or critics of literature, however, often you will be asked to explore literature from different genres. One such occasion might be the final examination or essay for a course, in which your teacher might ask you to answer thematic questions by referring to works in different genres or to discuss issues of literary history with examples of literature from a particular period that you have studied. Another common kind of writing assignment is the comparison-and-contrast paper, which can be done with works from different genres as well as with works within the same genre.

Writing about intertextual connections can be a particularly satisfying form of literary criticism because it allows readers and writers the opportunity to make original and unusual observations. Focused on two or three texts and looking for particular connections, students of literature have right in front of them the primary texts they need to construct their arguments. At a higher level, intertextual analysis can involve a consideration of historical events or social contexts, but the basic skill needed for this kind of work is close reading.

Writing about literary works in different genres, on the other hand, can also be a challenge. When faced with the task of discussing multiple texts, writers sometimes resort to plot summary rather than literary analysis, for the subtlety and close attention that you can bring to bear on a single text can be diffused when you are trying to discuss multiple texts. When dealing with texts from different genres, as well, it can prove difficult to pay attention to a writer's style or technique, since these features can differ greatly between genres. When writing about texts from different genres, think carefully about the reasons why you wish to group together this particular selection of texts: Do they have similar themes? Are there particular biographical or historical connections between the authors? Do the characters merit comparison? Are there formal similarities, in terms of plot or structure, style, or figurative language? In this way, you can focus your analysis in a way that allows you to deal with both form and content of the various texts.

THREE CASEBOOKS

One approach to intertextuality is to examine the works of a single author who works in different genres. In this way, student readers and writers can explore the writer's repeated themes, see how the writer's technique changes or remains the same when he or she works in different genres, or consider the writer's place in literary history. Here, we offer you three small casebooks. The first considers William Shakespeare, who is represented by his sonnets, a tragedy, and a romantic comedy. The second concerns Edgar Allan Poe, best known for his short stories, but also a well-known poet in his own time. The third considers contemporary multicultural writer Judith Ortiz Cofer, who is represented in this anthology by her poetry and prose; in some cases, the poems and short fiction are closely related to one another and meant to be read together. In each casebook, we offer one or two brief critical pieces as a "way in" to the author's work and conclude with a very brief list of useful and authoritative resources, some in print and some on the World Wide Web.

When working with the casebooks in *Prentice Hall Literature Portfolio* start by consulting the head notes for background information on each author and work. In reading closely the individual pieces of the casebook, you will want to refer as well to the discussions of genre in the chapters on "reading and writing about" short stories, poetry, and drama. Finally, use the brief critical pieces provided in the casebook to start thinking about ways to bring together the different pieces of literature under a common perspective or theme.

William Shakespeare

- Sonnet 18
- Sonnet 73
- Sonnet 116
- Sonnet 130
- *The Taming of the Shrew*
- *Hamlet*

- Rose, Mark. "*Hamlet*." *Homer to Brecht: The European Epic and Dramatic Tradition*. Ed. Michael Seidel and Edward Mendelson. New Haven: Yale UP, 1977. 239–43.
- Stanton, Kay. "*Hamlet*'s Whores." *New Essays on Hamlet*. Ed. Mark Thornton Burnett and John Manning. New York: AMS, 1994. 167–69.

Among Renaissance dramatists, Shakespeare was somewhat unusual, in that he wrote for a single company, the Lord Chamberlain's Men, which later became the King's Men. Shakespeare was both an actor and a shareholder in the company for which he wrote, which means that he understood both the medium of and the market for drama. In the middle and latter part of his career, he also wrote for specific theaters, the outdoor Globe and then the indoor theater, the Blackfriars. (*Hamlet* was performed at the Globe, but *The Taming of the Shrew* was not.) Given his business interests, it is no accident that later in his career he purchased New Place, the second largest house in Stratford-on-Avon and, after his retirement, became active in civic affairs. But given what he wrote, both in the *Sonnets* and plays, we must ask as well whether Shakespeare might have had a subversive streak. Did he uphold established values and wisdom; or does the presence of rebellious or skeptical characters in his plays suggest that Shakespeare questioned the status quo?

In the *Sonnets*, first published as a group in 1609, Shakespeare participated in a more rarified and aristocratic genre than one might expect from a participant in the growing, but still not-completely-respectable, professional theater: **sonnet** writing. Some of the *Sonnets* were published under his name in anthologies well before the 1609 collected *Sonnets*, suggesting that the poems may have been written before the plays printed in *Prentice Hall Literature Portfolio*. Shakespeare introduces several innovations to the sonnet tradition. In the first section of his sonnet cycle, the narrator addresses a fair young man rather than a woman, whose beauty and virtues exceed those of women (see Sonnet 18, for instance). The latter part of the cycle's narrative focuses on an older, more experienced "dark lady" (whose appearance is the subject of Sonnet 130); the narrator must deal with both the lady's cruelty and a rival poet. As in many sonnet cycles, most of the poems can be read independently, and some—in this case, Sonnet 73 and Sonnet 116—are related only tangentially to the main plot line.

Shakespeare also popularized a new structure and rhyming scheme for the sonnet. **Sonnets** are, by definition, fourteen lines long and generally written in **iambic pentameter**. The Shakespearean sonnet has three **quatrains** that rhyme according to the pattern *abab cdcd efef gg*. The three separate quatrains of the Shakespearean sonnet develop the argument more slowly, and often through analogy (see, for instance, Sonnet 73). The rhyming couplet either sums up the argument or offers a surprising twist. In either case, the rhyming **couplet** concludes the sonnet with a flourish. (For further discussion of the Shakespearean sonnet and a comparison with the Petrarchan sonnet, see the discussion in Chapter 6, "Reading and Writing about Poetry.")

The Taming of the Shrew, as a romantic comedy, and *Hamlet*, as a tragedy, pursue some of the same themes as do Shakespeare's *Sonnets*. If you want to understand the qualities of Petrarchan or sonnet love—falling in love at first sight, suffering fever and chills, pining away for love, and experiencing frustration—you need only look carefully at Lucentio's reaction to Bianca at the beginning of *The Taming of the Shrew*. Some readers have seen in Kate as well the fierce demeanor, but also the freedom from convention that characterizes Shakespeare's "dark lady." The attitude of *Hamlet* and Hamlet toward women is more like the cynical tone we associate with the later sonnets, where sexuality becomes a problem rather than a goal for the narrator. At the same time, however, we hear examples of love poems that Hamlet has written to Ophelia. Thus, while Shakespeare's plays address a wide range of social and political issues, they are tied to the *Sonnets* by virtue of their focus on the dynamics and ethics of love.

The Shakespeare casebook includes two brief critical excerpts that deal explicitly with *Hamlet*, but can provide a starting point for a wider discussion of human relationships in both the plays and *Sonnets*. The excerpt from Mark Rose's essay, "*Hamlet*," discusses how Hamlet is limited or "tethered" by the expectations others have for him. The second critical excerpt, from Kay Stanton's commentary on *Hamlet*'s "Nunnery Scene" (3.1), focuses on Ophelia, showing how she, too, is trapped by social perceptions of women and by Hamlet himself. We can see these same themes—the relationship of individuals to social expectations in the realm of love—at play in *The Taming of the Shrew* and the *Sonnets*. Furthermore, both plays and the *Sonnets* involve argument, or the attempt to persuade others of all kinds when love is at stake. For this reason, it is also possible to consider the relationship between sonnet structure and the structure of Shakespeare's plays about love.

Critical Resources for Shakespeare

Wells, Stanley, and Lena Cowen Orlin, eds. *Shakespeare: An Oxford Guide*. Oxford: Oxford University Press, 2003. Designed for students, this resource offers introductions to Shakespeare's genres and other topics that are both scholarly (accurate and up-to-date) and accessible (readable and digestible). You might consult Lois Potter on "Shakespeare's Life and Career" (9–19), Gabriel Egan on "Theatre in London" (20–31), Lynne Magnuson on the *Sonnets* (286–91 and 295–99), and Christy Desmet's essay on "Character Criticism" and *Hamlet* (351–72).

Best, Michael. *Internet Shakespeare Editions*. 4 Dec. 2005. http://ise.uvic.ca/index.html. A complete and accurate scholarly introduction to Shakespeare, his theater, and his times that is freely available over the Internet. The work of University of Victoria emeritus Michael Best, this is a great resource for students at different levels and also offers free, old-spelling online texts of the plays that can be searched through a Web browser.

Dolan, Frances E., ed. *The Taming of the Shrew: Texts and Contexts*. Boston: Bedford/St. Martin's, 1996. For students who want to delve further into the historical background of Shakespeare's comedy and the Renaissance phenomenon of shrew taming; the bibliography also directs readers to reputable sources.

Wofford, Susanne L. *Hamlet*. Boston: Bedford/St. Martin's, 1994. From the same publisher comes this thought-provoking casebook on Shakespeare's best-known tragedy. In addition to critical context and historical background, this collection of materials includes critical essays from different theoretical perspectives. The introductions to these different theoretical orientations also provide a handy reference for students wishing to write essays from a particular critical orientation.

Edgar Allan Poe

- "The Tell-Tale Heart"
- "The Cask of Amontillado"
- "The Black Cat"
- "The Purloined Letter"
- "Annabel Lee"
- "The Haunted Palace"
- "The Raven"
- "To Helen"
- Smith, Dave. "Edgar Allan Poe and the Nightmare Ode." *Southern Humanities Review* 29.1 (1995): 4–10.
- Poquette, Ryan D. "Critical Essay on 'The Purloined Letter.'" *Short Stories for Students*, 16. New York: Gale, 2003. Literature Resource Center.

In *Prentice Hall Literature Portfolio*, the head note to Edgar Allan Poe's short stories emphasizes the distinction between his **grotesque** tales, which privilege the irrational world of imagination, and the **ratiocinative** detective story "The Purloined Letter," in which reason prevails. It is possible, however, to see these principles as working together, or at least in tandem with one another, in different texts by Poe. The poems reproduced here offer us largely supernatural settings, hapless humans in conflict with malevolent forces, and a transparent poetic form. To see beneath this polished exterior, however, the reader need only look and listen carefully. Rhyme, rhythm, and sound patterns often will signal some irrationality beneath the matter-of-fact narration. Looking skeptically at the narrator and what he tells us is also a useful strategy. To some extent, to see beneath the bland exterior of Poe's poetic voice means to read his verse as one would his grotesque tales: "The Tell-Tale Heart," "The Black Cat," or "The Cask of Amontillado." One must wonder, for instance, why the speaker in "Annabel Lee," many years after losing the girl, still sounds so childish and persists so doggedly not only in mourning her, but also in perceiving the universe and angels as against him. Some readers think as well that Poe's elaborate versifying in "The Raven" signals that the poem parodies the romantic excesses of Anonymous Young Men like the narrator.

In "Edgar Allan Poe and the Nightmare Ode," Dave Smith compares Poe's poem—with its dark tone, mysterious setting, and anguished emotions—to a country song. Smith alludes to the disjunction between serious subject tone and excessive rhetoric that characterizes both genres. You might use Smith's observations about Poe's best-known poem to compare his themes and technique in the poems with his themes and technique in the short stories, where terror and destruction often destroy any possibility of irony. You might also think about how the voice of Poe's short-story narrators lures you into the rhythmic world of poetry. Try scanning, for instance, the very first sentence of "The Cask of Amontillado":

ˇ / ˇ / ˇ ˇ / ˇ /
The thousand injuries of Fortuna-
ˇ / ˇ / ˇ / ˇ / ˇ /
to I had borne as I best could, but when
ˇ / ˇ ˇ / ˇ / ˇ / ˇ /
he ventured upon insult, I vowed revenge.

With slight variation, the prose sentence reads as iambic pentameter.[1] What comparisons, then, might you make between not only the content, but also the form of Poe's poems and short stories? Are they all kinds of "country song"?

In his critical essay on "The Purloined Letter," Ryan D. Poquette suggests that in this detective story, Poe examines the "doubleness" of the human soul, part imagination and part reason. Poquette's clear analysis of this concept of the bipartite soul can be tried out as well on the grotesque tales and poetry. How do we see the principles of imagination and reason working either with or against one another in the pieces in the Edgar Allan Poe casebook?

Critical Resources for Poe

Kennedy, J. Gerald, ed. *A Historical Guide to Edgar Allan Poe*. Oxford: Oxford UP, 2001. The essays in this collection consider Poe in his historical context. The essay topics range from Poe's association with the American publishing industry to his personal relationships to gender constructions in his fiction. The volume also includes a bibliographic essay and a chronology of Poe's life.

Hayes, Kevin J., ed. *The Cambridge Companion to Edgar Allan Poe*. Cambridge: Cambridge UP, 2002. The essays in this collection are meant to address the needs of undergraduate students. The authors examine all of Poe's major writings in a variety of literary, cultural, and political contexts. Works of particular interest related to the selections in this anthology include Peter Thom's "Poe's Dupin and the Power of Detection" (133–47), Mark Neimeyer's "Poe and Popular Culture" (205–24), and Sandra Tomc's "Poe and His Circle" (21–41).

Poe Studies Association. 4 Dec. 2005. <http://www.poestudies.assn.org>. The Poe Studies Association "provides a forum for the scholarly and informal exchange of information on Edgar Allan Poe, his life, and works" and publishes the journal *The Edgar Allan Poe Review*, past issues of which are archived in full text on the site.

Judith Ortiz Cofer

- "More Room" / "Claims"
- "Tales Told Under the Mango Tree"
- "Arturo's Flight"
- "Cold as Heaven"
- "The Other"
- "The Woman Who Was Left at the Altar"
- "Learning to Walk Alone"
- "The Names of the Dead"
- Hernández, Carmen Delores. "Where Is Home? I Want to Go There" (Interview with Judith Ortiz Cofer). *Puerto Rican Voices in English: Interviews with Writers*. Westport, Conn.: Praeger, 1997. 98–103.

Describing herself as moving among cultures, Judith Ortiz Cofer spent her early childhood traveling back and forth between Paterson, New Jersey, and the island of Puerto Rico. The family later moved to Augusta, Georgia, and, after further dislocations, Ortiz Cofer has settled in Georgia, continuing her work as a writer while teaching as a Regents Professor at the University of Georgia. The stories (or *cuentos*) and poetry printed here attempt to represent the breadth of Cofer's sense of place; the settings for these pieces range from the New Jersey barrio and El Building to Mama's house on the Island, and finally to the mythical island of Ikaria, where Penelope waits for Odysseus. The selections also give us some sense of Ortiz Cofer's wide reading in literature. Finally, we get a sense of her command of a range of literary genres. The inclusion of "The Names of the Dead," as a **prose poem**, provides a touchstone for readers interested in the artistic borderline between story and poetry; the incorporation of phrases from the *New York Times* into that poem calls into question as well the boundary between how a catastrophic experience can be represented in the news and in art.

All of the pieces by Ortiz Cofer that you will find here can be read on their own terms. In one instance, however, a short story (or prose piece) and poem were originally printed together and therefore ask to be read as mirroring or commenting upon one another. The pair "More Room" / "Claims" comes from the collection *Silent Dancing: A Partial Remembrance of a Puerto Rican Childhood*. In her Preface, Ortiz Cofer explains that in this collection, which she does not quite want to call a memoir, "I wanted the essays to be, not just family history, but also creative explorations of known territory." As she further explains,

> Much of my writing begins as a meditation on past events. But memory for me is the "jumping off" point; I am not, in my poetry and my fiction writing, a slave to memory. I like to believe that the poem or story contains the "truth" of art rather than the factual, historical truth that the journalist, sociologist, scientist—most of the rest of the world—must adhere to. Art gives me that freedom. But in writing these "essays" (the Spanish word for essay, *ensayo*, suits my meaning here better—it can mean "a rehearsal," an exercise or practice), I faced the possibility that the past is mainly a creation of the imagination. (Cofer 12)

We might consider the paired essays and poems as approaching memory and communicating the "truth of art" through different perspectives and according to different literary conventions.

One of the pleasures of reading and writing about contemporary authors is the fact that the author is a person in process—still developing, changing, and moving in new directions. Furthermore, a living author is just that—living, breathing, thinking, and more directly accessible to readers than are authors from the past. While we should avoid the temptation to read any author's work strictly in terms of biography—as we have seen, Cofer herself talks about the creative dimension of reconstructing memories—some important resources for understanding a contemporary, living author are lectures, readings, and interviews. The Judith Ortiz Cofer casebook concludes with "Where Is Home? I Want to Go There," an interview conducted with Cofer (JOC) by Carmen Delores Hernández (CDH). In this discussion, Cofer talks about place, identity, language, and her goals as both a person and writer.

Critical Resource for Cofer

Cofer, Judith Ortiz. 4 Dec. 2005. <http://www.english.uga.edu/~jcofer/>. Like many authors, Cofer maintains a professional Web site. The site provides links to interviews, articles by and about Cofer, and access to other useful Web sites.

CONCLUSION

Intertextuality, as a concept, may seem abstract, but in fact, tracing connections between and among literary texts can be a fascinating journey into the interior of those texts and back out again into the personal and social forces that shape a writer's subject matter. Using the strategies for reading and writing that you have acquired in your engagement with *Prentice Hall Literature Portfolio*, you will find that you are well-equipped to understand the relationships between a text and its sources, writers and their predecessors, and the tradition of literary form. To return to one of our opening metaphors, when you explore intertextual relations among people and texts, you are able to see literature from both sides, as at once a rabbit and a duck. You truly will be reading "symbol-wise."

We hope that, as you conclude your reading of *Prentice Hall Literature Portfolio*, you enjoy literature even more than you did before you sat down with its writers; we hope also that the stories, poems, and plays contained within its covers give you a rich and varied view of the world. Like all literature, this text seeks both to teach and delight and to give you a lively window on the drama of life. We hope that on both counts, *Prentice Hall Literature Portfolio* has done its job well.

NOTE

1. We are indebted to Anne Williams for this observation.

WORKS CITED

Cofer, Judith Ortiz. "Preface: Journey to a Summer's Afternoon." *Silent Dancing: A Partial Remembrance of a Puerto Rican Childhood*. Houston: Arte Publico, 1990. 11–13.

Miller, Arthur. "Introduction to the *Collected Plays*." *The Theater Essays of Arthur Miller*. Rev. and expanded ed. Ed. Robert A. Martin and Steven Centola. New York: Da Capo, 1996. 113–70.

MARK ROSE

Hamlet

Classical and Elizabethan tragedy represent polar opposites in dramatic structure, the one tightly focused with few characters and a sharply defined action, the other loose and sprawling with many characters, multiple locales, and complex plots which may span years of narrative time. And yet all tragedies tend to share certain central concerns. Sophocles' Oedipus fled Corinth to prevent the oracle's prophecy from coming true, but in the process of trying to escape his fate he only succeeded in fulfilling it. Sophocles' play is concerned, we might say, with the degree to which our lives are not in our own control. The words of the player king in *Hamlet* are apposite:

> Our wills and fates do so contrary run
> That our devices still are overthrown;
> Our thoughts are ours, their ends none of our own.
>
> [3.2.317–19]

Hamlet, too, is concerned with the limits imposed upon mortal will, with the various restrictions that flesh is heir to; and it is upon this central tragic theme that I wish to dwell, suggesting how Shakespeare employs a characteristically Renaissance self-consciousness to transmute a popular Elizabethan dramatic form, the revenge play, into a tragedy the equal of Sophocles'.

Early in the play Polonius speaks to Ophelia of the "tether" with which Hamlet walks. The image is a useful one to keep in mind, for it suggests both that the prince does have a degree of freedom and that ultimately he is bound. Laertes cautions Ophelia in a similar manner and develops more explicitly the limits on Hamlet's freedom. The prince's "will is not his own," Laertes says,

> For he himself is subject to his birth,
> He may not, as unvalued persons do,
> Carve for himself; for on his choice depends
> The safety and the health of this whole state.
>
> [1.3.18–21]

What Laertes means is simply that Hamlet as heir apparent may not be free to marry Ophelia, but he says much more than he realizes. Hamlet is indeed subject to his birth, bound by being the dead king's son, and upon his "carving"—his rapier and dagger-work—the safety and health of Denmark do literally depend. Possibly Shakespeare has in mind the imagery of *Julius Caesar* and Brutus's pledge to be a sacrificer rather than a butcher, to carve Caesar as a dish fit for the gods, for, like Brutus, Hamlet is concerned with the manner of his carving. But the word is also Shakespeare's term for sculptor, and perhaps he is thinking of Hamlet as this kind of carver, an artist attempting to shape his revenge and his life according to his own standards. Yet here, too, Hamlet's will is not his own: there is, he discovers, "a divinity that shapes our ends,/Rough-hew them how we will" (5.2.10–11).

From the first scene in which the prince appears, Shakespeare wishes us to perceive clearly that Hamlet is tethered. He contrasts the king's permission to Laertes to return to France with his polite refusal of Hamlet's request to return

This essay originally appeared in slightly different form under the title "Hamlet and the Shape of Revenge" in *English Literary Renaissance* 1(1971): 132–43.

to Wittenberg. Denmark is in fact a prison for Hamlet, a kind of detention center in which the wary usurper can keep an eye on his disgruntled stepson. Claudius acclaims Hamlet's yielding as "gentle and unforced" and announces that he will celebrate it by firing his cannon to the heavens, but what he has done in fact is to cut ruthlessly the avenue of escape that the prince had sought from a court and a world he now loathes. One other, more desperate avenue still seems open, and as soon as the stage is cleared the prince considers the possibility of this course, suicide, only to remind himself that against this stands another sort of "canon," one fixed by God. Hamlet is tied to Elsinore, bound by his birth; on either side the road of escape is guarded and all that remains to him is his disgust for the world and the feeble wish that somehow his flesh will of itself melt into a puddle.

Hamlet's real prison is of course more a matter of mental than physical space. "Oh God," he exclaims to Rosencrantz and Guildenstern, "I could be bounded in a nutshell and count myself a king of infinite space, were it not that I have bad dreams" (2.2.258–60). The erstwhile friends suppose Hamlet means he is ambitious for the crown, but the bad dream the prince is thinking of, the insubstantial "shadow" as he calls it, is evidently the ghost and its nightmarish revelation. If Claudius has tied him to Elsinore it is of little consequence compared to the way the ghost has bound him to vengeance. Hamlet's master turns out to be even a more formidable figure than the king. Ironically, Laertes' and Polonius's remarks upon what they conceive to be the limits placed upon Hamlet's freedom immediately precede the scene in which the prince at last encounters the ghost and discovers what it means to be subject to one's birth. "Speak," Hamlet says to the ghost, "I am bound to hear," and the ghost in his reply picks up the significant word *bound* and throws it back at the prince: "So art thou to revenge, when thou shalt hear" (1.5.6–7). Hamlet cannot shuffle off his father's spirit any more than he can the mortal coil. The ghost's command is "Remember me," and after his departure Shakespeare dramatizes how from this charge there is no escape. Hamlet rushes about the stage seeking a place to swear his companions to secrecy, but wherever he makes his stand the ghost is there directly—"Hic et ubique," the prince says—its voice crying from the cellarage: "Swear!"

The ghost binds Hamlet to vengeance, but there is another and more subtle way in which the spirit of his father haunts the prince. It is one of the radical ironies of the tragedy that the same nightmarish figure who takes from Hamlet his freedom should also embody the ideal of man noble in reason and infinite in faculties—the ideal of man, in other words, as free. The ghost of King Hamlet, stalking his son dressed in the same armor he wore in heroic combat with Fortinbras of Norway, becomes a peripatetic emblem of human dignity and worth, a memento of the time before the "falling-off" when Hamlet's serpent-uncle had not yet crept into the garden, infesting it with things rank and gross in nature. It is no accident that Hamlet bears the same name as his father: the king represents everything to which the prince aspires. Hamlet, too, has his single-combats, his duels both metaphorical and literal, but the world in which he must strive is not his father's. The memory of those two primal, valiant kings, face to face in a royal combat ratified by law and heraldry, haunts the tragedy, looming behind each pass of the "incensed points" of the modern "mighty opposites," Hamlet and Claudius, and looming also behind the final combat, Hamlet's and Laertes' poisoned play, swaddled in a show of chivalry as "yeasty" as the eloquence of Osric, the waterfly who presides as master of the lists.

Subject to his birth, tethered by Claudius, and bound by the ghost, Hamlet is obsessed with the idea of freedom, with the dignity that resides in being master of oneself. One must not be "passion's slave," a "pipe for Fortune's finger/To sound what stop she please" (3.2.72–74)—nor for that matter a pipe for men to play. The first three acts are largely concerned with the attempts of Claudius and Hamlet to play upon each other, the king principally through Rosencrantz and Guildenstern, Hamlet through "The Mousetrap." It is Hamlet who succeeds, plucking out at last the heart of Claudius's mystery, pressing the king to the point where he loses his self-control and rises in a passion, calling for light. "Didst perceive?" Hamlet asks, and Horatio replies: "I did very well note him" (3.2.293, 296). I should like to see a musical pun in Horatio's word *note*, but perhaps it is far-fetched. At any rate, Hamlet's immediate response is to call for music, for the recorders to be brought, as if he thinks to reenact symbolically his triumph over the king. What follows is the "recorder scene" in which Rosencrantz and Guildenstern once again fail with Hamlet precisely where he has succeeded with the king:

> Why, look you now, how unworthy a thing you make of me! You would play upon me; you would seem to know my stops; you would pluck out the heart of my mystery; you would sound me from my lowest note to the top of my compass; and there is much music, excellent voice, in this little organ, yet cannot you make it speak. 'Sblood, do you think I am easier to be played on than a pipe? Call me what instrument you will, though you can fret me, you cannot play upon me. [3.2.371–80]

Immediately after speaking this, Hamlet turns to Polonius, who has just entered, and leads the old courtier through the game of cloud shapes, making him see the cloud first as a camel, then as a weasel, and finally as a whale. Though Claudius and his instruments cannot play upon him, Hamlet is contemptuously demonstrating that he can make any of them sound what tune he pleases.

Hamlet's disdain for anyone who will allow himself to be made an instrument perhaps suggests his bitter suspicion that he, too, is a kind of pipe. One of the most interesting of the bonds imposed upon Hamlet is presented in theatrical terms. Putting it baldly and exaggerating somewhat for the sake of clarity, one might say that Hamlet discovers that life is a poor play, that he finds himself compelled to play a part in a drama that offends his sense of his own worth. Hamlet is made to sound a tune that is not his own, the whirling and passionate music of the conventional revenger, a stock character familiar to the Elizabethans under a host of names, including Thomas Kyd's Hieronomo, his Hamlet, and Shakespeare's own Titus Andronicus. The role of revenger is thrust upon Hamlet by the ghost, and once again it is profoundly ironic that the figure who represents the dignity of man should be the agent for casting his son in a limited, hackneyed, and debasing role. That Hamlet should be constrained to play a role at all is a restriction of his freedom, but that it should be this particular, vulgar role is especially degrading.

KAY STANTON

from "Hamlet's *Whores*"

"Get thee to a nunnery" (III.i.121): in a play filled with memorable lines, this has been one of the most often quoted. As editors rarely fail to note in glosses, "nunnery" was Elizabethan slang for "brothel," so Hamlet *really tells* Ophelia to go to a whorehouse, where, he believes, she belongs. Why does the virtuous Ophelia belong, in Hamlet's judgement, in a whorehouse? A frequent answer has been that Hamlet so relegates her because of his disillusionment with women resulting from the revelation of his mother's lustfulness; *Gertrude* belongs in a whorehouse, since she has been "whor'd" by Claudius (V. ii. 64). Because Gertrude has become a whore, so will Ophelia—and so, in fact, will all women, in the estimation not only of Hamlet but also of those many men of various generations who have quoted—I would say prostituted—the line for the purpose of smugly concurring (and implying Shakespeare's concurrence) with Hamlet's estimation of woman's whorish nature.

A slightly more sophisticated reading of the passage in which the line occurs might recognize that both meanings of "nunnery" are operating: Ophelia is too virtuous for this corrupt world, which will prostitute her to its ways if she does not retreat into a cloistered religious life. Hamlet is "cruel only to be kind" (III. iv. 180). The world will corrupt Ophelia as it has corrupted Gertrude; Gertrude has become a whore, a fate that Hamlet wishes Ophelia to avoid, so he must therefore shock her, even by denying his feelings of love. This reading, however, still leaves Gertrude a whore, but it does also neatly reflect another comfortable misogynistic position that the play's commentators have often pandered it to; not all women are whores; some are Madonnas. Certainly the play as reflected through the male characters' perceptions seems to support this position. Women in *Hamlet* are allowed by the play's men to have two and only two choices: virgin or whore. Ophelia cannot, but Hamlet can, be "indifferent honest" (III. i. 122). So far as the play provides evidence, Gertrude has indulged in sexual activity only in marriage, yet even legalized expression of sexuality merits her the label of "whore": she suffers from the "plague" that Hamlet gives Ophelia for *her* dowry: "be thou as chaste as ice, as pure as snow, thou shalt not escape calumny" (III. i. 136–8). Thus the second position on women doubles back into the first: there may seem to be two choices for women of virgin or whore, but if a woman tries to be virtuous *and* sexual in monogamous marriage, or even if a woman remains an unmarried virgin, she cannot escape the "calumny" that will brand her a whore: all women are thus whores, either by action or by slander.

Of course, although it seems to warn against slander from others, the passage is itself an exercise in such "calumny." Ophelia's honour is verbally violated by Hamlet in his speech—and it may have already been done so in action: he may indeed have raped her in the offstage closet interlude that she reports, perhaps only in part, to her father in II. i. 75–110. The onstage Hamlet-woman-closet scene in III. iv. is usually staged, with good reason, to simulate a rape by Hamlet of

Gertrude. If both Gertrude and Ophelia are whores, it is Hamlet himself who has made them so, in words if not deeds, by *his* calumny. Although the other male characters may be seen to share Hamlet's misogyny, no male character not named "Hamlet," elder or younger, *calls* either woman a whore.

Perhaps it may be granted, however, that what makes a woman a whore in the Hamlets' estimation is her sexual use not by one man but by more than one man: Gertrude seems not to have been a whore in old Hamlet's judgement until she bedded Claudius; Ophelia, even if she has been sexually used by young Hamlet, is not seen by him as a whore until she has been employed as a sex object by Polonius, her "fishmonger" (II. ii. 174), or pimp. The rape of Ophelia by Hamlet may be more verbal than physical; the pandering of Ophelia by her father is more symbolic than literal, so its interpretation may be missed by the naive. Though I would concur with Hamlet that Polonius employs Ophelia's sexuality for his purposes, Polonius seems not to see himself as a "fishmonger" and Ophelia certainly does not see herself as a whore—it is, again, primarily Hamlet's Interpretation that makes them so, and, as he states later in the scene, "there is nothing either good or bad but thinking makes it so" (II. ii. 249–50).

DAVE SMITH

"Edgar Allan Poe and the Nightmare Ode"

"The Raven," unequivocally the most famous of Poe's small body of poetry, may be among our most famous *bad* poems. Americans are fond of saying we do not read and do not care for poetry. It may be so. Yet Americans commonly recognize Poe's bird as subject of a poem by a weird guy who drank himself to death. Written and published in 1845, in print steadily for 148 years, the stanzas of "The Raven" are sonic flashcards. We may not know Whitman, Dickinson, Frost, or Eliot. But we do know Poe. We know "The Raven."

A poem that might have been designed by Benjamin Franklin, "The Raven" purports to be explained by Poe's "Philosophy of Composition." Poe wrote his essay for crowds smitten by his bird. Interestingly, he does not justify poetry with morality, as Emerson and Whitman would. He pretends to expose the poet's trade. Some recent criticism has seen "The Raven" as a parody of Romantic poems of personal discovery. Perhaps. What Poe leaves unsaid peels, layer by layer, toward two questions answerable only by speculation. The first asks why "The Raven" has for fifteen generations commanded the imaginations of people who have often enough known it to be a bad poem. The second question asks if Poe is a Southern writer. They are related questions.

That "The Raven" is a bad poem is unacceptable to many readers, and Poe people are not swayed much by rational argument. Were they, the plot alone would convict Poe. A man sits late in a storm; he laments a lost lady love; a bird not ordinarily abroad at night, and especially not in severe weather, seeks entrance to the human dwelling; admitted, the bird betrays no fright, no panic, its attitude entirely focused on its host—an invited guest; the bird, then, enters into a ventriloquial dialectic with the host and is domesticated to become an inner voice; we might say it is the voice of the *innerground* as opposed to *underground*, which word means much to the American spirit with its reasons to run, to hide, to contain itself. Action then ceases.

Poe knew this one-man backlot production for the smoker it was. His embrace of gothic machinery includes a terrified, obsessed man, an inhospitable, allegorical midnight in December, a "gifted" animal, extreme emotional states, heavy breathing of both cadence and melodramatic signifers (*grim, gaunt*), the supernatural presence of inexplicables (perfume, Pallas, bird), all to portray a psychic battle in the mind. Poe assembles a version of saloon theater for the mind's ear. But his poem's form emerges from the unbuckled ways of the ode, the loosened metrics of which Poe knew in the work of Keats, Shelley, Coleridge, and Wordsworth. Poe's editorial slush pile was full of their imitators. Odes attracted people because, as Gilbert Highet has said, they "soar and dive and veer as the wind catches their wing." The capacity for passion, personal experience, ambitious public utterance, and a celebrative finish defines the ode. The boosterism, self-infatuation, and lyceum podiums of nineteenth-century America made Poe and the ode a natural match. . . .

Poe was attracted to the ode because, as English Romantics had used it, a classical rigor was maintained while a daring shift had begun which would result in lyric, singular, interior expression. . . .

That the language strategies Poe employs, largely yoked under the braided tropes of reiteration and interrogation, are distantly related to the Pindaric tradition of triadic movement which desires aesthetic completion as well as to the Horatian tradition of monody seems obvious enough. . . .

Poe wanted a rhythmic trance he felt was conducive to an impression of beauty but wanted the trance to dispossess the reader from tranquil stability. He relies on the catalectic, or broken pattern, a missing syllable that "bumps" our progression. Poe exploits a ballad half-line, with its comfortable lyric expectations, its mnemonic power, and its narrative momentum to tell a virtually plotless story, a story entirely interior and psychological. He has telescoped the ballad line into the ode's stanzaic regularity, controlling tropes, public address, and mixed dictions to accomplish what appears a personal complaint, not the ode's meditational tone for imponderables such as art, beauty, life, and death. The tale served by his machinery is the dispossessing myth of lost love, which Poe routinely furnishes with classical allusions to establish eternal resonance.

Our affection for Poe's bird must be, in some measure, due to his adaptations, clunky and juryrigged as they appear. Poe thought his work daring, and it is, in the presentation of the nightmare of absent consolation, or belonging-to. "The Raven" reverberates not with the usual flight-to-vision, return-enlightened celebration, but with the pyschic thrill of confronting despair, isolation, and the utter futility of lovely words. The nightmare vision made the poem an allegory of the darkest self in terror. . . .

Poe finds himself alone in the time and season of human intercourse at its lowest ebb; a time, indeed, when we remind ourselves that we had better change our ways, or else—as Dickens' Scrooge learns. A knock at his door should bring Poe a human visitor, if any, an emissary from the community; yet there is darkness, and then the Raven, the predator. And a predator who seems to know Poe is doomed to an absence of civil intercourse, a silence, and words which echo without effect. Poe understands and declares that even the bird will leave him, as all others have done, as hope has done. With this, Poe's poem has arrived at nightmare, the living isolation from fellowship that popular horror movies have turned into the ghoulish marches of the living dead. If Poe's bird seems deadly, the incantatory rhythms which evoked the birdspell are the forbidding stanzas which clank forth and enchant us as if the bird were enacting some chthonic ritual. The bird, in fact, makes no move after arrival. It does not threaten, seems entirely content, is a creature not unfamiliar to odes. Yet how different from, say, a nightingale so sweetly caged by a form which for Poe permits the witness to come close to his creature and yet keep safe, a glimpsed but not engaged threat. Still, having summoned the raven, Poe cannot so easily deny or repress it: he tells us the bird sits in the forever of that last stanza, a curse neither expiated nor escaped. . . .

This is a basic country-western song and it sells more than we may want to think about. Yet few country-western songs last in admiration or consciousness as "The Raven" does. Poe's addition of the nearly voiceless but intimidating bird employs Gothic machinery to touch unresolved fears of what's under the bed or behind the door. But Poe's bird has the power of knowledge—it knows *us*—and this makes the world a more slippery place than we had thought. It exposes our inside. That is a problem for Poe, and for all of us, because he knows that the inside without connection to an outside is an emptiness, a desert. No self can supply love's support, community sustenance, or the hope we once drew from an outside system. Poe's terrible fable sticks with us because no matter what our intellects conceive, our hearts believe we are alien, each of us, and there is a god-bird that knows it, too. . . .

Poe loved women who died, often violently, diseased. His mother went first; he was two and an orphan. He was taken in and raised as ward of John Allan and his wife Frances, a sickly woman who would die on him, but first there would be Jane Stanard, on whom he had a fourteen-year-old's crush. She was thirty-one when she died insane. Poe suffered the death of three women before he finished being a moody teenaged boy. . . .

Poe felt he had second-class treatment from his foster family. He felt himself orphaned. At eighteen he went to the University of Virginia, where he was undercapitalized and made to feel his inferior circumstance. He was pushed outside that society, too. Returned to Richmond, he found himself an outsider, and he embarked on one of his secret journeys. Wandering, turning up, writing, editing, trying to establish a domestic community, then wandering off—this was the pattern of Poe's life. In every relationship and in every circumstance, he was the outsider, the orphan. . . .

He was an artist, a truth-teller—nothing is more obsessive in his tales than that need. His truth was a nightmare.

If we read "The Raven," despite its absence of specific local details, as an "awareness" of the life of America in 1845, we see that Poe has conjectured the nightmare of the individual cut off from history, abandoned by family, place, and community love. . . .

This story is still the nightmare. Having seen it, Poe celebrates the sensibility or imagination that suffers and knows simultaneously, ultimately the figure of the artist. This figure will sit in the lost garden, knowing its lostness, without explanation, but aware that the change is hopeless and continuous. This poem will, in its late variations, become our outlaw song of the renegade, the cowboy in black, the rebel without a cause. "The Raven" is the drama of nightmare awakening in the American poetic consciousness where there is no history which is not dispossession, little reality to the American promise, and nothing of consequence to place trust in except the song, the ode of celebration. . . .

"The Raven" is the croaking and anguished nightmare ode of allegiance, and we have been finding ourselves in it ever since Poe began hearing "Nevermore."

RYAN D. POQUETTE

"Critical Essay on 'The Purloined Letter'"

Throughout his career, Poe was fascinated by the idea of a "bi-part" soul, half imagination, half reason—an idea that was expressed in many of his works. As Roger Asselineau noted about Poe in his entry for *American Writers*, "His works reflect this double aspect of his personality: the abandonment of the self-destructive romantic artist and the self-control of the conscious and conscientious craftsman." At first glance, somebody looking at Poe's stories may be tempted to label each one as either a horror story—emphasizing imagination—or a detective story, which emphasizes reason. However, with Poe, it is not always that simple, especially with Poe's detective stories. Kenneth Graham notes in the Introduction to *Selected Tales* that Dupin "is the most famous instance of the fusion of the faculties, in his Bi-part soul." The idea of the bi-part soul is especially prevalent in "The Purloined Letter," where Poe uses both characterization and dialogue to emphasize and demonstrate the possibilities of this duality.

While Dupin and the Minister engage in their intellectual battle, employing both their analytical and creative powers against their opponent, the Prefect and the narrator are completely out of the fight altogether.

Out of the four characters in Poe's "The Purloined Letter," only two of them, Dupin and the Minister, embody the author's idea of the "bi-part soul" Consequently, these two men are the political power brokers in the story, engaged in an intellectual war, while the other two—the narrator and the Prefect—trail along behind, oblivious to what is going on around them.

Dupin is a powerful character, who has a reputation for being able to use his logic to solve mysteries that others cannot. As a result, people like the Prefect seek him out when they have a case that gives them "a great deal of trouble." Still, although the Prefect praises him for his logical abilities, Dupin has admittedly romantic and illogical notions, like sitting in the dark when listening to the details of potential cases. Dupin believes that "If it is any point requiring reflection," then they can "examine it to better purpose in the dark." The

Prefect says this is one of Dupin's "odd notions," something that Dupin freely admits is "very true."

The Prefect cannot comprehend why somebody would choose illogical, artistic ideas over purely rational methods, and in fact disdains all things that are creative. The Prefect indicates that although the Minister is "not *altogether* a fool," "he is a poet, which I take to be only one remove from a fool." However, Dupin, who the Prefect respects, admits his own poetic side, saying, "I have been guilty of certain doggerel myself." In fact, it is precisely Dupin's ability to merge both the rational and the creative mindsets that allows him to solve the crime. As Stephen Marlowe notes in the Introduction to *The Fall of the House of Usher and Other Stories*, "[y]et for all his skill as a logician, Dupin is proof that success in detection needs the inspiration of a poet as well."

In Poe's view, both qualities are needed to make an effective criminal, too. Like Dupin, the Minister is both creative and analytical, something that neither the narrator nor the Prefect realizes. Says the narrator, "The Minister I believe has written learnedly on the Differential Calculus. He is a mathematician, and no poet." The Prefect is equally stumped as to the true nature of the Minister, focusing only on his mathematical side when trying to determine how and where the Minister might hide the letter. As Vincent Buranelli notes in *Twayne's United States Authors Series Online*, "The thief . . . successfully hides the letter from the police because he is both a poet and a mathematician." George Colton agrees, noting in *The American Review* that the Minister "identifies his own intellect with that of his opponents, and consequently understands what will be the course they will pursue in ferreting out the place where the letter is concealed." Only Dupin is aware of the truth, and he lets the narrator know of the Minister that "as poet *and* mathematician, he would reason well," and that "my measures were adapted to his capacity."

While Dupin and the Minister engage in their intellectual battle, employing both their analytical and creative powers against their opponent, the Prefect and the narrator are out of the fight altogether. Both men attempt to rely on purely rational thought. The Prefect is logical to a fault, and assumes that the letter can be found by logical methods alone. Says Dupin, "He never once thought it probable, or possible, that the minister had deposited the letter immediately beneath the nose of the whole world." The Prefect cannot comprehend why someone would want to hide something in plain view, so the letter becomes invisible to him.

The narrator is not much better off. Even though Dupin says that the Prefect's searching measures were "the best of their kind," and that they were "carried out to absolute perfection," he lets his friend know that this was not enough. "Had the letter been deposited within the range of their search, these fellows would, beyond a question, have found it." The narrator laughs at this statement, which flies in the face of the rational thought to which he is accustomed. If the Prefect's methods were perfect, then how could they not have found the letter? The narrator at first thinks that Dupin is joking, but soon realizes that Dupin "seemed quite serious in all that he said," and so listens some more. Dupin continues to explain that the defect in the search methods "lay in their being inapplicable to the case and to the man."

The narrator suffers, like the Prefect, from a tendency to rely totally on established systems of thought and past experience. The narrator is unaware of this, even though he had described this quality in the Prefect earlier in the story, when he noted that the Prefect "had the fashion of calling everything 'odd' that was beyond his comprehension, and thus lived amid an absolute legion of 'oddities.'" The narrator, too, is blinded to the possibilities of these "oddities," and so is unable to make the analogies that Dupin makes to solve the case. As Buranelli notes, "Dupin thinks by analogy when he solves the mystery . . . by inferring the behavior of the criminal from a knowledge of how human psychology operates." It is this duality of imagination and reason that places Dupin and the Minister ahead of the other two men.

The way in which dialogue is expressed in the story also helps to illustrate the duality of emotion and rationality. However, in this case, the model is flipped. Whereas in a person's thought processes, a touch of imagination and emotion affected reason in a good way, when dialogue becomes emotional, Poe shows it to be inferior. This is most notable in the dialogue of the Prefect and Dupin. Although the Prefect attempts to remain completely rational and unemotional in his thought processes, he uses emotional language at times. "Oh, good heavens! who ever heard of such an idea?" the Prefect says in response to Dupin's suggestion that the mystery may be too plain. This outburst shows the Prefect's tendency to get emotional in his speech, as well as his tendency, once again, to rule out any possibility that does not match his past experiences. In another instance, when Dupin asks the Prefect if he can describe what the letter looks like, the Prefect says, "Oh, yes!" and immediately pulls out a memo book with the description. His over eagerness in providing information to Dupin reflects his eagerness in his misguided search for the letter.

Dupin, on the other hand, is completely level-headed and rational throughout the tale. He remains calm, even indifferent—as when the narrator tells the Prefect to "proceed" in giving them details about the mystery, and Dupin says, "Or not." This cool behavior is evident throughout the story, as when Dupin gives the Prefect his advice to search again, and the Prefect says that it is not necessary. "I have no better advice to give you," says Dupin. He continues to keep his level demeanor when he tells the Prefect to make out the check to him: "you may as well fill me up a check for the amount mentioned. When you have signed it, I will hand you the letter."

Dupin is also rational as he walks the narrator through the lengthy deductive reasoning process that he used to figure out where the letter was, and as he tells the narrator how he recovered the letter, which could have been a potentially dangerous situation. Dupin notes that the Minister has "attendants devoted to his interests," and that if he had taken the letter outright—as the narrator suggested—Dupin "might never have left the Ministerial presence alive." In other words, although it is Dupin's ability to combine imaginative and rational thought processes that allows him to get inside the Minister's mind and leads to Dupin's discovery of the letter's hiding place, it is his purely rational outside demeanor, reflected in his language, that gives him the means to steal it back safely.

In Poe's "The Purloined Letter," the author illustrates the concept of the bi-part soul—combining reason and imagination in one person—an idea that dominated many of his works. In the story, Poe depicts two poet/mathematicians, embodiments of the idea of the bi-part soul, as people who are intellectually superior to both friends and foes. These creative and rational hybrids become, within *the context of a detective tale, political power brokers who can work the system* to their advantage, by operating outside of conventional society's rational thought and expectations.

CARMEN DELORES HERNÁNDEZ

"Where Is Home? I Want to Go There"

JOC: I grew up for the first fourteen years of my life in Paterson, New Jersey, and then we moved to Augusta, Georgia, where I lived from the time I was 16 till I went to college. I got married and moved to Florida with my husband, and now we're back in Georgia. I don't have a New York perspective; I know the New York–Puerto Rican writers, I teach the Nuyorican writers. They have provided a perspective. The thing is, however, that the Diaspora continues. It didn't get stuck in New York. There are Puerto Ricans all over the United States. I have found Puerto Ricans in Minnesota, in California, in Washington State, all over. There is a Puerto Rican Studies Association that groups professionals from all over the United States, with thirty-two states represented.

My vision is, therefore, a legitimate one. I didn't stop being Puerto Rican by changing locations. I use my language differently from other Puerto Ricans; my perspective has to be colored by those differences. There are all kinds of Puerto Rican writing. We don't have to consider ourselves Nuyorican in order to write. Puerto Rican writing does not come only out of Spanish Harlem. That is a colorful part of our heritage, but it's not the only part.

CDH: What has been your experience in the South, as a Puerto Rican?

JOC: I live on a farm in Georgia right now. It has been in my husband's family for many years. There are some similarities between this atmosphere and Puerto Rico. When I hear John's grandmother talking about the problems of the farm, I am reminded of my grandmother talking about "el cafetal."[1]

CDH: Have you had any problems with prejudice in the South?

JOC: Racism in the South is open. In the North, I'm treated in a particular way in which all Puerto Ricans are treated. Down here I'm more of an oddity, a curiosity. It's not a generalized prejudice. They ask me where I'm from and when I tell them, the reactions vary. I've learned the culture; I can deal with the culture.

CDH: So there are not many Latinos there?

JOC: Oh yes! In Atlanta there are over 100,000 Latinos. They even have a Spanish yellow pages for the phone book. There is much interest in Latino literature, even outside of Atlanta. I was recently invited to do a reading in a little town next to our farm. There are no Latinos there, but they want to learn more about that literature.

CDH: When did you decide to be a writer?

JOC: I started writing when I was already an adult. I had a child, I had finished graduate school and was teaching. I kept looking for what was missing in my life and discovered it was writing. It was a question of finding the time and the place to do it.

CDH: Do you feel you have been influenced by a specific literary tradition in terms of genre, language, and outlook?

JOC: What I realize now influenced me most were the strong storytelling narratives like the fairy tales and folk tales of different countries, and then also hearing my grandmother tell her *cuentos*.[2] I was fascinated by the power of the *cuento* to influence people and to move them and keep their attention, so in most of my stories there is a storyteller, and I use a frame story, like a grandmother telling a story or a woman telling a story.

Later, because I did not have any Latino models—being in the South, I was distant from Latino communities—all I knew was that I needed to read. There are lots of women writers in the South, like Flannery O'Connor and Eudora Welty, who wrap you up in a story. They come from a tradition of storytellers which is amazingly similar to the Puerto Rican *cuento*. "*Te voy a echar un cuento*," *eso era lo que Mamá decía*.[3]

CDH: The tradition of oral transmission is common among minorities, especially among immigrants.

JOC: Of course. When you read Flannery O'Connor, you almost hear her. It wasn't until I was an adult that I discovered Latino writers who do the same thing, but by that time I had been influenced by the storytellers of the South and by my grandmother. In my book, *Silent Dancing*, I go back and forth between Puerto Rico and the United States. Many of the pieces of the book are a combination of memory and imagination.

Immigrants transfer culture by oral transmission. When they came to the United States from Germany or whatever, the only way they had of letting their children know what was important in their culture was to tell stories.

CDH: Oral transmission is also something closely associated with women.

JOC: I think that with women it is solidarity. In *Silent Dancing* I use the way that my grandmother and my aunts talked about personal things when the boys were out playing baseball or something. They would begin to tell a story, and everybody would just laugh and my cousins and I looked at each other dumbfounded. Later I realized they were sharing their pain, sharing their problems and teaching us that there are ways to deal with life that women have, and so it is a way of not only passing the culture but of empowering each other.

When my mother moved to the United States, she took that with her. She would get together with the women in her building and they would do the same thing, except that then it became nostalgic: *cuando estaba en casa hacíamos esto y lo otro*.[4] They passed on not only culture but yearning. I grew up with my mother yearning for *la casa, la mamá, la isla*.[5] It's a part of the immigrant experience, this constant feeling of homesickness that you have; it's something that never quite goes away. That's why my work probably has an element of *Where is home? I want to go there.*

CDH: So Puerto Rico for you is bound up with memory and yearning.

JOC: Yes, and also with the knowledge that I can never come back to *la casa, la mamá y la isla* of my mother's *cuentos*. That doesn't exist anymore.

CDH: Is that the origin of your writing?

JOC: What I'm doing is examining the past and seeing what I can gather to explain where I came from. It's not a nostalgic journey; it's more of an exploration. For me writing is self-discovery.

The origin of my imaginative life was in Mama's *casa* [house]. That's where I learned about the power that women have; it wasn't from taking courses in the university. Another source of power is the language. Because I did not have access to the Spanish language, it appears in my work as a sort of energizing force. *Terms of Survival* is a book in which the titles are in Spanish and the poems are in English. It's like a dictionary. When I hear somebody say "la muerte,"[6] it rings bells in my head in a way that hearing somebody say "death" doesn't, because when I would hear my mother say something like *la muerte llegó a esta casa*,[7] it was a dramatic statement. The same as when they talked about "la maldad" or "el mal"[8] or something like that. Since I didn't grow up using Spanish all the time, Spanish is magical to me.

CDH: Because you only heard it in one context.

JOC: Yes, that's right, so Spanish connects me immediately to memory. People ask me, "Why do you use Spanish words?," and I answer, "Well, they're my magical formula for getting back in touch with my culture."

CDH: Would that be a kind of code-switching?

JOC: Not exactly, no. Code-switching is like what the Nuyoricans do when they mix Spanish and English. What I do is to use Spanish to flavor my language, but I don't switch. The context of the sentence identifies and defines the words, so my language is different from that; it's not code-switching. It is using Spanish as a formula to remind people that what they're reading or hearing comes from the minds and the thoughts of Spanish-speaking people. I want my readers to remember that.

CDH: It's a way of emphasizing the value of words.

JOC: Yes, when you hear a word three times in your life, it's not the same as if you hear it every day. So when my mother said something like "el olvido"[9]—I heard her say something one time about a child who had forgotten his mother, and she said, "el olvido"—that just gave me goose bumps because what she was saying was that he had fallen into this "el olvido" like into a pit or something. For someone who hears that all the time, it doesn't have the same power as for someone like me. Words are my medium.

CDH: So maybe to have two languages at your disposal can turn out to be especially enriching for a writer?

JOC: Definitely. It was hard being a bilingual child, but it opened my mind to two different realities, because I understood my mother's world and the world outside too.

CDH: Yet with Puerto Rican writers it is considered the other way around, both in relation to those who live in the States and those who live on the island. The ambivalence between the two languages is generally considered impoverishing.

JOC: For me it has not been impoverishing at all. You have to eventually choose, because I could not know both languages at the same level, living in one place most of my adult life, so I had to choose English as my literary language because I had more words in English. It's like I had more currency. If I had had more currency to spend in Spanish, I would have written in Spanish. But the longer I stayed away from Spanish, the fewer words I had, so I no longer can make metaphors in Spanish. I can make metaphors forever in English when I'm writing a poem. I don't have intimacy with Spanish anymore. I tell people: "My English is not a political choice, it's a choice of expediency."

CDH: You write poetry and you write prose, and in many books you combine poetry *and* prose. In *Silent Dancing* and in *The Latin Deli* you transmit one experience in both ways. Why is that?

JOC: They are different ways of seeing. Poetry allows you to delve into the depths of language. Prose is looser. Poetry is a probe to plumb the depths of language, to explore the hidden meaning of words.

Poetry is to me the first discipline. It empowers me. In a sense one is like a microscope, and the other like a telescope.

CDH: Do you think of your writing in terms of validating an experience?

JOC: Oh no, not validating. I'm not a politician or a philosopher or a historian; I'm a compulsive storyteller. I can't help myself: I make stories, I write stories, I tell stories. What I'm trying to do is something defined by Robert Frost: when he said "a poem is a momentary stay against confusion." When you write a poem you have a moment in which all confusion ceases and you understand one thing perfectly. I like that idea. When I write a story, I write it to try to see what I understand about a situation and what I don't understand. If it is successful, there's a momentary stay against confusion, at least for me. And if it is that for the reader, too, then we have art. If not, then I have it and it's a diary entry or something. I see art as a bridging, an understanding. I don't see it as speechmaking. I'm a very political person, but my politics are in the stories and the poems.

CDH: You mean your writing has a political result, but it is indirect.

JOC: Yes, we lead political lives. Every choice we make is a political choice, but we don't go around saying "I do this because I'm *estadista* or *nacionalista*."[10] I'm doing this because I'm human and I need it. So my characters make political choices that have to do with keeping their dignity and surviving.

CDH: And if you give an understanding of the Puerto Rican situation, that's political also.

JOC: Right, but that was my situation, so I'm not writing about things just because I'm interested in the political situation, but because it was what I witnessed, what I imagined. And it's not just autobiographical: I put myself in the place of the people. Knowing the people that I knew when I was growing up, I think this is the way they would have behaved. If I have a character modeled after my mother, I know how she feels about the Church, about children, about being *puertorriqueña*, so I use that. It's something that all authors do.

CDH: So in a roundabout way you *are* validating the dignity of Puerto Ricans in the United States.

JOC: Yes, in a roundabout way. I don't sit down in the mornings to write and say *I am validating the experience of Puerto Ricans*, because that would make me arrogant, like a politician. Nobody can give dignity to other people. What I can do is record in my stories what I feel are the true characteristics of the people around me, and if I put them in that context, it is the reader who tells me if I'm validating that experience or not. That's what I hope to hear.

I want to give a vision that is not a stereotypical vision of gangs and fallen women, and so on. That certainly exists but there are also decent men and women, and I've lived with them. We were aware of crime in the streets when we grew up, but my parents knocked themselves out trying to protect us from that. And they succeeded at the expense of their own lives, because my father didn't go to college, but he was determined that we go.

CDH: In a way it must have been a heroic enterprise.

JOC: Yes, but in a way that is not acknowledged. In our world heroics are in the movies, it is people with guns. It doesn't have to do with the fact that my father was one of the most intelligent people I knew and he would have made a fantastic college professor, but he didn't go to college. He had to spend his life alone in the Navy, missing us, getting sadder and sadder each year because he could not afford to have the life I have now. He gave up his future for us and that's tragic.

CDH: Yet that is the way immigrants get ahead in a new country.

JOC: Yes, and my daughter's life is already a hundred percent easier than my life, as mine has been a hundred percent easier than my father's and my mother's.

Some people make it out of the barrio,[11] some people stay in the barrio, but the barrio doesn't have to destroy you. My characters have an inner life; they think, they love, they suffer. I want my readers, no matter from where they are, to relate to them.

1. The coffee plantation.
2. Stories.
3. "I'll toss you a story," that's what my grandmother used to say.
4. "When I was at home we did this and that . . ."
5. Home, mother, the island.
6. Death.
7. Death came into this house.
8. Evil.
9. Forgetfulness,
10. Belonging to the pro-statehood party, or a nationalist with a pro-independence position in relation to the political status of Puerto Rico.
11. Generally used to signify Spanish Harlem but in a wider sense it refers, as used here, to any ghetto-like slum.

Glossary of Literary Terms

Abstract Realism: In drama, the term refers to the use of realistic furniture and props from ordinary life. This technique was used by designer Jo Mielziner in *Death of a Salesman.*

Accentual Meter: See Meter.

Accentual-Syllabic Meter: See Meter.

African American Folkways: Rituals and cultural practices of African Americans that trace back to the days of Southern slavery, but are African in origin. In *The Piano Lesson*, for instance, Berniece Charles and her husband jumped the broom at their wedding.

Allegory, Allegorical: A narrative that unfolds an abstract idea by representing it as an action played out by abstract or symbolically named persons. The allegory's characters, events, and even setting are coherent on a literal level, but at the same time suggest a second, more symbolic, level of significance. Allegories are often didactic, hammering home a particular moral, religious, or political lesson. The morality play *Everyman* is an allegory that dramatizes the state of death (an idea) as a voyage (an action). Everyman is the symbolic actor of this event, and the many personifications who abandon him externalize facets of his identity. In *Hamlet*, the death of the elder Hamlet through poisoning in a garden allegorizes the King's murder as a second fall in Eden.

Alliteration: The repetition of consonant sounds in nearby words, especially the words' beginnings, as in the repetition of the hard *g* in this selection from Sylvia Plath's poem "Daddy":

> Marble-heavy, a ba**g** full of **G**od
> **G**hastly statue with one **g**rey toe
> Bi**g** as a Frisco seal.

Allusion: An indirect or unidentified reference in a text to another work of literature, a historical event, a famous person, etc. The reference is meant to enhance the meaning of the work being read, but allusion is only effective if the reader recognizes the text, event, or person being alluded to. The speaker in T. S. Eliot's "The Love Song of J. Alfred Prufrock," for example, alludes to a famous Shakespeare character when he exclaims, "No! I am not Prince Hamlet, nor was meant to be."

American Gothic: The name Gothic traces back to the Goths, a medieval Germanic tribe, and was associated with a particular style of medieval architecture. Over the centuries, the style itself has been in and out of critical favor, but has always been defined by an elaborate, intricate, absorption in detail, undergirded by a dark fascination with the supernatural or fantastic. American writers Poe ("The Cask of Amontillado" and "The Raven") and Hawthorne ("Young Goodman Brown") tapped into the Gothic tradition. Later, a peculiarly American Gothic style began to develop, which included a darkly comic element, perhaps best evidenced by the painting, *American Gothic.* Batman, who lives in Gotham, presents a continuation of the American Gothic tradition. See Gothic.

Anagogic Metaphor: See Metaphor.

Anaphora: The repeated use of the same word at the beginning of consecutive verses of poetry. See, for example, the repeated use of "who" in Allen Ginsberg's poem "Howl":

> I saw the best minds of my generation destroyed by madness . . .
> . . . .

who poverty and tatters and hollow-eyed and high sat up smoking in the supernatural darkness of cold-water flats floating across the tops of cities contemplating jazz,
who bared their brains to Heaven under the El and saw Mohammedan angels staggering on tenement roofs illuminated,
who passed through universities with radiant cool eyes hallucinating Arkansas and Blake-light tragedy among the scholars of war,
who were expelled from the academies for crazy & publishing obscene odes on the windows of the skull,
who cowered in unshaven rooms in underwear, burning their money in wastebaskets and listening to the Terror through the wall. . . .

Annotate, Annotation: A comment or notation added to a literary text by the reader. Annotations can be used to explain or discuss particular words, phrases, or references; to add definitions; or to provide historical information.

Antagonist: The character who opposes the protagonist.

Anthropomorphic, Anthropomorphize: To attribute a human personality to anything nonhuman. See also Personification.

Antithesis: The joining together or juxtaposition of seemingly contradictory words or ideas. A well-known example comes from the first line of Hamlet's soliloquy, "To be or not to be."

Archaic (diction): Words and language characteristic of an earlier period or style. Shakespeare, Hawthorne, and other authors' use of words such as "thee," "thou," and "hath," for example, may seem archaic to modern readers.

Assonance: The repetition of vowel sounds in nearby words, as in this selection from Sylvia Plath's poem "Daddy":

In the p***i***cture I have of you,
A cleft ***i***n your ch***i***n ***i***nstead of your foot
But no less a dev***i***l for that . . .

Atmosphere: The mood (e.g., depressing, optimistic, hopeful) of a literary text. The setting often contributes to the atmosphere.

Aubade: A poem or song about lovers at dawn. The rising sun may signal that the lovers must go their separate ways. A warning about the approach of dawn is often given by a third person in the refrain.

Avant-garde: A French military term meaning front guard or vanguard. Avant-garde was first used as an artistic term in reference to a specific artistic movement in nineteenth-century France, but has since become a general term that is used to describe any literary, artistic, or musical work that is aggressively daring or innovative.

Ballad: A story in poetic form, which often is sung. "Bonny Barbara Allan," "Sir Patrick Spens," and "Lord Randall" are examples of early ballads. Dudley Randall's "Ballad of Birmingham" offers a more contemporary example. The literary ballad is exemplified by John Keats's "La Belle Dame sans Merci."

Beat Generation, Beat Movement: A counterculture group of poets and artists who eventually became involved with the peace and environmental movements and drug cultures of the 1960s and 1970s.

Bildungsroman: A coming of age story, such as James Joyce's "Araby" or John Updike's "A&P."

Black Power Movement: A 1960s initiative that developed from the civil rights movement, but stressed black self-reliance and solidarity as much as political and economic equality. The movement is associated politically with Malcolm X and aesthetically with playwright Amiri Baraka and others. August Wilson was influenced by the Black Power movement, about which he writes in his 1996 speech to the Theatre Communications Group National Conference, *The Ground on Which I Stand*.

Blank Verse: A poem written in iambic pentameter without end rhymes. "Ulysses," by Alfred, Lord Tennyson, is written in blank verse.

Cadence: A term for the underlying rising and falling rhythms of speech. Cadence is often used to describe the rhythms of free verse such as those found in Whitman's poetry and in the poetry of later adherents of open or free verse, such as Pound and Williams. Any rhythm not based on syllable counts and rhymes.

Canon, Canonical: The term *canon* can be used to refer to a collection of works indisputably written by a particular author or to refer to the broader literary canon, the collection of texts of authors whose works are commonly considered classics, are most frequently included in textbooks or anthologies, and are most often referred to by academics, literary critics, and historians.

Carpe Diem: A Latin phrase meaning "seize the day." A literary work with a *carpe diem* theme or motif suggests that because life is so brief and time passes so quickly one must make every moment as pleasurable as possible. The suggestion to seize the day is often made by a male speaker to his reluctant lover, as in Herrick's "To the Virgins, To Make Much of Time" and Marvell's "To His Coy Mistress."

Catachresis: See Metaphor.

Catharsis: A term used by Aristotle in the *Poetics* to explain the discrepancy between tragedy's usually disastrous conclusion and the audience's feelings of relief and exhilaration at the end of the drama. The catharsis purges the audience of pity (caused by the fact that the hero is too good to suffer his terrible fate) and fear (the feeling that follows the recognition that we too could suffer that fate). The purgation produces a feeling of pleasure and satisfaction.

Cavalier Poets: The Cavalier poets wrote in the mid-seventeenth century and are associated with Charles I and his exiled son. They are cavalier in their rejection of both Christian chivalry and poetic conventions. Their poems are marked by straightforward and colloquial language that is used to celebrate everyday life and love, not an idealized paradise and an unattainable love. Robert Herrick's "To the Virgins, To Make Much of Time" is a characteristic Cavalier poem.

Character, Characters: In general, the actors who engage in the events of a literary text. Minor or secondary characters are characters who are described with fewer details and who generally partake in less of the action. In short stories, a static character is one-dimensional and requires minimal description or development, since he or she remains relatively unchanged for the duration of the plot. A dynamic character, on the other hand, is multidimensional and complex and often undergoes some sort of change as the plot progresses. Because drama unfolds in time, dramatic characters tend to be dynamic. Even an allegorical character such as Everyman acquires knowledge of himself. In Aristotelian drama, there are specific guidelines for the tragic hero, who falls from high estate to death as a result of a wrong choice or mistake (hamartia).

Chiasmus: A mirrored inversion of words or phrases; a grammatical construction in which the first part is paralleled in reverse by the second part (**AB BA**). The final lines of Keats's "Ode on a Grecian Urn" contain an example of a chiasmus:

When old age shall this generation waste,
Thou shalt remain, in midst of other woe
Than ours, a friend to man, to whom thou say'st,

A B B A
Beauty is truth, truth beauty—that is all
Ye know on earth, and all ye need to know.

Chorus, Choric Character: The figures in ancient Greek drama who collectively voice the common opinion on the dramatic action and express traditional moral attitudes. In later drama, the chorus is often one character, either separated from the main action in a dramatic frame (as in Tennessee Williams's *The Glass Menagerie*) or embedded in the action as a dramatic character.

Climax: A crucial turning point in the plot of a literary work. See also Perepeteia.

Closet Drama: A play that is written in the same form as any other drama (e.g., including dialogue and stage directions), but intended by the author to be read, either silently or aloud in groups, rather than performed on stage.

Comedy: A work of fiction that interests and amuses us without creating serious or prolonged dramatic tension or suspense. With comedy, we expect a happy ending, often featuring a marriage or reconciliation. Most, if not all, comedy targets incongruities between expectation and reality. The common element between the many types of comedy—Romantic Comedy, Black Comedy, Comedy of Manners, Comedy of Humors, Farce—is this hopeful, but clear, focus on discrepancies between the god and the animal in all humans. Shakespeare's *The Taming of the Shrew* is a good example of comedy.

Complaint: A traditional theme of lyric poetry, a complaint is often directed at an inattentive lover, but can take on any topic, such as Chaucer's "Complaint to His Purse." Modern blues songs often echo this theme.

Conceit: Literally a "concept," a poetic conceit is a highly elaborated, often ingenious metaphor. The surprising nature of the equation between two dissimilar things is supported and justified by the clever logic of the elaboration. The metaphysical conceit, which Samuel Johnson famously described as the "yoking together" of dissimilar things "by violence," draws its comparisons from a wide range of subjects, including commerce, religion, and philosophy. Anne Bradstreet, John Donne, and George Herbert use metaphysical conceits in their poetry. See Metaphysical Poetry.

Concrete Poetry: Concrete poetry is also graphic art; it uses the visual appearance of a poem to further develop a theme. Richard Wilbur's "Junk" or George Herbert's "Easter Wings" are quite different examples of this type of poetry. See also Pattern Poem.

Confessional Poetry: A type of poetry that deals with intimate subject matter and experiences from the poet's own life. In the modern period, such poetry was often written as a response to and a rejection of the insistence on impersonality put forward by T. S. Eliot and others.

Conflict: A point in the plot during which the protagonist is challenged in some way. Conflict can apply to all literary genres, but is most prevalent in classical drama. In some of the best works, the protagonist must choose not merely between good and evil, but between two good values that nevertheless have become irreconcilably opposed to one another.

Connotation: The associations or emotions suggested by a particular word apart from that word's explicit definition. The word *spring*, for example, draws to mind such associations as renewal, rebirth, abundance, and growth. See also Denotation.

Consonance: The repetition of the same or similar consonant sounds in nearby words preceded by different vowel sounds, often found in the final or accented syllable. See, for example, the "s" consonance in Robert Frost's poem, "The Silken Tent":

She i*s* a*s* in a field a silken tent
At midday when the sunny summer bree*ze*

Has dried the dew and all its rope*s* relent,
So that in guy*s* it gently sway*s* at ea*se* . . .

Couplet: In a poem, two consecutive lines with the same end rhyme. The term heroic couplet was applied to poems written in couplets during the seventeenth century because couplets were used frequently in epic and heroic drama.

Creative Nonfiction: An approach to memoir that employs the narrative techniques—e.g., characterization, plot, and setting—that typically are associated with fiction.

Dactylic Meter: A poetic meter that features dactyls (a three-syllable foot consisting of a hard-soft-soft pattern, usually marked as / ˘ ˘). The first two lines of Alfred, Lord Tennyson's "The Charge of the Light Brigade" depend on a variation of dactylic meter:

/ ˘ ˘ / ˘ ˘
Half a league, half a league,
/ ˘ ˘ / ˘
Half a league onward,

Denotation: A word's literal or dictionary meaning. The denotation of spring, for example, is the season between winter and summer, which, in the northern hemisphere, runs from the month of March through the month of May. See also Connotation.

Dialect: A form of nonstandard English spoken by members of a particular region or socioeconomic class. Toni Cade Bambara's characters, in the short story "The Lesson," use the dialect of urban African Americans, for example, and in August Wilson's *The Piano Lesson*, Boy Willie uses a Southern rural African American dialect, but Avery and Berniece adapt their speech to their Northern, and largely white, surroundings.

Dialogue: A literary work in the form of a conversation; in drama, dialogue is the basis by which character is established and the plot advanced. August Wilson is noted for his skill in creating dialogue that is at once realistic and almost musical.

Diction: An author's choice of words. Because they are often limited in the length and form of their genre, poets, in particular, are concerned with their diction. See also Syntax.

Didactic Literature: Literature that seeks directly to inculcate moral values or to provide instruction. The morality play *Everyman* is an example, as are parables and fables and other children's literature.

Dramatic Frame: See Frame.

Dramatic Irony: See Irony.

Dramatic Lyric: A poem depicting a dramatic situation that the reader has access to only via the speech or monologue of a single character. John Donne's "The Flea" is a good example. The dramatic lyric differs from Robert Browning's dramatic monologue "My Last Duchess" in that the reader's attention falls less on the speaker than on the unfolding of the dramatic situation itself.

Dramatic Monologue. See Monologue.

Dramatic Unities: Aristotle's *Poetics* is usually cited as the source for the idea that a play should have unity of time (represent eight hours or a single day), unity of place (take place in a single location), and unity of action (be centered around a single crucial idea).

Dynamic Character: See Character.

Elegy, Elegiac: Elegiac poems contain mournful and meditative subject matter, particularly laments on death. Tichborne's, "My prime of youth is but a frost of cares," Walt Whitman's "O Captain! my Captain!," A. E. Housman's "To an Athlete Dying Young," and Randell "Jarrell's "The Death of the Ball Turret Gunner" are examples of elegiac poems.

Ellipsis, Elliptical: To leave out words normally required to complete a sentence. The adjective *elliptical* is used when describing an author who is using ellipsis, that is, who is leaving out words.

End-stopped: In a poem, a line that ends with a natural pause in the sense of the sentence, often signaled with a semicolon or a period.

Enjambment: In a poem, the carrying over of a sentence from one line to the next.

Envoy: Derived from the French term for a diplomatic messenger, the envoy of a poem, similar in function to a novel's epilogue, is a conventional final stanza that closes a *ballade* or a sestina. It may provide a concluding summary or send a message directly to a reader or patron. In Chaucer's "Complaint to His Purse," a *ballade*, the poem's envoy is directed to King Henry IV.

Epic: A lengthy, serious narrative poem, usually written in a lofty and elevated style, about a hero and the great deeds of cosmic significance that he accomplishes, despite the suffering and loss he inevitably experiences.

Epigram, Epigrammatic: A brief, witty statement in prose or verse. John Donne, Ben Jonson, and Robert Herrick are known for their use of the verse epigram. The dialogue of Oscar Wilde's play *The Importance of Being Earnest* is also epigrammatic in quality.

Epigraph: A quotation prefacing a longer work (e.g., poem, short story, or play) that offers a thematic perspective on that work.

Epiphany: A sudden revelation or visionary moment, such as Arturo's realization that he is in no mood anymore to run away after he has heard about Old Johann's life in Judith Ortiz Cofer's short story "Arturo's Flight."

Episodic: A work that consists of loosely connected occurrences.

Epistolary: In short fiction and novels, a narrative consisting of letters.

Epithalamium: A poem written to celebrate marriage.

Epitaph: From the Greek (*epi* = upon + *taph* = tomb), an epitaph is, literally, the memorial inscription on a tomb. As a literary term, an epitaph is any short memorial, poetic or otherwise, written in commemoration of the dead. This term is often confused with epigram, which is a brief quotation introducing a literary work, and epithet, which is an adjective used to point out a distinctive characteristic of a person or thing.

Epithet: An adjective or adjectival phrase that describes a notable characteristic of a person or idea. Caedmon's Hymn and Brian Henry's "Garage Sale" are structured around a series of epithets.

Ethos: The reputation or credibility an author or speaker establishes through speaking or writing.

Expressionist Drama: A movement most properly associated with German literature and art, expressionism is most simply a reaction against realism. Expressionist literature recognizes that objective reality cannot mirror inner states. The protagonists of expressionist drama tend to be alienated from society and are subject to psychological analysis. American dramatists who can be considered within the tradition of expressionism include Arthur Miller and Tennessee Williams.

Fable: A moralistic story, often featuring animals with human characteristics, that explicitly presents lessons about everyday behavior or manners.

Farce: A comedy or parts of a comedy that depend for humor on highly improbable situations, coarse gags and jokes, mistaken identities, and exaggerated characters. Often the plot line of a farce, because it is driven by the next gag or joke, is nonsensical. Parts of Shakespeare's comedy, *Taming of the Shrew*, can be considered as farce, as can much of the comedy found in modern television and film.

Feminine Ending: See Iambic Pentameter.

Feminine Rhyme. See Rhyme.

Feminism or Feminist: Works of literature that advocate women's social and political rights, highlight women's cultural achievements, and expose factors that limit women's social and cultural equality.

Figure of Speech: A noticeable alteration from ordinary diction, or common use of specific words and phrases. Although figures are common in poetry, they are also part of our everyday linguistic resources. There are two types of figure, tropes and schemes.

First-person Narrator: See Narrator.

Flashback: A familiar device in film, drama, and fiction, the flashback is a scene or narrative inserted into the main plot that explains events that took place before the beginning of the action. Sometimes, the information is presented as a dream, memory, or reminiscence. Flashbacks occur in Arthur Miller's *Death of a Salesman* to explain the father's alienation from his sons. Flashbacks are also crucial to understanding the relation of mother and daughter in Marsha Norman's *'Night, Mother.*

Foil: A minor or secondary character that is a contrast to or opposite of the main character in personality, attitude, or action. Hamlet's foil is Laertes, whereas Ismene is Antigone's foil.

Folklore: Stories and social customs that are initially passed along orally, rather than in writing, in such familiar forms as riddles, songs, superstitions, or nursery rhymes.

Folktale: A story or legend that reveals cultural superstitions and social rituals or draws on fantastic elements such as giants and witches, extraordinary transformations, and legendary heroes.

Foreshadowing: The use of signs (words, actions, gestures, etc.) to signal or look forward to a future event.

Frame; Dramatic Frame: Primarily in drama but sometimes in other genres, the device of representing the principal action as a fiction, presented and seen from the perspective of the characters in the fame. The Christopher Sly plot that frames William Shakespeare's *The Taming of the Shrew* is one example, although the frame device is dropped after a few scenes. The framing of *The Glass Menagerie* as Tom's memories also uses this device.

Free Verse: A type of verse that is not ordered in metrical form, often contains random line and stanza lengths, and typically lacks rhymes. See also Open Form.

Genre: A literary form such as a drama, poem, short fiction or short story, or novel. Different works of literature within any genre share a recognizable set of characteristics, although both authors and critics often seek to stretch generic boundaries. For instance, dramas are enacted on stage live before an audience, although closet dramas, which share the basic elements of other plays, are meant to be read. Short stories are defined by their length, although very short stories, such as Margaret Atwood's "Gertrude Talks Back," challenge that definition.

Gothic: A literary genre associated with horror, gloom, mystery, violence, and supernatural occurrences. See also American Gothic.

Grotesque: The use of the bizarre or of freakish and ridiculously absurd characteristics. The grotesque often revolves around physical abnormalities in characters (such as Joy/Hulga's artificial leg in Flannery O'Connor's "Good Country People") or stylized settings.

Haiku: A strict poetic form that originated in Japan made up of seventeen syllables ordered into three lines of five, seven, and five syllables, respectively.

Hamartia: The mistake or error committed by the tragic hero of Aristotelian drama that leads to his (or, in the case of Antigone, her) downfall. Later writers have mistranslated this word as "tragic flaw," which wrongly implies not a bad choice on the protagonist's part, but some inherent moral deficit or psychological excess. See also Character.

Harlem Renaissance: A creative movement during the 1920s and 1930s that was centered in Harlem and that gave African American writers, artists, and performers recognition as vital participants in American culture as they revealed many previously unknown aspects of black life through a black perspective.

Head Note: Head notes precede literary works and often provide biographical information about the author as well as additional information about the author and the work.

Heroic Couplet: See Couplet.

Hyperbole: An overstatement or exaggeration for effect. A hyperbole in common speech might be "I died a thousand deaths" as a way of expressing embarrassment. If we think Hamlet is not serious about wanting to die, we might interpret his statement, "O that this too too sullied flesh would melt," as hyperbole.

Hubris: In Greek drama, a term for a state of mind that has been translated most commonly as "pride." But hubris actually covers a broad range of excessive behaviors, from physical rape to overconfidence.

Iambic Pentameter: A ten-syllable regular poetic line composed of five iambs (a soft-hard pattern usually marked as ˘ /). When the meter is exact and ends on a strong beat, the line has a masculine ending. When there is an extra unstressed or soft beat (and therefore a total of eleven syllables), the line has a feminine ending.

Iambic Tetrameter: An eight-syllable regular poetic line composed of four iambs (a soft-hard pattern usually marked as ˘ /).

Identification: The effect of experiencing the similarity and difference between a literary and a real situation. Identification is often achieved through pathos, or a complex sense of identification with literary characters, as Aristotle's *Poetics* describes in its discussion of the tragic hero. But in other cases, identification may work through other elements, such as setting or language.

Image: A concrete literary representation of a sensory experience. A description that uses words evoking sight, sound, touch, smell, or taste to represent a thing or a moment. Images can be both literal and figurative; Adrienne Rich evokes the figurative image of a deep sea diver in "Diving into the Wreck," and William Carlos Williams, an Imagist poet, evokes the literal, still-life portrait of a wheelbarrow in the rain in "The Red Wheelbarrow."

Imagism, Imagist: A poetic movement led by Ezra Pound that called for an abandonment of traditional verse forms and subjects and called for precise, unemotional presentations of images and clear, concentrated descriptions of sensations.

Interpretation, Interpreting: The opposite of experiencing art and literature. After or apart from literary experience, interpretation focuses on such questions as "What does a work mean?" or "How does it communicate its meaning?" Interpretation often focuses on highly symbolic or ambiguous moments, seeking to unpack their meaning and significance to the work as a whole.

Intertextuality: In literary criticism, the idea that literary texts make reference to one another. These references can range from direct citation or quotation to allusion to strong structural and thematic similarity.

Irony, Ironic: A literary device in which the assumed state of affairs contrasts with the true state of affairs, or when there is a discrepancy between the apparent situation and the actual situation. Verbal irony is saying the opposite of what one means, often by understatement. It sometimes shades into sarcasm. An example would be Kate's willingness to call the sun the moon in Shakespeare's *The Taming of the Shrew*. Dramatic irony is a plot device in which the audience has knowledge that is denied to the main characters; an example would be Hamlet's decision not to kill Claudius at prayer based on the false assumption that his soul would go to heaven. Dramatic irony can also refer to a thematic contrast between characters or dramatic situations, sometimes for the purpose of parody—an example might be the contrast between the true and false Vincentios in *The Taming of the Shrew*.

Italian Sonnet: Otherwise known as the Petrarchan Sonnet. See Sonnet.

Jargon: A specialized vocabulary shared and understood by a limited group of people.

Limerick: A playful or nonsense verse containing five lines. The first, second, and fifth lines rhyme and have the same meter and length; the same is true of the third and fourth lines. This rhythm can be approximated with the rhythm of the nursery rhyme, "Hickory Dickory Dock."

Limited-omniscient Narrator: See Narrator.

Limited Third-person Narrator: See Narrator.

Local Color: A literary movement or effect characterized by the authors' detailed presentation of the characteristic setting, customs, clothing, and manner of speaking for a particular region. Mark Twain employs local color in his short story "The Celebrated Jumping Frog of Calaveras County."

Lyric: A short poem—originally meant to be sung with an accompaniment of a lyre, a musical instrument—that expresses a single speaker's state of mind, thoughts, and feelings.

Magic Realism, Magical Realism: A narrative mode of examining history, culture, and politics through an exploration of everyday events, as well as the imaginative dimensions of magic and myth. This movement is often associated with Latin American and Hispanic writers such as Gabriel García Márquez and Judith Ortiz Cofer.

Marginalia: The comments you write along the margins of the text as you read.

Marxist Criticism: A critical theory based on the economic and cultural ideology of nineteenth-century revolutionary and philosopher Karl Marx. Marxist literary critics argue that works of literature are inherently embedded within their historical, social, and economic contexts and that they reflect the values and ideals of the dominant social class of the time period in which they were written. In other words, cultural conditions and economic means of production influence, if they do not absolutely determine, what can and cannot be written about.

Masculine Ending: See Iambic Pentameter.

Masculine Rhyme: See Rhyme.

Memoir: As opposed to autobiography, which is an account of an author's own life, a memoir is an account of the events and people that the author witnessed.

Metadrama, Metadramatic: A play or moment in a play where the fictional nature of the plot is made apparent to the audience, encouraging in them self-consciousness about the artificial nature of the drama as an imitation of life. One example might be the instructions that Hamlet gives the visiting actors when he tells them not to saw the air with their gestures or let the actor who plays the Clown ad-lib with the spectators. Shakespeare's own audience would be aware that the company clown, Will Kemp, was famous for his unscripted banter with audience members. See also Metafiction.

Metafiction: Coined in 1970 by William H. Gass in his essay "Philosophy and the Form of Fiction," the term *metafiction* refers to fiction that is self-reflexive about its construction and its effects on the reader; in other words, metafiction is fiction about fiction. See also Metadrama and Postmodernism.

Metaphor: A form of figurative language in which a comparison between two things is understood; a metaphor is distinguished from a simile, in which the comparison is stated through the use of "like" or "as." The metaphor is supposedly based on a similarity between the two entities being compared (a strained metaphor is called a catachresis), but some linguists believe that in metaphor the tenor (the object being described—e.g., "love") and vehicle (the object being compared to the original object or tenor—e.g., a "rose") gain meaning through the interaction of their qualities. Some cognitive linguists believe that certain basic metaphors (such as life is a journey) are a product of human development and are essential to human meaning-making rather than merely poetic or decorative. Anagogic metaphor is an allegorical metaphor that leads to a transcendental or mystical truth that cannot be expressed in simple words alone; see Wallace Stevens's "Of Mere Being."

Metaphysical Conceit: See Conceit, Metaphysical Poetry.

Metaphysical Poetry: A group of seventeenth-century poets associated most closely with John Donne, who spurned the strict metrical conventions and idealized representations of love and humanity in Elizabethan poetry and embraced instead colloquial, often ironic or unusual, descriptions and metrically irregular lines. Poems by such writers such as John Donne, Andrew Marvell, and George Herbert are stylistically intricate, consider philosophical and spiritual subjects rationally, and often make what were considered unnatural comparisons (e.g., Marvell's reference to "vegetable love" in "To His Coy Mistress").

Meter: Meaning "to count," the term *meter* refers to the regular, rhythmic units that define a poem. Accentual meter, most common in English language poetry before Chaucer, counts the number of stresses in a line, regardless of the number of syllables. See also Metrical Foot, Feet, and Rhythm. Syllabic meter counts the number of syllables in a line. Accentual-syllabic meter sets up the expectation of a standard number of both accents and syllables within each line. Old English poetry is accentual; Dana Gioia's "California Hills in August" also can be considered as employing accentual meter (in a 3-3-4-3-3-4 pattern). Any of Shakespeare's *Sonnets* would be an example of syllabic meter. See also Rhythm.

Metrical Foot, Feet: The basic unit of measurement for poetry, consisting of a prescribed number of stressed and unstressed syllables. In iambic pentameter, for instance, a foot consists of two syllables, the first unstressed and the second stressed (i.e., ˘ /). A line of iambic pentameter verse therefore has five feet and ten syllables.

Minor Character: See Character.

Mnemonic: A system of words or letters used to enhance memory. Rhyme, rhythm, and repetition are all mnemonic aids commonly found in poetry.

Modernism, Modern: Literary works dating from the late nineteenth and early twentieth century, particularly the period after World War I, that are characterized by discontinuous and disconnected narratives, stream of consciousness, and other intentional subversions of the basic conventions of classical models and forms, as well as heightened reference to the creative process and to literature as a symbolic and complex construction of reality.

Monologue: A long speech by a single character, usually but not exclusively in drama. Margaret Atwood's very short story "Gertrude Talks Back" is a monologue intended to answer the diatribe Shakespeare's Hamlet levels against his mother in the closet scene of Act 4. A dramatic monologue is a lyric form perfected by Robert Browning (e.g., "My Last Duchess"). A single person, clearly distinguished from the poet, gives a speech that takes up the space of the whole poem; he speaks to an absent audience, whose reactions and interventions we must infer from the speaker's statements and comments. The reader's attention focuses less on the subject matter (what the speaker says) than on the speaker's character (how he presents his subject), often through ironic revelations of a discrepancy between his self-representation and of the speaker's true character. Related genres are the dramatic lyric and soliloquy.

Mood: See Atmosphere.

Morality Play: Unlike the medieval mystery plays and saints' plays, which were concerned with important events in Christian history from the Creation to the Last Judgment, the morality play offers an allegory of the life of Man. A morality play communicates general truths about the human condition in the personification of an Everyman. Morality plays, like sermons and other didactic literature, seek to educate audiences about temptations of the secular world that can endanger their chances for salvation.

Motif: A recurring theme, idea, or pattern in a literary work. Herrick's "To the Virgins" has a *carpe diem*, or "seize the day" motif.

Multiculturalism, Multicultural Literature: An alternative version of American cultural categories (particularly race, class, gender, and sexual orientation) that emphasizes the contributions groups other than the dominant group have made to America.

Muse: Traditionally, the nine muses were the daughters of Mnemosyne (memory). Each muse was the source of inspiration for humans in the following areas: Clio, history; Urania, astronomy; Calliope, epic or elegy; Melpomene, tragedy; Euterpe, music or flute playing; Erato, lyrics and love poems; Terpsichore, choral lyrics and dances; Thalia, comedy; and Polyhymnia, sacred music and dance. Some of the poets in this collection call on a muse for inspiration, either a traditional muse or a muse of the poet's choice.

Myth, Mythic, Mythology: The Greek word *mythos* means any story or plot, but has now come to mean a fiction used to explain worldly phenomena (e.g., the Persephone myth to explain the changing of the seasons) or cultural origins (e.g., the myth of Romulus and Remus to explain the origins of Rome). Myths are related to social rituals and customs. Many poets from the Medieval period (Chaucer) through the twentieth century (T. S. Eliot, H. D., Louise Glück) have used myths to generate fictions or to explore the contemporary human condition. Myth critics such as Robert Graves (*The White Goddess*) investigate the way in which literary works are modeled on mythic patterns.

Myth Critics: See Myth.

Narrator: The figure or voice who narrates a short story, or, in drama, a figure who talks to the audience, giving information about present or past events. A third-person narrator recounts the details from a position outside the story and refers to the characters by name or as "he," "she," or "they." A third-person narrator may be an omniscient narrator, a narrator who has access to the internal thoughts and feelings of all the characters and who can observe and comment on events happening in more than one place or at more than one time. A limited-omniscient third-person narrator may have the ability to access the thoughts and feelings of only one or two of the characters. A limited third-person narrator has no access to the internal thoughts and feelings of the characters and can only report and comment on his or her observations of a character's external actions and speech. A first-person narrator uses the pronoun "*I*" when speaking about him- or herself and refers to the other characters by name or "he," "she," or "they." A reliable narrator can be trusted to observe and report events accurately without obvious bias. An unreliable narrator's account, on the other hand, cannot be accepted at face value.

Naturalism, Naturalist Drama: Often conflated with realism in drama, naturalist drama puts more emphasis on social and historical setting and on character development. As a historical movement best represented by Henrik Ibsen's plays, naturalism reached its peak in the 1880s and 1890s. Naturalism demanded as well some concrete changes in theatrical practice, in particular a less broad and artificial style of acting.

Nature Writing: A work that presents nature as an incontrovertible influence on humanity and privileges descriptions of nature as much as descriptions of other characters.

New Formalism: A term designating a group of younger poets who experiment with rhyme, meter, and traditional poetic forms such as the sonnet, sestina, and villanelle. Dana Gioia's essay "Can Poetry Matter?" seeks to broaden the audience for poetry by returning to these traditional poetic concerns.

Octave: A stanza or poetic unit of eight lines. See Petrarchan Sonnet and Sonnet.

Ode: A long, formally complicated type of poetry characterized by seriousness of tone and subject matter and a stanza form that is internally consistent. Odes are often linked with public occasions, often involving important figures of state. John Keats's "Ode on a Grecian Urn" offers one example of the ode. Edgar Allan Poe's "The Raven" is an ode that employs multiple poetic techniques, including internal rhyme.

Omniscient Narrator: See Narrator.

Ontology, Ontologoical: The science or study of being.

Open Form: Another term for free verse.

Ottava Rima: In a poem, an eight-line stanza in iambic pentameter rhyming *abababcc*.

Oxymoron: See Paradox.

Parable: A story that provides nonspecific lessons about human behavior or imparts generalized religious, spiritual, or moral guidance. Many parables from the New Testament or Christian Bible are rather puzzling in literal terms and make sense only when their spiritual meaning is understood.

Paradox: A statement that seems, at first glance, to be illogical, but upon reflection makes sense. The metaphysical poets, such as John Donne, explored paradox in both secular (e.g., "The Flea") and sacred poetry (e.g., "Batter My Heart"). A dramatic example of paradox might be Hamlet's reiterated taunt to Claudius, in which he tells the King that since man and wife are one flesh by virtue of the marriage ceremony, then Claudius is Hamlet's mother. A condensed paradox (usually reduced to two words or a very short phrase) is an oxymoron: for instance, Antigone's crime of "holy reverence."

Parallelism: Using the same grammatical structure to link ideas, actions, or phrases.

Paraphrase: A rewording of an original text.

Parody: A work of literature that wittily mimics the style of another work, generally to achieve a comical or critical effect. Walter Ralegh's "The Nymph's Reply," for example, is a parody of Christopher Marlowe's "The Passionate Shepherd," and Anthony Hecht's "The Dover Bitch" is a parody of Mathew Arnold's "Dover Beach."

Passive Voice: A sentence formation in which the subject is acted upon, either in a *by* phrase following the verb or by omitting the actor entirely. The actor in this active voice sentence is clear: "I wrecked the car." In this passive voice sentence, "The car was wrecked," it is unclear who is responsible for the wreckage. Passive sentence constructions should generally be avoided because they not only conceal who is responsible for an action, but they also are harder for readers to understand.

Pastoral: Pastoral writing depicts rural life, particularly associated with shepherds and idyllic, uncomplicated natural settings.

Pastorelle: A medieval wooing dialogue poem in which an upper-class male tries to get a shepherdess to go out in the fields with him, but is usually interrupted by her brother or mother.

Pathos, Pathetic: In Greek, a term referring to the passions, or suffering, pathos is the quality of a literary work that evokes sympathy in the reader. In Aristotle's *Poetics*, pathos is aroused by the fact that the tragic hero does not deserve his harsh fate.

Patriarchy, Patriarchal: A commitment to the view that culture is controlled by men, keeping women in subordinate positions and relegating their points of view and values to an inferior status. Susan Glaspell's *Trifles* dramatizes the shortcoming of the patriarchal mindset.

Pattern Poem: Verse in which the lines are arranged to imitate a physical object or shape. George Herbert's "Easter Wings" offers a good example. See also Concrete Poetry.

Peripeteia: The turning point of an ancient or classical tragedy, in which the fortune of the tragic hero (and many other characters) takes a turn toward the worse or toward tragedy. See also Climax.

Persona: Literally, in Latin, the poet's "mask." The persona is the voice and tone the poet creates that is best able to convey a poem's ideas and themes.

Personification, Personify: A figure of speech that attributes human characteristics or emotions to nonhuman objects, beings, or ideas. Critics often see personifications as the rational transformation of mythic figures. See also Anthropomorphize.

Petrarchan Sonnet: Otherwise known as the Italian Sonnet. See Sonnet.

Picaresque: A literary text in which the life and exploits of a character with loose morals are recounted.

Plagiarism: The use of someone else's ideas or words without proper documentation. To avoid even the appearance of plagiarism, you must fully document all of your sources.

Plot: The events or actions of a literary work, which have been selected from the story (sum total of events that lie behind a particular plot) and then artistically shaped and arranged in a meaningful way. In Aristotle's *Poetics*, plot or action is the basic building block of drama.

Point of View: The perspective of the persona or narrator who recounts the poem or story.

Postcolonialism, Postcolonial: The study of effects of imperialism on the former colonies of Europe that rejects Eurocentric depictions of the colonial cultures as marginal and inferior.

Postmodernism: Participating in a literary movement dating from the end of World War II, postmodern works draw attention to themselves as works of fiction and privilege ambiguity over "totalization" and contingencies over truths. They reject "grand narratives" in favor of "little histories."

Prewriting: The early, informal, idea-generating phase of the writing process.

Prop: In drama, an object called for in the plot that is seen by the audience. The glass menagerie, in the play of that name, or the piano in *The Piano Lesson* are stage props that also take on symbolic meaning as the plot develops.

Prose Poem: A relatively short prose work that exploits all the available poetic devices without incorporating line breaks. Forché's "The Colonel" is a good example of this type of poem.

Protagonist: The central character with whom the reader is meant to empathize. See also Antagonist.

Psychoanalysis, Psychoanalytic Criticism: A field of literary criticism based on Freud's theories of the unconscious and the theories of later writers such as Jacques Lacan. Some psychoanalytic critics suggest that literary texts express an author's unconscious desires in the form of symbols and images and that writing fiction allows the author to displace his anxieties or to achieve his forbidden (usually sexual) fantasies. Other psychoanalytic critics are interested in how the dynamics of the unconscious are exhibited within literary texts rather than the author her- or himself.

Pun: A humorous play on words similar in sound but different in meaning. One example might be "What did one fly say to the other? Time to send in the swat team." A less light-hearted pun might be Hamlet's pun on "nunnery" as both convent and brothel when he attacks Ophelia in 3.1 of *Hamlet*.

Quatrain: A stanza of four lines.

Quintet: A stanza or poem of five lines that can be in any meter, have lines of any length, and be either rhymed or unrhymed.

Quotes, Quotations: When you quote a source, you integrate the source's exact words into your writing.

Ratiocination: The process of exact reasoning, often employed by crime investigators or detectives.

Rant: Any prolonged aggressively extravagant speech, the rant became a conventional poetic form after Allen Ginsburg's performance of his rant, "Howl."

Reader-Response Criticism: Criticism that focuses on an individual reader's creation of meaning for a literary text based on her distinctive characteristics (age, gender, race, religion, class, etc.) and asserts the impossibility of any single, authoritative interpretation of a text. The fact that different individuals can have similar readings of a text is due to their participation in an "interpretive community."

Realism, Realistic Drama: Literary works that present descriptions and details of daily life or that attempt to represent life "as it actually is." Realistic works are often opposed to romantic works, which depict life as we wish it would be. Realistic writers often focus on the commonplace and on everyday life.

Refrain: A line or group of lines that is repeated throughout the course of a poem. Refrains are particularly common in ballads or other sung poems. Poe's "The Raven" contains the single-word refrain, "Nevermore."

Reliable Narrator: See Narrator.

Resolution: The outcome of the plot; the point at which all loose ends are tied up.

Reverdie: A Medieval song celebrating the arrival of spring.

Rhetorical Question: A question asked simply for effect, without the expectation of an answer. Shakespeare begins Sonnet 18 with the rhetorical question, "Shall I compare thee to a summer's day?"

Rhetorical Triangle: The idea, usually attributed to Aristotle, that the reader, writer, and text constitute three points on a triangle, signifying that each of these forces plays a role in creating the text's meaning.

Rhyme: A property of much poetry, rhyme refers to the patterned repetition of the same sound at the end of poetic lines. Masculine rhymes involve one syllable (e.g., "cold" and "bold"); Feminine rhymes involve two syllables (e.g., "reader" and "feeder").

Rhythm: Recurring stressed and unstressed syllables at equal intervals, similar to meter. Two lines may have the same meter, but the lines' rhythms may differ.

Riddle: A literary genre that confronts the reader with a perplexing question or challenges the reader to discover a hidden meaning.

Romanticism, Romantic Movement: Romanticism was an artistic movement of the late eighteenth century characterized by a freedom of expression and a preference for innovative rather than traditional forms. In opposition to the rationality of classical and neoclassical authors and texts, the Romantics worshiped and admired the natural world, expressed emotion profusely, and sustained an interest in the mystic and supernatural. William Wordsworth, Samuel Taylor Coleridge, Percy Bysshe Shelley, George Gordon, Lord Byron, and John Keats are representative poets of the Romantic movement.

Runic Signature: Runes are alphabetic characters developed by Germanic tribes around the first century. They were often used in charms, spells, and other magical formulas and were carved into stones, weapons, and personal items, such as jewelry or cups. Later on, runes were used as a kind of code, and some poets, like the Old English poet, Cynewulf, would hide their names among the letters of their poetry, thus producing a runic signature.

Satire, Satiric: A literary device, related to irony, used to ridicule characters or subjects or to denounce and deride events or persons outside the work itself; satire is distinguished from comedy because it is meant to evoke an attitude rather than simply amusement. Poetic satires draw out the comic critique at great length.

Scan, Scansion: A close, critical reading of a poem or verse that analyzes and graphically indicates the meter; reading the rhythm, the music, of the poem or verse. Here is an example of a scan of two lines of verse from Hamlet's first soliloquy (1.2). The variations in meter convey Hamlet's agitation and disgust:

˘ / ˘ / / / ˘ / ˘ /

O, that this too too sullied flesh would melt

/ ˘ ˘ / ˘ / ˘ / ˘ /

Thaw and resolve itself into a dew!

Scene: In drama, the basic unit of action. A scene generally begins with a change of characters—some enter and others exit—and ends the same way. In Shakespearean drama, language may also be used to signal the end of a scene, when the dialogue ends in a rhyming couplet.

Scheme: A figure of speech that involves changing the normal word order or style of a group of words in order to create a particular effect. See also Trope.

Secondary Character: See Character.

Senex: In ancient Greek comedy, the figure of the old man who tries to prevent the young lovers from marrying or consummating their relationship. Both the father Baptista and the old wooer Gremio may be considered as *senex* figures in William Shakespeare's *The Taming of the Shrew*.

Serenade: A poem of praise for a lover meant to be sung under the beloved's window in the evening.

Sestet: A stanza or poem in units of six lines, which may be either rhymed or unrhymed. Chidiock Tichborne's "My Prime of Youth" is an example of the heroic sestet, which uses iambic pentameter and rhymes according to the pattern (*ababcc*). Dana Goia's "Unsaid" could be considered an experimental form of the sestet or perhaps a failed heroic sestet.

Sestina: A poetic form of thirty-nine lines and six stanzas, concluding with a three-line stanza (or *envoi*). The form has no rhymes, but employs the repetition of six end-words in a particular pattern—in which the first line ends with the end-word from the last line of the preceding stanza, the second line with the end-word of the first line of the preceding stanza, the third line with the end-word of the fifth line of the preceding stanza, the fourth line with the end-word of the second line of the preceding stanza, the fifth line with the end-word of the fourth line of the preceding stanza, and the sixth line with the end-word of the third line of the preceding stanza. The final three lines must use the end-words of the fifth, third, and first lines of the first stanza, in that order, and must also contain the other three end-words within the lines. This is a very complicated form: to see it concretely, read Elizabeth Bishop's poem, "Sestina."

Setting: The place, the historical time, the social and cultural situation, and the environment in which the actions of a story take place.

Shakespearean Sonnet: Otherwise known as the English sonnet. See Sonnet.

Short Story Cycle: An episodic collection of short stories featuring interrelated settings, characters, and themes.

Simile: A figure of speech that makes a comparison between two things using either "like" or "as." The speaker in Robert Burns's poem "A Red, Red Rose," for example, declares that his love is "*like* a red, red rose."

Soliloquy: In drama, an episode in which a character speaks aloud and at length to her- or himself. Often, the information is directed to the audience, although by convention the character seems to be thinking aloud. Usually, the character is alone on stage, although other characters may overhear him from the wings. In Shakespearean drama, villains (or sometimes revengers) also engage in soliloquy to explain or work out for the audience their evil plans. Both kinds of soliloquy can be found in *Hamlet*. In 2.2, Hamlet outlines his plan to "catch the conscience of the king" with the Mousetrap play (soliloquy as plan); in 3.1, he delivers his "To be or not to be" soliloquy (soliloquy as private thought) while being overheard by Polonius and Claudius.

Sonnet: A poem of fourteen lines in iambic pentameter with a variable rhyme scheme. Two types of traditional sonnets are the Italian or Petrarchan sonnet, with an octave and a sestet, and the Shakespearean or English sonnet, with three quatrains and a rhyming couplet. The rhyme scheme for the Petrarchan sonnet is often *abbaabba cdecde* (the sestet can vary in rhyme scheme). The rhyme scheme for the Shakespearean sonnet is usually *abab cdcd efef gg*.

Speech: In drama, the opposite of dialogue, in which characters speak formally and at length. Speeches may present arguments to other characters, analyze a character's state of mind, or provide the audience with information about a character's future plans. Shakespearean drama, especially *Hamlet*, is especially known for its soliloquies.

Sprung Rhythm: A term coined by poet Gerard Manley Hopkins to describe a poetic rhythm that imitates the rhythm of natural speech and music; each foot has one stressed syllable and an indefinite number of unstressed syllables. This poetic rhythm is demonstrated in Hopkins's poem "Pied Beauty."

Stanza: A group of lines in a poem that comprises a unit and often has a fixed pattern of rhyme or form.

Static Character: See Character.

Stichomythia: A dramatic exchange in which characters exchange one-line responses, often parallel in form and opposite in content. The device creates emotional tension through the rapid exchange of statements.

Story: The sum total of events that underlies the plot of a narrative or work of literature.

Stream of Consciousness: A narrative technique in which the ideas and consciousness of the character or narrator are unpredictable and shifting, rather than concrete and linear.

Style: In short fiction, how a story is written: that is, how the author uses words and structures sentences, the kinds of words and grammatical constructions the author uses, the language characters use to express themselves, and so forth.

Subjective Realism: In drama, a structural technique in which present life and memory exist on the same plane of reality and on the same stage. Arthur Miller uses this technique in *Death of a Salesman*.

Summary: A brief synopsis of the original text, written in your own words without any evaluative comments on the original.

Surreal, Surrealism: A literary movement that seeks to go beyond the real and into the worlds of the unconscious and the irrational. Magic realism is sometimes considered a further development of the surrealist movement that flourished in the 1920s.

Syllabic meter: See Meter.

Symbol, Symbolism: In the very broadest sense, a symbol is any word or object that stands for something else. In literature, words in a text and props on stage (such as Laura's glass menagerie in Tennessee Williams's play of that name) can become symbols by the attention readers and viewers are asked to give to these words. The meaning of symbols is usually complex. An example of an important symbol from a short story would be the quilt in Alice Walker's "Everyday Use." The albatross from Samuel Taylor Coleridge's "Rime of the Ancient Mariner" becomes a symbol precisely because its meaning cannot be pinned down.

Syntax: The rules governing the grammatical arrangement of words in a sentence.

Tenor: See Metaphor.

Tercet: A stanza of three lines.

Theme: A synopsis of the central idea or ideas a literary text explores and the issues it raises.

Thesis Statement: A focused, clearly defined, and arguable assertion. The thesis is the primary assertion about or the overall intended purpose of your argument.

Third-person Narrator: See Narrator.

Tone: Tone is the implied attitude of the author toward his characters and subjects as well as his or her attitude toward the audience.

Topic Sentence: In a paragraph, the topic sentence is the sentence that states the main idea of the paragraph. It acts as the thesis statement for the paragraph.

Tragedy: In specifically literary terms, a tragedy is a serious drama that ends in personal, social, or communal catastrophe. Shakespeare's *Hamlet* is considered a quintessential tragedy because all of the major characters die.

Tragic Hero: In classical tragedy, the figure who stands at the center of the dramatic action, who experiences the conflict, commits the tragic mistake or hamartia, and experiences a downfall. The tragic hero (or, occasionally heroine) is usually of aristocratic lineage and falls from high to low estate. The idea that a tragic hero has a personal, inherent "tragic flaw" is a modern misreading of the term hamartia, which refers to the hero's choice and actions rather than to internal and immutable qualities. Although originating with the drama, the term can be applied to other genres.

Trope: A figure of speech that changes, or turns a word from its usual, literal meaning. See also Scheme.

***Ubi Sunt*:** A literary motif bewailing the lost past, often in the form of a "Where are . . . ?" question.

Unity: A logical connection between successive events, places, or times. See also Dramatic Unities.

Unity of Action. See Dramatic Unities.

Unity of Place. See Dramatic Unities.

Unity of Time. See Dramatic Unities.

Unreliable Narrator: See Narrator.

Vehicle: See Metaphor.

Verbal Irony: See Irony.

Vernacular: A literary work written in the distinctive language of a particular place or people.

Verse: Metrical discourse or a text that is identified as poetry by its meter, rhyme scheme, or typography.

Villanelle: A form of poetry consisting of six stanzas comprised of nineteen lines (five tercets and a final quatrain). The first and third lines of the opening tercet rhyme and these rhymes are repeated in each successive tercet and in the last two lines of the quatrain. Lines 6, 12, and 18 are exactly the same as line 1, and lines 9, 15, and 19 are exactly the same as line 3. See Dylan Thomas's "Do Not Go Gentle into That Good Night," Marilyn Hacker's "Villanelle for D. G. B.," and John Yau's "Chinese Villanelle" for examples.

Voice Poem: A poem in which the speaker speaks normally, as if he or she is having a conversation.

Credits

Text

Achebe, Chinua, "Why the Tortoise's Shell is Not Smooth" from *Things Fall Apart* by Chinua Achebe. Reprinted by permission of Harcourt Education.

Akhmatova, Anna, "Biblical Poems 3, Lot's Wife" by Anna Akhmatova from *Anna Akhmatova, Selected Poems*, translated by Richard McKane (Bloodaxe Books, 1998). Reprinted by permission of the publisher.

Alexie, Sherman, "Reservation Love Song" from *The Business of Fancydancing*, copyright © 1992 by Sherman Alexie. Reprinted by permission of Hanging Loose Press.

Angelou, Maya, "Phenomenal Woman" and "Still I Rise" copyright © 1978 by Maya Angelou from *And Still I Rise* by Maya Angelou. Used by permission of Random House, Inc.

Anzaldua, Gloria, "Horse" from *Borderlands/La Frontera* by Gloria Anzaldua. Copyright © Gloria Anzaldua. Reprinted by permission of Aunt Lute Books.

Ashbery, John, "Paradoxes and Oxymorons" from *Shadow Train* by John Ashbery. Copyright © 1980, 1981 by John Ashbery. Reprinted by permission of Georges Borchardt, Inc. for the author.

Atwood, Margaret, "Gertrude Talks Back" from *Good Bones and Simple Murders* by Margaret Atwood, copyright © 1983, 1992, 1994 by O.W. Toad Ltd. A Nan A. Talese Book. Used by permission of Doubleday, a division of Random House, Inc. and McClelland & Stewart Ltd. "Siren Song" from *Selected Poems, 1965–1975* by Margaret Atwood. Copyright © 1976 by Margaret Atwood. Reprinted by permission of Houghton Mifflin Company and Oxford University Press, Canada. All rights reserved. "you fit into me" from *Power Politics* by Margaret Atwood, copyright © 1971, 1996 by Margaret Atwood. Reprinted by permission of House of Anasi Press, Toronto.

Auden, W. H., "As I Walked Out One Evening," "Musee des Beaux Arts," and "The Unknown Citizen" copyright 1940 and renewed © 1968 by W. H. Auden. From *Collected Poems* by W. H. Auden. Used by permission of Random House, Inc.

Bambara, Toni Cade, "The Lesson," copyright © 1972 by Toni Cade Bambara from *Gorilla, My Love* by Toni Cade Bambara. Used by permission of Random House, Inc.

Berry, Wendell, "Another Descent" from *Collected Poems* by Wendell Berry. Copyright © 1980 by Wendell Berry. Reprinted by permission of Farrar, Straus and Giroux, LLC. "The Peace of Wild Things" from *The Selected Poems of Wendell Berry* by Wendell Berry. Copyright © 1998 by Wendell Berry. Reprinted by permission of Counterpoint, a member of Perseus Books, L.L.C.

Bishop, Elizabeth, "The Fish," "One Art," and "Sestina" from *The Complete Poems 1927–1979* by Elizabeth Bishop. Copyright © 1979, 1983 by Alice Helen Methfessel. Reprinted by permission of Farrar, Straus and Giroux, LLC.

Bogan, Louise, "The Dream" and "Women" from *The Blue Estuaries* by Louise Bogan. Copyright © 1968 by Louise Bogan. Copyright © renewed 1996 by Ruth Limmer. Reprinted by permission of Farrar, Straus and Giroux, LLC.

Brooks, Gwendolyn, "We Real Cool," "The Bean Eaters," and "The Mother" from *Selected Poems* by Gwendolyn Brooks. Copyright © 1944, 1945, 1949, 1959, 1960, 1963 by Gwendolyn Brooks Blakely. Reprinted by consent of Brooks Permissions.

Carruth, Hayden, "An Apology for Using the Word 'Heart' in Too Many Poems" from *Collected Shorter Poems 1946–1991* by Hayden Carruth. Copyright © 1992 by Hayden Carruth. Reprinted with the permission of Copper Canyon Press, P.O. Box 271, Port Townsend, WA 98368-0271.

Chekhov, Anton, "Vanka" from *The Portable Chekhov* by Anton Chekhov, edited by Avrahm Yarmolinsky, copyright 1947, © 1968 by Viking Penguin, Inc., renewed © 1975 by Avrahm Yarmolinsky. Used by permission of Viking Penguin, a division of Penguin Group (USA) Inc.

Chin, Marilyn, "Turtle Soup" and "Autumn Leaves" from *The Phoenix Gone, The Terrace Empty* by Marilyn Chin. (Minneapolis: Milkweed Editions, 1994). Copyright © 1994 by Marilyn Chin. Reprinted with permission from Milkweed Editions.

Clifton, Louise, "at the cemetery, walnut grove plantation" from *Quilting: Poems 1987–1990*. Copyright © 1991 by Louise Clifton. Reprinted by permission of BOA Editions, Ltd., www.BOAEditions.org. "my mama moved among the days" and "this morning" from *Poems and a Memoir 1969–1980*. Copyright © 1987 by Louise Clifton. Reprinted by permission of BOA Editions, Ltd., www.BOAEditions.org.

Cofer, Judith Ortiz, "Arturo's Flight" from *An Island Like You* by Judith Ortiz Cofer. Published by Scholastic Inc./Orchard Books. Copyright © 1995 by Judith Ortiz Cofer. Reprinted by permission. "Claims," "The Woman Who Was Left at the Altar," "The Other," and "Cold as Heaven" from *Reaching for the Mainland and Selected New Poems*, copyright © 1987 by Judith Ortiz Cofer. Reprinted by permission of Bilingual Press/Editorial Bilingue, Arizona State University, Tempe, Arizona. "More Room" and "Tales Told Under the Mango Tree" are reprinted with permission from the publisher of *Silent Dancing: A Partial Remembrance of a Puerto Rican Childhood* by Judith Ortiz Cofer (Houston: Arte Publico Press – University of Houston © 1990).

Cullen, Countee, "From the Dark Tower" from *Copper Sun* by Countee Cullen. Copyright © 1927 by Countee Cullen. Reprinted by permission of GRM Associates.

cummings, e. e., "Buffalo Bill's." Copyright 1923, 1951 © 1991 by the Trustees for the E. E. Cummings Trust. Copyright © 1985 by George James Firmage from *Complete Poems: 1904–1962* by E. E. Cummings, edited by George J. Firmage. Used by permission of Liveright Publishing Corporation. "in Just-." Copyright 1923, 1951 © 1991 by the Trustees for the E. E. Cummings Trust. Copyright © 1985 by George James Firmage from *Complete Poems: 1904–1962* by E. E. Cummings, edited by George J. Firmage. Used by permission of Liveright Publishing Corporation. "next to of course god America I" Copyright 1926, 1954 © 1991 by the

Trustees for the E. E. Cummings Trust. Copyright © 1985 by George James Firmage from *Complete Poems: 1904–1962* by E. E. Cummings, edited by George J. Firmage. Used by permission of Liveright Publishing Corporation. "since feeling is first." Copyright 1926, 1954 © 1991 by the Trustees for the E. E. Cummings Trust. Copyright © 1985 by George James Firmage from *Complete Poems: 1904–1962* by E. E. Cummings, edited by George J. Firmage. Used by permission of Liveright Publishing Corporation.

Dickey, James, "The Heaven of Animals" from *Poems 1957–1967* by James Dickey (Wesleyan University Press, 1992). Copyright © 1992 by James Dickey and reprinted by permission of Wesleyan University Press.

Dickinson, Emily, "Because I Could Not Stop for Death," "Hope is a Thing with Feathers," and "I Heard a Fly Buzz When I Died" by Emily Dickinson. Reprinted by permission of the publishers and the Trustees of Amherst College from *The Poems of Emily Dickinson*, Thomas H. Johnson, ed., Cambridge, Mass.: The Belknap Press of Harvard University Press, copyright © 1951, 1955, 1983 by the President and Fellows of Harvard College.

Dunbar, Paul Lawrence, "We Wear the Mask" and "Sympathy" from The *Collected Poetry of Paul Lawrence Dunbar*, edited by Joanne M. Braxton. Copyright © 1993. Reprinted by permission of The University of Virginia Press.

Edelman, Bart, "Chemistry Experiment" from *The Gentle Man* by Bart Edelman. Copyright © 1997 by Bart Edelman. Reprinted by permission of Red Hen Press.

Elliot, T. S., "The Love Song of J. Alfred Prufrock" and "The Naming of Cats" from *Old Possum's Book of Practical Cats* by T. S. Eliot. Copyright © 1917 and 1939 by T. S. Eliot. Reprinted by permission of Harcourt, Inc.

Ellison, Ralph, "Battle Royal," copyright 1948 by Ralph Ellison, from *Invisible Man* by Ralph Ellison. Used by permission of Random House, Inc.

Erdrich, Louise, "A Love Medicine" and "The Red Convertible" from *Love Medicine*, New and Expanded Edition by Louise Erdrich, copyright © 1984, 1993 by Louise Erdrich. Reprinted by permission of Henry Holt and Company, LLC. "Family Reunion" and "Windigo" from *Jacklight* by Louise Erdrich. Copyright © 1984 by Louise Erdrich. Reprinted by permission of The Wylie Agency. "Family Reunion" and "Windigo" from *Jacklight* by Louise Erdrich. Copyright © 1984 by Louise Erdrich. Reprinted by permission of The Wylie Agency.

Faulkner, William, "A Rose for Emily," copyright 1930 and renewed © 1958 by William Faulkner, from *Collected Stories of William Faulkner* by William Faulkner. Used by permission of Random House, Inc.

Forche, Carolyn, All lines from "The Colonel" from *The Country Between* Us by Carolyn Forche. Copyright © 1981 by Carolyn Forche. Originally appeared in *Women's International Resource Exchange*. Reprinted by permission of HarperCollins Publishers.

Forman, Ruth, "Cancer" from *Renaissance* by Ruth Forman. Copyright © 1997 by Ruth Forman. Reprinted by permission of Beacon Press, Boston.

Frost, Robert, "Design," "Mending Wall," "The Silken Tent," "Acquainted with the Night," and "After Apple Picking" by Robert Frost. Copyright 1930, 1939, 1969 by Henry Holt and Company, copyright 1936, 1942 and © 1958 by Robert Frost, copyright © 1964, 1967, 1970 by Leslie Frost Ballantine. From *The Poetry of Robert Frost* edited by Edward Connery Lathem. Reprinted by permission of Henry Holt and Company, LLC.

Garcia, Richard, "Why I Left the Church" from *The Flying Garcias* by Richard Garcia, copyright © 1993. Reprinted by permission of the University of Pittsburgh Press.

Ginsberg, Allen, Part 1 from "Howl" from *Collected Poems 1947–1980* by Allen Ginsberg. Copyright © 1955 by Allen Ginsberg. Reprinted by permission of HarperCollins Publishers.

Glück, Louise, "Circe's Power" from *Meadowlands* by Louise Glück. Copyright © 1996 by Louise Glück. Reprinted by permission of HarperCollins Publishers. "Gratitude" and "The School Children" from *The First Four Books of Poems* by Louise Glück. Copyright © 1968, 1971, 1972, 1973, 1974, 1975, 1976, 1977, 1978, 1979, 1980, 1985, 1995 by Louise Glück. Reprinted by permission of HarperCollins Publishers.

Goia, Dana, "California Hills in August" copyright © 1986 by Dana Goia. Reprinted from *Daily Horoscope* with the permission of Graywolf Press, Saint Paul, Minnesota. "Unsaid" copyright © 2001 by Dana Goia. Reprinted from *Interrogations at Noon* with the permission of Graywolf Press, Saint Paul, Minnesota.

Graham, Jorie, "Reading Plato" from *The Dream of the Unified Field: Poems 1974–1994* by Jorie Graham. Copyright © 1995 by Jorie Graham. Reprinted by permission of HarperCollins Publishers.

Graves, Robert, "The Naked and the Nude" from *Complete Poems in One Volume* by Robert Graves. Reprinted by permission of Carcanet Press Limited.

Hacker, Marilyn, "Villanelle" copyright © 1974 by Marilyn Hacker, from *Selected Poems: 1965–1990* by Marilyn Hacker. Used by permission of W. W. Norton & Company, Inc.

Hardy, Thomas, "The Convergence of the Twain," "Ah, Are You Digging My Grave" and "The Ruined Maid" by Thomas Hardy reprinted with the permission of Scribner, an imprint of Simon & Schuster Adult Publishing Group, from *Complete Poems of Thomas Hardy* by James Gibson. Copyright © 1925 by The Macmillan Company; copyright renewed © 1953.

Harjo, Joy, "She Had Some Horses" and "The Woman Hanging from the Thirteenth Window" from the book *She Had Some Horses*, copyright © 1983, 1997 by Joy Harjo. Appears by permission of the publisher, Thunder's Mouth Press, a division of Avalon Publishing Group, Inc.

Hayden, Robert, "Those Winter Sundays." Copyright © 1996 by Robert Hayden, from *Collected Poems of Robert Hayden* by Robert Hayden, edited by Frederick Glaysher. Used by permission of Liveright Publishing Corporation.

HD, "Helen" by HD (Hilda Doolittle), from *Collected Poems 1912–1944*, copyright © 1982 by The Estate of Hilda Doolittle. Reprinted by permission of New Directions Publishing Corp.

Heaney, Seamus, "Digging" from *Death of a Naturalist* by Seamus Heaney. Copyright © 1966 by Seamus Heaney. Reprinted by permission of Farrar, Straus and Giroux, LLC. "Punishment" from *North* by Seamus Heaney. Copyright © 1975 by Seamus Heaney. Reprinted by permission of Farrar, Straus and Giroux, LLC.

Hecht, Anthony, "The Book of Yolek" copyright © 1990 by Anthony E. Hecht, from *The Transparent Man* by Anthony Hecht. Used by permission of Alfred A. Knopf, a division of Random House, Inc. "The Dover Bitch" from *Collected Earlier Poems* by Anthony Hecht, copyright © 1990 by Anthony E. Hecht. Used by permission of Alfred A. Knopf, a division of Random House, Inc.

Hemingway, Ernest, "A Clean, Well-Lighted Place" reprinted with permission of Scribner, an imprint of Simon & Schuster Adult Publishing Group from *The Short Stories of Ernest Hemingway.* Copyright © 1933 by Charles Scribner's Sons. Copyright © renewed © 1961 by Mary Hemingway.

Henry, Brian, "Garage Sale" from *Astronaut* by Brian Henry. Reprinted by permission of Carnegie Mellon University Press. Copyright © 2002 by Brian Henry.

Hernandez, Carmen Delores, Hernandez, Carmen Delores. "Where is Home? I Want to Go There" from *Puerto Rican Voices in English: Interviews with Writers* by Carmen Delores Hernandez. Copyright © Carmen Delores Hernandez. Reproduced with permission of Greenwood Publishing Group, Inc., Westport, CT.

Hughes, Langston, "Harlem" from *The Collected Poems of Langston Hughes* by Langston Hughes, copyright © 1994 by The Estate of Langston Hughes. Used by permission of Alfred A. Knopf, a division of Random House, Inc. "I, Too, Sing America" from *The Collected Poems of Langston Hughes* by Langston Hughes, copyright © 1994 by The Estate of Langston Hughes. Used by permission of Alfred A. Knopf, a division of Random House, Inc. "Theme for English B" from *The Collected Poems of Langston Hughes* by Langston Hughes, copyright © 1994 by The Estate of Langston Hughes. Used by permission of Alfred A. Knopf, a division of Random House, Inc.

Jarrell, Randall, "The Death of the Ball Turret Gunner" from *The Complete Poems* by Randall Jarrell. Copyright © 1969, renewed 1997 by Mary von S. Jarrell. Reprinted by permission of Farrar, Straus and Giroux, LLC.

Joyce, James, "Araby" from *Dubliners* by James Joyce, copyright 1916 by B. W. Heubsch. Definitive text copyright © 1967 by the Estate of James Joyce. Used by permission of Viking Penguin, a division of Penguin Group (USA) Inc.

Kafka, Franz, "The Metamorphosis", translated by Willa and Edwin Muir, from *Franz Kafka: The Complete Stories* by Franz Kafka, edited by Nahum N. Glatzer, copyright 1946, 1947, 1948, 1949, 1954, 1958, 1971 by Schocken Books. Used by permission of Schocken Books, a division of Random House, Inc.

Kincaid, Jamaica, "Girl" by Jamaica Kincaid. Copyright © 1978 by Jamaica Kincaid. Reprinted by permission of Farrar, Straus and Giroux, LLC.

Kinnell, Galway, "The Bear" from *Body Rags* by Galway Kinnell. Copyright © 1965, 1966, 1967 by Galway Kinnell. Reproduced by permission of Houghton Mifflin Company. All rights reserved. "Wait" from *Mortal Acts* by Galway Kinnell. Copyright © 1980 by Galway Kinnell. Reproduced by permission of Houghton Mifflin Company. All rights reserved.

Komunyakaa, Yusuf, "Facing It" and "Starlight Scope Myopia" from *Dien Kai Dau* by Yusef Komunyakaa (Wesleyan University Press, 1988). Copyright © 1998 by Yusef Komunyakaa and reprinted by permission of Wesleyan University Press. "My Father's Love Letters" from *Magic City* by Yusef Komunyakaa (Wesleyan University Press, 1992). Copyright © 1992 by Yusef Komunyakaa and reprinted by permission of Wesleyan University Press.

Lee, Li-Young, "The Gift" and "Persimmons" from *Rose.* Copyright © 1986 by Li-Young Lee. Reprinted with the permission of BOA Editions, Ltd., www.BOAEditions.org.

LeGuin, Ursula, "That Old Falling Down" from *Wild Oats and Fireweed* by Ursula LeGuin. Copyright © 1987 by Ursula LeGuin. First appeared in IO. Reprinted by permission of the author and the author's agents, the Virginia Kidd Literary Agency.

Levertov, Denise, "The Ache of Marriage" and "What Were They Like?" by Denise Levertov from *Poems 1960–1967*, copyright © 1966 by Denise Levertov. Reprinted by permission of New Directions Publishing Corp. "O Taste and See" from *Poems 1960–1967*, copyright © 1964 by Denise Levertov. Reprinted by permission of New Directions Publishing Corp.

Lewis, Trudy, "Limestone Diner" by Trudy Lewis. Originally appeared in *Meridian* 11 (2003) 28–48. Selected for *Best American Short Stories, 2004.* Reprinted by permission of Trudy Lewis.

Lorde, Audre, "Coping" and "Hanging Fire" from *The Black Unicorn* by Audre Lorde. Copyright © 1978 by Audre Lorde. Used by permission of W. W. Norton & Company, Inc.

Lowell, Robert, "Skunk Hour" from *Collected Poems* by Robert Lowell. Copyright © 2003 by Harriet Lowell and Sheridan Lowell. Reprinted by permission of Farrar, Straus and Giroux, LLC.

MacNeice, Louis, "Snow" from *Selected Poems of Louis MacNeice* by Louis MacNeice. Reprinted by permission of David Higham Associates.

Marquez, Gabriel Garcia, All text from "The Handsomest Drowned Man in the World" from *Leaf Storm and Other Stories* by Gabriel Garcia Marquez. Reprinted by permission of HarperCollins Publishers.

Mayers, Florence Cassen, "All-American Sestina" by Florence Cassen Mayers. First appeared in *The Atlantic Monthly*, 1996. Reprinted by permission of the author.

Millay, Edna St. Vincent, "What Lips My Lips Have Kissed" by Edna St. Vincent Millay. All rights reserved. Copyright © 1923, 1951 by Edna St. Vincent Millay and Norma Millay Ellis. Reprinted by permission of Elizabeth Barnett, Literary Executor, The Millay Society.

Miller, Arthur, From *Death of a Salesman* by Arthur Miller, copyright 1949, renewed © 1977 by Arthur Miller. Used by permission of Viking Penguin, a division of Penguin Group (USA) Inc.

Minty, Judith, "Conjoined" from *Walking With the Bear: Selected and New Poems* by Judith Minty. Copyright © 2000 by Judith Minty. Reprinted by permission of the author.

Mukherjee, Bharati, "A Wife's Story" by Bharati Mukherjee. Copyright © 1988 by Bharati Mukherjee. Reprinted by permission of Grove Publishing.

Nash, Ogden, "The Hunter," "Celery," and "Very Like a Whale" copyright 1948, 1941 by Ogden Nash. Reprinted by permission of Curtis Brown, Ltd.

Norman, Marsha, *'Night, Mother* by Marsha Norman. Copyright © 2004 by Marsha Norman. Reprinted by permission of Farrar, Straus and Giroux, LLC.

O'Brien, Tim, "Stockings" from *The Things They Carried* by Tim O'Brien. Copyright © 1990 by Tim O'Brien. Reprinted by permission of Houghton Mifflin Company. All rights reserved.

O'Connor, Flannery, "Good Country People" from *A Good Man is Hard to Find and Other Stories*, copyright © 1955 by Flannery O'Connor and renewed 1983 by Regina O'Connor, reprinted by permission of Harcourt, Inc.

Oates, Joyce Carol, "Loving" from *Love and Its Derangements* by Joyce Carol Oates. Copyright © 1970 by Ontario Review. Reprinted by permission of John Hawkins & Associates, Inc.

Olds, Sharon, "I Go Back to May 1937" and "On the Subway" from *The Gold Cell* by Sharon Olds, copyright © 1987 by Sharon Olds. Used by permission of Alfred A. Knopf, a division of Random House, Inc.

Ortiz, Simon, "Speaking" by Simon Ortiz. Copyright © by Simon Ortiz. Reprinted by permission of the author.

Owen, Wilfrid, "Dulce et Decorum Est" by Wilfred Owen from *The Collected Poems of Wilfred Owen*, copyright © 1963 by Chatto & Windus, Ltd. Reprinted by permission of New Directions Publishing Corp.

Parker, Dorothy, "Solace" and "One Perfect Rose" copyright 1926, renewed © 1954 by Dorothy Parker, from *The Portable Dorothy Parker* by Dorothy Parker, edited by Brendan Gill, copyright © 1928, renewed © 1956 by Dorothy Parker. Used by permission of Viking Penguin, a division of Penguin Group (USA) Inc.

Piercy, Marge, "Simple Song" and "Barbie Doll" from *Circles on the Water* by Marge Piercy, copyright © 1982 by Marge Piercy. Used by permission of Alfred A. Knopf, a division of Random House, Inc.

Plath, Sylvia, All lines from "Daddy" from *Ariel* by Sylvia Plath. Copyright © 1963 by Ted Hughes. Reprinted by permission of HarperCollins Publishers and Faber and Faber. All lines from "Metaphors" from *Crossing the Water* by Sylvia Plath. Copyright © 1960 by Ted Hughes. Reprinted by permission of HarperCollins Publishers and Faber and Faber.

Poquette, Ryan D., Critical Essay on "The Purloined Letter" by Ryan D. Poquette. Copyright © 2003. Reprinted by permission of Thomson/Gale.

Porter, Katherine Anne, "The Jilting of Granny Weatherall" from *Flowering Judas and Other Stories*, copyright 1930 and renewed 1958 by Katharine Anne Porter, reprinted by permission of Harcourt, Inc.

Pound, Ezra, "In a Station of the Metro" and "The River-Merchant's Wife: A Letter" by Ezra Pound from *Personae*, copyright 1926 by Ezra Pound. Reprinted by permission of New Directions Publishing Corp.

Randall, Dudley, "Ballad of Birmingham" by Dudley Randall. Copyright © 1966 by Dudley Randall. Reprinted by permission of Broadside Press.

Rankine, Claudia, "Him" by Claudia Rankine. Copyright © 1994 by Claudia Rankine. Reprinted by permission of the author.

Reed, Henry, "Naming of Parts" by Henry Reed. Reprinted by permission of Oxford University Press.

Rich, Adrienne, "Rape," copyright © 2002 by Adrienne Rich, copyright © 1973 by W. W. Norton & Company, Inc. "Aunt Jennifer's Tigers" copyright © 2002, 1951 by Adrienne Rich. "Diving Into the Wreck" copyright 2002 by Adrienne Rich, copyright © 1973 by W.W. Norton & Company, Inc. from *The Fact of a Doorframe: Selected Poems 1950–2001* by Adrienne Rich. Used by permission of author and W.W. Norton & Company, Inc.

Rios, Alberto, "Nani" from *Whispering to Fool the Wind* by Alberto Rios. Copyright © 1982 by Alberto Rios. Reprinted by permission of the author. "The Vietnam Wall" from *The Lime Orchard Women* by Alberto Rios. Copyright © 1989 by Alberto Rios. Reprinted by permission of the author.

Robinson, Edwin Arlington, Reprinted with the permission of Scribner, an imprint of Simon & Schuster Adult Publishing Group, from *The Collected Poems of Edwin Arlington Robinson* by Edwin Arlington Robinson (New York: Macmillan, 1937).

Roethke, Theodore, "My Papa's Waltz," "The Waking" and "Root Cellar" copyright 1942, 1953, 1943 by Modern Poetry Association, Inc. from *The Collected Poems of Theodore Roethke* by Theodore Roethke. Used by permission of Doubleday, a division of Random Hosue, Inc.

Rose, Mark, "Hamlet" by Mark Rose from *Homer to Brecht: The European Epic and Dramatic Tradition*, edited by Michael Seidel and Edward Mendelson. Reprinted by permission of Yale University Press.

Sandburg, Carl, "Fog" and "Chicago" from *Chicago Poems* by Carl Sandburg, copyright 1916 by Holt, Rinehart and Winston and renewed 1944 by Carl Sandburg, reprinted by permission of Harcourt, Inc. "Grass" from *Cornhuskers* by Carl Sandburg, copyright 1918 by Holt, Rinehart and Winston and renewed 1946 by Carl Sandburg, reprinted by permission of Harcourt, Inc.

Sexton, Anne, "To a Friend Whose Work Has Come to Triumph" from *All My Pretty Ones* by Anne Sexton. Copyright © 1962 by Anne Sexton, © renewed 1990 by Linda G. Sexton. Reprinted by permission of Houghton Mifflin Company. All rights reserved.

Shakespeare, William, *Hamlet,* edited by Stephen Orgel, copyright © 1957, 1970 by Penguin Books, Inc., copyright © 2001 by Penguin Putnam, Inc., from *The Pelican Shakespeare, 2nd Edition* by William Shakespeare, edited by Stephen Orgel and A. R. Braunmuller. Used by permission of Penguin, a division of Penguin Group (USA) Inc. *The Taming of the Shrew,* edited by Stephen Orgel, copyright © 1964, 1970 by Penguin Books, Inc., copyright © 2000 by Penguin Putnam, Inc., from *The Pelican Shakespeare, 2nd Edition* by William Shakespeare, edited by Stephen Orgel and A. R. Braunmuller. Used by permission of Penguin, a division of Penguin Group (USA) Inc.

Silko, Leslie Marmon, "Prayer to the Pacific" copyright © 1981 by Leslie Marmon Silko, permission of The Wylie Agency.

Simic, Charles, "Old Couple" by Charles Simic. Copyright © by Charles Simic. Reprinted by permission of the author.

Singer, Isaac Bashevis, "Gimpel the Fool" by Isaac Bashevis Singer. Copyright © 1945 by Isaac Bashevis Singer. Used by permission of Viking Penguin, a division of Penguin Group (USA) Inc.

Smith, Dave, "Edgar Allan Poe and the Nightmare Ode" by Dave Smith. Copyright © 1995 by Dave Smith. First appeared in *Southern Humanities Review.*

Song, Cathy, "Girl Powdering Her Neck" from *Picture Bride* by Cathy Song. Copyright © 1983. Reprinted by permission of Yale University Press.

Sophocles, "Antigone" by Sophocles, from *Three Theban Plays* by Sophocles, translated by Robert Fagles, copyright © 1982 by Robert Fagles. Used by permission of Viking Penguin, a division of Penguin Group USA.

Stafford, William, "Traveling Through the Dark" and "At the Bomb Testing Site" from *The Way it Is: New and Selected Poems* by William Stafford. Copyright 1960, 1962, 1998 by the Estate of William Stafford. Reprinted by permission of Graywolf Press, Saint Paul, Minnesota.

Stanton, Kay, "Hamlet's Whores" by Kay Stanton. Copyright © 1994 by AMS Press, Inc. Reprinted with permission.

Stanton, Maura, "Childhood" from *Cries from Swimmers* by Maura Stanton. Copyright © 1984 by Maura Stanton. Reprinted by permission of the author.

Steinbeck, John, "The Chrysanthemums," copyright 1937, renewed © 1965 by John Steinbeck, from *The Long Valley* by John Steinbeck. Used by permission of Viking Penguin, a division of Penguin Group (USA) Inc.

Stevens, Wallace, "The Emperor of Ice Cream," "Thirteen Ways of Looking at a Blackbird," and "Of Mere Being" from *The Collected Poems of Wallace Stevens* by Wallace Stevens, copyright © 1954 by Wallace Stevens and renewed 1982 by Holly Stevens. Used by permission of Alfred A. Knopf, a division of Random House, Inc.

Strand, Mark, "Eating Poetry" from *Selected Poems* by Mark Strand, copyright © 1979, 1980 by Mark Strand. Used by permission of Alfred A. Knopf, a division of Random House, Inc.

Thomas, Dylan, "Do Not Go Gentle Into That Good Night" from *The Poems of Dylan Thomas*, copyright © 1952 by Dylan Thomas. Reprinted by permission of New Directions Publishing Corp. "Fern Hill" from *The Poems of Dylan Thomas*, copyright © 1945 by Dylan Thomas. Reprinted by permission of New Directions Publishing Corp. "A Refusal to Mourn Death, by Fire, of a Child in London" from *The Poems of Dylan Thomas* by Dylan Thomas, copyright © 1945 by The Trustees for the Copyrights of Dylan Thomas. Reprinted by permission of New Directions Publishing Corp.

Updike, John, "The A & P" from *The Early Stories: 1953–1975* by John Updike, copyright © 2003 by John Updike. Used by permission of Alfred A. Knopf, a division of Random House, Inc.

Walker, Alice, "Everyday Use" from *In Love and Trouble: Stories of Black Women*, copyright © 1973 by Alice Walker, reprinted by permission of Harcourt, Inc.

Wideman, John Edgar, "What We Cannot Speak About We Must Pass Over in Silence" first published in *Harper's*, Vol. 307, Number 1843, December 2003. Copyright © 2003 by John Edgar Wideman, permission of The Wylie Agency.

Wilbur, Richard, "Junk" from *Advice to a Prophet and Other Poems*, copyright © 1961 and renewed 1989 by Richard Wilbur, reprinted by permission of Harcourt, Inc.

Williams, Tennessee, "The Glass Menagerie" by Tennessee Williams. Copyright © 1945 The University of the South. Reprinted by permission of Georges Borchardt, Inc. on behalf of the Tennessee Williams Estate.

Williams, William Carlos, "The Red Wheelbarrow" and "Spring and All" by William Carlos Williams from *Collected Poems: 1909–1939*, Volume I, copyright © 1938 by New Directions Publishing Corp. Reprinted by permission New Directions Publishing Corp. "This Is Just to Say" by William Carlos Williams, from *Collected Poems: 1909–1939, Volume I* copyright © 1938 by New Directions Publishing Corp.

Wilson, August, *The Piano Lesson* by August Wilson. Used by permission of Viking Penguin, a division of Penguin Group (USA) Inc.

Yau, John, "Chinese Villanelle" from *Sometimes: Poems by John Yau.* Copyright © 1979 by John Yau. Reprinted by permission of the author.

Yeats, William Butler, Reprinted with the permission of Scribner, an imprint of Simon & Schuster Adult Publishing Group, from *The Collected Works of W. B. Yeats, Volume I: The Poems, Revised*, edited by Richard J. Finneran. Copyright © 1928 by The Macmillan Company; copyright © renewed 1956 by Georgie Yeats.

Young, Kevin, "Langston Hughes" from *To Repel Ghosts* by Kevin Young. Copyright © 2001 by Kevin Young. Reprinted by permission of Zoland Books/Steerforth Press. "Nineteen Seventy-five" from *Giant Steps* by Kevin Young. Compilation copyright © 2000 by Kevin Young. Reprinted by permission of HarperCollins Publishers.

Photos

p. 9, Library of Congress; p. 11, United Media/United Feature Syndicate, Inc.; p. 27, Corbis/Bettmann; pp. 201, 226, Getty Images/Digital Vision; p. 277, Index Stock Imagery, Inc.; p. 305, Dorling Kindersley Media Library; p. 338, Getty Images/Photodisc; p. 418, Lebrecht Music & Arts Photo Library; p. 419, The Bridgeman Art Library International; p. 543, Art Resource, N.Y.; p. 657, Corbis/Stock Market; p. 666, Art Resource, N.Y.; p. 688, SuperStock, Inc.; p. 689, Creative Eye/MIRA.com; p. 696, Lebrecht Music & Arts Photo Library; p. 697, Picture Desk, Inc./Kobal Collection; p. 698, RSC Collection; p. 772, George E. Joseph; p. 670, Photofest; p. 1132, Paul Kolnik; p. 1178, Photofest; p. 1209, The Romare Howard Bearden Foundation, Inc.; p. 1275, King Features Syndicate.

Index of Authors and Titles